MANAGEMENT ACCOUNTING

STRATEGY AND CONTROL

CHARLES H. BRANDON
Roy E. Crummer School of Business
Rollins College

RALPH E. DRTINA
Roy E. Crummer School of Business
Rollins College

THE MCGRAW-HILL COMPANIES, INC.

New York St. Louis San Francisco Auckland Bogotá Caracas
Lisbon London Madrid Mexico City Milan Montreal New Delhi
San Juan Singapore Sydney Tokyo Toronto

McGraw-Hill

A Division of The **McGraw·Hill** Companies

Management Accounting
Strategy and Control

Copyright © 1997 by The McGraw-Hill Companies, Inc. All rights reserved. Printed in the United States of America. Except as permitted under the United States Copyright Act of 1976, no part of this publication may be reproduced or distributed in any form or by any means, or stored in a database or retrieval system, without the prior written permission of the publisher.

Material from Uniform CPA Examination Questions and Unofficial Answers, copyright © 1984, 1989, and 1991 by the American Institute of Certified Public Accountants, Inc., is adapted with permission.
Materials from the Certified Management Accountant Examinations, copyright © 1980, 1986, 1987, 1988, 1989, 1990, 1991, 1992, and 1993 by the Institute of Management Accountants, are reprinted and/or adapted with permission.
Material is reprinted, with permission, from the 1991 Certified Management Accountant Examination, published by the Society of Management Accountants of Canada.

This book was set in Trump Medieval by GTS Graphics, Inc.
The editors were Michelle E. Cox, Terri Varveris, and Linda Richmond;
the production supervisor was Kathryn Porzio;
the design manager was Charles A. Carson.
The designer was Robin Hessel Hoffmann.
Drawings were done by Vantage Art, Inc.
R. R. Donnelley & Sons Company, was printer and binder.

This book is printed on acid-free paper.

1 2 3 4 5 6 7 8 9 0   DOW   DOW   9 0 9 8 7 6

ISBN 0-07-017853-4

Library of Congress Cataloging-in-Publication Data

Brandon, Charles H.
  Management accounting: strategy and control / Charles H. Brandon, Ralph E. Drtina.
    p.   cm.
  Includes index.
  ISBN 0-07-017853-4
  1. Managerial accounting.   I. Drtina, Ralph E.   II. Title.
HF5657.4.B727   1997
658.15'11   dc20   96-15626

International Edition

Copyright © 1997. Exclusive rights by The McGraw-Hill Companies, Inc. For manufacture and export. This book cannot be re-exported from the country to which it is consigned by McGraw-Hill. The International Edition is not available in North America.

When ordering this title, use ISBN 0-07-114076-X.

*To my father, who thought I could do
anything—and my mother, who gave me
the strength to do it. The future lies
within my daughter, Suzanne, whom I love above everything.   C. H. B.*

*To my parents—who inspired me
to want to learn—and to my daughters,
Danielle and Erin—whom I hope
to inspire as well.   R. D.*

CONTENTS

CHAPTER 8 LONG-TERM DECISIONS—CAPITAL BUDGETING   434

CHAPTER 11 PROFIT VARIANCE ANALYSIS AND ENGINEERED COST CENTERS 618

CURRENT PRACTICE BOXES

PREFACE

PHILOSOPHY

We believe this textbook is unique, mainly because it is written to serve the needs of managers. Over the last 10 years, we both struggled to put together the right materials for our course in management accounting. The acid-test for our students—and ultimately for ourselves in selecting materials—always centered around one important question: "How will this course help students to further their jobs and careers?" In selecting materials, we borrowed from virtually every source imaginable. Our quest was to find resources that offered a broad-based manager's view of accounting in combination with sufficient analytical depth. In short, we wanted a text that offered managerial breadth, analytical depth, and a supply of real-world examples. No single text or source of materials ever seemed to meet our needs. Our frustration in finding relevant materials finally led us to write this book.

Our goal is to teach the fundamentals of management accounting as traditionally taught to accounting majors but not inundate students with procedural detail. Future managers need to know how they can use accounting concepts to shape thinking within their own organizations. They also must recognize that the world is a messy place, and all too often, unique single solutions to problems do not exist. Indeed, influencing the thought of others most often involves one's ability to communicate a series of arguments. Above all, it is our feeling that students should understand how decision-making information is constructed so that they can recognize faulty thinking in arguments presented to them.

Two themes guided us throughout the development of our text and explain our way of thinking:

- Accounting concepts guide decisions that determine organizational competitiveness.
- Our unwavering focus is on strategy and control.

DECISIONS ON COMPETITIVENESS

We believe that future managers will have the biggest impact on their organizations by making decisions that create shareholder value. They create value by searching for ways to improve products and processes and by creating sustainable competitive advantage in the marketplace. It is our conviction that management accounting offers the concepts and tools needed to make these value-creating decisions. Many tools—such as cost-volume-profit analysis, absorption costing, costs for decision making, and capital budgeting—have long been in use. However, today's process-oriented environment has given managers a new set of tools—such as activity-based costing, process improvement, strategic cost management, and multidimensional performance measurement. The key is to learn how best to use this new set of tools in conjunction with the traditional ones. Students should understand when the tools are appropriate and the advantages and shortcomings of each. These are concepts that we emphasize throughout the text.

We also emphasize global competition and technological advancements as catalysts for continuous change. Faced with these environmental conditions, managers focus on their organization's core competencies to create sustainable marketplace advantage. Management accounting, we believe, offers the tools to guide managers in evaluating decisions fundamental to this process, such as whether to downsize, outsource, or enter into strategic partnerships. We recognize that work teams, often represented by a multitude of separate functional areas, are taking on more decision authority. Moreover, operational techniques, like total quality management and just-in-time inventory management, are becoming commonplace. Here, too, we show, wherever appropriate, the impact of these methods on decision making.

FOCUS ON STRATEGY AND CONTROL

The goal of management accounting is to provide information that helps managers achieve the organization's objectives. One way to accomplish this is to prepare analytical models to determine which actions are preferable. This is largely the job of strategy formulation. The second way management accounting helps managers achieve organizational objectives is through strategy implementation, or management control. Throughout the text we emphasize the use of concepts and methods that serve this purpose, while drawing from the costing and decisions models developed earlier in the text. We place special importance on translating strategy into actions at the point where decentralized decisions take place. Budgets and financial reports are a fundamental part of this process. So too are specialized reports that promote continuous improvement and serve as a basis to compensate employees.

Unlike texts that develop each chapter as a stand-alone subject, our view is that management accounting represents an integrated set of tools—all of which support a manager's ability to formulate and implement strategy. This perspective leads us to integrate concepts from each chapter into a fabric supporting a strategy/control perspective. As a result of integrating concepts, students are well prepared to determine how best to achieve the organization's objectives. We believe that management accounting, more than any other business discipline, provides the concepts, methods, and tools to guide strategy formulation and implementation at every level in the organization.

KEY FEATURES AND PEDAGOGY

One way we carry out our objectives and bring management accounting concepts to life is through *examples of current practice.* Illustrations in each chapter allow us to show how managers deal with real-world, day-to-day problems. Examples cover a wide variety of organizations—including those which operate domestically and internationally, in manufacturing and service, and in the private and public sectors. These examples show how management accounting information is used across a rich spectrum of operating environments. In this way, we believe our readers are less likely to lose sight of the broad organizationwide issues.

The concepts in our book are given meaning through application. The end-of-chapter materials further extend this philosophy. We have included *three types of real-life assignment materials:* (1) discussion problems designed to elicit exploration of issues, (2) problems to illustrate how concepts are translated into calculations, and (3) cases that show the complexity of decisions made in the real world. We also recognize that end-of-chapter materials not corresponding to illustrations in the text lead to student frustration. Thus, we have written virtually all materials ourselves. Our goal, as always, is to align the logic and emphasis in the text with the application of the concepts. Nothing is more boring to students than end-of-chapter materials that are not grounded in reality. Accordingly, there are no XYZ corporations making widgets. Instead, we have tried to use real-life problems, drawing from our own research and consulting experiences as much as possible.

Employers seek job applicants with communication skills and the ability to work with others. To develop these skills—and to foster lively class discussions—*we have designed our assignment materials to promote student presentations, cooperative learning, group interaction, and critical thinking.* One-dimensional problems and cases, with a single numerical answer, don't develop these skills. Instead, students should be challenged with problems like the ones included in this book—problems that require balancing conflicting goals within the context of limited resources.

The complexity introduced by our assignment materials lends itself to *reliance on computer spreadsheets.* Building spreadsheet models allows both instructors and students to minimize time spent on procedural details. Models allow us to *focus on the process of problem solving* rather than emphasizing one-dimensional numeric solutions. We can then get to the issues more pertinent to the manager—what the numbers mean and what actions should be taken as a result.

Spreadsheet models are especially useful in dealing with unstructured, one-of-a-kind problems—those types of problems that typically have the greatest impact. *Models allow managers to prepare plans with multiple goals in mind.* Models can, for example, help managers make tradeoffs between improving profitability or enhancing product quality. Moreover, models allow managers to build into their computations limits imposed by resource constraints. In short, models play an important role in shaping plans and then altering them when events don't turn out as expected.

To create a focus on concepts rather than on procedural detail, we have made *all numeric exhibits and end-of-chapter materials available in spreadsheet form.* Instructors and students can use them several ways. For example, spreadsheets for exhibits in the text can be distributed to students so that they can see how each number is calculated and how the numbers relate to one another. Spreadsheets can also be used to distribute solutions for selected problems, thereby providing students a way to organize data. Still another use is spreadsheet templates to give students a head start in finding an effective way to solve problems.

ORGANIZATION

Chapter 1 provides students with an overview of the entire book. The remainder of the book is organized into three general sections. The first section, Chapters 2 through 5, is devoted to a *description of cost information provided by management accounting systems.* While we discuss traditional cost concepts for cost behavior, cost objects, and cost reporting, we also provide a comprehensive discussion of activity-based costing and its relation to process costing. Upon completing these chapters, students should understand how cost accounting information is accumulated and reported. But, just as importantly, they should be aware of its limitations, especially the cost of gathering and reporting more relevant data and the tradeoffs of settling for cost data that are second best.

The second section of the book, Chapters 6 through 8, *concentrates on how management accounting information is used for making short- and long-term decisions.* We describe the decision-making process and the kinds of information relevant for any type of decision. We illustrate the concepts with examples such as accepting offers for special orders; setting prices, using existing resources; managing inventories, outsourcing activities, evaluating underperforming products; and acquiring capital assets.

The third section, Chapters 9 through 15, *focuses on planning and control.* This part of the book ties together all of the concepts from the first two sections. It illustrates how management accounting information is used to achieve organizational goals and objectives. After introducing strategic planning and management control, we discuss how managers express expectations, compare actual results, and take corrective actions. One recurring concept throughout this discussion is the importance of multiple measures of performance applied throughout the organization as a means for influencing employee behavior and achieving goals.

SUPPLEMENTS

Instructor's Resource Manual (0-07-017854-2)
This is an instructor's manual with solutions. The instructor's manual portion, which complements the text, includes an overview for both the text and case material to help instructors prepare their lectures. The solutions manual portion contains complete answers to all of the end-of-chapter assignments: discussion problems, problems, and cases.

Test Bank (0-07-017855-0)
The *Test Bank*, written by Eric Carlsen of Kean College of New Jersey, is organized by chapter, with each chapter containing three categories of test questions: (1) true/false, (2) multiple-choice, and (3) short essay. Next to each question is a difficulty rating, ranging from 1 to 3 (easy to difficult), so that instructors can prepare tests that include all levels of questions. Answers immediately follow each question.

Computerized Test Bank—3.5" IBM (0-07-832773-2)
The *Computerized Test Bank* contains all of the questions included in the *Test Bank* by Eric Carlsen. This powerful system allows instructors to prepare a test quickly and easily. They can view questions as they are selected for a test; scramble questions; add, delete, and edit questions; select questions by type, objective, and difficulty; and view and save tests. The *Computerized Test Bank* is available in IBM 3.5", Windows, and Mac versions. A new feature of the Windows and Mac versions is on-line testing capabilities.

Overhead Transparencies (0-07-074566-8)
A complete set of numerical solutions to all end-of-chapter problems is available as transparencies.

Spreadsheet Disk
As discussed in the "Key Features and Pedagogy" section of this preface, a disk containing all of the numeric text exhibits and numeric end-of-chapter assignments in spreadsheet form will be made available to instructors.

ACKNOWLEDGMENTS

We wrote this book, first and foremost, for the students who will use it. We were fortunate enough to have support from our own students throughout the development and preparation of the book. Most helpful have been our graduate assistants, who worked on the end-of-chapter materials with perseverance. They helped us to develop, write, solve, check, and recheck our problems and cases, many of which were created expressly for this book. In particular, we would like to thank Kathy Hodges, Bella Villorante, Greg Goates, and Blane Huppert, who were instrumental in the creation and development of end-of-chapter materials. Diego Illingsworth and Marco Vannini also helped by rechecking, once again, the assignment materials and their solutions in the final stages of production.

We must also thank our MBA students. Over the past 3 academic years, they were assigned end-of-chapter materials during various phases of development. These students are from all three MBA programs—the full-time, professional, and executive programs at the Crummer Graduate School of Business, Rollins College. The feedback from these students helped us address issues, from strategic to operational, that most concern managers at all levels of an organization. The students' comments, suggestions, and frustrations helped us immensely in shaping the book into its current form.

We are especially grateful to Scott R. Colvin at Sacred Heart University and Robert P. Zwicker at Pace University, who carefully reviewed each of the end-of-chapter discussion problems, problems, and cases. They also reworked every solution to ensure accuracy and completeness.

We would like to thank the many external reviewers who have read and, in many cases, reread our material as it progressed. Their evaluations of the text helped us clarify our thinking and make sure we included topics that are at the core of management accounting. It has been quite helpful to see how our colleagues defined those concepts that they believe are essential and those that are peripheral for a book of this nature. Certainly, there was a broad range of comments on which items to add or delete and which to emphasize or deemphasize. The differing views of our colleagues helped us understand the diverse and dynamic nature of management accounting. Specifically, we would like to thank the following professors for their help: Wayne G. Bremser, Villanova University; Eric Carlsen, Kean College of New Jersey; Joseph R. Curran, Northeastern University; Frank P. Caroca, Loyola Marymount University; Kevin Devine, Xavier University; James M. Emig, Villanova University; Werner G. Frank, University of Wisconsin—Madison; Michael Haselkorn, Bentley College; Fred Jacobs, Michigan State University; Douglas H. Johnson, Arizona State University; Michael Kinney, Texas A&M University; Robert W. Koehler, Penn State University; Amy H. Lau, Oklahoma State University; Linda M. Marquis, Northern Kentucky University; William L. Mulvaney, Wayne State University; Joyce A. Ostrosky, Illinois State University; Eileen Peacock, Oakland University; Karl Putnam, University of Texas at El Paso; Gary S. Robson, Kansas State University; Paul J. Schlachter, Florida International University; Ali M. Sedaghat, Loyola College in Maryland; Douglas Y. Shin, University of Pittsburgh; Kenneth P. Sinclair, Lehigh University; Edward L. Summers, University of Texas at Austin; James Voss, Penn State University; and S. Mark Young, University of Colorado at Boulder.

We must also acknowledge the persistent support of many people at McGraw-Hill. Mickey Cox, as editor of our project, kept us on course while offering continuous encouragement. Our special thanks go to Terri Varveris, who provided us guidance at every stage of the project. Mike Elia and Ed Millman were crucial in transforming our early ideas into a book that is, thanks to their efforts, easier to read. And a great debt is owed to Linda Richmond, ZaZa Ziemba, and Diane Schadoff for making sure the final product met McGraw-Hill's uncompromising standards for publication quality. Our gratitude is extended to all of you.

Finally, we want to thank those with whom we work daily—our colleagues and coworkers. Foremost are Heather Bowers and Susan Crabill, who undertook many of the tasks in getting this book to the publisher. We would also like to acknowledge three faculty colleagues who have written successful textbooks. Sam Certo, Jim Higgins, and Barry Render have been terrific, both by providing materials from their disciplines and by offering guidance for success in textbook writing. We can't thank you enough.

Permission has been received from the Institute of Management Accountants, the American Institute of Certified Public Accountants, and the Society of Management Accountants of Canada to use questions and/or unofficial answers from past professional certification examinations.

Charles H. Brandon

Ralph E. Drtina

CHAPTER

1

MANAGEMENT ACCOUNTING: INFORMATION TO COMPETE

Today's managers are continually faced with decisions affecting their organization's ability to compete. We can't help noticing reports in the news about companies who, in response to competitive pressures, downsize operations, cut costs, and refocus their strategies. Consider IBM, an established company with a rich history of quality products and market success. IBM redefined the way it does business because of the decline in the market for mainframe computers. It pushed decisions down to lower levels in the organization and required product groups to compete against one another. Similarly, Boeing Corporation, after dominating the aircraft construction industry for decades, formed alliances with suppliers and competitors to maintain its market position. To sort out the costs and benefits of each of the possible alternative courses of action available to IBM and Boeing, decision makers required management accounting information.

Information provided by the management accounting system helps managers plan. It gives them the information they need to determine resource requirements for each action they take. Plus, it helps them prepare projections about the effect their actions are likely to have on the organization. A firm's management accounting system is the communication medium between senior corporate managers at the executive level and the managers of the organizational subunits responsible for enacting decisions.

Managers at all levels establish performance targets against which actual operating results are compared. In this way, senior managers can watch over the day-to-day operations to ensure they're making progress toward meeting the company's objectives.

Management accounting can also help motivate employees to improve their performance. Information provided by management accounting enables employees to understand the connection between what they do and the products or services that result from their efforts. Moreover, information is used to catalyze improvements in performance by linking workers' personal goals with those of their organization through rewards for accomplishments. In this way the management accounting system is a bridge between the efforts of employees at all levels and the plans initiated by senior corporate managers.

This chapter provides an overview of management accounting, introducing the key concepts that will be fully developed in later chapters. To begin, we look briefly at organizations, their objectives, and the general role played by management accounting. Then we introduce the specific functions of management accounting. Each broad function is explained and illustrated. Finally, we consider how today's business environment, the demands of the marketplace, and the opportunities created by technology are likely to affect each function.

ORGANIZATIONS: OBJECTIVES AND RESULTS

Organizations are made up of groups of people who come together to accomplish common objectives. Organizations can be classified by size. There are large multinational corporations like AT&T, Daimler-Benz, and Mitsubishi, or small neighborhood businesses such as mom-and-pop convenience stores, drugstores, or dry cleaners. Organizations may also be classified by the type of output they produce. Some make tangible products, such as autos, or convert crude oil into petroleum products, while others deliver services like transportation or consulting. And there's still a more basic way of classifying organizations—according to their purpose. While most companies are profit-seeking, like those listed on the New York Stock Exchange, others, like the American Heart Association, the United Nations, or the Environmental Protection Agency, strive for nonprofit objectives. Regardless of their purposes or how they are classified, all organizations must accomplish their objectives if they are to survive.

DEFINING OBJECTIVES

The first thing we need to understand about an organization is its objectives. **Objectives** are statements, usually expressed in quantitative terms, about what the organization wants to accomplish and when it should happen. For example, a firm's objective might be to attain a 30 percent market share by 1998. After objectives have been established, information can be gathered about the different ways the objectives can be accomplished. Only then can alternatives be evaluated, the best alternatives chosen, and plans formulated about how to carry out those objectives.

PROFIT-SEEKING BUSINESSES

All profit-seeking businesses strive to create sustainable shareholder value. *Creating shareholder value* means generating cash flows sufficient to cover all costs of operations plus provide an adequate return on invested capital. *Sustainable* means that the value created should benefit the organization for years into the future.

Every business decision must ultimately support this fundamental goal—the creation of long-term value for the shareholders of the organization. Past results do not necessarily ensure future value. Nor do past successes guarantee that long-term expectations will be met. Consider IBM. Despite its long history of success, IBM lost nearly half its stock value over a six-month period from 1992 to 1993. The capital markets reflected investors' concerns over the firm's declining ability to compete in a crowded market—a market shifting away from mainframe computers, IBM's basic product line.

To create value, managers identify short-term objectives that help guide their organizations toward long-term future success. Profitability is one measure of an organization's ability to meet its short-term objectives. And meeting those short-term objectives is surely a good indication of progress toward achieving long-term objectives. Equally good indicators are the detailed components of profit—such as revenue growth and cost containment. Both of these provide signals about management's ability to attain its objectives and to remain competitive in the markets it serves.

Financial measures are increasingly supplemented by nonfinancial measures such as quality, productivity, new product development, environmental impact, and employee satisfaction. These measures provide additional information about the organization's ability to achieve its objectives. It is the combination of short-term financial and nonfinancial measures that managers look at to decide which actions are most useful in achieving the long-term objective of creating sustainable shareholder value.

NONPROFIT ORGANIZATIONS

The objectives of nonprofit (or not-for-profit) organizations are defined in terms of the social needs the organizations strive to fulfill. Social objectives can be more complex than the objectives of for-profit businesses. (See "Current Practice: World Wildlife Fund.") For example, the objectives of a police department might include protecting citizens from crime and providing community services like traffic control or public education on crime prevention. Consider a private social service agency dedicated to helping the homeless. Its objectives might include supplying meals, providing temporary shelter, and assisting with employment. Unlike for-profit businesses, nonprofit organizations do not have a single objective—such as creating shareholder value. Nonprofits do, however, create social value by meeting the needs of the constituents they serve. Just as failing to meet objectives will lead profit-seeking entities to fail, consistently failing to meet these social needs will eventually lead nonprofits to fail, perhaps through the loss of funding.

Nonprofit firms, in achieving their objectives, must develop ways of conducting day-to-day operations that give them advantages relative to their competition, just as profit-seeking firms must do. For example, nonprofit organizations may create an advantage by delivering services at a low cost. Progress toward achieving the long-term objectives can be monitored by gathering data about current operating variables, many of which are the same as those for profit-seeking organizations—for example, the cost per unit of service. What something costs—like a unit of service—is a topic we will cover in the next three chapters.

World Wildlife Fund

The World Wildlife Fund, or WWF, believes that its primary objective is simple—the conservation of nature. However, the ways it strives to meet this challenge are diverse:

- *Protect species.* Develop international campaigns to save endangered species, halt global trade in endangered animals and plants, train and equip antipoaching teams, and relocate highly threatened animals.
- *Create and preserve protected areas.* Carve out permanent strongholds for irreplaceable plant and animal species. Safeguard protected areas from threats beyond their boundaries.

- *Link conservation and human needs.* Work with local leaders, groups of citizens, governments, and international funding institutions to improve living standards and integrate conservation into public and private-sector development programs.
- *Build effective institutions.* Use grants, training programs, and technical assistance to build institutions that can successfully sustain long-term conservation efforts.
- *Address global threats.* Focus on global changes that could wreak havoc on natural systems, and target toxic chemicals that pollute the air, poison the water, and endanger wildlife and humans.

Source: Adapted from the World Wildlife Fund, *Annual Report, 1992,* pp. 10–11.

Largely because they lack a profit measure, nonprofit organizations traditionally use nonfinancial measures, such as customer satisfaction and speed of service delivery, to measure their performance. As you will see, managers of nonprofit organizations need the same kinds of information to make the same (or similar) kinds of decisions made by managers of for-profit firms—information provided by management accounting.

INFORMATION AND DECISIONS

Managers go through a series of specific analytical steps in evaluating and reaching decisions aimed at achieving their organizations' objectives. Sometimes managers adhere strictly to these steps—for instance, when submitting a proposal to corporate executives for permission to proceed with a new project. At other times, managers may proceed less on prescribed analysis and more on intuition—for example, as when searching for ways to improve customer satisfaction. Either way, managers need information.

We now take a closer look at the decision-making process and some of the properties of information.

THE DECISION-MAKING PROCESS

There are seven steps in the formal process of managerial decision making:

1. Specify organizational objectives.
2. Find occasions to make decisions.
3. Identify alternative courses of action.
4. Choose among alternatives.
5. Implement the course of action chosen.
6. Gather information to compare actual results with objectives.
7. Correct the actions of employees in order to eliminate differences between actual results and objectives.

The first four steps constitute the process by which management defines its strategies, the organization's broad plans for action. The last three steps represent the control process that helps in implementing strategies. The seven steps are followed by all managers—regardless of their position within the firm's hierarchy. What differs among managers are their particular objectives and the way they attain them.

Consider the following example which illustrates the seven steps in the process of managerial decision making.

Senior managers, in creating long-term value for shareholders, establish an objective of increasing cash flow over a 3-year period. The managers are considering expanding distribution into new geographic areas. Three new markets are identified as possibilities: Brazil, Australia, and southeast Asia. Data are gathered showing projections for the amount of investment needed, revenue, and operating cost in each of the markets. Managers choose to expand into the Australian market because it offers the best cash flow. Implementation requires setting up an organizational subunit in Melbourne, Australia, and building an operating plan, or budget, with specific targets for revenue and cost. Each month, actual revenue and cost are compared against the targets in the budget. The manager in Melbourne, after identifying cost overruns, initiates cost-cutting actions.

This scenario illustrates the seven steps in the decision-making process. First, managers specify the organization's objective—increasing cash flow. When decision-making occasions occur—for instance, expanding distribution into new geographic areas—the actions managers take should be directed toward increasing cash flow. Alternative courses of action include expansion into three new markets. The alternative chosen (expanding into the Australian market) is implemented by creating an organizational subunit and building a budget for that subunit. After gathering monthly information, managers compare the actual results with targets established in the budget. When cost overruns are identified, cost-cutting actions are initiated.

PROPERTIES OF INFORMATION

The purpose of management accounting is to provide managers with information that guides them in reaching their objectives. Not all data, however, are considered information. The plant manager responsible for manufacturing a special order, for example, may receive literally thousands of individual pieces of data on materials prices and the quantities used in filling the order. *Data* becomes *information* when it is converted into a format that managers understand and is reported to them in time to ensure that the special order meets specifications.

A successful management accounting system provides only the information that is relevant to the decisions at hand. This means information must be delivered to the people who need it, when they need it, in a form they can use. Information must also be *cost-effective*—the benefits derived from the information should exceed the cost of collecting it. Irrelevant information should always be excluded.

Benefits Should Exceed Costs. Unlike goods, whose costs can be precisely measured, the cost of information is difficult to calculate. Moreover, the cost of information increases with the desired degree of accuracy, the amount of information requested, and the speed at which it is delivered. It is not uncommon for managers to request additional information in order to reduce uncertainties about the outcomes of various courses of action. They may request this information without being aware of the additional cost. Their decisions may be delayed while they gather additional information, even if it occasionally results in lost opportunities—another cost of additional information.

The value of information is not always well-understood. Its benefits might include an increased awareness of the subtleties of various alternatives or a better understanding of the impact of expected outcomes. Ultimately, information has value only if it causes a manager to make a decision that would not have been made without that information. At some point—admittedly not an easy point to identify—more information is not worth the additional cost of gathering it.

More Is Not Necessarily Better. Managers sometimes receive irrelevant information, often the product of an outdated system. As circumstances change, managers require new types of information and revised reporting formats. Rather than serving to replace irrelevant reports produced by outdated systems, new reports are sometimes merely added to the already crowded array of information available to managers. The result is "information overload," an overabundance of data. Overwhelmed managers aren't able to extract the information they need to make the best decisions. As a result, important objectives may not be realized and shareholder value may be lost.

PURPOSE AND NATURE OF MANAGEMENT ACCOUNTING

The purpose and nature of management accounting is introduced in this section by comparing management accounting with financial accounting. We then examine, in detail, the three primary functions that constitute management accounting.

WHAT IS MANAGEMENT ACCOUNTING?

Students who first encounter management accounting are often surprised at how it differs from financial accounting. Exhibit 1.1 offers an overview of some of the differences between the two. After looking at Exhibit 1.1, it should be clear that management accounting is intended for internal use by managers and employees who make decisions that affect the organization's future. In contrast, financial accounting is intended primarily for external use by investors, creditors, and financial analysts who evaluate the firm's past performance.

The purpose of management accounting is to supply information to meet the specific needs of managers and employees who are working to further the objectives of the organization. Historical information is of little benefit in this regard except to the extent that it can be used to predict future outcomes. The key word here is *future*. At all times, management accounting information must be "relevant"—it must help managers understand how future financial results are likely to differ as the result of pursuing alternative courses of action.

Financial accounting, on the other hand, is designed to communicate objective, verifiable information about the firm's historical financial performance. While management accounting is forward-looking, financial accounting's emphasis is on reliability in representing past performance.

One other way that managerial accounting differs from financial accounting is the degree of standardization of reports across companies. Generally accepted accounting principles (GAAP), described as the authoritative standards for financial reporting, provide guidelines for information that is given to external users. Management accounting, on the other hand, provides information in a variety of different formats, some custom-made for the purposes at hand.

Financial and management accounting also differ in the amount of detail reported. Financial accounting information is accumulated, summarized, and reported without the detail that managers need if they are

EXHIBIT 1.1   COMPARISON OF MANAGEMENT ACCOUNTING WITH FINANCIAL ACCOUNTING

Comparison Characteristic	Management Accounting	Financial Accounting
Closely related topics	Managerial economics, behavioral science, operations management	Corporate finance, financial analysis, financial investments
Purpose	To supply information useful for decisions	To report historical results
Primary users	Managers, employees	Investors, creditors, financial analysts
Time orientation	Future	Past
Reporting procedure	As needed, in standard and custom formats	Periodic, in standard GAAP format
Degree of detail reported	As needed	Aggregated and summarized

to direct operations. A hospital's financial statements, for example, may only show administrative cost broken out by functional area, such as salaries or supplies. Salary cost in management accounting reports might be broken down into activities like admissions or risk management. Moreover, the information might be organized in a variety of ways, each matching a specific need. For example, managers may want estimates of how admissions cost is likely to change if admission activities increase. Information organized in this way helps managers in planning and controlling day-to-day operations.

THE THREE FUNCTIONS OF MANAGEMENT ACCOUNTING

We now take a closer look at how information provided by the management accounting system is used for (1) determining what something cost, (2) providing information to support the evaluation of alternative courses of action, and (3) planning and controlling operations.

DETERMINING WHAT SOMETHING COSTS

Cost of Products. One function of management accounting is to determine what something costs. That something, called a cost object, can be anything managers want to collect costs for. Consider the cost of making a man's dress shirt, as shown in Exhibit 1.2. One shirt requires 1.5 yards of fabric at $4 per yard, or a total of $6 in materials cost per shirt. Labor time for cutting, sewing, and packing totals 15 minutes, or 0.25 hours, at a wage rate of $12 per hour, making the total labor cost $3 per shirt. In addition to materials and labor, producing the shirt entails use of the factory. The cost of operating the factory, called manufacturing (or factory)

EXHIBIT 1.2 MANUFACTURING COMPANY— SHIRT MANUFACTURER

Full Cost of Making a Man's Dress Shirt

		Cost per Shirt
Manufacturing cost:		
Materials (1.5 yards of fabric @ $4/yard)		$ 6.00
Labor: cutting, sewing, & packing (0.25 hr @ $12/hr)		3.00
Manufacturing overhead:		
Depreciation, utilities, repair & maintenance	$500,000	
Divided by number of shirts manufactured	100,000	
Manufacturing overhead per shirt		5.00
Total manufacturing cost per shirt		$14.00
Nonmanufacturing cost:		
Accounting, taxes, & advertising	$300,000	
Divided by number of shirts manufactured	100,000	
Total nonmanufacturing cost per shirt		$ 3.00
Full cost of making a man's dress shirt		$17.00

EXHIBIT 1.3 MANUFACTURING COMPANY— SHIRT MANUFACTURER

Income Statement

Sales revenue (100,000 shirts @ $20/shirt)	$2,000,000
Less cost:	
Cost of goods sold (100,000 shirts @ $14/shirt)	$1,400,000
Nonmanufacturing cost	300,000
Total cost	$1,700,000
Pretax operating income	$ 300,000

overhead, might include depreciation, utilities, and repair and maintenance.

In this example, manufacturing overhead cost totals $500,000 per
year. Assuming 100,000 shirts are made during the year, manufacturing
overhead averages $5 per shirt. Adding all manufacturing costs together
results in a total manufacturing cost of $14 per shirt. Nonmanufacturing
costs—such as accounting, taxes, and advertising—add $300,000 to total
cost, or another $3 per shirt. Therefore, the total cost—or the full cost—
of making a man's dress shirt is $17, comprising $14 in total manufacturing cost and $3 in total nonmanufacturing cost.

Exhibit 1.3 shows what the shirt manufacturer's income statement
for the year might look like. At a selling price of $20 per shirt, total sales
revenue for 100,000 shirts is $2 million. The cost of manufacturing a sin-
gle shirt is $14, or a total manufacturing cost—shown as *cost of goods
sold*—equal to $1,400,000 for all 100,000 shirts sold. After deducting the
nonmanufacturing cost—often called *selling, general,* and *administrative
costs*—equal to $300,000, the shirt-making firm generates a pretax oper-
ating income of $300,000.

Cost of Services.   Exhibit 1.4 shows what it might cost to supply a unit
of service—in this example, the use of a motel room for one night. As
with a man's shirt, costs are accumulated in categories for materials, labor,
and overhead. One obvious difference for the motel room is that materials cost is relatively minor, consisting primarily of complimentary sham-
poo and soap, which together cost $1 per day per room. Similarly, house-
keeping labor for each room consists of 0.25 hours at $12 per hour, or $3
per room per day. The cost of operating the motel building, called *operating overhead,* totals $800,000 for the year. It includes depreciation for the
motel building, furniture and equipment, utilities, and repair and maintenance costs. If 20,000 rooms are rented during the year, operating overhead averages $40 per room. Nonoperating cost includes accounting, taxes,
and advertising. Dividing nonoperating cost of $200,000 by 20,000 rooms
rented during the year gives a cost of $10 per room. Adding the operating
cost of $44 per room to the nonoperating cost of $10 gives us the full cost
of $54 per room.

EXHIBIT 1.4 SERVICE COMPANY—MOTEL OPERATOR

Full Cost of Renting a Motel Room

		Daily Cost per Room
Operating cost:		
Materials: complimentary soap, shampoo		$ 1.00
Labor: housekeeping services (0.25 hr @ $12/hr)		3.00
Operating overhead:		
Depreciation, utilities, repair & maintenance	$800,000	
Divided by number of rooms rented	20,000	
Operating overhead per room		$40.00
Total operating cost per room		$44.00
Nonoperating cost:		
Accounting, taxes, advertising	$200,000	
Divided by number of rooms rented per year	20,000	
Total nonoperating cost per room		$10.00
Full cost of renting a motel room		$54.00

EXHIBIT 1.5 SERVICE COMPANY—MOTEL OPERATOR

Income Statement—External Reporting Format

Sales revenue (20,000 rooms @ $60/room)	$1,200,000
Less operating cost:	
Materials (20,000 rooms @ $1/room)	$ 20,000
Labor (20,000 rooms @ $3/room)	60,000
Operating overhead	800,000
Nonoperating cost	200,000
Total cost	$1,080,000
Pretax operating income	$ 120,000

The income statement in Exhibit 1.5 shows what the motel's operating results might look like for the year. Based on a rate of $60 per room, revenue for 20,000 room rentals is $1,200,000. After deducting operating and nonoperating costs, the motel shows a pretax operating income of $120,000.

PROVIDING INFORMATION TO SUPPORT THE EVALUATION OF ALTERNATIVE COURSES OF ACTION

The second function of management accounting is providing information to support the evaluation of alternative courses of action. This means that we must look at information in a different way. Rather than examining what something costs, we must look at how revenue and cost are likely to change if managers choose one of the alternative courses of action. The change in revenue for each alternative is referred to as incremental (or *differential, or marginal*) revenue, while the change in cost is known as incremental (or differential, or marginal) cost. Incremental income for any alternative is simply the difference between incremental revenue and incremental cost. To maximize the firm's income, the alternative that is likely to ensure the highest level of attainment of company objectives is the course of action that managers should follow.

Correct decisions rely on separating from all available information only those revenues and costs that are relevant. Relevant revenues and costs are those that are likely to change as a result of the decision. Revenues and costs that do not change are not relevant and should not be considered in evaluating the decision.

To illustrate the decision-support function of management accounting using the motel example, assume the motel manager receives a request from a tour operator for 25 rooms. The tour operator plans to book the rooms as long as the motel manager is willing to accept a special rate of $50 per room. The rate offered by the tour operator is $10 less than the normal rate of $60 per room and $4 below the full cost of $54 (Exhibit 1.4). What should the motel manager do?

While the first inclination is to refuse the offer, the motel manager must try to determine if capacity will be available. That is, are there likely to be 25 rooms available on the date requested? After checking historical records, the manager is certain that at least 25 rooms will not be booked by guests paying the full $60 per night on the date requested.

After determining availability, the next step in the decision is to rearrange the cost information from Exhibits 1.4 and 1.5 into a format useful in making decisions. This internal decision-making format—called the contribution margin format—is shown in Exhibit 1.6. In that exhibit, costs

EXHIBIT 1.6　SERVICE COMPANY—MOTEL OPERATOR

Income Statement[a]—Internal Decision-Making Format

	Per Room	Total
Room rate per night	$60.00	$1,200,000
Variable cost:		
Materials: soap, shampoo	$ 1.00	$ 20,000
Labor: housekeeping services (0.25 hr @ $12/hr)	3.00	60,000
Total variable cost	$ 4.00	$ 80,000
Contribution margin	$56.00	$1,120,000
Fixed cost:		
Depreciation, utilities, repair & maintenance		$ 800,000
Accounting, taxes, advertising		200,000
Total fixed cost		$1,000,000
Pretax operating income		$ 120,000

[a]　Data are based on 20,000 rental days per year.

are organized in two broad groupings: costs that vary in direct proportion with the number of rooms rented, or **variable costs,** and costs that are unaffected by the number of rooms rented, or fixed costs. The difference between the normal room rate of $60 and the variable cost of $4 per room is $56. This difference is called the unit contribution margin and is defined as the unit selling price less unit variable costs. Multiplying the unit contribution by 20,000 rooms gives us the total contribution margin of $1,120,000. After deducting $1,000,000 in fixed costs, pretax operating profits for the year are $120,000, exactly the same profit figure shown in the income statement in Exhibit 1.5.

Managers use the contribution margin format in estimating the impact of changes in activity on operating income. For example, if the number of rental days were to fall from 20,000 to 18,000, total contribution would decline to $1,008,000 (18,000 days × $56 per room) and operating profit would decline to $8,000 ($1,008,000 in total contribution less fixed cost of $1 million). The $112,000 decrease in income (from $120,000 to $8,000) can be predicted directly by simply multiplying the reduced number of days the rooms are rented (2,000) by the per-room contribution margin ($56).

Exhibit 1.7 completes the example by showing how the special offer affects operating income. The incremental revenue is simply 25 rooms at $50 per room, or $1,250 in total. Incremental cost is equal to the variable cost of $4 per room multiplied by the number of rooms, or $100 in total. Note that we assume housekeeping labor varies in direct proportion with the number of rooms rented. That is, housekeeping labor is paid according to the number of rooms cleaned. This makes housekeeping a variable cost. None of the other costs change, regardless of whether or not the rooms are rented at the special rate of $50 per room. Because they do not change, these costs are irrelevant and should be ignored in evaluating the special offer decision.

The resulting net incremental contribution is $1,150. Since fixed cost is not affected, operating income also increases by this same amount. As

---

EXHIBIT 1.7 SERVICE COMPANY—MOTEL OPERATOR

Evaluation of a Special Offer for 25 Rooms[a]

	Per Room	Total
Incremental revenue	$50.00	$1,250
Less incremental cost:		
Materials: complimentary soap, shampoo	$ 1.00	$ 25
Labor: housekeeping services (0.25 hr @ $12/hr)	3.00	75
Total incremental cost	$ 4.00	$ 100
Incremental contribution margin	$46.00	$1,150

[a] Data are based on renting 25 rooms for 1 night.

long as the manager has 25 rooms that will not be rented to other guests at higher rates, and assuming that the price concession doesn't set a precedent whereby regular customers ask for similar price reductions, the motel is $1,150 better off by accepting the tour operator's offer.

The thing to remember is that management accounting provides relevant information in a form that is useful to the managers—as in Exhibit 1.7—when making decisions. Neither of the other two ways we have shown of organizing information—the form used in calculating the full cost of a motel room in Exhibit 1.4 and the form used for financial reporting in Exhibit 1.5—provides information useful in assessing the impact of the special room rates on operating income.

PLANNING AND CONTROLLING OPERATIONS

Senior managers must agree on an organization's **mission**—the reason for its existence. Only then can they formulate strategies that will guide them toward fulfilling that mission. The mission statement identifies the firm's customers, its products, and how it plans to achieve a competitive advantage. Mission statements are often stated in vague, sometimes visionary, language. For example, a company that makes breakfast cereal may say its mission is "to become the global leader in making wholesome food products at a good value for customers."

Managers at all levels of the organization work together to convert mission statements into goals and objectives. These are more-clearly defined statements about the organization's purpose. **Goals** are open-ended statements about how the company plans to fulfill its mission. Corporate goals may, for instance, emphasize shareholder value, product quality, customer satisfaction, cost competitiveness, or global markets. For example, the company that makes breakfast cereal may have a goal of "improving profitability by reducing costs."

Broadly defined goals are translated into more-specific objectives. As noted earlier, corporate objectives are statements about what the firm wants to accomplish and when the desired results should happen. For example, the company that makes breakfast cereal may state that its objective is to "reduce processing time by 5 percent by the end of the year in order to get products to market more quickly and to extend shelf life."

Strategies are the plans for action the firm will undertake in order to achieve each of its objectives. (See "Current Practice: Wendy's International, Inc.") For example, the breakfast cereal company may decide to install a computerized scheduling system that minimizes the amount of time unprocessed grain spends in company warehouses waiting to be converted into final products.

Management accounting affects the planning and control functions through a system of information flows designed to assure managers that strategies are being implemented. The system begins with the firm's corporate goals and objectives, which are transmitted to subunits within the organization responsible for achieving them. Each subunit develops plans for how it's going to achieve its goals and objectives. These plans then become part of the corporate strategy.

CURRENT PRACTICE

Wendy's International, Inc.

Wendy's International, Inc., operates in the "quick-service restaurant" industry. Its 1994 annual report contains a discussion about how it plans to compete against rivals like McDonald's, Burger King, and Hardee's. Excerpts from this report—selections from the mission statement, and from the goals, objectives, and strategies established by Wendy's managers for 1995—are listed below.

Corporate Mission
Our mission is to deliver total quality in our more than 4,400 restaurants worldwide by excelling in quality, variety, atmosphere, competitive prices, consistency (a familiar and predictable experience), and convenience.

Corporate Goals
Our corporate goal is to continue Wendy's growth rate by further penetrating the do-

mestic market and taking advantage of the even greater potential of the underserved international market.

Corporate Objectives

- Continue an annual 20 percent earnings growth rate.
- Grow to an estimated 5,000 restaurants by the mid-1990s.
- Increase the growth rate of new restaurants from 7 percent in 1994 to 9 percent in 1995.
- Remodel and retrofit 750 restaurants by the end of 1995.

Corporate Strategies

- Deliver a satisfying experience to customers.
- Build brand equity plus value.
- Grow a healthy system.
- Foster a performance-driven culture.

Source: Adapted from Wendy's International, Inc., *Annual Report, 1994*, pp. 1–7.

Exhibit 1.8 depicts an organizational structure for a multinational breakfast cereal producer. Operational plans are developed for each of its two major business units: the North American Group and the European Group. The exhibit illustrates several of the many possible ways subunits can be organized. For example, the North American Group is organized by type of customer (institutional or commercial), while the European Group is organized by product type (biscuits and crackers, and breads).

Each subunit prepares a financial plan called a budget. Managers use budgets as a basis for assigning resources. Budgets also form the basis for setting *targets*—the levels of revenue, cost, and profit that can realistically be accomplished in the forthcoming time period. Formal performance reports, typically prepared monthly, are sent back up through the organization, where they are reviewed by managers at successively higher levels in the organization. Managers review performance to compare actual performance against targets. The outcome of that review, referred to as feedback, is the identification of areas where performance can be improved and changes are needed. Feedback is necessary to control operations—to

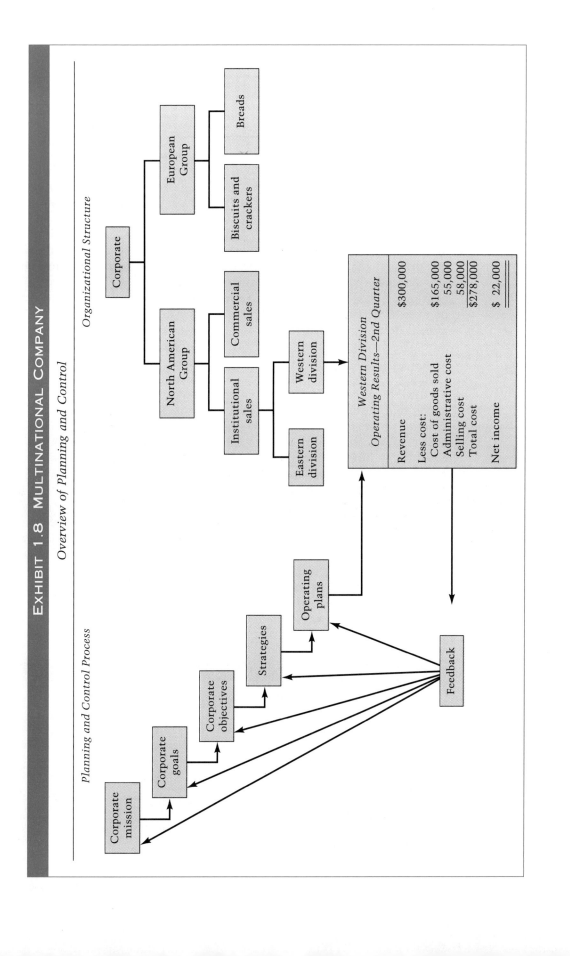

EXHIBIT 1.8 MULTINATIONAL COMPANY

Overview of Planning and Control

Organizational Structure

Planning and Control Process

Western Division
Operating Results—2nd Quarter

Revenue		$300,000
Less cost:		
Cost of goods sold	$165,000	
Administrative cost	55,000	
Selling cost	58,000	
Total cost		$278,000
Net income		$ 22,000

ensure that actions are consistent with plans. When necessary, plans may have to be reformulated to better match market conditions.

Exhibit 1.8 also illustrates the interaction between the organizational structure and the planning and control system of a multinational company. The operating results from the western division, for example, provide feedback, represented by the arrows pointing back to the strategy-setting process. Feedback about past performance provides important information for the next round of planning.

Exhibit 1.9 shows a quarterly performance report for the western division of the North American Group. Before the start of the year, the western division manager works with corporate officials to determine mutually agreeable budget targets for the year. The results are shown in the first column of data in Exhibit 1.9. Actual results are reported for the second quarter of the year and compared with one-fourth (three months) of the annual budget amounts.

The far-right column of Exhibit 1.9 shows the difference between actual performance and budget expectations. This difference is called a variance. For example, sales revenue exceeds budget by $50,000, shown as a positive variance, indicating an increase in operating income. Cost of goods sold is shown as a negative variance of $(40,000). The negative designation indicates an unfavorable effect on operating income. However, cost of goods sold is expected to increase as sales increase. Another relatively large unfavorable variance is selling cost, $(9,250) for the quarter. Like cost of goods sold, the unfavorable selling cost variance may be justified because it helped to stimulate an increase in sales activity. The total for all variance is $(500), indicating that the western division did not meet its budgeted profit expectations despite the increase in sales. Performance reports, like the one shown in Exhibit 1.9, are often accompanied by detailed explanations of the causes of variance and the likelihood that the subunit will be able to achieve its annual targets.

Besides planning and control, the management accounting information system provides a basis for evaluating and rewarding employees.

EXHIBIT 1.9   MULTINATIONAL COMPANY

Quarterly Performance Report for Western Division

	Year's Budget	2nd Quarter		
		Budget	Actual	Variance
Revenue	$1,000,000	$250,000	$300,000	$ 50,000
Less costs:				
Cost of goods sold	$ 500,000	$125,000	$165,000	$(40,000)
Administrative cost	215,000	53,750	55,000	(1,250)
Selling cost	$ 195,000	48,750	58,000	(9,250)
Total cost	$ 910,000	$227,500	$278,000	$(50,500)
Pretax operating income	$ 90,000	$ 22,500	$ 22,000	$ (500)

CURRENT PRACTICE

Forrest Gump

Stupid is as stupid does? Well, not exactly! The star of the movie *Forrest Gump*, Tom Hanks, and the film's director, Robert Zemeckis, both took a big gamble. Each agreed to give up part of their guaranteed salaries—reportedly $7 million for Hanks and $5 million for Zemeckis. In return, they took part of their compensation in the form of box-office receipts. With so much riding on their performances, Hanks and Zemeckis had every incentive to make the film a success.

The gamble paid off when *Forrest Gump* was nominated for Oscars in 13 categories and had worldwide receipts in excess of $525 million. For their efforts—and the giant gamble they took—Hanks and Zemeckis are each expected to pocket $35 million.

Source: John Lippman, "Star and Director of 'Gump' Took Risk, Reaped Millions," *The Wall Street Journal*, Mar. 7, 1995, pp. B1 and B9.

When managers agree to budgets, the targets included in the budgets can serve as yardsticks for measuring manager and employee accomplishments. If managers and employees achieve specified targets, they may be eligible for bonuses and advancement within the organization. In fact, some organizations have found that linking compensation to performance gives good results. (See "Current Practice: *Forrest Gump*.") Properly used, budgets can motivate actions that further the goals and objectives needed to accomplish the organization's mission.

MANAGEMENT ACCOUNTING IN A DYNAMIC BUSINESS ENVIRONMENT

Management accounting systems must adapt to the changing needs of the managers who rely on the information the system supplies. This is especially true today, as managers are constantly evaluating strategies and operating policies to meet the challenges of changing markets. We turn now to a discussion of how managers adapt to changes and the role played by the management accounting information. We'll also look at the ethical concerns facing managers and how those concerns affect the development of management accounting information.

A CONCEPTUAL MODEL

Changes in the global competitive environment are catalyzing changes in the management accounting system. Assessing and understanding the nature of these changes will be an integral part of this text. Exhibit 1.10

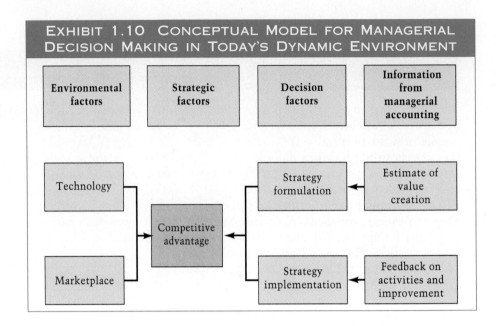

EXHIBIT 1.10 CONCEPTUAL MODEL FOR MANAGERIAL DECISION MAKING IN TODAY'S DYNAMIC ENVIRONMENT

represents an overview of linkages among environmental factors, management strategy, the process by which managers make decisions, and the managerial accounting information managers rely upon.

ENVIRONMENTAL FACTORS

The primary environmental factors transforming business operations today are technology and the changing marketplace. *Technology* involves the systematic application of knowledge. Advancements in process technologies, such as robotics and computer-aided design, have enabled manufacturers to deliver better-quality goods at lower prices, thus opening the door to greater market potential. Process technologies promote manufacturing flexibility, whereby design and production schedules respond quickly to changing market conditions. Flexible manufacturers are not locked into the standardized mass-production processes of the past. Products can be tailor-made, on short notice, to meet the unique demands of consumers within narrow market niches.

At the same time, advances in computers have opened channels of communication. These channels are especially important for global managers who share information on performance and emerging trends—information that can provide a competitive edge. (See "Current Practice: Riding the Data Highway.") Improved communication also creates demand among consumers, who are exposed to products from around the world.

Transformations in the marketplace are another big environmental force. More and more, markets are being fragmented by local tastes. Merchants, recognizing these "minimarkets," strive to identify and satisfy customer needs. Clothes designed for consumers in New York differ from clothes designed for consumers in, say, Rome or Los Angeles. Similarly,

CURRENT PRACTICE

Riding the Data Highway

Schneider National, of Green Bay, Wisconsin, has emerged as America's largest hauler of full-truckload freight. The company's rise from obscurity is built on the effective use of information.

When Procter and Gamble (P&G) advises the company that a truckload of detergent destined for Denver is ready at 3 p.m. in its Cincinnati plant, Schneider's computer lists all of the drivers headed for Cincinnati and their estimated arrival times. Arrival times are updated every 2 hours via a satellite link on each truck. Should driver A4378, who will be free at 1 p.m., pick up the load? The computer says no, because she has been on the road since 2 a.m. and is forced, by law, to take a break. What about driver B3967, who could pick up the load at 2:30 p.m.? Again, the computer says no, because this would mean extra pay for the driver for spending the weekend away from his Georgia home. Instead, driver B3967 is assigned an Atlanta-bound load while the Procter and Gamble freight goes to driver C5569, who is already on his way to Denver through Cincinnati.

The time and place for pickup is sent via satellite so that driver C5569 doesn't have to stop to call in. The computer monitors his speed all the way to Denver, making sure that he doesn't exceed the 55-mile-per-hour limit. This policy is intended to conserve fuel and minimize accidents. Plus, the drivers know that if they speed, they could lose their monthly bonuses. When driver C5569 stops for gas at one of Schneider's company-owned gas and maintenance centers, his fuel consumption is automatically recorded in the computer. This gives Schneider advanced warning of potential mechanical problems.

Schneider posted $1.25 billion in revenue in 1993, nearly double the figure it reported in 1989. While profits are not published, Mr. Schneider says his company's earnings provide enough capital to enable the firm to grow by as much as 20 percent per year.

Source: Marc Levinson, "Riding the Data Highway," *Newsweek,* Mar. 21, 1994, p. 43.

coming up with a single, universally popular automobile design—one that meets the tastes and needs of drivers in Japan, France, and the United States—may be virtually impossible.

Global businesses distribute key activities like product design and manufacturing to geographically dispersed subunits that can quickly respond to local customer needs. And changes in the world's political climate are fostering a freer flow of goods across national borders while creating greater potential in emerging markets like eastern Europe, South America, and southern Asia. However, narrowly focused marketing, specialized manufacturing, and geographically dispersed organizational subunits increase the complexity of operations, thereby creating a strain on the organization. Managers must schedule activities and amass the resources necessary to make a wide array of products in order to meet specific consumer needs.

To effectively deal with complexity and to make correct decisions—those that create value for shareholders—managers need information. Management accounting supplies that information—thereby allowing managers to understand where their opportunities lie and to identify strategies that are likely to take advantage of them.

STRATEGIC FACTORS

Given the uncertainties and changes facing all firms, managers pursue strategies that will generate competitive advantages for their firms, either by being recognized as the low-cost supplier for commodity items, such as Bic pens, or by being perceived by the market as different and better, as with Walt Disney theme parks. It is the manager's job to ensure that these advantages are sustained over the long term.

Meanwhile, a firm's competitors will try to mimic its market strengths and, if successful, will reduce or eliminate them. Consider, for example, the plight of Kmart, whose low-price strategy was improved upon by Wal-Mart, which then took over in the discount retail market as the industry leader. Similarly, Mercedes Benz saw its advantage of product image deteriorate in the United States as Japanese carmakers introduced their own highly successful lines of prestige autos such as Lexus (Toyota), Infiniti (Nissan), and Acura (Honda). A firm enjoying a competitive advantage today—whether because of low cost or better quality—must continually work on developing new competitive advantages for tomorrow. What constitutes today's advantages is likely to be copied and improved upon by the competition. (See "Current Practice: Changing Realities in the Worldwide Steel Industry.")

DECISION FACTORS

There are two steps in creating successful strategies. The first step is *strategy formulation*—deciding which products and services to pursue. This is also referred to as the **planning process.** The second step is *strategy implementation*—searching continually for ways to improve the delivery of products and services. This is also referred to as the **control process.**

Strategy Formulation. Much of the information essential in formulating strategies depends on environmental factors and market demand. Management accounting's job is to gather information about these factors to assist managers in evaluating alternative strategies. Often this means collecting information from such diverse sources—both within and outside the organization—as planning documents, marketing data, engineering designs, production plans, and employee work schedules. Management accounting also helps in measuring the impact—the benefits and costs—that strategies have on shareholder value. For example, management accounting information is useful in the preparation of estimates of revenue and potential cost savings likely to be derived from entering new markets, eliminating unprofitable product lines, adopting new technology, changing organizational structures, or constructing new facilities.

CURRENT PRACTICE

Changing Realities in the Worldwide Steel Industry

A good example of changing technologies and the search for new competitive advantages is illustrated by the steel industry.

Since the industrial revolution, the dominant firms have been, until recently, large companies with huge steel mills. Production was concentrated at a single site, whereby firms gained all the advantages of the scale of operations. First it was U.S. firms like U.S. Steel and Bethlehem that led world markets. Then, in the 1980s, Japanese firms such as Nippon and Kawasaki dominated the steel industry— largely through their investment in newer, more advanced equipment. Now, however, these behemoths are finding it difficult to compete with the efficient production techniques of the minimills. Minimills require far less labor and investment, and they generate much less water and air pollution. The new steel "giants" are smaller firms—for example, Nucor Corporation and Chaparral Steel Company, in the United States. Nucor and Chaparral run 4 of the world's 5 lowest-cost steel plants. Prices offered by these minimill operations can run 30 percent lower than those offered by the big steelmakers.

The downsizing of steel mills is indicative of the changes facing many old, established manufacturing industries. Cost advantage is now shifting to smaller operations that offer faster, more flexible production methods capable of quickly adjusting to fluctuations in demand. Old-style steel plants rely on blast furnaces and cost billions of dollars to build and maintain. They involve multistep processes that take days, if not weeks. The new minimills use electric furnaces that process scrap iron into finished products in minutes. Minimills are so efficient that they require as little as 1 hour of processing time per ton of output versus 5 hours for some of the older operations.

The latest technological advances permit minimills to expand beyond the narrow markets they once served. They have moved beyond their original niche of producing low-quality steel aimed mainly at the building and railway industries. New processes allow minimills to produce as good a quality steel as blast furnaces do, as well as to expand the types of steel they make. In their search for competitive advantage, big steel plants are now being forced to concentrate on specialty products—such as the galvanized sheets of steel used by the automobile industry—where the difference between the selling price and production cost is high. Nonetheless, changes in technology, coupled with the narrowness of steel market niches, have probably doomed forever the traditional big mill approach.

Source: Dana Milbank, "Changing Industry: Big Steel Is Threatened by Low-Cost Rivals, Even in Japan, Korea," *The Wall Street Journal Europe*, Feb. 3, 1993, pp. 1 and 8; "Japan's Steel Makers: Mini-Mills Roll," *The Economist*, Oct. 24, 1992, p. 72.

Consider the example in Exhibit 1.11. Assume managers are trying to decide whether to introduce a new product. An initial investment of $100,000 is needed to develop the product and to acquire new equipment. It is expected to generate sales over its four-year life cycle, with growth in the early years, followed by declining sales at the end of the product's life. After the fourth year, managers expect to withdraw the product from the market.

The initial investment of $100,000 is shown as a cash outflow in year 0—the year the project begins. Cash inflows from the sale of the product range from $50,000 during the first year of operations to a maximum of $120,000 in the third year. Cash outflows for operating costs range from $30,000 during the first year to a peak of $60,000 during the third year. After deducting cash outflows from cash inflows, the difference between them—*net cash flow*—starts at $20,000 in year 1 and reaches a maximum of $60,000 in year 3.

To determine the effect this proposal has on shareholder value, net cash flow in each of the five time periods is multiplied by a rate representing a *discount factor.* The reason for using a discount factor is that a dollar of cash flow in the future is "worth" less than a dollar of cash flow today. For example, $1,000 dollars put in the bank today, assuming bank accounts earn interest at a rate of 12 percent per year, will accumulate to a value of $1,120 at the end of one year. Conversely, $1,120 in cash received one year from now, assuming a rate of 12 percent, has an equivalent value of $1,000 today. We say that managers are "indifferent" to a choice of $1,120 one year from now and its present value equivalent of $1,000 today.

In the present example, assume the firm evaluates this new product proposal at a rate of 12 percent per year. Adding all of the individual discounted cash flows together we obtain the **net present value**, or **NPV**. The NPV is one indication of the value that the investment is expected to cre-

EXHIBIT 1.11 VALUE CREATION MEASURED BY DISCOUNTED CASH FLOW

Introduction of a New Product

		Year			
	0	1	2	3	4
Cash inflow from sale of product		$ 50,000	$ 90,000	$ 120,000	$ 40,000
Cash outflow for operating cost		(30,000)	(50,000)	(60,000)	(20,000)
Cash outflow for initial investment	$(100,000)				
Net cash flow	$(100,000)	$ 20,000	$ 40,000	$ 60,000	$ 20,000
Discount factor @ 12%	1.0000	0.8929	0.7972	0.7118	0.6355
Discounted cash flow	$(100,000)	$ 17,857	$ 31,888	$ 42,707	$ 12,710
Net present value (NPV) (sum of discounted cash flows)	$ 5,162				

ate. The positive net present value of $5,162 is the amount by which the investment is expected to increase shareholder value.

Strategy Implementation.   By resolving the firm's implementation of strategy into its component processes—the major elements of work performed by an organization, such as purchasing, production, and after-sales service—managers are able to understand where their competitive advantage comes from and how to maintain and improve it.

An organization's major processes, when taken together, constitute its value chain. An auto manufacturer's production process may, for example, yield a unit of output in 18 hours. Its two main rivals may require 22 and 25 hours to produce the same unit of output. A competitive advantage clearly lies with the most efficient producer. (See "Current Practice: GM's Labor Cost Disadvantage.")

IMPROVING INTERNAL ACTIVITIES

Many firms find that they perform internal activities that offer no competitive advantage. Sometimes these activities can be acquired at lower cost and better quality from outside vendors. Kodak Corporation, for example, gained attention in the late 1980s when it contracted an outside organization to perform its entire management information activity. Nike and Reebok, two giant shoe merchandisers, found that their competitive advantage was in marketing, not in making shoes. Each, recognizing that neither it nor its rival had a competitive advantage in manufacturing, found Asian companies to make its shoes.

Management accounting is the primary source of information for managers to use in improving operational activities. Exhibit 1.12, for

CURRENT PRACTICE

GM's Labor Cost Disadvantage

General Motors' employment levels place it at a $4 billion per year labor-cost disadvantage relative to Ford. It costs GM about $2,358 in labor cost to make a car, while it costs Ford only $1,563 in labor cost to make the same kind of car—a difference of $795 per car. GM's labor cost is also higher than Chrysler's $1,872 labor cost per car. This puts GM at a disadvantage when competing with Ford and Chrysler.

Ford, with the lowest labor cost of the three U.S. automakers, has about the same labor cost as its Japanese rivals Toyota and Honda. Ford's Kansas City, Missouri, plant, for example, requires about the same number of labor hours to make a car as the Toyota Georgetown, Kentucky, factory.

Source: Joseph B. White, "GM's Labor Cost Disadvantage to Ford Is Placed at $4 Billion a Year by Study," *The Wall Street Journal,* Oct. 6, 1992, p. A2.

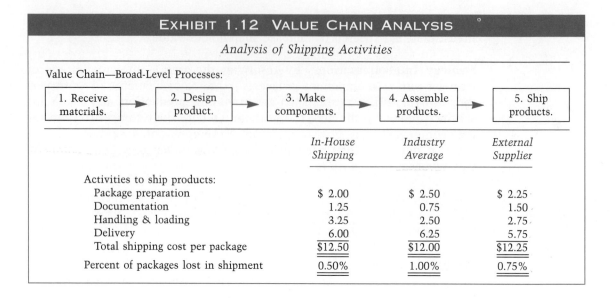

EXHIBIT 1.12 VALUE CHAIN ANALYSIS

Analysis of Shipping Activities

Value Chain—Broad-Level Processes:

| 1. Receive materials. | → | 2. Design product. | → | 3. Make components. | → | 4. Assemble products. | → | 5. Ship products. |

	In-House Shipping	Industry Average	External Supplier
Activities to ship products:			
Package preparation	$ 2.00	$ 2.50	$ 2.25
Documentation	1.25	0.75	1.50
Handling & loading	3.25	2.50	2.75
Delivery	6.00	6.25	5.75
Total shipping cost per package	$12.50	$12.00	$12.25
Percent of packages lost in shipment	0.50%	1.00%	0.75%

example, offers a value chain analysis of a company's shipping activities. Shipping is shown as the last process in the firm's value chain. Assume managers are trying to decide whether or not to continue to use company employees to ship products. The data shown in the bottom half of Exhibit 1.12 were gathered to compare the company's recent shipping cost, which totals $12.50 per package, with an average cost of $12.00 reported by an industry trade group. One option is to discontinue all internal shipping activities and let an outside contractor perform the activities instead. For example, a major national shipper has agreed to charge $12.25 per package if the firm commits to a long-term contract. On the basis of only cost considerations, the company should discontinue internal shipping activities and sign the contract with the national shipping firm.

However, cost may not be the only consideration. Performance data for the number of packages that are lost in transit relative to the total number of packages shipped by company employees reveal that their 0.50 percent rate is better than both the 1.00 percent industry average and the 0.75 percent rate of the outside shipper. If customer satisfaction is important in achieving company objectives, the firm may decide to retain in-house shipping activities. The cost of customer dissatisfaction arising from lost shipments may more than offset the cost saving derived from using an external supplier.

Besides providing data to support decisions, management accounting information produces reports useful in monitoring improvements in various activities. For example, assume the managers discussed above decide to continue shipping as an in-house activity. Management accounting reports might then list shipping cost together with the percentage of lost deliveries. Managers can thus compare the firm's actual percentages of shipments lost with those of the external shipper to track improvement. Furthermore, training sessions for shipping personnel may be initiated so that the employees can understand how to use the reports. Weekly meetings might be held for sharing information on problems and what to do about them.

The ultimate responsibility for problem solving and improvement, however, falls on the shipping employees themselves. They are the ones who are expected to meet and exceed targeted levels of performance. If they don't, the likely result will be the elimination of all in-house shipping activities and the hiring of an external supplier. Sharing information with employees, providing them with training, and holding them responsible for achieving their goals are all part of what's needed for a competitive advantage.

ETHICS, DECISION MAKING, AND MANAGEMENT ACCOUNTING

Management accounting is central to many business decisions that involve ethical considerations. Some decisions, such as whether or not to maintain an in-house shipping department, are purely *analytical*—that is, they are based solely on cost, benefit, and competitive advantage. Other decisions are not so analytical. These decisions involve human behavior—including such characteristics as power and greed. Consider the following examples that illustrate behavior involving ethical issues:

- Physicians who overcharge the government for medical services they never rendered
- Auto manufacturers who permit faulty designs that create the potential for injuries
- Companies who expose their employees to hazardous materials and dangerous working conditions
- Managers who tolerate or condone sexual harassment in the workplace.

Corporations are, increasingly, integrating ethics into the decision-making processes.[1] According to one estimate, 63 percent of Fortune 500 CEOs believe that a strong corporate social ethic results in a strategic advantage. Other surveys report that 30 percent to 44 percent of companies offer ethical training to their employees. The two most-often-cited objectives of ethics training are to develop employee awareness and draw attention to ethical issues to which the employee may be exposed.

One area where managers routinely confront ethical issues is in earnings management. Examples of earnings management include pulling revenue from future periods into the current year either through sales incentives, like cash-back premiums on new cars, or overloading distribution channels with more product than is likely to be demanded by customers in the short term. Another form of earnings management is income smoothing. General Electric, for example, offsets one-time gains from big

---

[1] This paragraph draws from an article by Susan J. Harrington, "What Corporate America Is Teaching About Ethics," *Academy of Management Executive*, Feb. 1991, pp. 21–30.

EXHIBIT 1.13 STANDARDS OF ETHICAL CONDUCT FOR MANAGEMENT ACCOUNTANTS

Management accountants have an obligation to the organizations they serve, their profession, the public, and themselves to maintain the highest standards of ethical conduct. In recognition of this obligation, the Institute of Management Accountants, formerly the National Association of Accountants, has promulgated the following standards of ethical conduct for management accountants. Adherence to these standards is integral to achieving the *Objectives of Management Accounting.*[a] Management accountants shall not commit acts contrary to these standards nor shall they condone the commission of such acts by others within their organizations.

COMPETENCE

Management accountants have a responsibility to:

- Maintain an appropriate level of professional competence by ongoing development of their knowledge and skills.
- Perform their professional duties in accordance with relevant laws, regulations, and technical standards.
- Prepare complete and clear reports and recommendations after appropriate analyses of relevant and reliable information.

CONFIDENTIALITY

Management accountants have a responsibility to:

- Refrain from disclosing confidential information acquired in the course of their work except when authorized, unless legally obligated to do so.

- Inform subordinates as appropriate regarding the confidentiality of information acquired in the course of their work and monitor their activities to assure the maintenance of that confidentiality.
- Refrain from using or appearing to use confidential information acquired in the course of their work for unethical or illegal advantage either personally or through third parties.

INTEGRITY

Management accountants have a responsibility to:

- Avoid actual or apparent conflicts of interest and advise all appropriate parties of any potential conflict.
- Refrain from engaging in any activity that would prejudice their ability to carry out their duties ethically.
- Refuse any gift, favor, or hospitality that would influence or would appear to influence their actions.
- Refrain from either actively or passively subverting the attainment of the organization's legitimate and ethical objectives.
- Recognize and communicate professional limitations or other constraints that would preclude responsible judgment or successful performance of an activity.
- Communicate unfavorable as well as favorable information and professional judgments or opinions.
- Refrain from engaging in or supporting any activity that would discredit the profession.

(continued)

asset sales with restructuring charges. This practice keeps earnings from rising to levels that can't be topped the following year. Another example is the Walt Disney Company, which re-releases classic films like *Snow White* whenever it needs the profits.[2]

A study found that most practicing managers use some form of earnings management.[3] While it may be legal, earnings management may not be ethical. Not all accountants agree, though, that it is unethical. In fact,

---

[2] Randall Smith, Steven Lipin, and Amal Kumar Raj, "How General Electric Damps Fluctuations in Its Annual Earnings," *The Wall Street Journal,* Nov. 3, 1994, pp. A1 and A6.
[3] William J. Bruns and Kenneth A. Merchant, "The Dangerous Morality of Managing Earnings," *Management Accounting,* Aug. 1990, pp. 22–25.

EXHIBIT 1.13 (CONTINUED)

OBJECTIVITY

Management accountants have a responsibility to:

- Communicate information fairly and objectively.
- Disclose fully all relevant information that could reasonably be expected to influence an intended user's understanding of the reports, comments, and recommendations presented.

RESOLUTION OF ETHICAL CONFLICT

In applying the standards of ethical conduct, management accountants may encounter problems in identifying unethical behavior or in resolving an ethical conflict. When faced with significant ethical issues, management accountants should follow the established policies of the organization bearing on the resolution of such conflict. If these policies do not resolve the ethical conflict, management accountants should consider the following course of action:

- Discuss such problems with the immediate superior except when it appears that the superior is involved, in which case the problem should be presented initially to the next higher managerial level. If satisfactory resolution cannot be achieved when the problem is initially presented, submit the issues to the next higher managerial level.

  If the immediate superior is the chief executive officer, or equivalent, the acceptable reviewing authority may be a group such as the audit committee, executive committee, board of directors, board of trustees, or owners. Contact with levels above the immediate superior should be initiated only with the superior's knowledge, assuming the superior is not involved.
- Clarify relevant concepts by confidential discussion with an objective advisor to obtain an understanding of possible courses of action.
- If the ethical conflict still exists after exhausting all levels of internal review, the management accountant may have no other recourse on significant matters than to resign from the organization and to submit an informative memorandum to an appropriate representative of the organization.

Except where legally prescribed, communication of such problems to authorities or individuals not employed or engaged by the organization is not considered appropriate.

Source: Management Accounting, Feb. 1994, p. 22.

[a] Institute of Management Accountants, formerly National Association of Accountants. *Statements on Management Accounting, Standards of Ethical Conduct for Management Accountants*, Statement No. 1C, June 1, 1983.

some accountants believe that earnings management is acceptable as long as it conveys a "fair" picture of the organization's long-term performance. Proponents of earnings management contend that a "smooth" stream of historical earnings may be the best indication of future earnings. Others are not so sure, because "managing" earnings can mislead investors by giving them inaccurate information. According to its opponents, earnings management produces questionable numbers, providing little indication of what the company is actually doing.

In providing information for decisions, management accounting is at the center of many considerations involving ethics. In response to the growing need for ethical standards, the Institute of Management Accountants, a leading organization for practicing and academic management accountants, issued the "Standards of Ethical Conduct for Management Accountants," shown in Exhibit 1.13. The statement defines the management accountant's ethical responsibilities and offers suggestions for resolving conflict. The consequences of ethical decisions must be borne both by the persons responsible for their outcomes and by the organization that created a corporate culture that allowed these actions to occur. We should be aware of the ethics lurking in any business decision and must learn how to include a consideration of ethics in each decision we make as managers.

SUMMARY

Management accounting, a discipline judged by its ability to help managers make better decisions, performs three basic functions:

1. It provides a way of determining what something costs.
2. It provides information to support the evaluation of alternate courses of action.
3. It provides a system that managers use for planning and controlling operations.

Unlike financial accounting, management accounting is not carefully guided by a set of generally accepted accounting principles that define how these functions must be accomplished. Instead, the information provided depends on the particular objectives of a firm's managers within the context of the organization and its operating environment. Ultimately, the particular information that management accounting will produce is determined by the nature of the data that managers need in order to create long-term value for the firm's shareholders.

Creating shareholder value begins with the expression of the organization's mission, the broad statement that identifies the firm's customers and the markets it expects to serve. Corporate mission statements are translated into goals, which are open-ended assertions of the organization's purpose, and objectives, which express in quantitative terms what the organization expects to accomplish and when it expects to accomplish it. Strategies represent the firm's game plan for how it will accomplish its objectives.

Through decision-support models, managers can determine which of their actions are likely to have the greatest potential for creating value. Once managers decide which actions they will pursue, budgets are prepared that express, in quantitative terms, what the organization and its subunits expect to accomplish in the current time period. As plans are set in motion, management accounting feedback helps managers monitor the firm's effectiveness and improve its operating activities. Feedback, the product of comparing actual results with plans, is important because managers must constantly revise their plans and search for more-productive operating methods in order to remain competitive.

The actual techniques and methods of management accounting are changing to meet the challenges of an increasingly competitive global market. The world's markets are largely driven by advancements in technology; thus, managers must develop and capitalize on their own particular competitive advantages if they are to survive in this arena. Information generated by a firm's management accounting system helps both in formulating and implementing the strategies that are necessary to compete in the global marketplace.

A business decision will be the right one only if, when carried out by those responsible for the actions, it furthers the long-term objectives of the organization. The people who are expected to help the organization achieve its objectives must have information to help them understand which actions are desirable. Furthermore, even if these individuals have the right information, they must be properly motivated if they are to choose the correct action. Finally, ethics should be an integral part of each action that managers take.

CHAPTER 1 ASSIGNMENTS

DISCUSSION PROBLEMS

D1.1 (Elements of Full Cost)

Blockbuster, well-known for video rentals, is moving into the audio business. The company recently announced plans with IBM to form a new kind of retail system to market audio CDs. The system could revolutionize marketing in the music industry.

The unique feature of the new system is that the disks are created on demand. Music stores will press CDs, on the spot, in several minutes. Besides giving consumers exactly what they want, when they want it, the plan saves costs. Blockbuster can now make the CDs one at a time, instead of making literally millions of copies of a recording and shipping them to its stores. Plus, the new system will cut down on lost sales from "stockouts." Customers may even be able to mix different artists on the same CD.[4]

The deal with IBM is in keeping with Blockbuster's philosophy, wherein technology is considered an ally. Blockbuster intends to continue devoting significant resources to entertainment-based technologies in order to carry out the company's commitment to being ". . . on the leading edge of the entertainment business."[5]

Required: Make a list of some of the elements of the full cost to Blockbuster of distributing a CD through the proposed marketing system.

D1.2 (Information for Decision Support)

Rolando Suarez owns a sandwich shop on Seventh Avenue in New York City called the Q-Ban Sandwich Shop. He specializes in only one item—a "Cuban sandwich" made with a crusty roll, cold cuts, and cheese. He puts a little mustard on the bread and then drizzles olive oil over the top of the sandwich. Finally, he heats the sandwich by pressing it between two hot plates in what looks like a waffle iron. After wrapping it in wax paper, Rolando sells the sandwich for $2.49.

The cost of making the sandwiches is shown in Exhibit D1.2. Rolando organizes cost into food cost (shown at the top of Exhibit D1.2) and operating cost (shown at the bottom of the exhibit). The two are separated by a subtotal Rolando

---

[4] Associated Press, "Blockbuster, IBM Form Innovative Team," *The Orlando Sentinel*, May 12, 1993, p. D1.
[5] Blockbuster Entertainment, *1992 Annual Report*, p. 5.

EXHIBIT D1.2   Q-BAN SANDWICH SHOP

Operating Profit at Different Volumes

Revenue:			
Sandwiches per year	40,000	50,000	60,000
Menu price	$2.49	$2.49	$2.49
Total revenue	$99,600	$124,500	$149,400
Food cost:			
Cold cuts	$0.45	$0.45	$0.45
Bread	0.18	0.18	0.18
Cheese	0.05	0.05	0.05
Mustard & olive oil	0.03	0.03	0.03
Lettuce, tomato & onions	0.07	0.07	0.07
Wrapping materials	0.02	0.02	0.02
Food cost per sandwich	$0.80	$0.80	$0.80
Sandwiches per year	40,000	50,000	60,000
Total food cost	$32,000	$ 40,000	$ 48,000
Excess of revenue over food cost	$67,600	$ 84,500	$101,400
Operating cost:			
Wages & benefits	$50,000	$ 50,000	$ 50,000
Rent	9,600	9,600	9,600
Utilities & security	2,400	2,400	2,400
Depreciation	12,000	12,000	12,000
Accounting & legal	2,000	2,000	2,000
Total operating cost	$76,000	$ 76,000	$ 76,000
Operating income	$ (8,400)	$ 8,500	$ 25,400

calls the "excess" or, more formally, the excess of revenue over food cost. Rolando measures volume in terms of the number of sandwiches he sells.

Required:

1. Are food costs variable or fixed? That is, do food costs increase and decrease with the number of sandwiches he sells or do they remain constant?
2. Are the operating costs variable or fixed? (They are expressed as totals rather than on a per-unit basis.) If Rolando were to divide the operating costs by the number of sandwiches, what would happen as more sandwiches were made?

D1.3   (Information for Decision Support)

Banner Airlines offers service between several midwestern cities. The airline doesn't own the three planes it flies nor does it operate maintenance facilities. Instead, Banner's planes are leased, and all maintenance work is performed by another airline. One of the company's primary routes provides nonstop jet service between Memphis and Topeka. The plane assigned to the route has a capacity of 200, but generally flies only 70 percent booked. The costs of operating the flight at 70 percent capacity are shown in Exhibit D1.3.

A small manufacturing company with offices in Memphis and Topeka uses one of the larger national airlines to fly four or five of its officials back and forth

EXHIBIT D1.3 BANNER AIRLINES

Flight Costs from Memphis to Topeka

Cost Component	Average Cost per Flight
Crew salaries & benefits	$ 3,250
Fuel cost	1,800
Meals & catering	1,680
Cleaning	275
Lease—plane	3,200
Maintenance	450
Gate & landing fees	225
Travel agent commissions	1,050
Ground crew	640
General & administrative	3,180
Total cost	$15,750
Number of passengers @ 70% load factor	140
Average cost per passenger	$112.50

between the two cities. However, because the plane makes an intermediate stop in Kansas City, service is slow.

The manufacturing company recently contacted Banner with a proposal. If Banner would lower its normal $125 price to $80, the company would guarantee five seats on every flight.

Required:

1. Which of the line-item costs are relevant in Banner's decision? Remember, relevant costs are those that change as a result of the decision. Therefore, the question is: Which line-item costs are likely to increase with five more passengers on the plane?
2. Assume that the total line-item cost that changes in requirement 1 is less than $400 ($80 times 5). Should Banner accept the manufacturing company's proposal? What are some of the qualitative measures of cost and benefit for the decision? How might the decision impact Banner's long-term goals?

D1.4 (Cost Information for Process Improvement)[6]

Switchgear Safety Design Inc. (SSDI) manufactures fire suppression devices that are a part of the switches that go into large power transformers. When an SSDI device senses an electrical fault, it shuts the transformer down. This greatly enhances safety, not to mention minimizing the cost of replacing burned-out transformers.

SSDI makes fire suppression devices two ways. Some models are made for stock based on standard designs. The others are custom designs based on the specialized needs of customers. Using computer software, custom designs can take as

---

[6] Adapted from John A. Chalker and Kim Bramer, "Speeding Up the Price Quote System," *Management Accounting*, Sept. 1993, pp. 45–49.

long as three months to complete. Because of the resources going into custom designs, SSDI cannot rely on price lists for these items. Instead, the company prepares individual price quotes based on the particular requirements for each device.

The amount of time it takes to prepare quotes has never been much of a concern—that is, until recently. After several customers complained, SSDI commissioned a study that compared the time it takes them to prepare a quote as compared with other firms in the industry. The results were alarming. Several of SSDI's competitors took less than three weeks to design and build custom devices.

SSDI put together a cross-functional team to look at the situation. The first task was to identify the problems. Some of the problems the team uncovered are listed below.

- Forms are filled out inaccurately or incorrectly.
- Single sources of information stop the system if key employees are absent.
- Process is not well-defined.
- Each department assigns its own priorities.
- Employees sometimes circumvent the system.
- Customer needs are not well-defined.
- Actual response time is not measured.
- There is no feedback when the system fails.
- Not everyone involved in the process is properly trained.

Next, the team looked for the fundamental, "root causes" of the problems. One technique they used is based on asking questions. For example:

- *Question:* Why is only one person capable of providing critical information?
  Answer: The task is assigned to only one person.
- *Question:* Why aren't more people assigned?
  Answer: Only one person has the experience to perform this job.
- *Question:* Why can't others be trained?
  Answer: Everyone else is busy.
- *Question:* Why can't training time be created by shifting work assignments?
  Answer: We have never done it before.

The team began flowcharting the entire price-quoting process. Two distinct cases emerged. The first case involved special pricing for devices that had been worked on before. The general opinion was that these quotes represent about 80 to 90 percent of the total. The sales department generally responds to these orders in less than a week. Everyone on the team felt satisfied with this part of the system. The second case generated much more diversity of opinion. It involved both internal and external quotes for devices SSDI had never worked on before. The volume of "second-case" quotes was quite low, only about two per day. The problem, though, was not the volume but the employees' frustration in dealing with incomplete or inaccurate information, confirming and reconfirming data, and finding the critical person needed to make key decisions.

After studying the problem, the team began to reach a consensus on a solution. The team members started looking at the process as a possible impediment to customer satisfaction. This examination was a necessary step if improvements were to be made. The proposed remedies included:

- Classify the second-case quotes as internal or external.
- Assign priority to external quotes.
- Revise price quote form.
- Get technical departments to review quote for capability and specifications.
- Improve training.

- Use a routing slip to help move quote through departments.
- Initiate a monthly report to summarize quote-processing time in each department.
- Use a form for sales personnel to submit when response time creates a problem.

Each of these recommendations was implemented within three months. Newly created reports showed processing time declining rapidly. Moreover, the forms prepared by sales personnel indicated fewer customer complaints.

Required:

1. What was the goal of the changes initiated by SSDI?
2. How can management accounting help in making changes needed to achieve this goal?

D1.5 (Information for Planning and Control)[7]

Kmart's overhead—what it spends on things like payroll, benefits, utilities, administration, depreciation, and other operating costs—is higher than Wal-Mart's. Analysts estimate that Kmart spends about 22.5 percent of each dollar of revenue on overhead while Wal-Mart spends only about 17.5 percent. This gives Wal-Mart a giant competitive edge by allowing it to offer lower prices.

Two other statistics help to pinpoint Wal-Mart's competitive advantage. The first is Wal-Mart's inventory *turns*, the number of times inventory turns over during the year. Wal-Mart data show about 4.5 turns in 1992 while Kmart data show only about 3.0. The second statistic is sales per square foot. Wal-Mart sells about $283 of merchandise per square foot. Kmart sells only $143.

Kmart points out that the comparison isn't exactly fair. The company's way of doing business evolved in the 1970s, when controlling costs was not as important as it is today. In direct contrast, Wal-Mart expanded in the 1980s, when being a low-cost merchandiser was commonly accepted. Wal-Mart's focus was on cost control from the very beginning.

In the end, the reasons for the differences between Wal-Mart and Kmart don't matter. What does count is the ability to offer low prices. To remain competitive, Kmart is going to have to become more efficient. Unfortunately, it is finding that it's easier to add costs than to get rid of them. To catch up, Kmart must spend more than Wal-Mart on capital expenditures to upgrade stores. But Kmart spent only 4.0 percent of 1992 sales revenue on capital investments while Wal-Mart spent 7.0 percent.

Required: How can Kmart change its way of doing business and drive down overhead cost so that it can be more competitive with Wal-Mart?

D1.6 (Setting Strategies)

Wendy's International, Inc., of Dublin, Ohio, operates the well-known Wendy's restaurants. With yearly sales averaging around $1.1 million per store, and stores costing about $950,000 to build, Wendy's restaurants generally do quite well. The company's success, in part, is built on creating an image of quality. Wendy's even

---

[7] Adapted from Stephanie Strom, "Kmart's Stock Surge Masks a Weakness at the Core," *The New York Times*, Oct. 10, 1993, Section 3, p. 5.

EXHIBIT D1.6.1 WENDY'S STRATEGIES

Building on a Highly Valued Brand

Today Wendy's stands as a highly valued brand among consumers—from a competitive standpoint, an enviable position. Our job is to first, protect that position and second, use it as a foundation for building customer and shareholder value. That's why it's emphasized in this year's report theme "Building on a Highly Valued Brand."

We have four very clear visions or major objectives. They are to be:

- The restaurant of choice for our customers
- A healthy, aggressively growing system
- The franchisor of choice for current and potential franchisees
- The employer of choice for our employees

Our ability to achieve these visions will depend on how successfully we maintain our momentum and execute our business strategies. We have worked hard to ensure that every employee understands those strategies. A consistent, focused approach to the business has brought a strong understanding of who we are and where we're going to all Wendy's people.

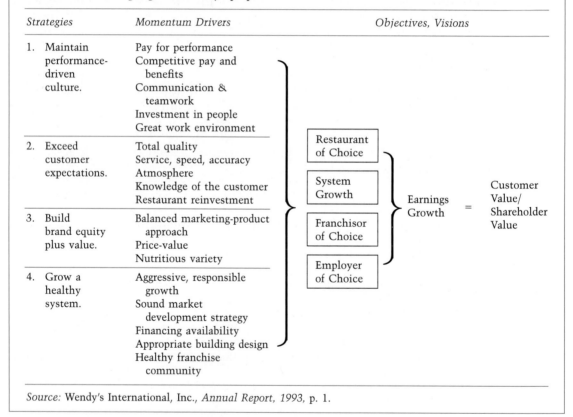

Strategies	*Momentum Drivers*	*Objectives, Visions*
1. Maintain performance-driven culture.	Pay for performance Competitive pay and benefits Communication & teamwork Investment in people Great work environment	
2. Exceed customer expectations.	Total quality Service, speed, accuracy Atmosphere Knowledge of the customer Restaurant reinvestment	Restaurant of Choice System Growth Franchisor of Choice Employer of Choice → Earnings Growth = Customer Value/Shareholder Value
3. Build brand equity plus value.	Balanced marketing-product approach Price-value Nutritious variety	
4. Grow a healthy system.	Aggressive, responsible growth Sound market development strategy Financing availability Appropriate building design Healthy franchise community	

Source: Wendy's International, Inc., *Annual Report, 1993*, p. 1.

refers to itself as a "quick-service" chain rather than a fast-food chain in order to drive home the quality difference. Wendy's overall satisfaction rating, according to the company's own surveys, is one of the highest in the industry.

Wendy's strategies are outlined in its *1993 Annual Report*, reproduced, in part, in Exhibit D1.6.1. One component of Wendy's strategy is based on building

EXHIBIT D1.6.2 THE POWER OF BRAND EQUITY

The Power of Brand Equity

By Roger D. Blackwell

There are many numbers in an annual report which attempt to describe a company's assets and shareholder equity. But one of the numbers you don't find is a number that may be a company's biggest asset—its brand equity.

Although not always apparent, the most important assets of a firm are intangible. These assets may include brands, symbols, slogans, training manuals, processes, people skills and other items which define the company and its position in the minds of consumers. Few, if any, of these show up on a firm's balance sheet, but when the asset value of these items exceeds the cost of developing them, a firm has valuable brand equity. Brand equity involves brand loyalty, brand awareness, perceived quality, brand associations and other brand assets.

Brand equity gives value to customers. This value is achieved by helping customers process information about the marketplace and gain confidence in their purchase decisions. Ultimately, brand equity enhances consumer satisfaction when using the product.

Brand equity gives value to the firm by increasing the effectiveness of marketing programs. The components of brand equity allow a firm to develop a competitive advantage over other firms. Ultimately, that leads to higher price earnings ratios and enhanced shareholder value, achieved because of the brand loyalty of customers.

Roger D. Blackwell is Professor of Marketing and Consumer Behavior at The Ohio State University. Known worldwide, he has written over 50 articles and 22 books on strategy and marketing including From Mind to Market, HarperCollins, *to be released in 1997, and* Consumer Behavior, *the most widely adopted textbook in the field.*

Source: Wendy's International, Inc., *Annual Report, 1993,* p. 7.

brand equity. Wendy's concept of brand equity is exemplified by the quote from Professor Roger D. Blackwell, shown in Exhibit D1.6.2.

Required:

1. What is Wendy's competitive advantage in the crowded fast-food market?
2. How does the management accounting system allow the broad strategies identified in the accompanying exhibits to be implemented?

D1.7 (Ethical Behavior)[8]

Do the securities markets place higher values on companies who demonstrate stable long-term growth? If the answer is yes, then it is reasonable to assume that some company officials may try to "manage" earnings by smoothing out periodic ups and downs. The incentive is even stronger if compensation is tied to market value through stock options.

Managing earnings consists of making decisions that maximize current earnings but are not necessarily good for the organization over the long term. In general, managing earnings means pushing costs forward and pulling sales from the future when the company appears headed for a bad year. Just the opposite happens

---

[8]   Based on an article by Kenneth Rosenzweig and Marilyn Fischer, "Is Managing Earnings Ethically Acceptable?" *Management Accounting,* Mar. 1994, pp. 31–34. The questionnaire used is a follow-up and extension of research conducted by William J. Bruns and Kenneth A. Merchant, "The Dangerous Morality," loc. cit.

in good years. An example might be an airline that decides to pump up current earnings by selling its international routes. The airline may show terrific short-term performance. But over the long haul, how will this impact its ability to generate cash flow? Another example is a cigarette manufacturer that decides to increase production at the end of a poor year. The increased volume of cigarettes is pushed off on distributors who, in turn, push the cigarettes off on retailers. The short-term impact is an improved bottom line. However, next year's income is reduced—perhaps even beyond the gains of the current year—because of returned cigarettes and increased inventory carrying costs.

Required: Is earnings management ethical? To find out your attitudes on the ethics of managing earnings, please respond to each of the 13 situations shown in Exhibit D1.7. Be sure to follow the directions shown at the top of the exhibit.

CASES

C1.1 (Carlito Brothers Farm)[9]

Benito and Luis Carlito own and operate the 5,000-acre Carlito Brothers Farm north of Sacramento, California. They grow almonds, walnuts, and plums. The brothers have been successful because of the businesslike way they manage their operations.

One thing the brothers do well is planning. The first big decision they face each year is whether or not to expand their land holdings. Then, they have to decide what kind of trees to plant. It usually takes about three to five years after planting before trees are productive. So the brothers have to decide where they are going to get the cash to pay for the trees, not to mention planting and caring for them until they reach maturity. Mature almond and plum trees yield crops for 20 to 25 years, while walnut trees are good for up to 60 years.

The Carlito Brothers Farm collects information by field. Each of its 25 fields is treated as a separate entity for both farming and accounting purposes. The fields are, in essence, treated as 25 small businesses. The fields all differ in size, soil composition, frost and flood exposure, and type of trees planted. The costs of operation, ranging from farm labor to interest on loans, are all assigned to individual fields. Revenues are also traced back to fields during harvesting.

The Production Process

The Carlitos employ two production managers. Under them are six supervisors, each of whom is responsible for managing a specific activity. Two supervisors manage each of the following activities: culture, harvest, and machine shop. Culture supervisors are responsible for activities ranging from land preparation to planting. However, their duties stop short of harvesting. Some of the culture activities are shown in Exhibit C1.1.1. The two culture supervisors are charged with growing trees at as low a cost as possible. However, low cost has to be balanced against effectiveness. Effectiveness means getting the most out of the trees—the largest possible quantity with the best possible quality.

Harvest activities differ from culture activities in several ways. First, harvesting is not year-round. It requires intense planning to keep labor cost at a minimum, to use limited farming equipment as efficiently as possible, and to get the crops to market in the best condition and as quickly as possible. Harvesting, unlike the culture activities, is not subject to weather and soil conditions.

---

[9]   Adapted from the description of the Peterson Ranch in Donald Keller and Paul Krause, "World Class Down on the Farm," *Management Accounting*, May 1990, pp. 39–45.

EXHIBIT D1.7 EARNINGS MANAGEMENT QUESTIONS

Directions: Assume you are the supervisor of the general manager (GM) of a division. For each of the thirteen questions below, decide whether, as the supervisor, you think the GM's actions are *clearly ethical* (E), involve *questionable ethics* (Q), or are *clearly unethical* (U). For example, if you believe that the GM's orders to defer discretionary expenses to the next accounting period are clearly ethical, then assign the letter E.

1. The division's headquarters building was scheduled to be painted in 1992. But since profit performance was way ahead of budget in 1991, the GM decided to have the work done in 1991. Amount: $150,000.

This information applies to the following two questions. The GM ordered division employees to defer all discretionary expenditures (e.g., postpone employee travel, advertising, hiring, maintenance) into the next accounting period so the division could make its budgeted profit targets. Expected amount of deferrals: $150,000.

2. The expenditures were postponed from February and March until April in order to make the first-quarter target.
3. The expenditures were postponed from November and December until January of next year in order to make the annual target.
4. On December 15, a clerk ordered $3,000 of office supplies, and the supplies were delivered on December 29. This order was a mistake because the GM had ordered that no discretionary expenses be incurred for the remainder of the fiscal year, and the supplies were not urgently needed. The company's accounting policy manual states that office supplies are to be recorded as an expense when delivered. The GM learned what had happened and, to correct the mistake, asked the accounting department not to record the invoice until February.

This information applies to the following three questions. In September, the GM realized the division would need strong performance in the fourth quarter to reach its budget targets.

5. The GM decided to implement a sales program offering liberal payment terms to pull some sales that normally would occur next year into the current year; customers accepting delivery in the fourth quarter would not have to pay the invoice for 120 days.
6. The GM ordered manufacturing to work overtime in December so that everything possible could be shipped by the end of the year.
7. The GM sold some excess assets and realized a profit of $40,000.

This information applies to the following two questions. At the beginning of December 1991, the GM realized the division would exceed its budgeted profit targets for the year:

8. The GM ordered the division controller to prepay some expenses (e.g., hotel rooms, exhibit expense) for a major trade show to be held in March 1992 and to book them as 1991 expenses. Amount: $60,000.
9. The GM ordered the division controller to write down the inventory due to obsolescence (i.e., reduce its asset value and record a corresponding loss in the income statement). By taking a pessimistic view of future market prospects, the controller was able to identify $700,000 worth of finished goods that conservative accounting would say should be written off even though the GM was fairly confident the inventory would still be sold at a later date at close to full price.

This information applies to the following two questions. The next year, the division sold 70% of the written-off inventory, and a customer had indicated some interest in buying the rest of that inventory the following year. The GM ordered the division controller to write the inventory back up to full cost. This would involve a $210,000 increase in the inventory asset value (which had been previously written down due to obsolescence) and a corresponding increase in net income. The GM's motivation for recapturing the profit was:

10. To be able to continue working on some important product development projects that might have been delayed due to budget constraints.
11. To make budgeted profit targets.

This information applies to the following two questions. In November 1991, the division was straining to meet budget. The GM called the consulting firm that was doing some work for the division and asked that the firm not send an invoice until next year. The firm agreed. Estimated work done but not invoiced:

12. $30,000
13. $500,000

Source: Kenneth Rosenzweig and Marilyn Fischer, "Is Managing Earnings Ethically Acceptable?" *Management Accounting*, Mar. 1994, p. 34.

EXHIBIT C1.1.1 CARLITO BROTHERS FARM

Culture Cost Activities

Planting
Pruning, grafting
Frost and flood control
Pollination
Fertilization
Insect and disease control
Irrigation
Ground preparation
Ranch supervision

The last two supervisors are responsible for shop operations. Shop duties involve primarily maintaining and operating all of the equipment used in the different phases of the farming. Equipment is scheduled for use in specific fields. Downtime has to be planned for preventive maintenance. The shop supervisors are also responsible for planning acquisition of new equipment and justifying the purchase to the Carlito brothers.

Product Mix
As noted earlier, Benito and Luis Carlito make decisions about the mix of trees. For example, the farm grows seven varieties of almond trees, each with different characteristics like maturity, soil requirements, pollination, and nut size. The mix of trees has to balance a number of different factors. For example, some trees mature faster than other varieties do but produce for fewer years. Some are hardier, less subject to freezes and insects. And each tree costs a different amount to establish and maintain. Furthermore, the Carlitos have to consider what the demand is likely to be many years down the road, not to mention guessing at what their competitors are likely to do. About 10 years ago they recognized that U.S. demographics showed that the population was growing older, so they decided to plant more plums that are processed as prunes. Today, that decision has really paid off.

Information Needs
In organizing costs by field, the Carlito brothers feel they have the information they need to manage their business. To get costs by field, they first collect costs by the three major activities: culture, harvest, and machine shop. These costs are then assigned to fields, as illustrated in Exhibit C1.1.2. For example, the shop figures that the cost of maintaining and operating a tractor is $54,000 per year. This includes depreciation, fuel, operator wages, and maintenance. Based on historical averages, the tractor is in use about 2,500 hours per year. Therefore, the tractor is charged out to fields at a rate of $21.60 per hour.

The Carlito Brothers Farm's information system generates reports in three broad areas. Field reports give the breakdown, by field, of revenues, costs, and crop quantities. Operations reports give information on production and cash flow while providing the basis for budgeting on a per-field basis. In addition, the system provides information for strategic planning—for instance, showing the history of equipment purchases, production mix, and product sales.

Required: Management accounting has three broad functions—determining what something costs, providing information to support decisions, and planning and control.

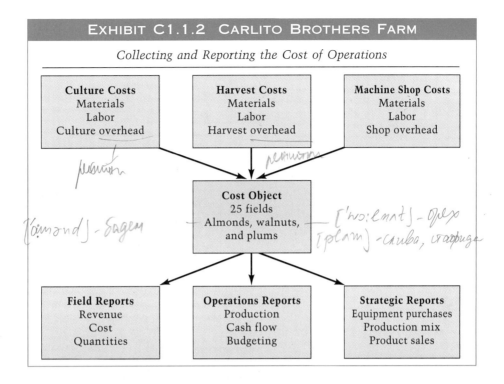

EXHIBIT C1.1.2 CARLITO BROTHERS FARM

Collecting and Reporting the Cost of Operations

1. Give some examples of how the Carlito Brothers Farm's information system provides data for product cost.
2. Give examples of how the Carlito Brothers Farm's information system provides data to support decisions.
3. Give examples of how the Carlito Brothers Farm's information system helps in planning and control.

C1.2 (Browning Copiers, Inc.)

Browning Copiers, Inc., is organized into three autonomous divisions—office software, photocopier, and service (Exhibit C1.2.1). The focus of this case is the interaction between the photocopier and service divisions. The photocopier division concentrates on manufacturing and selling copiers. The service division assumes all responsibility for after-sales customer service. This relationship has worked well in the past, and Browning Copiers has built a strong reputation for product dependability and for prompt and reliable service. Research has shown that the company's service network differentiates Browning Copiers from its competitors in this crowded market.

Nature of the Sales-Service Arrangement

The marketing department of the photocopier division develops and implements the divisional sales strategy. An important selling point is the inexpensive lifetime-warranty coverage available to customers. Copiers are sold with a full one-year warranty against all failures and defects. When the original warranty expires, customers are given the option to buy, at a reduced price, a one-year extension of the full-coverage warranty. The warranty extensions can be renewed at the same reduced price by the original owner for the entire life of the copier.

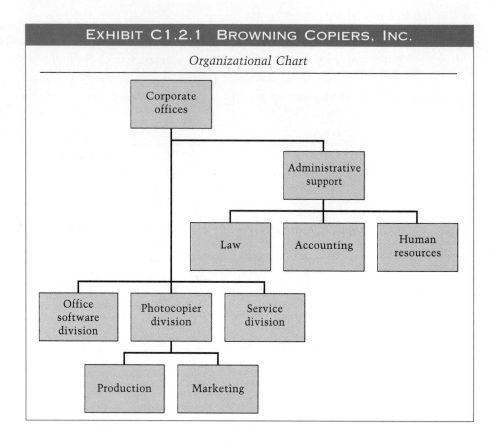

EXHIBIT C1.2.1 BROWNING COPIERS, INC.

Organizational Chart

When a copier is sold, the photocopier division pays the service division for the first year of warranty coverage. The service division assumes all responsibility for maintaining photocopiers once they have been delivered to customers. Subsequent to the first year, the service division will sell the customer a warranty extension at the price specified in the original copier purchase contract. The profitability of warranty extensions is solely the responsibility of the service division, which is credited with the sale of extension warranties and is charged for all costs of service maintenance and repair.

This sales-service arrangement has been very successful in the past and is considered a key success factor in explaining the company's high percentage of return buyers. More recently, however, problems are beginning to surface, with customers complaining that they are not receiving prompt responses to their service calls. Whereas, in the past, service calls were always answered the same day—and often within 1 or 2 hours—customers are now having to wait until the next day, or even longer.

The problem stems from the new emphasis put on the service division's need to generate additional revenues through the sale of generic maintenance-service contracts on all photocopiers, whether made by Browning or not. This has become a highly lucrative source of new revenue for the service division, but has caused a backlog of service requests for Browning Copier owners—who typically experience the greatest delays. The issue has been brought to the attention of the corporate-level senior managers, who believe that any threat to the company's service reputation will undermine future copier sales.

Examining the Effects of One Sales Transaction

To demonstrate how management accounting reports affect manager actions, the following example portrays the sale and warranty arrangements on one model, a Desk-Max copier.

Financial Results for Servicing a Desk-Max Copier

As shown in Exhibit C1.2.2, this sale generates revenue of $21,000 and profit of $10,250 for the photocopier division. The cost of the photocopier includes all costs needed to make the product—even those, like building rent, that cannot be directly traced to any one product. Thus, the $10,000 cost to manufacture the copier (cost of goods sold) includes charges for direct materials ($5,000) and direct labor ($1,000), both of which can be traced to the product. Also included are charges for factory overhead ($4,000)—which represent an assignment of manufacturing costs, such as depreciation, rent, and power. Besides the cost of the product, the photocopier division receives an additional charge of $750 to cover the cost of the manufacturer's one-year warranty.

Exhibit C1.2.3 presents the projected effects of this sale on the service division. The $750 warranty charge to the photocopier division is credited as revenue to the service division for providing first-year warranty coverage. Based on an estimate of 15 service calls during the first year, it is expected that the cost of service delivery will total $375, which includes labor and normal maintenance supplies, like toner and oil. An additional $50 is allowed for replacement parts needed as the result of defect or excessive wear. The projected gross profit earned by the service division for the first year is $325.

Virtually all customers purchase the extended full-coverage warranty, which is priced according to the original sales contract at $900 per year—25 percent below market price. The average life for the Desk-Max is four years; customers thus purchase three years of additional warranty. As seen in the columns for years 2 through 4 in Exhibit C1.2.3, the service division will profit in each of the successive three contract years. Gross profit is expected to be $325 in year 2 but will deteriorate thereafter, falling to $300 in year 3 and $150 in year 4. These reduced profits can be explained by an increase in the number of service-hours and replacement parts needed in later years. Nonetheless, total gross profit over the four-year

---

EXHIBIT C1.2.2 BROWNING COPIERS, INC.

Financial Results from Sale of a New Desk-Max Photocopier

Sales revenue		$21,000
Cost of production:		
Direct materials	$5,000	
Direct labor	1,000	
Overhead	4,000	
Total cost of goods sold		10,000
Gross profit		$11,000
Less warranty cost (one-year coverage)		750
Profit from sale after cost of warranty		$10,250

Note: Warranty cost = 15 hours of service × $50 cost per hour paid to the service division.

EXHIBIT C1.2.3 BROWNING COPIERS, INC.

Projected Financial Results for Servicing a Browning Desk-Max Photocopier

	Year 1 Original Warranty	Year 2	Year 3	Year 4	Total
		Optional Extended Warranty			
Expected service-hours per year	15	20	20	25	80
Revenue	$750	$900	$900	$900	$3,450
Less expenses:					
Cost of service delivery	$375	$500	$500	$625	$2,000
Average replacement parts cost	50	75	100	125	350
Total cost	$425	$575	$600	$750	$2,350
Gross profit	$325	$325	$300	$150	$1,100
Average profit per service-hour					$13.75

EXHIBIT C1.2.4 BROWNING COPIERS, INC.

Projected Financial Results from Sale of a Generic One-Year Maintenance Contract

	Year				
	1	2	3	4	Total
Expected service-hours per year	20	20	25	30	95
Revenue per contract	$1,200	$1,200	$1,200	$1,200	$4,800
Less expenses:					
Cost of service delivery	$500	$500	$625	$750	$2,375
Average replacement parts cost	125	125	150	200	600
Total cost	$625	$625	$775	$950	$2,975
Gross profit	$575	$575	$425	$250	$1,825
Average profit per service-hour					$19.21

period is expected to be $1,100, which averages to $13.75 gross profit for each of the 80 service-hours worked.

Financial Results for Servicing a Copier Under a Generic Contract
Exhibit C1.2.4 presents data on the generic, 1-year maintenance contracts sold by the service division. These contracts are extended warranties and are available for most copiers on the market. They begin at the end of the original manufacturer's 1-year warranty period and can be renewed yearly for up to 3 additional years at $1,200 per year. The exhibit reports the results of a maximum-length contract, which shows the expected number of service hours beginning at 20 hours in year 1 and increasing to 30 hours by year 4. After allowing for the cost of service delivery and for the cost of replacement parts, the service division expects to generate gross profits of $575 in years 1 and 2. As the cost of maintenance increases with

the photocopier's age, profits are expected to fall in years 3 and 4 to $425 and $250, respectively. Still, the total four-year gross profit of $1,825, or $19.21 per hour, far exceeds the $1,100 gross profit, or $13.75 per hour, earned over the same period for servicing one of the company's own Desk-Max copiers.

The difference between the financial results shown in Exhibits C1.2.3 and C1.2.4 is at the heart of Browning's service problems. Division managers are evaluated on the profits they generate, and the manager of the service division is trying to maximize divisional profits. Since more can be earned by selling generic maintenance contracts, the service division manager gives first priority to fulfilling maintenance orders under generic contracts. However, the success of the service division is beginning to erode the repeat-customer base of the photocopier division and is thus threatening to undermine Browning Copiers' primary business activity, its photocopier sales.

Required:

1. The total cost of goods sold for a Desk-Max photocopier includes an overhead charge of $4,000 (see Exhibit C1.2.2). Included in this cost are charges for items like depreciation, rent, and power. However, excluded are selling and administrative charges, such as marketing. Explain this apparent discrepancy.
2. Do you think managers should be evaluated based on divisional profit? Can division managers be expected to think first of the long-term best interests of the corporate entity? Or do you think they will seek only to maximize performance outcomes that increase individual rewards?
3. Assume that senior corporate management is considering adopting one of the following three methods to motivate more goal-congruent actions between the sales and service functions. Choose the method you think will be most effective for achieving long-term corporate goals. Be ready to defend your answer.
   a. Merge the photocopier and service divisions into one combined division that will handle both sales and service functions.
   b. Keep the two divisions as separate entities but evaluate managers on measures besides profit—like customer satisfaction or productivity.
   c. Keep the two divisions separate but base only 50 percent of manager rewards on divisional profit. Base the other 50 percent on the profitability of Browning Copiers, Inc.

CHAPTER 2

COST BEHAVIOR AND PROFITS

The U.S. automobile industry reported record losses in 1992. The cause was foreign competition, afflicting virtually every industry. The U.S. auto industry eventually rebounded, but not without fundamentally changing the way it does business. Rather than maintain costly facilities capable of making more products than can be sold, many companies are deciding to restructure their operations. Anticipating shrinking market share and increased competition, some managers are downsizing capacity. Other managers shorten product-planning cycles and redesign their manufacturing processes to get products out the door more quickly.

Restructuring operations and redesigning production facilities have long-term implications for executing strategies. There are also routine, day-to-day decisions managers must attend to. For example, managers have

to prepare budgets, participate in facility planning, determine work assignments, decide on product mixes, and establish market prices. Managers need management accounting information in order to forecast the likely results of their decisions in any of these areas. Since one measure affecting any decision is cost—often *the* measure—information enabling managers to predict how costs are likely to change helps them to make decisions that will better achieve intended results and create value for their organizations. Consequently, in this chapter we will:

- Illustrate the ways costs can change in response to managers' actions
- Determine an appropriate mixture of different kinds of costs
- Show how to predict costs

COST BEHAVIOR

Cost behavior refers to how costs change as a result of a manager's actions. One way of illustrating cost behavior is by graphs, like the one shown in Exhibit 2.1. This graph shows the actual total cost incurred by Orlando Printing Company, a commercial printer, at each of a number of different levels of activity (expressed in pages printed per month). Note that total cost increases as more pages are printed.

Exhibit 2.2 shows how actual observed data can be used to help managers *estimate* relationships between total cost and activity. The way they estimate these relationships will be introduced later in this chapter. For now, we want you simply to recognize that it is easier to see and describe cost behavior patterns as solid, continuous lines like the one in Exhibit 2.2. It would be difficult to predict the results of a given level of activity without straight-line estimates of how cost changes in response to changes in activity. Fortunately, each of the cost behavior patterns described in this chapter can be represented in a similar straight-line format. However, predictions of costs based on an estimated relationship are subject to uncertainty and deviation from the theoretical straight line representing the relationship. Nevertheless, it's possible to quantify the degree of uncertainty and extent of deviation and represent it as a measure of the confidence that managers can place on the predictions they make.

In Exhibit 2.2, the horizontal axis, measured in thousands of printed

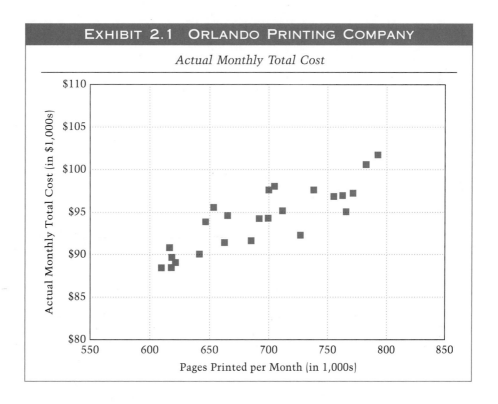

EXHIBIT 2.1 ORLANDO PRINTING COMPANY

Actual Monthly Total Cost

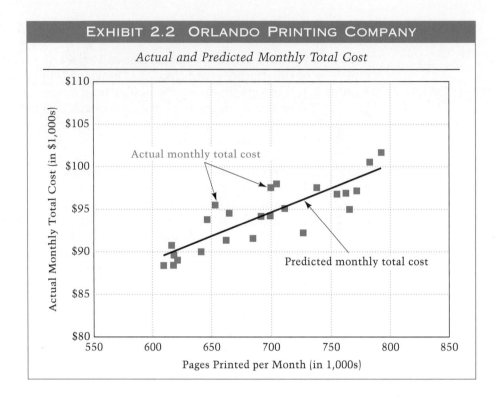

EXHIBIT 2.2   ORLANDO PRINTING COMPANY

Actual and Predicted Monthly Total Cost

pages per month, represents the **independent variable.** Independent means the variable is free to assume virtually any value within a given range of activity. Typically, in managerial accounting applications, independent variables represent activities. Activities are usually volume-based measures such as units of production, the number of labor-hours, or, as in our example, the number of pages printed per month. The vertical axis represents the **dependent variable,** so named because any value represented on the vertical axis depends on a corresponding value of the independent variable. The value of the independent variable is presumed to cause, or **drive,** the value of the dependent variable. In our example, levels of the independent variable (pages printed per month) drive the level of the dependent variable (total cost). That is, printing more pages causes more cost to be incurred. Since managers are often concerned with predicting costs, independent variables are sometimes referred to as **cost drivers.**

TYPES OF COST BEHAVIOR PATTERNS

Some costs are constant, unchanging over a wide range of activity. In contrast, other costs vary in direct proportion with changes in activity. While there are many different kinds of cost behavior between these two extremes, they can be classified into four basic patterns: (1) fixed, (2) step (semifixed), (3) variable, and (4) mixed (semivariable).

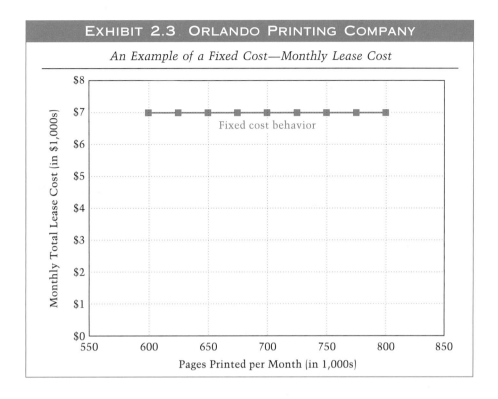

EXHIBIT 2.3 ORLANDO PRINTING COMPANY

An Example of a Fixed Cost—Monthly Lease Cost

FIXED COSTS

Costs that do not change *in total* as the activity levels driving them increase or decrease are **fixed costs.** Often referred to as *capacity costs*, fixed costs are unresponsive to changes in activity. Illustrations of fixed costs include leases, depreciation, managers' salaries, charges for basic utility service, accounting fees, advertising, research and development, and insurance. In each of these examples, increasing activity levels has no impact on total cost.

Monthly lease cost, shown in Exhibit 2.3, represents one of the fixed costs encountered by Orlando Printing Company. Lease cost is $7,000 per month, or $84,000 each year, regardless of the number of pages printed per month. This should be evident by looking at the graph in Exhibit 2.3.

Another way of describing this relationship is by looking at the slope of the line. The line in Exhibit 2.3 is flat—it has no slope. A fixed cost is graphically represented by a line having no slope. Any change in printing activity within the range indicated—between 600 and 800 pages[1]—does not cause a change in the lease cost.

---

[1]   The number of pages printed is expressed in thousands.

RELEVANT RANGE

A range of activity over which the theoretical cost behavior pattern is assumed to describe actual cost is called the **relevant range.** Generally, the relevant range represents the range of historical levels of activity over which the cost behavior pattern has been estimated. For Orlando Printing Company, the range of observed values in Exhibit 2.1 falls between approximately 600 and 800 printed pages per month.

What might happen if Orlando Printing Company's activity dropped to 400 pages per month? If such a low level of activity were sustained, managers might choose to relocate to smaller facilities, incurring lower levels of costs and thereby reducing total fixed cost.

Let's consider another possibility. What is the cost behavior pattern if Orlando Printing Company's lease agreement requires rent payments that are linked to the number of pages printed, subject to a maximum payment of $7,000 per month? Under this agreement, lease payments are fixed only after printing activity reaches the upper limit of $7,000. Before this point, lease cost increases proportionally with the number of pages printed.

Two possible cost behavior patterns outside of the relevant range are shown in Exhibit 2.4. Note several things about this exhibit. First, actual observations of lease cost are found only within the elliptical area representing the relevant range. The cost behavior for leases, which we identified earlier as fixed, is estimated from the actual observations within the relevant range. Second, cost behavior outside of the relevant range is

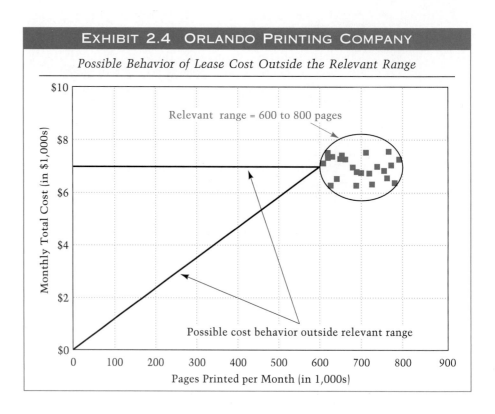

EXHIBIT 2.4   ORLANDO PRINTING COMPANY

Possible Behavior of Lease Cost Outside the Relevant Range

unknown, since managers have no experience at those activity levels. Without data from observations, actual cost behavior cannot be accurately assessed. Actual cost could follow virtually any cost behavior pattern, such as the two shown below the starting point (600 pages) of the relevant range.

The lesson to learn here is that managers cannot automatically assume that costs will behave in the same way outside of the relevant range as they do within the range. From this point on we will no longer show data with activity levels starting at zero. Instead, we will always show only the cost behavior pattern within the relevant range.

STEP COSTS

Costs that are fixed over one range of activity and shift abruptly to a different level, where they are fixed over the adjacent range of activity, are called **step costs.** Any graphical representation of fixed costs that shift in this way, such as the depiction in Exhibit 2.5, suggests why they are called "step" costs. It's evident from the graphical representation that the level at which step costs are fixed varies—discretely—over different ranges of activity, which is why they are sometimes referred to as *semifixed* costs.

Fixed costs can be referred to as *capacity costs*, since they represent the resources that provide the capability of making goods and services. As activity levels approach the limits of capacity, managers are forced to

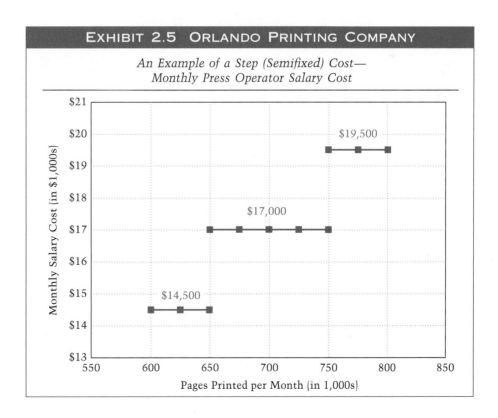

EXHIBIT 2.5 ORLANDO PRINTING COMPANY

An Example of a Step (Semifixed) Cost—
Monthly Press Operator Salary Cost

decide whether to make additional investments that expand capacity and increase output. Many companies use *models*—mathematical formulas—to determine when the next step in fixed costs is required. For example, some commercial airlines, as illustrated in "Current Practice: Airline Staffing Formulas," use this approach to determine crew size. With each additional increase in capacity, managers must recognize they have made a commitment to a higher level—the next higher step—in fixed costs.

Exhibit 2.5 shows total monthly printing press operator salaries at Orlando Printing Company. Assume the firm employs six operators who collectively earn salaries of $14,500 per month. These six operators provide capacity—enough total hours, skill, and experience—to print up to 650 pages per month. To increase printing activity above that level, Orlando Printing Company would have to hire an additional operator who would earn an annual salary of, say, $30,000 ($2,500 per month). With the addition of one more operator, total monthly salary cost increases to $17,000 ($14,500 + $2,500) while capacity is boosted to 750 pages per month. Beyond 750 pages per month, an eighth operator is required at a cost of $2,500 per month, thereby increasing salary cost to $19,500 ($17,000 + $2,500) per month. Each additional operator causes fixed cost to step up to a higher level.

The three levels of fixed salaries for printing press operators, over each of the three successive ranges of activity, illustrate the behavior of

CURRENT PRACTICE

Airline Staffing Formulas

Airlines used to employ lots of flight attendants, whose job was to make passengers comfortable. Today, that level of comfort has been "squeezed out" by competition. Some commercial airlines use what are known as *variable staffing formulas* to determine the number of attendants needed for any given flight. For example, USAir reduced the minimum number of attendants from four to three on its Boeing 737-300s. The addition of a fourth is supposed to be triggered by several factors, such as flights longer than 2½ hours and having 90 or more passengers. According to these airlines, this method allows them to better align services with demand.

Nevertheless, according to some people in the industry, service suffers. With smaller crews, passengers wait longer for meals and beverages. Carts clog up aisles and empty trays sit in front of passengers, inhibiting their movement. Obtaining a pillow or magazine is now, for many passengers, a "do-it-yourself" experience. Worse, some flights never get the needed additional staff member because of the airlines' inability to predict certain load factors, such as passengers arriving immediately prior to departure.

Source: James S. Hirsch, "With Fewer Attendants Aboard Jets, Mood of Passengers Turns Turbulent," *The Wall Street Journal,* July 23, 1993, pp. B1 and B6.

step costs. As printing capacity is approached in any range of activity, where capacity is measured in terms of operator-hours, managers must decide whether or not to hire more operators. If they do hire additional operators, they commit to a higher level of fixed cost.

While the increase in capacity may be justified by higher levels of printing, the additional fixed cost might be difficult to avoid if printing activity were to decline or not to materialize at all. Therefore, each additional step adds more risk, since fixed operator salaries must be covered regardless of the number of pages printed. An alternative to hiring more operators and committing to higher levels of fixed cost is to sign a contract with a temporary employment agency. Temporary workers are dismissed when activity declines. While the pros and cons of these two alternatives will be discussed later, recognize that each alternative exposes managers to different risks.

VARIABLE COSTS

Variable costs change continually and in direct proportion with changes in activity. Materials like the paper, ink, glue, and cardboard used in making books represent a good example. As more copies of a book are printed, more paper, ink, and other materials are used. At one extreme, if no books were printed, no materials would be required and total materials cost would drop to zero. Other examples of costs that vary directly and continually with activity include labor, electricity charges tied to kilowatt-hours of utilization, supplies, and sales commissions.

Exhibit 2.6 illustrates total paper cost for Orlando Printing Company. As more pages are printed, total paper cost increases by $33 per page. Note that total paper cost in the relevant range varies continually starting at $19,800 (600 × $33). However, no paper costs are shown below this point. The reason is that managers may not be able to describe cost behavior at lower levels of printing activity. Were activity to decline below the lower boundary of the relevant range, the product mix might change, altering the types and quality of paper used. For example, during economic downturns, demand may shift from higher-quality printing, such as glossy brochures and stationery, to bulk mail printed on lower-quality paper. With a larger proportion of lower-quality bulk mail printing, the slope of the total materials cost line might decrease. This is yet another example of the importance of limiting estimates of cost behavior to activity levels within the relevant range.

Labor cost may actually be described by several different behavior patterns. For many organizations, labor cost is variable, increasing in direct proportion with increases in activity. For labor cost to be truly variable though, managers would have to pay workers by the "piece." Increasing the number of pieces made translates directly into increases in total labor cost. For example, for salaries at Orlando Printing Company to be variable, worker compensation would have to be linked to the number of pages printed. While piecework may have been common earlier in this century, it is not as common today. Instead, employees are typically paid hourly

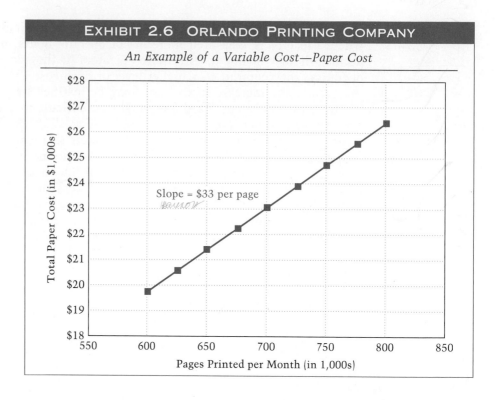

EXHIBIT 2.6 ORLANDO PRINTING COMPANY

An Example of a Variable Cost—Paper Cost

Slope = $33 per page

(Y-axis: Total Paper Cost (in $1,000s), values $18 to $28)
(X-axis: Pages Printed per Month (in 1,000s), values 550 to 850)

wages. Total labor cost, under these circumstances, depends on the number of hours worked, not on the number of units produced. If the number of hours worked is unaffected by changes in activity, then total labor cost is fixed.

Some fast-food restaurants pay their employees on the basis of *shifts*—a fixed number of hours worked. A shift may include a peak period during which there is a surge in the number of hamburgers cooked and served. Other shifts may have lulls during which employees prepare for the next surge or perform housekeeping chores such as cleaning equipment. Regardless of their duties and which shifts they work, employees are not paid by the number of hamburgers they cook and sell. Managers who schedule employees for shifts commit to steps, although small ones, in total fixed labor cost.

Taking a closer look, total labor cost may be more variable than it seems. When revenue increases, total labor cost is likely to increase, since more workers are needed during peak periods. Total labor cost goes down in slower periods, when revenue declines and fewer workers are needed. This cost behavior is shown in Exhibit 2.7, where total labor cost is graphed, along with total revenue, for each hour during a representative workday. This nearly variable cost behavior is reinforced when a manager has the authority to release employees before the end of their shift because of slowdowns in activity.

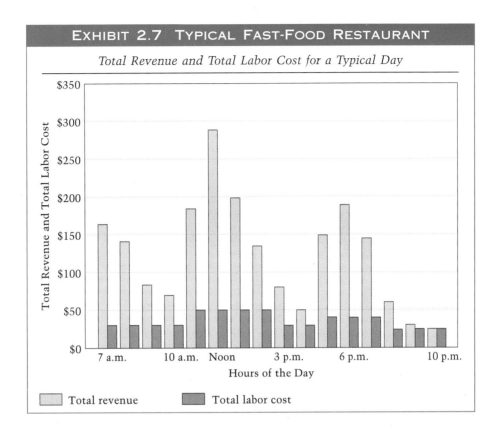

EXHIBIT 2.7 TYPICAL FAST-FOOD RESTAURANT

Total Revenue and Total Labor Cost for a Typical Day

MIXED COSTS

Mixed costs, sometimes called *semivariable costs,* are made up of both fixed and variable components. Utilities cost, such as electricity, gas, and water, provides a good example of a mixed cost. One part of utilities cost, representing charges for basic monthly service, is fixed—it is incurred each month regardless of how much energy is used. The other part is variable—it depends directly on the amount of energy used each month.

Mixed costs are illustrated in Exhibit 2.8. The (solid) total cost line begins at the low end of the relevant range and slopes upward, indicating that total cost increases with the number of pages printed. The mixed cost behavior illustrated here looks very much like the variable cost behavior shown in Exhibit 2.6. However, there is a big difference. The line graphically representing variable costs in Exhibit 2.6, if extended downward through decreasing activity, would cross the origin at a cost of zero when there is no activity. That is, a purely variable cost has no fixed component. Mixed costs pass through the vertical axis when activity is zero at a point representing the fixed portion of total cost. For example, if the solid line in Exhibit 2.8 were extended back from 600 pages to an activity level of zero, represented by the unconnected dotted line, total utilities cost would equal $2,000—the fixed portion of the mixed cost. Total

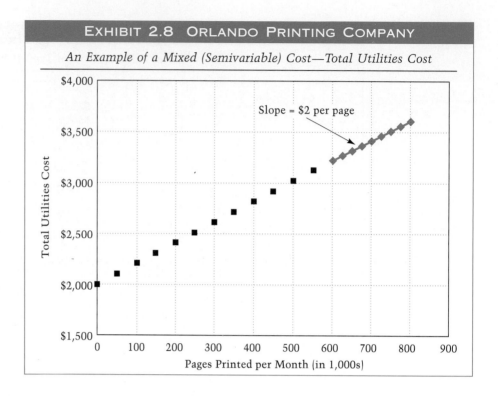

EXHIBIT 2.8 ORLANDO PRINTING COMPANY

An Example of a Mixed (Semivariable) Cost—Total Utilities Cost

utilities cost, then, is composed of a fixed monthly hookup charge of $2,000, plus variable charges calculated by multiplying the number of printed pages by the variable utilities cost of $2 per page. At 700 pages, for example, total utilities cost is $3,400, which is the sum of the $1,400 variable cost (700 × $2 per page) and the $2,000 fixed cost.

NONLINEAR COST BEHAVIOR

In each example thus far, cost behavior patterns have been represented by a constant slope—a straight line—over the entire relevant range. But it's possible for total cost to behave in a nonlinear way. The cost of commissions paid to sales representatives is a good example. Consider the sales commission table shown in Exhibit 2.9. Over a range of 600 to 624 pages, the total commission is $2,500. From 625 to 649 pages, the commission is $3,500, an increase of $1,000 over the previous level. From 650 to 674 pages, the commission is $4,250, or an increase of $750. Each successive increment in the number of pages printed brings an increase in sales commission. However, each increase in sales commission is less than the increase at the previous level. Costs that increase at a decreasing rate, such as sales commissions, lead to nonlinear cost behavior. The nonlinear behavior of sales commissions is easily seen when the data in Exhibit 2.9 are placed in a graph, like the one shown in Exhibit 2.10.

We can predict costs that behave nonlinearly in exactly the same way as we predict linear costs. The problem is establishing a mathematical

EXHIBIT 2.9 ORLANDO PRINTING COMPANY

Sales Commission Schedule

Pages (in 1,000s)	Commission
600	$2,500
625	$3,500
650	$4,250
675	$4,625
700	$4,900
725	$5,150
750	$5,350
775	$5,500
800	$5,600

EXHIBIT 2.10 ORLANDO PRINTING COMPANY

An Example of Nonlinear Cost Behavior—Sales Commission Cost

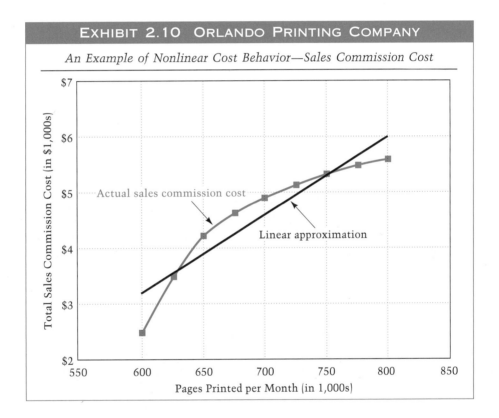

function or graph that represents closely enough the nonlinear cost behavior. Rather than working with nonlinear functions, many managers approximate them with straight lines. In doing so, they assume that linear predictions produce results that are good enough within the relevant range. Linear approximations are likely, however, to yield cost estimation errors such as those illustrated in Exhibit 2.10. Using the straight-line approximation, total commission cost is overestimated at both extremes of the relevant range and underestimated in the middle ranges of activity. Linear approximations of nonlinear relationships should be used only after it has been determined that the economic "consequences" from the discrepancies between them are not likely to be significant. Unfortunately, there are no general guidelines for determining what is significant. Ultimately you, as the manager, will have to decide what is significant and what is not.

One application of nonlinear cost behavior is known as a **learning curve.** Learning curves represent increases in productivity that result when employees, through repetition and experience, become more efficient at performing a task. The more they perform the task, the less time it takes. And the less time it takes to do a task, the lower the cost. Learning curves are discussed, in detail, in the appendix to this chapter.

COST BEHAVIOR WITH DECREASING ACTIVITY

Managers generally presume that decreases in activity cause costs to follow the same behavior pattern that increases in activity follow. For some costs, such as materials, this may be a realistic assumption. For other costs, though, decreases in activity may cause costs to follow an entirely different path. One example is labor, where a "ratchet effect" may result from downsizing labor cost—that is, it may cost more to release employees than to hire them, perhaps because of corporate cultures, labor contracts, or government regulations. An example is given in "Current Practice: GM and Ford Labor Agreements."

SHORT-TERM VERSUS LONG-TERM COST BEHAVIOR

Strategic decisions are likely to exert their influence over a relatively long period of time. In contrast, day-to-day, "tactical" decisions have an impact for a relatively short period of time. Over short time horizons, many costs are likely to exhibit fixed cost behavior. Salaries and leases may be difficult to alter in the short term. But, over longer time horizons, managers have the ability to convert short-term fixed costs into long-term variable costs. Labor costs that are fixed over a one-month period may vary in rough proportion to long-term production activity. Therefore, *when the time horizon is extended to the long term, all costs are variable.*

UNIT COST

One way cost information is reported is in the form of a **unit cost**—the cost of a single unit of product or service. Managers use unit cost in a number of ways, one of which is to determine market prices. Determining unit cost starts by adding together all the costs of producing a given level of output, as illustrated in column 1 of Exhibit 2.11. The variable costs, shown in column 2 of Exhibit 2.11, total $35,000. Variable costs include materials, sales commissions, the variable portion of utilities (a mixed cost), temporary labor, and supplies. Similarly, the fixed costs shown in column 3 of Exhibit 2.11 total $60,000. Among the various fixed

CURRENT PRACTICE

GM and Ford Labor Agreements

General Motors (GM) converted some salaries from variable to fixed costs when it signed an agreement with the UAW (United Auto Workers) union in the late 1980s. The agreement guaranteed workers 95 percent of their salaries for up to two years if they were laid-off. GM wanted to boost workers' morale, improve loyalty, and retain skilled workers despite lapses in volume.

The United Auto Workers, in contract negotiations with Ford, requested specific employment levels be maintained for each plant. Although the UAW accepted programs that protect employees who might lose jobs because of tech-nological changes or as a result of work transferred to outside companies (outsourcing), the union is still concerned about protecting jobs lost through attrition. However, the UAW is expected to permit the elimination of jobs as a consequence of reductions in volume. In effect, it was revealed during contract negotiations that employees would like to see a minimum level for their salaries while participating in profits when activity picks up. Automobile manufacturers such as Ford might want just the opposite—labor cost that is variable when activity drops and fixed when activity increases.

Source: Jacob M. Schlesinger, "UAW Is Expected to Ask Ford Today to Keep Work Force at Current Levels," *The Wall Street Journal*, Sept. 8, 1987, p. A7.

EXHIBIT 2.11 ORLANDO PRINTING COMPANY

Total Printing Cost—Variable and Fixed

Monthly Component Cost	(1) Total Cost	(2) Variable Cost	(3) Fixed Cost
Materials—paper*	$23,100	$23,100	
Labor—press operator salaries*	17,000		$17,000
Administrative salaries	12,600		12,600
Office salaries	9,400		9,400
Lease*	7,000		7,000
Sales commissions*	4,900	4,900	
Labor—preprint art work	4,000		4,000
Supervision & inspection	3,800		3,800
Utilities*	3,400	1,400	2,000
Temporary labor	3,150	3,150	
Supplies	2,450	2,450	
Office supplies	2,400		2,400
Materials acquisition & handling	1,800		1,800
Total cost	$95,000	$35,000	$60,000
Pages printed	700	700	700
Unit cost	$135.71	$50.00	$85.71

Note: An asterisk (*) denotes component costs discussed in this chapter.

			EXHIBIT 2.12 ORLANDO PRINTING COMPANY		

Unit Cost and Billing Rates at Different Activity Levels

			Activity, 1,000s of pages		
	650	675	**Expected 700**	725	750
Total cost:					
Printed pages	650	675	700	725	750
Unit variable cost	$ 50.00	$ 50.00	$ 50.00	$ 50.00	$ 50.00
Total variable cost	32,500	33,750	35,000	36,250	37,500
Total fixed cost	60,000	60,000	60,000	60,000	60,000
Total cost	$92,500	$93,750	$95,000	$96,250	$97,500
Unit cost:					
Variable	$ 50.00	$ 50.00	$ 50.00	$ 50.00	$ 50.00
Fixed	92.31	88.89	85.71	82.76	80.00
Unit cost	$142.31	$138.89	$135.71	$132.76	$130.00
Total cost as percentage of expected	104.86%	102.34%	100.00%	97.82%	95.79%

costs are the fixed portion of utilities (a mixed cost) and the fixed cost for press operator salaries (a step fixed cost).

Unit cost is calculated by dividing the sum of the total variable and fixed costs by the number of units produced. For example, for Orlando Printing Company variable cost is $50.00 per page, fixed cost is $85.71 per page, and the combined unit cost is $135.71 per page. (See the bottom three lines of Exhibit 2.11.)

What if printing activity were to increase to 750 pages? Can we predict total printing cost by multiplying 750 by the $135.71 unit cost? The answer is no! To see why this is so, consider Exhibit 2.12, which shows total cost and unit cost at different levels of activity. The first row lists printing activity levels between 650 and 750 pages. Total variable cost is calculated by multiplying the number of pages printed by the $50 per page variable cost. Adding total variable cost to total fixed cost of $60,000 yields total costs that range from $92,500 to $97,500. Also, don't forget that fixed cost is lower by $2,500 at activity levels of under 650 pages. That's because fixed cost steps down, since fewer printing press operators are needed at lower activity level ranges. Similarly, fixed cost steps up by $2,500, representing the additional printing press operator required when printing activity exceeds 750 pages.

Unit cost is calculated by dividing total cost at each activity level by the number of printed pages. For example, the unit fixed cost at 650 pages is $92.31, calculated by dividing $60,000 by 650. The combined variable and fixed cost is $142.31 per unit. Similarly, the combined variable and fixed cost decreases to $130.00 per page when 750 pages are printed. At the expected level of activity—700 pages—unit cost is $135.71.

We can conclude from Exhibit 2.12 that:

- Variable costs are *constant* on a per-unit basis.
- Fixed costs per unit *change* inversely (in the opposite direction) with changes in activity. They increase as activity decreases, and decrease as activity increases.

The *correct way to predict total cost* is to multiply variable unit cost by the number of units and add total fixed cost. The total cost to print, say, 740 pages is $97,000, calculated by first multiplying 740 pages by the $50 variable cost per page and then adding fixed cost of $60,000. Unit cost is calculated by dividing the total cost of $97,000 by 740. The result is $131.08 per page.

ECONOMIES OF SCALE

We have seen that fixed cost per unit decreases as activity increases. This effect is called **economies of scale.** Over a relatively short time, fixed cost cannot be altered even if activity levels decrease. Therefore, at any given level of fixed cost, managers achieve the lowest unit cost by using fixed resources to the fullest extent possible. Economies of scale explains why unit cost in Exhibit 2.12 decreased from $142.31 to $130.00 as activity increased.

Fast-food restaurants offer an example of economies of scale. Years ago, many served only lunch and dinner. Once managers recognized that many of their costs were fixed, they decided to open for breakfast. Their logic—breakfast could add to profits as long as the food items were sold at prices greater than the variable cost to produce it. They argued that since the restaurant was already committed to a given level of fixed cost, profits could be increased by spreading fixed cost over more and more units. Similarly, the cost of new labeling laws can be minimized by spreading it over many units, as shown in "Current Practice: New U.S. Labeling Law."

UNIT FIXED COST CAVEATS

The general rule to follow when calculating unit cost is to always start with fixed cost expressed as a total and then divide by the units of activity. Some of the reasons for doing it this way include:

- Changes in activity change unit fixed cost. On a per-unit basis, fixed cost is not constant. Total fixed cost, on the other hand, is unchanged by changes in activity.
- Fixed costs are averaged over all units when total fixed cost is divided by units of activity. The result is not a variable cost. Remember, fixed costs do not change in total as a result of changes in activity. Only variable costs do! *An increase in activity causes only total variable cost to change.* Printing an additional page using the data in Exhibit 2.12, for example, causes cost to increase by an amount equal to the variable cost of $50.00 per page—not by the combined fixed and variable cost of $135.71.

New U.S. Labeling Law

The Nutrition Labeling and Education Act of 1990 requires clearer disclosure of nutritional and health information on food packaging. However, fulfilling the new labeling requirements can be expensive. For example, labeling costs might include such components as laboratory analysis, design work, and new label production. It could cost a small company as much as $6,250 per product to switch to the new, required labeling. A company with 100 products might incur a relabeling cost of $625,000. If volume is low— say, 10,000 units per product per year— relabeling cost spread over 10 years might add 6.25 cents per container ($625,000/ 10,000,000). If volume is high—say, 1 million units per product per year—then relabeling only adds 0.0625 cents per container ($625,000/1,000,000,000 labels).

Source: Brent Bowers, "Small Food Makers Seek to Fatten Labeling Law's Exemptions," *The Wall Street Journal,* June 2, 1993, pp. B1 and B2.

- Averaging fixed costs over units of activity assumes each unit is homogeneous. For example, each page printed by Orlando Printing Company is assumed to require the same utilization of fixed costs. If this assumption is incorrect, averaging fixed costs may distort unit cost. In effect, products that use disproportionately large amounts of fixed resources are "subsidized" by other products that use relatively lower amounts. To illustrate the problem, what if one of Orlando Printing Company's printing presses occupies five times the floor space and requires two times as much of the supervisor's time to manage? Jobs printed on the first press should cost more than the same jobs printed on the second. Otherwise, bid prices for jobs using the expensive press may be too low. Under these circumstances, it may make sense to find ways of attaching fixed cost to units in proportion to the benefit the units derive. This is the topic of the next chapter.

MEASURING ACTIVITY

So far we have used a single measure of activity. In practice, many activities drive the cost of a product or service, thus increasing the complexity of predicting its cost. For example, Orlando Printing Company's total printing cost for one year might be caused by a variety of cost drivers, two of which might be paper costs, driven by the number of printed pages, and setup costs, driven by the number of times the press is prepared. We will introduce multiple cost drivers in Chapter 4.

COST STRUCTURES

The mixture of variable and fixed costs as proportions of the organization's total cost is known as its **cost structure.** Managers should determine an appropriate cost structure, selecting a mixture of fixed and variable costs that matches their organization's strategic needs. A strategy of risk avoidance and flexibility for a start-up company might translate into a cost structure dominated by variable costs. Recall that variable costs change in direct proportion with activity. Managers of start-ups may want to avoid risk, electing not to commit their organizations to high levels of fixed cost until they are sure of what they can expect in the future. In contrast, managers who pursue a low-cost strategy may decide to invest in assets that create high levels of fixed cost. Fixed cost–dominated cost structures allow their organizations to take advantage of economies of scale and to drive unit costs down. Unfortunately, committing to fixed costs exposes managers to risks from downturns in activity.

In general:

- *High variable, low fixed* cost strategies avoid risk and enhance flexibility. The downside is that unit cost may be relatively high.
- *Low variable, high fixed* cost strategies offer low unit cost because of economies of scale. However, they expose the organization to high risks from downturns in activity. That's because fixed costs still have to be covered even when there is little revenue coming in to pay for them.

TOTAL REVENUE

We can use formulas to help sort out the costs and benefits of alternative cost structures. We'll start by presenting a **total revenue** function that will help make the analysis clearer. Total revenue represents resources derived from the sale of products and services. It is driven by the number of units of product sold or units of service delivered to customers. In the Orlando Printing Company example, revenue is calculated by multiplying the number of pages printed by the selling price per page.

The slope of the total revenue function is typically assumed to be constant—the price of each unit sold is the same. That is, total revenue is usually represented as a straight line. However, it is easy to identify situations that might cause the slope to deviate from a straight line. For example, if demand exceeds capacity, market forces may push prices higher. In that case, the slope of the total revenue function increases to reflect higher prices. Conversely, the slope of the total revenue function might decrease when suppliers offer price breaks for the purchase of large quantities.

PROFIT EQUATION

If costs are driven by a single activity, such as printing pages, then the relationship between total revenue, total cost, and profit can be expressed mathematically as

Profit = total revenue − total cost

= total revenue − total variable cost − total fixed cost

= (unit selling price × activity) − (unit variable cost × activity) − total fixed cost

Rearranging the first two terms on the right to factor out activity,

Profit = [(unit selling price − unit variable cost) × activity] − total fixed cost

= (unit contribution margin × activity) − total fixed cost

Where: Unit contribution margin = unit selling price − unit variable costs

As noted in Chapter 1, *unit contribution margin* is defined as the "unit selling price less unit variable costs." Since profit is measured in terms of totals, not individual units, total contribution margin (or simply "total contribution") is calculated by multiplying the unit contribution margin by activity. In other words, total contribution margin is the difference between total revenue and total variable cost. The term *contribution margin* is descriptive because it indicates the contribution each unit makes toward covering fixed costs. If enough units are sold, the total contribution margin is large enough to cover all fixed costs. At relatively high levels of activity, the excess of total contribution margin over total fixed cost represents profit. Alas, when activity levels are too low, total fixed cost exceeds total contribution margin, resulting in losses.

To illustrate the role played by contribution margin, assume Orlando Printing Company's variable cost is $50 per page and fixed cost is $60,000 per month. Also assume it plans to print 700 pages. If the price is $150 per page, then

Unit contribution margin = unit price − unit variable cost

= $150 − $50

= $100

Total contribution margin = unit contribution margin × activity

= $100 × 700

= $70,000

and Profit = total contribution margin − total fixed cost

= $70,000 − $60,000 = $10,000

Exhibit 2.13 illustrates cost behavior and profit at five activity levels. The data in Exhibit 2.13 are arranged in the contribution margin format. In this application, the format begins with total revenue. Then, variable costs are deducted from revenue to derive total contribution margin. Next, fixed costs are deducted from total contribution margin to yield profit.

EXHIBIT 2.13 ORLANDO PRINTING COMPANY

Revenues, Costs, and Contribution Margin at Different Activity Levels

	Activity, 1,000s of pages				
	650	675	Expected 700	725	750
Revenue:					
Printed pages	650	675	700	725	750
Revenue per page	$ 150	$ 150	$ 150	$ 150	$ 150
Total revenue	$97,500	$101,250	$105,000	$108,750	$112,500
Less variable cost:					
Printed pages	650	675	700	725	750
Variable cost per page	$ 50	$ 50	$ 50	$ 50	$ 50
Total variable cost	32,500	33,750	35,000	36,250	37,500
Equals total contribution margin	65,000	67,500	70,000	72,500	75,000
Less fixed cost	60,000	60,000	60,000	60,000	60,000
Equals (pretax) profit	$ 5,000	$ 7,500	$ 10,000	$ 12,500	$ 15,000
Unit data:					
Revenue	$150.00	$150.00	$150.00	$ 150.00	$ 150.00
Variable cost	50.00	50.00	50.00	50.00	50.00
Contribution margin	100.00	100.00	100.00	100.00	100.00
Fixed cost	92.31	88.89	85.71	82.76	80.00
(Pretax) profit per page	$ 7.69	$ 11.11	$ 14.29	$ 17.24	$ 20.00
Printed pages	650	675	700	725	750
(Pretax) profit	$ 5,000	$ 7,500	$10,000	$ 12,500	$ 15,000
Percent change from expected activity:					
Change in activity level	−7.14%	−3.57%	0.00%	3.57%	7.14%
Change in (pretax) profit	−50.00%	−25.00%	0.00%	25.00%	50.00%

To reiterate, the contribution margin format is organized as follows:

- Revenue (unit selling price × activity)
- Less variable cost (unit variable cost × activity)
- Equals contribution margin (unit contribution margin × activity)
- Less fixed cost (total)
- Equals (pretax) profit

Notice that total contribution margin in Exhibit 2.13 increases in direct proportion with activity. Each additional 25 pages of print causes total contribution to increase by $100 per page, an amount exactly equal to the contribution margin. For example, increasing activity from 650 to 675 pages causes total contribution margin to increase from $65,000 to $67,500, or a total of $2,500. From the unit data at the bottom of Exhibit 2.13, we can see that this same figure can be derived by multiplying the unit contribution margin ($100) by the additional number of pages printed (25).

OPERATING LEVERAGE

Contribution margin helps illustrate the concept of operating leverage. **Operating leverage** is the change in operating profit relative to a change in revenue. The driving force behind operating leverage is economies of scale. Highly leveraged companies—those with a high proportion of fixed cost relative to total cost—achieve much higher increases in net profit from an increase in activity. Unfortunately, operating leverage works both ways. Companies with high operating leverage are subject to larger losses when activity declines. Therefore, operating leverage can be used as a measure of relative risk. For example, the percent change in activity and the percent change in net profit for Orlando Printing Company are shown at the bottom of Exhibit 2.13. An increase of 3.57 percent in the volume of printed pages (from 700 to 725 pages) causes a 25.00 percent increase in profit (from $10,000 to $12,500). Conversely, a 3.57 percent decline in activity causes a 25.00 percent decrease in profit.

BREAKEVEN ACTIVITY

Decreasing activity causes the total contribution margin to decline. At some point, total contribution is just barely sufficient to cover fixed cost. At the activity level where total contribution margin just equals fixed cost, neither a profit nor a loss is realized. The precise point where breakeven activity is achieved—where profit is zero—is called the **breakeven point**. (See "Current Practice: Chrysler Corporation's Breakeven Volume.") For

CURRENT PRACTICE

Chrysler Corporation's Breakeven Volume

Chrysler Corporation reported an increase in its breakeven point to 1.9 million units in 1991—up from 1.8 million units in 1990. Chrysler explained that this increase was the result of poor industry conditions, especially in the first half of 1991, when it sold relatively more automobiles to rental fleets, thus yielding lower unit contribution margins.

Chrysler said its breakeven point is influenced by several factors. First comes the level of operating costs. Higher fixed cost simply increases the number of cars the carmaker has to sell to break even.

Next comes the product and option mix. Building low-margin cars packaged with low-margin options simply increases the number of cars that have to be sold to reach breakeven. After that comes the proportion of lower-margin rental car sales. Finally, changes in sales incentives influence the breakeven point. In years when consumer demand is low or competition stiff, Chrysler offers sales incentives to help move vehicles. The result is lower contribution margins, again increasing the number of cars that have to be sold to achieve breakeven.

Source: Adapted from Chrysler Corporation, *Report to Shareholders, Management's Discussion and Analysis of Financial Conditions and Results of Operations,* 1991, p. 17.

activity levels greater than the breakeven point, total contribution margin exceeds total cost. The result is profit. Activity levels below the breakeven point generate total contribution insufficient to cover fixed costs. The result is loss!

At breakeven, profit is zero and total contribution margin equals total fixed cost. Mathematically, we can represent the breakeven point as follows:

Profit = (unit contribution margin × activity) − total fixed cost

Because profit is equal to zero at breakeven, we can express the equation as follows:

0 = (unit contribution margin × activity) − total fixed cost

And

(unit contribution margin × activity) = total fixed cost

Therefore

$$\text{Breakeven activity} = \frac{\text{total fixed cost}}{\text{unit contribution margin}}$$

Using the data from Exhibit 2.13,

$$\text{Breakeven activity} = \frac{\$60,000}{\$100 \text{ per page}}$$

$$= 600 \text{ pages}$$

We can prove that profit is zero at 600 pages as follows:

Profit = (unit contribution margin × breakeven activity) − total fixed cost

= ($100 per page × 600 pages) − $60,000

= 0

CAVEATS WHEN USING BREAKEVEN

Here are several things to watch out for when using breakeven:

- Separating total cost into fixed and variable components is not an exact science. We will illustrate this point later in the chapter.
- When using breakeven as a planning tool, remember that the contribution margin and fixed cost are based on estimates. Breakeven serves as a rough guideline for managers to use when planning activities. So it may not make sense to try to be overly precise and carry breakeven computations to several decimal places.
- Breakeven, as a planning tool, provides managers with a mechanism for predicting the impact of their actions on organizational strategies. If managers are not satisfied with what they anticipate in the future, they should look for ways to change it.
- Breakeven is based on a single cost driver. In real life there are many cost drivers, making identification of a single breakeven point difficult.

- Activity is typically expressed in terms of a single product. Since most organizations offer a variety of products and services, identification of a single breakeven point may not be very useful.
- When cost structures are complex, breakeven may yield misleading results. For example, mixed and step costs are not accounted for in the breakeven equations shown above.

Because of some of the problems associated with the breakeven formula, you may want to build a spreadsheet model. The breakeven point is found by varying volume up or down by "trial and error" until a profit of zero is attained. If the model includes multiple cost drivers, the breakeven volume for each driver is found through trial and error by holding all of the other cost drivers constant. Also, spreadsheet models can accommodate complex cost structures by using conditional "if" statements and "look-up" tables. One other benefit of spreadsheet models is that they indicate the degree of change in profit relative to a change in volume. Known as sensitivity analysis, a topic we will cover in Chapter 7, this benefit gives managers an indication of the risks they face when actual volume differs from breakeven volume.

GRAPHING TOTAL REVENUE AND TOTAL COST

Total revenue and total cost can be graphed to illustrate the relationship between activity and profit. Exhibit 2.14 shows the total revenue line for

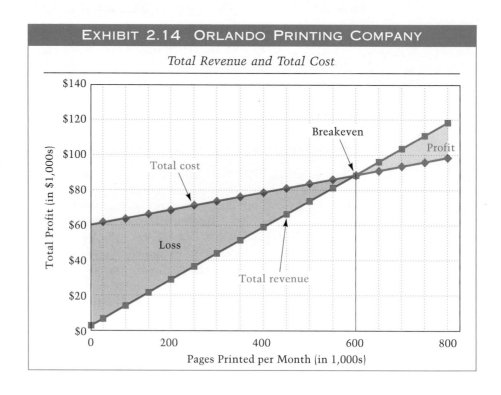

EXHIBIT 2.14   ORLANDO PRINTING COMPANY

Total Revenue and Total Cost

Orlando Printing Company increasing at a rate of $150 per page. The total cost function starts where total fixed cost is $60,000 and activity is zero and increases at a slope equal to the variable cost of $50 per page. The total revenue and total cost functions cross at 600 pages, which is breakeven activity. Breakeven revenue is equal to $90,000 (600 pages × $150 revenue per page). To the right of the breakeven point, total revenue is greater than total cost, and profits are achieved. Activity levels to the left of the breakeven point don't generate revenue sufficient to cover fixed cost. The result is loss.

PROFIT GRAPH

Total revenue and total cost can be combined in what is known as a **profit graph**, like the one shown in Exhibit 2.15, for Orlando Printing Company. The horizontal line represents zero profit. Values above the line represent profit. Below the line are losses. At zero activity, loss equals fixed cost, since no contribution is generated to cover fixed cost. The slope of the profit graph starts at a loss equal to the total fixed cost and increases at a rate equal to the unit contribution margin. For example, Orlando Printing Company's profit graph starts at a loss equal to $60,000 at zero pages and increases at a rate of $100 ($150 revenue − $50 variable cost) for each page printed. If, say, 200 pages are printed, Orlando Printing Company shows a

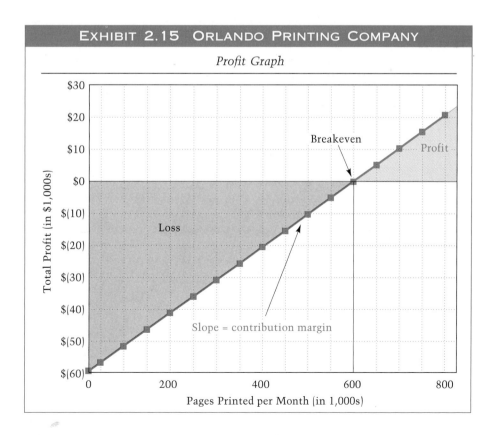

EXHIBIT 2.15 ORLANDO PRINTING COMPANY

Profit Graph

loss of $40,000 (200 pages at $100, or $20,000 total contribution margin − $60,000 fixed cost). When 600 pages are printed, total contribution equals fixed cost, and breakeven is achieved. Every page above breakeven brings $100 in profit. For example, 700 pages generate operating profits of $10,000 ($100 in contribution × 100 pages above breakeven).

EVALUATING ALTERNATIVE COST STRUCTURES

Profit graphs can be used to analyze the trade-off between risk for alternative cost structures. To illustrate, Exhibit 2.16 shows two possible cost structures for Orlando Printing Company. The first is its existing cost structure, represented by the following equation:

Existing cost structure = ($50 × no. of pages) + $60,000

Assume the alternative cost structure is as follows:

Alternative cost structure = ($100 × no. of pages) + $20,000

Note that the alternative cost structure has higher variable cost per page ($100 vs. $50) but lower fixed cost ($20,000 vs. $60,000). Contribution margins for the two cost structures, assuming an average billing rate of $150 per page, are

Contribution margin for existing cost structure = $150 − $50 = $100 per page

Contribution margin for alternative cost structure = $150 − $100 = $50 per page

You should recognize three things after looking at Exhibit 2.16. First, the alternative cost structure achieves breakeven at 400 pages ($20,000 fixed costs/$50 per-page contribution margin), a volume considerably lower than the existing breakeven point. This decreases the likelihood of sustaining losses. Second, the alternative cost structure generates higher profits at printing levels of less than 800 pages. Conversely, the existing cost structure yields higher profits at printing levels greater than 800 pages because of economies of scale. And, third, at 800 pages—the **indifference point**—profits arising from both cost structures are equal.[2]

In general:

• At low levels of activity, cost structures dominated by large proportions of variable costs are desirable. This may be appropriate for risk-averse start-up companies that face widely fluctuating demand.

---

[2] The point where profits are equal is found by setting the two profit equations equal to one another. In the present example, the point of indifference, or *crossover point*, is calculated as follows:

Contribution margin − fixed cost of present structure = contribution margin − fixed cost of alternative structure
($100 × no. of pages) − $60,000 = ($50 × no. of pages) − $20,000
($50 × no. of pages) = $40,000
Indifference pages = $40,000/$50 = 800

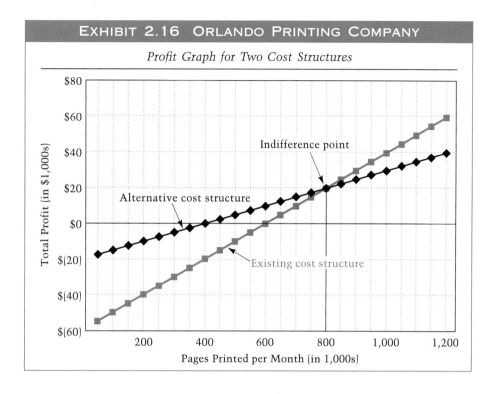

EXHIBIT 2.16   ORLANDO PRINTING COMPANY

Profit Graph for Two Cost Structures

- At high levels of activity, cost structures dominated by fixed costs make low unit costs possible as the result of economies of scale. This may be appropriate for companies that produce large volumes of products and that compete based on price. However, such companies may be less flexible and have greater exposure to losses from downturns in activity.
- When activity declines, managers may convert fixed cost dominated structures into variable structures by outsourcing. (See "Current Practice: Outsourcing Fixed Labor Cost.") An example is maintenance. Managers may opt to disband the maintenance department and hire an outside maintenance service organization to take its place. When activity increases again, they may reverse the process. Previously outsourced activities are brought back in-house, converting variable costs back into fixed costs to achieve economies of scale.
- Over the long term, all costs are variable.

SEGMENT CONTRIBUTION MARGINS

Managers group costs in a number of different ways. They can organize costs by cost behavior (as shown in this chapter), characterizing them as fixed or as variable. Or they may organize costs along many other dimensions, such as work functions, business units, geographic regions, departments, distribution channels, or product lines. Each of the different components within a grouping of costs is called a *segment*. For example, the northwestern district might be one of the segments for costs organized by geographic region.

CURRENT PRACTICE

Outsourcing Fixed Labor Cost

One recent example of converting fixed cost into variable is the "sale and lease-back" of employees whose contracts are signed over to labor-management companies. The benefit to the outsourcing company is reduced labor cost when activity levels are relatively low. Labor cost, under this arrangement, is directly linked to activity. Labor is contracted only as needed, avoiding labor cost when there is no work to be done. It's a form of just-in-time, "accordion-style" employment, where the right amount of workforce is delivered at the exact point it is needed. When their services aren't needed, employees are simply dismissed and their cost avoided.

Employers may end up paying higher labor rates under this arrangement. But they may not mind because labor cost is incurred only when revenue is coming in. This premium for labor cost, for some firms, is viewed as a form of insurance against underutilization of labor capacity.

Source: John Dickerson, Jane Van Tassel, and William McWhirter, "Disposable Workers," *Time Magazine,* Apr. 19, 1993, p. 41.

Consider Exhibit 2.17, where the total costs of Orlando Printing Company are organized by product line. The company's two lines of business are web printing and sheetfed printing. *Web* refers to jobs run on high-speed printers fed continuously with large rolls of paper. *Sheetfed* presses print one sheet of precut paper at a time. With costs separated in this way, managers can make decisions and predict how their actions may impact specific parts of the business. For example, what will happen if the web segment manager lowers prices? How would this affect the web line and company profits?

Exhibit 2.17 is organized in a contribution margin format, with costs classified by cost behavior (fixed, step, variable, and mixed). Deducting variable cost from total revenue yields total contribution margin. Then fixed cost is subtracted from total contribution margin to obtain profit. The web segment prints 450 of the total of 700 pages and shows a total contribution margin of $53,000, or $117.78 per page. The sheetfed segment shows a total contribution margin of $17,000, or $68 per unit.

MULTIPRODUCT BREAKEVEN

At what level should breakeven be calculated in multiproduct settings? Should breakeven points be calculated for each segment? Or should breakeven be determined for the organization as a whole? While both approaches are possible, each requires different assumptions. To calculate organizationwide breakeven we need to make an assumption about product mix. First, we determine the organizationwide contribution margin by weighing the web and sheetfed unit contributions by the product mix.

EXHIBIT 2.17 ORLANDO PRINTING COMPANY						
Segment Contribution Margins, Profits, Breakeven Points, and Desired Page Rates						
	Web and Sheetfed		Web		Sheetfed	
	Total	Page	Total	Page	Total	Page
(Pretax) profit:						
Printed pages, 1,000s		700		450		250
Total revenue	$105,000	$150.00	$75,000	$166.67	$30,000	$120.00
Variable cost	35,000	$ 50.00	22,000	$ 48.89	13,000	$ 52.00
Contribution margin	70,000	$100.00	53,000	$117.78	17,000	$ 68.00
Fixed cost	60,000	$ 85.71	42,000	$ 93.33	18,000	$ 72.00
(Pretax) profit (loss)	$ 10,000	$ 14.29	$11,000	$ 24.45	$ (1,000)	$ (4.00)
Breakeven pages:						
Total fixed cost		$60,000		$42,000		$18,000
Divided by page						
contribution margin		$100.00		$117.78		$ 68.00
Breakeven pages, 1,000s		600		357		265
Desired price:						
Variable cost		$ 50.00		$ 48.89		$ 52.00
Fixed cost		$ 85.71		$ 93.33		$ 72.00
Total cost		$135.71		$142.22		$124.00
Desired profit (15% of						
total cost)		$ 20.36		$ 21.33		$ 18.60
Desired price (1,000 pages)		$156.07		$163.56		$142.60
Prevailing market price		$150.00		$166.67		$120.00
Excess (deficiency) of						
market price to desired price		$ (6.07)		$ 3.11		$ (22.60)

Orlando Printing Company's $100 weighted-average unit contribution margin is calculated by multiplying the web unit contribution ($117.78) by the relative number of pages sold (450/700, or 64.3%) and adding the results to the sheetfed unit contribution ($68) multiplied by the relative number of pages (250/700, or 35.7%) sold. Thus, we get the organization-wide weighted-average unit contribution margin, which is $100 per unit. Next, we can determine the organizationwide breakeven point by dividing the fixed cost ($60,000) by the weighted-average contribution margin ($100). The result is a breakeven of 600 pages.

Altering the mix changes the breakeven point. For example, increasing the product mix to, say, 80 percent web and 20 percent sheetfed increases the weighted-average contribution margin to $107.82 and decreases the breakeven point to 556 units ($60,000/$107.82). To recap, *breakeven for a firm that produces multiple goods and services is determined by dividing fixed cost for the organization as a whole by the weighted-average unit contribution margin.*

Breakeven becomes more complicated where output is measured in heterogeneous units. In the Orlando Printing Company example, printing pages is an activity common to both the web and sheetfed segments. How would you express breakeven for an organization having such diverse activities as manufacturing automobile parts, providing information services, and offering commercial financing? In such cases, one answer is to express breakeven in terms of dollars of revenue rather than units of product. The breakeven calculation expressed in dollars rather than units becomes

$$\text{Breakeven (dollars)} = \frac{\text{total fixed cost}}{\text{contribution margin ratio}}$$

Where: $$\text{Contribution margin ratio} = \frac{\text{unit contribution margin}}{\text{unit sales price}}$$

Using the combined web and sheetfed data from the Orlando Printing example,

$$\text{Contribution margin ratio} = \frac{\$100}{\$150} = 66.67\%$$

And $$\text{Breakeven (dollars)} = \frac{\$60,000}{0.6667} = \$90,000$$

SEGMENT BREAKEVEN POINTS

The alternative to an organizationwide breakeven point is individual segment breakeven points. When calculating individual segment breakeven points, all of the variable and fixed costs have to be broken down and assigned to specific segments. For example, we need to determine how much of the $35,000 of total variable cost and how much of the $60,000 of fixed cost in Exhibit 2.17 to assign to the web and sheetfed segments. Methods for making these assignments will be introduced in the next chapter. But for now, assume that $22,000 of variable cost and $42,000 of fixed cost are assigned to the web segment and $13,000 of variable cost and $18,000 of fixed cost are assigned to the sheetfed segment.

Both segments show positive contribution margins. However, the sheetfed segment shows a loss of $1,000, while the web segment shows a profit of $11,000, after deducting fixed cost. Losses from the sheetfed product line may prompt managers to consider options such as increasing sheetfed prices, reducing costs, or discontinuing sheetfed operations altogether. Making correct decisions about each of these options assumes that the fixed costs have been assigned to segments accurately—an assumption that is not always justified. We will show how to sort out and evaluate these alternatives in Chapter 7. For now, remember that fixed costs, regardless of how they are assigned to segments, are not likely to go away in the short term. Therefore, if managers decided to discontinue sheetfed activities, there's a good chance the web line will end up absorbing most, if not all, of the $60,000 in fixed cost. That's because the sheetfed's fixed cost will not immediately drop to zero.

The middle section of Exhibit 2.17 shows breakeven activity for both segments. Breakeven for the web segment is 357 pages, while breakeven for sheetfed is 265 pages. Note that the two segment contributions don't add up to the organizationwide breakeven of 600 pages. That's because each segment's contribution margin has to be multiplied by the relative number of pages sold (64.3% for web and 35.7% for sheetfed) to get the organizationwide breakeven point.

The bottom section of Exhibit 2.17 shows billing rates based on a desired 15 percent markup on total cost. From the viewpoint of the organization as a whole, the average billing rate of $150 per page doesn't generate the desired level of profit. Segment information gives insight into the reasons. While the web segment generates an excess of the prevailing market price relative to the desired price, the sheetfed segment shows a deficiency. We will discuss how to remedy this situation in Chapter 6.

ESTIMATING COST BEHAVIOR

Earlier we indicated that historical data provide a basis for predicting future cost. We use historical data to *estimate* a relationship between cost (dependent variable) and cost driver (independent variable). The result is an equation that can be used to predict cost at different levels of cost-driver activity. Four steps should be followed to estimate this relationship: (1) identify the component of cost to be estimated, (2) identify a cost driver, (3) estimate the relationship between cost and cost driver, and (4) predict cost for a given level of the cost driver.

1: IDENTIFY THE COMPONENT OF COST TO BE ESTIMATED

We can use individual components of total cost as a basis for predictions. The resulting prediction of total cost is derived by adding together the predictions for each individual component. Or we can prepare predictions of total cost directly based on historical values of total cost. To understand these two approaches, consider a beverage distributor's costs, as shown in Exhibit 2.18. The organizationwide cost of $13,592,834 is broken down into departments—delivery, selling, warehouse, transport, and general and administrative. Transport department cost, representing the cost of trucking beverages from the manufacturer to the distributor's warehouses, is then broken into functional areas, one of which is repairs and maintenance. Repairs and maintenance cost, which equals $541,596, can be, in turn, broken down into even further levels of detail.

The first step, then, is to determine the level of aggregation of the cost to be predicted. For example, if managers want to predict firmwide total cost, they can use any one of the following approaches:

- Estimate firmwide cost using firmwide cost data.
- Estimate firmwide cost by adding together estimates of department costs.
- Estimate firmwide cost by adding together estimates of individual components of cost.

2: IDENTIFY A COST DRIVER

Cost drivers represent activities that cause costs. One way to identify cost drivers is by exploiting the knowledge and experience of employees familiar

EXHIBIT 2.18 BEVERAGE DISTRIBUTOR

Operating Costs

Operating Cost, by Department

Operating Department	Cost
Delivery	$ 3,675,214
Selling	2,543,178
Warehouse	1,023,456
Transport	2,280,320
General & administrative	4,070,666
Total operating cost	$13,592,834

Transport Operating Cost

Function	Cost
Salaries	$ 667,543
Benefits	86,682
Payroll taxes	44,978
Equipment & supplies	29,345
Fuel & oil	385,910
Repairs & maintenance	541,596
Tires	100,264
Rental vehicles	17,657
Repairs—building & equipment	84,387
Uniforms	13,678
Licenses & fees	89,515
Depreciation	218,765
Total transport cost	$2,280,320

with operations. They are likely to understand the fundamental activities that cause costs. In choosing among alternative cost drivers, consider the following:[3]

- Cost drivers should have a logical relationship with the activity.
- Cost drivers should be highly correlated with cost.

For example, assume that the repair and maintenance department is responsible for the trucks that transport beverages from the manufacturer to the distributor. Potential cost drivers might include the number of miles driven, the number of trips, or the number of visits to the repair shop. Each of these cost drivers has a logical relationship with repair and maintenance activities, and data for each are readily available.

When several cost drivers are available, employees familiar with the activity should be able to help identify the most meaningful one. The selection is aided by quantitative tools, like the **coefficient of determination (r^2)**, which provide an objective measure of how closely costs are correlated with cost drivers.

The coefficient of determination measures the amount of variation in the dependent variable (cost of repair and maintenance) explained by the independent variable (miles driven). For example, a coefficient of determination equal to 0.8992 is interpreted to mean that 89.92 percent of variations in repair and maintenance cost can be explained by miles driven.

---

[3] Michael Ostrenga, Terrence Ozan, Robert McIlhattan, and Marcus Harwood, *The Ernst & Young Guide to Total Cost Management.* New York: John Wiley & Sons, 1992, p. 170.

When coupled with the judgment and experience of employees familiar with operations, the coefficient of determination can be used to select appropriate cost drivers.

Caution: A high coefficient of determination does not establish causation. That is, a high coefficient of determination cannot be interpreted to mean that the miles driven directly cause repair and maintenance cost. Instead, it measures the degree of association of observed changes in one variable (cost of repair and maintenance) with observed changes in another variable (miles driven).

3: ESTIMATE THE RELATIONSHIP BETWEEN COST AND COST DRIVER

After the cost to be predicted is identified and an appropriate cost driver selected, the relationship between the two can be estimated. Remember, the objective is to develop an equation that can be used to describe how costs behave in response to changes in the cost driver. Two methods can be used to develop prediction equations: account analysis and regression analysis.

ACCOUNT ANALYSIS

The account analysis method requires relatively little data. Essentially it's subjective, depending on the analyst's knowledge and experience as gleaned from studies, surveys, observations, and interviews with other employees. The procedure is straightforward: Each element of cost is evaluated in light of its cost driver and classified as either fixed or variable. When the analyst believes a cost is mixed, that cost is separated into fixed and variable components, based on judgment. We'll show in the next section how regression analysis can be used in conjunction with account analysis to help separate mixed costs into fixed and variable components.

To illustrate account analysis, example data representing total transport costs for a beverage distributor are separated into fixed and variable components in Exhibit 2.19. Each element of cost is evaluated to determine its nature, the activities it represents, and whether or not it is likely to change in conjunction with changes in its cost driver. For example, salaries represent monthly compensation paid to truck drivers. Since salaries are neither logically linked nor correlated with miles driven, they are considered fixed. Because fuel and oil cost varies in direct proportion with miles driven, it is classified as a variable cost.

The results of account analysis are an equation that can be used to predict each individual component of cost, such as the cost of repair and maintenance, and an equation to predict total cost, such as the total cost of the transport department. For example, assume that miles driven is the cost driver for repairs and maintenance cost and that 600,000 miles are driven during the year. Dividing total annual variable repair and maintenance cost of $316,596 by 600,000 gives a variable cost per mile of $0.528 and the following prediction equation:

EXHIBIT 2.19   BEVERAGE DISTRIBUTOR

Account Analysis of Transport Cost

Function	Year 1993 Total	Fixed	Variable
Salaries	$ 667,543	$ 667,543	
Benefits	86,682	86,682	
Payroll taxes	44,978	44,978	
Equipment & supplies	29,345	29,345	
Fuel & oil	385,910		$385,910
Repair & maintenance	541,596	225,000	316,596
Tires	100,264		100,264
Rental vehicles	17,657	17,657	
Repairs—building	84,387	84,387	
Uniforms	13,678	13,678	
Licenses & fees	89,515	89,515	
Depreciation	218,765	218,765	
Total transport cost	**$2,280,320**	**$1,477,550**	**$802,770**

Repair and Maintenance Cost

Variable cost
   = $316,596/600,000 miles
   = $.528/ mile
Fixed cost = $225,000
Prediction equation
   = $225,000 + $.528 per mile

Transport Cost

Variable cost = $802,770/600,000 miles
             = $1.338/mile
Fixed cost = $1,477,550
Prediction equation = $1,477,550 + $1.338 per mile

Repair and maintenance cost = fixed cost + variable cost

Repair and maintenance cost = $225,000 + ($0.528 × no. of miles driven)

Transport department cost can be predicted in a similar fashion, by dividing $802,770 in total variable cost by 600,000 miles. The results are variable cost of $1.338 per mile and the following prediction equation:

Transport cost = fixed cost + variable cost

Transport cost = $1,477,550 + ($1.338 × no. of miles driven)

Note that transport department cost can be predicted by using the departmentwide equation or by adding together the predictions for the individual cost functions.

The advantage of account analysis is simplicity. And it incorporates the judgment of those most familiar with operations. Among its disadvantages is the arbitrary separation of mixed costs into fixed and variable components. And it often relies on only a single observation of cost, such as that shown in Exhibit 2.19. While the arbitrariness of separating mixed costs is hard to avoid with account analysis, the problem of relying on a single observation can be remedied by observing total cost at different activity levels, perhaps by gathering monthly data and observing whether or not the cost changes in response to changes in activity. Both short-comings of account analysis can be reduced by using regression analysis, as we shall see next.

REGRESSION ANALYSIS

The objective of regression analysis is precisely the same as that of account analysis—identifying an equation that can be used to predict cost at different levels of activity. Unlike account analysis, which can be performed using very little data—such as that for a single period—regression requires multiple observations of historical cost and cost drivers. Since costs have to be accumulated over a period of time—for example, months, quarters, or years—care should be taken to ensure that underlying conditions haven't changed during the term of observation. For example, if the cost driver reflects labor and labor is being displaced by some sort of automated machinery, that's going to change the fundamental relationship between cost and the cost driver.

PLOT MATCHED DATA PAIRS

The first step in regression analysis is to plot matched pairs of data in the form of a scattergram. A matched pair requires two values—value of an independent variable and the corresponding value of the dependent variable. The scattergram is formed by plotting the points where each matched pair intersects. The purpose is to see if there's a relationship between cost (dependent variable), located along the vertical axis, and the cost driver (independent variable), placed on the horizontal axis. If there appears to be a relationship, then it can be represented as an equation and used to make predictions.

To illustrate, let's consider the 24 historical observations of monthly repair and maintenance costs and miles driven shown in Exhibit 2.20. These data are graphed as a scattergram in Exhibit 2.21. After looking at Exhibit 2.21, it appears that there is a straight-line relationship between miles driven and repair and maintenance cost.

ESTIMATING REGRESSION PARAMETERS

To accomplish the objective of regression analysis and produce an equation that can be used to predict total cost, the analyst positions a "best fit" line through the data points. To understand what *best fit* means, consider how you might draw a straight line through the scattergram of data points in Exhibit 2.21. Visualize moving a hypothetical line up or down among all the data points, and, at the same time, rotating it clockwise *and* counterclockwise. One objective way to position the line is to connect the highest and lowest data points. In fact, use any straight edge and connect these two points. While it's easy to position the line by connecting the highest and lowest points, this approach ignores all of the information contained in the data lying in-between.

The idea of regression is to use the available information in *all of the data points.* If the distances of the actual data points from a hypothetical straight line (measured perpendicular to the horizontal axis) are added

EXHIBIT 2.20 BEVERAGE DISTRIBUTOR

Repair and Maintenance Cost and Miles Driven

1992	Miles Driven	Repair and Maintenance Cost
January	31,924	$ 31,343
February	35,359	34,718
March	55,473	46,337
April	37,365	34,071
May	49,382	44,553
June	35,914	32,846
July	47,947	46,019
August	36,634	35,738
September	44,098	38,787
October	46,589	45,022
November	39,179	38,892
December	42,268	40,867
Total year	502,132	$469,192

1993		
January	43,055	$ 37,256
February	45,240	41,288
March	51,188	45,069
April	56,741	49,674
May	49,507	47,033
June	40,754	40,805
July	48,823	44,990
August	52,358	43,922
September	51,336	46,758
October	54,149	48,109
November	49,275	43,171
December	57,574	53,521
Total year	600,000	$541,596

together, the sum of these distances (called *deviations*) above the line should exactly equal the sum of the deviations below it. If that's the case, then the line drawn through the data might be considered the best possible fit.

Using this approach, the distance of each data point from the hypothetical line, no matter how far above or below, would count the same as any other data point in positioning the line. However, the computational method actually used in regression assigns less weight to data points close to the line and more weight to points farther away. Squaring the deviations provides a way of assigning disproportionate weight to large deviations. For example, 1 unit of deviation equals only 1 unit of squared deviation (1^2) while another data point—say, 5 units of deviation away from the line—equals 25 (5^2) units, or 25 times as much. As a result, points far away from the line count more heavily in positioning the line than points

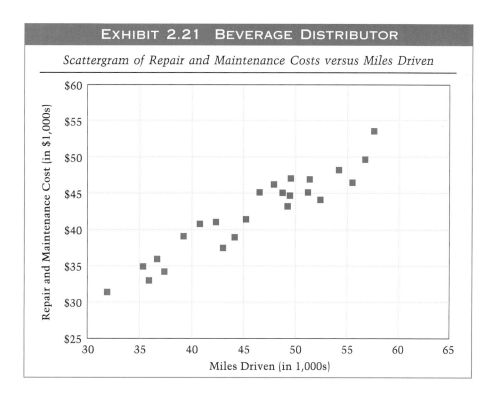

EXHIBIT 2.21 BEVERAGE DISTRIBUTOR

Scattergram of Repair and Maintenance Costs versus Miles Driven

located close by do. Therefore, the line should be selected to *minimize the squared distances* of each data point from the line. That's why this form of regression is called *least-squares regression.*

Least-squares regression, built on these assumptions, positions a straight line that is described by two **parameters:**[4]

- **Intercept** (also called the constant, *alpha,* often represented by the Greek letter "α"), the starting point of the line
- **Slope** (also called *beta,* often represented by the Greek letter "β"), the rate of change in the dependent variable for a unit change in the independent variable

In reality, the true values of these two parameters can never be known, since it is impossible to observe every occurrence of the independent variable and the corresponding values of the dependent variable. Instead, the parameters are *estimated* from a sample of data.[5]

Estimates of intercept and slope parameters, based on the historical observations of repair and maintenance using the data in Exhibit 2.20, are

---

[4] *Parameters* are numerical measures of a population.

[5] Parameters, usually denoted by Greek letters, like α and β, are estimated by drawing a sample and calculating a statistic. In financial settings, there may be very few opportunities to draw samples. In our example, there are infinite combinations of repair and maintenance costs and miles driven. We have gathered only a few of these possible combinations and generalized the relationship between them.

EXHIBIT 2.22 BEVERAGE DISTRIBUTOR	
Regression of Repair and Maintenance Cost on Miles Driven	
Regression Output	
Constant	8,055
Standard error of y estimate	1,852
r squared	0.8992
Number of observations	24
Degrees of freedom	22
x Coefficient	0.7417
Standard error of x coefficient	0.0529

shown in Exhibit 2.22. This exhibit represents the **regression output panel** from a computer spreadsheet. The dependent variable, or the *y* range used in estimating the parameters, is repair and maintenance cost, while the independent variable, or *x* range, is miles driven. The intercept (constant) equals $8,055, and the slope coefficient equals $0.7417. That is, monthly fixed costs are equal to $8,055—or, on an annual basis, $96,660 ($8,055 × 12) plus $0.7417 for every mile driven.

CHECKING HOW WELL THE ESTIMATED REGRESSION LINE "FITS" THE DATA

The last phase in identifying a prediction equation using regression analysis is to evaluate *goodness of fit*. While there is no precise formula, several tools are useful in determining how accurately the equation is likely to predict cost. One tool, the coefficient of determination (r^2), equal to 0.8992, is found in the regression output panel on the line reading "*r* squared" in Exhibit 2.22. Values for r^2 should be relatively high, indicating that cost and its cost driver are highly correlated.[6] Unfortunately, there are no guidelines that quantify what constitutes a relatively high coefficient of determination. Instead, it is determined by comparing r^2 for alternative cost drivers. Recall that a high r^2 indicates that a large proportion of variation in the variable being projected is explained by the dependent variable. Many analysts would say an r^2 of 0.8992 indicates a good fit, adding confidence in the usefulness of the prediction equation obtained from our regression.

Another test of goodness of fit is to see whether or not the slope coefficient is located far enough away from zero. The reason is that a regression equation with a slope coefficient close to zero adds nothing to the

---

[6] The standard error of the *y* estimate, equal to 1,852 in Exhibit 2.22, is computationally connected to the coefficient of determination. This figure summarizes the variation in the actual values of cost around the regression line. In unusual cases, the standard error will equal exactly zero, indicating a perfect fit between actual and predicted values. Correspondingly, r^2 will equal 1.00. While the lower limit of the standard error is zero, there is no upper limit. As disagreement between actual and predicted costs increases, the standard error increases, driving r^2 closer to zero.

ability to predict total cost. If the slope is close to zero, then the prediction for any value of the independent variable is simply equal to the intercept. The test for "far enough away" from zero is calculated by dividing the value of the slope coefficient by the standard error of the slope coefficient. The results are expressed in units of standard error. A general guideline[7] is that the (absolute value of) units of standard error should be greater than a critical value of 2. Using the Regression Output panel in Exhibit 2.22 and dividing the value of the slope coefficient (0.7417) by the standard error of the slope (x) coefficient (0.0529) yields a statistic equal to 14.02. Since the (absolute value of) units of standard error (14.02) exceed the critical value (2), the slope coefficient is considered far enough away from zero, increasing the confidence level of the usefulness of the prediction equation.

Another way to assess goodness of fit is from a visual inspection of the scattergram. Check to see that the line fits through the data points and that the scatter of the data points is relatively homogeneous over the entire range of values. Exhibit 2.23 shows three graphs that illustrate this point. The graph in panel A has the desired homogeneous scatter. The graph in panel B shows nonhomogeneous scatter, called *heteroscedasticity*. The dispersion of observed values around the regression line in panel B increases as activity increases. While nonhomogeneous scatter may not affect predictions of values over the range of observed data, it should be obvious that predictions at lower activity levels are subject to less uncertainty than are predictions at higher levels of activity.

Panel C illustrates nonlinearity. Note that the data points generally fall below the regression line at the very low and very high levels of activity, while falling above the line in the middle range. Using the linear estimate will produce costs that are overestimated at either extreme, while underestimated in the midranges of activity. Under these conditions, a nonlinear prediction equation should be used. Estimation of nonlinear cost functions is illustrated in the appendix to this chapter, using learning curves as an example.

4: PREDICT COST FOR A GIVEN LEVEL OF THE COST DRIVER

POINT ESTIMATES

The results, whether from account analysis or regression analysis, can be used to predict exact values of repair and maintenance cost for any number of miles driven within the relevant range. These exact values are

---

[7] This guideline is based on values from the student's *t* distribution. In general, values from this table center around approximately 2 for all but the smallest *degrees of freedom* and lowest *levels of significance*. Degrees of freedom, taken from the regression output panel in Exhibit 2.22, equal the sample size less the number of parameters estimated in the regression equation. In simple linear regression, the method illustrated in this chapter, two parameters are estimated—one for the intercept and one for the slope. The level of significance represents the risk that managers are willing to accept if they *incorrectly* conclude that the slope coefficient is significantly different from zero. The most common significance levels are 1 percent, 5 percent, and 10 percent.

EXHIBIT 2.23 THREE SCATTERGRAMS ILLUSTRATING
DIFFERENT CONDITIONS AFFECTING GOODNESS OF FIT

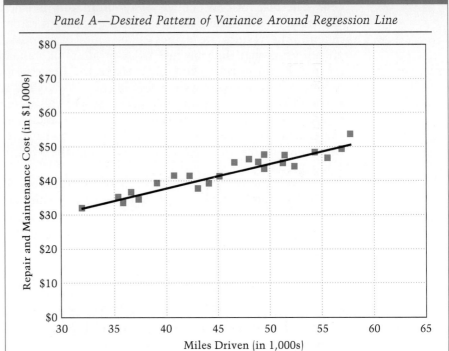

Panel A—Desired Pattern of Variance Around Regression Line

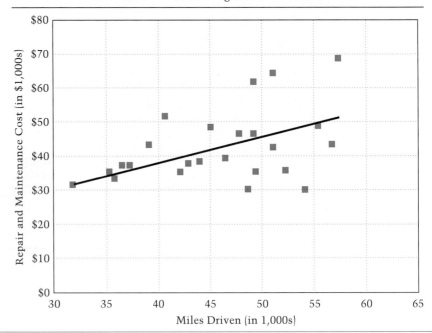

Panel B—Nonhomogeneous Variance

(continued)

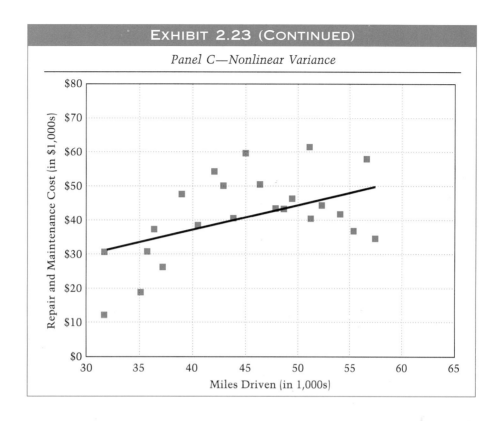

EXHIBIT 2.23 (CONTINUED)

Panel C—Nonlinear Variance

known as **point estimates.** For example, assume that the slope and intercept parameters are estimated using regression analysis. A point estimate of total repair and maintenance cost for any month can be prepared using the following equation:[8]

$$y = a + (b \times x)$$

Where:

y = estimate of the value of the dependent variable.

a = estimate of the intercept parameter.

b = estimate of the slope parameter.

x = value of the independent variable (cost driver) expected during the period for which the prediction is being prepared. Note that x should fall within the values in the relevant range.

At, say, 50,000 miles driven, a point estimate of repairs and maintenance cost is

$$\text{Repair and maintenance cost} = \$8,055 + (\$0.7417 \times 50,000)$$

$$= \$8,055 + \$37,085$$

$$= \$45,140$$

---

[8] You may have noted that we changed the notation from the Greek letters "α" and "β" to the alphabetic characters "a" and "b". The reason is that "α" and "β" refer to known population parameters while "a" and "b" represent *estimates* of these parameters.

This prediction can be modified, as deemed necessary, to reflect events or conditions that managers believe have changed or are likely to change in the future. For example, recent labor contracts may require a cost-of-living adjustment. Or perhaps some repair and maintenance activities have been outsourced to an independent contractor. These events change the conditions under which the parameters were originally estimated. One way to deal with changing conditions, other than by making judgmental modifications, is to periodically reestimate parameters. Old, outdated data points are eliminated and replaced by current data. Then the regression parameters are estimated again using the new data set.

CONFIDENCE INTERVALS

The probability of a prediction's exactly equaling an actual value is quite small. Fortunately, the standard error of the y estimate extracted from the regression output panel (1,852 in our example) can be used to create upper and lower boundaries, called **confidence intervals**. For example, the estimate of repair and maintenance cost at 50,000 miles (calculated above) is $45,140. Without explaining where the numbers come from, managers can be confident that, 95 percent of the time, the actual cost will fall within an interval bounded at the upper level by $49,087 and at the lower level by $41,195. Computation of confidence intervals is beyond the scope of this book but can typically be found in introductory statistics textbooks.

One rough approximation of confidence intervals is found by multiplying the standard error of the y estimate (found in the regression output panel, Exhibit 2.22) by the number 2. Then this quantity is added to the point estimate to obtain the upper boundary of the confidence interval. That is,

$$\text{Upper boundary of confidence interval} = \text{estimated } y + (\text{standard error of } y \text{ estimate} \times 2)$$
$$= \$45,140 + (\$1,852 \times 2)$$
$$= \$45,140 + \$3,704$$
$$= \$48,844$$

Similarly, subtract the quantity from the point estimate to obtain the lower boundary of the confidence interval:

$$\text{Lower boundary of confidence interval} = \text{estimated } y - (\text{standard error of } y \text{ estimate} \times 2)$$
$$= \$45,140 - (\$1,852 \times 2)$$
$$= \$45,140 - \$3,704$$
$$= \$41,436$$

That is, repair and maintenance cost is likely to fall within an interval ranging from $48,844 on the upper boundary to $41,436 on the lower boundary. Remember that confidence intervals calculated this way are not statistically valid. In particular, they tend to underestimate the upper and lower boundaries for values of the independent variable located at both extremes of the relevant range.

SUMMARY

Costs behave with respect to changes in activity in four ways, according to which of four cost types they are: fixed, step (semifixed), variable, and mixed (semivariable). While total variable costs increase with activity, unit variable costs remain constant. Fixed costs, which do not change in total in response to changes in activity, decrease on a per unit basis when activity increases. The behavior of unit fixed costs gives rise to the concept of economies of scale, where the lowest cost is achieved when fixed resources are used to their fullest extent. In fact, some managers build cost structures that are predominately fixed so that they can take advantage of economies of scale. Unfortunately, higher levels of fixed costs also expose the organization to higher breakeven points and greater probability of loss.

Breakeven is the activity level where there is neither a profit nor a loss. It is the activity level where just enough units are sold for the total contribution margin—the difference between total revenue and total variable cost—to just equal fixed cost. Breakeven is calculated by dividing total fixed cost by the unit contribution margin.

Contribution margin formats organize costs by their cost behavior. Total variable cost is deducted from total revenue to determine total contribution margin. Fixed cost is deducted from total contribution margin to determine net income. Income statements in this format are more helpful to managers in assessing the impact of changes in activity on cost than financial accounting statements are.

There are two methods for identifying cost behavior: (1) account analysis, which is more subjective, relying upon the knowledge and experience of the analyst; and (2) regression analysis, which is more objective, although it requires more information to implement. Managers use these tools to separate total cost into fixed and variable costs.

APPENDIX

LEARNING CURVES

As employees gain work experience, their skill at performing operations increases. The results are improvements in efficiency, better-quality products, and overall reduction in cost. The relationship between experience and improvements can be represented graphically in the form of a learning curve. Learning curves are used in several ways. One way is in estimating costs, especially life-cycle costs. Organizations whose products compete based on price, for example, may rely on learning-curve effects to bring costs down and achieve economies of scale over the life of the product. Another use of learning curves is in competitive analysis—for example, in negotiations with a supplier. Estimates of the supplier's learning rate might permit purchasing managers to obtain better prices. Moreover, the impact of learning curves may transcend a single product, bringing about synergistic, firmwide improvements.

Learning curves capture the relationship between the average amount of time it takes to accomplish a task and the cumulative number of units produced. For example, suppose managers start making a new product and the first unit takes 200 labor-hours to produce. Assume that production is likely to experience an 80 percent learning rate. As cumulative production doubles from 1 to 2 units, the average number of labor-hours (per unit) declines to 80 percent of the average labor-hours it took to produce 1 unit. Increasing output from 2 to 4 units causes the average number of labor-hours per unit to again decline to 80 percent of the average number of labor-hours required to produce 2 units. These results are shown in tabular form in Exhibit 2.24.

The first column of Exhibit 2.24 shows the cumulative number of units. The second column shows the average number of hours per unit. The third column shows the cumulative hours it takes to make the number of units shown in column 1. For example, it takes 200 hours to make the first unit. When the output doubles to 2, it takes an average of 160 hours (80% of 200) for both the first and second units. That is, it takes a total of 320 hours (2 × 160) to make the first 2 units. When output doubles again to 4 units, it takes an average of 128 hours (80% of 160) for all 4 units. That is, it takes a total of 512 hours (4 × 128) to make the first 4 units. The progressive reduction in the average hours per unit, represented in graph form, is shown in Exhibit 2.25. Note that, as more units are produced, the reduction in the average number of labor-hours becomes smaller and smaller. That is, the biggest benefits are realized in the early stages of production.

Evidence from actual applications indicates that learning rates, such as those tabulated in Exhibit 2.26, can be quite high. Each organization

EXHIBIT 2.24 80 PERCENT LEARNING CURVE		
(1) Cumulative Number of Units	(2) Average Hours per Unit	(3) Cumulative Hours
1	200.0	200
2	160.0	320
4	128.0	512
8	102.4	819
16	81.9	1,311
32	65.5	2,097
64	52.4	3,355
128	41.9	5,369
256	33.6	8,590
512	26.8	13,744

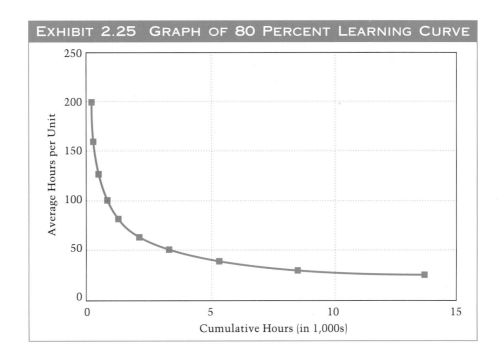

EXHIBIT 2.25 GRAPH OF 80 PERCENT LEARNING CURVE

EXHIBIT 2.26 EXAMPLES OF LEARNING CURVES

Example	Improving Factor	Cumulative Activity	Learning Curve	Period Effected
Model T production	Price	Units produced	86%	1910 to 1926
Aircraft assembly	Direct labor-hours per unit	Units produced	80%	1925 to 1957
Equipment maintenance	Avg. time to replace parts	Number of replacements	76%	Around 1957
Labor-hours per barrel of oil	Avg. direct labor-hours per barrel	Barrels refined in U.S.	84%	1860 to 1962
Electric power generation	Miles per kilowatt-hour	Millions of kilowatt-hours	95%	1910 to 1955
Steel production	Labor-hours per unit	Units produced	79%	1920 to 1955
Integrated circuits	Avg. price per unit	Units produced	72%	1964 to 1972
Handheld calculators	Avg. selling price	Units produced	74%	1975 to 1978
Disk memory drives	Avg. price per bit	Number of bits	76%	1975 to 1978

Source: J. A. Cunningham, "Using the Learning Curve as a Management Tool," *IEEE Spectrum*, June 1980, p. 45. Copyright © 1980 IEEE. Used with permission.

encounters a different learning rate based on different factors. Examples of these factors include product characteristics, activities required in making the product, skill level, labor-saving equipment, innovations in technology, process improvements, corporate culture, and incentives offered for improvements. Changes in any of these factors can influence the learning rate. For example, introduction of automated equipment, simplification of product design, or elimination of non-value-added activities can cause improvements.

Failure to recognize the potential decline in labor requirements attributable to learning curves may result in lost opportunities. For example, what if the market price for the product represented in Exhibit 2.24 were based on the assumption that, say, only 30 units would be sold. If the prevailing market price allows for only 50 hours of labor per unit, then the managers are likely to decide not to enter the market. That's because each of the first 30 units are expected to require an average of 81.9 hours per unit to make. Sales would have to increase to above 64 units before the average number of labor-hours declined to below 50.

If learning rates are not known, they may be estimated based on historical data, and then the estimates may be used to make predictions. To illustrate, consider the data in Exhibit 2.27, which represents monthly auto loan applications processed by a bank. The first column is the month and the second column is the number of loan applications processed during that month. Total loan applications are accumulated in the third column. The fourth column represents the number of labor-hours required to process all of the applications for a particular month. Cumulative labor-hours are shown in the fifth column. Column 6 shows the average labor-hours per loan application, derived by dividing cumulative loan applications processed (column 3) by the cumulative labor-hours (column 5).

Were the data in Exhibit 2.27 to be plotted, they would exhibit nonlinear behavior. A nonlinear prediction equation—specifically, an *exponential function* useful in describing learning curves—takes the following general form:

$$y = ax^b$$

The two parameters in the exponential equation are the same as in linear regression. The *a* in the equation is an estimate of the intercept (constant), while *b* represents an estimate of the slope. Fortunately, the data can be transformed from a nonlinear form to a linear form and the parameters of the equation estimated using linear regression.[9] The transformation is accomplished by taking logarithms of both sides of the equation:[10]

$$\text{Log } y = \text{Log } a + [b \times \text{Log}(x)]$$

Using the data in Exhibit 2.27, the seventh column in Exhibit 2.27 represents (base 10) logarithms of the values in column 3. For example, the log of 1,450 is 3.1614. The eighth column is similarly transformed by taking the logarithm of each value in column 5. The two transformed data columns, shown now as logarithms in columns 7 and 8, are the independent (x) and dependent (y) variables, respectively. After performing a lin-

---

[9]   Some statistical software packages allow direct estimation of parameters. In addition, nonlinear optimizers in some spreadsheets allow direct estimation of parameters in nonlinear equations by minimizing the sum of the squared errors.
[10]   Logs are easily calculated in spreadsheets by using the @Log function.

EXHIBIT 2.27 AUTO LOAN APPLICATIONS PROCESSED IN BANK

Estimating Learning Curve Parameters

							Average Labor-Hours per Application		
(1) Month	(2) Monthly Applications Processed	(3) Cumulative Applications Processed	(4) Monthly Labor-Hours	(5) Cumulative Labor-Hours	(6) Average Labor-Hours per Application	(7) Log of Cumulative Applications Processed (x Range)	(8) Log (y range)	(9) Log Prediction	(10) Antilog Prediction
1	1,450	1,450	3,575	3,575	2.47	3.1614	0.3919	0.4279	2.68
2	1,465	2,915	3,422	6,997	2.40	3.4646	0.3802	0.3633	2.31
3	1,525	4,440	2,766	9,763	2.20	3.6474	0.3422	0.3243	2.11
4	1,537	5,977	2,516	12,278	2.05	3.7765	0.3127	0.2968	1.98
5	1,645	7,622	2,339	14,617	1.92	3.8821	0.2828	0.2743	1.88
6	1,328	8,950	1,811	16,428	1.84	3.9518	0.2638	0.2594	1.82
7	1,545	10,495	2,376	18,804	1.79	4.0210	0.2533	0.2447	1.76
8	1,581	12,076	2,105	20,909	1.73	4.0819	0.2384	0.2317	1.70
9	1,765	13,841	1,907	22,817	1.65	4.1412	0.2171	0.2191	1.66
10	1,867	15,708	2,022	24,839	1.58	4.1961	0.1990	0.2073	1.61
11	2,011	17,719	1,872	26,711	1.51	4.2484	0.1782	0.1962	1.57
12	2,156	19,875	2,749	29,460	1.48	4.2983	0.1709	0.1856	1.53
Prediction 13	1,980	21,855				4.3396		0.1768	1.50

Regression Output

Constant		1.102
Standard error of *y* estimate		0.017
r squared		0.952
Number of observations		12.000
Degrees of freedom		10.000
x coefficient	−0.213	
Standard error of *x* coefficient	0.015	

ear regression on the data in columns 7 and 8, estimates of the intercept and slope coefficients are found in the Regression Output panel, located at the bottom of Exhibit 2.27. Specifically, the intercept is 1.102, while the slope is −0.213. Converting this data into a prediction equation,

$$\text{Prediction of log } y = 1.102 + (-0.213 \times \log x)$$

Predictions of the average labor-hours for each of the 12 actual observations, in logarithmic form, are shown in the ninth column. Each value is calculated by using the prediction equation above, multiplying values in column 7 by −0.213, and adding 1.102. Finally, antilogs[11] of the logarithmic predictions in column 9 are shown in column 10. These values represent estimates of the average number of hours per loan application. They can be compared with the actual values in column 6 to assess goodness of fit.

An example of predictions of average labor-hours is found at the bottom of Exhibit 2.27. For example, what if managers believe that approximately 1,980 applications are likely to be processed next month? How many hours should they budget for this level of activity? Cumulative applications, shown in column 3, are expected to increase from 19,875 to 21,855. The log of 21,855 (the cumulative number of applications) is shown in column 7. The prediction, in log form, of the average number of hours, using the prediction equation, is 0.1768. Finding the antilog of 0.1768 yields 1.50 hours, an estimate of the average time it will take to process each of the applications.

CHAPTER 2 ASSIGNMENTS

DISCUSSION PROBLEMS

D2.1 (Economies of Scale)

Exhibit D2.1 shows a consolidated statement of income, containing revenue and selected expenses, taken from the 1990 annual report of American Express. The upper section shows the dollar amounts of revenue and expense. The middle section shows expenses, expressed as a percent of revenue. For example, human resources represented 22.15 percent of revenue ($5,390/$24,332) in 1990. The bottom section shows the percent changes for revenue and expense from the previous year, calculated by dividing the figures for the current year by that of the previous year and subtracting one. For example, revenue in 1990 declined 2.85 percent from 1989 [($24,332/$25,047) − 1].

Required:

1. Would you expect expenses to increase proportionally with increases in revenues? For example, if revenue increased by 10 percent, would you expect

---

[11] Some spreadsheets include antilog functions. However, you can find base 10 antilogs by simply raising the number 10 to the power of the log. For example, 2.68, the first number in column 10, is derived by raising 10 to the exponent 0.4279.

EXHIBIT D2.1 AMERICAN EXPRESS COMPANY

Consolidated Statement of Income
Revenue and Selected Expense ($ millions)

	1990	1989	1988
Revenues[a]	$24,332	$25,047	$20,895
Expense—dollar amounts:[a]			
Human resources	$ 5,390	$ 5,322	$ 4,988
Occupancy & equipment	$ 1,473	$ 1,390	$ 1,259
Advertising & promotion	$ 1,032	$ 1,079	$ 1,022
Expense—percent of revenue:			
Human resources	22.15%	21.25%	23.87%
Occupancy & equipment	6.05%	5.55%	6.03%
Advertising & promotion	4.24%	4.31%	4.89%

	1990/1989	1989/1988
Percent change [(year/previous year) − 1]:		
Revenue	−2.85%	19.87%
Human resources	1.28%	6.70%
Occupancy & equipment	5.97%	10.41%
Advertising & promotion	−4.36%	5.58%

Source: American Express Company, *1990 Annual Report*, p. 41.

[a] Dollar figures in millions.

human resources cost to increase by 10 percent? If not, list some of the reasons why costs shouldn't increase proportionally.

2. Which of the three categories of cost—human resources, occupancy and equipment, and advertising and promotion—do you think are more likely to change proportionally with increases in revenue? Which of the three are less likely to change proportionally?

D2.2 (Trading Variable for Fixed)

Time Magazine[12] reports a trend in American companies whereby permanent workers are released and temporary workers, or "temps," hired in their places. Every day, nearly 1.5 million temps are dispatched from labor agencies, up over 300 percent from 10 years ago. An additional 34 million workers start their day as "contingent" workers, paid on an hourly basis for part-time work or for full-time projects of short duration. Nearly 1 out of every 3 workers has a part-time position, with the ranks of part-time workers growing so quickly that they are likely to exceed the number of permanently employed workers by the turn of the century.

Time Magazine considers this one of the most important trends in American business, a trend fueled by poor economic conditions, growing global competition, and uncertainties about the future. Employers want to have just the right

---

[12] Janice Castro, "Disposable Workers," *Time*, Apr. 19, 1993, pp. 40–41.

number of employees—no more and no fewer than needed—a form of "just-in-time" employment. Managers are leaning more and more toward staffing core activities—those operations at the heart of their businesses—with full-time workers and leaving all noncrucial functions to contingent workers.

While this strategy may help in the short term, it may cause unexpected long-term costs. Not only does temporary employment disrupt the lives of contingent workers, but it fails to build human capital, one of the most important assets a nation can possess. In fact, Labor Secretary Robert Reich believes that the skills and ideas of the employees are the key resource of any organization.

Required: Why do managers replace full-time workers with part-time workers? Discuss the pros and cons of this strategy with respect to cost structures, risk, and ability to compete.

PROBLEMS   **P2.1** **(Basic Cost—Volume—Profit Analysis)**

Matoney Manufacturing makes a single product that's sold primarily through a nationally known discount house. Last year's performance, reflected in the income statement shown in Exhibit P2.1, was considered a normal year. All materials and direct labor cost, plus $0.80 of the $2.50 manufacturing overhead cost, vary in direct proportion with the number of units sold. In addition, commissions vary with the dollar amount of revenue. All other costs are fixed.

Next year, however, managers expect volume to increase temporarily to 220,000 units because of an unusually large order anticipated from the discount house. Since Matoney has excess capacity, none of the managers believe that fixed cost will increase.

Required: What is Matoney Manufacturing's expected operating income if it sells 220,000 units? Prepare your solution in a contribution margin format.

P2.2 **(Breaking Costs into Fixed and Variable)**

Hornsby Frames, located in Dothan, Alabama, makes a single line of upscale metal eyeglass frames. The total cost of operations for the current year, extracted from

---

EXHIBIT P2.1   MATONEY MANUFACTURING

Income Statement

Volume (in units)		200,000
Revenue	$7.40	$1,480,000
Cost of goods sold:		
Materials	1.35	270,000
Direct labor	1.25	250,000
Manufacturing overhead	2.50	500,000
Total cost of goods sold	$5.10	$1,020,000
Gross profit		$ 460,000
Operating expense:		
Commissions (based on revenue)	5.00%	74,000
Administrative		190,000
Total operating expense		$ 264,000
Operating income		$ 196,000

EXHIBIT P2.2 HORNSBY FRAMES	
Total Cost of Operations	
General Ledger Account	*Total Cost*
Direct materials	$125,000
Manufacturing salaries & benefits	87,500
Office salaries & benefits	46,300
Marketing salaries	44,800
Depreciation—building	19,100
Office supplies	18,500
Manufacturing utilities	11,200
Depreciation—manufacturing equipment	8,700
Total cost	$361,100

Hornsby's general ledger, is shown in Exhibit P2.2. The firm's accountant, when asked about cost behavior, stated that most of the costs are fixed. However, there are three exceptions. All of the direct materials cost, 20 percent of manufacturing salaries and benefits cost, and 35 percent of manufacturing utilities cost varies with the number of frames manufactured. Hornsby manufactured and sold 6,422 frames in the current year.

Required: Prepare an estimate of total cost for next year assuming Hornsby sells 7,000 frames.

P2.3 (Profit with Two Cost Structures)

Lake Nona Products manufactures a product that costs $250,000 per year plus $4.10 for each unit made. Lake Nona's president is considering replacing the production equipment with a newer, more efficient system. While the new equipment reduces variable cost to $3.80 per unit, fixed cost increases to $325,000. The selling price of Lake Nona's product is $5.60 per unit.

Required:

1. Calculate the number of units (crossover point) where the total cost is the same for both the old and the new equipment.
2. If Lake Nona Products makes 50,000 *fewer* units than the number of units indicated by the crossover point, what are the pretax operating profits on the basis of using (*a*) the old equipment and (*b*) the new equipment?
3. If Lake Nona Products makes 50,000 *more* units than the number of units representing the crossover point, what are the pretax operating profits on the basis of using (*a*) the old equipment and (*b*) the new equipment?

P2.4 (Breakeven for a Single Product)

Almo Canopies manufactures adjustable canopies that attach to motor homes and trailers. Almo sells both new and replacement canopies in a variety of colors. Its business plan for the current year is based on the assumption that the unit retail price of its single line of canopies will be $400. Canopies are made by cutting canvas into pieces using standard forms. The pieces are then sewn together using commercial-grade sewing machines. The completed canopies are wrapped in plastic, then placed in cardboard boxes for shipment. Almo has always paid workers according to the number of units they produce, resulting in a labor cost of $60 per unit. Almo's accountant estimates that materials will cost about $120 per unit, while other variable manufacturing and nonmanufacturing costs are about $20 per unit.

Fixed costs at Almo are nominal, since the firm uses relatively low-tech production methods. Annual fixed cost includes a $30,000 lease payment for the warehouse, $25,000 for the manufacturing supervisor, $15,000 for utilities, $12,000 for bookkeeping services, and about $38,000 for all other fixed costs.

Almo's president is considering leasing state-of-the-art fabric-cutting tables and other equipment that would increase worker productivity. The equipment would be leased for $30,000 per year. The benefit comes from the reduction in the amount of time it takes to make each canopy. With the new equipment, labor cost falls from $60 to $35 per unit. Unfortunately, the new equipment causes more waste, increasing materials cost by about $5 per unit.

Required: How many units have to be sold at a price of $400 each to achieve before-tax breakeven for the year using the present equipment? How many units would have to be sold to achieve before-tax breakeven using the new, state-of-the-art equipment?

(CMA Adapted)

P2.5 (Setting Selling Prices)

Morgan Ball began making Vivant Merlot, a full-bodied red wine, in the Russian River area of California in the early 1970s. The market considers Morgan's wines upscale, an image she enhances by using a distinctively shaped bottle. This brand "value" allows Morgan to charge a little more per case than her competitors do. Under normal conditions, she sells about 30,000 six-bottle cases each year. However, Morgan is concerned about changes she sees in consumer attitudes. For example, excess capacity in the industry may lead to price competition. She is also worried about the impact of declining disposable income, not to mention the rumors that foreign wine merchants are going to increase exports to the United States. All of this has Morgan wondering about how to price her wine.

Morgan buys grapes from area growers at a cost of about $1.25 per bottle of wine. The bottles themselves, together with corks, cost about $0.30. The cost of all other materials is $0.25 per bottle. Besides incurring fixed utilities cost, each bottle of wine causes utilities cost to increase by $0.15.

Morgan employs a core group of employees, most of whom have been with her for many years. Their salary cost, together with management's, is $320,000. Benefits and other related costs add another 25 percent to payroll cost. When production activity picks up, Morgan's agreement with her employees is that everyone pitches in and works harder to get the job done. Then, when activity slackens, she gives everyone time off. Other annual fixed costs include $72,000 for the fixed portion of utilities cost, $140,000 for facilities and equipment, $125,000 for marketing cost, and $225,000 for administration.

Required:

1. Morgan believes that a 15 percent return on all of her costs (before income taxes) is reasonable. She wants to know what the selling price per case must be, including a 15 percent return on total cost. Prepare a schedule showing case selling prices for 20,000, 25,000, 30,000, 35,000, and 40,000 six-bottle cases.

2. Assume Morgan settles on a case price of $50 and publishes it in the price list sent to her distributors. What are her expected pretax profits and percent return on total cost if sales volume equals the normal volume of 30,000? What happens to Morgan's pretax net income if sales volume decreases to 25,000 cases?

P2.6 (Breakeven with Two Cost Structures)

In its 1991 annual report, General Motors disclosed information relating to the automotive segment, some of which is presented in Exhibit P2.6. During the year, GM sold 7,268,000 vehicles worldwide. Cost and expense for this level of activity are also shown in Exhibit P2.6. While General Motors does not disclose details of its costs, assume that cost and expense are decomposed into fixed and variable as follows:[13]

- Materials—100 percent variable
- Direct labor—85 percent fixed
- Manufacturing overhead—72 percent fixed
- Selling, general, and administrative expense—84 percent fixed
- Depreciation and amortization—100 percent fixed

Required:

1. How many vehicles have to be sold to achieve breakeven with the hypothetical cost structure outlined above? What is pretax operating profit (loss)

---

[13]   The breakdown of costs by behavior is purely hypothetical. However, an article by Doron P. Levin, "GM Forecasts Operating Loss for 3rd Quarter," *The Wall Street Journal*, July 23, 1986, quotes James McDonald, GM's president at that time, as stating that fixed cost for plant, equipment, and administration was 26 percent of the total cost structure in 1980, 30 percent in 1986, and expected to rise to 35 percent in 1990.

EXHIBIT P2.6   GENERAL MOTORS

Breakdown of Costs for Automotive Products, 1991
(in $ millions)

Net sales of automotive products		$ 94,607
Cost and expense:		
Cost of sales	$37,327	
Materials	26,908	
Direct labor	22,150	
Manufacturing overhead		
Total cost of sales		86,385
Selling, general, & administrative expenses		9,745
Depreciation & amortization		4,671
Total cost & expense		$100,801
Operating loss (Before income taxes)		$ (6,194)

Source: Net sales of automotive products, depreciation and amortization, and operating loss (before income taxes) are taken from: General Motors, *1991 Annual Report*, p. 41. The other figures are estimates.

if 7 million vehicles are sold? What is pretax operating profit (loss) if 9 million vehicles are sold?

2. Independent of your answer to requirement 1, assume General Motors signed a new contract with its labor unions linking pay with productivity. Also assume the new contract reduces the fixed proportion of direct labor from 85 to 20 percent. With this change in cost structure, and assuming no other changes in the data shown in Exhibit P2.6, how many vehicles have to be sold to achieve breakeven? What is operating profit (loss) before tax if 7 million vehicles are sold? What is operating profit (loss) before tax if 9 million vehicles are sold?

3. What do you need to know in order to determine which of the two cost structures is better?

P2.7   (Single Product Breakeven; Downward-Sloping Demand Curve)

Mainland Manufacturing makes small power generators that are used in the production of automobiles. Mainland has the theoretical capacity to produce nearly 75,000 units per year but normally makes only around 40,000. There is considerable global competition in both the generator and the automotive industry, and Mainland's products are considered commodities. Management feels that small changes in price can cause sizeable swings in volume. Mainland tested the reaction of volume to changing prices by lowering its present unit price of $250 to $200. The market's response surprised nearly everyone! Reducing price caused volume to increase 20,000 units, from 40,000 to 60,000 units.

Armed with this information, managers began to wonder what price would generate the largest operating profit. To help answer this question, they gathered the following information:

- Sales commissions of 3.5 percent are paid on every dollar of revenue.
- Production materials cost is $75 per unit.
- Transportation cost is $2.75 per unit.
- Packing materials and supplies cost is $10 per unit.
- Production labor, provided by permanent salaried employees is $85 per unit at normal production (40,000 units). These core employees are protected by a contract that provides for guaranteed minimum hours.
- Part-time workers are used to supplement permanent production labor for volumes greater than 40,000 units. Part-time workers are provided by an independent contractor who is paid according to the following schedule:

Units	Total Part-Time Labor Cost
0–40,000	$0
40,001–45,000	$350,000
45,001–50,000	$675,000
50,001–55,000	$975,000
55,001–60,000	$1,250,000
60,001 or more	$1,500,000

- Building lease cost is $375,000 per year.
- Base salaries for sales personnel are $400,000 per year.
- Administrative cost is $480,000 per year.

Required: What price maximizes Mainland's pretax profit? Assume the equation for the demand curve is [Units demanded = a + (b × price)]. Use this equation to predict how sales volume is affected by changes in price. That is, generalize the relationship between price (independent variable) and units demanded (dependent variable) so that you can insert any price between $200 and $250 in the equation and come up with an estimate of the number of units demanded.

P2.8 (Basic Multiple Product Breakeven)

Kalifo Company manufactures a line of electric garden tools that are sold in general hardware stores. The company's controller, Sylvia Harlow, has just received the sales forecast for the coming year for Kalifo's three products: hedge clippers, weeders, and leaf blowers. Kalifo has experienced considerable variations in sales volumes and variable costs over the past two years. The preliminary budget information for next year is shown in Exhibit P2.8.

Kalifo's fixed manufacturing cost is budgeted for $2 million next year. The company also expects fixed selling and administrative cost to be $600,000. Kalifo pays income taxes at a rate of 40 percent.

Required:

1. Determine Kalifo Company's budgeted after-tax profit for next year if they sell 50,000 hedge clippers, 50,000 weeders, and 100,000 leaf blowers.
2. Assuming the sales mix remains as budgeted, determine how many units of each product Kalifo Company must sell next year in order for the company, as a whole, to achieve breakeven.

(CMA Adapted)

P2.9 (Multiple Products; Breakeven)

Sunnyvale Correctional Healthcare (SCH) provides medical care for inmates at county, state, and federal correctional facilities. Born out of the privatization movement, SCH's mission is to meet the health care needs of prison inmates. Government agencies, facing exploding prison populations, have discovered they are unprepared to meet medical needs of the inmates, most of whom are considerably less healthy than the general public. While some authorities approach the problem with an in-house medical staff, others have turned to local hospitals. However, with growing occupancy rates and the negative visual impact of guarded rooms, hospital officials are increasingly reluctant to accept prisoners. As a result, many correctional boards began to search for alternatives. Not only do third-party

EXHIBIT P2.8 KALIFO COMPANY

Preliminary Budget Data for the Year

	Hedge Clippers	Weeders	Leaf Blowers
Unit sales	50,000	50,000	100,000
Unit selling price	$28.00	$36.00	$48.00
Variable manufacturing cost per unit	$13.00	$12.00	$25.00
Varibable selling cost per unit	$5.00	$4.00	$6.00

providers such as SCH deliver better health care, they do so, in many cases, at a lower cost. Furthermore, exposure to many of the risks associated with in-house medical solutions is greatly reduced by using providers like SCH.

SCH is currently negotiating a contract with the Tangelo County Correctional Facility, geographically encompassing one of the largest metropolitan areas in the southwest. The proposed contract calls for SCH to provide three basic kinds of service for the following fees: $50 per rapid in-out encounter, $400 per bed-day for psychiatric care, and $400 per bed-day for medical-surgical care. Rapid in-out care clearly represents the highest patient load, with encounters estimated to run about 85 percent of the number of daily inmate visits. Rapid in-out encounters range from the treatment of headaches to minor cuts and dental care. Psychiatric bed-days are expected to constitute around 10 percent of the total patient visits, while the remaining 5 percent is likely to represent bed-days for inmates requiring medical or surgical treatment. In return, SCH will agree to provide qualified medical personnel, meals, and supplies. However, for the convenience of Tangelo County, SCH will use existing space located adjacent to the booking facility. This leaves SCH in the enviable position of having no facilities cost, although this advantage is reflected in its lower rates to the county.

The average daily population at the Tangelo County Correctional Facility is currently running around 4,000 inmates per day. The uncertainty facing SCH is the number of inmates who will require medical attention. While expectations are that an average of 5 percent of the prison population will visit the health care facility each day, other institutions report daily visits at a rate as high as 10 percent of the average daily population. That is, SCH might expect as many as 400 Tangelo County inmates (4,000 times 10 percent) to require some form of medical attention or hospitalization during an average day.

SCH has a pretty good lock on costs based on data from their other installations. Drug and medicine costs, for example, averages $8 per encounter for rapid in-out, $4 per day for psychiatric inmates, and $45 per day for medical-surgical. SCH is also responsible for feeding some of the prisoners. Rapid in-out patients are not fed in the health care facility. However, food will cost SCH $3.75 per day for both psychiatric and medical-surgical inmates. Supplies are estimated at $8 per encounter for rapid in-out, $10 per day for psychiatric, and $14 per day for medical-surgical inmates.

The costs of fixed salaries and wages for medical personnel are projected at $750,000 for rapid in-out, $450,000 for psychiatric, and $1,150,000 for medical-surgical. These staffing levels should provide adequate capacity to handle the expected patient load. In addition, benefits and payroll-related cost adds another 26 percent to salary cost. Since Tangelo County requires dental care, SCH plans to sign a contract with a dental provider that will cost a flat $290,000 per year. SCH gets compensated for dental care through the $50 charge it receives for rapid in-out encounters. In addition to costs directly associated with each of the three medical service areas, SCH will incur costs necessary to support the overall medical facility, including fixed costs for administration ($840,000), insurance ($230,000), pharmacy ($270,000), records management ($220,000), and equipment leases and maintenance ($325,000). These fixed costs are common to all activities and are not assigned to any one of the three medical services.

Required:

1. Assuming that 5 percent of the inmates, on the average, require medical attention each day and the mix between the three areas of medical service is 85 percent rapid in-out, 10 percent psychiatric, and 5 percent medical-surgical, calculate the pretax operating profit for SCH.

2. What percent of prison population, on the average, must visit the medical facility each day in order for SCH to achieve breakeven pretax operating profit? Assume the same mix of services as in requirement 1.

P2.10   (Separating Costs into Fixed and Variable; Cost-Volume-Profit Analysis)

Doris Peace, D.V.M., owns and operates the Peace River Animal Hospital. Her hospital is located on a divided highway in a predominantly residential section on the outskirts of a large city. Dr. Peace offers services for small animals that fall into two broad categories: (1) medical services, including routine checkups, vaccinations, minor surgery like neutering, and major surgery for dogs and cats who have been injured in accidents; and (2) boarding and grooming.

Most clients typically call Dr. Peace's office to make an appointment. However, she also accepts walk-ins. When a client brings in an animal, the receptionist pulls his or her record from a computerized database and notifies one of the medical assistants. The medical assistant escorts the client and the animal to one of three treatment rooms, where they determine the reason for the visit. Most treatments, including minor surgery, are carried out by Dr. Peace's assistant. Known as a *contract vet*, the assistant is a fully certified veterinarian who works for Dr. Peace as an outside contractor until he or she can open his or her own clinic. Dr. Peace, in addition to performing major surgery, supervises the work of the contract vet, not only to ensure quality but to pass along her many years of experience. Dr. Peace also supervises office activities, including medical records, billing, payroll, and accounts payable.

Dr. Peace owns most of the medical equipment she needs for her practice. However, she leases some of the more-specialized pieces. While she maintains a basic laboratory and x-ray facility, she also sends work to outside labs. Animals receiving medical treatment require medical supplies, like drugs and syringes, that vary in rough proportion to the volume of animals seen at the clinic during the year.

Dr. Peace's second major source of revenue comes from boarding. Clients usually make appointments for this service, since the number of kennel spaces is limited. This is especially true on weekends and around holidays. When an animal arrives, it is immediately dipped for fleas and parasites. Peace River Animal Hospital offers grooming services for all animals, whether boarded or not. Any animal boarded overnight must be fed. Dr. Peace also provides pickup and delivery services for boarded and groomed animals.

Operating revenue and expense for the current year, including salaries and benefits, are shown in Exhibit P2.10. Most of these expenses are fixed. Exceptions are (1) animal food and supplies, (2) credit card expense, (3) laboratory and x-ray fees, and (4) medical supplies. Dr. Peace spends about 40 percent of her time on the medical side of the business, while 10 percent of her time is spent managing boarding and grooming activities. The remaining 50 percent of her time is spent supervising the reception area, records, accounting, and other office activities. Credit card expense, which is proportional to revenue from medical services as well as boarding and grooming represents fees paid for processing credit card transactions. Records indicate that a total of 9,506 animals were seen during the current year, comprising 5,450 for medical reasons and 4,056 for boarding and grooming.

Required:

1. Separate the operating expense and salaries and benefits expense in Exhibit P2.10 into fixed and variable. Assume there are no mixed expenses, only fixed

EXHIBIT P2.10 PEACE RIVER ANIMAL HOSPITAL

Operating Revenue and Expenses for the Current Year

Operating revenue:	
Medical	$234,567
Boarding & grooming	83,456
Total revenue	$318,023
Operating expense:	
Advertising	$ 2,612
Alarm & security	414
Animal food & supplies	14,311
Bank charges	116
Contributions	2,208
Credit card expense	8,331
Depreciation—delivery truck (pickup for boarding)	1,333
Depreciation—medical equipment	3,763
Depreciation—boarding & grooming equipment	1,823
Depreciation—general & office equipment	988
Dues & subscriptions	621
Insurance—building & contents	4,568
Laboratory & x-ray fees	5,150
Legal & accounting	3,888
Liability insurance	9,217
License & permits	447
Medical supplies	18,976
Office expense	2,758
Rent for facility	24,900
Rental equipment—medical	8,320
Repairs & maintenance	1,793
Telephone	3,854
Utilities	4,518
Total operating expense	$124,909
Salaries & benefits expense:	
Salary & benefits—Doris Peace	56,200
Contract veterinarian	24,765
Office salaries & benefits	23,442
Medical assistant's salaries & benefits	22,186
Boarding & grooming salaries & benefits	27,890
Total salaries & benefits	$154,483
Pretax operating income	$ 38,631

and variable. Also assume that Dr. Peace believes that variable costs are driven by the number of animals she sees.

2. Separate the operating expense and salaries and benefits expense another way: medical, boarding and grooming, and general and office expenses. Once you have separated the expenses into the three categories, organize them into the fixed and variable categories you created in requirement 1. When you are finished, you will have the total costs categorized two ways: (a) by medical, boarding and grooming, and general and office and (b) by fixed and variable.

3. Using the contribution margin format, prepare an income statement. Break the contribution margin income statement into three columns: a total col-

umn, a column for medical, and a column for boarding and grooming. Assign the general and office expense calculated in requirement 2 to medical and to boarding and grooming. Assume that 70 percent of the total general and office expense is assigned to medical and 30 percent to boarding and grooming. Finally, calculate the revenue per visit, variable cost per visit, contribution per visit, and operating profit per visit for both the medical and the boarding and grooming segments.

P2.11 (Regression; Overhead)

Christoph Courdieret opened Christoph's Bistro several years ago. The restaurant, serving upscale cajun and continental food, boasts an average customer check of almost $18. This relatively high check average is driven, in part, by wine sales. In fact, Christoph believes that high markups on wine may have masked marginal profits—or perhaps even losses—on food. Christoph's success is based on using only fresh ingredients—for example, chefs make all of their own sauces. This adds considerably to food preparation time and is rarely identifiable with a particular meal.

Christoph's general rule of thumb is to take food cost and multiply by 3 to arrive at menu price. For example, the Redfish d'Christoph, one of the restaurant's specialties, includes 6 ounces of redfish and is served with potatoes, sauce, and garnish. Food cost totals about $3.50. The menu price is $10.50, derived by multiplying $3.50 by a factor of 3.

Christoph believes that wine consumption may be declining, and he wants to make sure that food is properly priced to earn a fair return. The ingredients going into cach dish are relatively easy to identify. So is cooking and preparation time. Actual food prep and cooking times were sampled, averaged, and then multiplied by hourly labor rates. The real problem, though, is not food cost or kitchen labor. Instead, Christoph believes that kitchen overhead, which includes food preparation and readying the kitchen, may be the culprit. All of these activities—such as cleaning, storing leftover food, preparing vegetables, cutting meats, making condiments, and assembling side dishes—are very time-consuming and not considered explicitly in the cost of a dish. To help sort things out, Christoph's office manager gathered the weekly kitchen overhead data shown in Exhibit P2.11.

Required:

1. Prepare two regression analyses:
   a. Regress kitchen overhead cost (y) against the number of meals (x_1).
   b. Regress kitchen overhead cost (y) against kitchen hours (x_2).
2. Which of the two regressions in requirement 1 would you choose?
3. Assume Christoph believes that the normal volume of weekly meals is 900 and the normal level of kitchen hours is 290. Prepare estimates of kitchen overhead costs with both of the regression models. Assume that predicted kitchen overhead is assigned to meals based on the normal volume of weekly meals. What is the average kitchen overhead cost per meal with both of the estimates?
4. Assume food cost for a particular dish is $3.50 and direct labor cost is $2.75. What would you add to the cost of the meal for kitchen overhead using both models developed above? Assume Christoph wants a 20 percent markup on cost to cover other overhead and a small profit. What is the menu price of the meal using this approach? How does the menu price calculated these two ways compare with Christoph's rough "3 times-food-cost" rule of thumb?

| | EXHIBIT P2.11   CHRISTOPH'S BISTRO | | |
| | Weekly Kitchen Overhead Data | | |

Week	Number of Meals (x_1)	Kitchen Hours (x_2)	Kitchen Overhead Cost (y)
1	671	278	$5,487
2	451	293	5,039
3	860	214	5,790
4	910	207	5,815
5	545	290	5,274
6	121	276	3,687
7	684	287	5,885
8	811	254	5,706
9	907	312	6,669
10	973	288	6,925
11	1,075	291	7,033
12	832	266	5,928
13	798	271	5,823
14	1,058	307	7,127
15	1,162	257	6,794
16	890	265	6,017
17	459	256	4,758
18	904	307	6,424
19	768	304	6,135
20	1,180	259	7,347
21	851	310	6,312
22	693	298	5,632
23	974	253	6,302
24	896	277	6,469
25	1,056	275	6,939
26	934	252	6,202

P2.12   (Regression)

Annual operating expenses and the numbers of passengers enplaned for Delta Airlines for the nine-year period of 1982–1990 are shown in Exhibit P2.12.

Required:

1. Assume activity, measured by the number of passengers enplaned, drives operating expense:
   a. Estimate the relationship between these two variables. Plot both the observed data pairs (xy graph) and predicted values for operating expense for actual values of passengers enplaned using the linear equation $y = \alpha + (\beta \times x)$.
   b. How good is the fit between these two variables? Identify and describe each of the ways goodness of fit can be measured, and comment on the values.
   c. Comment on the value and interpretation of the slope coefficient. Is it significant? The intercept is negative. What does this mean?

EXHIBIT P2.12 DELTA AIRLINES		

Operating Expense and Passengers Enplaned

Year	Operating Expense (in $1,000s)	Revenue Passengers Enplaned
1982	$3,625,679	34,169,927
1983	3,823,747	35,666,116
1984	4,052,339	36,319,567
1985	4,318,105	39,340,850
1986	4,425,574	39,582,232
1987	4,913,647	48,172,626
1988	6,418,293	58,564,507
1989	7,411,159	64,242,212
1990	8,162,719	67,240,233

Source: Delta Airlines, Inc. *1990 Annual Report*, pp. 32–33.

2. Suppose Delta expected to enplane 69 million passengers in 1991:
   a. Predict operating expense (point estimate) for 1991.
   b. Delta actually enplaned 69,127,249 passengers in 1991 and operating expense reported in its 1991 annual report was $9.621 billion. How close was your point estimate to the actual value?
3. The position of the actual 1991 data point may make it easier to see that one of the goodness-of-fit assumptions may have been violated. To determine if this is the case, calculate the differences (called *residuals*) between the actual and predicted operating expenses for each year between 1982 and 1990. Plot these values (dependent variable) against passengers enplaned (independent variable). What is your conclusion?
4. What do you conclude about Delta's management of operating expense? What are some possible factors that may have contributed to Delta's performance?

P2.13   (Lost Contribution from Fire; Linear Regression)

The Walter Brewing Company opened for business in Seattle in January 1993. Founded by Walter Fagan, Walter Brewing manufactures a single line of amber ale. After the ale, known locally as Walter's Best, is brewed and bottled, it is sold to a local beer distributor for $100 per barrel. The distributor then sells the ale for about $105 a barrel to bars, restaurants, hotels, and other retailers who serve ale on draft.

For nearly a year before selling his first barrel, Walter perfected the brew. In the meantime, he went to virtually every bar, restaurant, and hotel in town to line up business once production started. As a result of his efforts, sales of Walter's Best were a success from the very first day. Since that time, volume has grown with each passing month.

Early in July 1994 the brewing facility suffered a fire. In addition to ruining some of the ale inventory, water and smoke damage slowed the pace of operations. Since the brewmaster had to deal with fire damage, he had difficulty keeping production up to normal levels. However, he was able to keep most of the brewery's accounts satisfied, with the production shown in Exhibit P2.13.1. As hard as it

EXHIBIT P2.13.1 · WALTER BREWING COMPANY

Monthly Beer Production

Month	Barrels of Beer
January 1993	1,051
February	1,790
March	2,117
April	2,213
May	2,858
June	3,135
July	3,390
August	3,194
September	3,351
October	3,602
November	3,954
December	3,791
January 1994	4,069
February	4,363
March	4,367
April	4,434
May	4,586
June	5,112
July (fire)	4,098
August	4,354
September	4,842
October	5,214

EXHIBIT P2.13.2 WALTER BREWING COMPANY

Income Statement
For the Year Ending June 30, 1994

Revenue:		
Number of barrels sold	48,213	
Selling price per barrel	$100	
Total revenue	$4,821,300	100.00%
Cost of goods sold:		
Grains, hops, & other materials	$1,157,112	24.00%
Direct labor	1,482,130	30.74%
Brewery overhead	850,000	17.63%
Cost of goods sold	$3,489,242	72.37%
Gross profit	$1,332,058	27.63%
General & administrative expense	650,000	13.48%
Operating income (before tax)	$ 682,058	14.15%

			EXHIBIT P2.13.3 WALTER BREWING COMPANY				
			Estimated Loss of Operating Income				
			Fire Loss for July–October 1994				
Month	Barrels Sold in June	Actual Barrels Sold	Lost Barrels	Selling Price per Barrel	Lost Revenue	Percent of Operating Income	Lost Income
July 1994	5,112	4,098	1,014	$100	$101,400	14.15%	$14,345
August	5,112	4,354	758	$100	$75,800	14.15%	$10,723
September	5,112	4,842	270	$100	$27,000	14.15%	$3,820
October	5,112	5,214	(102)	$100	$(10,200)	14.15%	n.a.
Operating income (before tax) lost as result of fire							$28,888

tried, Walter Brewing sold only 4,098 barrels of beer in July, down from 5,112 barrels in June.

After the fire, Walter filed a claim with his insurance company. At the insurance company's request, Walter submitted the income statement shown in Exhibit P2.13.2, which covers the 12 months immediately prior to the fire.

After submitting the data, Walter received the settlement offer shown in Exhibit P2.13.3. The offer, totaling $28,888, was based on production lost during the four-month period from July 1, 1994 through October 31, 1994. The insurance company's estimator used barrels sold in June 1994, the month immediately before the fire, as a basis for predicting what production should have been had the fire never occurred. After subtracting actual production, lost production was multiplied by the per-barrel selling price to determine lost revenue. Finally, the insurance company's estimator multiplied lost revenue by the percent of operating income relative to total revenue to determine lost profit.

Walter's first reaction to the offer was anger. He felt that sales volume would surely have grown beyond the level experienced in June 1994. Furthermore, Walter intuitively knew that multiplying lost revenue by the operating profit percentage didn't fully compensate for all that he had lost as a result of the fire.

Required:

1. Number the months from 1 to 22, starting with January 1993. Using the data from Exhibit P2.13.1, regress barrels of beer produced monthly (dependent variable) against months (independent variable). However, use only the first 18 observations in your regression equation. That is, use only January 1993 through June 1994 data to estimate the slope and intercept parameters. Use the results of the regression to predict the number of barrels of beer that Walter Brewing is likely to have sold in July through October 1994 (months 19 through 22).

2. Estimate Walter's lost contribution using the data in Exhibit P2.13.2 and your projections from requirement 1. Assume that grains, hops, and other materials costs vary in proportion with the number of barrels and that $875,000 of the direct labor cost is fixed. Assume brewery overhead and general and administrative expense are fixed.

3. Which estimate of loss is more accurate? The insurance company's or Walter's?

CASES

C2.1 (Nuline Tubs)[14]

Bill Beckland developed a new bathtub design that provides handicapped and elderly people with the ability to take a bath independently. The improved design allows access through a door in the side and provides a molded seat 18 inches above the floor. Bill invented the tub, constructed out of fiberglass, while he was working as an independent manufacturer's representative selling products to nursing homes and hospitals.

Bill's initial design was refined to meet architectural and mechanical standards. He received help from an engineer friend to make sure that the tub's design and safety features conformed to industry specifications. After applying for a patent, Bill took his design to Charlie Green at Lathe Manufacturing to build a prototype.

While still working as a manufacturer's representative, Bill sunk nearly $25,000 of his own money into the project to pay for legal fees and to build a prototype. Bill knew he would have to raise capital in order to get his tub to market. His strategy was to create a joint venture, called Nuline Tubs, between himself and Lathe Manufacturing. Bill planned to quit his current job and turn his efforts toward selling Nuline tubs. Lathe Manufacturing, for its part, would purchase equipment, hire workers, and make the tubs.

Before either party was willing to go any further, each wanted to see what kind of profits the new business might generate. Bill contacted a local certified public accountant, who agreed to build a business plan that included projections of costs and revenue. The results, based on data provided by Bill Beckland and Charlie Green, are shown in Exhibit C2.1. While the net income looked great, both Bill and Charlie wanted to know what was likely to happen if the sales volume they anticipated didn't materialize. In Charlie's words, "I'm not going to bet on sales revenue that high! If it turns out to be that good, well, all the better. What I want to know is just how low sales can be before we start losing money. The CPA's figures don't give me a clue as to where that point is."

---

[14] This case is adapted from Leonard E. Stokes, III (Siena College), Case No. 92-10, "Independent Tub Co.," New York: The American Institute of Certified Public Accountants, 1992, pp. 1–3.

EXHIBIT C2.1 NULINE TUB	
Projected Income Statement	
Total revenue	$13,350,000
Cost of goods sold	9,062,160
Gross margin	$ 4,287,840
Operating Expense:	
Selling & promotion	$ 1,167,500
General & administrative	115,125
Total operating expense	$ 1,282,625
Operating income	$ 3,005,215
Income taxes	841,460
Net income	$ 2,163,755

To answer these questions, Bill and Charlie sat down with the CPA and identified the following assumptions used in preparing the projections:

- 15,000 tubs are sold at a net price of $890 per tub.
- Materials cost $425 per tub.
- Each tub takes 12.5 labor-hours to make.
- Nuline will hire a core of 20 skilled workers. Each core employee will be paid $8.25 per hour (plus 30 percent for benefits) for 40 hours a week, 52 weeks per year. However, because of breaks and vacation time, Nuline assumes an average productivity of only 37.5 hours of work per employee per week for 50 weeks per year.
- Part-time workers will be contracted through a temporary employment agency. These part-time workers are not required to have any special skills, since their job is basically to assist salaried employees. Temps boost the productivity of salaried employees, so that, based on the efforts of all employees, including the contribution of core employees, Nuline can still average 12.5 hours per tub. Temps are paid on the basis of the number of tubs they make. They are called in the evening and show up for work the next morning. If work slows down at any point during the day, the temps are released and sent home. The cost of temps, including fees to the employment agency, runs $6.75 per hour, with no benefits.
- Variable overhead is $65 per tub.
- After Bill establishes a network for marketing Nuline tubs, sales representatives are to be hired for the day-to-day selling. Bill plans to pay sales representatives by straight commission at a rate of 5 percent of each dollar of revenue they generate.
- Product liability insurance is 0.75 percent (¾ of 1%) of each dollar of revenue.
- Charlie will have to hire a plant supervisor at $76,000 and a secretary at $24,000 per year (both salary figures include benefits).
- Fiberglass mixing equipment will be purchased at a cost of $250,000. Straight-line depreciation over 10 years will be used, with no provision for residual value.
- After fiberglass is mixed, it must be quickly placed in forms using automated equipment called "quick-molders." One form, costing $75,000, is required for every 5,000 tubs. Based on a decision to build capacity for 15,000 tubs, Nuline plans to buy three forms. In addition, one quick-molder is all Nuline will need. It will cost $400,000, including shipping and installation. Both the forms and the quick-molder will be depreciated using the straight-line method over 10 years, with no provision for salvage value.
- Repair and maintenance will be provided by an outside contractor at a cost of $18,000 per year.
- Liability insurance for production workers is a fixed $48,000 per year, regardless of the number of full- and part-time workers.
- Advertising and promotion expense, including travel costs, phone bills, entertainment, media charges, and brochures, is budgeted at $500,000 per year.
- Office expense is estimated at $15,000 per year.
- The income tax rate is expected to be 28 percent of taxable income.

Required:

1. Prepare a projected income statement in the contribution margin format. For this and the remaining requirements, include depreciation in your computations. Also, ignore Bill's $25,000 investment in your computations.

2. Assume Nuline decides to acquire capacity sufficient to make 15,000 tubs. How many tubs have to be sold to achieve breakeven?

3. Assume Bill decides to acquire capacity sufficient to make 15,000 tubs. If Bill believes that the lowest number of tubs that Nuline is likely to sell is 10,000, how low can he set the price in order to just break even?

C2.2 (Camp Challenge)

Dan Webster recently retired from the U.S. Marine Corps. After talking with several civilian friends, he decided to use his military training to start a leadership and team-building camp. With $75,000 in retirement funds and $125,000 pledged by his friends, Dan started working on operating plans.

He selected business executives and children as target groups for his camp. Dan felt he could attract executives and their staffs to a five-day wilderness adventure through advertisements placed in selected business periodicals. The camp's objective is to transform interpersonal relationships by breaking down barriers and increasing the desire to work together as a group for common organizational goals. He also felt that he could market the same concept to children in several of the close-by metropolitan areas. Rather than offering participants sports and crafts, Dan felt he could create a different experience for them by building the children's confidence and self-reliance through rock-climbing, canoeing, and cave-exploring exercises.

Dan selected a 10-acre base-camp site in mountainous north Georgia that would cost about $75,000. Dan then obtained estimates, averaging about $125,000, to construct a rustic-looking headquarters where he could stage trips and administer camp operations. In addition, Dan figured he needed office equipment, furniture, computers, and phone systems costing about $45,000. He also decided he needed a van costing about $14,000 and two canoes at $1,400 apiece.

Dan's plan was to greet campers at the base camp, and then transport them by van to a wilderness area in a nearby state park. He had already obtained permission to use specific areas of the park, at no cost, from the state's park commission. Accompanied by trained counselors, campers would sleep in tents for five nights, hiking or canoeing from one area to another. For example, a group might spend the first night learning how to pitch tents and set up camp. In the morning, they would canoe to the next site, where they might, for example, practice scaling the side of a mountain. After five days, the campers would return to the base camp by van for a debriefing before returning to their homes. Dan had already contacted several college students who he felt he could train to guide groups. The camp would only operate for about eight months a year, from spring through fall, a schedule suitable to potential counselors.

With this overall plan, Dan began putting together the data needed to justify an investment in Camp Challenge. After reviewing camp fees and brochures for other organizations offering team-building experiences, Dan was convinced that he could charge $350 for each person in executive groups and $300 per person for children. These fees included all meals, use of camping equipment, and transportation into wilderness campsites for five nights.

Dan felt that he would average 12 campers in the executive groups and 7 campers in the children's groups. Each group would be accompanied by two counselors, both of whom would be paid $200 per five-day trip. Food costs are projected at $7.50 per day per person for executive groups (including food for two counselors) and $6.00 per day per person for children's groups (including food for two counselors). Gas used by the van in transporting the groups from base camp to the wilderness areas is expected to be about $5 each way, or $10 round-trip.

After contacting several ad agencies, Dan budgeted $18,000 annually for advertising to executives and $15,000 for advertising to children's groups. In addition, Dan will purchase camping equipment, including backpacks, tents, cooking utensils, emergency medical kits, portable telephones, ropes, and other miscellaneous supplies. Dan plans to purchase 5 sets of equipment for the executives, at $2,250 per set, plus 10 sets for children's groups, at $2,000 per set.

To manage all of these activities, Dan expects to incur the following annual cash operating outlays:

- Bookkeeper and payroll preparation—$40 per week for 52 weeks per year
- Insurance for contents and liability—$18,000 per year
- Advertisements for counselors—$2,000
- Telephone and utilities—$650 per month for 12 months
- Answering service—$50 per week for 52 weeks per year
- Van maintenance—$500 per year
- Secretary—$1,000 per month for 9 months
- Head Counselor—$1,250 per month for 9 months
- Director's Salary (Dan Webster)—$25,000 per year

For accounting purposes, Dan's accountant suggested depreciating the base camp structure over 25 years, using straight-line depreciation with no salvage value. Similarly, the base camp equipment, van and canoes will be depreciated over five years, again, using straight-line depreciation with no salvage value. The camping equipment is expected to last only three years, after which it will be replaced. It, too, will be depreciated using straight-line depreciation with no salvage value.

Required:

1. Prepare projections of annual pretax operating cash flows (cash inflows less cash outflows, excluding depreciation) assuming 80 groups per year, composed of 24 executive and 56 children's groups. Use the contribution margin approach.
2. Assuming that the mix of groups is 30 percent executive and 70 percent children, how many groups does Dan have to book for the year in order to achieve breakeven cash flows (excluding depreciation). Assume it is possible to have a fraction of a group.
3. Recalculate the number of groups needed to break even after including depreciation. Which is the correct breakeven? With or without depreciation?

CHAPTER 3

FULL COST

One of the most important uses of accounting information is to measure what something costs. That something, called a **cost object**, can be virtually anything that managers want to collect cost for. The most broadly defined cost object is the organization as a whole. There is a wide range of intermediate cost objects below the organizational level. Examples of these midlevel cost objects include departments, distribution channels, product lines, projects, business segments, and activities. At the lower end of the spectrum, costs can be collected for objects as detailed as a single unit of **product** or service.[1]

Costs can be identified by their relationship to cost objects. A **direct cost**, for example, is a cost that is directly traceable to a specific object. In contrast, costs incurred for the common benefit of multiple objects are called **indirect costs**. Indirect costs are spread over the benefiting objects by assigning a share of indirect cost to each. The **full cost** of an object, then, is its direct cost plus an assignment of indirect cost.[2]

Before we can begin to describe costs, we must first understand what costs are. To explain costs we must begin by describing **resources**. Resources refer to all assets available for use by an organization. They include both tangible and intangible assets. Some of these assets are easy to measure, such as the value of materials inventory. Other assets, though, are not so easy to measure, such as technological know-how or workforce experience. Regardless of whether or not assets can be easily measured, they still represent resources available for use by the organiza-

---

[1] *Product* is used throughout this text to mean both physical products and services.
[2] The term *full cost* can also be defined as "variable costs plus a fair share of fixed costs." In theory, full cost should be exactly the same—no matter how the data are collected.

tion. So, when we say "cost" we mean *both the measurable and hard-to-measure resources available for making goods and delivering services.*

The goals of this chapter, then, are to:

- Illustrate how costs are collected by cost objects
- Evaluate the adequacy of the system of collecting costs by cost objects in providing useful information

COLLECTING COSTS BY COST OBJECTS

Exhibit 3.1 illustrates how resources flow into the organization from suppliers and exit as products and services. The cost of the resource inputs is represented by the rectangles at the top of the exhibit, while the cost of resources associated with each product and service is shown at the bottom. In-between are the activities required to transform resource inputs into output products and services.

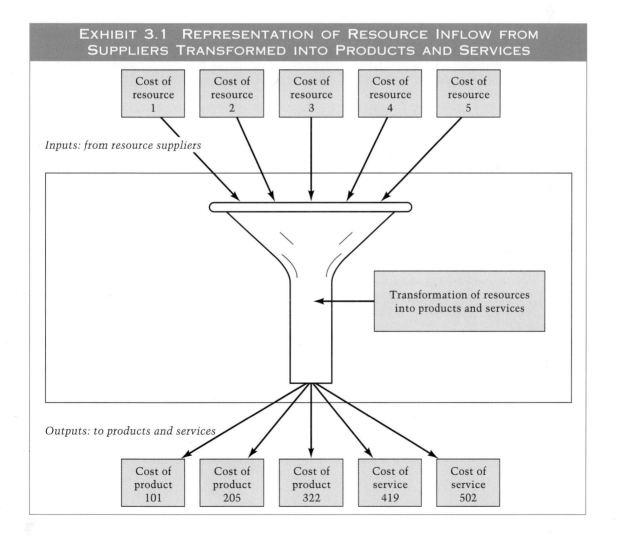

EXHIBIT 3.1   REPRESENTATION OF RESOURCE INFLOW FROM SUPPLIERS TRANSFORMED INTO PRODUCTS AND SERVICES

If resource inputs could be matched directly with specific units of output, the task of tracing costs to specific cost objects would be relatively easy. However, in actual practice, resource inputs are often shared when products and services are made. In fact, the more narrowly defined the cost object is, the greater the likelihood that resource inputs will be shared.

Suppose a manufacturing company makes only a single product. The task of assigning costs to the company's product is easy—there is only one product, and all costs flow directly to it. Consider the salary cost of the manager who supervises all operations. Because the manager's efforts are directed solely to a single product, salary cost is easily traceable directly to the product. That is, the manager's salary is a direct cost of the product. However, if there are five models rather than just one, the manager's salary cost is incurred for the common benefit of all five models. In that case, the manager's salary is an indirect cost shared by all models.

DIRECT MATERIALS

Direct costs are generally traced directly to a specific cost object. Direct materials, for example, can be traced directly to the organization, the division, or the department—whatever unit is responsible for the use of the materials. Moreover, materials can often be traced to an individual unit of product. That makes materials cost a direct cost with respect to the unit of product.

DIRECT LABOR

If the cost object is a single unit of product, then labor cost is generally considered direct as long as employee time can be traced to that unit. If the cost object is an organizational unit, then direct labor cost is assigned to the organizational unit where the employee works.

OTHER DIRECT COSTS

Materials and labor costs are the most common kinds of direct costs. But there are others. For example, depreciation on equipment used solely for the benefit of a specific organizational unit is considered a direct cost of that unit.

INDIRECT COSTS

Costs that must be incurred in order to make an object or render a service and that are not directly traceable to the product or service are indirect costs. They are sometimes called **common costs**, or **overhead**. An older, perhaps more descriptive, term for indirect costs is **burden**, since indirect costs encumber (or weigh down) cost objects. Sometimes common costs include items that you might not think of. For example, consider some of the costs involved in a traffic fatality, as shown in "Current Practice: The Cost per Vehicle Fatality."

One characteristic of indirect costs is that they cannot be traced directly to a specific cost object, as noted above. Another type of costs comprises those that *can* be traced to cost objects, but only at great expense. These costs, too, are considered indirect costs. For example, assume commercially processed potato chips pass through room-size vats

The Cost per Vehicle Fatality

Vehicle crashes represent a staggering national economic burden, according to a study by the National Highway Traffic Safety Administration. Each of the 44,531 traffic fatalities in 1990, as shown in the table at the right, cost an average of $702,281. The cost of some of the items in the table is relatively easy to measure. Take medical expense and funeral cost. Data for these costs are relatively easy to gather. The table also includes intangible, difficult-to-measure costs, such as the value of household work and the cost of traffic delayed as the result of an accident.

The Cost per Vehicle Fatality, 1990	
Lost wages and benefits	$458,606
Value of household work	101,658
Legal and court cost	70,934
Administering insurance	48,336
Property damage	8,058
Overtime and employee replacement	6,679
Medical expense	3,705
Funeral cost	2,988
Police, fire, and ambulance	930
Traffic delay	387
Total cost per vehicle fatality	$702,281

Source: National Highway Traffic Safety Administration statistics, quoted in Lori Sharn and James R. Healey, "Cost of Vehicle Crashes 'Staggering,'" *USA Today*, Oct. 9, 1992, p. A1. Copyright 1992, USA TODAY. Reprinted with permission.

of cooking oil. There is no cost-effective way of tracing molecules of oil to an individual bag of chips. Nor would there be much benefit in doing so. Instead, cooking oil is considered an indirect cost shared by each bag of chips processed.

Another example of indirect cost is the cost of services provided by one organizational unit to another. Consider the human resource department, which advertises, screens, and hires employees to work in other departments. The cost of operating the department is considered an indirect cost of all departments, since each receives benefits from it. The full cost of each department, then, should include a share of the cost of the human resource department.

Depreciation for equipment used solely for the benefit of a single product is a direct cost of that product. However, if the equipment is used in making many products, then depreciation is an indirect cost of each product. Suppose a motion picture studio bought film-making equipment for a specific film. Depreciation for the equipment would be a direct cost of that film. However, depreciation for equipment used in making many films is an indirect cost of each film.

Indirect costs must be absorbed into the cost of each product and service. As indicated above, in addition to absorbing direct costs, each product and service must assimilate a share of indirect cost. *The full cost of any cost object, then, is the cost of resources used directly for that object plus a share of the cost of resources used in common in making all objects.*

Software Support

Nintendo, maker of nearly 900 video games, uses video-game play counselors to answer customers' questions—questions like "Where is the sword in the Legend of Zelda?" With sales at nearly 76 million games in 1992, Nintendo maintains troubleshooting lines that operate 20 hours a day, 360 days a year. But during the week after Christmas, Nintendo answers 170,000 calls. Counselors generally have two screens on their desks—one for displaying solutions and another on which they can play along with the caller.

The cost of this service is high and must be absorbed into the selling price of each game Nintendo sells. The company spends $15 to $20 million each year but feels it is a crucial investment given the fiercely competitive, but very profitable, video game industry.

Source: Bill Richards, "A Prisoner of Zelda and Two Lost Pilots Are on the Line: Video-Game Makers Face Rash of Christmas Callers Who Can't Run Their Presents," *The Wall Street Journal,* Dec. 30, 1992, pp. A1 and A2.

If indirect costs are a small part of the total, how they are shared by products and services may not make much difference. But if indirect costs represent a large part of total cost, then the way they are shared will affect the full cost of each. One such example of a high proportion of direct cost in relation to total cost is Nintendo's software support cost, as shown in "Current Practice: Software Support."

COLLECTING COSTS BY PRODUCTS

We turn now to a discussion of how resource costs are ultimately collected by products and services. The process entails the three broad steps outlined in Exhibit 3.2. We'll use a hypothetical music video production company called Music Video Partners (MVP) to illustrate the process. Assume MVP has five departments, each with its own manager. Two of the departments (rock/pop and country) produce and promote revenue-generating products (music videos). The other three departments supply internal services that support video production. Administration's activities include accounting, personnel, finance, and contract negotiation. Facility's activities include managing the physical plant, studios, and equipment. Finally, recording's activities include coordinating the production staff, scheduling artists, and arranging sets.

1: ASSIGN RESOURCE COSTS TO RESPONSIBILITY CENTERS

Resource inputs, shown at the top of Exhibit 3.2, are provided by resource suppliers. They include direct labor, direct materials, purchased services, and all the other resources necessary to make the firm's products and deliver services. The cost of resource inputs is assigned, as indicated by

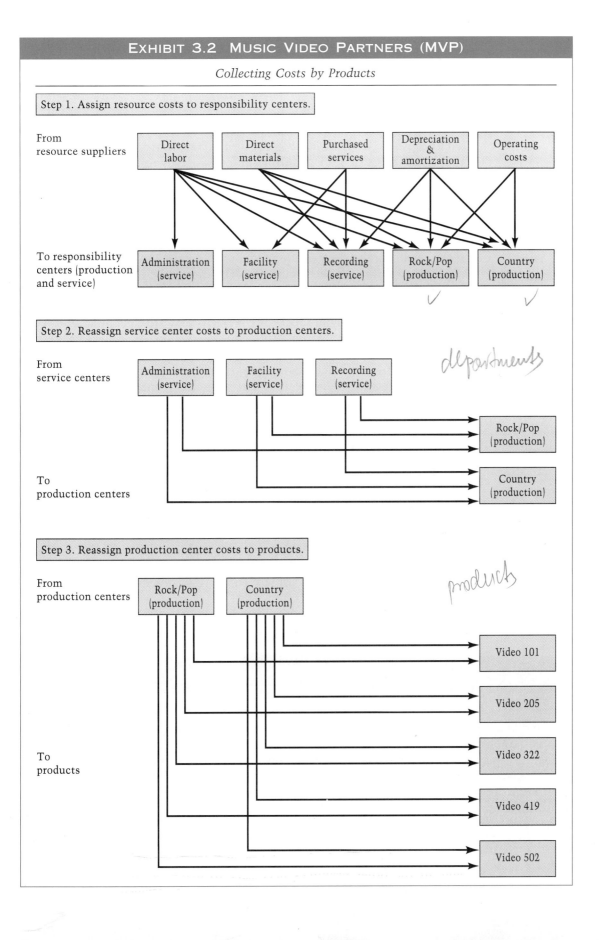

Exhibit 3.2 Music Video Partners (MVP)

Collecting Costs by Products

Step 1. Assign resource costs to responsibility centers.

From resource suppliers

| Direct labor | Direct materials | Purchased services | Depreciation & amortization | Operating costs |

To responsibility centers (production and service)

| Administration (service) | Facility (service) | Recording (service) | Rock/Pop (production) | Country (production) |

departments

Step 2. Reassign service center costs to production centers.

From service centers

| Administration (service) | Facility (service) | Recording (service) |

To production centers

Rock/Pop (production)

Country (production)

Step 3. Reassign production center costs to products.

products

From production centers

| Rock/Pop (production) | Country (production) |

To products

Video 101

Video 205

Video 322

Video 419

Video 502

the arrows, to responsibility centers. Responsibility centers *are any organizational unit for which a manager is responsible.* They represent the points where costs enter into the organization. This is where the responsibility resides for managers who make resource acquisition decisions. The two broad types of responsibility centers are production centers and service centers.

Production Centers.   The production centers (rock/pop and country in the example) make saleable goods and services. Managers of production centers make decisions about the kinds of products they offer, quantities they make, and selling prices of the products. They decide which resources are needed and how to make products in the most efficient way possible.

Service Centers.   Service centers (administration, facility, and recording in the example) supply products and services that are consumed internally by other responsibility centers. In addition to supporting production centers, service centers may also support other service centers. For example, a data processing service center may supply information for service centers such as personnel, as well as for production centers.

Service centers are created for several reasons. They consolidate activities of a common nature, as in the example of Walt Disney's Imagineering Division in the Current Practice box. Another reason is that service centers accomplish common tasks. Finally, service centers provide an opportunity to take advantage of economies of scale by spreading fixed cost over many users.

2: REASSIGN SERVICE CENTER COSTS TO PRODUCTION CENTERS

The costs of resources assigned to service centers are reassigned to production centers in the second step. This process is represented in the middle panel of Exhibit 3.2 by arrows pointing from service centers to pro-

---

CURRENT PRACTICE

Walt Disney's Imagineering Division

Walt Disney's Imagineering Division is a service center comprising several thousand employees—among them, engineers, designers, architects, and ride system specialists. They develop the many different theme parks and attractions "... that bring fantasy to life for people the world over." Imagineering's work is internal—its clients are other responsibility centers within the Disney organization. The cost of maintaining Imagineering—salaries, benefits, occupancy, and equipment—is shared by all projects receiving benefits from Imagineering's services.

Source: The Walt Disney Company, *1991 Annual Report,* p. 36.

duction centers. Production centers, therefore, consume resources from two types of sources—directly from resource suppliers and indirectly from internal service centers.

3: REASSIGN PRODUCTION CENTER COSTS TO PRODUCTS

At this point, all costs have been collected in production centers. The third and last step is to assign production center costs to products and services. Note that the cost objects have changed—while they were responsibility centers in the first two steps, the cost objects are now products.

The third step is represented in the bottom panel of Exhibit 3.2. Arrows show the assignment of resources from production centers to products. Some production center costs, such as materials and labor, can be assigned directly to videos. They flow directly to the production centers and then directly to specific products. All other costs—indirect production center costs—are pooled together and assigned to products on the basis of some measure of activity.

Let's take a look at each of the three steps in more detail.

1: ASSIGN RESOURCE COSTS TO RESPONSIBILITY CENTERS

Collecting costs by responsibility centers begins with the general ledger. Costs, recorded in general ledger accounts, are assigned to responsibility centers on the basis of attribution. *Attribution* means "tracing a cost to its source or origin." To illustrate, we will consider the costs for Music Video Partners (MVP), shown in the income statement in Exhibit 3.3.

Each cost in the income statement can be attributed to a production or service center. Attribution is based on determining which production or service center is responsible for the incurrence of the cost. Direct materials, for example, can be traced through materials requisition forms to the responsibility center that ordered them. Similarly, direct labor can be attributed to responsibility centers through payroll records. So, also, can

EXHIBIT 3.3 MUSIC VIDEO PARTNERS (MVP)	
Income Statement	
Revenue	$650,000
Operating cost:	
Direct labor	$220,000
Direct materials	35,000
Purchased services	110,000
Depreciation & amortization	80,000
Other operating cost	55,000
Total operating cost	$500,000
Operating income	$150,000

EXHIBIT 3.4 MUSIC VIDEO PARTNERS (MVP)

Assignment of Resource Costs to Responsibility Centers by Attribution

Resource	Total Cost	Service Center			Production Center	
		Admin.	Facility	Recording	Rock/Pop	Country
Direct labor	$220,000	$ 24,000	$15,000	$37,000	$ 84,000	$ 60,000
Direct materials	35,000				20,000	15,000
Purchased services	110,000	18,000			30,000	62,000
Depreciation & amortization	80,000	3,000	35,000	3,000	16,000	23,000
Other operating cost	55,000	55,000				
Total operating cost	$500,000	$100,000	$50,000	$40,000	$150,000	$160,000

we attribute purchased services such as technical consultants, as well as costs like depreciation and operating expense. The result of attributing all costs to responsibility centers is shown in Exhibit 3.4.

2: REASSIGN SERVICE CENTER COST TO PRODUCTION CENTERS

Cost collected in service centers is reassigned to production centers. That's because only production centers generate revenue. Production centers collectively must set prices for products and services such that the prices are sufficient to cover all costs of the organization. If each production center set prices to cover only its own direct costs, the cost of the service centers might never be recovered. Therefore, *revenue from the production centers must be sufficient to cover not only their direct costs but also a fair share of the indirect cost of internal services supplied by service centers*. In determining a production center's "fair share" of indirect costs, we must be aware that unfairly, or arbitrarily, assigned cost may generate false signals and lead to incorrect actions.

Service center costs can be assigned to production centers in several ways, each resulting in a different degree of fairness. The three ways of assigning service center costs to production centers, listed in order of preference, are (1) attribution, (2) direct assignment, and (3) allocation.

ATTRIBUTION *there must be a relationship! → clear way how to*

The method providing the highest degree of fairness is attribution. Attribution is possible where there is no question as to who is the sole recipient of services, where costs are ". . . unambiguously associated with a particular cost object."[3] For example, MVP's recording service center might support only one production center, or a hospital laboratory may provide services dedicated to only one user—the emergency room.

→ attribute the price

---

[3]   Robert S. Kaplan and Anthony A. Atkinson, *Advanced Management Accounting*, 2d. ed. Englewood Cliffs, N.J.: Prentice-Hall, Inc., 1989, p. 240.

sharing resources → Direct major

DIRECT ASSIGNMENT

When attribution is not possible, and several responsibility centers jointly share benefits from a service center, its cost is reassigned by direct assignment. Some organizations use the term *direct charges* or *chargebacks* rather than *direct assignment.* Whatever term is used, direct assignment describes a system whereby service centers charge production centers fees for services provided.

The primary goal of direct assignment is to assign costs in a way that reflects the relative amount of services each responsibility center consumes. In effect, direct charges serve as an internal pricing mechanism, where responsibility centers pay the equivalent of market prices for the services they receive.

Illustrations of direct assignment include photocopy centers that charge by the page, computer service centers that charge for each minute of processing time, or company cafeterias that charge based on the dollar amount of food consumed by employees. In each of these examples, the direct charges are likely to provide a fair assignment of cost. Each presumes availability of measures that capture the actual utilization of the service—for example, the number of photocopies, minutes of processing time, or the dollar value of food consumed. If easily obtainable measures of the service center's output are unavailable, input measures provide a reasonable alternative. For example, the photocopy center might use labor-hours, an input measure, rather than pages photocopied as the basis for internal charges.

ALLOCATION — *indirect measures*

When neither attribution nor direct assignment is possible, or each is too expensive to administer, the alternative is allocation. Allocation assigns service center cost based on indirect measures, commonly known as allocation bases. The goal in selecting allocation bases is to capture relative resource consumption when direct measures aren't available.

For example, assume electricity cost is collected in a service center. One way to assign electricity cost might be through direct charges, perhaps by metering kilowatt-hours and charging electricity cost directly to the consuming responsibility center. What if metering is not possible, perhaps because all activities take place in a large, open facility? In that case, some other indirect measure—such as the square feet occupied by the responsibility center—might be used as an allocation base. Unfortunately, allocation bases may show little correspondence to actual energy consumption. For example, using square feet occupied as the measure may underassign electricity cost to high-intensity electronic equipment occupying a relatively small space.

Some other examples of allocation bases include dollar amounts of sales (for allocating marketing cost), the number of projects (for allocating research and development cost), the number of purchase orders (for allocating purchasing cost), and the number of maintenance hours (for allocating maintenance cost). (See "Current Practice: Allocations at a Community Bank" for another example of allocation bases.)

CURRENT PRACTICE

Allocations at a Community Bank

One community bank, with eight branches and $248 million in assets, has never yet been able to come up with a yardstick for measuring branch profitability. The bank's board wants to be able to compare the performance of each branch and determine the relative contribution of each. The problem is, how do you fairly assign general, systemwide costs incurred in common for all eight branches?

One method the bank tried was assigning common costs on the basis of each branch's percentage of average deposits. A problem with that method is deciding whether a deposit account opened at a particular branch is actually being serviced at that branch. One suburban branch might have weekend hours that are attractive for customers wishing to come in and open accounts while a downtown branch might be more conveniently located for day-to-day transactions. Another problem is that one branch might be located in a prime area that generates a lot of profitable loans but is inconvenient for depositors to visit on a day-to-day basis.

Source: Deborah L. Fish, "What to Do About Allocations," *CFO*, Nov. 1994, pp. 9–10.

Recall that we identified three ways of assigning service center cost to production centers. In order of "fairness" they are attribution, direct assignment, and allocation. If assignment is by allocation, there are also three methods of assignment. In ascending order of computational complexity, they are:

1. Direct
2. Step-down
3. Reciprocal services

The choice among methods depends on the *degree of recognition of services that service centers provide to one another*. Recall that earlier we stated that service centers sometimes provide services to other service centers. For example, maintenance service center workers who maintain the company cafeteria may also eat in the cafeteria. Therefore, the choice of an allocation method depends on the extent to which managers want to recognize inter-service center activities.

The **direct method**, illustrated in Exhibit 3.5, *does not recognize* services provided by one service center to another. Note that the arrows representing allocations from service centers point only to production centers—the arrows do not point to other service centers.

The **step-down method**, illustrated in Exhibit 3.6, *partially recognizes* services provided by one service center to another. The first panel (step 1) in Exhibit 3.6 shows allocation of the administration service center to two other service centers (facility and recording) and two production centers

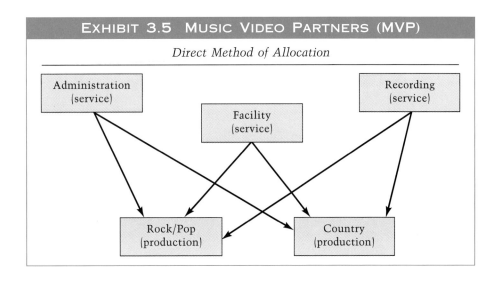

EXHIBIT 3.5 MUSIC VIDEO PARTNERS (MVP)

Direct Method of Allocation

(rock/pop and country). The next step in the step-down procedure is to assign facility, the second service center, to the remaining service center (recording) and to the two production centers. The final step is to assign the remaining service center (recording) to the two production centers. As service centers are allocated, they are *closed out;* that is, costs from other service centers cannot be reallocated to them. For example, recording service center costs in step 3 cannot be allocated back to administration or facility (step 1), since those service centers have been eliminated. That's why we stated that the step-down method only partially recognizes service interactions between service centers.

The third and most complex method, **reciprocal services,** is illustrated in Exhibit 3.7. It *fully recognizes* services flowing back and forth between service centers. Note that the arrows representing allocations point both ways between service centers. The administration service center, for example, provides services to the facility service center and vice versa. Also note that the reciprocal services method, unlike the step-down method, does not involve steps. That's because allocations are determined simultaneously.

Let's take a closer look at how each of the three allocation methods works.

Direct Method of Allocation. First, allocation bases are selected. Then, the cost of each service center is assigned to each production center, according to the center's relative proportion of the total allocation base. To illustrate, let's assume that MVP selected the allocation bases listed below and shown in Exhibit 3.8:

- Administration service center—number of employees
- Facility service center—square feet occupied
- Recording service center—recording hours

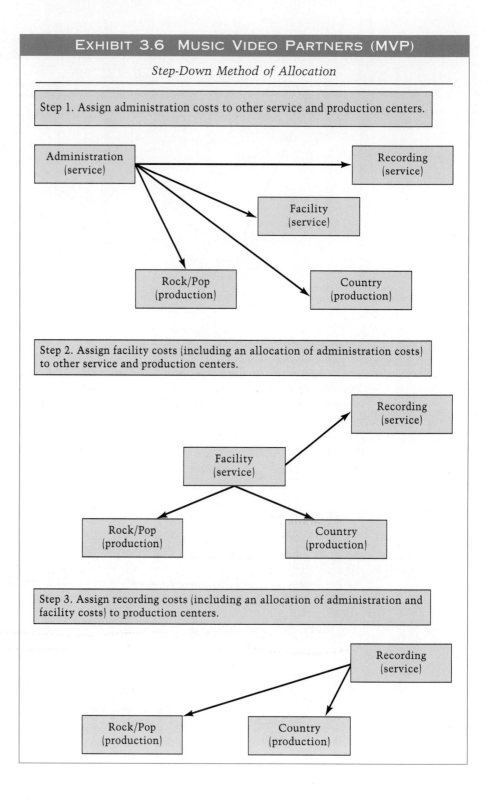

EXHIBIT 3.6 MUSIC VIDEO PARTNERS (MVP)

Step-Down Method of Allocation

Step 1. Assign administration costs to other service and production centers.

Step 2. Assign facility costs (including an allocation of administration costs) to other service and production centers.

Step 3. Assign recording costs (including an allocation of administration and facility costs) to production centers.

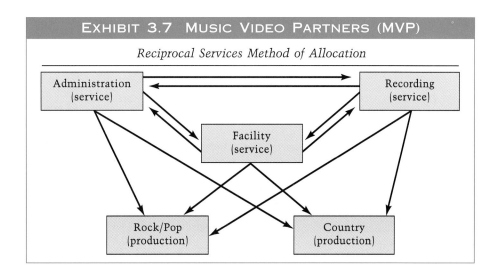

EXHIBIT 3.7 MUSIC VIDEO PARTNERS (MVP)

Reciprocal Services Method of Allocation

EXHIBIT 3.8 MUSIC VIDEO PARTNERS (MVP)

Allocation Bases

Allocation Base	Service Center			Production Center		
	Admin.	Facility	Recording	Rock/Pop	Country	Total
Employees (administration)	2	1	2	3	2	10
Square feet occupied (facility)	4,000		1,000	2,000	3,000	10,000
Recording-hours (recording)			500	3,500	1,500	5,500

Details of the direct method of allocation are shown in Exhibit 3.9. The top panel summarizes the results, while the middle and bottom panels show where the numbers come from. For example, the total cost attributed to the facility service center is $50,000. The goal is to reassign facility service center cost directly to production centers. The total square feet occupied—the allocation base chosen for the facility service center—by the two production centers is 5,000 square feet: 2,000 square feet for rock/pop and 3,000 square feet for country. Rock/pop occupies 40 percent (2,000/5,000) of the total square feet. As a consequence, rock/pop receives 40 percent of the total facility service center cost, or a total of $20,000 (40% of $50,000).

Note that no service center costs are allocated to other service centers when using the direct method. The allocation bases in the middle panel of Exhibit 3.9 exclude bases for other service centers. Note that the 4,000 square feet occupied by the administration service center and the 1,000 square feet occupied by the recording service center (Exhibit 3.8) are eliminated when calculating the total square feet to be used as a base in allocating facility cost. We actually *do* show those square feet figures but cross them out with an X in Exhibit 3.9. Instead, the total includes only

EXHIBIT 3.9 MUSIC VIDEO PARTNERS (MVP)

Allocation of Service Center Cost Using the Direct Method of Allocation

Allocation of Service Center Cost

	From Service Centers			To Production Centers		
	Admin.	Facility	Recording	Rock/Pop	Country	Total
Responsibility center cost (from Exhibit 3.4)	$100,000	$50,000	$40,000	$150,000	$160,000	$500,000
Allocation of service center costs:						
Administration service center	(100,000)			60,000	40,000	
Facility service center		(50,000)		20,000	30,000	
Recording service center			(40,000)	28,000	12,000	
Total	$ 0	$ 0	$ 0	$108,000	$ 82,000	
Total cost (production center cost plus allocations)				$258,000	$242,000	$500,000

Allocation Bases

	Admin.	Facility	Recording	Rock/Pop	Country	Total
Administration service center:						
Employees (from Exhibit 3.8)	X̶	X̶	X̶	3	2	5
Percent of total				60.00%	40.00%	100.00%
Facility service center:						
Square feet occupied (from Exhibit 3.8)	4̶,̶0̶0̶0̶		1̶,̶0̶0̶0̶	2,000	3,000	5,000
Percent of total				40.00%	60.00%	100.00%
Recording service center:						
Recording-hours (from Exhibit 3.8)			5̶0̶0̶	3,500	1,500	5,000
Percent of total				70.00%	30.00%	100.00%

Allocation Computations

	Rock/Pop	Country	Total
Administration service center:			
Direct cost to be allocated	$100,000	$100,000	
Percent of total employees	60.00%	40.00%	
Administration service cost allocated	$ 60,000	$ 40,000	$100,000
Facility service center:			
Direct cost to be allocated	$50,000	$50,000	
Percent of total square feet occupied	40.00%	60.00%	
Facility service cost allocated	$20,000	$30,000	$50,000
Recording service center:			
Direct cost to be allocated	$40,000	$40,000	
Percent of total recording-hours	70.00%	30.00%	
Recording service center cost allocated	$28,000	$12,000	$40,000

the square footage occupied by the two production centers. This means that, even though some of a service center's cost is used by other service centers, all of any one service center's cost is allocated directly to—and only to—production centers. That's how the direct method completely ignores services provided by one service center to another.

After all service center cost is allocated, the full cost of rock/pop is $258,000. This figure includes $150,000 in cost attributed directly to it and a total allocation of $108,000 from the service centers. The $500,000 of total cost, originally spread among five responsibility centers, is now collected in only two production centers.

Step-Down Method. Unlike the direct method, the step-down method partially recognizes services provided between service centers. Once cost is assigned from a particular service center, that service center is eliminated from further consideration. That is, no costs can be allocated "backward" to a service center once it has been considered. In this way, the step-down method captures some, but not all, of the interactions between service centers.

The suggested *sequence of steps* to assign cost is in descending order of the dollar amount of service center costs. In the MVP example, the sequence of steps is first, administration, with a cost of $100,000; followed by facility, with a cost of $50,000; and finally, recording, with a cost of $40,000.

The key to understanding the step-down method is found in the allocation bases shown in the middle of Exhibit 3.10. Administration, because it has the highest cost, is allocated first, using the number of employees as the base. Adding together all of the employees in each of the service and production centers, with the exception of administration, gives a total of 8. Why not include administration in the total? Because of the first of three rules for the step-down method. *Rule 1: Bases are always ignored for the service center currently being allocated.* This is because the step-down method closes out one service center at a time. If bases for the service center being allocated are included in the total, then cost can never be closed out and is continually reassigned to that center.

Administration's cost is allocated to other responsibility centers by multiplying administration's $100,000 in total cost by the percent of employees in each service and production center. For example, 12.50 percent (1/8 employees) of administration's $100,000 total cost, or $12,500, is allocated to the facility service center. The next step is to allocate the cost of the facility service center to recording—the only remaining service center—and to the two production centers. Since the facility service center uses square feet as an allocation base, total square feet is calculated by adding together all of the square feet in the remaining service and production centers, exclusive of the square feet from the service centers already allocated in prior steps. Note that bases not used are crossed out with Xs.

This illustrates the second step-down rule. *Rule 2: Bases are ignored for any service center already allocated.* Using the allocation data in Exhibit 3.8, the square feet used as a base to allocate facility cost is 1,000

EXHIBIT 3.10 MUSIC VIDEO PARTNERS (MVP)

Allocation of Service Center Cost Using the Step-Down Method of Allocation

| | Allocation of Service Center Cost | | | | | |
| | From Service Centers | | | To Production Centers | | |
	Admin.	Facility	Recording	Rock/Pop	Country	Total
Responsibility center cost (from Exhibit 3.4)	$100,000	$50,000	$40,000	$150,000	$160,000	$500,000
Allocation of service center costs:						
Administration service center	(100,000)	12,500	25,000	37,500	25,000	
Facility service center		(62,500)	10,417	20,833	31,250	
Recording service center			(75,417)	52,792	22,625	
Total	$ 0	$ 0	$ 0	$111,125	$ 78,875	
Total cost (production center cost plus allocations)				$261,125	$238,875	$500,000

| | Allocation Bases | | | | | |
	Admin.	Facility	Recording	Rock/Pop	Country	Total
Administration service center:						
Employees (from Exhibit 3.8)	~~X~~	1	2	3	2	8
Percent of total		12.50%	25.00%	37.50%	25.00%	100.00%
Facility service center:						
Square feet occupied (from Exhibit 3.8)	~~4,000~~		1,000	2,000	3,000	6,000
Percent of total			16.67%	33.33%	50.00%	100.00%
Recording service center:						
Recording-hours (from Exhibit 3.8)			~~500~~	3,500	1,500	5,000
Percent of total				70.00%	30.00%	100.00%

(continued)

square feet for recording, 2,000 square feet for rock/pop, and 3,000 square feet for country, or a total of 6,000 square feet. The cost to be allocated in the second step—and all subsequent steps—consists of the direct cost of the service center currently being allocated *and* any allocations to that service center from prior steps. This brings us to the third step-down rule. *Rule 3: Total cost to be allocated is the sum of the service center's direct cost and allocations to it from all prior steps.* We must then add $12,500 allocated to the facility service center from the administration service center to facility's own $50,000 in direct cost. Thus, the total facility service center cost to be allocated is $62,500. Multiplying $62,500 by each of the percentages of total square feet shown in the middle panel of Exhibit 3.10 produces allocations to the one remaining service center and to the two production centers. For example, 16.67 percent of $62,500, or $10,417 of facility's cost, is allocated to recording.

EXHIBIT 3.10 (CONTINUED)

Allocation Computations

	Admin.	Facility	Recording	Rock/Pop	Country	Total
Administration service center:						
Direct cost to be allocated	$100,000	$100,000	$100,000	$100,000	$100,000	
Percent of total employees		12.50%	25.00%	37.50%	25.00%	
Administration service cost allocated		$ 12,500	$ 25,000	$ 37,500	$ 25,000	$100,000
Facility service center:						
Direct facility service center cost to be allocated		$ 50,000				
Allocation from administration service center		12,500				
Cost to be allocated		$ 62,500	$ 62,500	$ 62,500	$ 62,500	
Percent of total square feet occupied			16.67%	33.33%	50.00%	
Facility service cost allocated			$ 10,417	$ 20,833	$ 31,250	$62,500
Recording service center:						
Direct recording service center cost to be allocated			$ 40,000			
Allocation from administration service center			25,000			
Allocation from facility service center			10,417			
Cost to be allocated			$ 75,417	$ 75,417	$ 75,417	
Percent of total recording-hours				70.00%	30.00%	
Recording service center cost allocated				$ 52,792	$ 22,625	$75,417

Read This—Note on Rounding

Each exhibit in this textbook was prepared using a spreadsheet. None of the numbers in any of the exhibits is rounded—all computations are carried out to the full precision allowed by the spreadsheet. However, the numbers used for computations are all formatted, making them appear as though they are rounded. As a result, if you were to check the computations, you might come up with answers slightly different from those that appear in the exhibits.

For example, the 16.67 percent figure shown toward the bottom of Exhibit 3.10 represents one-sixth of the total square feet occupied by recording. The amount of cost allocated to recording in Exhibit 3.10 ($10,417) is calculated by multiplying 0.1666666667 by $62,500. In fact, $10,417 itself appears rounded—the actual number is $10,416.67. If you were to multiply $62,500 by 16.67% you would get $10,418.75—slightly more than the $10,417. Again, that's simply because the numbers are formatted to make them easier to read. Carrying numbers out to, say, 10 decimal places simply detracts from our examples. These discrepancies may appear to be trivial—and in most cases, they are. But the discrepancies become larger as the scale of the numbers increases. You will find this to be particularly true in later chapters when dealing with large unit volumes.

We continue to repeat the steps in the same fashion until all service centers' costs have been allocated to production centers. In the end, all $190,000 in service center cost is collected in the two production centers. That is, all of the original $500,000 in total cost is eventually collected in rock/pop and country. For example, the full cost of the rock/pop production center comprises $150,000 of direct cost and $111,125 of allocated cost, or a total of $261,125.

The order in which the steps are performed in the step-down method is important. You'll get different results if you change the sequence. While the suggested sequence is to proceed in descending order of the dollar amount of service center cost, other sequencing rules can be followed. One alternative is to allocate service center cost in descending order of the percentage of services provided by service centers to other service centers.

Reciprocal Services Method.   Earlier we said the step-down method only partially captures the cost of services provided between service centers. The reason this method does not fully recognize interservice costs originates in the second step-down rule. The rule states that bases for any service center allocated in prior steps are ignored. If this rule were not invoked, step-down allocations would never be complete, since costs would always be reallocated to prior steps. The reciprocal services method permits full recognition of the cost of services between service centers by employing a system of simultaneous equations. For complex organizations with many responsibility centers, allocations using the reciprocal services method would become quite complex.

While the mechanics of the reciprocal services method are only presented in the appendix to this chapter, the results are shown in Exhibit 3.11. This exhibit also summarizes the results of allocations using the direct and step-down methods.

COMPARISON OF THREE ALLOCATION METHODS

We see by looking at Exhibit 3.11 that both the direct and step-down methods allocate lower amounts of service center cost to rock/pop and higher amounts to country than are allocated using the reciprocal services method. Several factors might cause these differences. One is the amount of service center cost relative to total cost. All service center costs together represent 38 percent ($190,000/$500,000) of MVP's total cost. As the percentage of the aggregate service center cost becomes larger, the differences

EXHIBIT 3.11 MUSIC VIDEO PARTNERS (MVP)		
Comparison of Three Allocation Methods		
Allocated Service Center Cost	*Rock/Pop*	*Country*
Direct method (from Exhibit 3.9)	$108,000	$82,000
Step-down method (from Exhibit 3.10)	$111,125	$78,875
Reciprocal services method (from Exhibit 3.17)	$115,237	$74,763

in the dollar amount of costs allocated with each of the three methods become larger. Another factor is the allocation base. Selection of one base over another can shift the proportions of costs allocated to responsibility centers.

3: REASSIGN PRODUCTION CENTER COSTS TO PRODUCTS

We have shown how all service center costs are reassigned to production centers. The goal of the third and final step is to assign production center costs to units of product. Consequently, the focus of cost collection shifts from responsibility centers to units of product as cost objects.

Some production center costs can be traced directly to units of product. Materials, labor, and any other costs attributable directly to individual units are attached to those units. All other costs, meaning production center costs that cannot be assigned directly to individual units of product, are considered indirect costs or overhead. They are collected together in what are known as overhead cost pools. Costs in an overhead cost pool are then assigned to units using allocation bases.

ALLOCATION BASES FOR OVERHEAD

Unlike service center allocations, where different bases are selected for each service center, a single, volume-related base is typically used when assigning overhead cost to units of product. A number of different terms are used to describe these bases, including *allocation bases*, *activity bases*, and *overhead bases*. We will use the term *activity bases* to distinguish them from *allocation bases*, used earlier.

Activity bases commonly used in practice include units of product, direct labor-hours, direct labor dollars, materials dollars, and measures of utilization, such as machine-hours. As with any allocation base, an activity base should reflect how indirect resources are consumed in making products and services. For example, if production is labor-driven, then either direct labor-hours or direct labor dollars might be a good activity base. Ideally, activity bases should also drive costs. For example, increasing the number of direct labor-hours should, ideally, cause overhead cost to increase.

Once overhead cost pools are formed and activity bases chosen, the next step is to allocate overhead to each unit of product. One way is to calculate the percent of total activity base used for each unit (as we did in step 2, when service center costs were allocated to other responsibility centers). However, since units of product are often homogeneous, we can simply divide total overhead cost by the total activity base. The result is a rate—commonly referred to as the overhead rate—per unit of activity base.

In formula form, the overhead rate is expressed as follows:

$$\text{Overhead rate} = \frac{\text{overhead cost}}{\text{total activity base}}$$

To illustrate, let's assume the activity base selected for the rock/pop production center is the number of recording hours for the year. The full cost of rock/pop, as shown in Exhibit 3.12, is $261,125, assuming the step-down

---

EXHIBIT 3.12 MUSIC VIDEO PARTNERS (MVP)

Computation of Overhead Rate for the Rock/Pop Production Center

	(1) Total Rock/Pop Cost	(2) Direct Costs Attributable to Specific Rock/Pop Videos	(3)[a] Indirect (Overhead) Costs for All Videos
Direct cost of rock/pop (from Exhibit 3.4):			
Direct labor	$ 84,000	$32,900	$ 51,100
Direct materials	20,000	2,750	17,250
Purchased services	30,000	3,200	26,800
Depreciation & amortization	16,000	3,525	12,475
Other operating cost	0	0	0
Total direct cost of rock/pop	$150,000		
Costs allocated to rock/pop assuming step-down method (from Exhibit 3.10):			
Administration service center	$ 37,500		37,500
Facility service center	20,833		20,833
Recording service center	52,792		52,792
Total cost allocated to rock/pop	$111,125		
Total rock/pop responsibility center cost	$261,125	$42,375	$218,750
Number of rock/pop recording-hours			3,500
Rock/pop overhead rate (per recording-hour)			$62.50

[a]   The figures in column 3 are obtained by subtracting the figures in column 2 from those in column 1.

---

method of allocation. Without showing the details, let's assume $42,375 of total cost is directly attributed to specific rock/pop video projects. The remaining $218,750 represents indirect cost that cannot be attributed to any specific video. If rock/pop logged 3,500 recording-hours for the year, the overhead rate is $62.50 per recording-hour ($218,750/3,500 recording hours). Overhead cost is absorbed into the cost of rock/pop videos by charging each at a rate of $62.50 per recording-hour.

PREDETERMINED OVERHEAD RATES

Overhead rates are calculated at the end of the year when actual overhead cost and the actual volume of the activity base are known. Alternatively, overhead rates can be estimated at the beginning of the year. If the second method is used, the rate is referred to as a **predetermined overhead rate**, calculated by dividing **estimated overhead** by **estimated units of the activity base.** Predetermined overhead rates provide managers with an important tool—a way of estimating full cost without having to wait until the end of the year.

To estimate the cost of producing a video at any time during the year—say, in February—rock/pop's manager would predict direct materials, direct labor, and other direct costs for producing a video and then add an amount for predetermined overhead. For example, assume MVP wants to estimate the cost of making a new video, coded video no. 107. As shown

EXHIBIT 3.13 MUSIC VIDEO PARTNERS (MVP)

Full Cost of Rock/Pop Video No. 107

Direct cost attributed to video:		
Direct labor		$1,500
Direct materials		120
Purchased services		430
Depreciation & amortization for equipment used on video		150
Total direct cost attributable to video		$2,200
Rock/pop overhead:		
Overhead rate per recording-hour (from Exhibit 3.12)	$62.50	
Recording hours	120	
Total overhead assigned		$7,500
Full cost of rock/pop video no. 107		$9,700

in Exhibit 3.13, estimates of direct labor, direct materials, and other direct costs total $2,200. Managers expect the video to take 120 hours of recording time. Adding predetermined overhead of $7,500 (120 hours × $62.50 per hour) to direct cost yields $9,700, an estimate of the full cost to produce the video.

The kinds of indirect costs pooled together to form an overhead cost pool may include different items:

- For manufacturing companies, overhead costs generally include only indirect manufacturing costs, called **manufacturing (factory) overhead.** Indirect manufacturing costs are essential in making products but cannot be traced directly to individual units. Examples include plant supervisor salaries, depreciation for manufacturing equipment, and utilities used in manufacturing products. Nonmanufacturing costs—such as personnel, marketing, accounting, and any other costs that might be classified under the heading of Selling, General, and Administrative Cost—are *not* included as part of manufacturing overhead. So, when we refer to *full manufacturing cost,* we mean all the direct and indirect costs to make a product. Nonmanufacturing overhead would have to be added to full manufacturing cost to obtain full cost.

- For companies that process materials, indirect costs might include costs that are similar to those of a manufacturing firm. For example, a commercial printer may pool together all indirect costs of its printing operations—such as press depreciation and the print supervisors' salaries—and assign those costs to printing jobs, using an overhead rate. Nonprocessing costs—such as personnel, marketing, accounting, and any other costs that might be classified under the heading of Selling, General, and Administrative Cost—are *not* included as part of processing overhead. So, when we refer to *full processing cost,* we mean all the direct and indirect costs of processing products. Nonprocessing overhead would have to be added to full processing cost to obtain full cost.

- For companies that offer only services, most of the total costs are indirect with respect to the service and are included in one comprehensive overhead rate. In a law firm, for example, perhaps the only direct cost of a case is the attorney's time and costs such as telephone charges, travel costs, and professional fees for experts assigned to the case. Virtually all other costs—such as marketing and general and administrative costs—*are* included as part of overhead. So, when we refer to *full cost for a service organization*, we mean all the direct costs plus all overhead.

SEGMENT DIRECT MARGINS

Segment contribution margin, introduced in Chapter 2, is calculated by subtracting variable cost from revenue. Fixed cost is then subtracted from the segment contribution margin to derive segment profit. When a segment's total cost is separated into direct and indirect cost, we *deduct the segment direct cost from the segment revenue to get the segment direct margin.* Managers can define segments in virtually any way they want—by product lines, geographic regions, customer groups, or distribution channels, for example. Segment information helps managers sort out the contribution each segment makes—in the form of direct margin—toward coverage of indirect cost.

Segment profit is calculated by subtracting the segment indirect cost from the segment direct margin. Of course, that means that indirect cost must be assigned to a segment using the methods discussed earlier in this chapter. As long as the sum of all segments' direct margins exceeds the total organizationwide indirect cost, the firm as a whole will show a profit.

Consider the segment data shown in Exhibit 3.14. Both of MVP's production centers show positive direct margins—namely, $275,000 for rock/pop and $65,000 for country. Note that indirect cost is assigned to each production center using the step-down method (Exhibit 3.10). Segment profit is calculated by deducting allocations of indirect cost from direct margin. While the organization as a whole shows a $150,000 profit, segment data indicates that rock/pop generates a profit of $163,875 while country shows a loss of $(13,875). If the assignment of indirect cost fairly represents resource consumption—an assumption that we will challenge

EXHIBIT 3.14   MUSIC VIDEO PARTNERS (MVP)

Segment Direct Margins and Profits

	Rock/Pop	Country	Total
Segment revenue	$425,000	$225,000	$650,000
Direct cost (from Exhibit 3.4)	(150,000)	(160,000)	(310,000)
Segment direct margin	$275,000	$ 65,000	$340,000
Allocated costs using step-down method (from Exhibit 3.10)	(111,125)	(78,875)	(190,000)
Segment profit (before tax)	$163,875	$ (13,875)	$150,000

in the next chapter—then country's loss might be caused by a number of different factors, ranging from low selling prices to excessive costs. Segment data indicate areas that managers may need to investigate and where they may want to consider corrective action.

We must sound a note of caution when interpreting segment data, however. We cannot conclude that Music Video Partners should discontinue producing country videos. As indicated in Chapter 2, that kind of decision should be based on how organizationwide costs are likely to change. Since the data in Exhibit 3.14 offer no insight into cost behavior, we cannot draw conclusions about whether or not Music Video Partners should discontinue making country videos.

Managers may confuse direct cost with variable cost. Some costs, such as materials, are both direct and variable. On the other side of the coin, other costs, such as labor, may be direct but may have cost behavior that is fixed. Even though managers are probably aware of the differences between direct and indirect, and variable and fixed, they may still use direct costs as an approximation of variable costs, especially if they don't have access to costs classified by cost behavior. So the important lesson here is, *don't confuse direct costs with variable and indirect costs with fixed!*

EVALUATION OF FULL COST

By this point you should have a good idea of how costs are collected by cost objects. But how accurate are the results? Does collecting costs by cost objects provide managers with useful information? Here are some factors that should be considered in determining how accurate and how useful the cost information is:

- How broad should overhead cost pools be?
- Do allocation-based full costs realistically represent cost behavior?
- Under what conditions do allocations produce accurate measures of full cost?
- Do allocations guide managers in making decisions that will benefit their organizations?
- What are the alternatives to allocations?

HOW BROAD SHOULD OVERHEAD COST POOLS BE?

As shown above, indirect production costs are added to one another to form cost pools before they are assigned to units of product. How broad should these overhead cost pools be? Should there be only one organizationwide overhead cost pool? Or should there be many narrowly defined overhead cost pools, each with its own activity driver?

The overhead rate calculated based on a single cost pool is referred to as the plantwide overhead rate. Music Video Partners might create a single, plantwide overhead rate that could be used for both rock/pop and country. Such a rate would be derived by combining indirect costs from both rock/pop and country into a single cost pool and dividing the total by a common activity driver. Alternatively, indirect costs can be broken down into a number of lower-level cost pools, each having its own activity base and its own overhead rate. Since cost pools are often formed for departments, lower-level overhead rates are often called departmental overhead rates—for example, the $62.50 per recording-hour rate for rock/pop (Exhibit 3.12).

Production center overhead can be pooled at even lower, subdepartmental levels. For example, rock/pop may create two overhead cost pools rather than one: the first, for labor (perhaps using direct labor-hours as an activity base), and the second, for all other indirect costs. Obviously, even-more-narrowly defined cost pools are possible. How, then, are managers to decide how broadly or narrowly to define the overhead cost pools? The answer comes from an analysis of the trade-off between the value derived from the additional detail against the cost of gathering the additional information.

To illustrate departmental overhead rates, let's consider the auto parts manufacturer represented in Exhibit 3.15. Manufacturing comprises three activities: grinding, assembly, and finishing. Total organizationwide overhead is $232,000. Let's assume the auto manufacturer uses a plantwide manufacturing overhead rate based on the combined direct labor-hours for all three departments. If there are 15,000 combined direct labor-hours for the three departments, the plantwide manufacturing overhead rate is $15.47 per direct labor-hour ($232,000/15,000 hours).

We will assume, without showing the details of where the data came from, that $29,000 in manufacturing overhead cost is assigned to grinding, $157,000 to assembly, and $46,000 to finishing. As shown in Exhibit 3.15, departmental overhead rates are calculated by dividing departmental overhead by the amount of the activity base. The overhead rate for the fin-

EXHIBIT 3.15 AUTO PARTS MANUFACTURER

Departmental Overhead Rates

	Grinding	Assembly	Finishing	Plantwide Total
Manufacturing overhead:				
Utilities	$ 5,000	$ 44,000	$11,000	$ 60,000
Supplies	6,000	27,000	9,000	42,000
Depreciation	18,000	86,000	26,000	130,000
Total manufacturing overhead	$29,000	$157,000	$46,000	$232,000
Base used for manufacturing overhead rates:				
Plantwide—labor-hours				15,000
Grinding department—labor-hours	3,000			
Assembly department—machine-hours		1,800		
Finishing department—labor-cost			$26,000	
Manufacturing overhead rate:	$9.67 per labor-hour	$87.22 per machine-hour	176.92% of labor cost	$15.47 per labor-hour

ishing department, for example, is 176.92 percent of finishing labor cost. That is, a product requiring, say, $100 of finishing labor will be assigned $176.92 of indirect manufacturing cost. Full manufacturing cost for an automobile part is calculated by adding overhead for each department involved in processing the part to direct materials and direct labor costs.

To illustrate departmental overhead rates, let's consider the bids for auto parts for two different customers, as shown in Exhibit 3.16. The middle columns (under Volume Customer) represent a part routinely manufactured in large quantities for a long-standing customer. The right-hand columns (under Special Order) represent a low-volume, one-time custom order for a new customer. While the total labor-hours are the same for both jobs, the distribution of hours among the three departments might be considerably different.

Using departmental rates, $1,316 in total manufacturing overhead is assigned to the part for the volume customer. In contrast, $1,547 is assigned to the volume customer using the plantwide rate. If full manufacturing cost is marked up by, say, 35 percent to cover nonmanufacturing cost and provide for profit, then the bid price ought to be $2,820 if

EXHIBIT 3.16 AUTO PARTS MANUFACTURER

Bid Price for Two Automobile Parts Jobs Using Departmental and Plantwide Overhead Rates

Using Departmental Overhead Rates

Manufacturing Cost	Base	Volume Customer			Special Order		
		Quantity	Rate	Total	Quantity	Rate	Total
Materials & labor				$773			$ 773
Manufacturing overhead:							
Grinding	Labor-hours	85	$9.67	$ 822	20	$9.67	$ 193
Assembly	Machine-hours	5	$87.22	436	20	$87.22	1,744
Finishing	Labor cost	$32.50	176.92%	57	$162.50	176.92%	287
Total overhead assigned				$1,316			$2,225
Total manufacturing cost				$2,089			$2,998
Desired markup	Mfg. cost		35.00%	731		35.00%	1,049
Bid price using departmental rates				$2,820			$4,048

Using Plantwide Overhead Rate

Materials & labor				$ 773			$ 773
Manufacturing overhead	Labor-hours	100	$15.47	1,547	100	$15.47	1,547
Total manufacturing cost				$2,320			$2,320
Desired markup	Mfg. cost		35.00%	812		35.00%	812
Bid price using plantwide rate				$3,132			$3,132

Summary

Bid price using departmental rates	$2,820	$4,048
Bid price using plantwide rate	$3,132	$3,132
Ratio of departmental to plantwide bid price	90.02%	129.24%

departmental rates are used or $3,132 if the plantwide rate is used. Assuming departmental rates provide a more accurate basis for assigning manufacturing overhead, then the part for the volume customer is likely to be overcosted and the price overbid if the plantwide overhead rate is used. The likely result using the plantwide rate is the loss of work from the volume customer because the price is too high.

Just the opposite happens for the special-order part. Using departmental rates, $2,225 in manufacturing overhead is assigned to the special-order part. In contrast, $1,547 of manufacturing overhead is assigned using the plantwide rate. After the special-order part is marked up by 35 percent of manufacturing cost, the desired bid price is $4,048 using departmental rates and $3,132 using the plantwide rate. Assuming departmental rates are more accurate, the special-order part is undercosted, with the likely result that the market price will be underbid if the plantwide overhead rate is used. Customers know a bargain when they see one. More and more special orders are likely to be received, since the price is relatively low. The likely result from using the plantwide rate is a decline in direct margins.

DO ALLOCATION-BASED FULL COSTS REALISTICALLY REPRESENT COST BEHAVIOR?

Most managerial accounting information is based on financial accounting systems designed primarily to meet the needs of external users. Since the focus of these systems is external reporting, costs are typically collected according to whether they are direct or indirect rather than according to their cost behavior. For many managers, identification of costs as direct or indirect may be the only form of cost information routinely available. As we mentioned before, *managers may incorrectly use direct costs as approximations of variable costs.*

UNDER WHAT CONDITIONS DO ALLOCATIONS PRODUCE ACCURATE MEASURES OF FULL COST?

In general, allocations are likely to provide accurate estimates of full cost when:

- *The proportion of allocated costs is small compared to total cost.* Products with high direct materials and direct labor costs contain relatively low proportions of allocated costs. With indirect cost representing only a small percentage of the total cost, the impact of poorly allocated costs may be minimal. But as competition increases and direct margins shrink, improved allocations may become a necessity.
- *The variety of products is small and the scope of operations narrow.* Allocations among similar products, each requiring nearly the same kinds of resources, may have little impact on the unit cost of any of those products. However, if the number of products is large, or diversity among products is high, whereby each product draws dissimilar amounts of shared resources, then there's a greater likelihood of misallocations and distortions in unit costs.

DO ALLOCATIONS GUIDE MANAGERS IN MAKING DECISIONS THAT WILL BENEFIT THEIR ORGANIZATIONS?

Poor allocations of overhead cost cause inaccurate measures of full cost. This may lead to poor decisions. If they are to guide managers in making decisions that add value to their organizations, allocations of indirect costs should provide an accurate pricing system whereby internal consumers pay the equivalent of market prices for services they receive. If indirect cost allocations do not accurately reflect the cost of resource consumption and are perceived as arbitrary, then:[4]

- *Other production and service centers may demand more services than can be economically justified.* If maintenance cost, for example, is allocated based on square feet occupied rather than utilization, internal consumers may demand more maintenance services than they need. That's because cost is not linked to utilization. Since the number of square feet is *static*—that is, it doesn't change with utilization—the cost allocated to users is unaffected by the volume of services requested. Thus, there is no penalty for overuse. As a consequence, overall maintenance cost may increase as more and more services are demanded.

- *Managers will not be able to determine whether the service center is operating efficiently.* It is difficult to determine whether service centers can provide services at lower cost when internal consumers are not charged the equivalent of market prices for the services they receive. That is, allocations provide a poor basis for comparison of relative efficiency.

- *Managers cannot determine whether services should be provided internally or externally.* Without meaningful measures of costs, managers may find it difficult to determine whether services should be purchased from external suppliers. Service center costs based on indirect cost allocations may not sufficiently represent the full cost of providing internal services. Managers may not make the right decisions when trying to compare the relative cost of services provided internally versus the cost of outsourcing.

- *Managers may intentionally make allocations unfair.* In some circumstances, managers may not intend allocations to be fair. Sometimes costs are deliberately shifted from one group to another, as illustrated in "Current Practice: Cost Shifting—Three Examples."

WHAT ARE THE ALTERNATIVES TO ALLOCATIONS?

- One alternative to allocations is to regard service centers as though they were production centers. Instead of allocating costs, internal products and services are transferred—perhaps by using chargeback systems—between responsibility centers at approximate market

---

[4] This section is based on materials found in Robert S. Kaplan and Anthony A. Atkinson, *Advanced Management Accounting*, 2d ed. Englewood Cliffs, N.J.: Prentice-Hall, 1989, pp. 241–243.

CURRENT PRACTICE

Cost Shifting—Three Examples

Managers may intentionally shift costs from one group of customers to another. Here are three examples:

1. Some hospitals allocate more costs and increase prices for services provided to selected groups of customers. Shifting costs helps compensate for shortfalls in reimbursements from insurance companies, government agencies, and programs that support indigent care.

2. Some contractors allocate as much overhead to government jobs as contracts will allow. This permits the contractor to offer lower, more competitive prices to other customers.

3. Some international companies shift overhead charges for corporate activities such as research and development to operations in countries with the highest income tax rates, thereby minimizing the companywide tax burden.

[handwritten annotation: Tindidzong - degen 6 ugatuva uppge]

prices, thereby linking cost with utilization. Each production center then *contracts* for services with other organizational units, just as it would with outside suppliers. Service centers failing to show a profit are targeted for cost reductions or for outsourcing.

- Another alternative is to reorganize service centers as dedicated subunits of production centers. General Motors offers an example of consolidating services in the Current Practice box. For example, rather than relying on an organizationwide human resource department, each operating unit might supply its own human resource department. All costs of the human resource department are then assigned

CURRENT PRACTICE

General Motors' Restructuring of a Restructuring Plan

General Motors created separate staffs for its three North American vehicle manufacturing groups and its U.S.-based corporate headquarters in a 1984 reorganization. Each staff performed functions such as planning, purchasing, personnel, marketing, labor relations, and finance. Their costs were directly attributed to the seg-

ment they served. However, GM reversed its policy in 1992, when it announced that separate staffs would no longer be maintained. The move was intended to centralize corporatewide functions, reduce labor costs, and eliminate duplication of effort.

Source: Paul Ingrassia and Joseph B. White, "GM Is Planning to Consolidate Group Staffs: Recent Decision to Shrink Work Force Could Undo Reorganization of 1984," *The Wall Street Journal,* Feb. 7, 1992, pp. A3 and A4.

to production centers by attribution, thus eliminating the need for allocations. Unfortunately, the use of redundant localized service centers, each providing the same service as the others, negates economies of scale—one of the principal reasons for creating centralized service centers in the first place.

- A third alternative is to improve the accuracy of the cost accumulation system. Tracing costs more accurately minimizes the proportion of allocated costs. *Activity-based costing*, or *ABC*, is one such system. ABC systems, introduced in the next chapter, trace costs to activities rather than to responsibility centers. Activities, and their costs, are then traced to products and services.

SUMMARY

Costs that can be traced directly to cost objects are direct costs. Indirect costs are costs that are incurred in common for many cost objects. To calculate unit cost, resources are traced to the responsibility centers where they were incurred. Responsibility centers include both service centers, which provide internal services, and production centers, which sell products or services to external customers. Full cost for a production center comprises direct cost and a fair share of the cost of service centers.

There are three methods of allocating service center costs to other responsibility centers. In ascending order of computational difficulty, they are the direct, step-down, and reciprocal services methods. It is generally assumed that the reciprocal services method provides the most accurate results.

Each production center collects its costs—direct and indirect—and assigns them to units of product. Direct costs are attributed directly to units. Production departments' indirect costs are assigned to units using overhead rates.

Overhead rates are calculated by pooling together all indirect costs and dividing the sum by the activity base. The choice of an activity base should parallel the relative consumption of resources by each unit of product. Full cost of a unit comprises direct costs, such as materials and labor, and overhead reflecting the amount of the allocation base that the unit consumes.

The direct margin of a segment is calculated by deducting direct cost from revenue. The direct margin is the amount that segment contributes to cover indirect cost. A segment margin must not be confused with a contribution margin, which is revenue less variable cost.

When the different products a firm produces are homogeneous, requiring little variation in the use of resources, indirect cost allocations may provide reasonable approximations of full cost. However, for companies with a variety of products and services, requiring vastly different resource inputs, indirect cost allocations may result in distorted full cost. In these situations, other, more-detailed systems may be needed in order to provide more accurate estimates of full cost. These systems are the subject of the next chapter.

APPENDIX

RECIPROCAL SERVICES METHOD OF COST ALLOCATION

The reciprocal services method fully captures interactions between a service center and other responsibility centers. The first step in the approach is to create a schedule, like the one shown in the top portion of Exhibit 3.17. (Data for this exhibit are taken from Exhibit 3.8.)

Using these allocation bases, the percentages of services provided by each of the service centers to other responsibility centers are calculated. (Make sure they total 100 percent.) The next step is to rearrange the percentages in a **matrix format**, like the one shown in step 1 (Exhibit 3.17).

EXHIBIT 3.17 MUSIC VIDEO PARTNERS (MVP)

Reciprocal Services Method for Allocating Service Center Costs*

	Service Center			Production Center		
	Admin.	Facility	Recording	Rock/Pop	Country	Total
Employees	2	1	2	3	2	10
Percent of total	20.00%	10.00%	20.00%	30.00%	20.00%	100.00%
Square feet occupied	4,000		1,000	2,000	3,000	10,000
Percent of total	40.00%		10.00%	20.00%	30.00%	100.00%
Recording-hours			500	3,500	1,500	5,500
Percent of total			9.09%	63.64%	27.27%	100.00%

Step 1. Rearrange percentage data by provider or receiver of services.

	Provider of Services			Direct Cost
	Admin.	Facility	Recording	(from Exhibit 3.4)
Services received by:				
Administration	20.00%	40.00%	0.00%	$100,000
Facility	10.00%	0.00%	0.00%	$ 50,000
Recording	20.00%	10.00%	9.09%	$ 40,000
Total to other service	50.00%	50.00%	9.09%	$190,000
Rock/pop	30.00%	20.00%	63.64%	$150,000
Country	20.00%	30.00%	27.27%	$160,000
Total to production	50.00%	50.00%	90.91%	$310,000
Total service provided	100.00%	100.00%	100.00%	$500,000

Step 2. Put services provided to service centers (step 1) in matrix format.

Service Center Matrix

20.00%	40.00%	0.00%
10.00%	0.00%	0.00%
20.00%	10.00%	9.09%

Step 3. Put services provided to production centers (step 1) in matrix format.

Production Center Matrix

30.00%	20.00%	63.64%
20.00%	30.00%	27.27%

(continued)

The columns represent percent of services provided, first to other service centers and then to production centers. For example, administration provides 20 percent of its services to itself, 10 percent to facility, 20 percent to recording, 30 percent to rock/pop, and 20 percent to country. The last column represents direct costs of each service and production center (data are taken from Exhibit 3.4).

The steps, in more detail, are:

1–4. In the first four steps, simply rearrange the data and convert it into matrices. Step 1 rearranges the data at the top of Exhibit 3.17 by the service centers providing services (in columns) and by the service and production centers receiving services (in rows). For example, administration receives 40 percent of the services provided by facility. Step 2 simply repeats the services provided by service centers to other service centers taken from step 1. Step 3 repeats the services provided by service centers to production centers taken from step 1. Next, the

---

EXHIBIT 3.17 (CONTINUED)

Step 4. Put direct costs of service centers (step 1) in matrix format.

Service Center Direct Cost
$100,000
$ 50,000
$ 40,000

Step 5. Create an identity matrix.

Identity Matrix		
1	0	0
0	1	0
0	0	1

Step 6. Subtract service center matrix (step 2) from identity matrix (step 5).

Identity Matrix Minus Service Center Matrix		
0.8000	−0.4000	0.0000
−0.1000	1.0000	0.0000
−0.2000	−0.1000	0.9091

Step 7. Find inverse of matrix created in step 6.

Inverse of Identity Matrix Minus Service Center Matrix		
1.3158	0.5263	0.0000
0.1316	1.0526	0.0000
0.3039	0.2316	1.1000

Step 8. Multiply the inverse matrix created in step 7 by the service center direct cost matrix (step 4).

Service Center Total Cost Matrix
$157,895
$65,789
$85,974

Step 9. Multiply production center matrix (step 3) by the matrix created in step 8.

Cost Allocated to Production Centers
$115,237
$74,763

Step 10. Add costs allocated to production centers (step 9) to direct production center costs (step 1).

	Direct Cost (Step 1)	Allocated Cost (Step 9)	Total Cost
Rock/pop	$150,000	$115,237	$265,237
Country	$160,000	$ 74,763	2234,763
			$500,000

* *Note:* Data are from Exhibit 3.8.

total direct cost is repeated for each of the service centers, also taken from step 1.

5. Create an identity matrix, with the number of rows equal to the number of service centers.
6. Subtract the service center matrix, from step 2, from the identity matrix in step 5.
7. Find the inverse of the matrix created in step 6. Most electronic spreadsheets have a data/matrix/inverse command.
8. Multiply the inverse matrix created in step 7 by the service center direct cost matrix, from step 4.
9. Multiply the production center matrix, from step 3, by the service center total cost matrix in step 8.
10. Add allocated service center costs, from step 9, to direct production center costs, found in step 1. The results are $265,237 for rock/pop (composed of $150,000 of direct cost and allocations of $115,237), and $234,763 for country (composed of $160,000 of direct cost and allocations of $74,763).

CHAPTER 3 ASSIGNMENTS

DISCUSSION PROBLEMS

D3.1 (What's Included in Full Cost)

You may have read in the newspaper about seemingly low-cost, everyday items that are sold at exaggerated prices. One example is an aspirin. You might be able to buy a bottle of 100 aspirins at the drugstore for, say, $3.50, or $0.035 per aspirin. But, if you "bought" that aspirin at a hospital—that is, had it delivered to your bedside—it is likely to cost a whole lot more. In fact, the price might be as high as $3.50 for a pair of aspirins. That's about 50 times the amount you would pay in the drugstore! Why the difference?

Consider the breakdown of the direct and indirect costs of delivering aspirins to a hospital patient, as shown in Exhibit D3.1.

Required:

1. What is the cost object? Is it a product, a service, or both?
2. Do you think that physician, pharmacist, and nurse labor costs are really direct? What characteristic makes a cost direct or indirect?
3. What are shared and shifted costs? Do you think they should be included in the cost of an aspirin? If so, do you think that they are accurately allocated?

D3.2 (Allocated Costs)

A *U.S. News & World Report*[5] article indicated that Stanford University is battling allegations that it "... seriously and habitually overbilled taxpayers for research-related expenses throughout the 1980s."[6] This allegation has led to fed-

---

[5] Thomas Toch, "The Pitfalls of Big Science: Stanford's Curious Bookkeeping Points to More Basic Problems," *U.S. News & World Report,* Mar. 4, 1991, p. 52.
[6] Ibid., p. 52.

EXHIBIT D3.1 WHAT DOES IT COST TO DELIVER AN ASPIRIN AT A HOSPITAL?

	Unit Measure	Unit Cost	Total Units	Total Cost
Direct materials:				
Aspirin	Each	$0.006	2	$0.012
Paper cup	Each	0.020	1	0.020
Direct labor:				
Physician	Hour	60.000	0.0083	0.500
Pharmacist	Hour	30.000	0.0201	0.602
Nurse	Hour	20.000	0.0056	0.111
Indirect labor:				
Orderly	Hour	12.000	0.0167	0.200
Recordkeeping	Hour	12.000	0.0167	0.200
Shared & shifted cost:				
Unreimbursed medicare		0.200	1	0.200
Indigent care		0.223	1	0.223
Uncollectible receivables		0.084	1	0.084
Malpractice insurance		0.068	1	0.068
Excess bed capacity		0.169	1	0.169
Other operating cost		0.056	1	0.056
Other administrative cost		0.112	1	0.112
Equipment & employee downtime		0.074	1	0.074
Total product cost				$2.632
Hospital overhead	Percent product cost	32.98%	$2.632	$0.868
Full cost				$3.500

Source: David W. McFadden, "The Legacy of the $7 Aspirin," *Management Accounting,* Apr. 1990, p. 39.

eral investigations; preliminary findings indicate that Stanford may have received as much as $150 million in payment for illegally charged overhead.

The problem stems from identifying overhead cost that is legitimately charged to government contracts. While scientists' salaries and lab equipment cost can be clearly attributed to specific contracts, other indirect cost cannot be traced to government contracts at all. Good examples are student placement and admissions. In-between these two extremes are costs—such as utility bills and the expense of running the library—that may indirectly benefit the government but are incurred primarily for students.

Overhead costs chargeable to contracts are controlled by government cost-accounting regulations, but the regulations are subject to interpretation. Stanford University is accused of deliberately pushing the limits of what is allowable by billing as much for indirect research costs as possible. Stanford's alleged abuses include charging Uncle Sam for, among other things, upkeep on its golf course and depreciation on a sailing-club yacht. As a result, Stanford has been charging as much as 70.0 percent of its total funding for overhead, one of the highest rates in the United States. In Stanford's defense, it appears to have charged overhead that is technically permitted. Moreover, its overhead rates may actually be less than those charged by private contractors.

Required:

1. Do you think it's appropriate for a university to bill the government for indirect costs? If so, do you believe it's appropriate to charge for depreciation on research facilities? Is it appropriate to charge an allocation of the university's admissions department?
2. Some accountants refer to the practice illustrated above as *cost shifting*. Do you think cost shifting is ethical?
3. Can allocations of costs create cost shifting?

PROBLEMS   P3.1 (Basic Allocations)

Leisure Boats is organized into three departments. The first is new boat production, where Leisure manufactures new fiberglass boats. The second department is repairs and rebuilding, where company employees fix used boats for customers. Both of these production departments are supported by administration, the only service department. Data for Leisure's current year are shown in Exhibit P3.1.

Leisure is trying to decide between square feet occupied and the number of employees as a basis for allocating the cost of administration to new boat production and repairs and rebuilding. Once it decides on an allocation base, Leisure plans to divide total overhead in each of the two production departments by the number of boats each works on to come up with an overhead cost per boat. It expects to use the overhead figure for pricing.

Required:

1. Calculate the overhead costs per boat for new boat production and for repairs and rebuilding using square feet occupied as the base for allocating administration cost.
2. Calculate the overhead costs per boat for new boat production and for repairs and rebuilding using the number of employees as the base for allocating administration cost.

P3.2 (Departmental vs. Organizationwide Overhead Rates)

The Community Bank of Winter Park (CBWP) offers four basic banking services: (1) checking accounts, (2) savings accounts, (3) consumer loans, and (4) certificates of deposit (CDs). Each month CBWP incurs $800,000 in processing charges to handle these four types of accounts. On the average, there are about 250,000 active accounts each month.

CBWP has been attaching a service charge of $3.20 per month to cover pro-

EXHIBIT P3.1 LEISURE BOATS

Current Year Data

Cost & Other Data	Administration	New Boat Production	Repairs & Rebuilding	Total
Department overhead	$4,000,000	$15,000,000	$6,000,000	$25,000,000
Square feet occupied	5,000	60,000	20,000	85,000
Number of employees	10	40	60	110
Number of boats		4,000	2,500	6,500

EXHIBIT P3.2 COMMUNITY BANK OF WINTER PARK					
Monthly Processing Costs					
	Checking Accounts	*Savings Accounts*	*Consumer Loans*	*CDs*	*Total*
Monthly processing costs	$340,000	$120,000	$280,000	$60,000	$800,000
Number of accounts	120,000	80,000	40,000	10,000	250,000

cessing costs. The charge was determined by dividing total processing cost ($800,000) by the average number of accounts (250,000). Several managers have challenged the fairness of assigning cost in this way. Instead, they propose breaking down the total cost into cost for each of the four basic service categories. To help support their proposal, the managers collected the data shown in Exhibit P3.2.

Required:

1. Calculate the processing cost per account for each of the four basic services.
2. Based on the results of your computations in requirement 1, which of the four basic services have been receiving subsidies and which have been giving subsidies to other services?

P3.3 (Allocation Mechanics)

Local Manufacturing makes electronic components. It uses relatively expensive materials, acquired from a variety of vendors. To meet the high standards of its customers, Local feels that it must conduct extensive quality tests on both inbound materials and outbound completed components. Because of limited resources, Local must carefully schedule production and quality testing.

Local's operations are organized into five departments. Three of the departments (plant administration, scheduling, and quality testing) support the activities of Local's two production departments (assembly and soldering). After inbound materials are tested, they are inserted into prepunched slots on assembly boards. Lead lines sticking from the underside of assembly boards are connected using equipment known as wave-solderers. Finally, completed components are tested to ensure that all electrical connections are complete and that components function as intended. In addition to scheduling and quality testing, Local provides plant administrative support. Plant administration's job is to supervise production and collect common manufacturing costs, such as depreciation for the manufacturing facility. Budgeted direct costs for all five departments and estimates for several measures of activity are shown in Exhibit P3.3.

Local wants to assign the costs of the three service departments—plant administration, scheduling, and quality testing—to the two production departments in order to calculate the cost of making components. Presently, its managers are considering two allocation methods—direct and step-down—to assign service department costs to production departments. After looking at alternative allocation bases, managers decide to allocate plant administration cost based on direct labor-hours, scheduling cost based on scheduling hours, and quality testing costs based on testing hours. The sequence of steps, if Local decides to use the step-down method, is plant administration first, followed by scheduling, and quality testing last.

EXHIBIT P3.3 LOCAL MANUFACTURING

Service and Production Departments

	Service Department			Production Department	
	Plant Administration	Scheduling	Quality Testing	Assembly	Soldering
Cost component:					
Materials	$ 25,000	$ 15,000	$ 85,000	$1,100,000	$220,000
Labor	210,000	85,000	180,000	400,000	295,000
Overhead	140,000	75,000	60,000	350,000	125,000
Direct departmental costs	$375,000	$175,000	$325,000	$1,850,000	$640,000
Measure of activity:					
Direct labor-hours		3,750	1,200	55,000	74,000
Scheduling hours			12,500	6,500	8,750
Testing hours				845	650

Once service department costs are allocated to production departments, Local uses direct labor-hours to assign manufacturing overhead to electronic components.

Required:

1. Calculate an hourly overhead rate for assembly and soldering, using the direct method of allocation.
2. Calculate an hourly overhead rate for assembly and soldering, using the step-down method of allocation.

P3.4 (Basic Allocations)

The Parker Manufacturing Company has two production departments (fabrication and assembly) and three service departments (general factory administration, factory maintenance, and factory cafeteria). Parker allocates the cost of general factory administration on the basis of direct labor-hours. The cost of factory maintenance is allocated based on the number of square feet occupied. Factory cafeteria cost is allocated based on the number of employees. A summary of the actual cost and other data for each department prior to the allocation of service department cost is given in Exhibit P3.4.

Required:

1. Assuming Parker allocates service department cost using the direct method, calculate the total cost of both production departments after service department cost is allocated.
2. Assuming Parker allocates service department cost using the step-down method, calculate the total cost of both production departments after service department cost is allocated. Assume the sequence of steps is in descending order of total service department cost.
3. Assume fabrication assigns production departmental overhead to products using a predetermined overhead rate based on direct labor-hours. Calculate a

EXHIBIT P3.4 PARKER MANUFACTURING COMPANY

Cost and Other Data for Service and Production Departments

	Service Department			Production Department	
	General Factory Administration	Factory Maintenance	Factory Cafeteria	Fabrication	Assembly
Cost component:					
Direct materials		$65,000	$91,000	$3,130,000	$950,000
Direct labor	$90,000	$82,100	$87,000	$1,950,000	$2,050,000
Manufacturing overhead	$70,000	$56,100	$62,000	$1,650,000	$1,850,000
Measure of activity:					
Direct labor-hours	31,000	27,000	42,000	562,500	437,500
Square feet occupied	1,750	2,000	4,800	88,000	72,000
Employees	12	8	20	280	200
Machine-hours				51,000	35,000

predetermined overhead rate per direct labor-hour for fabrication, assuming service department cost is allocated using the step-down method.

4. Assume assembly assigns production departmental overhead to products using a predetermined overhead rate based on machine-hours. Calculate a predetermined overhead rate per machine-hour for assembly, assuming service department cost is allocated using the step-down method.

5. Assume full manufacturing cost is marked up by 35 percent to cover non-manufacturing cost and a reasonable profit. Calculate the desired selling price for a product requiring direct materials costing $30,000, direct labor of $20,000, a total of 4,000 direct labor-hours in fabrication, and 350 machine-hours in assembly. Assume Parker uses the step-down method of allocation.

(*AICPA Adapted*)

P3.5 (Predetermined Overhead)

The law firm of Rendor, Rendor & Veit charges clients on an hourly basis. Once clients are assigned account numbers, any costs that can be traced to a specific client are charged to that account. Examples of direct costs include attorney and secretarial time, travel, phone calls, and photocopies. All other costs—those that can't be traced directly to a specific client—are pooled together in what Rendor, Rendor & Veit calls "administrative services." An estimate of the total administrative services cost is prepared at the beginning of the year. Then the cost is spread among all clients using an overhead rate based on the estimated number of hours billed by the attorneys.

A breakdown of total administrative services cost for next year, estimated at $600,000, is presented in Exhibit P3.5. Rendor, Rendor & Veit expects to bill a total of 10,000 hours for the year.

Required:

1. Calculate the predetermined overhead rate. Then assume all costs in Exhibit P3.5 are fixed and that 12,000 hours of attorney time is actually billed. Also

EXHIBIT P3.5 RENDOR, RENDOR AND VEIT, ATTORNEYS

Estimated Administrative Services Cost for 1997

Salaries & benefits	$176,000
Facility lease	216,000
Advertising	120,000
Supplies	42,000
Equipment depreciation	31,000
Utilities	15,000
Total	$600,000

assume that $600,000 in administrative services cost is actually incurred. What is the effect on pretax operating income? If only 8,000 hours are actually billed, what is the effect on pretax operating income?

2. What if half of the costs in Exhibit P3.5 are fixed and half are variable? Assume that the actual variable administrative services cost per hour and the total fixed administrative services cost are exactly as estimated. Also assume that 12,000 hours of attorney time is actually billed. What is the effect on pretax operating income? What is the effect if only 8,000 hours are actually billed?

P3.6 (Plantwide vs. Departmental Overhead Rates)

Wynona makes the interior speaker components that are used in the manufacture of hearing aids. Several years ago, it manufactured the entire hearing aid system. When a number of domestic and international hearing aid manufacturers began to flood the market, Wynona decided to pull back and focus on what it does best—making miniature interior speaker systems. Using technology developed over the years and employing a highly trained workforce, Wynona was able to capture a large share of the market. Today, many of the hearing aid manufacturers rely on outsourcing speakers to Wynona. Unfortunately, the more Wynona grows, the worse it seems to do. While the dollar revenue actually increased last year, the return on sales fell steadily. All of this has Benny King, CEO of Wynona, determined to figure out what the problem is.

Wynona makes eight basic speaker designs, some of which are modified to suit client requirements. Some clients mass-produce hearing aids and compete on price. They generally require no design changes, but want the lowest possible price. Other customers, however, require significant design modifications.

Wynona factors quality control into the cost of its speakers, since every contract specifies allowable defect rates. In general, mass manufacturers are less concerned about quality. In contrast, some of Wynona's other customers require rigid testing, even putting significant penalties in contracts for high defect rates.

Wynona collects costs in two production departments—component assembly and quality testing. Four service centers provide support for production. They are plant administration, factory maintenance, cafeteria, and materials handling. Production overhead costs for the two production departments and the four service centers, together with selected measures of activity, are shown in Exhibit P3.6.1.

Wynona sets speaker prices by marking production cost up by 40 percent to cover nonproduction overhead and provide a reasonable profit. The current cost

EXHIBIT P3.6.1 WYNONA HEARING AIDS

Overhead Costs for Service and Production Departments

	Service Department			Production Department			
	Plant Administration	Factory Maintenance	Cafeteria	Materials Handling	Component Assembly	Quality Testing	Total
Estimated production overhead	$180,000	$500,000	$150,000	$62,500	$650,000	$170,000	$1,712,500
Measure of activity:							
Square feet occupied		8,000	22,000	6,000	85,000	7,000	128,000
Maintenance hours	1,200		350	200	6,200	2,100	10,050
Number of employees	7	3	6	2	43	3	64
Materials transactions					1,800	400	2,200
Labor-hours	14,000	6,500	11,800	4,200	90,000	7,500	134,000
Machine-hours					24,500		24,500
Testing hours						4,300	4,300

system traces materials and labor directly to each job. In addition to materials and labor, production cost includes a charge for predetermined production overhead based on direct labor-hours.

The predetermined production overhead rate is calculated by adding all production overhead costs, including production overhead for component assembly and quality testing departments, to the production overhead for all four of the service centers. Total production overhead, estimated at $1,712,500 for next year, is then divided by the estimated total direct labor-hours in the two production departments to derive a single predetermined production overhead rate. When Benny is asked to submit a bid for a batch of speakers, he simply estimates direct labor and direct materials and multiplies the predetermined production overhead rate by the estimated direct labor-hours. He then adds the direct materials, direct labor, and production overhead together and multiplies by 140 percent to get the bid price.

After discussing the problem with some of his friends, Benny asked Wynona's accountant to devise another approach. After several weeks of study, the accountant suggested using the step-down procedure to collect service center cost in the two production departments. The accountant also suggested use of different overhead rates for component assembly and quality testing. Since component assembly is primarily machine-driven, Wynona decided to use machine-hours as a base for the overhead rate. Testing hours were chosen as the base for quality testing.

The accountant indicated that the sequence of steps for the step-down procedure should be plant administration first, followed by factory maintenance, cafeteria, and, finally, materials handling. She also indicated that the following allocation bases should be used:

	Job A-33		Job B-87	
	Component Assembly	Quality Testing	Component Assembly	Quality Testing
Materials	$16,800	$3,500	$2,000	$750
Direct labor	$33,600	$3,000	$4,000	$380
Labor-hours	2,800	310	330	30
Machine-hours	166		57	
Testing hours		22		58
Units in batch	21,000	21,000	2,500	2,500

EXHIBIT P3.6.2 WYNONA HEARING AIDS

Data for Two Batches of Hearing Aids

- Plant administration—square feet occupied
- Factory maintenance—maintenance hours
- Cafeteria—number of employees
- Materials handling—number of materials transactions

To see if this method makes any difference, Benny asked Wynona's accountant to supply data on two recently completed jobs. The results are shown in Exhibit P3.6.2. Job A-33 was performed for one of Wynona's larger customers who typically does not request customization, nor does it require stringent quality testing. Job B-87 represents work completed for a smaller client, one who is particularly adamant about quality control.

Required:

1. Reconstruct the bid prices for jobs A-33 and B-87 using Wynona's present system of assigning production overhead to jobs.
2. Recalculate the bid prices for the two jobs based on the new system as outlined by Wynona's accountant.

P3.7 (Direct Charging)

Marfrank Corporation is composed of six functional departments that include finance, marketing, personnel, production, research and development (R&D), and information systems. Each department is administered by a vice president. The information systems department (ISD) was established in 1995 when Marfrank decided to acquire a mainframe computer and develop a new information system.

While systems development and implementation is an ongoing process at Marfrank, many of the basic systems needed by each of the functional departments were operational at the end of 1996. Thus, calendar year 1997 is considered the first year when the ISD costs can be estimated with a high degree of accuracy. Marfrank's president wants the other five functional departments to be aware of the magnitude of the ISD costs by reflecting the allocation of ISD costs in the reports and statements prepared at the end of the first quarter of 1997. The allocation of ISD costs to each of the departments was based on their actual use of ISD services.

Jon Werner, vice president of ISD, suggested that the actual costs of ISD be

EXHIBIT P3.7.1 MARFRANK CORPORATION

Allocation of ISD Costs

Department	Percent	Allocated Cost
Finance	50.00%	$112,500
Marketing	30.00	67,500
Personnel	9.00	20,250
Production	6.00	13,500
R&D	5.00	11,250
Total	100.00%	$225,000

allocated on the basis of the pages of actual computer output. This basis was suggested because reports are what all of the departments use in evaluating their operations and making decisions. The use of this basis resulted in the allocation for the first quarter 1997 presented in Exhibit P3.7.1.

After the quarterly reports were distributed, the finance and marketing departments objected to this allocation method. Both departments acknowledged that they were responsible for most of the output in terms of reports, but they believed that these output costs might represent a relatively small proportion of ISD total costs and requested that a more equitable allocation basis be developed.

After meeting with Werner, Marfrank's controller, Elaine Jergens, concluded that ISD provided three distinct services—systems development, computer processing represented by central processing unit (CPU) hours, and report generation. She recommended that a predetermined rate be developed for each of these services from budgeted annual activity and costs. The ISD costs would then be assigned to the other functional departments using the predetermined rate times the actual activity used. Any difference between actual costs incurred and costs allocated to the other departments would be absorbed by ISD.

Jergens and Werner concluded that systems development could be charged on the basis of hours devoted to systems development and programming, computer processing based on CPU hours used for operations (exclusive of database development and maintenance), and report generation based on pages of output. The only cost that should not be included in any of the predetermined rates would be purchased software; these packages were usually acquired for a specific department's use. Thus, Jergens concluded that purchased software would be charged at cost to the department for which it was purchased. In order to revise the first-quarter allocation, Jergens gathered the information on ISD costs and services shown in Exhibits P3.7.2 and P3.7.3.

Required:

1. Develop predetermined rates for each of the service categories of ISD—systems development, computer processing, and report generation.
2. Using the predetermined rates developed in requirement 1, determine the amount each of the other five functional departments would be charged for services provided by ISD during the first quarter of 1997.

(CMA Adapted)

EXHIBIT P3.7.2 MARFRANK CORPORATION

Information Systems Department Cost

	Estimated Annual Cost	Actual 1st-Quarter Costs	Percent Devoted to:		
			Systems Development	Computer Processing	Report Generation
Wages & benefits:					
Administration	$100,000	$25,000	60.00%	20.00%	20.00%
Computer operators	55,000	13,000		20.00	80.00
Analysts/programmers	165,000	43,500	100.00%		
Maintenance:					
Hardware	24,000	6,000		75.00	25.00
Software	20,000	5,000		100.00	
Output supplies	50,000	11,500			100.00
Software purchases[a]	45,000	16,000			
Utilities	28,000	6,250		100.00	
Depreciation:					
Mainframe computer	325,000	81,250		100.00	
Printers	60,000	15,000			100.00
Building improvements	10,000	2,500		100.00	
Total department costs	$882,000	$225,000			

[a] All software purchases in the 1st quarter were for the production department.

EXHIBIT P3.7.3 MARFRANK CORPORATION

Information Systems Department Services

	Systems Development (in hours)	Computer Processing (in CPU hours)	Report Generation (in pages)
Estimated annual usage	4,500	360	5,000,000
Actual usage for 1st quarter:			
Finance	100	8	600,000
Marketing	250	12	360,000
Personnel	200	12	108,000
Production	400	32	72,000
R&D	50	16	60,000
Total usage	1,000	80	1,200,000

P3.8 (Allocations; Plantwide vs. Departmental Rates)

Custom Ultrasound, headed by Susan Allen, is a major medical equipment man-ufacturer. It makes ultrasound imaging devices in an industry long served by small firms such as itself.[7] However, the industry is about to change. Three medical

---

[7] Descriptions of the ultrasound industry are based on Amal Kumar Naj, "Big Medical-Equipment Makers Try Ultrasound Market," *The Wall Street Journal*, Nov. 30, 1993, p. B4.

equipment giants—General Electric, Siemens AG of Germany, and the Dutch firm Philips Electronics NV—recently entered the market.

Custom Ultrasound uses high-frequency sound waves to create images of the human body. Because imaging requires alternative scanning methods, different machines are produced for different tasks. A heart-imaging system, for example, is quite different from a machine used for urological-imaging applications.

Custom Ultrasound equipment prices range from $15,000 to $250,000. In contrast, MRI imaging equipment costs between $1 and $2 million. X-ray-based CT, or "cat," scanners usually cost between $350,000 and $1 million. Because of the high cost of CTs and MRIs, and because of the health care industry's determination to contain costs, the market for ultrasound equipment is expected to expand quickly. Growth is projected at about 15 percent annually, with domestic ultrasound sales expected to reach $1 billion.

Custom Ultrasound's niche in the market is blood-flow-monitoring devices. It offers two standard configurations—the professional model and the office model. The professional model is designed for large hospitals and imaging centers, while the less expensive office model is intended for small hospitals and group practices. The main functional difference between them is that the professional model measures both quantity and velocity of blood flow, while the office model measures only blood flow. Custom Ultrasound rarely builds equipment for stock. Customers ordering ultrasound equipment generally specify their own configurations and options.

Manufacturing at Custom Ultrasound is arranged in two production departments—component assembly and final assembly. Electronic parts are put together to create subassemblies in the component assembly department. The final assembly department takes subassemblies and pieces them together in the desired configuration. Both component and final assembly operations rely on four manufacturing support departments:

1. General manufacturing support
2. Materials handling
3. Setup
4. Testing

Costs and measures of activity for all of the support (service) and production departments are shown in Exhibit P3.8.1.

At a recent planning meeting, Custom Ultrasound's marketing manager urged Susan Allen to refocus marketing efforts on the professional model in order to take advantage of an increasing trend in sales. In support of his recommendation, the marketing manager noted that sales representatives seemed to just miss winning contracts for the office model. Based on follow-up interviews and anecdotal information, it appeared as though Custom Ultrasound lost contracts not because of product features or quality, but because of price. He concluded that other manufacturers were able to make devices comparable to the office model more cheaply. With industry giants like GE about to enter the market, the marketing manager argued that Custom Ultrasound needed to secure market share by concentrating on the professional model.

Susan Allen is not quite sure and has questioned the wisdom of concentrating on the professional model. One reason for her uncertainty stems from how costs are determined. Currently, Custom Ultrasound uses a single, plantwide manufacturing overhead rate. Overhead costs are assigned to products on the basis of direct labor-hours. With this system, costs of all four manufacturing support departments and indirect manufacturing cost for both the component and the final assembly departments are pooled together. The results are then divided by the

	General Mfg. Support	Materials Handling	Setup	Testing	Component Assembly	Final Assembly	Total
EXHIBIT P3.8.1 CUSTOM ULTRASOUND							
Departmental Costs and Measures of Activity							

	General Mfg. Support	Materials Handling	Setup	Testing	Component Assembly	Final Assembly	Total
Departmental manufacturing cost:							
Direct materials	$ 70,000	$ 25,000	$ 20,000	$ 50,000	$1,350,000	$ 860,000	$ 2,375,000
Direct labor	670,000	485,000	320,000	305,000	2,780,000	1,685,000	6,245,000
Indirect manufacturing cost	110,000	140,000	135,000	5,000	370,000	620,000	1,380,000
Total manufacturing cost	$850,000	$650,000	$475,000	$360,000	$4,500,000	$3,165,000	$10,000,000
Measure of activity:							
Materials transactions			8,000	5,000	10,000	17,000	40,000
Number of setups					12,000	8,000	20,000
Testing minutes					20,000	120,000	140,000
Direct labor-hours	35,000	28,000	22,000	15,000	150,000	130,000	380,000
Machine-hours					25,000	50,000	75,000

combined direct labor-hours for both component and final assembly. Manufacturing overhead cost is charged to ultrasound machines based on the number of direct labor-hours required in both production departments. Manufacturing overhead cost is added to direct materials and direct labor costs to determine full manufacturing cost. Selling price is calculated by multiplying full manufacturing cost by 150 percent to cover general, administrative, and marketing cost and provide a fair profit.

Susan Allen is considering an alternative system for assigning manufacturing overhead cost to ultrasound models. With this system, the total cost of each of the four manufacturing support departments is allocated to the two assembly departments using the step-down method. The sequence of the four steps is determined by the descending order of total cost and in the four manufacturing support departments and allocated on the following bases:

1. General manufacturing support—direct labor dollars
2. Materials handling—materials transactions
3. Setup—number of setups
4. Testing—testing minutes

Once costs are collected in the two assembly departments, total production department manufacturing cost is assigned to ultrasound models using two different bases: direct labor-hours for component assembly and machine-hours for final assembly.

In order to evaluate the impact of the step-down method, Susan Allen requested cost and production data for a typical professional model and a typical office model. The results are shown in Exhibit P3.8.2.

Required:

1. Calculate a plantwide manufacturing overhead rate. Calculate the selling price for each model, based on the plantwide manufacturing overhead cost and using the data in Exhibit P3.8.2.

EXHIBIT P3.8.2 CUSTOM ULTRASOUND

Cost and Production Data for Professional and Office Models

	Professional Model		Office Model	
	Component Assembly	Final Assembly	Component Assembly	Final Assembly
Direct materials	$22,000	$19,000	$16,000	$12,000
Direct labor	$15,750	$ 9,450	$12,000	$ 9,450
Direct labor-hours	1,050	700	800	700
Machine-hours	400	500	400	150

2. Allocate the cost of the four manufacturing support departments to the two production departments using the step-down method. Then calculate manufacturing overhead rates for the two assembly departments. Finally, calculate the selling price for each model, based on these plantwide manufacturing overhead rates using the data in Exhibit P3.8.2.

P3.9 (Allocation Mechanics)

GloStar Electronics is a large discount electronics warehouse with locations in four major Pennsylvania metropolitan areas. The company started seven years ago in Reading, Pennsylvania, as the Electronics' Warehouse. Headed by Doug Vestal, the store was successful from the start. Its primary product line, stereos and televisions, has evolved to where, today, a significant proportion of revenue also comes from the sale of camera equipment.

After the Reading store had been open for about two years, Vestal decided to expand. To achieve rapid growth, he created a holding company called GloStar Electronics, which sold 49 percent of the Reading store to a local investor-operator. Each of the next three stores was organized using similar arrangements— GloStar tendered about 25 percent of the capital but received 51 percent of the voting common stock. In return, the minority shareholders got substantial salaries as compensation for operating the store—plus generous incentive-based bonuses. A second store was opened in Pittsburgh under this arrangement. The third store opened shortly thereafter in Harrisburg, followed by a fourth in Philadelphia.

Corporate Services

As part of its agreement, GloStar is responsible for providing supporting services for each of the four stores. Administration, the first of the three support services, handles all accounting records and payroll, with data transferred electronically to the corporate offices from each of the retail locations. Administration also negotiates and manages leases for each of the stores.

Purchasing, the second service provided by GloStar, acquires all of the electronics and camera equipment from the manufacturers. As a result, it is able to buy in large quantities, take advantage of significant price breaks, and buy better-quality products. Purchasing also manages all paperwork and arranges shipments from the suppliers to the retail stores. Centralized purchasing permits GloStar to stay on top of the rapidly changing electronics, camera, and video products market.

Advertising-promotion is responsible for maintaining GloStar's name and presence in Pennsylvania's markets. The four stores advertise cooperatively—at football games, over regional TV and radio stations, and through various print media. In addition, the advertising-promotion staff runs local campaigns, as the need arises, designed for individual stores.

Recent Events

Even though competition was already tough when Vestal started, it intensified with every passing year. Today, GloStar is facing extremely stiff price competition. While its basic pricing strategy is built on low cost, management recognizes differences in regional competition. In Philadelphia, for example, rivalry appears to be much more fierce than in the other areas, resulting in tighter profit margins.

Corporate services are charged to each store based on a formula used ever since the second store opened in Pittsburgh. The formula is quite simple. Total corporate overhead, comprising the cost of the three service centers, is estimated at the beginning of each year, and projections of the total cost of merchandise purchases are made. Overhead from the three service centers is divided by the number of expected merchandise purchases in order to determine a corporate overhead rate. Overhead is then assigned to each store based on the expected dollar volume of merchandise purchases.

Each store bases prices on merchandise purchase cost. After a store receives its allocation of overhead, the store manager adds it and all other nonmerchandise cost together. That is, nonmerchandise cost includes direct labor, indirect costs, and assignments of service center cost. The total is divided by the store's projected merchandise-purchase cost to determine a store-specific markup that can be used to estimate full cost. Store managers then have a method for pricing products. For example, assume the Reading store receives an assignment of corporate overhead equal to $825,000. If direct labor cost is $1,000,000 and indirect cost for the Reading store is $600,000, then total nonmerchandise cost is $2,425,000. If merchandise purchases total $4,500,000, then each dollar of merchandise cost need simply be marked up by 53.9 percent ($2,425,000/$4,500,000) to obtain an estimate of full cost. A CD player, for instance, purchased by the Reading store for $100 would carry a full cost of $153.90.

While this system seemed to work during the early years, several of the store owners started voicing concern over its accuracy. Mike Gooch, from Philadelphia, for example, increasingly complained about the fairness of the formula. According to Gooch, his store has been charged for services he believes were, in fact, provided to other stores. While he couldn't be specific, he felt that a system that charged each store for corporate services based on relative merchandise cost was not fair, since some stores benefited more from corporate activities than others. Mike repeatedly stated that of the four locations, the Philadelphia store probably faced the keenest competition. Since his margins were already razor thin, he felt he could no longer afford—in his own words—"to subsidize the other stores."

Gooch, with the encouragement of the owner of the Pittsburgh store, requested a study by GloStar to look into alternatives. After a couple of weeks, several alternatives were suggested, including use of the step-down allocation method. Budgeted data for next year and square feet of occupancy are shown in Exhibit P3.9.

The step-down method, if adopted, will assign service center cost in the following order: advertising-promotion first, allocated on the basis of square feet occupied; administration second, allocated on the basis of direct labor dollars; and purchasing third, allocated on the basis of merchandise purchase cost.

Required:

1. Allocate corporate service cost to the four stores using the present method. Determine the percent markup on merchandise cost for each store.

EXHIBIT P3.9 GLOSTAR ELECTRONICS

Estimated Service and Production Center Costs

	Service Center			Production Center				
	Administration	Purchasing	Advertising-Promotion	Reading	Pittsburgh	Harrisburg	Philadelphia	Total
Merchandise purchase cost				$4,500,000	$5,800,000	$3,000,000	$ 8,500,000	$21,800,000
Direct labor	$200,000	$ 400,000	$ 300,000	1,000,000	1,400,000	700,000	2,000,000	6,000,000
Media			1,200,000					1,200,000
Indirect cost	500,000	1,000,000	400,000	600,000	1,500,000	600,000	1,400,000	6,000,000
Total cost	$700,000	$1,400,000	$1,900,000	$6,100,000	$8,700,000	$4,300,000	$11,900,000	$35,000,000
Square feet occupied	18,000	22,000	6,000	35,000	75,000	55,000	85,000	296,000

2. Allocate corporate service cost to the four stores using the step-down method. Determine the percent markup on merchandise cost for each store.
3. Is there merit to Mike Gooch's claim that the existing method of allocation is unfair? In the presence of strong price competition for electronics equipment, how might unfair allocation of service center cost impact profits?

P3.10 (Allocation Mechanics)

InterPharm, a U.S.-based research lab, develops pharmaceutical products for sale in Germany, Italy, England, and Austria. Its headquarters, located in Atlanta, houses a research facility and manufacturing operation. The Atlanta office is also responsible for managing a centralized warehouse located in Italy. After a pharmaceutical product is developed in the Atlanta research lab, governmental agencies in each of the four countries undertake lengthy reviews of the drug's benefits and risks. Upon government approval, InterPharm manufactures and ships the drug to the Italian warehouse. Since drug inventories must be built up to minimum levels at retail outlets, maintaining a large initial supply of inventory in the Italian warehouse is deemed essential. After stocking up to meet the initial surge in demand, InterPharm manufactures products in large batches as the need arises.

Marketing and local distribution are left to nationals in each of the four countries. Their activities take place through wholly owned subsidiaries, incorporated in each country.

There are six service centers, each of which performs a different function. Central offices, located in Atlanta, perform three basic service functions:

1. *Administration.* Manage personnel, accounting, domestic legal matters, and other corporate activities.
2. *Research and development.* Find new drugs and new applications of existing products.
3. *Corporate liaison.* Obtain government approval and determine legal and tax implications for InterPharm products.

The warehouse in Italy performs three basic service activities:

1. Warehouse occupancy, representing depreciation and utilities cost
2. Shipping and receiving
3. Delivery

Projected revenue and cost for the support activities and each of the four subsidiaries are shown in Exhibit P3.10.1.

While wholly owned by InterPharm, the U.S. parent, the subsidiary corporations must pay income taxes according to the tax regulations in their respective countries. For planning purposes, InterPharm assumes that pretax operating losses, if any, result in a zero tax liability. Since no other InterPharm operations exist in each of these countries, no credit against any past or future taxes is given for losses. Assume the effective income tax rates in the four countries are:

Germany	35%
Italy	48%
England	27%
Austria	34%

As part of the cost of operations, each of the four foreign subsidiaries must absorb a portion of the cost of the Atlanta corporate headquarters and Italian warehouse service center. Reasonable charges against revenue for indirect cost for the

EXHIBIT P3.10.1 INTERPHARM

Revenue and Cost

| | Service Center | | | | | Revenue-Generating Center | | | | |
	Admin.	R&D	Corporate Liaison	Warehouse Occupancy	Shipping & Receiving	Delivery	Germany	Italy	England	Austria	Total
Revenue							$4,850,000	$2,760,000	$2,375,000	$1,015,000	$11,000,000
Cost of goods sold							1,870,000	890,000	1,280,000	210,000	4,250,000
Gross margin							2,980,000	1,870,000	1,095,000	805,000	6,750,000
Direct operating cost							1,150,000	720,000	310,000	140,000	2,320,000
Direct operating profit							$1,830,000	$1,150,000	$ 785,000	$ 665,000	$ 4,430,000
Service center cost	$1,240,000	$460,000	$700,000	$220,000	$410,000	$260,000					$ 3,290,000
Pretax operating income											$ 1,140,000

purpose of determining taxable income are acceptable in the tax codes of all four countries.

InterPharm is considering how much to charge each of these subsidiaries for the cost of the Atlanta corporate headquarters and Italian service center. Two plans are under consideration for allocating the service center costs to each of the four countries. The first is the direct method of allocation, while the second approach relies on the step-down procedure. The bases chosen to allocate service center costs are as follows:

- Administration—number of employees
- Corporate liaison—number of transactions
- Warehouse occupancy—square feet occupied
- Research and development—total revenue
- Shipping and receiving—cost of goods sold
- Delivery—delivery-miles

The order of steps for the step-down method is as listed above, starting with administration and ending with delivery. The number of transactions, the number of employees, square feet occupied, and delivery-miles are presented in Exhibit P3.10.2.

Required:

1. Allocate service center cost to the four countries using the direct method. Calculate the income taxes paid in each of the four countries and the total amount of income taxes.
2. Allocate service center cost to the four countries using the step-down method. Calculate the income taxes paid in each of the four countries and the total amount of income taxes.
3. Assuming income tax minimization is the goal, which of the two allocation methods should be chosen?
4. If manager performance is based on after-tax net income, how do you think managers in each of the four countries are likely to respond to allocations based on income tax minimization?

(AICPA Adapted)

EXHIBIT P3.10.2 INTERPHARM				
Selected Bases for Allocation				
	Number of Transactions	*Number of Employees*	*Square Feet Occupied*	*Delivery-Miles*
Administration	11,400	12	3,400	
Research & development	4,300	46	18,700	
Corporate liaison	6,500	8	14,200	
Warehouse occupancy	3,200	16	26,200	
Shipping & receiving	2,800	7	18,500	
Delivery	11,900	11	14,600	
Germany	124,000	33	122,000	168,000
Italy	100,900	18	97,500	128,000
England	92,000	27	108,900	116,000
Austria	143,000	22	176,000	88,000
Total	500,000	200	600,000	500,000

P3.11   (Predetermined Overhead Rate)

Franzel Company manufactures several different models of luggage in its three manufacturing (production) departments. Luggage production begins in the molding department, where the product's basic shape is formed on automated molding machines. Molded parts are assembled and other hardware attached in the assembly department. Fully assembled luggage is transferred to finishing/packing, where Franzel's logo is attached, the luggage is inspected for quality, and the product is placed in cartons for shipment. The three production departments are supported by equipment maintenance, the only service department. Franzel uses a separate departmental overhead rate for each of its three manufacturing departments.

Franzel is in the process of reviewing its operations at the end of June 1996 as a basis for preparing budgets for the manufacturing departments for the coming fiscal year. Franzel's fiscal year runs from July 1st to June 30th. The molding department is being reviewed first. Its cost and operating data for the last six months of the current fiscal year are presented in Exhibit P3.11.1.

All of the costs in Exhibit P3.11.1 are variable costs except for equipment maintenance and the allocation of corporate overhead. Equipment maintenance is a mixed cost, while the allocation of corporate overhead is fixed. The allocation of corporate overhead cost includes common building and operating costs assigned to each manufacturing department on the basis of square feet occupied. The equipment maintenance department charges the molding department for services rendered. These charges represent the actual cost of parts and supplies, plus a charge of $50 per maintenance hour. The actual cost of parts and supplies for the molding department during the current fiscal year totals $150,000. The volume of parts and supplies is expected to remain unchanged for the coming fiscal year. The manager of the equipment maintenance department determines the preventive maintenance schedule for each of the production departments. All other repairs are made on a "first-come, first-served" basis.

Management is expecting cost increases and is requesting the following adjustments for the coming year:

EXHIBIT P3.11.1   FRANZEL COMPANY—MOLDING DEPARTMENT

Actual Cost and Operating Data for Last 6 Months of Fiscal Year 1995/96

	1996					
	January	February	March	April	May	June
Activity measure:						
Pounds of material	25,000	27,000	30,000	24,000	20,000	22,000
Machine-hours	11,500	13,500	12,500	8,500	9,500	10,000
Units produced	50,000	45,000	52,000	42,000	48,000	40,000
Machine setups	15	20	16	18	19	21
Overhead cost:						
Materials-handling cost ($1.40/lb)	$ 35,000	$ 37,800	$ 42,000	$ 33,600	$ 28,000	$ 30,800
Setup cost	12,200	15,250	12,000	14,000	14,500	15,100
Indirect labor ($5/machine-hour)	57,500	67,500	62,500	42,500	47,500	50,000
Power ($0.20/kilowatt-hour)	21,250	24,250	22,750	16,750	18,250	19,000
Equipment maintenance	15,000	18,000	12,000	19,000	16,000	35,000
Allocation of corporate overhead cost	335,000	335,000	335,000	335,000	335,000	335,000
Total overhead	$475,950	$497,800	$486,250	$460,850	$459,250	$484,900

EXHIBIT P3.11.2 FRANZEL COMPANY— MOLDING DEPARTMENT

Number of Setups and Monthly Setup Cost

Month	Number of Setups	Actual Monthly Setup Cost
July 1995	14	$12,400
August	19	$14,100
September	16	$12,750
October	20	$14,500
November	18	$13,100
December	17	$13,600
January 1996	15	$12,200
February	20	$15,250
March	16	$12,000
April	18	$14,000
May	19	$14,500
June	21	$15,100

EXHIBIT P3.11.3 FRANZEL COMPANY— MOLDING DEPARTMENT

Projected Activity for 1996/97 Fiscal Year

Activity Measure	Estimated Annual Amount	
Material	280,000	pounds
Machine-hours	135,000	hours
Units produced	520,000	units
Machine setups	225	setups
Power usage	2.50	kilowatt-hours/unit
Equipment maintenance	1,600	hours

- Indirect labor cost increase of 8 percent
- Equipment maintenance cost increase of 10 percent for parts, supplies, and hourly charge
- Allocation of corporate overhead cost increase to $360,000 per month

In addition, management plans to change the way setup costs are estimated. The managers collected the data shown in Exhibit P3.11.2 which represent the number of setups and total setup cost for the last 12 months. Management plans to use this data to regress monthly setup costs (y) against the number of setups (x). The resulting regression equation will serve as a basis for predicting setup costs in the future.

Total manufacturing overhead for the molding department is applied to the different models of luggage on a predetermined basis, using machine-hours. Based on the production budgets, the activity measures for the molding department are expected to be at the levels shown in Exhibit P3.11.3 for the coming fiscal year.

Required:

1. Estimate the relationship between monthly setup cost and the number of setups, using regression analysis.
2. Using the cost data presented for the last six months of the current fiscal year, adjusted for the estimated changes expected to occur and the estimated activity measures, develop a manufacturing overhead budget for the molding department for the 1996/97 fiscal year.
3. Develop the predetermined overhead rate that should be used in the molding department for the coming 1996/97 year.

(CMA Adapted)

P3.12 (Loss from Cancellation of Contract)

Construction Rental Associates (CRA) leases heavy equipment to construction companies. Many contractors have found that it is cheaper to lease equipment than it is to own it. One major advantage of leasing is that contractors don't have to carry the salaries of machine operators when equipment is not in use. They simply call rental companies such as CRA and reserve the equipment for when they need it. Then they pay on an hourly basis for an operator and equipment. Leasing allows contractors to avoid covering fixed cost, especially during downturns in construction activity. In effect, these arrangements let contractors shift capacity risks to the leasing companies. In turn, CRA leases much of its equipment from manufacturers such as John Deere and Caterpillar.

Alexander Brothers Construction Company is one of CRA's clients. Last year, it approached CRA about the possibility of leasing three pieces of heavy earthmoving equipment it needed for a job: a front-end loader, a grader, and a dump truck. CRA gathered the data shown in Exhibit P3.12 to serve as a basis for preparing the quote. Variable cost, driven by hours of operations, consists of machine operators, benefits, and fuel. Fixed cost directly attributable to each piece of equipment over the term of the lease include insurance, equipment lease cost, and maintenance. CRA will incur these costs only if Alexander Brothers signs a contract. If Alexander Brothers decides to sign a contract, these costs are eliminated when the lease is over.

In addition to costs directly traceable to each piece of equipment, CRA incurs other indirect costs in managing the business. For example, considerable scheduling and dispatching time is required to coordinate equipment utilization. Administrators have to manage contracts, while supervisors must check job sites to ensure proper equipment utilization. And garage space must be leased to house equipment not being used. CRA's practice has been to assign indirect cost to equipment for the purpose of determining hourly rates based on the estimated total hours of operation for all equipment. Another indirect cost of managing the business is office and administration cost. For the present year, CRA expects to lease equipment to all of its clients for a total of 18,000 hours.

Based on the estimates in Exhibit P3.12, CRA calculated the total cost of each piece of equipment and added its standard 18 percent markup for profit. On the basis of these computations, CRA negotiated a one-year "take-or-pay" type of contract with Alexander Brothers that specified minimum operating hours: 800 front-end loader hours, 1,000 grader hours, and 3,200 dump-truck hours.

Midway through the year, Alexander Brothers lost the contract for which it was using CRA's equipment. Alexander Brothers had several other jobs on which it could use the equipment, but by year-end it was able to log only 430 front-end loader hours, 625 grader hours, and 2,160 dump-truck hours. Since the total num-

EXHIBIT P3.12 CONSTRUCTION RENTAL ASSOCIATES

Annual Cost for Three Pieces of Construction Equipment

	Front-End Loader	Grader	Dump Truck	Total
Contracted operating hours	800	1,000	3,200	5,000
Variable cost (per operating hour):				
Machine operator	$12.50	$12.50	$10.75	
Benefits (22%)	2.75	2.75	2.37	
Fuel	8.00	6.50	3.50	
Total variable cost per hour	$23.25	$21.75	$16.62	
Fixed cost attributable to equipment:				
Insurance	$ 4,800	$ 3,700	$ 2,500	$ 11,000
Equipment lease	42,200	37,500	18,300	98,000
Maintenance	6,500	4,400	3,100	14,000
Total attributable fixed cost	$53,500	$45,600	$23,900	$123,000
Annual indirect (fixed) cost for all equipment:				
Scheduling & dispatching				$ 30,500
Contract administration				42,000
Supervision				57,500
Garage rental				27,800
Office & administration				123,000
Total indirect cost				$280,800

ber of hours fell considerably short of what Alexander Brothers had contracted for, CRA demanded compensation. However, before any further discussion took place, CRA had to quantify its loss.

Required:

1. Reconstruct the total value of the contract. Then determine the billing rate per hour of operation for each of the three pieces of equipment.
2. Assume CRA's agreement stipulates that if Alexander Brothers doesn't fulfill the contract, Alexander Brothers is responsible only to the extent of its actual losses, including lost profit. What is CRA's actual loss?

CASES

C3.1 (Homestead Family Clinic)

Part A

Bethany (Beth) Brauner grew up in Miami during the 1960s. When many of her friends shed their bell-bottom jeans and lovebeads for power suits and dresses, Beth held steadfast in her deep personal commitment to helping those who could not help themselves. During summer vacations, for example, Beth chose to work with grassroots community health organizations. When it came time to select a major at college, she chose health care administration. At graduation, she took a low-paying job in Miami's fledgling Homestead Free Clinic, whose mission was to provide family planning and pregnancy counseling services. With an annual operating budget of less than $200,000, the clinic was supported by grants and funding from government agencies. Its clients were mainly poverty-level families and migrant farmworkers. Its fees for service were based on clients' ability to pay.

Today, Beth runs the Homestead Family Clinic (the "Family Clinic"), which evolved from the earlier Homestead Free Clinic. With an annual operating budget of $11 million, the Family Clinic is an important player in the area's health care arena. Recognizing the key role played by family planning and prenatal care in a healthy society, Beth provided the leadership and drive that made the Family Clinic what it is today. She persuaded the Free Clinic's executive board to expand by assimilating other community health organizations into what was to eventually become the Family Clinic. The guiding principal in each acquisition, however, was to maintain a clear focus on the physical and mental health of the family. As a result, the Family Clinic now encompasses five broad family health care services: women's health services, family planning, a birthing center, infant care, and physical therapy.

Beth observed that fee-based private hospitals often engage in what is known as *cost shifting.* Cost shifting began when the federal government changed the way it reimbursed hospitals. Instead of refunding actual cost, a method that provided no inducement for cost containment, the government established a fixed payment schedule based on procedures known as diagnostic-related groups (DRGs). As a result, pressure was placed on hospitals to deliver services at a cost that would yield a profit. With no control on the revenue side of the equation for government-insured patients, hospitals began to charge more to other classes of patients— namely, HMOs and private paying patients. The end result was shifting the burden for health care from the government to the private sector.

The health care industry, in addition to growing public awareness of cost shifting, is facing still another challenge. Health care cost represents a sizeable portion of national expenditure. Between 1970 and 1990, for example, personal health care expenditure increased at an annual rate of between 10 and 12 percent. As a result, much of the national agenda has focused on how to deal with health care costs and on finding ways to create public-private partnerships to solve the problem.

In light of the changing health care environment, and in keeping with a trend toward privatization, the agencies funding the Family Clinic indicated that they could no longer continue to provide the same level of support that they had in the past. Instead, their long-term plan is to discontinue budget-based support and to adopt DRG-type reimbursement formulas.

At present, the Family Clinic's budget is based on the number of anticipated clinic visits. For this year and the immediate future, about 50,000 clinic visits are expected annually. Based on a budget of $11 million, the cost per visit is calculated at $220. This is what the Family Clinic charges for each clinic visit regardless of the patient center visited or services rendered. While this figure seems high, patients end up paying what they can afford. In general, the Family Clinic receives less than half of what it bills. The rest is made up from other sources. For example, the Family Clinic is seeking about $6 million in funding from state and federal agencies.

Beth, in response to this changing environment, has asked the Family Clinic's accountant, Michael Ryans, to prepare an immediate short-term plan to deal with the expected changes in funding. While this year's $11-million budget is not in jeopardy, it is unclear what the formula will be next year. However, it is clear to both Beth and Michael that the Family Clinic needs to develop a more accurate way of determining the cost of a clinic visit, since the present method does not distinguish between the costs for each of the five patient centers.

Michael produced the budgeted data shown in Exhibit C3.1.1. It shows the costs directly associated with each of the five service centers: (1) facilities and utilities, (2) administration, (3) housekeeping, (4) medical records, and (5) lab. These

EXHIBIT C3.1.1   HOMESTEAD FAMILY CLINIC

Budgeted Cost and Activity Data

	Budgeted Costs					Expected Activity Levels				
Responsibility Center	Salaries & Benefits	Materials & Supplies	Contract Services	Equipment Rental & Deprec.	Total Cost	Square Feet Occupied	Number of Employees	Housekeeping Hours	Clinic Visits	Lab Visits
Service Center:										
Facilities & utilities	$ 250,000	$ 85,000		$1,800,000	$ 2,135,000		45	88		
Administration	750,000	40,000	20,000	50,000	860,000	100,000	17	54		
Housekeeping	850,000	80,000	30,000	140,000	1,100,000	35,000	15			
Medical records	375,000	50,000		270,000	695,000	25,000	12	232		
Lab	275,000	145,000	50,000	740,000	1,210,000	60,000	5	441		
Patient Center:										
Women's health services	450,000	90,000		150,000	690,000	80,000	12	219	9,300	2,261
Family planning	875,000	60,000		260,000	1,195,000	50,000	20	118	15,500	1,799
Birthing center	650,000	130,000		170,000	950,000	65,000	18	244	4,100	1,521
Infant care	900,000	95,000		320,000	1,315,000	45,000	30	389	7,450	2,189
Physical therapy	625,000	125,000		100,000	850,000	40,000	21	107	13,650	480
Total	$6,000,000	$900,000	$100,000	$4,000,000	$11,000,000	500,000	195	1,892	50,000	8,250

service centers provide support for the five patient centers delivering health care: (1) women's health services, (2) family planning, (3) birthing center, (4) infant care, and (5) physical therapy. Michael proposes that this data be used in conjunction with the step-down procedure to assign the cost of the five service centers to the five revenue-generating patient centers. The service centers are listed below according to the sequence of steps in the step-down procedure, together with the allocation bases selected by Michael:

- Facility and utilities—square feet occupied
- Administration—number of employees
- Housekeeping—housekeeping hours
- Medical records—clinic visits
- Lab—lab visits

Required: Calculate the cost per visit to each of the patient centers. Compare this cost with the average cost per visit. Which patient centers provide subsidies and which patient centers receive subsidies?

Part B
After completion of cost data derived using the step-down method, several patient center directors asked for a meeting with Michael. As it turned out, their centers were the ones receiving subsidies. Michael listened to their concerns about the future for their centers. One specific area of dissatisfaction was the way lab cost is allocated under the step-down procedure. The directors stated that many of the patients receiving care require low-intensity lab assistance. Regardless of lab utilization, and whatever the lab resources used, these centers end up paying the same rate as everyone else under the new step-down procedure. They felt that other patient centers ordered visits to the lab that used expensive lab equipment and required more time of highly paid lab technicians. Furthermore, the directors felt that because these centers received subsidies under the step-down procedure and paid less than their fair share of lab cost, they might order more tests than necessary, driving up the cost for everyone.

To help sort out the arguments, Michael asked Suzanne Gibson, the lab administrator, to convert last year's lab visits into procedures and then rank them according to level of intensity—low, medium, and high. Intensity, according to Michael's directions, should be measured in terms of the amount of lab materials, labor, and equipment used in performing a procedure.

Suzanne was then asked to recast next year's 8,250 anticipated lab visits into intensity levels. The results are shown in Exhibit C3.1.2. In addition, Suzanne gave

EXHIBIT C3.1.2 HOMESTEAD FAMILY CLINIC

Lab Visits and Intensity Levels

	Low Intensity	Medium Intensity	High Intensity	Total Lab Visits
Women's health services	1,001	118	1,142	2,261
Family planning	1,456	289	54	1,799
Birthing center	532	478	511	1,521
Infant care	1,835	322	32	2,189
Physical therapy	328	65	87	480
Total	5,152	1,272	1,826	8,250

Michael a rough scale to convert intensity into relative costs. The results are as follows: low intensity, 1; medium intensity, 2; and high intensity, 4. That is, a high-intensity procedure should cost roughly 4 times as much as a low-intensity procedure.

Required: Recalculate your results for Part A. However, for this part of the case, exclude the lab. Develop a formula the lab can use to charge patients fees based on the intensity weights. What are some of the behavioral implications that might be expected if lab cost is charged in this manner rather than allocated using the step-down method?

C3.2   (CraftMasters Cabinets, Inc.)

CraftMasters Cabinets, Inc., manufactures a full line of kitchen cabinets for new home installations and renovations. Its products are sold through a network of independent retail custom cabinet shops located primarily on the East Coast. Secondary sources of sales are contractors and home improvement superstores. The cabinet industry experienced relatively strong competition over the last couple of years. However, the market is becoming even more competitive after the entry last year of a nationally known woodworking company. While historical profit margins for CraftMasters have averaged 15 percent, pressure from the national woodworking company and price-cutting by smaller firms drove CraftMasters' 1996 net income down to only 9 percent of sales revenue.

Ron Plane, president of CraftMasters, attributes declining income to changes in demand and increases in competition. He notes that CraftMasters used to sell about the same number of standard and custom-made cabinets. Some years it would sell fewer custom and more standard cabinets. But any decline in sales of one model of cabinet would reverse in the years that followed. So, over the long run, CraftMasters sold about the same number of custom and standard cabinets. Today, Ron Plane believes that the historical pattern is changing. Records indicate that CraftMasters is selling more and more high-end custom cabinets. Since custom cabinets sell at higher prices than standard models do, Ron expected to see net income rise. Instead, he is puzzled by the decline in the actual profit margins, as shown in Exhibit C3.2.1.

Homeowners typically visit kitchen stores or work with contractors to select cabinets. The salesperson or contractor fills out a standardized bid sheet to request a quote from the cabinet manufacturer. CraftMasters' bid sheet shows pictures of

EXHIBIT C3.2.1   CRAFTMASTERS CABINETS, INC.

Common-Sized Income Statement

	1994	1995	1996
Revenue	100.00%	100.00%	100.00%
Cost of goods sold	63.00%	63.00%	69.00%
Gross profit	37.00%	37.00%	31.00%
Less operating expense	22.00%	22.00%	22.00%
Net income before tax	15.00%	15.00%	9.00%

Note: All figures are stated as a percent of revenue.

each type of cabinet, the range of finishes, and the external dimensions. Bid sheets are then faxed to CraftMasters and completed by one of the estimators. Using the bid sheets, materials quantities and price are estimated, along with the number of labor-hours needed to complete the job. Over the years, CraftMasters estimators have become quite good at their job. In fact, their estimates are typically within 5 percent of actual cost.

Materials quantities needed are calculated by multiplying the estimated quantity of materials by unit cost. For example, a job might call for 350 linear feet of 12-in. oak at a cost of $2.37 per foot. Once total materials cost is determined, estimators apply a multiplication factor of 1.6 (160%) to the total materials cost to determine the materials component of the bid. Estimates of total labor-hours are multiplied by $22 per hour to determine the labor component of the bid. The final bid, then, is the combination of the materials and labor components. For example, the bid for a job requiring materials costing $1,000 and 100 hours of labor would be $3,800 [$1,000 × 160% = $1,600 + (100 × $22) = $2,200].

Exhibit C3.2.2 shows the actual wage rates paid to the three levels of skilled woodworkers. On top of the hourly wage, CraftMasters pays 20 percent of the hourly rate for benefits.

To identify the causes of falling profit margins, Ron Plane asked CraftMasters' accountant to gather data from a recent bid. Exhibit C3.2.3 shows the estimated and actual quantities of materials for job 96-107. Exhibit C3.2.4 shows estimated and actual labor-hours for the job.

EXHIBIT C3.2.2 CRAFTMASTERS CABINETS, INC.

Labor Classifications and Hourly Pay Rates

Labor Classification	Hourly Rate
Apprentice woodworkers	$6.87
Woodworkers	$9.24
Master woodworkers	$18.26

EXHIBIT C3.2.3 CRAFTMASTERS CABINETS, INC.

Materials Cost for Job No. 96–107

Material	Material Format in Inches	Estimated Linear Feet	Actual Linear Feet	Estimated & Actual Cost per Linear Foot
Oak	12	350	367	$2.37
Oak	8	40	37	$2.06
Oak plywood	1/4	30	32	$1.57
Oak trim	1	30	27	$0.85
Oak veneer	1/4	120	118	$1.86
Oak trim	1/2	50	50	$0.85
Total		620	631	

EXHIBIT C3.2.4 CRAFTMASTERS CABINETS, INC.

Labor-Hours for Job No. 96–107

Labor Classification	Estimated Labor-Hours	Actual Labor-Hours
Apprentice woodworkers	22	23
Woodworkers	24	23
Master woodworkers	74	76
Total	120	122

Required:

1. Reconstruct the bid price for job 96-107. Determine the gross profit (loss) for job 96-107. Also calculate the markup percentage on direct (materials and labor) cost.
2. What is causing profit margins to fall? Why is CraftMasters getting more and more custom cabinet orders? Develop an improved bidding system that rectifies the problem.

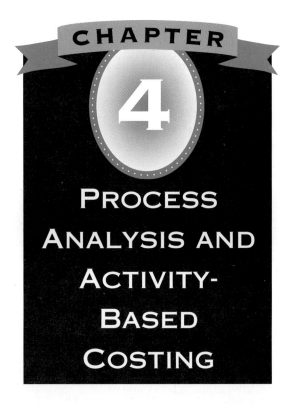

CHAPTER 4

PROCESS ANALYSIS AND ACTIVITY-BASED COSTING

At the completion of the last chapter, we questioned the accuracy and usefulness of allocation-based full cost. We concluded by stating that one way to improve accuracy and reduce potential distortions is to decrease the proportion of indirect costs requiring allocations. For many companies, the trend is in just the opposite direction—toward greater proportions of indirect costs. One reason is that many managers, prompted by competition and the quest for global markets, have expanded—not contracted—already high levels of customer support by:

- Offering a broad range of products and options
- Expanding inventories and suppliers to reduce disruptions in production
- Increasing capacity to allow for product variety
- Designing new products to meet customers' specifications

- Installing quality assurance programs
- Extending product warranties and return policies
- Expanding prepurchase and postpurchase customer support

Adding service and customer support in any of these ways increases total indirect costs that ultimately must be assigned to products. As we have shown, traditional allocation-based costing methods may not reliably reflect a product's share of these additional costs.

One system replacing traditional allocation-based costing is called **activity-based costing**, or **ABC**. Activity-based costing attaches costs to activities, whereas traditional costing methods attach costs to responsibility centers. Activity-based costing systems start with collecting costs by activities. Once this is completed, the cost of activities is assigned to products and other cost objects on the basis of the amount of each activity the cost object consumes.

Before ABC systems can be implemented, managers must look at their organizations in a different way. Rather than viewing the firm as a collection of responsibility centers—the focal point for cost collection in the last chapter—managers must view the firm as a system of interrelated activities. Isolating activities begins with identifying broad, organizationwide processes. *Processes represent the major elements of work performed by an organization.*

Activity-based costing provides a way for managers to understand the processes by which an organization serves its customers, to *manage the firm's activities* and the resources the activities consume, and, ultimately, to focus on results—customer satisfaction.

The purposes of this chapter, then, are to:

- Identify the impact of a changing business environment
- Introduce process analysis and ways of identifying activities
- Describe activity-based costing
- Illustrate how activity-based costing systems can be used to identify opportunities for improving customer satisfaction and reducing cost.

THE CHANGING BUSINESS ENVIRONMENT

The way many businesses will operate in the future is likely to be quite different from how they are operating today. Most will have to face stronger competition in an environment that requires increasing attention to rapidly changing markets, changing technology, and increasing consumer demands.

TRADITIONAL BUSINESS ENVIRONMENT

STABLE ENVIRONMENTS

Many companies now operate in relatively stable environments, some with day-to-day activities that have not changed significantly over several decades. To aid in understanding what keeps these operating environments from changing, some of the key characteristics of the traditional view of the business environment are illustrated in Exhibit 4.1.[1]

Competitive Environment. In the traditional setting, organizations compete in relatively stable markets, where each firm enjoys a relatively secure market share. New products are expected to generate revenues and profits over long product life cycles.

Organizational Environment. Traditional organizational structures are hierarchical, with decision making concentrated at the top. Layers of middle managers translate directives from top management into actions at the operational level. Manufacturing resources are entrusted to operational units or functional departments, and managers responsible for the resources are held accountable for their use.

---

[1] This classification scheme is adapted from Peter Turney and Bruce Anderson, "Accounting for Continuous Improvement," *Sloan Management Review,* winter 1989, pp. 37–47.

EXHIBIT 4.1 TRADITIONAL BUSINESS ENVIRONMENT

Competitive Environment

Stable markets, known competitors, secure market share
Long product life cycle

Organizational Environment

Hierarchical organization
Focus on departments and functions

Manufacturing Environment

Batch production
Maximum volume, economies of scale
Quality as secondary issue
Inventory buffers
Labor-driven costs
High direct and low indirect cost
Stable technology
Variability accepted, scrap and rework tolerated
Periodic improvement

Engineering Environment

Design for engineering features
Elimination of direct labor

Marketing Environment

Low concern for customer preferences
Prices based on buildup of cost

Accounting Environment

External financial reporting perspective
Accounting as source of information
Characteristics of information:
  Focus on inventory valuation
  Control over transactions
  Use of work orders
  Adherence to standards
  Labor-efficiency variances
  Allocation of overhead

Source: Adapted from Peter Turney and Bruce Anderson, "Accounting for Continuous Improvement," *Sloan Management Review,* winter 1989, pp. 37–47, by permission of the publisher. Copyright 1989 by the Sloan Management Review Association. All rights reserved.

Manufacturing Environment. Products are manufactured in batches, focusing on maximizing volume to drive down unit cost. Quality is secondary. Inventories serve as buffers to eliminate downtime in production and to protect against fluctuations in the day-to-day demand. Production is labor-intensive. Variability in production is implicitly accepted through provisions for scrap, rework, and defects. Improvements in efficiency and productivity are gradual since, in the absence of strong competition, increases in costs are simply passed along to customers.

Engineering Environment. Technology improves only gradually. Products are designed to conform to what manufacturers believe customers expect and to suit factory production schedules. Since labor costs are generally significant, products and production processes are engineered to reduce labor content.

Marketing Environment. Marketing's job is to convince customers to purchase products. Customer preferences are often secondary to manufacturing schedules. Products are delivered with relatively little customer support. Prices are based on a buildup of costs, especially where price competition is weak.

Accounting Environment. Managerial accounting is a by-product of the financial reporting system. Managers focus on controlling input costs rather than creating customer value. Inventory costs often provide the only source of information for product decisions. Materials and labor are charged to products, together with overhead allocated on the basis of direct labor content. Costs are controlled by comparing actual performance with standards and by using the data obtained as the basis for devising corrective actions.

EMERGING BUSINESS ENVIRONMENT

EVENTS CHANGING THE TRADITIONAL BUSINESS ENVIRONMENT

Changes in the traditional business environment began to appear in the 1970s. High interest rates shifted attention from the income statement to cash flow management. With high financing costs, companies began to shorten their view of the future in order to maximize cash flow, thereby requiring quicker paybacks on investments. Investors in the stock market focused on short-term performance. At the same time, the Japanese emerged as formidable global competitors, joining the strengthening alliance of European countries in challenging U.S. producers. Bolstered by an array of technological advances, information technology surfaced as a strategic weapon. Characteristics of this emerging view of the business environment are shown in Exhibit 4.2.

Competitive Environment. Changing global business conditions have forced many businesses to become more competitive. With prices determined by the marketplace, products whose costs are too high to yield reasonable profits are dropped from production or are targeted for cost reduction. Product life cycles are generally shorter, placing pressure on product design and process engineering to help ensure low costs and immediate profits.

Organizational Environment. Alliances between workers and management are changing what formerly were adversarial relationships. Linking pay to performance gives workers a stake in the success of their companies. Organizational structures, historically formed around functions such as production, marketing, and finance, are restructured to focus on cus-

---

EXHIBIT 4.2 EMERGING BUSINESS ENVIRONMENT

Competitive Environment

Global competition
Short product life cycle

Organizational Environment

"Flattened" organizations
Focus on process and activities
Empowerment of employees

Manufacturing Environment

Continuous flow
Customization, units of one, flexibility
Quality as fundamental philosophy
Elimination of inventory and use of JIT
Activities drive costs
High indirect and low direct cost
Dynamic technology
Variability and waste unacceptable
Continuous process improvement

Engineering Environment

Design for manufacturability
Design for customer value

Marketing Environment

Meet customer needs
Market-driven and target pricing

Accounting Environment

Internal decision-making perspective
Accounting part of a team
Characteristics of information:
   Focus on information for strategy and control
   Efficiency and productivity
   Performance measured by quality and customer satisfaction
   Information for continuous improvement
   Identifying and controlling value-adding activities
   Overhead associated with activities

Source: Adapted from Peter Turney and Bruce Anderson, "Accounting for Continuous Improvement," *Sloan Management Review*, winter 1989, pp. 37–47, by permission of the publisher. Copyright 1989 by the Sloan Management Review Association. All rights reserved.

tomers, distribution channels, and products. Tomorrow's big companies, according to the experts, will abandon traditional hierarchical structures for "flatter" organizations with fewer middle managers, and will ". . . consist of tens or hundreds of small, highly decentralized units, each with a laserlike focus on a market or a customer."[2]

---

[2] Brian Dumaine, "Is Big Still Good?" *Fortune*, Apr. 20, 1992, p. 51.

CURRENT PRACTICE

Procter & Gamble

Procter & Gamble Company (P&G) simplified its pricing system in the early 1990s. Instead of offering promotional discounts, which effectively reduce prices, P&G instituted what the industry called "everyday low prices." Under the old system, grocery stores took advantage of promotions by stockpiling products on special discount, disrupting P&G production schedules. Many grocery store chains, over the years, spent millions of dollars constructing warehouses just to stock inventory bought specially in order to take advantage of discounts. For some products, stores bought enough to allow them to go as long as 6 months before reordering.

P&G hoped to end the system of stockpiling and even out the flow of orders. Under the old pricing system, factories had to work around the clock for as long as four weeks to build inventories and then operate at less than full capacity for several months until the supermarkets used up their stocks of inventory. The new policy was designed to allow improvements in inventory management and to lower operating costs. Equally as important, shoppers were to receive consistently low prices that—it was hoped—would be returned in the form of brand loyalty to P&G.

Source: Eben Shapiro, "P&G Takes on the Supermarkets with Uniform Pricing," *The New York Times,* Apr. 26, 1992, section 3, p. 5.

Manufacturing Environment. New manufacturing philosophies are emerging, fusing traditional methods with new technology. Supported by new organizational structures, the new approach to manufacturing requires a commitment to total quality. *Quality,* which refers to the character of a product with "... respect to excellence, fineness, etc., or grade of excellence,"[3] is typically measured in terms of how well products are suited for their intended use. The direct cost of poor quality—manifested in rework, defective units, idle time, and customer returns—leads to the indirect cost of customer dissatisfaction. Inferior-quality products are rejected before ever reaching customers. Variability in product quality is minimized as companies reengineer processes to build products right the first time.

The new manufacturing environment is based on a philosophy of **just in time,** or **JIT,** where raw materials are delivered to production only a moment before they are needed and final products are placed on retailer's shelves only when customers demand them. While one of the reasons U.S. manufacturing companies are adopting JIT is to minimize inventories, the philosophy is more ambitious. Some of the goals of JIT include reducing

---

[3] Jess Stein, editor, *The Random House Dictionary of the English Language.* New York: Random House, 1967, p. 175.

inventory, (See "Current Practice: Procter & Gamble") improving flexibility, eliminating production defects, keeping lead times short, and making vendors or subcontractors a part of the team.

Engineering Environment.   Engineering, in the new business environment, coordinates design with manufacturing. Engineers start with market research indicating features consumers want and then design products that both meet customer needs and are easy to make.

Marketing Environment.   Marketing efforts are based on giving customers what they want. After delivery, customers require assistance, ranging from help offered by employees staffing customer service hot lines to receipt of immediate refunds when product quality is less than expected. While support services costs are traditionally added to the buildup of a product's costs, managers are less able to pass along these services costs because of stiff competition. Instead, managers either accept lower profits, redesign products, or withdraw the products from the market altogether. In contrast, managers in the new environment will start with prices that the market is most likely to accept and work backward to determine allowable costs.

Accounting Environment.   Managerial accounting systems are likely to expand the type and scope of information available to managers. Moreover, managerial accountants themselves will increasingly be viewed as members of the teams that make decisions and solve problems.

PROCESS ANALYSIS

One system designed to provide more-accurate information—information required in the rapidly changing environment described above—is activity-based costing. The ABC system traces costs to activities, since activities reflect what employees actually do. However, before introducing activities we must first look at processes.

PROCESS ANALYSIS[4]

Processes are the major elements of work performed by an organization— things that people do to convert resource inputs into output products and services. Generally, an organization's processes transcend departmental boundaries. That's because employees in different parts of the organization often work together to accomplish common tasks. Engineers, for example, collaborate with marketing when developing specifications for new products. Given the importance of these interrelationships between workers,

---

[4]   This section relies on Michael R. Ostrenga, Terrence R. Ozan, Robert D. McIlhattan, and Marcus D. Harwood, *The Ernst and Young Guide to Total Cost Management.* New York: John Wiley & Sons, 1992.

CURRENT PRACTICE

A New Tool for Managing Costs

According to *Fortune*, traditional accounting systems look at business in the same way Charlie Chaplin did in his film *Modern Times*. The company is like a huge machine made up of departments such as human resources, purchasing, and maintenance. They all work together with employees as the cogs to make products and provide services.

In contrast, activity-based costing views businesses as groups of individuals performing all kinds of activities—for example, training employees, processing purchasing orders, and fixing machines. Their common goal is satisfying customer demand. The point of view is more like, say, that of the cowhands in the movie *City Slickers*, who share the common tasks that are required in driving cattle to market.

Source: Terence P. Pare, "A New Tool for Managing Costs." *Fortune*, June 14, 1993, pp. 124–128.

organizations can be viewed as a ". . . collection of processes rather than as a hierarchy of departments"[5] (see "Current Practice: A New Tool for Managing Costs").

Looking at the organization this way provides a powerful advantage—it's the way customers view the business. Customers interact with the organization, not through its departments but ". . . through its business processes—entering into contracts, receiving goods and services, paying for these goods and services, and requesting after-sales support."[6] These two views of the organization—the responsibility center/departmental view versus the process view—are represented in Exhibit 4.3.

Some examples of broad, organization-level processes, as shown at the top of Exhibit 4.4, include:

- Corporate-level support
- New customer and new business acquisition
- Product design and introduction
- Operations
- Customer support

SUBPROCESSES

Subprocesses are lower-level processes. They are simply more narrowly defined tasks. For example, one subprocess of operations is procurement, as illustrated in Exhibit 4.4. Subprocesses themselves can be decomposed into even lower-level tasks. One subprocess of procurement, for example, might be warehouse materials. In general, processes are broken into sub-

---

[5] Ibid., p. 22.
[6] Ibid., p. 62.

EXHIBIT 4.3 RESPONSIBILITY CENTER/DEPARTMENTAL VIEW VERSUS PROCESS VIEW OF THE ORGANIZATION

Responsibility Center/Departmental View of the Organization

	Department 1	Department 2	Department 3	Department 4
Process A				
Process B				
Process C				
Process D				
Process E				

Process View of the Organization

EXHIBIT 4.4 ORGANIZATION-LEVEL PROCESSES AND SUBPROCESSES

Processes:

Corporate-level support	New customer/new business acquisition	Product design and introduction	Operations	Customer support

Subprocesses:

Personnel	Research & development	Design research	Forecasting	Packing
Legal	Advertising-promotion	Product planning	Procurement	Distribution
Accounting	Proposals-quotations	Product design	Manufacturing	Customer training
Financial planning	Order processing	Development	Assembly	Technical assistance
Information systems	Staff training	Process engineering	Maintenance	Repair-service
Planning-budgeting		Product testing		
Community relations				
Shareholder relations				

See details in Exhibit 4.5.

processes and subprocesses themselves are broken into even lower level subprocesses. Each step reveals more detail than the previous step did. Narrowing continues until managers isolate subprocesses at an "appropriate" level of detail. These last-step subprocesses are then broken down into activities, like those shown in Exhibit 4.5.

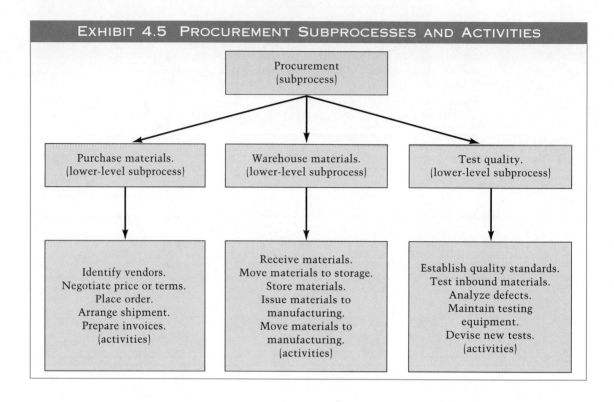

EXHIBIT 4.5 PROCUREMENT SUBPROCESSES AND ACTIVITIES

How narrowly subprocesses are broken down before reaching an "appropriate" level of detail is a matter of management discretion. Managers may decide to identify very narrowly defined subprocesses, thereby creating a large amount of information. However, the information may not be very useful. For example, the subprocess warehouse materials might be broken down into lower-level subprocesses such as receive materials. In turn, the subprocess receive materials may be broken into even lower-level subprocesses such as off-load delivery vehicle. Assume managers decide that off-load delivery vehicle is the lowest level subprocess and that one activity of off-load delivery vehicle is to pick up a box of raw materials from the bed of the truck and place it on the loading dock. Information about activities collected at this level of detail may not be very useful. It entails costly data collection that is likely to yield only marginal benefit. On the other hand, activities identified too broadly may not capture day-to-day work. Ultimately, the decision is based on balancing the cost of gathering the additional detail against the value the data create.

One way of isolating activities within a subprocess is to focus on who the customers of the subprocess are and what outputs they receive. After identifying customers, subprocess inputs are identified. In-between are the activities required to convert inputs into outputs. For example, the primary customer of the subprocess warehouse materials is manufacturing, an internal customer. Outputs supplied to manufacturing from the warehouse materials subprocess might include receive materials, store materials until needed, document material flow, and other services such as maintain inventory records. Based on this analysis, the procurement subprocess (warehouse materials) might be broken into the five activities listed below and shown in the lower-middle section of Exhibit 4.5.

1. Receive materials
2. Move materials to storage
3. Store materials
4. Issue materials to manufacturing
5. Move materials to manufacturing

ACTIVITY-BASED COSTING

We saw in Chapter 3 that the traditional system for assigning costs to cost objects relies on collecting costs by responsibility centers and then reassigning service center cost to production centers. Service center costs that cannot be either attributed to or charged directly to other responsibility centers are allocated using methods like the step-down procedure. Once all costs are collected in production centers, direct costs are charged to specific products, while indirect costs are assigned to products using overhead rates.

Activity-based costing works in a similar way. The key difference is the focal point of cost collection. Instead of assigning costs to responsibility centers (as illustrated in "Current Practice: Materials Control Department at Dana"), ABC systems assign costs to activities. Once costs are collected by activities, they are charged to products and services. The charge depends on the amount of the activity the product or service consumes.

An important cornerstone of activity-based costing is linking resource use to activity consumption. In this way, products are charged for the cost of activities they consume. For example, assume one activity is to move materials to storage. Each time a product is moved it receives a materials-moving charge. Moving products drives—or causes—activities to happen. In turn, activities cause costs. It is only fair that products and services be charged for the cost of activities they cause.

An overview of activity-based costing is shown in Exhibit 4.6. The top part of the exhibit portrays the cost of inputs (represented as rectangles) from resource suppliers into the organization. The flow of resources (represented by arrows) is from suppliers to activities such as receive materials and move materials to storage. After collecting costs by activities, each product or service is charged for the cost of activities it consumes.

The steps in assigning costs to products and other cost objects in ABC systems are (1) assign general ledger costs to activities, (2) identify activity drivers, (3) calculate unit activity cost by dividing the total cost for each activity by its activity driver, and (4) charge costs to products based on the amount of activities the products consume.

1: ASSIGN GENERAL LEDGER COSTS TO ACTIVITIES

As noted in the previous chapter, assigning input resource costs to activities relies on a preferred order. The order is as follows:

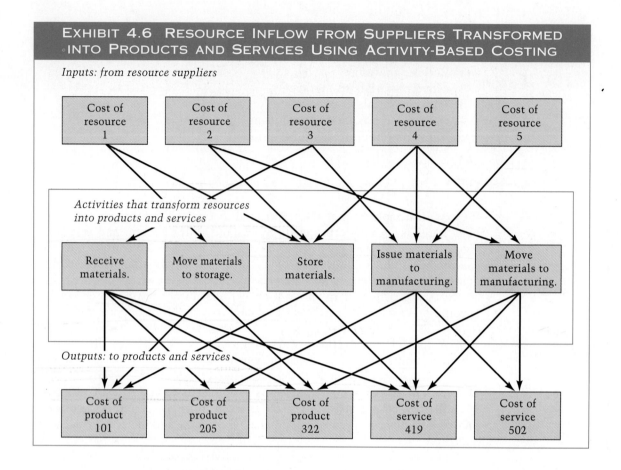

EXHIBIT 4.6 RESOURCE INFLOW FROM SUPPLIERS TRANSFORMED INTO PRODUCTS AND SERVICES USING ACTIVITY-BASED COSTING

1. Attribution
2. Direct assignment (direct charge)
3. Indirect assignment (allocation)

ATTRIBUTION

We saw in Chapter 3 that attribution is possible only when cost is unequivocally identified with a specific activity. For example, the cost of materials used exclusively for a particular activity is attributed to that activity. Depreciation for a forklift used exclusively to off-load materials from supplier's delivery trucks, for example, is attributed to the activity for which the equipment is used. If costs are shared by multiple activities—costs that cannot be identified, unequivocally, with a single activity—then we can use the next best method, direct assignment.

DIRECT ASSIGNMENT

Direct assignment, often referred to as *chargebacks* or *direct charges*, relies on measures called **resource drivers** that reflect the amount of shared resources used by a specific activity. For example, depreciation for a fork-lift used in several activities might be charged to those activities based on hours of operations, where hours of operations is the resource driver. An

CURRENT PRACTICE

Materials Control Department at Dana

Several years ago, Dana, a Minnesota auto parts manufacturer, installed an ABC accounting system. Dana's old system collected costs in categories such as salaries, fringe benefits, and supplies, as shown in the first table below. While Dana still reports the same cost, today its accounting system is organized differently. The new ABC system focuses on the cost of performing specific tasks such as processing sales orders, purchasing parts, and the other activities listed in the second table below. The cost of a product is simply the summation of the cost of all the activities required to make it. Not only can Dana determine product profitability better, but the new system provides a focal point—activities—for controlling costs.

COST UNDER DANA'S OLD ACCOUNTING SYSTEM	
Resource	*Total Cost*
Salaries	$371,917
Fringe benefits	118,069
Supplies	76,745
Other cost	23,614
Total cost	$590,345

COST WITH DANA'S NEW ABC ACCOUNTING SYSTEM	
Activity	*Total Cost*
Process sales orders	$144,846
Purchase parts	136,320
Expedite supplier orders	72,143
Expedite internal processing	49,945
Resolve supplier quality	47,599
Reissue purchase orders	45,235
Expedite customer orders	27,747
Schedule intracompany sales	17,768
Request engineering changes	16,704
Resolve problems	16,648
Schedule parts	15,390
Total cost	$590,345

Source: Terence P. Pare, "A New Tool for Managing Costs," *Fortune,* June 14, 1993, pp. 125–128, © 1993 Time Inc. All rights reserved. Reprinted with permission.

activity using, say, 40 percent of the available forklift hours should be assigned 40 percent of the depreciation cost. If depreciation were $6,000 per year and the forklift is expected to operate for 200 hours, the direct charge is $30 for each hour of use.

INDIRECT ASSIGNMENT, OR ALLOCATION

When it's not possible to identify specific costs with a specific activity (attribution) or identify resource drivers that assign costs of a shared resource proportional to its use (direct assignment), then we must allocate costs. For example, if depreciation for a forklift shared by multiple activities cannot be charged to those activities using direct assignment—say, based on hours of use—then it must be allocated. However, as we indicated in Chapter 3, allocations increase the likelihood of arbitrary assignments of indirect cost. If so, how can allocations be consistent with the principles of activity-based costing?

One reason they are consistent is that activity-based costing makes it easier to identify appropriate resource drivers. It is more likely that managers will be able to isolate resource drivers that capture the relative share of resources used for a relatively narrowly defined activity, such as move materials to storage, than it is to capture the relative share of resources for a department such as procurement, which has lots of diverse activities. Moreover, the goal of ABC is to reduce the amount of costs that require allocation in the first place. Over time, the system can be improved by increasing the proportion of costs that are assigned using attribution or direct assignment. Ultimately, though, ABC systems cannot entirely escape the use of allocations.

ILLUSTRATION OF ASSIGNING COSTS TO ACTIVITIES

Exhibit 4.7 illustrates how general ledger costs may be assigned to activities. The first column shows the total cost of the organization as a whole—in this case, $25 million. The middle column shows the methods used to assign organizationwide costs to activities. Resource drivers are found in the third column. We see, for example, that the salaries and wages cost of $17,150,000 can be traced to specific activities on the basis of an employee's work assignment. Therefore, salaries and wages cost is *attributed* (the method of assignment) to activities based on work assignment. Similarly, depreciation—facility is *allocated* (the method of assignment) to activities based on the number of square feet occupied (the resource driver).

The first box in Exhibit 4.8 shows the results after assigning general ledger costs to activities. The activity receive materials, for example, ends up with total cost—called total activity cost—of $145,340. Note that we show the detail for only the five activities introduced earlier. Details for assignment of the remaining $24.5 million in cost are omitted. However, these costs are assigned to activities in exactly the same way.

EXHIBIT 4.7 METHODS OF ASSIGNING GENERAL LEDGER COSTS TO ACTIVITIES

General Ledger Account	Total Cost	Method of Assignment	Resource Driver
Salaries & wages	$17,150,000	Attribution	Work assignment
Direct materials	4,610,000	Attribution	Materials requisitions
Benefits	1,540,000	Attribution	Work assignment
Depreciation—facility	560,000	Allocation	Square feet occupied
Supplies	370,000	Attribution	Supply requisitions
Depreciation—equipment	250,000	Direct charge	Operating hours
Maintenance	190,000	Direct charge	Maintenance hours
Utilities	130,000	Direct charge	Kilowatt-hours
Other accounts	200,000	Allocation	Other drivers
Total cost	$25,000,000		

EXHIBIT 4.8 GENERAL LEDGER COSTS ASSIGNED TO ACTIVITIES

General Ledger

Account	Receive Materials	Move Materials to Storage	Store Materials	Issue Materials to Manfg.	Move Materials to Manfg.	Other Activities	Method of Assignment	Resource Driver
Salaries & wages	$108,000	$52,000	$ 83,000	$40,000	$57,000	$16,810,000	Attribution	Work assignment
Direct materials	0	0	0	0	0	4,610,000	Attribution	Materials reqs.
Salary benefits	23,500	10,800	18,000	8,500	12,200	1,467,000	Attribution	Work assignment
Depreciation—facility	1,400		22,400	4,200		532,000	Allocation	Square feet occupied
Supplies	2,800	1,100	2,800	900	400	362,000	Attribution	Supply reqs.
Depreciation—equipment	3,100	1,400	6,500	1,800	1,200	236,000	Direct charge	Operating hrs
Maintenance	4,000	2,600	7,100	2,400	1,900	172,000	Direct charge	Maintenance hrs
Utilities	600	200	5,700	1,200	300	122,000	Direct charge	KWh
Other accounts	1,940	720	3,980	3,440	920	189,000	Allocation	Other drivers
Activity cost	$145,340	$68,820	$149,480	$62,440	$73,920	$24,500,000		

Payroll Register

Employee	Wages	Benefits	Work Assignment	Activity
Caen, J.	$ 15,600	$ 3,432	Receiving clerk	Receive materials
Russell, L.	13,800	2,898	Materials handler—off-loading	Receive materials
Other	78,600	17,170	Other	Receive materials
Subtotal	$ 108,000	$ 23,500		
Cocker, J.	$ 18,260	$ 3,652	Forklift operator—receiving	Move materials to storage
Laval, C.	14,500	2,755	Materials handler—off-loading	Move materials to storage
Other	19,240	4,393	Other	Move materials to storage
Subtotal	$ 52,000	$ 10,800		
Mustafa, J.	$ 16,400	$ 3,936	Records clerk—stores warehouse	Store materials
Spielberg, S.	9,700	1,455	Stores warehouse clerk	Store materials
Other	56,900	12,609	Other	Store materials
Subtotal	$ 83,000	$ 18,000		
Betts, R.	$ 18,100	$ 3,620	Records manager—manufacturing	Issue materials to manufacturing
Other	21,900	4,880	Other	Issue materials to manufacturing
Subtotal	$ 40,000	$ 8,500		
Trucks, B.	$ 18,400	$ 4,232	Materials handler—manufacturing	Move materials to manufacturing
Day, D.	16,700	3,006	Forklift operator—manufacturing	Move materials to manufacturing
Other	21,900	4,962	Other	Move materials to manufacturing
Subtotal	$ 57,000	$ 12,200		
Other	$16,810,000	$1,467,000	Other duties	Other activities
Total labor	$17,150,000	$1,540,000		

Facility Depreciation

Activity	Square Feet	% of Total Square Feet	Facility Deprec.	Activity Cost
Receive materials	14,000	0.25%	$560,000	$ 1,400
Move materials to storage	0	0.00	560,000	0
Store materials	224,000	4.00	560,000	22,400
Issue materials to manufacturing	42,000	0.75	560,000	4,200
Move materials to manufacturing	0	0.00	560,000	0
Other activities	5,320,000	95.00	560,000	532,000
Total	5,600,000	100.00%		$560,000

Maintenance

Activity	Maint. Hours	Charge per Hour	Total Charges
Receive materials	160	$25.00	$ 4,000
Move materials to storage	104	25.00	2,600
Store materials	284	25.00	7,100
Issue materials to manufacturing	96	25.00	2,400
Move materials to manufacturing	76	25.00	1,900
Other activities	6,880	25.00	172,000
Total	7,600		$190,000

You can see the detail on how several of the general ledger costs are assigned to activities by looking at the three lower boxes in Exhibit 4.8. For example, work assignments are taken from the payroll register, part of which is shown in the second box of Exhibit 4.8. J. Caen, a receiving clerk, compares shipping invoices with purchase orders for goods taken from inbound delivery vehicles. His salary, along with the salaries of other employees whose job is to receive materials, is attributed to the receive materials activity.

Facility depreciation is shown in the third box in Exhibit 4.8. The activity issue materials to manufacturing occupies 42,000 square feet, or 0.75 percent of total square feet. The issue materials activity is assigned (by allocation) $4,200 of the facility cost. Maintenance cost is shown in the box at the bottom of Exhibit 4.8. Activities consuming maintenance resources are charged at a rate of $25 per hour based on the number of maintenance hours used.

2: IDENTIFY AN ACTIVITY DRIVER FOR EACH COST POOL

Activity drivers are bases used to assign activity costs to products and other cost objects. An activity driver should meet these three criteria:[7]

1. It should reflect the demand the product (or other cost object) places on the activity.
2. It should be correlated with the underlying cost driver.
3. It should be quantifiable.

The first criterion implies that activity drivers should reflect relative resource use. For example, assume that the number of receipts is the activity driver for receive materials. The number of receipts should increase proportionally with increases in the demand for services from the receive materials activity.

The second criterion suggests that the fundamental cause of the cost, called the root cause, should be strongly associated with the activity driver. For example, the root cause of costs for the receiving materials activity might include workload, the variety of parts, the number of deliveries, and the size of shipping containers. Each of these factors may contribute toward causing receiving costs to increase. However, the number of receipts might be chosen as the activity driver because it is highly correlated with changes in the cost of the receiving materials activity.

And, third, activity drivers must be quantifiable if they are to have value in assigning costs.

Resource drivers should also be cost drivers. Increasing the amount of the resources used causes the cost of the activity to increase. In such a case, a resource driver can be used not only to reflect the amount of resources consumed by an activity but also to predict its cost behavior. Unfortunately, it is not always possible to find measures of activity that satisfy both objectives. For example, forklift hours may be a logical activ-

---

[7] Ibid., pp. 182–183.

ity driver, meeting all three of the criteria listed above. However, forklift hours may not clearly reflect cost behavior. Here's why not: Since depreciation is a fixed cost, increasing forklift utilization will have no effect on the cost of the activity. One solution is to separate the cost of forklift operations into several activities, one of which might be driven by utilization.

FOUR-LEVEL HIERARCHY OF ACTIVITY DRIVERS

One way of looking at activity drivers is to break them down by their cost behavior:[8]

Unit Level.   Activity drivers that change proportionally with the number of units of product are unit-level activity drivers. Example: For a hypothetical commercial airline, food and beverage cost and the cost of commissions paid to travel agents, as shown in Exhibit 4.9, increase proportionally with the number of passengers enplaned.

Batch Level.   Batch-level activity drivers increase proportionally with the number of batches. Activity drivers such as the number of setups, material movements, purchase orders, or inspections may increase with the number of batches. Example: A batch-level activity driver for a commercial airline might be the "number of flights." Each flight causes increases in jet fuel, gate fees, and contract cleaning. Batch-level costs are caused by operating a flight, regardless of the number of passengers enplaned.

Product Level.   Product-level activity drivers increase proportionally with the number of products an organization offers. As the number of products expands, product-level activity drivers parallel increases in cost for new product development, marketing, and product-specific customer service. Example: A product-level activity driver for a commercial airline might be the number of routes. Each additional route the airline flies causes an increase in costs such as marketing, airplane leases, flight crews, gate agents, and maintenance. Adding a new route—say, to Mexico City— requires another layer of product-level costs.

Corporate Level.   Corporate-level activity drivers reflect support for the organization as a whole, regardless of the number of units produced, the number of batches, or the number of products and services. These drivers parallel activities such as corporate planning, personnel, legal services, marketing, information systems, research and development, and other centralized activities. Example: Corporate-level cost drivers at a commercial airline cause an increase in costs required to sustain the organization as a whole, including systemwide marketing, personnel, reservation systems, depreciation for corporate facilities, and accounting systems.

Activity drivers separated into this four-level hierarchy may help in identifying cost behavior. As mentioned above, one desirable characteristic

[8]   This hierarchy is based on Robin Cooper and Robert Kaplan, "Profit Priorities from Activity-Based Costing," *Harvard Business Review*, May–June 1991, pp. 130–136.

EXHIBIT 4.9 ACTIVITY DRIVERS FOR A HYPOTHETICAL COMMERCIAL AIRLINE

Activity	Activity Driver	Number of Units	Cost per Unit	Total Cost
Passenger Level				
Food & beverages	No. of passengers	1,868,800	$20.00	$37,376,000
Commissions	Revenue, $s	$280,320,000	5.00%	14,016,000
Total passenger-level cost				$51,392,000
Flight Level				
Jet fuel	No. of flights	14,600	$5,500	$ 80,300,000
Gate fees	No. of flights	14,600	$2,000	29,200,000
Contracted cleaning	No. of flights	14,600	$200	2,920,000
Total flight-level cost				$112,420,000
Route Level				
Marketing	No. of routes	10	$1,500,000	$15,000,000
Airplane leases	No. of routes	10	$1,250,000	12,500,000
Maintenance	No. of routes	10	$ 750,000	7,500,000
Flight crews	No. of routes	10	$1,750,000	17,500,000
Ground crews	No. of routes	10	$ 800,000	8,000,000
Gate agents	No. of routes	10	$ 450,000	4,500,000
Total route-level cost				$65,000,000
Corporate Level				
Marketing				$ 7,000,000
Personnel				1,250,000
Reservations				8,500,000
Facility depreciation				2,500,000
Accounting & information systems				3,250,000
Total corporate-level cost				$22,500,000
Total Cost				
Total cost				$251,312,000

of activity drivers is that they are also cost drivers. Unit-level cost drivers are likely to provide good estimates of volume-related, short-term variable costs. Batch-level costs are probably either short- or intermediate-term variable costs. Product-level costs are generally short- to intermediate-term step or fixed costs, depending on how frequently product lines are changed. Finally, corporate-level costs are likely to be mainly long-term fixed costs, since they represent ongoing support for corporatewide activities.

RESOURCE DRIVERS, ACTIVITY DRIVERS, OR COST DRIVERS?

How do resource drivers, activity drivers, and cost drivers differ? Resource and activity drivers are similar since they both provide the basis for assigning costs. Cost drivers, on the other hand, refer to cost behavior.

- *Resource drivers* provide the basis for assigning general ledger costs to activities. Example: The cost of the general ledger account maintenance is assigned (by direct assignment) to activities such as receive materials. The resource driver is maintenance hours.
- *Activity drivers* are the basis for assigning activity costs to products and other cost objects. Example: The activity cost for the receive materials activity is assigned to units of product (or other cost objects) using an activity driver such as the number of receipts.
- *Cost drivers* reflect activities that cause costs to increase or decrease. Example: The activity driver number of receipts is also a cost driver if the total cost of the receive materials activity increases proportionally with the number of receipts. Suppose the receive materials activity cost is composed predominately of salary and wages and employees are paid based on the number of material receipts. In that case, the number of receipts is both an activity driver and a cost driver.

3: CALCULATE UNIT ACTIVITY COST BY DIVIDING THE TOTAL COST OF AN ACTIVITY BY ITS ACTIVITY DRIVER

Activity costs are sometimes pooled together when they share a common activity driver. In fact, when making a decision among several activity drivers, one criterion guiding the selection might be which of the activity drivers can best be used to form activity cost pools. For example, consider the activities in Exhibit 4.10. The receive materials activity cost is pooled together with the move materials to storage activity cost because both share a common activity driver—the number of receipts. Similarly, the issue materials to manufacturing activity cost and the move materials to manufacturing activity cost form an issue materials cost pool based on the activity driver number of requisitions.

Exhibits 4.11 through 4.13 show unit activity costs calculated by dividing the activity cost pools by the activity driver. Exhibit 4.11 shows the cost per receipt for the receive materials cost pool. Each product is charged with $85.66 per receipt associated with that product for the cost of off-loading materials from delivery vehicles and moving them into storage. In addition, each batch of product is charged $1.49 per cubic meter for storage (from Exhibit 4.12) and $136.36 per requisition for issuing materials to production (from Exhibit 4.13).

4: CHARGE COSTS TO COST OBJECT BASED ON UTILIZATION

The last step is to charge products and other costs objects with the costs of activities they consume. Exhibit 4.14 shows activities and activity costs for a batch of typical product, say, a 400-unit batch of product no. 33211. The full cost of the batch is $47,334, or $118.34 per unit. Note two other things about Exhibit 4.14. First, full cost includes both manufacturing and nonmanufacturing costs. And, second, the activity costs are organized in the four-level hierarchy.

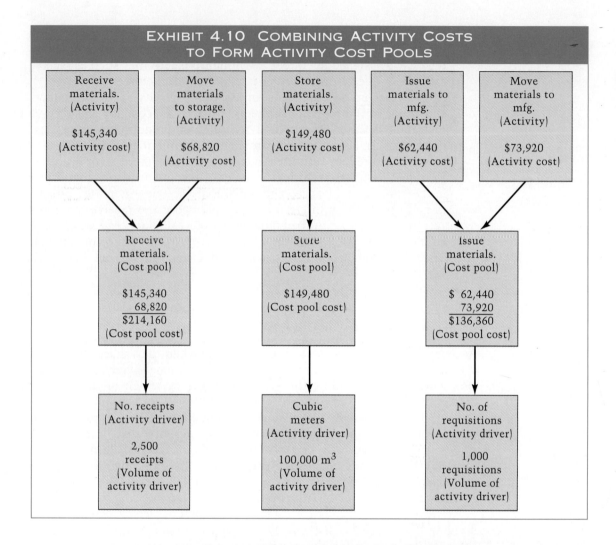

EXHIBIT 4.10 COMBINING ACTIVITY COSTS
TO FORM ACTIVITY COST POOLS

Receive materials. (Activity)	Move materials to storage. (Activity)	Store materials. (Activity)	Issue materials to mfg. (Activity)	Move materials to mfg. (Activity)
$145,340 (Activity cost)	$68,820 (Activity cost)	$149,480 (Activity cost)	$62,440 (Activity cost)	$73,920 (Activity cost)

Receive materials. (Cost pool)

$145,340
 68,820
$214,160
(Cost pool cost)

Store materials. (Cost pool)

$149,480
(Cost pool cost)

Issue materials. (Cost pool)

$ 62,440
 73,920
$136,360
(Cost pool cost)

No. receipts (Activity driver)

2,500 receipts (Volume of activity driver)

Cubic meters (Activity driver)

100,000 m^3 (Volume of activity driver)

No. of requisitions (Activity driver)

1,000 requisitions (Volume of activity driver)

EXHIBIT 4.11 ACTIVITY COST—RECEIVE MATERIALS

Activity Cost Pool	Receive materials
Activity Driver	Number of receipts
Part No.	*No. of Receipts*
1101	230
1105	195
1119	769
3402	88
3448	835
4321	18
4487	210
5689	67
5760	88
Total no. of receipts	2,500
Receive materials cost pool (from Exhibit 4.10)	$214,160
Cost per receipt	$85.66

CHAPTER 4/PROCESS ANALYSIS AND ACTIVITY-BASED COSTING

EXHIBIT 4.12 ACTIVITY COST—STORE MATERIALS

Activity Cost Pool			Store Materials
Activity Driver			Cubic Meters
Part No.	Average Units in Inventory	Cubic Meters per Unit	Cubic Meters
1101	4,000	0.75	3,000
1105	84,040	0.73	61,350
1119	22,000	0.25	5,500
3402	13,000	0.40	5,200
3448	6,000	0.05	300
4321	2,000	3.25	6,500
4487	7,000	1.70	11,900
5689	1,000	1.75	1,750
5760	1,000	4.50	4,500
Total cubic meters			100,000
Store materials cost pool (Exhibit 4.10)			$149,480
Cost per cubic meter			$1.49

EXHIBIT 4.13 ACTIVITY COST—ISSUE MATERIALS

Activity Cost Pool	Issue Materials
Activity Driver	No. of Requisitions
Part No.	No. of Requisitions
1101	125
1105	198
1119	87
3402	107
3448	86
4321	15
4487	107
5689	84
5760	191
Total no. of requisitions	1,000
Issue materials cost pool (from Exhibit 4.10)	$136,360
Cost per requisition	$136.36

COMPARING ACTIVITY-BASED COSTING WITH RESPONSIBILITY-CENTER COSTING BASED ON ALLOCATIONS

Exhibit 4.15 illustrates the differences in full cost of a unit of product calculated using the allocation-based, responsibility-center approach introduced in Chapter 3 and in full cost of that same unit of product using costs calculated with activity-based costing. While direct materials and direct labor costs are the same under both approaches, a total of $15,228 in overhead is assigned to the batch using ABC, while only $6,533 of overhead is assigned using the allocation approach.

EXHIBIT 4.14   PRODUCT COST USING ACTIVITY-BASED COSTING

Cost for a 400-Unit Batch of Product 33211

Level	Activity	Activity Driver	Rate	Quantity	Total
Unit:	Direct material 1119	Pounds	$ 11.23	200	$ 2,246
	Direct material 3402	Pounds	$ 4.08	280	1,142
	Direct material 4321	Unit	$ 12.90	800	10,320
	Direct material 4487	Unit	$ 4.32	400	1,728
	Direct material 5689	Unit	$ 2.47	275	679
	Total unit-level cost				$16,115
Batch:	Direct labor—subassembly 1	Hours	$ 22.15	125	$ 2,769
	Direct labor—subassembly 2	Hours	$ 18.72	80	1,498
	Direct labor—assembly	Hours	$ 16.44	400	6,576
	Direct labor—packing	Hours	$ 12.87	400	5,148
	Forecasting product demand	Hours	$ 30.00	3	90
	Receiving (from Exhibit 4.11)	Receipts	$ 85.66	5	428
	Storing (from Exhibit 4.12)	m³	$ 1.49	3,923	$ 5,845
	Issuing (from Exhibit 4.13)	Requisitions	$ 136.36	5	682
	Quality control	Inspections	$ 173.40	5	867
	Quality assurance	Inspections	$ 86.93	5	435
	Total batch-level cost				$24,338
Product line:	Obtaining customers	Sales reps	$ 475.00	1	$ 475
	Product design	Designers	$1,400.00	1	1,400
	Customer support	Head count	$2,200.00	1	2,200
	Purchasing	Parts	$ 456.00	1	456
	Total product-line cost				$ 4,531
Corporate:	Corporate-level cost	Batches	$2,350.00	1	$ 2,350

Full cost—batch of product 33211	$47,334
No. of units in batch	400
Full cost per unit	$118.34

Summary:

Direct materials	$16,115
Direct labor (subassembly 1 and 2, assembly, and packing)	15,991
Overhead (batch-level, product line, and corporate-level)	15,228
Full cost	$47,334

Adding overhead cost to direct materials and direct labor cost, then dividing that sum by 400 units yields full activity-based cost of $118.34 per unit. The comparable full-cost figure based on allocations is $96.60 per unit.

Assume the selling price of product 33211 (Exhibit 4.15) is determined using a markup of, say, 15 percent added to full cost. With activity-based costing, the product should be priced at $136.09 per unit, while the price based on allocations should be $111.09 per unit. If the prevailing market price is, say, $115 per unit, managers using allocation-based, responsibility center costs are likely to erroneously believe that the selling price yields operating profit at a rate greater than 15 percent. If activity-based costing generates more-accurate estimates of cost, then the pre-

EXHIBIT 4.15 COMPARISON OF ACTIVITY-BASED COST VS. RESPONSIBILITY CENTER COST

Full Cost for a Batch of Product 33211

	Activity-Based Costing	Responsibility Center Allocations
Resource:		
Direct materials	$16,115	$16,115
Direct labor	$15,991	$15,991
Overhead based on allocations:		
Direct labor-hours		1,005
Overhead rate per direct labor-hour		$ 6.50
Total overhead applied		$ 6,533
Overhead based on ABC (from Exhibit 4.14)	$15,228	
Full cost	$47,334	$38,639
Divided by units in batch	400	400
Full cost per unit	$118.34	$ 96.60
Desired price:		
Full cost per unit	$118.34	$ 96.60
Desired profit (15% of full cost)	$ 17.75	14.49
Desired selling price	$136.09	$111.09
Prevailing market price	$115.00	$115.00
Excess (deficiency) of market price over desired price	$(21.09)	$3.91

vailing market price is actually below the full cost of $118.34. Assuming that activity-based costing is more accurate, there is a deficit of $21.09 for each unit sold. While full-cost pricing will be discussed in detail in Chapter 6, the point here is that inaccurate assignments of costs can lead to inaccurate decisions—for example, opting to incorrectly promote sales of product 33211.

COSTING SERVICES WITH ACTIVITY-BASED COSTING

The case of a securities broker illustrates the role that activity-based costing can play in providing information for service-oriented firms.[9] The broker's principal business is executing securities transactions for institutional investors. Transactions, performed by account executives, are grouped together as product lines based on the instruments traded—for example, over-the-counter securities or options. Revenues are derived from commissions levied on each transaction.

[9] This is the Steward and Company example found in Robin Cooper, Robert Kaplan, Lawrence Maisel, Eileen Morrissey, and Ronald Oehm, *Implementing Activity-Based Cost Management: Moving from Analysis to Action.* Montvale, N.J.: Institute of Management Accountants, 1992, pp. 179–208.

Some of the activities necessary to support account executives are shown in the first column of Exhibit 4.16. The costs of these activities are assigned to the product lines listed across the top of Exhibit 4.16. Managers may use this information in several ways. For example, they can evaluate relative product-line profitability. Three of the products contributed most of the profit—listed securities ($25,942), options and futures ($10,151), and taxable fixed income ($27,414). On the other hand, managers may question whether to continue trading unprofitable products, such as convertibles (−$989) and international (−$2,328).

WHEN IS AN ACTIVITY-BASED COSTING SYSTEM JUSTIFIED?

An Institute of Management Accountants study reports 29 percent of companies surveyed use activity-based costing instead of traditional systems. Moreover, 56 percent of the respondents use activity-based costing to help analyze and solve problems.[10] However, ABC systems are costly when compared with traditional allocation-based systems. In another survey, 40 percent of the large companies responding to questions about the cost of ABC management systems had out-of-pocket costs exceeding $100,000, while 16 percent reported costs in excess of $500,000.[11] All ABC systems don't have to be so expensive, however. But they take a significant commitment of time and energy. Given these cost considerations, under what circumstances is an investment in activity-based costing systems justified?

The answer depends on the value of the information the system provides. As indicated earlier in this chapter, organizations offering few products and having costs dominated by direct materials and direct labor may be able to derive sufficient information from allocation-based full costs to make appropriate decisions. However, as managers face stronger competition, more-accurate knowledge of product costs becomes increasingly necessary.

Firms with a wide variety of products that share common services are candidates for ABC systems. The potential for distortions in full cost increases when indirect costs constitute a sizeable proportion of total cost. Distortions in full costs are likely to be aggravated when products draw from indirect resources at different rates. Perhaps more important than the impact on product costs, poorly allocated costs can lead to incorrect decisions.

IDENTIFYING OPPORTUNITIES TO REDUCE COSTS

Activity-based costing is designed to provide managers with a system for measuring the cost of products and services. But it also provides them with a powerful tool for managing costs. That tool is activities—managers control costs by controlling activities.

---

[10] "More Companies Turn to ABC," *Journal of Accountancy*, July 1994, p. 14.

[11] Jonathan Schiff, "How to Succeed at Activity-Based Cost Management," *Management Accounting*, Mar. 1992, pp. 64–65.

EXHIBIT 4.16   PROFIT AND LOSS FROM SECURITIES TRANSACTIONS

Type of Security

	Listed	Over-the-Counter	Options and Futures	Technology-Trading	Convertibles	Euro-Convertibles	International	Taxable Fixed Income	Corporate Finance
Revenue	$69,832	$19,464	$17,133	$11,555	$5,705	$3,254	$7,245	$44,999	$7,758
Direct cost	24,816	10,312	4,945	7,302	5,270	1,880	6,769	15,559	6,844
Direct profit	$45,016	$9,152	$12,188	$4,253	$435	$1,374	$476	$29,440	$914
Indirect (activity) cost:									
Sales office & support	$7,334	$3,835	$323	$1,230	$249	$191	$828	$656	$252
Sales promotion	4,873	419	45	36	35	34	54	36	38
Trade comparison & settlement	1,225	681	372	342	124	100	555	197	3
Account maintenance	236	88	33	87	10	2	34	10	0
Human resource management	159	105	22	29	4	23	23	59	50
Legal & compliance support	577	435	321	333	272	306	301	271	423
Account executive support	373	183	68	18	20	21	14	12	15
Accounting support	363	309	203	203	204	173	256	170	169
Data processing	944	526	82	316	18	10	87	114	11
Portfolio management support	928	500	0	0	0	0	0	0	0
Telecommunications	372	175	36	18	16	15	30	20	28
Trade processing	1,193	640	105	406	54	23	195	37	0
General management support	196	196	196	196	196	196	196	196	196
Facilities sustaining support	301	276	231	235	222	232	231	248	233
Total indirect (activities) cost	$19,074	$8,368	$2,037	$3,449	$1,424	$1,326	$2,804	$2,026	$1,418
Net earnings	$25,942	$784	$10,151	$804	$(989)	$48	$(2,328)	$27,414	$(504)

Source: Robin Cooper, Robert Kaplan, Lawrence Maisel, Eileen Morrissey, and Ronald Oehm, *Implementing Activity-Based Cost Management: Moving from Analysis to Action.* Montvale, N.J.: Institute of Management Accountants, 1992, p. 194.

One approach to controlling activities and, ultimately, cost is based on the following sequence of logic: First, decide whether or not an activity adds value. If it *doesn't add value*, then consider reducing or eliminating it. For those activities that *do add value*, decide whether or not you should perform them internally. Then figure out ways to perform value-adding activities better.

The first step, then, is to identify whether or not an activity creates value. To help sort out what's valuable from what's not, consider placing activities in one of the following categories:[12]

- *Real value-adding activities.* Activities that help provide the output customers are expecting are called **real value-adding activities**. Example: a grinding operation in making a bicycle part.
- *Business value-adding activities.* Activities that add no value from the customer's perspective but are required by the organization are **business value-adding activities**. Example: keeping payroll records for production workers.
- *Non-value-adding activities.* Activities that are neither required by the customers nor the organization are called **non-value-adding activities**. Example: moving inventory from one location in a factory to another.

Separating activities into these three categories helps managers focus clearly on what's important—the customer. In fact, the following questions might help in sorting out value determination from the customer's point of view:[13]

- Given a choice, would customers be willing to pay for the activity?
- If you quit performing the activity, would the output still meet customer requirements?
- If you eliminated the activity altogether, would customers care or notice?

Consider the following description of steps in a manufacturing process:[14]

- *Processing*—Activities involved in actually making products
- *Inspection*—Activities involved in making sure that products meet quality standards
- *Rework*—Activities required to bring defective products to acceptable levels of quality
- *Move*—Activities devoted to moving products from one location to another
- *Queue*—Activities where products wait before being processed, moved, or inspected
- *Storage*—Activities involved in storing products before further processing or shipment

[12] Ostrenga et al., op. cit., p. 111.
[13] Adapted from Ostrenga et al., ibid., p. 110.
[14] Adapted from Robert D. McIlhattan, "The JIT Philosophy," *Management Accounting*, Sept. 1987, pp. 20–26.

Only "processing" activities add value from the customer's point of view. The other activities contribute little or nothing toward meeting customer needs. Moving products from one location to another, for example, or inspecting inventory adds nothing of value.

Separating activities into value-adding and non-value-adding may seem clear-cut. But it's not! Making the distinction between the two relies on the experience, judgment, and intuition of the team making the evaluation. The problem is that everyone may have a different idea about what's valuable to customers. Consider a pharmaceutical company. An obvious value-adding activity is manufacturing final products. But the company also provides some important services you might not think of—like answering inquiries from doctors about side effects of drugs, discovering new pharmaceutical products through research and development, obtaining patents, constructing legal defenses against patent infringements, gaining clearance through regulatory bodies, and creating new distribution networks.[15] All of these activities may be required by the pharmaceutical company, although customers may assign them relatively low values. Wherever possible, managers should reduce or eliminate non-value-adding activities and turn their attention to performing value-adding activities more efficiently.

Once managers have identified value-adding activities, they must decide which of those activities to perform internally. Since resources are always limited, they have the option of outsourcing less critical activities. If outside suppliers can perform an activity at a lower cost, or perhaps with higher levels of service or improved reliability, then the activity should be outsourced.

In sorting out candidates for outsourcing, managers might want to consider the following questions:[16]

- Is the activity relatively costly?
- Does the activity increase process complexity?
- Does the activity require long processing times?
- Does the activity involve lots of people and participation in many functional areas?
- Are multiple approvals and additional paperwork required?

If the answer is yes to any of these questions, then the activity might be a good candidate for outsourcing. In fact, answers to these questions may help prioritize which of the activities to evaluate first. That is, activities with the highest cost—those that are the most complex, take the longest time to process, require participation by lots of people, and require the most paperwork—are the first candidates for outsourcing.

One important step in an outsourcing evaluation is **benchmarking**—looking at how other organizations perform an activity. Benchmarking can be described as finding out how other companies do something better than

---

[15]   James B. Quinn, Thomas L. Doorley, and Penny C. Paquette, "Technology in Services: Rethinking Strategic Focus," *Sloan Management Review*, winter 1990, p. 79.

[16]   Adapted from Ostrenga et al., op. cit., pp. 93–97.

CURRENT PRACTICE

Benchmarking at L. L. Bean's Warehouse

Xerox managers, looking for faster ways to fill customer orders, decided to use L. L. Bean, known for quick service, as a benchmark. A visit to Bean's warehouse in Maine found that workers could "pick and pack" items 3 times faster than Xerox workers could. The secret to their speed was in the layout of the warehouse. Instead of storing items by category, L. L. Bean stored according to "velocity." That is, the fastest-selling items were located closest to the desk where orders came in, saving time and motion. In contrast, slow-moving items were stored farthest away. L. L. Bean's computer system also played a role by sorting orders, which came in randomly, so that workers could combine trips to pick up the same item for different orders.

Source: Jeremy Main, "How to Steal the Best Ideas Around," *Fortune,* Oct. 19, 1992, pp. 103–104.

your company does. Then you imitate and perhaps improve upon the other company's techniques. One application of benchmarking is physically tearing down other companies' products, as Ford did when it redesigned the Taurus. Ford formed a list of 400 items that customers said were the most important features about a car. It then searched the market for the best examples of each feature—for instance, door handles from the Chevy Lumina—and regarded them as standards. Then engineers tried to design features that beat these standards. (See "Current Practice: Benchmarking at L. L. Bean's Warehouse" for another example of benchmarking.)

We assume managers have no strategic interest in an activity when they make an outsourcing decision. In some cases they may retain activities for a very simple reason—to maintain control over those activities. For example, a law firm would probably not outsource photocopying of sensitive documents. Or consider an organization whose competitive advantage is the training, skills, and experience of its employees. Outsourcing activities that use these skills may place the firm at a strategic disadvantage in the future. We will return to a discussion of outsourcing in Chapter 6. But for now, remember the general rule: Organizations should outsource activities when others can perform them better unless, in doing so, they give up a strategic competitive advantage.

ILLUSTRATION OF VALUE- AND NON-VALUE-ADDING ACTIVITIES

We can illustrate value- and non-value-adding activities with the example of the processes involved in making a bicycle part. We will focus on the amount of time it takes to process the part, called "cycle time." Cycle time refers to the length of time it takes from the start to completion of

CURRENT PRACTICE

General Motors' Concept-to-Production Cycle

General Motors recognized that its "concept-to-production" cycles, spanning two to three years, put it at a disadvantage with respect to its Japanese counterparts. By the time GM developed a working prototype, consumer preferences often had changed. Furthermore, features added after the initial design phase to satisfy customer preferences required additional manufacturing steps. As a result, GM changed the way it designed new cars, creating integrated teams rather than relying on the more traditional, functional approach.

Source: Author's unpublished research.

an entire process or activity. It is calculated by following work and keeping track of the time it takes all the way through the process or activity. (See "Current Practice: General Motors' Concept-to-Production Cycle" for an illustration of the importance of cycle time.)

The bicycle manufacturing process is shown in a factory-floor layout format in Exhibit 4.17. A brief description of the process is as follows: Materials for the bicycle part are delivered to the manufacturing area from the warehouse. The parts are stored until the milling machine operator is ready. After undergoing the milling operation, the parts are stored on carts until the grinding operator is ready for the next step. After the initial grinding operation, the parts go through a second grinding operation, after which they are painted. Partially completed parts are stored temporarily between each step. Upon completion, the parts are transferred by cart to packing.

The process described above clearly adds value—there would be no saleable product without it. But what are the value-adding and non-value-adding activities, and can they be improved? We start by converting the factory-floor layout in Exhibit 4.17 to the tabular format in Exhibit 4.18. The first column in Exhibit 4.18 assigns step numbers to each activity. The second column indicates the nature of each activity using one of the four symbols shown in the box at the bottom of the exhibit. The third column gives a description of each activity.

The fourth and fifth columns separate each activity into value-adding and non-value-adding functions, expressed in minutes. For example, the first activity—storing parts—requires an average of 30 minutes. Storage time adds no value from the customer's standpoint. However, it increases processing time, plus it ties up funds in inventories. After processing times for all 19 activities are added together, the total—the *cycle time*—is 104 minutes. Only 18 minutes, or 17.31 percent, of the cycle time is expended for value-adding activities. The percentage of value-adding time (in minutes) relative to total cycle time is known as **cycle efficiency.**

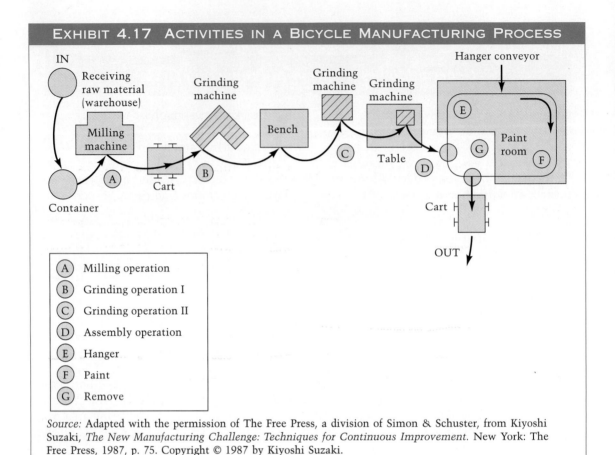

EXHIBIT 4.17 ACTIVITIES IN A BICYCLE MANUFACTURING PROCESS

(A) Milling operation

(B) Grinding operation I

(C) Grinding operation II

(D) Assembly operation

(E) Hanger

(F) Paint

(G) Remove

Source: Adapted with the permission of The Free Press, a division of Simon & Schuster, from Kiyoshi Suzaki, *The New Manufacturing Challenge: Techniques for Continuous Improvement.* New York: The Free Press, 1987, p. 75. Copyright © 1987 by Kiyoshi Suzaki.

Cost figures are shown in the last three columns of Exhibit 4.18. Only $64 out of a total process cost of $180, or 35.56 percent of the total, is expended for value-adding activities. Relatively low cycle efficiency and a low percentage of value-adding figures indicate opportunities for improvement.

Non-value-adding activities are considered waste. In fact, *waste* can be described as "anything other than the minimum amount of equipment, materials, parts, space and worker's time which are [*sic*] absolutely essential to add value to the product."[17] Consider some of the sources of waste listed below and depicted by the figures in Exhibit 4.19:[18]

- *Overproduction*—Getting ahead of work
- *Waiting time*—Waiting for material to work on or watching machines operate
- *Transportation*—Excess handling of inventory
- *Process*—Inefficient use of equipment or personnel

[17] Fujio Cho of Toyota, as quoted in Kiyoshi Suzaki, *The New Manufacturing Challenge: Techniques for Continuous Improvement.* New York: The Free Press, 1987, p. 8.
[18] Kiyoshi Suzaki, op. cit., pp. 9–10.

EXHIBIT 4.18 VALUE-ADDING AND NON-VALUE-ADDING ACTIVITIES IN A MANUFACTURING PROCESS

Step Number	Process Symbol	Activities	Value-Adding, min.	Non-Value-Adding, min.	Total min.	Value-Adding, Cost	Non-Value-Adding, Cost	Total Cost
1	▽	Storage		30.00	30.00		$ 37.50	$ 37.50
2	▽	Transfer by cart		0.50	0.50		$ 1.75	$ 1.75
3	▽	Storage		4.00	4.00		$ 5.00	$ 5.00
4	Ⓐ	Milling operation	7.00		7.00	$23.00		$ 23.00
5	▽	Storage		8.00	8.00		$ 10.00	$ 10.00
6	▽	Transfer		0.50	0.50		$ 1.75	$ 1.75
7	▽	Storage		14.00	14.00		$ 17.50	$ 17.50
8	Ⓑ	Grinding operation I	1.50		1.50	$ 4.50		$ 4.50
9	▽	Storage		5.00	5.00		$ 6.25	$ 6.25
10	Ⓒ	Grinding operation II	0.75		0.75	$ 3.00		$ 3.00
11	▽	Transfer		0.50	0.50		$ 1.75	$ 1.75
12	▽	Storage		3.00	3.00		$ 3.75	$ 3.75
13	Ⓓ	Assembly operation	4.50		4.50	$12.00		$ 12.00
14	☐	Inspection		0.75	0.75		$ 6.00	$ 6.00
15	▽	Storage		4.75	4.75		$ 6.25	$ 6.25
16	Ⓔ	Hanger	0.50		0.50	$ 2.00		$ 2.00
17	Ⓕ	Paint	3.25		3.25	$18.00		$ 18.00
18	Ⓖ	Remove	0.50		0.50	$ 1.50		$ 1.50
19	▽	Storage in cart		15.00	15.00		$ 18.50	$ 18.50
		Total	18.00	86.00	104.00	$64.00	$116.00	$180.00

Process Symbols:

◯ = operation
▽ = transfer
▽ = store
☐ = inspect

Cycle efficiency = $\dfrac{18.00}{104.00}$ **17.31%**

Percent value adding = $\dfrac{\$\ 64.00}{\$180.00}$ **35.56%**

Source: Adapted with the permission of The Free Press, a division of Simon & Schuster, from Kiyoshi Suzaki, *The New Manufacturing Challenge: Techniques for Continuous Improvement.* New York: The Free Press, 1987, pp. 75–78. Copyright © 1987 by Kiyoshi Suzaki.

EXHIBIT 4.19 WASTE IN A FACTORY

Source: Adapted with the permission of The Free Press, a division of Simon & Schuster, from Kiyoshi Suzaki, *The New Manufacturing Challenge: Techniques for Continuous Improvement.* New York: The Free Press, 1987, pp. 9–10. Copyright © 1987 by Kiyoshi Suzaki.

- *Inventory*—Too much inventory
- *Motion*—Time not spent adding value
- *Product defects*—Time spent on rework and correcting defects

IDENTIFYING ROOT CAUSES

After non-value-adding (wasteful) activities are identified, managers must evaluate whether or not these activities can be eliminated. For example, activities such as storing materials (in step 1 of Exhibit 4.18) or transferring materials by cart (in step 2) add no value. The next question is, how can the manufacturing process be improved without sacrificing product quality or compromising customer satisfaction? The answer lies in the identification of the reasons for inefficiency, or the root cause. The root cause of inefficiency can be traced to a variety of sources, including poor process design, poor product design, inadequate training, processes not functioning in accordance with design, poor organizational structures, and inappropriate measures of performance. To illustrate finding the root cause, consider the following scenario:

> Let's say you identified moving the product between two processes as very inefficient or perhaps even nonessential. The customer doesn't care how you move the product from one process to another because moving the product doesn't affect what's received. So moving the product is a non-value-adding activity.
>
> But how to you eliminate or make more efficient the moving activity? You can't, not while there is distance between the two processes. Failure to move the product would result in piles of inventory at the end of the first process and no work for the second process.
>
> The distance between the two processes—a part of the plant layout—is the moving activity's cost driver. If you reorganize the plant to place the two processes next to each other, the cost driver is eliminated. It's no longer necessary to move the products over a distance.[19]

Understanding root causes can lead to eliminating waste and improving efficiency (see "Current Practice: Gillette Company"). By eliminating unnecessary activities and improving the activities that remain, managers are better able to achieve organizational objectives and satisfy customers' demands.

REDUCING ROOT CAUSES OF WASTE

Once root causes of waste are identified, they offer opportunities for improvement. "Current Practice: Hallmark Cards" offers an example of how processes can be improved. Other examples include:

- Processes can be reengineered.
- Products can be redesigned to reduce the number of parts or to reduce assembly time.
- Plants can be redesigned to reduce the distance between operations.
- Inspections can be reduced or eliminated.
- Production can be reorganized to eliminate inventory buildup.

---

[19] Peter Turney, "Activity-Based Management," *Management Accounting*, Jan. 1992, p. 22.

CURRENT PRACTICE

Gillette Company

Gillette Company uses advanced technology in manufacturing a flexible twin-blade razor—the Sensor razor. Gillette has to fit 10 parts together with microscopic precision—to one 25,000th of an inch. Moreover, this exacting level of precision has to be achieved at high production volumes—hundreds of millions of blades each year.

Gillette has been able to "shave off" fractions of cents from the cost of producing each unit. In the two years after the blade was first introduced, unit costs were cut by 30 percent. The goal was to reduce costs by another 10 percent over the next two years.

Gillette is unusual in U.S. industry—a low-cost, high-quality producer. Besides using laser welds and cameras that scan distances between the twin blades, Gillette's engineers learned how to make molded plastic parts faster and with even greater quality. In its pursuit of continuous improvement, Gillette started with a list of 30 problems whose solutions managers believed would improve productivity and reduce costs for the Sensor blade. Of the original 30 items, only 15 have been solved. However, the list now stands at 35, because other problems have been added. But that was not unexpected. According to the Sensor's production manager, improvement is a matter of constant evolution, a process that never ends.

Source: Lawrence Ingrassia, "The Cutting Edge: Using Advanced Technology, Gillette Has Managed an Unusual Feat: It Has Become Both the Low-Cost and High-Quality Manufacturer," *The Wall Street Journal*, Apr. 6, 1992, p. R6.

CURRENT PRACTICE

Hallmark Cards

The lifeblood of Hallmark Cards, with 1991 sales of $2.9 billion, is new greeting cards. Hallmark comes up with around 40,000 new cards each year, produced by 700 writers, artists, and designers. The process of developing new cards used to take nearly 2 years. In the meantime, employees nearly choked on a backlog of sketches, approvals, cost estimates, and proofs—all this while customer preferences were changing.

Starting in the spring of 1992, about half of the staff began working in teams on cards destined for a particular holiday. Teams are supported by artists, writers, lithographers, merchandisers, and accountants assigned to each holiday. Team members from all over the United States relocated to a 2-million-square-foot building in Kansas City so that they could work together in the same place at the same time. Hallmark expects the redesigned process to cut cycle time in half. Moreover, managers believe that the reorganization will not only save money but will make the company more responsive to changing consumer tastes.

Source: Rahul Jacob, "The Search for the Organization of Tomorrow," *Fortune*, May 18, 1992, pp. 92–98.

- Production can be redesigned to smooth product flow.
- New technology can be introduced.
- Workers can be trained to operate more efficiently.

Consider improvements in the layout of the bicycle manufacturing process first shown in Exhibit 4.17. Assume that the process is changed to the one shown in the factory-floor layout in Exhibit 4.20 and in tabular form in Exhibit 4.21. The machinery is rearranged in a tighter, U-shaped configuration. Workstations are moved closer together and inventory storage eliminated between stations. Overall cycle time declines from 104 minutes to 21.75 minutes, increasing cycle efficiency from 17.31 to 82.76 percent. As a result, activity cost decreased from $180 to $93.50, while the percent of value-adding cost increased from 35.56 to 68.45 percent.

The impact non-value-adding activities have on product cost and market prices is illustrated in Exhibit 4.22. The first column shows the full cost of making a batch of 100 units of a typical product. After adding a markup of, say, $50.00 per unit, the desired selling price comes to a total

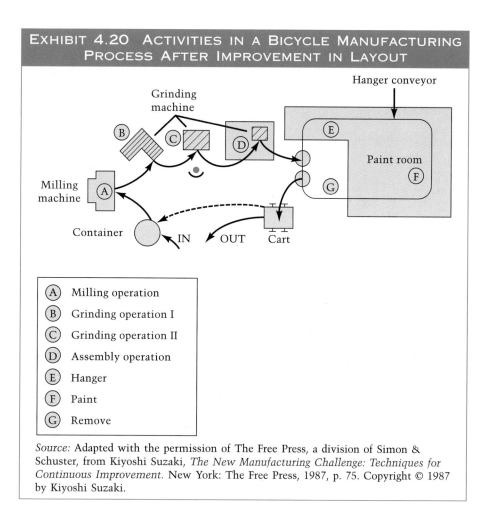

EXHIBIT 4.20 ACTIVITIES IN A BICYCLE MANUFACTURING PROCESS AFTER IMPROVEMENT IN LAYOUT

(A) Milling operation
(B) Grinding operation I
(C) Grinding operation II
(D) Assembly operation
(E) Hanger
(F) Paint
(G) Remove

Source: Adapted with the permission of The Free Press, a division of Simon & Schuster, from Kiyoshi Suzaki, *The New Manufacturing Challenge: Techniques for Continuous Improvement.* New York: The Free Press, 1987, p. 75. Copyright © 1987 by Kiyoshi Suzaki.

EXHIBIT 4.21 VALUE-ADDING AND NON-VALUE-ADDING ACTIVITIES IN A MANUFACTURING PROCESS AFTER IMPROVEMENT IN LAYOUT

Step Number	Process Symbol	Activities	Value-Adding, min.	Non-Value-Adding, min.	Total min.	Value-Adding, Cost	Non-Value-Adding, Cost	Total Activity Cost
1	▽	Storage		2.00	2.00		$ 5.00	$ 5.00
2	Ⓐ	Milling operation	7.00		7.00	$23.00		$23.00
3	Ⓑ	Grinding operation I	1.50		1.50	$ 4.50		$ 4.50
4	Ⓒ	Grinding operation II	0.75		0.75	$ 3.00		$ 3.00
5	Ⓓ	Assembly operation	4.50		4.50	$12.00		$12.00
6	☐	Inspection		0.75	0.75		$ 6.00	$ 6.00
7	Ⓔ	Hanger	0.50		0.50	$ 2.00		$ 2.00
8	Ⓕ	Paint	3.25		3.25	$18.00		$18.00
9	Ⓖ	Remove	0.50		0.50	$ 1.50		$ 1.50
10	▽	Storage in cart		1.00	1.00		$18.50	$18.50
		Total	18.00	3.75	21.75	$64.00	$29.50	$93.50

Cycle efficiency = $\frac{18.00}{21.75}$ **82.76%**   Percent value adding = $\frac{$64.00}{$93.50}$ **68.45%**

Process Symbols:
○ = operation
▽ = transfer
▽ = store
☐ = inspect

Source: Adapted with the permission of The Free Press, a division of Simon & Schuster, from Kiyoshi Suzaki, *The New Manufacturing Challenge: Techniques for Continuous Improvement.* New York: The Free Press, 1987, pp. 75–78. Copyright © 1987 by Kiyoshi Suzaki.

of $259.50. This represents the maximum price. The second column shows only those costs that contribute value. Eliminating non-value-adding costs reduces total cost from $209.50 to $152.70 and the desired selling price from $259.50 to $202.70. The desired selling price can be as much as 20 percent lower, while the profit margin of $50 per unit remains the same. Or, conversely, the company can make more profit on products whose price is determined by the market.

SUMMARY

Changing competition and changing technology have intensified the need for information. Traditional labor-driven allocation systems may be unable to provide the information that managers need in order to compete successfully. That's why new cost management systems are emerging. These

EXHIBIT 4.22 IMPACT OF VALUE-ADDING AND NON-VALUE-ADDING COSTS ON SELLING PRICE

Costs for a Batch of Product

	Maximum Price	Minimum Price
Value-adding cost:		
Materials	$ 9,000	$ 9,000
Packaging	600	600
Direct manufacturing labor	2,400	2,400
Shipping	1,200	1,200
Sales order taking	850	850
Scheduling	220	220
Sales promotion & commissions	1,000	1,000
Total value-adding cost	$15,270	$15,270
Non-value-adding cost:		
Scrap & spoilage loss	$ 1,200	
Setup	500	
Quality inspection	750	
Engineering changes	375	
Raw material moves	300	
Work-in-process material moves	325	
Finished goods moves	280	
Wait time	600	
Sales returns	850	
Warranty claims	500	
Total non-value-adding cost	$ 5,680	$ 0
Total cost of batch	$20,950	$15,270
Units in batch	100	100
Unit cost	$209.50	$152.70
Desired profit per unit, $s	50.00	50.00
Desired selling price	$259.50	$202.70

Source: Robert J. Campbell, *Competitive Cost-Based Pricing Systems for Modern Manufacturing.* Westport, Conn.: Quorum Books, 1992, p. 39. Copyright © 1992 by Quorum Books. Reproduced with permission of Greenwood Publishing Group, Inc., Westport, CT.

systems take a holistic view of the business by providing information for product costing and for finding opportunities for improvement.

The first step in activity-based costing is to identify activities. This begins with classifying high-level processes in an organization and translating them into more and more detail, until activities are identified. Once activities are identified, costs are attached to the activities through activity drivers. Cost of products, or any other cost object, is calculated by determining how much of each activity is included in the object.

Processes and activities can also be used as a basis for improving efficiency. Activities that add cost—but no benefit for customers—are reduced or eliminated. Activities that either directly or indirectly benefit customers are evaluated for improvement, often by comparing these activities with the best practices of other organizations by benchmarking.

CHAPTER 4 ASSIGNMENTS

DISCUSSION PROBLEMS

D4.1 (Identifying Activities)[20]

A water treatment facility at an oil well in Alaska provides a good example of identifying activities. The primary purpose of the water treatment facility is to provide water for drinking, although it is also used to prepare water for injection into oil formations. Untreated water contains elements that can affect both the formation and the pipes through which the oil flows. The water treatment plant in this example was so far from base camp that the workers ate and slept at the treatment facility.

Some of the primary activities performed at the facility included:

- Desalination of water
- Deoxygenation of water
- Chlorination of water
- Catering food for workers
- Providing living quarters for workers

Some people might argue that these are really subprocesses and that each group might be broken into even lower levels of detail. For example, the activity of providing living quarters for workers might include lower-level activities such as:

- Cleaning rooms
- Maintaining rooms
- Washing laundry

Based on the more broadly defined activities, managers decided to use the following activity drivers:

Activity	Activity Driver
Desalination of water	Gallons of water desalted
Deoxygenation of water	Barrels processed
Chlorination of water	Barrels processed
Catering food for workers	People fed
Providing living quarters for workers	Occupants

As the seasons changed, so did the processing requirements. For example, construction occurred in the summer, which meant less water was treated. If a field required more treated water, managers would see their total cost increasing for each gallon of treated water they used. If the incoming water quality changed, as it usually did, or if the desired outgoing quality changed, the cost per gallon processed changed.

The company identified the resource drivers that cause cost to increase or to decrease. Under these circumstances, activity drivers are also cost drivers. That is, as activity increases, total cost increases in proportion to increases in the activity driver. For example, the cost drivers for chlorinating water might include:

---

[20] Adapted from John Antos, "Activity-Based Management for Service, Not-for-Profit, and Government Organizations," *Cost Management*, summer 1992, pp. 13–23.

- Cost of materials
- Bacteria levels
- EPA (Environmental Protection Agency) requirements
- Weather
- Age of equipment
- Preventive and unscheduled maintenance
- Training of employees
- Fish going into intake tanks
- Water input and output quality

Itemizing these resource drivers gave the company insight into what drivers caused use of resources. Managers could focus on ways to eliminate or reduce the cost of the activities by reducing the cost drivers. For example, the company used screens to prevent fish from being introduced into intake tanks. This action increased the cost of preventive maintenance, but the cost was more than offset by reducing cost associated with unscheduled breakdowns.

As an oil field matures and production volume decreases, the amount of water treated increases, because more water is needed to replace the oil that has been pumped out of the ground. Therefore, budgeting water treatment based on production volume would not make any sense. Budgeting based on activities helps managers of the water treatment facilities understand the operation better and find ways to reduce cost.

Not all activities, however, create value. For example, the oil production company considers the following activities to be non-value-adding:

- Cleaning up the chemicals sprayed from halon fire extinguishers in cases of false alarms
- Drilling holes incorrectly, requiring additional oil field services
- Engaging in litigation because of spills and violations
- Reworking wells because the field is not being operated properly
- Handling accidents
- Failing to build housing or production facilities correctly

Required: What are some of the ways managers might use this information about the water treatment facility at an oil well?

D4.2 (Process Improvement)[21]

Process improvements began at Henry Ford Hospital, a 903-bed not-for-profit hospital in downtown Detroit, with an analysis of the hospital's financial performance. After an evaluation of some of the more common procedures, chemotherapy stood out as a good candidate for improvement, says William Scramm, Ford's vice president for management services. Chemotherapy cost jumped 14 percent in 1990. That's compared with an increase of only 2% in reimbursement that the hospital receives. Rather than arbitrarily cutting costs, Ford assembled a team of doctors, nurses, and administrators with instructions to look for ways to reduce outlays without sacrificing the quality of care.

Based on its initial study, the team found that about 30 percent of the hospital's 800 chemotherapy patients are treated with high doses of a tumor-killing drug called *cisplatin*. Unfortunately, cisplatin has two severe side effects. It ravages

[21] Ron Winslow, "Health-Care Providers Try Industrial Tactics to Reduce Their Costs," *The Wall Street Journal,* Nov. 3, 1993, pp. A1 and A6.

the kidneys, and it causes vomiting. Vomiting creates serious problems, since it reduces the patient's intake of fluids that help protect the kidneys from the drug. The team zeroed in on the average 3- to 4-day stay at the hospital for a typical cancer patient. After being admitted the day before treatment, patients begin to "bulk up" on liquids. Then they stay another 2 days after treatment taking anti-nausea drugs.

Using quality improvement techniques, the team mapped out the entire treatment process from admission to discharge. Nurses on the team offered the first important suggestion, based on the insight they gained from the map. Why couldn't patients be given detailed instructions on how to take fluids at home the day before coming to the hospital and keep a record of their liquid consumption? That way chemotherapy could start the day the patient entered the hospital.

Doctors figured that if they could control nausea, patients could be discharged in one day after treatment rather than two. However, they needed a blood test in the afternoon of the day of discharge to make sure that the patient's kidneys had stood up to the side effects of cisplatin. But getting the afternoon test taken and the results in the doctor's hands created yet another problem. The test itself only took 2 minutes. However, ordering the test, transcribing the order, drawing blood, delivering it to the lab, and notifying the doctor all added up to an extra day. The team's task was to trim the process down to 2 hours.

Lab managers, responsible for more than 1,200 routine tests each day, were, at first, reluctant to agree to afternoon tests. They did agree, though, that early afternoon would be a good time to perform the test. With this breakthrough concession, the team recommended drawing blood from patients at 1 p.m. Blood samples would be tagged with special red stickers to alert the lab to expedite the test and get it back to the doctors by 3 p.m. With this new procedure, patients could go home by 5 p.m.

Another change the team suggested was getting admittance counselors to set aside beds for chemotherapy patients. That way, treatment wouldn't be delayed. Also, nurses were to be required to call patients at home the day after discharge to ensure that they were taking enough liquids.

None of this would have been possible without a new antinausea drug made by Glaxo. Although the drug costs the hospital about $130 per dose, it is more effective and cheaper than another day in the hospital.

Today, nearly 80 percent of chemotherapy patients are successfully discharged after only one night in the hospital. Henry Ford has benefited as well. The margin of revenue over expense for all chemotherapy patients has averaged about $750 per patient, nearly $350 above that for 1990.

Required: Cite some examples of how analysis of the chemotherapy process helped the Henry Ford Hospital.

PROBLEMS   **P4.1 (Activity Drivers)[22]**

Davidson Pharmaceutical's marketing research department recently conducted a study to determine the nature and cost of its primary activities. The results, shown in Exhibit P4.1.1, represent data for the current year. For example, handling technological resources cost Davidson $320,000 per year.

---

[22] Adapted from "Minicase: Applying ABC to Market Research," *Cost Management Update,* Apr. 1994, pp. 1–2.

EXHIBIT P4.1.1 DAVIDSON PHARMACEUTICALS

Marketing Research Department Costs

| | Activity | | | | | |
General Ledger Account	Information Retrieval	Reports & Presentations	Market Research	Business Analysis	Technological Resource Handling	Total
Salaries & benefits	$ 90,000	$135,000	$100,000	$255,000	$220,000	$800,000
Dues & subscriptions	2,000	3,000	5,000	7,000	8,000	25,000
Travel & entertainment	0	22,000	35,000	45,000	23,000	125,000
Hardware	5,000	2,000	2,000	4,000	12,000	25,000
Software	18,000	35,000	9,000	16,000	12,000	90,000
Outside services	61,000	0	5,000	35,000	24,000	125,000
Training & development	0	6,000	7,000	0	7,000	20,000
Miscellaneous	4,000	7,000	7,000	8,000	14,000	40,000
Total	$180,000	$210,000	$170,000	$370,000	$320,000	$1,250,000

EXHIBIT P4.1.2 DAVIDSON PHARMACEUTICALS

Activity Drivers for Marketing Research Department

Activity	Activity Driver	Volume of Activity Driver
Information retrieval	No. of requests	7,400
Reports & presentations	No. of presentations	320
Market research	No. of projects	125
Business analysis	No. of prospects, studies	180
Technological resource handling	No. of workstations	14

Activity drivers for marketing research are shown in Exhibit P4.1.2. Information retrieval activity, for instance, is measured by the number of requests, which totals 7,400 in the current year.

Required: Calculate the unit cost of performing each activity.

P4.2 (Activity Costs)

Cleaning Compounds, Inc. makes private-label commercial cleaning products. Recently, the sales staff received a request for quote from Power Chemical, which wants 400 bottles of cleaning agent. Before quoting a price, Cleaning Compounds, Inc. gathered the manufacturing cost data shown in Exhibit P4.2. These costs include all direct labor and manufacturing overhead. For example, the remove compounds from storage activity costs Cleaning Compounds, Inc. $147,775 per year and is assigned to products based on the number of material requisitions. Since 5,750 requisitions are anticipated for next year, each requisition is expected to cost $25.70. Manufacturing cost is estimated by adding direct materials cost to activity cost.

Managers estimate that the Power Chemical job will require $112.75 in raw materials and will entail the following manufacturing activities:

EXHIBIT P4.2   CLEANING COMPOUNDS, INC.

Cost Data by Activity for Manufacturing

Activity	Activity Driver	Activity Cost	Volume of Activity	Unit Activity Cost
Remove compounds from storage	No. of materials requisitions	$147,775	5,750	$25.70
Move compounds to mixing	No. of moves	40,740	8,400	$4.85
Mix chemical	No. of mixing minutes	253,200	60,000	$4.22
Bottle, label, & package	No. of labor-hours	78,750	4,500	$17.50
On-load delivery truck	No. of packages	95,760	6,300	$15.20
Total		$616,225		

- Remove compounds from storage—7 materials requisitions ×25.70
- Move compounds to mixing—2 moves ×4.85
- Mix chemical—32 mixing minutes × 4.22
- Bottle, label, and package—2.4 labor-hours ×17.50
- On-load delivery truck—4 packages ×15.20

Required: What is the manufacturing cost per bottle for the Power Chemical job?

P4.3   (Costing Two Products)

Zion Trailers makes several different kinds of vehicle trailers. Two of its most popular models are for boats and motorcycles. Under the current costing system, manufacturing overhead is assigned to trailers based on machine-hours. Next year, Zion expects manufacturing overhead to total $1,413,600 and machine-hours to total 35,340 hours.

Zion recently adopted a new ABC system, with the activity costs shown in Exhibit P4.3.1. In order to gauge the accuracy of the new ABC system, Zion prepared the data shown in Exhibit P4.3.2. These data represent activities required in building a typical motorcycle and boat trailer.

Required: Calculate the manufacturing overhead cost for a typical motorcycle and boat trailer using the current machine-hour–based costing system and the new ABC system.

P4.4   (Resource Drivers)[23]

Selma Mortgage Company offers mortgage services to home buyers. Most of the interaction with customers is over the phone. In fact, virtually all calls represent activities in one of three categories:

---

[23]   Adapted from Gilbert Y. Yang and Roger C. Wu, "Strategic Costing and ABC," *Management Accounting,* May 1993, pp. 33–37.

EXHIBIT P4.3.1 ZION TRAILERS

Activity Cost

Activity	Total Activity Cost	Activity Measure	Volume of Activity	Unit Activity Cost
Move materials	$ 140,800	No. moves	3,520	$40.00
Set up equipment	156,600	No. setups	783	$200.00
Fabrication	358,600	No. welds	71,720	$5.00
Move to assembly	68,100	No. moves	3,405	$20.00
Assembly	625,400	labor-hours	25,016	$25.00
Prepare for shipment	64,100	No. shipments	1,282	$50.00
Total	$1,413,600			

EXHIBIT P4.3.2 ZION TRAILERS

Activities for Motorcycle and Boat Trailer

Activity	Activity Measure	Volume of Activity	
		Motorcycles	Boats
Move materials	No. moves	12	5
Set up equipment	No. setups	2	4
Fabrication	No. welds	322	270
Move to assembly	No. moves	10	4
Assembly	labor-hours	118	90
Prepare for shipment	No. shipments	2	1
Machine-hours		125	125

1. Home buyers seeking mortgages typically call in to determine current interest rates. If the quoted rates are acceptable, callers then make an appointment with a loan representative to begin filling out the paperwork.
2. After meeting with loan representatives, customers make frequent calls to determine the status of their application. Applications typically take several weeks to complete because of the paperwork, such as credit reports and appraisals, that must be received before an approval can be authorized.
3. After the loan is made, customers call in with inquiries about loan service—for example, the current balance, whether or not payments have been received, or the balance in the escrow account.

Selma Mortgage Company, while trying to improve the way it prices services, gathered data on resource drivers for the phone center activities shown in Exhibit P4.4. For example, the $318,000 in salaries and benefits is attributed to activities based on dollars of salary cost. Another example is the telephone charge of $179,000, which is assigned to activities based on the number of minutes operators are on the phone.

Required: Assign the $600,000 in phone center cost to the three activities.

EXHIBIT P4.4 SELMA MORTGAGE COMPANY

Phone Center Activity Report

General Ledger Account	Total Cost	Assignment	Resource Driver	Total Resource Driver	Activities		
					Interest Rate Inquiries	Application Status Inquiries	Loan Service Inquiries
Salaries & benefits	$318,000	Attribution	Salary, $s	$318,000	$190,000	$89,000	$39,000
Telephone charge	179,000	Direct as-signment	Phone minutes	275,000	225,000	40,000	10,000
Management salaries	46,000	Allocation	Hours	1,400	420	630	350
Office rent	34,000	Allocation	Square feet	22,000	7,000	9,000	6,000
Equipment depreciation	23,000	Attribution	Depreciation, $s	$23,000	$6,500	$12,500	$4,000
Total	$600,000						

P4.5 (Activity Costs)

The Wellness Center began operations nearly five years ago with funds donated by a local benefactor.[24] Operating in a large leased facility crammed full of exercise equipment, the Wellness Center offers three basic activities:

1. *Weight training and exercise.* The 9,000-square-foot area devoted to weight training and exercise is packed with equipment. Training is self-directed, although staff members provide instructions on how to use each piece of equipment.
2. *Personal training.* Staff trainers in the weight training and exercise area are available to provide personal instruction.
3. *Weight loss.* An area within the Wellness Center is set aside for 30-minute sessions on weight loss. In addition to receiving instruction, weight loss clients are taught how to use the appropriate equipment in the weight training and exercise area.

The monthly cost of operating the Wellness Center is shown in Exhibit P4.5. Monthly charges for each of the three basic training activities include part of the Wellness Center overhead, assigned to each activity based on the amount of square feet occupied. Unit activity cost is calculated by dividing total activity cost, including the assignment of overhead cost, by the following activity drivers:

- Weight training and exercise—total number of clients (including personal training and weight loss clients)
- Personal training—training hours
- Weight loss—number of sessions

---

[24] The local benefactor is, in real life, Philip Crosby. Mr. Crosby's generous support in starting the Wellness Center in Winter Park, Florida, is a natural extension of his quest for quality—in every aspect of life.

EXHIBIT P4.5 THE WELLNESS CENTER

Operating Costs and Other Data

General Ledger Account	Wellness Center Overhead	Weight Training and Exercise	Personal Training	Weight Loss	Total
Salaries & benefits	$ 45,000	$15,000	$32,000	$26,000	$118,000
Maintenance contracts	7,000	6,000	1,000		14,000
Equipment depreciation		16,000		4,000	20,000
Facility lease	125,000				125,000
Utilities	23,000				23,000
Total	$200,000	$37,000	$33,000	$30,000	$300,000

Resource Driver

Square feet occupied (Wellness Center overhead)		9,000	0	1,000	10,000

Activity Drivers

Number of clients (weight training & exercise)		10,000	600	250	10,850
Training hours (personal training)			1,200		1,200
Number of sessions (weight loss)				1,000	1,000

Note that the monthly cost of both personal training and weight loss includes the cost of using the weight training and exercise area.

Required: Calculate the unit cost for each activity.

P4.6 (Basic Activity-Based Costing)[25]

Allen Chemical, located near the intersection of I-285 and I-75 on the outskirts of Atlanta, Georgia, operates a warehouse/distribution center designed specifically for carpet mills and textile manufacturers. Because of increasing competition, some of the manufacturers decided to concentrate on their core businesses. It seemed that many of them no longer wanted to carry costly inventories nor deal with the distractions such inventories create.

Textile company purchasing agents order chemicals, yarns, and dyes from suppliers and have them shipped directly to Allen. Upon receipt, Allen unloads the materials, prepares appropriate documentation, and confirms payment. Materials are stored until the textile company notifies Allen that it wants the materials delivered. Allen confirms the request, packages the materials in the size and quantity requested, repacks remaining materials, and makes delivery before 9 a.m. the following morning.

Allen Chemical bills customers by adding together the annual warehouse facility costs and all other costs of warehouse operations. Then it divides this sum

---

[25] Adapted from an article by Harold P. Roth and Linda T. Sims, "Costing for Warehousing and Distribution," *Management Accounting*, Aug. 1991, pp. 42–45.

by the number of pounds of materials normally processed each year. After a 25 percent markup is added to cover administrative cost and profit, customers receive bills for the number of pounds handled. The billing rate is currently $12.80 (per 1,000 lbs. handled). While this method worked well at the start, Allen is now looking at billing methods that don't average costs over all customers. Its goal is to charge companies for only those services they request.

Allen identified the major warehousing activities shown in Exhibit P4.6.1. Costs were then collected for each activity for the year, with the results shown in Exhibit P4.6.2.

To test the reasonableness of the warehouse activity costs, Allen pulled an order for carpet dye from its files at random. According to company records, warehousing costs for the order under the existing system totaled $1,920. This amount was calculated by multiplying the number of pounds handled (150,000 lbs.) in the

---

EXHIBIT P4.6.1 ALLEN CHEMICAL

Warehouse Activities

Activity	Description
Receipt of materials	Chemicals, yarns, and dyes are received via common carrier or boxcar and are unloaded by warehouse personnel.
Storage	Chemicals, yarns, and dyes are physically stored in warehouse bays.
Shipment of materials	Office personnel account for chemicals, yarns, and dyes shipped to the client's customers by company truck, customer's truck, or common carrier.
Inventorying	Inventories are physically counted by warehouse personnel and compared with the perpetual inventory records.
Deliveries	The company truck is used for deliveries to the client's local customers.
Repackaging	Materials are repacked upon request from the client.
Restencilling	Product labels are changed by removing old labels and replacing them with new ones.

Source: Adapted from Harold P. Roth and Linda T. Sims, "Costing for Warehousing and Distribution," *Management Accounting,* Aug. 1991, p. 44.

EXHIBIT P4.6.2 ALLEN CHEMICAL

Cost of Warehouse Activities for the Year

Activity	Total Cost, $s	Activity Driver	Units of Driver
Receipt of materials	$175,000	lbs. (000s)	118,000
Storage	430,000	Square feet	25,000
Shipment of materials	220,000	Bills of lading	6,740
Inventorying	140,000	No. of items	840
Deliveries	190,000	Bills of lading	1,750
Repackaging	45,000	lbs. (000s)	11,640
Restenciling	8,000	No. of drums	3,190

EXHIBIT P4.6.3 ALLEN CHEMICAL		
Warehouse Activities for an Order of Carpet Dye		
Activity	*Activity Driver*	*Units of Driver*
Receipt of materials	lbs. (000s)	150
Storage	Square feet	35
Shipment of materials	Bills of lading	4
Inventorying	No. of items	1
Deliveries	Bills of lading	2
Repackaging	lbs. (000s)	18
Restenciling	No. of drums	3

order by the billing rate of $12.80 (per 1,000 lbs. handled). The volume and type of activities relating to the order are shown in Exhibit P4.6.3.

Required: Calculate the cost of warehousing the sample order for carpet dye using ABC.

P4.7 (Comparing Plantwide Overhead Rates with ABC)

Richard (Dick) Mojena owns and operates a large commercial print shop in Salt Lake City. Dick's shop bids out jobs based on client specifications. He has been around the printing business long enough to know what kinds of bids have a good chance of winning contracts. To help assure keeping his largely fixed-cost facilities operating at full capacity, Dick generally gives a little more service than his competitors, whether faster turnaround times or higher-quality paper than specified. As a result, Dick has been very successful. That is, up until the last 3 or 4 years.

What changed things was a decline in advertising expenditures experienced by the printing industry. Several national magazines, mail-order catalogues, and mass mailers who send work to Dick suffered a downturn in business. With the loss of discretionary print dollars, some of these clients cut back the volume of work they send Dick. Even after their business started returning, many of Dick's clients were reluctant to return to their previous print levels. To make matters worse, excess capacity and fierce price competition kept Dick's profits low. According to Dick, scrambling for low-margin jobs became a way of life.

Dick's bidding system is based on estimates of direct labor and materials costs. Once he estimates these figures, he adds a markup on direct labor costs for production overhead. Production overhead for next year is expected to total $900,000, while direct labor cost should be around $600,000. Dick then adds a 25 percent markup on estimated production cost to get a bid price. The markup on production cost is intended to cover nonproduction overhead and yield a reasonable profit.

While Dick's bidding system worked fine for years, he's not so confident that he can trust the results anymore. Recently, he has been surprised by some of the bids it produced. Intuitively, Dick knows that some jobs are overcosted. While under- or overcosting jobs may not have mattered much in the past, overcapacity and strong competition have changed that. Today, Dick is forced to watch every penny.

EXHIBIT P4.7.1 MOJENA PRINT

Overhead Activities and Activity Drivers

Production Overhead	Total Cost	Activity Drivers	Volume of Activity
Print preparation	$320,000	Labor-hours	6,400
Printer setup	120,000	No. of setups	800
Equipment depreciation	120,000	Machine-hours	5,000
Materials setup	200,000	Purchase orders	4,000
Cleaning & maintenance	140,000	Labor-hours	4,000
Total production overhead	$900,000		

EXHIBIT P4.7.2 MOJENA PRINT

Two Sample Printing Jobs

	Job A37	Job B654
Type of client	Low volume Special order	High volume Normal production
Direct materials	$8,000	$112,000
Direct labor	$1,500	$18,000
Pages printed	100,000	1,400,000
Print preparation labor-hours	30	100
Printer setups	4	2
Machine-hours	8	112
Purchase orders	12	4
Cleaning & maintenance labor-hours	4	8

To get to the bottom of the problem, Dick asked a local CPA to make a study of his costing system and suggest ways it could be improved. After several weeks of work, the CPA came up with the data shown in Exhibit P4.7.1. Total production overhead cost is organized into five cost pools: print preparation, printer setup, equipment depreciation, materials setup, and cleaning and maintenance. Each cost pool has its own allocation base (activity driver). For example, the CPA felt that print preparation is best captured by the total hours of print preparation labor.

To see how well this system worked, Dick took data from two representative jobs he recently completed. One was a low-volume special order (job A37) while the other was a high-volume, normal production job (job B654). Data for these two sample jobs are shown in Exhibit P4.7.2.

Required: Calculate the bid price for jobs A37 and B654.

1. Use the existing direct labor dollar basis for assigning production overhead.
2. Use the ABC method.

P4.8   (Activity Costs for Reservation System)

Western Pacific Airways (WPA) operates flights to midsize cities west of the Rocky Mountains. Its strategy is to be *the* low-cost carrier while still offering basic ameni-

EXHIBIT P4.8.1   WESTERN PACIFIC AIRWAYS

Income Statement

Operating revenue:	
Passenger	$500,000,000
Cargo	2,000,000
Less agency commissions	(47,500,000)
Net revenue	$454,500,000
Operating cost & expense:	
Salaries, wages, & benefits	$220,000,000
Airplane fuel	85,000,000
Leased airplanes	24,500,000
Passenger services	26,800,000
Repairs & maintenance on aircraft	18,700,000
Depreciation	45,000,000
Other operating expense	67,000,000
Total operating cost & expense	$487,000,000
Operating income	$ (32,500,000)
Gain on disposal of aircraft	27,200,000
Net loss before income taxes	$ (5,300,000)

ties like reserved seating and in-flight meals. Unfortunately, because of a variety of internal, industrywide, and economic factors, WPA has not shown a profit, as indicated in the income statement in Exhibit P4.8.1.

One key piece of WPA's strategy was the creation of an internal reservation system called *AirNet*. WPA's directors felt that a reservation system would give the airline better access to potential customers, and an edge over competitors. AirNet was modeled after systems such as Sabre and Worldspan.[26] While AirNet is expensive, the directors felt that the volume of calls it generated and reservations for seats on WPA planes that it resulted in would justify the investment. WPA's plan from the very beginning, though, was to sell AirNet once it was up and operating. In fact, WPA had already organized a consortium of regional airlines, itself included, that would acquire and operate AirNet.

WPA's organizational chart is shown, in part, in Exhibit P4.8.2. The AirNet reservation system is treated as a service center under administration. AirNet operations are centralized in a facility near Seattle. The heart of the reservation center is an IBM mainframe linked to sophisticated communications networks. Phones tied to the computer are staffed by crews of reservation agents and supervisors, 24 hours a day, 365 days a year. After peak hours in the day, the number of agents on duty declines in conjunction with the volume of calls. Calls into the system are automated, branching to the appropriate destination based on the Touch-Tone choice of the caller. In fact, many flight status inquiries are handled by computer-simulated voices. While this feature reduces the load on reservation agents, they must still handle questions about flight times and ticket prices. AirNet's computer system monitors each call, keeps track of the elapsed time, and allows agents to assign the call to one of three categories:

---

[26]   Worldspan is a limited partnership between Delta, Northwest, and TWA.

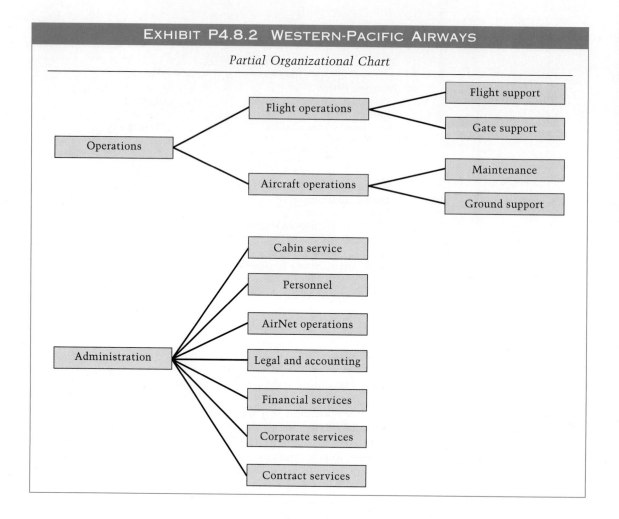

EXHIBIT P4.8.2 WESTERN-PACIFIC AIRWAYS

Partial Organizational Chart

1. Flight time, rate, and restrictions inquiries
2. Booking requests
3. After-booking inquiries

Calls to AirNet come from three types of customers. The first are individuals who place calls for themselves, either for pleasure or business. The second kind of calls come from individuals seeking reservations for a group, which WPA defines as 10 or more people traveling together. Typically, WPA offers discounts ranging between 5 and 10 percent of published fares for groups formed by individuals. The third kind of calls are from tour operators and travel agents who seek individual or group seats. Depending on the volume of seats booked by the travel agent, and the size and destination of the group, WPA can offer even larger discounts, sometimes as much as 15 percent below published fares.

WPA's costs include not only direct flight costs—such as crew wages, fuel, meals, and depreciation—but indirect costs. One of the indirect costs is the cost of operating the AirNet reservation system, currently budgeted at $15 million. With 700,000 bookings anticipated next year, each ticket price carries a booking fee of $21.43. WPA, though, is beginning to receive complaints from travel agents who demand larger discounts for group bookings. After reviewing their requests, it has become obvious that WPA needs to see if there is a better way of assigning reservation costs to ticket prices.

WPA gathered the data in Exhibit P4.8.3. The first column shows budgeted costs for AirNet operations, while the percentages represent the proportion of total budgeted costs consumed by each activity. For example, 23 percent of the total costs associated with inbound calls are for the automated flight arrival system.

WPA commissioned a study to determine whether or not individuals, non-tour-operated groups, and tour group operators require different services from the reservation system. These results, shown in Exhibit P4.8.4, represent typical activities

---

EXHIBIT P4.8.3 WESTERN PACIFIC AIRWAYS

Budgeted Costs and Utilization, by Activities

Budgeted Cost	Total Cost	Automated Flight Time & Information	Agent-Assisted Flight Time & Information	Book Seat	After-Booking Inquiry	Total
Direct charges:						
Inbound communications	$ 1,450,000	23.00%	28.00%	37.00%	12.00%	100.00%
Reservation agents & supervisors	6,710,000	3.00%	52.00%	32.00%	13.00%	100.00%
Computer operations	580,000	23.00%	28.00%	37.00%	12.00%	100.00%
Allocations:						
Facility cost	680,000	8.00%	39.00%	46.00%	7.00%	100.00%
Computer equipment	430,000	27.00%	26.00%	44.00%	3.00%	100.00%
Depreciation & amortization	3,750,000	31.00%	28.00%	37.00%	4.00%	100.00%
Corporate overhead	1,400,000	10.00%	22.00%	56.00%	12.00%	100.00%
Total cost	$15,000,000					
Activity driver	Bookings	Inquiries	Minutes	Minutes	Inquiries	
Volume of driver	700,000	2,500,000	3,285,000	1,872,000	158,000	

EXHIBIT P4.8.4 WESTERN PACIFIC AIRWAYS

Activities for Three Groups of Users

Product	Activity Driver	Volume
Individual:		
Automated flight time & information	Inquiries	3
Agent-assisted flight time & information	Minutes	4
Book seat	Minutes	6
After-booking inquiries	Inquiries	2
Groups formed by individuals:		
Agent-assisted flight time & information	Minutes	10
Book seat	Minutes	22
After-booking inquiries	Inquiries	18
Tour operator groups:		
Book seat	Minutes	46
After-booking inquiries	Inquiries	18

for each of the three customer groups. For example, a typical call by an individual might, on the average, entail three inquiries into the automated flight time and information system, 4 minutes of an agent's time for flight times and information, 6 minutes of an agent's time to book a seat, and two after-booking inquiries. Calls for this category of customers result in bookings for an average of two seats. Calls from individuals forming nontour groups require 10 minutes of agent-assisted flight time and information, 22 minutes to book seats, and 18 minutes of after-booking inquiries. These customers typically book an average of 12 seats. Tour operators, who have access to reservation systems in their offices, almost never use the automated system nor do they require agents' help other than to book seats. Group booking by a tour operator requires an average of 46 minutes of an agent's time. Furthermore, tour agents require considerably more after-booking assistance. On the average, 18 minutes are typically required to correct errors or to accommodate group members who change their minds. Tour operators, on the average, book 18 seats.

Required: What does it cost to provide reservation system assistance to each of the three groups of users with ABC? How does this compare with the $21.43 per ticket WPA is currently charging? Do these results provide WPA a justification for reducing reservation charges for groups formed by tour operator groups?

P4.9   (Introductory ABC; 4 Levels of Cost)[27]

Chicken Delicious operates a network of 250 fast-food restaurants throughout the United States. Its primary product is deep-fried chicken. With the current trend toward more-healthful food, competing chains like KFC (Kentucky Fried Chicken) and Church's have been experimenting with rotisserie-cooked chicken. With about 40 percent less fat than fried, rotisserie chicken is receiving lots of attention. But healthfulness is not the only appeal! The way chicken is roasted can seal in juices, making it more tender and flavorful. Plus, customers like seeing the open glass-and-steel rotisseries where chickens are cooked. Chicken cooked in this manner, however, has a downside. Uncooked chicken has a shorter shelf life. Another disadvantage is that it takes 75 minutes to rotisserie cook versus 30 minutes for fried chicken, limiting the ability to meet demand during peak lunch and dinner hours. Still another disadvantage is that rotisserie chicken spoils if kept under warming lights too long.

Regardless of its shortcomings, rotisserie chicken has been introduced by some of the major players in the chicken business. And for good reason! During its recent introduction of rotisserie chicken, KFC saw a substantial (15 percent) jump in sales volume. Today, KFC reports that nearly 25 percent of its sales in its company-owned stores are from rotisserie chicken. While the $700 million in sales from nonfried chicken is small when compared with the $6-billion fried chicken market, rotisserie chicken still represents a significant opportunity. And industry experts expect the gap to narrow within the next 10 years. Not to be left behind, Chicken Delicious's test kitchen is working on developing a rotisserie chicken recipe. In the meantime, the finance department is evaluating the impact of installing rotisserie equipment in all 250 restaurants in the chain.

Before making a decision about whether or not to put rotisserie chicken on the menu, company officials gathered the data shown in Exhibit P4.9. Some costs

---

[27]   Based on an article by Daniel M. Gold, "Big Bets on Roasted Chicken," *The New York Times,* Oct. 17, 1993, section 3, p. 7.

EXHIBIT P4.9 CHICKEN DELICIOUS

Data for Rotisserie Chicken Equipment

Sales volume:		
Number of stores		250
Estimate of the customers per store		
per day who will order rotisserie chicken		40
Menu price per whole chicken		$6.95
Food cost:		
Chicken	$1.15	per order
Basting spices	$0.12	per order
Condiments	$0.15	per order
Packaging	$0.07	per order
Labor and overhead cost:		
Utilities	$9,000	Per store, per year
Depreciation on rotisserie equipment	$10,000	Per store, per year
Preparation labor	$19.50	Once per day
Cleaning rotisserie oven	$4.75	Twice per day
Rotisserie setup	$12.75	Once per day
Labor cost to order chicken	$25.00	50 times per year
Advertising and promotion	$4,000,000	Product line per year
Amortization of R&D	$300,000	Product line per year
Corporate overhead	10.00%	Gross revenue

are incurred for each order of chicken, such as the cost of the chicken itself. Other costs are incurred for each of Chicken Delicious's restaurants. For example, rotisseries and other equipment have to be installed at a cost of $50,000 (depreciated over 5 years) for each store. Other costs represent product-level costs necessary to sustain the product line. Finally, corporate-level costs represent those incurred at headquarters to administer the new product line.

Required:

1. Prepare a projected income statement for the chain, reflecting the expected change in pretax operating profits from introducing rotisserie chicken. Assume restaurants are open 365 days per year. Organize costs in the four-level format introduced in this chapter. Use the following descriptions for the four levels: unit (order) level, store level, product level, and corporate level.
2. What does the average number of rotisserie chicken orders per store, per day, have to be in order to break even for the 250-store chain?

P4.10 (Assigning Costs to Activities)

CadieWay Products makes a thin, flexible, plastic-based film that is installed in automobile windows to protect against the sun. The product comes in a variety of different gauges, widths, and colors. While the company's primary focus is manufacturing, Mr. Cadie, the founder and president of CadieWay, created a distribution center several years ago. Organized as a service center with its own staff and manager, the distribution center is charged with responding quickly to customer needs. Almost all of CadieWay's accounts are local and regional distributors who purchase film in large rolls, rebundle the film in smaller packages, and distribute it to installers. Mr. Cadie believes his business adds value by delivering just the right film, just when the distributor needs it. CadieWay receives calls late in the afternoon for deliveries the next day. Distributors specify a desired delivery time, which CadieWay guarantees within one hour.

CadieWay recently installed an ABC system on the recommendation of Rolando Hall, the newly hired comptroller. In deciding where to start implementation, Hall focused on the distribution center. His first task was to trace costs from the general ledger to the distribution center, with the results shown in Exhibit P4.10.1. Simultaneously, Hall worked with a team of managers and employees to identify activities within the distribution center. After careful study, the team identified the following four activities:

1. *Preparing boxes for delivery.* Film is shipped in boxes. Distributors specify film length, width, and color, which determine box size. The film, stored on large bulk rolls, has to be transferred to smaller rolls and placed in boxes. Individual boxes are loaded onto pallets. When a shipment is complete, pallets are labeled and invoices attached. The activity driver is the number of boxes prepared for shipment. Normal activity is 20,000 boxes per year.
2. *Arranging for shipment.* Common carriers are contacted, and pickup times arranged. Information on carriers, schedules, and payment terms is maintained in CadieWay's databases. Invoices are prepared, tracked, and linked back to the accounting system. The activity driver is the number of shipments. Normal activity is 3,000 shipments per year.
3. *On-loading trucks.* Pallets are moved from the area where boxes are prepared for shipment and loaded onto delivery trucks. The activity driver is the number of labor-hours on-loading trucks. Normal activity is 5,000 labor-hours per year.
4. *Accepting returns.* Returned shipments are placed back in storage and credit slips prepared. Credit slips and other shipping documents are routed to shipping and to accounting. The activity driver is the number of returns. Normal activity is 300 returns per year.

EXHIBIT P4.10.1 CADIEWAY PRODUCTS

General Ledger Assigned Costs for Distribution Center

General Ledger Account	Assignment Base	Total Cost
Salaries & wages	(See Exhibit P4.10.2.)	$172,400
Benefits	20% of salaries & wages	34,480
Supplies expense	(See Exhibit P4.10.3.)	14,200
Liability insurance	No. of nonmanagement employees	21,700
Utilities expense	(See Exhibit P4.10.3.)	33,100
Depreciation—office equipment	Equipment used 95% for arranging shipping; 5% for returns	10,500
Depreciation—forklifts	Equipment used only to on-load trucks	13,500
Depreciation—facilities	Square feet (20% prepare; 10% arrange; 65% on-load; 5% returns)	45,000
Corporate—information support	Same as for depreciation—office equipment	23,000
Corporate—personnel	No. of nonmanagement employees	28,000
Corporate—administration	Based on nonmanagement salaries & wages	38,000
Total distribution center cost		$433,880

After identifying activities, Rolando Hall assigned costs from the general ledger to activities, using the assignment bases shown in the middle columns of Exhibit P4.10.1. Hall also collected data on salaries and wages for distribution center employees, as shown in Exhibit P4.10.2, and prepared a breakdown of supplies and utilities costs by activity, as shown in Exhibit P4.10.3.

EXHIBIT P4.10.2 CADIEWAY PRODUCTS

Analysis of Salaries and Wages for Distribution Center

Employee	Title	Job Description	Salary or Wage
Brown, D.	Shipping clerk	Contact common carriers. Arrange shipping pickup dates & times.	$ 22,100
Cohen, E.	Forklift operator	Move pallets from storage. On-load trucks.	18,000
Elizawan, K.	Shipping clerk	Maintain database of carrier schedules to arrange shipments.	24,500
Fitzgerald, T.	Shipping clerk	Prepare products for shipping. Attach delivery labels & invoice.	16,500
Gauthier, S.	Forklift operator	Move pallets from storage & on-load trucks.	18,700
Kerr, R.	Shipping clerk	Accept returns. Prepare credit slips.	20,400
Setti, S.	Manager	Manage distribution center. Spends 5% time in preparation to ship, 60% on arranging shipping, 30% on on-loading, & 5% on returned orders.	37,600
Stephens, P.	Forklift operator	Move pallets from storage & on-load trucks.	14,600
Total distribution center salaries & wages			$172,400

EXHIBIT P4.10.3 CADIEWAY PRODUCTS

Distribution Center Supplies and Utilities

Activity	Supplies Expense
Preparing for shipping	$ 8,750
Arranging shipping	1,200
On-loading trucks	3,800
Accepting returns	450
Total supplies	$14,200

Activity	Utilities Expense Base Charge	Metered kWh[a]
Preparing for shipping	$ 2,500	1,000
Arranging shipping	5,400	3,700
On-loading trucks	3,600	2,100
Accepting returns	600	200
Total base charges	$12,100	7,000
Metered utilities cost	21,000	
Total utilities cost	$33,100	

[a] kilowatt-hours

Required:

1. Assign the costs in the distribution center's general ledger to activities. Then calculate unit cost for each activity.
2. Assume a typical shipment requires preparation of 20 boxes, arrangements for 2 shipments, 2.5 hours to on-load trucks, and accepting returns for 1 box. What is the distribution cost for this typical shipment?

P4.11 (Comprehensive Product Costing Using ABC)[28]

Earthmovers, Inc., manufactures a wide range of industrial and commercial construction equipment. Its products range from tractors and front-end loaders to graders, backhoes, and fork-lift trucks. While Earthmovers' original market was the United States, it quickly became a global company. Today, Earthmovers has sales offices and manufacturing operations throughout the world.

Unfortunately, expenditures for heavy equipment slowed down in 1996 because of a glut in worldwide production capacity. Consequently, Earthmovers' sales declined from $976 million in 1995, with a pretax profit of $68 million, to sales of $938 million in 1996 and a loss of $55 million. These results are shown in Exhibit P4.11.1. In addition, Earthmovers began negotiating a new contract with its labor union in 1996. During the negotiations, it became clear to the directors that the new contract was likely to compromise Earthmovers' ability to compete against companies like Deere and Caterpillar. Moreover, Earthmovers was facing increasing protectionism in some of the countries where its products were sold.

Earthmovers expects demand to fall in the future for virtually all of its lines of heavy equipment, especially in logging and environmentally impacted markets. In addition, Earthmovers' relation with the labor union is expected to adversely affect worker productivity. Fortunately, company directors had begun a restructuring program in 1995 with goals of downsizing capacity and eliminating unprofitable operations. Their first move was to close outdated manufacturing facilities, causing writeoffs of $87 million in 1996. After that, the directors reviewed prod-

---

[28] Adapted from Lou F. Jones, "Product Costing at Caterpillar," *Management Accounting,* Feb. 1991, pp. 34–42.

EXHIBIT P4.11.1 EARTHMOVERS, INC.		
Consolidated Results of Operations		
	1996	*1995*
Revenue	$938,000	$976,000
Operating costs:		
Cost of goods sold	636,000	656,000
Selling, general & administrative expenses	118,000	108,000
Research & development expenses	152,000	144,000
Provision for plant closing & consolidation costs	87,000	0
Total operating costs	$993,000	$908,000
Operating profit (before tax)	$ (55,000)	$ 68,000

Note: Figures in $1,000s.

uct strategies to identify opportunities for price increases and areas where costs could be reduced. In addition, Earthmovers' directors began implementing an improved cost management system.

The new cost management system tracks direct materials costs to individual units of equipment. Similarly, direct labor costs are attached to products using a new bar-coding system. Manufacturing overhead, which was previously applied using a plantwide rate based on direct labor-hours, is now divided into four manufacturing overhead cost pools: (1) logistics, (2) manufacturing overhead, (3) assembly overhead, and (4) a catch-all category for hard to trace overhead costs called general manufacturing overhead. The cost of goods sold for 1996 is broken down into the cost pools and activity bases shown in Exhibit P4.11.2.

Logistics

Heavy equipment is made from large amounts of unformed materials, castings, forging, and purchased materials. Raw materials, like steel plate, are purchased and cast or forged into parts. Not only are the materials themselves expensive, but moving these heavy, bulky materials around inside the factory is costly. Logistics overhead includes costs associated with operating shipping docks, receiving areas, storage, freight, materials receiving, inspection, cleaning, purchasing, depreciation, utilities, insurance, property taxes, and maintenance.

Logistics overhead is divided into the following activities:

- Unformed weight based: Purchase unformed materials.
- Casting/forging weight based: Make castings and forgings.
- Unformed move: Move unformed materials within the factory.
- Casting/forging move: Move formed castings and forged materials within the factory.
- Purchased finished: Purchase finished parts and components from external suppliers.

EXHIBIT P4.11.2 EARTHMOVERS, INC.

Cost of Goods Sold for 1996 Divided into Manufacturing Departments

Cost of Goods Sold	Total	Logistics	Manufacturing Overhead	Assembly Overhead	General Manufacturing Overhead
Direct materials	$237,000	$47,000	$118,000	$72,000	
Direct labor	206,000	21,000	111,000	74,000	
Overhead:					
Indirect materials	48,000	3,000	28,000	17,000	
Indirect labor	37,000	2,000	22,000	13,000	
Supervision	29,000	2,000	17,000	8,000	$2,000
Equipment depreciation	41,000	2,000	28,000	10,000	1,000
Occupancy cost	38,000	4,000	27,000	6,000	1,000
Total overhead	$193,000	$13,000	$122,000	$ 54,000	$4,000
Total cost of goods sold	$636,000	$81,000	$351,000	$200,000	$4,000
Direct labor-hours	7,500	500	4,350	2,650	
Activity drivers for overhead cost pools		exhibit	labor-hrs.	exhibit	material $s
Units of activity driver		various	4,350	various	$237,000

Note: All figures in 1,000s.

Exhibit P4.11.3 shows data used to assign logistics costs to the five cost pools.

The basis for assigning costs to activities are called resource drivers at Earthmovers. For example, machine-hours are used to assign equipment depreciation to each of the five logistics cost pools. Once costs are collected in one of the five cost pools, they are assigned to products using activity drivers. The cost of unformed moves, for instance, is assigned to products based on the number of pounds of unformed materials moved.

Manufacturing Overhead
Manufacturing overhead includes the cost of operating machines, manufacturing cells, and work stations. Since all of these costs are assigned to products based on direct labor-hours, manufacturing overhead is not broken into separate activities. Instead, it is lumped together in one cost pool and assigned to products using labor-hours as the activity driver.

Assembly Overhead
Assembly overhead is organized into the five cost pools shown in Exhibit P4.11.4. Assembly overhead includes such activities as:

- Frame assembly: Assemble the frame, or backbone, of the equipment.
- Drivetrain assembly: Assemble and install the wheels, axles, drive shafts, motors, and transmissions.
- Finish assembly: The cab structure is placed over the drivetrain assembly; then wiring, glass, seating, and final components are installed.
- Paint: Paint the assembled equipment.
- Test: Test the equipment.

EXHIBIT P4.11.3 EARTHMOVERS, INC.

Logistics—Cost Pools and Activity Drivers

Direct Costs	Resource Driver	Unformed Weight Based	Casting/ Forging Weight Based	Unformed Move	Purchased Finished	Casting/ Forging Move	Total
Direct materials	attributed	$8,500	$10,500	$7,200	$14,200	$6,600	$47,000
Direct labor	attributed	$3,800	$6,100	$4,100	$2,700	$4,300	$21,000
Basis for Assigning Overhead to Activities							
Indirect materials	attributed	$540	$1,020	$660	$270	$510	$3,000
Indirect labor	hours	32,100	109,800	48,300	20,700	22,100	233,000
Supervision	$s direct labor	$3,800	$6,100	$4,100	$2,700	$4,300	$21,000
Equipment depreciation	machine-hours	2,700	19,800	4,400	2,200	4,500	33,600
Occupancy cost	square feet	31,000	75,000	49,000	29,000	56,000	240,000
Activity Drivers							
Activity driver for overhead cost pools	pounds	pounds	pounds	pounds	purchase $		
Units of activity driver		9,500	6,060	3,650	4,870	$2,100	

EXHIBIT P4.11.4 EARTHMOVERS, INC.

Assembly Overhead—Cost Pools and Activity Drivers

Direct Costs	Resource Driver	Frame Assembly	Drivetrain Assembly	Finish Assembly	Paint	Test	Total
Direct materials	attributed	$19,800	$27,600	$18,500	$4,600	$1,500	$72,000
Direct labor	attributed	$22,800	$21,700	$23,600	$4,300	$1,600	$74,000
Basis for Assigning Overhead to Activities							
Indirect materials	attributed	$5,400	$4,200	$3,600	$3,400	$400	$17,000
Indirect labor	hours	650	825	875	280	70	2,700
Supervision	$s direct labor	$22,800	$21,700	$23,600	$4,300	$1,600	$74,000
Equipment depreciation	machine-hours	73,000	104,800	63,600	4,500	19,100	265,000
Occupancy cost	square feet	175,000	212,500	168,750	56,000	12,750	625,000
Activity Drivers							
Activity driver for overhead		hours	hours	hours	hours	hours	
Units of activity driver		850	675	650	350	125	

The resource drivers used in assigning the cost to assembly overhead activities are shown in Exhibit P4.11.4. For example, dollars of direct labor costs is used to assign supervision costs to activities. Once costs are collected in cost pools, they are then assigned to products based on direct labor-hours, shown at the bottom of Exhibit P4.11.4.

General Manufacturing Overhead

The final component, general manufacturing overhead, includes costs such as manufacturing accounting, production control systems, employee relations, plant administration, medical services, scheduling, and inventory control. General manufacturing overhead is organized in a single cost pool and assigned to products using direct materials dollars as the activity driver.

Using this system, Earthmovers' accountants gathered the data shown in Exhibit P4.11.5. These data represent all of the manufacturing activities required to make a typical front-end loader, no. A-131.

Required: Calculate the cost to manufacture one no. A-131 front-end loader using the new cost system. Assume that manufacturing costs are the same as those experienced by Earthmovers in 1996.

P4.12 (ABC and Process Value Analysis)[29]

Part A:

Located in Sebring, Florida, SteelMan Corporation has been making free-standing carports for central Florida homes for nearly 30 years. SteelMan uses high-quality prepainted corrugated aluminum on all carports because of its light weight,

---

[29] Based on an article by Michael R. Ostrenga and Frank R. Probst, "Process Value Analysis: The Missing Link in Cost Management," *Cost Management*, fall 1992, pp. 4–13.

EXHIBIT P4.11.5 EARTHMOVERS, INC.

Manufacturing Costs for Front-End Loader, No. A-131

Cost Element	Base	Quantity	Unit Cost
Materials	various		$37,760
Direct labor	hours	1,528	$24.75
Logistics overhead:			
Unformed	pounds	1,820	
Casting/forging	pounds	960	
Unformed move	pounds	2,000	
Casting/forging move	pounds	3,500	
Purchased finished	material $s	$8,660	
Manufacturing overhead	hours	1,234	
Assembly overhead:			
Frame assembly	hours	54	
Drivetrain assembly	hours	89	
Finish assembly	hours	124	
Paint	hours	19	
Test	hours	8	
General manufacturing overhead	material $s	$37,760	

strength, and durability. Most of SteelMan's products generally sell between $2,500 and $7,500, although custom designs can sell for as much as $25,000.

Manufacturing Carports

SteelMan distributes carports to homeowners through a network of sales representatives. After closing a deal, representatives fax dimensions, materials, and target delivery dates to SteelMan's administrative offices. Computers schedule the design and a preliminary production date. On the design date, job specifications are plugged into the computer, which generates fabrication schematics and a bill of materials. On the fabrication date, workers build the carport using two distinct processes: metal cutting and assembly. Metal-cutting activities begin by gathering all the parts and the appropriate size sheets of corrugated aluminum from inventory. The aluminum is cut to custom size by workers using high-speed metal saws. Before moving to assembly, the shop manager inspects the materials for quality and to see that dimensions conform to customer specifications.

The sheets of aluminum are moved across the factory floor to an assembly area where they are placed in a large, flexible frame that holds all the pieces in place. The flexible frame must be broken down before each job and rebuilt (called a *changeover*) to meet the dimensions of the carport being assembled. Workers then attach structural supports to the corrugated aluminum pieces that form the top and sides. Upon completion, the carport is broken down for shipment and reassembly at the construction site. Details of metal-cutting and assembly activities, as well as activity drivers, are shown in Exhibit P4.12.1.

Cost System

Manufacturing cost includes materials, direct labor, and manufacturing overhead. Manufacturing overhead includes the metal-cutting and assembly activities described above and is charged to jobs based on direct labor dollars. The overhead rate SteelMan plans to use next year is 300 percent of direct labor cost, calculated by dividing $2,735,000 in projected manufacturing overhead by an estimated $912,000 in direct labor dollars.

Competitive pressures have prompted SteelMan to consider a more sophisti-

EXHIBIT P4.12.1 STEELMAN CORPORATION

Manufacturing Processes, Activities, and Costs

Process	Activity	Cost	Activity Driver	Quantity
Metal cutting	Materials handling	$ 300,000	Pieces	50,000
	Setup scheduling	200,000	Work orders	1,000
	Conversion	800,000	Labor-hours	8,000
	Inspection	100,000	Work orders	1,000
	Maintenance	150,000	Machine-hours	4,000
	Total	$1,550,000		
Assembly	Materials handling	$ 200,000	Pieces	10,000
	Changeover	100,000	Work orders	1,000
	Conversion	720,000	Labor-hours	6,000
	Inspection	90,000	Work orders	1,000
	Breakdown	75,000	Work orders	1,000
	Total	$1,185,000		
Total manufacturing overhead		$2,735,000		

EXHIBIT P4.12.2 STEELMAN CORPORATION

Activities and Costs for Two Sample Jobs

		Rey Job	Stone Job
		Direct Costs	
Direct materials		$1,150	$1,550
Direct labor		810	567
Total direct cost		$1,960	$2,117

Activity	Activity Driver	Volume of Activity Driver	
Metal cutting:			
Materials handling	Pieces	13.00	9.00
Setup scheduling	Work orders	1.00	2.00
Conversion	Labor-hours	7.50	5.25
Inspection	Work orders	1.00	2.00
Maintenance	Machine-hours	0.50	1.00
Assembly:			
Materials handling	Pieces	6.00	4.00
Changeover	Work orders	2.00	2.00
Conversion	Labor-hours	5.00	3.50
Inspection	Work orders	2.00	2.00
Breakdown	Work orders	2.00	2.00

cated way of costing jobs. After talking to the firm's CPA, SteelMan decided to evaluate ABC software by conducting a pilot study. Its goal was to see if manufacturing costs for several typical jobs are substantially different from costs generated by the present system. With manufacturing overhead already broken down into activities, SteelMan needed only to calculate activity costs to see if there were any differences. Two jobs were selected (the Rey job and the Stone job) and the volume of activities recorded, as shown in Exhibit P4.12.2.

EXHIBIT P4.12.3 STEELMAN CORPORATION

Elapsed Time for Value-Adding and Non-Value-Adding Activities

Process	Activity	Activity Driver	Elapsed Time, Hours per Unit	VA or NVA[a]
Metal cutting	Materials handling	Pieces	5.7	NVA
	Setup scheduling	Work orders	3.4	NVA
	Conversion	Labor-hours	38.0	VA
	Inspection	Work orders	0.4	NVA
	Maintenance	Machine-hours	1.5	NVA
Assembly	Materials handling	Pieces	9.2	NVA
	Changeover	Work orders	4.6	NVA
	Conversion	Labor-hours	34.6	VA
	Inspection	Work orders	1.3	NVA
	Breakdown	Work orders	3.7	NVA

[a] VA indicates value-adding; NVA indicates non-value-adding.

Required:

1. Calculate activity costs for each of the activities in Exhibit P4.12.1.
2. Calculate the manufactured costs for the two sample carport jobs, using SteelMan's current labor-based system and the new ABC system.

Part B:

Process Value Analysis

After calculating costs for the two sample jobs, managers decided to adopt ABC. After several months of working with the new system, SteelMan's controller began asking the software representative about other uses of the system. Specifically, the controller had heard the representative mention process value analysis in her sales pitch. She stated that ABC could help separate value-adding from non-value-adding activities. Non-value-adding activities could be eliminated, while value-adding activities could be targeted for improvement.

Using the metal-cutting and assembly activities, SteelMan managers calculated total elapsed time (in hours) required to complete a typical carport. They also classified activities according to whether or not they felt the activity created value in the eyes of the carport's owner. The results are shown in Exhibit P4.12.3.

Required: Separate metal-cutting and assembly activities into value-adding and non-value-adding hours. Next, calculate cycle efficiency for each of the two processes.

CASES

C4.1 (Masters Manufacturing)[30]

Masters Manufacturing, located in Princeton, New Jersey, makes residential gas cooktops. Its products, distributed nationwide, are sold through a network of appli-

---

[30] Adapted from William D. J. Cotton, "The Factory in Transition," *Cost Management*, fall 1993, pp. 65–68.

ance dealers. Most cooktops on the market are electric, leaving a niche for those few manufacturers, like Masters, with gas-fed products. While it enjoys little direct competition, the firm's market is small. Masters sold only about 18,000 ranges last year. With the slowdown in housing construction, it expects volume to decline to around 17,000 cooktops for the coming year.

Cooktops, unlike free-standing stoves, don't include ovens. This allows more flexibility in arranging kitchen layouts—plus it gives homeowners the ability to mix different brands of appliances. A negative feature of gas cooktops is that installation is more difficult than simply plugging in a free-standing electric stove. An opening has to be created for the cooktop by either leaving a space in the counter or by cutting a hole after the counter is installed. Ventilation systems are built right into the cooktops but require outside ducts and electrical hookups. Finally, gas lines have to be connected by certified technicians. As a result, installation costs can easily add several hundred dollars to the cost of the cooktop itself.

Masters cooktops are associated with an image of quality. Each model has an industrial, "restaurant" look that many homeowners find attractive. All cooktops are made from heavy-gauge stainless steel with cast-iron metal burners. Heavy construction adds durability and enhances the image associated with professional chefs ("True masters use Masters"). There are four models in Masters' line:

1. *4BS.* Standard, 36-in. by 22-in. model with four burners.
2. *6BS.* Standard, 36-in. by 22-in. model with six burners.
3. *6BC.* Commercial, six-burner model made from heavier-gauge stainless steel. It includes a "superburner," larger than the other five, that puts out almost twice the BTUs. Commercial six-burners come in three different, standard sizes.
4. *6BCU.* Custom, six-burner model with superburner. Sized in any dimensions customers want. It is available in two different finishes (bright or burnished) and in burner configurations specified by the customer. For example, customers may want all six burners pushed up against one side, leaving an open area for hot pots and pans.

All four models are fabricated with automated equipment that shapes the cooktop and punches all burner openings. Standard models (4BS and 6BS) require no change in standard production settings. The major difference between the two is materials and the installation of two more burners in the 6BS. Lower-volume commercial (6BC) and custom models (6BCU) require stopping the automated equipment, changing standard settings, and inserting stainless steel with the appropriate gauge and finish.

At a recent meeting, Masters's executive committee, composed of Ron Masters (president and CEO), Charlie Edmondson (controller), Ted Veit (marketing director), and Susan Higgins (vice president—manufacturing) discussed their plans for the coming year:

Ron Masters (CEO): OK, you all know that Charlie is working on a new cost system. I'll talk about that in a few minutes. To get started, I want to remind everyone that our policy is to add 22 percent on top of full manufacturing cost to cover nonmanufacturing cost. Then we add another 8 percent of full cost—that's including nonmanufacturing—to give us a fair return.

Ted Veit (marketing director): I'll agree with the 8 percent, since we still control a niche in the market. As you are aware, there are only a few of us in gas appliances. However, I know some of the major appliance manufacturers are looking at gas as a way to fill excess capacity. What I'm saying is that we can still pass along our costs, but we have to be careful. If our prices are outrageous, we either lose customers or invite competition.

Charlie Edmondson (controller): Speaking of costs, let's take a look at next year's manufacturing overhead. I've got it broken down into six major manufacturing cost pools and a catch-all category called "general manufacturing overhead." For next year, my best estimate is that manufacturing overhead ought to be right around $5.39 million. You can see the details in Exhibit C4.1.1. My second

EXHIBIT C4.1.1 MASTERS MANUFACTURING

Details of Manufacturing Overhead Cost

Machine setup cost:	
Setup salaries	$ 670,000
Indirect materials	93,000
Total machine setup cost	$ 763,000
Machine operations cost:	
Repairs & maintenance	$ 653,000
Utilities & power	103,000
Supplies, lubricants, & tools	75,000
Insurance	82,000
Depreciation	840,000
Total machine operations cost	$1,753,000
Occupancy cost:	
Repair & maintenance	$ 99,000
Custodial	46,000
Utilities & heat	38,000
Insurance	20,000
Property taxes	41,000
Facility depreciation	155,000
Total occupancy cost	$ 399,000
Materials acquisition & handling cost:	
Purchasing	$ 145,000
Materials handling	119,000
Warehousing	228,000
Utilities	97,000
Repair & maintenance	44,000
Equipment depreciation	321,000
Total materials acquisition & handling cost	$ 954,000
Process control cost:	
Supervision	$ 60,000
Indirect materials	34,000
Quality control & inspection	104,000
Depreciation of testing equipment	76,000
Total process control cost	$ 274,000
Engineering cost:	
Industrial engineers	$ 374,000
Product development	439,000
Depreciation of equipment	26,000
Total engineering cost	$ 839,000
General manufacturing overhead:	
Payroll & benefits	$ 65,000
Data processing	259,000
Security	84,000
Total general manufacturing overhead	$ 408,000
Total manufacturing overhead cost	$5,390,000

EXHIBIT C4.1.2 MASTERS MANUFACTURING

Pricing for Gas Cooktops

	4BS, Standard Four-Burner	6BS, Standard Six-Burner	6BC, Commercial Six-Burner	6BCU, Custom Six-Burner
Component cost:				
Direct materials	$ 90.00	$120.00	$150.00	$180.00
Direct labor	30.00	30.00	30.00	40.00
Manufacturing overhead (See rate below.)	310.96	310.96	310.96	414.62
Total manufacturing cost	$430.96	$460.96	$490.96	$634.62
Nonmanufacturing (22% of manufacturing cost)	94.81	101.41	108.01	139.62
Full cost	$525.77	$562.37	$598.97	$774.23
Profit (8% of full cost)	42.06	44.99	47.92	61.94
List price	$567.83	$607.36	$646.89	$836.17
Manufacturing overhead rate:				
Manufacturing overhead	$5,390,000			
Direct labor cost	$520,000			
Overhead rate per dollar of direct labor (rounded)	1,037%			

exhibit (Exhibit C4.1.2) shows target selling prices for next year. I've done what we always do in assigning overhead to products. That is, I've divided manufacturing overhead by direct labor cost to get an overhead burden rate. Next year, I'm planning on using 1,037 percent—a little more than last year. The results show target prices ranging from $567.83 for the 4BS (four-burner, standard) to $836.17 for the 6BCU (six-burner, custom).

Susan Higgins (VP—manufacturing): I certainly appreciate what you're doing, Charlie, but I think we are clueless about the real resources we consume in making each of our products. Commercial and custom models, for example, take a lot more time to set up. And, because they are nonstandard, they require more inspections. Moreover, it takes a lot of engineering time to see to it that everything fits together when you customize sizes and burner configurations—vents, electronics, and all the mechanicals. What I'm saying is, from a manufacturing point of view, I think the commercial and custom models ought to sell for more.

Ted Veit: Hold on, Susan. You're getting me worried. We are experiencing an increasing trend in sales of custom models. I'm afraid that raising prices might just shut off some of that demand.

Ron Masters: Ted! Let's go ahead and let Charlie talk about his new way of costing products.

Charlie Edmondson: OK, here's how it works. I've already collected costs for the primary manufacturing processes that you saw in Exhibit C4.1.1. General manufacturing overhead, found at the bottom of Exhibit C4.1.1, is assigned to the six manufacturing processes using the allocation bases shown in Exhibit C4.1.3. Then, costs for the six remaining manufacturing activities—after allocating general manufacturing overhead—are assigned to products using the activity drivers shown in Exhibit C4.1.4. I've gathered the data I think I need, but am not quite finished with the computations. So I'm not really prepared today to tell you if this is going to change costs and have any impact on prices.

Ron Masters: Why don't we adjourn and give Charlie a chance to finish. In fact, I'd like Charlie and the rest of you to be prepared to answer two important questions when we reconvene: What are prices with the new system and will it change our priorities?

EXHIBIT C4.1.3 MASTERS MANUFACTURING

Allocation Bases for Assigning General Manufacturing Overhead to Other Activities

General Manufacturing Overhead	Total Cost	Basis	Total	Machine Setup	Machine Operations	Occupancy	Materials Acquisition	Process Control	Engineering
Payroll & benefits	$ 65,000	Employees	130	4	16	10	40	40	20
Data processing	259,000	CPU hours	3,700	800	1,000	200	1,000	300	400
Security	84,000	Square feet	42,000	2,000	5,000	20,000	4,000	2,000	9,000
	$408,000								

EXHIBIT C4.1.4 MASTERS MANUFACTURING

Manufacturing Data

Activity	Activity Driver	Total Activity	4BS, Standard Four-Burner	6BS, Standard Six-Burner	6BC, Commercial Six-Burner	6BCU, Custom Six-Burner
Machine setup	Setups	1,200	200	100	400	500
Machine operations	Machine-hours	23,000	4,000	10,000	5,000	4,000
Occupancy	Production, in units	17,000	4,000	10,000	2,000	1,000
Materials acquisition	Raw materials cost	$2,040,000	$360,000	$1,200,000	$300,000	$180,000
Process control	Inspections	20,000	4,000	10,000	4,000	2,000
Engineering	Engineering hours	2,800	400	400	800	1,200
Other Data						
Units sold			4,000	10,000	2,000	1,000
Unit direct materials cost			$90.00	$120.00	$150.00	$180.00
Direct labor cost per unit ($20/hour × labor hours)			$30.00	$30.00	$30.00	$40.00
Direct labor-hours per unit			1.50	1.50	1.50	2.00

Required:

1. What are the costs and target prices for each of the four cooktop models under the new system?
2. Does this information change product priorities?

C4.2 (Marsicano Trucking)[31]

Ed Marsicano operates Marsicano Trucking out of San Francisco. While the trucking industry is quite competitive, Ed has found a niche. He recognized that moving relatively small amounts of perishable, temperature-sensitive products by truck created serious logistical problems for merchants. Putting small loads on large refrigerated trucks was usually impractical and almost always too expensive. Ed combined container technology he had observed on intermodal transport with refrigeration technology. He created lockable, insulated containers with microprocessor-controlled, liquid carbon-dioxide cooling systems.[32] The refrigerated containers, which look pretty much like large commercial refrigerators, can hold up to 2,000 pounds at precisely controlled temperatures as low as minus 40 degrees Fahrenheit (−40°F).

Ed transports refrigerated containers in his fleet of trailers, along with other types of freight. He specializes in next-day delivery in a market known as *less than truckload* (LTL). Ed's advantage is his scheduling staff, which is quite good at arranging multiple LTLs to make up a full load. A typical trailer can hold up to 20,000 pounds, or as many as 10 refrigerated containers. Ed's fleet, which he operates from a warehouse located near an interstate highway, consists of about 15 trucks and 40 trailers. The warehouse has 20 loading bays and about 25,000 square feet of dock space. The facility also contains nearly 20,000 square feet of warehouse

---

[31] Adapted from Jerry Jackson, "Shipping Small Loads No Big Problem for Company," Central Florida Business, *The Orlando Sentinel*, Oct. 18, 1993, p. 5.

[32] The individual refrigerated containers are built by Pallet Reefer Co. of Houma, Louisiana.

space, some of which is refrigerated. Ed employs about 25 people, including office staff, dock crews, warehouse personnel, and truckdrivers.

Last year's pretax operating income, as shown in Exhibit C4.2.1, fell to about 6.5 percent on revenue of $7.25 million. Ed knew that other truckers earned as much as 20 to 22 percent on revenue, and he felt that part of the reason for low returns was his outdated system of quoting prices for jobs.

Ed's pricing system is relatively simple. First, he estimates the weight of the load in tons and then figures out the number of miles it has to be hauled. Price quotes are determined by multiplying the number of tons by the number of miles the cargo is transported. This gives him the number of ton-miles that he multiplies by a standard rate. For example, a 1,000-mile trip with 2.5 tons of freight translates into 2,500 ton-miles. This figure is multiplied by the standard ton-mile rate to derive the quote.

Calculating the standard ton-mile rate starts with an estimate of total operating cost, generally around $6.775 million. Ed multiplies total cost by 18 percent—his desired return on cost—and adds this amount to total cost to get target revenue. That gives him the numerator in the standard-rate equation. He then estimates the number of miles his trucks are likely to drive for the year. Next year, Ed figures total mileage will be about the same as this year's 1.85 million miles. Then he multiplies the average load factor by the trailer capacity to get an average cargo weight. Since the load factor is generally around 80 percent and trailer capacity is 20,000 pounds, the average load is around 16,000 pounds, or 8 tons. Then he multiplies the average 8-ton load by the miles he expects his trucks to drive to get total ton-miles. The last step is to divide the desired total revenue by the estimated ton-miles. The result is the standard rate per ton-mile that Ed uses in his pricing equation.

Recently, Ed noticed that he was doing more and more short hauls rather than the longer-distance trips that were common several years ago. Ed is convinced that his costing system is to blame and has asked Lou Maraczk, his controller, to sort things out. One of the first things Lou did was to review the organization chart shown in Exhibit C4.2.2.

Using the current year's data, Lou broke general ledger accounts into variable and fixed costs, which he then spread to activities. The results are shown in Exhibit C4.2.3 and described below:

1. *Truck operations.* Truckdrivers' wages, plus travel expenses for multi-day trips.
2. *Trucks and equipment.* Oil, gas, and upkeep on trucks. Includes equipment depreciation.
3. *Scheduling.* Schedule freight and refrigerated loads for outbound trucks, usually multiple LTL. Schedule remote pickups for inbound return trips.

EXHIBIT C4.2.1 MARSICANO TRUCKING	
Income Statement for Last Year	
Trucking revenue	$7,250,000
Cost & expense:	
Truck operations	$3,045,000
Trucks & equipment	2,299,000
Scheduling, docking, & warehouse	935,000
Administration	496,000
Total	6,775,000
Operating income	$ 475,000

4. *Docking.* On-loading and off-loading containers and freight from trucks to loading dock.
5. *Warehouse.* Moving freight between docks and warehouse. Stacking and maintaining freight in warehouse.
6. *Administration.* Manage business activities, including legal, accounting, information systems, documents, personnel, payroll, insurance, and fees functions.

In addition, Lou identified bases that could be used to gauge activity; he also identified normal volumes for activity drivers. The results are shown in Exhibit C4.2.4.

Finally, Lou came up with two typical jobs that Ed could use in evaluating his pricing system. One was a typical 4-ton short haul of 250 miles, while the other was a 3-day, 1,500-mile, 8-ton long haul. The results are shown in Exhibit C4.2.5.

EXHIBIT C4.2.2 MARSICANO TRUCKING

Organization Chart

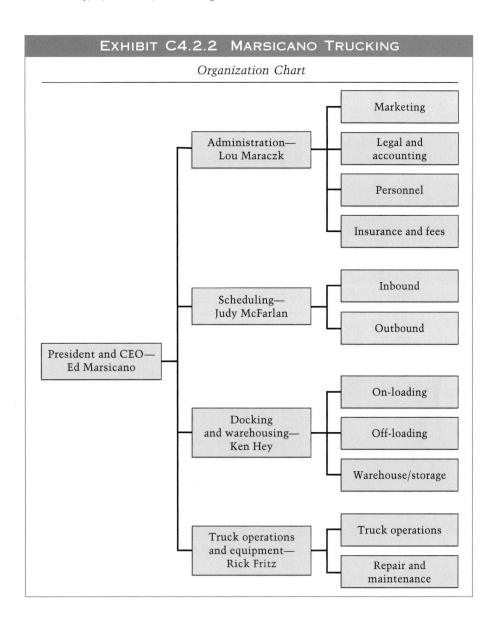

EXHIBIT C4.2.3 MARSICANO TRUCKING

Variable and Fixed Costs for Activities

General Ledger Account	Truck Operations	Trucks and Equipment	Scheduling	Docking	Warehouse	Administration	Total
Variable cost:							
Salaries, wages, & benefits	$2,340,000		$ 65,000	$240,000	$110,000		$2,755,000
Fuel & oil		$1,050,000					1,050,000
Tolls & fees		430,000					430,000
Travel expense	425,000						425,000
Total variable cost	$2,765,000	$1,480,000	$ 65,000	$240,000	$110,000		$4,660,000
Fixed cost:							
Salaries, wages, & benefits	$ 280,000	$ 450,000	$ 85,000	$165,000	$ 60,000	$225,000	$ 815,000
Equipment depreciation		124,000	25,000	80,000	50,000	45,000	650,000
Insurance & fees						36,000	160,000
Accounting						80,000	80,000
Personnel						65,000	65,000
Utilities						20,000	20,000
Repair & maintenance		245,000			55,000	25,000	325,000
Total fixed cost	$ 280,000	$ 819,000	$110,000	$245,000	$165,000	$496,000	$2,115,000
Total cost	$3,045,000	$2,299,000	$175,000	$485,000	$275,000	$496,000	$6,775,000

Required:

1. Calculate Ed's present ton-mile rate, and price the two typical jobs shown in Exhibit C4.2.5.
2. Prepare a quote for the two typical jobs using activity-based costing. Compare these quotes to the quotes based on standard ton-mile rates.
3. Why do you think Ed is getting more short-haul work?

EXHIBIT C4.2.4 MARSICANO TRUCKING

Activities and Activity Drivers

Activity	Activity Driver	Volume of Activity Driver
Variable cost:		
Truck operations	Driving days	5,475
Trucks & equipment	Miles driven	1,850,000
Scheduling	Trips	4,320
Docking	Labor-hours	26,000
Warehouse	Labor-hours	14,000
Fixed cost:		
Truck operations	Trips	4,320
Trucks & equipment	Trips	4,320
Scheduling	Stops	29,450
Docking	On-loads/off-loads	7,000
Warehouse	Transfer orders	13,500
Administration	Trips	4,320

EXHIBIT C4.2.5 MARSICANO TRUCKING

Activities for Two Typical Jobs

	Activity Driver	Short-Haul Units of Activity	Long-Haul Units of Activity
Number of tons hauled		4	8
Variable costs:			
Truck operations	Driving days	1	3
Trucks & equipment	Miles driven	250	1,500
Scheduling	Trips	1	1
Docking	Labor-hours	1	4
Warehouse	Labor-hours	0	0
Fixed costs:			
Truck operations	Trips	1	1
Trucks & equipment	Trips	1	1
Scheduling	Stops	3	8
Docking	On-loads/off-loads	6	16
Warehouse	Transfer orders	1	1
Administration	Trips	1	1

CHAPTER 5

PRODUCT COSTING AND FINANCIAL REPORTING

We concentrated on information for internal uses in the preceding chapters. Now we turn our attention to reporting the results of operations to **external users.** Our first step is to identify the information provided to external users and to contrast it with that provided to internal users. Financial information for external users must:

- *Focus on historical financial performance.* External reports include information about cost of goods sold (shown on the income statement) and the value of inventory (shown on the balance sheet). Income statements reflect actual, historical performance—actual revenues and actual costs. Similarly, balance sheets show assets and equities at historical values. Managerial accounting reports, on the other hand, supply prospective, forward-looking information. They are used to guide managers' actions in the future. The results of managers' actions show up in income statements and balance sheets in future periods.

- *Be based on measurable revenues and costs.* External reports are limited to financial information, such as revenues and costs, which are measurable in dollars and cents. Managerial accounting takes a broader view. It encompasses all data pertaining to resources available for use by the organization—whether financial or nonfinancial, measurable or immeasurable.

- *Rely upon authoritative standards.* Financial accounting relies upon standards that specify the kinds of information to be given to external users. In contrast, managerial accounting has no regulations that stipulate the kinds of information internal decision makers must receive. Managers need different kinds of information, supplied in different formats and tailored to meet the needs of particular situations.

We indicated earlier, in Chapters 2, 3, and 4, that managerial accounting information can be organized in different ways to meet different needs. External financial reports are, on the other hand, only designed to provide information that meets the needs of external users. However, managers may want, for example, costs organized by cost behavior in order to predict how their actions are likely to impact cost. Information in external reports doesn't provide costs organized that way.

As a result, managers using financial reporting systems as their only sources of information for internal decisions have two fundamental choices. They can (1) build supplementary, dedicated internal managerial accounting systems or (2) modify existing, externally oriented financial reporting systems to provide the information they need.

The first four chapters illustrated the kinds of information that managers need to make decisions. Some organizations have managerial accounting systems that are entirely separate from their financial reporting systems. Activity-based costing is one example of a system designed to supplement accounting information in order to improve decision making. However, many—and perhaps even most—managers don't have access to dedicated managerial accounting systems. Instead, they must rely upon information derived from the data provided for external reporting.

The purpose of this chapter is to show how information—information concerning cost—is collected for use in financial accounting systems. By understanding the way cost data are collected, managers using this information to support internal decisions are more likely to recognize its limitations and initiate changes to assure that they get the information they need.

PRODUCT COSTING FOR EXTERNAL REPORTING

Accounting systems designed to collect costs for products are called **product costing systems**. Their primary job is to capture product-related costs and separate them into costs that have the potential of creating value in the future (i.e., costs considered assets) and costs whose value has expired (i.e., costs considered expenses). Although, we'll usually refer to *products*, remember that costs can also be collected for services. For example, costs can be collected for a printing job or an engineering project, just as they can be for a batch of manufactured product.

PRODUCT COSTING SYSTEMS

PRODUCT COSTS FOR MANUFACTURING COMPANIES

Product costs represent the cost of resources required in making the organization's product. Consider the examples shown in Exhibit 5.1. The costs of an auto parts manufacturer, a printing firm, and an engineering firm are all separated into direct product costs, indirect product costs, and nonproduct costs. In the case of the auto parts firm, product costs are those incurred in making auto parts, such as direct materials and direct labor. Indirect product costs, or manufacturing (factory) overhead, for the auto parts firm include, for example, indirect materials, indirect labor, manufacturing utilities, depreciation for manufacturing equipment, and supervisors' salaries. Nonproduct costs have nothing to do with manufacturing

EXHIBIT 5.1 ILLUSTRATIONS OF DIRECT AND INDIRECT COSTS FOR THREE KINDS OF PRODUCTS AND SERVICES

Auto parts manufacturer Batch of auto parts	Printing firm Print job	Engineering firm Engineering project
Direct Product Costs		
Direct materials Direct labor	Direct materials Direct labor	Direct materials Direct labor
Indirect Product Costs		

Manufacturing overhead:
  Indirect materials
  Indirect labor
  Manufacturing utilities
  Depreciation—manufacturing
    equipment
  Supervisors' salaries
	Processing overhead:
	  Printing ink & supplies
	  Indirect labor
	  Printing utilities
	  Depreciation—printing
	    equipment
	  Supervisors' salaries
		Project overhead:
		  Indirect materials
		  Indirect labor
		  Engineering utilities
		  Depreciation—engineering
		    equipment
		  Supervisors' salaries

Nonproduct Costs		

General & administrative:
  Marketing labor
  Administrative labor
  Office supplies
  Administrative utilities
  Depreciation—office
    equipment
	General & administrative:
	  Marketing labor
	  Administrative labor
	  Office supplies
	  Administrative utilities
	  Depreciation—office
	    equipment
		General & administrative:
		  Marketing labor
		  Administrative labor
		  Office supplies
		  Administrative utilities
		  Depreciation—office
		    equipment

auto parts but are, nevertheless, incurred in order to administer the organization and bring its products to market.

Excerpts from the financial statements of the Sara Lee Corporation, shown in "Current Practice: Sara Lee Corporation," help illustrate product costs. Costs for product sold during the year, such as direct materials, direct labor, and indirect product costs (such as equipment depreciation) make up Sara Lee's cost of sales even though we don't see the details. Selling, general, and administrative expenses are considered nonproduct costs. Direct and indirect product costs—such as direct materials, direct labor, and indirect manufacturing costs for goods not yet sold—are considered assets. They are found in the balance sheet in the inventory section.

PRODUCT COSTS FOR SERVICE COMPANIES

Two examples of product costs for service organizations are also found in Exhibit 5.1. The first is a printing firm whose product is a service—processing sheets of paper into printed pages. A printing firm's service is often organized into print jobs. Print-related costs, such as paper (direct materials) and press operator salaries (direct labor), are product costs, directly traceable to specific print jobs. Indirect product costs, considered processing overhead, include the cost of performing printing activities not directly related to specific jobs, such as printing ink and supplies, indirect labor,

CURRENT PRACTICE

Sara Lee Corporation

The Sara Lee Corporation, with headquarters in Chicago, is a global manufacturer of consumer products. Best known for food items such as its pecan coffee cake, Sara Lee also makes coffee, hosiery, and knit products. In the excerpts from Sara Lee's 1993 annual report (shown below), the line labeled "Cost of Sales" on the partial consolidated statement of earnings includes both direct and indirect product costs for all items Sara Lee sold. Cost of sales includes flour, sugar, butter, and all other direct materials, plus direct labor and depreciation on equipment where conversion of direct materials into products took place. Product costs for items not sold are found under inventory on the partial consolidated balance sheet. All other costs are nonproduct costs—namely selling, general, and administrative expense—found on the income statement beneath cost of sales.

Partial Consolidated Statement of Income (in millions)

| | For Year Ended | | |
	July 3, 1993	June 27, 1992	June 29, 1991
Net sales	$14,580	$13,243	$12,381
Cost of sales	$9,039	$8,306	$8,072
Selling, general, & administrative expenses	$4,377	$3,891	$3,359

Product costs (direct and indirect)

Nonproduct cost

Partial Consolidated Balance Sheet, in millions

| | Inventory | | |
	1993	1992	1991
Finished goods	$1,413	$1,311	$1,017
Work in process	322	325	208
Materials & supplies	545	524	482
Total inventories	$2,280	$2,160	$1,707

Source: Sara Lee Corporation, *Annual Report*, 1993, p. 33.

printing utilities, depreciation for printing equipment, and supervisors' salaries. These costs are shared by all print jobs. Nonproduct costs, those not associated with printing activities, include marketing labor, administrative labor, office supplies, administrative utilities, and depreciation for office equipment.

The second example of product costs for service organizations (Exhibit 5.1) shows data for an engineering firm. Engineers typically organize costs around jobs or projects. Product costs might include engineers' salaries (direct labor) and materials (direct materials)—all of which are directly traceable to specific engineering jobs or projects. Indirect product costs, classified as project overhead, include the engineering costs that cannot be traced to specific jobs or projects, such as indirect materials, indirect labor, engineering utilities, depreciation for engineering equipment, and supervisors' salaries. All costs not involved in providing engineering services, shown as general and administrative costs in Exhibit 5.1, are considered nonproduct costs.

PRODUCT COSTS AND INVENTORIES

A big difference between companies that make tangible products and companies that provide services is the ability of the former to store costs in inventories. Manufacturing costs can be attached to tangible products and stored in conjunction with the physical inventories. Manufacturing costs stay with the inventories until the goods are sold. After the goods are sold, the product costs are released as cost of goods sold.

The salary cost of an employee who makes auto parts illustrates how costs can be stored in inventories. The employee's wages are added to inventory accounts until the automobile parts are sold. Only then are the employee's wages released against income as cost of goods sold. In contrast, service companies cannot store product costs in inventories. By their very nature, these costs expire and are deducted from revenue as the services are rendered.

PRODUCT AND PERIOD COSTS

The purpose of inventory accounts is to collect and store all costs that can be attached to the product—that's why they're called *product costs*. Then, in the period when the product is sold, total product cost is released against income as cost of goods sold. Then, and only then, is the cost deducted from revenue.

In contrast, all nonproduct costs are released immediately. That's because they cannot be associated with specific products. Because nonproduct costs are released in the time period for which they are incurred, they are commonly referred to as **period costs**. Period costs are never found in inventories. For example, the marketing manager's salary is a cost of the period during which the manager works, not of the period when the product is sold.

FLOW OF COSTS IN A PRODUCT COSTING SYSTEM

Product costs flow through a series of successive inventory accounts that parallels the tangible product's progress toward completion. The cost flow begins with three primary resource inputs—direct materials, direct labor, and indirect manufacturing overhead costs. Direct materials cost is added to the direct materials inventory as it is acquired. When a new batch of product is started, for example, direct materials are physically transferred to production. At the same time, the cost of the materials issued to production is transferred from the direct materials inventory to an inventory called **work in process**. While in production, direct materials are converted into finished products by applying direct labor and manufacturing over-head. Costs associated with converting materials into finished products are included, along with direct materials, in work in process. When process-ing is complete, finished products are moved from the production area to storage, where they wait for delivery. Along with the physical move of completed goods to storage, manufacturing costs are transferred from the work-in-process inventory to a third inventory, called finished goods. As completed products are sold, they are moved from storage and delivered to customers. Physically removing products from the finished-goods inven-tory triggers a corresponding transfer of costs from finished goods to cost of goods sold.

The cost flow for an auto parts manufacturer is shown in Exhibit 5.2. Note that the three accounts along the left-hand side of the exhibit rep-resent resource inputs. Direct materials and direct labor are direct prod-uct costs, while manufacturing overhead represents indirect product cost. Resources from these three sources flow into the work-in-process inven-tory as direct materials are physically converted into finished auto parts by applying direct labor and manufacturing overhead. When the parts have been completed, their cost is transferred from work in process to finished goods. There, direct materials, direct labor, and manufacturing overhead costs are stored until the auto parts are sold. Before leaving Exhibit 5.2, we'll make one final observation. Note that there is no reference to non-product costs. As we stated earlier, nonproduct costs never enter the prod-uct costing system. Nonproduct costs are never inventoried, since they are deducted from the revenue for the time period in which they are incurred.

DIRECT MATERIALS

The direct materials inventory in Exhibit 5.2 shows a beginning balance of $32,400. Assume our example covers a 1-month period of time—the month of July. Therefore, this balance represents the cost of the materials that were on hand at the end of June. Material purchases during the month are $68,850, making the total cost of materials available for use $101,250. Materials totaling $76,750 are issued to production and transferred to work in process. After removing the costs of materials transferred to work in process, $24,500 of direct materials is left in the materials inventory at the end of July.

DIRECT LABOR

The cost of wages for production workers—a direct labor cost of $80,000—is transferred directly to work in process. Unlike materials, direct labor cannot be stored in its own inventory account. As workers apply their labor, direct materials are converted into finished products. At the same time, labor cost is added to work in process. In effect, labor is transformed into an inventory.

MANUFACTURING (FACTORY) OVERHEAD

Indirect product cost (manufacturing overhead) includes costs such as indi-rect production materials, indirect production labor, factory equipment

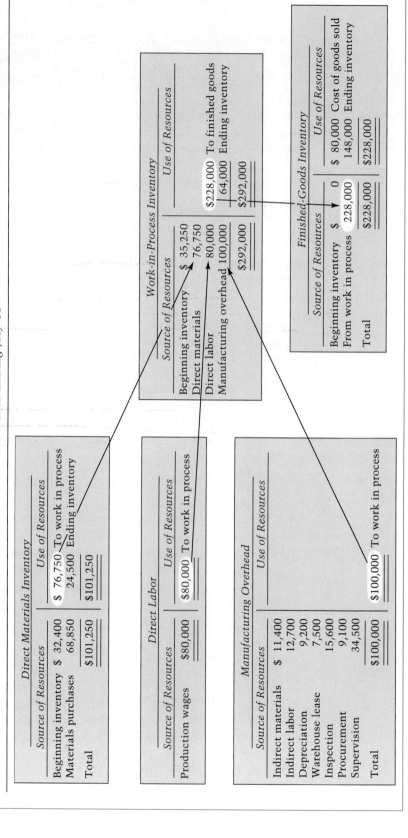

EXHIBIT 5.2 FLOW OF MANUFACTURING COSTS THROUGH PRODUCTION

For the Month Ending July 31

Direct Materials Inventory

Source of Resources		Use of Resources	
Beginning inventory	$ 32,400	$ 76,750	To work in process
Materials purchases	68,850	24,500	Ending inventory
Total	$101,250	$101,250	

Direct Labor

Source of Resources		Use of Resources	
Production wages	$80,000	$80,000	To work in process

Manufacturing Overhead

Source of Resources		Use of Resources	
Indirect materials	$ 11,400		
Indirect labor	12,700		
Depreciation	9,200		
Warehouse lease	7,500		
Inspection	15,600		
Procurement	9,100		
Supervision	34,500		
Total	$100,000	$100,000	To work in process

Work-in-Process Inventory

Source of Resources		Use of Resources	
Beginning inventory	$ 35,250	$228,000	To finished goods
Direct materials	76,750	64,000	Ending inventory
Direct labor	80,000		
Manufacturing overhead	100,000		
	$292,000	$292,000	

Finished-Goods Inventory

Source of Resources		Use of Resources	
Beginning inventory	$ 0	$ 80,000	Cost of goods sold
From work in process	228,000	148,000	Ending inventory
Total	$228,000	$228,000	

depreciation, factory warehouse lease, materials inspection, materials procurement, factory supervision, and any other cost necessary to support production activities. As manufacturing overhead cost is incurred—$100,000 in our example—it is transferred to the work-in-process inventory. As with direct labor, manufacturing overhead cannot be stored in its own inventory account.

Direct materials cost is transferred to the work-in-process inventory when materials are physically issued to production. Similarly, direct labor cost is added to work in process when payrolls are recorded. There is no similar physical event that triggers the transfer of manufacturing overhead to work in process. We will show how to overcome this problem later in the chapter.

WORK IN PROCESS

The work-in-process inventory beginning balance (as of July 1st) is $35,250. The beginning balance in the inventory of work-in-process represents the cost of partially completed products carried forward from June. Assume that the beginning inventory of work in process represents a single batch of automobile parts that was still being worked on at the end of June. Additional direct materials ($76,750), direct labor ($80,000), and manufacturing overhead ($100,000) costs are added to production during July. Adding the cost of the beginning inventory of work in process to the costs introduced during July gives a total cost of $292,000, representing manufacturing resources available for the month. These costs are incurred for two reasons: (1) to complete the batch of automobile parts carried over from June and (2) to start several new batches of automobile parts in production.

A statement called cost of goods manufactured, such as the one shown in Exhibit 5.3, accounts for all of the costs in work in process and the disposition of those costs at the end of the month. After removing $64,000 of cost associated with goods still in work in process at the end of the month, work in process is left with a balance of $228,000, representing the cost of goods manufactured for the month of July.

EXHIBIT 5.3 COST OF GOODS MANUFACTURED	
For the Month Ending July 31	
Beginning work in process, July 1	$ 35,250
Resources added to production in July:	
Direct materials	$ 76,750
Direct labor	80,000
Manufacturing overhead	100,000
Total resources added to production in July	$256,750
Total resources available for production	$292,000
Less ending work in process, July 31	(64,000)
Cost of goods manufactured for July	$228,000

FINISHED GOODS

The finished-goods inventory (Exhibit 5.2) contains the costs of completed products. It is similar to the cost of inventory purchased from outside suppliers. In Exhibit 5.2, the finished-goods inventory increases by $228,000, representing the cost of auto parts (cost of goods manufactured) transferred from work in process during the month of July. Note that there are no completed-but-unsold batches of automobile parts in the beginning inventory of finished goods. As products are sold and removed from finished goods, their cost is transferred to cost of goods sold. The cost that remains in finished goods represents completed-but-unsold product as of the end of the month. In the auto parts example shown in Exhibit 5.2, the ending inventory of finished goods is $148,000.

Financial statements summarizing the flow of costs through the inventories are shown in Exhibits 5.4 and 5.5. Exhibit 5.4 is an income

EXHIBIT 5.4 INCOME STATEMENT

For the Month Ending July 31

Revenue	$140,000
Cost of goods sold:	
Beginning finished goods, July 1	0
Cost of goods manufactured (from Exhibit 5.3)	228,000
Cost of goods available for sale	$228,000
Less ending finished goods, July 31	(148,000)
Total cost of goods sold	$ 80,000
Gross profit	$60,000
Operating expense:	
Administration	$20,000
Marketing	15,000
Research & development	10,000
Total operating expense	$45,000
Operating income for month of July	$15,000

EXHIBIT 5.5 PARTIAL BALANCE SHEET

As of July 31

Current assets:		
Cash & equivalents		$15,000
Accounts receivable		30,500
Inventory:		
Direct materials	$ 24,500	
Work in process	64,000	
Finished goods	148,000	
Total inventory		236,500
Other current assets		35,000
Total current assets		$317,000

statement reflecting the cost of goods sold for the month of July. Note that the cost of goods sold section contains only the cost of auto parts actually sold. All costs incurred for auto parts yet unsold are found in inventories (as illustrated in Exhibit 5.5). In Exhibit 5.4 you also see, for the first time, nonproduct costs under the heading "Operating Expense." These costs, totaling $45,000, were incurred and released as expenses during the month of July. Exhibit 5.5 shows a partial balance sheet summarizing the costs remaining in inventories as of the end of July. We show only the current assets section of the balance sheet, since it is there that product cost data are disclosed. There are three inventories on the balance sheet—direct materials, work in process, and finished goods.

DIFFERENT WAYS OF COLLECTING COSTS

Product costs flow through the product costing system in many different ways. Fortunately, product costing systems can be classified in one of two ways, according to: (1) how costs move through the system and (2) how costs are measured.

HOW COSTS MOVE THROUGH PRODUCT COSTING SYSTEMS

Understanding the way work is organized when a product is made or a service provided helps in understanding how costs move through the product costing system. There are two basic ways manufacturing work is structured.

One method is to organize work by job order. This method is used when the product is a single unit, such as a Boeing 777 or a new house built by a contractor. Another example of such a unit is a commercial printing company's print job. In job-order costing, work is characterized by a "jumbled" flow, with intermittent stops and starts as jobs are completed and new ones started. The volume of products is typically low, and each product is one of a kind, made to customer specifications using general-purpose equipment.[1] Another characteristic of job orders is that workers and equipment are usually organized in work centers.

The other way work is organized is based on continuous-flow processes. In this method, a relatively small array of commodity-type products is manufactured at high volume—the exact opposite of job-order work. An example of a firm that relies on continuous-flow processes might be Gillette, which manufactures razor blades, or a refinery that processes sugar cane into granulated sugar. Work in continuous-flow processes is identifiable with the process itself rather than with units of product. Direct materials, for example, can be identified with a specific job—a Boeing 777—when work is organized in jobs. In contrast, direct materials are

---

[1] The descriptions of job order systems and processes are adapted from Roger G. Schroeder, *Operations Management: Decision Making in the Operations Function*, 2d ed., New York: McGraw-Hill Book Company, 1985, pp. 134–153.

D.M. are identified with a specific process—refining sugar—in continuous-flow processes. Work and materials in continuous-flow processes are generally standardized, usually requiring repetitive tasks on highly specialized equipment. Continuous-flow processes generally take advantage of economies of scale.

Between job-order work and continuous-flow processes are other ways that manufacturing work can be structured. Closer to the job-order end of the spectrum is batch work, where **batches** represent a small array of custom-designed products made in relatively low volumes. An example is a batch of special-order auto parts. Between batch work and continuous flow are **assembly lines**, where relatively few products are made using specialized equipment. Work on assembly lines is typically organized around highly structured jobs. An automobile manufacturer offers an example of an assembly-line operation.

Accounting systems are designed to accommodate each of these different manufacturing environments. **Job-order costing systems** are used for products manufactured in jobs or batches. After costs are traced to a specific job or batch, the total cost of each job or batch is divided by the number of units in order to get unit cost. **Process costing systems** capture product costs for goods made on assembly lines or in continuous-flow processes. In process costing, it's the cost of the process that we want to know. For example, the annual cost of operating an automated bottle-labeling line might total $250,000. If 100 million bottles are labeled during the year, the labeling cost is $0.0025 per bottle.

All of the examples in this chapter assume costs are collected in a job-order costing system. Discussion of process costing is deferred to the appendix.

JOB-ORDER COSTING SYSTEMS

Job-order costing systems are characterized by the following features:

- Work is organized around individual jobs or batches. (Note: We will hereafter use the terms *job* and *batch* interchangeably).
- Costs are collected by jobs. Direct materials are issued to and direct labor is traced to specific jobs. Manufacturing overhead is assigned to all jobs, since it cannot, by definition, be traced to specific jobs.
- Completed jobs are transferred from work in process to finished goods. The cost of incomplete jobs remains in work in process.
- The cost of completed jobs remains in finished goods until the products are sold. When they are sold, their cost is transferred from finished goods to cost of goods sold.

The key to understanding job-order costing systems is to recognize that all direct and indirect product costs must be attached to specific jobs. The status of a particular job determines whether its costs belong in work in process, finished goods, or cost of goods sold. The cost of jobs that are physically completed, for example, is transferred from the work-in-process inventory to the finished-goods inventory. Similarly, the cost of jobs sold is transferred from finished goods to cost of goods sold.

Costs in job-order costing systems are collected in documents known as **job cost sheets**, such as the one shown in Exhibit 5.6. Materials are released to a job on the basis of materials requisition forms. Assume the automobile parts manufacturer used in the earlier examples specializes in making fuel injectors. The job cost sheet for job 101, a batch of no. 456 fuel injectors, includes 2,050 units of housing materials issued to the job

EXHIBIT 5.6 JOB COST SHEET

Actual Costing—Fuel Injector No. 456

Job number:	101
Product description:	Fuel injector no. 456
Units in batch:	2,000
Date started:	June 29
Date completed:	July 3

Actual Direct Materials

Date	Requisition	Material	Quantity	Unit Price	Cost
June 29	C113	Housing	2,050	$3.18	$ 6,519
June 30	F378	Screws	9,840	0.21	2,066
June 30	C198	Valves	3,200	3.52	11,264
July 1	C198	Valves	780	3.50	2,730
July 1	F378	Screws	3,136	0.19	596
July 2	G807	Jets	1,620	1.96	3,175
Total					$26,350

Actual Direct Labor

Date	Task	Grade	Hours	Hourly Rate	Cost
June 29	Setup	4	498.0	$ 9.60	$ 4,781
June 30	Assembly	5	188.1	11.80	2,219
July 1	Assembly	5	418.5	11.80	4,938
July 1	Assembly	5	867.5	11.80	10,237
July 2	Finish	3	235.5	7.75	1,825
Total					$24,000

Actual Manufacturing Overhead Applied

Date	Basis	Grade	Labor Cost	Rate	Cost
June 29	Labor $s	4	$ 4,781	120.00%	$ 5,737
June 30	Labor $s	5	2,219	120.00%	2,663
July 1	Labor $s	5	4,938	125.00%	6,173
July 1	Labor $s	5	10,237	125.00%	12,796
July 2	Labor $s	3	1,825	125.00%	2,281
Total					$29,650

Summary	June	July	Total
Direct materials	$19,850	$ 6,500	$26,350
Direct labor	7,000	17,000	24,000
Manufacturing overhead applied	8,400	21,250	29,650
Total manufacturing cost	$35,250	$44,750	$80,000
Number of units			2,000
Unit cost			$40.00

during June. Direct labor is also attached to jobs through the job cost sheet. By keeping track of how employees spend their time, perhaps by using time cards, labor cost can be traced to specific jobs. Finally, manufacturing overhead is assigned to jobs based on direct labor dollars. Note that overhead is applied at different rates in June and July, a point we will return to shortly. By the time job 101 is completed at the end of July, 2,000 units have been finished and $80,000 in manufacturing cost, or an average of $40 per unit, has been accumulated. These results are summarized at the bottom of Exhibit 5.6.

Using costs organized by job allows product costs to be tracked as they flow through the production system. Continuing the example of the auto parts manufacturer, Exhibit 5.7 shows the details of the cost of three jobs passing through work in process during the month of July. Job 101 is incomplete at the beginning of July; at the same time, two new jobs (105 and 107) are started. By the end of July, two of the three jobs in work in process (jobs 101 and 105) have been completed. The costs of these two completed jobs are transferred from the work-in-process inventory to the finished-goods inventory. The costs associated with job 107 are in the inventory of work in process at the end of July.

The cost in the beginning inventory of work in process ($35,250) represents the cost of job 101 incurred prior to the start of July. Direct materials costing $76,750, direct labor costing $80,000, and manufacturing overhead costing $100,000 are added to costs in the beginning inventory ($35,250) to bring the total cost of resources placed in production during July to $292,000.

How much of the three jobs' aggregate product cost of $292,000 should be transferred from work in process to finished goods? And how much should be left in the ending inventory of work in process? Job-order costing provides the answers. The amount in the ending inventory of work in process is determined by simply adding together all of the costs accumulated for jobs not yet completed. Because only job 107 is incomplete at the end of July, it remains in work in process, at a cost of $64,000. Since jobs 101 and 105 have been completed, their combined cost ($80,000 + $148,000, or $228,000) is transferred to finished goods.

Exhibit 5.8 shows the costs of the two jobs completed as of the end of July. Jobs 101 and 105 were completed and transferred to finished goods. However, only job 101 is sold. Its cost of $80,000 is transferred out of finished goods and into cost of goods sold. This leaves only job 105, at a cost of $148,000, in the ending inventory of finished goods at the close of July.

HOW COSTS ARE MEASURED

As jobs pass through the product-costing system, how are their costs measured? There are three fundamental ways: (1) actual costing systems, (2) normal costing systems, and (3) standard costing systems.

ACTUAL COSTING SYSTEMS

Actual costing systems, as the name implies, record manufacturing activities at actual cost. Direct materials issued to production are charged to

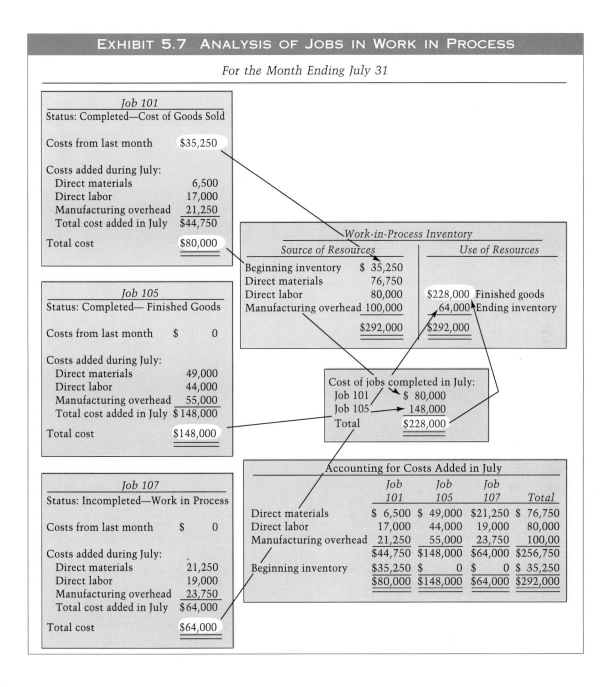

EXHIBIT 5.7 ANALYSIS OF JOBS IN WORK IN PROCESS

For the Month Ending July 31

work in process at the actual number of units—for example, pounds or square feet—multiplied by the actual price per unit. To illustrate, the first direct material listed on the job cost sheet for job 101 in Exhibit 5.6 is 2,050 fuel injector housings. The actual unit cost for each fuel injector housing is $3.18. Multiplying the actual quantity issued to production (2,050) by the actual unit cost ($3.18) gives a total cost of $6,519. Similarly, direct labor cost is charged to work in process at the actual hourly rate paid to employees multiplied by the actual number of labor-hours they worked.

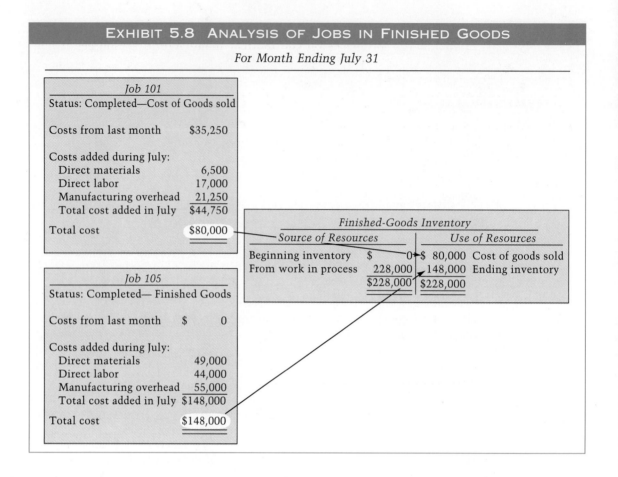

EXHIBIT 5.8   ANALYSIS OF JOBS IN FINISHED GOODS

For Month Ending July 31

Job 101

Status: Completed—Cost of Goods sold

Costs from last month	$35,250
Costs added during July:	
Direct materials	6,500
Direct labor	17,000
Manufacturing overhead	21,250
Total cost added in July	$44,750
Total cost	$80,000

Job 105

Status: Completed— Finished Goods

Costs from last month	$ 0
Costs added during July:	
Direct materials	49,000
Direct labor	44,000
Manufacturing overhead	55,000
Total cost added in July	$148,000
Total cost	$148,000

Finished-Goods Inventory

Source of Resources		*Use of Resources*	
Beginning inventory	$ 0	$ 80,000	Cost of goods sold
From work in process	228,000	148,000	Ending inventory
	$228,000	$228,000	

While direct materials and direct labor costs can be traced to specific jobs, manufacturing overhead has to be assigned to jobs using an overhead rate. The overhead rate, introduced in Chapter 3, is calculated by dividing total actual manufacturing overhead cost by the actual volume of the activity base:

$$\text{Actual manufacturing overhead rate} = \frac{\text{actual manufacturing overhead cost}}{\text{actual volume of activity base}}$$

When calculating the manufacturing overhead rate we need to consider two things: (1) an appropriate activity base and (2) at what point the overhead rate is to be calculated.

What Is an Appropriate Activity Base?   Some of the activity bases commonly used in determining manufacturing overhead rates include:

- Actual direct materials dollars
- Actual direct labor dollars
- Actual direct labor-hours
- Actual machine-hours

The activity base we decide to use should be the one that best reflects the demand a job places on the indirect manufacturing resources it consumes. For example, suppose a large percentage of manufacturing cost is tied up in direct materials. If manufacturing overhead consumed by a job parallels the job's materials content, then direct materials dollars offer a logical basis for applying manufacturing overhead to jobs. On the other hand, if production cost is largely made of labor cost, then either actual labor-hours or actual labor dollars should be the activity base. Similarly, if manufacturing activities are highly automated, measures such as actual machine-hours or actual processing time may offer a fairer reflection of manufacturing overhead cost.

As indicated in Chapter 3, activity bases such as actual direct materials dollars or actual direct labor-hours aren't always good measures of relative resource consumption. Nor do they offer fair ways of assigning overhead cost to products. That's why we introduced activity-based costing (Chapter 4) as an improved way of assigning costs. If the purpose of product costing is external reporting, then assignment of manufacturing overhead costs using bases such as actual direct materials dollars or actual direct labor-hours may provide reasonably accurate measures of product costs.

Managers relying on information derived from the external reporting system as a basis for decisions must be aware of the potential for distortions in costs. As we indicated in Chapter 3, products with poorly allocated indirect costs are either under- or overcosted, depending upon whether too little or too much indirect cost is allocated to them. This may not be a significant problem if the purpose of the allocations is external reporting. If, however, product costs are used by managers for decision-making purposes, such as in product pricing, then improper assignment of costs may lead to poor decisions.

When Is the Manufacturing Overhead Rate Calculated? Manufacturing overhead rates can be calculated at either the beginning or end of a period. When calculated at the end of the period—say, at the end of each month—manufacturing overhead rates are referred to as actual overhead rates. Actual overhead rates can only be determined after recording actual manufacturing overhead costs and collecting the actual volume of the activity base. Managers who want to use actual manufacturing overhead rates won't know what the rates are until the end of the accounting period. For example, Exhibit 5.9 shows the actual manufacturing overhead rate on a month-by-month basis for the auto parts manufacturer. Note that the activity base used is direct labor cost, and that June's rate is 120 percent of actual direct labor cost, while July's rate increases to 125 percent.

Changes in production activity are likely to cause changes in the activity base. For example, increased production activity is likely to cause actual direct labor cost—the activity base—to increase. If a large percentage of manufacturing overhead cost is fixed, dividing manufacturing overhead cost by larger activity levels when total costs aren't changing much causes the overhead rate to decline. Exhibit 5.9 indicates that October has the highest level of the activity base ($97,000) and, therefore, the lowest

		Actual	Manufacturing
Month	Actual Direct Labor Cost	Manufacturing Overhead	Overhead Rate
January	$ 75,800	$ 97,900	129.16%
February	78,060	99,030	126.86%
March	93,250	106,625	114.34%
April	85,100	102,550	120.51%
May	77,620	98,810	127.30%
June	85,710	102,855	120.00%
July	80,000	100,000	125.00%
August	83,400	101,700	121.94%
September	89,090	104,545	117.35%
October	97,000	108,500	111.86%
November	94,400	107,200	113.56%
December	60,570	90,285	149.06%
Total year	$1,000,000	$1,220,000	122.00%

EXHIBIT 5.9 EFFECT ON OVERHEAD RATE FROM CHANGES IN VOLUME

rate (111.86%) for the year. Low rates are attributable to economies of scale, wherein largely fixed manufacturing overhead costs are spread over more units. In contrast, the highest manufacturing overhead rates are associated with months of relatively low activity—in our example, December.

In the example illustrated by Exhibit 5.9, different manufacturing overhead rates exist for each month. In such cases, month-to-month unit costs are also going to change. For example, Exhibit 5.7 shows that job 105 was assigned $55,000 in manufacturing overhead cost during July (125% × direct labor cost of $44,000). What if job 105 had been manufactured in December, when the overhead rate was 149.06% rather than in July? In that case, job 105 would have been assigned $65,586 ($44,000 × 149.06%) in manufacturing overhead, 19 percent more than in July. It is highly improbable that customers buying automobile fuel injectors would agree to pay more for parts made in December than in July.

NORMAL COSTING SYSTEMS

Normal costing systems are similar to actual costing systems. They are similar in that both systems use actual direct materials and actual direct labor. They differ in the way in which they treat manufacturing overhead. Actual costing systems use actual manufacturing overhead rates, whereas normal costing systems rely on rates that normalize—or "smooth out"—the month-to-month fluctuations in volume. So, the answer to the question—when the manufacturing overhead rate is to be calculated—is, it can be either at the end of the month or year (for actual costing) or at the beginning of the year (for normal costing).

Suppose in Exhibit 5.9 the manufacturing overhead and direct labor costs are based on projections for the year—not on actual month-to-month costs. Then we can calculate a projected—or predetermined—manufacturing overhead rate that can be used for any month during the year. The rate is calculated by dividing projected annual overhead cost by the normal annual volume of activity:

$$\frac{\text{Predetermined manufacturing}}{\text{overhead rate}} = \frac{\text{projected manufacturing overhead}}{\text{normal volume of activity base}}$$

Normal volume is the average volume of the activity base that managers expect over the long term. Assume that direct labor cost in a normal year averages $1 million. If manufacturing overhead for the coming year is projected at, say, $1,220,000, then the predetermined overhead rate is 122 percent of direct labor cost.[2] That is, every time a dollar of direct labor cost is added to work in process, 122 percent, or $1.22, is added for manufacturing overhead.

Earlier, we stated that manufacturing overhead, unlike direct materials and direct labor, has no specific event that triggers its introduction to work in process. To solve this difficulty, normal costing systems "piggyback" manufacturing overhead on top of costs such as direct labor or direct materials or onto measures such as direct labor-hours or machine-hours. After the rate has been determined at the beginning of the year, it can be used at any time during the year, even though volume may change from month to month. Normal cost, then, comprises actual direct materials, actual direct labor, and estimated (normal) manufacturing overhead.

What if the auto parts manufacturer who makes fuel injectors were to use normal costing for job 101 rather than actual costing? Direct materials and direct labor costs would be exactly the same under either approach. Under an actual costing system, as shown in Exhibit 5.6, manufacturing overhead is assigned to jobs at the rate of 120 percent of direct labor cost in June and 125 percent of the rate in July. Normal costing, on the other hand, assigns manufacturing overhead cost to all jobs, during any month, at the rate of 122 percent of direct labor cost.

So, what is the advantage of normal costing? It allows managers to prepare cost quotes for jobs at any time during the year. All they have to do is estimate the amount of the activity base for any job—in this case, direct labor cost—and simply multiply it by the predetermined rate. The resulting estimate of manufacturing overhead is then added to actual direct materials and actual direct labor costs to derive an estimate of full manufacturing cost.

An example of the auto parts manufacturer's job cost sheet using normal costing is shown in Exhibit 5.10. The total manufacturing cost for a batch of 2,000 fuel injectors is $79,630, or $39.82 per unit. Note that the only difference between Exhibit 5.10, prepared using normal costing, and Exhibit 5.6, prepared using actual costing, is manufacturing overhead. Specifically, $29,650 in actual manufacturing overhead is assigned to job 101 over a 2-month period when two different monthly rates are used: 120 percent in June and 125 percent in July. In contrast, $29,280 in overhead

---

[2] Some companies calculate separate predetermined rates for both fixed and variable manufacturing overhead.

EXHIBIT 5.10 JOB COST SHEET

Normal Costing—Fuel Injector No. 456

Job number:	101
Product description:	Fuel injector no. 456
Units in batch:	2,000
Date started:	June 29
Date completed:	July 3

Actual Direct Materials

Date	Requisition	Material	Quantity	Unit Price	Cost
June 29	C113	Housing	2,050	$3.18	$ 6,519
June 30	F378	Screws	9,840	0.21	2,066
June 30	C198	Valves	3,200	3.52	11,264
July 1	C198	Valves	780	3.50	2,730
July 1	F378	Screws	3,136	0.19	596
July 2	G807	Jets	1,620	1.96	3,175
Total					$26,350

Actual Direct Labor

Date	Task	Grade	Hours	Hourly Rate	Cost
June 29	Setup	4	498.0	$ 9.60	$ 4,781
June 30	Assembly	5	188.1	11.80	2,219
July 1	Assembly	5	418.5	11.80	4,938
July 1	Assembly	5	867.5	11.80	10,237
July 2	Finish	3	235.5	7.75	1,825
Total					$24,000

Normal Manufacturing Overhead Applied

Date	Basis	Grade	Labor Cost	Rate	Cost
June 29	Labor $s	4	$ 4,781	122.00%	$ 5,833
June 30	Labor $s	5	2,219	122.00%	2,707
July 1	Labor $s	5	4,938	122.00%	6,024
July 1	Labor $s	5	10,237	122.00%	12,489
July 2	Labor $s	3	1,825	122.00%	2,227
Total					$29,280

Summary	June	July	Total
Direct materials	$19,850	$ 6,500	$26,350
Direct labor	7,000	17,000	24,000
Manufacturing overhead applied	8,540	20,740	29,280
Total manufacturing cost	$35,390	$44,240	$79,630
Number of units			2,000
Unit cost			$39.82

is assigned to job 101 when a single, normal, manufacturing overhead rate of 122 percent is used. Don't forget that the full cost of job 101 must include a share of nonproduct cost, a topic we will cover in Chapter 6.

Manufacturing Overhead Applied. Normal costing systems create a month-to-month imbalance between the actual manufacturing overhead incurred and the manufacturing overhead assigned to jobs using predetermined rates. Consider the data shown in Exhibit 5.11. (*Note:* The first two columns of Exhibit 5.11 are taken from Exhibit 5.9.) Manufacturing overhead is *applied* to all jobs throughout the year at a predetermined rate of 122 percent of direct labor cost. Look at the month of July, highlighted in Exhibit 5.11. Note that $80,000 in actual direct labor cost is incurred for all jobs during the month. Based on the $80,000 of actual direct labor cost, $97,600 ($80,000 × 122%) in manufacturing overhead cost is added to work in process. Assume that the actual manufacturing overhead cost for July turned out to be $100,000. The $2,400 difference between the actual manufacturing overhead cost and the manufacturing overhead cost applied using the predetermined overhead rate is called underapplied manufacturing overhead. *Underapplied* means that less manufacturing overhead is charged to jobs going into work in process than was actually incurred. As you can see in Exhibit 5.11, months of relatively low activity, such as December, cause manufacturing overhead to be underapplied, while months of relatively high activity, such as October, cause manufacturing overhead to be overapplied.

EXHIBIT 5.11 OVERAPPLIED (UNDERAPPLIED) MANUFACTURING OVERHEAD

Month	(1) Actual Direct Labor Cost	(2) Actual Manufacturing Overhead	(3) Manufacturing Overhead Applied (122% of Direct Labor Cost)	(4) Overapplied (Underapplied) Manufacturing Overhead	(5) Cumulative Overapplied (Underapplied) Manufacturing Overhead
January	$ 75,800	$ 97,900	$ 92,476	$ (5,424)	$(5,424)
February	78,060	99,030	95,233	(3,797)	(9,221)
March	93,250	106,625	113,765	7,140	(2,081)
April	85,100	102,550	103,822	1,272	(809)
May	77,620	98,810	94,696	(4,114)	(4,922)
June	85,710	102,855	104,566	1,711	(3,211)
July	80,000	100,000	97,600	(2,400)	(5,611)
August	83,400	101,700	101,748	48	(5,563)
September	89,090	104,545	108,690	4,145	(1,418)
October	97,000	108,500	118,340	9,840	8,422
November	94,400	107,200	115,168	7,968	16,390
December	60,570	90,285	73,895	(16,390)	$ 0
Total year	$1,000,000	$1,220,000	$1,220,000	$ 0	

Note: Some figures may contain rounding errors.

The balance in manufacturing overhead cost, as shown in column 4 of Exhibit 5.11, begins with underapplied manufacturing overhead in January and in February, when direct labor costs are less than the average monthly direct labor cost of $83,333 ($1,000,000/12 months). However, the cumulative underapplied manufacturing overhead cost, shown in column 5, decreases during March and April because direct labor costs in those months are higher than average.

The numbers in Exhibit 5.11 were carefully chosen so that the cumulative manufacturing overhead applied for the year ($1,220,000, in column 3) is exactly equal to the actual manufacturing overhead ($1,220,000, in column 2). By year-end, all of the manufacturing overhead is added, in full (fully absorbed) into the cost of products. However, the chances of preparing such exact predictions for both the total manufacturing overhead and the volume of the activity base are quite small. In realistic applications, manufacturing overhead may be either over- or underapplied by year-end. Waiting until the end of the month to calculate a precisely accurate manufacturing overhead rate, as is done with actual costing, eliminates this inaccuracy. However, the result is different manufacturing overhead rates during the year. Many managers believe that the nominal decrease in accuracy with normal costing is more than offset by the system's benefits.

One disadvantage of normal costing is the impact it may have on managers' behavior. A cumulative underapplied manufacturing overhead balance at any point during the year may make them nervous. They may feel they are not incorporating enough overhead into the cost of their products, prompting them to take actions that may be inappropriate. For example, the net underapplied overhead of $9,221 at the end of February (Exhibit 5.11) might cause managers to increase prices. Higher prices, though, may cause sales to decline, perhaps even triggering another round of potentially disastrous price increases.

STANDARD COSTING SYSTEMS

Normal costing systems help managers cope with fluctuating manufacturing overhead rates caused by month-to-month changes in activity. However, there may also be fluctuations in both the quantity and unit cost for direct materials and direct labor. Jobs completed during months when, for example, unit materials costs are relatively high cost more than jobs completed in months when materials costs are low. Worse, keeping records of unit costs for all of the individual purchases and tracing them to specific jobs can be daunting.

One solution is to establish norms for direct materials and direct labor costs, just as norms are created for manufacturing overhead in normal costing systems through the use of predetermined overhead rates. Such norms, representing expectations about what costs ought to be under normal conditions, are called standard costs. Work in process is charged with the standard cost of direct materials, direct labor, and manufacturing overhead each time work on a new job begins. This makes routine the transfer of resource costs into production and makes the task of accounting for these resources considerably easier. Exhibit 5.12 illustrates an auto parts manufacturer's standard cost for fuel injector no. 456—$13.70 for

EXHIBIT 5.12 STANDARD COST

Fuel Injector No. 456

Direct Materials

Material	Description	Quantity	Unit Price	Cost
C113	Housing	1	$ 3.20	$ 3.20
C198	Valves	2	3.50	7.00
F378	Screws	7	0.20	1.40
G807	Jets	1	2.10	2.10
Total				$13.70

Direct Labor

Activity	Grade	Hours	Hourly Rate	Cost
Setup	4	0.25	$ 9.50	$ 2.38
Assembly	5	0.75	11.75	8.81
Finish	3	0.10	8.00	0.80
Total				$11.99

Manufacturing Overhead

Activity	Base	Volume	Rate	Cost
Overhead	Labor $s	$11.99	122.00%	$14.62
				$40.31

direct materials, $11.99 for direct labor, and $14.62 for manufacturing overhead—or a standard manufacturing cost of $40.31 per unit.

The standard cost of material C113, for example, is derived by multiplying the **standard quantity** of material C113 (one housing unit for each fuel injector) by its **standard price** ($3.20 per housing). The result is a standard cost for material C113 of $3.20 per fuel injector. Standard quantities can be expressed in lots of ways, such as in units, pounds, square feet—whatever measure is appropriate for the particular material. Similarly, the standard cost for grade 4 setup labor is derived by multiplying the standard quantity (0.25 hours for each fuel injector) by its standard price (the labor rate of $9.50 per hour). The result is a standard cost for grade 4 setup labor of $2.38 per fuel injector. Manufacturing overhead is applied using the standard volume of the activity base—in this case, the total direct labor cost. For this example, standard manufacturing overhead cost is derived by multiplying the total direct labor cost ($11.99 per fuel injector) by its standard price (the predetermined overhead rate of 122%). The result is a standard manufacturing overhead cost of $14.62 per fuel injector.

Flow of Cost in a Standard Costing System.   Standard costs flow through the job-order costing system in much the same way as actual costs and normal costs flow through it. The difference is that direct materials, direct labor, and manufacturing overhead costs are all recorded at their respective standard cost.

Exhibit 5.13 shows standard costs for job 101, a batch of no. 456 fuel injectors. The first direct material listed is C113 (fuel injector housings). Job 101 is charged for the standard quantity of 2,000 fuel injector housings multiplied by the standard cost of $3.20 per housing. This results in

EXHIBIT 5.13 JOB COST SHEET

Standard Costing—Fuel Injector No. 456

Job number: 101
Product description: Fuel injector no. 456
Units in batch: 2,000
Date started: June 29
Date completed: July 3

Standard Direct Materials

Date	Requisition	Material	Quantity	Unit Price	Cost
June 29	C113	Housing	2,000	$3.20	$ 6,400
June 30	F378	Screws	10,000	0.20	2,000
June 30	C198	Valves	3,200	3.50	11,200
July 1	C198	Valves	800	3.50	2,800
July 1	F378	Screws	4,000	0.20	800
July 2	G807	Jets	2,000	2.10	4,200
Total					$27,400

Standard Direct Labor

Date	Task	Grade	Hours	Hourly Rate	Cost
June 29	Setup	4	500.0	$ 9.50	$ 4,750
June 30	Assembly	5	200.0	11.75	2,350
July 1	Assembly	5	500.0	11.75	5,875
July 1	Assembly	5	800.0	11.75	9,400
July 2	Finish	3	200.0	8.00	1,600
Total					$23,975

Standard Manufacturing Overhead Applied

Date	Base	Grade	Labor Cost	Rate	Cost
June 29	Labor $s	4	$4,750	122.00%	$ 5,795
June 30	Labor $s	5	2,350	122.00%	2,867
July 1	Labor $s	5	5,875	122.00%	7,168
July 1	Labor $s	5	9,400	122.00%	11,468
July 2	Labor $s	3	1,600	122.00%	1,952
Total					$29,250

Summary	June	July	Total
Direct materials	$19,600	$ 7,800	$27,400
Direct labor	7,100	16,875	23,975
Manufacturing overhead applied	8,662	20,588	29,250
Total manufacturing cost	$35,362	$45,263	$80,625
Number of units			2,000
Unit cost			$40.31

$6,400 of total standard cost for material C113. Material C113 is charged to job 101 at standard cost even though the actual quantity of fuel injector housings required (2,050, from Exhibit 5.6) is greater than the standard quantity (2,000) and the unit cost of parts purchased was lower ($3.18, from Exhibit 5.6) than standard ($3.20). Remember that standards represent norms, and actual costs fluctuate around these norms. If the norms don't change, then actual costs will, on the average, equal the standard costs. Part C113, for example, which may be purchased below standard cost at one point during the year, may cost more than standard at other times of the year. But the average day-to-day prices should be reasonably close to standard. If they aren't, it may mean that prices have changed permanently or, perhaps, that those responsible for buying material C113 may not be getting the best price.

WHAT HAPPENS WHEN THERE ARE DIFFERENCES BETWEEN STANDARD AND ACTUAL COSTS?

If work in process is charged for standard costs, what happens to actual costs in the accounting system? For example, the total cost of job 101 based on actual cost is $80,000 (Exhibit 5.6), while the total cost based on standard cost is $80,625 (Exhibit 5.13). That is, actual cost is $625 less than standard cost. For external reporting purposes, *generally accepted accounting principles require that inventories and cost of goods sold be recorded at actual, not standard, costs.*[3] Differences between actual costs and standard costs, known as **variances,** are calculated for direct materials, direct labor, and manufacturing overhead. Variances are disposed of by determining the status of each job at the end of the period. Then the variance is assigned to either work in process, finished goods, or cost of goods sold, depending on the job's status. For example, since job 101 is in cost of goods sold, its net (favorable) variance of $625 reduces the standard cost of goods sold from $80,625 to the actual cost of $80,000.

Actual costs don't have to be collected for individual jobs in a standard costing system. Collecting actual costs for individual jobs would defeat one of the purposes of using a standard costing system. Instead, actual costs are collected and variances calculated when manufacturing resources are placed into production. At the end of the year, variances are added to standard costs in order to reconstruct actual cost. This process makes recording the hundreds of day-to-day transactions much easier— each transaction is simply recorded at its standard cost.

There's another way of disposing of net variances—a way that makes good theoretical sense and requires less work. Some managers simply charge all variances to cost of goods sold, thereby deducting them from current income. The method discussed above, where variances are assigned to inventories, carries them forward to be charged against income in future periods. The obvious question, then, is which period should be charged with operating inefficiencies or credited with operating efficiencies?

---

[3]   An exception to the general principle is that standard cost can be used for external reporting if it is not materially different from actual cost.

Should a variance be charged against current income when the inefficiency occurs or should it be carried forward in inventory until the product is sold? We already mentioned that generally accepted accounting principals require that cost of goods sold, work in process, and finished goods be reported at actual cost. Therefore, the answer to the question about which period should be charged with operating efficiencies is resolved, for external reports, by financial accounting theory: Variances are assigned back to inventory accounts, thereby converting them to actual cost.

Then why use standard costs in the first place? Some of the reasons are that standard costs:

- Provide managers with product costs that don't fluctuate with changes in input prices and quantities.
- Allow managers to prepare estimates of manufacturing costs for decision-making purposes.
- Provide data, in the form of variances, that can be used to control costs, as we will show in Chapter 11.
- Make the accountant's job easier. Each time a new job is started, work in process is charged for the standard cost per unit multiplied by the number of units.

SUMMARY OF ACTUAL, NORMAL, AND STANDARD COSTS

Exhibit 5.14 summarizes the actual, normal, and standard costs for job 101. Actual and normal costs differ only in manufacturing overhead. However, standard cost differs in direct materials, direct labor, and manufacturing

EXHIBIT 5.14 COMPARISON OF ACTUAL, NORMAL, AND STANDARD COSTING			
Job 101—Batch of 2,000 Fuel Injectors (No. 456)			
	Exhibit 5.6— Actual	Exhibit 5.10— Normal	Exhibit 5.13— Standard
Direct materials:			
Actual direct materials	$26,350	$26,350	
Standard direct materials			$27,400
Direct labor:			
Actual direct labor	$24,000	$24,000	
Standard direct labor			$23,975
Manufacturing overhead:			
Actual manufacturing overhead	$29,650		
Predetermined manufacturing overhead (applied on actual direct labor cost)		$29,280	
Standard manufacturing overhead (applied on standard direct labor cost)			$29,250
Total manufacturing cost:			
Total manufacturing cost	$80,000	$79,630	$80,625
Number of units in batch	2,000	2,000	2,000
Manufacturing cost per unit	$40.00	$39.82	$40.31

overhead. Note that normal and standard costing systems both use predetermined manufacturing overhead rates. Normal manufacturing overhead is applied on actual measures of activity, while standard manufacturing overhead is applied on standard measures. To illustrate this last point, let's consider the data in Exhibit 5.14. Here, manufacturing overhead under normal costing is applied based on $24,000 of actual direct labor cost. In contrast, standard manufacturing overhead is applied based on $23,975 of standard direct labor cost.

VARIABLE COSTING

Financial reports for external users are designed to provide information that conforms with generally accepted accounting principles. They are not designed to provide information for day-to-day decisions. One reason for this is that managers may not want to disclose internal information to external users. How, then, do organizations satisfy the information needs of both external and internal users?

Some organizations maintain separate systems. One system, based on generally accepted accounting principles, provides information for external users. The other system, based on costs collected by cost objects and cost behavior, provides information for internal decision makers. Another approach altogether is to modify existing financial reporting systems to satisfy simultaneously both kinds of users. But is it possible for the same system to fully meet the information needs of both external and internal users? (See "Current Practice: Chrysler Corporation.") Before answering, let's consider the impact on gross profit and inventories from changes in volume.

CURRENT PRACTICE

Chrysler **Corporation**

The primary purpose of Chrysler's old cost accounting system was to help monitor operations and to place a value on inventory. However, few people outside the finance department felt that the system gave an accurate portrayal of the company's costs.

One skeptic, Robert A. Lutz, chairman and chief operating officer, was annoyed when his creative proposals for new product designs and changes in manufacturing processes were turned down. Chrysler's financial system focused on direct costs and relied on arbitrary allocations of overhead. Lutz felt the system made it impossible for a fair evaluation of proposals.

Eventually, under Lutz's leadership, Chrysler implemented activity-based costing to help reinforce the importance of a "process" view of the organization. The new system helped show how much each process actually cost. It also exposed inefficiencies and, eventually, led to improvements in operations.

Source: Joseph A. Ness and Thomas G. Cucuzza, "Tapping the Full Potential of ABC," *Harvard Business Review*, July–Aug. 1995, p. 132.

EFFECTS OF PRODUCTION AND SALES ON OPERATING INCOME

Suppose managers are reasonably certain that sales are going to be 40,000 units for the year. Let's say they decide to make 40,000 units, just enough to meet sales expectations, as shown in the base case column of Exhibit 5.15. With production equal to sales, there is no change in the inventory of finished goods. If manufacturing costs consist of $2.50 per unit of variable cost and $250,000 of fixed cost, then the cost of making and selling 40,000 units is $350,000 [(40,000 units × $2.50) + $250,000], or $8.75 ($350,000/40,000 units) per unit. If each unit is sold for $10, then total revenue is $400,000 and gross profit is $50,000.

Managers may misjudge demand and inadvertently build up inventory. Or, facing the realities of an uncertain marketplace, they may build

EXHIBIT 5.15 EFFECTS OF CHANGES IN VOLUME ON GROSS PROFIT AND INVENTORY

	Base Case	Build-Inventory Case
Physical units:		
Units in beginning inventory—finished goods	0	0
Number of units manufactured	40,000	50,000
Number of units sold	40,000	40,000
Units in ending inventory—finished goods	0	10,000
Manufactured cost:		
Unit variable manufacturing cost	$2.50	$2.50
Number of units manufactured	40,000	50,000
Total variable manufacturing cost	$100,000	$125,000
Total fixed manufacturing cost	250,000	$250,000
Total manufacturing cost	$350,000	$375,000
Total unit manufacturing cost	$8.75	$7.50
Income Statement		
Revenue:		
Number of units sold	40,000	40,000
Unit selling price	$10.00	$10.00
Total revenue	$400,000	$400,000
Cost of goods sold:		
Number of units sold	40,000	40,000
Unit cost	$8.75	$7.50
Cost of goods sold	$350,000	$300,000
Gross profit	$50,000	$100,000
Balance Sheet		
Units in ending inventory	0	10,000
Unit cost	$8.75	$7.50
	$0	$75,000

inventory just in case demand suddenly becomes greater than anticipated. (See "Current Practice: Philip Morris's Inventory.") And there's one more possibility—managers may intentionally build inventories to influence gross profit, an action that many consider unethical.

Building inventories can improve short-term performance in two ways. First, because of economies of scale, unit fixed costs decline as production activity increases. And, second, manufacturing costs for unsold units are pushed forward into the future in the form of work-in-process and finished-goods inventories.

To illustrate, let's consider the build-inventory scenario shown in the second numerical column of Exhibit 5.15. Assume managers decide to manufacture at levels well above what they expect to sell—say, 50,000 units—instead of planning production output to meet current needs. If the cost structure is the same, where variable cost is $2.50 per unit and fixed cost is $250,000, then total manufacturing cost is $375,000 [($2.50 per unit × 50,000 units) + $250,000]. Average unit manufacturing cost drops from $8.75, at 40,000 units, to $7.50 ($375,000/50,000 units) at 50,000 units. The net effect, as shown in the income statement in Exhibit 5.15, is to double gross profit from $50,000 to $100,000. Note that none of the additional output is sold, so the excess 10,000 units of inventory, costing $75,000, are carried forward to the next year. Since total revenue is the same ($400,000) under both scenarios, the increase in gross profit comes solely from reducing average manufacturing cost and deferring fixed manufacturing cost to the future through stockpiling inventory.

As you might suspect, stockpiling inventory cannot continue every year. Gross profit will decline when—as must inevitably occur—production schedules are scaled back to deplete the oversupply of inventory. In the meantime, operating income and cash flows may be adversely

▶ **CURRENT PRACTICE** ◀

Philip Morris's Inventory

Philip Morris, regarded by many as one of the best-run U.S. tobacco companies, reported "imbalances" in shipments of trade inventories in 1992 relative to the amount of cigarettes actually sold. Philip Morris disclosed that distributors' inventories of cigarettes had grown to between 16 billion and 20 billion cigarettes, nearly double what industry analysts consider desirable. One possible reason was the lower-than-expected levels of demand for the company's products.

Philip Morris was not the only U.S. tobacco manufacturer that continued to aggressively ship cigarettes while facing declining demand. R. J. R. Nabisco, the maker of Winston, Salem, and Camel cigarettes, took a $360-million charge after it was revealed that it had flooded the market at year-end with the equivalent of 6 weeks' supply of cigarettes.

Source: George Anders and Suein L. Hwang, "Big Cigarette Inventories Weigh Down Philip Morris," *The Wall Street Journal*, Oct. 22, 1992, p. B4.

impacted because of increased warehouse cost, finance cost for the additional inventory, and the increased costs of recordkeeping, insurance, theft, and obsolescence.

VARIABLE COSTING

Variable costing—also called direct costing—is a way of modifying externally oriented financial accounting reports for internal use. Although variable costing is not acceptable for external reporting, some managers believe that it can provide useful decision-making information. Plus, variable costing helps overcome the problems associated with shifting fixed manufacturing overhead cost to future periods through inventories, as we just illustrated in Exhibit 5.15.

Variable costing differs from the product costing systems presented earlier in this chapter in only one fundamental way—the treatment of fixed manufacturing cost. *Under variable costing, all fixed manufacturing costs, including fixed portions of direct labor and manufacturing overhead, are released as period costs in cost of goods sold during the time period in which they are incurred.* As a result, work-in-process and finished-goods inventories contain only variable direct materials, variable direct labor, and variable manufacturing overhead costs. Variable costing systems provide managers with an estimate of variable manufacturing cost—important information they can use for decision-making.

In contrast, product costs used for external reporting are referred to as full-absorption costs. They "absorb" a fair share of all manufacturing overhead costs—both fixed and variable—into the cost of each unit of product. Since variable costing excludes fixed manufacturing overhead from work-in-process and finished-goods inventories, it is not acceptable for external reporting.

We return to the auto parts manufacturer example to illustrate variable costing. Look at Exhibit 5.16, and assume that:

- Direct materials cost is variable.
- Direct labor cost is variable.
- All manufacturing overhead cost is fixed.
- Costs are measured at actual cost using the data in Exhibit 5.7.

The upper section of the first numerical column in Exhibit 5.16 shows the total manufacturing cost for the month of July under full-absorption costing. Total manufacturing cost to be accounted for in July ($292,000) includes the cost from June carried forward to July ($35,250), plus manufacturing cost added in July ($256,750).

Total manufacturing costs are accounted for, as shown in the bottom part of the first numerical column in Exhibit 5.16, by tracing them to jobs. The cost of all three jobs—$64,000 (job 107), $148,000 (job 105), and $80,000 (job 101)—equals the total cost to be accounted for ($292,000).

The upper section of the second numerical column in Exhibit 5.16 shows total manufacturing cost to be accounted for under variable costing. Total manufacturing cost to be accounted for in July ($283,600) includes cost from June carried forward to July ($26,850), plus the total

EXHIBIT 5.16 COMPARISON OF FULL-ABSORPTION AND VARIABLE COSTING

Costs to Account for	Full-Absorption Costing	Variable Costing
Work-in-process inventory—June 30 (Job 101):		
Direct materials	$19,850	$19,850
Direct labor	7,000	7,000
Manufacturing overhead	8,400	0
Total manufacturing cost carried forward to July	$35,250	$26,850
Costs added during July (Jobs 101, 105, and 107):		
Direct materials	$ 76,750	$ 76,750
Direct labor	80,000	80,000
Manufacturing overhead	100,000	100,000
Total manufacturing cost added in July	$256,750	$256,750
Total manufacturing cost to account for in July:	$292,000	$283,600
Costs Accounted for		
Work-in-process inventory—July 31 (Job 107):		
Direct materials	$21,250	$21,250
Direct labor	19,000	19,000
Manufacturing overhead	23,750	0
Total manufacturing cost carried forward to August	$64,000	$40,250
Finished goods inventory—July 31 (Job 105):		
Direct materials	$ 49,000	$49,000
Direct labor	44,000	44,000
Manufacturing overhead	55,000	0
Total manufacturing cost carried forward to August	$148,000	$93,000
Cost of goods sold for month ending July 31 (Job 101):		
Direct materials	$26,350	$26,350
Direct labor	24,000	24,000
Manufacturing overhead	29,650	0
Total manufacturing cost in cost of goods sold for July	$80,000	$50,350
Period cost—fixed manufacturing overhead:	$ 0	$100,000
Total cost of goods sold for July	$80,000	$150,350
Total manufacturing cost accounted for in July	$292,000	$283,600

Note: Data in this exhibit are based on actual cost from Exhibit 5.7. Assume all manufacturing overhead is fixed.

manufacturing cost added in July ($256,750). Note that the total costs to be accounted for in July under variable and full-absorption costing differ in only one respect—manufacturing overhead cost in the beginning inventory of work in process ($8,400).

Recall that we assumed that all manufacturing overhead cost is fixed. Also recall that we stated that, under variable costing, fixed costs are released against cost of goods sold in the month in which they are incurred. Therefore, the $8,400 of fixed manufacturing overhead shown in the full-absorption costing column is excluded from the beginning inventory of work in process in the variable costing column. The reason is that it was released as part of cost of goods sold during June. As a result, the total cost to be accounted for in July is $8,400 less under variable costing than it is under full-absorption costing.

Total manufacturing costs are accounted for by tracing them to jobs, as shown in the lower section of the second numerical column in Exhibit 5.16. Note that no fixed manufacturing overhead cost is assigned to any of the jobs under variable costing. However, *total fixed manufacturing overhead cost for the month of July ($100,000) is treated as a period cost, and is added, in its entirety, to July's cost of goods sold.* The variable cost of all three jobs [$40,250 (job 107), $93,000 (job 105), and $50,350 (job 101)] plus the fixed manufacturing overhead cost for the month ($100,000) equals the total cost to be accounted for ($283,600) under variable costing.

Exhibit 5.17 should help reconcile the differences between full-absorption and variable costing. Note that cost of goods sold is $70,350 less under full-absorption costing than it is under variable costing. That means that net income under full absorption is $70,350 higher than it is under variable costing. The difference can be explained by looking at how fixed manufacturing overhead cost is treated under full-absorption costing. First, $8,400 of fixed manufacturing cost is carried forward from June to July under full-absorption costing. Since job 101, carried forward from June, is sold in July, $8,400 of fixed manufacturing overhead is included in the cost of goods sold for July. Then, to offset the release of June's fixed manufacturing cost to cost of goods sold in July, some of the fixed manufacturing cost incurred in July is pushed forward into August. Specifically, the work-in-process inventory consists of $23,750 (job 107) and the finished-goods inventory consists of $55,000 (job 105) of fixed manufacturing overhead. Combining the $8,400 released to cost of goods from June with the deferral of $78,750 ($23,750 + $55,000) to August yields a net deferral, under full-absorption costing, of $70,350 in fixed manufacturing overhead cost. A net deferral of $70,350 in fixed manufacturing overhead means that, under full-absorption costing, the cost of goods sold is lower and gross profit is higher by that amount than would be the case under variable costing.

EXHIBIT 5.17 RECONCILIATION OF FULL-ABSORPTION AND VARIABLE COSTING

For the Month Ending July 31

Difference in cost of goods sold (from Exhibit 5.16):	
Cost of goods sold for month of July using variable costing	$150,350
Cost of goods sold for month of July using full-absorption costing	(80,000)
Reduction in cost of goods sold using full-absorption costing	$ 70,350
Effect on cost of goods sold from fixed cost in inventory:	
Fixed cost released in July from June 30 work-in-process inventory (job 101)	$ (8,400)
Fixed cost in July 31 inventory of work in process (job 107), deferred to August	23,750
Fixed cost in July 31 inventory of finished goods (job 105), deferred to August	55,000
Net deferral of fixed cost to August in July 31 inventory using full-absorption costing	$ 70,350

The impact of full-absorption costing relative to variable costing can be categorized in one of three ways, as follows:

- *Net increase in inventories (ending inventory > beginning inventory).* When there is a net increase in inventories, the result is a net deferral of fixed manufacturing overhead until subsequent time periods. Cost of goods sold is lower under full-absorption costing and gross profit is higher.
- *No net change in inventories (ending inventory = beginning inventory).* When there is no change in inventories, there is no net deferral of fixed manufacturing overhead. Cost of goods sold and gross profit are the same under both full-absorption and variable costing.
- *Net decrease in inventories (ending inventory < beginning inventory).* When there is a net decrease in inventories, the result is a net release of fixed manufacturing overhead. Cost of goods sold is higher under full-absorption costing and gross profit is lower.

EVALUATION OF VARIABLE COSTING

Variable costing represents a modification of the external reporting system. Unlike full-absorption costing, which is geared to external reporting, the goal of variable costing is to support internal decisions. However, a recent study reports that only 12.1 percent of the companies surveyed used variable costing in their pricing decisions.[4] The arguments for and against variable costing, which are listed below, may give insight into why it is not widely used.

- Variable costing assumes that all variable manufacturing costs—direct materials, direct labor, and variable manufacturing overhead—are caused by volume, as measured in units of product. As we have shown, manufacturing costs may vary with multiple cost drivers. As a result, reliance on a single cost driver limits the usefulness of variable-costing information.
- Variable costing relies on an accurate division of manufacturing cost into fixed and variable. In some cases, managers may not have access to this information.
- Managers may use full-absorption costs for some decisions, such as for long-term pricing, and variable costs for other decisions. If managers have access to only variable costs, they may not have all the information they need to make correct decisions.
- Managers who focus on variable manufacturing costs may forget to consider nonmanufacturing costs when making their decisions.
- Modifying full-absorption costing systems for variable costing may be expensive. As a result, some managers may not be able to justify the cost of developing variable-costing systems.
- Variable costing is not acceptable for external reporting.

---

[4] Eunsup Shim and Ephraim F. Sudit, "How Manufacturers Price Products," *Management Accounting*, Feb. 1995, pp. 37–39.

SUMMARY

Accounting systems used by manufacturing firms in the preparation of financial statements destined for external users come in different forms:

Component	Actual Cost	Normal Cost	Standard Cost
Direct materials	Actual	Actual	Standard
Direct labor	Actual	Actual	Standard
Manufacturing overhead	Actual	Predetermined	Standard

Overhead rates under actual costing systems can change dramatically in response to changes in production. Normal costing systems use predetermined overhead rates rather than the actual rates. Predetermined overhead rates are calculated by dividing predicted manufacturing overhead by normal activity. Standard costing systems record all component costs at standard cost. Variance accounts reflect the difference between actual costs and standard costs. Standard costing systems are used because they make it easier to record production transactions, since standard "bills of materials" form the basis of each entry. Since generally accepted accounting principles stipulate the use of actual cost, standard costs must be converted back to actual costs by distributing all manufacturing variances to work-in-process and finished-goods inventories and to cost of goods sold.

While costing systems are designed to meet external reporting requirements, many managers use the information to support decisions. Some managers may use full-absorption product costing, unmodified, extracted directly from the financial accounting system. One modification of the financial reporting system is called *variable costing*. Full-absorption costing differs from variable costing in the treatment of fixed manufacturing overhead. Under full-absorption costing, fixed overhead is attached to inventories and released when products are sold. Variable costing, in contrast, releases all fixed manufacturing overhead costs in the period in which they are incurred, leaving only variable costs in inventories.

Recent data indicate a movement away from full-absorption product costs as the basis for decisions. One reason for this trend is that full-absorption product costing typically uses single cost drivers—for example, direct labor-hours, direct labor dollars, or machine-hours—to assign overhead costs to products. While these measures may provide an acceptable basis for allocating manufacturing overhead for financial reporting purposes, they may fail to capture differing amounts of overhead associated with each product. Applying overhead averaged over a single activity base to products may undercost some products and overcost others. Averaging profits over all product lines may be acceptable for companies operating in the absence of strong competition. Unfortunately, companies facing fierce competitive environments may make incorrect decisions when using inaccurate cost data.

APPENDIX

PROCESS COSTING

Process costing systems reflect work organized and collected by continuous processes rather than by batches and jobs. Process costing can be characterized as follows:

- Work is organized around processes.
- Costs are collected by processes. Direct materials are issued and direct labor is traced to specific processes. Manufacturing overhead is assigned to a process using an overhead rate.
- The cost of goods completed and transferred from work in process to finished goods is based on equivalent "whole" units of work performed. Total cost is divided by equivalent whole units to determine unit cost. Costs of goods completed are transferred from work in process to finished goods at the equivalent whole-unit cost.
- The cost of completed units is maintained in finished goods at the equivalent whole-unit cost until the product is sold.

Cost collection begins by attributing costs to processes. For example, imagine a continuous production line where one specific model of microwave oven is assembled. Assume that the line is always moving. It would be difficult, and probably not worth the effort, to track the number of labor-hours spent in assembling each individual microwave oven. Labor-hours and costs are, instead, attached to the assembly process rather than to individual units. At the end of each period—say, at the end of each month—the number of partially completed ovens is counted and converted into an equivalent number of completed ovens. A unit cost is calculated by dividing the total cost accumulated during that period by the number of equivalent units.

The key to process costing is the conversion of partially completed units into **equivalent whole units.** For example, assume there are no microwave ovens in process on January 1, and that 1,000 microwave ovens are started in production during the month. A physical count reveals that there are 250 ovens still in process at the end of January. Furthermore, the ovens still in process are considered to be 20 percent complete, on the average, with respect to their direct labor content. Therefore, of the 1,000 oven units started during January, 750 pass all the way through production, each receiving 100 percent of the required direct labor. The remaining 250 units, having received only 20 percent of the required direct labor, are left in the inventory of work in process.

As shown in Exhibit 5.18, each of the 250 units in the ending inventory receives, on the average, 20 percent of the labor content. The number of equivalent whole units—that is, ovens that are the equivalent of 100 percent complete with respect to direct labor in the ending inventory of work in process—is equal to 50 (20% × 250). In total, 800 equivalent whole units of direct labor (750 "wholly" completed units and 50 "equivalently wholly" completed units in the ending inventory) are expended during January. If January labor cost is $12,000, then each equivalent whole

EXHIBIT 5.18 PROCESS COSTING—DIRECT LABOR

Physical Units and Cost Data	Physical Units	Degree of Completion	Cost
Units in process at beginning of July	0		
Units started during July	1,000		$12,000
Total units available in July	1,000		
Units completed during July	750	100%	
Units in ending inventory	250	20%	

Computation of Equivalent Units	Physical Units	Degree of Completion	Equivalent Units
Units completed during July	750	100%	750
Units in ending inventory	250	20%	50
Total equivalent units			800
Direct labor cost			$12,000
Direct labor cost per equivalent unit			$15.00

Cost Accounted for	Equivalent Units	Cost per Equivalent Unit	Total Cost
Direct labor cost of units completed	750	$15.00	$11,250
Direct labor cost of units in ending inventory	50	$15.00	750
Total direct labor cost			$12,000

unit of labor costs $15 ($12,000/800 equivalent whole units). Ovens completed and transferred to finished goods are charged $11,250 (750 completed ovens × $15 per unit) for direct labor, while the ending inventory of work in process is left with the remaining $750 ($12,000 − $11,250 transferred to finished goods). We can double-check this $750 by multiplying the 50 equivalent whole units of labor in the ending inventory of work in process by $15 per equivalent unit of labor.

We can extend this process costing example from only direct labor to all manufacturing costs, including direct materials and manufacturing overhead. Assume the following:

- Microwave ovens are manufactured on a continuous production line.
- There is no work-in-process inventory on July 1, the beginning of the month.
- During the month of July, 1,000 microwave ovens are started.
- A physical count reveals 250 ovens still in process on July 31, the end of the month.
- Manufacturing overhead is applied on the basis of direct labor-hours.
- The ending inventory of 250 microwave ovens is considered 100 percent complete for materials but only 20 percent complete with respect to direct labor and manufacturing overhead.

The data representing the physical completion status of the units and the respective costs are shown in the top section of Exhibit 5.19. A total

EXHIBIT 5.19 PROCESS COSTING

For the Month Ending July 31

Physical Units and Cost Data	Physical Units	Degree of Completion	Cost
Units in process at beginning of July	0		
Units started during July	1,000		
Total units available in July	1,000		
Cost added during July:			
Direct materials			$ 5,000
Direct labor			12,000
Manufacturing overhead			18,000
Total cost to account for			$35,000
Units completed during July	750	100%	
Units in ending inventory:	250		
Direct materials		100%	
Direct labor		20%	
Manufacturing overhead		20%	
Total ending inventory			

			Equivalent Units		
Computation of Equivalent Units	Physical Units	Degree of Completion	Direct Materials	Direct Labor	Manufacturing Overhead
Units started & completed	750	100%	750	750	750
Units in ending inventory, July 1:					
Direct materials	250	100%	250		
Direct labor	250	20%		50	
Manufacturing overhead	250	20%			50
Total equivalent units of production in July			1,000	800	800
Total cost added in July			$5,000	$12,000	$18,000
Cost per equivalent unit of production			$5.00	$15.00	$22.50

Cost Accounted for	Physical Units	Degree of Completion	Equivalent Units	Cost per Equivalent Unit	Total Cost
Units started & completed:					
Direct materials	750	100%	750	$ 5.00	$ 3,750
Direct labor	750	100%	750	15.00	11,250
Manufacturing overhead	750	100%	750	22.50	16,875
Total cost of units started & completed					$31,875
Units in ending inventory:					
Direct materials	250	100%	250	5.00	$1,250
Direct labor	250	20%	50	15.00	750
Manufacturing overhead	250	20%	50	22.50	1,125
Total cost of units in ending inventory					$3,125
Total cost accounted for					$35,000

of $35,000 in direct materials, direct labor, and manufacturing overhead is introduced in July, when 1,000 microwave ovens are started. Of the 1,000 ovens started, 750 ovens are completed and transferred to finished goods. Each of the 750 units started and finished during July contains 100 percent of the per-unit direct materials, direct labor, and manufacturing overhead costs.

The middle section shows the computation of equivalent units. Each of the 750 units started and completed receives 100 percent of the per-unit direct materials, direct labor, and manufacturing overhead costs. A problem arises with the ending inventories, since direct materials, direct labor, and manufacturing overhead each received different degrees of processing. For example, each of the 250 units in the ending inventory received all of the direct materials. There are, as a consequence, 1,000 equivalent units of direct materials, including 750 equivalent units started and completed, plus 250 equivalent units of direct materials in the ending inventory. Dividing $5,000 of direct materials cost by 1,000 equivalent units produces a $5 cost per equivalent unit of materials.

The 250 partially completed physical units in the ending inventory are also only partially completed with respect to direct labor and manufacturing overhead. As we just explained, these physical units are converted into 50 equivalent whole units of direct labor by multiplying 250 by 20 percent, the degree of completion of the ending inventory of work in process with respect to direct labor. Adding the 50 equivalent units in the ending inventory to the 750 equivalent units started and finished during July yields a total of 800 equivalent units of direct labor for the month. Dividing $12,000 of direct labor cost by 800 equivalent units produces a $15 cost per equivalent unit of direct labor. Since manufacturing overhead is applied on the basis of direct labor-hours, the number of equivalent units is the same for manufacturing overhead as for direct labor. Dividing $18,000 of manufacturing overhead cost by 800 equivalent units produces a $22.50 cost per equivalent unit of manufacturing overhead.

The bottom section illustrates how the $35,000 in cost introduced in July is accounted for. Since 750 units were started and completed in July, each unit is complete with respect to direct materials, direct labor, and manufacturing overhead, at a cost of $42.50 ($5.00 in direct materials + $15.00 in direct labor + $22.50 of manufacturing overhead) per equivalent unit. Therefore, $31,875 (750 equivalent units × $42.50 per unit) of cost is transferred from work in process to finished goods. The remaining $3,125 in the ending inventory of work in process is composed of 250 equivalent units of direct materials at $5.00 per unit, 50 equivalent units of direct labor at $15.00 per unit, and 50 equivalent units of manufacturing overhead at $22.50 per unit.

DISCUSSION PROBLEMS

D5.1 (Different Kinds of Costing Systems)

An article in *The Hollywood Reporter* lists the costs of making a typical ($25.2-million) film.[5] The costs, reproduced in Exhibit D5.1, are broken down into those "above the line," meaning talent and producing fees, and those "below the line," meaning everything else. However, a number of different conditions influence what a film ultimately costs. For example, a thriller (e.g., *True Lies*) might require a special location or a period drama (e.g., *Schindler's List*) might require heavy set expenditures, while an adventure film (e.g., *Jurassic Park*) might require lots of special effects.

Required:

1. What kind of cost system would a film studio probably use?
2. On its 1992 balance sheet, the Walt Disney Company lists an asset called "Film and Television Cost" that totals $760.5 million. What kinds of costs do you think are included in film and television cost? That is, what kinds of costs are considered product costs for films?

D5.2 (Different Kinds of Costing Systems)

Caterpillar Inc., a multinational company with headquarters in Peoria, Illinois, has three primary lines of business:[6]

1. The design, manufacture, and marketing of earthmoving, construction, and materials-handling machinery. Examples include the familiar track-and-wheel tractors, lift trucks, and log skidders.
2. The design, manufacture, and marketing of engines. Examples include diesel, spark-ignited, and turbine engines for on-highway trucks, and marine and locomotive engines.
3. The provision of financial products, primarily financial services in acquiring both equipment made by Caterpillar and noncompeting equipment.

Caterpillar, which reported revenue of nearly $11.6 billion in 1993 versus $10.19 billion in 1992, sells more than 40 percent of its output in the United States and employs over 50,000 people worldwide.

Caterpillar unveiled a new "300" series of excavators designed for worldwide distribution. The 325 hydraulic excavator, the first in the new series, moved from the computer screen to production in 1991.

Required:

1. What kind of cost system do you think Caterpillar uses?
2. In addition to direct costs, what kinds of costs do you think are included in manufacturing overhead for the 325 hydraulic excavator?

---

[5] Frank Spotnitz, "Go Figure," *The Hollywood Reporter*, 1993 Craft Series, p. S6.

[6] Information on Caterpillar was taken from its 1991 annual report and from Robert L. Rose, "Labor Strife Threatens Caterpillar's Booming Business," *The Wall Street Journal*, June 10, 1994, p. B4.

EXHIBIT D5.1   THE COST OF MAKING A TYPICAL HOLLYWOOD MOVIE

Talent & producing cost:

Story rights	$ 304,000
Producers	927,000
Director	1,900,000
Cast	9,900,000
Total talent & producing cost	$13,031,000

Production cost:

Production staff	$ 767,000
Extra talent	769,000
Set design	340,000
Set construction	648,000
Set rigging & striking	60,000
Set operations	315,000
Special effects	638,000
Set dressing	449,000
Property	289,000
Wardrobe	356,000
Picture vehicles & animals	165,000
Makeup & hairdressing	197,000
Set lighting	350,000
Camera	124,000
Production sound	124,000
Transportation	1,500,000
Location	1,800,000
Production film & lab	373,000
Production video	29,000
Special unit	500,000
Tests	50,000
Production facilities	150,000
Total production cost	$9,993,000

Postproduction cost:

Photo effects & stock shots	$ 45,000
Editorial & projection	813,000
Music	300,000
Postproduction sound	322,000
Postproduction film & lab	106,000
Titles	30,000
Postproduction video	10,000
Total postproduction cost	$1,626,000

Other cost:

Publicity	$ 89,000
Insurance	209,000
General expense	213,000
Fees & charges	32,000
Total other cost	$543,000
Total cost	$25,193,000

Source: Frank Spotnitz, "Go Figure," *The Hollywood Reporter,* 1993 Craft Series, p. S6.

EXHIBIT P5.1 BETT BROTHERS MANUFACTURING

Actual Costs for the Month of May

Inventory Account	Beginning of May	End of May
Raw materials inventory	$23,600	$18,700
Work in process	$345,000	$387,200
Finished goods	$78,000	$86,300

Other Data	Month of May
Raw material purchases	$202,900
Direct labor cost incurred	$411,900
Manufacturing overhead incurred	$531,600

PROBLEMS

P5.1 (Statement of Cost of Goods Manufactured and of Cost of Goods Sold)

Bett Brothers Manufacturing, which makes office furniture, gathered the cost data shown in Exhibit P5.1 for the month of May. All accounting records are based on actual cost.

Required: Prepare a statement of cost of goods manufactured and a statement of cost of goods sold for the month of May.

P5.2 (Normal Job-Order Costing)

Norwood Electronic Products manufactures high-tech electronic switchgear for a variety of industrial applications. Norwood, which uses a normal job-order costing system, based its predetermined overhead rate on an estimate of $486,000 in annual manufacturing overhead. Managers estimated that direct labor-hours, the base used in applying manufacturing overhead, would equal 9,000 hours for the year.

Actual data for the month of January are shown in Exhibit P5.2. These data represent jobs that were started during the month. Norwood, whose year starts on January 1, had no beginning inventories of work in process or finished goods.

Required: Calculate the total cost of each job. What is the amount of overapplied (underapplied) overhead at the end of January? What happens to the overapplied (underapplied) overhead at the end of January?

EXHIBIT P5.2 NORWOOD ELECTRONIC PRODUCTS

Manufacturing Data for January

Actual Data for Jobs Started in January	Job A11	Job B04	Job C33	Total
Actual materials issued to jobs	$33,200	$18,700	$56,100	$108,000
Actual direct labor-hours	320	60	280	660
Actual hourly labor rate—all jobs				$12.45
Actual manufacturing overhead—all jobs				$43,200

EXHIBIT P5.3.1 CHEN MANUFACTURING

Standard Cost

Manufacturing Cost	Standard	Standard Cost
Direct materials	3 lb @ $4.50/lb	$13.50
Direct labor	2.5 hr @ $12.70/hr	31.75
Manufacturing overhead	2.5 hr @ $18.00/hr	45.00
Standard unit manufacturing cost		$90.25

EXHIBIT P5.3.2 CHEN MANUFACTURING

Jobs in Production and Actual Costs for January

	Job Number			
Jobs in Production	A-005	B-231	C-087	All jobs
Status of job	Completed	Completed	Completed	
Inventory account	Cost of goods sold	Finished goods	Finished goods	
Units placed in production	2,500	22,000	13,500	38,000
Actual Cost for January				
Actual direct materials cost	$35,407	$286,543	$193,459	$ 515,409
Actual direct labor cost	77,540	722,390	431,865	1,231,795
Actual manufacturing overhead cost				1,754,000
Total actual cost for January				$3,501,204

P5.3 (Basic Standard Cost)

The standard manufacturing cost for Chen Manufacturing's only product is shown in Exhibit P5.3.1. Chen started the current year with no inventory in work in process or in finished goods. During January, three new jobs were started. The status of the jobs at the end of January and actual manufacturing cost for the month are shown in Exhibit P5.3.2. Company policy is to net manufacturing variances against one another at the end of each month. Any net favorable or unfavorable manufacturing variance is charged to cost of goods sold.

Required: Calculate the cost of goods sold for January.

P5.4 (Cost of Goods Manufactured)

Mat Company's cost of goods sold for the month ending March 31 was $345,000. The ending work-in-process inventory was 90 percent of the beginning work-in-process inventory. Manufacturing overhead was applied at 50 percent of direct labor cost. Inventories and direct materials purchases are shown in Exhibit P5.4. Mat Company uses a normal costing system.

EXHIBIT P5.4 MAT COMPANY	
Data for March	
Beginning inventories (March 1):	
Raw materials	$20,000
Work in process	$40,000
Finished goods	$102,000
Direct materials purchases during March	$110,000
Ending inventories (March 31):	
Raw materials	$26,000
Work in process	?
Finished goods	$105,000

Required:

1. Prepare an analysis of the finished-goods inventory. Calculate the cost of goods manufactured for the month of March.
2. Prepare an analysis of the work-in-process inventory. Calculate the cost of direct labor and manufacturing overhead applied during March.

(AICPA Adapted)

P5.5 (Basic Job-Order Costing, Actual Cost)

Bobbitt Boats makes sailboats. After being in the boat-building business for nearly 50 years, Bobbitt has established a reputation for excellent designs and quality of work. Most of the boats it builds are in the 20- to 30-ft range. Potential customers pick out a design, make whatever modifications they want, and then decide how the boat is to be equipped. When Bobbitt doesn't have firm orders and is left with excess capacity, it builds boats for inventory.

Bobbitt uses a job-order costing system to keep track of the costs for each boat it makes. Manufacturing overhead is assigned to jobs using an actual costing system. At the end of each month, Bobbitt determines actual manufacturing overhead and divides it by the total direct labor cost for the month to get an actual overhead rate. The rate is then multiplied by the direct labor cost to determine the amount of overhead to assign to each boat.

Production data for the month of March are shown in Exhibit P5.5.1. A report on the status of the various jobs during March is shown in Exhibit P5.5.2.

Required:

1. Calculate the cost of each job processed during March.
2. Calculate the cost of the ending inventory for raw materials, work in process, and finished goods.

P5.6 (Job-Order Costing, Normal Cost)

Northcoast Manufacturing Company, which makes parts used in appliances, has just completed its first year of operation. The company's controller, Vic Trainor, has been preparing estimates of manufacturing overhead for next year. Trainor's estimates are shown in Exhibit P5.6.

Northcoast applies factory overhead using a predetermined, plantwide rate that is based on direct labor-hours. Trainor believes that normal activity for the next couple of years is going to be right around 600,000 units of product.

EXHIBIT P5.5.1 BOBBITT BOATS

Production Data for the Month of March

Beginning inventories—March 1:	
Raw materials	$47,600
Work in process:	
Job A-13	2,340
Job B-14	3,870
Finished goods—job C-24:	6,750
Total beginning inventories	$60,560
Raw material purchases in March	$13,450
Materials issued to jobs in March:	
Job A-13	$ 2,320
Job B-14	1,870
Job D-39	3,450
Job E-44	5,620
Job F-54	4,580
Total materials	$17,840
Direct labor cost for jobs in March:	
Job A-13	$ 5,870
Job B-14	3,460
Job D-39	7,820
Job E-44	5,490
Job F-54	1,870
Total direct labor cost	$24,510
Manufacturing overhead cost incurred in March:	
Supervision	$37,400
Materials handling & warehousing	22,100
Depreciation—facility	8,650
Depreciation—equipment	3,280
Utilities	1,890
Indirect materials	1,090
Total manufacturing overhead cost	$74,410

EXHIBIT P5.5.2 BOBBITT BOATS

Status of Jobs—March 31

Job	Status
A-13	Completed, sold
B-14	Completed, finished-goods inventory
C-24	Sold
D-39	Incomplete, work-in-process inventory
E-44	Completed, sold
F-54	Incomplete, work-in-process inventory

Required: Assuming that actual overhead for next year turns out to be $920,000 and that actual direct labor-hours turn out to be 35,000, determine the dollar amount of overapplied or underapplied factory overhead. What happens to overapplied or underapplied factory overhead?

(CMA Adapted)

EXHIBIT P5.6 NORTHCOAST MANUFACTURING COMPANY

Budgeted Annual Costs—Manufacturing Overhead

Activity measure:			
Units of product	360,000	540,000	720,000
Direct labor-hours	21,600	32,400	43,200
Manufacturing overhead cost:			
Plant supervision	$ 70,000	$ 70,000	$ 70,000
Plant rent	40,000	40,000	40,000
Depreciation—equipment	378,000	378,000	378,000
Maintenance	43,200	64,800	86,400
Utilities	115,200	172,800	230,400
Indirect materials	86,400	129,600	172,800
Other manufacturing overhead	16,000	16,000	16,000
Total manufacturing overhead cost	$748,800	$871,200	$993,600

P5.7 (Actual Cost; Affect of Volume on Unit Cost)

Vicki Surez lives in Key West, Florida. With all of the tourist attractions as potential clients, she decided to start selling custom-designed T-shirts. After founding Terrific T's, she immediately began capturing market share because of her innovative designs and high-quality materials.

When Surez receives an order she calls her T-shirt supplier and has the shirts sent directly to the shop. She negotiated a fixed price in January based on the number of T-shirts she expects to sell for the whole year. This arrangement allows her to buy shirts in virtually any lot size yet get the same unit price. After receiving the shirts, she puts her two full-time employees to work printing the designs.

One of Surez's first clients, Attractions, Inc., ordered 1,350 shirts in April. Not only was it pleased with the quality of work, but the unit price of $5.21 was less than the usual price of $5.75. As soon as it ran out of stock, Attractions, Inc., placed another order, this time for 2,250 T-shirts to be delivered in mid-December. The owners were shocked when they received a bill in January for $13,807, or $6.14 per shirt. They requested a meeting with Surez to discuss price and—in their words—to "reevaluate a continued relationship with Terrific T's."

Surez keeps track of costs using a job-order costing system that consists of two components: materials and production overhead (labor is included in overhead). Each T-shirt costs $2.80, the amount Surez pays to her supplier. Surez assigns production overhead cost to jobs based on materials cost. She waits until the end of each month, when she knows the actual overhead and materials costs. Then, Vicki divides actual overhead by actual materials cost to come up with an actual overhead rate for that particular month. After adding production overhead to materials, Surez multiplies the total by 135 percent to cover office expense and advertising and to provide a reasonable profit for her efforts.

Surez knows almost to the penny what production overhead is going to be each month. Rent, utilities, equipment rental, salaries, and the fixed part of production overhead cost a total of $11,500 each month. The variable part of production overhead changes in direct proportion with materials cost. Based on past experience, every dollar increase in materials cost causes a $0.25-increase in production overhead.

Surez prepared a schedule of actual materials cost for the year, as shown in Exhibit P5.7, to help her sort out why the job costs were so different in April and December.

EXHIBIT P5.7 TERRIFIC T'S

Actual Direct Materials Cost

Month	Direct Materials Cost
January	$ 42,000
February	50,400
March	61,600
April	89,600
May	39,200
June	67,200
July	44,800
August	78,400
September	84,000
October	58,800
November	50,400
December	30,800
Total year	$697,200

Required:

1. Reconstruct Surez's calculation of the billing price for the April and December batches of T-shirts.
2. How would the use of a normal costing system have changed the amount Surez billed Attractions, Inc., in April and December? Assume the normal level of direct materials is $697,200 per year.

P5.8 (Job-Order, Normal Costing; Cost of Goods Manufactured)

Valport Company uses a normal job-order costing system. Manufacturing overhead is applied on the basis of machine-hours, using a predetermined overhead rate. The current rate of $15 per machine-hour for the fiscal year ending November 30 was based on an estimated manufacturing overhead cost of $1,200,000 and an estimated activity level of 80,000 machine-hours. Valport's policy is to charge any overapplied or underapplied manufacturing overhead to the cost of goods sold.

Operations for the year have been completed. Managers are now trying to determine how much manufacturing overhead to apply to jobs worked on during November. In addition, they have to figure out how much cost to transfer from work in process to finished goods for the jobs completed in November. Finally, they have to calculate the amount of costs to transfer from finished goods to cost of goods sold for the jobs sold during November.

Data accumulated from the firm's accounting records as of October 31 and for the month of November are presented in Exhibit P5.8.

Jobs N11-007, N11-013, and N11-015 were completed during November. All completed jobs—except job N11-013—had been turned over to customers by the close of business on November 30.

Required:

1. How much manufacturing overhead would Valport have applied to jobs through October 31? How much manufacturing overhead would be applied to jobs by Valport during November? What is the amount of manufacturing overhead overapplied or underapplied as of November 30?

EXHIBIT P5.8 VALPORT COMPANY

Production Data

Work in Process		November		
Job No.	Balance, October 31	Direct Materials	Direct Labor	Machine-Hours
N11-007	$ 87,000	$ 1,500	$ 4,500	300
N11-013	55,000	4,000	12,000	1,000
N11-015	0	25,600	26,700	1,400
D12-002	0	37,900	20,000	2,500
D12-003	0	26,000	16,800	800
Total work in process	$142,000	$95,000	$80,000	6,000

Operating Activity	Through October 31	Month of November
Manufacturing overhead incurred:		
Indirect materials	$ 125,000	$ 9,000
Indirect labor	345,000	30,000
Utilities	245,000	22,000
Depreciation	385,000	35,000
Total manufacturing overhead	$1,100,000	$96,000
Other data:		
Materials purchases (direct & indirect)	$965,000	$98,000
Direct labor cost	$845,000	$80,000
Machine-hours	73,000	6,000

Inventory Balances	At Beginning of Fiscal Year, December 1	At End of Fiscal Year, November 30
Materials (excluding indirect materials)	$105,000	$85,000
Work in process	$60,000	
Finished goods	$125,000	

2. Determine the balance in Valport Company's finished-goods inventory at November 30.
3. Prepare a statement of cost of goods manufactured for Valport Company for the year ending November 30. (*Note:* Be careful of your treatment of indirect materials.)

(*CMA Adapted*)

P5.9 (Comprehensive Job-Order Costing, Standard Cost)

Southwest Outdoor Furniture started operations on January 1, 1995. Gloria Zahn founded Southwest when she recognized that inexpensive but durable outdoor furniture was hard to find. After conducting an informal market survey, Zahn leased a warehouse, bought equipment, hired permanent employees, and started making outdoor-quality chairs under the logo "S-O-F."

Her chair-manufacturing process is simple. It begins with 3-in PVC pipe that employees cut to form the chair's frame. Then the chair frame is pieced together with adhesives. Next, the pieces that form the top and bottom of the chair's cushions are cut from cloth and sewn together after being stuffed with a nylon filling.

The firm's logo is attached to the products, and the chairs are placed in cartons for shipment.

Zahn sells chairs to large furniture retailers. Since orders come in batches, she uses a standard job-order costing system based on the data shown in Exhibit P5.9.1. Each chair requires $20.65 of standard materials and $8.44 in direct labor. Manufacturing overhead is applied on the basis of direct labor-hours. Zahn estimates that manufacturing overhead will be $135,000 next year and expects to operate at 9,000 normal direct labor-hours. The estimates result in a standard manufacturing overhead rate of $15 per direct labor-hour, or $18 per chair.

Zahn landed the four big jobs shown in Exhibit P5.9.2 during 1995, her first year of operation. Three of the four jobs started in 1995 were completed by year-end (jobs 01, 02, and 03). Job 04 received all of the materials but was only about halfway completed with respect to direct labor and manufacturing overhead. Of the three completed jobs, two were sold (jobs 01 and 03), leaving only job 02 in the ending inventory of finished goods. Zahn started operations with no beginning inventories of materials, work in process, or finished goods.

Actual materials purchased and the amount of materials issued to production during the year are shown in Exhibit P5.9.3. In addition, actual direct labor and manufacturing overhead costs for the year are shown at the bottom of Exhibit P5.9.3.

Zahn maintains the direct materials inventory at actual cost. All materials acquisitions are recorded at actual quantity multiplied by actual price. Materials

---

EXHIBIT P5.9.1 SOUTHWEST OUTDOOR FURNITURE

Standard Costs for Chairs

Direct Materials

Material	Measure	Quantity	Price	Total
PVC—straight	Linear feet	24.00	$0.46	$11.04
Nylon & filling	Square yards	6.50	1.26	8.19
Supplies	Chair	1.00	1.42	1.42
Total materials				$20.65

Direct Labor

Activity	Grade	Hours	Rate	Total
Cut PVC	A	0.20	$6.80	$1.36
Sew pads	B	0.40	7.50	3.00
Assemble frame	A	0.60	6.80	4.08
Total direct labor		1.20		$8.44

Manufacturing Overhead

Activity	Variable	Fixed	Total
Normal overhead	$36,000	$99,000	$135,000
Normal direct labor-hours			9,000
Normal overhead rate per hour			$ 15.00
Direct labor-hours per chair			1.20
Manufacturing overhead per chair			$ 18.00
Standard manufactured cost per chair			$47.09

EXHIBIT P5.9.2 SOUTHWEST OUTDOOR FURNITURE

Jobs in Production

Job No.	Units	Standard Units of Materials	Standard Units of Labor & Overhead	Status at End of Year
01	900	900	900	Completed—sold
02	2,200	2,200	2,200	Completed—finished goods
03	3,600	3,600	3,600	Completed—sold
04	1,300	1,300	650	Incomplete—work in process
Total	8,000	8,000	7,350	

EXHIBIT P5.9.3 SOUTHWEST OUTDOOR FURNITURE

Production Data for Chairs

Raw Materials Purchases

Material	Measure	Actual Quantity	Actual Price	Total Actual
PVC—straight	Linear feet	200,000	$0.45	$ 90,000
Nylon & filling	Square yards	60,000	1.30	78,000
Supplies	Chair	8,500	1.48	12,580
Total materials				$180,580

Raw Materials Issued—Actual

Material	Measure	Actual Quantity	Actual Price	Total Actual
PVC—straight	Linear feet	195,000	$0.45	$ 87,750
Nylon & filling	Square yards	51,000	1.30	66,300
Supplies	Chair	8,200	1.48	12,136
Total materials				$166,186
Direct labor cost—actual				$ 60,000
Manufacturing overhead—actual				$142,500

issued to production are taken out of the raw materials inventory at actual quantity multiplied by actual price. Materials going into work in process, however, are recorded at standard quantity multiplied by standard price. As a result, materials variances are recognized when materials are issued to production. Work in process and finished goods are both recorded at standard cost. Any differences between standard and actual costs—that is, all variances—are charged against cost of goods sold in the current year.

Required:

1. Calculate the inventory of direct materials at the end of 1995 using actual cost. Also calculate the standard cost of direct materials issued to production.

2. Calculate the standard direct labor and manufacturing overhead costs that were charged to work in process during the year.
3. Calculate the standard cost of jobs 01, 02, 03, and 04.
4. Calculate the dollar amount of ending inventory of work in process and finished goods at standard cost. Calculate cost of goods sold, assuming all differences between standard and actual costs are charged against the current period (e.g., charged against cost of goods sold).

P5.10 (Variable vs. Full Absorption Costing)

Com\Plex Computing, based in Dublin, Ireland, developed an accounting software package several years ago that sells for $75. The customer base is a small but dedicated group of European users. Orders are sent to Com\Plex's Dublin office from throughout Europe and Great Britain. The company's central computer aggregates orders, upon receipt, by language. Once enough orders in a common language—say, in Spanish—are received, a production time is scheduled. At the same time, the computer sends an electronic message to a printing company to which Com\Plex outsources user's manuals.

To prepare the software, an employee inserts a blank floppy disk in equipment that simultaneously formats the disk and transfers the computer code from a master file in the appropriate language onto the blank disk. It takes only about 80 seconds per disk. Next, the floppy disks are placed in an electronic device that compares the newly coded software disks with the master file for discrepancies. Finally, several test transactions are executed to ensure that the software is functioning properly.

After passing quality control, the disks are moved to another work area, where they are inserted into protective paper sleeves and the packages shrink-wrapped. Then, the packages, containing disks and user's manuals, are placed in display boxes labeled in the appropriate language. Finally, the display boxes are wrapped in plastic film and placed in cartons for shipment.

Com\Plex currently employs a full-absorption costing system based on actual overhead rates. Full costs for three different volumes are shown in Exhibit P5.10.

The cost of Com\Plex's product and its $75 selling price are based on a normal volume of 30,000 units. At the beginning of the current year, Com\Plex's managers decided to make 33,000 units—the same number of units they sold the year before. However, the unexpected entry of a competing software package into the market and downturns in general economic conditions caused sales to reach only 24,000 units by year-end. Because they started the current year with no inventory, managers were left with 9,000 units in inventory at year-end.

Required:

1. Calculate pretax operating profit under full-absorption and variable costing, assuming Com\Plex makes 33,000 units, sells 24,000, and has 9,000 completed units in the ending inventory. Also assume that actual costs are exactly equal to budgeted costs. Over- or underapplied overhead, if any, is charged to cost of goods sold.
2. Calculate the cost of the ending inventory of finished goods under full-absorption and under variable costing. Show that the difference between these two inventory costs is the same as the difference in pretax operating profits from requirement 1.

EXHIBIT P5.10 COM\PLEX COMPUTING			
Full Cost at Different Volumes			

	Volume (in Units)			Unit Cost at Normal Volume
	25,000	Normal— 30,000	35,000	
Direct materials:				
Floppy disk	$ 20,000	$ 24,000	$ 28,000	$ 0.80
Paper sleeve	1,500	1,800	2,100	0.06
Computer manual	294,000	352,800	411,600	11.76
Packaging	15,500	18,600	21,700	0.62
Total materials cost	$ 331,000	$ 397,200	$ 463,400	$13.24
Direct labor:				
Computer code	$ 106,250	$ 127,500	$ 148,750	$ 4.25
Assemble packages	85,000	85,000	85,000	2.83
Total direct labor cost	$ 191,250	$ 212,500	$ 233,750	$ 7.08
Manufacturing overhead:				
Heat, light, & power	$ 3,500	$ 4,200	$ 4,900	$ 0.14
Supervision	127,500	127,500	127,500	4.25
Leased equipment	56,250	56,250	56,250	1.88
Depreciation—facility	94,000	94,000	94,000	3.13
Other manufacturing	85,000	85,000	85,000	2.83
Total manufacturing overhead	$ 366,250	$ 366,950	$ 367,650	$12.23
Selling & administrative cost:				
Marketing	$ 175,000	$ 175,000	$175,000	$ 5.83
New product development	235,000	235,000	235,000	7.83
Administration	310,000	310,000	310,000	10.33
Technical assistance	115,000	115,000	115,000	3.83
Total selling & administrative cost	$ 835,000	$ 835,000	$ 835,000	$27.83
Full cost	$1,723,500	$1,811,650	$1,899,800	$60.39

P5.11 (Basic Process Costing; Direct Labor)

Smitt's Toasters makes upscale countertop toasters. It offers a single, standard model toaster with a suggested selling price of $89.95. Smitt's toasters are old-fashioned in appearance, heavy, and durable—just the qualities that some consumers are looking for. Smitt's makes the toasters on a continuous production line. The process begins when all of the materials are delivered in a container for the first operation. An employee places the electric heating elements in the bottom of the toaster frame. As partially assembled toasters move down the production line, the next employee installs a spring mechanism that holds the bread in place inside the toaster. The third operation entails placing the chrome exterior housing over the frame. In the final step, an employee attaches an electrical cord to the unit and places the finished toaster in a box for shipping.

Production began on May 1 of the current year. During this first month of operation, 18,400 toasters were started. A total of 2,730 toasters were still in process by the end of May. The toasters still in process were 100 percent complete with respect to materials but only 18 percent complete with respect to labor and manufacturing overhead. Total conversion cost (direct labor and manufacturing overhead) for the month was $112,600.

Required: Calculate the conversion cost (direct labor and manufacturing overhead) transferred to finished goods and the conversion cost in the ending inventory of work in process, using process costing.

P5.12   (Process Costing)

Gregg Industries manufactures a variety of plastic products, including a series of molded chairs. The three models of molded chairs, which are all variations of the same design, are:

1. Standard model
2. Deluxe model, which is the standard model with the addition of arms
3. Executive model, which is the deluxe model with the addition of padding

Gregg employs an extrusion operation and other processes to form, trim, and finish the chairs. Plastic sheets are produced by the extrusion operation. The sheets that are not used in making chairs are sold to other manufacturers. During the forming operation, plastic sheets are molded into chair seats and the legs are added. The standard model is ready for sale after this operation. During the trim operation, the arms are added to the deluxe and executive models, and the chair edges are smoothed. After this operation, the deluxe model is ready for sale. Only the executive model enters the finish operation. The finish operation adds padding to the deluxe model in order to convert it into the executive model. All of the units manufactured are subject to the same steps in each of the operations, although the number of operations undergone varies according to model.

May production resulted in a manufacturing cost totaling $898,000. The number of units produced and direct materials cost together with direct labor cost and manufacturing overhead cost are shown in Exhibit P5.12. Gregg uses process costing to keep track of production cost.

EXHIBIT P5.12   GREGG INDUSTRIES

Units Produced and Direct Materials Cost

| | | Materials, by Operation | | | |
	Units Produced	Extrusion	Form	Trim	Finish
Plastic sheets	5,000	$60,000			
Standard model	6,000	72,000	$24,000		
Deluxe model	3,000	36,000	12,000	$9,000	
Executive model	2,000	24,000	8,000	6,000	$12,000
Total	16,000	$192,000	$44,000	$15,000	$12,000

Manufacturing Costs Applied during May

| | Operation | | | |
	Extrusion	Form	Trim	Finish
Direct labor	$152,000	$60,000	$30,000	$18,000
Manufacturing overhead	$240,000	$72,000	$39,000	$24,000

Required:

1. Assuming each product made by Gregg Industries during May was started and completed during the month, determine the total and unit costs.
2. Without prejudice to your answer in requirement 1, assume that 1,000 units of the deluxe model remain in work in process at the end of the month. These units are 100 percent complete as to material cost and 60 percent complete with respect to direct labor and manufacturing overhead in the trim operation. Determine the value of the 1,000 units of the deluxe model in Gregg Industries' work-in-process inventory at the end of May.

(CMA Adapted)

CASES

C5.1 (Chow, Dragovitz and James)

Chow, Dragovitz and James are attorneys. The firm's specialty is condemnation work, which it performs for companies operating retail businesses. When a government agency starts a road improvement project, for example, the changes can have a dramatic impact on the businesses along the project's path. In this example, widening the road may alter the way customers enter a business or it may possibly eliminate parking spaces. Chow, Dragovitz and James represents clients in proceedings against the agencies in which they seek to gain compensation for their losses.

Debra Manos, the office manager for Chow, Dragovitz and James, does the billing. She relies on a normal job-order costing system for the data she needs. The general procedure Manos follows is described below:

- She traces actual direct costs—such as phone calls, consultant's fees, and travel—to specific jobs, without markup.
- Attorney costs are billed to specific clients based on the number of hours charged to the job. The sum of the attorney's annual salary cost and benefits cost is divided by the estimated number of billable hours to get an hourly billing rate.
- Indirect costs—that is, those not chargeable to specific clients—are grouped together under the heading office and administration cost (O&A). Whenever Manos charges a client for the number of hours an attorney worked on its case, she includes a charge for O&A.

Calculating the O&A rates starts with an estimate of office and administration cost for the coming year. Then Manos adds a pretax profit goal—which, for 1995, is $150,000. Next, she divides the combined O&A cost and profit goal by the total estimated billable hours.

Attorneys at Chow, Dragovitz and James billed a total of 4,500 hours in 1994 but expect to bill 5 percent more hours in 1995. Operating income for 1994, broken down by direct and O&A cost, is shown in Exhibit C5.1.1.

All of the O&A cost is fixed, with the exception of the copy equipment lease, office expense, and office payroll and taxes. The copy equipment lease calls for a base fixed monthly charge of $1,000, with an additional charge for each page copied. The additional charge tends to vary with billable hours. Office expense and office payroll and taxes also vary in rough proportion with the number of billable hours. Manos believes that fixed O&A cost is likely to increase in 1995 by 10 percent above 1994 levels. The rates for variable cost, on the other hand, are not expected to change in 1995.

Actual hours billed and O&A cost for 1995 are shown in Exhibit C5.1.2.

EXHIBIT C5.1.1 CHOW, DRAGOVITZ AND JAMES

Income Statement for the Year 1994

Professional fees	$1,225,000
Direct costs:	
Chargeable attorney salaries	$523,400
Attorney benefits	87,600
Phone charges	22,600
Transportation	57,200
Meals & lodging	58,200
Consultants & experts	65,100
Other direct costs	23,200
Total direct cost	$837,300
Direct profit	$387,700
Office & administrative (O&A) cost:	
Advertising	$24,300
Amortization & depreciation	8,400
Bank charges	1,500
Copy equipment lease	22,800
Insurance	9,200
Legal & accounting	8,700
License & permits	4,800
Office expense	84,600
Office payroll & taxes	64,800
Repair & maintenance	2,700
Telephone	18,600
Utilities	4,600
Total office & administration	$255,000
Operating income (before tax)	$132,700

EXHIBIT C5.1.2 CHOW, DRAGOVITZ AND JAMES

Actual Hours and Office & Administration (O&A) Costs for 1995

Month	Attorney Hours Billed	Actual O&A Costs
January	281	$ 19,830
February	360	21,670
March	326	21,380
April	409	22,210
May	427	23,750
June	315	21,360
July	327	23,560
August	317	21,100
September	403	23,290
October	471	26,430
November	422	24,900
December	362	23,690
Total year	4,420	$273,170

Required:

1. Calculate the predetermined O&A overhead rate that Manos used in 1995.
2. One of Chow, Dragovitz and James's clients is a company called Brown/Webber. Direct cost for Brown/Webber during 1995 included 23.5 hours of Alex Dragovitz's time. Dragovitz makes $87,000 per year plus 25 percent for benefits and is expected to bill a total of 1,500 hours. Other direct costs for Brown/Webber include $108.60 in phone charges; $489.50 in travel, food, and lodging; and $86.50 in filing fees. Calculate the charges to Brown/Webber.

C5.2 (Pot O' Gold Electronics)

Pot O' Gold is a wholly owned division of Damon Electronics. Damon created Pot O' Gold in late 1990 in order to develop, manufacture, and sell gaming devices for video draw poker, or VDPs. The event that catalyzed creation of Pot O' Gold was the introduction of a bill in the Louisiana legislature that would legalize VDPs.

Damon Electronics has been manufacturing video game electronics for the last 6 years. It recognized an opportunity when South Dakota legalized video poker in 1989. From an initial base of 800 machines, the number of devices in South Dakota grew to an estimated 6,000 units by 1992. Damon, whose prototype was late to market, put its VDP project on hold. However, when talk of the Louisiana legislation surfaced, Damon quickly completed its prototype and created the Pot O' Gold division.

Damon's new division, headed by Patrick Smeenge, was organized as a separate company in order to enable Damon to clearly measure its profitability. If, by the end of 3 years, his division doesn't show reasonable pretax operating profits, Smeenge knows that Damon is likely to discontinue Pot O' Gold.

Smeenge helped lobby for VDPs in Louisiana while he continued to pursue business in other states. To his surprise, the 1991 session of the Louisiana legislature adopted the Video Draw Poker Device Control Law. Under the new law, players can win up to $500 in cash or prizes. By law, VDPs can be placed in bars, restaurants, hotels, clubs, or any other place of business permitted to sell alcoholic beverages. The legislation also allows VDPs at race tracks, OTB (off-track betting) facilities, and even at truck stops. Machines are linked to a centralized computer controlled by the Louisiana State Police.

In order to elevate the image of the new VDPs and to reduce the potential for illegal activities, the Louisiana legislature requires strict control over licensing and set rigid manufacturing specifications for VDPs. Not only was Pot O' Gold prepared to meet the specifications, but a small batch of 10 prototype machines was already available to demonstrate the machine's capabilities. After a successful demonstration of the prototypes, Smeenge signed an exclusive agreement with one prominent promoter of VDPs in Louisiana who planned to install as many as 7,000 devices in the first year of operation.

With an agreement between Pot O' Gold and the VDP operator in his pocket, and bolstered by an initial order for 500 units, Smeenge began operations. He selected suppliers, the most prominent of which is Damon, which provides electronics boards and hired a small core of employees to manufacture the devices. After training for 3 weeks at Damon, new employees were given 2 more weeks of instruction at Pot O' Gold. After that, production began, and the first machines were boxed and shipped. In the meantime, Smeenge's representatives had made several sales in South Dakota. Smeenge felt that the Pot O' Gold device was superior to those already installed and hoped that the few units sold in South Dakota would lead to even more sales in the future. In addition, Smeenge was able to adapt the machine for nongaming applications, primarily for use in video game parlors. His hopes were that this would open up an entirely new—and perhaps even larger—market for the products.

The cost of manufacturing VDPs is shown in Exhibit C5.2. Variable cost totals $133 per unit, while fixed cost—calculated at 5,000 units, the level of production Smeenge expected for the year—totals $250. This results in a full manufacturing cost of $383 per unit. Fixed selling and administrative cost adds another $80 per unit, bringing the full cost to a total of $463. Adding a desired markup of 15 percent on full cost, Smeenge arrived at a selling price of $532.45, which he rounded down to $525 per unit.

Unfortunately, in November 1991, as the end of the first full year of operation approached, the volume of sales anticipated never materialized. Smeenge's revised projections placed expected sales at just about 4,000 units, rather than 5,000 units, which he originally projected. With these disappointing results, Smeenge tried to decide how many units to make by the end of the year. Pot O' Gold's accountant urged him to make only what he expected to sell—that is, 4,000 units. Smeenge, however, decided to build inventory in anticipation of the following year's sales. Rather than making only 4,000 units, Smeenge decided to add 1,000 units to the ending inventory of finished goods, for a total production of 5,000 units.

Required:

1. Calculate the pretax operating profit for 1991 using full-absorption costing under two assumptions. First, assume that Smeenge made and sold 4,000 units. Then, calculate pretax operating profit assuming he made 5,000 units but sold only 4,000 units. Reconcile the differences between the two. Do you think it's ethical for Smeenge to make 5,000 units when he is virtually certain to sell only 4,000 units?

EXHIBIT C5.2 POT O' GOLD ELECTRONICS

Cost to Manufacture VDPs

	Total	Unit
Expected activity for the year, units		5,000
Variable cost:		
Direct materials		$ 90.00
Variable labor		25.00
Variable manufacturing overhead		18.00
Total variable cost		$133.00
Fixed cost:		
Direct labor	$ 150,000	$ 30.00
Manufacturing overhead	1,100,000	220.00
Total fixed cost	$1,250,000	$250.00
Full manufacturing cost		$383.00
Fixed selling & administrative cost	$400,000	80.00
Full cost		$463.00
Desired markup on full cost (15 percent)		69.45
Target selling price		$532.45

2. What are the implications of each of the 1991 production strategies on 1992 if sales in 1992 were only 4,000 units? Assume that the cost structure was exactly the same in 1992 as in 1991. Calculate the pretax operating profit for 1992 under two assumptions, using full-absorption costing. First, assume that Smeenge made 4,000 units in 1991 and that he made and sold 4,000 units in 1992. Then, calculate pretax operating profit assuming he made 3,000 units in 1992 but sold 4,000, including 1,000 units left over from 1991.

3. Recalculate pretax operating income for 1991 assuming production of 4,000 and of 5,000 units, only this time using variable costing. Reconcile your answer with your data from requirements 1 and 2, above.

CHAPTER 6

SHORT-TERM DECISIONS AND PRICING

In the preceding chapters, we focused on what something cost, how costs are measured, and where cost data come from. We now turn to how managers use cost information in making decisions.

Whether planning for the future or coordinating what employees do, managers manage by making decisions. If they make the right decisions, they create value for their organizations. If they don't, and their decisions turn out to be wrong, then managers destroy value.

To show how cost information is used to make value-creating decisions, we will:

- Discuss the decision-making process
- Develop principles affecting short-term decisions
- Elaborate on the role played by cost in pricing decisions

MAKING DECISIONS

How do managers make decisions? In order to make decisions, managers must know how to:[1]

- Find appropriate occasions for decision making
- Identify alternative courses of action
- Choose among alternatives

FINDING OCCASIONS FOR DECISION MAKING

Successful decision making consists of making the right decision about the right problem or opportunity.[2] The first step in the decision-making process, then, is for managers to identify the right problem or opportunity—the right occasion for decision making. The right problems and opportunities are those with the greatest impact on the organization. Identifying these high-impact problems and opportunities starts with collecting information.

INFORMATION FROM DIFFERENT SOURCES

Some information sources are formal, systematic, and quantitative, like the information routinely collected in the financial accounting system. Other sources may be less formal, as is the information they provide, such as qualitative information about employee attitudes or customer satisfaction. Qualitative information such as this may never enter any formal reporting system. However, managers may still use it to supplement whatever quantitative data are available.

To deal with problems and take advantage of opportunities—whether they are discovered through formal or informal sources of information—requires making decisions that fall into one or more of the following categories:

- **Tactical decisions.** Decisions about day-to-day operations
- **Program decisions.** Decisions about projects and products
- **Strategic decisions.** Decisions about the long-term objectives of the organization

Tactical Decisions. Tactical decisions are often identified by the organization's formalized management control system. They generally focus on deployment of the firm's resources—for example, on assigning employees or equipment to specific tasks. Since tactical decisions are concerned with utilization of existing resources, they are not likely to affect the capacity of the organization nor are they immediately likely to impact its long-term future. Because tactical problems arise out of repetitive operations, they

[1] Herbert A. Simon, *The New Science of Management Decision*, revised ed., Englewood Cliffs, N.J.: Prentice-Hall, Inc., 1977, pp. 40–41.
[2] Alexander Cornell, *The Decision Maker's Handbook*, Englewood Cliffs, N.J.: Prentice-Hall, 1980, p. 13.

are generally well-understood by managers and can be assessed using quantitative data.

A common way of identifying problems whose solutions require tactical decision making is based on establishing standards for performance. For example, L. L. Bean, a mail-order retailer, processes phone orders within hours. By monitoring *thru-put time*—the time that elapses between receiving an order and shipping it—the company can immediately identify potential service problems and take appropriate actions. While some factors critical to the success of an organization can be quantified, such as L. L. Bean's thru-put time, other factors may be more difficult to translate into numbers. For example, regular meetings with employees may provide managers with warnings of potential problems and provide suggestions about how to avoid such problems before they arise. However, the benefits of such meetings may be difficult to quantify.

Program Decisions.   *Programs* generally refer to products and services. A commercial printer, for example, may decide to initiate a program offering printing services to a government agency. Or an auto parts manufacturer may initiate a 3-year program to convert production from carburetors to fuel injectors. Programs may also involve operations, such as a quality improvement program, or they may involve an organization's structure, such as a program to eliminate unnecessary layers of management. In each of these examples, program decisions have impacts on the organization over a relatively long period of time.

Identifying opportunities for program decisions generally comes about through monitoring long-term trends. For example, a commercial printer may notice that state agencies are eliminating internal printing operations. Based on this information, managers may decide to invest in new equipment and hire additional personnel—decisions that have long-term effects. Just as organizations may start new programs, they may also initiate programs that allow them to exit markets.

Strategic Decisions.   Decisions requiring strategic considerations are likely to have long-term impacts on an organization. It's not likely that formalized, quantitative sources will provide the data that signal problems in any of these areas. Rather, the signals will come from the recognition of other problems, from environmental scanning, or from the intuition and instincts—the "gut feelings"—of managers.

Strategic decisions are based on an organization's competitive advantage—that is, on what it does better than anyone else. Competitive advantage comes from adopting one of the two fundamental competitive strategies—*low cost* or *product differentiation*. Companies adopting a strategy of low cost sell the same products as their competitors, only at a lower cost and of the same or better quality. Southwest Airlines is a good example. It offers rock-bottom prices for basic, no-frills service. Differentiated products, on the other hand, either offer unique characteristics or deliver higher levels of service—extras that customers are willing to pay for. Air France, for example, is known for pampering its customers. In return, Air France's passengers expect to pay more for the service they receive.

EXHIBIT 6.1 VALUE CHAIN

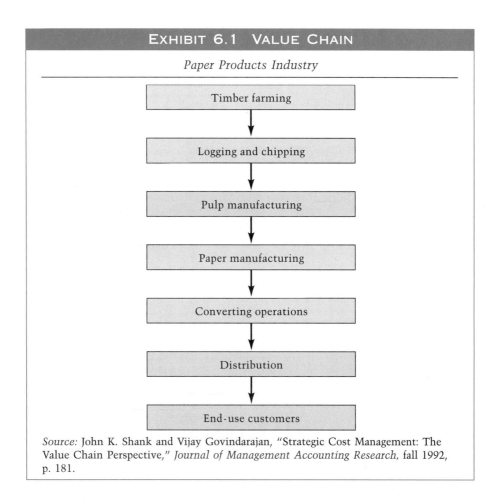

Paper Products Industry

Timber farming

↓

Logging and chipping

↓

Pulp manufacturing

↓

Paper manufacturing

↓

Converting operations

↓

Distribution

↓

End-use customers

Source: John K. Shank and Vijay Govindarajan, "Strategic Cost Management: The Value Chain Perspective," *Journal of Management Accounting Research*, fall 1992, p. 181.

Obtaining a competitive advantage—and keeping it—requires understanding the value chain for the industry within which the firm competes. The value chain concept was first introduced by Michael Porter.[3] According to Shank and Govindarajan, it is the "... set of value-creating activities all the way from basic raw material sources through the ultimate end-use product delivered into the final customers' hands."[4] For example, the value chain for the paper industry might include the broad-scale links shown in Exhibit 6.1. There are two types of links that make up the value chain—external links and internal links. External links lie outside of the boundary of the organization. Internal links, on the other hand, represent links within the organization. What's external and internal depends upon the position of the organization within the value chain. For example, a

[3] Michael E. Porter, *Competitive Advantage: Creating and Sustaining Superior Performance*, Glenwood, Ill.: The Free Press, 1985.
[4] John K. Shank and Vijay Govindarajan, "Strategic Cost Management: The Value Chain Perspective," *Journal of Management Accounting Research*, fall 1992, pp. 179–97.

firm engaged in pulp and paper manufacturing in the paper products industry occupies the third and fourth links in the value chain in Exhibit 6.1.
You may recall that we referred to internal links in Chapter 4 as processes.
Processes are subsequently broken down into lower-level processes and
ultimately into activities. External links are everything else in the value
chain. Timber farming, and logging and chipping, are considered *upstream*
links in the value chain while converting operations, distribution, and end-
use customers are considered *downstream* links. Understanding each of
the external links is important, since the organization depends upon
upstream suppliers and, in turn, is depended upon by downstream users
in later stages of the value chain.

IDENTIFYING ALTERNATIVE COURSES OF ACTION

Before trying to figure out what to do—regardless of whether the decision
concerns tactics, programs, or strategies—you must first determine how
the results are to be judged. That is, the search for a solution requires
establishing criteria that delineate what constitutes a good decision. In
many cases, the criteria are explicit—for example, improving thru-put
time or reducing costs. In other cases, the criteria are vague—for example, improving service or satisfying customers. Performance based on a single criterion, even when the criterion is vague, may be relatively easy to
measure. However, when multiple criteria have to be evaluated, it's more
difficult to measure performance. (See "Current Practice: Memory Products Division of Stolle Corporation.") Beware that satisfying one criterion
may come at the expense of doing so for other criteria. For example, choosing a course of action because of its favorable impact on customer satisfaction may result in not meeting another criterion—cost containment.

PREDICTION MODELS

Decisions are always about the future. That's why managers must always
anticipate what impacts are likely to result from their decisions. One way
to consider the likely outcomes of alternative courses of action is to build
prediction models. Prediction models are simplified representations of
complex activities. They capture important interactions among key variables—without the clutter of irrelevant details.

An example of a prediction model is shown in Exhibit 6.2. The Base
Case section represents existing conditions. Changes in the values of key
variables are introduced in the model to show what impacts those changes
have on the decision criteria. For example, what if the number of units
sold were to increase from 50,000 to 60,000? How would that change affect
net operating profit—the decision criterion? Based on this anticipated
increase in volume, managers might predict an increase in operating profit
from $250,000 to $450,000.

Prediction models can also be used to evaluate the impact of changes
in the organization's cost structure. For example, suppose new laborsaving
equipment is installed. Assume that unit variable cost decreases from $60
to $50, reflecting an increase in productivity. Also assume that the
decrease in variable cost, however, is offset by an increase in fixed cost—

CURRENT PRACTICE

Memory Products Division of Stolle Corporation

The Stolle Corporation's memory products division, which makes hard disks for personal computers, saw an opportunity to increase sales. A team was formed to identify an initial project that would take advantage of the opportunity. However, before the project could be evaluated, the team had to identify the criteria by which increased sales were to be judged. The best project, they argued, would be one with the largest favorable impact on:

- Product quality
- Cost
- Thru-put time
- Work-in-process inventories

- Percentage of handling damage

In addition, the team identified secondary selection criteria. The project should also:

- Minimize nonvalue-adding steps— such as scrap, defective work, and idle time
- Reduce distances between operations
- Improve process flow
- Reduce downtime
- Improve traceability of parts
- Encourage cooperation among employees
- Make the area where parts are polished a safer place to work

Source: Nabil Hassan, Herbert Brown, Paula Saunders, and Nick Koumoutzis, "Stolle Puts World Class into Memory," *Management Accounting*, Jan. 1993, pp. 22–25.

say, from $750,000 to $1 million. The change in cost structure, assuming 50,000 units are sold, causes a predicted increase in operating profit of $250,000 ($500,000 versus the base case profit of $250,000).

EVALUATE ALTERNATIVES

Alternative courses of action are evaluated by predicting the effect each has on the selection criteria. For problems occurring regularly—problems whose solutions entail making tactical decisions—managers are likely to have access to quantitative data that are helpful in generating dependable predictions of the impact on selection criteria. These routine, structured problems—such as daily work assignments—are called programmed decisions.[5] In fact, many programmed decisions can be reduced to rules or simple decision models that indicate how to solve the problems.

Decisions at the program level are often less structured than are programmed decisions. They often involve complex solutions. Alternative solutions to program-level problems are subject to a series of evaluation cycles. The idea is to reduce a large number of complex alternatives to a few simpler ones. The surviving alternatives are subject to extensive scrutiny. Behavioral considerations—ranging from the limited ability of

---

[5] Herbert A. Simon, op. cit., p. 45.

EXHIBIT 6.2 PREDICTION MODEL	
Base Case	

Revenue:	
Units sold	50,000
Unit selling price	$80
Total revenue	$4,000,000
Variable cost:	
Unit variable cost	$60
Total variable cost	$3,000,000
Total contribution margin	$1,000,000
Fixed cost	750,000
Net operating profit	$250,000

Change in Variables

Revenue:	
Units sold	60,000
Unit selling price	$80
Total revenue	$4,800,000
Variable cost:	
Unit variable cost	$60
Total variable cost	$3,600,000
Total contribution margin	$1,200,000
Fixed cost	750,000
Net operating profit	$450,000

Change in Structure

Revenue:	
Units sold	50,000
Unit selling price	$80
Total revenue	$4,000,000
Variable cost:	
Unit variable cost	$50
Total variable cost	$2,500,000
Total contribution margin	$1,500,000
Fixed cost	$1,000,000
Net operating profit	$500,000

managers to handle large volumes of information, to risk aversion, to factors such as group dynamics, individual biases, ethical values, and corporate cultures—ultimately limit the potential of achieving optimal solutions. (See "Current Practice: Johnson & Johnson's New Product Decisions.")

Problems requiring strategic decisions have virtually the same characteristics as those requiring program decisions. Strategic decisions generally involve one-of-a-kind threats or opportunities. It is often difficult, if not impossible, to measure all of the costs and benefits of strategic decisions. For example, managers evaluating entry into an entirely new market—a market they have no experience in—may be able to prepare accurate predictions of revenues and costs. But they may be less successful in measuring the impact of the decision on factors such as service quality

CURRENT PRACTICE

Johnson & Johnson's New Product Decisions

After investing millions of dollars in Medipren over 6 years, Johnson & Johnson took the nonprescription pain reliever off the shelves because of disappointing sales. In the dynamic health care industry, according to Elyse Tanouye, ". . . staying on top means scrambling relentlessly for new products, equipment and technology—and accepting occasional failures." In fact, a third of the company's sales in 1991 came from products introduced in the preceding 5 years. What distinguishes Johnson & Johnson is its ability to adapt quickly to changing market demands.

To create an organizational environment conducive to change, Johnson & Johnson decentralized its corporate structure into autonomous operating units. Under this arrangement, midlevel managers have the authority to make decisions that pursue new products—even though their own higher-level managers may not agree. Sometimes these deci-

sions don't work out successfully. Medipren is a good example. But, according to top management, more winning products are generated than are losing products. In the mid-1980s, for example, Paul Bowman, an international vice president, proposed creation of a subsidiary to sell products in Turkey. Some executives felt that the Turkish economy was unstable and argued against the project. Mr. Bowman prevailed, and the project was approved.

According to Mr. Bowman, 99 percent of his belief in the idea was based on "gut feel." And his instincts were correct. Chief executive Ralph Larsen, conceding that he was wrong, says that Johnson & Johnson has a strong business in Turkey today as the result of the persistence of Mr. Bowman. Since 1986, sales in Turkey have grown 30 to 40 percent, producing profits for the last 2 years.

Source: Elyse Tanouye, "Johnson & Johnson Stays Fit By Shuffling Its Mix of Businesses," *The Wall Street Journal,* Dec. 22, 1992, p. A1.

and response time—not to mention the impact that poor performance in each of these areas might have on the firm's other products. While it may be difficult to accurately predict these factors, they are, nevertheless, important in reaching a correct decision.

CHOOSING AMONG ALTERNATIVES

Decisions about routine tactical problems are likely to involve few variables, each with reasonably predictable outcomes. However, decisions associated with program-level and strategic problems expose the organization to high levels of risk. The outcomes of these decisions are likely to be evaluated according to multiple—often conflicting—criteria. It is not unlikely, then, that managers will often make less-than-optimal decisions. Managers simply cannot consider every conceivable option, a situation referred to as **bounded rationality.**[6] The effect may be decisions that are only satisfactory:

> Because the search for a course of action that will yield the highest possible payoff is often impractical, most people settle for a course of action that is "good enough," one that offers a sufficient rather than a maximum payoff. Not only does the use of "satisficing" as a decision rule fit the severe limitations of man's capacity to process information . . . it is also an appropriate way of adjusting to the fact that to apply an "optimizing" decision rule requires enormous quantities of information and analytical resources such as are often simply not available or could be obtained only at great cost.[7]

SHORT-TERM DECISIONS

Decisions that have no long-lasting impact are considered **short-term decisions.** *Short-term decisions generally involve the best use of the firm's currently available resources.* Described in terms of what they are not, short-term decisions:

- Do not impact the firm's capacity to make products or deliver services
- Do not affect the firm's cost structure
- Do not impact markets, product quality, or internal processes
- Do not affect pricing for primary products and customers
- Do not cause increases in indirect support

COSTS RELEVANT FOR SHORT-TERM DECISIONS

Managers making short-term decisions need only consider the costs and benefits that change. *As long as the change in benefits exceeds the change in costs, the short-term decision should be adopted.* For example, a government agency may offer a commercial printing company a contract for $34,800 if it will print 435 pages[8] of material. As long as the increase in costs such as materials, utilities, temporary labor, and supplies is less than the increase in benefits ($34,800), and assuming the job has no long-term impact, then the printer should accept the government agency's offer.

Costs that change as a result of a decision are called **incremental costs.** Any cost that is incremental is also considered relevant to a decision. So, incremental costs are always relevant to a decision. On the other hand, costs that do not change are not relevant and should be ignored. For example, assume that accepting the government agency's offer will cause paper cost to increase. Paper cost is, therefore, an incremental cost, one

---

[6]   Herbert A. Simon, *Models of Man,* New York: John Wiley, 1957, p. 198.
[7]   Alexander L. George, *Presidential Decisionmaking in Foreign Policy,* Boulder, Colo.: Westview, 1980, p. 40.
[8]   Throughout this chapter, all page amounts in printing-industry examples are expressed in thousands of pages.

that is relevant to the decision. On the other hand, assume that salaries for full-time workers are not affected by the agency's proposal—all work for the contract will be performed by temporary workers. Since total salary cost for full-time workers does not change, it is irrelevant to the decision. The cost of the temporary workers, however, does increase as a result of the contract and is relevant to the decision.

Short-term decisions may also involve *decreases* in costs. Costs associated with decreasing activity are called avoidable costs. For example, if the commercial printer were to eliminate a line of business, revenue for the firm as a whole would decrease. To offset loss of revenue, managers may release part of the salaried workforce, thereby avoiding their cost. Other costs, though, may not be avoidable—at least, not in the short term. An example of an unavoidable cost is the lease cost for the facility housing all printing operations. Assume that the printer has signed a long-term lease agreement. The lease cost must be paid even though activity has declined. In contrast, the lease cost may be avoidable if the printing company has an agreement that allows it to use the facility on a month-to-month basis. (See "Current Practice: The GOP's Lesson in the Reality of Making a Structural Change.")

As long as the costs avoided are greater than the decrease in benefits, the short-term decision to decrease activity should be adopted. Unavoidable costs are not incremental to the decision and are not relevant. Focusing on only those benefits and costs that change allows managers to isolate those factors that impact a short-term decision. All other information should be ignored.

CURRENT PRACTICE

The GOP's Lesson in the Realities of Making a Structural Change

To show the U.S. public that the cost-cutting revolution is real, the GOP wanted to shut down an office complex known as "House Annex II." Talk of selling the building began in the fall of 1994, when Newt Gingrich indicated in a speech to the Republican Conference that cuts in staff ought to trigger the sale of a House-owned building.

Unfortunately, avoiding the cost of House Annex II turned out to be more difficult than it had, at first, appeared to be.

Experts advised that moving the occupants out of the annex and into another facility would be very expensive. Just turning off and cooling the computers would cost $3 million. Determining alternative uses for an old building whose only utility is its proximity to the Capitol was another problem. Just getting the raw data needed to evaluate alternatives offered the GOP a "cruel lesson in navigating Washington's bureaucracy."

Source: Jill Abramson, "GOP Gets Mini-Lesson in Realities of Making a Structural Change," *The Wall Street Journal*, Jan. 17, 1995, p. A1.

VARIABLE COSTS

The first kind of cost that you normally think of as changing in response to any kind of decision is variable cost. *The general rule is that variable costs are always relevant for short-term decisions.* Increases in direct materials, direct labor, or any other cost that changes are relevant to the decision. But not *all* variable costs are relevant. For example, assume managers are considering an offer presented to them for a special, one-time order. Manufacturing the special order may be combined with that of other batches of the same product, already scheduled for production, thereby avoiding additional setup costs. Or perhaps the special order is negotiated without incurring any additional sales commissions. Setup cost and commissions cost, normally variable with respect to activity, are not relevant and should not be considered in the special-order decision, because they do not change.

FIXED COST

Fixed costs, as a general rule, are not relevant for short-term decisions. Since fixed costs represent the cost of maintaining long-term capacity, they are not likely to change as the result of a short-term decision about how capacity is used. To illustrate treatment of a fixed cost in short-term decisions, consider Exhibit 6.3. Assume a company has full manufacturing cost equal to $200 per unit. Suppose that managers receive a special, one-time order for 100 units at a price of, say, $175 per unit—a price that is $25 below full manufacturing cost. Also assume that the special order has no impact on either existing customers or the organization's primary business. The fixed manufacturing overhead cost of $65 per unit is not relevant to the special-order decision, because total fixed manufacturing cost does not change. If the special order is accepted—the correct decision—then total contribution increases by $40 for each unit sold ($175 selling price − variable manufacturing cost of $135). This results in a total benefit of $4,000 ($40 per unit × 100 units). Therefore, fixed costs are not relevant for short-term decision unless the total fixed manufacturing cost changes.

Managers making short-term decisions must be careful with the treatment of fixed costs expressed on a per-unit basis. That's because unit fixed costs appear to be variable. For example, suppose all direct fixed cost for a commercial printing company is $300,000, composed of $250,000 in

EXHIBIT 6.3 MANUFACTURING COST	
Variable manufacturing cost:	
Direct materials	$ 35
Direct labor	$ 40
Manufacturing overhead	$ 60
Total variable cost	$135
Fixed manufacturing overhead	$ 65
Full manufacturing cost per unit	$200

CHAPTER 6/SHORT-TERM DECISIONS AND PRICING

salaries for employees involved directly in printing activities and $50,000 in depreciation for printing equipment. If a total of 8,400 pages is normally printed each year, then the direct fixed cost per page is $35.71 ($300,000/8,400). In considering the proposed contract, the unit direct fixed cost of $35.71 is not relevant unless total direct fixed cost ($300,000) changes. Therefore, direct fixed cost—or any fixed cost, for that matter— is only relevant when it changes because of a decision.

Another example of an incorrect treatment of fixed cost in short-term decision making is when managers try to recalculate unit fixed cost based on the increase in the volume of activity. For example, assume that the proposed printing contract with the government agency calls for 435 printed pages. If the contract is accepted, the total number of pages printed increases from 8,400 to 8,835, and the unit direct fixed cost declines from $35.71 to $33.96 ($300,000/8,835). Neither of these unit fixed cost figures is relevant. That's because total fixed cost ($300,000) does not change, regardless of whether the agency's contract is accepted or not. Total direct fixed cost declines from $35.71 to $33.96 simply because it is averaged over more units.

OTHER COST DRIVERS

Costs caused by drivers other than units of product are also relevant for short-term decisions. For example, incremental costs, such as the cost of ordering materials or the cost of additional handling, can also change as the result of a decision. Batch-level costs, such as leasing equipment or the cost of hiring a special crew, are examples of relevant costs. At the end of a job, as long as costs return to the prejob levels—for example, when equipment cost is brought to prejob levels by returning equipment to the lessor or labor cost reduced by dismissing a special crew—these costs are relevant for short-term decisions.

SUNK COSTS

Sunk costs represent the costs of resources acquired in prior periods. Since the decision to incur these costs has already been made, *sunk costs are never relevant for short-term decisions.* To illustrate, let's assume that $100,000 worth of electronic components were purchased for the materials inventory in prior years and that the inventory has now been made obsolete by faster, more powerful components. The cost of these components is a sunk cost—irrelevant for any decision concerning their disposition. For example, what if managers are offered $5,000 for the components? Turning down the offer—arguing that $5,000 is lower than the $100,000 acquisition cost—would be incorrect.

ALLOCATED COSTS

Allocated costs typically do not change as the result of a short-term decision. Consequently, *allocated costs are generally not relevant for short-term decisions.* For example, total depreciation cost does not change as more or fewer units are manufactured. But if the total cost to be allocated changes, then allocated cost *is* relevant.

For example, assume that managers are considering altering a firm's product mix. Data for the present and proposed product mix are shown in Exhibit 6.4. Under the new production plan, volume for product A will double from 25,000 to 50,000 units, while volume for the other two products remains unchanged. Also assume that the plant manager's salary ($75,000) is assigned to products based on relative units produced. Because of the increase in volume, a large proportion of the plant manager's salary will be allocated to product A even though her total salary has not changed. It would be incorrect to decide not to increase the volume of product A because of the $12,500 increase in allocated costs. The $75,000 salary cost to be allocated is the *same*, regardless of how it is assigned among products.

Another example of the irrelevance of allocated costs for short-term decisions is when costs are shifted from one responsibility center to another. If total cost for the organization as a whole does not change, then the shifted costs within the organization are irrelevant. Managers held accountable for the performance of responsibility centers, though, may see this issue differently. For example, what would happen if managers, relying on the data in Exhibit 6.5, were to consider letting an outside firm process the firm's payroll? By contracting with an outside organization to process the payroll (i.e., by outsourcing) salary and benefit cost for three employees is avoided, saving $54,000 annually. Moreover, assume the payroll manager will be transferred to another operating unit within the same organization, saving the division another $24,000 in salary and benefit cost. Outsourcing also avoids $18,000 in materials and supplies, bringing the cost saving—cost avoided—to a total of $96,000. The net benefit—after deducting $74,000 to pay for the cost of payroll-processing services performed by the outside firm—is $22,000.

However, is it correct to consider the manager's $24,000 salary and benefits as an avoided cost? While it may be reasonable to shift account-

---

EXHIBIT 6.4   EVALUATION OF ALLOCATED COSTS

Change in Allocation of Plant Manager's Salary

| | Product | | | |
Present production plan	A	B	C	Total
Units produced under present product mix	25,000	37,500	12,500	75,000
Percent of total units	33.33%	50.00%	16.67%	100.00%
Allocation of manager's salary	$25,000	$37,500	$12,500	$75,000
New production plan				
Units produced under new product mix	50,000	37,500	12,500	100,000
Percent of total units	50.00%	37.50%	12.50%	100.00%
New allocation of manager's salary	$37,500	$28,125	$9,375	$75,000
Change in allocation of manager's salary	$12,500	$(9,375)	$(3,125)	$0

EXHIBIT 6.5 EVALUATION OF PROCESSING PAYROLL EXTERNALLY

Incorrect Analysis

Cost avoided by outsourcing:	
Salaries & benefits of employees released	$54,000
Salaries & benefits of manager transferred	$24,000
Materials & supplies	$18,000
Total cost avoided	$96,000
Increase in cost because of outsourcing	(74,000)
Net benefit from outsourcing	$22,000

ability for the payroll manager's cost to another responsibility center, it is not correct to assume that her salary is avoided. The reason is that the total cost for the organization as a whole has not changed. In reality, total firmwide cost avoided is only $72,000 ($54,000 in salaries and benefits for three released employees, plus $18,000 in materials and supplies), not $96,000. That means it will cost $2,000 more ($74,000 vs. $72,000) to have the payroll prepared by an outside service firm than it will cost to process the payroll internally.

OPPORTUNITY COSTS

Opportunity costs represent benefits foregone when one course of action is chosen over another. For example, the capacity of a repair shop at an automobile dealership is expressed in terms of the number of repair bays available to service customers' cars. Let's assume that all repair bays are fully booked weeks in advance. That is, the repair shop is working at full capacity. Now let's assume the used car manager wants exclusive use of one of the repair bays to recondition trade-ins for resale. That means the repair shop will sacrifice a benefit that it could have earned from serving external customers. For instance, assume the repair bay regularly generates an average contribution of, say, $100 per hour from external customers. Also assume that the used car manager cannot be charged more than $75 per hour if he is to make a profit on used cars. If the repair shop manager agrees to the used car manager's request, the repair shop incurs an opportunity cost of $25 for each hour spent reconditioning trade-ins— $75 earned from used car repairs less $100 that it would have earned from external customers.

Opportunity costs are not relevant for short-term decisions when there is excess capacity. However, when capacity is limited, as in the repair bay example, managers must make short-term decisions about how best to use it. As a result, *opportunity costs are relevant and should be included in the analysis of short-term decisions when capacity is limited.* They are relevant because limited capacity used in one way would create real value if used in another way. (See "Current Practice: The Cost of Quality.")

FOCUS ON MEASURABLE COSTS

While we offer general guidelines about what kinds of costs are relevant, the reality is that *relevance always depends on the situation*. Managers must evaluate each situation independently if they are to fully understand which costs are likely to change. As a practical matter, managers may not even be able to identify all of the different categories of costs that might be relevant to a particular decision. Nor will they always have access to accurate estimates of how costs are likely to change. For example, managers may be aware that behavioral considerations such as employee morale have an important impact on a decision. But placing a dollar value on the cost of low morale is another matter.

SHORT-TERM DECISIONS ILLUSTRATED

To illustrate short-term decisions, we return to the Orlando Printing Company example introduced in Chapter 2. Orlando Printing Company's primary business is commercial printing, and its revenue comes from two primary printing processes. Sheetfed printing presses are used for small-volume, frequent-setup jobs, while a giant newspaper-style web press is used for longer runs. As shown in Exhibit 6.6, Orlando Printing Company expects to print 8,400 pages during the coming year, at an average selling price of $150 per page. Variable cost is expected to equal $420,000, or an average of $50 per page. As a result, the expected contribution margin is $100 per page, and the total contribution margin is projected to be $840,000. After deducting the fixed cost of $720,000, management anticipates $120,000 in before-tax operating profit, or a profit of $14.29 per page.

SPECIAL ORDER

A new opportunity has been presented to Orlando Printing Company by a local government agency. In planning for an informational brochure, the agency has asked Orlando Printing Company to print 435 pages on the web press. Although Orlando Printing Company has never worked with

EXHIBIT 6.6 ORLANDO PRINTING COMPANY

Expected Revenue, Cost, and Profit for Coming Year

Printed pages (in 1,000s)		8,400
	Total	Per 1,000 Pages
Total revenue	$1,260,000	$150.00
Variable cost:		
Paper	$254,100	$30.25
Utilities	9,660	1.15
Temporary labor	98,700	11.75
Supplies	11,340	1.35
Commissions	46,200	5.50
Total variable cost	$420,000	$50.00
Contribution margin	$840,000	$100.00
Fixed cost:		
Labor—sheetfed	$75,000	$8.93
Labor—web press	175,000	20.83
Labor—art work	80,000	9.52
Supervision-inspection	40,000	4.76
Materials acquisition and handling	25,000	2.98
Depreciation—equipment	50,000	5.95
Depreciation—facility	44,000	5.24
Utilities	22,000	2.62
Administrative salaries	84,000	10.00
Office salaries	90,000	10.71
Office supplies	35,000	4.17
Total fixed cost	$720,000	$85.71
Operating profit (before tax)	$120,000	$14.29

the agency before, it is optimistic about the prospect. Unfortunately, the agency's offer of $80 per page is well below the $150 price that Orlando Printing Company normally gets for web work. Several managers suggest turning the offer down, arguing that it is below the full cost of $135.71 ($50.00 in variable cost + $85.71 in fixed cost, as shown in Exhibit 6.6). However, before any decision could be reached, managers felt they needed a breakdown of costs between product lines. The results, shown in Exhibit 6.7, indicate that web jobs are typically billed at an average rate of $166.67 per page. Variable cost averages $48.89 for web jobs and fixed cost traceable to web jobs equals $36.57 per page. With this new information, managers prepared predictions of how costs are likely to change if the special order is accepted. The results are shown in Exhibit 6.8.

The first column of data in Exhibit 6.8 shows the expected results if the special order is not accepted—this is the base case. It simply repeats the data from Exhibit 6.7. The second column of data shows the predicted outcome if the special order is accepted. The last column, highlighted and labeled "Changes Caused by Special Order," shows only the data relevant to the decision—the expected changes in total and per-page revenue and in variable cost. The data shown in the bottom of the first two columns

EXHIBIT 6.7   ORLANDO PRINTING COMPANY

Departmental Revenue and Cost

	Sheetfed		Web Press		Total: Sheetfed and Web	
Printed pages (in 1,000s)	3,000		5,400		8,400	
	Total	Per 1,000 Pages	Total	Per 1,000 Pages	Total	Per 1,000 Pages
Total revenue	$360,000	$120.00	$900,000	$166.67	$1,260,000	$150.00
Variable cost:						
Paper	$96,390	$32.13	$157,710	$29.21	$254,100	$30.25
Utilities	3,360	1.12	6,300	1.17	9,660	1.15
Temporary labor	35,550	11.85	63,150	11.69	98,700	11.75
Supplies	3,450	1.15	7,890	1.46	11,340	1.35
Commissions	17,250	5.75	28,950	5.36	46,200	5.50
Total variable cost	$156,000	$52.00	$264,000	$48.89	$420,000	$50.00
Contribution margin	$204,000	$68.00	$636,000	$117.78	$840,000	$100.00
Direct fixed cost:						
Labor—sheetfed and web	$75,000	$25.00	$175,000	$32.41	$250,000	$29.76
Depreciation—equipment	27,500	9.17	22,500	4.17	50,000	5.95
Total direct fixed cost	$102,500	$34.17	$197,500	$36.57	$300,000	$35.71
Direct profit	$101,500	$33.83	$438,500	$81.20	$540,000	$64.29
Indirect fixed cost:						
Labor—art work					$80,000	$9.52
Supervision-inspection					40,000	4.76
Materials acquisition & handling					25,000	2.98
Depreciation—facility					44,000	5.24
Utilities					22,000	2.62
Administrative salaries					84,000	10.00
Office salaries					90,000	10.71
Office supplies					35,000	4.17
Total indirect fixed cost					$420,000	$50.00
Operating profit (before tax)					$120,000	$14.29

Note: Some figures reflect rounding errors.

are irrelevant because they do not change. It doesn't matter what the dollar amount of the fixed costs is—or any other cost, for that matter—if it is not affected by the decision. In fact, information about costs that do not change simply clutters the decision, obscuring relevant data.

Revenue is expected to increase by $34,800 (435 pages × $80), while variable cost is expected to increase by $18,936, yielding a net incremental contribution of $15,864. Since this order will cause *no changes in fixed cost*, operating profit before tax increases by an amount equal to the increase in total contribution.

EXHIBIT 6.8 ORLANDO PRINTING COMPANY

Analysis of Special Order

	Before—As Planned (Exhibit 6.7)	After—Special-Order Accepted	Changes Caused by Special Order — Total	Changes Caused by Special Order — Per 1,000 Pages
Printed pages (in 1,000s)	8,400	8,835		435
Total revenue	$1,260,000	$1,294,800	$34,800	$80.00
Variable cost:				
Paper	$254,100	$266,806	$12,706	$29.21
Utilities	9,660	10,169	509	1.17
Temporary labor	98,700	103,785	5,085	11.69
Supplies	11,340	11,975	635	1.46
Commissions	46,200	46,200	—	—
Total variable cost	$420,000	$438,936	$18,936	$43.53
Contribution margin	$840,000	$855,864	$15,864	$36.47
Direct fixed cost:				
Labor—sheetfed & web	$250,000	$250,000		
Depreciation—equipment	50,000	50,000		
Total direct fixed cost	$300,000	$300,000	$0	$0
Direct profit	$540,000	$555,864	$15,864	$36.47
Indirect fixed cost:				
Labor—art work	$80,000	$80,000		
Supervision-inspection	40,000	40,000		
Materials acquisition & handling	25,000	25,000		
Depreciation—facility	44,000	44,000		
Utilities	22,000	22,000		
Administrative salaries	84,000	84,000		
Office salaries	90,000	90,000		
Office supplies	35,000	35,000		
Total indirect fixed cost	$420,000	$420,000	$0	$0
Operating profit (before tax)	$120,000	$135,864	$15,864	$36.47

Note: Some figures reflect rounding errors.

EVALUATION OF THE SPECIAL ORDER

Because fixed costs are presumably unaffected by short-term decisions, *accept the special order as long as there is an increase in total contribution.* An increase in total contribution means that the net increase in (incremental) revenue exceeds the net increase in (incremental) cost. Remember that the relevance of each cost in short-term decisions is situational. Variable costs may be irrelevant (e.g., commissions cost that doesn't have to be paid for a special order) and fixed costs may be relevant (e.g., the cost of part-time workers hired to process a special order).

Based on the analysis shown in Exhibit 6.8, managers at Orlando Printing Company decide that accepting the special order is likely to improve operating profits. But in order to consider the full impact of the decision on the organization and to be sure that the decision is consistent with the firm's long-term goals and objectives, Orlando Printing Company managers identified the additional pros and cons of accepting the special order, as listed below, before reaching a final conclusion:

Measurable Advantages of the Special Order

- Operating profit before tax increases.
- Revenue per employee, a key measure of performance, increases.
- Capacity utilization increases.

Other Benefits of the Special Order

- Investment in relationship with government agency and contact with key officials increases the probability of future work.
- Reductions in the cost per printed page are likely as the result of economies of scale.
- Competitors will likely accept the offer if Orlando Printing Company doesn't.

Disadvantages of the Special Order

- The new business represents a distraction from primary businesses.
- The workload for salaried personnel increases.
- Special pricing may undermine the pricing structure for primary customers.
- The range of activities with a third customer group increases.
- Venturing into an unknown area increases exposure to risk.
- Operating nearer capacity reduces flexibility.
- The need for preventative maintenance on equipment increases.

ORLANDO PRINTING COMPANY'S DECISION

The advantages and disadvantages shown in these lists should make clear that decisions typically involve a variety of conflicting criteria. Managers at Orlando Printing Company, after evaluating all of these factors, decided to accept the contract. Although improvements in operating profit are more than acceptable, managers based their final decision, in part, on considerations that could not be quantified. For example, they are certain that a competitor will accept the agency's offer if they do not; therefore, refusing the work amounts to creating an opportunity for another firm. While there was no attempt to quantify the impact of the future loss of business, Orlando Printing Company felt that not accepting the offer would result in a significant opportunity cost.

On the negative side, Orlando Printing Company is concerned about the increase in complexity that comes with new clients. However, managers are more worried about the potential risk of declining service quality for primary customers. This concern prompts Orlando Printing to monitor turnaround time and customer satisfaction. While managers have concerns about the new contract, they feel that the opportunities it creates more than offset the costs it incurs.

Orlando Printing Company's Decision Revisited—Use of Multiple Cost Drivers. Prediction models are often based on single, volume-related cost drivers. For example, Orlando Printing assumes that costs are driven only by the number of pages printed. In reality, there are many cost drivers.

Consider the multiple cost drivers listed in Exhibit 6.9. The only unit-level cost is paper, which is driven by the number of pages. Job-level costs include setup cost, driven by the number of setups; test run and adjustment cost, driven by the number of machine-hours; processing, driven by the number of machine-hours; and cleanup, driven by the number of jobs. There are no relevant product- and corporate-level costs—none of these costs are expected to change if the government agency's proposal is

EXHIBIT 6.9 ORLANDO PRINTING COMPANY

Analysis of Government Agency's Proposal Using Multiple Cost Drivers

Unit Level	Cost Behavior	Activity Driver	Units of Activity Driver	Cost per Unit of Activity Driver	Total Cost
Paper	Variable	Pages	435	$29.21	$12,706
Job Level					
Setup job	Variable	Setups	2	$875	$1,750
Test run/adjustment	Variable	Machine-hours	.5	$900	450
Processing	Variable	Machine-hours	6	$1,300	7,800
Cleanup	Variable	Jobs	1	$573	573
Total job-level cost					$10,573
Product Level					
Direct Labor	Step	Number of shifts	0	$350.00	
Material Acquisition, handling	Fixed	Items ordered	0	$38.50	
Inspection/supervision	Fixed	Number of jobs	0	$78.00	
Total product-level cost					
Corporate Level					
Depreciation—web equipment	Fixed	Pages	0	$3.20	
Depreciation—indirect	Fixed	Pages	0	$5.40	
Utilities	Fixed	Machine-hours	0	$3.65	
Administrative salaries	Fixed	Pages	0	$8.80	
Office salaries	Fixed	Pages	0	$10.24	
Supplies	Fixed	Setups	0	$12.00	
Total corporate-level cost					
Incremental cost					$23,279
Incremental revenue—435 pages (in 1,000s) @ $80 per page					$34,800
Incremental operating profit (before tax)					$11,521

accepted. Incremental cost based on multiple cost drivers is $23,279—considerably higher than $18,936, the incremental cost shown in Exhibit 6.8 for a single cost driver. As a result, the predicted incremental operating profit is lower—and (presumably) more accurate—when multiple cost drivers are used as compared with a single cost driver.

USING COST DATA IN PRICING DECISIONS

Companies offer products and services in a variety of different market environments. At one extreme are companies with little or no control over the prices of their products. As "price takers," their products' prices are set by the market. At the other extreme are companies that control prices. As "price setters," they establish a price for themselves and their competitors. Managers have a number of strategies that determine their pricing decisions within these extremes, including industry strategies, product strategies, and customer strategies.[9]

INDUSTRY STRATEGIES

Basic supply and demand for products and the prices they are likely to be sold for are often determined at the industry level. Managers influence prices at the industry level through industry strategies—decisions about the amount of product they will supply. They might add capacity, for example, by constructing new facilities or by outsourcing noncritical activities, thereby freeing space in existing facilities. Or managers may reduce capacity by closing plants when demand falls. They must also devise strategies that respond to new government regulations or to the entry of competitors in the market. Simultaneously, the prices of products are affected by consumer demand, shifts in market and consumer attitudes, changes in demographics, and the emergence of substitute products.

PRODUCT STRATEGIES

Product strategies refer to how managers react to the actions of competitors. All product strategies can be reduced to two generic types: products offered with different features and different levels of service (*a strategy of differentiation*) or low-cost products with acceptable levels of quality (*a strategy of low cost*). Products that customers feel offer more value or better service—products differentiated from their competitors, such as Mercedes-Benz autos—often command higher prices in the marketplace. In contrast, consumers may base their purchasing decisions solely on price—such as when choosing to shop at Wal-Mart, which sells brand-name products at low prices.

---

[9] Adapted from Michael V. Marn and Robert L. Rosiello, "Managing Price, Gaining Profit," *Harvard Business Review,* Sept.–Oct., 1992, pp. 84–94.

CUSTOMER STRATEGIES

At the most basic level, managers set pricing strategies for individuals, or for groups of customers. Strategies at this level, called customer strategies, often start with list prices, which are determined by adding a "reasonable" profit to cost. From this base, managers may increase prices when, for example, short-term supply decreases and the availability of goods is limited. Or they may decide to decrease prices in response to actions by competitors. They also influence the amount sold through a number of individual pricing actions, such as offering quantity discounts, sales incentives, or early payment discounts.

USING COSTS IN PRICING DECISIONS

Recognizing that prices are influenced by a wide range of market forces, some managers determine prices strictly on the basis of cost. One reason for this is that cost information is often readily available. Moreover, cost data are organized in formats that are easily understood. Yet another reason is that if prices determined on the basis of cost are too high by market standards, cost gives managers a starting point from which they can gauge improvement. Cost also provides a convenient reference point for determining list prices. Starting from a cost-based list price, actual market prices are derived by adjusting list prices upward or downward to reflect prevailing market conditions.

PRICING USING FULL COST

Long-term prices, especially for primary products and services, should be based on full cost. For organizations to achieve long-term profitability, prices must be at levels high enough to generate revenue that equals or exceeds full cost plus a reasonable profit. The full cost of a product, as outlined in Chapter 3, consists of direct cost and a fair share of total indirect cost—both manufacturing and nonmanufacturing costs. We will discuss what constitutes a reasonable profit later in this chapter.

We can represent this mathematically in what is known as the *full-cost pricing model:*

Long-term price = full cost + reasonable profit

Earlier in this chapter, we introduced the idea that fixed costs are irrelevant in special, short-term decisions. They are irrelevant because fixed costs do not change. The example we used to illustrate this point assumed that accepting or not accepting a special order had no impact on permanent customers or on the organization's primary products. Both of these conditions—the assignment of existing resources and the lack of impact on primary products—are what makes special orders short-term decisions. However, over the long term, primary products must recover all costs—not just incremental costs. Otherwise, fixed costs would never be recovered through the price of products.

To reiterate, special orders and one-time, short-term actions need not cover all costs—only those costs that change as a result of the decision.

The reason is that fixed cost is covered by revenue from the sale of the firm's primary products. A short-term decision may cause the firm to enter a new market, as Orlando Printing Company does when it accepts the government agency's proposal. New products and services may eventually become primary products. When they do, they are incorporated into the firm's plans and are expected to recover a fair share of indirect fixed cost.

DIFFERENT BASES FOR CALCULATING MARKET PRICES

Different starting points—called *bases* or *platforms*—can be used in calculating market prices. Manufacturing companies often use product cost—direct materials, direct labor, and manufacturing overhead—as a base for pricing. For example, a product cost of $100 might be marked up by adding 35 percent of the product cost to the base in order to obtain a market price of $135. The markup would include two components: one to cover nonmanufacturing overhead (say, 20%), and a component representing a reasonable profit (e.g., 15%). Alternatively, managers may decide to apply markup percentages to full cost, which comprises both product cost—direct materials, direct labor, and manufacturing overhead—and nonmanufacturing cost. For example, assume product cost is $100 and nonmanufacturing cost is $25, for a full cost of $125. Adding a markup percentage of 8 percent to the full cost of $125 produces the same selling price of $135 (108% × $125 = $135).

Another approach is to use cost components as a pricing platform. For example, products with large proportions of direct materials cost and relatively small amounts of direct labor and manufacturing overhead costs may use direct materials cost as a pricing base. For instance, a materials cost of $60 multiplied by a markup of 225 percent yields a market price of $135. The 225 percent markup covers not only direct materials but direct labor, manufacturing overhead, nonmanufacturing overhead, and a reasonable profit.

If costs are predominately labor-driven, then direct labor-hours may be used as a pricing platform. For example, assume direct labor cost is $50, composed of 5 hours of direct labor at $10 per hour. Direct labor cost can be marked up by 270 percent, to derive a selling price of $135. Direct labor is billed to customers at a rate of $27 per hour ($135/5 hours). Each hour billed covers not only direct labor but direct materials, manufacturing overhead, nonmanufacturing overhead, and a reasonable profit.

ORLANDO PRINTING COMPANY— FULL-COST PRICING

To illustrate full-cost pricing and several pricing platforms, we return to Orlando Printing and the data in Exhibit 6.7, expanded as Exhibit 6.10. The purpose of Exhibit 6.10 is to illustrate just three of the many different ways of determining the desired selling price for sheetfed printing.

The top panel of Exhibit 6.10 shows the calculation of the desired price based on a markup of full cost. Full cost is calculated first, and then a reasonable profit, expressed as a percentage return on full cost, is added.

EXHIBIT 6.10 ORLANDO PRINTING COMPANY

Alternative Full-Cost Pricing Bases—Sheetfed Printing

Price Based on Markup of Full Cost

	Total
Full cost—sheetfed printing:	
Total variable cost (from Exhibit 6.7)	$156,000
Total direct fixed cost (from Exhibit 6.7)	102,500
Indirect fixed cost allocated to sheetfed	
[(3,000 sheetfed pages/8,400 total pages) × $420,000]	150,000
Full cost of sheetfed printing	$408,500
Desired profit:	
Desired rate of return on full cost	15.00%
Reasonable profit (15% × $408,500)	$61,275
Desired price—full cost plus reasonable profit	$469,775
Number of pages—sheetfed printing	3,000
Desired price per page (in 1,000s) for sheetfed printing	$156.59

Price Based on Markup of Direct Cost

	Total
Direct cost—sheetfed printing:	
Total variable cost (from Exhibit 6.7)	$156,000
Total direct fixed cost (from Exhibit 6.7)	102,500
Total direct cost	$258,500
Desired price—full cost plus reasonable profit (from above)	$469,775
Desired markup on direct cost (desired price/total direct cost)	181.73%

Price Based on Markup on Materials and Labor Cost

	Total
Direct materials & direct labor cost—sheetfed printing:	
Direct materials (from Exhibit 6.7)	$ 96,390
Direct labor (from Exhibit 6.7)	75,000
Total direct materials & direct labor cost	$171,390
Desired price—full cost plus reasonable profit (from above)	$469,775
Desired markup on direct materials & direct labor cost (desired price/total direct materials & direct labor cost)	274.10%

Full cost comprises variable cost ($156,000), direct fixed cost ($102,500), and an allocation of indirect fixed cost ($150,000). This results in a full cost of $408,500. Indirect fixed cost is allocated to sheetfed printing based on the relative number of pages printed (3,000/8,400) multiplied by the total dollar amount of indirect fixed cost to be allocated ($420,000). Assuming that a 15 percent markup for profit is reasonable, an additional $61,275 (15% × $408,500) is added, to achieve a desired price of $469,775.

Dividing $469,775 by 3,000 pages results in a desired price of $156.59. At this price, full cost is recovered, and a 15 percent return obtained.

Direct cost is used as the pricing platform in the middle panel of Exhibit 6.10. Assume the desired revenue from sheetfed printing is $469,775 (taken from the top panel of Exhibit 6.10). In that case, a 182 percent markup on direct cost would be required. The markup percentage is derived by dividing the desired price for all sheetfed printing ($469,775) by the total direct cost (variable cost of $156,000 and direct fixed cost of $102,500), for a total of $258,500. The markup percentage is multiplied by the total direct cost to derive a price. For example, a printing job with $5,000 in direct cost—say, $3,000 of variable cost and $2,000 in direct fixed cost—would be priced at $9,100 (182% × $5,000).

The bottom panel of Exhibit 6.10 shows how a combination of direct materials cost and direct labor cost can be used as a pricing platform. Total direct materials cost, taken from Exhibit 6.7, is $96,390, while direct labor cost is $75,000, or a combined total of $171,390. Assume the desired revenue from sheetfed printing is $469,775 (taken from the top panel of Exhibit 6.10). In that case, a 274 percent markup on these two cost components would be required. The markup percentage is derived by dividing the desired price for all sheetfed printing ($469,775) by the total combined direct materials and direct labor cost ($171,390). A job with a combined total of $4,000 in direct materials and direct labor cost, for example, would be priced at $10,960 (274% × $4,000).

MARGINAL PRICING

In practice, the goal of recovering full cost and obtaining a reasonable profit may not always be achieved. One reason is that managers may not have access to what they consider to be accurate measures of full cost, especially when full cost includes a large proportion of allocated cost. Another reason is that managers may be able to charge prices based on full cost only when operating at or near full capacity. If demand is high and short-term capacity is limited, managers may be able to sell everything they make. Under these conditions, there is no reason to reduce price. In contrast, excess capacity may arise because of overbuilding in the industry, process improvements that "free up" capacity, downturns in general business activity, or permanent shifts in consumer preferences. Managers with excess capacity are stuck, at least in the short term, with the fixed cost that must be covered by revenue from the sale of fewer products. With the reality of shrinking revenue and unavoidable fixed cost, plus the uncertainty of not knowing when markets are likely to recover, some managers choose to accept prices for their products that are lower than full cost. Prices under these conditions—at less than full cost plus a reasonable profit—are referred to as marginal prices.

RANGE OF PRICES

Prices lower than full cost plus a reasonable profit are considered marginal prices. *The lowest possible marginal price is equal to variable cost.* The reason is that a price equal to variable cost provides no profit, nor does it

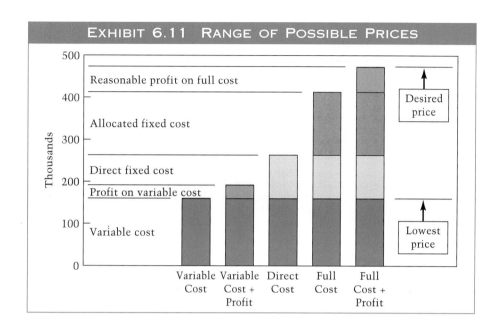

EXHIBIT 6.11　RANGE OF POSSIBLE PRICES

make a contribution to covering fixed cost. Between this minimum price (variable cost) and the desired upper range of prices (full cost plus a reasonable profit) is a wide band of price possibilities. This range of pricing options is shown in Exhibit 6.11. The next step above the minimum price is based on variable cost plus a reasonable profit. The step above that is a price that recovers variable and direct fixed costs. The next step is a price based on full cost—variable, direct fixed cost plus allocated fixed cost. The last step is a desired price derived by adding a reasonable profit to full cost.

We will illustrate the range of possible cost-based prices using data from the Orlando Printing Company's sheetfed operation. As shown in the top panel of Exhibit 6.12, the lowest possible ("floor") price is $52. This price is simply equal to total variable cost of $52 per page ($156,000 in total variable cost/3,000 pages). The next-higher price is $59.80. It is based on variable cost plus a desired 15 percent markup on variable cost. The next step up is a price of $86.17. It is based on total direct cost—variable cost plus direct fixed cost. Full-cost price is the next step. It is $136.17 per page and covers variable cost plus a fair share of both direct fixed cost and allocated fixed cost. Finally, a price of $156.59 per 1,000 pages covers full cost *and* contributes a markup of 15 percent for profit.

PRICING IN ACTUAL PRACTICE

How do managers determine prices in actual practice? A study of U.S. industries indicates that 59.5 percent of the manufacturers surveyed base market prices on full cost.[10] Only 12.1 percent base prices on variable cost. The remaining 17.7 percent use market-based competitive pricing.

---

[10]　Eunsup Shim and Ephraim F. Sudit, "How Manufacturers Price Products," *Management Accounting*, Feb. 1995, pp. 37–39.

EXHIBIT 6.12   ORLANDO PRINTING COMPANY

Range of Selling Prices for Sheetfed Printing

	Total	Selling Price per Page
Number of pages printed—sheetfed printing (in 1,000s)		3,000
Minimum price = variable cost:		
Total variable cost (from Exhibit 6.7)	$156,000	$52.00
Variable cost plus reasonable profit:		
Total variable cost (from Exhibit 6.7)	$156,000	$52.00
Reasonable profit (15% of variable cost)	23,400	7.80
Variable cost plus reasonable profit	$179,400	$59.80
Direct cost:		
Total variable cost (from Exhibit 6.7)	$156,000	$52.00
Total direct fixed cost (from Exhibit 6.7)	102,500	34.17
Total direct cost	$258,500	$86.17
Full cost:		
Total variable cost (from Exhibit 6.7)	$156,000	$52.00
Total direct fixed cost (from Exhibit 6.7)	102,500	34.17
Indirect fixed costs allocated to sheetfed		
[(3,000 sheetfed pages/8,400 total pages) × $420,000]	150,000	50.00
Full cost—sheetfed printing	$408,500	$136.17
Desired price = full cost plus reasonable profit:		
Total variable cost (from Exhibit 6.7)	$156,000	$52.00
Total direct fixed cost (from Exhibit 6.7)	102,500	34.17
Indirect fixed cost allocated to sheetfed		
[(3,000 sheetfed pages/8,400 total pages) × $420,000]	150,000	50.00
Full cost—sheetfed printing	$408,500	$136.17
Reasonable profit (15% of full cost)	61,275	20.43
Full cost plus reasonable profit for sheetfed printing	$469,775	$156.59

Of those manufacturing companies using full cost as a base for pricing, 57.1 percent use full manufacturing cost, while 42.9 percent define full cost in terms of both manufacturing cost and nonmanufacturing cost. Of those manufacturing companies that base prices on variable cost, 47.1 percent use only variable manufacturing cost, while 52.9 percent use both variable manufacturing cost and variable nonmanufacturing cost.

PRICES DEPEND UPON ACCURATE ESTIMATES OF COST

In each pricing situation, managers must have access to accurate measures of product costs. Since full cost includes allocations of indirect cost, managers must be confident of the data's accuracy. In competitive markets, managers may learn by the reactions of their customers that cost data are inaccurate. For example, prices based on full cost that contain overallocations of indirect cost are likely to meet with customer resistance. Customers will perceive that prices are too high and will simply not buy the products. If, on the other hand, prices are set by the market, and managers are price takers, products with overallocated costs may appear to be unprofitable. As a result, managers may erroneously decide to exit the market when it is, in fact, generating a profit. Conversely, managers may have products with underallocations of indirect cost. If managers are price takers, prevailing market prices may indicate that undercosted products are more profitable than they really are. If so, managers may incorrectly assign resources to the undercosted products in order to make more of them, believing the products yield higher-than-actual profits. In reality, the margins on undercosted products may not be sufficient to cover full cost.

OTHER APPROACHES TO PRICING

EMERGING PRICING TRENDS

There may be a long-term trend toward declines in real, inflation-adjusted prices for some industries.[11] As more and more competitors enter markets, high-price manufacturers are likely to be driven out, leaving only the low-cost, high-quality firms. One survival strategy in these highly competitive markets is to differentiate products in order to command higher prices. When differentiation is not possible, then managers should try to drive costs down through process improvements. If costs cannot be driven down to levels that yield profits at prevailing market prices, then managers should consider finding substitute products that yield higher profit margins. (See "Current Practice: Holding the Line on Prices at KFC.") The last resort is to exit the market entirely.

---

[11] Bill Saporito, "Why the Price Wars Never End," *Fortune,* Mar. 23, 1992, pp. 68–78.

TARGET PRICING

One way to set prices is by using a technique called target pricing. Using prices determined by the market as a starting point, manufacturers work backward to identify the level of costs that will allow a desired level of profitability. For example, assume managers of a TV manufacturer believe that large volumes of high-definition televisions (HDTVs) can be sold at a target price of, say, $1,800. Their job, then, is to find ways to make HDTV sets, with a given level of quality, at a full cost of less than $1,565, assuming a 15 percent profit margin ($1,800/1.15) is desired. Engineers, product designers, production workers, and managers all have to work together to find ways of achieving the target cost implied by the target price.

The biggest opportunity to reduce costs generally comes during the design phase. Using a technique called value engineering, employees work together across functional areas to design products that meet customer specifications while reducing costs. Value engineering seeks savings by means such as simplifying materials specifications, increasing output for a given level of input, reducing the number of parts, reducing labor tasks, and enhancing the interaction between workers and equipment.[12]

Once production begins, and after the efforts to reduce costs through value engineering are complete, continuous improvement takes over. The goal of continuous improvement is to reduce costs to below standard cost. Even after companies find the best product design and manufacturing strategy, they may have to settle for setting prices below full cost until they are able to increase volume or decrease costs through continuous improvement. (See "Current Practice: Target Pricing in the Automobile Market" for an example of value engineering and target pricing.)

Target pricing can be coupled with what is known as life-cycle costing. In contrast with traditional methods, where product costs are calculated for only the current period, life-cycle costing plans for costs over all phases of a product's service life. This broader view includes the cost of activities such as design, development, new product introduction, and product support. Another example of life-cycle costs are those associated with exiting the market at the end of the life of the product—for example, the cost of dismantling production facilities. Costs such as environmental cleanups or carrying parts for models no longer sold are often overlooked by traditional costing methods. Life-cycle costing encourages coordination between design and engineering to ensure that high-quality products are manufactured at the lowest possible cost. For example, planners using life-cycle costing can make early design changes that will save production costs later.

Consider the example shown in Exhibit 6.13, which illustrates target pricing for a typical product. The target price for a new model of the product is based on adjusting the current price ($5.50) of an existing model. Assume planners believe consumers are willing to pay $0.50 more for the added features in the new model, or a total of $6.00. The target cost of

---

[12] Takao Tanaka, "Target Costing at Toyota," *Journal of Cost Management*, spring 1993, p. 10.

CURRENT PRACTICE

Target Pricing in the Automobile Market

A critical technique of the system that Japanese automobile makers use to keep their costs down is to reduce or eliminate costs during the planning and design stage. After that point, the automakers contend that virtually all costs are locked-in. This technique, *target costing*, begins with the efforts of a team in charge of bringing the new product to market. The team first determines a price that is likely to appeal to potential buyers and then deducts a desired profit margin. What is left are the costs allowed for each of the elements that make up the product's total cost, including the costs of design, engineering, manufacturing, sales, and marketing.

Each part or function of the product is treated as a component. Physical components may range from windshields to engine blocks. Even the space in the trunk is considered a component. Each component is assigned a target cost, which is ". . . where the battle begins." The *battle* refers to the intense negotiations between the company as a whole, its suppliers, and the various departments contributing to the product. The sum of the initial estimates of the cost of components may exceed target cost by 20 percent or more. But by the time the battle is over, compromises and trade-offs bring the product cost close enough to the target cost.

In contrast, U.S. companies, in the past, transferred product designs from one department to the next. At the end of the design phase, product specifications were given to accountants, who determined what the product would cost by simply adding up the costs of individual components. Unfortunately, resulting prices often didn't add up to marketable products. What the product *ought* to cost was missing in this approach. Today, U.S. automobile manufacturers have adopted many of the Japanese costing techniques, resulting in significant improvements in productivity, quality, and profitability.

Source: Ford S. Worthy, "Japan's Smart Secret Weapon," *Fortune,* Aug. 12, 1991, pp. 72–75.

$5.22 is determined by dividing the $6.00 target price by 1.15, assuming the firm expects to earn a 15 percent return on cost. Deducting target cost from target price leaves a desired profit of $0.78. That is, target cost cannot exceed $5.22 if the firm is to achieve the 15 percent profit goal. Using the cost of the current model as the base figure, the cost of the improvements is added, bringing the estimated total cost of the new model to $5.40. A comparison of the estimated cost with the target cost indicates a difference, or cost gap, of $0.18. This is where the hard work begins. Designers, engineers, accountants, and other employees must find ways to reduce costs and close the $0.18 gap. One way to do so is through design changes during the value-engineering phase initiated prior to production. Assume value engineering, according to estimates by company employees, should close, say, $0.15 of the gap. After production begins, costs must be driven down another $0.03 through continuous improvement. Cost reduc-

EXHIBIT 6.13 TARGET PRICING

Target Price

Price of current model	$5.50
Value of improvements to customers	0.50
Target price	$6.00

Target Cost

Target price (from above)	$6.00
Less profit (forced)	(0.78)
Target cost ($6.00/1.15)	$5.22

Estimated Cost

Cost to make current model	$5.00
Cost of improvements	0.40
Estimated cost	$5.40

Cost Gap

Estimated cost (from above)	$5.40
Target cost (from above)	5.22
Cost gap	$0.18

Closing Cost Gap

Cost gap (from above)	$0.18
Gap closed by value engineering	(0.15)
Gap closed by continuous improvement	$0.03

tions to be targeted are set at the beginning of each time period, and employees arc cmpowered to find ways of achieving those goals.

Exhibit 6.14 shows the various phases of a product's service life. After two years of design and development, the new product is "rolled out" and brought to market during the third year. Manufacturing continues until the seventh year. At that time, managers plan to withdraw the product from the market after introducing a new model. Target costs are identified at the outset of the project, and value engineering is implemented to help close cost gaps. During the first years of production, workers are expected to sustain initial levels of productivity. As workers gain experience, targets become tighter.

Life-cycle cost includes development cost and manufacturing cost, broken into fixed and variable costs. Initial levels of fixed and variable manufacturing costs are reduced as workers find better, more efficient ways of making the product. Operating losses in early years are offset by profits as the product achieves market maturity. In addition, up-front costs, such as development, are recovered later in the project revenue. Note that the expected return is 14.7 percent over the life cycle—slightly less than the desired 15 percent. If calculations indicate a shortfall in expected return, managers can go back to the drawing board and encourage employees to "push" even more costs out of the product. As a last resort, they may compromise by permitting a small increase in market price.

EXHIBIT 6.14 TARGET PRICING AND LIFE-CYCLE COSTING

	Year 1	2	3	4	5	6	7	Total Over Product Life Cycle (Years 1–7)
Activity	Design	Develop	Rollout	Manufacture	Manufacture	Manufacture	Withdraw	
Costing basis	Target	Target	Sustain	Sustain	Improve	Improve	Improve	
Projected unit sales			250,000	400,000	500,000	500,000	175,000	1,825,000
Revenue:								
Target price			$6.00	$6.00	$6.00	$6.00	$6.00	
Total revenue	$0	$0	$1,500,000	$2,400,000	$3,000,000	$3,000,000	$1,050,000	$10,950,000
Cost:								
Development cost	$200,000	$300,000	$50,000					$550,000
Fixed cost			$750,000	$725,000	$700,000	$680,000	$550,000	$3,405,000
Unit variable cost			$3.25	$3.15	$3.00	$2.75	$2.50	
Total variable cost			$812,500	$1,260,000	$1,500,000	$1,375,000	$437,500	$5,385,000
Total cost	$200,000	$300,000	$1,612,500	$1,985,000	$2,200,000	$2,055,000	$987,500	$9,340,000
Average unit cost								$5.12
Operating profit	$(200,000)	$(300,000)	$(112,500)	$415,000	$800,000	$945,000	$62,500	$1,610,000
Return on sales								14.70%

Continuous improvement

EFFECTS OF INFLATION AND EXCHANGE RATES

The effects of anticipated inflation should be accounted for in the determination of market prices. For goods and services sold internationally, regular changes in exchange rates also have to be accounted for when setting the prices of products (See "Current Practice: Japan Airlines.")

BASES FOR MEASURING REASONABLE RETURNS

What base should be used to measure costs when determining a reasonable return? One alternative, illustrated earlier (Exhibit 6.10), is to add a markup to full cost to cover a reasonable profit. Using this approach, the dollar amount of profit increases proportionally with increases in product cost.

An alternative approach relies on using the cost of assets employed in making the product as a pricing base. Called *return-on-investment pricing*—or simply, ROI pricing—the cost of total assets is multiplied by a desired percent markup. To illustrate ROI pricing, let's assume full cost consists of $4,250,000 in fixed cost and $40 per unit in variable cost. Let's also assume that assets costing $6,250,000 are employed in making 50,000

CURRENT PRACTICE

Japan Airlines (JAL)

The ethnic composition of Japan Airlines (JAL) crews, once all Japanese, is changing. On a recent flight from Tokyo to Honolulu, the crew included a dozen Thai flight attendants—who earn one-twentieth of the pay of their Japanese counterparts. The crew also included an Irish captain, a Canadian copilot, and an Irish flight engineer—all of whom work for 50 percent less than the Japanese employees who perform the same jobs. Overall, by 1998, one out of four JAL workers will be non-Japanese.

The reason for these changes is the strong Japanese yen. Even though the wages of Japanese flight attendants have risen only 12 percent since 1985, when measured in yen, salaries have risen 70 percent when measured in terms of dollars. Japanese flight attendants' salaries are about $85,000 a year—vastly higher than salaries paid to attendants by overseas competitors.

To survive, JAL must either raise prices, cut costs, or reduce profit margins. With an intensely competitive airline industry, it's unlikely JAL is going to raise its prices. The pressure is going to be on costs. As a result, some services may disappear—although traditions die hard. Some flights still have attendants whose primary job is to keep the toilets clean and tidy after each use—this includes making sure there is a fresh fold in the first sheet of the roll of toilet tissue.

Source: Valerie Reitman and Jathon Sapsford, "Unchartered Course: To See Issues Vexing Japanese Business Now, Consider JAL Flight 76," *The Wall Street Journal,* Aug. 9, 1994, p. A1.

EXHIBIT 6.15 ROI PRICING		
	Historical Cost	Replacement Cost
Desired profit:		
Assets employed:		
Historical cost	$6,250,000	
Replacement cost		$7,500,000
Desired return on assets	8.00%	8.00%
Desired profit	$500,000	$600,000
Cost:		
Fixed cost	$4,250,000	$4,250,000
Desired profit (from above)	500,000	600,000
Total fixed cost & desired profit	$4,750,000	$4,850,000
Estimated unit sales	50,000	50,000
Unit fixed cost & profit	$95.00	$97.00
Unit variable cost	40.00	40.00
Desired selling price	$135.00	$137.00

units of product. Finally, we will assume that an 8 percent return on assets is considered fair in the industry. The total dollar amount of return, as shown in the historical cost column in Exhibit 6.15, equals $500,000 ($6,250,000 × 8%). Adding the desired dollar amount of profit to fixed cost yields a total of $4,750,000. When this sum is divided by 50,000 units, fixed cost plus desired profit comes out to $95 per unit. Adding a variable cost of $40 per unit yields a desired selling price of $135.

An issue related to ROI pricing is the method of measuring asset costs. Should assets be measured using historical cost or replacement cost? Historical costs may not provide profits sufficient to replace assets in the future if real, price-level-adjusted asset costs are increasing. An alternative is to use **replacement cost** rather than historical cost. Let's assume the replacement cost for assets employed (in Exhibit 6.15) amounts to $7,500,000. A return of 8 percent on replacement cost yields a desired selling price of $137.

SUMMARY

The three steps in making a value-creating decision are (1) finding the right occasions to make decisions, (2) identifying possible courses of action, and (3) choosing among alternatives. Managerial accounting's role is to collect data needed in each of these steps. Specifically, the data that managerial accounting provides to help identify opportunities for decisions come from monitoring the internal and external business environments. Managerial accounting organizes these data in such a way as to provide predictions of the likely outcomes of various alternative courses of action and of the impact each alternative will have on measures of performance. Corrective action, carried out through the organization's control structure, is based on the divergence of actual from planned results, as captured by measures of performance.

Predictive models are used to estimate how costs are likely to change with each different course of action. In addition, predictive models show how these changes affect shareholders' value. Not all costs change as a result of a decision. Only those costs that change are relevant. Costs that do not change are not relevant and are not considered in the decision-making process.

Variable costs are presumed to change with changes in activity and are generally considered relevant for short-term decisions. Fixed costs are assumed to be unchanged by activity over a relatively short period of time. As a result, fixed costs are presumed irrelevant for short-term decisions. In the long term, all costs—both fixed and variable—have the potential to change.

To determine which costs are relevant and which are not, we have to look at costs in different ways. While allocated costs are useful in determining full cost, they are generally not relevant for decisions, because the total amount to be allocated does not change.

Other cost concepts include sunk costs and opportunity costs. Sunk costs, representing assets previously acquired, are never relevant to such decisions. Opportunity costs, representing benefits foregone when one course of action is chosen over another, are relevant only when the firm is operating at full capacity.

Full cost, for many companies, is the basis used for pricing products. Pricing strategies, though, depend upon a number of factors—such as competition and utilization of capacity. In general, prices should reflect full cost plus a reasonable profit. When full cost includes allocations, managers should try to gain assurance that allocated costs reflect relative resource use. Otherwise, inappropriate pricing decisions will result. In some circumstances, marginal pricing may be used, yielding market prices that range between variable and full cost.

CHAPTER 6 ASSIGNMENTS

DISCUSSION PROBLEMS

D6.1   (Costs for Product Pricing)[13]

Wyeth-Ayerst, a unit of American Home Products Corporation, launched a new, long-acting contraceptive product called Norplant in 1991. Packaged together with a kit doctors use to insert Norplant, the product sells in the United States for about $350. In other countries, Wyeth-Ayerst sells Norplant for as little as $23.

Family-planning clinics in the United States were stunned by Norplant's price, since many of their clients are low-income or on Medicaid. Plus, Norplant is one of the first important new women's drugs. Many worry that the pricing scheme is an indication of things to come for women's health products. Some clin-

[13]   Elyse Tanouye, "Norplant's Maker Draws Sharp Criticism on Pricing of Long-Acting Contraceptive," *The Wall Street Journal*, Aug. 30, 1993, p. B1.

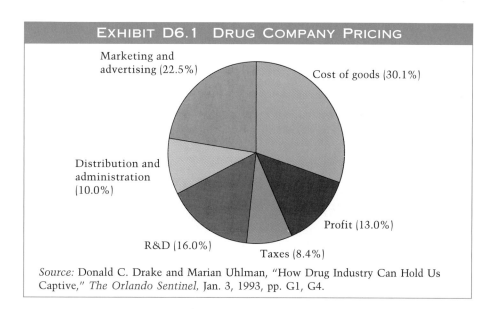

EXHIBIT D6.1   DRUG COMPANY PRICING

Marketing and advertising (22.5%)

Cost of goods (30.1%)

Distribution and administration (10.0%)

Profit (13.0%)

R&D (16.0%)

Taxes (8.4%)

Source: Donald C. Drake and Marian Uhlman, "How Drug Industry Can Hold Us Captive," *The Orlando Sentinel,* Jan. 3, 1993, pp. G1, G4.

ics claim they lose money on Norplant because Medicaid will not reimburse them for the full cost of the drug. As a result, several family-planning doctors have called the pricing scheme misguided and challenged Wyeth-Ayerst to deeply discount the drug to clinics.

Another reason that some in the family-planning community are unhappy with Norplant's pricing stems from the way the contraceptive was developed in the first place. Norplant originated at the nonprofit Population Council, which used $10 million in government and philanthropic grants to develop the contraceptive. Wyeth-Ayerst got the rights to it because Norplant contains the company's patented hormone Levnorgestrel. The Population Council receives only a small royalty from Wyeth-Ayerst for the sale of Norplant.

Wyeth-Ayerst responded to this issue by claiming that it is only earning a fair return on its investment. It backs up its claim by asserting that:

- High prices reflect high costs. (See the pie chart in Exhibit D6.1, which represents a breakdown of pricing for a typical drug company.) For example, training physicians and nurses in how to use Norplant cost Wyeth-Ayerst $26 million over the last several years. Training costs are included as part of cost of goods sold.
- High profits are limited to the patent protection period. When that's over, the availability of generic drugs is likely to sharply reduce prices.
- Profits are plowed back into research and development of new versions of Norplant and other women's health products.
- Some other companies charge more in the United States than in other countries, for the same products. Wyeth-Ayerst points to Upjohn's Depro-Provera as an example.
- Five years' protection by Norplant is cheaper than 5-years' worth of oral contraceptives. Market research indicates that the price could have been even higher.
- In the first 2½ years since its introduction, Norplant has been inserted in 780,000 women in the United States, an indication of the market's acceptance

of the price. Critics counter that women who want long-term protection have no other choice. There are currently no other competing products, since Norplant is protected by patents.

Required:

1. What kinds of costs does Wyeth-Ayerst have to recover in its price?
2. Do you think Norplant's pricing is fair?

D6.2   (Opportunity Cost)[14]

The banking industry sometimes has to take giant losses on loans to developing countries. For example, in 1992 banks restructured $44 billion in debt from Brazil, the world's second-largest debtor nation. However, debt restructuring may not be as bad as it appears. For one thing, the high interest rates charged before loans go bad can help offset losses. For another thing, debt is sometimes swapped for equity. In July 1992, J. P. Morgan reported a $124-million gain on Mexican securities acquired in an earlier Mexican loan restructuring. In addition, loan-loss provisions sometimes create tax advantages.

However, there are other costs that increase the losses. The estimated $26-billion net loss on the Brazilian bank loans doesn't take into account opportunity costs—what banks could have earned had the money been put to other uses. In addition, the loss doesn't take into account the higher interest rates developing countries end up paying when they borrow money. On top of all that, the stock market penalizes banks that make loans to developing countries. One way to measure the penalty is to compare stock market returns for banks with and without such loans. A sampling of banks with outstanding loans to developing countries had stock market returns of about 19 percent from 1982 through 1986. In contrast, banks without loans to developing countries had returns of 28.8 percent over the same period.

Required: What is an opportunity cost? Do opportunity costs differ from real costs? When are opportunity costs relevant for decisions?

PROBLEMS   P6.1   (Special Order)

Dane Manufacturing makes a single line of plastic skylights. While capacity is around 80,000 units per year, Dane's current projections are for demand of between 60,000 and 65,000 units. In March, Janet Dane, CFO of Dane Manufacturing, received an order for 3,000 units from a distributor in Venezuela, a country where the company does not normally sell its product. Unfortunately, the Venezuelan distributor offered only $15 per unit, a price below the full-cost figures shown in Exhibit P6.1 and considerably lower than the normal selling price of $17. While the distributor is responsible for all shipping costs, Dane managers argue that the price is still too low.

Required: What is the financial impact if Dane decides to accept the offer?

---

[14]   Steven Lipin, "Banks Escape the Latin Debt Crisis with Little Damage," *The Wall Street Journal,* July 16, 1992, p. B4.

EXHIBIT P6.1 DANE MANUFACTURING			
Manufacturing Cost			
	Volume, in Units		
	50,000	*60,000*	*70,000*
Direct materials	$250,000	$300,000	$350,000
Direct labor	400,000	480,000	560,000
Depreciation	50,000	50,000	50,000
Utilities	25,000	30,000	35,000
Supervision	80,000	80,000	80,000
Supplies	10,000	12,000	14,000
Manufacturing cost	$815,000	$952,000	$1,089,000
Unit manufacturing cost	$16.30	$15.87	$15.56

P6.2   (Incremental, Full, and Opportunity Costs)

Jane Cordray has been making fried fruit-stuffed pies—a snack food found mainly in the South—for years. After encouragement from friends, Cordray leased space from a local restaurant and began selling pies to a food distributor at $0.60 apiece. The cost of making the pies is shown in Exhibit P6.2.

Cordray's pies are so popular that she is working at 100 percent capacity, producing approximately 300,000 pies each year. Recently, she received an offer for an order of 5,000 pies from the owner of a Seattle-based restaurant chain who read about her in a newspaper article. The restauranteur's offer was for $0.72 per pie, a price 20 percent higher than normal. While all costs in making pies for the special order are the same as her typical cost, Cordray is leaning toward turning the restauranteur down, since she doesn't have the extra capacity.

EXHIBIT P6.2 JANE'S FRIED PIES			
Operating Profit at Different Volumes			
	Volume (Number of Fried Pies)		
	250,000	*275,000*	*300,000*
Revenue	$150,000	$165,000	$180,000
Costs:			
Direct materials	$ 50,000	$ 55,000	$ 60,000
Direct labor	15,000	15,000	15,000
Depreciation	5,000	5,000	5,000
Utilities	12,500	13,750	15,000
Office expense	15,000	15,000	15,000
Kitchen lease	8,000	8,000	8,000
Full cost	$105,500	$111,750	$118,000
Pretax operating profit	$44,500	$53,250	$62,000

Required:

1. If Cordray had the capacity, what is the incremental cost of the special order?
2. What is the full cost of a pie at full capacity?
3. What is the opportunity cost if Cordray decides not to accept the special order?

P6.3 (Cost Buildup)

An income statement for Starr Manufacturing is shown in Exhibit P6.3. The cost of goods sold contains $750,000 in fixed costs, while the fixed portion of operating expense is $250,000.

Required:

1. Calculate the markup percent required on variable cost (both cost of goods sold and operating cost) in order to achieve the pretax net income shown in Exhibit P6.3.
2. Calculate the markup percent required on direct cost in order to achieve the pretax net income shown in Exhibit P6.3.
3. Calculate the markup percent required on full cost (both cost of goods sold and operating cost) in order to achieve the pretax net income shown in Exhibit P6.3.

P6.4 (Incremental and Opportunity Costs, Special Order)

Dawat Products manufactures a single product in a facility that has the capacity for producing 50,000 units per year. Dawat's managers prepared the estimate of pretax operating income for 1995, based on estimated sales of 35,000 units, as shown in Exhibit P6.4.

At the beginning of 1995, Dawat received an offer for a 20,000-unit order from an offshore distributor. The units requested in the offer are identical in every respect to those Dawat sells to its regular customers. Dawat will incur the same selling and administrative costs as it does with units sold through regular channels. The offer requires that all 20,000 units be delivered by the end of 1995. Unfortunately, the offshore distributor is willing to pay only $32.50 per unit, well below Dawat's $50.00 regular selling price. If it accepts the special order, all production activities will take place at its present facility. Since capacity is limited, Dawat will have to give up some of its business with regular customers if it accepts the special order.

EXHIBIT P6.3 STARR MANUFACTURING

Income Statement for the Year

Units manufactured and sold	100,000
Revenue	$2,420,000
Cost of goods sold	1,750,000
Gross profit	$ 670,000
Operating expense	450,000
Pretax net income	$ 220,000

EXHIBIT P6.4 DAWAT PRODUCTS

Projected Operating Income for 1995

Revenue:		
Units sold	35,000	
Selling price	$50	
Total revenue		$1,750,000
Variable cost:		
Manufacturing	$735,000	
Selling	175,000	
Administrative	70,000	
Total variable cost		$980,000
Contribution margin		$770,000
Fixed cost		475,000
Pretax operating income		$295,000

Required:

1. What is the total incremental contribution from the special order, given present capacity?
2. Dawat can lease additional equipment for $50,000 that will temporarily add 10,000 units of capacity. What is the incremental contribution from the special order, assuming Dawat leases the equipment?

(AICPA Adapted)

P6.5 (Relevant-Cost Basics)

The Mowerson Division of Brown Instruments manufactures testing equipment for the automobile industry. Mowerson's equipment is installed in several places along an automobile assembly line for component testing. It is also used for recording and measurement purposes during track and road tests. Mowerson's sales have grown steadily, and, in 1995, revenue will exceed $20 million for the first time in the division's history.

Mowerson designs and manufactures its own printed-circuit boards (PCBs) for use in the test equipment. The PCBs are pieced together by hand by 45 technicians in the assembly department. Because of the lack of plant capacity and a shortage of skilled labor, Mowerson is considering outsourcing the printed-circuit boards to Tri-Star, a specialist in this field. However, the cost of outsourcing the circuit boards is higher than the cost of manufacturing them in-house. Mowerson's managers think that the higher cost might be offset by other savings.

Jim Wright, a recently hired cost analyst, was asked to prepare an evaluation of the costs and benefits of outsourcing the PCBs. His report, shown in Exhibit P6.5, includes the assumptions he used in this analysis, along with his recommendation. The notes and detailed assumptions Wright used in his analysis are presented below:

Personnel

The number of assembly department technicians will be reduced by 40, at an annual saving (salary plus benefits) of $28,500 each. The remaining 5 technicians—

EXHIBIT P6.5 MOWERSON DIVISION

Annual Cost Saving for Tri-Star Contract

Saving:

1. Reduction in assembly technicians		
($28,500 × 40)		$1,140,000
2. Assembly supervisor transferred		35,000
3. Floor space savings		
[(1,000 × $9.50) + (8,000 × $6.00)]		57,500
4. Purchasing clerk		
(1/2 time on special project)		6,000
5. Purchase order reduction		
(2,000 orders @ $1.25 each)		2,500
6. Reduced incoming freight and issuing costs		7,500
Total saving		$1,248,500

Cost:

7. Outsourcing to Tri-Star		
[($60.00 − $52.00) × 100,000 units]		$800,000
8. Hire junior engineer		20,000
9. Hire quality-control inspector		22,000
10. Increased storage cost for safety stock		
(4,200 units @ $2.00/unit)		8,400
Total cost − 1800		$850,400
Net annual saving		$398,100

5 assemblers who have always assisted in repair work—will remain on Mowerson's payroll and will assist the field service department with repair work on the boards. The supervisor of the assembly department will remain with Mowerson because he has only 2 years until retirement. A position will be created for him in the machining department, where he will serve as a special consultant.

Because purchasing and stocking the component parts for PCB assembly will no longer be needed, one purchasing clerk will be reassigned half-time to a special project until his time can be more fully utilized. The clerk will still earn the same salary.

A junior engineer will be hired to act as liaison between Mowerson and the manufacturer of the PCBs. In addition, a third quality-control inspector will be needed to monitor the vendor's adherence to quality standards.

Floor Space

For the past 2 years, to accommodate the overflow of assembly work, Mowerson has rented, on a month-to-month basis, 1,000 square feet of space for $9.50 per square foot in a neighboring building. The 8,000 square feet currently being used in Mowerson's main plant by the assembly department will be used for temporary stockroom storage. However, this space could be reclaimed for manufacturing use without overloading the stockroom facilities. This floor space is valued at $6 per square foot.

Production Cost and Volume

Mowerson's standard cost for manufacturing PCBs is as follows:

Direct materials	$24.00
Direct labor (including assembly department technicians)	12.50
Variable overhead	6.25
Fixed overhead	9.25
Total cost	$52.00

It is taken into account

its included on the direct material

The direct materials cost includes normal scrap and other such materials-related costs as incoming freight and issuing costs. Mowerson's annual cost for incoming freight attributed to PCBs is $7,500. Tri-Star will charge $60 per board, including the cost of delivery.

Mowerson's production volume of printed-circuit boards for the past 2 years has been 80,000 and 90,000 boards, respectively. Projected production volume for next year is 100,000 units.

Storage Costs

Because Mowerson will not have direct control over the manufacture of the PCBs, the level of safety stock will be increased over the current level of 1,800 boards. Because of the uncertainty in manufacturing and delivery schedules, the supervisor of the assembly department expects to increase safety stock to 4,200 if the PCBs are outsourced to Tri-Star. The variable cost to store the PCBs is $2 per board per year.

Other

The variable cost of executing a purchase order at Mowerson is $1.25 and comprises the cost of items such as postage, forms, and telephone charges. Since Mowerson will no longer have to purchase all the component parts required for the PCBs, the number of purchase orders prepared annually will be reduced by 2,000. The equipment used in making PCBs has negligible value. Any proceeds from its sale will be offset by the cost of disposal.

Recommendation

Based on the annual saving of $398,100 projected above, Mowerson should enter into an agreement with Tri-Star to manufacture the PCBs.

Required:

1. Determine whether or not Wright's analysis is correct. If not, prepare a schedule of the costs relevant to the outsourcing decision.
2. What other factors might Mowerson consider before reaching a final decision on the Tri-Star contract?

(*CMA Adapted*)

P6.6 (Incremental Costs)

Helene's Clothing, a high-fashion women's dress manufacturer, is planning to market a new cocktail dress for the coming season. Helene's supplies retailers in New England and in the mid-Atlantic states.

Four yards of material are required in order to lay out the dress pattern. After the cutting operation, some materials remain that can be sold as remnants. The leftover material can also be used to make a matching cape and handbag. However, if the leftover material is to be used for the cape and handbag, more care is required in the cutting operation, thereby increasing cutting cost.

EXHIBIT P6.6.1 HELENE'S CLOTHING	
Sales of Various Combinations of Clothing Items	
Complete sets of dress, cape, & handbag	70.00%
Dress & cape	6.00%
Dress & handbag	15.00%
Dress only	9.00%
Total	100.00%

EXHIBIT P6.6.2 HELENE'S CLOTHING		
Selling Prices and Costs to Complete Items		
Item	*Selling Price per Unit*	*Unit Cost to Complete*[a]
Dress	$200.00	$80.00
Cape	$27.50	$19.50
Handbag	$9.50	$6.50

[a] Excludes materials and cutting operations.

The company expects to sell 1,250 dresses if it decides not to sell the matching cape and handbag. Helene's market research reveals that dress sales will be 20 percent higher if a matching cape and handbag are available to customers. The market research indicates that the cape and handbag will not be sold individually but only as optional accessories with the dress. The various combinations of dresses, capes, and handbags that are expected to be sold by retailers are shown in Exhibit P6.6.1.

The material used in the dress costs $12.50 a yard, or $50.00 for each dress. The cost of cutting the dress if the cape and handbag are not manufactured is estimated at $20 per dress. The resulting remnants can be sold for $5 for each dress cut out. However, if the cape and handbag are manufactured, cutting cost will increase by $9 per dress. There will be no saleable remnants if the capes and handbags are manufactured in the quantities estimated.

Selling prices and the costs to complete the three items once they are cut are shown in Exhibit P6.6.2.

Required: Calculate Helene's incremental (differential) profit or loss from manufacturing the capes and handbags in conjunction with the dresses.

(CMA Adapted)

P6.7   (Calculating Selling Price)

Fiore Company manufactures office equipment for sale through a network of retail outlets. Tim Lucas, vice president of marketing, proposed that Fiore introduce two new products, an electric stapler and an electric pencil sharpener. Lucas asked the accounting department to develop preliminary selling prices for both new products. The company's standard policy specifies that it use all available data in making its pricing recommendations. The results are shown in Exhibit P6.7.1.

EXHIBIT P6.7.1 FIORE COMPANY

Data Used for Pricing Two New Products

	Electric Stapler	Electric Pencil Sharpener
Estimated annual demand, in units	12,000	10,000
Estimated unit manufacturing cost:		
Variable	$3.50	$5.75
Fixed	$6.50	$6.25
Estimated unit selling & administrative cost		
Variable	$2.40	$2.40
Fixed	$1.60	$1.60
Assets employed in manufacturing	$180,000	$225,000

EXHIBIT P6.7.2 FIORE COMPANY

Budgeted Income Statement

Revenue	$4,800,000
Cost of goods sold	2,880,000
Gross profit	$1,920,000
Selling & administrative expense	1,440,000
Operating profit (before tax)	$ 480,000

Fiore plans to use an average of $2,400,000 in assets to support its operations in the current year, before consideration of either new product. The budgeted income statement for the year is shown in Exhibit P6.7.2. It represents Fiore's planned goals for the year with respect to cost and return on investment (ROI) across all products.

Required:

1. Calculate selling prices for both new products using cost-based pricing. Assume Fiore wants to achieve a target return on investment equal to its projected ROI. *Note:* Return on investment equals pretax operating profit divided by assets employed.
2. Calculate the selling price for each new product using cost-based pricing. Assume Fiore wants to achieve a target return on full cost (both manufacturing and nonmanufacturing) based on its budgeted income statement.
3. Calculate the minimum selling price for each new product. Assume that minimum means the price that will neither increase nor decrease profit.

(CMA Adapted)

P6.8 (Alternative Ways to Make Circuit Boards)

The Gytechnics Company was recently awarded a contract to supply an electronic component used in monitoring commercial aircraft movement. The original contract is with the Federal Aviation Administration (FAA). Gytechnics, serving as a subcontractor, is to make a total of 12,800 of the devices. The controllers include a circuit board whose manufacture requires a number of complex steps. Gytechnics is considering three alternative ways of making the boards: (1) using the current, labor-intensive process, (2) leasing automatic insertion machinery in order to eliminate the learning-curve effect and reduce the labor content in the circuit boards, and (3) purchasing the boards from another manufacturer.

Gytechnics manufactures specialized products to order in a job-shop environment. As noted above, its current manufacturing processes are labor-intensive. Since Gytechnics makes a variety of different products, it typically experiences an 80 percent learning curve on new production runs. That is, each time cumulative production doubles, the average amount of time for all units is only 80 percent of the time it took to make the preceding lot. For example, assume production of the first lot of 100 units takes an average of 2 direct labor-hours per unit, or a total of 200 hours. When production doubles to 200 units (the original lot of 100 units and a second lot of 100 units), the average amount of labor time declines to about 1.6 hours (80% × 2.0) per unit, or 320 hours for all 200 units. That is, the second lot of 100 units takes an increment of 120 hours to make (320 − 200 hours), or 1.2 incremental hours per unit.

Gytechnics' learning rate applies to direct labor and variable overhead through the fifth production run. After that, production of all the rest of the units should take the same amount of incremental hours as the fifth lot took. Gytechnics' manufacturing engineers plan to make the components in lots of 100 units. They estimate that the first lot of 100 circuit boards should cost $20,460, as shown in Exhibit P6.8.

An automatic insertion machine to make the 12,800 boards can be leased at a cost of $250,000. The annual lease cost includes installation, tryout, removal, and all maintenance. If the machine is leased, cash fixed cost will decline by $75,000 for the length of the run. Only 2,000 direct labor-hours, at $12 per hour, will be required to operate the machinery. Since Gytechnics has a backlog of work, the direct labor-hours released by the automatic insertion machine will be used on other, similar projects. The materials cost, labor rate, overhead rate, and the selling and administrative allocation are unchanged if the insertion machine is leased.

The boards can also be acquired from a specialty electronics manufacturer at a cost of $130 apiece. If Gytechnics chooses this option, cash fixed cost will decline

---

EXHIBIT P6.8 GYTECHNICS COMPANY

Cost to Manufacture First Lot of 100 Circuit Boards

Cost Component	Total
Direct materials ($102 per unit)	$10,200
Direct labor (2 hours/unit @ $12/hour)	2,400
Variable overhead (50% of direct labor cost)	1,200
Fixed overhead[a]	4,800
Total manufacturing cost	$18,600
Selling & administrative cost[b]	1,860
Total cost of first lot of 100 units	$20,460

[a] Fixed overhead is applied on a per-unit basis.
[b] Selling and administrative cost is allocated to products on the basis of revenue.

by $256,000. This figure includes the $75,000 cash fixed cost avoided in the machine lease alternative. Gytechnics has purchased components from the supplier in the past and is satisfied with both their quality and service.

Required: What are the relevant costs of making 12,800 circuit boards under each of the three alternatives?

(CMA Adapted)

P6.9   **(Relevant Costs, Allocations)**

CedarMade is one of the three product divisions of Carolina Products, Inc. Carolina Products formed CedarMade to concentrate on the outdoor patio furniture segment of the market. Carolina Products supports all administrative and selling functions, charging each of its three divisions corporate overhead based on the number of units sold.

CedarMade's only product is a rectangular, trestle-like table. Standard costs for the table are shown in Exhibit P6.9.1. Direct materials cost represents the purchase of pressure-treated cedarwood, as needed, from independent suppliers. Direct labor reflects CedarMade's 10 workers, each of whom is salaried. When the workforce was hired, CedarMade planned on making more tables than it is making today. Instead of releasing unneeded workers, CedarMade's managers decided to keep them on the payroll. Not only would CedarMade retain the workers' skills, but the no-layoff policy encouraged loyalty. In return, CedarMade's workers are expected to increase production whenever activity picks up without demanding overtime pay. Manufacturing overhead, which is totally fixed, is $116,000 per year and is applied to tables based on 18,000 normal direct labor-hours. Corporate overhead is assigned on the basis of the total number of units sold companywide, as indicated at the bottom of Exhibit P6.9.1.

EXHIBIT P6.9.1   CAROLINA PRODUCTS, INC.— CEDARMADE DIVISION

Standard Cost for Trestle Table

Cost Component	Measure	Units	Cost	Unit Cost
Direct materials	Board feet	50.00	$0.35	$17.50
Direct labor	Labor-hours	2.25	$12.75	28.69
Manufacturing overhead	Labor-hours	2.25	$6.44	14.50
Total manufactured cost				$60.69
Corporate overhead (see below)				22.50
Full cost				$83.19

Corporate Overhead—Carolina Products, Inc.

	Fixed	Variable (with Units Sold)	Total
Corporate overhead	$375,000	$75,000	$450,000
Units manufactured & sold companywide	20,000	20,000	20,000
Corporate overhead per unit	$ 18.75	$ 3.75	$ 22.50

Until recently, sales of the trestle tables have been relatively stable at around 8,000 units, well below the facility's 15,000-unit capacity. However, CedarMade just received a one-time offer from Standpointe, a national furniture warehouse that sells a similar table. Safety violations at Standpointe's manufacturing plant temporarily interrupted production. It turned to CedarMade with an offer for 4,000 tables at $72 per unit, considerably below CedarMade's normal selling price of $100. While Standpointe's offer is below full cost, the tables will be sold in the southwestern United States, an area where CedarMade doesn't normally compete.

The special tables, if CedarMade decides to make them, will be identical to existing tables, except that they will need less finishing labor. While the Standpointe tables will use the same materials, only 1.75 hours of direct labor will be required to produce them. Overhead, which is assigned on the basis of direct labor-hours, will also be lower. The only other change is the temporary transfer of a production manager to CedarMade from another Carolina Products division. The manager, whose salary and benefits total $48,000, will be temporarily assigned to CedarMade for the year. At the end of that period, the manager will return to his own division. In the meantime, the assistant manager will fill in.

When CedarMade's managers worked out the numbers on the special order, they found, as expected, that the new product lowered operating income. Their analysis is shown in Exhibit P6.9.2.

Required: Review CedarMade's evaluation of the special offer, shown in Exhibit P6.9.2. Do you agree with the analysis? If not, recalculate operating income to include only those items you believe are relevant to the special order.

P6.10 (Make or Buy Decision)[15]

Martin Electronics manufactures fuel injection systems for automobiles. The company experienced explosive growth over the last 10 years, as automakers switched from mechanical carburetors to electronic fuel injection systems. While fuel injectors add to the sticker price of new cars, they save money in the long run by minimizing maintenance, improving performance, and reducing fuel expense.

Martin makes fuel injectors in a highly automated factory. Many of the parts that go into making fuel injectors are purchased from outside suppliers. Once materials and other components are transferred to production, the entire manufacturing process takes place virtually automatically. Production employees serve as machine operators; they monitor production and make sure that the fuel injectors fall within quality standards.

Recently, Chanel Machining, one of Martin's suppliers, sent notice that it would be unable to deliver 10,000 components needed by Martin for production of fuel injectors scheduled 2 months from now. Chanel has always been reliable in the past, providing high-quality components on time and at a reasonable cost. After discussions with Chanel, Martin managers are convinced that the situation is temporary and plan to continue their relationship. However, Martin must still find a temporary source for the components. Because of competitive pressures, they simply cannot afford to deviate from their production schedule. Nor can they fail to meet promised delivery dates for customers.

The materials handling manager located an alternative supplier that agreed

---

[15] Based on an article by Linda F. Christensen and Douglas Sharp, "How ABC Can Add Value to Decision Making," *Management Accounting*, May 1993, pp. 38–42.

EXHIBIT P6.9.2 CAROLINA PRODUCTS, INC.— CEDARMADE DIVISION

Evaluation of Special Order

	Reject Special Order	Accept Special Order
Revenue:		
Normal units expected to be sold	8,000	8,000
Number of special-order units		4,000
Total unit sales	8,000	12,000
Selling price for normal units	$100.00	$100.00
Selling price for special order		72.00
Total revenue	$800,000	$1,088,000
Costs for normal units:		
Standard cost	$83.19	$83.19
Normal units expected to be sold	8,000	8,000
Total cost of normal units	$665,500	$665,500

	Units	Unit Cost	Total Cost
Costs for special order:			
Direct materials (board-feet)	50.00	$0.35	$17.50
Direct labor (hours)	1.75	$12.75	22.31
Manufacturing overhead (hours)	1.75	$6.44	11.28
Total manufacturing cost			$51.09
Corporate overhead			22.50
Unit cost			$73.59
Units sold			4,000
Total cost of special order			$294,360
Manager transferred from another division			48,000
Total cost of special order			$342,360
Total cost	$665,500		$1,007,860
Operating income	$134,500		$ 80,140

to make the 10,000 units and meet the desired delivery date. While Martin pays Chanel $235 for each component, the new supplier is charging $283 per component, including inbound shipping and delivery. That's a hefty increase—about $480,000 for 10,000 components. The supplier is inflexible, unwilling to negotiate price because it sees the transaction as a one-time deal.

A second alternative is for Martin to make the component. It has the technical capability and equipment, plus it is operating at less than full capacity. Manufacturing activities at Martin consist of:

- *Materials handling.* Ordering, storing, and supplying production with materials and components.
- *Production scheduling.* Scheduling manufacturing operations, coordinating manufacturing activities with materials handling, and packaging and shipping.
- *Setup.* Changing over manufacturing between different injector lines.

EXHIBIT P6.10.1 MARTIN ELECTRONICS

Activities, Activity Costs, and Activity Drivers

Activity	Activity Driver	Volume of Activity Driver	Total Cost	Percent Variable
Materials handling	Parts	646,000	$260,000	40.00%
Production scheduling	Production orders	570	$115,000	0.00%
Setup labor	Production setups	200	$625,000	25.00%
Automated machinery	Machine-hours	117,000	$3,000,000	0.00%
Finishing	Direct labor-hours	54,600	$1,100,000	60.00%

EXHIBIT P6.10.2 MARTIN ELECTRONICS

Data for Making Component

Units produced	10,000
Direct materials cost per unit	$120.00
Number of parts per unit	3
Production orders	10
Number of setups	10
Machine-hours per unit	0.70
Direct labor-hours per unit in finishing	0.25

- *Automated machinery operations.* Operating the factory using automated machinery as well as staff such as equipment operators and process monitors.
- *Finishing.* Physical inspection and preparation for shipping.

Martin, which uses an activity-based costing (ABC) system, developed the production data shown in Exhibit P6.10.1. Costs and activities shown in the exhibit are based on normal levels of activity. Exhibit P6.10.1 also shows estimates of the cost-behavior relationship between activity drivers and total cost. For example, approximately 40 percent of materials-handling cost is variable.

Martin gathered the data shown in Exhibit P6.10.2 to use in evaluating the alternatives.

Required:

1. Calculate the cost of each manufacturing activity. Split activity costs into variable and fixed.
2. Calculate the relevant costs of making the components and of buying them from the outside supplier. What is the net incremental benefit (cost) if Martin makes the components?
3. What should Martin do? Should it buy the components from the alternative supplier at $283 or should it make the components? What are some of the nonfinancial factors Martin should consider?

P6.11 (Pricing Platforms)

Geraldo Daspin opened Daspin Motors nearly 10 years ago. At that time Daspin, who sold cars for a Volvo dealership in Houston, decided to open his own used car lot. Daspin decided to deal only in used Volvos. His second-most-important decision was to create an on-site repair shop. His plans were to repair used Volvos for his own lot and to fill excess repair shop capacity with external repair work. When Daspin Motors was formed, Daspin created two departments—car sales and service, each with its own manager. The focus in each department, as evidenced by the way performance is measured, is on customer satisfaction.

Daspin Motors initially grew at a dramatic pace. To meet increasing demand for service work, Daspin expanded the repair shop capacity several years ago by adding a second hydraulic lift. Unfortunately, current economic conditions and the entry of a new Volvo dealer into the market have left him with excess capacity.

Daspin has been able to sell some of the excess capacity to several major customer groups. For example, he does a lot of the overflow work for the new Volvo dealership. In addition, some of the other used car shops have verbal agreements with Daspin to send their repair work to him. Another source of work is insurance companies, which include Daspin Motors on their preferred list of repair shops. However, each of these customer groups expects to pay less than what it would pay at the authorized Volvo dealer. Moreover, Daspin has to closely monitor repair costs for cars that are to be sold on his own lot. If these repair costs become too high, Daspin could easily price himself right out of a very competitive used car market.

Daspin decided to work out a formula that provides different ways of determining prices for repair work. His plan is to charge each repair job for the actual cost of parts and materials. All other costs, including salaries of repair mechanics, service department overhead, allocated corporate overhead (occupancy, marketing, and administrative costs), and a desired markup on cost are assigned to jobs based on mechanics' labor-hours.

Daspin started with the 1994 income statement for the service department, shown in Exhibit P6.11.1. After reviewing the income statement, he believes that it will serve as a good basis for expressing the desired relationships between costs and customer charges. Next, he determined the changes in costs expected for 1995. These changes, plus a breakdown of costs by the percent variable, are shown in Exhibit P6.11.2. Daspin uses practical capacity to determine the normal level of

EXHIBIT P6.11.1 DASPIN MOTORS— SERVICE DEPARTMENT

Income Statement for the Year 1994

Charges to customers		$628,458
Cost & expense:		
Auto parts & materials		$254,585
Mechanics' salaries		114,320
Service department overhead:		
Indirect materials	$23,190	
Heat, light, & power	14,512	
Depreciation	62,400	
Supervisors' salaries	38,900	
Direct service department overhead		139,002
Allocated corporate overhead		
(8.5% of charges to customers)		53,419
Total cost		$561,326
Operating income—service department		$67,132

EXHIBIT P6.11.2 DASPIN MOTORS— SERVICE DEPARTMENT

Service Department Data Projected for 1995

Cost Component	Projected Growth in Cost in 1995	Percent That Varies with Mechanics' Hours
Auto parts & materials	0.00%	100.00%
Mechanics' salaries	2.25%	20.00%
Indirect materials		0.00%
Heat, light, & power	4.00%	15.00%
Depreciation		0.00%
Supervisors' salaries	$2,500	0.00%
Allocated corporate overhead	Note 1	0.00%

Note 1: Revenue for the service department is expected to increase by 5.5% in 1995.

labor-hours for his five mechanics. Each mechanic is normally expected to charge 35 hours per week, 50 weeks per year, to jobs.

To test how the pricing alternatives might work, Daspin pulled a typical job from his files. The job incurred 6.25 hours of mechanics' time and $137.50 in materials cost.

Required:

1. Determine separate fixed and variable rates for 1995 for:
   a. Mechanics' labor
   b. Direct service department overhead
   c. Corporate overhead
   Note: All rates are based on practical capacity expressed in chargeable mechanics' hours.
2. Determine the buildup of cost for a typical job with 6.25 hours of mechanics' time and $137.50 in materials based on the following:
   a. Variable cost
   b. Direct cost
   c. Full cost
   d. Full cost plus desired profit

P6.12 (Pricing with Downward-Sloping Demand Curve)

Schenck Chemical manufactures lubricants used in a wide variety of high-speed machinery. Its primary product, referred to as BF-12, is sold in 1-gallon containers. Since BF-12 is an indirect material used in manufacturing and several substitutes are available, Schenck finds that it has to compete on price. The current price for a gallon of BF-12 is $7, calculated based on the standard costs shown in Exhibit P6.12. Standard costs assume a normal volume of 4 million gallons per year. Last year Schenck sold just about 4 million gallons at an average unit price of $7. Next year should be about the same, with no changes in price, volume, or cost anticipated. Schenck marks up full cost by 20 percent. This margin is intended to pro-

EXHIBIT P6.12 SCHENCK CHEMICAL

Unit Cost for BF-12

Normal Volume = 4 million gallons

Manufacturing	Cost per Gallon
Variable cost:	
Chemicals	$1.86
Labor	0.65
Processing overhead	0.22
Fixed cost:	
Labor	0.56
Processing overhead	1.16
Research, Selling, and Administration	
Variable cost:	
Selling	0.25
Administration	0.08
Fixed cost:	
Research	0.62
Selling	0.17
Administration	0.26
Full cost	$5.83
Markup on full cost (20%)	1.17
Selling price	$7.00

vide for income taxes, estimated at 35 percent of pretax income, and to allow a reasonable profit.

Menter Schenck, president of Schenck Chemical, is trying to finalize a pricing strategy for next year. She is considering a proposal to raise the price of a gallon of BF-12 to $9. However, estimates prepared by industry consultants indicate that sales volume is likely to fall from 4 million to 2.9 million gallons if Schenck raises its price from $7 to $9.

Required:

1. Calculate after-tax net income at a price of $7. Repeat your calculations at a price of $9.
2. Develop a demand curve using the two paired price-quantity observations. Assume that price drives demand. That is, Schenck sets prices that, in turn, determine the demand for BF-12. Using the demand curve, calculate after-tax net income at selling prices ranging from $6.00 to $13.00, in $0.25 increments. Then plot the prices on the *x*-axis and the after-tax net income amounts on the *y*-axis. What is the optimum price? *Note:* The demand curve takes the form: Quantity sold = intercept + (slope × price). The slope parameter is estimated by calculating the change in volume relative to the change in price. After the slope is determined, the intercept is calculated by substituting either one of the price-quantity pairs into the demand curve and solving for the intercept.

EXHIBIT C6.1.1 HUGHES TEXTILES		
Utilization of Capacity[a]		
Year	Industry	Hughes Textiles
1984	80.5	85.2
1985	80.0	86.8
1986	87.0	87.0
1987	91.0	93.3
1988	84.5	90.1
1989	85.7	75.2
1990	82.0	48.8
1991	85.0	50.4

[a] Full capacity = 100.

CASES

C6.1 (Hughes Textiles)[16]

Charles Hughes is president of Hughes Textiles. The son of the company's founder, Charles built the present-day manufacturing facilities in his hometown of Greenville, South Carolina. Hughes competes in the textile industry against well-known companies such as Fieldcrest, Cannon, Burlington Industries, and Galey & Lord. Textile products are consumed both indirectly by other manufacturers and as finished consumer goods such as sheets, towels, draperies, and carpets. While textile plants are located in virtually every part of the United States, they tend to be concentrated in southern states such as the Carolinas and Georgia.

Textile product manufacturing begins with fibers such as cotton, wool, and synthetics. Conversion of materials into finished products is not always simple, often requiring multiple, complex steps. Cotton yarns, for example, must be textured and spun, knitted, and woven, and then dyed or printed. In the final stages of processing, finished fabrics are converted into clothing and household goods.

Textiles are heavily dependent on *basic demand*—consumer spending on clothing and semidurable items such as home furnishings. In the past, textile prices have "trended" higher, primarily because of increasing materials and labor costs. When the basic demand slackens, operating rates—and profits—fall dramatically. As a result, textile manufacturers experience considerable variation in profit margins. This is exemplified by the utilization of capacity for Hughes Textiles and the textile industry, as shown in Exhibit C6.1.1.

Textile manufacturers commit huge sums of capital to improving productivity and enhancing flexibility by investing in new equipment. Industry experts, in fact, predict equipment investments of $2 billion or more. A good example of one such investment is the shutterless loom, which improved the speed and efficiency with which fabrics were woven by almost 4 times. As a side benefit, new machinery also reduces floor space requirements. Not only do capital investments improve operating efficiency, they also boost U.S. competitiveness. Even though the United States is a net importer of textiles, the growth in exports appears to be picking up (Exhibit C6.1.2).

---

[16] Materials for the textile industry are taken from *Standard and Poor's Industry Surveys,* "Textiles, Apparel, & Home Furnishings," Mar. 18, 1993, pp. T61–T77, and Nov. 26, 1992, pp. T78–T95.

EXHIBIT C6.1.2 HUGHES TEXTILES

Textile Industry Imports and Exports, Millions of Pounds

Year	Imports	Exports
1984	2,765.8	703.9
1985	3,343.8	681.5
1986	3,875.8	785.9
1987	4,293.7	910.9
1988	4,078.9	1,043.1
1989	4,393.8	1,628.1
1990	4,451.6	2,056.0
1991	4,671.4	2,222.2

Source: Standard & Poor's Industry Surveys. "Textiles, Apparel and Home Furnishings." Nov. 26, 1992, p. T78. Reprinted by permission of Standard & Poor's, a division of The McGraw-Hill Companies.

EXHIBIT C6.1.3 HUGHES TEXTILES— TERRY WOVEN TOWEL INDUSTRY

Market Share, Millions of Dozens

Year	Terry Woven Towels Market[a]	Hughes Textiles' Terry Woven Division	Hughes Textiles' Market Share	Hughes Textiles' Capacity
1984	48.0	9.2	19.17%	10.8
1985	44.9	9.9	22.05%	11.4
1986	49.9	10.0	20.04%	11.5
1987	52.4	11.1	21.18%	11.9
1988	47.2	10.9	23.09%	12.1
1989	62.4	9.1	14.58%	12.1
1990	42.4	5.9	13.92%	12.1
1991	43.2	6.1 M	14.12%	12.1

[a] Data are from Standard & Poor's Industry Surveys. "Textiles, Apparel and Home Furnishings." Nov. 26, 1992, p. T80. Reprinted by permission of Standard & Poor's, a division of The McGraw-Hill Companies.

Home textiles, the segment in which Hughes Textiles competes, accounts for over one-third of all textile output. Home textiles are sold in four primary market segments: carpeting, drapes and upholstery, sheets and towels, and all other uses (encompassing products such as bedspreads, tablecloths, and napkins).

One of Hughes Textiles' operating divisions, the Terry Woven division, in Greenville, manufactures dish towels for home use. Towel manufacturing occupies nearly 40 percent of the factory's total square footage. Committing such a large proportion of the plant's capacity to Terry Woven is justified by market share, because, at one point, Hughes Textiles captured over 23 percent of total market volume (see Exhibit C6.1.3).

Hughes, as one of the industry leaders, raised its prices to $3.75 per dozen towels at the end of 1988. When other major towel producers failed to follow suit, Terry Woven quickly lost market share. Managers justified the price increase on the basis of input prices. In addition to rising materials cost, Hughes Textiles experienced increases in wage rates for nearly a decade. All of Terry Woven's employees are salaried and are represented by a strong textile workers union. Another justification for price increases was the belief that Hughes towels are better, with more absorbing power than other dish towels. Unfortunately, consumers either did not recognize product quality or were not willing to pay for it.

Charles Hughes, concerned about the pricing problem, commissioned an independent market research study. The study reported that Hughes Textiles was likely to sell the indicated quantities at the prices shown in Exhibit C6.1.4.

To help evaluate the impact on the bottom line, the company's accountant prepared estimates of the unit cost of making towels at each of the five volumes, as shown in Exhibit C6.1.5.

Required: On the basis of the data in the case, what price should Hughes Textiles select?

EXHIBIT C6.1.4 HUGHES TEXTILES— TERRY WOVEN DIVISION

Projected Sales Volumes at Selected Prices (in Millions of Dozens)

Price	Volume
$4.55	6,000,000
$4.25	7,000,000
$4.00	8,000,000
$3.80	9,000,000
$3.40	10,000,000

EXHIBIT C6.1.5 HUGHES TEXTILES— TERRY WOVEN DIVISION

Unit Manufacturing Cost—Terry Woven Towels

	6,000,000 (normal)	7,000,000	8,000,000	9,000,000	10,000,000 (capacity)
			Volume[a]		
Revenue	$4.550	$4.250	$4.000	$3.800	$3.400
Manufacturing cost:					
Materials	$1.4800	$1.4800	$1.4800	$1.4800	$1.4800
Labor	.5000	.4286	.3750	.3333	.3000
Direct division overhead	0.2710	0.2710	0.2710	0.2710	0.2710
Indirect plant overhead	0.6067	0.5200	0.4550	0.4044	0.3640
Total manufacturing cost	$2.8577	$2.6996	$2.5810	$2.4887	$2.4150
General & administrative cost	0.5000	0.4286	0.3750	0.3333	0.3000
Total cost	$3.3577	$3.1282	$2.9560	$2.8220	$2.7150
Operating income	$1.193	$1.122	$1.044	$0.978	$0.685

[a] Volume figures are in dozens.

C6.2 (Aeiran Motors)[17]

Aeiran Motors makes cars. It is one of the newest players in the automotive market—at least, compared to long-established companies such as Ford and GM. Aeiran, a U.S.-owned company, decided to build its assembly plant in Ireland. In part, Ireland was chosen because of its highly skilled workforce. A second reason for choosing Ireland was its access to European markets and proximity to North Atlantic shipping routes.

Aeiran's niche is compact cars. Currently, it is considering introducing a new model in an existing line of cars. The new model will have a redesigned body but will use the same frame and interior as other cars in the line. Engineers have completely reworked the engine block, adding another 15 horsepower, and are incorporating an innovative four-wheel steering system. Designers are putting in active suspension and, for safety, a rider's side air bag.

Aeiran's new-car planning process is built around the team concept. People from all the functional areas are brought together to design the car. Teams include engineers, production workers, accountants, and sales representatives. Aeiran decided to bypass the old, sequential way of designing cars, where ideas were passed back and forth between functional areas. Managers felt that designs were never coordinated and all new cars were essentially compromises. Plus, it took forever to get the car out the door using the old approach.

With Aeiran's approach, teams work together in a central design facility. The team members stay together for the entire product development cycle, not just during the phase affecting their functional area. For example, team members from manufacturing are involved in phases such as product definition and development well before production trials ever start (see Exhibit C6.2.1). One benefit is that team members are able to spot problems early. Once cars are in production, engineering changes are extraordinarily expensive. So catching problems before production begins saves big-time dollars. Plus, car designs can be truly innovative, with everyone pitching in to make them work. Sean Colahassen, CEO at Aeiran, points to his company's cars as proof of how well this approach to new car development works. According to Sean, team members "buy into" the new car concept. And when they run into problems, team members find ways to make final design consistent with the original concept.

A second car-making technique used by Aeiran is target costing. The old way of costing cars was called *cost buildup*. Materials and labor costs were added together and then "burdened" with manufacturing overhead. After adding general, administrative, and selling cost to manufacturing cost, the total was marked up by the firm's profit margin to arrive at a price. Sometimes prices derived this way were more than buyers were willing to pay.

In contrast, Aeiran's approach starts with a target price most likely to fit the market it is going after. In deriving the target selling price, Aeiran's marketing team starts with the list price of the closest existing model. Then, the price is increased to cover the cost of features that add value in the eyes of the customers. For example, the older model sells for $13,200. After adding the features shown in Exhibit C6.2.2 to the car—and the prices marketing believes car buyers are willing to pay for the features above the base cost—Aeiran plans to sell the new car for $13,800. After the target selling price is determined, Aeiran deducts 15 percent of the target selling price to provide for pretax profit. The difference between the

---

[17]Takao Tanaka, "Target Costing at Toyota," *Journal of Cost Management,* spring 1993, pp. 4–11. Also, see Yasuhiro Moden and John Lee, "How Japanese Auto Maker Reduces Costs," *Management Accounting,* Aug. 1993, pp. 22–26.

EXHIBIT C6.2.1 AEIRAN MOTORS

Responsibility and Involvement of Functions in Product Programs

	Generation	Definition	Development	Production Trials	Scale–Up	Rollout	Tracking	Withdrawal
Program management	Light	Heavy	Heavy	Heavy	Heavy	Heavy	Light	Light
Product strategy & planning	Heavy	Heavy	Medium	Light	Light	Light	Light	Heavy
Research & development	Heavy	Heavy	Heavy	Light	Light	Light	Light	Light
Manufacturing	Light	Light	Light	Heavy	Heavy	Heavy	Heavy	Medium
Sales & marketing	Light	Heavy	Light	Light	Light	Heavy	Heavy	Heavy
Procurement	Light	Medium	Medium	Medium	Medium	Light	Medium	Medium
Service & support	Light	Medium	Light	Light	Light	Light	Medium	Medium
Finance	Light	Medium	Medium	Medium	Medium	Medium	Medium	Light

Functional involvement: Heavy   Medium   Light

Source: Peter B. Scott Morgan "Managing Interfaces: A Key to Rapid Product Development," p. 58. Excerpted with permission from the Second Quarter 1991 issue of *Prism*, the quarterly journal for senior managers, published by Arthur D. Little, Inc.

EXHIBIT C6.2.2 AEIRAN MOTORS

Selling Price of New Model

Selling price of current model	$13,200
Price customers are willing to pay for added features:	
Four-wheel steering	$125
Increase in horsepower	180
Active suspension	60
Rider's side air bag	235
Total value of design changes	$600
Target selling price	$13,800

target selling price and the 15 percent pretax profit, or the target cost, represents those costs that have to be covered over the model's entire life cycle.

Next, managers figure another cost, the *estimated cost*. The estimated cost for the new model is shown in Exhibit C6.2.3. Estimated cost starts with the cost of the existing model. Using this figure as a base, Aeiran adds what it thinks it will cost for each of the new features. For example, including four-wheel steering adds $375 in manufacturing cost. Once costs are added for all of the new features, the result is the estimated cost. For the new model, the estimated cost is $12,510.

EXHIBIT C6.2.3 AEIRAN MOTORS

Estimated Cost of New Model[a]

Cost of current model	$11,600
Cost of design changes:	
Four-wheel steering	$375
Increase in horsepower	175
Active suspension	120
Rider's side air bag	240
Total cost of design changes	$910
Estimated cost	$12,510

[a] Normal volume = 8,000 units per month.

EXHIBIT C6.2.4 COST REDUCTION OF A BRACKET VIA VALUE ENGINEERING AND VALUE ANALYSIS

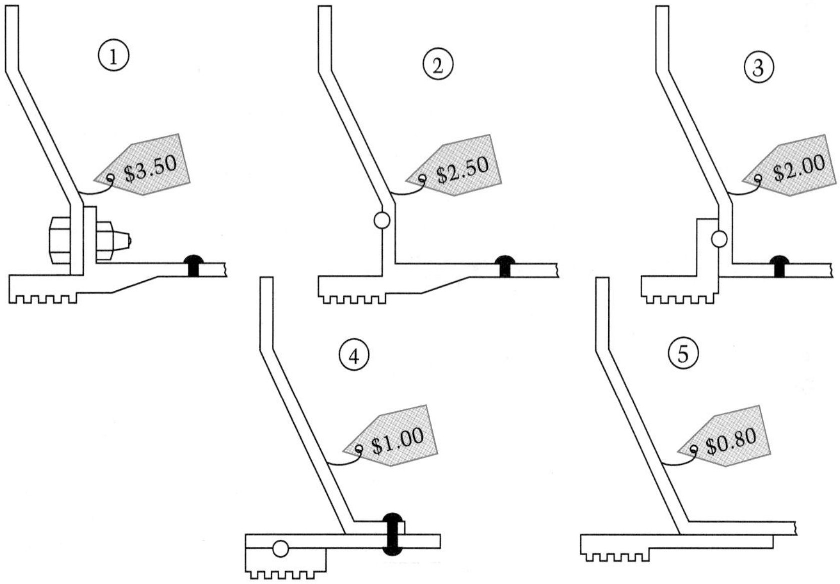

Source: Robert Goodell Brown, *Management Decisions for Production Operations,* Hinsdale, Ill,: The Dryden Press, 1971, p. 353.

The difference between estimated cost and target cost represents the gap that Aeiran has to close in order to achieve its profit target. That's when the real work begins. Everyone on the team knows that they have to figure out how to close the gap so that Aeiran can earn the desired profit.

Opportunities to close the gap come in two forms. The first opportunity, value engineering, is the design team's responsibility. Working together, team members find ways to make the car better and cheaper before production ever begins. An example of a design change is shown in Exhibit C6.2.4. While there is no formula, there are several common areas that Aeiran looks at. For example, the team considered material specifications, number of parts, and manufacturability. As a result of value engineering, Aeiran found several ways to reduce estimated cost, saving a total of $236. Aeiran calculates what it calls *startup cost* by deducting preproduction cost reductions created through value engineering from estimated cost. An opportunity to close the remaining gap comes from continuous improvement after production begins.

Cost-reduction targets are established for 6-month periods, and workers are expected to drive costs down to meet these goals. For example, workers may increase their speed in performing certain tasks or eliminate production steps by finding new, innovative ways to accomplish tasks.

The six 6-month cost-reduction goals for the new model are shown in Exhibit C6.2.5. There are no cost-reduction goals for the first 6 months. This gives workers a chance to learn the process. After that, the cost of an engine, for example, is slated to decrease by 1.5 percent, or $28.05, as of the start of the second 6 months. Details of the makeup of the cost-reduction goal for engines in three different models of the new car during the second 6 months are shown in Exhibit C6.2.6.

The production schedule for the new model is shown in Exhibit C6.2.7 on page 358.

Required:

1. Calculate the gap between estimated cost and target cost. Then break the gap into the parts closed by value engineering and by continuous improvement. What is the startup cost for the new model?
2. Prepare estimates of costs and operating profits for each of the six 6-month periods. Be sure to incorporate planned cost reductions derived from continuous improvement.
3. Does Aeiran achieve its overall target return of 15 percent?

EXHIBIT C6.2.5   AEIRAN MOTORS

Cost-Reduction Targets per Vehicle

		Cost-Reduction Targets[a,b]					
Component	Startup Cost	First 6 Months	Second 6 Months	Third 6 Months	Fourth 6 Months	Fifth 6 Months	Sixth 6 Months
Engine	$ 1,870	0.00%	1.50%	0.75%	0.50%	0.30%	0.15%
Body	3,240	0.00%	2.75%	1.50%	0.85%	0.50%	0.20%
Chassis	2,270	0.00%	1.85%	0.90%	0.50%	0.30%	0.10%
Drive train	1,960	0.00%	2.25%	1.80%	0.65%	0.40%	0.20%
Electronics	610	0.00%	1.60%	0.85%	0.45%	0.20%	0.05%
Interior	1,240	0.00%	1.00%	0.70%	0.40%	0.20%	0.05%
All other cost	1,084	0.00%	3.50%	2.50%	1.50%	0.50%	0.25%
Total startup cost	$12,274						

[a] Percentages are applied by multiplying the cost-reduction target by the cost of the previous 6-month period. For example, engine cost should decline by $28.05 (1.5% × $1,870), or a cost of $1,841.95 ($1,870 − $28.05), by the start of the second 6 months. The cost-reduction target for the start of the third 6 months is 0.75% of $1,841.95.
[b] Reduction targets are assumed to be implemented at the beginning of each 6-month period.

EXHIBIT C6.2.6 AEIRAN MOTORS

Example of Process Involvement for Engines—Second 6 Months

Model	Labor-Hours per Car Before Improvement	Units Produced	Total Hours Before Improvement	Cost-Reduction Target	Labor-Hours per Car After Improvement	Total Hours After Improvement	Reduction in Labor-Hours	Labor Rate per Hour	Labor Cost Saving
S1	15.50	27,000	418,500	2.00%	15.19	410,130	8,370	$22.75	$190,418
S2	17.75	11,250	199,688	1.30%	17.52	197,100	2,588	$22.75	58,877
S3	19.25	6,750	129,937	0.50%	19.15	129,263	674	$22.75	15,334
Total		45,000	748,125			736,493	11,632		$264,629

Total units produced—second 6 months   45,000
Engine labor savings per car manufactured $5.88
Saving in direct materials (details not shown) $8.68
Other process improvements (details not shown) $13.49
Targeted cost reduction for engines for second 6 months $28.05

EXHIBIT C6.2.7   AEIRAN MOTORS

Production Schedule for New Model

First 6 months	36,000
Second 6 months	45,000
Third 6 months	48,000
Fourth 6 months	53,000
Fifth 6 months	53,000
Sixth 6 months	53,000
Total life-cycle units	288,000

CHAPTER

7

APPLICATIONS OF SHORT-TERM DECISION MODELS

We now show how management accounting supplies relevant information for use in decision models. We start with information needed for short-term decisions, but as we proceed, we begin to relax some of the assumptions implicit in such models. In relaxing these assumptions, we provide a transition into long-term decision theory (the subject of the next chapter). In addition, we will look at ways of dealing with uncertainty—where the revenues and costs of alternative courses of action are not completely known.

The applications of short-term decision models that we will illustrate in this chapter are:

- Product mix decisions
- Inventory decisions
- Outsourcing decisions
- Decisions for nonperforming products and services

PRODUCT MIX DECISIONS

Managers assign resources such as facilities, personnel, and equipment in ways they expect will provide the maximum benefits to their organizations. One way is by making product or service mix decisions—choosing the quantities of each product the firm will make and sell. As with all short-term decisions, the data relevant to product mix decisions are limited to only those revenues and costs that change as a result of the decision. Generally, revenues and variable costs are presumed relevant for product mix decisions while fixed costs are not. However, as with any short-term decision, relevance is determined by the situation.

BREWS BROTHERS MICROBREWERY— EXAMPLE OF A PRODUCT MIX DECISION

Product mix decisions are based on choosing the combination of individual products that is likely to generate the highest overall total contribution—the greatest difference between total revenue and total variable cost. For example, assume that a company called Brews Brothers Microbrewery makes three kinds of beer—lager, ale, and stout. Suppose managers are considering several different combinations of beer they can make, three of which are shown in Exhibit 7.1. Multiplying the individual product-line contribution margins, shown in the top section of Exhibit 7.1, by the quantity managers expect to make gives the total contribution for that kind of beer. Adding the total contribution for all three beers together gives the total contribution for the company as a whole.

EXHIBIT 7.1 BREWS BROTHERS MICROBREWERY

Total Contribution from Three Product Mix Plans

	Lager	Ale	Stout	Total
Selling price per batch	$5,000	$4,500	$4,250	
Variable cost per batch	500	500	450	
Contribution per batch	$4,500	$4,000	$3,800	
Product mix 1:				
Number of batches brewed & sold	10	10	59	79
Contribution per batch	$4,500	$4,000	$3,800	
Total contribution	$45,000	$40,000	$224,200	$309,200
Product mix 2:				
Number of batches brewed & sold	59	10	10	79
Contribution per batch	$4,500	$4,000	$3,800	
Total contribution	$265,500	$40,000	$38,000	$343,500
Product mix 3:				
Number of batches brewed & sold	59	20	20	99
Contribution per batch	$4,500	$4,000	$3,800	
Total contribution	$265,500	$80,000	$76,000	$421,500

The first product mix plan (mix 1) anticipates making 10 batches of lager, 10 batches of ale, and 59 batches of stout. This product mix generates a total contribution of $309,200. By simply shifting more production resources to lager and reducing the quantity of stout—as in the second product mix plan (mix 2)—managers can increase the total contribution to $343,500. One generalization that managers might make, after seeing the results of product mix 2, is that increasing quantities of products with high contributions, such as lager, at $4,500 per batch, and decreasing quantities of products with low contributions, such as stout, at $3,800 per batch, increases total contribution.

A second conclusion managers might draw from Exhibit 7.1 is that total contribution increases by making more beer. The more beer the firm brews and sells, the more total contribution it will make. For example, the third product mix plan (mix 3) adds another 20 batches of beer to what managers already plan to make, bringing the total to 99 batches. Total contribution under this plan increases to $421,500. It is only logical for managers to continue increasing production until they reach the limits of the microbrewery's capacity to make and sell beer.

Limits imposed by the amount of resources currently available—called **constraints**—establish the upper boundary of how much product a firm can make. For example, managers may have limited access to raw materials or skilled labor. And there are always physical limits to the amount of product that can be made in the organization's facilities. Still another constraint is the number of products consumers are likely to buy.

To illustrate limitations imposed by the amount of resources currently available, let's continue with the Brews Brothers Microbrewery example. Assume that the microbrewery makes its beer in stainless-steel vessels called conditioning tanks. Ingredients such as malted barley, hops, yeast, and water are converted into beer over several weeks' time in the conditioning tanks. The microbrewery has five conditioning tanks, giving it a total of 1,825 conditioning days per year (5 tanks × 365 days). That is, production of all types of beer is limited—constrained—to no more than 1,825 conditioning days per year.

Consider the impact that the third product mix (mix 3) has on the total number of conditioning days currently available for making beer. As shown in Exhibit 7.2, a batch of lager takes 25 days in the conditioning

EXHIBIT 7.2 BREWS BROTHERS MICROBREWERY

Feasibility of Making Product Mix 3 with Limit on Conditioning Days

	Lager	Ale	Stout	Total
Number of days in conditioning tank	25	20	15	
Number of batches brewed & sold—Product mix 3	59	20	20	
Total conditioning days required	1,475	400	300	2,175
Total conditioning days available for all products				1,825
Excess of required days over days available				350

Conclusion: Product mix is not feasible!

tanks, a batch of ale takes 20 days, and a batch of stout takes 15 days. The total number of conditioning days required under the third product mix plan is 2,175. The demand placed on the conditioning tanks by this production plan exceeds the 1,825 conditioning days currently available. Unless managers can obtain 350 more conditioning days of capacity or, perhaps, reduce the number of days it takes to make a batch of beer, possibly affecting product quality, then the proposed product mix plan is not feasible—it cannot be implemented.

In general, then, product mix decisions entail choosing quantities of individual products that, when combined with all other products, generate the largest total contribution—subject to the constraints imposed by the short-term availability of resources.

Assume that managers tentatively decide to make 59 batches of lager, 10 batches of ale, and 10 batches of stout. The impact of this plan—a total contribution of $343,500 and an operating income of $193,500—is shown in Exhibit 7.3. After direct and allocated fixed costs are subtracted from each product's contribution margin, product-line operating incomes are $3,139 per batch of lager, $1,421 per batch of ale, and $1,700 per batch of

EXHIBIT 7.3 BREWS BROTHERS MICROBREWERY

Operating Results with Proposed Product Mix

	Lager		Ale		Stout		All Products	
	Total	*Batch*	*Total*	*Batch*	*Total*	*Batch*	*Total*	*Batch*
Number of batches		59		10		10		79
Total revenue	$295,000	$5,000	$45,000	$4,500	$42,500	$4,250	$382,500	$4,842
Variable cost:								
Malted barley	$16,225	$275	$2,350	$235	$2,200	$220	$20,775	$263
Hops	2,950	50	750	75	500	50	4,200	53
Yeast	1,475	25	400	40	300	30	2,175	28
Supplies	1,475	25	500	50	400	40	2,375	30
Utilities	7,375	125	1,000	100	1,100	110	9,475	120
Total variable cost	$29,500	$500	$5,000	$500	$4,500	$450	$39,000	$494
Contribution margin	$265,500	$4,500	$40,000	$4,000	$38,000	$3,800	$343,500	$4,348
Direct fixed cost:								
Brewmaster	$20,000	$ 22	$2,500	$ 29	$2,500	$ 50	$25,000	$316
Depreciation	14,000	237	3,000	300	3,000	300	20,000	253
Total direct fixed cost	$34,000	$259	$5,500	$329	$5,500	$350	$45,000	$570
Allocated fixed cost:								
Lease & utilities	$30,000	$ 508	$12,000	$1,200	$12,000	$1,200	$ 54,000	$ 684
Maintenance & cleaning	25,000	424	8,000	800	3,000	300	36,000	456
Insurance	6,000	102	1,500	150	1,000	100	8,500	108
Supplies	4,000	68	1,000	100	1,500	150	6,500	82
Total allocated fixed cost	$65,000	$1,102	$22,500	$2,250	$17,500	$1,750	$105,000	$1,329
Total fixed cost	$99,000	$1,361	$28,000	$2,579	$23,000	$2,100	$150,000	$1,899
Operating income	$166,500	$3,139	$12,000	$1,421	$15,000	$1,700	$193,500	$2,449

stout. Have managers made the best use of resources with this plan? And have they assigned capacity to its optimum use?

As we indicated above, *the general rule for short-term decisions is to assign resources to making products in a manner that will generate the highest total contribution.* This rule means that the product with the highest contribution margin is made first, followed by the product with the second-highest contribution margin, and so forth. Using this rule, managers should assign capacity first to making lager, with a contribution margin of $4,500 per batch, then to ale, with a contribution margin of $4,000 per batch, and finally, to stout, with a contribution margin of $3,800 per batch.

Product mix decisions based solely on the impact of the product mix on total contribution do not consider the demands that each product places on capacity. Different products place different demands on the firm's resources. If an organization's resources are unlimited, then the proportion of capacity used by each product is irrelevant and doesn't enter into the product mix decision. However, in real life, resources are always limited. So, resource allocations among products in a mix must be made according to each product's contribution to operating income relative to its consumption of finite resources.

We alter the general rule stated above, which holds when there are no constraints on capacity, to the following general rule, which applies when resources are limited: *Make the most of the product with the highest contribution margin per unit of limited resource, followed by the product with the second-highest contribution margin per unit of limited resource, and so forth.*

For example, a batch of lager requires 25 days in the conditioning tanks. It yields a $180 contribution margin per conditioning day ($4,500/25 days). Similarly, ale, which takes 20 days in the conditioning tanks, yields a contribution margin of $200 ($4,000/20 days) per conditioning day. Stout, which takes only 15 days, yields the largest contribution margin—$253 ($3,800/15 days)—per conditioning day.

Using the decision rule that is based on limited capacity, production priorities change from those that are based on contribution margin alone. Lager, which was first in priority when the decision was based solely on contribution margin ($4,500), drops to last priority when it is based on contribution margin per conditioning day ($180). Stout, which was last based solely on contribution margin ($3,800), changes to first priority based on contribution margin per conditioning day ($253). And, ale, which was second in priority based solely on contribution margin ($4,000), remains at second priority based on contribution margin per conditioning day ($200).

Consider a second resource—the total number of brewmaster hours—and each product's use of that resource. Assume the brewmaster puts in 2,000 hours (40 hours per week × 50 weeks) each year. Also assume that a batch of lager takes 18 hours of the brewmaster's time, a batch of ale takes 20 hours, and a batch of stout takes 24 hours. The contribution margin per hour of the brewmaster's time is $250 ($4,500/18 hours) for lager, $200 ($4,000/20 hours) for ale, $158 ($3,800/24 hours) for stout.

Looking only at the brewmaster's capacity, expressed in the number of hours of availability each year, and ignoring the capacity of the conditioning tanks, the highest priority is lager, with $250 in contribution margin per brewmaster hour, followed by ale, and then stout, at $200 and $158 in contribution margin per brewmaster hour, respectively.

When the capacity of each resource is evaluated individually in order to determine its allocation among products, it is not difficult to determine and set priorities. However, when there are many products and many resources of limited capacities, priorities conflict and resource allocation decisions become quite complex.

One way to solve short-term resource allocation problems having conflicting priorities is to build a model such as the one shown in Exhibit 7.4.[1]

Three types of information are required for the model:

1. *Decision variables*—What variables do managers change in order to achieve their objective?
2. *Objective*—What is the criterion by which the results of the decision will be judged?
3. *Constraints*—What are the resources that limit the ability to achieve the objective?

First we need to identify the decision variable. In our example, the managers must decide how many batches of each type of beer to produce. Therefore, the decision variable is batches of beer. Next we must identify the objective of the decision—the criterion is to maximize total contribution margin. Finally, we have to consider the constraints imposed by the limited capacity of each resource. Constraints in our example include days in conditioning tanks and brewmaster hours, plus four more that we will introduce shortly.

To choose the best mix of lager, ale, and stout (the decision variable) we must adjust proposed quantities of each up and down until the total contribution margin from all three types of beer (the objective) is as large as possible.[2] Assume managers decide to make 7.14 batches of lager, 63.57 batches of ale, and 25.00 batches of stout, a product mix that happens to be optimal. (The term *optimal* means that there is no other product mix with a higher total contribution margin.)

Observe that the optimal product mix assumes divisibility, meaning that products can be made and sold in fractions of whole units. In our example, divisibility means that it is possible to make seven 100 percent full batches of lager plus one 14 percent full batch, or a total of 7.14 batches.

The first constraint, shown in the bottom panel in Exhibit 7.4, rep-

---

[1] An alternative approach, one that yields exactly the same results, is to use computer packages known as *linear programming*.

[2] Most spreadsheets have built-in functions that identify the optimal solution—the value of the variables that maximizes the objective subject to the constraints—automatically. In addition, linear programming software also identifies optimal solutions without having to use trial and error.

EXHIBIT 7.4 BREWS BROTHERS MICROBREWERY

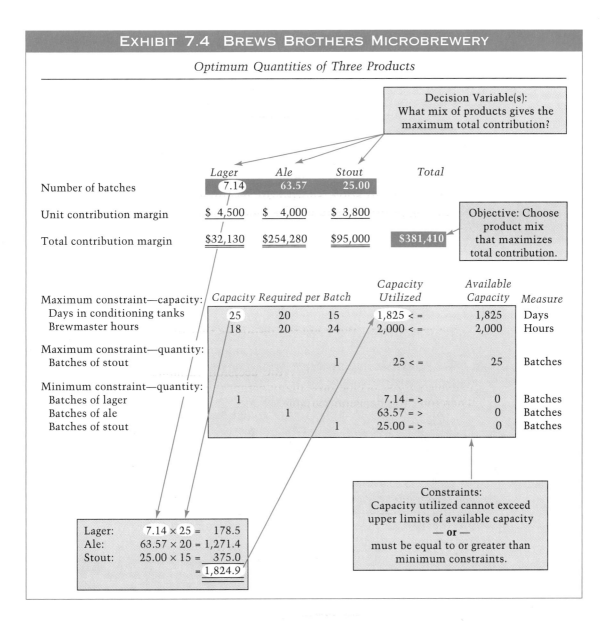

Optimum Quantities of Three Products

Decision Variable(s):
What mix of products gives the
maximum total contribution?

	Lager	Ale	Stout	Total
Number of batches	7.14	63.57	25.00	
Unit contribution margin	$ 4,500	$ 4,000	$ 3,800	
Total contribution margin	$32,130	$254,280	$95,000	$381,410

Objective: Choose
product mix
that maximizes
total contribution.

	Capacity Required per Batch			Capacity Utilized	Available Capacity	Measure
Maximum constraint—capacity:						
Days in conditioning tanks	25	20	15	1,825 < =	1,825	Days
Brewmaster hours	18	20	24	2,000 < =	2,000	Hours
Maximum constraint—quantity:						
Batches of stout			1	25 < =	25	Batches
Minimum constraint—quantity:						
Batches of lager	1			7.14 = >	0	Batches
Batches of ale		1		63.57 = >	0	Batches
Batches of stout			1	25.00 = >	0	Batches

Constraints:
Capacity utilized cannot exceed
upper limits of available capacity
— **or** —
must be equal to or greater than
minimum constraints.

Lager:	7.14 × 25 =	178.5
Ale:	63.57 × 20 =	1,271.4
Stout:	25.00 × 15 =	375.0
	=	1,824.9

resents conditioning days. Earlier, we saw that conditioning days are limited to 1,825 per year. The product mix shown in Exhibit 7.4 uses all 1,825 days, with no unused (excess) capacity.

The second constraint represents the limited availability of brewmaster hours, which cannot exceed 2,000 per year. Again, the product mix shown in Exhibit 7.4 fully utilizes all hours currently available from the brewmaster.

The third constraint, referred to as a marketing constraint, requires that production of stout not exceed 25 batches. Past experience indicates that no more than this quantity is likely to be sold.

The last three constraints limit production to minimum quantities. When the minimum quantities are zero, they are referred to as nonnegativity constraints. Their purpose is to ensure that the decision variable—batches of beer—is never less than zero. This simply prohibits a product mix with "negative" batches of beer—a situation that cannot exist in real life.

Looking at the solution in Exhibit 7.4—a solution that we have identified as optimal—we see that it is not what we expected! Lager, with the highest contribution margin ($4,500 per batch), is assigned the fewest batches of beer (7.14) while ale is assigned the most batches of beer (63.57). The total contribution derived from this product mix plan is $381,410—$37,910 more than the $343,500 in contribution margin that would be obtained by making 59 batches of lager, 10 batches of ale, and 10 batches of stout. Since neither direct fixed cost nor allocated fixed cost is affected, net operating income is also $37,910 greater with this product mix.

ADDING CAPACITY

The model shown in Exhibit 7.4 provides a framework for planning, especially in evaluating the impact that constraints have on total contribution. For example, what would happen if managers were able to obtain more capacity? While adding capacity is considered a long-term decision—a topic we will introduce in the next chapter—the impact of additional capacity can still be evaluated here.

Assume the microbrewery can lease another conditioning tank for $20,000 per year. The new tank increases the total number of conditioning days from 1,825 to 2,190 (6 tanks × 365 conditioning days) per year. Also, assume that it is possible to increase the total number of brewmaster hours by hiring a part-time assistant at a salary cost of $10,000 per year. The assistant would add another 1,000 hours of brewing time, bringing the total to 3,000 hours per year. The new optimal solution, reflecting the two changes in capacity—increasing conditioning days to 2,190 and adding another 1,000 brewmaster hours—is shown in Exhibit 7.5.

The new optimal product mix, reflecting the two increased capacities, provides a total contribution of $458,000—an increase of $76,590 over the total contribution that was based on the original capacity and product mix shown in Exhibit 7.4.

The conclusion is that capacity should be expanded as long as the increase in total contribution exceeds all of the increases in cost. In our example, the net increase in total contribution is $46,590. It's made up of $76,590 in additional contribution less $30,000 in additional costs—$20,000 for the conditioning tank and $10,000 in salary cost for the part-time assistant. Managers should go ahead and lease the sixth conditioning tank and hire the part-time assistant.

Note that there is slack in the number of brewmaster hours in Exhibit 7.5. Slack represents unused capacity—the difference between capacity available for production and capacity used in a product mix. In fact, only 2,415 brewmaster hours are used—585 fewer hours than the 3,000 hours available if the part-time assistant is hired. This means that

EXHIBIT 7.5 BREWS BROTHERS MICROBREWERY

Optimum Quantities of Three Products with Increase in Capacity

	Lager	Ale	Stout			
Number of batches	0.00	90.75	25.00			

				Total		
Unit contribution margin	$4,500	$ 4,000	$ 3,800			
Total contribution margin	$ 0	$363,000	$95,000	$458,000		

				Capacity Utilized	Available Capacity	Measure
Maximum constraint—capacity:	Capacity Required per Batch					
Days in conditioning tanks	25	20	15	2,190 < =	2,190	Days
Brewmaster hours	18	20	24	2,415 < =	3,000	Hours
Maximum constraint—quantity:						
Batches of stout			1	25 < =	25	Batches
Minimum constraint—quantity:						
Batches of lager	1			0.00 = >	0	Batches
Batches of ale		1		90.75 = >	0	Batches
Batches of stout			1	25.00 = >	0	Batches

Unused Capacity (Slack)	
Brewmasters hours available	3,000
Brewmasters hours utilized	2,415
Unused capacity (slack)	585

the number of hours required from the brewmaster's assistant can be reduced, or perhaps the assistant can be assigned other duties.

Before leaving product mix decisions, we want to warn you of one common mistake—managers may assign resources to products on the basis of their product-line operating incomes rather than on their product-line contribution margins. For example, lagers have the highest operating income per batch ($3,139), while stout is second ($1,700), and ale is third ($1,421). Each of these product-line operating income figures includes fixed cost on a per-unit basis. These unit fixed costs are often incorrectly assumed to be variable costs. As a result, attempting to maximize total operating income by choosing a product mix based solely on product-line operating incomes is likely to lead to an incorrect assignment of capacity.

What if the optimal number of batches of each type of beer was incorrectly chosen using product-line operating income figures? The result would be a decision to make 73 batches of lager and no batches of either ale or stout, based on the original constraints found in Exhibit 7.4. This product mix generates a total contribution of $328,500, well below the total contribution of $381,410 achieved with the optimum product mix. Again, the solution using product-line operating income is incorrect, because total fixed cost does not change, regardless of the quantities of beer managers choose to make.

INVENTORY DECISIONS

Inventories, in the form of raw materials, work in process, and finished goods, often constitute a sizeable investment in resources. Inventories also represent a factor in the organization's competitive strategy. An inventory policy that provides adequate levels of service is crucial to meeting the organization's goals and objectives. (See "Current Practice: Inventories and Competitive Strategy.")

RELEVANT COSTS FOR INVENTORY-ORDERING DECISIONS

Managers try to balance two conflicting goals when devising an inventory policy. One goal is to provide customers with high levels of service. This means high costs as the result of large, costly investments in inventory. The conflicting goal is to provide services at a relatively low cost. Costs can be kept low, in part, by maintaining relatively low investments in inventories.

To help understand the kinds of activities associated with inventories—and the costs these activities cause—consider the floor plan of a typ-

---

CURRENT PRACTICE

Inventories and Competitive Strategy

The average car dealership stocks about $250,000 worth of parts. One Cadillac dealer keeps more than $1 million in parts. His goal is to fill 90 percent of parts orders from on-site inventories. He maintains such large inventories because it costs between $25 and $40 an hour to interrupt work while waiting for parts to be delivered. In contrast, Lexus dealers generally carry only about $30,000 worth of parts. Since the Lexus line is relatively new and has fewer models, the dealers' need for parts is less. Also, Lexus's strategy of locating its showrooms and shops at premium, high-visibility sites makes the space where parts are housed relatively costly. As a result, Lexus dealers typically carry a broad range of inventory, stocked at shallow levels. When a part is removed from inventory, it is replaced immediately using next-day delivery.

Source: Adam Bryant, "Turning a Source of Headaches into a Source of Profits: Stocking Up—The Cost of Keeping Parts on Hand," *The New York Times*, Jan. 26, 1992, section 3, p. 10.

EXHIBIT 7.6 INBOUND MATERIALS

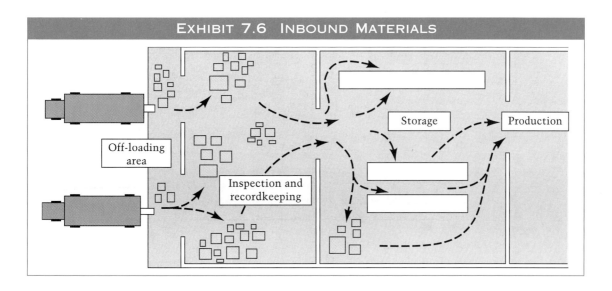

Off-loading area

Inspection and recordkeeping

Storage

Production

ical materials-handling area, shown in Exhibit 7.6. When a materials order is received, it is off-loaded from the delivery truck and moved into the warehouse. There, materials are inspected and compared with the type and quantity specified in the original purchase order. Bulk materials are broken down and repackaged into smaller containers. Repackaged materials are then moved by forklift to storage, typically located between receiving and production, where they wait to be issued to production.

ORDER QUANTITY

One decision that managers must make concerns the amount of inventory to order, called the <u>order quantity.</u> They can either order small quantities relatively frequently, or large quantities infrequently. Receiving frequent, small orders results in small average inventories, while large orders create large average inventories.

The graph in <u>Exhibit 7.7 portrays</u> the decline in inventory levels from the time an order is received until the time the inventory level reaches zero. Assume that managers purchase inventory in order quantities of 1,200 units and that customers require an average of 120 units each day. By the end of the tenth day—or, equivalently, the start of the eleventh day—all inventory has been completely depleted. On the morning of the eleventh day, a new order of 1,200 units arrives, replenishing the inventory to its previous level. Midway between the receipt of a new order (i.e., the time when the inventory is fully stocked) and the complete depletion of the inventory, the average level of inventory, equal to 600 units, is reached.

Consider Exhibit 7.8, which shows the relationship between order quantity, number of orders, and average inventory. The first data column represents inventory ordered in quantities of 600 units, while the second data column represents order quantities of 1,200 units. If 30,000 units are

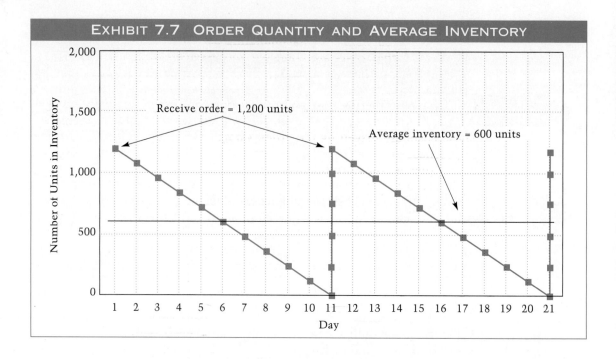

EXHIBIT 7.7 ORDER QUANTITY AND AVERAGE INVENTORY

EXHIBIT 7.8 RELATIONSHIP BETWEEN ORDER QUANTITY, NUMBER OF ORDERS, AND AVERAGE INVENTORY

Order quantity (in units)	600	1,200
Number of orders per year:		
Annual demand (in units)	30,000	30,000
Divided by order quantity	600	1,200
Equals number of orders per year	50	25
Average inventory:		
Maximum inventory level (order quantity)	600	1,200
Divided by 2	2	2
Equals average inventory	300	600

required during the year, then buying inventory in order quantities of 600 units means that 50 orders have to be placed during the year. When inventory is purchased in lots of 600 units, the average inventory is 300 units, which is derived by dividing the order quantity by 2.

Alternatively, managers may choose to buy inventory in quantities of 1,200 units. If so, they will place 25 orders each year—half as many as when the order quantity is 600. But the quantity ordered each time will be twice as large, causing the average inventory to increase from 300 units to 600 units. In general, the number of orders placed each year is equal to the annual demand divided by the order quantity. And the average inventory for any order quantity is simply the order quantity divided by 2.

INVENTORY COSTS

Costs associated with materials-handling activities are shown in Exhibit 7.9. Observe that costs are collected and assigned to one of two departments—ordering and warehousing. Costs broken down between these two departments are then separated into their fixed and variable components.

Variable ordering cost comprises order processing, delivery charges, direct labor, benefits, materials and supplies, and contents insurance. These costs are driven by (i.e., they vary in proportion with) the number of purchase orders placed during the year. All other ordering costs are fixed—that is, they are unaffected by the number of purchase orders. As with any other short-term decision, costs are not relevant unless they change. Since fixed costs are unaffected by order quantity, they are not relevant and should not be considered in short-term inventory decisions.

EXHIBIT 7.9 COMPUTATION OF VARIABLE ORDERING AND WAREHOUSING COST

Department Measure of activity	Ordering Purchase orders			Warehousing Inventory units		
	Total Cost	Fixed	Variable	Total Cost	Fixed	Variable
Direct cost:						
Order processing	$ 1,250		$ 1,250			
Delivery charges	45,000		45,000			
Direct labor	88,200		88,200	$128,000	$128,000	
Benefits	17,400		17,400	85,600	85,600	
Materials & supplies	49,000	$45,000	4,000	27,000	11,000	$16,000
Contents insurance	6,000	4,000	2,000	15,000	5,900	9,100
Interest charges				900		900
Total direct cost	$206,850	$49,000	$157,850	$256,500	$230,500	$26,000
Indirect cost:						
Depreciation—equipment	$57,000	$57,000		$175,300	$175,300	
Intangible property taxes	12,000	12,000		78,000	59,000	$19,000
Maintenance	11,000	11,000		46,000	46,000	
Data processing charges	12,000	12,000		28,000	28,000	
Total indirect cost	$92,000	$92,000	$0	$327,300	$308,300	$19,000
Allocated cost:						
Depreciation—facility	$22,000	$22,000		$148,000	$148,000	
Security	6,000	6,000		87,200	87,200	
Corporate overhead	21,000	21,000		58,000	58,000	
Total allocated cost	$49,000	$49,000	$0	$293,200	$293,200	$0
Total cost	$347,850	$190,000	$157,850	$877,000	$832,000	$45,000

Measure of activity − order quantity = 600 units:
Ordering—number of orders (30,000/600)   50
Warehousing—average inventory in units (600/2)   300

Variable cost per unit of activity driver	$3,157	$150
Activity driver	Purchase order	Unit of inventory

Variable warehousing cost comprises materials and supplies, contents insurance, interest charges, and intangible property taxes. These costs are driven by the size of the average inventory. Again, all other warehousing costs are fixed and should not be considered in determining the quantity of inventory to be ordered.

The data in Exhibit 7.9 reflect costs for a typical year when 50 orders are placed. If total variable ordering cost is $157,850 for 50 orders, then the average variable ordering cost is $3,157 per purchase order. Similarly, if total variable warehousing cost—called carrying cost—is $45,000, and the average number of units in the inventory is 300, then the average variable carrying cost for one unit in inventory for one year is $150.

Can increasing or decreasing the order size reduce inventory-related costs? Fortunately, the relationships represented in Exhibit 7.8 and the variable costs in Exhibit 7.9 can be combined for different order quantities to help identify a unique quantity that minimizes the total combined ordering and carrying cost. The results are shown in Exhibit 7.10.

Ordering Cost.   Order quantities ranging from 100 to 2,500 units per order, in increments of 100 units, are shown in column 1 of Exhibit 7.10. Column 2 shows how many orders would need to be placed during the year for each order quantity, assuming that annual demand is 30,000 units. The number of orders is calculated by dividing annual demand by each of the different order sizes in column 1. For example, an order size of 1,124 units requires placing 27 (26.69) orders during the year (30,000 units/1,124 units) or 1 order approximately every 9.4 days (250 working days/26.7 orders). Note that the numbers in column 2 are rounded to the nearest whole number.

Total variable ordering cost is calculated by multiplying the variable cost of placing an order ($3,157, from Exhibit 7.9) by the number of orders (column 2). For example, placing 27 (26.69) orders per year at a variable cost per order of $3,157 results in a total variable ordering cost equal to $84,262 per year.

Carrying Cost.   Small order sizes translate into small average inventories, since average inventory (column 4) is calculated by dividing order quantity (column 1) by 2. Multiplying the average inventory by the unit variable carrying cost ($150, from Exhibit 7.9) gives the total variable carrying cost (column 5). For example, carrying an average inventory of 562 units at a variable cost of $150 per unit results in a total variable carrying cost of $84,300 per year.

Total Cost.   The combined variable ordering and carrying cost (column 6) is calculated by adding total variable ordering cost (column 3) to total variable carrying cost (column 5).

ECONOMIC ORDER QUANTITY DECISIONS

The inventory decision managers must make is to select the economic order quantity (EOQ). The economic order quantity is the order quantity in column 1 that produces the lowest total variable cost (column 6). In

EXHIBIT 7.10 COMPUTATION OF ORDERING, CARRYING, AND TOTAL COST FOR SELECTED ORDER QUANTITIES

(1)	(2)	(3)	(4)	(5)	(6)
Order Quantity (in Units)	Number of Orders 30,000/ (col. 1)	Variable Ordering Cost $3,157 × (col. 2)	Average Inventory (col. 1) /2	Variable Carrying Cost $150 × (col. 4)	Total Cost (col. 3)+(col. 5)
100	300	$947,100	50	$ 7,500	$954,600
200	150	473,550	100	15,000	488,550
300	100	315,700	150	22,500	338,200
400	75	236,775	200	30,000	266,775
500	60	189,420	250	37,500	226,920
600	50	157,850	300	45,000	202,850
700	43	135,300	350	52,500	187,800
800	38	118,388	400	60,000	178,388
900	33	105,233	450	67,500	172,733
1,000	30	94,710	500	75,000	169,710
1,100	27	86,100	550	82,500	168,600
1,124	27	84,262	562	84,300	168,562
1,200	25	78,925	600	90,000	168,925
1,300	23	72,854	650	97,500	170,354
1,400	21	67,650	700	105,000	172,650
1,500	20	63,140	750	112,500	175,640
1,600	19	59,194	800	120,000	179,194
1,700	18	55,712	850	127,500	183,212
1,800	17	52,617	900	135,000	187,617
1,900	16	49,847	950	142,500	192,347
2,000	15	47,355	1,000	150,000	197,355
2,100	14	45,100	1,050	157,500	202,600
2,200	14	43,050	1,100	165,000	208,050
2,300	13	41,178	1,150	172,500	213,678
2,400	13	39,463	1,200	180,000	219,463
2,500	12	37,884	1,250	187,500	225,384

Note: The numbers in column 2 above are rounded to the nearest whole number.

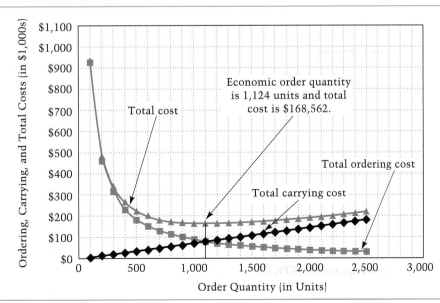

this example, the EOQ is equal to 1,124 units. Order quantities more or less than 1,124 units cause total inventory related costs to increase.

Alternatively, the EOQ can be found by using the following formula:

$$EOQ = \sqrt{\frac{(2 \times \text{annual demand} \times \text{unit ordering cost})}{\text{unit carrying cost}}}$$

Using the data in our example

$$EOQ = \sqrt{\frac{(2 \times 30{,}000 \times \$3{,}157)}{\$150}}$$

$$= \sqrt{1{,}262{,}800}$$

$$= 1{,}124 \text{ units}$$

To understand the relationship between ordering and carrying costs, we will consider the graph shown at the bottom of Exhibit 7.10. The horizontal axis (the independent variable) represents order quantity—the decision that managers must make. The vertical axis (the dependent variable) represents ordering, carrying, and total costs. Note that the objective is to find the order quantity that minimizes the total combined ordering and carrying cost. Total cost is lowest at an order size of 1,124 units. No other order size produces a lower total cost. In other words, ordering in lot sizes of 1,124 units minimizes the total cost of ordering and carrying inventory. Note that if full-cost data—including fixed cost—rather than variable cost data were used, the result would be an EOQ of 378 units,[3] considerably smaller than the correct order quantity of 1,124.

JUST-IN-TIME INVENTORY SYSTEMS

Many managers strive to minimize their investment in inventory while maintaining adequate levels of service. (See "Current Practice: Procter & Gamble.") The traditional approach to determining inventory size, as shown above, is to identify the order quantity yielding the lowest combined ordering and carrying cost. Another approach to lowering inventory costs is to eliminate nonvalue-adding activities, perhaps by adopting the just-in-time, or JIT, philosophy of inventory management. By working with suppliers, many companies find they can use JIT to reduce ordering costs without sacrificing customer service. Consider Exhibit 7.11, which contains data that are basically the same as the data in Exhibit 7.9. The only difference is that ordering costs are treated as fixed costs rather than as variable. After recalculating total variable ordering cost, the cost per purchase order declines to $120 (from $3,157).

The impact on the EOQ of converting variable ordering costs into fixed costs can be seen in the top part of Exhibit 7.12. These results are

---

[3] Ordering cost equals $6,957 ($347,850/50 orders) and warehousing cost equals $2,923 ($877,000/300 units) per unit. Using the formula approach, then

$$EOQ = \sqrt{\frac{(2 \times 30{,}000 \times \$6{,}957)}{\$2{,}923}}$$

$$= 378$$

Procter & Gamble

A time-honored practice called *trade loading* is largely responsible for an estimated $60 to $80 billion each year in grocery products sitting in trucks, railway cars, and distribution centers. Carrying that extra inventory adds between $1.6 billion and $2.9 billion to food costs each year. In fact, the average grocery product takes 84 days to travel from the factory floor to retail store shelves. Grocers have spent millions of dollars to build gigantic warehouses simply to hold the goods they buy on special discounts.

In the past, manufacturers slashed prices and offered promotional discounts to induce stores to stock up on their products. Shoppers benefit when these low-cost items are sold at special discounts. Unfortunately, production of unusually large quantities of special items plays havoc with manufacturing, warehousing, and distribution.

Procter & Gamble tried to stop the practice of trade loading. It offered stores what it calls *value pricing* on many of its products. Value pricing translates into prices that are 8 to 25 percent below list. P&G hoped that its new policy would not only lower manufacturing costs by stabilizing production but would also translate into happier customers who buy products at everyday low prices.

Source: Patricia Sellers, "The Dumbest Marketing Ploy," *Fortune,* Oct. 5, 1992, pp. 88–94, and Eben Shapiro, "P&G Takes on the Supermarkets with Uniform Pricing," *The New York Times,* Apr. 26, 1992, section 3, p. 5.

also shown as a graph at the bottom of the exhibit. The economic order quantity drops to 219 units, considerably lower than the 1,124 units we saw in Exhibit 7.10.

While looking at the graph, note that the economic order quantity shifts to the left. That's because virtually all ordering costs are fixed—increasing the number of orders does not cause an increase in total ordering cost. There is little or no penalty for ordering frequently. Since carrying cost is minimized with small order sizes, the obvious conclusion is that total cost is reduced by holding small quantities of inventory that is replenished at relatively frequent intervals. These insights form the foundation for the just-in-time philosophy.

One way of implementing the JIT approach to inventory management is to create long-term relationships with suppliers who agree to provide frequent deliveries. In return for the increase in service, they become members of a small group of suppliers, or perhaps the only supplier, allowed to meet the firm's inventory needs. Ford, for example, reported that it dropped 47,000 of the 52,000 firms who provided everything from toilet paper to stamping presses. This move saves Ford an estimated $1.6 billion annually.[4] Those firms who survive the cut are often given access to planning schedules and other inventory information, allowing them better

---

[4] "Automakers," *The Orlando Sentinel,* Oct. 22, 1994.

EXHIBIT 7.11 COMPUTATION OF VARIABLE ORDERING AND CARRYING COST PER UNIT ASSUMING ORDERING COSTS ARE PREDOMINATELY FIXED

Department Measure of activity	Ordering Purchase orders			Warehousing Inventory units		
	Total *Cost*	*Fixed*	*Variable*	*Total* *Cost*	*Fixed*	*Variable*
Direct cost:						
Order processing	$ 1,250	$ 1,250				
Delivery charges	45,000	45,000				
Direct labor	88,200	88,200		$128,000	$128,000	
Benefits	17,400	17,400		85,600	85,600	
Materials & supplies	49,000	45,000	$4,000	27,000	11,000	$16,000
Contents insurance	6,000	4,000	2,000	15,000	5,900	9,100
Interest charges	0	0		900	0	900
Total direct cost	$206,850	$200,850	$6,000	$256,500	$230,500	$26,000
Indirect cost:						
Depreciation—equipment	$57,000	$57,000		$175,300	$175,300	
Intangible property taxes	12,000	12,000		78,000	59,000	$19,000
Maintenance	11,000	11,000		46,000	46,000	
Data processing charges	12,000	12,000		28,000	28,000	
Total indirect cost	$92,000	$92,000	$0	$327,300	$308,300	$19,000
Allocated cost:						
Depreciation—facility	$22,000	$22,000		$148,000	$148,000	
Security	6,000	6,000		87,200	87,200	
Corporate overhead	21,000	21,000		58,000	58,000	
Total allocated cost	$49,000	$49,000	$0	$293,200	$293,200	$0
Total cost	$347,850	$341,850	$6,000	$877,000	$832,000	$45,000

Measure of activity − order quantity = 600 units:

Ordering—number of orders (30,000/600)			50			
Warehousing—average inventory in units (600/2)						300
Variable cost per unit of activity driver			$120			$150
Activity driver			Purchase order			Unit of inventory

control over their own costs. These kinds of arrangements create opportunities for both the producers and suppliers to reduce or eliminate non-value-adding activities and to shed unnecessary costs. For example, materials may no longer require inspection, because goods are delivered at consistently high levels of quality; invoices may no longer need to be compared with shipping orders, because of electronic data sharing; and internal material moves may no longer be needed.

There are, however, downsides to JIT systems. One problem occurs when suppliers reduce their capacity. Inventory is harder to find, and market prices are likely to be higher. Managers may decide to hold larger-than-normal levels of inventory when they expect such a decrease in the supply of goods. They may also hold larger inventories than needed as a way of protecting themselves from price increases.

EXHIBIT 7.12 COMPUTATION OF ORDERING, CARRYING, AND TOTAL COST FOR SELECTED ORDER QUANTITIES ASSUMING ORDERING COSTS ARE PREDOMINATELY FIXED

(1)	(2)	(3)	(4)	(5)	(6)
Order Quantity (in Units)	Number of Orders 30,000/ (col. 1)	Variable Ordering Cost $120 × (col. 2)	Average Inventory (col. 1) /2	Variable Carrying Cost $150 × (col. 4)	Total Cost (col. 3)+(col. 5)
100	300	$36,000	50	$ 7,500	$ 43,500
200	150	18,000	100	15,000	33,000
219	137	16,438	110	16,425	32,863
300	100	12,000	150	22,500	34,500
400	75	$9,000	200	30,000	39,000
500	60	$7,200	250	37,500	44,700
600	50	$6,000	300	45,000	51,000
700	43	$5,143	350	52,500	57,643
800	38	$4,500	400	60,000	64,500
900	33	$4,000	450	67,500	71,500
1,000	30	$3,600	500	75,000	78,600
1,100	27	$3,273	550	82,500	85,773
1,200	25	$3,000	600	90,000	93,000
1,300	23	$2,769	650	97,500	100,269
1,400	21	$2,571	700	105,000	107,571
1,500	20	$2,400	750	112,500	114,900
1,600	19	$2,250	800	120,000	122,250
1,700	18	$2,118	850	127,500	129,618
1,800	17	$2,000	900	135,000	137,000
1,900	16	$1,895	950	142,500	144,395
2,000	15	$1,800	1,000	150,000	151,800
2,100	14	$1,714	1,050	157,500	159,214
2,200	14	$1,636	1,100	165,000	166,636
2,300	13	$1,565	1,150	172,500	174,065
2,400	13	$1,500	1,200	180,000	181,500
2,500	12	$1,440	1,250	187,500	188,940

Note: The numbers in column 2 above are rounded to the nearest whole number.

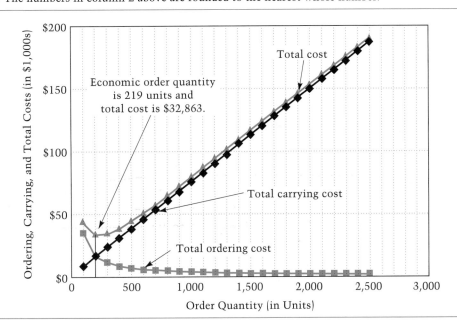

Still another problem with JIT implementations occurs when customers expect faster delivery. Unless goods are on hand, some suppliers cannot meet their customers' delivery expectations. Even some Japanese firms that pioneered JIT are having to increase their inventories. They found that delivering small orders is costly, and, in some cases, is not worth the effort. And another, totally unexpected problem has emerged— the Japanese are reporting traffic jams caused by the multitudes of trucks and vans attempting to deliver small orders.

ECONOMIC ORDER QUANTITY AND SETUPS

We can determine the optimum number of setups—the activities needed to change over production from one product to another—in much the same way as we determined the optimum order quantity. One example of setup activities is the preparation of a printing press for the next run, including steps such as removing master printing sheets, cleaning rollers, removing ink from the previous run, inserting new master printing sheets, loading a new roll of paper, applying the new run's ink, adjusting machine settings, and making a trial run.

Setup costs generally increase in conjunction with any increase in the number of setups. To counter large setup costs, some manufacturing companies make big batches of product, thereby reducing the total number of setups. However, making big batches of product creates large inventories and high inventory carrying costs. Optimal batch size, then, is determined by balancing two opposing costs—setup cost and carrying cost—in exactly the same way as ordering and carrying costs are balanced in making EOQ decisions. The approach that is used to find the lowest combined ordering and carrying cost can also be used to determine the optimum number of setups by merely substituting setup cost for ordering cost in the EOQ formula.

Economic order quantity

Improving Setup Efficiency. Consider the difference between manual and automated setup times, shown in Exhibit 7.13. Assume that, when changing over production from one model to the next, the mold used in forming a product is removed and a new mold is inserted in its place. Workers disconnect supply lines, remove the old mold, and move it to storage. Then the process is reversed as a new mold is inserted and equipment reconnected. During setup, production comes to a standstill—workers and equipment stand idle. The changeover from the old mold to the new requires three workers and takes 13.75 hours.[5]

Assume new equipment can automate the changeover process, eliminating the need for physical mold changes. Setup time is reduced from 13.75 hours to 0.75 hour. In addition, automated setups create operating efficiencies that translate into the cost savings shown in Exhibit 7.14. Batch sizes are smaller, decreasing from 2,500 units with manual setup to

---

[5] Adapted from A. Faye Borthick and Harold P. Roth, "Accounting for Time: Reengineering Business Processes to Improve Responsiveness," *Journal of Cost Management*, fall 1993, pp. 4–14.

EXHIBIT 7.13 MANUAL VERSUS AUTOMATED SETUP ACTIVITIES AND TIMES

Sequence	Activity	Manual Setup Time, (in Minutes)
1	Disconnect supply lines	2.50
2	Remove old mold	0.25
3	Transfer old mold to storage	1.50
4	Retrieve new mold from storage	0.75
5	Insert new mold	6.75
6	Reconnect supply lines	0.25
7	Perform trial run	0.50
8	Adjust settings	1.25
	Total setup	13.75

		Automated Setup Time, (in Minutes)
Steps 1 through 8	Automated changeover—all in one step	0.75

EXHIBIT 7.14 SETUP COST

Manual versus Automated Setup

	Manual Setup	Automated Setup	Cost Saving— Automated vs. Manual Setup
Setup labor:			
Annual production (in units)	750,000	750,000	
Batch size	2,500	500	
Number of setups (production/batch size)	300	1,500	
Batch setup time (from Exhibit 7.13)	13.75	0.75	
Total setup hours	4,125	1,125	
Workers required per setup	3	1	
Total labor-hours	12,375	1,125	
Labor cost per hour	$15	$15	
Annual setup labor cost	$185,625	$16,875	$168,750
Carrying cost:			
Average inventory (batch size/2)	1,250	250	
Unit material & labor cost	$225	$225	
Cost of average inventory	$281,250	$56,250	
Carrying cost as a percent of average inventory	18.00%	18.00%	
Annual carrying cost	$50,625	$10,125	$40,500
Operating cost:			
Facility lease	$ 24,000	$ 24,000	
Equipment depreciation	15,000	45,000	
Materials handling	22,000	8,000	
Inspection	42,000	6,000	
Recordkeeping	15,000	28,000	
Annual operating cost	$118,000	$111,000	$7,000
Total cost	$354,250	$138,000	$216,250

500 units with automated setup. Since setup times are shorter, products can be made in smaller batch sizes. Smaller batch sizes permit greater flexibility and speed in responding to changing consumer demands. And average inventory levels decline, thereby reducing carrying cost. In addition, operating costs are lower for activities such as materials handling and inspection. But some costs increase, such as equipment depreciation and recordkeeping. The net result is a substantial reduction in total cost—from $354,250 for manual setup to $138,000 for automated setup—a net saving of $216,250 per year.

OUTSOURCING DECISIONS

Rather than attempting to provide internally all of the services the organization needs in order to function, managers instead concentrate on providing in-house only those activities they believe add value. These internal value-adding activities contribute to an organization's competitive advantage. However, not all activities are value-adding. Those activities that are not essential—and that don't contribute to creating a competitive advantage—should be evaluated as candidates for outsourcing. (See "Current Practice: Core Activities at Sun Microsystems.")

Some of the advantages of letting outside contractors perform internal activities—or outsourcing—include:[6]

- Increasing efficiency
- Reducing the cost of benefits and administration
- Decreasing overhead and debt
- Easing the burden of regulatory compliance
- Making up for any lack of skills among in-house staff

---

[6] Adapted from a survey conducted by Coopers & Lybrand and reported in "How and Why Firms Use Outside Contractors," *Nation's Business,* Oct. 1994, p. 14.

- Giving access to the latest technology
- Enhancing flexibility
- Providing opportunities to participate in innovation

CREATING PARTNERSHIPS

"Strategic" partnerships are alliances among noncompeting companies. For example, a medical supplies vendor may receive daily information directly from a hospital. The information describes the hospital's inventory status and its needs for medical supplies. The hospital benefits from the partnership by shifting inventory control activities to the vendor while still receiving inventory on a timely basis. The vendor, in turn, benefits from the arrangement through guaranteed sales.

Air freight companies such as Federal Express often "partner" with hospitals to keep high-cost, low-demand items such as artificial hearts at central locations. The hospital, rather than having to maintain costly inventories, relies on Federal Express to deliver the artificial hearts mere hours before surgery.

Some final assembly manufacturers are finding that they can cut product development costs by "farming out" (outsourcing) design tasks to suppliers. The idea is that parts manufacturers ought to be the ones best able to conceive new parts. One benefit is that assemblers pass along engineering tasks to suppliers, thereby reducing their own need for engineers. Moreover, using suppliers that sell parts to an entire industry often facilitates the rapid transfer of new technology from one manufacturer to another. (See "Current Practice: Rockwell International–Boeing Partnership.")

CANDIDATES FOR OUTSOURCING

Based on a self-evaluation using measures of an internal service—such as its cost, flexibility, and quality—an organization can compare how well its service stacks up against an outside firm's provision of that same service. If the comparison favors the outside firm, then the service should be transferred to that outside source. Called benchmarking, this comparison is illustrated in Exhibit 7.15.

Benchmarking is also a way for companies to identify processes and activities that they do well compared to outside firms. The bottom line for this kind of evaluation is to determine whether value added by services generated internally is greater than value added when this service is provided by external suppliers. If a firm can't perform an activity faster or better than an outside contractor can, then the activity becomes a viable candidate for outsourcing.

RELEVANT COSTS FOR OUTSOURCING DECISIONS

What are the relevant costs of outsourcing decisions—sometimes called *make-or-buy* decisions? As with all short-term decisions, only those costs

CURRENT PRACTICE

Rockwell International–Boeing Partnership

One example of a mutually beneficial partnership is that between Rockwell International and Seattle-based Boeing. When Boeing began developing its all-new 777, the design-build team included suppliers such as Rockwell in the computer design phase. Even suppliers not physically located at the design center were tied into the design process by computer links. The impact of the partnership was noted when the first 777 rolled off the assembly line. Parts from various suppliers snapped together with such precision that the nose-to-tail measurement was off by less than 23/1,000 of an inch.

Boeing benefited from the partnership by reducing its development costs and building better planes. Moreover, Boeing believes that costly parts rework has been cut in half. Boeing's suppliers also benefited from the partnership. Perhaps their biggest benefit of all was learning how to collaborate with companies such as Boeing.

Source: Neal Templin and Jeff Cole, "Manufacturers Use Suppliers to Help Them Develop New Products," *The Wall Street Journal*, Dec. 19, 1994, p. A1.

EXHIBIT 7.15   TYPICAL COMPANY

Benchmarking Procurement Activities

	Performance Measures— Company Performing Services Internally	Benchmark Measures— Company with Best Practices
Cost factor:		
Suppliers per purchasing agent	34	5
Purchasing agents per $100 million of purchases	5.4	2.2
Purchasing cost as a % of purchases made	3.30%	0.80%
Time factor:		
Supplier evaluations (in weeks)	3	0.4
Supplier lead times (in weeks)	150	8
Time spent placing an order (in weeks)	6	0.001
Quality of deliveries:		
Percent late	33.00%	2.00%
Percent rejected	1.50%	0.01%
Materials shortages (instances per year)	400	4

Source: McKinsey and Co., as quoted in Otis Port and Geoffrey Smith, "Quality: Small and Midsize Companies Seize the Challenge—Not a Moment Too Soon," *Business Week*, Nov. 30, 1992, pp. 66–75.

that change are relevant. Outsourcing focuses on the costs that would not be incurred—avoidable costs—should the organization stop performing that service internally. Avoidable costs are compared with the cost of purchasing the service from an outside supplier. Typically, it's the variable costs that affect the make or buy decision. And, as always, fixed costs that don't change are not relevant.

Consider an organization that is trying to decide whether it should maintain its own fleet of 625 delivery vehicles or purchase fleet maintenance services from an external supplier. Assume that fleet maintenance is neither a core activity nor an activity directly affecting the firm's customers. That means the analysis is driven only by the amount of costs avoided by outsourcing. Other factors—such as quality of maintenance service, turnaround time, and frequency of mechanical failure—are also important. But in this example, assume that the outside supplier can meet or exceed internally provided service in each of these areas.

Exhibit 7.16 illustrates the costs relevant in this outsourcing decision. We see the cost of in-house maintenance in the first numerical column in the top portion of the exhibit. The total, after-tax cost of in-house maintenance is $430,089. Are all of the components of this cost avoided if maintenance is outsourced?

In the second numerical column we see which costs are avoided if maintenance is performed by an outside supplier. These are the costs that are relevant to the decision. For example, the variable cost avoided for parts and supplies represents a cost saving of $293,750. Of the five workers and one manager assigned to maintenance, four are to be released, thereby reducing salary and benefits cost by $137,500. After managers look at the duties of the two remaining employees, they decide to reassign the mechanic to another department and to change the shop manager's role to supervisor of the outside contractor. Space presently occupied by fleet maintenance cannot be used by other activities. With no change in facility occupancy, allocated occupancy cost is not relevant and should not be considered. Other fixed costs avoided consist of insurance, outside cleaning service, and utilities.

Total cost avoided equals $298,914, while the total cost of outsourcing equals $358,875. The net result: Overall cost *increases* by $59,961 when fleet maintenance is outsourced.

Costs that appear to be avoided are sometimes not—they are simply shifted to other operating units within the same organization. For example, what if a salaried maintenance worker reassigned to another division takes the place of someone who would have been hired from outside the organization? The salary that would have been paid to hire someone from outside is an avoidable cost, and the worker's salary is relevant to the decision. On the other hand, if the reassigned worker does not offset another cost or replace another worker, then total cost does not change. In that case, the cost is not avoided and is irrelevant to the decision. Reallocated or shifted costs that do not result in an overall reduction in total cost for the organization as a whole are not avoided and, therefore, are not relevant.

EXHIBIT 7.16 OUTSOURCING DECISION

Relevant Fleet Maintenance Costs

In-House Fleet Maintenance

	In-House Maintenance Cost	Relevant Costs— Costs Avoided If In-House Maintenance Is Discontinued
Fleet size: 625 vehicles		
Variable cost—maintenance:		
Parts ($430/vehicle)	$268,750	$268,750
Supplies ($40/vehicle)	25,000	25,000
Total variable cost—maintenance	$293,750	$293,750
Direct fixed cost—maintenance:		
Payroll & benefits—maintenance workers	$206,250	$137,500[a]
Depreciation—maintenance facility	100,000	0
Insurance on maintenance facility	7,500	7,500
Cleaning service	8,750	8,750
Utilities	5,400	5,400
Total direct fixed cost—maintenance	$327,900	$159,150
Allocated administrative cost—maintenance	30,000	0
Total cost—maintenance	$651,650	$452,900
Less income tax (Rate = 34%)	(221,561)	(153,986)
Net cost after tax—maintenance	$430,089	
In-house cost avoided by outsourcing fleet maintenance		$298,914

[a] Maintenance employs five mechanics and one shop manager. Four mechanics will be released. The fifth mechanic will be reassigned to another department. The shop manager will supervise the outside contractor to assure quality.

Outsourced Fleet Maintenance

	Cost of Outsourcing Maintenance
Service cost—external maintenance supplier ($870 per vehicle)	$543,750
Less income tax (Rate = 34%)	(184,875)
Cost of outsourcing fleet maintenance	$358,875

Summary

	Total Cost
Cost of outsourcing fleet maintenance	$358,875
In-house cost avoided by outsourcing fleet maintenance	(298,914)
Cost saving from performing fleet maintenance in-house	$ 59,961

Conclusion: it will cost $59,961 more to outsource fleet maintenance. Therefore, maintenance should be performed internally.

DISADVANTAGES OF OUTSOURCING

Some outsourcing decisions are reversed when managers recognize the full cost of outsourcing. Poor outsourcing decisions can be made for a number of reasons. One is faulty data—managers may not be able to identify all of the costs that are likely to change. Another is that managers may not have experience working with outside contractors, especially when outsourcing abroad. Language differences, cultural differences, and the difficulty of managing foreign currency all require extra attention, and, in some cases, learning new skills. Another problem encountered in outsourcing is the missed opportunities for building in-house expertise. Plus, the organization has to work with a larger number of subcontractors—this entails better organizational coordination and adds to the complexity of operations.[7]

CHANGES IN COST STRUCTURE

Outsourcing can have a big impact on an organization's cost structure. In general, outsourcing involves trading fixed costs for variable ones. The effect of outsourcing on the firm's cost structure is to reduce the breakeven point and decrease the risks of covering fixed costs when activity declines. This is especially important to managers during sustained downturns in business activity, when they decide to shed high levels of fixed costs by downsizing (decreasing) the firm's capacity to match the decline in demand.

To see the impact of outsourcing on an organization's cost structure, consider Exhibit 7.17. Assume total fixed cost is $2,000,000 and total variable cost is $250 per unit before outsourcing. After outsourcing, fixed cost declines to $750,000, since some fixed cost is avoided. However, variable cost increases to $450 per unit, because services formerly performed internally are provided by outside contractors who charge fees based on each unit of service they supply. After looking at Exhibit 7.17, note that the net impact of outsourcing is to reduce the breakeven point from 4,000 to 2,500 units.

At lower volumes of output, the cost structure with outsourced services is preferable. It yields higher operating income, with improved prospects for reaching breakeven. However, if volume increases, managers may return to their former cost structure by adding back fixed costs. The point where managers consider changing is called the crossover volume or point of indifference. It is where operating incomes for both alternatives are the same. In the present example, the crossover volume is 6,250 units. Below this crossover volume, managers prefer a cost structure dominated by variable cost. Above the crossover volume, fixed-cost-dominated structures are preferred because of their potential to realize economies of scale.

Not all outsourcing decisions turn out the way they are supposed to. A recent study found that many companies "... doomed themselves by

---

[7] Edward Davis, "Global Outsourcing: Have U.S. Managers Thrown the Baby Out with the Bath Water?" *Business Horizons*, July–Aug. 1992, pp. 58–65.

EXHIBIT 7.17   COST STRUCTURE BEFORE AND AFTER OUTSOURCING

		Cost Structure Before Outsourcing			Cost Structure After Outsourcing		
Selling price	$750	Fixed cost Variable cost	**$2,000,000** **250**		Fixed cost Variable cost	**$750,000** **450**	
Volume	Total Revenue	Total Cost	Unit Cost	Operating Income	Total Cost	Unit Cost	Operating Income
0	$ 0	$2,000,000		$(2,000,000)	$ 750,000		$(750,000)
500	375,000	2,125,000	$4,250	(1,750,000)	975,000	$1,950	(600,000)
1,000	750,000	2,250,000	2,250	(1,500,000)	1,200,000	1,200	(450,000)
1,500	1,125,000	2,375,000	1,583	(1,250,000)	1,425,000	950	(300,000)
2,000	1,500,000	2,500,000	1,250	(1,000,000)	1,650,000	825	(150,000)
2,500	1,875,000	2,625,000	1,050	(750,000)	1,875,000	750	**0**
3,000	2,250,000	2,750,000	917	(500,000)	2,100,000	700	150,000
3,500	2,625,000	2,875,000	821	(250,000)	2,325,000	664	300,000
4,000	3,000,000	3,000,000	750	**0**	2,550,000	638	450,000
4,500	3,375,000	3,125,000	694	250,000	2,775,000	617	600,000
5,000	3,750,000	3,250,000	650	500,000	3,000,000	600	750,000
5,500	4,125,000	3,375,000	614	750,000	3,225,000	586	900,000
6,000	4,500,000	3,500,000	583	1,000,000	3,450,000	575	1,050,000
6,500	4,875,000	3,625,000	558	1,250,000	3,675,000	565	1,200,000
7,000	5,250,000	3,750,000	536	1,500,000	3,900,000	557	1,350,000
7,500	5,625,000	3,875,000	517	1,750,000	4,125,000	550	1,500,000
8,000	6,000,000	4,000,000	500	2,000,000	4,350,000	544	1,650,000
8,500	6,375,000	4,125,000	485	2,250,000	4,575,000	538	1,800,000
9,000	6,750,000	4,250,000	472	2,500,000	4,800,000	533	1,950,000
9,500	7,125,000	4,375,000	461	2,750,000	5,025,000	529	2,100,000
10,000	7,500,000	4,500,000	450	3,000,000	5,250,000	525	2,250,000

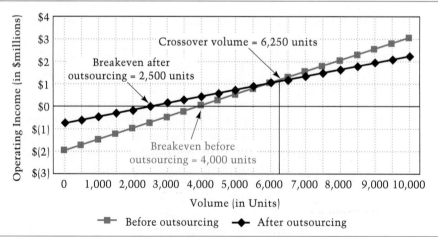

Crossover Volume (Where Total Operating Income Is Equal with Two Alternative Cost Structures):

Operating Income Before Outsourcing = Operating Income After Outsourcing

$$[(\$750 - \$250) \times volume] - \$2,000,000 = [(\$750 - \$450) \times volume] - \$750,000$$
$$[(\$500 \times volume] - \$2,000,000 = [\$300 \times volume] - \$750,000$$
$$\$200 \times volume = \$1,250,000$$
$$Crossover\ volume = \$1,250,000/\$200$$
$$Crossover\ volume = \boxed{6,250\ units}$$

restructuring the wrong way."[8] For example, some companies who release employees lose key skills when workers depart. Worse, the expected cost saving from downsizing the organization may never materialize. Managers may be forced to rely on consultants or end up training new employees. While early retirements help some companies shrink payrolls, other companies are discovering that shrinking payrolls by laying off workers can lead to lawsuits that increase costs.[9]

ELIMINATING NONPERFORMING PRODUCTS

Another type of short-term decision that requires management accounting information involves dropping or replacing product lines whose operating incomes are below what managers expect. One aspect of this kind of decision is that not only are costs avoided but revenues are also lost. Variable costs, as usual, are relevant. And unlike short-term product mix and inventory decisions, fixed costs may be avoided when product lines are discontinued. Moreover, the total amount of costs allocated to different product lines may change when the products are discontinued.

In general, *products are candidates for elimination when avoidable costs exceed avoidable revenues.* However, long before having to decide whether a product should be eliminated, managers should consider:

- Reducing costs by making processes more efficient and eliminating waste
- Raising prices, perhaps by finding ways to differentiate products and services

If neither of these alternatives is possible, or if their implementation does not provide the expected results, then managers should:

- Consider dropping the product
- Look for a suitable replacement (as Porsche did in Current Practice: "Porsche Pursues Work from Other Automakers")

To illustrate how to evaluate products that are performing below expectations, we introduce the Alameda Engineering Company. Projected revenues and costs for the firm, shown in the top panel of Exhibit 7.18, are broken down by product line—commercial, residential, and government. While direct margins, calculated by subtracting direct costs from segment revenues, are positive for all three client groups, government contracts show a $5,000 segment operating loss after deducting allocated cost. Based on this information, should Alameda discontinue working on government contracts?

---

[8] Gilbert Fuchberg, "Why Shake-Ups Work for Some, Not for Others," *The Wall Street Journal*, Oct. 1, 1993, p. B1.

[9] Don Boroughs, "Amputating Assets: Companies That Slash Jobs Often End Up with More Problems Than Profit," *U.S. News & World Report*, May 4, 1992, pp. 50–52.

CURRENT PRACTICE

Porsche Pursues Work from Other Automakers

Porsche, a manufacturer of luxury sports cars, has more production capacity than it can use. Although its sales increased by 20 percent in the last 6 months of 1993, Porsche still incurred a loss of DM 114 million (about $80 million). Rather than shedding capacity and losing highly skilled workers, Porsche decided to expand its business by building cars for other manufacturers.

Porsche had contracted to make the Mercedes model 500 E for Daimler-Benz, but that agreement expired in 1994. To fill the gap, Porsche now makes the Avant RS2 for Audi. Porsche expects to make about 2,000 cars, including the RS2s. That's in addition to the 16,000 Porsches it plans to make.

Source: Christopher Parkes, "Porsche to Pursue Work for Other Makers," *Financial Times* (European ed.), Mar. 22, 1994.

DROPPING A PRODUCT LINE

Assuming that neither lowering costs nor increasing prices is possible, what is the net impact of Alameda's dropping all government contracts? Managers may, at first, assume that all costs associated with government contracts are avoided. That is, $95,000 of direct cost and $85,000 of allocated cost, or a total cost of $180,000, are eliminated if Alameda discontinues its work on government contracts. Avoiding $180,000 in cost while giving up $175,000 in revenue yields a net increase in total, firmwide operating income of $5,000. However, the real question is, will discontinuing government contracts actually result in avoiding $180,000 in cost?

Exhibit 7.19 shows a thorough analysis of the costs that are likely to be avoided. The column headed "Revenues and Costs Avoided by Dropping Government Contracts" indicates those costs that will not be incurred as a result of the decision to discontinue working on the contracts. To predict which costs are likely to change, managers must first identify all of the costs associated with the department or activities involved in making the product or service being considered for elimination. This information, in some cases, may be extracted from the accounting system, perhaps using departmental or product-line performance reports. After identifying costs affected by the decision, the next step is to decide which costs are likely to be avoided.

If all government contracts are discontinued, then all of the revenue from this segment will be eliminated. To balance the loss of revenue, Alameda Engineering may be able to reduce some of its costs. For example:

- The employee assigned to government contracts will be given duties in another department within Alameda Engineering. The employee's

EXHIBIT 7.18 ALAMEDA ENGINEERING

Product-Line Segment Margins and Operating Income

Before Dropping Government Contracts

	Commercial	Residential	Government	Total
Revenue by segment	$350,000	$125,000	$175,000	$650,000
Direct cost	(175,000)	(40,000)	(95,000)	(310,000)
Direct margin	$175,000	$ 85,000	$ 80,000	$340,000
Allocated cost	(80,000)	(25,000)	(85,000)	(190,000)
Segment operating income (loss)	$ 95,000	$ 60,000	$ (5,000)	$150,000
Return on revenue (income as a % of revenue)	27.14%	48.00%	−2.86%	23.08%

After Dropping Government Contracts—Incorrect Analysis

	Commercial	Residential	Government	Total
Revenue by segment	$350,000	$125,000	$0	$475,000
Direct cost	(175,000)	(40,000)	$0	(215,000)
Direct margin	$175,000	$ 85,000	$0	$260,000
Allocated cost	(80,000)	(25,000)	$0	(105,000)
Segment operating income	$ 95,000	$ 60,000	$0	$155,000
Return on revenue (income as a % of revenue)	27.14%	48.00%		32.63%

cost is not avoided, since direct labor cost does not change for the organization as a whole.

- All direct materials and purchased services attributed to government clients are avoided. Since these costs will be eliminated, they are relevant to the decision.
- Drafting costs, directly charged to internal clients based on drafting hours, will be reduced. Since the total number of drafting hours decreases, one part-time employee will be released and $12,000 in direct charges—representing the released employee's salary and benefits cost—will be eliminated.
- The full-time employee currently assigned to administration who manages government contracts will be released, not transferred or reassigned to a different department. As a result, $22,000 in salary cost is eliminated.

Altogether, Alameda will be able to avoid $115,000 in cost if it discontinues its work on government contracts. However, the cost avoided is offset by the loss of $175,000 in revenue. If managers were to go ahead with the plan, operating income would *decline* by $60,000 per year. Therefore, managers should continue working on government contracts. As always, other quantifiable, but nonfinancial, factors (together with nonquantifiable factors) should play a role in this decision.

EXHIBIT 7.19 ALAMEDA ENGINEERING

Impact from Discontinuing Government Contracts

	Segment			Total Before	Revenues and Costs Avoided by Dropping Government Contracts	Total After
	Commercial	Residential	Government			
Revenue	$350,000	$125,000	$175,000	$650,000	$(175,000)	$475,000
Direct cost:						
Direct labor	$110,000	$20,000	$14,000	$144,000	$ 0[a]	$144,000
Direct materials	18,000	5,000	12,000	35,000	(12,000)	23,000
Purchased services	47,000	15,000	69,000	131,000	(69,000)	62,000
Total direct cost	$175,000	$40,000	$95,000	$310,000	$(81,000)	$229,000
Direct charge—drafting	$16,000	$12,000	$12,000	$40,000	$(12,000)	$28,000
Allocated cost:						
Administration	$40,000	$ 5,000	$55,000	$100,000	$(22,000)[b]	$ 78,000
Occupancy & depreciation	24,000	8,000	18,000	50,000	0[c]	50,000
Total allocated cost	$64,000	$13,000	$73,000	$150,000	$(22,000)	$128,000
Total cost	$255,000	$65,000	$180,000	$500,000	$(115,000)	$385,000
Operating income	$95,000	$60,000	$(5,000)	$150,000	$(60,000)	$ 90,000

[a] The employee assigned to government contracts is on salary. The employee will be reassigned to commercial or residential work.

[b] Dropping government work caused the release of one employee, saving $22,000 in salary cost.

[c] No occupancy or depreciation cost is avoided by dropping government activities.

While retaining government contracts may be the best short-term action, is it the correct decision over a longer time horizon? If revenue fails to cover full cost, including an allocation of common cost, then *managers must either downsize, by reducing capacity, or find opportunities for more-promising uses of existing facilities.* That is, if managers eliminate activities, they may be stuck in the short-term with the cost of excess capacity. They must either eliminate the excess capacity or find ways of using it. Therefore, *over a longer planning horizon, all cost, including allocated common cost, must be reduced if no replacement products are found.* When managers must drop products without finding replacements, they should work toward eliminating the full cost associated with those products.

ALAMEDA ENGINEERING REVISITED

Our evaluation of the data in Exhibit 7.19 indicated that managers should continue working on government contracts, since the contracts make a positive contribution to operating income. However, government contracts do not cover full cost, and Alameda Engineering should begin to look for other opportunities. For example, the firm's managers may see environmental engineering as an emerging field and begin building expertise in that area. If the managers cannot identify other opportunities and can neither increase the billing rates nor reduce cost, Alameda Engineering should exit the government market, shedding the full $180,000 of cost in the process.

DEALING WITH UNCERTAINTY

NATURE OF UNCERTAINTY

Decisions about what to do today result in actions that affect the organization in the future. These decisions rely on estimates of revenues and costs, many of which cannot be made with complete accuracy. (See "Current Practice: Amtrak Plans to Slash Service.")

Assume Alameda Engineering is considering the addition of a new line of business—environmental engineering—to take the place of government contracts. In evaluating the prospects for this new line of business, Alameda Engineering's managers aren't sure how many environmental engineering jobs they are likely to get. Moreover, they are uncertain about the value of each contract, although they believe that the average contract will be worth about $15,000. While managers know how much they will have to pay environmental engineers, they don't know how many engineers they will need.

Uncertainty is generally expressed in terms of a range of values for each variable affecting the decision. For example, assume Alameda Engineering expects the number of environmental engineering contracts to vary between, say, 18 and 22 per year. The uncertainty associated with projecting this range of values is a lot less than if the range were between, say, 15 and 25 contracts per year. Both ranges have a mean—called the

CURRENT PRACTICE

Amtrak Plans to Slash Service

Amtrak, facing a budget deficit of about $200 million, decided to cut its passenger train service by 20 percent, reduce the frequency of departures, and eliminate three routes. These cutbacks are eventually expected to avoid about $430 million in operating cost while eliminating $66 million in revenue, a net saving of $364 million per year.

While some analysts praised the plan, others warned that such sweeping reductions in service would expose Amtrak to considerable risk. According to William Withuhn, transportation curator at the Smithsonian Institution, "The risk is that the cuts will reduce revenues more than expected and drive Amtrak below the threshold of viability into a death spiral."

Source: Daniel Machalaba and Daniel Pearl, "Amtrak Plans to Slash Service, Cut 5,500 Jobs," *The Wall Street Journal,* Dec. 15, 1994, p. A3.

expected value—of 20 contracts. But the range of possibilities for the second is much greater. It is, therefore, subject to greater uncertainty, as measured by the standard deviation.[10]

SENSITIVITY ANALYSIS

Sensitivity analysis offers one way of incorporating uncertainty into decisions. It is so named because it consists of assessing the degree of change (the *sensitivity*) of the criterion, such as operating income, used in evaluating any decision relative to a change in a variable subject to uncertainty, such as the number of environmental engineering contracts. Sensitivity analysis begins with the creation of a spreadsheet model, like the one found in Exhibit 6.2 (in Chapter 6), that captures the important relationships among the variables affecting a decision. Then, the uncertainty can be assessed by changing the values of each variable to determine its impact on the criterion (or criteria) used in evaluating alternative courses of action.

Recall that, often, multiple—sometimes conflicting—criteria are used in judging a decision. For example, Alameda Engineering's managers may state that their objective is to increase current operating income. The cost of getting started—for example, the expense of training employees, marketing environmental engineering, and carrying the salary cost of engineers until the volume of work increases—may have the effect of reducing operating income. Moreover, focusing the organization's energy on

---

[10] The range of values—and, hence, the degree of uncertainty—can be measured quantitatively by standard deviation. Activities with wider ranges of values—that is, with larger standard deviations—present greater exposure to risk than activities with narrower ranges and lower standard deviations do.

environmental engineering may have a negative impact on customer satisfaction in Alameda Engineering's other lines of business.

Consider the following sequence of steps in model building, steps that we have illustrated previously:

- Build a model.
- Insert expected values for all variables in the model.
- Use the model to focus on data collection.
- Identify criteria used in evaluating the decision.

For sensitivity analysis, rather than inserting expected values (the second step in typical model building), managers can deal with uncertainty by substituting the following steps:

Perform Sensitivity Analysis.   Values for variables in the model are altered to determine their impact on the criteria used in evaluating the decision. The different values of the variables selected can be based on judgment and past experience. Or the values can be varied, systematically, by starting at the low end of the range of possible values and adding small increments, or steps, until the upper limit of the range of values is reached.[11]

Identify High-Leverage Variables.   Variables with the greatest impact on the criteria used in evaluating alternatives are called high-leverage variables. *High leverage* means that a small change in the value of the variable has a disproportionately large impact on the evaluation criteria. High-leverage variables expose the decision to high levels of risk. For example, assume that reducing the number of environmental engineering contracts from an expected value of 20 per year to 15 causes operating income to change from a positive $15,000 to a loss of $45,000. As a consequence, the number of contracts qualifies as a high-leverage variable.

Some managers focus only on what are known as "downside" risks by evaluating the worst-case scenario. They calculate the impact on the criteria used by selecting the lowest realistic estimates of revenues and the highest possible estimates of cost. For example, assume Alameda Engineering realistically expects to sign a minimum of 18 contracts, with an average contract value of $13,500. Also assume that all other costs are evaluated at the upper limit of what managers realistically expect to happen. Operating income—under these worst-case assumptions—is, say, $10,000. That's the worst operating income that managers can realistically expect.

Collect More Data.   Managers may decide to collect more data regarding high-leverage variables. The reason is that more-accurate estimates allow them to reduce the range of values for these variables, thereby reducing

---

[11]   Data tables, or "what-if" tables, as they are called in some spreadsheets, provide a systematic way of conducting sensitivity analysis.

uncertainty. For example, managers may commission a study of the market for environmental engineering or conduct surveys to determine the average value of environmental engineering contracts. This information helps narrow the range of values for these variables, thereby reducing risk.

However, managers may decide not to collect additional information for some variables, especially those with relatively small impact on the criteria used in evaluating alternatives. That's because the cost of gathering the information is likely to exceed the benefits derived from reducing the range of values.

Find Ways to Reduce or Eliminate Risks.   One important feature of sensitivity analysis is that it prompts managers to look for ways to reduce or eliminate the exposure to risk posed by high-leverage variables. For example, potential variations in material prices may lead to contracts that guarantee prices at a given level for months or years into the future. Or, perhaps, the steps in assembling a product can be standardized and guidelines established for the amount of time considered acceptable for performing certain tasks. Another option for reducing risk is to improve manufacturing processes, perhaps by acquiring automatic equipment that eliminates the variability inherent in manual labor. In the Alameda Engineering example, managers may be willing to accept jobs at lower-than-going contract prices in return for gaining long-term agreements that guarantee work in the future.

SENSITIVITY ANALYSIS ILLUSTRATED

To illustrate sensitivity analysis, let's assume that Alameda Engineering managers settle on the estimates of variables shown in the model at the top of Exhibit 7.20. They expect to win 20 contracts during their first year of offering environmental engineering services, with an average contract value of $15,000. Managers believe additional materials and supplies will total about 20 percent of contract revenues and that five new employees will have to be hired at a salary cost of about $25,000 each. In addition, other incremental fixed cost will be about $100,000 per year. Based on these "best guess" assumptions, managers expect environmental engineering to yield an operating income of $15,000 during the first year.

To assess the impact of uncertainty on the expected operating income, Alameda Engineering managers performed sensitivity analysis for the following variables:

- Number of contracts awarded—between 15 and 25
- Value of contracts—between $12,500 and $16,000
- Materials and supplies—between 18 and 22 percent of total revenue
- Wages of new employees—between $22,000 and $28,000 per year, per employee

The results of the sensitivity analysis are shown in the bottom part of Exhibit 7.20. Each variable begins at the low end of the range. Small increments in the value of the variables are added in steps until the upper end of the range is achieved. Operating income is recalculated with each step. For example, the lowest number of contracts that Alameda believes

EXHIBIT 7.20 ALAMEDA ENGINEERING

relevant

^ change as a result of a decision

Sensitivity Analysis for Environmental Engineering

	Expected
Incremental revenue:	
Number of contracts awarded	20
Value of contracts	$15,000
Total incremental revenue	$300,000
Incremental cost:	
Materials & supplies (20% of gross revenue)	$ 60,000
Salary cost—environmental engineers (5 @ $25,000)	125,000
Other fixed cost	100,000
Total incremental cost	$285,000
Incremental operating income	$15,000

Variable	Value of Variable	Operating Income	Sensitivity[a]
Number of contracts awarded:	15	$(45,000)	−300.00%
	16	$(33,000)	−220.00%
	17	$(21,000)	−140.00%
	18	$(9,000)	−60.00%
	19	$3,000	20.00%
	20	$15,000	100.00%
	21	$27,000	180.00%
	22	$39,000	260.00%
	23	$51,000	340.00%
	24	$63,000	420.00%
	25	$75,000	500.00%
Value of contracts:	$12,500	$(25,000)	−166.67%
	$13,000	$(17,000)	−113.33%
	$13,500	$(9,000)	−60.00%
	$14,000	$(1,000)	−6.67%
	$14,500	$7,000	46.67%
	$15,000	$15,000	100.00%
	$15,500	$23,000	153.33%
	$16,000	$31,000	206.67%
Materials & supplies:	18.00%	$21,000	140.00%
	18.50%	$19,500	130.00%
	19.00%	$18,000	120.00%
	19.50%	$16,500	110.00%
	20.00%	$15,000	100.00%
	20.50%	$13,500	90.00%
	21.00%	$12,000	80.00%
	21.50%	$10,500	70.00%
	22.00%	$9,000	60.00%
Salary cost for environmental engineers:	$22,000	$30,000	200.00%
	$23,000	$25,000	166.67%
	$24,000	$20,000	133.33%
	$25,000	$15,000	100.00%
	$26,000	$10,000	66.67%
	$27,000	$5,000	33.33%
	$28,000	$0	0.00%

[a] Sensitivity calculated by dividing operating income by $15,000 (expected operating income).

will be awarded is 15. Inserting 15 into the model, while holding all other variables constant, produces an operating loss of $45,000. Next, operating income is recalculated for 16 contracts. This process continues through the range of possible values.

It should be clear from the sensitivity analysis that relatively small changes in either the number of contracts awarded or the value of an average contract will have a big impact on projected operating income. For example, if Alameda wins only 18 contracts, operating income—the criteria used in evaluating the decision—shows a loss of $9,000. Each of the other variables is evaluated in the same way. The same change in either the cost of materials and supplies or the salary cost of environmental engineers does not have the same proportional impact on operating income.

Even though environmental engineering poses significant risks, Alameda Engineering managers may still be willing to enter the environmental engineering field. One reason is that operating income reflects only the first year of operations. If the firm expects environmental engineering to grow, the number of contracts awarded may be expected to increase, thereby reducing exposure to losses. However, its managers may want to look for ways to reduce downside risks before committing themselves to that course of action.

EXPECTED VALUE

Another way to deal with uncertainty is to calculate the expected value. Expected value is defined as "the value of a variable that is most likely to occur." As illustrated in Exhibit 7.21, expected value is calculated by multiplying each possible outcome of a variable, such as the number of environmental engineering contracts that Alameda Engineering might win, by the chances (likelihood) of that outcome's occurring. This is called the *weighted value of that outcome.* The sum of the weighted values for all outcomes is the expected value. (See "Current Practice: Big Risks for Division I-A Football.") In the present example, the expected value of contracts awarded to Alameda is 20.75.

EXHIBIT 7.21 ALAMEDA ENGINEERING

Expected Value for the Number of Contracts Awarded

(1) Number of Environmental Engineering Contracts	(2) Probability	(3) (1 × 2) Weighted Value
15	25.00%	3.75
20	35.00%	7.00
25	40.00%	10.00
	100.00%	20.75
		Expected value

Big Risks for Division I-A Football

The University of Central Florida (UCF) in Orlando, Florida, faced a big decision in 1995. Rated the no. 1 football team in the I-AA division by *Sports Illustrated* before the 1994 season began, UCF considered the opportunity to move from division I-AA, where it was a powerhouse, to the elite ranks of I-A teams, where it might not enjoy the same status.

UCF cites a National Collegiate Athletic Association (NCAA) study of 1993 football teams that puts the financial risks of fielding a football team in perspective. The study indicates that only 5 percent of the I-AA football teams make a profit. Even if the teams are profitable, the average profit is only $75,000. The remaining 95 percent of the teams lose an average of $664,000 each. In contrast, the odds are much better for I-A teams, where 67 percent of the teams make an average profit of $3,883,000. Of the 33 percent of teams that lose money, the average loss is $1,020,000.

According to *The Sporting News*, UCF's goal of joining I-A football is unrealistic: "Attribute it to ambition or dreams, but certainly not reality." However, UCF's president, John Hitt, is confident that his team will receive an invitation to join an NCAA conference by the year 2000. If so, its chances of making a profit will be greatly enhanced—conference membership gives teams a share of conference proceeds, especially when games are shown on television. According to Hitt, "We've got a 70,000-seat stadium (the Citrus Bowl), a great sports-minded city and the 23rd largest television market in the nation."

Source: Gene Yasuda, "UCF Bid for Big-Time Football Could Turn Out to Be a TD—Or a Fumble," *The Orlando Sentinel*, Sept. 11, 1994, pp. A1 and A7.

SHORT-TERM OR LONG-TERM DECISIONS?

In every example in this chapter, we assumed that decisions have no long-lasting impacts. The product mix and inventory examples both focused on using existing capacity—capacity that managers cannot change in the short-term. However, when we introduced outsourcing decisions and the option of dropping products that perform below expectations, we began to approach the limit of what constitutes a short-term decision.

In each of these short-term decision applications we assumed several things—admittedly without stating them:

- We used a decision's impact on operating income as the criterion for evaluating the various courses of action. When decisions have an impact on future years, operating income is an inadequate measure. That's because revenues may not be collected immediately. Cash inflows are collected in future years, while cash outflows for expenses that affect the future are paid right away. Consequently, all long-term decisions require conversion of costs and benefits to cash flows.

- We assumed that no additional long-term resources were required for any of the decisions. For example, changing the product mix or implementing a just-in-time inventory system requires no long-term investment. Clearly, this is not always the case. Converting to a JIT inventory system, for example, is likely to require sizeable cash outlays for software, physical modifications to the manufacturing facility, employee training, and salary cost during the conversion to the new system. Similarly, both outsourcing services and dropping product lines may require changes in the firm's long-term resources.

When either of these implicit assumptions are violated, then the decision is long-term and should be evaluated using the capital budgeting techniques described in the next chapter.

SUMMARY

Short-term decisions affect only current resources. They do not commit the organization to future actions. In general, short-term decisions involve a determination of the best use of existing resources in order to create the most value for shareholders. Short-term decisions generally focus on measurable costs. Relevant costs are those that change in the short-term as a result of the decision. Generally, variable costs are relevant, while fixed and allocated costs are not. However, each situation is different, and these general rules may not necessarily apply.

One of the factors that makes a decision short-term is the focus on maximizing contribution margin rather than full cost. The implications of a focus on contribution margin are that:

- The only relevant costs are those that change.
- Costs driven by cost drivers other than volume, such as product-line or corporate-level drivers, are generally assumed to remain unaffected by short-term decisions.
- Fixed costs are presumed to be unaltered by resource allocation decisions. However, fixed costs, too, may change, but only temporarily.
- Capacity is unaffected by short-term decisions. Changing capacity involves long-term commitments that entail, by definition, long-term decisions.
- Not only do short-term decisions leave capacity unchanged, but they do so with no long-lasting impact on other parts of the organization. That is, short-term decisions do not cause changes in markets, quality, flexibility, organizational structures, production methods, or any other factor that might affect the firm over a longer time horizon. As a result, short-term decisions must be consistent with the long-term goals and objectives of the organization.

Product mix decisions assign capacity in a way that maximizes benefits to the organization. Examples of product mix decisions include assignment of facilities, equipment, and personnel. The goal in product mix decisions, since fixed costs are presumed unaffected, is to determine how much of each product to produce so that the product mix will maximize total contribution margin. By maximizing total contribution, net income is also maximized.

Where there are alternative uses of capacity, contribution margin is maximized by making the most of the product with the highest contribution per unit of capacity.

Inventories offer another illustration of a short-term decision application. The first step in making short-term inventory decisions is to separate costs that are likely to change and are, therefore, relevant to the decision from costs that do not change. The lowest-cost order quantity, an important short-term determination that managers make, is the one that minimizes the combined cost of ordering and carrying inventory. Order costs increase with the frequency of ordering, while carrying costs decline with order frequency.

A just-in-time inventory system offers an alternative way of looking at a firm's investment in inventories. It has the potential of lowering costs and improving product quality but requires cooperation with suppliers.

Outsourcing is when organizations have external contractors perform services previously performed in-house by company employees. Outsourcing permits managers to focus on those activities that give the organization a competitive advantage and to let others perform noncrucial activities. In general, outsourcing involves trading fixed costs for variable costs. The guiding principle in outsourcing decisions is that the internal cost avoided should be greater than the cost of the service provided by the outside supplier. The downside of outsourcing includes the loss of key skills and market presence. In some cases, outsourcing decisions are reversed when activity levels increase.

Another example of short-term decisions relates to nonperforming products and services. The first step in such decisions is to determine whether or not prices can be increased or costs lowered. As always, managers should gain assurance that costs, especially allocated costs, are accurate before making a decision. If neither pricing nor cost improvement efforts are possible, then managers should consider dropping the product or service.

Dropping a product may leave unused capacity that must be filled by a suitable replacement. If no replacement product is found, then capacity should be reduced. Decisions such as dropping product lines are likely to have ramifications for future periods, requiring assessments based on capital budgeting techniques, which are introduced in the next chapter.

Finally, methods of dealing with uncertainty were introduced. Uncertainty is present in any decision where the outcomes of various courses of action are unknown. Uncertainty is often measured by the range of potential values for important variables in a decision. One way of dealing with uncertainty is to obtain more information—this reduces the range of values, thereby reducing the uncertainty. Another way of dealing with uncertainty is to identify high-leverage variables—those revenues and costs that, when changed, cause disproportionately large changes in the criterion (or criteria) by which the decision is to be judged. Sensitivity analysis helps identify variables that require more of management's attention, either in gathering more information to decrease the range of possible values or in finding ways to reduce or eliminate uncertainty.

The last approach to uncertainty introduced in this chapter is expected value. <u>*Expected value* is</u> defined as the "value of a variable that is most likely to occur."

CHAPTER 7 ASSIGNMENTS

DISCUSSION PROBLEMS

D7.1   (Short- or Long-Term Decisions)[12]

Robert Crandall, chairman and chief executive of AMR Corporation, the parent company of American Airlines, recently told employees he was about to reduce flights out of American's San Jose hub, where American was losing about $50 million a year. Crandall's announcement came in response to Southwest Airlines' plans to invade two markets served by American. Abandoning San Jose to get out of the way of Southwest Airlines was an uncharacteristic move for the scrappy Crandall. Seven weeks later, it happened again. Only this time, it was tiny, 11-month old Reno Air challenging American's routes from San Jose to four West Coast cities. As Crandall pulls back from competitors such as Southwest and Reno, he is planning to abandon routes and retire planes. His goal is to get American out of the business of flying because, in his own words, "Unless the world changes, we will never buy another airplane."

What happened to cause this tough competitor—someone whom the co-chairman of Northwest Airlines called a "bully in the schoolyard"—to take such unprecedented steps? His aggressive expansion plans, costing American nearly $20 billion, were to have increased its domestic market share from 14.4 to 20.4 percent. But Crandall's plans didn't materialize—and prospects are not much brighter. Ticket prices driven down by fare wars are 20 percent below the prices of a decade ago, when adjusted for inflation. And there is little hope for increases in the future. New, low-cost carriers are entering the market all the time. And other airlines keep cutting costs and lowering prices—some from the shelter of bankruptcy.

With high costs, American can't match the competition. However, American is not alone. Collectively, the airline industry reported losses of $10.5 billion over the last three years, with American's share at $1.2 billion. And, with large amounts of debt used to fuel American's expansion and high-interest payments, the prospects of raising additional capital seem dim.

For American, the real fear is that it built the wrong kind of airline for the 1990s. Assuming customers wanted plenty of service, the company crafted American into a full-service, high-cost carrier. But, with declining disposable income and cutbacks in business travel, customers have shown that they would prefer "... paying $59 for a seat on Southwest Airlines and to hell with the tarragon chicken."

American's prospects look better in the international arena, where service is still important. But international routes are still heavily regulated. If these routes were deregulated, relatively efficient U.S.-based carriers would probably dominate the market, even competing successfully against government-subsidized airlines

---

[12]   Adapted from Stephen D. Solomon, "The Bully of the Skies Cries Uncle," *The New York Times Magazine,* September 5, 1993, section 6, p. 13.

such as Air France and Germany's Lufthansa. But American will probably never get the chance, since most governments are tightening, rather than loosening, regulations. So, for now, American will have to live or die by its domestic routes. With its high costs and full service, American is not postured to compete against the low-cost, no-frills fares passengers want. Seats today are seen as commodities, sold on the basis of price.

Looking back, American recognized early the advantages of Sabre, its computerized reservation system. With Sabre, American was able to control the "channel of distribution" for airline tickets. American's Sabre system put terminals right on the desks of travel agents. Computers also helped American to devise the frequent-flyer program, the only successful way the airlines have found to create brand loyalty. Computers also helped American get the most out of its resources. Through the use of large customer databases and sophisticated mathematical software, American can predict the demand for seats at various fares or the mix of fares that is likely to generate the most revenue.

The origin of American's problems may be traced back to the deregulation of the industry in 1978. Airlines became free to add routes and price seats as they saw fit. While this was believed to be good for the industry, deregulation also brought new competition. Low-cost Federal Express is a good example—it started from scratch with mostly nonunion workers. Fast growth after deregulation meant American needed to reduce its operating cost. In the hope of doing so, Crandall created a two-tier wage structure that protected salaries for existing employees but paid "new hires" at lower wage rates. The idea, which is based on the concept of economies of scale, was that the faster American grew, the lower the average wage would become. Crandall's growth plans also meant adding more planes. And, to fuel the company's expansion, Crandall needed hubs throughout the country. Passengers would be fed from outlying areas, such as Amarillo, Texas, into an American hub such as Dallas–Ft. Worth. American built seven of the more than two dozen U.S. hubs.

During the second half of the 1980s the plans seemed to gel, and, of all the domestic carriers, American garnered the largest market share. American achieved after-tax profit margins of 4 to 5 percent, solid for the airline industry. However, by 1990 it was clear that Crandall's plans were falling apart. American, cost-competitive with other major American carriers such as United and Delta, was no match for low-cost carriers such as Southwest. Operating costs started creeping up, led by a sharp rise in fuel prices. But perhaps the biggest blow came when the two-tier wage system collapsed from pressure applied by organized labor. Rather than seeing a decline in their average wages, American's employees enjoyed some of the highest wages in the country. And, to make matters worse, American was left with more facilities than it needed. For example, a new maintenance center constructed outside of Ft. Worth was based on a design capacity of 800 planes, far more than current plans would justify. American's massive investment in hubs also became a burden, since they are expensive to operate.

These investments made sense when growth was expected. According to one analyst, Crandall ". . . was looking for tremendous economies of scale as he added more flights into his hubs. That didn't work." Southwest Airlines, in contrast, didn't use hubs. Since its planes don't have to wait for passengers to be collected from outlying areas, they're back in the sky in just 15 or 20 minutes. American, on the other hand, may take an hour or more to gather passengers in a hub and board them again for their destination. As a result, Southwest's "factory" is in operation more hours each day than American's is.

Crandall recently tried a simplified pricing system, called *value pricing*, whereby coach fares were cut back by as much as 38 percent and discounts eliminated. In response, competing airlines offered discounts, taking market share away from American. Value pricing was abandoned and, with it, Crandall's plans. He was persuaded there was no way out.

Today, American is cutting back capital spending. It plans to gradually withdraw from shorter routes, retire planes, cancel new plane orders, and lay off employees. Its new plan is to use resources on longer routes, where service is still important. However, focus will shift to expanding profitable subsidiary businesses. Sabre, for example, is expected to earn $240 million in operating profit on revenue of $1.7 billion. But even Sabre is feeling increased pressure, as low-cost airlines such as Valujet bypass the traditional travel agent-reservation system network altogether.[13] Another indication of Crandall's new strategy is a 20-year, $20-billion deal with Canadian Airlines, which would allow the latter to use American's computers to maximize revenue, and to run its reservations, ticketing, and frequent-flyer programs. In another deal, American is creating a reservations system for the French high-speed rail network and another system for the Chunnel, the tunnel beneath the English Channel.

Required:

1. Are American's decisions short-term or long-term?
2. Do American's and Southwest's strategies translate into different cost structures?

D7.2 (Inventory)[14]

Steve Seide, a general manager in Houston with Baxter International, and Dave Render, his operations manager, meet every day with nurses and executives in two local hospitals. "We talk about everything from a request to stock the new Diet Dr. Pepper to a complaint that a pest control truck is taking too long at the loading dock," Mr. Render said.

Seide and Render run a service that Baxter calls Valuelink at St. Luke's Episcopal Hospital and Hermann Hospital. Using a stockless system, Baxter fills precise orders for supplies and delivers them just as they are needed, directly to the departments that place the orders.

"We have become their warehouse, their central supply—we're it," Seide said. As the hospitals phase in the stockless system, he said, "all they have left is two to three days of supplies. Then it's all up to us."

Among other economies, stockless service has enabled Hermann Hospital to eliminate a 68,000-square-foot warehouse and St. Luke's to get rid of a 20,000-square-foot warehouse. Baxter keeps enough supplies for both institutions in an automated warehouse with only 44,000 square feet of storage space.

Baxter has used the stockless system to become a virtual partner with St. Luke's and Hermann in managing their supply flows. "We formed teams in the hospital units, with leaders and steering committees to deal with problems," Render said.

Seide said Baxter can tailor its services according to the wishes of a hospital's staff. "Seventy percent of it is good communications," he said. A suggestion from the operating rooms led Baxter to become part of the telephone voice mail system at St. Luke's. Anyone in an operating room can now dial the letters *RSVP* to reach the company.

---

[13]   Bridget O'Brian, "Ticketless Plane Trips, New Technology Force Travel Agencies to Change Course," *The Wall Street Journal*, Sept. 13, 1994, p. B1.

[14]   Milt Freudenheim, "Removing the Warehouse from Cost-Conscious Hospitals," *The New York Times*, Mar. 3, 1991, section 3, p. 5. Copyright © 1991 by The New York Times Company. Reprinted by permission.

Another suggestion by an operating room nurse at St. Luke's has helped Baxter prevent surgical mix-ups. Seide said the nurse had noticed that Baxter's blue labels on Pentalyte liquid, used to moisten and clean surgical incisions, closely resembled the blue labels on sterile water. Baxter, which says it was already planning to remedy the problem, promptly started putting black labels on Pentalyte.

Seide and Render have good reasons for boasting of their progress at Hermann and St. Luke's. They are hoping to attract other Houston hospitals to their service. Analysts say that as more hospitals join, the greater the economies for Baxter will be.

Required: What benefits does the Valuelink partnership bring to Hermann and St. Luke's hospitals and to Baxter International?

PROBLEMS

P7.1   (Basic Product Mix Decisions)

Home Cooking Company offers monthly service plans providing prepared meals that are delivered to the customers' homes and that need only to be heated in a microwave or conventional oven. The target market for these meal plans includes double-income families with no children and retired couples in the upper-income brackets.

Home Cooking offers two monthly plans—Premier Cuisine and Haute Cuisine. The Premier Cuisine plan provides frozen meals that are delivered twice each month. This plan generates a contribution of $120 for each monthly plan sold. The Haute Cuisine plan provides freshly prepared meals delivered on a daily basis and generates a contribution of $90 for each monthly plan sold. Home Cooking's reputation assures the company of a market that will purchase all the meals that it can prepare.

All meals go through food preparation and cooking steps in the company's kitchens. After these steps, the Premier Cuisine meals are flash-frozen. The time requirements for each monthly meal plan and the hours available per month are presented below:

	Preparation	Cooking	Freezing
	Hours Required		
Premier Cuisine	2	2	1
Haute Cuisine	1	3	0
Hours Available	60	120	45

Required:

1. Build a model like the one shown in Exhibit P7.1. Through trial and error, identify the combination of Premier Cuisine and Haute Cuisine meal plans that maximizes total contribution. Make sure that your solution falls within the constraints.
2. Assume that Home Cooking is looking for ways to eliminate preparation time, perhaps by outsourcing preparation to another firm. What is the maximum Home Cooking would be willing to pay each month to eliminate preparation? (*Hint:* Eliminate the preparation constraint by making the hours available very large. Then find a new optimal solution.)

(CMA Adapted)

EXHIBIT P7.1 HOME COOKING			
Model with Decisions, Objective, and Constraints			
Decision	*Premier Cuisine*	*Haute Cuisine*	*Total*
Meal plans to produce	10	10	
Unit contribution	$120.00	$90.00	
Total contribution	$1,200	$900	$2,100

Constraints			*Hours Used*		*Hours Available*
Hours:					
Preparation	2	1	30	≤	60
Cooking	2	3	50	≤	120
Freezing	1	0	10	≤	45
Non-negativity:					
Premier cuisine	1	0	10	≥	0
Haute cuisine	0	1	10	≥	0

P7.2 (Use of Capacity; Product Mix Decisions)[15]

Schatz Staplers manufactures three lines of staplers: an economy model selling for $8.95, a standard model selling for $12.50, and its top-of-the-line deluxe model selling for $14.95. Each model has three primary components: a base, a cartridge that holds the staples, and a handle for the stapling action.

While planning for next year, managers at Schatz prepared the pro forma income statement shown in Exhibit P7.2.1. They also calculated the unit costs and total costs shown in Exhibit P7.2.2, based on normal volumes. Schatz anticipates no buildup in inventories, since it plans on selling everything it makes.

In reviewing unit cost data, the managers noted that the economy model achieved the highest unit operating profit of all three models. In fact, the $2.48 operating profit is over 10 times that of Schatz's deluxe model. Based on this observation, Schatz's managers tentatively decided to shift production priorities to the economy model.

Schatz uses automated equipment in making stapler components. However, the number of hours available on each piece of equipment is limited. The number of machine-hours required to produce each component, by model, is shown in Exhibit P7.2.3. For example, it takes 0.3 machine-hours (18 minutes) to make the base for an economy stapler. With a total of 42,000 machine-hours available to make bases, Schatz can produce a maximum of 140,000 economy staplers (42,000/0.3), assuming neither of the other two models is made.

After reviewing machine-hour requirements, managers decide that the data in Exhibit P7.2.3 indicated that production of the economy model requires less total time than production of either of the other two. As a result, Schatz's managers are even more convinced that they can maximize operating profit by devoting all of their capacity to producing the economy model. Before changing pro-

---

[15]   Adapted from David Anderson, Dennis Sweeney, and Thomas Williams, *An Introduction to Management Science: Quantitative Approaches to Decision Making*, 4th ed., St. Paul, Minn.: West Publishing Company, 1985, pp. 209–213.

EXHIBIT P7.2.1 SCHATZ STAPLERS

Pro Forma Income Statement

	Model			
	Economy	Standard	Deluxe	Total
Revenue:				
Selling price	$8.95	$12.50	$14.95	
Number of staplers sold	40,000	80,000	20,000	140,000
Total revenue	$358,000	$1,000,000	$299,000	$1,657,000
Cost of goods sold	$234,000	$780,000	$285,000	$1,299,000
Gross profit	$124,000	$220,000	$14,000	$358,000
Selling & administration	25,000	90,000	10,000	125,000
Operating profit	$99,000	$130,000	$4,000	$233,000
Operating profit per unit	$2.48	$1.63	$0.20	

EXHIBIT P7.2.2 SCHATZ STAPLERS

Breakdown by Cost Behavior

	Model		
	Economy	Standard	Deluxe
Direct materials (variable)	$4.35	$6.50	$7.75
Direct labor (fixed)	1.00 40%	2.50	5.00
Manufacturing overhead (fixed)	0.50 20%	0.75	1.50
Total manufacturing cost	$5.85	$9.75	$14.25
Normal activity (units)	40,000	80,000	20,000
Total manufacturing cost	$234,000	$780,000	$285,000
Selling & administration (fixed)	25,000	90,000	10,000
Total cost	$259,000	$870,000	$295,000

duction schedules, however, they prepared the revised income statement shown in Exhibit P7.2.4, based on the assumption that they would make 140,000 units of the economy model. Net total operating profit increases from $233,000 to $309,000, clinching their decision to concentrate all of their efforts on the economy model.

Required:

1. Build a model organized by cost behavior and include a section for constraints. Use Exhibit 7.4 (in the text) as a guide. Enter the original volumes (40,000, economy; 80,000, standard; and 20,000, deluxe) and confirm the operating profit of $233,000.
2. Using the model from requirement 1, change volume to 140,000 units of the economy model and 0 units for the standard and the deluxe models. What happens to net income? Which is correct—your version or the $309,000 shown in Exhibit P7.2.4?

EXHIBIT P7.2.3 SCHATZ STAPLERS

Production Constraints

	Machine-Hours Required			Total Hours Available
Constraint	Economy	Standard	Deluxe	
Base	0.30	0.30	0.30	42,000
Cartridge	0.20	0.25	0.40	40,000 8 000
Handle	0.10	0.20	0.30	40,000 4 000

EXHIBIT P7.2.4 SCHATZ STAPLERS

Revised Pro Forma Income Statement

	Model			
	Economy	Standard	Deluxe	Total
Revenue:				
Selling price	$8.95	$12.50	$14.95	
Number of staplers sold	140,000	0	0	140,000
Total revenue	$1,253,000	$0	$0	$1,253,000
Cost of goods sold:				
Units sold	140,000	0	0	
Unit cost of goods sold	$5.85	$9.75	$14.25	
Total cost of goods sold	$819,000	$0	$0	$819,000
Gross profit	434,000	0	0	434,000
Selling & administration	125,000	0	0	125,000
Operating profit	$309,000	$0	$0	$309,000

3. Using the model from requirement 1, change volumes to 0 units of the economy model, 106,667 units of the standard model, and 33,333 units of the deluxe model. Confirm that these are optimal values for the number of each model sold. Are these results feasible? That is, does Schatz have the machine capacity to make this combination of models?

P7.3 (Optimal Use of Capacity; Constraints)

Missy Barnett makes potato chips. She makes three kinds: traditional, thick-cut potato chips ("chips"); thin potato sticks ("sticks"); and cross, or "grid," cuts ("grids"). Her Missy's Best Chips products have a distinctive taste, primarily because she uses only the best cooking oils. However, Barnett makes sure her chips are going to taste good by getting them on the shelf within 24 hours. She sells them in 6-ounce bags to specialty food shops, health food stores, and local grocery stores, all within a 250-mile radius of her San Francisco-based company.

    Barnett leases 10,000 square feet of warehouse space, where all of the activities required to make chips takes place:

- *Peeling and sorting.* Raw potatoes are fed into an automatic peeling machine. Peeled potatoes are sorted according to size and suitability for one of the three products.
- *Slicing.* Peeled and sorted potatoes are placed in stainless steel containers until enough are collected for a batch: 100 lb for a batch of chips; 110 lb for a batch of sticks; and 140 lb for a batch of grids. The potatoes are transferred from the containers to the automatic slicer, where they are cut into the desired shape. Chips require only a single pass on the slicer, while sticks and grids require additional passes to get the desired size and shape.
- *Frying.* Sliced potatoes are submersed in a large cooking vessel and deep-fried. Cooking time is about the same for all three products. Any variations in cooking time are due to moisture content and potato density rather than to the type of cut. Cooking oils are replenished periodically—typically one or two times a month—to replace oil removed with the chips. Once a year, the cooking vessel is completely drained, and the oil replaced. Three or four batches of potatoes are processed each working day.
- *Bagging.* Chips exiting the fryer are cooled and then packed in 6-ounce foil bags using automated machinery. Bagged chips are placed in 24-count cardboard containers and moved to the loading bay, where they await delivery.

In addition to using four primary pieces of equipment (peeler, slicer, fryer, and bagger), Barnett incurs fixed costs, as shown at the bottom of P7.3.1.

Barnett is currently preparing plans for next year. Based on the production information shown in Exhibit P7.3.1, she plans on making 250 batches of chips, 600 of sticks (her best-seller), and 50 of grids. She can sell all the product she can make, with the exception of grid cuts, where the upper limit is 100 batches.

Barnett, aware of the limitations created by her operations, gathered the data shown in Exhibit P7.3.2 in order to assess the cost of adding capacity. She can, for example, extend capacity in peeling and sorting by adding 500 machine-hours and the part-time labor to run the machinery at a combined cost of $5,375. In contrast, adding bagging capacity entails securing 200 additional machine-hours at a cost of $2,500. Labor capacity, provided by part-time workers, can be added one hour at a time.

Required:

1. Prepare a contribution margin income statement. Show the contribution by product line as well as for the total. Include a section for constraints, containing production constraints, a maximum-quantity constraint (100 batches) for grids, and a nonnegativity constraint for each of the three products. Calculate the total contribution margin for Barnett's present production plan (250 chips, 600 sticks, 50 grids). How much unused capacity is left in each of the four processes?
2. Change Barnett's original mix to 0 chips, 800 sticks, and 100 grids. What is the change in total contribution? (*Note:* If you have access to linear programming, prove that this combination of products optimizes total contribution.) How much unused capacity is left with each of the four machines? This plan eliminates production of chips. Does this make sense?
3. Add 200 machine-hours of capacity to bagging, bringing the total to 2,000 hours (1,800 + 200). Next, change the product mix to 0 chips, 1,000 sticks, and 0 grids. What is the change in total contribution from requirement 2, above? (*Note:* If you have access to linear programming, prove that this combination of products optimizes total contribution, subject to the new

Production Data

	Potato Chips	Potato Sticks	Grid Cuts	Total
Selling price:				
Selling price per batch	$192	$240	$288	
Sales commissions (2.5% × selling price)	$4.80	$6.00	$7.20	
Potatoes:				
Potatoes required per batch, lbs	100	110	140	
Price per pound of potatoes	$0.22	$0.22	$0.22	
Variable cost per processing hour:				
Peeling & sorting	$3.00	$3.00	$3.00	
Slicing	$4.00	$4.00	$4.00	
Frying	$9.00	$9.00	$9.00	
Bagging	$4.00	$4.00	$4.00	
Processing hours per batch:				
Peeling & sorting	3.0	3.0	4.0	
Slicing	1.5	2.5	3.0	
Frying	0.5	0.5	0.5	
Bagging	2.0	2.0	2.0	
Total machine-hours available:				
Peeling & sorting				3,000
Slicing				3,000
Frying				1,000
Bagging				1,800
Fixed cost:				
Peeling & sorting				$25,000
Slicing				$15,000
Frying				$45,000
Bagging				$8,000
Marketing				$12,000
Administration				$10,000

Cost of Adding One Unit of Capacity

	Cost Behavior	Hours in 1 Unit of Capacity	Cost per Unit
Peeling & sorting:			
Machine capacity—additional machine-hours	Fixed	500	$2,500
Labor capacity—part-time labor	Fixed	500	$2,875
Slicing:			
Machine capacity—additional machine-hours	Fixed	500	$2,500
Labor capacity—part-time labor	Variable	1	$6.75
Frying:			
Machine capacity—additional machine-hours	Fixed	500	$2,500
Labor capacity—part-time labor	Fixed	500	$6,000
Bagging:			
Machine capacity—additional machine-hours	Fixed	200	$2,500
Labor capacity—part-time labor	Variable	1	$6.50

constraints.) How much unused capacity is left on each of the four machines? Note that this plan eliminates production of chips and sticks. What is the incremental benefit of this plan?

P7.4 (Inventory)

AgriCorp manufactures farm equipment that is sold by a network of distributors throughout the United States. A majority of the distributors also serve as repair centers for AgriCorp equipment and depend on AgriCorp's service division to provide a timely supply of spare parts.

In an effort to reduce the inventory costs incurred by the service division, Richard Bachman, division manager, implemented a just-in-time (JIT) inventory program on June 1, 1994, the beginning of the company's fiscal year. Since the JIT inventory has now been in place for a year, Bachman has asked the division controller, Janice Grady, to determine the effect the program has had on the service division's financial performance. Grady has been able to document the following results of the JIT implementation:

- The service division's average inventory declined from $550,000 to $150,000.
- Projected annual insurance cost of $80,000 declined to 60 percent of its previous level as a result of the lower average inventory.
- A leased 8,000-square-foot warehouse, previously used for raw material storage, was not used at all during the year. The division paid $11,200 annual rent for the warehouse and was able to sublet three-quarters of the building to several tenants at $2.50 per square foot, while the balance of the space remained unoccupied.
- Two warehouse employees whose services were no longer needed were transferred on June 1, 1994, to the purchasing department to assist in the coordination of the just-in-time program. The annual salary expense for these two employees totaled $38,000 and continued to be charged to the indirect labor portion of fixed overhead.
- Despite the use of overtime to manufacture 7,500 spare parts, lost sales as the result of stock-outs totaled 3,800 spare parts. The overtime premium incurred amounted to $5.60 per part manufactured. The use of overtime to fill spare-parts orders was immaterial prior to June 1, 1994.

Prior to the decision to implement the just-in-time inventory program, Agri-Corp's service division had completed its 1994–1995 fiscal budget. The division's pro forma income statement, without any adjustments for JIT inventory, is presented in Exhibit P7.4. Agricorp's incremental borrowing rate for inventory is 15% before income taxes. All AgriCorp's budgets are prepared using an effective tax rate of 40 percent.

Required:

1. Calculate the after-tax cash saving (loss) for AgriCorp's service division that resulted during the 1994–1995 fiscal year from the adoption of the just-in-time inventory program.
2. What are some nonfinancial factors that AgriCorp might have considered before adopting the just-in-time inventory system?

(CMA Adapted)

EXHIBIT P7.4 AGRICORP

Pro Forma Income Statement for the Year Ending May 31, 1995

Sales (280,000 units)		$6,160,000
Cost of goods sold:		
Variable	$2,660,000	
Fixed	1,120,000	3,780,000
Gross profit		$2,380,000
Selling & administrative expense:		
Variable	$ 700,000	
Fixed	555,000	1,255,000
Operating income		$1,125,000
Other income		75,000
Income before interest & income taxes		$1,200,000
Interest expense		150,000
Income before income taxes		$1,050,000
Income taxes		420,000
Net income		$ 630,000

P7.5   (Inventory; Process Improvement)[16]

Biojoint distributes synthetic parts used in replacements for damaged joints—such as elbows, hips, and knees—in humans. Typically, hospitals maintain very small inventories of these parts, relying on firms such as Biojoint to supply items they themselves don't have. In turn, Biojoint adds value by carrying relatively large inventories as buffers against variations in demand. Usually hospitals have adequate lead time before elective surgery to secure needed joints. However, emergency joint replacements are relatively common. Consequently, hospitals often need parts in a hurry.

Time has always been a critical component in Biojoint's competitive strategy. Getting the right part to the hospital at the right time is crucial to its success. It cannot risk being out of any item a hospital requests. However, carrying and ordering costs take a big bite out of Biojoint's net income. As a result, managers are looking for ways to streamline the investment in inventory.

For the vast majority of inventory items, lead times average 25 days. For an inventory item with average daily demand of, say, 400 units, Biojoint reorders when the inventory level reaches 10,000 units (400 units per day × 25 days). Biojoint works 250 days per year.

Biojoint organized a small team of employees charged with identifying ordering activities and searching for ways to reduce cycle time. The results of their study confirmed the 25-day lead time, based on the following sequence of activities:

- *Company preparation—4 days in preparation.* Whenever the inventory count drops below the reorder point, the computerized materials management system issues a report to the inventory manager. The manager then authorizes

[16]   Based on an article by A. Faye Borthick and Harold P. Roth, "Accounting for Time: Reengineering Business Processes to Improve Responsiveness," *Cost Management*, fall 1993, pp. 4–14.

EXHIBIT P7.5.1 BIOJOINT

Inventory Data

Part Number	Annual Usage	Unit Cost	Total Cost
S33—knee joint	100,000	$65.00	$6,500,000
L56—elbow joint	60,000	$58.00	3,480,000
Total	160,000		$9,980,000

the purchase and "cuts" a four-part purchase order. The purchasing secretary verifies that the manager's request and purchase order agree, sends one copy to the supplier, one to accounts payable, and one to receiving, and retains one for the firm's files.
- *Order in mail—3 days in transit.* The supplier receives the purchase order.
- *Supplier receipt—4 days for receipt.* The supplier opens the mail and enters the data into its information system.
- *Supplier processing—5 days in process.* The supplier creates a purchase order report, verifies the credit status, and mails an order request confirmation back to Biojoint.
- *Supplier confirmation—5 days for supplier confirmation.* The supplier confirms prices, shipping date, and mode of transportation. Shipping documents are prepared and forms sent to the warehouse to release the requested items from inventory.
- *Supplier delivery—4 days for delivery.* The supplier loads the delivery truck, dispatches the truck, and delivers the items to Biojoint's receiving dock.

Because of the long lead time, Biojoint began to look into automating the entire system. One promising option is EDI, or electronic data interchange. With EDI, all transactions between Biojoint and a supplier are transferred electronically, thereby reducing response time. To explore the benefits of EDI, Biojoint contracted a consultant who outlined the costs and benefits of EDI.[17] According to the consultant, EDI would shorten Biojoint's inventory replenishment cycle from the present 25 days by sending and receiving purchase orders electronically. After a preliminary study, the consultant estimated that, using EDI, Biojoint could reduce elapsed times as follows: company preparation, 0.3 day; order in transit, 0.1 day; supplier receipt, 0.2 day; supplier processing, 0.1 day; supplier confirmation, 0.2 day; supplier delivery, 3.6 days.

Projected demand and other inventory data for the firm's two primary products are shown in Exhibit P7.5.1.

Exhibit P7.5.2 shows cost data for Biojoint's two primary products under the present system and using EDI. In addition to producing changes in variable costs, the EDI system reduces the levels of supplies used in ordering. Furthermore, reduced inventory levels will permit Biojoint to vacate 2,000 square feet of space, thereby reducing lease payments to the owner of the building as allowed in the lease agreement. Adoption of EDI will permit reductions in staffing levels for both move labor and maintenance.

---

[17] A. Faye Borthick and Harold P. Roth, "EDI for Reengineering Business Processes," *Management Accounting*, Oct. 1993, pp. 32–37.

EXHIBIT P7.5.2 BIOJOINT

Cost of Ordering and Carrying Inventory

	Present System			EDI System
	Activity Cost	Activity Driver	Activity Cost	Activity Driver
Variable ordering cost:				
Forms & supplies	$10.00	No. of orders		
Materials management system	$15.00	No. of orders	$15.00	No. of orders
Phone, communication	$25.00	No. of orders	$75.00	No. of orders
Variable carrying cost:				
Insurance	2.00%	% of avg. $ value of inv.	2.00%	% of avg. $ value of inv.
Interest	14.00%	% of avg. $ value of inv.	14.00%	% of avg. $ value of inv.
Security	$2.00	per $100 of inv.	$2.00	per $100 of inv.
Intangible property taxes	5.00%	% of avg. $ value of inv.	5.00%	% of avg. $ value of inv.
Fixed ordering cost:				
Salaries (including 35% benefits)		$72,900		$72,900
Supplies		$3,500		$1,500
Fixed carrying cost:				
Occupancy (leased @ $8/square foot)	6,000	square feet	4,000	square feet
Equipment (depreciation)		$10,000		$10,000
Move labor ($6.75 per hour)	2,500	move labor-hr	1,500	move labor-hr
Maintenance ($8.50 per hour)	500	maintenance hr	300	maintenance hr

Required:

1. Calculate the following under the present system and the proposed EDI system for Biojoint's two primary products:
   a. Average daily usage (annual usage/250 days)
   b. Order quantity (average daily usage × lead time)
   c. Orders per year (annual usage/order quantity)
   d. Average inventory (order quantity/2)
   e. Average inventory cost (average inventory × unit cost)
2. Calculate the net benefit (loss) of EDI over the present system.

P7.6 (Inventories; EOQ)

Part I

Porter Chemicals, a division of LaGustrum Industries, manufactures a petroleum-based product used in manufacturing a paint solvent. After several dry ingredients are added to a petroleum base, the final product is packaged in drums and sold directly to paint manufacturers. Porter Chemicals uses several raw materials. However, one ingredient, called B403, accounts for nearly all of the total dollar and physical volume of materials. Porter, which normally uses 50,000 drums of B403 each year, employs two people whose sole responsibilities are to negotiate prices and deal with B403 suppliers. Over the last 2 years, B403 has cost Porter an average of $32 per drum. Because B403 plays such a key role in manufacturing, Porter maintains a small warehouse and staff to manage inventories of the ingredient.

Porter currently places 48 orders per year for B403. However, several managers have suggested that an economic order quantity (EOQ) approach to order size might help reduce costs. Current ordering and carrying costs are shown in Exhibit P7.6.

An explanation of each line item (general ledger account) in Exhibit P7.6 is as follows:

Ordering Cost

- *Direct labor and benefits.* Porter employs two full-time workers. Each is paid by salary. One earns $30,000 including benefits, while the other earns $24,000 including benefits.
- *Supplies.* Supplies vary directly with the number of B403 orders placed.
- *General liability insurance.* Rates charged by the insurance company are based on the number of square feet in the warehouse.
- *Equipment depreciation.* Depreciation for office equipment, phone systems, and computers.
- *Maintenance.* Routine, scheduled maintenance on facility and equipment.
- *Data processing/IS.* The data processing and information system services are provided by LaGustrum. The cost of maintaining and operating the system is fixed. The charges from LaGustrum to Porter are based on the number of computer minutes Porter uses. Computer minutes are directly related to the number of orders for B403.

EXHIBIT P7.6 PORTER CHEMICALS

Selected General Ledger Accounts

Ordering Cost	
Direct labor & benefits	$54,000
Supplies	1,500
General liability insurance	15,000
Equipment depreciation	6,500
Maintenance	660
Data processing/IS	2,500
Phone/data communications	4,000
Facility depreciation	3,600
Security	2,250
Corporate overhead	5,400
Total annual ordering cost	$95,410

Carrying Cost	
Direct labor & benefits	$ 71,000
Supplies	12,000
Contents insurance	8,000
Interest	12,000
Equipment depreciation	20,000
Maintenance	4,400
Data processing/IS	1,250
Facility depreciation	18,000
Security	11,250
Corporate overhead	7,100
Total annual carrying cost	$165,000

- *Phone/data communications.* Phone and network linkup charges are driven by the volume of orders for B403.
- *Facility depreciation.* Facility depreciation is the square-foot charge for space utilization.
- *Security.* Security costs are based on square feet occupied.
- *Corporate overhead.* Corporate overhead is charged to Porter at 10 percent of direct labor and benefits costs.

Carrying Costs

- *Direct labor and benefits.* Direct labor and benefits comprises two full-time salaried workers at $22,000 each, including benefits, plus two part-time workers. The part-time workers, who are paid on an hourly basis, are called in when needed to help salaried employees off-load deliveries of B403 and move materials into the warehouse. When there is no work, the part-time workers are sent home. Each part-time worker earns an average of about $13,500 per year.
- *Supplies.* Supplies vary in direct proportion with the size of the average inventory.
- *Contents insurance.* Warehouse insurance is based on the average dollar amount of inventory.
- *Interest.* Financing charges are based on the average dollar amount of inventory.
- *Equipment depreciation.* Depreciation for warehouse equipment.
- *Maintenance.* Scheduled, routine maintenance for the facility and equipment.
- *Data processing/IS.* Data processing and information system services are provided by LaGustrum. The cost of maintaining and operating the system is fixed. Charges from LaGustrum to Porter are based on the number of computer minutes Porter uses. Computer minutes are directly related to the average number of units in the inventory.
- *Facility depreciation.* The square-foot charge for use of space.
- *Security.* Security costs are based on square feet occupied.
- *Corporate overhead.* Overhead is charged to Porter at 10 percent of direct labor and benefits costs.

Required:

1. Separate total ordering and carrying cost into fixed and variable components. Calculate the cost per order and the carrying cost per unit.
2. Calculate the EOQ for B403 based on full ordering and carrying cost. That is, include both variable and fixed costs in your computations. Use the approach shown in the text rather than the EOQ formula. Create a column for order size, starting at 250 and ending at 1,000, in steps of 25 units. Then calculate the number of orders, total ordering cost, average inventory, carrying cost, and total cost.
3. Recalculate the EOQ, using only variable cost. Use the same approach as in requirement 1, above. Which EOQ computation is correct—the EOQ based on full cost or that based on variable cost?
4. Calculate the cost to Porter of ordering using an EOQ based on full cost rather than on variable cost.

Part II
Assume Porter, prior to making any changes in its ordering system, decides to form a long-term, sole-source arrangement with Brown Industrial Products, one of its

suppliers. Rather than delivering B403 in the quantities calculated according to the EOQ in requirement 1, above, Brown has agreed to make deliveries on each of Porter's 250 working days.

As a result of the arrangement with Brown, Porter expects to release the lower-paid, full-time ordering worker. In addition, Porter believes general liability insurance will decrease to about half of its present level. Equipment depreciation and maintenance will be unaffected. Data processing/IS charges for ordering are expected to decline to $400. Facility depreciation and security costs will be unaffected by the new arrangement with Brown. Charges for corporate overhead will decrease, because of the release of the ordering worker. However, no changes in total cost is expected at the corporate level. Variable carrying cost will change to reflect the new level of inventory. Fixed carrying cost will remain unchanged.

Required: Calculate the incremental benefit (cost) of the delivery arrangement with Brown.

P7.7 (Special Order)

Auerbach Industries received an order for a piece of special machinery from Jay Company. Just as Auerbach completed the machine, Jay Company declared bankruptcy, defaulted on the order, and forfeited the 10 percent deposit paid on the seling price of $72,500.

Auerbach's manufacturing manager identified the costs already incurred in the production of the special machinery for Jay Company, as shown in Exhibit P7.7.1.

Kaytell Corporation is willing to buy the special machinery if it is reworked to Kaytell's specifications. Auerbach offered to sell the reworked machinery to Kaytell as a special order for $68,400. Kaytell agreed to remit the full price when it takes delivery, in 2 months time. The additional identifiable costs to rework the machinery to Kaytell's specifications consist of direct materials costing $6,200 and direct labor of $4,200.

A second alternative available to Auerbach is to convert the special machinery to the standard model, which sells for $62,500. The additional identifiable costs for this conversion include direct materials costing $2,850 and a direct labor cost of $3,300.

A third alternative for Auerbach is to sell the machine "as is" for a price of $52,000. However, the potential buyer of the unmodified machine does not want it for 60 days. This buyer has offered a $7,000 down payment, with the remainder due upon delivery.

EXHIBIT P7.7.1 AUERBACH INDUSTRIES	
Cost Incurred for Special Machinery	
Direct materials	$16,600
Direct labor	21,400
Manufacturing overhead applied:	
Variable	10,700
Fixed	5,350
Selling & administrative—fixed	5,405
Total cost	$59,455

EXHIBIT P7.7.2 AUERBACH INDUSTRIES		
Allocation Rates		
Cost	Rate	Allocation Basis
Variable manufacturing overhead	50.00%	Direct labor cost
Fixed manufacturing overhead	25.00%	Direct labor cost
Fixed selling & administrative	10.00%	Total direct materials, direct labor, & manufacturing overhead cost

The following additional information is available regarding Auerbach's operations:

- The sales commission rate on sales of standard models is 2 percent, while the rate on special orders and "as is" sales is 3 percent.
- Normal credit terms for sales of standard models are 2/10, net/30. This means that a customer receives a 2 percent discount if payment is made within 10 days, and payment is due no later than 30 days after billing. Most customers take the 2 percent discount. Credit terms for a special order are negotiated with the customer.
- Normal time required for rework is 1 month.
- The allocation rates for manufacturing overhead and fixed selling and administrative costs are shown in Exhibit P7.7.2.

Required:

1. Determine the total contribution from each of the three alternatives.
2. If Kaytell makes Auerbach a counteroffer, what is the lowest price Auerbach should accept for the reworked machinery from Kaytell?

(CMA Adapted)

P7.8   (Make or Buy Decision)

Sportway Inc. is a wholesale distributor supplying a wide range of moderately priced sporting equipment to large chain stores. About 60 percent of Sportway's products are purchased from other companies; the remainder of the products are manufactured by Sportway. The company has a plastics department that is currently manufacturing molded fishing tackle boxes. Sportway is able to manufacture and sell 8,000 tackle boxes annually, making full use of its direct labor capacity at available workstations. Sportway's workers are paid according to the number of boxes they make. However, no overtime is available, and, due to the special skills required to make the tackle boxes, no additional hours are available from any other workers. Exhibit P7.8.1 shows the selling price of and costs associated with Sportway's tackle boxes.

Sportway believes it could sell as many as 12,000 tackle boxes if it had sufficient manufacturing capacity. Consequently, one of the alternatives the company has looked into is the possibility of purchasing the tackle boxes from another manufacturer. Maple Products, a steady supplier of quality products, would be able to provide as many tackle boxes per year as Sportway needed at a price of $68 per box.

EXHIBIT P7.8.1 SPORTWAY INC.

Unit Selling Price and Cost of a Tackle Box

Selling price per box	$86.00
Cost per box:	
Molded plastic	$ 8.00
Hinges, latches, & handle	9.00
Direct labor ($15 per hour)	18.75
Manufacturing overhead	12.50
Selling & administrative cost	17.00
Total cost per box	$65.25
Profit per box	$20.75

EXHIBIT P7.8.2 SPORTWAY INC.

Unit Selling Price and Cost of a Skateboard

Selling price per skateboard	$45.00
Cost per skateboard:	
Molded plastic	$ 5.50
Wheels & hardware	7.00
Direct labor ($15 per hour)	7.50
Manufacturing overhead	5.00
Selling & administrative cost	9.00
Total cost per skateboard	$34.00
Profit per skateboard	$11.00

Bart Johnson, Sportway's product manager, has suggested that the company could make better use of its plastics department by manufacturing skateboards. To support his position, Johnson has provided a market study that indicates an expanding market for skateboards and a need for additional suppliers. Johnson believes that Sportway could expect to sell 17,500 skateboards annually at a price of $45 per skateboard. Johnson's estimate of the cost to manufacture the skateboards is presented in Exhibit P7.8.2.

In the plastics department, Sportway uses direct labor-hours as the basis for applying manufacturing overhead. Included in the manufacturing overhead for the current year is $50,000 of factorywide, fixed manufacturing overhead. For each unit of product that Sportway sells, regardless of whether the product has been purchased or is manufactured by Sportway, there is an allocated $6 fixed overhead cost per unit for distribution. This cost is included in the selling and administrative cost for all products. Total selling and administrative cost for the purchased tackle boxes would be $10 per unit.

Required: Prepare an analysis that will show which product or products Sportway Inc. should manufacture and/or purchase in order to maximize the company's profitability and that will show the associated financial impact.

(CMA Adapted)

P7.9   (Discontinue Product Line)

Sporto Products manufactures four related product lines. Each product is made at one or more of the firm's manufacturing facilities. The product-line income statement, shown in Exhibit P7.9.1, indicates a net loss for the baseball equipment in 1995. A loss of similar magnitude is expected for 1996.

All of the baseball equipment is manufactured at Sporto's Evanston plant. In addition, some of the football equipment and miscellaneous sports items are manufactured at the Evanston plant. A separate production line is used at the Evanston plant to manufacture each product line.

The data shown in Exhibit P7.9.2 present the operating cost incurred at the Evanston plant in 1995. Inventories at the end of the year were identical to those at the beginning of the year.

As a result of the year-end financials, Sporto's management requested a study of baseball equipment in order to determine if the line should be discontinued. Marketing and accounting developed the following additional data to use in the study:

- If the baseball equipment line is discontinued, the company will lose approximately 10 percent of its sales in each of the other lines.
- If baseball equipment is discontinued, the machinery used in making baseball equipment will be scrapped. The equipment has no salvage value and a book value of zero.
- The plant space now occupied by the baseball equipment line will be segregated from the rest of the plant and rented out for $175,000 per year.
- If the baseball equipment line is discontinued, the supervisor of the line will be reassigned to the hockey equipment production line.
- All production line workers on the baseball equipment line will be released if Sporto decides to stop making baseball equipment. None of these workers is eligible for severance pay.

Required: Should Sporto discontinue its baseball equipment line?

(CMA Adapted)

P7.10   (Eliminating a Product Line)

GaugeCore makes three different kinds of gauges, identified internally as D-gauges, P-gauges, and T-gauges. For years GaugeCore has been profitable, almost always operating at or near practical capacity. However, in the last 2 years GaugeCore has had to reduce its prices on all gauges and to increase selling expenses to meet competition. As a result of these efforts, GaugeCore has been able to keep the plant operating at capacity. The operating results for the current year, shown in Exhibit P7.10.1, typify its recent experience.

Roberta Diaz, GaugeCore's president, is concerned about the firm's future. She has requested a review of the company's policies on pricing, selling, and production. After receiving the operating results of the current year, she asked her managers to consider the financial impact of the following suggestions:

- Discontinue the T-gauge line immediately. T-gauges would not be returned to the product line unless the problems with the gauges can be identified and resolved. Eliminate all advertising and promotion costs on T-gauges.
- Increase advertising and promotion costs by $100,000 per year on the P-gauge product line. This should increase sales volume of P-gauges by 15 percent.

EXHIBIT P7.9.1 SPORTO PRODUCTS

Product-Line Profit for the Year 1995

	Football Equipment	Baseball Equipment	Hockey Equipment	Miscellaneous Sports Items	Total
Sales	$2,200,000	$1,000,000	$1,500,000	$500,000	$5,200,000
Cost of goods sold:					
Direct materials	$ 400,000	$175,000	$ 300,000	$ 90,000	$965,000
Direct labor & variable overhead	800,000	400,000	600,000	60,000	1,860,000
Fixed overhead	350,000	275,000	100,000	50,000	775,000
Total cost of goods sold	$1,550,000	$850,000	$1,000,000	$200,000	$3,600,000
Gross profit	650,000	150,000	500,000	300,000	1,600,000
Selling expense:					
Variable	440,000	200,000	300,000	100,000	1,040,000
Fixed	100,000	50,000	100,000	50,000	300,000
Corporate administration expense	48,000	24,000	36,000	12,000	120,000
Total expense	$ 588,000	$274,000	$436,000	$162,000	$1,460,000
Total profit	$62,000	$(124,000)	$64,000	$138,000	$140,000

EXHIBIT P7.9.2 SPORTO PRODUCTS

Cost of Operating the Evanston Plant for the Year 1995

	Football Equipment	Baseball Equipment	Miscellaneous Sports Items	Total
Direct materials	$100,000	$175,000	$90,000	$365,000
Direct labor	$100,000	$200,000	$30,000	$330,000
Variable overhead:				
Supplies	$85,000	$60,000	$12,000	$157,000
Power	50,000	110,000	7,000	167,000
Other	15,000	30,000	11,000	56,000
Total variable overhead	$150,000	$200,000	$30,000	$380,000
Fixed overhead:				
Supervision[a]	$25,000	$30,000	$21,000	$76,000
Depreciation[b]	40,000	115,000	14,000	169,000
Plant rentals[c]	35,000	105,000	10,000	150,000
Other[d]	20,000	25,000	5,000	50,000
Total fixed overhead	$120,000	$275,000	$50,000	$445,000
Total cost	$470,000	$850,000	$200,000	$1,520,000

[a] Supervision represents salary & benefits cost for supervisors for each product line.

[b] Depreciation for machinery & equipment is charged to the product line on which the machinery is used.

[c] The Evanston plant is leased. Lease rental cost is charged to product lines based on square feet occupied.

[d] Other fixed overhead represents the cost of plant administration. It is charged to product lines based on product-line revenue.

- Cut production on the D-gauge line by 50 percent. Cut advertising and promotion on the D-gauge line by $20,000. That is, reduce advertising and promotion on the D-gauge line from $100,000 to $80,000.

Julia Lemon, GaugeCore's controller, indicated that Diaz's suggestions provided a useful starting point for dealing with some of the company's problems. However, she suggested a more careful study be made in order to determine the possible effects of Diaz's proposals on GaugeCore's operating results. After listening to Lemon, Diaz agreed and assigned preparation of such an analysis to Mike McKeskil, the assistant controller. Part of the information McKeskil gathered is as follows:

- All three gauges are manufactured with common equipment and facilities.
- Direct labor costs are variable.
- Unit selling prices, unit manufacturing costs, and selling and administrative expense are shown in Exhibit P7.10.2.
- The company is operating its manufacturing facility at capacity and is selling all the gauges it produces.

Required: What is the financial impact of each of the three suggestions? Support your opinion with an analysis that shows the net impact on pretax operating income for each of the three suggestions.

(AICPA Adapted)

EXHIBIT P7.10.1 GAUGECORE

Income Statement for the Year

	D-Gauge	P-Gauge	T-Gauge	Total
Sales	$900,000	$1,600,000	$ 900,000	$3,400,000
Cost of goods sold	770,000	1,048,000	940,000	2,758,000
Gross margin	$130,000	$ 552,000	$ (40,000)	$ 642,000
Selling & administrative expense	185,000	370,000	135,000	690,000
Income before taxes	$ (55,000)	$ 182,000	$(175,000)	$ (48,000)

EXHIBIT P7.10.2 GAUGECORE

Unit Selling Prices, Manufacturing Cost, and Special Selling Expense

	D-Gauge	P-Gauge	T-Gauge
Selling price (per unit)	$90.00	$200.00	$180.00
Manufacturing cost (per unit):			
Raw materials	$17.00	$ 31.00	$ 50.00
Direct labor	20.00	40.00	60.00
Variable manufacturing overhead	30.00	45.00	58.00
Fixed manufacturing overhead	10.00	15.00	20.00
Total manufacturing cost (per unit)	$77.00	$131.00	$188.00
Selling & administrative expenses:			
Advertising & promotion (total)	$100,000	$210,000	$40,000
Shipping expense (per unit)	$4.00	$10.00	$10.00
Other fixed expenses (total)	$45,000	$80,000	$45,000

P7.11 (Dealing with Uncertainty)

Putt Trainer, a startup company, plans to manufacture a new line of golfing products. Putt's founder, Robert Alvarez, invented a mechanism that helps golfers improve their putt by keeping the swing of their club straight. Putt Trainer will offer two models, each having the same basic design. The deluxe model, known as the Maxi-Putt, uses electronics to guide the golfer's swing, while the lower-priced Mini-Putt is based on a mechanical design.

Putt Trainer is preparing a business plan for potential investors that outlines expected performance. In light of the risks, potential investors are interested in the likelihood that the new company will achieve at least pretax breakeven profit. Alvarez gathered the following data as a basis for evaluating the likelihood of achieving breakeven profit:

- The price for the Maxi-Putt is expected to be $125 but could range from a low of $110 to a high of $135. The price of the Mini-Putt is expected to be $25, with a range of $20 to $30.
- Estimates of sales volume for the Maxi-Putt are dependent on price. Alvarez believes that Putt Trainer will sell 162,500 units less 500 units multiplied by the price. That is, the number of units sold is equal to $162,500 - (500 \times \text{price})$. For example, at a price of $125, Alvarez expects a sales volume of 100,000 units [$162,500 - (500 \times \$125)$]. In contrast, sales volume for the Mini-Putt should equal about 55,000 units but could range between 50,000 and 60,000 units.
- Each Maxi-Putt requires two units of materials. Material cost is expected to equal $30, with a minimum of $25 per unit and a maximum of $40 per unit. The Mini-Putt requires only one unit of materials, at a known cost of $12.50 per unit.
- The rate paid to production workers is fixed through a long-term contract at $7.50 per hour. Workers are expected to make about 0.5 Maxi-Putt units per hour, but production rates could range between 0.4 and 0.6 units per worker per hour. Similarly, workers can make about 1.25 Mini-Putts per hour, with a range of 1.0 to 1.5 units per worker per hour.
- Managers are certain about variable manufacturing and nonmanufacturing overhead. It should average $6.75 per unit for the Maxi-Putt and $2.75 for the Mini-Putt. In addition, fixed overhead for both products combined is expected to total $1.75 million.
- Alvarez negotiated a lease that allows the landlord to participate when revenue exceeds $12.5 million. The lease calls for a base payment of $250,000 per year, plus 2 percent of the total combined revenue from both product lines in excess of $12.5 million.
- Income taxes are 38 percent of pretax profit. If Putt Trainer shows an operating loss, the tax saving will be passed on to investors to offset income from other investments. Assume the average tax rate for investors is also 38 percent.

Required:

1. Calculate after-tax net income for the company as a whole using the expected values (*Note:* Use the contribution margin format for all requirements of this problem.)
2. Calculate after-tax net income for the company as a whole for both the best-case and worst-case scenarios.

3. Perform sensitivity analysis. Calculate after-tax net income for each value of each variable subject to uncertainty. Follow the format in Exhibit 7.20 (in the text). After selecting a variable, start at the low end of the range, and increase each value using the following steps:

Steps in Increasing Values

	Maxi-Putt	Mini-Putt
Price	$5	$1
Volume	Not applicable	1,000 units
Materials price	$1	Not applicable
Production rate	0.05 units per hour	0.05 units per hour

Note: Make sure you leave the value of all other variables—those not being stepped—at their expected values!

4. What are the high-leverage variables?
5. Did any of the results of the sensitivity analysis in requirement 3 come near the results of the worst-case scenario? Why or why not?

P7.12   (Alternative Cost Structures for Two Investments; Uncertainty)[18]

The BigSteel Corporation owns several steel mills in Pennsylvania and Ohio. The company directors are currently considering acquisition of another plant. Several of the well-known U.S. steel producers recently pulled out of traditional markets, while others have gone out of the steelmaking business altogether. This offers unique opportunities for BigSteel. The problems steelmakers are having don't stem from demand, although recent soft economic conditions have not helped. The problem is supply. Overcapacity has plagued the industry, especially after the Japanese and Koreans entered the market after World War II. For example, Korea's Pohang Iron & Steel Company—or Posco, for short—built the third-largest mill in the world 20 years ago. With new equipment and labor costs of about $11 per hour, it represents a formidable global competitor.

BigSteel is looking at investment in two existing U.S. Mills. Since changes in the industry have made investment necessary to become a world-class competitor, BigSteel believes that now is the right time to acquire another U.S. mill. The trouble is, what kind of facility offers the best potential for profitability and long-term growth?

At a recent board meeting, the discussion about new plant acquisitions began with a presentation by Bill Hobby:

Bill Hobby (VP—manufacturing): Before we can make any kind of decision, I think it's important to review what's happening in the industry. You all have heard about integrated mills, and some of you are aware of the newer minimills. But, to make sure, let me quickly review how they operate.

First of all, the conventional mills—the ones we all think about when we

---

[18]   This problem relies on materials from *Standard & Poor's Industry Surveys: Steel, & Heavy Machinery*, Dec. 24, 1992; Dana Milbank, "Minimill Inroads in Sheet Market Rouse Big Steel," *The Wall Street Journal*, Mar. 9, 1992, p. B1; Dana Milbank, "Big Steel Is Threatened by Low-Cost Rivals, Even in Japan, Korea," *The Wall Street Journal*, Feb. 2, 1993, p. A1.

hear the words *steel mill*—are referred to as *integrated plants.* In these facilities, lumps of iron ore, limestone, and coke are charged together in a blast furnace to make pig iron. The next step is to refine the pig iron into steel by removing the carbon. That's done in another furnace. The resulting steel is cast into ingots, which are then broken down into different sizes and shapes—including slabs, billets, and blooms. These shapes then go into "rolling mills," where they are formed into products, such as sheets of steel. At some plants, slabs are transported from the refining furnace to other parts of the factory—perhaps as far as 2 miles away—where rolling mills are located. In some of the older mills, this process can take as long as a week.

One improvement in traditional processing methods is called *continuous casting,* where molten steel is converted directly into the solid shapes. This greatly improves efficiency by knocking out steps and increasing thru-put time. Many of the Japanese and European mills have already adopted this technology, allowing them to lower prices. Americans, however, with older mills, have resisted investments in new technology for several reasons, one of which is the disincentive for managers to make new investments when they have high ROIs (returns on investment). However, that changed in the 1980s, and the Americans are beginning to catch up. Production of continuous cast steel, representing 75 percent of the total 1991 industry production, is up from 15 percent in 1980. At present, more than 80 percent of the EEC (European Economic Community) mills and 90 percent of the Japanese mills use continuous castings. In 1992, U.S. Steel, the largest American steelmaker, achieved a 100 percent continuous-casting rate. Both Inland Steel and Armco are also at 100 percent, with the remaining U.S. producers close behind. Predictions are that the United States will soon be at parity with its global rivals.

The biggest challenge, though, comes from minimills. Minimills accounted for about 25 percent of industry production in 1992. Minimills produce steel by melting recycled scrap in electric arc furnaces. They are generally smaller than traditional integrated mills and operate more efficiently. Moreover, the investment in a minimill is about one-fourth the cost of an integrated mill. And that's not all. Labor costs are often lower at minimills, since they need fewer workers to make a ton of steel. And most of these workers are nonunion, compensated based on productivity. For example, it takes Nucor, a minimill, between 0.7 and 1.3 worker hours to produce a ton of steel, while it takes U.S. Steel's 86-year-old Gary, Indiana, plant nearly 3 hours to do so.

There's a downside to minimills, though. Typically, they make only a limited line of commodity products, such as steel bars or structural beams used in construction. In other steel markets, the minimills have not yet achieved the quality levels of the integrated mills. A good example is sheet steel production, where quality is important in making the wide, high-quality, coated sheet steel used for auto bodies. Minimills leave excess scale on the metal. As a result, rejection rates can run as high as 10 percent, considerably higher than those typical for integrated mill products.

Pat Fishback (president, CEO): Thanks, Bill, that was a great background. It sounds like we need to decide which direction we want to take. The integration path leads us one way, while the minimills take us in another direction.

Bill Hobby: Well, not necessarily. The distinction between the two is blurring. Minimills are starting to enter markets dominated by the integrators. To do so successfully—unless they discover some new technology—they are going to have to invest in some of the processes that integrated mills use. I'm not ruling out new technology, since the minimills spend a lot in that area. So it's quite possible they'll find a way. Labor costs are coming down through automation, the use of continuous casting, and union concessions. And, to cut costs, some integrated mills are planning to incorporate minimills into their operations.

Susan Webster (VP—marketing): Well, perhaps some market data will help. I've put together figures on steel production, capacity, and utilization, plus some price data for the years 1982 through 1991 (Exhibit P7.12.1). By the way, I'll use industry shipments as a base for measuring market share. Projections for 1992 shipments are 80 million tons. For 1993, the estimate increases to 83 million tons. As you can see, average prices have fluctuated from as low as $346 to as high as $389. But, remember, these are only averages—prices may be as high as $450 to $475 per ton for some products. Recently, prices have been relatively low because of the problem of overcapacity. With changes in the industry, and consolidations such as those we are planning, capacity might decline and prices increase.

Pat Fishback: OK. Now, with that background, let's talk about the two specific mills under consideration, both of which are known to be for sale. The first is Pittsburgh-National (PN), a traditional integrated mill. It is currently running at about 95 percent continuous casting and has one of the best thru-put times of all American mills. PN is an older mill located in Indiana, near many of the automobile manufacturers. The other choice is NuSteel, one of the newer minimills. It has relatively low labor-hour requirements per ton and is located near a good, steady source of recyclable materials. Bill (Bill Hobby, VP—manufacturing), can you jump in here and give us more-specific data on both of these mills?

Bill Hobby: Sure can, Pat! I can add to Susan's figures with some rough production and cost data. You will see it all in a schedule I have prepared (Exhibit P7.12.2).

Pat Fishback: OK, I think the next step is to figure this all out. Dave (David Perez, controller), will you put together an analysis of potential pretax profitability based on market predictions for 1993?

EXHIBIT P7.12.1 STEEL INDUSTRY PRODUCTION, CAPACITY, UTILIZATION, AND PRICES (IN MILLIONS OF TONS)

For the Years 1982 through 1991

Year	Industry Capacity	Industry Production	Industry Shipments	Exports	Imports	Apparent Supply	Sales (Millions of $s)	Average Price per Ton
1982	154.1	74.6	61.6	1.80	16.70	76.4		
1983	150.6	84.6	67.6	1.20	17.10	83.5		
1984	135.3	92.5	73.0	1.00	26.20	98.2		
1985	133.5	88.3	72.7	0.90	24.30	96.0	$28,272.3	$389
1986	127.9	81.6	70.3	0.90	20.70	90.0	$24,875.2	$354
1987	112.1	89.2	76.7	1.10	19.90	95.4	$26,932.7	$351
1988	112.0	99.9	84.0	2.10	20.90	102.8	$32,465.7	$386
1989	115.9	97.9	84.1	4.60	17.30	96.8	$31,524.9	$375
1990	116.7	98.0	85.0	4.30	17.20	110.9	$30,635.2	$360
1991	117.7	87.3	78.9	6.30	15.70	96.7	$27,270.2	$346
1992 estimated			80.0					
1993 estimated			83.0					

Source: Standard & Poor's Industry Surveys: Steel & Heavy Machinery, Dec. 24, 1992, pp. S20–S29.

EXHIBIT P7.12.2 PITTSBURGH-NATIONAL AND NuSTEEL		
Production and Cost Data		
Production Data	NuSteel	Pittsburgh-National
Capacity (in tons)	1,000,000	3,500,000
Sales in 1991 (shipments in tons)	420,000	2,750,000
Total 1991 market (shipments in tons)	78,900,000	78,900,000
1991 market share (sales/total 1991 market)	0.5323%	3.4854%
Revenue and Cost Data		
Selling price (per ton)	$375	$400
Labor-hours (per ton)	1.00	2.75
Labor cost (per hour)	$28.00	$30.00
Percent Labor cost variable	45.00%	25.00%
Materials cost (per ton)	$220.00	$210.00
Plant overhead, excluding depreciation (% of materials & labor cost)	10.00%	25.00%
Percent plant overhead variable	25.00%	10.00%
Research & development (fixed)	$12,600,000	$9,400,000
Selling & marketing (35% variable)	$9,000,000	$12,600,000
Administration (10% variable)	$3,500,000	$11,500,000
Investment in plant (depreciated over 20 years)	$330,000,000	$1,240,000,000

Required:

1. Calculate pretax operating profit (including depreciation) for both mills, based on their 1991 operations, using the data in Exhibit P7.12.2. Use the contribution margin format. In addition, calculate:
   a. Return on sales (pretax operating profit/total revenue)
   b. Return on investment (pretax operating profit/investment in plant)
   c. Manufacturing cost per ton
   d. Full cost per ton
   e. Contribution margin per ton
   f. Total fixed cost
2. Prepare a schedule that estimates pretax operating profit for both mills at different industry volumes (shipments). Vary industry volume from 75 to 90 million tons in steps of 1 million tons. Assume that market share for both mills will not change from their respective 1991 shares. For both mills, calculate:
   a. Percent market share
   b. Pretax profit
   c. Percent of capacity utilized
3. Based on your analysis, and disregarding the acquisition price of the mills, what would you recommend to BigSteel's board?

CASES

C7.1 (Great Southern Bank)

Great Southern Bank, with headquarters in Richmond, Virginia, has 10 regional banking centers spread throughout Virginia, North Carolina, and Tennessee. Its assets, totaling about $60 million dollars, are made up mostly of loan and mortgage notes. Interest revenue stands at $7.2 million, with outlays for interest

EXHIBIT C7.1.1   GREAT SOUTHERN BANK

Condensed Income Statement

Interest margin:	
Interest revenue	$7,200,000
Interest expense	(5,400,000)
Interest margin	$1,800,000
Other income:	
Financial services	650,000
Fees & other charges	375,000
Net revenue:	$2,825,000
Operating expense	(2,075,000)
Net income before taxes	$ 750,000

expense at $5.4 million. Net income before tax, as shown in Exhibit C7.1.1, is $750,000 after adding revenue from other services and deducting operating expense.

One important internal service that Great Southern performs is auditing. According to Roy Kerr, Great Southern's VP for internal auditing (IA), internal audits are a good management practice, especially for banks, in safeguarding against fraud and theft. In addition, IA reviews alterations in computerized software and monitors the firm's management control system. Any changes in procedure that involve "who does what and how" are evaluated by IA for their impact on asset management. Finally, IA plays an important role in assuring compliance with state and federal banking regulations.

Great Southern is currently reviewing an internal study aimed at outsourcing IA.[19] It is not the first organization to consider outsourcing internal auditing. Other nonbanking companies, such as Clark Equipment, have successfully outsourced IA by selling the functions to the firm's IA management group. In Clark's case, a separate private corporation was created—now staffed by 75 people—that provides Clark with fee-based internal auditing and accounting-related management services.

CPA firms, which face declining audit fees, are looking for new markets. IA provides a logical niche for them. Besides supplying traditional internal auditing services, CPAs suggest that they can bring objectivity, consistency, and quality to IA, while giving clients a way of controlling costs. Objectivity is enhanced, according to the CPAs, by avoiding the employee-employer relationship. The cost advantage to Great Southern comes, in part, from the CPAs' ability to squeeze out more productive hours from their staff. For example, they save salary costs and overtime by requiring that travel be done outside working hours.

Sara Whiting, Great Southern's controller, is worried. Not only is she concerned about IA personnel, many of whom are her friends, but she is also concerned about the effect of outsourcing on the bank. Whiting concedes that firms in other industries might find benefits in outsourcing IA but asks how her bank will benefit. And, how will the regulators feel about it? Furthermore, who will provide the service?

---

[19]   The discussion of outsourcing internal auditing relies on an article by Curtis C. Verschoor, "Evaluating Outsourcing of Internal Auditing," *Management Accounting*, Feb. 1992, pp. 27–30.

Sue Crabill, VP for finance, is heading the outsourcing study. She knows of two other banking organizations that use CPAs for internal auditing—First American Corporation in Nashville and First Bank System in Minneapolis. In fact, First American, with $6 billion in assets, outsourced IA to its CPAs and eliminated 30 positions. Similarly, First Bank System eliminated 54 staff positions by outsourcing IA to its auditors. While it retained some IA functions in-house—such as compliance evaluations and special investigations—First Bank System decided to make the outsourcing move as part of its continuing efforts toward controlling costs.

In addition to some of the benefits already discussed, Crabill put together a list of pros and cons for outsourcing:[20]

Advantages of Outsourcing
- Costs are lower because of reduced billing rates. Much of the work will be performed during the CPAs' slow season. Furthermore, CPAs generally offer fewer benefits to their employees.
- CPAs will provide liability insurance to back up the quality of their work.
- CPAs can provide specialized expertise that is not available internally.
- If Great Southern uses its auditors, Cooper's & Ernst, as IA suppliers, combined fees for external and internal auditing might be lower than the going rate.
- The CPAs' reputation might enhance Great Southern's own reputation and the confidence of regulators.

Disadvantages of Outsourcing
- IA staff are available year-round, not just during the CPAs' slack season.
- Knowledge about Great Southern's operations is better retained with an internal staff, rather than being entrusted to CPAs, who experience high turnover.
- Changes may disrupt organizational harmony. Employees may be afraid of losing their jobs, with declines in morale and productivity.
- Use of external services may increase the likelihood that knowledge of Great Southern's business practices and strategies will reach outsiders.

After listing these pros and cons, Crabill began gathering the cost information she knew would be required by the bank's board in order to make a final decision. She started by obtaining a quote from Cooper's & Ernst. Based on a list of duties and activities to be performed by IA staff, Cooper's & Ernst quoted an average hourly rate of $65. Most of the work would be performed by the junior audit staff, to keep rates low. Cooper's & Ernst would require a 3-year contract guaranteeing a minimum of 750 hours each year. On the upside, Cooper's & Ernst is willing to place a cap on fees at 1,000 hours.

Gathering the costs of running IA was the next step. Details from the general ledger outlining operating costs, by function, are shown in Exhibit C7.1.2. The details of IA's costs are shown in Exhibit C7.1.3.

Crabill requested a breakdown of IA salaries from personnel. The results (Exhibit C7.1.4) indicate that IA employed three staff members, besides Kerr. With this information, Crabill began to sort out likely cost savings:

- *Salaries and benefits.* Benefits are 20 percent of salaries. After 15 years of service, employees are eligible for early retirement. Early retirement amounts are one-time payments calculated by dividing years of service by 15 and mul-

---

[20] Ibid., p. 29.

EXHIBIT C7.1.2 GREAT SOUTHERN BANK

Operating Expenses, by Function

Savings & time deposits	$ 385,000
Mortgage department	274,700
Commercial services	195,000
Trust department	140,200
Legal & title	210,000
Information systems	221,100
Internal auditing	174,800
Corporate offices	474,200
Total	$2,075,000

EXHIBIT C7.1.3 GREAT SOUTHERN BANK

Operating Expenses—Internal Auditing Department

	Total
Salaries & benefits:	
Salaries	$ 98,000
Benefits (20% of salaries)	19,600
Travel cost	11,900
Utilities cost	1,800
Paper & supplies	1,200
Depreciation—equipment	3,200
Facilities	12,000
Allocations:	
Information systems	7,500
Corporate (20% of salaries)	19,600
Total internal auditing department costs	$174,800

EXHIBIT C7.1.4 GREAT SOUTHERN BANK

Internal Auditing Department Personnel

Employee	Position	Salary	Years of Service
Kerr, Roy	VP—Internal auditing	$32,000	22
Gray, Jan	Senior auditor	27,500	17
Matulich, Serge	Junior auditor	20,000	3
Trifts, Jack	Junior auditor	18,500	2
Total		$98,000	

tiplying the results by the current annual salary (excluding benefits). Kerr, with 22 years of service, is likely to take early retirement and accept a job offer with Cooper's & Ernst. Jan Gray intends to stay with Great Southern and spend half of her time overseeing the contract with Cooper's & Ernst.

The other half of her time will be spent working with the information systems group, another department within Great Southern. Matulich and Trifts will be released.

- *Travel cost.* Since Cooper's & Ernst has offices in cities close to Great Southern's regional operations, travel cost will be cut in half.
- *Utilities cost.* One-half of the utilities cost will be eliminated.
- *Paper and supplies.* Eliminated in full.
- *Depreciation—equipment.* Equipment, consisting solely of computers, will be sold for $8,000, an amount equal to book value. No gain or loss will be recognized for tax purposes.
- *Facilities.* IA occupies 1,200 square feet in Great Southern's headquarters. The space will be used for storage.
- *Allocations—Information Systems.* Operations of information systems will not be affected by IA's departure.
- *Allocations—Corporate.* Corporate overhead, representing organizationwide activities, such as personnel, is charged to IA at a rate equal to 20 percent of salary cost. Outsourcing IA will result in the release of one secretary, who is ineligible for early retirement. Salary and benefits cost for the secretary is $14,500.

In addition, Crabill noted that outsourcing would cause a one-time payment of $9,000 to the firm's legal counsel. First, attorneys would structure employee-release documents in order to minimize litigation risks. Second, they would structure a contract and negotiate terms with Cooper's & Ernst.

Required:

1. Calculate the measurable avoidable and unavoidable cash costs and benefits. Make your computations without consideration of income taxes. Break them down into recurring and one-time costs and benefits. Then calculate how many years it will take to recover one-time costs.
2. What are some of the nonfinancial factors that Great Southern should consider in making its decision?
3. Is this a short-term or long-term decision?

C7.2 (Lawn Masters)

Harriet Nelson, president of Lawn Masters, recently received an offer from Values, a major national discount chain. While Nelson is excited by the prospect of selling products through national outlets, she is concerned about the long-term impact on Lawn Masters' future. Together with the firm's CFO, Barry Allen, Nelson is trying to determine what benefits Lawn Masters is likely to derive from the deal.

Lawn Masters, which has been in business for over 30 years, specializes in top-of-the-line lawn mowers. In the past, Lawn Masters offered a wide range of commercial and residential models. Based on a strategy of product diversity, it felt it could capture market share and compete with industry leaders. With the entry of strong competitors, the market quickly became overcrowded. As a result, some of the less efficient manufacturers decided to call it quits. In order to concentrate on what it felt was its core business, Lawn Masters scaled back operations. Today, it offers no commercial models and only two residential models: the 30-in, self-propelled Lawn Master and the 42-in riding Lawn King.

Lawn Masters sells its mowers through a network of independent lawn shops. Each shop is granted an exclusive distributorship covering a specific geographical area. In return, shop owners agree to limit their sales of other brands and to contribute 1 percent of their gross revenue from Lawn Masters' products to a national advertising fund. While the network has been successful in the past, Lawn Masters began to feel the pinch from competition by national discounters such as Kmart and Target. Consumers find it easier to shop at warehouse-type stores, where they can purchase mowers at deep discounts.

Nelson recognized that the trend in mowers is based on price competition. Accordingly, she felt that the role played by independent lawn mower shops, whose primary contribution is service, might be changing. Some shop owners, when questioned, felt their future was in repairs. In contrast, other shop owners had already built large lawn superstores, selling a wide variety of mowers and lawn care products. In fact, several of these superstores had violated their agreements with Lawn Masters, and their contracts were immediately dropped. But the future of the independents and the trends they represented clearly worried Nelson.

The Values offer is for 4,500 low-cost Lawn Masters at $175 per mower. Several of Lawn Masters' managers wanted to cease all discussions with Values, since the Values offer was well below the full cost of $195. However, Nelson tried to negotiate price with Values' representatives. Her efforts were unsuccessful. Values simply would not budge. Values stated that the offer was based on market research indicating that enough mowers would sell at around $220 to justify carrying the Lawn Master model. Working backward, Values felt that $175 was the most it could pay if it was to make the kind of return it required on the deal. On the positive side, Lawn Masters would not incur any marketing costs, since the deal came directly to Nelson. In addition, Lawn Masters has sufficient capacity to make as many as 40,000 mowers annually, well above the 25,000 mowers it normally makes each year.

Mowers made for Values would require only minor modifications. Specifically, Values models would be painted a different color from Lawn Masters' mowers and would carry the Values brand name. Other than these changes, the Values model would be exactly the same as the Lawn Master model. These changes cause virtually no change in cost as compared with the present Lawn Master model.

In evaluating the offer, Nelson asked Barry Allen to collect data on the standard costs to make and distribute the company's two models. The results are shown in Exhibit C7.2.1. Allen also supplied a copy of the budgeted income statement, without including the Values deal, shown in Exhibit C7.2.2. When asked about cost behavior, Allen stated that all materials costs (components and parts) are variable, as is 20 percent of the forming and assembly labor cost. Indirect manufacturing cost contains both fixed and variable components. All other manufacturing costs and all selling and administrative cost are fixed with respect to the number of mowers manufactured and sold.

Even though several of the managers at Lawn Masters still wanted to terminate negotiations, Nelson decided to continue the talks with Values. Their discussions now focused on the mechanics of how and when mowers were to be delivered. At present, Lawn Masters holds inventories of finished goods averaging about 15 percent of the annual demand. This is the result of a decision, made several years ago, to adopt level production. During the winter months, Lawn Masters builds inventories that are then "drawn down" as the weather warms and demand picks up.

During the discussions, Values representatives indicated they would require inventories of finished lawn mowers at levels enabling them to take delivery on as many as 50 percent of the total annual demand at any one time. Values requires this feature in all contracts because of its distribution network, which uses large regional distribution centers. Clearly, additional finished-goods inventories

EXHIBIT C7.2.1 LAWN MASTERS		
Standard Cost per Unit		
	Lawn Master	Lawn King
Revenue	$250.00	$500.00
Manufacturing cost:		
Raw materials (components & parts)	$ 73.50	$137.75
Forming & assembly labor	62.50	179.00
Manufacturing overhead:		
Depreciation—facility & equipment	3.00	4.00
Supervision	0.75	0.75
Indirect manufacturing	15.25	18.50
Total manufacturing overhead	$ 19.00	$ 23.25
Total manufacturing cost	$155.00	$340.00
Gross profit	$95.00	$160.00
Selling & administrative cost:		
Sales & promotion salaries	$14.00	$24.00
Administrative salaries	9.50	16.50
Administrative facilities	16.50	44.50
Total selling & administrative cost	$40.00	$85.00
Full cost	$195.00	$425.00
Net income:		
Net income before income taxes	$55.00	$75.00
Income taxes (34%)	18.70	25.50
Net income	$36.30	$49.50
Return on sales	14.52%	9.90%

increase the costs to Lawn Masters and reduce the attractiveness of the contract. When combined with the average inventories of raw materials, parts, and components, which are normally maintained at 20 percent of annual demand, and work-in-process inventories normally equal to 10 percent of annual demand, the resulting total additional cost of inventories alone might jeopardize the deal. Ending inventories of work in process, on the average, are 100 percent complete with respect to raw materials and 50 percent complete with respect to direct labor and manufacturing overhead.

To help assess the impact on inventories, Allen commissioned an in-house evaluation of costs related to carrying inventories for the Lawn Master model. All inventory-related costs are classified as indirect manufacturing cost. The results, together with data on cost behavior, are shown in Exhibit C7.2.3. Some of the costs—off-loading, moving, forklift depreciation, recordkeeping, and pilferage—vary with the number of units in the average inventory. Other costs vary with the dollar value of the average inventory, such as interest (11.41% of average materials, work-in-process, and finished-goods inventories) and intangible property taxes (2.2 percent of average finished-goods inventory). The cost of all other activities contained in indirect manufacturing is fixed.

Nelson asked Allen to assess the impact of the Values deal on existing sales of the Lawn Master models. According to Allen, who had spoken to the marketing director, a reasonable estimate of the number of units that would be lost as

EXHIBIT C7.2.2 LAWN MASTERS

Budgeted Income Statement (at Normal Volume)

	Lawn Master	Lawn King	Total
Revenue:			
Selling price	$250	$500	
Units sold	16,450	8,550	25,000
Total revenue	$4,112,500	$4,275,000	$8,387,500
Manufacturing cost:			
Raw materials (components & parts)	$1,209,075.00	$1,177,762.50	$2,386,837.50
Forming & assembly labor	1,028,125.00	1,530,450.00	2,558,575.00
Depreciation—facility & equipment	49,350.00	34,200.00	83,550.00
Supervision	12,337.50	6,412.50	18,750.00
Indirect manufacturing	250,862.50	158,175.00	409,037.50
Total manufacturing cost	$2,549,750.00	$2,907,000.00	$5,456,750.00
Gross profit	$1,562,750	$1,368,000	$2,930,750
Selling & administrative cost:			
Sales & promotion salaries	$230,300	$205,200	$ 435,500
Administrative salaries	156,275	141,075	297,350
Administrative facilities	271,425	380,475	651,900
Total selling & administrative cost	$658,000	$726,750	$1,384,750
Net income before income taxes	$904,750	$641,250	$1,546,000
Income taxes (34%)	$307,615	218,025	525,640
Net income	$597,135	$423,225	$1,020,360
Return on sales	14.52%	9.90%	12.17%

customers bought Lawn Master models from Values rather than through traditional outlets was about 5 percent.

Nelson's approach to decision making starts by looking at all of the solid, quantifiable factors. As long as they look promising, she is then willing to assess the nonquantifiable ramifications. One downside of the Values opportunity, other than the low price, is that the contract covers only one year. However, if the relationship proves agreeable to both parties, Nelson feels that Values would probably offer Lawn Masters a long-term contract.

Required:

1. Calculate the average number of units presently carried in materials, work in process, and finished goods for the Lawn Master model. Then calculate the average total cost of the raw materials, work-in-process, and finished goods inventories for the Lawn Master model. (*Hint:* Calculate equivalent whole-unit cost for direct labor and manufacturing overhead in the work-in-process inventory).
2. Calculate the variable carrying cost for the raw materials, work-in-process, and finished goods inventories for the Lawn Master model. Express the variable cost (including carrying costs that vary with the dollar value of the average inventory) as a unit cost based on the average levels of raw materials, work-in-process, and finished goods inventories.

EXHIBIT C7.2.3 LAWN MASTERS

Analysis of Indirect Manufacturing Costs Carrying Costs for Lawn Master Model

	Total Cost	Percent Variable	Inventory Effected[a]
Costs that vary with the no. of units in average inventory:			
Off-loading	$ 70,000	60.00%	Materials
Moving goods to storage	17,500	75.00%	Materials
Depreciation fork lift	5,000	0.00%	Materials
Recordkeeping	7,500	0.00%	Materials, WIP, & FG
Pilferage	2,000	50.00%	FG
Total	$102,000		
Costs that vary with dollar value of average inventory:			
Interest (11.41% of all inventories)	$92,674	100.00%	Materials, WIP, & FG
Intangible property taxes (2.2% of finished-goods inventory)	8,414	100.00%	FG
Total carrying costs	$101,088		
Other indirect manufacturing costs (all fixed)	47,775		
Total indirect manufacturing cost Lawn Master model	$250,863		

[a] "WIP" is work in process and "FG" is finished goods.

---

3. Calculate (a) the increase in costs caused by carrying the additional 4,500 units of the Lawn Master model in the inventories if the Values contract is accepted and (b) the decrease in carrying cost arising from the projected loss in sales of the Lawn Master model through normal channels.
4. Calculate the after-tax net benefit (cost) of the Values special order.
5. What are some of the long-term strategic factors that Lawn Masters might want to consider before reaching a final decision? What should Lawn Masters do?

CHAPTER

8

LONG-TERM DECISIONS— CAPITAL BUDGETING

In this chapter, we leave our discussion of routine, short-term decisions—the ones having little or no impact beyond the immediate future—and turn our attention to decisions that have long-lasting impacts.

Organizations have a *general* idea of the direction in which they are headed, which is often expressed in abstract mission statements. However, it is the long-term programs and projects that identify and define specifically the strategic markets the firm will pursue. (See "Current Practice: RJR Nabisco Plans New Ovens.") Building a new facility, funding research, investing in laborsaving devices, downsizing operations, creating a new organization—all of these are long-term decisions requiring investments aimed specifically at the markets in which the firm will participate.

Loosely defined, **capital budgeting** is the linkage between the corporate vision and the resources—the personnel, materials, and equipment—necessary to translate the vision into reality. Capital budgeting, then, is a *systematic approach to deciding among long-term investment opportunities that further an organization's strategies.*

Therefore, capital budgeting plays a prominent role in decision making. It is an important tool enabling managers to carry out the strategies of their organizations. With the importance of capital budgeting in mind, our goals are to:

- Discuss the role played by discounted cash flow in capital budgeting
- Describe the capital budgeting process

CURRENT PRACTICE

RJR Nabisco Plans New Ovens

RJR Nabisco spent $62 million to install three large ovens in its Chicago bakery. The new ovens gave Nabisco the capacity to make more cookies than it had been able to make in its old ovens—but in the same amount of time and using fewer workers. In all, Nabisco plans to realize $12 million in cost savings and benefits from the installation of the new equipment in the first year of operation.

Source: Fred R. Bleakley, "As Capital Spending Grows, Firms Take a Hard Look at Returns from the Effort," *The Wall Street Journal,* Feb. 8, 1994, p. A2.

OPERATING VERSUS CAPITAL ASSETS

To help visualize the impact of capital-budgeting decisions, consider the graphical representation of a firm's balance sheet, shown in Exhibit 8.1, in which items are shown as relative proportions of total assets and total equities.

Current assets—such as cash, marketable securities, receivables, and inventories—generally represent a relatively small proportion of total assets. They are the resources the firm requires in order to meet its day-to-day operating needs.

Fixed assets, the shaded area in Exhibit 8.1, represent the firm's long-term investments. These investments—also called **capital assets**—are what capital-budgeting decisions are all about. Capital assets—such as land, buildings, and equipment—have the potential of creating value for

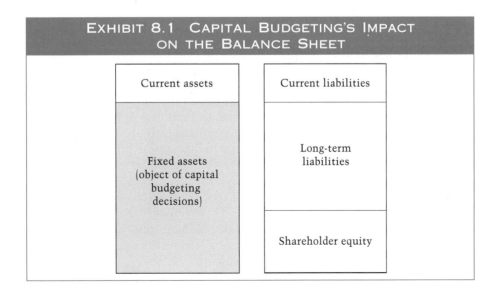

EXHIBIT 8.1   CAPITAL BUDGETING'S IMPACT ON THE BALANCE SHEET

Current assets	Current liabilities
Fixed assets (object of capital budgeting decisions)	Long-term liabilities
	Shareholder equity

the organization in the future. Since they usually represent the largest proportion of total assets, making decisions about capital assets is an important part of what managers do.

The right-hand side of Exhibit 8.1 represents the firm's *equities*—the sources of funding for assets. Equities include current liabilities, such as accounts and salaries payable; long-term liabilities, such as mortgages and bonds payable; and shareholder equity, including capital stock and retained earnings.

Our focus in this chapter, then, is on the decisions that determine the makeup of fixed capital assets. By acquiring and disposing of these capital assets, managers determine the long-term resources available to implement the organization's strategies. Where the funds come from to pay for the capital assets is a topic that is covered in finance textbooks.

Capital-budgeting decisions affect not only the balance sheet but also the income statement. That's because capital-budgeting decisions determine an organization's cost structure—the particular mix of fixed and variable costs. Recall that a firm's cost structure should match its strategies. For example, companies who compete based on low cost will sometimes have cost structures that are predominately fixed. This allows them to achieve lower unit costs through economies of scale. In contrast, companies who differentiate their products might want cost structures with relatively high proportions of variable costs.

What if managers are considering acquiring equipment that will automate activities formerly performed by hand? Their goal is to reduce variable labor costs and to release production workers—thereby reducing the cost of labor. But when the managers achieve the goal, fixed costs, such as depreciation and maintenance, will increase and take the place of reducing the variable costs. Capital-budgeting decisions, then, determine the firm's cost structure through the addition and deletion of fixed assets.

Don't forget—high levels of fixed costs don't come without a price. In adding long-term assets that increase fixed costs, managers raise the breakeven point, thereby increasing the firm's exposure to risk.

IMPORTANCE OF CASH FLOWS

Capital-budgeting decisions are based on *expected future cash flows*. To seek why cash flows are used instead of net income, consider the projected income statement shown in Exhibit 8.2. The projections, prepared for Walter Company, will be used to evaluate the acquisition of $3 million in equipment needed to introduce a new product. Assume that Walter Company's **planning horizon**—the period over which it will evaluate the potential investment—is 5 years.

The project begins with the purchase of the equipment needed to produce the new product. This point in the planning horizon is designated as "year 0." After the equipment is put in service, the costs and benefits anticipated from that project start accumulating. By the end of the first year of operations, designated as "year 1," Walter Company expects to sell 25,000 units of product at a per-unit price of $25, generating $625,000 in

	EXHIBIT 8.2 WALTER COMPANY						

Projected Income Statement

	(Start-up) Year 0	Year 1	Year 2	Year 3	Year 4	Year 5	Total
Revenue:							
Units sold		25,000	100,000	125,000	150,000	100,000	
Selling price per unit		$ 25	$ 25	$ 25	$ 25	$ 25	
Total revenue		$ 625,000	$2,500,000	$3,125,000	$3,750,000	$2,500,000	
Operating cost:							
Variable cost (@ $11 per unit)		$ 275,000	$1,100,000	$1,375,000	$1,650,000	$1,100,000	
Fixed cost (excluding depreciation)		550,000	550,000	550,000	550,000	550,000	
Depreciation ($2.5 million cost/5 years)		500,000	500,000	500,000	500,000	500,000	
Total operating cost		$1,325,000	$2,150,000	$2,425,000	$2,700,000	$2,150,000	
Income before taxes		$ (700,000)	$ 350,000	$ 700,000	$1,050,000	$350,000	
Income taxes (@ 30%)		(210,000)	(105,000)	(210,000)	(315,000)	(105,000)	
Net income		$ (490,000)	$ 245,000	$ 490,000	$ 735,000	$ 245,000	$1,225,000

total revenue. Sales are projected to increase annually for years 1 through 4, reaching a peak at the end of year 4. Managers anticipate that sales will decline in the fifth year, as competitors gain market share. The equipment will be sold and the new product abandoned at the end of the 5-year planning horizon.

Variable production cost is $11 per unit, while fixed cost (excluding depreciation) is estimated at $550,000 each year. Equipment depreciation, based on the equipment's original cost of $3,000,000, is reduced by $500,000 in *estimated residual value*—the value Walter Company expects to receive from the liquidation of the equipment at the end of the planning horizon. This leaves $2,500,000 in cost to be spread over 5 years. Thus, the annual depreciation charge, assuming the straight-line method, is $500,000 [($3,000,000 − $500,000)/5 years] each year.

Net income, after deducting income taxes, ranges from a loss of $(490,000) in the first year of the project to a maximum profit of $735,000 in the fourth year. Adding the annual after-tax net income figures together over the project's 5-year planning horizon gives a total net income of $1,225,000.

As a manager of Walter Company, would you accept or reject the investment proposal? Before you answer, consider the two investments shown in Exhibit 8.3. Assume both cost the same, both have the same net income, and both are equally risky. The only difference between them is the timing of cash flows.

Looking at Exhibit 8.3, observe that the net income and total cash flow for each project is exactly the same—$3,000. However, project A generates cash flow sooner than project B does. Assume the (positive) $250

EXHIBIT 8.3 TWO INVESTMENTS WITH DIFFERENT CASH FLOW PATTERNS

| | Project A | | | | Project B | | | | Difference | |
| | Net Income | Cash Flow | Present Value Factor @ 15% per Year | Present Value of Cash Flow | Net Income | Cash Flow | Present Value Factor @ 15% per Year | Present Value of Cash Flow | Cash Flow | Present Value of Cash Flow |
Year										
1	$1,000	$ 250	0.86957	$ 217	$1,000	$ 0	0.86957	$ 0	$ 250	$217
2	1,000	1,250	0.75614	945	1,000	0	0.75614	0	1,250	945
3	1,000	1,500	0.65752	986	1,000	3,000	0.65752	1,973	(1,500)	(986)
Total	$3,000	$3,000		$2,148	$3,000	$3,000		$1,973	$ 0	$176

difference in cash flow generated by project A in the first year is placed in an interest-earning investment at a rate of 15 percent per year. Another $1,250 is added to the investment in the second year. Meanwhile, project B generates no cash flow in years 1 and 2. Then, in the third year, project B produces $1,500 more cash flow than project A does, reversing the differences of the first 2 years. While the net cash flow over the 3-year period is exactly the same for each project, the present value of the cash flow for project A is $2,148, while it is only $1,973 for project B. The difference is that project A earns interest on the additional cash flow during the first 2 years. The conclusion is that projects generating cash flow earlier in their planning horizons create more total cash flow.

The concept represented in Exhibit 8.3 is the **time value of money.** The point to remember is that cash flows received sooner are preferred to the same cash flows received later. Thus, a dollar today is worth more than the same dollar in the future. For example, $1.00 invested at 15 percent per year accumulates to $1.15 ($1.00 principal + $0.15 interest) by year-end. Conversely, $1.15 at the end of 1 year has the present value equivalent of $1.00 today, assuming it generates a return of 15 percent.

The table in Appendix A, located at the end of this chapter, translates rates and the number of periods for which the cash flow is received in the future into present value equivalents.[1] For example, find 15 percent along the top row of the table and the number 1 along the first column. At the intersection of these two coordinates is a number—0.86957— referred to as a **present value factor.** This factor represents the present value equivalent of $1 received one year from today at a rate of 15 percent per year. We can calculate the present value for any dollar amount received one year from now, assuming that the investment earns interest at 15 percent per year, by multiplying that dollar amount by the present

---

[1] An alternative to using the table is to embed a formula in spreadsheets that calculates a present value factor. The formula is $[1/((1 + \text{rate})^{\text{Period}})]$, where *rate* refers to a cell containing the desired discount rate and *period* represents a cell containing the number for a specific time period, such as 0, 1, or 2. Most spreadsheets include built-in present value functions.

value factor 0.86957. In other words, the present value of $1.15 received one year from now at an annual rate of 15 percent has a present value equivalent of $1.00 ($1.15 × 0.86957).

NET PRESENT VALUE

The data in Exhibit 8.4 shows the impact of Walter Company's $3-million equipment decision from a different perspective. Exhibit 8.4 is similar to Exhibit 8.2, only the data are stated in terms of cash flow. The first line in Exhibit 8.4 (net income) simply repeats the net income line from Exhibit 8.2. The next line in Exhibit 8.4 shows depreciation added back to net income to approximate cash flow from operations. Recall that depreciation is a noncash expense—that is, it reduces net income without reducing cash outflow. Since depreciation is a deductible expense for income tax purposes, it reduces Walter Company's obligation to pay taxes and, thereby, reduces its cash outflow.

The third line in Exhibit 8.4 shows the annual net cash flow from operation for years 1 through 5. The next line shows the initial outlay of $3 million in cash for the equipment at the start of the project—year 0. The line after that, residual value at the end of project, represents $500,000 in cash received from the sale of the equipment at the end of the fifth year. The line labeled "net cash flow" summarizes, by year, the net benefit from the new project—the cash inflows and outflows generated by the new product. The net cash flow ranges from the $(3,000,000) cash outflow at the start of the project to a net cash inflow of $1,245,000 in the fifth year. If you were to sum net cash flow over the 5-year planning horizon, the result would be $1,225,000—*an amount exactly equal to the sum of the annual net incomes* in Exhibit 8.2. This is worth repeating: The sum

	(Start-up) Year 0	Year 1	Year 2	Year 3	Year 4	Year 5	Total
EXHIBIT 8.4 WALTER COMPANY							
Projected Cash Flows							
Net Income (from Exhibit 8.2)		$(490,000)	$245,000	$490,000	$ 735,000	$ 245,000	
Add depreciation (from Exhibit 8.2)		500,000	500,000	500,000	500,000	500,000	
Net cash flow from operations		$ 10,000	$745,000	$990,000	$1,235,000	$ 745,000	
Initial outlay at start-up	$(3,000,000)						
Residual value at end of project						$ 500,000	
Net cash flow	$(3,000,000)	$ 10,000	$745,000	$990,000	$1,235,000	$1,245,000	$1,225,000
Present value factor (15%)	1.00000	0.86957	0.75614	0.65752	0.57175	0.49718	
Present value of net cash flow	$(3,000,000)	$ 8,696	$563,324	$650,945	$ 706,111	$ 618,989	$ (451,935)

Net present value (NPV)

of cash flows and the sum of net incomes are precisely the same over the life of the project. Differences between cash flow and net income arise only in the context of timing, not in the context of total amount.

The next-to-last line of data in Exhibit 8.4 shows present value factors for the value of $1 received in each of the respective periods at a rate of 15 percent—a rate, that, for now, we will call the **discount rate.** The final line of data in Exhibit 8.4 shows net cash flows in each year discounted to their present value. For example, the present value of the $3-million initial outlay is simply $3,000,000 ($3,000,000 × a present value factor of 1.0000, the factor for any rate of interest for year 0). That is, the present value of a $3-million outlay today is $3 million. The present value of $10,000 received at the end of year 1—a year after the initial investment—is equivalent to $8,696 ($10,000 × the present value factor for 15%—0.86957, from Appendix A).

Net cash flows for each year, after being multiplied by their respective present value factors, are added together for all of the years in the planning horizon. The total is the **net present value (NPV).** In our example, the NPV is negative—$(451,935). While we will discuss the NPV in more detail shortly, *the decision rule regarding whether to invest in capital assets or not based on NPV is quite simple: Accept only those proposed projects with NPVs greater than zero.* A positive NPV means that the present value of all cash inflows *exceeds* the present value of all cash outflows. On the other hand, a negative NPV indicates that the present value of all cash inflows *does not exceed* the present value of all cash outflows—the project should be rejected. As a result of a consideration of the data, Walter Company should not invest $3 million in new equipment. If it does, its assets—and its shareholder value—will decrease by $451,935.

To reiterate: When accounting-based net income supports one decision while the net present value supports another, let the decision be based on the net present value. Accounting-based net income should not be used for decision-making purposes. However, net income based on generally accepted accounting principles (GAAP) still has a role to play—namely, in providing information needed to assess performance of the project—*but this activity is not needed until after an investment decision (favoring such investment) has been made.*

In a broader context, the general financial model for the firm as a whole is based on the creation of shareholder value. Since the value of any business is determined by its expected future cash flow, decisions that increase net cash flow add value for shareholders. Projects whose discounted cash inflows exceed the discounted cash outflows—that is, projects with positive NPVs—increase the present value of total assets by the amount of the NPV. This increase in value accrues to shareholders.

Now let's see how all this fits into the process of capital budgeting.

THE CAPITAL BUDGETING PROCESS

Capital budgeting focuses on how managers decide which opportunities they will take advantage of (i.e., invest in) and which they will forego. The capital budgeting process is described by the following steps:

- Identifying investment opportunities
- Establishing selection criteria
- Gathering data
- Performing a capital-budgeting evaluation
- Evaluating project costs and benefits
- Performing a postaudit evaluation

The list above should not be considered a strict sequence of steps to be followed. Rather, it is an illustration of how an idea about an opportunity progresses to a point where sufficient information is gathered to support a consensus among those who are making the decision. As more information is collected, the impact of the investment on the organization becomes better understood. Momentum is built as coalitions of individuals with stakes in the project lend their support to one side or another.

IDENTIFYING INVESTMENT OPPORTUNITIES

PROGRAMMING

Programming is the process whereby managers evaluate the major activities their organization will pursue in the future. *Programs* generally refer to products and services the organization plans to offer. But programs also involve operations (e.g., a quality improvement program) or an organization's structure (e.g., a program to eliminate layers of management).

Programs are generally translated into a series of **projects.** Projects, which are shorter in duration than programs are, usually focus on specific investments that help move a program closer to its objectives. Projects are undertaken for a variety of reasons—for example, enhancing revenue, lowering costs, improving customer satisfaction, building employee skills, or developing new technology. General Motors, for example, initiated a program to shorten the time it takes to design and build new automobiles. As part of this program, GM implemented projects ranging from reorganizing the design team to acquiring automated equipment. These projects served to carry out different phases of the program. (For an example of the program-project relationship, see "Current Practice: Georgia-Pacific's Spending Spree.")

One way to evaluate projects is to classify them according to the risks to which they expose their organizations. An example of such a classification scheme is as follows:

- *Is the investment required by government regulation?* Projects mandated by government regulations are intended to minimize the risks of noncompliance. Examples of such investments include smoke stack scrubbers, safety equipment, and provision of facilities access for the handicapped. The consequences of failing to satisfy government regulation may include, for example, fines, litigation costs, and adverse publicity. The risks associated with these kinds of projects are generally relatively small, since the organization typically has no viable choice other than compliance. To illustrate, the EPA recently required dry cleaners to reduce emissions of harmful chemicals; in

CURRENT PRACTICE

Georgia-Pacific's Spending Spree

Georgia-Pacific, the U.S. forest products giant, is flush with cash because of the surge in pulp and paper prices, a booming world economy, and tight supplies. Georgia-Pacific plans to use some of its newfound cash to purchase offshore timberlands and manufacturing facilities. At present, Georgia-Pacific chooses to locate all of its manufacturing facilities in the United States. The decision to keep operations at home was based on the company's original strategy of supplying the world's paper needs by efficiently managing the more than 6 million acres it owns in North America.

Georgia-Pacific's strategy is changing for two reasons. First, the United States is running out of new forestland. And, second, Georgia-Pacific wants to be close to its growing overseas markets. Demand for pulpwood and paper in South America, for example, has grown by about 200 percent per year over the past 5 years while demand in the United States and Europe has grown at a modest 2 to 3 percent a year. As a result, a good part of Georgia-Pacific's $1.75 billion to be spent on capital assets will likely go to Brazil, Chile, or Argentina, where softwoods such as pine grow quickly and abundantly.

Source: Emory Thomas, Jr., "Georgia-Pacific May Embark on a Spending Spree," *The Wall Street Journal,"* Dec. 12, 1994, p. B4.

many cases, compliance entailed the purchase of several machines costing from $30,000 to $75,000 each.[2]

- *Is the project mandated by competitors' actions?* The risk of not remaining competitive includes loss of revenue, higher costs, or, in the worst case, withdrawal from markets. (Again, as with meeting government regulations, managers may have little choice in whether or not they undertake these kinds of projects.) Such investments include, for example, projects that modernize equipment, improve productivity, enhance customer service, or strengthen product quality. In each case, the organization must decide what kinds of projects, if any, it must undertake in order to remain competitive.

- *Is the expenditure necessary for existing projects or products?* The risk associated with investment in existing products or projects is moderate, because managers have experience with them and know what the costs and benefits are likely to be. Examples of such investments include expenditures for replacing existing equipment, installing laborsaving devices, and extending existing product lines.

- *Is the investment necessary for new product, process, or technology start-ups?* Start-up projects are undertaken to explore or begin new

---

[2]   Joanne Ball Artis, "Dry Cleaners Face Strict New U.S. Rules," *The Boston Globe,* June 1, 1993, p. 17.

U.S. Steel and Nucor Plan Joint Venture

U.S. Steel and Nucor, rivals in the huge steelmaking business, have joined to explore a new technology. The new process, whereby steel is manufactured directly from iron carbide, bypasses raw materials currently used in mills such as those owned by U.S. Steel. The new technology's advantage is twofold: Not only are the raw materials currently used expensive, they may create environmental headaches. The new process eliminates the need for the scrap metal used by many of the smaller mills—or minimills—such as those operated by Nucor. Taking scrap out of the process not only sidesteps the risk entailed by volatile scrap metal prices but eliminates the exposure to periodic supply shortages.

The first step in evaluating the project is to prepare a study that outlines the expected costs and benefits of the new process. Then, the partners plan to build a test plant. On top of its investment in the test plant, U.S. Steel plans to appropriate funds for developing the new technology, building technical expertise, providing design and development assistance, and supplying start-up support for the new plant. When added together, these direct and indirect investments in the new technology are substantial.

Source: Erle Norton, "Rivals U.S. Steel and Nucor Plan Joint Venture," *The Wall Street Journal*, Oct. 13, 1994, p. A4.

programs, typically programs that fall outside of what managers have experienced in the past. Examples include projects involving research in new technology, experimental manufacturing processes, and organizational restructuring. In general, such projects entail relatively high levels of risk. While some projects may end up yielding extraordinary above-market returns, others may prove unsuccessful, representing a sacrifice of time and money. (See "Current Practice: U.S. Steel and Nucor Plan Joint Venture.")

Relying on categories such as these helps managers to characterize projects by their impact on risk. Projects involving new technology, for example, may fundamentally alter operations, change the corporate culture, forge new relationships with suppliers, or change the way products and services are delivered to customers. Projects such as any of these should be subject to much more stringent scrutiny than, for example, projects that merely replace existing equipment.

ESTABLISHING SELECTION CRITERIA

Organizations should clearly specify how capital projects are to be evaluated. This entails specifying the criteria by which the projects are to be judged. Such criteria might include the project's impact on such factors as

8

cash flow, shareholder value, product quality, market position, flexibility, and productivity. These criteria establish priorities that help focus managers' attention on what the organization considers important to achieve its long-term objectives.

GATHERING DATA

Data may come from a variety of internal and external sources, such as historical financial records, publicly available data, analysis of the results of similar projects undertaken by competitors, or special studies commissioned for a particular project. These initial sources of data may indicate that the project does not meet minimum expectations. An equipment replacement decision with negative net cash flow, for example, might fail to *qualify* for further analysis. Managers may decide to drop the project rather than expending more time and resources on evaluating it and may choose to turn their attention, instead, to alternatives that have better prospects.

For those projects passing an initial qualification, additional data is gathered in order to provide managers with more detail and to allow them to fill in values for unknown variables. For example, projected cash flow from a new project may be based on estimates of growth derived from the sales history of a similar product. If the project data meets the initial criteria, the marketing department might commission studies to validate the estimates of the new product's growth. In the process of gathering additional data, the costs, benefits, and exposure to risk become better understood by everyone involved in the project. Thus, proposals move forward in phases until the managers responsible for the decision feel they can defend or reject the project's costs and benefits.

PERFORMING A CAPITAL-BUDGETING EVALUATION

Recall that at the beginning of this chapter, we made the case that all decisions relating to the acquisition of long-term capital assets are based on cash flows derived from that asset. And all investments in capital assets have three kinds of cash flow in common: (1) an outlay of cash at the outset of the project, (2) cash flow derived from the assets over the project's planning horizon, and (3) cash flow when the assets are sold—a process called **disinvestment**—at the end of the project's planning horizon. Planning horizons can be as short as 3 years, especially for products with short life cycles or for projects involving new technology. Or for projects with predictable, long-term benefits, planning horizons might look ahead as far as 10 years or more.

Five categories serve as the basis for a five-step framework to organize data for each of the three types of cash flow. The steps consist of calculating each of the following category's cost:

1. Incremental cash inflow and outflow (net benefit) from operations
2. Incremental cash inflow from depreciation
3. Incremental cash inflow from disinvestment

4. Incremental cash outflow for the initial investment outlay
5. Summary of incremental cash flow using net present value

Note that each of these categories is based on **incremental cash flow.** Since new projects often replace existing projects, it is the *change* in cash flow—the incremental cash flow—that we are interested in. For example, if the cash flow expected from operating a new piece of equipment is, say, $100,000 each year, and it replaces an existing piece of equipment having an operating cash flow of $25,000, then the incremental cash flow is $75,000 per year. Even if the project is entirely new and there is no existing project to compare it against, its cash flow is still considered incremental. The new project is simply compared against zero—doing nothing at all. In that case—when there is no existing project—all cash flow from the new asset is incremental.

By concentrating on *changes in cash flows,* only those cash flows that differ are considered relevant to the decision. That is, as always, we ignore those costs and benefits that do not change. We will refer to this as a *challenger-versus-defender* perspective, since the net benefit of the new project (the challenger) must overcome the net benefit of the existing project (the defender) if it is to gain approval.

The first step in the evaluation framework is to focus on the incremental operating costs and benefits associated with projects. These costs and benefits may enhance revenues by adding production capacity or by introducing new products. Or projects may reduce costs by improving productivity, enhancing flexibility, or increasing operating efficiency (See "Current Practice: Monsanto's Fibers Division.") Thus, projects may increase revenue, or reduce cost—or do both.

Proposals for projects in areas where managers have little or no expertise are sometimes difficult to justify. For example, a pharmaceutical company may want to consider research in new drug delivery systems. How does it measure the benefits? Or a firm may wish to consider installing a new information system or undertaking a corporate reorganization. While it may be difficult to quantify costs and benefits for such projects, it is clear that some managers find ways of incorporating difficult-to-quantify factors in their decisions.

The second step in the evaluation framework based on the categories outlined above concentrates on the role played by depreciation. Recall that depreciation is a deductible expense for income tax purposes—but that it does not entail a cash outflow. It therefore creates cash inflow by reducing the amount of cash paid for income taxes. As with all steps in the evaluation framework, it is the incremental depreciation that we are interested in—depreciation used in calculating income taxes for an existing project subtracted from depreciation for a new project. The incremental depreciation expense is multiplied by the marginal tax rate to derive the incremental tax savings.

The third step is to calculate net cash proceeds from the disposal—the disinvestment in the assets at the end of the project's planning horizon. Since it may be difficult to predict exactly when projects will be phased out, a future point at which the project is expected to be terminated

CURRENT PRACTICE

Monsanto's Fibers Division

Monsanto's Fibers Division plant in Pensacola, Florida, produces nylon yarn for carpeting and tires. With the slump in the housing industry and the market inroads being made by steel-belted radial tires, the demand for nylon yarn had been shrinking. In response, management implemented a three-part plan emphasizing employee involvement, quality, and automation. The division was charged with improving productivity by 50 percent.

The response plan consisted of a capital expenditures program to improve productivity by installing new processing equipment, a computer network to help the different functional groups transfer and share information, and an automated office system. The cost of all this was approximately $37 million.

The new control system reduced variations in the process of making a product, which improved product uniformity. This allowed Monsanto's fiber division to skip steps in the carpet-manufacturing process and reduce overall manufacturing cost by approximately 1 to 2 percent. A second benefit was a 30 percent reduction in "off-grade" (below-specification) fibers. Production of the highest-grade fibers increased by more than 5 percent after installation of the automated control system. Finally, the system generated reductions in working capital by minimizing the amount of inventory needed to safeguard against variations in production.

Source: R. Cole, Jr., and H. Lee Hales, "Automation," *Management Accounting*, Jan. 1992, pp. 39–43.

is identified for planning purposes. At that point, proceeds from the disposal of any of the project's tangible assets—such as buildings and equipment, net of any income taxes—are subtracted from proceeds that would have been realized from the disposal of the old equipment.

The fourth step is to quantify the cash outlay required to secure the net benefits from the project. The initial outlay includes cash outflows not only for tangible assets but also for start-up costs such as employee training or organizational changes. When a new project replaces one already in place, the amount of the initial outlay is reduced by the cash proceeds from the disposal of existing assets, net of any tax effect. Just as occurs in a trade-in, disposal values from existing assets reduce the amount of cash required for the initial outlay.

The fifth and last step in the evaluation framework simply consists of adding together all the incremental cash inflows and outflows for each of the first four steps for every year in the planning horizon. Then, net cash flows in each year are converted to their present value equivalents by multiplying each by its present value factor. Finally, the discounted cash flows for all years are added together. The result is the net present value. If the net present value is greater than zero, the project qualifies for further consideration.

INCREMENTAL CASH FLOW

To illustrate how incremental cash flows are calculated, we introduce a case study of Great Northern Food Store, a small chain of retail grocery stores.

GREAT NORTHERN FOOD STORE

In the early 1970s, IBM and NCR, among others, were developing bar code systems. When coupled with evolving laser technology, the bar code systems had the potential of significantly improving labor productivity. One logical application was at grocery store checkout counters. A laser beam could read the bar code on a food package, look up its previously stored price in the computer system, and automatically record the price in the checkout register. Today, this technology is accepted, and its costs and benefits known. However, in the early 1970s, the conversion of traditional cash register systems to this unknown technology—while representing potentially significant cost savings for the stores adopting it—was fraught with uncertainty. It is within this setting that we will illustrate capital-budgeting procedures.

The management of Great Northern Food Store, after visiting a model bar code installation, began considering conversion of its manual cash register system to the new bar code checkout technology. If a trial installation was successful, company managers intended to convert all stores to the bar code system. They felt that the new equipment—which would cost $165,000 per store—would enhance Great Northern Food Store's image and would help the company expand its customer base.

The manager responsible for evaluating the bar code project identified the benefits expected from the new system. They included increased revenue, reduction in errors in keying in prices, improved labor productivity among cashiers, and reduced recordkeeping cost. The results of the evaluation are shown in Exhibit 8.5.

Samples of the current checkout process (using the manual cash register system) indicated, on the average, that about 10 checkouts per register took place each hour. Using past sales data, management determined that population growth in the neighborhood would cause physical checkout volume to increase at a rate of about 1 percent each year.

Management believes that Great Northern Food Store's market share would increase by about 3.5 percent each year if the new bar code system were installed. Current checkout totals average $42 and are expected to grow in parallel with general price-level increases, estimated at about 5 percent each year. No increase in revenue is projected for the first year after installation (year 1). However, the net increase in gross profit is projected at $13,336 for the second year, based upon an increase in revenue of $47,628 and a 28 percent gross profit rate.

The second area of potential benefit from the new bar code system is the elimination of errors. Based on the projected total number of checkouts and an estimated average error rate of 4.25 percent of the items on each customer's bill, 1,836 errors for cashiers using the old system were anticipated for the first year. Estimates were also prepared for the amount

EXHIBIT 8.5 GREAT NORTHERN FOOD STORE

Incremental Benefits of Bar Code System Over Manual System

Increased Revenue	(Start-up) Year 0	Year 1	Year 2	Year 3	Year 4	Year 5
Average checkouts per hour— new equip. (growth @ 3.5%)		10.00	10.35	10.71	11.09	11.48
Average checkouts per hour— old equip. (growth @ 1%)		10.00	10.10	10.20	10.30	10.41
Increase in checkouts per hour		0.00	0.25	0.51	0.78	1.07
Operating hours per day		12	12	12	12	12
Days open per year		360	360	360	360	360
Annual increase in checkouts		0	1,080	2,209	3,388	4,619
Average checkout amount (growth @ 5%)		$ 42.00	$ 44.10	$ 46.31	$ 48.62	$ 51.05
Annual increase in revenue		$ 0	$47,628	$102,269	$164,706	$235,801
Gross profit percentage		28.00%	28.00%	28.00%	28.00%	28.00%
Increase in gross profit		$ 0	$13,336	$ 28,635	$ 46,118	$ 66,024
Elimination of the Cost of Errors						
Average checkouts per hour—old equipment		10.00	10.10	10.20	10.30	10.41
Operating hours per day		12	12	12	12	12
Days open per year		360	360	360	360	360
Total checkouts		43,200	43,632	44,068	44,509	44,954
Average error rate per checkout		4.25%	4.25%	4.25%	4.25%	4.25%
Estimated errors per year		1,836	1,854	1,873	1,892	1,911
Cost per error:						
Cost to correct errors (growth @ 5%)		$ 0.35	$ 0.37	$ 0.39	$ 0.41	$ 0.43
Cost of manager's time (growth @ 5%)		$ 1.25	$ 1.31	$ 1.38	$ 1.45	$ 1.52
Cost per error		$ 1.60	$ 1.68	$ 1.76	$ 1.85	$ 1.94
Reduction in cost of errors		$ 2,938	$ 3,115	$ 3,304	$ 3,504	$ 3,717
Reduction in Labor Cost						
Total number of checkouts per year		43,200	43,632	44,068	44,509	44,954
Average time per checkout (in minutes)		6	6	6	6	6
Total checkout time (in minutes)		259,200	261,792	264,410	267,054	269,725
Reduction in checkout time (growth @ 4%)		20.00%	20.80%	21.63%	22.50%	23.40%
Reduced checkout minutes		51,840	54,453	57,197	60,080	63,108
Reduced checkout hours (checkout minutes/60)		864	908	953	1,001	1,052
Cost of checkout labor:						
Hourly rate for checkout labor (growth @ 5%)		$ 6.50	$ 6.83	$ 7.17	$ 7.52	$ 7.90
Benefits (18% of payroll)		$ 1.17	$ 1.23	$ 1.29	$ 1.35	$ 1.42
Total hourly cost		$ 7.67	$ 8.05	$ 8.46	$ 8.88	$ 9.32
Total reduction in labor cost from increase in productivity		$ 6,627	$ 7,309	$ 8,061	$ 8,891	$ 9,806
Reduced bookkeeping cost (growth @ 5%)		$18,000	$18,900	$ 19,845	$ 20,837	$ 21,879

Note: Figures may reflect rounding errors.

of time it would take checkout staff and supervisors to correct errors. Multiplying the expected error rate by the employee and supervisor wage rates produced a cost per error, which is expected to grow at about 5 percent each year. With the new system, errors are essentially zero, occurring only when items have no bar codes or when lasers fail to read bar codes. When multiplying the number of errors and the cost per error, the project manager was surprised to find a reduction in the cost of errors per store with the new system. The reduction ranges from $2,938 in the first year to $3,717 by the fifth year.

Improved labor productivity and subsequent reductions in labor cost would come as a result of increased speed and the elimination of checkout errors. Total checkout minutes were projected for each year, based on an average checkout time of 6 minutes. Using existing installations as examples and time-and-motion studies conducted by the equipment manufacturers, the project manager expects the average per-customer checkout process to take 20 percent less time at start-up and improve each year at a rate of 4 percent. When multiplying the reduced checkout time by the hourly wage rate, which is expected to increase at a rate of 5 percent along with benefits of 18 percent, the total cost saving from improved labor productivity ranges from $6,627 per store in the first year to $9,806 by the fifth year.

Finally, one bookkeeper who keeps track of the daily checkout tapes would be released, reducing total salary cost and benefits by $18,000. Since salaries are anticipated to increase at a rate of 5 percent annually, this saving would grow to $21,879 by the fifth year.

Armed with this basic operational data, the manager assigned to the bar code project began preparing the capital-budgeting proposal according to company policy. The policy dictates that capital-budgeting proposals must be prepared in an incremental format where changes in costs and benefits are measured relative to existing conditions. In addition, the policy states that the primary criterion by which projects will be judged is cash flow. Secondary criteria include the proposed project's impact on profitability, market share, and customer satisfaction.

1: CALCULATE THE INCREMENTAL NET BENEFIT FROM OPERATIONS

In order to evaluate the benefits sought from the new equipment, we need to consider how its installation will affect operations. Benefits generally either lower costs by improving productivity or raise revenue from new or existing products. In Great Northern Food Store's case, the benefit is a combination of both of these mechanisms. The expected net changes in operational cash flow each year are shown in Exhibit 8.6.

The benefits of the bar code system, taken from Exhibit 8.5, are shown in the first four lines of Exhibit 8.6. In addition, the cost of training employees to use the new equipment is estimated at $12,000 per year. Training sessions are planned throughout the first year of installation. A maintenance contract required by the bar code equipment manufacturer would cost $7,500 each year, without escalation for changes in prices.

EXHIBIT 8.6 GREAT NORTHERN FOOD STORE

Step 1: Incremental Net Benefit from Operations

	(Start-up) Year 0	Year 1	Year 2	Year 3	Year 4	Year 5
Increase in revenue (from Exhibit 8.5)	$ 0	$13,336	$28,635	$46,118	$66,024
Elimination of cost of errors (from Exhibit 8.5)		2,938	3,115	3,304	3,504	3,717
Reduction in labor cost (from Exhibit 8.5)		6,627	7,309	8,061	8,891	9,806
Reduced bookkeeping cost (from Exhibit 8.5)		18,000	18,900	19,845	20,837	21,879
Training cost		(12,000)	0	0	0	0
Annual maintenance cost		(7,500)	(7,500)	(7,500)	(7,500)	(7,500)
Incremental net benefit before income taxes		$ 8,065	$35,160	$52,345	$71,850	$93,926
Income taxes (rate @ 38%)		(3,065)	(13,361)	(19,891)	(27,303)	(35,692)
Incremental net benefit after income taxes (new vs. old)		$ 5,000	$21,799	$32,454	$44,547	$58,234

The yearly total increase in profit before depreciation, including outlays for training and maintenance, ranges from $8,065 in the first year to $93,926 by the fifth year. After deducting income taxes at a rate of 38 percent, the expected incremental annual net benefits per store ranges from $5,000 in the first year to $58,234 in the fifth year.

2: CALCULATE THE INCREMENTAL CASH INFLOW FROM DEPRECIATION

Depreciation is a noncash expense that impacts cash flow through income taxes. Since depreciation reduces net income subject to taxation, it reduces or "shields," the outflow of cash. For this reason, tax savings from depreciation are called a depreciation **tax shield.** It is the *difference* in depreciation between the proposed and existing equipment that is multiplied by the income tax rate to derive the incremental cash flow from depreciation. To understand how depreciation shields cash flow from income taxes, consider the data shown in Exhibit 8.7.

The base used in calculating depreciation for the new bar code equipment called the *cost basis* is $165,000. Depreciation is calculated using rates established by the Internal Revenue Service. Examples of these rates, called the *Modified Accelerated Cost Recovery System (MACRS)* rates, are reproduced in Appendix B, at the end of this chapter. Instead of making choices among depreciation methods, residual values, and estimated useful lives, business taxpayers simply place assets into one of several classes, based on the IRS guidelines.

Under the 5-year class in Appendix B, you will find six percentages. There are six percentages because of the presumption that new assets are placed in service in the middle of the year. As a result, one-half year's depreciation is taken in the first year, and four full years of depreciation

EXHIBIT 8.7 GREAT NORTHERN FOOD STORE						
Step 2: Incremental Cash Inflow from Depreciation Tax Shield						
	(Start-up) *Year 0*	*Year 1*	*Year 2*	*Year 3*	*Year 4*	*Year 5*
MACRS depreciation rates (from Appendix B)		20.00%	32.00%	19.20%	11.52%	11.52%
Cost basis for depreciation— new equipment		$165,000	$165,000	$165,000	$165,000	$165,000
Depreciation expense—new equipment		$ 33,000	$ 52,800	$ 31,680	$ 19,008	$ 19,008
Depreciation expense—old equipment		(10,000)	(10,000)	(10,000)	(10,000)	(10,000)
Incremental depreciation expense (new vs. old)		$ 23,000	$ 42,800	$ 21,680	$ 9,008	$ 9,008
Incremental depreciation tax shield (rate = 38%) (new vs. old)		$ 8,740	$ 16,264	$ 8,238	$ 3,423	$ 3,423

are taken after that, followed by one-half year's depreciation in the last year of the asset's life. Since Great Northern Food Store is using a 5-year planning horizon, the one-half year's depreciation in the last year will not be included in the analysis of the new bar code system. Note that MACRS rates are applied to the cost of the asset without reduction for estimated residual (disposal) value.

Multiplying the $165,000 cost of the bar code system by the 20 percent MACRS first-year rate results in depreciation expense of $33,000 for the new bar code system in its first year of operation. The depreciation expense for the bar code equipment is highest in the second year ($52,800) and lowest in the fifth year ($19,008).

Depreciation for the old cash register system is based on current book value (historical cost less its accumulated depreciation) of $50,000. Assuming Great Northern Food Store uses straight-line depreciation and assuming no provision for salvage value, depreciation expense is $10,000 in each of the 5 years [($50,000 − $0 salvage)/5 years].

The incremental depreciation—the difference between depreciation expense for the new bar code system and depreciation for the old cash registers—is $23,000 ($33,000 for the bar code system − $10,000 for the old equipment) in the first year of operation. Incremental depreciation expense increases to $42,800 in the second year, but declines to $9,008 in the fifth year. When multiplied by the income tax rate of 38 percent, the cash saving associated with reduced income tax payments ranges from $8,740 in the first year to a maximum of $16,264 in the second, and declines to $3,423 in the fifth year.

3: CALCULATE INCREMENTAL CASH FLOW FROM DISINVESTMENT

Incremental cash flow from disinvestment is calculated in the third step. Other terms for the cash value received from the disinvestment in a project include *residual value, liquidation value,* and *disposal value.* We have conveniently chosen disinvestment in the new bar code system at the end of 5 years so that it coincides with disinvestment in the existing equipment. In reality, there is little likelihood of a common disinvestment date. To place investments on a comparable footing, capital-budgeting theory suggests that projects with unequal lives be evaluated by viewing them as a series of replacements, known as a **replacement chain**, over a common time horizon. For example, the common time horizon for an 8-year project and a 5-year project is 40 years. The 8-year project would be replaced five times, while the 5-year project would be replaced eight times. For simplicity's sake, we assume a common disinvestment date for both the new and the old projects, eliminating the need to consider replacement chains.

Great Northern Food Store's projected cash inflow from disinvestment is presented in Exhibit 8.8. Assume the new bar code system is sold after 5 years for $75,000. Also assume the bar code system has a book value at disposal of $9,504—the original cost of $165,000 reduced by $155,430 in accumulated depreciation ($33,000 + $52,800 + $31,680 + $19,008 + $19,008, from Exhibit 8.7). Alternatively, book value can be calculated by taking the MACRS depreciation rate for any year not included in the planning horizon—the sixth year, in our example—and multiplying it by the cost of the project. In other words, the book value of $9,504 can be calculated by multiplying the sixth-year rate (5.76% found in Appendix B under the 5-year investment class) by the project cost ($165,000).

The difference between the cash proceeds from the disposal of a project's assets and the asset's book value (original cost less accumulated

EXHIBIT 8.8 GREAT NORTHERN FOOD STORE

Step 3: Incremental Cash Inflow from Disinvestment

New Equipment	(Start-up) Year 0	Year 1	Year 2	Year 3	Year 4	Year 5
Estimated net disposal value						$75,000
Book value for tax purposes						9,504
Gain on disposal						$65,496
Additional taxes (38% rate × gain on disposal)						(24,888)
Net cash flow:						
Estimated net disposal value						75,000
Less additional taxes						(24,888)
Net cash flow—new equipment						$50,112
Old Equipment						
Estimated net disposal value						$20,000
Book value for tax purposes						0
Gain on disposal						$20,000
Additional taxes (38% rate × gain on disposal)						(7,600)
Net cash flow:						
Estimated net disposal value						20,000
Less additional taxes						(7,600)
Net cash flow—old equipment						$12,400
Incremental disinvestment cash inflow (new vs. old)						$37,712

depreciation) is considered a gain for tax purposes. The gain in our example is $65,496 ($75,000 − $9,504). Remember, too, that gains and losses are not cash flows. They do, however, impact cash flows through income taxes. A gain of $65,496 causes a $24,888 cash outflow for income taxes (38% × $65,496). After deducting the cash outflow for taxes, the net cash flow from disposal of the new bar code system at the end of 5 years is $50,112 ($75,000 cash from the sale of the bar code equipment − $24,888 in taxes on the capital gain).

A similar computation has to be made for the cash flow arising from the sale of the old cash registers. By the end of the fifth year, the old cash registers are fully depreciated, with a book value of zero. If we assume that they are sold for $20,000, then Great Northern Food Store will recognize a gain of $20,000. The gain is calculated by subtracting the book value of zero ($20,000 in cost − $20,000 in accumulated depreciation) from the proceeds of the sale ($20,000). Recognizing a $20,000 gain causes Great Northern Food Store's tax liability to increase by $7,600 (38% tax rate × $20,000) and net after-tax cash flow to increase by $12,400 ($20,000 in cash proceeds from the sale − $7,600 for additional tax liability).

The net incremental disinvestment cash flow ($37,712) is calculated by comparing net disinvestment cash flow for the bar code system ($50,112) with that for the old cash registers ($12,400).

4: CALCULATE INCREMENTAL CASH OUTFLOW FOR THE INITIAL INVESTMENT OUTLAY

The fourth step in evaluating capital-budgeting proposals is to calculate the incremental cash outflow required to obtain the benefits estimated in the three preceding steps. This outlay is assumed to take place at the very beginning of the planning horizon (year 0). The upper part of Exhibit 8.9 shows the initial outlay for the new equipment: $135,000 for the bar code scanners, $14,000 for modifications to the store's checkout area, and $16,000 for new checkout counters, for a total cost of $165,000.

We assume that if the new bar code system is acquired, then the old cash registers will be sold. If so, the after-tax cash flows from disposal of the old equipment reduces the cash outlay required for the new bar code system. So, again, we have to calculate the disposal value of the old cash registers, only this time at the beginning of the 5-year planning horizon.

Assume the cash registers were placed in service 3 years ago, at an original cost of $80,000. At that time, straight-line depreciation was selected, disposal value was estimated as zero at the end of an 8-year economic life, and $10,000 depreciation was deducted from taxable income for each of the 3 years. Today (year 0) the cash registers have a book value of $50,000 ($80,000 original cost − $30,000 in accumulated depreciation).

If the cash registers were sold for $45,000, net of removal and disposal cost, Great Northern Food Store would recognize a $5,000 loss for tax purposes ($45,000 cash proceeds from disposal − $50,000 in book value). Losses associated with the *sale* of capital assets are used to offset capital gains, thereby reducing the firm's income tax liability. In contrast, losses on the **exchange** (trade-in) of like-kind assets generally do not result in an immediate tax saving. Instead they increase the cost basis for the

EXHIBIT 8.9 GREAT NORTHERN FOOD STORE

Step 4: Incremental Investment Outflow

Cost of New Equipment	(Start-up) Year 0	Year 1	Year 2	Year 3	Year 4	Year 5
Equipment cost	$(135,000)					
Physical modifications	(14,000)					
New checkout counters	(16,000)					
Cost of new equipment	$(165,000)					
Disposal of Old Equipment						
Estimated net disposal value	$ 45,000					
Book value for tax purposes	50,000					
Loss on disposal	$ (5,000)					
Tax saving (38% rate × loss on disposal)	$ 1,900					
Net cash flow:						
Estimated net disposal value	45,000					
Plus tax savings	1,900					
Net cash flow—old equipment	$ 46,900					
Incremental investment outflow (new vs. old)	$(118,100)					

new asset and are recognized for tax purposes only at the termination of the series of replacements. To keep our example as uncomplicated as possible and to focus on capital-budgeting issues rather than on the tax codes, we have assumed that the transaction is a sale and that Great Northern Food Store has gains against which losses can be offset.

From an accrual accounting standpoint, the $5,000 capital loss—less a tax saving of $1,900 (38% tax rate × $5,000)—results in a net after-tax loss of $3,100. However, for capital-budgeting purposes, accrual accounting losses—just as accounting gains—are only relevant to the extent they effect cash flows for income taxes. Proceeds from the disposal of the old cash registers is equal to $45,000 plus the $1,900 in income taxes that Great Northern Food Store *does not have to pay.* Thus, the result of the disposal of the old cash registers is a net cash inflow of $46,900—the cash proceeds from the sale *plus* the taxes Great Northern Food Store doesn't have to pay. This point bears repeating: Cash flow from the sale of an asset has two components—actual cash proceeds from disposal and any tax effect.

The inflow from the sale of the old cash registers offsets the cash outflow required for the new system. The net incremental cash outflow, after the proceeds from liquidation of the cash registers are deducted, comes to $(118,100). This outflow is required at the beginning of the project—year 0 in Exhibit 8.9.

One item that is sometimes included in the initial outlay is *working capital.* We chose not to include working capital in the Great Northern Food Store example in order to keep our illustration as simple as possible.

CURRENT PRACTICE

Working Capital in Capital-Budgeting Proposals

Net working capital as a percent of total assets is shown at the right for several industries. Net working capital—defined as current assets minus current liabilities—includes cash outlays for accounts receivables, inventories, accounts payables, and salaries payables. Sometimes, investments in working capital can be substantial. Unfortunately, working capital is often ex- cluded from the evaluation of projects, sometimes with disastrous results.

Chemicals	21.9%
Wood furniture	26.6%
Industrial machinery	25.6%
Auto manufacturers	24.3%
Aircraft parts	30.4%
Manifold business forms	18.3%

Source: Robert Morris Associates' 1986 Annual Statements. Adapted from Harry Wolk, Gary Porter, and Daniel Vetter, "Net Working Capital Investment and Capital Budgeting Analysis: Some Pedagogical Insights," *Journal of Accounting Education*, vol. 7 (1989), pp. 253–262.

However, working capital often causes a significant increase in the total investment required for capital assets. (See "Current Practice: Working Capital in Capital-Budgeting Proposals.")

Working capital, defined as "current assets minus current liabilities," consists of incremental investments in cash, receivables, inventories, and other current operating assets, less any offsetting current liabilities. Investments in working capital are generally required at the outset of any project in order to get the project started. However, working-capital investments may be needed even after projects start in order to keep them going until enough cash flow to cover initial losses is generated.

Working-capital investments are always assumed to be recovered at the end of the planning horizon, at which point they are treated as additional cash inflow. Working capital is not subject to capital gains tax nor to any other form of taxation, either when the investment is made or when it is recovered. Since we assumed that Great Northern Food Store's proposal did not require any change in working capital, there was no necessity to include working capital in the initial outlay.

5: SUMMARIZE CASH FLOWS AND NPV

The fifth and final step is to add together the incremental cash flows from each of the four preceding steps. As shown in Exhibit 8.10, the first four lines reflect the net incremental cash flow figures for each of those steps. (The numbers in the first four lines of Exhibit 8.10 are taken from Exhibits 8.6 through 8.9.) Combining them yields net incremental cash flow in each year, ranging from an initial outlay of $(118,100) at the start-up of the project to $99,369 in the fifth year.

EXHIBIT 8.10 GREAT NORTHERN FOOD STORE

Step 5: Summary of Cash Flows and Net Present Value (NPV)

	(Start-up) Year 0	Year 1	Year 2	Year 3	Year 4	Year 5
Step 1: incremental net benefit (from Exhibit 8.6)		$ 5,000	$21,799	$32,454	$44,547	$58,234
Step 2: incremental depreciation tax shield (from Exhibit 8.7)		8,740	16,264	8,238	3,423	3,423
Step 3: incremental disinvestment (from Exhibit 8.8)						37,712
Step 4: incremental investment outflow (from Exhibit 8.9)	$(118,100)					
Net cash flow	$(118,100)	$13,740	$38,063	$40,692	$47,970	$99,369
Present value factor (@ 18% discount rate)	1.0000	0.8475	0.7182	0.6086	0.5158	0.4371
Present value of cash flow	$(118,100)	$11,645	$27,337	$24,765	$24,743	$43,434

Net present value (NPV)—sum of present value of cash flow $13,824

Next, net cash flow for each year is multiplied by a present value factor at a discount rate of 18 percent in order to obtain the *present value of cash flow*, or the **discounted cash flow.** The discount rate used in capital budgeting is called the **hurdle rate.** While we will discuss the hurdle rate in detail later in this chapter, it can be loosely defined here as the rate of return managers would expect on other investments having similar risks. The sum of the present value of cash flow for all years—the sum of the discounted cash flow—is equal to the net present value (NPV).

The *decision rule here is to accept all projects with positive NPVs.* In Great Northern Food Store's case, the NPV is positive—$13,824. Recall that the primary criterion in evaluating capital-budgeting projects at Great Northern Food Store is cash flow. Assuming the impact on cash flow from the bar code project is captured in the five-step framework outlined above and assuming it has a positive impact on the other selection criteria, then the project should be accepted.

ALTERNATIVES TO THE NET PRESENT VALUE METHOD

Net present value is one way of summarizing the costs and benefits associated with long-term investments in capital assets. However, it is not the only method used in actual practice. Other methods serve as supplements or alternatives to the NPV method. They include calculations based on:

- Internal rate of return (IRR)
- Present value index (PVI)
- Payback period (PB)
- Return on investment (ROI)

INTERNAL RATE OF RETURN

Another way of evaluating long-term investments is called the **internal rate of return (IRR).** In order to illustrate the internal rate of return, we must return to the present value concepts introduced at the beginning of this chapter. Recall that we showed how a $1.00 investment today accumulates to $1.15 by the end of the year, assuming that the investment earns interest at a rate of 15 percent per year.

Now, suppose we don't know what the interest rate is. We are only told that an investment of $1.00 today will yield $1.15 one year from now. We can work backward to find that rate of interest—the rate of return—implied by the investment's cash flows. By trying different rates—perhaps by using trial and error—we can find a rate that equates the investment's initial outlay with the present value of the investment's cash inflows. That rate is the interest rate that is "implicitly" earned on the investment.

For example, the present value factor, from Appendix A, for one period at a rate of 14 percent is 0.87719. Multiplying 0.87719 by $1.15 gives a present value of $1.0088, a value higher than the investment outlay of $1.00. Similarly, the present value factor for 16 percent for one period is 0.86207. Multiplying 0.86207 by $1.15 gives a present value of $0.9914, a value lower than the initial outlay. Since the present value of the future cash flow from the investment is more than the initial outlay for that investment at 14 percent ($1.0088) and less than the initial outlay at 16 percent ($0.9914), it stands to reason that the rate of return implicitly earned by the investment falls between 14 and 16 percent. We can show that 15 percent is the precise implicit internal rate of return by multiplying the present value factor for 15 percent—0.86957—by $1.15. The result confirms that the present value of $1.15, discounted at 15 percent, is exactly equal to the initial outlay. We conclude that this rate—the internal rate of return—for an investment of $1.00 today that is expected to yield a cash inflow of $1.15 at the end of 1 year is equal to 15 percent. *The internal rate of return, then, is the discount rate that equates the sum of the present value of all future cash inflows with the initial cash outflows.*

An alternative way of identifying internal rate of return is to find the *difference* between the initial outlay and the present value of all future cash inflows. When the difference is zero, we have the internal rate of return. For example, the present value of $1.15 at 14 percent is equal to $1.0088 (0.87719 × $1.15). Subtracting $1.0088 (the present value of future cash inflows) from $1.0000 (the initial outlay) gives a positive net present value of $0.0088. Similarly, the present value of $1.15 at 16 percent is $0.9914 (0.86207 × $1.15). Subtracting $0.9914 from $1.0000 gives a negative NPV of ($0.0086). The present value of $1.15 at 15 percent is $1.0000 (0.86957 × $1.15). Subtracting $1.0000 from $1.0000 gives a net present value of $0.0000. Since the NPV is zero at 15 percent, the internal rate of return is 15 percent. Thus, *a second way of defining the internal rate of return is "the discount rate that causes the net present value to equal zero."*

Exhibit 8.11 shows the NPV for Great Northern Food Store's bar code project at a discount rate of 18 percent. We can try different discount rates, recalculating the NPV each time, until we find the rate where the NPV switches from positive to negative. In our example, the NPV is positive at 21 percent ($2,911) and negative at 22 percent (− $435). The conclusion is that the IRR falls between 21 and 22 percent. Were we to choose smaller

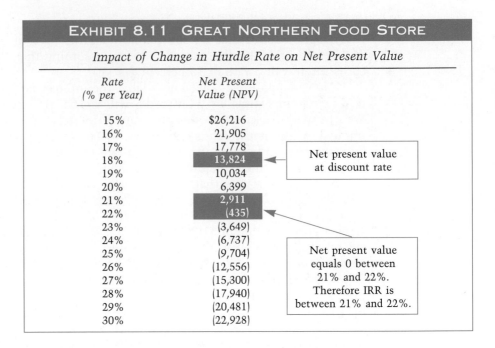

EXHIBIT 8.11   GREAT NORTHERN FOOD STORE

Impact of Change in Hurdle Rate on Net Present Value

Rate (% per Year)	Net Present Value (NPV)
15%	$26,216
16%	21,905
17%	17,778
18%	13,824
19%	10,034
20%	6,399
21%	2,911
22%	(435)
23%	(3,649)
24%	(6,737)
25%	(9,704)
26%	(12,556)
27%	(15,300)
28%	(17,940)
29%	(20,481)
30%	(22,928)

Net present value at discount rate

Net present value equals 0 between 21% and 22%. Therefore IRR is between 21% and 22%.

increments in the discount rate, we could eventually narrow down the positive and negative values until the NPV reached zero. The discount rate when the NPV equals zero is 21.87—the internal rate of return for Great Northern Food Store's proposed investment in a new bar code system.[3]

The *decision rule* for accepting and rejecting projects based on the internal rate of return is as follows: *Accept any project whose internal rate of return is greater than the rate of return (hurdle rate) specified to evaluate the investment proposal.* Note that the hurdle rate (18%), which we will discuss in detail shortly, is the same rate that we used to calculate net present value.

As illustrated in Exhibit 8.11, the internal rate of return for the bar code project is between 21 and 22 percent (21.87%), while the discount (hurdle) rate is 18 percent, so the decision should be to accept the project. In fact, in most situations, both the NPV and IRR will support the same decision. That is, a project with an NPV greater than zero (meaning that it is acceptable) will normally have an IRR greater than the discount (hurdle) rate (again, meaning that it is acceptable). While both criteria normally indicate the same accept-reject decision, there are assumptions built into the IRR that can cause projects to be evaluated differently.

For example, it is possible to have multiple IRRs when net cash flows switch from positive in one year to negative in another, and back once

---

[3] Most spreadsheets have built-in functions that automatically compute the IRR, eliminating the necessity of finding it by trial and error. However, a table such as the one in Exhibit 8.11 is easily created using a data ("what-if") table at different rates of interest. The advantage of the table is that we can see how quickly or slowly the NPV changes at different rates.

again to positive. That means there is more than one IRR. These multiple rates have no economic meaning.[4] For example, suppose net cash flows are as follows: ($100,000) in year 0, $10,000 in year 1, ($20,000) in year 2, $30,000 in year 3, ($40,000) in year 4, and $150,000 in year 5. When net cash flows switch back and forth in this manner, it means that the project has more than one IRR. We won't show how the multiple IRRs are calculated, but the fact that a project can have multiple IRRs raises questions about its validity for evaluating capital-budgeting projects.

Another assumption limiting the usefulness of IRR relates to the rate of return assumed when cash inflows from one project are invested in subsequent projects—known as the reinvestment rate. While the NPV approach assumes reinvestment at the hurdle rate, the IRR method assumes reinvestment at the IRR. For example, the NPV method assumes that all net cash inflow from Great Northern Food Store's bar code project is reinvested at 18 percent per year, while the IRR method assumes it is reinvested at 21.87 percent per year. In theory, investments in projects with the same risks should be evaluated at the same discount rates. That's not the case with IRR.

Another difference between the NPV and the IRR approaches concerns how the net cash flows are expressed—either as a rate or as an amount. Consider two projects with the following characteristics:

	Project A	Project B
IRR	16%	35%
NPV	$1,000,000	$1,000

Assume that the discount (hurdle) rate is 10 percent for each project. Thus, both projects are acceptable, regardless of whether we use the IRR or the NPV. Both have NPVs greater than zero and both have IRRs greater than the discount (hurdle) rate.

What happens if only one project can be chosen? This situation arises when projects are *mutually exclusive*, meaning that one project precludes the other. Great Northern Food Store, may, for example consider two bar code projects, each acquired from a different bar code equipment manufacturer. Only one of the projects will be chosen. Another situation is when managers have limited funds to invest in projects—a situation called capital rationing.

When acceptable projects are forced to compete—whether because they are mutually exclusive or because funds are limited—managers must choose between them. In such cases, managers may be forced to rely on other criteria in making the choice. And these criteria often reflect the way the organization measures a manager's performance. For example, what if performance is measured in terms of cash flow, as it is in the Great

---

[4] J. Fred Weston and Thomas E. Copeland, *Managerial Finance,* 8th ed., Chicago: The Dryden Press, 1986, p. 119.

Northern Food Store example? In that case, the manager is likely to select project A, since it yields the most cash flow. If, on the other hand, performance is based on maximizing rates of return, then Project B is likely to be selected. That's because project B's IRR is higher than project A's. In choosing project B, a perfectly acceptable project is rejected—one whose cash flow is significantly higher than that of the project selected.

Because of the assumptions implicit in IRR—the more-aggressive reinvestment rate assumption, the possibility of multiple IRRs, and the potential for managers to choose among competing projects based on rates rather than on dollar amounts—*the best method to use in evaluating competing capital-budgeting proposals is the NPV* approach.

PRESENT VALUE INDEX

Another alternative to the NPV method relies on the **present value index (PVI)**, where:

$$\text{Present value index} = \frac{\text{sum of present value of future cash inflows}}{\text{initial outlay}}$$

The PVI is found by adding together the present value of all the future cash flows, exclusive of the initial outlay, and dividing that sum by the initial outlay. For example, the discounted cash flows for Great Northern Food Store's bar code project, taken from Exhibit 8.10, are reproduced at the top of Exhibit 8.12. We can add all of the positive present values of cash flow together ($11,645 + $27,337 + $24,765 + $24,743 + $43,434), or we can take the sum of the present values of all future cash flow ($13,824) and add back the initial outlay of $118,100. In either case, we get the same figure ($131,924). Dividing $131,924 by $118,100, the initial outlay, yields a PVI of 1.12.

The PVI shows the present value of benefits per dollar of initial cash outlay. The PVI will equal 1 when the NPV is zero. When the PVI is greater than 1, the sum of the present values of all future cash flow exceeds the present value of the initial outlay—that means the NPV is greater than zero. *The decision rule is to accept projects with PVIs greater than 1.*

Some managers rank projects in descending order by PVI. The project with the greatest PVI is accepted first, followed by the project with the second-highest PVI, and so forth, for all projects with PVIs greater than 1. If there are enough funds for all projects, then a PVI-based evaluation will achieve the same results as an NPV-based approach. However, in situations where funds are limited (i.e., where capital is rationed) and where the objective is to maximize the combined NPV of the available funds, ranking projects by their PVIs may yield less total cash flow than the maximum possible combined NPV.

PAYBACK PERIOD

Another alternative to the NPV approach is based on the **payback period (PB)**. The payback period is the number of years it takes before the cost of the project is recovered through **nondiscounted cash flows**. Data needed to calculate Great Northern Food Store's payback period are found in the

EXHIBIT 8.12 GREAT NORTHERN FOOD STORE

Other Measures of Investment Performance

Present Value Index (PVI)

	(Start-up) Year 0	Year 1	Year 2	Year 3	Year 4	Year 5
Present value of cash flow (from Exhibit 8.10)	$(118,100)	$ 11,645	$ 27,337	$ 24,765	$ 24,743	$43,434
Cumulative present value of cash flow	$(118,100)	$(106,455)	$ (79,118)	$ (54,353)	$ (29,610)	$13,824
Cumulative present value of cash flow—year 5	$13,824					
Plus initial outlay	$ 118,100					
Present value of total cash flow	$ 131,924					
Divided by initial investment	$ 118,100					
Equals present value index (PVI) ($131,924/$118,100)	**1.12**					

Payback Period (PB)

Net cash flow (from Exhibit 8.10)	$(118,100)	$ 13,740	$ 38,063	$ 40,692	$ 47,970	$ 99,369
Cumulative net cash flow	$(118,100)	$(104,360)	$ (66,297)	$ (25,605)	$ 22,365	$121,734
Calculation of payback period:						
Cumulative cash flow in year 4	$22,365					
Less cumulative cash flow in year 3	(25,605)					
Increase in cash flow during year 4	$47,970					
Divide cumulative cash flow in year 3 by increase in cash flow during year 4	(25,605)					
Proportion of year (absolute value)	0.53					
Plus years before cash turns positive	3.00					
Payback period (in years)(PB)	**3.53 years**					

Return on Investment (ROI)

		Year 1	Year 2	Year 3	Year 4	Year 5
Net benefit before income taxes (from Exhibit 8.6)		$ 8,065	$ 35,160	$ 52,345	$ 71,850	$93,926
Less straight-line depreciation— ($165,000 − $75,000 residual value)/5 years)		(18,000)	(18,000)	(18,000)	(18,000)	(18,000)
Net income before taxes		(9,935)	17,160	$ 34,345	$ 53,850	$75,926
Less income taxes (rate @ 38%)		3,775	(6,521)	(13,051)	(20,463)	(28,852)
Net income using straight-line depreciation		$ (6,160)	$ 10,639	$ 21,294	$ 33,387	$47,074
Investment—average book value:						
Book value—beginning of period		$ 165,000	$147,000	$129,000	$111,000	$93,000
Less depreciation (see above)		(18,000)	(18,000)	(18,000)	(18,000)	(18,000)
Book value—end of period		$ 147,000	$129,000	$111,000	$ 93,000	$75,000
Average book value		$ 156,000	$138,000	$120,000	$102,000	$84,000
ROI (net income/average book value)		**−3.95%**	**7.71%**	**17.74%**	**32.73%**	**56.04%**

middle panel of Exhibit 8.12. Cumulative cash flows are calculated by adding all the nondiscounted cash flows for each period over the project's life. For example, the initial cumulative cash flow in Exhibit 8.12 is $(118,100), representing the initial cash outlay. Cash inflow for the first year of operations—$13,740—partially offsets the initial outlay, resulting in a cumulative cash flow of $(104,360). Continuing to add each year's net cash flow to the accumulating total causes the total to turn positive between the third and fourth year or, more precisely, at 3.53 years.

Payback period is often used as a measure of risk, since investments in projects with longer payback periods are perceived as more risky than investments with shorter payback periods. The payback period for an investment is calculated and compared with a desired, or *threshold*, payback period. A project whose payback period exceeds the threshold is deemed too risky and is likely to be rejected. If, for example, Great Northern Food Store had imposed a 3-year payback maximum, the bar code system proposal would have been rejected.

Using payback as an investment criterion forces managers to take a short-term perspective. Few investments with long-term benefits—even though they may have NPVs greater than zero—are likely to gain acceptance when the payback period method is used to evaluate them.

RETURN ON INVESTMENT

Another alternative to the NPV method is an approach based on the accounting rate of return, or **return on investment (ROI)**. The ROI is calculated by dividing the net income—not net cash flow—generated by a project by its investment cost, typically measured in terms of book value, as follows:

$$ROI = \frac{\text{net income derived from project}}{\text{amount invested in project}}$$

The numerator in the ROI equation (net income) is measured in terms of accrual-based accounting revenue and expense—not in terms of cash flow. If the project's costs and benefits are already expressed as cash flow, then conversion to accrual-based revenue and expense is required. One of the expenses that has to be converted is depreciation. MACRS rates are not used in calculating depreciation for the ROI method. Rather, depreciation used in calculating ROI is often the same as that reported on the firm's financial statements.

For example, Great Northern Food Store's revenue and expense—the net benefit before depreciation and income taxes—from the bar code project are shown in the bottom section of Exhibit 8.12. Accrual-accounting-based net income is determined by subtracting straight-line depreciation and recalculating income taxes. For example, if the bar code equipment costs $165,000, has a useful life of 5 years, and has a residual value of $75,000, then straight-line depreciation is $18,000 per year [($165,000 − $75,000 in salvage value, or $90,000)/5 years]. Deducting depreciation ($18,000) from the net benefit before income taxes ($8,065) gives a pretax net loss of $(9,935) in the first year and an after-tax loss of $(6,160) in the first year.

The investment part of the ROI—the denominator in the equation—reflects the project's cost. Investment cost can be measured in two ways—as either gross book value ($165,000, the original cost of the project) or net book value (original cost less accumulated depreciation). Net book value is calculated either:

1. At the *beginning of the year*—$165,000 − $0 in accumulated depreciation, or $165,000
2. At the *end of the year*—$165,000 − $18,000 in accumulated depreciation, or $147,000
3. For the *average for the year*—the average of the net book value at the beginning of the year and the book value at the end of the year or $156,000 [($165,000 + $147,000)/2]

Assume Great Northern Food Store measures the cost of investments based on average book value. If so, the ROI is negative (3.95%) in the first year of operations. It increases to 7.71 percent in the second year and reaches its highest point in the fifth year.

As mentioned in the Walter Company example at the beginning of this chapter, accrual-based accounting measures such as net income should not be used in evaluating capital-budgeting projects, because such measures do not reflect the time value of money. Moreover, managers have more discretion over when revenue and expense show up in net income than they do over the timing of cash flows, giving them more opportunities to influence ROI.

Another problem with ROI is that it is frequently used to *measure the performance* of managers responsible for making capital-budgeting decisions—*after* the managers have made the decisions. ROI is a logical choice as a measure of performance, since both the numerator (net income) and denominator (book value) are routinely collected as a part of the financial accounting system.

While ROI should not be used to make capital-budgeting decisions, managers whose performance is measured by ROI may look ahead and estimate a project's impact on their future ROI. If the project isn't likely to improve their ROI beyond what would have been expected without the project, then the project is likely to be rejected. For example, assume the manager evaluating Great Northern Food Store's bar code project expects to earn an average ROI next year of 15 percent based on existing investments. By accepting the project, the manager's average ROI would decrease below 15 percent, pulled down by the bar code project's first-year ROI of (3.95) percent. As a result, projects with perfectly acceptable NPVs may be rejected because of their anticipated short-term impacts on ROI. We will address this dilemma of lack of goal congruence, where measures of performance should motivate employees to act in ways that serve both the needs of the individuals and those of the organization, in later chapters.

We conclude this section by affirming the validity of NPV—*NPV is better for evaluating capital-budgeting projects than the alternative methods* are. The alternative methods can be used as supplements to an NPV approach but should not replace it as the primary evaluation criterion.

HURDLE RATE

The hurdle rate mentioned earlier in this chapter is the rate of return used to discount future cash flows to present value. The term *hurdle* is used because it represents an obstacle, or a barrier, that a project has to overcome in order to be accepted. Therefore, the hurdle rate is the minimum level of return needed from an investment, at a given level of risk, for the investment to be considered acceptable.

The hurdle rate is a measure of what the organization expects to earn on its best opportunities. It is not a single rate for all projects, nor is it constant from year to year. It changes according to a project's perceived level of risk. From a base used for virtually riskfree projects, the hurdle rate is adjusted upward to reflect increasing levels of risk. Investments in replacement equipment, for example, where costs and benefits are generally known, will be evaluated at relatively low hurdle rates. In contrast, projects involving investments in new product lines or evolving technology, where costs and benefits are largely unknown, are typically evaluated at higher hurdle rates.

Hurdle rates start from a base known as the **weighted-average cost of capital.** Capital for new investments comes from a pool of sources—consisting of debt financing, undistributed cash flow from operations, and newly issued stock. The weighted average cost of capital is determined by multiplying the relative proportions of each of these three sources of funds by the after-tax cost of funds from that source. For example, assume the before-tax cost of debt is, say, 12 percent. Then the after-tax cost is 7.44 percent if the tax rate is 38% [(100% − 38%) × 12%]. If 25 percent of the total funds used to finance all capital-budgeting projects is expected to come from debt, then the weighted-average after-tax cost of debt is 1.86 percent (25% × 7.44%).

Recall that cash flow from operations can be used to pay dividends. If, instead, cash flow from operations is reinvested in capital projects, the undistributed (retained) earnings carry an opportunity cost equal to the current dividend rate—in this case, equal to, say, 13.50 percent. Since dividends are not tax deductible, there is no tax effect. So, the before- and after-tax costs of internally generated funds are the same. When multiplied by 50 percent (the proportion of financing we assume comes from retained earnings) the weighted-average after-tax cost of retained earnings is 6.75 percent. Similarly, funds for capital-budgeting projects can be raised by issuing new stock. The rate for newly issued stock is typically higher than retained earnings because the company must pay someone to issue the stock. The cost of stock is measured in terms of dividends relative to the amount the firm receives from the issuance of that stock. Again, dividends are not deductible for tax purposes. Therefore, the before- and after-tax cost of new stock is 14 percent. When multiplied by 25 percent (the proportion of financing we assume comes from the issuance of new stock), the weighted-average after-tax cost of the new stock is 3.50 percent. Adding the after-tax cost of all three components together gives a weighted-average cost of capital equal to 12.11 percent. The results of these calculations are shown in Exhibit 8.13 for the Great Northern Food Store example.

EXHIBIT 8.13 GREAT NORTHERN FOOD STORE

Weighted-Average Cost of Capital

Source of Capital	Before-Tax Rate	Tax Effect (38%)	After-Tax Rate	Weight[a]	Weighted Rate for Each Source of Capital
Debt	12.00%	4.56%	7.44%	25.00%	1.86%
Retained earnings	13.50%	0.00%	13.50%	50.00%	6.75%
New issue of common stock	14.00%	0.00%	14.00%	25.00%	3.50%
Weighted-average cost of capital					12.11%

[a] Weights are based on desired proportions of capital from each source. In our example, 25 percent of the long-term financing will come from bonds, 50 percent from retained earnings, and 25 percent from a new issue of common stock.

The weighted-average cost of capital forms a "floor" discount rate. From this floor, discount rates are adjusted upward to reflect risks inherent in each project. *The cost of capital adjusted to reflect a project's risk, then, is the hurdle rate.* For example, Great Northern Food Store's 18 percent hurdle rate for the bar code project starts with the weighted-average cost of capital of 12.11 percent and adds an adjustment of 5.89 percent to compensate for the relative risk associated with the project. We do not show how the risk adjustment is determined—that's a topic for finance textbooks.

In general, higher hurdle rates make it more difficult to justify investments in new projects. This is especially true for projects with higher-than-normal levels of risk. For example, consider a pharmaceutical company that invests in a new or emerging technology, such as genetic engineering. The benefits and costs of this technology are largely unknown. However, it is often investment in such high-risk projects that positions an organization for growth in the future. In contrast, lower hurdle rates make it possible for managers to take a long-term view in evaluating major projects. We are not arguing for a reevaluation of rate structures here; we are simply pointing out the impact that discount rates have on the acceptance and rejection of long-term projects, especially those whose benefits are hard to quantify. Ultimately, the choice of hurdle rates is important, as is the way a manager's performance is measured. Both factors should induce managers to take risks that are appropriate for their organizations.

We have stated throughout this text that the primary goal of any organization is to create shareholder value. *As long as the return on each project exceeds its hurdle rate, shareholder value will be created.*

EVALUATING PROJECT COSTS AND BENEFITS

Besides costs and benefits measured in dollars, there are nonfinancial quantitative and qualitative factors that influence the decision to accept or reject a project. (See "Current Practice: Justifying Pollution Prevention Projects.") The degree to which these factors will affect an investment decision should be established as part of an organization's capital-budgeting procedures. For example, the criteria used by Great Northern Food Store places the greatest weight on short-term cash flow. Other strategic categories of costs and benefits include profitability, market share, and customer satisfaction, as noted earlier.

Profitability.   With demographics indicating reduced availability of skilled workers where its stores are located, Great Northern Food Store believes conversion to bar code technology, which requires lower skill levels, will provide access to larger labor pools. The bar code system offers a form of insurance against future labor shortages and a means of reducing future payroll cost. Hence, the new technology reflects cost reductions and productivity improvements not captured quantitatively in the formal capital-budgeting procedures.

Market Share.   Great Northern Food Store's management believes the new equipment will permit tighter day-to-day control of inventory reordering. As a result, managers plan to stock fewer units on the shelves and to use the extra space to display a wider assortment of products. While they are not able to quantify the impact of increased variety, managers firmly believe that offering a wider assortment of products will improve the company's future market share. In addition, the new equipment will indicate

CURRENT PRACTICE

Justifying Pollution Prevention Projects

Many of the costs and benefits of pollution prevention projects are difficult to measure. That makes them difficult to justify. A recent EPA publication listed categories of costs that might be considered when evaluating projects with environmental ramifications. Some categories comprise costs such as equipment, site preparation, start-up, and training. Other costs might include:

- Compliance costs, such as the costs of permits, reporting, and monitoring
- On-site waste management, soil removal, and groundwater treatment

- Liability costs, such as penalties for noncompliance, and similar fines
- Legal claims, awards, settlements for remediation, personal injury, and property damage as the result of routine or accidental release of hazardous material

These costs may be partially offset by hidden benefits:

- Increased revenues from improved public image
- Reduced health costs from improved working conditions
- Better employee relations

Source: U.S. Environmental Protection Agency, Office of Pollution Prevention and Toxics, *Total Cost Assessment: Accelerating Industrial Pollution Prevention through Innovative Project Financial Analysis,* May 1992.

to Great Northern Food Store's customers that it is modern and up-to-date. Moreover, Great Northern Food Store managers predict that the new bar code technology is inevitable and that they should be among the first to adopt it.

Customer Satisfaction. Customer satisfaction is measured in terms of three dimensions: (1) checkout cycle time, (2) employee turnover, and (3) ease of access to checkout counters. Surveys show that customers want fast checkout. Friendly, efficient employees are a key to customer satisfaction; and managers believe that projects that improve customers' access to the checkout counters will also contribute to customer satisfaction.

Since the evaluations indicate that the project will have a positive impact on all of the selection criteria, Great Northern Food Store managers decide to invest in the new bar code system. At this point, the decision may be considered nothing more than a formality, since a consensus may have already been achieved.

POSTAUDIT EVALUATION

After a project has been selected and implemented, postaudit evaluations—or simply, "postaudits"—provide managers with a systematic way of assessing the project's progress, and the programs constituting it. Postaudits can be used to compare actual performance against the costs and benefits estimated during the capital-budgeting process. Furthermore, postaudits serve as a way of holding those managers who are responsible for making capital-budgeting decisions accountable for the results of their decision. Depending on the outcome of a postaudit evaluation, projects can be redirected or, if necessary, abandoned should benefits not materialize or costs be greater than originally estimated.

Information gathered from the postaudit evaluation can:

- Foster management learning by providing the basis for understanding causes of deviations from projections
- Encourage managers to prepare realistic estimates of project costs and benefits
- Reduce managers' aversion to risky investments
- Provide the data necessary in order to make the decision to abandon a project
- Furnish managers with the information they need in order to improve future capital-budgeting proposals[5]

A well-designed postaudit system should:[6]

- Indicate which projects are to be reviewed
- Identify those who will conduct the review
- Specify the frequency of postaudit evaluations

---

[5] Adapted from Kimberly J. Smith, "Postauditing Capital Investments," *Financial Practice and Education*, spring-summer 1994, pp. 129–137.

[6] This section is based upon an article by Lawrence Gordon and Mary D. Myers, "Postauditing Capital Projects," *Management Accounting*, Jan. 1991, pp. 39–42.

- Stipulate the assessment method and evaluation criteria
- Modify the accounting system so that it is able to provide the requisite information
- Communicate evaluation results and make appropriate modifications to existing policies and procedures

A POSTAUDIT EXAMPLE: CATERPILLAR, INC.

Caterpillar, Inc., monitors its capital expenditures by gathering projects in "bundles."[7] Bundles may be manufacturing processes (e.g., machining, welding, assembly, heat treating, or press shop), commodities (e.g., axle factory bundle, which includes gear line and integrated heat treatment, wheel and drum line, axle-machining line, and axle assembly area), or activities and expenditures related to new products (e.g., R&D and new equipment to produce a new product).

Caterpillar uses the bundles approach because it is easier to identify costs and benefits for bundles of products or services than it is to do so for individual machines. Moreover, monitoring bundles places the focus on the strategic marketing and manufacturing goals of the firm.

Each project bundle is monitored every 6 months, usually by the team involved in the original planning and justification of that bundle. The team selects the characteristics to be monitored, determines current values of those characteristics, and estimates what the values are likely to be in the future. The team may also recommend modifications when a bundle's performance is not up to expectations. In addition, the management accountant on the team analyzes alternatives for improving performance and calculates the resulting reduction in product cost.

Approved in 1986 and implemented in 1987, Caterpillar's "structures bundle" comprises projects that weld and machine heavy structures for medium and large equipment. The postaudit of the structures bundle, as of June 1991, is shown in Exhibit 8.14.

The first numerical column of Exhibit 8.14 indicates values of key characteristics prior to the organization of Caterpillar's structures bundle in August 1986. The second column represents projections made in August 1986 showing where management wanted the key characteristic values for structures bundle to be by the end of 1994. The third column represents the status of the structures bundle during an evaluation in June 1991. The remaining four columns represent revised annual projections, prepared in June 1991, for the end of 1991 through 1994.

The rows in Exhibit 8.14 are the structures bundle's characteristics that managers decided to monitor, as well as the project's IRR. The data obtained from the monitoring resulted in the revised projections. For example, the June 1991 evaluation caused managers to revise the original target IRR of 30 percent downward to 27 percent. According to the structures-bundle managers, the downward adjustment in IRR is necessary because of:

---

[7]   J. Hendricks, R. Bastian, and T. Sexton, "Bundle Monitoring of Strategic Projects," *Management Accounting*, Feb. 1992, pp. 31–35.

EXHIBIT 8.14   CATERPILLAR'S STRUCTURES BUNDLE

Postaudit Evaluation

Key Characteristics	As is— 8/86	Original Target— 12/94	Current— 6/91	Revised Projections			
				12/91	12/92	12/93	12/94
Total capital spent (in $ millions)	$4	$42	$40	$42	$45	$45	$45
Start-up expense (in $ millions)	$0	$12	$13	$14	$16	$17	$17
Manpower:							
Direct, hourly	623	497	568	543	525	504	504
Indirect, hourly	200	160	184	184	175	165	165
Salaried	77	63	74	73	68	63	63
Total manpower	900	720	826	800	768	732	732
In-process inventory (in $)	65	34	34	34	27	27	27
In-process inventory (days)	30	15	16	16	12	12	12
Average throughput (days)	12	6	9	8	6	6	6
Floor space (1,000s of square feet)	450	410	430	425	420	415	410
Dies & fixtures	2,800	850	1,930	1,775	1,450	1,125	845
Scheduling	Forecast	Demand	Forecast	Forecast	Forecast	Demand	Demand
Production cost reduction		13.00%	6.00%	8.00%	8.00%	10.00%	11.00%
Internal rate of return (IRR)		30.00%	27.00%				

Source: J. Hendricks, R. Bastian, and T. Sexton, "Bundle Monitoring of Strategic Projects," *Management Accounting,* Feb. 1992, pp. 31–35.

- A total of $3 million more of capital that was expended in order to acquire a life-arm flexible machining system
- Delays in implementation and in achieving savings
- Additional start-up expenditures of $5.4 million
- Increase of seven direct labor employees involved in the installation of a robot weld bank
- The addition of five indirect employees for unanticipated materials handling and maintenance
- An offsetting $7 million decrease in work-in-process inventory

Based on the postaudit evaluation, the structures-bundle team recommended the following actions:

- Investigate and correct the problem of parts that do not fit properly on the robot weld bank, thereby eliminating rework.
- Increase the workload on underutilized robot welders and machining systems by evaluating structures that are currently purchased in a finished state. Consider making some of these structures internally.
- Review the purchase of a $2-million conveyor shuttle system scheduled for 1992, since the revised estimate of savings results in an unacceptable IRR.
- Ask that suppliers deliver oversized materials into the building directly to the point of use, thereby eliminating the need for three materials handlers.
- Eliminate temporary contracted programming for the robot weld system (at a cost saving of $60 per hour) by using in-house programmers.

The goal of bundle monitoring at Caterpillar, Inc., and for all postaudit evaluations is to keep the key characteristics of a project—and, hence, cash flows—on target.

SUMMARY

Capital budgeting is a systematic approach to determining the quantitative and qualitative consequences of an investment expected to help fulfill the firm's strategic mission. Capital budgeting begins with the identification of appropriate investment projects and the collection of both quantitative and qualitative data needed in order to evaluate and make an accept/reject decision.

The organization should establish policies specifying how the evaluation process is to be conducted and how costs and benefits are to be measured. Once data representing the project have been gathered, the project's net benefit can be estimated by calculating the net present value (NPV).

NPV represents the difference between a project's discounted cash inflows and its discounted cash outflows. If all inflows exceed all outflows, the NPV will be positive, and the project, at least quantitatively, should be deemed acceptable.

Other quantitative measures of a project include IRR, payback period, and accounting rate of return. Each of these approaches has limitations and should not be used as the primary decision-making model.

After project's estimated quantitative and qualitative data have been assembled, a decision is reached by weighing them in accordance with the firm's previously established selection criteria.

Accepted projects, once implemented, are revisited in the form of a postaudit review that evaluates the impact of the project on shareholder value. The postaudit review also helps improve decision making in the future.

Capital budgeting should be viewed not as a final product, but as a process—a series of steps taking a project proposal from an idea to implementation. Since many proposals have strategic implications, this careful evaluation of a project's future impact on the firm acts as an important link in the firm's overall planning and control system.

APPENDIX A SELECTED PRESENT VALUE FACTORS FOR $1

Discount Rate

Periods	5%	6%	8%	10%	12%	14%	15%	16%	18%
1	0.95238	0.94340	0.92593	0.90909	0.89286	0.87719	0.86957	0.86207	0.84746
2	0.90703	0.89000	0.85734	0.82645	0.79719	0.76947	0.75614	0.74316	0.71818
3	0.86384	0.83962	0.79383	0.75131	0.71178	0.67497	0.65752	0.64066	0.60863
4	0.82270	0.79209	0.73503	0.68301	0.63552	0.59208	0.57175	0.55229	0.51579
5	0.78353	0.74726	0.68058	0.62092	0.56743	0.51937	0.49718	0.47611	0.43711
6	0.74622	0.70496	0.63017	0.56447	0.50663	0.45559	0.43233	0.41044	0.37043
7	0.71068	0.66506	0.58349	0.51316	0.45235	0.39964	0.37594	0.35383	0.31393
8	0.67684	0.62741	0.54027	0.46651	0.40388	0.35056	0.32690	0.30503	0.26604
9	0.64461	0.59190	0.50025	0.42410	0.36061	0.30751	0.28426	0.26295	0.22546
10	0.61391	0.55839	0.46319	0.38554	0.32197	0.26974	0.24718	0.22668	0.19106
11	0.58468	0.52679	0.42888	0.35049	0.28748	0.23662	0.21494	0.19542	0.16192
12	0.55684	0.49697	0.39711	0.31863	0.25668	0.20756	0.18691	0.16846	0.13722
13	0.53032	0.46884	0.36770	0.28966	0.22917	0.18207	0.16253	0.14523	0.11629
14	0.50507	0.44230	0.34046	0.26333	0.20462	0.15971	0.14133	0.12520	0.09855
15	0.48102	0.41727	0.31524	0.23939	0.18270	0.14010	0.12289	0.10793	0.08352
16	0.45811	0.39365	0.29189	0.21763	0.16312	0.12289	0.10686	0.09304	0.07078
17	0.43630	0.37136	0.27027	0.19784	0.14564	0.10780	0.09293	0.08021	0.05998
18	0.41552	0.35034	0.25025	0.17986	0.13004	0.09456	0.08081	0.06914	0.05083
19	0.39573	0.33051	0.23171	0.16351	0.11611	0.08295	0.07027	0.05961	0.04308
20	0.37689	0.31180	0.21455	0.14864	0.10367	0.07276	0.06110	0.05139	0.03651
21	0.35894	0.29416	0.19866	0.13513	0.09256	0.06383	0.05313	0.04430	0.03094
22	0.34185	0.27751	0.18394	0.12285	0.08264	0.05599	0.04620	0.03819	0.02622
23	0.32557	0.26180	0.17032	0.11168	0.07379	0.04911	0.04017	0.03292	0.02222
24	0.31007	0.24698	0.15770	0.10153	0.06588	0.04308	0.03493	0.02838	0.01883
25	0.29530	0.23300	0.14602	0.09230	0.05882	0.03779	0.03038	0.02447	0.01596
26	0.28124	0.21981	0.13520	0.08391	0.05252	0.03315	0.02642	0.02109	0.01352
27	0.26785	0.20737	0.12519	0.07628	0.04689	0.02908	0.02297	0.01818	0.01146
28	0.25509	0.19563	0.11591	0.06934	0.04187	0.02551	0.01997	0.01567	0.00971
29	0.24295	0.18456	0.10733	0.06304	0.03738	0.02237	0.01737	0.01351	0.00823
30	0.23138	0.17411	0.09938	0.05731	0.03338	0.01963	0.01510	0.01165	0.00697
31	0.22036	0.16425	0.09202	0.05210	0.02980	0.01722	0.01313	0.01004	0.00591
32	0.20987	0.15496	0.08520	0.04736	0.02661	0.01510	0.01142	0.00866	0.00501
33	0.19987	0.14619	0.07889	0.04306	0.02376	0.01325	0.00993	0.00746	0.00425
34	0.19035	0.13791	0.07305	0.03914	0.02121	0.01162	0.00864	0.00643	0.00360
35	0.18129	0.13011	0.06763	0.03558	0.01894	0.01019	0.00751	0.00555	0.00305
36	0.17266	0.12274	0.06262	0.03235	0.01691	0.00894	0.00653	0.00478	0.00258
37	0.16444	0.11579	0.05799	0.02941	0.01510	0.00784	0.00568	0.00412	0.00219
38	0.15661	0.10924	0.05369	0.02673	0.01348	0.00688	0.00494	0.00355	0.00186
39	0.14915	0.10306	0.04971	0.02430	0.01204	0.00604	0.00429	0.00306	0.00157
40	0.14205	0.09722	0.04603	0.02209	0.01075	0.00529	0.00373	0.00264	0.00133
41	0.13528	0.09172	0.04262	0.02009	0.00960	0.00464	0.00325	0.00228	0.00113
42	0.12884	0.08653	0.03946	0.01826	0.00857	0.00407	0.00282	0.00196	0.00096
43	0.12270	0.08163	0.03654	0.01660	0.00765	0.00357	0.00245	0.00169	0.00081
44	0.11686	0.07701	0.03383	0.01509	0.00683	0.00313	0.00213	0.00146	0.00069
45	0.11130	0.07265	0.03133	0.01372	0.00610	0.00275	0.00186	0.00126	0.00058
46	0.10600	0.06854	0.02901	0.01247	0.00544	0.00241	0.00161	0.00108	0.00049
47	0.10095	0.06466	0.02686	0.01134	0.00486	0.00212	0.00140	0.00093	0.00042
48	0.09614	0.06100	0.02487	0.01031	0.00434	0.00186	0.00122	0.00081	0.00035
49	0.09156	0.05755	0.02303	0.00937	0.00388	0.00163	0.00106	0.00069	0.00030
50	0.08720	0.05429	0.02132	0.00852	0.00346	0.00143	0.00092	0.00060	0.00025

(continued)

APPENDIX A (CONTINUED)

20%	22%	24%	25%	26%	28%	30%	35%	40%	50%
0.83333	0.81967	0.80645	0.80000	0.79365	0.78125	0.76923	0.74074	0.71429	0.66667
0.69444	0.67186	0.65036	0.64000	0.62988	0.61035	0.59172	0.54870	0.51020	0.44444
0.57870	0.55071	0.52449	0.51200	0.49991	0.47684	0.45517	0.40644	0.36443	0.29630
0.48225	0.45140	0.42297	0.40960	0.39675	0.37253	0.35013	0.30107	0.26031	0.19753
0.40188	0.37000	0.34111	0.32768	0.31488	0.29104	0.26933	0.22301	0.18593	0.13169
0.33490	0.30328	0.27509	0.26214	0.24991	0.22737	0.20718	0.16520	0.13281	0.08779
0.27908	0.24859	0.22184	0.20972	0.19834	0.11764	0.15937	0.12237	0.09486	0.05853
0.23257	0.20376	0.17891	0.16777	0.15741	0.13878	0.12259	0.09064	0.06776	0.03902
0.19381	0.16702	0.14428	0.13422	0.12493	0.10842	0.09430	0.06714	0.04840	0.02601
0.16151	0.13690	0.11635	0.10737	0.09915	0.08470	0.07254	0.04974	0.03457	0.01734
0.13459	0.11221	0.09383	0.08590	0.07869	0.06617	0.05580	0.03684	0.02469	0.01156
0.11216	0.09198	0.07567	0.06872	0.06245	0.05170	0.04292	0.02729	0.01764	0.00771
0.09346	0.07539	0.06103	0.05498	0.04957	0.04039	0.03302	0.02021	0.01260	0.00514
0.07789	0.06180	0.04921	0.04398	0.03934	0.03155	0.02540	0.01497	0.00900	0.00343
0.06491	0.05065	0.03969	0.03518	0.03122	0.02465	0.01954	0.01109	0.00643	0.00228
0.05409	0.04152	0.03201	0.02815	0.02478	0.01926	0.01503	0.00822	0.00459	0.00152
0.04507	0.03403	0.02581	0.02252	0.01967	0.01505	0.01156	0.00609	0.00328	0.00101
0.03756	0.02789	0.02082	0.01801	0.01561	0.01175	0.00889	0.00451	0.00234	0.00068
0.03130	0.02286	0.01679	0.01441	0.01239	0.00918	0.00684	0.00334	0.00167	0.00045
0.02608	0.01874	0.01354	0.01153	0.00983	0.00717	0.00526	0.00247	0.00120	0.00030
0.02174	0.01536	0.01092	0.00922	0.00780	0.00561	0.00405	0.00183	0.00085	0.00020
0.01811	0.01259	0.00880	0.00738	0.00619	0.00438	0.00311	0.00136	0.00061	0.00013
0.01509	0.01032	0.00710	0.00590	0.00491	0.00342	0.00239	0.00101	0.00044	0.00009
0.01258	0.00846	0.00573	0.00472	0.00390	0.00267	0.00184	0.00074	0.00031	0.00006
0.01048	0.00693	0.00462	0.00378	0.00310	0.00209	0.00142	0.00055	0.00022	0.00004
0.00874	0.00568	0.00372	0.00302	0.00246	0.00163	0.00109	0.00041	0.00016	0.00003
0.00728	0.00466	0.00300	0.00242	0.00195	0.00127	0.00084	0.00030	0.00011	0.00002
0.00607	0.00382	0.00242	0.00193	0.00155	0.00100	0.00065	0.00022	0.00008	0.00001
0.00506	0.00313	0.00195	0.00155	0.00123	0.00078	0.00050	0.00017	0.00006	0.00001
0.00421	0.00257	0.00158	0.00124	0.00097	0.00061	0.00038	0.00012	0.00004	0.00001
0.00351	0.00210	0.00127	0.00099	0.00077	0.00047	0.00029	0.00009	0.00003	0.00000
0.00293	0.00172	0.00102	0.00079	0.00061	0.00037	0.00023	0.00007	0.00002	0.00000
0.00244	0.00141	0.00083	0.00063	0.00049	0.00029	0.00017	0.00005	0.00002	0.00000
0.00203	0.00116	0.00067	0.00051	0.00039	0.00023	0.00013	0.00004	0.00001	0.00000
0.00169	0.00095	0.00054	0.00041	0.00031	0.00018	0.00010	0.00003	0.00001	0.00000
0.00141	0.00078	0.00043	0.00032	0.00024	0.00014	0.00008	0.00002	0.00001	0.00000
0.00118	0.00064	0.00035	0.00026	0.00019	0.00011	0.00006	0.00002	0.00000	0.00000
0.00098	0.00052	0.00028	0.00021	0.00015	0.00008	0.00005	0.00001	0.00000	0.00000
0.00082	0.00043	0.00023	0.00017	0.00012	0.00007	0.00004	0.00001	0.00000	0.00000
0.00068	0.00035	0.00018	0.00013	0.00010	0.00005	0.00003	0.00001	0.00000	0.00000
0.00057	0.00029	0.00015	0.00011	0.00008	0.00004	0.00002	0.00000	0.00000	0.00000
0.00047	0.00024	0.00012	0.00009	0.00006	0.00003	0.00002	0.00000	0.00000	0.00000
0.00039	0.00019	0.00010	0.00007	0.00005	0.00002	0.00001	0.00000	0.00000	0.00000
0.00033	0.00016	0.00008	0.00005	0.00004	0.00002	0.00001	0.00000	0.00000	0.00000
0.00027	0.00013	0.00006	0.00004	0.00003	0.00001	0.00001	0.00000	0.00000	0.00000
0.00023	0.00011	0.00005	0.00003	0.00002	0.00001	0.00001	0.00000	0.00000	0.00000
0.00019	0.00009	0.00004	0.00003	0.00002	0.00001	0.00000	0.00000	0.00000	0.00000
0.00016	0.00007	0.00003	0.00002	0.00002	0.00001	0.00000	0.00000	0.00000	0.00000
0.00013	0.00006	0.00003	0.00002	0.00001	0.00001	0.00000	0.00000	0.00000	0.00000
0.00011	0.00005	0.00002	0.00001	0.00001	0.00000	0.00000	0.00000	0.00000	0.00000

APPENDIX B MACRS DEPRECIATION RATES FOR TANGIBLE PROPERTY

| | Investment Class | | | | | |
Year	3-Year	5-Year	7-Year	10-Year	15-Year	20-Year
1	33.33%	20.00%	14.29%	10.00%	5.00%	3.75%
2	44.45%	32.00%	24.49%	18.00%	9.50%	7.22%
3	14.81%	19.20%	17.49%	14.40%	8.55%	6.68%
4	7.41%	11.52%	12.49%	11.52%	7.70%	6.18%
5		11.52%	8.93%	9.22%	6.93%	5.71%
6		5.76%	8.92%	7.37%	6.23%	5.29%
7			8.93%	6.55%	5.90%	4.89%
8			4.46%	6.55%	5.90%	4.52%
9				6.56%	5.91%	4.46%
10				6.55%	5.90%	4.46%
11				3.28%	5.91%	4.46%
12					5.90%	4.46%
13					5.91%	4.46%
14					5.90%	4.46%
15					5.91%	4.46%
16					2.95%	4.46%
17						4.46%
18						4.46%
19						4.46%
20						4.46%
21						2.23%
	100.00%	100.00%	100.00%	100.00%	100.00%	100.00%

Example

Assume purchase of equipment that costs $165,000. The purchase qualifies as a 5-year class with an estimated disposal value of $75,000. Note that the disposal value is not used in the computation.

Year	Rate	Basis	Deprec.
1	20.00%	$165,000	$ 33,000
2	32.00%	$165,000	52,800
3	19.20%	$165,000	31,680
4	11.52%	$165,000	19,008
5	11.52%	$165,000	19,008
6	5.76%	$165,000	9,504
			$165,000

CHAPTER 8 ASSIGNMENTS

DISCUSSION PROBLEMS

D8.1 (Capital Budgeting at an Oil Field)[8]

Phillips Petroleum brought Norway into the league of countries with a stake in the oil industry when it discovered the Ekofisk field 180 miles off the coast of Norway in 1969. (*Ekofisk* is a Norwegian-based word referring to the underseas

---

[8] Adapted from Agis Salpukas, "For 'This Old Field,' a Costly Renovation Project," *The New York Times*, Feb. 6, 1994, section 3, p. 13.

seismic readings that engineers used to find the field.) At the time, Phillips planned to abandon Ekofisk before the year 2011. However, Phillips is currently thinking about investing another $3 to $4 billion to extend the life of the field to the year 2031.

After Phillips began drilling at Ekofisk in the early 1970s, at levels as deep as 15,000 feet below the surface of the North Sea, it realized there were reserves estimated at more than 1 billion barrels. At first, Phillips used tankers to get the oil ashore. But the severe North Sea conditions, with waves sometimes as high as 40 feet, prompted Phillips to install a 1-million barrel on-site storage tank that also served as a central processing operation. In 1972, Phillips began laying 220 miles of 34-inch pipe from Ekofisk to a processing facility in Teesside, England.

Phillips expected oil production to decline by the 1980s. In fact, production hit a peak of 624,000 barrels per day in 1980, which sank to 150,000 barrels by 1986. Engineers then made the happy discovery that the porous chalk ocean floor sucks up water, displacing more oil for recovery. Phillips began to help this natural process along by injecting hundreds of thousands of barrels of water a day deep into the oil field to keep pressure constant and maintain a continuous flow of oil.

Extracting this oil, unfortunately, created a problem. The seabed itself was sinking, bringing some of the platforms closer to the sea. To solve the problem, Phillips spent $400 million to jack six of the platforms 20 feet higher and $300 million to erect a concrete wall around the storage tank. The investments paid off. Production today has rebounded, averaging about 270,000 barrels per day.

To extend the Ekofisk oil field into the twenty-first century, Phillips will have to deal with increased operating costs, stricter environmental regulations, and rising safety standards, and will have to convince the Norwegian government to extend its license to the year 2031. Phillips, for its part, will construct three new platforms, at a cost of $4 billion. With no wells beneath them, the new platforms will be less vulnerable to sinking. Moreover, Phillips will abandon its giant storage tank and use pipelines instead. To make all this happen, Phillips is asking Norway to forego its oil royalties until 2031, currently running at about 10 percent of the price of a barrel of oil. Norway, though, will still be able to collect corporate income taxes at rates as high as 70 percent.

Required: What are some of the reasons the Norwegian government might want to use capital budgeting in reaching a decision? What are some of the costs and benefits that it may want to consider relative to granting Phillips an exemption from royalties?

D8.2 (Capital Budgeting and Financial Statements)[9]

Where do the funds come from to finance capital projects? To gain insight into funding, consider the information selected from Chrysler Corporation's 1992 Annual Report. Exhibit D8.2.1 shows Chrysler's statement of cash flow for 1992, while Exhibit D8.2.2 contains a discussion of Chrysler's liquidity and capital resources. Note that the cash flows for Chrysler Finance Corporation (CFC), a wholly owned subsidiary of Chrysler, are included in the figures.

Required: What are some of the long-term investments Chrysler made? Where did the funds for these investments come from?

---

[9] Adapted from: Chrysler Corporation, *1992 Chrysler Corporation Report to Shareholders,* pp. 24–25, and 32.

EXHIBIT D8.2.1   CHRYSLER CORPORATION

Consolidated Statement of Cash Flows (in millions of dollars)

	Chrysler Corporation and Consolidated Subsidiaries Year Ending December 31,		
	1992	*1991*	*1990*
Cash flows from operating activities:			
Net earnings (loss)	$ 723	$ (795)	$ 68
Adjustments to reconcile to net cash provided by operating activities:			
Depreciation & amortization	1,610	1,465	1,398
Provision for restructuring charges	101	–	(101)
Equity in earnings of unconsolidated subsidiaries & affiliates	–	–	–
Plant capacity adjustment	–	(391)	–
Provision for credit losses	345	579	339
Deferred income taxes	229	(288)	55
Gain on equity investment transactions	(142)	(205)	–
Cumulative effect of changes in accounting principles	(218)	257	–
Change in accounts receivable	100	1,801	1,311
Change in inventories	535	(167)	(188)
Change in prepaid expense & other assets	(51)	(492)	(138)
Change in accounts payable & accrued liabilities	525	1,152	(258)
Dividends received from subsidiary	–	–	–
Other	(8)	(22)	93
Net cash provided by operating activities	$ 3,749	$ 2,894	$ 2,579
Cash flows from investing activities:			
Purchases of marketable securities	$(18,084)	$(8,001)	$(7,480)
Sales & maturities of marketable securities	17,786	8,788	7,189
Proceeds from sale of Gulfstream Aerospace Corporation, net of expense	–	–	820
Proceeds from sale of equity investments, net of expense	215	100	–
Finance receivables acquired	(17,290)	(17,476)	(19,973)
Finance receivables collected	10,605	13,652	15,683
Proceeds from sales of finance receivables	8,034	6,465	8,354
Proceeds from sales of nonautomotive assets	903	–	–
Sales of property & equipment	48	81	37
Expenditures for property & equipment	(1,417)	(1,553)	(1,131)
Expenditures for special tools	(872)	(708)	(663)
Change in property held for lease	204	(87)	(251)
Other	(303)	(235)	345
Net Cash provided by (used in) investing activities	$ (171)	$ 1,026	$ 2,930

(continued)

	EXHIBIT D.8.2.1 (CONTINUED)		

	Chrysler Corporation and Consolidated Subsidiaries Year Ending December 31,		
	1992	1991	1990
Cash flows from financing activities:			
Change in short-term debt (less than 90-day maturities)	$ (110)	$ (635)	$(8,996)
Proceeds under revolving lines of credit and long-term borrowings	65,963	68,231	29,361
Payments on revolving lines of credit and long-term borrowings	(69,700)	(71,058)	(25,037)
Proceeds from issuance of preferred stock, net of expense	836	–	–
Proceeds from issuance of common stock, net of expense	–	385	–
Proceeds from issuance of subsidiary preferred stock, net of expense	–	–	123
Redemption of subsidiary preferred stock	(75)	(210)	(215)
Dividends paid	(225)	(169)	(269)
Other	49	5	24
Net cash provided by (used in) financing activities	$ (3,262)	(3,451)	(5,009)
Change in cash & cash equivalents	$316	$ 469	500
Cash & cash equivalents at beginning of year	2,041	1,572	1,072
Cash & cash equivalents at end of year	$ 2,357	$ 2,041	$ 1,572

Source: Chrysler Corporation, *1992 Chrysler Corporation Report to Shareholders*, p. 32. Used with permission of Chrysler Corporation.

PROBLEMS   **P8.1   (Net Benefit for CIM Equipment)**

Magruder Industries manufactures automobile components. The company has three large production facilities and is debating the benefits of implementing computer-integrated manufacturing (CIM) in one of its factories. The CIM system will be installed at the beginning of 1997 and will produce benefits over the 5-year period ending on December 31, 2001. After discussions with the vice president of marketing, the corporate controller compiled the following list of benefits, along with comments on how they might be quantified:

- *Increased manufacturing flexibility.* The equipment can be programmed for process and design changes and from one product line to another. This capability will reduce the number of setups by 100 in 1997, by 200 in 1998, and by 250 in 1999 and each year thereafter. Cost avoided when a setup is not required is $2,500 per setup.
- *Improved product quality.* CIM reduces the risk of poor-quality production by making output more uniform and decreasing rework. The number of units requiring rework will decrease by 2,000 in 1997, by 3,000 in 1998, and by 5,000 for each year thereafter. Variable rework cost is $125 per unit.
- *Less required floor space.* The computer-controlled equipment will replace the conventional equipment and eliminate the need for inventory storage. As a result, Magruder will no longer need to lease 10,000 square feet and will

EXHIBIT D8.2.2 CHRYSLER CORPORATION

Liquidity and Capital Resources

Liquidity and Capital Resources

During 1992, the company generated cash flow from operations of $3.0 billion, which slightly exceeded its funding requirements for capital expenditures, which were $2.2 billion, and for debt repayments, which were $662 million.

Chrysler's combined cash, cash equivalents, and marketable securities totaled $3.65 billion at December 31, 1992 (including $766 million held by CFC), an increase of $614 million from December 31, 1991. The increase in 1992 was the result of cash generated from operating activities and cash provided by external financing actions, including the private offering of preferred stock to institutional investors for net cash proceeds of $836 million and the sale of 43.6 million shares of MMC stock for $215 million. A $211 million payment was made to Regie Nationale des Usines Renault, as required by the AMC acquisition agreement. CFC's cash, cash equivalents, and marketable securities decreased $54 million during 1992.

For the period from 1989 to 1991, the company had been unable to generate sufficient cash flow from operations to finance its funding requirements, which included substantial capital expenditures relating to the development of new products and the modernization of facilities. In addition, Chrysler's ability to access the credit markets had become severely restricted due to the lack of investment-grade debt ratings from Moody's Investors Service, Inc., ("Moody's") and Standard & Poor's Corporation ("S&P"). As a result, Chrysler relied increasingly on its cash position, external equity, and other financing actions and asset sales to finance its cash requirements.

The Company's long-term profitability

CAPITAL EXPENDITURE
(*In billions of dollars*)

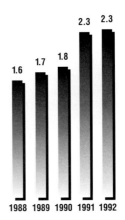

will depend on its ability to introduce and market its products successfully and on its ability to generate sufficient cash to fund its new product development and facility modernization programs. Chrysler has planned expenditures in the 1993–1997 period of approximately $17.5 billion (including $0.2 billion for its nonautomotive subsidiaries) for the development of new products and the modernization of facilities. Of this amount, approximately $10.1 billion is for capital expenditures, which are expected to be $2.2 billion in 1993, $2.3 billion in 1994, $1.7 billion in 1995, and $3.9 billion in the remaining two years. The balance of the planned expenditure is principally for engineering, research and development, preproduction and launch, and certain facility expenses, which are charged to operations in the year incurred. Chrysler (excluding CFC) also has contractual debt maturities of $159 million in 1993, $694 million in 1994, and $199 million in 1995.

Source: Chrysler Corporation, *1992 Chrysler Corporation Report to Shareholders,* pp. 24–25. Use with permission of Chrysler Corporation.

thus avoid a lease cost of $12.00 per square foot per year and a utilities cost of $2.50 per square foot per year.

Magruder has a 40 percent effective tax rate.

Required: Calculate the net after-tax benefit associated with an investment in computer-integrated manufacturing (CIM) in one of Magruder's factories.

(CMA Adapted)

P8.2 (Net Present Value for CIM Equipment)

After discussions with the vice president of manufacturing, the corporate controller of Magruder Industries (see P8.1) felt that the benefits from CIM included increased manufacturing flexibility, improved product quality, and less required floor space. Dollar estimates of these after-tax benefits are as follows:

1997	$400,000
1998	$500,000
1999	$600,000
2000	$600,000
2001	$600,000

The CIM equipment will cost $1.5 million, including installation. The equipment will qualify as a 5-year asset for tax purposes and will be depreciated using the following MACRS rates: 0.33 in 1997, 0.45 in 1998, 0.15 in 1999, and 0.07 in 2000. The equipment is expected to have no residual value at the end of its useful life on December 31, 2001. Magruder uses a 20 percent discount rate and has a 40 percent effective tax rate.

Required: Determine whether Magruder Industries should implement the computer-integrated manufacturing in one of its factories by calculating the net present value (NPV) of the investment.

(CMA Adapted)

P8.3 (Depreciation Tax Shield)

Mayhem Management works crowd control at country-western concerts. With their business growing rapidly, Mayhem's managers are considering buying a mobile command center. The vehicle is expected to cost about $500,000 and will have no residual value at the end of its 5-year life.

Mayhem plans to use straight-line depreciation over a 5-year period at a rate of 20 percent each year. Mayhem's argument for adopting the straight-line method is based on its simplicity. Mayhem's accountant, on the other hand, recommends using MACRS depreciation spread over 5 years. Assume the MACRS rates are 20 percent in year 1, 32 percent in year 2, 18 percent in year 3, 15 percent in year 4, and 15 percent in year 5.

Mayhem uses a discount (hurdle) rate of 15 percent and pays income taxes at a rate of 40 percent.

Required: What is the difference in the NPVs for the mobile command center if Mayhem decides to use MACRS depreciation rather than straight-line depreciation for tax purposes?

P8.4 (Disposal Value)

The Doodah Company is estimating disposal value for equipment it is considering buying. The equipment will be used to support a 5-year project scheduled to begin on January 1, 1997. The project is expected to end on December 31, 2001. The equipment will cost $100,000 and qualify as a 7-year asset for tax purposes. However, it will be evaluated over the 5-year planning horizon using the following MACRS rates: 14.3 percent in year 1 (1997), 24.5 percent in year 2 (1998), 17.5 percent in year 3 (1999), 12.5 percent in year 4 (2000), and 8.9 percent in year 5 (2001). All gains and losses are taxed at a rate of 40 percent.

Managers believe that the disposal value of the equipment will decline at a compound rate of about 30 percent each year. The decline in value is expected to begin as soon as the equipment is purchased. Disposal value will not be considered in calculating the MACRS depreciation tax shield.

Required: What are the estimated cash disposal proceeds on December 31, 2001?

P8.5 (Basic NPV Computations)

DiaBolical Industries is considering offering a new line of products. The following facts, data, and projections were gathered to assist managers in evaluating the project's potential:

- New equipment costing $100,000 will be acquired and placed in operations on January 1, 1996 (year 0). The equipment will require installation costing $35,000.
- The new line of products, expected to have a 4-year life, will generate revenue of $150,000 in 1996 (year 1), $175,000 in 1997 (year 2), $250,000 in 1998 (year 3), and $100,000 in 1999 (year 4). Current plans are to withdraw the new product line from the market at the end of 1999.
- Cash variable cost is expected to equal 30 percent of revenues, while fixed cost (excluding depreciation) is projected at $50,000 each year.
- The equipment and installation qualify as 5-year assets. These assets will be depreciated using the following MACRS rates: 20 percent in 1996 (year 1), 32 percent in 1997 (year 2), 19.2 percent in 1998 (year 3), and 11.5 percent in 1999 (year 4). *Note:* Equipment and installation have a book value greater than zero at the end of year 4.
- The equipment is expected to be sold for $10,000, net of disposal costs, on December 31, 1999.
- Income is taxed at a rate of 35 percent.
- DiaBolical will use a discount rate of 18 percent.

Required: What is the NPV for the investment in the new line of products?

P8.6 (NPV, IRR, PVI, Payback)[10]

Sparrow Airlines, which provides jet service from Orlando to the Bahamas, flies three leased, 128-seat Boeing 737-300s. Sparrow is trying to decide what to do with

---

[10] Adapted from Adam Bryant, "New Jet-Age Wrinkle: The Propeller Plane," *The New York Times*, May 23, 1994, section A, p. 1.

the Boeings when the lease expires next year. The most attractive option appears to be the purchase of smaller, propeller-driven planes. Sparrow has some concerns about changing over from jets though. Industry surveys indicate that some passengers refuse to fly propeller-driven planes, citing their safety record, stability in turbulence, and lack of amenities. The impact of this consumer attitude is offset, in some cases, by the advantages of better service. Smaller planes offer customers more frequent schedules, reducing the amount of time they have to wait. But the bottom line for many travelers is that they may have no other choice—major carriers simply don't serve their market.

Like many other airlines, Sparrow flies with empty seats. But with smaller, 30-passenger "prop" planes, such as Embraer Aircraft's EMB-120 Brasilia turboprop, Sparrow's load factors should increase dramatically over those obtained with the Boeings. With higher load factors, operating cost goes down and profit goes up. Sparrow believes it will save $321 per flying hour in crew cost plus $344 per flying hour in fuel and oil for each of the EMB-120s it buys. Next year, Sparrow expects each of its planes to fly about 1,800 hours. In addition, Sparrow estimates that each year a turboprop should save $673,200 in airport facility rental, $12,600 in insurance, $27,000 in property taxes, and $376,200 in maintenance relative to the cost of the Boeings.

Sparrow will look at the $5.7-million investment required for an EMB-120 over a 7-year planning horizon and deduct depreciation for tax purposes at rates of 16 percent, 25 percent, 18 percent, 14 percent, 9 percent, 9 percent, and 9 percent. The EMB-120s will require a major overhaul at the end of 7 years. Sparrow's plan is to get rid of the planes right before they need the overhaul. Unfortunately, the planes are expected to be virtually valueless, generating no cash flow for Sparrow when they are sold at the end of the seventh year.

Sparrow uses an 18 percent discount rate in evaluating capital projects and a marginal tax rate of 36 percent.

Required:

1. Calculate the following for one EMB-120:
   a. Net present value (NPV)
   b. Internal rate of return (IRR)
   c. Present value index (PVI)
   d. Payback period (PB)
2. What should Sparrow do?

P8.7 (NPV)

Jacquie Barrett makes fabulous cookies. She used to make them only for her kids, in the family kitchen. But the cookies were so good her friends wanted to be able to buy them. So Barrett decided to go into business for herself and leased space in a commercial warehouse. In January 1994, she purchased a machine that took a lot of the drudgery out of making cookies. The machine, which mixes and cuts cookies, has been in service for 3 years. Today, Barrett is considering the purchase of a machine that represents the next generation of cookie-making technology. One attractive feature of the new machine is that it requires less energy, decreasing the variable cost of making a dozen cookies from $0.25 to $0.18 by reducing utilities cost. However, annual fixed cash operating costs will increase from $15,000 to $28,000. If she decides to get the new machine, she will have it installed and ready for service on January 1, 1997. With either machine, Barrett believes she will make about 400,000 dozen cookies per year at a price of $3 per dozen. Some of the oper-

EXHIBIT P8.7 BARRETT'S FABULOUS COOKIES

Operating Costs and Data for Cookie-Cutting Machines

	Old Machine	New Machine
Original cost of machine at acquisition	$90,000	$120,000
Salvage value at the end of useful life for depreciation purposes	$10,000	$0
Useful life at date of acquisition	8 years	5 years
Expected annual cash operating expense:		
Variable energy cost per dozen	$0.25	$0.18
Total cash fixed cost	$15,000	$28,000
Depreciation method used for tax purposes	Straight-line	MACRS
Estimated cash value of machines as of:		
January 1, 1997	$35,000	
December 31, 2001	$ 8,000	$27,000

ating costs and data Barrett gathered to aid her in making her decision are shown in Exhibit P8.7.

The old machine, acquired in January 1994, originally cost $90,000. At the time, Barrett deducted $10,000 in estimated salvage value in calculating depreciation for reporting to the IRS. If she decides not to acquire the new machine and continues to use the old one, Jacquie will keep the same depreciation schedule. That is, she will still deduct the original $10,000 estimate of salvage value and continue to use straight-line depreciation. However, if Barrett buys the new machine, she will adopt the MACRS method, depreciating the new machine over 5 years, starting in 1997. She will use the following depreciation rates: 20 percent in 1997, 32 percent in 1998, 18 percent in 1999, and 15 percent in 2000 and 2001. Even though the new machine will have an estimated salvage value of $27,000 on December 31, 2001, Barrett will not use it in calculating MACRS depreciation.

Barrett pays taxes on income at a rate of 40 percent. Any gains or losses on the sale of either cookie machine are taxed at the same 40 percent rate. Barrett will use 16 percent as a discount rate in evaluating the investment in the new machinery.

Required:

1. Calculate the incremental NPV of the new machine relative to that of the old.
2. What does the variable energy cost per dozen cookies have to be for the new machine in order for Barrett to be indifferent in choosing between the two alternative pieces of equipment?

(CMA Adapted)

P8.8 (NPV for New Office Equipment)[11]

Metronic Mail Metering, manufacturers of automated mailing systems, is developing a new generation of high-volume mail processors. Code-named Premier, the new computerized system is designed to reduce labor and improve efficiency. After polling nearly 4,000 customers, Metronic discovered that mail room managers are frustrated by the number of steps required with existing mass-mailing systems.

---

[11] Adapted from Gautam Naik, "After Years of R&D, Pitney Bowes Now Seeks the Sale," *The Wall Street Journal,* Feb. 25, 1993, p. B4.

These extra steps not only create unnecessary work but reduce thru-put time. To complete a major mailing, for example, some mail room managers have to manually fold pieces of mail, stuff envelopes, weigh each piece, and attach postage. Metronic, on the basis of the survey, decided to use one of its technological platforms to build a better machine, one that would eliminate all handling and would be difficult for competitors to replicate.

Initial designs of the Premier system use a patented "weigh-on-the-way" technology to weigh and meter 90 items of mail of assorted sizes and shapes or 240 pieces of uniform mail per minute. The Premier system, at the beginning, was considered an ambitious project by some Metronic officials because of the technological barriers that had to be overcome. While engineers had occasionally run into roadblocks in the design phase, hurdles were ultimately overcome, and a prototype of the Premier system was finished.

Now that the prototype has been completed, Metronic managers are working with marketing and engineering to come up with the right price—a price that will cover full cost and contribute a reasonable return on investment. One pricing approach used in justifying new generations of equipment is based on identifying a breakeven price for a typical customer. At breakeven, the sum of equipment cost and installation cost just equals the estimated benefit, which is discounted to present value.

A typical Metronic customer processes an average of 1,500 pieces of mail each day, 250 working days per year. Currently, it takes about 0.25 minutes (15 seconds) to weigh and meter a piece of mail. The Premier, in automating the complete process, will eliminate some tasks, bringing the average time down to 0.15 minutes (9 seconds) per piece. Mail room workers who perform mailing tasks are usually paid by the hour, typically at a rate of $6.75, plus 20 percent benefits.

The working price that Metronic managers are using for planning purposes is $12,000. Installation of the Premier system requires physical and electrical modifications estimated at about $1,800 for a typical site. In addition, Metronic plans to charge a maintenance fee of $250 during the first year of operations, which will escalate to $350 for the second year of operation and all subsequent years. Metronic knows that managers evaluating equipment such as the Premier usually employ a discount rate of 15 percent. While the system will provide benefits for many years, the typical planning horizon for such equipment is 5 years. As part of the deal, Metronic is planning to guarantee 25 percent of the equipment cost (excluding installation) as a buyback at the end of the fifth year. Unamortized installation costs are written off at the end of the fifth year, resulting in a loss for tax purposes. Marginal tax rates for an average client are about 28 percent. The IRS has set depreciation rates for equipment such as the Premier system at 20 percent in year 1, 32 percent in year 2, 19.2 percent in year 3, 11.52 percent in years 4 and 5, and 5.76 percent in year 6. The IRS requires capitalization of installation cost, which is amortized using the same rates as those used for the equipment.

Required:

1. Prepare an estimate of the NPV for a typical installation, assuming that equipment cost for the Premier is $12,000.
2. Identify the price Metronic should charge for the Premier (assuming installation cost is $1,800) so that a typical customer will just break even on its investment.
3. What are some possible costs and benefits of the Premier that have been excluded from the numerical analysis?

P8.9 (New Product with Working Capital)[12]

Devices that monitor blood pressure come in two forms: *invasive* and *noninvasive*. Invasive monitors, which are inserted into a patient's artery, measure pressure continuously, from heartbeat to heartbeat. The downside of invasive units is the risk of bloodstream infections or clotted arteries. Noninvasive monitors, on the other hand, measure blood pressure without invading the patient's body. They monitor pressure intermittently, usually every 2½ to 5 minutes. While the risk of infections and clotting is eliminated with the use of noninvasive units, such units don't provide feedback quickly enough to pick up dramatic, and potentially lethal, changes in blood pressure. It is estimated that, regardless of the risk, 85 percent of the blood pressure monitors in actual use are noninvasive. Several companies recently closed the gap by developing noninvasive monitors that measure blood pressure continuously. These units employ a wide variety of technology, ranging from infrared to ultrasound and piezoelectric sensors.

SangTeck, a division of PharmoSute, is one of the companies working on a new, noninvasive continuous-monitoring unit, which it calls Pegasus-NI. SangTeck's Pegasus-NI depends on sensors that generate electrical currents. They react to pressure created by the patient's pulse. The monitor, which is attached around the patient's wrist, will be ready for market by the end of 1995. All R&D work is complete, with no additional cash outflows necessary prior to production. SangTeck, a newly created division of PharmoSute organized to manufacture and market the device, believes it will ultimately capture as much as 15 percent of the total market.

While development is expected to be completed by the end of 1995, SangTeck plans to buy an existing manufacturing facility on January 1, 1996, for $25 million. During 1996, it will prepare for production. However, no units will be manufactured, nor will any significant costs be incurred until January 1997. The reason for the delay is to allow SangTeck time to submit tests to the FDA in order to gain permission to sell Pegasus-NI. After gaining FDA approval, which is expected in January 1997, SangTeck will start production and begin selling the monitors. Looking ahead, managers are planning an orderly exit from the market in December 2000. At that time, low-cost competitors are likely to take away virtually all of SangTeck's market share.

The primary market for Pegasus-NI is hospitals, of which there are estimated to be around 183,000 in the United States. Research indicates that about 70 percent of these hospitals use intermittent, noninvasive monitors. SangTeck expects to sell one monitor to each of about 10 percent of the hospitals that now use the intermittent, noninvasive monitors in 1997 and 15 percent in 1998 and 1999. They expect market share to fall to 5 percent in 2000 because of increasing competition. The initial selling price in 1997 will be $4,500 and is expected to increase annually by 4 percent starting in 1998.

Production, selling, and administrative costs are expected to remain stable—that is, there will be no cost increases during the life of the project. Estimates of the annual costs are as follows:

Variable materials	$1,800 per unit
Variable labor	$375 per unit
Variable overhead	$120 per unit
Fixed overhead (excluding depreciation)	$15 million

---

[12] Adapted from Robert E. Calem, "Monitoring Blood Pressure without Skipping a Heartbeat, *The New York Times*, Mar. 28, 1993, section 3, p. 16.

The manufacturing facility SangTeck plans to acquire in January 1996 will cost $25 million and will be depreciated for tax purposes over 25 years. Because of the delay in production while waiting to gain FDA approval, SangTeck won't start claiming depreciation on its tax returns until 1997. Then it will use the following rates: 12 percent in 1997, 18 percent in 1998, 9 percent in 1999, and 7 percent in 2000.

In addition to capital outlays, managers at SangTeck must make provisions to meet working-capital requirements for the Pegasus-NI. While day-to-day cash needs will be supplied by corporate headquarters, SangTeck must set aside funds to finance receivables and inventories. Fortunately, funding requirements for working capital are partially offset by the firm's suppliers, in the form of accounts payable. Furthermore, employees are paid at the end of each month, which helps to conserve cash flow. Forecasts for working-capital needs are based on the following items:

- *Accounts receivable.* Collections on accounts receivables are expected to average 45 days. During each year of operations, starting in January 1997 and continuing through December 1999, an amount of working capital is to be set aside equal to 45 days (based on 365 days per year) of sales for the current year.
- *Materials inventory.* SangTeck plans to hold substantial inventories of materials in order to ensure meeting delivery dates. Materials inventory is expected to turn over four times per year. That is, average material inventory will equal 25 percent of the variable materials cost for the year. Therefore, during each year of operations, starting in January 1997 and continuing through December 1999, an amount of working capital is to be set aside equal to 25 percent of the variable materials costs for the current year. Since SangTeck's manufacturing processes are relatively quick and completed units are shipped almost immediately, no working capital is required for the work-in-process or finished-goods inventories.
- *Wages payable.* Workers are paid wages at the end of the month in which they work. During each year of operations, starting in January 1997 and continuing through December 1999, working capital is reduced by an amount equal to 1 month of the expected average variable labor cost for the current year.
- *Accounts payable.* Payment on account for materials purchases is expected to average 45 days. During each year of operations, starting in January 1997 and continuing through December 1999, working-capital requirements are reduced by an amount equal to 45 days of the expected average variable materials costs for the current year.
- *Overhead.* Variable and fixed overhead costs are paid when incurred. As a result, SangTeck will not make provision for working capital to cover these costs.
- *Working capital summary.* During the year 2000, as the project draws to a close, SangTeck plans to cease operations and expects to fully recover all of its net working-capital outlays. A summary of SangTeck's working-capital needs over the entire life of the project (rounded to the nearest $1,000) is presented in Exhibit P8.9.

The manufacturing facility will be sold for an estimated $10 million, net of all disposal fees and costs, at the end of the year 2000. SangTeck will evaluate the Pegasus-NI project at a discount rate of 15 percent. Marginal tax rates are 30 percent. Since PharmoSute's other divisions are profitable, any capital or operating loss will be used to offset capital gains or operating income for the organization as a whole.

EXHIBIT P8.9 SANGTECK

Working-Capital Requirements[a]

Current Asset or Liability	1/1/96	12/31/96	12/31/97	12/31/98	12/31/99	12/31/00
Accounts receivable:						
Beginning of the year				$ 7,107,000	$11,087,000	$11,530,000
End of the year	$0	$0	$7,107,000	$11,087,000	$11,530,000	$ 0
Materials inventory:						
Beginning of the year				$ 5,765,000	$ 8,647,000	$ 8,647,000
End of the year	$0	$0	$5,765,000	$ 8,647,000	$ 8,647,000	$ 0
Direct labor—accrued wages:						
Beginning of the year				$ 400,000	$ 600,000	$ 600,000
End of the year	$0	$0	$ 400,000	$ 600,000	$ 600,000	$ 0
Accounts payable:						
Beginning of the year				$ 2,843,000	$ 4,264,000	$ 4,264,000
End of the year	$0	$0	$2,843,000	$ 4,264,000	$ 4,264,000	$ 0

[a] Figures are rounded to the nearest thousand.

Required:

1. Calculate the NPV and IRR for this proposed investment. Assume that the start of the project is January 1, 1996, even though operations do not begin until 1997. Also calculate the cumulative net discounted cash flow. (*Hint:* The net outlay for any component of working capital is equal to the change in that component during the year. For example, the outlay for accounts receivable for 1998 (year 3) is $3,980,000. Also assume that the net working capital is fully recovered on December 31, 2000. Finally, assume that the working capital requirements presented in Exhibit P8.9 are correct. Use these figures rather than calculating the working capital requirements based on the description of working capital components presented in the problem.)
2. Should PharmoSute fund the SangTeck project?
3. What would happen to the NPV and IRR if SangTeck could obtain immediate approval from the FDA and start production in January 1996, immediately after acquiring the manufacturing facility? Assume that the length of the project is unchanged, and that it will end 1 year earlier—on December 31, 1999—rather than on December 31, 2000.

P8.10 (Investment Assessment for Health Care Project at a Jail)

Corrections Health Care (CHC) is a newly formed division of a national conglomerate specializing in construction. Since one of its primary strengths is a presence in the corrections industry through jail construction, CHC decided to explore the possibility of providing health care for prison inmates. While this is a risky extension of its business, fraught with potential (and largely unknown) exposure to risk, recent downturns in the construction industry have prompted managers to rethink the future of construction and to look for new markets.

CHC's plan is to relieve local municipalities of the burden of managing prison inmates' heath care. With explosive growth in average daily populations (in some states as high as 18% per year), an increasing proportion of inmates who require health care—often as the result of court decisions and increasing liability exposure—and double-digit increases in health care costs, the potential for a new market for CHC is clearly evident. After a brief study, CHC identified Dade County, Florida, and the city of Miami as its first target site and an appropriate test case for determining the viability of the concept.

CHC proposes to take over all health care needs of the inmates at the Webster Correctional Facility, located in the Hialeah section of Miami. The determination of appropriate rates and the acceptance of the concept of the project has already been worked out with members of the corrections division at both the city of Miami and Dade County. At this point, CHC must decide how to structure the delivery of health care, prior to making a formal proposal.

CHC has identified two basic alternatives—only one of which it will advocate in its presentation. The first, referred to as the "outside contractor" option, relies upon area hospitals to provide health care, producing a predominately variable-cost-driven solution. On the other hand, CHC can build a residential facility on county-owned land that will provide all of the requisite health care services on-site. CHC will charge Dade County the same rate for each inmate—regardless of which of the two alternative plans Dade County chooses. In order to determine which option to pursue, CHC commissioned a study to develop appropriate data it will need in order to evaluate the two alternatives.

CHC began with data on historical population statistics and demographics as a basis for estimates of inmate population over the 5-year project horizon. For planning purposes, operations will start at the beginning of 1997 and extend through the end of December 2001. The choice of such a short planning horizon is the result of the parent company's desire for immediate returns and the relatively short tenures of the elected city officials working with CHC.

During 1997, CHC estimates that the average daily population (ADP) at Webster will be around 4,000 inmates. The ADP is expected to grow by 15 percent in 1998, 12 percent in 1999, 10 percent in 2000, and 8 percent in 2001. Historical data reveal that about ½ of 1 percent (0.5%) of the inmate population will require hospitalization each day. For example, 20 inmates per day (4,000 ADP × 0.005), 365 days per year are expected to require hospitalization during 1997.

Under the outside contractor option (sending inmates to area hospitals) CHC must administer delivery of health care by establishing and monitoring contracts with outside suppliers. There would be no necessity to construct a facility, since currently employed personnel in the parent company's Orlando office would be utilized. CHC would then negotiate contracts with outside suppliers, such as physicians, at rates that would provide sufficient margins.

Three major cost categories were identified under this option: (1) transportation, (2) hospital day-charges, and (3) physician fees. It is anticipated that 27 percent of the inmates will require one-way emergency transport at an average charge of $325 per trip. The other 73 percent of the inmates requiring health care would be either transported by correctional officers, in nonemergency situations, or taken directly to the hospital by the arresting officers. The rate negotiated with area hospitals is $695 per inmate per day, and physician fees are expected to average $1,650 per inmate requiring health care per day.

The second alternative requires construction of a correctional health care facility at a cost of $18 million and the purchase of equipment costing $5.5 million. There are no land costs, since Dade County already owns the proposed site, as noted earlier. Construction, using a new method called "tunnel forms," can be completed relatively quickly, with opening scheduled for January 1st, 1997. Because of rapid construction, virtually all of the construction cash "draws" will occur near the opening date, in January 1997.

Once the facility is completed, operations will begin, and the following annual fixed operating costs will be incurred: transportation personnel, $700,000; physicians and nurses, $4,500,000; nonmedical materials and supplies, $800,000; insurance, $2,000,000; contract services, $1,250,000; utilities, $650,000; and maintenance and repair, $450,000. In addition, medical supplies are estimated at $285 per inmate requiring health care per day. Finally, food and clothing cost is estimated at $25 per inmate per day.

The health care facility will be depreciated for tax purposes, with no provision for salvage, using rates of 5 percent the first year, 7 percent in the second, 4.5 percent in the third, and 4 percent in the fourth and fifth years. Similarly, equipment depreciation rates for tax purposes are 20 percent, 32 percent, 19 percent, 14.5 percent, and 14.5 percent. For planning purposes, and to emphasize the requirement of immediate capital recovery, CHC estimates it can sell the facility in five years (at the end of the year 2001) for $12 million. Salvage value of the equipment at that time is estimated at $2.5 million.

The parent company requires a minimum of 18 percent return on new projects. All gains, losses, and operating income are taxed at a marginal rate of 30 percent. The parent company typically has operating income and capital gains with which losses, if any, can be offset.

Required:

1. Evaluate the two CHC proposals and determine which of the two options CHC should evaluate further. Calculate the incremental NPV of the outside contractor option relative to the residential option.
2. CHC is relatively confident about all of the projections except the assumption of a 0.5 percent proportion of inmates requiring care. Determine the sensitivity of this assumption by recalculating the NPV for proportions ranging from 0.0 percent to 1.0 percent, in steps of 0.1 percent. At what proportion are the two alternatives equal?
3. Which of the two options would you recommend to CHC?

P8.11 (Leasing versus Buying Airplanes)[13]

Aeroflot Russian International Airlines recently signed a letter of intent to lease four new Boeing 767s. Aeroflot plans to use the planes on its North Atlantic routes. Currently, it flies Soviet-built Ilyushins, with service to Montreal, New York, San Francisco, Chicago, and Washington. The new 767s will be configured to seat as many as 260 people in two classes. With the Russian economy in shambles, Aeroflot has reportedly sought Boeing 767s because of the difficulty of obtaining airplanes from Russian factories.

Aeroflot plans to lease the planes through the GPA Group, PLC, of Shannon, Ireland, one of the world's foremost airplane-leasing companies. Backed by GE Capital Aviation Services, which manages GPA's assets, the deal is likely to receive the green light. The primary stumbling block, though, is how Aeroflot will pay for the equipment.

While Aeroflot will make its decision according to Russian economic criteria, assume for the purposes of this problem that its evaluation process for the decision will conform to the way U.S. commercial airline companies acquire

---

[13] The Aeroflot deal with GPA is described by Brian Coleman, "Aeroflot to Lease Boeing 767s from GPA Group," *The Wall Street Journal*, Jan. 19, 1994, p. A14. However, the numerical example used in the problem is not reported in the article and is purely fictional.

planes. Also assume that factors such as the impact the transaction has on U.S. federal income taxes will be similar in the Russian context. Moreover, assume that Aeroflot has two ways to structure the deal. The first, called an *operating lease,* is what you normally think of when you hear the term *lease.* GPA, the lessor, will retain ownership of the airplanes. Aeroflot, the lessee, will secure the right to use the planes by making periodic lease payments. Payments are treated as operating expenses by Aeroflot and are fully deductible from revenue on its income statement.

The second option is called a *capital lease.* This option effectively transfers the risks and rewards of plane ownership to Aeroflot. One way to look at a capital lease is to view it as a means of financing a purchase. For accounting purposes, capital leases create assets on the balance sheet that are subject to depreciation. On the equity side of the balance sheet, capital leases give rise to long-term liabilities equal to the present value of future lease obligations. As a consequence, each lease payment reduces the long-term liability, giving rise to tax-deductible interest charges. Thus, one of the benefits of capital leases is that interest on the lease payments, depreciation, and all costs of ownership are deductible for tax purposes.

Companies with lots of debt may find capital leases unattractive because they increase already high debt-to-equity ratios. They may instead prefer operating leases that offer "off-balance-sheet" financing, which keeps debt off the balance sheet altogether.

Assume that, under the proposed operating lease agreement, Aeroflot will acquire four airplanes at a cost of $41,251,788 each. It will make six $31-million payments, the first of which is scheduled for January 1, 1998, the beginning of the lease term. The tax benefit, however, for this initial payment won't be realized until the end of 1998, the end of the first year of the lease. The second payment is due on December 31, 1998, and the tax benefit will be realized immediately. The third payment and subsequent payments are all due on December 31 of each successive year. As in 1998, the tax benefit will be realized immediately. At the end of the lease term, the airplanes revert back to GPA. Ownership costs, such as taxes, maintenance, and insurance, are borne by GPA. Aeroflot is certain that the lease will be a deductible operating expense for IRS tax purposes.

Assume that Aeroflot purchases four airplanes at $41,251,788 each under the capital lease arrangement. Aeroflot must make an initial payment of $2 million for each plane, or a total payment of $8 million for all four airplanes, on January 1, 1998, the outset of the lease term. In addition to the initial payment, Aeroflot must make six $35-million payments, the first of which is on December 31, 1998, and each year thereafter through December 2003. The interest rate that is "implicit" in the lease is 9 percent.[14] It has also agreed to sign a 6-year maintenance contract with Boeing and to pay all costs of ownership. Together, the maintenance agreement and ownership costs add $600,000 per plane to the annual year-end payment. At the end of the sixth year, Aeroflot expects to sell the planes for $3.5 million each, net of disposal cost. Aeroflot will use the following depreciation rates for federal income tax purposes: 20.0 percent in the first year, 32.0 percent in the second, then 19.2 percent, 11.5 percent, 11.5 percent, and 5.8 percent. The depreciation rates are applied to the original cost of the planes, without reduction for residual value.

---

[14] Interest is deductible for tax purposes on capital leases at the lessee's incremental borrowing rate or at the lessor's implicit interest rate, if it is lower. Assume that the implicit rate for Aeroflot is lower than the incremental borrowing rate for GPA.

Assume cash flows are discounted at 12 percent and that all operating income, operating losses, capital gains, and capital losses are taxed at 34 percent.

Required:

1. What is the present value to Aeroflot of the net after-tax cash flows for the operating lease option?
2. What is the present value to Aeroflot of the net after-tax cash flows for the capital lease option?
3. Assuming Aeroflot has relatively high financial leverage (i.e., a large proportion of debt relative to shareholder's equity) and that the airline industry is one of the least stable industries, what are some of the other factors Aeroflot might want to consider before reaching a decision?

P8.12 (Evaluating an Environmental Project)[15]

Donnis Gelb's business, called Gelb Gold, is making gold electroplated jewelry. He has been making jewelry for over 30 years. Gelb, who learned the process from his father, still uses one of the traditional methods whereby pure gold is first plated onto a nickel base. Then metal settings are dipped into the liquified-nickel solution. The end results are gold-plated rings, earrings, and bracelets.

Present Process

Before plating, the metal settings have to be cleaned at room temperature using a process known as *cold cleaning*. Gelb uses a chlorinated solvent (TCA), which is applied to the settings in an open-top vapor degreaser. After cleaning, the settings are dipped in the gold-plating bath. In the second major phase, the settings are dipped into two consequently "still" rinse baths. The process is completed when the settings go through a running rinse bath.

The gold-plating process requires Gelb to maintain good housekeeping. For one reason, the materials and chemicals he uses are very expensive. A second reason is to maintain a continuous flow of product. A third, and increasingly important, reason is to meet the environmental regulations imposed on the metal-finishing industry. For example, the gold-plating bath is subject to continuous filtration to prevent contamination. Another example is Gelb's treatment of the chemicals in the two still baths. Gold and cyanide, one of the chemicals used in the process, plus other contaminants, accumulate in the bath rinse water. Gelb recycles the rinse water back into the gold-plating bath. In performing this operation, he recovers much of the cyanide and some of the gold. Recycling also reduces the cyanide to levels that allow him to discharge the rinse water into the city sewer system.

Gelb uses about 60,000 pounds of TCA, the cold-cleaning solvent, each year. After processing, the TCA, together with other suspended solids and nickel, is reduced to about 2,350 gallons of waste per year. This residue is classified as a hazardous waste under the Resource Conservation Recovery Act (RCRA). Since Gelb cannot put the waste in a landfill, he stores the liquid in an off-site 600-gallon container. At least once every 90 days, the tank is emptied and the hazardous waste is transported to a treatment facility.

The filters on the gold-plating bath are changed biweekly and sent to an outside contractor, who attempts to reclaim the gold and clean the filter for reuse. At

[15] Adapted from Paul E. Bailey, "Full Cost Accounting for Life Cycle Costs: A Guide for Engineers and Financial Analysis," *Environmental Finance,* spring 1991, pp. 13–29.

least once every 90 days, the solids are placed in a drum and sent off-site to a reclamation facility. The solids—other than the gold—are listed as hazardous waste under the RCRA regulations. However, the regulations apply only if Gelb Gold exceeds certain volume limits. Unfortunately, by adding together the physical volume of rinse water and solid hazardous wastes, Gelb's process exceeds the minimum limits. As a result, his operations are subject to RCRA regulations.

The still-rinse-water discharges into the city sewer system fall under the jurisdiction of the Clean Water Act (CWA). Currently, Gelb meets the standards; thus he is permitted to discharge the liquid waste into the public utility.

New Process

Gelb is considering a new process that reduces the amount of hazardous waste generated. He intends to substitute the TCA used in the open-top vapor degreaser with a spray-cleaning system. This new system, which does not use TCA, will eliminate the necessity of disposing of the 2,350 gallons of hazardous waste each year. This leaves only the solids reclaimed from cleaning the filters to be dealt with as hazardous waste. But because use of the new system eliminates the need for TCA, Gelb Gold's discharges will fall under the minimum quantities outlined by the RCRA and be conditionally exempt from its regulations. The net effect is that Gelb will be able to dispose of the solid-waste filtrate as a nonhazardous waste. Furthermore, the wastewater effluent from the new equipment can be discharged directly into the sewer system.

Economics of the New Process

Gelb's accountant gathered the following information to help Gelb make the decision:

- The old equipment (open-top vapor degreaser) is fully depreciated. After consideration of disposal cost, the equipment has an expected cash salvage value of zero.
- The new system's costs are $100,000 for equipment, $40,000 for a dryer, and $15,000 for installation.
- The new system will be evaluated over a 7-year planning horizon. Depreciation rates for tax purposes are 14.3 percent, 24.5 percent, 17.5 percent, 12.5 percent, 8.9 percent, 8.9 percent, and 8.9 percent. (*Note:* The eighth-year rate is 4.5 percent.) These rates are applied to the full $155,000 cost of the new system, including installation, without reduction for estimated salvage value.
- Salvage, less disposal cost for the new equipment, is estimated at $38,750 at the end of seven years.
- The operating cost of the present process consists of the following costs: 60,000 pounds of TCA per year at $0.75 per pound; quarterly equipment maintenance of $1,000, or $4,000 per year; recovery of cost for 2,350 gallons of by-product per year at $0.94 per gallon. The by-product reduces the cost of operating the present system. The cost of each of these three items is assumed to escalate at 4 percent per year, beginning with the second year of operations.
- The new process eliminates all use of TCA, as noted earlier. The open-top vapor degreaser is replaced by the new spray-cleaning system. Operating costs for the new system comprise the following: water and chemicals of $5,000 per year, maintenance for the new equipment of $12,000 per year, waste disposal costs of $2,000 per year, and energy costs of $10,000. Each of these costs is assumed to escalate at 4 percent per year, beginning with the second year of operations.
- Since waste under the new system falls below minimum standards, Gelb will be able to eliminate costs associated with environmental regulation compli-

ance and reporting. These costs comprise a reporting cost of $930 per year, an inspection cost of $1,800 per year, and other miscellaneous regulatory costs totaling $870 per year. Each of these costs is also expected to escalate at 4 percent per year, beginning with the second year of operations.

- The old system requires disposal of hazardous wastes that are eliminated under the new system. This disposal consists of the cost of treatment or storage in 600-gallon holding tanks, $4,750 per year; transportation of hazardous waste, $1,300 per year; and disposal at the landfill, $3,530 per year. Each of these costs is also expected to escalate at 4 percent per year, beginning with the second year of operations.

- Gelb believes that using the new system may generate additional revenue or perhaps may cut other unanticipated costs. For example, if he decides to acquire the new equipment, he plans to advertise to his clients about the change. This may result in some increase in revenue. Also, he would be eligible for an environmental award given by his industry. Gelb also believes that he can negotiate a better lease rate for his facilities based on the reduction in the use of hazardous wastes caused by the new system. While he is not quite sure how all of these components add up, his best guess is that they will bring in additional cash flow of $4,000 per year. These benefits are expected to escalate at 4 percent per year, beginning with the second year of operations.

- The old process exposed Gelb to fines and even the potential of litigation. However, he cannot place estimates on these costs. But as long as he complies with existing laws, Gelb feels that his exposure is quite small.

- Gelb uses NPV as an investment criterion and discounts net cash flows at a rate of 15 percent.

- Gelb Gold's tax rate is 44 percent, including 34 percent for federal taxes and a "piggyback" state tax of 10 percent. The same rate is applied to operating incomes and losses, as well as to capital gains and losses.

Required: Calculate the NPV for the difference between the new and the old processes. What should Gelb do?

CASES

C8.1 (Barnett Boats)[16]

Part 1

Barnett Boats has been making several models of fiberglass fishing boats for over 20 years at its plant near Charleston, South Carolina. Its manufacturing process entails several stages. The first stage begins when fiberglass cloth is inserted in the bottom half of a mold used to form the boat's hull. After the top half of the mold is attached, a mixture of quick-setting resin is injected. When the hull hardens, the rough edges are sanded and the fittings attached. Each finished boat is moved from the production area to a storage area. When an order is received, the boat is moved from the storage area, loaded onto a motor transport, and delivered to the dealer.

Barnett makes boat hulls in batches of 250. At the end of a run, workers prepare the equipment for the next batch. Each time production is changed over to a new model, workers must remove the old mold. It is first disconnected from the

---

[16] Adapted from A. Faye Borthick and Harold P. Roth, "Accounting for Time: Reengineering Business Processes to Improve Responsiveness," *Cost Management*, fall 1993, pp. 4–14.

resin injection machinery, cleaned, and then placed in storage. A mold for the next run's model is removed from storage, maneuvered into place, and reconnected to the injection machinery. Once the new mold is in place, Barnett workers make a test run to see that the top and bottom mold halves are properly aligned. If the test hull meets standards, it is discarded and production begins. Otherwise, the model positions are corrected, without the necessity of a second test run. All of these steps take time, but experienced Barnett workers can complete a setup in just about 5 hours.

Setup cost, the cost of changing over production from one boat model to another, entails primarily labor and materials costs. Next year, setup cost is expected to total $120,000. About 40 percent of this amount varies in direct proportion with the number of setup hours. At normal levels of production, Barnett makes about 10,000 boats each year.

Barnett boats, known for quality, are beginning to catch on. While Barnett believes that sales in 1997 will stay at the normal level of 10,000 units, it fully expects to see volume in 1998 and the foreseeable future increase by 500 boats each year. As a result, Barnett managers believe that the time has come to modernize the changeover process. Some of the managers attending a recent trade show saw equipment that essentially automates changeovers, thereby reducing overall setup time. After speaking with the equipment vendor sales representatives, Barnett managers believe that the equipment can eventually reduce setup times from 5 hours to 1 hour.

To help justify the investment, a team of managers at Barnett formulated a 6-year plan. Starting in January 1997, with acquisition and installation of the new equipment, the plan assumes initial setup times of 2 hours. After that, setup times decline by 15 minutes each year until they reach 1 hour—the minimum obtainable with the new equipment. Variable setup costs for the new equipment is expected to equal about $100 per setup-hour.

With faster production changeovers, Barnett plans to reduce the size of production runs. During the first year, until workers get used to the new equipment, Barnett plans to leave the number of hulls in each run at 250. But, starting in 1998, and each year thereafter, it will reduce run length by 25 units. In 1998, for example, production should be 225 hulls per run.

Smaller production runs also mean that average inventory levels decline. Since demand for Barnett boats is fairly even throughout the year, the average inventory is typically equal to production batch size divided by 2. Since each boat in production costs about $50 per year to carry in inventory, reductions in inventory cost represent yet another way of justifying the new equipment.

The new equipment will cost $132,500, plus an installation cost of $12,500, or a total of $145,000. In addition, Barnett will pay the equipment vendor $7,500 at the end of the first year of operations for training. Training sessions are planned for Sunday afternoons throughout the first year of operations in order to minimize interruption of normal work schedules. Overtime pay for employees receiving training is expected to total $20,000. Barnett's accountant believes that the equipment as well as the installation qualify as a 6-year asset for tax purposes, with depreciation rates equal to 20.0 percent, 32.0 percent, 19.2 percent, 11.5 percent, 11.5 percent, and 5.8 percent. Training cost, including both payments to the equipment vendor and overtime pay, will not be capitalized. Instead, it will be written off at the end of the first year of operations for tax purposes. The current plan is to replace the equipment at the end of 6 years. However, no residual value is anticipated from the disposal of the equipment in the year 2002. The existing equipment is fully depreciated and has no residual value. Barnett's tax rate is 36 percent. All new investment proposals are evaluated at 18 percent.

Required: What is the NPV of the new equipment proposal? Start by calculating total setup cost with and without the new equipment. Next, calculate the total carrying cost by multiplying the average inventory (batch size/2) by the carrying cost per unit under both the present conditions and with the new equipment. Then, complete the capital-budgeting model.

Part 2

Reliance on NPV as the sole criterion for justifying investments may lead to overemphasis on short-term results. When capital-budgeting decisions are based only on NPV, investments yielding difficult-to-quantify benefits may never see the light of day. For example, investments in new technology, such as Barnett Boats is considering, may create considerable value in the future. But if their immediate dollar benefits cannot be demonstrated by Barnett managers, such investments may never gain approval. Baxter-Travenol's investment in transdermal technology is a case in point. At the time the firm committed resources for research, the health benefits and ultimate revenues from this new technology were largely unknown. Today, its investment appears to provide Baxter-Travenol with a platform for another generation of profitable pharmaceutical products. Another example is the Vindicator Company, which built a $6.8-million irradiation plant in Florida in 1992.[17] Irradiation is the use of low-level gamma rays to kill insects and bacteria, such as salmonella, on food. Uncertainty about the health impact of the process has kept some food retailers from stocking irradiated products. Even though the plant is operating at less than capacity, with losses of $325,000 in 1992, the investment may eventually give Vindicator an important foothold in an emerging industry.

To remedy this potential shortfall of NPV, new approaches have been advocated that offer systematic ways of incorporating nonquantitative factors into investment decisions. For example, Shank and Govindarajan advocate a value chain analysis.[18] Under their approach, managers evaluate investments over a broader range of benefits and costs by asking questions such as the following: How does the investment impact other business units? What are future growth opportunities brought by the investment? How does it give us a competitive advantage? How does the investment impact economies of scale? Does it effect suppliers, production, throughput time, or technology?[19]

To help organize an approach for incorporating difficult-to-quantify costs and benefits into the capital-budgeting decision, Bromwich and Bhimani offer a framework useful for evaluating the potential strategic impact of investments in new technology.[20]

    I. Marketing strategies
      A. Product enhancements
        1. Enhancing corporate image
        2. Response to fluctuating demand
        3. Lower cost of meeting demand
        4. Improved quality

---

[17] "The Food Irradiation Plant in Polk County," *The Orlando Sentinel,* Jan. 23, 1994.
[18] John K. Shank and Vijay Govindarajan, "Strategic Cost Analysis of Technological Investments," *Sloan Management Review,* fall 1992, pp. 39–51.
[19] Kevin Cherry, "Why Aren't More Investments Profitable?" *Cost Management,* summer 1993, pp. 28–37.
[20] Michael Bromwich and Al Bhimani, "Strategic Investment Appraisal," *Management Accounting,* Mar. 1991, pp. 45–48.

B. Diversification
1. Expanded product portfolio
2. New products with new skills
3. New skills in new areas
C. Risk reduction
1. Stronger skill base
2. Better control
3. Better planning
4. Reduced working capital and inventory
5. More-flexible responses
II. Internal strategies
A. Cost advantages
B. More control over production systems
C. Improved organizations
D. Beneficial interactions

Required: Identify the potential marketing and internal strategies that might be impacted by Barnett's investment in automated setup equipment.

C8.2 (Columbia Forest Products)[21]

Part 1

Columbia Forest Products is considering investing in two alternative kinds of technology for logging its 450,000 acres of timberland in the Virginia tidewater region. Conventional logging technology, one that Columbia has used successfully for many years, is based on *clear-cutting* (removal of all trees in a stand of timber) with equipment known as feller/bunchers. Feller/bunchers are similar to large farm tractors, except they have heavy-duty attachments that shear off bunches of trees at ground level. The tempo and pace at a clear-cut site might best be described as pandemonium. Felled trees are dragged to staging areas by equipment called "skidders." There, workers with chain saws remove tree limbs as best as they can. From staging areas, logs are loaded onto flatbed trucks and transported to woodyards, where they are sorted and cut into sections for processing. The primary benefit of this approach to logging is the high volume of throughput. However, productivity comes at a cost— serious damage to the forests and land, plus hard, dangerous conditions for workers.

A second form of logging technology, called the *harvester/forwarder* method, is beginning to be adopted in the United States. Using this method, sophisticated machinery, called a harvester, moves carefully through the forests, selecting specific trees for harvesting based on the needs of the processing mills. Each tree is felled with a smooth saw cut, precisely delimbed, and cut into predetermined lengths. Sections of logs are moved to the roadside by another piece of equipment, called a forwarder, and then loaded onto trucks to be taken to processing mills. In direct contrast with traditional logging methods, harvester/forwarders do minimal damage to the forest and land. In addition, workers are relatively safe and comfortable when using this kind of equipment.

The issue facing Kim Price, CEO of the logging division of Columbia, is whether to use the traditional feller/buncher approach or to adopt the harvester/forwarder technology. Price first observed this new process while traveling in Germany several years ago. Because of the importance of the decision to her

[21] Adapted from John K. Shank and Vijay Govindarajan, "Strategic Cost Analysis of Technological Investments," *Sloan Management Review,* fall 1992, pp. 39–51.

division and because of her first-hand knowledge of the harvester/forwarder technology, Price was asked to head a team charged with evaluating the benefits and costs of the two types of equipment on a test tract consisting of 25,000 acres. The data gathered from the test site are shown in Exhibit C8.2.1.

Required: Prepare a separate analysis of the NPV for each of the two options. Based solely on quantifiable costs, which approach should Price's logging division adopt?

Part 2
Assume Price's calculations indicate that the cost of conventional feller/buncher technology is less than that of the newer harvester/forwarder approach. During the data-gathering stage, Price's team identified several important, yet difficult-to-quantify, factors favoring continued use of the conventional technology. For example, harvester/forwarders rely on highly skilled labor rather than on the day laborers required in conventional logging. Dependability is a second issue. Just keeping harvester/forwarder equipment in the field may be more difficult. In addition, Price

EXHIBIT C8.2.1   COLUMBIA FOREST PRODUCTS

Logging Division

	Harvester/ Forwarder (New Technology)	Feller/Buncher (Conventional Technology)
Equipment configuration	1 harvester-forwarder pair	1 feller-buncher with 2 skidders and 1 crane
Cost	$608,000	$370,000
Number of shifts	2	1
Annual Output (cubic units of wood)	17,600	17,600
Cash operating cost:		
Labor	$ 94,000	$105,000
Fuel	15,000	75,000
Supplies, repair, & maintenance	91,000	91,000
Insurance & taxes	3,000	3,000
Supervision	50,000	35,000
Total cash operating cost	$253,000	$309,000
Depreciation:		
Method	MACRS	MACRS
Depreciation rates:		
Year 1	0.15	0.15
Year 2	0.22	0.22
Year 3 through 5	0.21	0.21
Salvage value (end of year 5)	$ 60,000	$ 18,000
Other data:		
Discount rate	12.00%	12.00%
Income tax rate	36.00%	36.00%

Source: Reprinted from John K. Shank and Vijay Govindarajan, "Strategic Cost Analysis of Technological Investments," *Sloan Management Review*, fall 1992, p. 46, by permission of the publisher. Copyright 1992 by the Sloan Management Review Association. All rights reserved.

was well aware that orchestrating the flow of work with the new technology requires changes in management style and job tasking. Finally, Price was concerned about the impact on the community if low-wage laborers were released. On the other side of the coin, the new technology was much kinder to the environment.

Before making a recommendation to Columbia's executive board, Price decided to look at all stages of Columbia's involvement in forest products. Columbia, like other major forest product companies, is vertically integrated, adding value all the way along the value chain. Its operations range from genetic seedling research, through processing, to distribution of paper and solid wood products, and, finally, to end users. Price urged the team to look at the process as a whole and to identify costs and benefits at all stages. Its results, based on the test site, shown in Exhibit C8.2.2, cast a very different slant on the problem. Although Price's logging division would never get credit for these savings, it was clear that harvester/forwarder technology produced significant savings for other divisions in Columbia. For example, neatly felled, delimbed, and precisely sorted trees will save an estimated $12,000 annually in processing costs at Columbia's processing division pulp mills.

As a final step, the members of Price's team initiated discussions with the company officials responsible for strategic planning. From these discussions, they learned that Columbia had embarked on a "differentiation" strategy over 20 years ago. Central to the strategy is growing genetically improved trees that will yield a higher mixture of wood at maturity. This is important, since trees in the Virginia tidewater region have a 35-year growth cycle. With this strategy in mind, the team developed short- and intermediate-range projections of how each of the two technologies would impact forest management. The results are shown in Exhibit

EXHIBIT C8.2.2   COLUMBIA FOREST PRODUCTS

Annual Benefits of Harvester/Forwarder Relative to Feller/Buncher

	Annual Benefit
After-tax value added for forest division:	
Improved product mix selection	$ 6,000
Saved stem damage waste (saw cut better than shear cut)	3,000
Saved cost for site repair (less damage to land)	4,000
Total value for land	$13,000
After-tax value added for logging division:	
Quantifiable costs & benefits (reflected in Exhibit C8.2.1)	
After-tax value added for processing division:	
Saved processing costs at pulpmills from precise sorting	$12,000
Saved cost of sawing trees to logs in woodyards	5,000
Saved trim loss in woodyards	3,000
Saved costs from logs misapplied by saw operators at woodyards	4,000
Saved wood loss from woodyard saw spacing	8,000
Saved downtime from delivering type of wood when needed	3,000
Kiln-drying savings from more-precise sorting	2,000
Savings by using lighter-duty debarkers	1,000
Savings from double handling of off-grade logs	1,000
Total value for processing mills	$39,000
Annual after-tax value added from adopting harvester/forwarder	$52,000

C8.2.3. The bottom-line conclusion is that the new technology will permit Columbia to obtain 90 percent of the wood it needs from its own timberlands rather than the 80 percent obtained with conventional technology. This will save Columbia's sawmills and plywood mills more than $5 million each year for the full tract of 450,000 acres. Columbia will be that much closer to self-sufficiency in supplying the sawmills and plywood mills with the high-grade logs needed to meet growing consumer demand.

Required:

1. Calculate the difference in the net cash flow for the harvester/forwarder equipment relative to the feller/buncher equipment. Then calculate the NPV for the differences in net cash flow. Include the benefits from the forest and processing divisions shown in Exhibit C8.2.2 in your computations. Does this change your decision from part 1?
2. Without making any computations, do the data in Exhibit C8.2.3 influence your decision? If so, how?

EXHIBIT C8.2.3 COLUMBIA FOREST PRODUCTS		
Estimated Wood Supply and Demand		
1995	*Pulp Mills*	*Sawmills/ Plywood Mills*
Demand (in cubic units of wood)	1,500,000	300,000
Supply from Columbia Timberlands	600,000	200,000
Percent of demand supplied by Columbia	40.00%	66.67%
2010		
Demand (in cubic units of wood)	1,500,000	500,000
Supply from Columbia timberlands using:		
Conventional technology	500,000	400,000
Percent of demand supplied by Columbia	33.33%	80.00%
Harvester/forwarder technology	500,000	450,000
Percent of demand supplied by Columbia	33.33%	90.00%

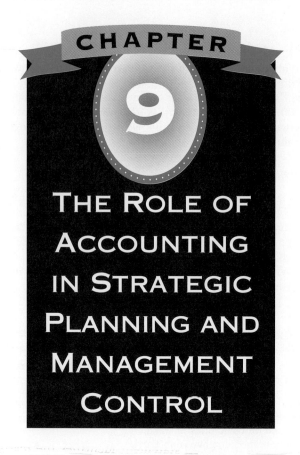

THE ROLE OF ACCOUNTING IN STRATEGIC PLANNING AND MANAGEMENT CONTROL

We have been focusing on two of the purposes of management accounting—costing and the provision of data for decision making. Now we shift to the third purpose—<u>planning</u> and <u>controlling</u>—translating broad, corporate-level goals into specific operating plans.

We begin by investigating how a firm goes about achieving its mission. Senior managers decide what the firm will produce and in what markets it will compete—in other words, <u>the firm's strategic plans</u>. Accounting provides a framework for evaluating the relative strengths of the firm's resources and operations in accomplishing these strategic plans. For example, a chemical firm, Green Earth Chemicals, Inc., may find that its low-cost U.S. production activities—when combined with its existing worldwide delivery networks—offer an advantage for entering a low-toxicity herbicide market in South America. Such decisions rely on the cost and decision-making principles discussed in the first eight chapters.

Let's assume Green Earth Chemicals decides to enter the market in South America. What's next? It's evaluating issues such as the following:

- Will a new organizational unit need to be created? If so, where should it be located?
- Who will develop the operating plans?
- How will information be gathered?
- What reports and inducements are necessary for employees who produce, sell, and deliver the product to ensure their motivation and success?

Asking questions such as these and evaluating the answers is the job of the management control system.

The interaction between strategic planning and management control is represented in Exhibit 9.1. It depicts control as an ongoing system that both depends upon and helps to shape company plans. Management control is also a reporting mechanism that links the firm's operations back to its strategic intent. We will see in this chapter how management accounting is expected to provide information needed for decision making throughout this strategy-control-operations cycle.

This chapter will:

- Define the various meanings of *strategy* and discuss different types of strategies
- Explain the relationship between organizational and reporting structures
- Examine the five phases of management control
- Introduce incentive compensation plans
- Offer alternatives to formal control systems

INTRODUCTION TO STRATEGY

Since management accounting helps managers plan and carry out a given strategy, we must be clear about the various meanings of *strategy* in our discussions. In its broadest context, *strategy* means a plan of organizational action designed to attain organizational goals—essentially a game plan for running the organization.

STRATEGIC PLANNING AT THE CORPORATE LEVEL

CORPORATE MISSION

The corporate mission statement identifies the reason a firm exists, or its *mission*. It identifies the firm's external focus—its targeted customers and

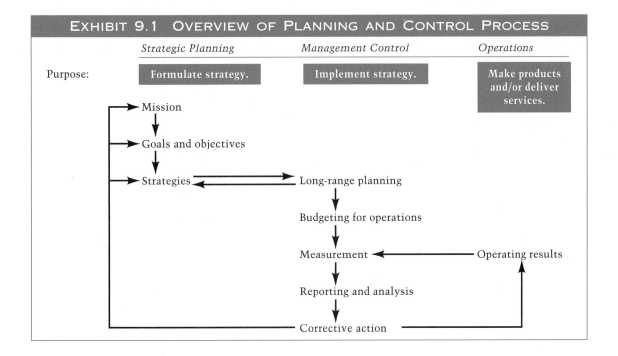

EXHIBIT 9.1 OVERVIEW OF PLANNING AND CONTROL PROCESS

	Strategic Planning	Management Control	Operations
Purpose:	Formulate strategy.	Implement strategy.	Make products and/or deliver services.

Mission
↓
Goals and objectives
↓
Strategies ⇄ Long-range planning
↓
Budgeting for operations
↓
Measurement ← Operating results
↓
Reporting and analysis
↓
Corrective action

market—and its internal focus—the products, technologies, and functions through which it will serve that market. A well-designed mission statement will contain a central theme that helps managers identify new products or business acquisitions as good strategic fits. Consider these two examples:

> *Saturn Corporation:* "Market vehicles developed and manufactured in the United States that are world leaders in quality, cost and customer satisfaction through the integration of people, technology and business systems and to transfer knowledge, technology and experience throughout General Motors."[1]

> *IBM:* "IBM develops, manufactures, and sells advanced information processing products, including computers and microelectronic technology, software, networking systems and information technology-related services. We offer value worldwide—through our United States, Canada, Europe/Middle East/Africa, Latin America and Asia Pacific business units—by providing comprehensive and competitive product choices."[2]

While imprecise because it is visionary, the corporate mission statement should be regarded as the basis for developing every plan and action in the organization.

CORPORATE GOALS AND OBJECTIVES

The broad corporate mission statement must be converted into clear, specific statements of purpose. Goal statements identify outcomes that the firm wants to achieve but still are broad in tone. Objective statements express goals in quantifiable terms, stating *what* is to be accomplished and *when* it will happen. For example, in 1991 Xerox defined the following customer goal:[3]

> Our customer goal is to become an organization with whom customers are eager to do business.

The following is Xerox's 1991 customer objective statement:

> Achieve progress toward our 1993 goal of 100 percent customer satisfaction by improving all of our work processes.

Thus, the objective statement says what will be accomplished (100 percent satisfaction) and when it will occur (by 1993).

A firm will normally identify several goals that it must achieve in order to accomplish its mission. Unlike the "profit maximization" objective that dominates models used in the study of economics, real-world models used by actual firms include other goals that are vital for long-term survival. In addition to profitability and customer satisfaction, these aims address issues such as market position, productivity, employee development, and public responsibility, among others.

---

[1]   Gilbert Fuchsberg, "'Visioning' Missions Becomes Its Own Mission," *The Wall Street Journal,* Jan. 7, 1994, pp. B1–B2.
[2]   IBM *1993 Annual Report,* p. 1.
[3]   Xerox Corporation, internal corporate documents, entitled "Managing for Results," compiled for the budget year 1991.

Corporate Strategy. The corporate strategy is the firm's game plan in which it defines *how* it will accomplish its objectives. Strategy begins with the identification of the types of business in which the firm will compete. The result of this process is often referred to as the firm's *business portfolio.* For example, assume a bank announces a 10 percent market growth objective. It might reach its objective by expanding its mortgage business while cutting back on its stock brokerage business. How this strategy will be accomplished is addressed in specific terms at lower organizational levels.

Formulating a corporate strategy requires that senior management make decisions about the relative emphasis among the firm's business lines for establishing its business portfolio. A strategy formulated at the corporate, or highest, management level will affect how a firm directs the strategies of its business units. Senior management communicates these strategies to business unit managers through the process of setting objectives and allocating resources. There are three strategies a firm can execute at the business-unit level in order to pursue its broader corporate strategy—whether it be to grow, hold, or harvest, or a combination of these.[4]

- *Grow.* A growth strategy places emphasis on building market share and bringing new products to market. A growth strategy can mean sacrificing profit or cash flow—although cost advantage is gained thereby when fixed costs are spread over increased production. A firm in an industry that enjoys the benefits of growth will generally choose a growth strategy. For example, Anheuser-Busch took advantage of its existing investment in beer delivery networks in implementing its growth strategy for the Eagle Snack unit. The decision to pursue a growth strategy was made as the snack food industry itself grew in the 1980s and early 1990s. (See "Current Practice: Multimedia Inc. Entertainment.")
- *Hold.* A firm protects its market share and competitive position by means of a hold strategy. A hold strategy is especially appropriate for a successful business in an industry with little or no growth. Managers using this strategy emphasize *productivity gains*—gains made through process improvement or capital investment—as a means to increase profitability. For example, General Motors' Cadillac division competes in an overcrowded luxury car market that has experienced a sales slowdown in the 1990s. Cadillac has sought to reduce production costs by adopting productivity improvements realized by GM's Saturn division.
- *Harvest.* The idea of the harvest strategy is to maximize cash flow and earnings, even if this results in sacrificing market share. The business is seen as having a limited useful life; therefore, capital investment is generally inappropriate. This is a useful strategy in

---

[4] These same three types of strategies also apply to products. For example, a strategic business unit may try to grow one product, such as high-definition TV, while harvesting another, such as analog electrical components.

CURRENT PRACTICE

Multimedia Inc. Entertainment

Multimedia Inc. is composed of five lines of business that, in 1993, generated a combined net income of $100 million on sales of $635 million. One Multimedia business, entertainment, has pursued a growth strategy by producing television talk shows. It acquired the rights to Phil Donahue's talk show in 1976, when daytime TV was dominated by game shows and soap operas. When it began, the *Donahue* show was brash and highly differentiated. It was also very profitable—one hour-long show cost about $50,000 to produce and generated $400,000 in revenue. In 1983, Multimedia expanded further by creating a TV talk show for Sally Jesse Raphael, who until then had been a radio celebrity. The tide began to turn, however, as competition emerged. The Oprah Winfrey show, which began in 1986, had overtaken Donahue in the ratings by the early 1990s. Other TV talk-show hosts, such as Geraldo Rivera, began to appear. And some of their shows produced an even greater shock value than the show that Donahue first introduced. Meanwhile, Multimedia's corporate strategy for its entertainment business began to shift from a growth to a hold position.

Source: Adapted from Anita Sharpe, "Sedate Multimedia Inc., Home of Phil and Sally, Faces Unclear Future," *The Wall Street Journal*, May 10, 1994, pp. A1, A12.

mature industries where growth is not possible. For example, as the mainframe computer market is being replaced by local area networks, IBM is beginning to harvest its mainframe business unit. It has diverted the unit's resources to other independent business units—such as personal computers, software, and networks—in order to compete in growth markets.

When designing a management control system, we will need to focus on these three corporate strategies as they are carried out at the business level. Through them, it's possible to measure how well the managers at that level are fulfilling the broader corporate strategies devised by senior management. For example, a manager placed in charge of a new South American herbicide business should set market position and sales growth as indicators of a business growth strategy. The manager's performance should be measured accordingly. It would be misleading (and unfair) for senior management to evaluate the manager according to such measures as meeting profit and ROI targets at levels comparable to those used for mature chemical business lines.

LOWER-LEVEL STRATEGIES

Corporate strategies are implemented by subunits within the organization. Exhibit 9.2 presents a breakdown of three levels of strategy: (1) corporate, (2) business, and (3) functional. When a subunit pursues a strategy, its

EXHIBIT 9.2 LEVELS OF STRATEGY

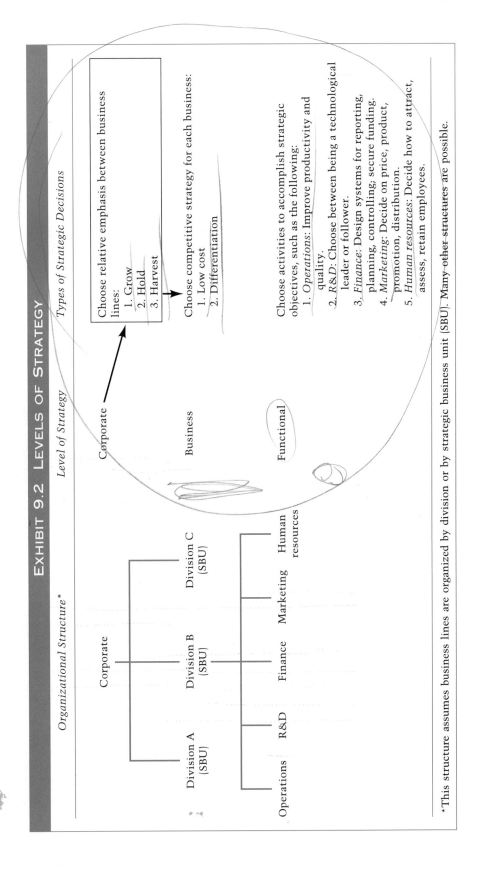

Organizational Structure*	Level of Strategy	Types of Strategic Decisions

Corporate — Choose relative emphasis between business lines:
1. Grow
2. Hold
3. Harvest

Business — Choose competitive strategy for each business:
1. Low cost
2. Differentiation

Functional — Choose activities to accomplish strategic objectives, such as the following:
1. *Operations:* Improve productivity and quality.
2. *R&D:* Choose between being a technological leader or follower.
3. *Finance:* Design systems for reporting, planning, controlling; secure funding.
4. *Marketing:* Decide on price, product, promotion, distribution.
5. *Human resources:* Decide how to attract, assess, retain employees.

Corporate

Division A (SBU) Division B (SBU) Division C (SBU)

Operations R&D Finance Marketing Human resources

*This structure assumes business lines are organized by division or by strategic business unit (SBU). Many other structures are possible.

actions should help senior-level organizational units achieve their strategies, as well. If, for example, senior management seeks to build market share by introducing new and innovative products, then the R&D subunit strategy should be geared to creating new products, rather than adding features to existing products. In this and succeeding chapters, we will find that management accounting information enables managers to coordinate strategies between various levels of the organization.

BUSINESS STRATEGIES

Corporate management decides which businesses are to be grown, held, or harvested. Hence, the objective of business strategy is to establish a sustainable competitive position from which to successfully implement the corporate strategy. That's why business-level managers examine their activity through questions about target market, product, promotion, distribution, and price. To establish an advantage in the marketplace, business managers choose between two competitive strategies—low cost and differentiation.[5]

Low Cost. A manager establishes a cost advantage by setting the prices of the unit's products or services below those of its competitor's products or services in order to gain market share. Low cost production is necessary to sell at a low price. A low-cost strategy must be central to the business unit's philosophy and be a recurring theme throughout its operations. Pursuit of a low-cost-leadership strategy requires "aggressive construction of efficient-scale facilities, vigorous pursuit of cost reductions from experience, tight cost and overhead control, avoidance of marginal customer accounts, and cost minimization in areas like R&D, service, sales force, advertising, and so on."[6] Examples of businesses well-known for low-cost leadership in their markets include Bic (ballpoint pens), Wal-Mart (discount retailing), and Hyundai (passenger cars). All of these firms produce and distribute their products at low cost, and in turn, have built market share by offering products priced lower than comparable products offered by their competitors. (See "Current Practice: ValuJet Airlines' Low-Cost Strategy.")

Differentiation. The strategy of differentiation focuses on creating a product or service that is perceived by customers as unique. It can take many different forms, such as brand image (Levi's jeans), product technology (Coleman in camping equipment), distribution channels (Tupperware), engineering design and performance (Mercedes-Benz), and product taste (Dr. Pepper, Listerine). Differentiation is recognized as a viable strategy for

---

[5] Michael E. Porter, *Competitive Strategy*, New York: The Free Press, 1980, pp. 35–40. We limit our discussion to two of Porter's three competitive strategies. The third strategy, called *focus*, combines aspects of the other two strategies but is directed at various portions of a product line or geographic area, or at segments of a defined market. For more information, refer to Porter or to a strategic management text.
[6] *Ibid.*, p. 35.

CURRENT PRACTICE

ValuJet Airline's Low-Cost Strategy

Within the first year of going public, ValuJet Airlines' share price quadrupled. The firm's early success is due to its narrowly focused, low-cost competitive strategy. In fact, evidence of a low-cost approach can be spotted in every aspect of the company culture. Corporate headquarters are small and spartan. Top executives occupy window offices that are fitted out with furniture bought at Office Depot and assembled by the executives themselves. Fixed pay is low—pilots earn only $45,000 per year, flight attendants $11 per hour; ticket agents are hired at $6 per hour from a temporary agency. Passengers feel the effects of a low-cost strategy, too. There is no in-flight meal service, and the availability of flights is limited—no more than four daily flights to any of the 30 cities that ValuJet serves. And fares are nonrefundable. Nonetheless, with ticket prices as low as $39, the customers keep coming back!

Source: Adapted from Bridget O'Brian and Rick Brooks, "No Frills Approach Propels ValuJet to Quick Success," *The Wall Street Journal*, May 4, 1995, p. B4.

earning above-average returns for a business, mainly because customers are willing to pay a premium for brand loyalty. That's the upside of differentiation. On the downside, attempts to achieve differentiation often increase operating costs. A business-level manager pursuing a differentiation strategy must still control costs—otherwise, the result could be prices that are higher than the market will bear.

FUNCTIONAL STRATEGIES

Managers at each of the firm's functional-activity levels—operations, marketing, R&D, finance, human resources—spell out the specific tasks, or functional strategies, that help managers to implement business strategy. What actions, for example, should human resources take to ensure that an innovative firm is hiring creative people? Accounting provides information that measures the success of these functional activities—including how well they are coordinated with each other. It also shows senior management whether lower-level subunits are working in harmony to implement the chosen business strategy. An example of functional strategies and related decisions facing an R&D manager is shown in Exhibit 9.3.

One fundamental functional-strategy decision is whether to be a technological leader or follower. This choice must be framed within the context of the higher-level competitive strategy—low cost or differentiation. If the decision is to be a follower and the business is pursuing a strategy of low cost, the R&D manager may decide either (1) to learn from the leader's experience how to help lower the cost of the product or (2) to avoid R&D costs by imitating the leader (e.g., by using the same product design). Each functional strategy must be derived from the business strategy that

EXHIBIT 9.3 FUNCTIONAL STRATEGIC DECISIONS FACING AN R&D MANAGER		
Competitive Strategy	Technological Leadership	Technological Followership
Low Cost	Pioneer the lowest-cost product design. Be the first firm down the learning curve. Create low-cost ways of performing activities.	Lower the cost of the product by learning from the leader's experience. Avoid R&D costs through imitation.
Differentiation	Pioneer a unique product that increases buyer value. Innovate activities to increase buyer value.	Adapt the product or delivery system more closely to buyer needs by learning from the leader's experience.

Source: Adapted with the permission of The Free Press, a division of Simon & Schuster, from Michael E. Porter, *Competitive Advantage: Creating and Sustaining Superior Performance,* New York: The Free Press, 1985, p. 181.

it supports. An integrated accounting system should provide information that helps to coordinate the R&D manager's plans with the overall business plans and with other functional areas, such as operations and finance, upon which R&D will depend.

MANAGEMENT CONTROL SYSTEMS

We now turn from how strategies are chosen to how they are implemented. We take a broader view of how an organization uses information for motivating, evaluating, and rewarding employee performance.

A **management control** system is a *system designed to ensure that organizational strategies are implemented.* The accounting information system provides the information necessary to make the management control system work. You just saw that corporate-level strategies initiate action first at the business level and then at the functional level. Employees at each level must understand what they are expected to do; then they need feedback indicating whether they are doing it. However, feedback from the most complete and accurate accounting system may not be enough to ensure that employees will attain their strategic objectives. Accomplishing strategic objectives depends on the firm's ability to inspire its employees to take appropriate actions.

GOAL CONGRUENCE

Goal congruence, as noted earlier, exists when employees are motivated to act in ways that serve their own needs as individuals and, at the same time, the needs of the organization. A management control system's success is determined by its ability to motivate employees to strive for corporate goals.

As we discuss various aspects of management control, we can always rely on goal congruence as the acid test of an acceptable control alternative. Will a proposal—whether it affects organizational structure, reporting systems, reward systems, or whatever—encourage employees to strive toward accomplishing corporate goals? While many dimensions of human behavior may not be predictable, it's likely employees will act in the best interests of the organization if their motivation to do so is aligned with their own self-interest.

The management control system consists of two fundamental elements: structure and process. We will spend the rest of this chapter examining them.

MANAGEMENT CONTROL STRUCTURE

Management accounting results are reported by **responsibility center** (Chapter 3)—any organizational unit for which a manager is responsible. All an organization's responsibility centers together constitute its structure. The accounting system provides the information for measuring each responsibility center's activity and its contribution to achieving the organization's goals.

TYPES OF ORGANIZATIONAL STRUCTURE

Exhibit 9.4 provides charts for three common types of organizational structure.

Functional Structure. A **functional structure** comprises units that specialize in a designated function. One of its first users was Moses, who sought better work efficiency from the multitudes he led. He thus organized people into units of tens, fifties, hundreds, and thousands. In functional structures, the managers of each unit are responsible for decisions within their own units, although the decisions of all units must be coordinated with one another in order to achieve the goals of the organization as a whole. The chain of decisions is highly centralized, with all the important ones rising to the top. In the example of a functional structure shown in Exhibit 9.4, production, marketing, and finance operate as separate units altogether, although each relies on the efforts of the others. For example, production coordinates its plans with marketing's plans. Typically, each unit's planning and coordination of interunit activity must be approved by higher-level management.

Because each unit's employees focus on one activity, the functional structure offers the advantage of *efficiency*. A common activity, such as human resources, can be centralized. Instead of each unit's having to carry out its own human resource function, one human resources unit can serve all personnel needs of the others. Also, the organization will enjoy economies of scale, as those who work in the human resources department become specialists in areas such as applicant testing, training, or benefits. However, this structure can lead to control problems if employees become so narrowly focused that they lose sight of the larger, organizationwide purpose. For example, a production department solely concerned with cost and output may neglect quality, which it sees as the

EXHIBIT 9.4   TYPES OF ORGANIZATIONAL STRUCTURES

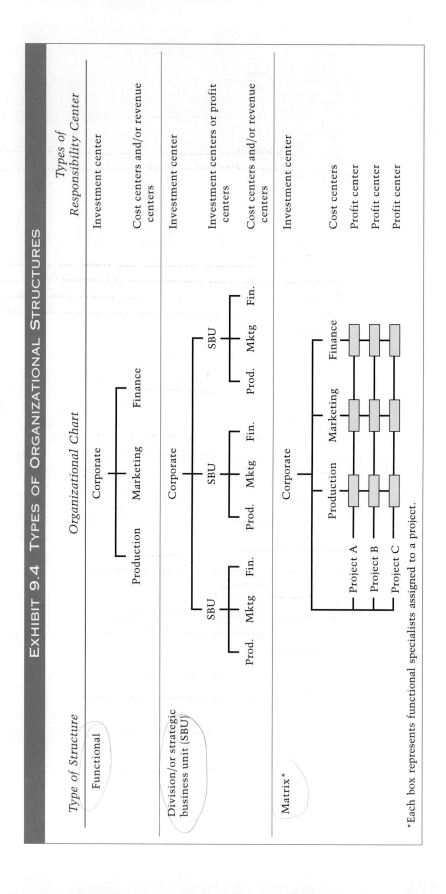

*Each box represents functional specialists assigned to a project.

responsibility of another department, to the detriment of the firm's purpose as a whole.

Division or Business Unit Structure.   One way organizations avoid the control problems inherent to the functional structure is by creating independent business units that combine production and marketing activities. These are frequently called divisional structures or strategic business units (SBUs). In the divisional or business-unit structure, divisions are made up of one or more business units organized along some common dimension—such as geography, customer type, or product. An SBU represents a grouping of business units organized along a more strategic dimension, such as technologically related opportunities or an overlapping set of competitors. For our purposes, the terms *divisions* and *SBUs* are used interchangeably.

In this structure, decisions are made by managers down at levels closely involved with markets and operations. Each division or business unit is an independent responsibility center that makes its own decisions and determines its own survival. This differs from the functional structure, in which each subunit manager is assigned resources and then is held accountable for the way the resources are consumed, but not for any derived benefits. Resource decisions made by divisions are driven by the marketplace, whereas those made by functional subunits are driven by the desire to bargain for more resources from senior management.

While divisional structures were used by General Motors and Du Pont Corporation as early as the 1920s, they did not become widely popular until after World War II. At that time, U.S. companies grew dramatically in size, and better accountability was needed. Today probably more than 90 percent of Fortune 500 firms operate with this structure.[7] (See "Current Practice: Ford's Global Restructuring.")

Divisionalization is successful because of the clear accountability that comes with ownership. Division managers are free to make their own decisions, and their success (or failure) is easily measured in terms of profit (or loss). A manager needs this autonomy in order to read and react quickly to changes in today's dynamic markets. However, this structure can create friction between various division managers, all of whom are motivated to act in their own division's best interest—sometimes without regard to the interests of their corporate organizations. The problem can be made worse when divisions must share resources or when they buy goods from one another.

Matrix Structure.   Combining the features of both the functional and division or business unit structures, the matrix structure is used primarily for project-based or joint venture firms, such as defense contractors, management consultants, and construction companies. This structure offers flexibility, since it allows employees to be assigned to jobs on a when-needed basis. Employees' first allegiance is to a functional area—such as manufacturing, marketing, or finance—that takes on the characteristics of a specialty

---

[7]   Charles W. L. Hill, Michael Hitt, and Robert E. Hoskisson, "Declining U.S. Competitiveness: Reflections on a Crisis," *The Academy of Management Executive*, Feb. 1988, p. 54.

CURRENT PRACTICE

Ford's Global Restructuring

Ford Motor Company reorganized in 1994 in order to compete more in the global market. For decades, Ford comprised three geographic business units: North America, Europe, and Asia Pacific. Now, Ford wants to develop vehicles—such as the European Mondeo—that, with minor modifications, can be sold in many different parts of the world. Thus, its North American and European operations now are combined into a single group that encompasses employees on both sides of the Atlantic. The chief goals of this new business unit are to speed new vehicle development and to cut costs by eliminating overlaps and duplication.

Sources: Paul Ingrassia and Jacqueline Mitchell, "Ford to Realign with a System of Global Chiefs," *The Wall Street Journal*, Mar. 31, 1994, pp. A3 and A5; Neal Templin, "Ford's Trotman Gambles on Global Restructuring Plan," *The Wall Street Journal*, Apr. 22, 1994, p. B4.

subunit in a functional structure. The functional areas serve as resource pools that loan employees to projects, which are similar to divisions in that they must prove their competitiveness in the marketplace. Each employee reports to two managers: one in his or her functional area and one who directs the project the employee has been assigned to.

In matrix structures the focus for control is the project, which can be evaluated for the profit it produces. The advantage of matrix structures is that they facilitate creation of new organizational units as needed in order to focus resources on strategic opportunities as they arise. Problems are inevitable, however, in coordinating the assignment of employees to projects and in the accountability of employees to two separate managers. For example, an employee may be requested to leave one project for a new project, but the current project manager may refuse the reassignment. The functional manager can assign the employee to the new project anyway, thus putting the employee in the middle of interunit hostilities. Still, proponents of this structure point to its versatility in distributing the best mix of employee talent to any job for the benefit of the overall organization.

TYPES OF RESPONSIBILITY CENTERS

The firm's organizational structure defines its responsibility centers—the units for which managers are responsible. The job of the accounting information system is to translate the function and performance of a responsibility center into measurements that indicate whether the unit has achieved its strategic objective. Each responsibility center is assigned resource inputs and is expected to provide outputs. The responsibility center converts these inputs to outputs through the work it does, as shown in the following table:

Inputs	→	Work	→	Outputs
Labor Materials Capital		Processes Activities		Products Services

In Exhibit 9.4, we see that for any type of corporate structure, the organizational units constituting it also represent responsibility centers. What type of responsibility center an organizational unit is depends on the objective it is expected to fulfill, as we shall now see. Exhibit 9.5 provides a summary of the types of responsibility centers and their financial-reporting characteristics.

Cost Centers. The primary responsibility of managers of organizational units considered cost centers is to control cost. There are two types of cost center.

In an **engineered cost center,** very precise expectations are formed about the relationship between inputs and outputs. For example, a production center uses inputs—material, labor, and machinery—to manufacture an output, such as men's dress shirts. It can carefully predetermine engineering-based standards and use variance from standard cost as an evaluation measure. The manager's primary financial objective is to minimize cost.

In a **discretionary cost center,** such as a legal department, little is known about the relationship between inputs—the costs of operating the

[handwritten margin notes: "Prod center" and "legal dept"]

EXHIBIT 9.5 RESPONSIBILITY CENTERS AND THEIR FINANCIAL-REPORTING CHARACTERISTICS

Financial Report Characteristics

Type of Responsibility Center	Example	Primary Objective	Information Needs	Primary Measure
Engineered cost center	Production center	To minimize cost	Costs	Cost variance from standard
Discretionary cost center	Legal department	To constrain spending	Costs (or expenses)	Costs (or expense) vs. budget
Revenue center	Sales department	To maximize revenue	Revenue	Revenue vs. budget
Profit center	Branch office	To maximize profit	Revenue and expenses	Profits vs. budget
Investment center	Business line	To maximize profit relative to investment	Revenue, expense, and investment	ROI or residual income vs. budget

Source: Adapted from William Rotch, Brandt R. Allen, and C. Ray Smith, *The Executive's Guide to Management Accounting and Control Systems*, 4th ed., Houston, Tex.: Dame Publications, Inc., 1991, p. 177.

department—and outputs—the amount and quality of legal services provided. The manager is given a *cost budget*—a plan that details available resources—that serves as a constraint on spending. The primary measure for determining whether spending has been properly controlled is to compare actual cost with the budget. Discretionary cost centers are mainly service-related but may also include custom production.

Revenue Centers. The results obtained by organizational units such as sales or marketing departments, whose function it is to generate revenue, are measured against planning targets. No attempt is made to relate inputs (e.g., salaries, travel expenses, and promotions) against their outputs (the revenue they produced). That's because the responsibility of a **revenue center** is to meet its sales expectations. Managers of revenue centers must meet a cost budget, but cost control is a separate—and secondary—issue.

Profit Centers. Managers of **profit centers** have autonomy in deciding what types and amounts of costs are incurred in order to generate revenue. The manager of a profit center is considered to be closest to the market and, therefore, in the best position to decide what trade-offs are necessary to meet profit targets. Profit centers are expected to motivate entrepreneurial behavior and stimulate a strategic perspective.

Investment Centers. Managers of **investment centers** are responsible not only for achieving profit but also for containing the amount of investment their profit centers require. Investment center managers have even more authority in deciding cost trade-offs, because they are responsible for the level of assets needed to generate profits. *Return on investment (ROI)* Is the most common measure of an investment center's performance.

LINKING FINANCIAL REPORTS TO THE ORGANIZATION'S STRUCTURE

Thus far we have seen how the structure of an organization—as well as the responsibilities of the units constituting it—begins to form a management control system. Now we take a look at the financial performance reports—which are needed to link organizational units. It is these linkages that make the management control system work.

Exhibit 9.6 offers an example for Consolidated Paints, Inc., a firm structured into two autonomous business units—paint production and decorating. Panel 1 shows the firm's organizational structure. We will focus on those organizational units that are highlighted in the chart to see how the financial reports are integrated between the four levels.

At the bottom of panel 2, we find the functional unit marketing, which is a cost center. Its performance report indicates a cost budget overrun of $7,000 for the current period. Marketing's report is "folded into" the income statement of the domestic division, to which it reports. Note that the domestic division, a profit center, has exceeded by $75,000 its target profit of $2,635,000. The domestic division reports to the paint production business, an investment center. Its report shows that the combined results of the domestic and international divisions fell short of the

Exhibit 9.6 Consolidated Paints, Inc.

Hierarchy of Responsibility Centers

1. Organizational Structure

Level of Corporate Structure

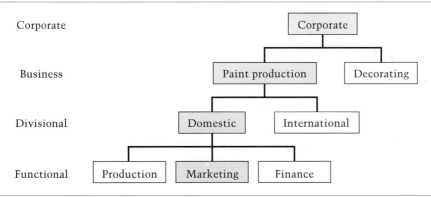

Corporate	Corporate
Business	Paint production — Decorating
Divisional	Domestic — International
Functional	Production — Marketing — Finance

2. Organizational Reports

Type of Responsibility Center	Corporate Level	Performance Report (in 000's)		
		Budget	Actual	Variance
Investment Center	Net income from:			
	Paint Production	$3,850	$3,640	$(210)
	Decorating	–	–	–
	Corporate	$6,280	$6,310	$30
	ROI	14.5%	15.3%	0.8%
	Paint Production—Business Level			
	Net income from:	Budget	Actual	Variance
Investment Center	Domestic	$2,635	$2,710	$75
	International	–	–	–
	Paint Production Business	$3,850	$3,640	$(210)
	ROI	12.9%	11.2%	–1.7%
	Domestic—Divisional Level			
		Budget	Actual	Variance
Profit Center	Revenue	$4,680	$4,830	$150
	Expense:			
	Manufacturing	–	–	–
	Marketing	$329	$332	$(7)
	Finance	–	–	–
	Other	–	–	–
	Net income	$2,635	$2,710	$75
	Marketing–Functional Level			
	Expense:	Budget	Actual	Variance
Cost Center	Salaries	–	–	–
	Occupancy	–	–	–
	TV ads	–	–	–
	Promotion	–	–	–
	Total expense	$329	$332	$(7)

12.9 percent target ROI by 1.7 percent. Last, we find the corporate level, a responsibility center whose objective is an ROI of 14.5 percent. The combined figure for the paint production and decorating business units has surpassed this target by 0.8 percent.

MANAGEMENT CONTROL PROCESS

We now examine the mechanism for implementing corporate strategy at each responsibility center. We will explore the five steps of implementing the strategy that are under management's control; these steps are shown in Exhibit 9.1. They are (1) long-range planning, (2) budgeting for operations, (3) measurement, (4) reporting and analysis, and (5) corrective action.

1: LONG-RANGE PLANNING

Formulating the long-range plan is the first step in the management control process. The plan outlines the actions the firm will take to achieve its strategy. Prior to devising the long-range plan, the firm has to formulate a strategy. Then management must identify and evaluate alternative means for implementing it. Admittedly, the process of formulating and implementing strategy is iterative; the strategy itself may change.

Let's look at an example. Green Earth Chemicals has decided to enter a low-toxicity herbicide market in South America. This is a business-level decision made by senior managers in the firm's agricultural chemicals business unit and endorsed by corporate management. Many questions concerning implementation must now be addressed:

- Which countries should be included in the plan?
- Should goods be manufactured in the United States or in South America?
- What types of marketing and delivery channels should be used?
- Which specific products should be included?
- What type and size of organization is needed on-site? Where will the unit be located?

Evaluating the answers to questions such as these is the purpose of long-range planning.

Capital Budgeting.   We can use capital budgeting as an analytical tool to express in measurable terms the results of long-term decisions. Let's see how capital budgeting works in our example of the agricultural chemicals business unit by examining one of the decisions the unit faces: Should inventory be manufactured in the United States or in South America? Exhibit 9.7 presents a capital-budgeting analysis of the differential costs related to each of the two alternatives. In panel 1, we see estimates reflecting:

- A five-year projection of unit production and sales, showing growth from 10,000 units in year 1 to 26,000 units in year 5
- Inventory manufactured in the United States using existing facilities and machinery

EXHIBIT 9.7 AGRICULTURAL CHEMICALS BUSINESS UNIT

Projected Cash Flows for Two Inventory Production Alternatives

1. Incremental Cash Outflows If Manufactured in the United States

	Year 1	Year 2	Year 3	Year 4	Year 5
Units expected to be produced and sold	10,000	16,000	21,000	24,000	26,000
Variable manufacturing cost (@ $1 per unit)	$10,000	$16,000	$21,000	$24,000	$26,000
Transportation per unit (@ $0.25 per unit)	2,500	4,000	5,250	6,000	6,500
Net cash outflow	$12,500	$20,000	$26,250	$30,000	$32,500
Present value factor (@ 15% hurdle rate)	0.8696	0.7561	0.6575	0.5718	0.4972
Discounted cash outflow	$10,870	$15,123	$17,260	$17,153	$16,158
Net present value	$76,563				

2. Incremental Cash Outflows If Manufactured in La Paz, Bolivia

	Year 1	Year 2	Year 3	Year 4	Year 5
Units expected to be produced and sold	10,000	16,000	21,000	24,000	26,000
Variable manufacturing cost (@ $0.50 per unit)	$5,000	$8,000	$10,500	$12,000	$13,000
Facility rental (@ $8,000 per year)	8,000	8,000	8,000	8,000	8,000
Equipment purchase	45,000	0	0	0	0
Net cash outflow	$58,000	$16,000	$18,500	$20,000	$21,000
Present value factor (@ 15% hurdle rate)	0.8696	0.7561	0.6575	0.5718	0.4972
Discounted cash outflow	$50,435	$12,098	$12,164	$11,435	$10,441
Net present value	$96,573				

- The variable production cost of $1 per unit, which is the only cost for manufacturing in the United States that differs from the cost of manufacturing in South America
- The variable cost of transporting the goods to South America, at $0.25 per unit

Panel 2 shows estimates for the second alternative, reflecting the following factors:

- Manufacturing in La Paz, Bolivia, a distribution point agreed upon in the planning process
- The variable production cost of $0.50 per unit (vs. $1.00 in the United States)
- No transportation cost (vs. $0.25 per unit if made in the United States)
- The cost of production plant setup in La Paz—comprising the costs of renting a facility ($8,000 per year) and of purchasing equipment ($45,000)

Cash flows under the two alternatives are discounted to the present at 15 percent, the firm's hurdle rate for long-term investment decisions. Income tax effects are ignored to simplify the illustration. The net present value (NPV) of the cost of alternative 1 is lower ($76,563 vs. $96,573), indicating that manufacturing in the United States is the lower-cost alternative.

This approach can be useful for sorting out other long-range planning issues—such as marketing channels, choice of product lines, and organization size.

Long-Range Planning Process.   Long-range planning can take many forms. In the most structured form, each division or business unit prepares, early in the year, a plan that must be evaluated and approved by corporate staff. At a minimum, this plan should include financial projections for the planning period, *normally 3 to 5 years,* and estimates for resources required, such as facilities and personnel. (See "Current Practice: A One-Page 5-Year Plan.")

Each division's plan is shared with other divisions, either in written summary form or verbally during joint meetings. This enables the divisions to make a coordinated effort toward achieving the company's goals and indicates how objectives will be accomplished. Plans from all divisions are combined into a master corporate plan. If senior executives determine that the corporate plan will attain the corporate objectives, great! If they decide that some divisions' long-range plans do not fit in with the corporate objectives, the plans must be revised.

Preparing formal long-range plans is costly and time-consuming. This step may not be needed by all firms. The capital budget alone may be sufficient to represent formal long-range plans. Divisions or business units are expected to submit a capital budget request that justifies in detail what they need and why. Corporate funds are allocated accordingly. Together, the preparation of the capital budget and the allocation of funds represent the entire long-range planning process.

Also serving the same purpose as corporate long-range plans are interdivisional meetings, where managers share their long-range plans with

---

CURRENT PRACTICE

A One-Page 5-Year Plan

Bob Frey, CEO of Cin-Made, a maker of paper and packaging materials, sought new applications for his products. He found that trying to keep track of product strategies in his head was not nearly as effective as doing it on paper. He began preparing one-page summaries of the corporate strategy. The summaries are 5-year plans that are updated as often as weekly—but no less frequently than monthly—and distributed to all employees and to the board of directors. Included for each of six product lines are assessments of the market future, market strategy, management attention, price strategy, capital investment strategy, quality strategy (i.e., an action plan to attain a desired level of product quality), and operational tactics.

Source: Terri Lummers, "The One-Page Strategy Guide," *Inc.,* Sept. 1992, pp.135–138.

other managers. The idea is for each manager to share information, as well as to seek opportunities for ventures with other divisions.

Another substitute for corporate long-range planning is to let each division operate as a freestanding business unit that sinks or swims on its own merit. Long-range planning is left to managers at the divisional or business-unit level. Division managers share their plans through reports and discussions with corporate-level management, which need neither revise nor approve divisional plans.

2: BUDGETING FOR OPERATIONS

The second step in the management control process is preparation of the operating budget. Budgets translate the company's long-range plan into short-term operating targets. The budget is the manager's plan of action for the upcoming time period, normally one year for U.S. firms. It shows in detail the amounts of resources needed by the manager in order to accomplish his or her responsibility center's objectives. The budget contains targets—revenue, costs, and profit—against which the manager's actual results can be compared.

Let's see how the agricultural chemical business unit in our example implements its long-range South America product plan. Assume that the decisions have been made concerning the channels of production, marketing, and distribution of the low-toxicity herbicide. Responsibility for outcomes must now be assigned and operating targets set. The budget communicates these targets to the organizational units and assigns the resources needed to hit these targets. Questions that must be answered in the budget are:

- Who will be assigned the responsibility for meeting sales, production, delivery, and quality expectations?
- What resources are needed, and by which managers are they needed?
- How are budget targets to be set? What steps will be taken to ensure that targets are met?
- What mechanism will be used to transfer goods and services between responsibility centers and what prices will be set for such transactions?
- To what extent are managers' evaluations to be based on the differentials between outcomes and budget targets?

Translating a Long-Range Plan into a Budget. Exhibit 9.8 shows how the agricultural chemical business unit assigned responsibility for entering the South American market. In panel 1, we find a new operations unit, called South America, that reports to the packaged chemicals product line. South America is to take full responsibility for implementing the long-range plan and will operate as a profit center.

In panel 2, we see South America's income statement for its first year of operations. The statement incorporates unit sales projections from the capital-budgeting analysis (Exhibit 9.7). Inventory (low-toxicity herbicide) will be supplied by the Houston plant, also a profit center, at a price of $2.50 per unit, comprising Houston's normal markup of $0.75 per unit,

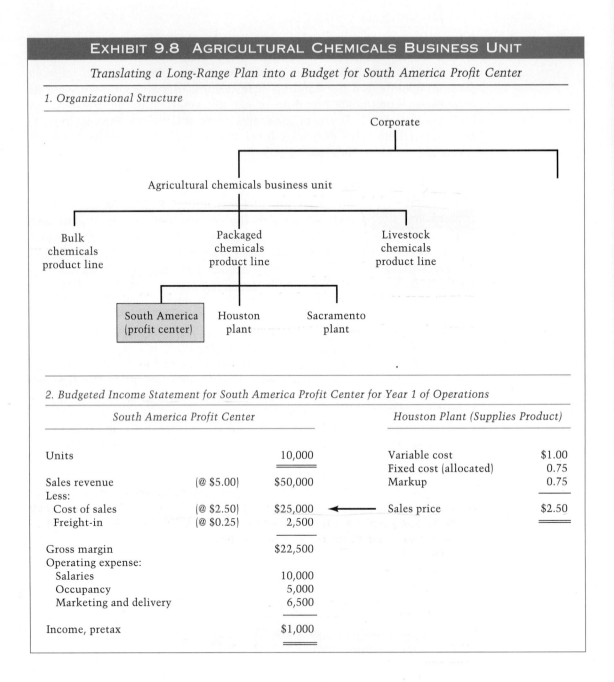

EXHIBIT 9.8 AGRICULTURAL CHEMICALS BUSINESS UNIT

Translating a Long-Range Plan into a Budget for South America Profit Center

1. Organizational Structure

2. Budgeted Income Statement for South America Profit Center for Year 1 of Operations

South America Profit Center			Houston Plant (Supplies Product)	
Units		10,000	Variable cost	$1.00
			Fixed cost (allocated)	0.75
Sales revenue	(@ $5.00)	$50,000	Markup	0.75
Less:				
Cost of sales	(@ $2.50)	$25,000 ←	Sales price	$2.50
Freight-in	(@ $0.25)	2,500		
Gross margin		$22,500		
Operating expense:				
Salaries		10,000		
Occupancy		5,000		
Marketing and delivery		6,500		
Income, pretax		$1,000		

$1.00 in variable cost, and $0.75 in fixed cost. South America includes in its budget $0.25 per unit for freight-in charges, plus operating expenses for salaries, occupancy, and marketing and delivery. The South America profit center's target income is $1,000. This return, only 2 percent of sales revenue, represents the results for the first year of a 5-year growth strategy.

Setting Targets.   The budget commits managers to their operating targets and commits the firm's resources to reaching those targets. The targets represent the managers' realistic assessment of what can be accomplished in the forthcoming period. Managers from all levels must coordinate and negotiate their plans with managers from other organizational units. The targets evolve from plans. As we saw in the herbicide example, the budget enables the manager of the Houston production plant to plan on producing inventory to meet the needs of the South America distribution center.

3: MEASUREMENT

The next step in the control process is to compare the actual results with the targets—which are what the manager aimed at. Determining which numeric criteria, or measures, a manager should focus on is critical to the success of a control system. The measures chosen to gauge the performance of employees, managers, and executives will *influence their behavior*, particularly when measurements are linked to rewards. The measures used to gauge a responsibility center's performance must motivate performance that is congruent with the center's strategic objective.

Evaluating Performance.   Efficiency and effectiveness are the criteria for evaluating operating performance. *Efficiency* reflects the relationship between a responsibility center's outputs and its inputs. An example of an efficiency measurement for a manufacturing department is the cost per unit. *Effectiveness* is a broader criterion that reflects the relationship between a responsibility center's outputs and its objectives. For example, a manufacturing department might be measured on its success in meeting its production target—say, production of 10,000 dress shirts per month.

Profit is a measure of performance that reflects both the efficiency and effectiveness of operations. Revenues are the outputs of a responsibility center, and expenses are the inputs. Since profit is the difference between revenue and expense, profit is a measure of efficiency. When profit is compared to a targeted objective, as is done in the budget, then profit becomes an indicator of effectiveness.

Efficiency and effectiveness are attained independently of one other. A responsibility center may perform better than expected regarding one, while performing worse than expected regarding the other. For example, a sales center can be evaluated by examining expense ratios and sales variances. If selling expense was only 17 percent of sales revenue, while it was budgeted at 20 percent, then we can conclude the sales center was more efficient than expected. But if actual sales revenue was only $95,000, yet $100,000 was budgeted, then we can also conclude the sales center was less effective than planned.

Linking Measures to Strategy.   One way to ensure that managers focus on the right outcomes is to align the measures of their performance with their responsibility centers' strategies. For example, the projected budget for the South America profit center (from Exhibit 9.8) represents the first year of its operations and was derived from the long-range (5-year) plan. The long-range plan, in this example, relies on a growth strategy based on a differentiated product line. Even though the South America unit is structured as a profit center, the measure motivating its success in the first year or two is not profit. Rather, long-term success will depend on its developing a market presence as a platform for future sales. Although the measures for this kind of success will include revenue and sales growth, they will also include nonfinancial measures—such as the number of sales calls or training workshops—that are geared toward opening this market potential.

As the South America market becomes established and the objective switches to protecting—rather than building—market share, performance measures should change as well. When sales have begun to flatten and the strategy shifts to "hold," management's concern becomes one of cost-efficiency and profit. Nonetheless, it may still be appropriate to include some nonfinancial measures—such as customer retention or market share—in order to provide an early warning of changes in the business climate.

4: REPORTING AND ANALYSIS

The fourth step in the control process is reporting and analysis. Besides playing an important role in planning, the budget provides feedback for *monitoring results, making corrections, and evaluating performance.* Actual results are commonly reported in comparison with targets for the budgeted time period. Differences between actual results and budget targets are reported as variances. Reacting to budget variances as symptoms of operational problem areas is frequently referred to as **management by exception.**

Reports for Financial Objectives.   Financial reports differ according to the type of responsibility center for which they have been prepared. Cost center managers regularly receive financial reports covering brief intervals. Such reports indicate whether or not their spending is within budget.

For example, the financial report of an engineered cost center, such as manufacturing, normally presents detailed variances from budget costs for every input—materials, labor, and overhead. The purpose of reporting detailed variances is to pinpoint problems—such as faulty raw materials or poorly maintained machinery—that might cause inefficiencies in the production line.

On the other hand, variances for discretionary cost centers, such as marketing or product design, typically report spending variances in less detail and cover the current period—and, often, the year to date. The purpose of this type of report is to inform managers of their spending limits.

Reports for profit centers and investment centers serve a different function. As with cost center reports, profit and investment center reports identify variances of actual results from budget targets, in detail. However, in such reports the bottom-line measure, either profit or ROI, is more meaningful than the variances are. The reason is that managers of profit or investment centers have authority to make trade-offs between cost categories or to incur greater expense in order to generate even greater revenue. For example, a manager who exceeds the advertising budget is still likely to be praised, despite that variance, if profit exceeds expectations.

Competitive Benchmarking. Managers find that the comparison between operating results and budgeted targets may not be the best measure of success in the marketplace. One way to make reported results more meaningful is to compare them with the results of operations of companies considered to have the best business practices in the industry—a technique called benchmarking. When negative differences are identified, managers must begin to determine the causes and to seek solutions. For example, in late 1991 General Motors received praise for implementing many cost-efficiency improvements, including reductions in component prices, in the cost of metal-stamping dies, and in time elapsed from the initial auto design phase to actual production. Alas, compared with the benchmark of Ford, it still took GM 30 percent longer to build a comparable compact car.[8]

Frequency of Reports. Financial reports are distributed regularly, usually monthly, to all responsibility center managers. Some reports, however, are prepared more frequently because of the costs of *not* immediately taking corrective action, as noted earlier. This is especially characteristic of repetitive, lower-level operations that rely mainly on nonfinancial feedback. For example, production-line managers who run a tightly controlled operation may require daily reports on pounds of spoiled raw materials. Computerized manufacturing systems may even report certain key measures on an hourly, or even a real-time, or continuous, basis. At Cummins Diesel Engines, for example, quality-inspection failures are immediately entered into the computer and monitored by managers and their employees on the factory floor.

5: CORRECTIVE ACTION

The fifth control step consists of taking corrective action. The control system first must help to identify what needs corrective action. Then it must provide the information that will enable management to determine which is the best corrective action. Next, it must prompt management to take action. Responsibility center managers can use decision tools, such as differential-cost models and capital budgeting, to determine what needs fixing and how best to fix it. However, the final part of this control step is not nearly so analytical. Managers and their subordinates must be motivated to take the correct action.

TYPES OF CORRECTIVE ACTION

Let's look at the possible actions a manager can take when performance results do not meet budgeted targets.

Change Operations. The objective of changing operations is to improve the way work is accomplished; various approaches are possible. A manager

---

[8] Joseph B. White, "GM's Problems Have Overtaken Stempel's Go-Slow Approach," *The Wall Street Journal*, Dec. 16, 1991, p. B1.

could try to improve inputs—for example, by purchasing better materials or by increasing the amount of training given to employees. Alternatively, changes could be made to the capital equipment that is used to convert inputs to outputs. New and better equipment could be introduced, or human labor might be replaced by machinery. Also, the work procedures could be changed—for example, sales inquiries could be redirected to the production department instead of the sales department, thus saving an extra round of sales-order reviewing.

Change the Budget Model.   The manager may find that the problem is not the result of faulty operations but rather the result of poor correlation between expected results (the budget) and actual results. For example, the relationship between an activity and the resources consumed in that activity may not be well understood. Thus, increases in sales may cause higher production costs than are provided for in the budget, because the relationship between sales and production costs is not clear. In another example, managers may not understand the causal connection between marketing activity and sales revenue, especially when sales are influenced by environmental factors, such as inflation and consumer income. In these cases, corrective action must be focused on preparing a budget with more-accurate linkages between cost and revenue behaviors.

Change Objectives.   Finally, the manager may find the problem arises neither from the operations nor the budget model but rather from the objectives of the firm or responsibility center. In this case, the entire planning-control model may need rethinking. On the strategic-planning side, this may entail reviewing the appropriateness of the firm's mission, goals and objectives, or strategies. From a perspective of control, management will need to readjust either its long-range plans at the corporate level or its budget targets at the responsibility-center level. This process of changing objectives reflects the closed loop of the planning-control model, since information gathered in trying to improve the firm's operations and budget model can lead to a better understanding of how well the firm can compete. Management must go back and forth between evaluating market opportunities and assessing company strengths, while it challenges the targets it has set at every organizational level. (See "Current Practice: Sun Microsystems Inc.")

MOTIVATION AND EVALUATION

A manager must feel that taking the appropriate corrective action needed by his or her responsibility center will at the same time serve his or her self-interest. For example, a manager may realize that employees require additional training in order to increase their productivity. However, much of what they might learn from the training will not begin paying benefits until the longer term. Moreover, the manager expects to be promoted within the year to another responsibility center. Since the expense of the training will cause current profit to fall, and the manager will not be around when the training pays off, what motivation is there for the man-

Sun Microsystems Inc.

Sun Microsystems Inc., the pioneer of workstation computing, offers an example of a company whose corrective action was to effectively change its strategic objectives. When the number of units sold fell in each of the first two quarters of fiscal year 1994, the company looked for ways to rebound. One big cause of Sun's poor performance was the failure of its strategy of selling low-end workstations to companies that might otherwise buy PCs. Sun then changed its strategy to one of targeting the mainframe computer market. It focused its efforts on increasing the sales of midrange computer network servers capable of linking large numbers of workstations and PCs. Thus it offered companies a low-cost option to multimillion-dollar mainframes.

Source: Joan E. Rigdon, "Sun Microsystems Finds Growth Difficult to Sustain," *The Wall Street Journal,* May 10, 1994, p. B4.

ager to incur the cost? Mixed signals such as these will always occur when performance evaluation and, particularly, compensation are tied to financial results.

INCENTIVE COMPENSATION PLANS

We began this chapter with a discussion of strategies, goals, and objectives; then we considered how to translate them into operating plans and how to measure the success of those plans—all within the context of control for lower-level responsibility centers. Now we find that the success of the control system depends largely on the motivations of managers and their employees. Compensation systems help to motivate employees to act in ways that support corporate goals.

Compensation consists of salary and fringe benefits—including health plans, pensions, and life insurance. And perquisites, such as a company car, merit additional consideration. These elements, combined with bonus payments, are intended to motivate a manager's efforts and reinforce his or her commitment to corporate goals. However, the results of relying on compensation systems as motivators can sometimes fall far short of the intended results!

DEFINING GOALS AND NEEDS

A well-developed management control system should link the corporate mission to the performance of each responsibility center and to how that performance is measured. The measurements chosen should reflect and reinforce desirable actions and outcomes for which managers and their employees can be evaluated.

CURRENT PRACTICE

Monsanto's Compensation Plan

In 1987, Monsanto began to believe that if its compensation plan increased worker commitment, the company could thereby gain a competitive advantage. More than 40 different pay plans were put in place to meet the strategic objective of each company work group. The plans differed in many ways—such as measures, targets, amount of payouts, time frames, and levels of employee participation. Each plan was designed by a team of 12 to 15 employees, who represented their various work groups. Every plan was given an expiration date, so the specifics of each plan could be reviewed and revised as needed.

Source: Michael J. Verespej, "Pay-for-Skills: Its Time Has Come," *Industry Week,* June 15, 1992, pp. 22–29.

Determining employees' needs is complex, because each individual's wants and desires differ. Pay is a motivator for all employees, up to a point. But beyond that point are other, often diverse, things that motivate some employees more effectively. That point is different for each person, depending on his or her hierarchy of needs.[9] For example, each person has lower-level personal needs, such as safety and compensation, and higher-level needs, such as social interaction and self-esteem. Employers should understand the needs of employees if they are to motivate them and gain their commitment. This understanding of employee needs can then be used to help define pay plans that offer a balance of sufficient pay and a work environment that promotes individual growth and development, for examples.

There is no uniform solution for matching corporate strategies and individual needs. Rather, each firm tends to design its own unique compensation system and then scrutinize and amend it as seems to be warranted. (See "Current Practice: Monsanto's Compensation Plan.")

DESIGNING A PAY PLAN

One trend in U.S. pay plans is to compensate employees on the basis of individual contributions. These "pay-for-performance" plans attempt to reward behavior and outcomes the firm wishes to encourage. While pay for performance has long been used to compensate managers, especially at the senior level, it is now beginning to be used for lower-level managers and even rank-and-file workers. Where once employee pay was entirely fixed, it now tends to comprise a fixed component and a variable compo-

[9] Abraham H. Maslow, *Motivation and Personality,* New York: Harper & Row, Publishers, Inc., 1954.

nent, both tied to performance—the fixed shrinking and the variable growing. Let's examine some of the considerations and trade-offs in designing this kind of pay plan.

Individual versus Team Performance. When pay is based on individual performance, it is critical that supervisors give accurate and discriminating ratings for each person's contributions. This has proved to be difficult, as managers are often unwilling or unable to make distinctions between their workers. Furthermore, efforts to express distinctions among employees are sometimes based on a frequency distribution (such as a bell curve) of employee evaluations within a responsibility center. These have proved to be highly unpopular—and of questionable validity—since they end up classifying some productive workers in a successful center as low-level performers.

Many compensation specialists favor basing performance on the results obtained by small groups. This structure was designed to encourage employees to work together and find innovative work solutions. One survey reports that 55 percent of firms currently have or plan to add such a program.[10] However, "group plans" are susceptible to the "free rider" problem, where the burden of unproductive members is carried by the efforts of others.

Financial or Nonfinancial Measures. Assessing success at meeting financial targets is the traditional way to measure performance. Managers focus on achieving bottom-line results and are rewarded for their contributions toward maximizing profit and investment return. This system relies on the budget for goal setting and for coordinating the work among responsibility centers. It emphasizes meeting financial performance expectations of creditors and investors in the marketplace.

Another method measures the performance of nonfinancial activity and usually supplements analysis of financial results. A growing criticism of reliance on financial measures alone is that this approach motivates behavior that produces quick, positive results that have often long-term negative effects. Managers may be unwilling to invest in maintenance, training, or research if the current period's income would be negatively affected. On the other hand, if measures are not only financial but include qualitative considerations—such as customer satisfaction, product quality, or employee development—both short- and long-term corporate interests will be served.

Uniformity or Flexibility. A question arises regarding whether managers at similar organizational levels should be measured against the same yardstick. For instance, should all division managers be evaluated by income and sales growth? This approach makes it easier to compare the performances of managers. Problems arise, however, when the same financial

---

[10] Edward J. Ost, "Team-Based Pay: New Wave Strategic Incentives," *Sloan Management Review,* spring 1990, p. 20.

measures are used to compare managers who are pursuing different business-line strategies—growth versus hold versus harvest. Profit and sales growth measures will also be unfair to good managers placed in troublesome responsibility centers.

To avoid problems such as these, target setting and measurement must be custom-tailored to meet each manager's circumstances and to reflect his or her unit's strategic objectives. Thus, we might expect a manager of a start-up unit to be evaluated by sales growth and number of customer leads, whereas a manager of a unit scheduled for harvest would be judged against income and cash flow.

Immediate or Delayed Payment. Some pay-plan designers have suggested that the best way to motivate personnel is to identify appropriate behavior and reward it on the spot. For example, if an employee comes up with a laborsaving work improvement, then immediately give him or her a bonus check for a portion of the company's expected savings. Even in the case of periodic rewards based on performance, an argument can be made that prompt payment demonstrates to employees a clear connection between action and reward.

Other incentive plans are built on deferred compensation specifically to encourage positive results in the long term. This has been a popular way to motivate and reward executives, as in the use of stock option plans in which the options cannot be converted to stock until a number of years have elapsed. In recent years several corporations, including Du Pont and PepsiCo, have experimented with deferring some portion of pay for workers on the shop floor. The purpose is to encourage all employees to feel a commitment to the company's development and to feel that they share its prosperity and failures. (See "Current Practice: ValuJet Airlines' Profit-Sharing Plan.")

CURRENT PRACTICE

ValuJet Airlines' Profit-Sharing Plan

Recall the success of ValuJet Airlines' low-cost strategy? This included paying pilots only $45,000 and flight attendants $11 per hour, but these amounts represent only the fixed portion of compensation. Employees also participate in a profit-sharing plan, which delays payment until after financial results for the year are reported. Profit sharing can boost pay significantly. In the first year after the firm went public, the firm's 900 employees earned an extra $3.5 million dollars, or an average of nearly $3,900 per employee. Of course, profit bonuses are not guaranteed, and some workers are making it known they would prefer seniority-based pay increases instead.

Source: Adapted from Bridget O'Brian and Rick Brooks, "No Frills Approach Propels ValuJet to Quick Success, *The Wall Street Journal,* May 4, 1995, p. B4.

GUIDELINES FOR INCENTIVE COMPENSATION

An effective compensation plan is one of the things needed if a management control system is to work. What specifically will constitute the compensation plan most likely to succeed will depend on each firm and its situation. But there are two things that apply to all firms in every situation. First, employees should _perceive the compensation system as fair._ Pay systems can fail in this regard, for several reasons. Defining performance can be difficult, especially when performance is tied to an individual who provides services. How, for example, can the performance of one bank teller be considered better or worse than that of another? Measuring performance results is complex and often relies on subjective judgment. How can the performance of an audit manager be measured? Further, employees may perceive the size of rewards as inadequate or unfair, particularly in comparison with the huge bonuses reported for corporate officers.

Second, employees should see rewards as _a result of their actions._ Compensation experts have noted that plans work only if employees feel they can influence outcomes that measure their performance. This suggests that only those results that are controllable should be measured, while those that are not controllable—such as the influence of nonperformers in a group or the impacts of a troubled economy—should be eliminated.

Finally, some argue that the obstacles to incentive plans are too great and that such plans should not be used. Dr. W. Edwards Deming, the architect of the Japanese quality approach to manufacturing and service, asserts that incentive systems are demoralizing, since performance measures will always fail to show an individual's contributions. He prefers that all employees, from the CEO on down, be paid only by salary.[11]

ALTERNATIVES FOR CONTROL

So far in this chapter we have concentrated on the relationship between strategy and formal control systems. Now we look briefly at two other types of control mechanisms—rules and culture. Any organization will likely have some elements of both, in addition to its formal system that is built on budgets and performance reports. Refer to Exhibit 9.9 for highlights of the three control alternatives.

RULES

The rules-based approach to control specifies—within carefully defined limits—how employees are expected to act in a given situation. As its name implies, _management control through rules_ requires that management know what specific actions are desirable and that it be able to assess

---

[11] Dana Wechsler Linden and Vicki Contavespi, "Incentivize Me, Please," _Forbes,_ May 27, 1991, pp. 208–212.

EXHIBIT 9.9 CONTROL ALTERNATIVES

Management Control	Rules-Based	Culture

Set formal target.
 	
Measure process and results.
 	
Take corrective action.
	Use behavioral constraints:
	  Locks
	  Security guards
	  Separation of duties
	      or
	Conduct preaction review:
	  Direct supervision
	  Approval limits
	      or
	Institute action accountability:
	  Work rules
	  Standing instructions
	  Policies and procedures
		Select, train, and assign employees so that the culture is inculcated in all employees.
		
		Clarify work expectations and
		  provide feedback for learning.
		
		Encourage commitment—
		  shared beliefs, values, and action.

Source: Adapted from Kenneth A. Merchant, "The Control Function of Management," *Sloan Management Review*, summer 1982, p. 45, by permission of the publisher. Copyright 1982 by the Sloan Management Review Association. All rights reserved.

whether these actions were taken. This is a very centralized, bureaucratic type of control, whereby employees are essentially told what to do. Three ways to control employees' behavior by rules are presented in the central column in Exhibit 9.9.

The first method relies on use of *behavioral constraints*. This approach involves methods that seek to prevent employee actions that run contrary to the goal of achieving corporate objectives. The most common types of constraints are those intended to safeguard company assets. For example, locks and security guards are useful for restricting access to assets—thereby preventing their misuse. Another constraint is separation of duties—for example, preventing the bookkeeper from handling cash. This basic rule prevents an employee from stealing cash and covering up the theft with falsified journal entries.

The second type of rules-based approach, using *preaction reviews*, requires that employees receive formal approvals before taking action. This may mean that employees are closely supervised and that managers have preset spending limits that cannot be exceeded without approval. For example, a department head may not be allowed to purchase any supply item that exceeds $50 without approval.

Finally, controlling employees through rules may encompass all sorts of *action-accountability* measures, such as work rules, standing instructions, and policies and procedures. For example, fast-food workers typically must follow precise instructions on how to take customer orders, how to handle cash, and even when to offer water or ketchup.

Rules-oriented methods of controlling employee behavior are commonly used to supplement the management control system. Virtually all firms that carry inventory and cash require employees to follow prescribed procedures in order to ensure that the firm's money and goods don't stray or get lost or stolen. We must be careful, however, that such rules do not work against achievement of the firm's strategic objectives. For example, a firm that wishes to encourage its workers to innovate will not be successful if those workers are required to get so many levels of approval for every action that their ability to innovate is smothered by the system.

CULTURE

Culture is the pattern of shared beliefs and expectations that shapes group behavior. To control employees through their culture, it's necessary to create a culture wherein the members of the organization provide direction and guidance to each other. Fellow workers try to live up to socially created standards, or *norms*, to gain acceptance from coworkers. In a corporate culture, members might be expected to take action—even in new and unpredictable situations—in a way that furthers the corporation's goals.

A strong corporate culture can be created, as shown in Exhibit 9.9. First, select, train, and assign employees in such a way that each individual will develop an outlook to fit the culture. Second, make clear to employees the work that is expected of them, and provide them with feedback so that they will better understand their roles within the group. Next, encourage each employee's commitment to the group's task by developing a sense of shared beliefs, values, and actions among all workers.

As organizations adjust to meet the challenges of changing technology and dynamic markets, they seem to rely increasingly on corporate culture. Examples of successful corporate cultures are 3M Corporation, which is often cited for its innovative spirit, and Delta Airlines, which is said to have developed a "family feeling" among its committed employees. A corporate culture consistent with the corporate strategy can mean that each worker is "under control" in the presence of coworkers. The guidance of coworkers and the need for acceptance by the group thus influence employee actions. In a firm whose business decisions are made by managers and workers at lower and lower levels, culture becomes an unwritten guide to behavior.

In the ideal situation, rules and measures become secondary, as employees share a commitment for actions—such as innovation and continuous improvement—that move the organization toward achieving its mission.

SUMMARY

Planning and control determine where an organization is going and how it will get there. Senior managers formulate corporate strategies to meet the firm's missions and goals. Corporate strategies identify the types of businesses—growth, hold, and harvest—in which the firm will compete. Business strategies are the means by which corporate strategies are implemented at the firm's lower levels. Businesses create competitive advantage by distinguishing their products through either low cost or differentiation. Functional strategies then spell out the tasks that must be performed in order to accomplish business-level strategy. The implementation and coordination of strategies depend on accounting information—the foundation of the management control system. Management control is effected through both structure and process. Structure is based on a firm's interlocking responsibility centers—each of which must meet the firm's strategic objectives. Process refers to the means by which managers set targets, receive feedback, and initiate corrective action. Control includes budgeting and performance reporting, as well as taking corrective action and reexamining strategies. The control process is ongoing and connects business operations to attainment of the firm's strategic objectives. The continual recycling of information for improving strategy and operations constitutes the control loop.

Goal congruence binds together planning and control systems. Employees should be able to satisfy their own needs when acting in the corporate interest. Accounting information seeks to make goal congruence occur by linking corporate strategies to performance measures at the operational level.

Managers identify and track meaningful performance measures, including some—such as quality—that are nonfinancial. Feedback from measures enables managers and their employees to identify areas needing improvement and helps them to evaluate alternatives for corrective action. Managers and their employees need to be motivated if they are to meet financial and nonfinancial performance expectations.

Various types of incentive compensation plans can be instituted in order to motivate employees to act in ways intended to satisfy themselves *and* to fulfill corporate objectives. Compensation plans can include both a fixed-pay and a variable-pay component; the right mix of components depends on the situation of the firm. For any motivating plan to be successful, employees must perceive it as fair and they should see a linkage between their actions and the rewards for those actions.

CHAPTER 9 ASSIGNMENTS

DISCUSSION PROBLEMS

D9.1 (Identifying Organizational Structure Type)

Lawrence Corporation develops and manufactures pharmaceutical products. The company has a line of standard products that have been the mainstay of the company for many years, and sales and profits from these products have remained steady. Five years ago, Lawrence moved into the field of genetically engineered drugs, which it considers to represent the future of the company in the long run. Profits from these new products rose dramatically for the first few years but have leveled off recently. Lawrence's board of directors has been disappointed with the company's recent operating performance. Under increasing pressure from the board, Lawrence's president, Mark Pine, recently resigned.

The board selected Jeff Nichols, a top executive with Progressive Drugs, a competitor of Lawrence, to be the new president. He was given the authority to take whatever steps were necessary to boost the sales of and profits from the new drug line. Six months after taking office, Nichols announced a major reorganization of Lawrence, which included replacing the controller and two other employees. Nichols explained that the changes were being made to improve management control, productivity, and efficiency. Lawrence's old and new organizational structures are shown in Exhibit D9.1.

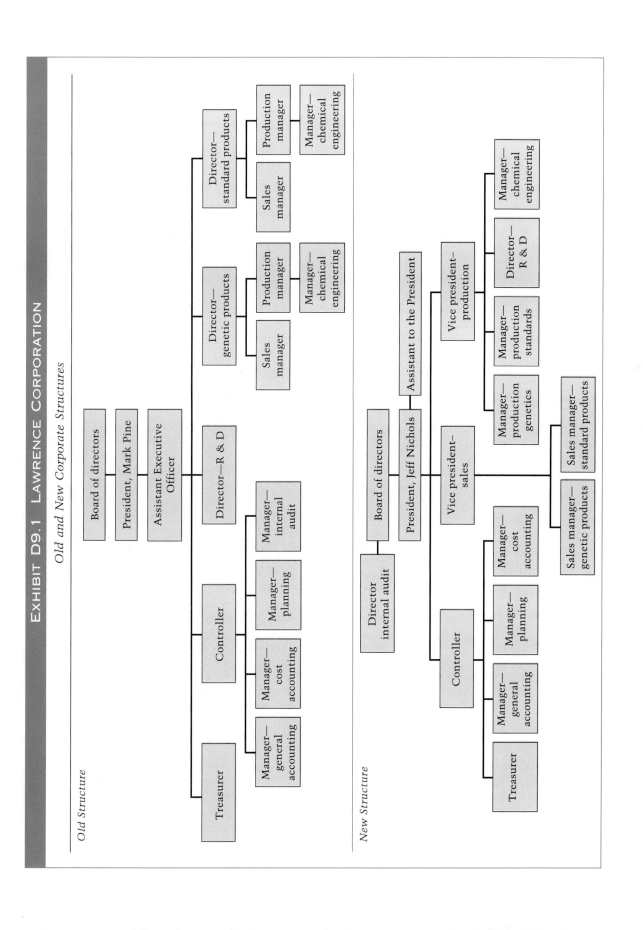

EXHIBIT D9.1 LAWRENCE CORPORATION

Old and New Corporate Structures

Old Structure

Board of directors
President, Mark Pine
Assistant Executive Officer

Treasurer — Manager—general accounting
Controller — Manager—cost accounting, Manager—planning, Manager—internal audit
Director—R & D

Director—genetic products — Sales manager, Production manager — Manager—chemical engineering

Director—standard products — Sales manager, Production manager — Manager—chemical engineering

New Structure

Board of directors
President, Jeff Nichols
Assistant to the President

Director internal audit

Vice president—sales — Sales manager—genetic products, Sales manager—standard products

Controller — Manager—general accounting, Manager—planning, Manager—cost accounting

Treasurer

Vice president—production — Manager production genetics, Manager—production standards, Director—R & D — Manager—chemical engineering

Required:

1. What type of organizational structure existed at Lawrence before and after the reorganization? Are the firm's departments more likely to be structured as profit centers or as cost centers?
2. What is the new structure's (a) main advantage and (b) main disadvantage?

(*CMA Adapted*)

D9.2 (Controlling Decentralized Business Units)[12]

In late 1991, Paul H. O'Neill, CEO and chairman of Aluminum Co. of America (Alcoa), announced a major restructuring. He attributed many of the firm's problems to the existing structure. Managers had to negotiate their way through layers of approval in order to implement new programs and embark on joint ventures. Managers of business units would now be given the freedom to make their own decisions, even though separate units might end up competing with each other for the same sale. As O'Neill explained, "We cannot succeed if we persist in our use of the traditional command-and-control system."

The purpose behind these moves was to push decision making down to lower corporate levels. Changes in competition and in technology required faster response times than the traditional hierarchy could provide. Under the new structure, business unit managers were given the authority to move quickly to meet their customers' expectations.

Alcoa comprises 25 business units, which had been reporting to business-group vice presidents who were overseen by the corporate president. Thus, O'Neill's office had controlled the entire structure. In the past, business unit plans would be delayed for months as they went through scrutiny and awaited approval at the many layers of management. Under the new plan, however, all business managers report directly to O'Neill. In fact, the positions of president and group vice president have been eliminated.

The 25 business unit managers now have automatic spending authority for up to $5 million, and they are now only required to seek approval from O'Neill for larger programs. The business unit managers are charged with handling their own strategic plans, budgeting, purchasing, and sales. They are also charged with setting 2 year targets designed to close 80 percent of the gap between their units' performance and that of the industry leaders. Business unit managers are kept in line by the corporate requirement that they maintain a minimum 15 percent return on equity (ROI).

The company put together several teams to counter the potential problems of decentralization. It created a new advisory team of executive vice presidents to present a unified view of Alcoa when necessary. Employees were organized into a number of self-directed teams in order to speed up product development and to help transfer technology among business units. Other cross-functional teams were created to improve the manufacturing processes for all business units.

Required:

1. Decentralized operations should engender an entrepreneurial spirit among managers without creating chaos and backbiting. How do you propose that

---

[12] Adapted from Dana Milbank, "Changes at Alcoa Point Up Challenges and Benefits of Decentralized Authority," *The Wall Street Journal*, Nov. 7, 1991, p. B1.

Alcoa, for example, prevent competing business units from undercutting each other?

2. With each manager acting independently, what mechanism will help managers see opportunities for joint action? How will each manager know what the other business units are doing? Should they know?

3. Each business unit is required to meet a 15 percent ROI target. Comment on short-term actions that managers could take to reach this financial goal. What assurance does corporate management have that business unit managers are acting in the corporate entity's long-term best interest?

D9.3 (Incentive Compensation Pay Plan)[13]

The fibers division is Du Pont's largest operating business unit. In 1988 it reported earnings of $705 million, more than double the 1985 figure of $250 million. During this 3-year period, the division had restructured its workforce in order to become more competitive and to encourage broader employee participation and team management. As a result, total employment fell from 27,000 in 1984 to 20,000 in 1988. Those employees who remained were expected to acquire new work and technology skills. They also were encouraged to become involved in business strategy and to develop the new interpersonal skills needed to work effectively in self-directed teams.

In January 1989, an innovative incentive-pay plan was introduced to support the participative team culture that the fibers division was creating. Two central features stood out. First, employees would share in both gains and losses; second, the plan would focus on one specific business target—earnings growth of 4 percent per year.

The plan was to be phased in over a 5-year time frame. Under the plan, employees would forego a standard increase of 6 percent of their earnings in return for the promise of potentially higher pay should their units surpass their earnings expectations. If the division met its budget, employees would receive their 6 percent shortfall. If it exceeded the budget by 150 percent, employees would earn a 12 percent bonus, but if it reached only 80 percent of the budget, they would get only a 3 percent raise. Below 80 percent, there would be no bonus—in other words, no raise. For example, an employee earning $30,000 per year before the plan's implementation could earn between $28,200 and $33,600 under the new system.

Early reports about results of the pay plan were encouraging. Workers at all levels were changing the ways they thought and behaved in order to cut costs and improve efficiency. For example, a marketing representative found that her secretary had routed her business travel through "Godforsaken parts of the country" to save $300 on airfare. In another case, a marketing manager began reexamining the value of holding an annual customer outing in Aspen, Colorado, each February. Was this promotion really needed? Was it effective in accomplishing its objective? Generally, employees questioned their own work efforts, as well as those of fellow employees and management, in order to improve earnings.

The importance of organizing workers into teams was considered paramount in achieving division targets. Team members were expected to pull their own

---

[13] Adapted from Laurie Hays, "All Eyes on Du Pont's Incentive-Pay Plan," *The Wall Street Journal*, Dec. 5, 1988, p. B1; Amanda Bennett, "Paying Workers to Meet Goal Spreads, but Gauging Performance Proves Tough," *The Wall Street Journal*, Sept. 10, 1991, pp. B1, B4; and Edward J. Ost, "Team-Based Pay: New Wave Strategic Incentives," *Sloan Management Review*, spring 1990, pp. 19–27.

weight, and employees sometimes pressured each other to become more productive. In one case, workers complained about a loafing worker whose machine was under repair. In another situation, an employee reprimanded a fellow worker who disposed of still-usable safety gloves. A number of conflicts between team workers began to arise.

Other problems became apparent. Some employees became discouraged over their inability to influence profits, while others expressed concern about the difficulty of finding ways to become more efficient. Hard decisions had to be made about meeting current earnings targets, particularly when quality and greater future profits became potential trade-offs. Some employees distrusted management and complained about loopholes, such as management's deciding to take an unexpected write-off that would affect current profits.

The plan's death knell came 2 years after the program was started. The incentive program was abruptly halted after it became clear the division's profit—and, thus, employees' pay—was expected to drop. As one employee noted, "I could use that money"—implying that she would have preferred not to gamble with her raise. One of the plan's designers, Robert McNutt, said people wanted more choice. Increasingly the choice became clear—they wanted out of the plan.

Required: Discuss the reactions you would expect from employees who were compensated by the fibers division's pay plan. Consider the following issues as part of your analysis:

- Trade-offs in basing rewards on divisional outcomes as opposed to basing them on individual merit
- The use of a financial measure, profit, without consideration of nonfinancial measures
- The implications of having employees surrender part of their normally expected pay raise in hopes of receiving a higher bonus
- Equity concerns of highly productive employees whose bonuses would be the same as those of noncontributing workers

PROBLEMS   **P9.1   (Long-Range Plan for a Distribution Center)**

Eastern Food Supply Company is in need of a warehousing and distribution location for its Caribbean operations. Senior management has narrowed the choice to two locations: Kingston, Jamaica, or St. Thomas, U.S. Virgin Islands. The site that is chosen will be used for a minimum of 5 years. Cost projections (in U.S. dollars) for the two sites are shown in Exhibit P9.1.

Both alternatives involve long-term operating leases that cover the cost of all necessary warehouse equipment and shelving, and, thus, neither choice will require any capital outlay. However, tax effects are expected to differ for the two locations. Eastern Food Supply already has a subsidiary company in each location, and the expense associated with the new distribution site will become fully deductible against existing revenue. The tax rate in St. Thomas is 36 percent, whereas the rate in Kingston is 40 percent. Cash flow will be evaluated using the corporate cost of capital, which is 16 percent.

Required: Determine which location is the better choice, and calculate the discounted cash saving used to justify your answer.

P9.2   (Building Operating Budgets from a Capital Budget)

Chromatic Sinogram produces a wide variety of products with life cycles that range from 1 to 5 years. The company has reorganized and assigned profit responsibility

EXHIBIT P9.1   EASTERN FOOD SUPPLY COMPANY

Comparative Expenditure Analysis for Two Alternative Distribution Centers

| | End of Year Cash Flows | | | | |
	Year 1	Year 2	Year 3	Year 4	Year 5
Kingston, Jamaica					
Warehouse lease	$ 84,000	$ 89,040	$ 94,382	$100,045	$106,048
Distribution expense	200,000	220,000	242,000	266,200	292,820
Other expenditure	105,000	113,400	122,472	132,270	142,851
	$389,000	$422,440	$458,854	$498,515	$541,719
St. Thomas, U.S.V.I.					
Warehouse lease	$100,000	$104,000	$108,160	$112,486	$116,986
Distribution expense	180,000	198,000	217,800	239,580	263,538
Other operation expense	115,000	121,900	129,214	136,967	145,185
	$395,000	$423,900	$455,174	$489,033	$525,709

to its product managers. However, senior management has encountered some resistance on the part of product managers to introduce new products. The lower-level managers have argued that their profits—and, thus, their bonuses—are often reduced when they agree to promote a new product. Bonuses for product managers are calculated based on a percentage of their product incomes.

One recent example of such a conflict involved the capital budget shown in Exhibit P9.2, which was prepared by the corporate committee charged with initiating new products. This product seems to be highly profitable, generating a net present value of $11,957 after cash flows are discounted at a 15 percent rate. Still, the product manager who would be expected to take on this new project says it will kill her bonus potential for the upcoming year.

Required: Using the data given in the new product capital budget, prepare a product income statement, based on accrual accounting methods, for years 1, 2, and 3.

P9.3   (Correcting Budget Overruns for a Cost Center)

The cost center for product design and testing at Miramar Boat Manufacturing is encountering significant problems. The performance report (Exhibit P9.3) for the first 6 months of operations reports a cost overrun of $26,700—a variance of almost 12 percent above the amount budgeted. Nonetheless, the budget for the second 6 months was not changed. It remained the same as the budget for the first 6 months.

The cost center manager initiated improvements for the second half of the year. Most important, all phases of design, prototype construction, and testing now require early approval by the production and marketing departments. This change has resulted in a large decrease in the amount of corrective work needed after a prototype is made. The cost center has shown the following cost improvements for the second half of the year:

1. Wages, made up mainly of the cost of part-time workers, fell by 35 percent based on actual cost incurred the first 6 months.
2. Overtime was reduced to $2,500.

EXHIBIT P9.2 CHROMATIC SINOGRAM

Capital Budget Related to the New Product

	Year 0	Year 1	Year 2	Year 3
Operations:				
Cash revenue		$250,000	$350,000	$300,000
Cash expenditure:				
Production		100,000	125,000	90,000
Sales		45,000	35,000	30,000
Administration		25,000	25,000	25,000
Total		$170,000	$185,000	$145,000
Cash proceeds before tax		$ 80,000	$165,000	$155,000
Tax @ 35.0%		(28,000)	(57,750)	(54,250)
Net cash proceeds		$ 52,000	$107,250	$100,750
Tax shield:				
Investment		250,000	250,000	250,000
Depreciation rate		50.0%	30.0%	20.0%
Depreciation expense		125,000	75,000	50,000
Tax @ 35.0%		43,750	26,250	17,500
Disposal				0
Investment	$(250,000)			
Net cash flow	$(250,000)	$ 95,750	$133,500	$118,250
Discount @ 15.0%	1.0000	0.8696	0.7561	0.6575
Present value	$(250,000)	$ 83,261	$100,945	$ 77,751
NPV	$ 11,957			

3. Supplies were reduced by 25 percent over the cost incurred in the first half of the year.
4. Rework fell $2,000 below the budget allowance.

Other costs incurred in the second half of the year include computer software

EXHIBIT P9.3 MIRAMAR BOAT MANUFACTURING

Product and Design Center Performance Report
for the First Six Months of the Year

	Budget	Actual	Variance
Salaries & bonuses	$150,000	$146,600	$ 3,400
Wages	25,000	34,500	(9,500)
Overtime	2,000	9,300	(7,300)
Computer software	22,000	20,000	2,000
Supplies	12,500	16,500	(4,000)
Rework	8,000	19,600	(11,600)
Occupancy	10,200	9,900	300
Total	$229,700	$256,400	$(26,700)

($22,500) and occupancy ($10,300). Salaries and bonuses in the last 6 months resulted in full payment of the amount budgeted for the year.

Required: Prepare a performance report for the second 6 months of the year.

P9.4 (Alternative Incentive Plans)

Total Auto Parts, Inc., is an expanding business with 14 retail outlet locations. Senior management is in the process of revising the store manager incentive plan, which is now based solely on each site's pretax profit. Managers have complained that bonuses based on profit fail to take into account differences in the strategies of each location.

An example of differences between two stores' performance is given in Exhibit P9.4. The growth business has exceeded both budgeted revenue and budgeted profit. The mature business has also exceeded its budget for revenue and profit, but only by a relatively small incremental amount. Managers argue that the existing system, which rewards managers by giving them a bonus equal to 2 percent of actual pretax profit, favors large store managers and disregards sales accomplishments. To counter these objections, senior management is considering five alternative bonus proposals. The bonuses would be equal to one of the following percentages:

1. 25 percent of pretax profit over budget
2. 0.25 percent of actual sales revenue
3. 5 percent of sales revenue in excess of budget
4. 0.50 percent of gross profit
5. 10 percent of gross profit over budget

Required: Calculate the bonus for each manager using the current bonus plan and using each of the alternative bonus proposals.

P9.5 (Competitive Strategy and Product Pricing)

Len & Barry's Homemade, Inc., is a "niche" maker of very rich, high-quality, specialty ice creams. Its products, which are sold by U.S. grocery stores, offer intriguing

---

EXHIBIT P9.4 TOTAL AUTO PARTS, INC.

Financial Results for the First 6 Months of the Year

	Growth Business		Mature Business	
	Budget	*Actual*	*Budget*	*Actual*
Revenues	$200,000	$214,600	$432,500	$435,000
Cost of goods sold	110,000	116,957	237,875	236,205
Gross profit	$ 90,000	$ 97,643	$194,625	$198,795
Operating expense:				
Salaries	$ 45,000	$ 44,650	$ 80,800	$ 80,200
Occupancy	33,100	33,550	43,200	46,700
Marketing	13,250	13,500	21,560	22,500
Total	$ 91,350	$ 91,700	$145,560	$149,400
Pretax profit	$ (1,350)	$ 5,943	$ 49,065	$ 49,395
Percent of revenues	−0.7%	2.8%	11.3%	11.4%

EXHIBIT P9.5.1 LEN & BARRY'S HOMEMADE, INC.		
Projected Cost of Raw Materials		
	Cost per Gallon	
	Fresh Fruit	*Frozen Fruit*
Milk	$0.77	$0.77
Sugar	0.17	0.17
Fruit	0.55	0.39
Other ingredients	0.28	0.28
	$1.77	$1.61

EXHIBIT P9.5.2 LEN & BARRY'S HOMEMADE, INC.		
Expected Price-Volume Relationships		
	Gallons of Fruit Used	
Price	*Fresh*	*Frozen*
$4.00	470,000	420,000
3.90	500,000	455,000
3.80	530,000	488,000
3.70	560,000	519,000
3.60	590,000	548,000
3.50	620,000	575,000
3.40	650,000	600,000

blends of exotic flavors, such as Peanut Butter Explosion and Rainforest Scrunch. Now Len & Barry's is considering the introduction of a new tropical flavor, Magnificent Mango Mix, but it is running into difficulty lining up a steady supply of fresh mangoes. These are very sweet fruits imported from the tropics, mainly from South and Central American countries. The mangoes must be used at the height of freshness if the product is to be successful. Timing is difficult, because the window of opportunity for best flavor is very small. A proposal has been made to purchase frozen fruit instead of fresh fruit, but some concern has been expressed about compromising the firm's high-quality focus by doing so.

Because the firm is operating at capacity, virtually all of its production costs are fixed, other than the materials cost for each container of ice cream. If senior management decides to go with the frozen mango, it will save about $0.16 per gallon in materials cost. As shown in Exhibit P9.5.1, the materials cost per gallon using fresh mangoes is projected at $1.77, while the materials cost using frozen mangoes is expected to be $1.61. Some marketing tests have been conducted in order to determine the market's sensitivity to the use of the frozen mangoes. Exhibit P9.5.2 reports on the price-volume relationships as projected by the marketing department. These data support the argument that Len & Barry's customers do expect only the very best in ingredients and that use of the frozen mangoes will result in lower sales volume.

Required:

1. Determine the expected profit contribution for each of the listed price options, assuming the firm uses fresh fruit in the production process. Repeat these calculations, assuming that the firm uses frozen fruit. Which combination of fruit and price generates the highest profit?
2. Should senior management choose the product strategy that generates the highest profit? For a specialty firm such as Len & Barry's, to what extent should other considerations, such as quality and freshness, be considered in product decisions?

P9.6 (Reporting Structures: Cost vs. Profit Centers)

Arrowhead Shirts, Inc., is a company that concentrates its activities on only one product—men's dress shirts—which it makes in many different styles and sizes.

The firm is composed of three divisions, each designated by its location: New Orleans, Salt Lake City, and Cleveland (see Exhibit P9.6.1). While only the Cleveland division manufactures the product, all three divisions operate as regional centers for warehousing, marketing, and distribution. Each division is evaluated as a profit center and is judged on its ability to meet profit targets for the year. Because only Cleveland manufactures shirts, however, New Orleans and Salt Lake City must buy all their merchandise from Cleveland, whose charges for intercompany sales are set by the corporate-level managers.

At the Salt Lake City division, the manager has been under intense pressure during 1996 to meet his budget. The problem does not seem to be with sales revenue, which was $3,885,000 in 1996, or with the cost of sales, which have averaged 55 percent. Rather, the problem stems from the firm's highly centralized organization structure. All operating expenditures now fall under the division manager's direct control, and frequent spending delays slow decisions at the department level, thereby adding to costs. Now the division manager wants to push greater responsibility down to the three operating departments: administration, warehousing and distribution, and marketing. He wants to divide all operating costs along these organizational lines by making the manager of each functional department responsible for his or her own budget. The new departmental cost center structure is also shown in Exhibit P9.6.1.

Detailed operating data for the year ending December 31, 1996, are presented in Exhibit P9.6.2. Some of the spending, such as that for personnel, can be divided very cleanly into departmental subunits. Apportioning other expenses, such as telephone and utilities, is more arbitrary, particularly because the division has not tracked the association of operating expenditures with departments. Additional information, presented in Exhibit P9.6.3, has been prepared to help guide the distribution of these costs. You have been called upon to help the division reconstruct cost center reports so that department managers will have a baseline for budgeting their expenditures for next year.

Required:

1. Prepare an income statement for the Salt Lake City division for the year ending December 31, 1996.

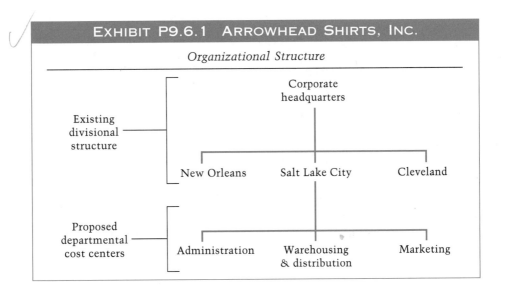

EXHIBIT P9.6.1 ARROWHEAD SHIRTS, INC.

Organizational Structure

EXHIBIT P9.6.2 ARROWHEAD SHIRTS, INC.

Detail of Salt Lake City Operating Results
for the Year Ending December 31, 1996

	Number of Employees	Total Wages	Fringe Benefits	Total Payroll
Personnel:				
Administration	5	$ 262,500	$ 63,000	$ 325,500
Warehousing & distribution	15	300,000	54,000	354,000
Marketing	8	329,600	92,288	421,888
	28	$ 892,100	$209,288	$1,101,388

		Cost	Deprec. Expense	
Plant assets:				
Office equipment		$ 157,000	$ 31,400	
Furniture & fixtures		93,700	13,386	
Warehouse equipment		575,000	57,500	
Building		1,375,000	45,833	
Land		650,000	0	
		$2,850,700	$148,119	
Other operating expense:				
Office supplies		$ 8,600		
Warehouse supplies		13,560		
Advertising		86,700		
Travel		43,500		
Repairs & maintenance		21,200		
Telephone & utilities		32,750		
Training		7,600		
		$ 213,910		

2. Prepare expense reports for each of the three departments—administration, warehousing and distribution, and marketing—for the year ending December 31, 1996. Exclude the cost of sales, which, along with sales revenue, will remain the responsibility of the division manager.
3. Do you think it is a good idea to assign all operating expenditures to departments in the upcoming year? Can you foresee problems that might develop as managers try to minimize expenses charged to their respective departments?

P9.7 (Preparing Operating Budget from Capital Budget)

We Are Toys, Inc., is a large retail chain outlet that currently has 97 store locations in the United States. The northeast division, one of four divisions, has just completed a capital budget for adding the ninety-eighth store, which would be located in Montreal, Canada. This information, shown in Exhibit P9.7.1, is based on a 5-year analysis, which is the maximum long-range horizon permitted by corporate management. Projections assume a 15 percent growth rate in sales revenue

EXHIBIT P9.6.3 ARROWHEAD SHIRTS, INC.

*Information for Distributing Operating Expense to Departments
for the Year Ending December 31, 1996*

	Asset Cost Basis, by Department			
	Admin.	Warehousing & Distribution	Marketing	Total
Plant assets:				
Office equipment	$97,000	$ 34,000	$26,000	$157,000
Furniture & fixtures	$38,600	$ 6,200	$48,900	$ 93,700
Warehouse equipment	$ 0	$575,000	$ 0	$575,000

	Square Footage, by Department			
	Admin.	Warehousing & Distribution	Marketing	Total
Building	2,500	25,000	2,500	30,000

	Approximate Percent of Use		
	Admin.	Warehousing & Distribution	Marketing
Other operating expense:			
Office supplies	80%	10%	10%
Warehouse supplies		100%	
Advertising			100%
Travel	25%	10%	65%
Repairs & maintenance	4%	92%	4%
Telephone & utilities	25%	45%	30%
Training	25%	35%	40%

and a tax rate of 40 percent. Results show a positive net present value (NPV) of $498,800, after discounting at a 15 percent after-tax corporate hurdle rate.

The northeast division has already prepared a budgeted income statement for 1998, without consideration of the proposed Montreal store. The budget is based on the combined results of 42 retail toy stores under divisional control. As seen in Exhibit P9.7.2, northeast's target for before-tax earnings is $507,000. You are asked to recompute northeast's 1998 budgeted income statement under the assumption that the Montreal store is operational, as projected in the capital budget.

Consider the following information in calculating the revised budget:

- The cost of sales is determined by the LIFO inventory method. (Recall that LIFO charges cost of sales with the cost of the most recent inventory items purchased.) Inventory additions shown in the Montreal capital budget are considered base inventory stock and are not used in computing the cost of sales.

EXHIBIT P9.7.1 WE ARE TOYS, INC.

Capital Budget for Adding Store 98 in Montreal, Canada (in thousands)

			End of Year			
Operations	1997	1998	1999	2000	2001	2002
Revenue:		$6,664	$7,664	$8,813	$10,135	$11,655
Cost of sales		(3,920)	(4,508)	(5,184)	(5,962)	(6,856)
Salaries		(1,125)	(1,215)	(1,312)	(1,417)	(1,531)
Occupancy		(740)	(770)	(800)	(832)	(866)
Other		(480)	(499)	(519)	(540)	(562)
Cash from operations		$ 399	$ 672	$ 997	$ 1,384	$ 1,841
Tax @ 40%		(160)	(269)	(399)	(554)	(737)
Net cash flow		$ 239	$ 403	$ 598	$ 830	$ 1,105
Tax Shield						
Depreciation rate		20%	20%	20%	20%	20%
Annual depreciation		170	170	170	170	170
Savings @ 40%		68	68	68	68	68
Disinvestment						
Residual value						0
Book value						0
Gain & cash flow						0
Investment						
Purchase of equipment	$ (850)					
Inventory additions	(490)	(74)	(85)	(97)	(112)	(129)
Net cash flow	(1,340)	234	387	569	786	1,044
Present value factor @ 15%	1.000	0.870	0.756	0.658	0.572	0.497
Discounted cash flow	$(1,340)	$ 203	$ 292	$ 374	$ 450	$ 519
Net present value	$ 498.8					

EXHIBIT P9.7.2 WE ARE TOYS, INC.— NORTHEAST DIVISION

Budgeted Income Statement for 1998 (in thousands)

	Without Montreal
Sales revenue	$150,000
Cost of sales	88,235
Gross margin	$ 61,765
Operating expense:	
Salaries	$ 22,500
Occupancy	11,250
Other	7,500
Depreciation	6,000
Total expense	$ 47,250
Earnings before interest and tax	$ 14,515
Interest charged by corporate offices @ 25%	14,007
Earnings before tax	$ 507
Assets for determining interest charge:	
PPE—beg. of yr. book value	$ 45,000
Inventory (@ cost of sales/8)	11,029
Total assets	$ 56,029

- Montreal equipment is to be depreciated over 5 years, using the straight-line method.
- Division income includes an imputed pretax interest charge of 25 percent levied by the corporate offices on plant and inventory carried by the division. These assets are valued as follows:

    Plant—at beginning-of-year book value

    Inventory—at ⅛ cost of sales (inventory is expected to turn 8 times per year)

Required:

1. Prepare the northeast division's 1998 budgeted income statement, assuming the Montreal store's financial projections are included as indicated by the capital budget.
2. For years 1998 through 2002 calculate the differential earnings projected for the northeast division if it adds store 98. (Earnings are calculated before tax and after the corporate interest charge.)
3. Based on your answers above, how do you think the northeast divisional manager will react to opening the Montreal store?

P9.8   (Financial Objectives and the Budget)

Healthful Foods Inc., a manufacturer of breakfast cereals and snack bars, has experienced several years of steady growth in sales, profits, and dividends, while maintaining a relatively low level of debt. The board of directors has adopted a long-run strategy aimed at maximizing the value of the shareholders' investment. In order to achieve this goal, the board of directors established the following 5-year financial objectives:

- Increase sales by 12 percent per year.
- Increase income before taxes by 15 percent per year.
- Increase dividends by 12 percent per year.
- Maintain long-term debt at a maximum of 16 percent of assets.

These financial objectives have been attained for the past 3 years. At the beginning of last year, the president of Healthful Foods, Andrea Donis, added a fifth financial objective: Maintain the cost of goods sold at a maximum of 61 percent of sales. This goal was attained last year.

The budgeting process at Healthful Foods is to be directed toward attaining these goals for the forthcoming year—a difficult task with the economy in a prolonged recession. In addition, the nation's increased emphasis on eating healthful foods has driven up the price of ingredients used by the company at a rate significantly higher than the expected rate of inflation.

John Winslow, cost accountant at Healthful Foods, is responsible for preparing the profit plan for next year. Winslow assured Donis that he could present a budget that achieved all of the financial objectives. Winslow believed that he could overestimate the ending inventory and reclassify fruit and grain inspection cost as administrative rather than manufacturing cost in order to attain the desired objective. Exhibits P9.8.1 and P9.8.2 present the actual statements for 1996 and the budgeted statements for 1997 that Winslow prepared

The company paid dividends of $27,720 in 1996 and expects to pay dividends of $29,695 in 1997. The expected tax rate for 1997 is 34 percent.

EXHIBIT P9.8.1 HEALTHFUL FOODS INC.

Income Statement

	1996 (Actual)	1997 (Budget)
Sales	$850,000	$947,750
Variable cost:		
Cost of goods sold	510,000	574,725
Selling & administrative	90,000	87,500
Contribution margin	$250,000	$285,525
Fixed cost:		
Manufacturing	85,000	94,775
Selling & administrative	60,000	70,000
Income before taxes	$105,000	$120,750

EXHIBIT P9.8.2 HEALTHFUL FOODS INC.

Statement of Financial Position (in thousands)

	1996 (Actual)	1997 (Budget)
Assets:		
Cash	$ 10	$ 17
Accounts receivable	60	68
Inventory	300	365
Plant & equipment (net)	1,630	1,600
Total assets	$2,000	$2,050
Liabilities:		
Accounts payable	$ 110	$ 122
Long-term debt	320	308
Shareholder equity:		
Common stock	400	400
Retained earnings	1,170	1,220
Total	$2,000	$2,050

Required:

1. Determine whether Winslow's budget attains each of the five financial objectives established by the board of directors and the president of Healthful Foods Inc. Support your conclusion in each case by presenting appropriate calculations. Use the following format for your answer:

Objective	Attained or Not Attained	Calculations
a.		
b.		
c.		
d.		
e.		

2. Do you feel the adjustments contemplated by Winslow are ethical? Explain your answer.

(CMA Adapted)

P9.9 (Using a Monthly Budget Variance Report)

Senior management of Allied Computer Supply Co. is thinking about changing the way its division managers are evaluated. The firm is made up of four divisions—computer furniture, computer supplies, computer service, and the newly created virtual reality division. During its 22 years of operation, Allied has always used the annual budget as the key element for controlling divisional performance. With the addition of the virtual reality division in late 1996, however, problems began to arise. The virtual reality division manager has struggled continually with corporate management over the division's budget targets, and, every month, he argues that the variance reports have no meaning.

Allied's budget process is critical to the firm's success in meeting its strategic objectives. Division managers are expected to submit realistic plans to corporate management by November 1 for the next calendar year. Divisional plans are then consolidated at corporate headquarters and revised to ensure that profit objectives will be met. Some negotiation between corporate and division managers is necessary in order to close the gaps between the original plans and corporate objectives. After a workable consolidated plan is agreed upon, division managers are expected to meet their budgeted profit targets for the year. Senior management keeps a close watch on each division's progress by having division managers submit monthly reports explaining revenue and expense variances between the plan and actual results achieved.

The latest results, for September 1997, are typical and highlight recent problems with the virtual reality division. The division's 1997 annual budget sets a target operating income of $86,250 (Exhibit P9.9.1). Actual results through September 1997 show a year-to-date operating loss of $26,326, although results for the month of September were positive, with a profit of $16,076 (Exhibit P9.9.2).

Recent control problems with the virtual reality division can be traced to two separate issues. First, as explained by the division manager, corporate management must give more consideration to business strategy when evaluating divisional performance. He has repeatedly argued that the virtual reality division is inherently different from the other three divisions, which are mature and well-established in the markets they serve. He further explains that the division is a start-up operation whose main focus is building market share and generating *sales*—not profit. Senior management has countered by pointing out that the budgeted profit margins for the virtual reality division are only about 30 to 40 percent of returns targeted for the other divisions. They also note that business strategy was already taken into consideration when profit targets were set.

The second issue concerning virtual reality's control problems addresses the seasonal nature of product sales and the division's predominately fixed cost structure. The virtual reality manager notes that most sales in this business occur in

EXHIBIT P9.9.1 ALLIED COMPUTER SUPPLY CO.— VIRTUAL REALITY DIVISION

Annual Budget for 1997

Revenue		$2,300,000	100.0%
Cost of goods		324,300	14.1%
Gross margin		$1,975,700	85.9%
Operating expense:			
Software development	$514,050		22.4%
General administration	211,600		9.2%
Warehousing	239,200		10.4%
Distribution	282,900		12.3%
Marketing & advertising	377,200		16.4%
Other sales expense	264,500		11.5%
Total operating expense		$1,889,450	82.2%
Operating income		$ 86,250	3.8%

EXHIBIT P9.9.2 ALLIED COMPUTER SUPPLY CO.— VIRTUAL REALITY DIVISION

Actual Results through September 1997

	Year to Date		Month of September	
Revenue	$1,621,500	100.0%	$214,390	100.0%
Cost of goods	239,982	14.8%	31,087	14.5%
Gross margin	$1,381,518	85.2%	$183,303	85.5%
Operating expense:				
Software development	$ 389,650	24.0%	$ 43,694	20.4%
General administration	159,758	9.9%	17,563	8.2%
Warehousing	177,965	11.0%	21,050	9.8%
Distribution	202,688	12.5%	26,799	12.5%
Marketing & advertising	289,690	17.9%	34,325	16.0%
Other sales expense	188,094	11.6%	23,797	11.1%
Total operating expense	$1,407,844	86.8%	$167,228	78.0%
Operating income	$ (26,326)	−1.6%	$ 16,076	7.5%

the last part of the year, as retailers get ready for the Christmas season. Consequently, he expects a tremendous spurt in sales and profit over the last quarter of the year. September, he points out, is just the beginning of the seasonal boom. Comparing monthly performance against an average of budgeted annual sales does little to guide improvement, since seasonal sales fluctuations are not being considered. On this point, senior management has remained silent.

Required:

1. Using data from Exhibits P9.9.1 and P9.9.2, prepare a report for the virtual reality division at September 30, 1997. Show performance for the month and for the year to date, using the following format:

Year to Date			Month		
Budget	*Actual*	*Variance*	*Budget*	*Actual*	*Variance*

2. Comment on the virtual reality manager's statement that monthly reports used to track performance of his division are not meaningful. Specifically, do you agree that performance for the virtual reality division should be evaluated differently from that of the other three divisions? Should virtual reality receive a more specialized type of report, given the seasonal nature of its business?
3. Does the performance report prepared in requirement 1 help you to resolve these issues?

P9.10 (**Creating Goal Congruence between Departments**)

Bonnie O'Hara, the managing partner for advertising at Universal Media Promotions, cannot understand why her three department managers are acting so childishly. Universal has always prided itself on having a workforce that is committed to seeing the organization prosper and grow. But lately it seems that the personal self-interests of the managers have gotten in the way of the firm's overall success. O'Hara has heard several complaints from clients who say it is impossible to get their account managers to share information on the firm's alternative advertising programs.

Universal's advertising division is divided into three departments—broadcast, print, and direct mail. Each is run as both a cost center and a revenue center. Department managers request the resources they believe are needed to run their departments for the upcoming budget year, and, after some discussion, O'Hara decides upon the spending limits allowed. Staying within these limits is not normally an issue, since most costs are fixed in nature. When expense overruns are necessary, the manager must first receive O'Hara's approval. A breakdown of actual department expenses for 1996 is given in Exhibit P9.10.1.

The success of department operations depends much more on revenue earned—a situation which seems to have created many of the interdepartmental problems that O'Hara is now confronting. Revenues generated by each department for the past 2 years—1995 and 1996—are shown in Exhibit P9.10.2. Results have shifted substantially during this period, with broadcast revenue increasing by 15 percent and direct mail revenue increasing by nearly 60 percent, but print revenue has fallen by 6 percent. Managers' compensation is partially determined by the amount of revenue their units generate. All three managers make a base salary of $50,000, but their commission rates vary. The broadcast manager earns 6 percent of department revenues, while the print manager earns 5 percent and the direct mail manager 7 percent.

As managers have tried to boost their departments' revenues, they have begun to view the other forms of advertising offered by the firm as competition. For example, a client working with the broadcast department on a television commercial had asked the broadcast manager for help in putting together a print advertising campaign for magazines. The broadcast manager saw this print campaign as a potential threat to generating future television commercials and, therefore, dissuaded the client from pursuing the print option. Some of the firm's long-term clients, who are good friends of O'Hara, candidly expressed their displeasure over the arguments with Universal managers that have resulted from such situations. O'Hara fears that this treatment—judging from the intensity of the feedback she has received—may well result in a loss of business. She is determined to put a stop to such self-interested actions by her managers in the future.

After some discussion with staff from human resources and accounting, O'Hara is considering changing the department manager compensation plan. She

EXHIBIT P9.10.1 UNIVERSAL MEDIA PROMOTIONS— ADVERTISING DIVISION

1996 Department Expense

	Broadcast	Print	Direct Mail
Office expense	$145,799	$ 287,190	$120,176
Salaries	240,568	449,514	233,676
Travel	131,219	212,271	126,853
Promotion	87,479	112,379	66,765
Entertainment	123,929	187,298	120,176
Total expense	$728,993	$1,248,650	$667,645

EXHIBIT P9.10.2 UNIVERSAL MEDIA PROMOTIONS— ADVERTISING DIVISION		
Department Revenues for 1995 and 1996		
	Revenue	
Department	*1995*	*1996*
Broadcast	$ 895,750	$1,026,750
Print	1,560,000	1,469,000
Direct mail	689,750	1,094,500
Total revenue	$3,145,500	$3,590,250

EXHIBIT P9.10.3 UNIVERSAL MEDIA PROMOTIONS— ADVERTISING DIVISION	
Proposed Compensation Structure	
Base salary	$50,000
Commission rates on department sales:	
Broadcast	3.0%
Print	2.5%
Direct mail	3.5%
Bonus on total advertising revenue	1.0%

thinks managers would be more inclined to work together if part of their commission depended on revenues generated by all of advertising. The proposed plan would maintain the $50,000 base salary, but would cut in half the rates of the commission that is based on department revenues. To counter the lower commission, the plan would create a 1 percent bonus based on overall revenue for the advertising division. Details of the plan are given in Exhibit P9.10.3.

Required:

1. Calculate the total compensation amount for each department manager for 1995 and for 1996 under the existing plan.
2. Calculate the department manager commissions for 1996 under the proposed plan.
3. What are the advantages of adopting the new compensation plan proposal? What are the disadvantages?
4. Each department is now structured as both a cost center and a revenue center. If departments were restructured as profit centers, would you expect interdepartmental competition to decrease?

P9.11 (Identifying Performance Measures for a Social Service Organization)

Children's Support Services (CSS) is a nonprofit organization whose mission is to provide readily available support for children living under stressful conditions. The organization is divided into three service departments—foster care, adoption, and counseling and therapy—each structured as a cost center. Recently, CSS has come under close reporting scrutiny by its third-party funding sources, which include the state government, the United Way, and several other private foundations. These external parties are now requesting verifiable measurements that indicate the levels of service effectiveness being attained by CSS. Specifically, these third-party sources want information indicating the organization's level of operating efficiency and of effectiveness.

The executive director of CSS has asked the head of the foster care service department to construct such measures. Foster care is run by Sarah Earnest, a former social welfare caseworker who switched to administrative work three years ago. Earnest is examining performance results collected for the first 6 months of 1997. Her first source of information is the cost report (Exhibit P9.11.1), which shows that foster care service has overspent its budget by $5,080 for this time period. She explains that the overruns are small—generally, less than 5 percent of budget—and were largely out of her control.

Earnest believes that the report on department performance measures (Exhibit P9.11.2) provides justification for these overruns. She points out that the number of foster care cases actually handled exceeds the budgeted caseload by 32 cases. (Each case represents the processing of one child.) She also notes that department performance exceeds budget targets in the number of children placed in foster care (+8) and in the number of children reunited with their natural families (+33). The department has established objectives of placing 70 percent of all cases handled in foster care and reuniting 20 percent of all cases with their natural families. However, Earnest has not considered these goals in her analysis.

When Earnest offered these explanations to CSS's executive director, she was told that she needed to devise more-concrete measures. The director reiterated the need for measures of efficiency and effectiveness and explained that agencies such as theirs would now have to report data in a convincing manner in order to receive funding in the future.

Required:

1. Calculate the variances for foster care service (Exhibit P9.11.1) as percentages of the year-to-date budget.
2. Calculate the following actual and, where possible, budgeted amounts for foster care service:
   a. Workload variance = actual cases/budgeted cases
   b. Cost per case handled = total cost/number of cases

EXHIBIT P9.11.1   CSS—FOSTER CARE SERVICES

Cost Report for the Six Months Ending June 30, 1997

	Budget		YTD Actual Expenses	Variance
	1997	*YTD*		
Professional fees	$ 55,000	$ 27,500	$ 29,540	$(2,040)
Insurance	21,000	10,500	13,900	(3,400)
Salaries & benefits	125,600	62,800	61,800	1,000
Conferences & travel	10,400	5,200	5,150	50
Transportation	3,500	1,750	2,440	(690)
Total cost	$215,500	$107,750	$112,830	$(5,080)

EXHIBIT P9.11.2   CSS—FOSTER CARE SERVICES

Performance Measures for Six Months Ending June 30, 1997

	Budget		YTD Actual Results	Variance
	1997	*YTD*		
Number of foster care cases	425	213	245	32
Number of children placed in foster care	298	149	157	8
Number of children reunited with their natural families	84	42	75	33

      c. Placement-success ratios:
         1) Foster care placement/actual cases
         2) Natural family placements/actual cases
    3. Using the information obtained in requirements 1 and 2, evaluate the efficiency and the effectiveness of the foster care service department.

CASES

C9.1 (Johnston Banking Corporation)[14]

Mike Johnston sat quietly at his desk contemplating. Another company holiday party had come and gone. This year, the Johnston Banking Corporation (JBC) year-end financial reports did not show the high profits he was accustomed to seeing. Instead, his desk was covered with reports of losses at two of his company's six banks. As he reflected on the past 37 years, he realized that his company today was a far cry from what it had been when he started working there after graduating from college. When his father had passed on to him the leadership responsibility for Johnston Banking Corporation, the family's company consisted only of the Fairview State Bank. Now Johnston stood at the head of a holding company that owned six northwestern Oklahoma banks, each with its own individual market, management, and challenges.

Although he was managing the firm using the same methods he had always used in the past, Johnston now found himself immersed in detailed decisions that were taking too much of his time. He often had to spend long hours at work after the bank had closed and then go home with his briefcase full of additional paperwork. While he felt confident in the management abilities of his senior executives at each of the banks, he was not sure that they were receiving adequate guidance to assure their reaching his goals for the company. He realized that, in order for the banks to achieve the level of performance he expected, his New Year's resolution would have to include a resolve to change his current style of management and control.

History of Johnston Banking Corporation

In 1934, at age 25, James Johnston purchased the Fairview State Bank. He was reported to be the youngest bank president in the United States, and he continued to work in the bank until his death in 1987. His son, Mike Johnston, started working at the bank at age 22 and later became the bank's president, at which time he acquired two more banks and built three additional branches. (See the organizational chart in Exhibit C9.1.1.) The Johnston family currently owns 100 percent of the bank's stock.

James Johnston had been involved with managing every aspect of the bank, from making individual loan decisions to strategic planning for the future. His son, Mike, has continued in the same manner. This owner-management style has created a distinct culture within the bank. It has resulted in a group of loyal, long-term employees who have contributed to the bank's strong financial performance over the years. Returns average 15 percent ROA and 17.5 percent ROE. This style of management, which allows customers and employees to meet with the CEO one-on-one and to get immediate decisions, has been effective in the bank's rural market locale.

The creation of JBC's strong, familylike culture is a result of Mike Johnston's emphasis on quick, direct customer service and on openness among bank employees. The company culture has developed over many years—primarily because the CEO, a self-described "benevolent dictator," makes practically every decision and

---

[14] Prepared by Dena Aloian and Tim Morris under the direction of Ralph Drtina.

South-Central Virginia

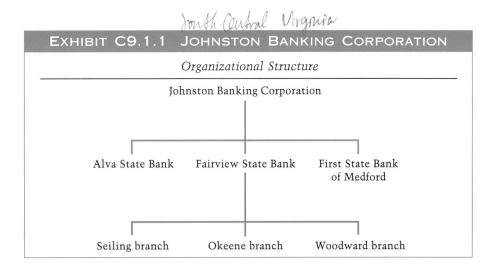

EXHIBIT C9.1.1 JOHNSTON BANKING CORPORATION

Organizational Structure

Johnston Banking Corporation

Alva State Bank   Fairview State Bank   First State Bank
of Medford

Seiling branch   Okeene branch   Woodward branch

EXHIBIT C9.1.2 JOHNSTON BANKING CORPORATION

Mission Statement

The mission of Johnston Banking Corporation is to be the dominant independent banking system in the northwestern region of Oklahoma. We will concentrate on fulfilling the banking needs of our customers, retaining well-
trained and satisfied employees, reaching financial performance goals, and
acting as a responsible business leader in the community. Johnston Banking
Corporation will provide reliable and courteous banking services and will
strive to have a completely satisfied customer at the end of each transaction.

---

values employees who are loyal and mirror his customer-oriented and profit-cen-
tered approach. The very fact that customers and employees deal directly with
Johnston results in an effective, although highly centralized, management control
system.

Current Banking Environment
While JBC's banks have enjoyed a market share nearing 70 percent in the past,
competition is increasing, as new banks enter their areas. In order to position itself
for the future, JBC has developed a formal strategic plan that includes a mission
statement, which outlines goals and objectives for the next 5 years. The bank's
primary mission has always been to be the dominant independent banking system
in the region by focusing on four areas. In order of importance these areas are (1)
customers, (2) employees, (3) profit, and (4) the community. Traditionally, this mission statement was informally conveyed to staff and understood by them through
the corporate culture. It has only now been issued as a formal, written statement
(see Exhibit C9.1.2). In addition, the 5-year strategic plan includes a competitive
analysis and sets out specific financial goals.

The current evaluation system is extremely informal and subjective. In the
past, Johnston has either issued equal bonuses to senior managers or has distributed bonuses of different amounts based on personal discretion and with no measurable tie to performance. One manager described this annual bonus process as
similar to receiving an IRS refund, "You aren't sure during the year whether or not
you will receive any money back at the end of the year." Still, this system had

been effective because of Johnston's complete understanding of each manager's effectiveness and the unique situation each faced.

The changes in JBC's structure and in the banking environment have made it increasingly difficult for Johnston to maintain his high level of personal involvement. Although he wants to maintain his strong, centralized control, he realizes that the bank's expansion has created the need for more-decentralized decisions. After years of hands-on, detail-oriented management, it is personally challenging for him to trust others to act in the best interest of his family's business. One of his primary concerns is how to determine the most effective system for achieving desired performance in senior managers at JBC without losing the familylike orientation that has defined the bank's success until now.

Designing the System

Johnston sat at his desk debating what type of system would be most appropriate, given his company's unique makeup. He knew that, because he alone currently dictated the culture, whatever system he designed most not only motivate senior managers to achieve company goals but must also instill in them the values so important for the bank's success. He wanted to make sure that the control system would relieve him of the burden of making *every* decision, yet allow him to retain adequate authority and flexibility in making decisions at the appropriate level. He decided that the steps to be taken in developing the best system for motivating, evaluating, and rewarding senior managers at JBC were as follows.

1: Set Goals and Objectives That Address the Mission Statement

Johnston felt that the goals should reflect the mission of the organization, including its profit and customer objectives. Formerly, the goals of JBC addressed only market share and financial returns and were both set and used only by Johnston. He would have to set new goals and measurable objectives that address the customer and profitability aspects of the mission and then communicate these companywide goals to senior managers.

2: Set Strategies for Each Individual Bank

Johnston felt that he should work with the senior managers of each bank to set local strategies for meeting the established goals and objectives. Allowing senior managers to help set the local strategies would not only ensure a sense of ownership on their part, but it would also enable each bank to maintain autonomy by letting the different strategies reflect each bank's specific market and environment.

3: Develop a Formal Evaluation and Reward System for Senior Managers

Johnston knew that his current, informal evaluation system was not an effective tool for motivating desired performance from his senior managers. On several occasions, he had even heard managers comment that they "wished they knew what it was that their evaluations were based upon."

The evaluation system he designed would provide structure to the evaluation process by addressing customer service and financial returns based on the following measures:

Customer Service	*Financial Returns*
Customer satisfaction	Return on assets (ROA)
Retention of customers	Return on equity (ROE)
Market share	Capital-asset ratio
Personalized customer service	
Maintaining familylike company culture	

The evaluation system that Johnston developed was based on both qualitative and quantitative measurements. He felt that, as CEO, he should conduct annual evaluations with senior managers based on information obtained from two sources:

1. *Self-evaluations,* which would give senior managers the opportunity to rate themselves on their achievement of the bank's objectives. These self-evaluations would allow managers to explain some of the more qualitative aspects of their performance, such as actions they had taken in order to retain customers.
2. *Quantitative reports,* which would relate directly to the bank's specific goals. They would include reports on financial performance, customer satisfaction surveys, and market share.

Johnston was pleased with his plan. Managers would know at the beginning of the year how they would be evaluated at year-end. They would have worked with him to develop a strategy to meet their respective bank's goals and objectives. The end-of-year bonuses would consist of a monetary award and corporate stock and would be directly related to manager performance in the two key areas of customers and profitability. The amount of each reward would be determined by a given manager's evaluation rating, which would range from *Adequate* (75 percent of the annual bonus base) to *Exceptional* (125 percent of the annual bonus base). Johnston felt that the bonus structure (one-half cash and one-half stock) would be an effective incentive for managers, because the cash would serve as an immediate monetary award for their efforts, while the stock offering would encourage them to make decisions that would not only raise the ROA and the ROE but also increase the overall value of the corporation in the long term.

Required:

1. Will the proposed control system motivate senior managers to act in ways that are consistent with obtaining the CEO's desired results?
2. How should the control system be designed in order to achieve goal congruence between the CEO and senior managers?
3. What are some concerns in shifting from a control system with no formal measures to a system that has multiple measures?

C9.2   (FineFabriks, Inc.)[15]

Background

FineFabriks, Inc., is a midsize manufacturer of textile products headquartered in a small city on the North Carolina-Virginia border. Its main product lines are cotton and cotton blends. Many of the company's middle- and upper-level management personnel have been with the company for a long time, and it's not unusual for retirees to have been with FineFabriks for their entire careers. Contributing to FineFabriks' role as a leader in the industry is its ability to develop successful new products, such as new weave styles and new print designs. While company profits have shown slight but steady increases over most of the company's history, in the last 5 years or so they have been unpredictable—with one year even showing a loss (see Exhibit C9.2.1).

FineFabriks' profit picture may have been affected by its decision not to buy into some of the significant technological advancements that occurred in the tex-

---

[15]   From AICPA Care Development Program. Copyright 1992 by The American Institute of Certified Public Accountants, Jersey City, NJ. Reprinted with permission of the publisher.

EXHIBIT C9.2.1 FINEFABRIKS, INC.

Results of Operations (in thousands)

	For the Year Ending December 31,		
	1995[a]	1994	1993
Operating revenue	$752,964	$684,808	$667,397
Operating expense:			
Cost of goods sold	$618,282	$585,274	$552,680
Selling & administrative	74,802	68,768	65,241
Depreciation	20,789	20,586	19,792
Bonuses:			
Top management	5,612	5,510	5,285
Production management	7,593	6,287	6,851
Total operating expense	$727,078	$686,425	$649,849
Income before tax	$ 25,886	$ (1,617)	$ 17,548

[a] Does not include results of operations for CuttingEdge in 1995.

---

tile industry in the 1980s. The biggest development was new equipment that could make the changeover from producing one color fabric or type of weave to another in a fraction of the time previously required for the process. The new equipment made it possible for the firms to change colors or weaves almost immediately in response to customer demand. Thus, a company with the new equipment would benefit by having significantly reduced setup costs as well as by being able to be more responsive to the needs of its customers. However, in spite of the benefits of the new equipment, FineFabriks, like many other established companies, felt the cost of purchasing and installing it was prohibitive and thus decided not to make the investment.

In September 1995, FineFabriks acquired CuttingEdge Co., a relatively new one-plant, privately held manufacturer that had taken full advantage of the innovations in machinery design developed in the 1980s. CuttingEdge's principal product is Lyco, a revolutionary new fiber used primarily in women's clothing. When Lyco is combined with cotton or linen fibers, the result gives the wearer the best of both worlds—a fabric that "breathes" but doesn't wrinkle, that can be machine washed and dried, and that doesn't fade after repeated washings. Demand for this fiber has increased rapidly since its introduction in late 1991. Over its short 5-year life, CuttingEdge has had a remarkable history of earning profits in excess of those obtained by even the leading companies in the industry—partly, at least, because of its state-of-the-art equipment and technology. Prior to its acquisition by Fine-Fabriks, its profits for 1995 showed a 200 percent increase over the same period in 1994, and profit for 1994 was twice that for 1993.

After the acquisition, FineFabriks eliminated the top management positions at CuttingEdge but left the remainder of the organizational structure pretty much as it was, allowing the plant to continue producing Lyco in the same way. The acquisition was expected to improve FineFabriks' profit picture in 1996 and thereafter.

FineFabriks has made few major changes since 1980 in its organizational structure, its accounting and costing policies, and its employee incentive policy (see Exhibit C9.2.2). One change it did make was to install a new computer system a few years ago. This new system enabled information to be input more effi-

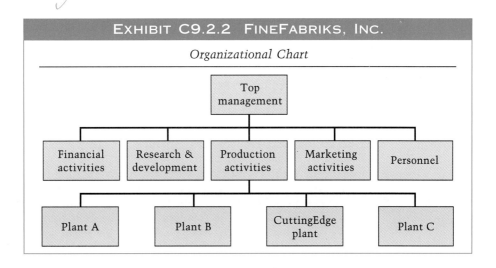

EXHIBIT C9.2.2 FINEFABRIKS, INC.

Organizational Chart

ciently. Terminals are now located in all departments and department heads can input data about their areas from these terminals. The system also allows department heads and other management personnel to extract virtually any information they desire from the system in order to prepare periodic reports for upper-level management. While the system has the capability to validate any information extracted from it, it is not set up to dictate specifically *what* information should be used for a given purpose. This decision is left to the individual preparing the various reports required by upper management. Information on materials usage and labor-hours worked are entered in the system daily by production department heads. Overhead items are entered when costs are incurred, and predetermined overhead rates are in the system and accessible when reports are prepared.

FineFabriks' top managers historically have felt they were well-informed about all important aspects of the company, both financial and operating. They have stressed to department managers the importance of keeping top management up-to-date on company business. In keeping with this policy, they require monthly reports from all production department heads. Before the new computer system was installed, much of this reporting was done orally, with top management and production and auxiliary personnel sitting around the conference table discussing last month's results. When the new computer system was installed, much of the information that previously had been shared at the monthly meetings could now be quickly and easily generated by computer. As a result, top management discontinued most of the meetings and began requiring submission of monthly paper reports from the various departments. Production departments report product costs and production levels, the sales department reports sales figures, and the auxiliary departments—such as personnel and maintenance—report relevant information about their departments.

The Issues

It is now early in 1997, and top management has just received a copy of the financial statements for 1996. It is shocked by the low net income figure that appears on the income statement. Of particular concern is an item on the statement entitled *Loss due to market decline of inventory*, an item with which the top managers are unfamiliar—it has never before appeared on their statements. The monthly sales reports showed sales for 1996 (in terms of yards sold) to be higher than they were last year. The monthly production reports showed favorable production figures, and reports from the auxiliary departments showed 1996's operating expenses to be in line with budgeted figures. Additionally, the acquisition of CuttingEdge was expected to boost profits. Because top management had always felt it was on top of what was going on in the company, it wondered where the lines of communication had failed and what gave rise to these unexpected results.

Further investigation revealed the following. Early in 1996, a competitor began producing an improved blend of Lyco and cotton, which was an immediate success and sold for $4.05 per yard. Since the Lyco-cotton fabric had been one of FineFabriks' major product lines, FineFabriks had a warehouse full of the old blend. Because of the popularity of the new blend, sales of the old declined significantly for both FineFabriks and the other manufacturers selling it. FineFabriks realized it would have to cut the selling price of the old blend from $3.75 per yard to $1.80 per yard in order to be able to sell the fabric. The old blend cost FineFabriks $2.20 per yard to manufacture. In February 1996, when FineFabriks recognized the need to cut its selling price for the blend, the company had approximately 3.2 million yards in stock. It then recorded an inventory valuation loss of $1,280,000 [($2.20 − $1.80) × 3,200,000 yards].

Fortunately for FineFabriks, the research and development department was able to quickly make the changes necessary to begin producing the new blend. In fact, by October 1996, the company was up to full production and had begun selling the new product. Thus, sales figures for the year ended up being close to what had been budgeted. While top management was aware of the new product and the decline in demand for the old, none of the monthly reports submitted to it made explicit reference to the cost-quantity information just described. This omission was not intentional on the part of production and auxiliary personnel; rather, it was a result of the lack of communication between top and middle management. Since FineFabriks had not had problems with inventory obsolescence in the past, the reports were not designed to include such information, and no department manager had been given the responsibility of passing this information along to top management.

Second, during the 1996 year-end audit performed by the Jamison Rollins CPA firm, the auditor began to suspect that all was not well with the management bonus figures shown in the accounting records. Since this CPA firm had just recently been hired to conduct the annual audit, the auditor was not really familiar with company policy regarding bonuses. She became concerned when FineFabriks showed a very small profit in 1996—in spite of the expectation that acquisition of CuttingEdge would boost its profits. Still, bonuses seemed to be in line with what they had been in the past. The auditor found it even stranger that past bonuses for production managers had been fairly stable, even though profits over the last 5 years had been erratic. She discovered that production managers' bonuses were a percent of the difference between budgeted amounts and actual amounts for each department (assuming the actual amounts were favorable when compared to budgeted figures). She suspected some budget manipulation was being done by these managers in order to ensure that they received their "fair shares" in the form of bonuses. Additionally, she found that year-end bonuses for top management were a fixed percent of their annual salaries. Of particular interest to her was the fact that production managers at the former CuttingEdge plant received no bonuses, even though it appeared that their plant was operating more efficiently and productively than the other three plants were.

The auditor's investigation revealed that even though company policy lets production managers have pretty much a free hand in preparing their departments' budgets, the managers associated with CuttingEdge had their budgets prepared for them by longtime employees of FineFabriks. Top management said it did this because CuttingEdge managers had not been with FineFabriks long and might not be adept at budgeting, because none of them had prepared budgets before the acquisition. However, because FineFabriks employees were unfamiliar with CuttingEdge's equipment and processes, and because they had been told that CuttingEdge's equipment was state-of-the-art, they had materially underestimated setup and run times when they prepared the 1996 budgets. This resulted in an overall underestimation of manufacturing costs in these departments.

CuttingEdge production managers did not protest the budgetary process initially, because they were not fully aware of the bonus policy and had not prepared budgets in the past. Besides, they had enough other changes to deal with as a result of the acquisition and the associated changes in management. Even though they operated as efficiently as they had in the past, their costs exceeded what was budgeted, and they received no year-end bonuses. When they heard managers in other departments and at other plants talking about their own bonuses, CuttingEdge managers became angry and felt they were victims of the system. They felt that, as they had not participated in the budgetary process, they should not suffer as a result of the arbitrary production cost variances that resulted in their overall cost figures' exceeding what was budgeted.

Probably as a result of the many years of steadily increasing profits (prior to 1991), top management of FineFabriks had become very complacent about productivity and profits. It had adopted a "leave well enough alone" attitude. Top managers saw no reason to question either the budgets developed by the different departments or the bonus policy and resulting bonus amounts. (After all, they were still receiving their bonuses!) However, after this year's results were reported, top management feels it needs to reexamine several aspects of the business. Of particular concern are the budgeting policies, the bonus policies, and the means by which top management is to be kept informed about what is going on—both internally and externally.

Required:

1. What do you think was the major factor contributing to the low profits reported on 1996's income statement?
2. With respect to the bonus policy:
   a. Why is the auditor concerned about the bonus figures? What problems do you see with the bonus policy as it currently exists?
   b. What changes would you recommend be made to the bonus policy? Why would you recommend them?
   c. Who is most likely to be affected by the changes recommended in requirement *b* above and in what way will these people be affected?
3. What suggestions do you have for top management regarding its involvement with the budget process?
4. What steps could top management take to improve the quality of information it receives and to prevent future year-end surprises? (Recall that top management expected 1996 profits to be much higher than they were, and that it received the required monthly reports from all departments.)

CHAPTER 10

BUDGETING FOR OPERATIONS AND CASH FLOW

Any management control system is only as good as the budgeting it depends on. The budget is a short-term plan coordinating the firm's long-range strategies with the day-to-day activities of responsibility centers. Managers set the upcoming period's goals in the budget, which then becomes the yardstick for evaluating performance—that is, for assessing the degree to which those goals have been achieved.

In Chapter 8, we saw how managers use capital budgets to evaluate alternative long-range programs and projects. The discounted projected cash flows in capital budgets provide estimates of increases in shareholder value. Managers thus have a basis for selecting investments and large-scale programs that offer the highest returns. Selecting what seems to be the best investment from a number of alternatives is only the first step in implementing long-range corporate plans.

The budget serves to translate discounted cash projections into short-term ac-

crual-accounting goals at the operational level. We already saw that capital budgets focus on analysis of investment alternatives. Now we'll see how operating budgets concentrate senior managers' attention on influencing employees in order to accomplish specific tasks and outcomes. Since programs and projects approved in the capital budget may span many responsibility centers, the budget offers managers a means to coordinate the firm's energy and resources in the short term, while senior management directs long-term corporate strategy.

In this chapter we explore the philosophy, mechanics, and behavioral implications of the budgeting process. Recall that budgeting is the second of the five steps constituting management control:

1. Long-range planning
2. **Budgeting**
3. Measurement
4. Reporting and analysis
5. Corrective action

We will examine what activities are involved in setting budget targets, how to construct a detailed budget aimed at those targets, and what's involved in gaining corporate approval of the budget. We will explore the role played by the personal commitment of responsibility center managers in all of these activities; especially, we will look into gamesmanship behavior in the budget process. We will conclude with a brief introduction to how budget data is used to guide corrective action, which will be explored in depth in Chapter 11.

OVERVIEW OF BUDGETING

Generally, a discussion of the budget involves few new accounting concepts or techniques. The budget process, shown in Exhibit 10.1, results in a set of projected (or pro forma) financial statements. Preparation of these statements involves many of the same procedural steps needed to prepare financial statements at the end of the period. While the mechanics of budgeting are important to accountants, managers are more concerned with the budget as a plan of action for the upcoming time period.

USES OF BUDGETING

Budgets are used to direct short-term actions within responsibility centers in the following ways:

PLANNING

The budget serves as a means for refining financial expectations at every operating level. A firm's budget differs from its strategic plan. The budgeting process directly involves all responsibility center managers. The strategic plan is normally prepared by only the top level of corporate or business unit managers. Since the budget is prepared after the strategic plan, it depends on more up-to-date information and, thus, enables preparation of more-realistic short-term targets. (See "Current Practice: Photon Technology.") Through the use of budgets, managers at lower levels prepare functional strategies that support higher-level corporate and business-unit strategies.

For firms that do not prepare a formal strategic plan, the budget is the planning document. For these firms, usually small ones, the budget can include an analysis of the external environment—including the economy, societal trends, politics, regulation, and technology—that would normally fall into the domain of strategic planning. In such cases, budgeting requires that high-level management make strategic decisions identifying which business units are to follow a growth strategy and how product lines are expected to build competitive advantage (i.e., by low cost or by differentiation).

CONTROLLING

The process of developing the budget provides a measure of control as responsibility center managers commit their units to certain levels of operating activity. The main elements of control are the targets contained in

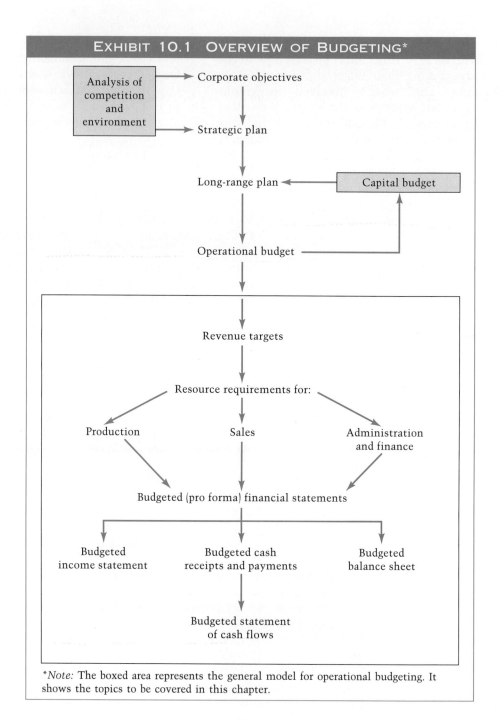

EXHIBIT 10.1 OVERVIEW OF BUDGETING*

Note: The boxed area represents the general model for operational budgeting. It shows the topics to be covered in this chapter.

the budget—they provide financial yardsticks against which actual results are compared. Feedback on differences between actual results and budgeted estimates alert managers that they must intervene in troublesome areas of operations. A system that provides signals for taking corrective action when needed is the basis for management by exception. At higher levels

Photon Technology

Photon Technology develops and manufactures high-tech electro-optical instrumentation—for example, a spectrofluorometer that measures calcium ions in living cells. The firm's potential for success has been tied to the ability of its R&D department to develop new products and the ability of its production department to make them and get them "out the door." Product delivery schedules make planning critical, especially since most customers are research or medical institutes that sometimes take 12 months to receive approval to purchase new equipment. The company relies on its budget to plan sales, cash flows, and resource needs. To handle the uncertainty of R&D outcomes, the budget is prepared according to three "what-if" product development scenarios: (1) best case, (2) most likely case, and (3) worst case. By understanding the consequences of these three possible R&D outcomes, Photon's management has been well-prepared to take corrective action, such as securing emergency financing.

Source: Janine S. Pouliot, "High-Tech Budgeting," *Management Accounting*, May 1991, pp. 30–31.

of the firm, unfavorable feedback may result in decisions to change strategic plans—or even corporate objectives. At lower levels, feedback from operating results usually results in fine-tuning operations in order to improve productivity.

COORDINATION

In order to determine the firm's resource needs for the upcoming budget period, managers must coordinate activities among responsibility centers. Therefore, developing the budget requires communication among responsibility centers. Consider, for example, a manufacturing cost center that has little or no communication with the sales department. Clearly, this is not a good situation. The manufacturing cost center must have access to sales forecasts if it is to plan its needs for human labor, facilities, and materials. And that's why the individual budgets for every responsibility center must be communicated and coordinated to converge in an overall budget intended to meet corporate financial objectives. If the individual budgets do not successfully converge to meet these objectives, then either they must be resolved through better coordination or the strategy or objectives must be revised.

MOTIVATION AND EVALUATION

The success of the budget process depends on managers' success in setting appropriate targets—for which they are held accountable. After the reporting period is complete, the budget is used to measure whether targets were achieved. In that sense, it becomes a tool for evaluating manager performance. And, in the same way, the budget is a tool that motivates manager actions. The common example is financial rewards for profit center managers who meet or exceed their profit targets. This bottom-line approach has proved a successful way to encourage entrepreneurial thinking by managers in decentralized firms. But the success of a profit goal depends on setting the correct profit target to begin with.

SETTING TARGETS

Based on findings from psychological research, business theorists argue that an ideal budget is one that sets challenging, but achievable, targets. They recommend that, in such a budget, goals should not be achievable more than 50 percent of the time. Managers will be inspired by a difficult (but attainable) goal; they will also be better motivated, and hence more productive.[1]

NEED FOR NEGOTIATION

Upper-level management can specify a target intended to satisfy overall strategic objectives, but management may fail to consider lower-level managers' understanding of local competitive conditions. On the other hand, when lower-level managers have sole responsibility for setting targets, they tend to set goals that understate planned revenue or overstate planned expenses—goals that are more easily attainable.

Upper and lower management need to negotiate and agree on lower-level goals. Budget targets imposed by top management may be regarded by lower-level managers as impossible. Such targets can lead managers to feel frustrated and even to manipulate data. To make budgets work as motivational tools, a sense of ownership and commitment to targets must be instilled in lower-level managers.

TARGET TIME PERIODS AND SUBSEQUENT REVISION[2]

Operating budgets in large U.S. companies normally cover 1 year. Since responsibility center targets are the basis of budgets, target time periods generally coincide with the budget period. Most senior managers are reluctant to allow revisions to budget targets during the year, particularly when the budget is used to control operations and evaluate performance. Revising targets during the budget period would permit more-accurate planning

---

[1] K. A. Merchant and J. F. Marzoni, "The Achievability of Budget Targets in Profit Centers: A Field Study," *Accounting Review*, July 1989, pp. 539–558. This article reviews the literature on goal setting, and it reports an interesting contradiction. In a study of 12 companies, managers achieved their budgets 80 to 90 percent of the time, despite top management's statements suggesting a philosophy more in line with 50 percent achievability.

[2] This section draws from comments by Neil C. Churchill, "Budget Choice: Planning vs. Control," *Harvard Business Review*, July–Aug. 1984, pp. 150–164; and John E. Rehfeld, "What Working for a Japanese Company Taught Me," *Harvard Business Review*, Nov.–Dec. 1990, pp. 167–176.

over the period, but making the changes would effectively eliminate the usefulness of the budget as a control mechanism.

The 1-year budget doesn't work well for all firms. Small entrepreneurial companies that rely on budgets mainly as planning tools revise targets as needed. For these firms, managers rely on other control methods, including informal feedback and personal observation. Japanese firms often prepare budgets on 6-month cycles, in accordance with their *kaizen* (or *continuous-improvement*) philosophy, whereby new targets are set at shorter intervals to meet expected shifts in the markets. Frequent revision is also seen as a chance to wipe the slate clean and start over—a policy that can help motivate managers by changing goals that no longer seem achievable.

THE BUDGET PROCESS

Preparation of the operating budget will depend on the structure of the organization and the extent to which a strategic planning program is in place.

TIES TO LONG-RANGE PLANNING

We saw, one chapter earlier, that a multibusiness or multidivisional firm has three levels of strategy:

1. *Corporate level*—to determine which business lines are to be grown, held, or harvested
2. *Business level*—to develop competitive advantage by emphasizing either a low-cost or a differentiation strategy
3. *Functional level*—to develop feasible action programs by operating units in a manner that supports business strategy

Through preparation of long-range plans, top management chooses those programs, products, and projects that best satisfy its higher-level—that is, corporate-level and business-level—strategies. As strategies become more concrete, capital-budgeting techniques are used to compare the alternative ways of implementing the strategies. For example, analysts discount long-term projected cash flows that represent alternative means of production or channels of product distribution. This not only helps management decide how it will compete but also helps management select the best means for production and distribution.

In its most complete form, the long-range plan includes annual projections of financial statements for 3 to 5 years. The operating budget is the first-year "slice" of the long-range plan. For the many firms that do not prepare comprehensive long-range plans, their annual capital and operating budgets form the basis of their higher- and lower-level strategies.

PHASES OF BUDGET PROCESS

There are many ways firms prepare their budgets. Some or all of the following steps may be part of the preparation:[3]

---

[3] Adapted from Churchill, *ibid.*, p. 154.

- *Guidelines.* Top management communicates the strategic directives, financial objectives, economic assumptions, and resource constraints to lower levels.
- *First submission.* Operating-unit managers offer an initial plan that includes broadly defined targets and resources.
- *Combination and review.* Top management evaluates each unit's initial plans and combines them to form a companywide plan.
- *Negotiation and revision.* Top management negotiates changes to targets and resources with operating-unit managers.
- *Detailed plan submission.* Operating-unit managers prepare and submit a complete plan based on negotiated changes.
- *Approval.* Top management combines detailed plans into a companywide plan and continues to revise and renegotiate until final approval is granted.

This ongoing interaction between top management and lower-level managers permits both to satisfy their budget needs. Top management implements its long-range plan, while it adjusts the budgets to reflect up-to-date information on competition, products, and markets. At the same time, operating managers are closely involved in defining targets, and they are more likely to feel committed to their attainment. (See "Current Practice: Emerson Electric Co.")

BUDGET TIMETABLE

The budget is prepared according to a tightly prescribed timetable overseen by a corporate budget director. Two to three months' time is needed to complete the budget for a single business firm. It can take twice as long for companies composed of multiple business units, starting with first submission, review, negotiation, and so on. The budgeting process can begin as early as July for a fiscal year that starts the following January 1.

BUDGET ILLUSTRATION: HEALTHFIRST YOGURT COMPANY

Let's see how a detailed operating budget is prepared, including the financial statements and the supporting schedules that show where data in the statement comes from. A financial document comprising this information is referred to as the **profit plan** or **master budget**. To illustrate the calculations that go into creating such integrated plans, we'll see how it's done for a single-product firm, HealthFirst Yogurt Co., which operates as an independent division within a larger, multiproduct organization.

The budget model for HealthFirst Yogurt is very detailed and is best prepared on a computer spreadsheet. However, rather than plunge into the details, you should begin by trying to get an overall feel for the types of exhibits needed to build the budget model. For now, you should regard the following exhibits from a manager's perspective, focusing on how the detail provided can help in planning the allocation of company resources.

CURRENT PRACTICE

Emerson Electric Co.

Emerson Electric Co. makes electric, electromechanical, and electronic products, including such brand names as Skil, Craftsman power tools, and U.S. Electric Motors. The company, made up of 40 independent divisions, has increased profits every year for 34 consecutive years. According to CEO Charles F. Knight, the reason for this success is a careful annual planning process in which each divisional manager has a personal commitment to meeting operating-budget targets.

Each division hosts a 1- or 2-day planning conference with senior corporate management. The mood is confrontational as the division presents and defends a 5-year plan that must prove it is stretching to reach its goals. As a minimum, a division must generate returns greater than its cost of capital—that is, create shareholder value. Using the most recent data, each division also prepares estimated income statements for the current year, plus actual income statements, or "actuals," for the past 5 years and pro formas for the next 5 years—making income statements for a total of 11 years. Divisional managers are then given time to rework plans and budgets to close any shortfalls. As the current fiscal year nears its end, each division meets again with corporate officials to review the current year's results and to submit a final budget.

Upon receipt of all 40 budgets from the divisions, corporate management consolidates them into a corporate budget. It then holds an annual planning conference in order to share the results of this highly decentralized process. With top managers of all divisions in attendance, senior corporate officers present the 5-year plan and next year's budget for the company as a whole.

Source: Charles F. Knight, "Emerson Electric: Consistent Profits, Consistently," *Harvard Business Review,* Jan.–Feb. 1992, pp. 57–70.

COMPANY BACKGROUND

HealthFirst Yogurt runs a specialized food production system in a mature industry. It supplies only one size of product, an 8-ounce yogurt, but offers a variety of yogurt products, each having different fresh fruit ingredients. HealthFirst competes in a regional market and has distinguished itself both by the quality of its products and its timely delivery service.

ORGANIZATIONAL STRUCTURE

As shown in Exhibit 10.2, HealthFirst Yogurt is one of three independent divisions constituting HealthFirst Foods, Inc. Divisions are organized around products or services. Both the yogurt and the cheese divisions are seen as marketing mature products, each with slow, long-term growth targeted at 5 percent per year. In the strategic plan, the refrigerated transport division has been slated for much faster growth.

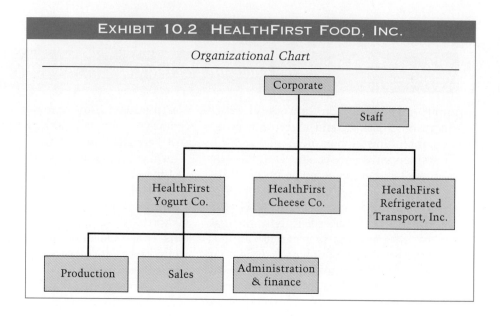

EXHIBIT 10.2 HEALTHFIRST FOOD, INC.

Organizational Chart

PRODUCT AND PROCESS

HealthFirst Yogurt has refurbished its production and organizational processes to include the latest in technology and employee involvement. Over the past 2 years, it has invested heavily in new equipment and factory floor redesign to enable shorter production cycle time. Previously, one flavor, such as strawberry, would be "run" for 1 week, and then production would close down. Equipment was washed out to prepare for the next flavor—say, blueberry. In the meantime, the strawberry product would be stored. This process would continue until enough different flavors were available for shipment. This caused problems in stores when customers saw yogurt arrive with 20 to 25 days of its 40-day shelf life already expired.

Advanced manufacturing equipment now makes it possible to fill each 8-ounce cup with successively different flavors (e.g., strawberry, blueberry, and lemon). This eliminates the need for batch production runs, as well as most yogurt storage and handling. Moreover, stores can now order mixed cases of yogurt that reflect their consumers' buying patterns. Freshly manufactured yogurt is shipped within 48 hours of order (and production), increasing its actual shelf life to 38 days.

PROFIT PLAN COMPONENTS

HealthFirst Yogurt is organized along functional lines, with three separate responsibility centers—production, sales, and administration and finance. Managers of each center must prepare a cost (or expense) budget; the sales manager not only must meet her or his expense budget but also must meet sales targets.

Exhibit 10.3 is a detailed breakdown of all the components of the firm's profit plan. This diagram begins to flesh out the bones of the general model for the operating budget (Exhibit 10.1). Here we see the statements

EXHIBIT 10.3 HEALTHFIRST YOGURT CO.

Detailed Statements and Schedules Constituting the Profit Plan

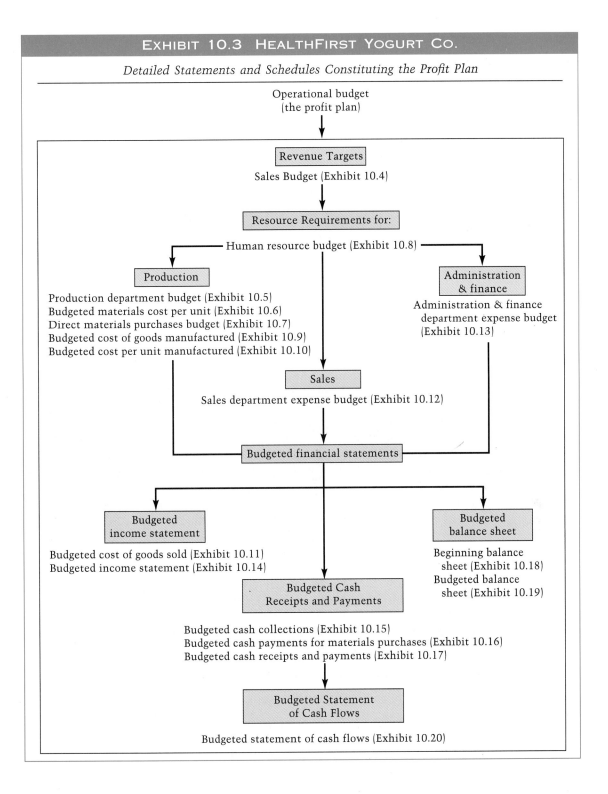

Operational budget
(the profit plan)

Revenue Targets

Sales Budget (Exhibit 10.4)

Resource Requirements for:

Human resource budget (Exhibit 10.8)

Production

Production department budget (Exhibit 10.5)
Budgeted materials cost per unit (Exhibit 10.6)
Direct materials purchases budget (Exhibit 10.7)
Budgeted cost of goods manufactured (Exhibit 10.9)
Budgeted cost per unit manufactured (Exhibit 10.10)

Administration
& finance

Administration & finance
department expense budget
(Exhibit 10.13)

Sales

Sales department expense budget (Exhibit 10.12)

Budgeted financial statements

Budgeted
income statement

Budgeted cost of goods sold (Exhibit 10.11)
Budgeted income statement (Exhibit 10.14)

Budgeted
balance sheet

Beginning balance
sheet (Exhibit 10.18)
Budgeted balance
sheet (Exhibit 10.19)

Budgeted Cash
Receipts and Payments

Budgeted cash collections (Exhibit 10.15)
Budgeted cash payments for materials purchases (Exhibit 10.16)
Budgeted cash receipts and payments (Exhibit 10.17)

Budgeted Statement
of Cash Flows

Budgeted statement of cash flows (Exhibit 10.20)

and schedules needed to complete the firm's budget. Exhibit 10.3 shows the "big picture" of HealthFirst Yogurt's budget preparation and the supporting calculations, which follow in Exhibits 10.4 to 10.20.

PREPARING THE PROFIT PLAN

Corporate management has positioned the HealthFirst Yogurt division on a hold strategy. The corporation has communicated preliminary budget guidelines to all divisions. The divisions responded by submitting their initial, broad-based target and cost plans. Corporate management negotiated targets with each division and combined the divisional plans.

We focus now on preparing HealthFirst Yogurt's detailed 1997 profit plan, which is based on a quarterly breakdown of revenue and cost data.

Sales Budget.   The process of preparing the sales budget (Exhibit 10.4) begins with a commitment by management to attain its sales target. For HealthFirst Yogurt, this goal reflects a series of negotiations whose purpose is to meld corporate strategic plans with divisional sales plans. Using the tools of strategic planning, top management decides on the firm's opportunities and the relative long-term strengths of its business lines. Making these decisions is largely a qualitative exercise. But the decisions are not reached without some help from quantitative models. Broad-based variables, including consumer income, spending patterns, and regional economic strength, are often part of these models.

The divisional manager's forecast depends on an understanding of customer demands. Individual salespersons in close contact with customers will prepare sales targets—usually targeted sales within a designated geographic territory—that are combined with all other sales targets to obtain the target for the entire division. In HealthFirst Yogurt's case, division-level targets have been reconciled with corporate management's plans in earlier stages of planning negotiations. Companies may set and reconcile sales targets in different ways. Lack of formal strategic planning prior to putting together the budget may mean that more time must be devoted to developing long-term plans and setting targets.

We'll now turn to the yogurt division's sales budget for the upcom-

EXHIBIT 10.4 HEALTHFIRST YOGURT CO.

Sales Budget for 1997

	Quarter				
	1	*2*	*3*	*4*	*Total*
Sales in units of yogurt (8-oz. cup)[a]	1,204,375	1,332,500	1,435,000	1,153,125	5,125,000
Price per unit	$ 0.55	$ 0.55	$ 0.55	$ 0.55	$ 0.55
Sales revenue	$662,406	$732,875	$789,250	$634,219	$2,818,750
Quarterly percent breakdown of annual sales	23.5%	26.0%	28.0%	22.5%	100.0%

[a] Unit sales expected to grow by 5% over 1997.

ing year, as is shown in Exhibit 10.4. Sales targets include adjustments, by quarter, to provide for seasonal demand. Unit sales are expected to grow at a moderate rate of 5 percent per year, reflecting the mature nature of the yogurt product line.

Production Budget. Each quarter's production schedule, or production budget, shown in Exhibit 10.5, is derived directly from the sales budget. Adjustments in production will be made in order to reflect management's desire to increase or decrease existing inventory levels. The desired level of one quarter's ending finished-goods inventory then becomes the beginning inventory of the next quarter. HealthFirst Yogurt's use of the latest technology now enables it to custom-tailor production orders and reduce the need for storage. Consequently, desired inventory levels are expected to be maintained at a 2-day supply, the minimum level of inventory considered acceptable by management

Budgeted Materials Cost per Unit. The budgeted materials cost per unit is shown in Exhibit 10.6. Three direct materials are needed in order to produce the yogurt: (1) containers, (2) whole milk, and (3) fresh fruit. The small amount of active dairy culture used to make yogurt is borrowed and

EXHIBIT 10.5 HEALTHFIRST YOGURT CO.

Production Budget, in Units, for 1997

	Reference	1	2	3	4	Total
				Quarter		
Budgeted sales in units:	Exh. 10.4	1,204,375	1,332,500	1,435,000	1,153,125	5,125,000
Plus desired ending inventory in units[a]		29,286	31,196	25,068	28,102	28,102
Total unit needs		1,233,661	1,363,696	1,460,068	1,181,227	5,153,102
Less beginning inventory in units	Exh. 10.11	26,764	29,286	31,196	25,068	26,764
Budgeted production in units		1,206,897	1,334,410	1,428,872	1,156,159	5,126,338

[a] Inventory needs based on carrying levels of 2 days' inventory for the next quarter: 29,286 units = (2 days/91 days) × (1,332,500 units).

EXHIBIT 10.6 HEALTHFIRST YOGURT CO.

Budgeted Materials Cost per Unit for 1997

	Budgeted Cost	Need per Unit	Cost per Unit
Item description:			
Container	$0.026 each	1	$0.0260
Whole milk	$2.650 gal	2/3 cup	0.1104
Fresh fruit	$1.850 lb	1/2 oz	0.0578
			$0.1942

replenished from the finished-goods inventory, so it is not accounted for as a direct cost. Nor does the accounting system trace the use of water, which is treated as part of overhead.

Direct Materials Purchases Budget. Purchases of each raw materials item must be adjusted for levels of inventory desired at the end of each quarter. This is shown in the **direct materials purchases budget** (Exhibit 10.7). Thus, we find that desired ending containers inventory is expected to run at 20 percent of the next quarter's production. Carrying such a large containers inventory is costly in terms of storage space and working-capital needs. But management maintains large supplies in order to earn quantity discounts and to avoid stockout problems. No inventory is carried for whole milk and fresh fruit, because suppliers deliver them daily.

EXHIBIT 10.7 HEALTHFIRST YOGURT CO.

Direct Materials Purchases Budget for 1997

		Quarter				
	Reference	*1*	*2*	*3*	*4*	*Total*
Number of containers						
@ 1 per unit of output:						
Containers needed for production	Exh. 10.5	1,206,897	1,334,410	1,428,872	1,156,159	5,126,338
Add desired ending inventory[a]		266,882	285,774	231,232	253,448	253,448
Total needed		1,473,779	1,620,184	1,660,104	1,409,607	5,379,787
Less beginning inventory[b]		241,379	266,882	285,774	231,232	241,379
Required purchases		1,232,399	1,353,302	1,374,330	1,178,376	5,138,407
Cost per container		$ 0.026	$ 0.026	$ 0.026	$ 0.026	$ 0.026
Total cost of purchases		$ 32,042	$ 35,186	$ 35,733	$ 30,638	$ 133,599
Gal. of whole milk (no inventory)						
@ ⅔ cup per unit						
Gallons needed for production[c]		50,287	55,600	59,536	48,173	213,597
Cost per gallon		$ 2.65	$ 2.65	$ 2.65	$ 2.65	$ 2.65
Total cost of purchases		$ 133,262	$ 147,341	$ 157,771	$ 127,659	$ 566,033
Lbs. of fresh fruit (no inventory)						
@ ½ oz. per unit						
Pounds needed for production[d]		37,716	41,700	44,652	36,130	160,198
Cost per pound		$ 1.85	$ 1.85	$ 1.85	$ 1.85	$ 1.85
Total cost of purchases		$ 69,774	$ 77,146	$ 82,607	$ 66,840	$ 296,366
Total direct materials purchases		$ 235,078	$ 259,673	$ 276,111	$ 225,137	$ 995,998

[a] The ending containers inventory is 20% of the next quarter's production: 266,882 containers = 0.20 × 1,334,410 containers (see Exhibit 10.5).

[b] Container beginning inventory is 20% of current qtr production: 241,379 = (0.20) (1,206,897).

[c] One gallon of whole milk is based on 16 cups per gal: 50,287 gal = ⅔ cup/unit yogurt × 1/16 cups/gal × 1,206,897 units.

[d] An ounce of fresh fruit is based on 16 oz per lb: 37,716 lb = 0.5 oz/unit yogurt × 1/16 oz/lb × 1,206,897 units.

Human Resource Budget. A human resource budget (Exhibit 10.8) is prepared along the lines of the three responsibility centers constituting the yogurt division. The budget includes both base pay (and commission for sales staff) and a direct charge for payroll tax and benefits expense. The latter includes legislated employer costs (such as workers' compensation, unemployment compensation, and social security, or FICA, taxes) and company benefits (such as health and life insurance, and pension benefits). The human resource needs of each responsibility center are reviewed by top management early, as the budget is developed. Later, lower-level managers incorporate the new, approved human resource positions into their individual responsibility center budgets.

Budgeted Cost of Goods Manufactured. The production manager summarizes all costs charged to the production department in the budgeted cost of goods manufactured schedule (Exhibit 10.9). The cost of goods manufactured is equal to the production cost of the current period—comprising materials, labor, and overhead—adjusted for changes in work in process. For HealthFirst Yogurt there is no such adjustment, because it does not maintain any work-in-process inventory. Notice in Exhibit 10.9

EXHIBIT 10.8 HEALTHFIRST YOGURT CO.

Human Resource Budget for 1997

	Number	Base	Commission	Payroll Tax, Benefits	Total
Production:					
Plant manager[a]	1.0	$ 85,000		$ 23,800	$108,800
Direct labor[b]	5.0	132,000		31,680	163,680
Materials handling[b]	1.0	23,100		5,544	28,644
Maintenance[b,c]	1.5	36,850		8,844	45,694
Purchasing, shipping, & receiving[b,c]	1.5	34,650		8,316	42,966
Sales:					
Sales manager[a,e]	1.0	45,000	$28,188	20,493	93,680
Salespersons[b,e]	2.0	40,000	28,188	16,365	84,553
Secretary[b]	1.0	16,000		3,840	19,840
Administration & finance:					
President[d]	1.0	125,000		43,750	168,750
Controller[a]	1.0	75,000		21,000	96,000
Clerical worker[b]	1.0	15,000		3,600	18,600
Secretary[b]	1.0	20,000		4,800	24,800
	18.0	$647,600	$56,375	$192,032	$896,007

[a] Payroll tax and benefits @ 28% × (base + commission).

[b] Payroll tax and benefits @ 24%.

[c] 1.5 employees includes one full-time and one half-time worker.

[d] Payroll tax and benefits @ 35%.

[e] Sales commissions @ 1% of sales revenue.

EXHIBIT 10.9   HEALTHFIRST YOGURT CO.

Budgeted Cost of Goods Manufactured, 1997 (No Work in Process)

		Quarter					Fixed Cost per Quarter	Variable Cost per Unit	Activity Base
	Reference	1	2	3	4	Total			
Direct materials usage[a]	Exh. 10.6	$234,415	$259,181	$277,529	$224,560	$ 995,684		$0.1942	Units produced
Direct labor[b]	Exh. 10.8	40,920	40,920	40,920	40,920	163,680	40,920		
Total		275,335	300,101	318,449	265,480	1,159,364			
Manufacturing overhead:									
Plant manager[b]	Exh. 10.8	27,200	27,200	27,200	27,200	108,800	27,200		
Materials handling[b]	Exh. 10.8	7,161	7,161	7,161	7,161	28,644	7,161		
Repair & maintenance payroll[b]	Exh. 10.8	11,424	11,424	11,424	11,424	45,694	11,424		
Purchasing, shipping, & receiving[b]	Exh. 10.8	10,742	10,742	10,742	10,742	42,966	10,742		
Insurance		8,000	8,000	8,000	8,000	32,000	8,000		
Supplies, parts, & tools		12,741	13,506	14,073	12,437	52,758	5,500	0.0060	Units produced
Power & water		26,172	28,251	29,791	25,345	109,559	6,500	0.0163	Units produced
Depreciation—factory		9,500	9,500	9,500	9,500	38,000	9,500		
Depreciation—machinery		20,500	20,500	20,500	20,500	82,000	20,500		
Total manufacturing overhead		133,440	136,283	138,390	132,308	540,421	$147,446		
Total cost of goods manufactured		$408,774	$436,385	$456,839	$397,788	$1,699,786		$0.2165	Units produced

[a] $234,415 = 1,206,897 units (from Exhibit 10.5) × $0.19422917 (rounded here to $0.1942).

[b] Quarterly payroll cost = annual payroll cost (from Exhibit 10.8) divided by 4: $40,920 = $163,680/4.

that we have already determined from previous schedules the unit production costs for materials (Exhibit 10.6) and total human resource cost (Exhibit 10.8). Overhead costs for items such as insurance, power and water, and depreciation will be detailed in Exhibit 10.9. Information showing expected variable cost and fixed cost is provided on the right-hand panel of the schedule.

Budgeted Cost per Unit Manufactured.   The budgeted cost per unit manufactured (Exhibit 10.10) for the year equals the total cost of goods manufactured divided by the total number of units budgeted for production (from Exhibit 10.5). We need this unit cost to determine the budgeted cost of goods sold.

Budgeted Cost of Goods Sold.   The budgeted cost of goods sold is shown in Exhibit 10.11. HealthFirst Yogurt expects to add 1,338 units to its finished-goods inventory by year-end. Assuming HealthFirst uses a LIFO (last-in, first-out) cost flow, it will determine the value of this new inventory layer by using the unit cost for the most recent time period. Thus, Health-First's ending finished goods is composed of two layers: 26,764 units carried over from 1996 at the beginning unit cost of $0.315 and 1,338 units added in 1997 at the unit cost of $0.332.

Sales Department Expense Budget.   The sales manager prepares a sales department expense budget (Exhibit 10.12) on a quarterly basis. As with the production department budget, human resource costs for this department are taken from the human resource budget (Exhibit 10.8). Additional operating expenses (which include such items as advertising, shipping costs, and travel) complete the sales department budget. As shown on the right-hand panel of this exhibit, all costs are fixed, except for variable payroll costs and shipping.

EXHIBIT 10.10   HEALTHFIRST YOGURT CO.

Budgeted Cost per Unit Manufactured

	Reference	
Direct materials	Exh. 10.9	$ 995,684
Direct labor	Exh. 10.9	163,680
Manufacturing overhead	Exh. 10.9	540,421
Total cost of goods manufactured		$1,699,786
Units produced	Exh. 10.5	5,126,338
Budgeted cost per unit		$ 0.332[a]

[a] $0.332 is rounded for ease of illustration. The exact budgeted cost per unit is $0.331579, which will be used for calculating inventory and cost of goods sold.

EXHIBIT 10.11   HEALTHFIRST YOGURT CO.

Budgeted Cost of Goods Sold (LIFO Cost Flow)

	Reference	Units	Unit Cost	Inventory Layers	Total Cost
Beginning finished goods[a]	Exh. 10.18	26,764	$0.315		$ 8,431
Cost of goods manufactured	Exh. 10.10	5,126,338	$0.332[c]		1,699,786
Available		5,153,102			$1,708,216
Ending finished goods[b]		26,764	$0.315	$8,431	
		1,338	$0.332[c]	444	
		28,102			8,874
Cost of goods sold		5,125,000			$1,699,342

[a] Beginning finished goods is taken from the December 31, 1996, balance sheet (Exhibit 10.18).

[b] The added layer of ending inventory, 1,338 units, is costed at current unit cost, $0.332, using the LIFO cost-flow method.

[c] The exact unit cost used for calculation is $0.331579.

What we need to realize is that many selling costs are discretionary in nature. It is impossible to link discretionary expenses, such as advertising and travel, directly to income—that is, as a cause that affects income. Nonetheless, this is an inferential relationship. The sales manager should be able to justify these expenses as having effects that will add to sales value. (See "Current Practice: Determining a Marketing Budget.")

Administration and Finance Department Expense Budget.   The **administration department expense budget** is shown in Exhibit 10.13. The department is under the direction of the division president. Administration and finance payroll expense is taken from the human resource budget (Exhibit 10.8). Administrative operating expenses—such as travel, rent, and supplies—are all considered fixed. As in the case of the sales department, the activities and costs of administration and finance are largely discretionary.

Budgeted Income Statement.   The budget schedules prepared thus far are the building blocks for the quarterly **budgeted income statement**, shown in Exhibit 10.14. The sales manager provided a budget that includes commitments for sales revenue and sales expense. The production manager budgeted production costs and the cost of goods sold. The division president submitted the administration and finance budget. Combining these budgets results in a quarterly budget for operating income before interest and taxes.

To complete the income statement, we need the quarterly interest expense, which we will calculate later in the quarterly budget for cash receipts and payments. We will see next that, in order to budget cash flows, we must rely on information contained in the income statement. Thus, there is a simultaneous need for information to calculate budgeted income and to calculate cash flows.

EXHIBIT 10.12   HEALTHFIRST YOGURT CO.

Sales Department Expense Budget for 1997

	Reference	Quarter 1	Quarter 2	Quarter 3	Quarter 4	Total	Fixed Costs per Quarter	Variable Costs	Activity Base
Sales payroll:									
Sales manager[a,b]	Exh. 10.8	$ 22,879	$ 23,781	$ 24,502	$ 22,518	$ 93,680	$14,400	1.28%	Sales revenue
Salespersons[a,b]	Exh. 10.8	20,614	21,488	22,187	20,264	84,553	12,400	1.24%	Sales revenue
Secretary[a]	Exh. 10.8	4,960	4,960	4,960	4,960	19,840	4,960		
Advertising		33,000	37,000	40,000	30,000	140,000	Seasonal		
Shipping cost		15,055	16,656	17,938	14,414	64,063		$0.0125	Units sold
Travel		5,000	5,000	5,000	5,000	20,000	5,000		
Facility rent		2,400	2,400	2,400	2,400	9,600	2,400		
Supplies & utilities		775	775	775	775	3,100	775		
Depreciation—furniture & fixtures		600	600	600	600	2,400	600		
Total selling expense		$105,282	$112,660	$118,362	$100,931	$437,235	$40,535 + advertising		
Budgeted cash payments:[c]									
Total selling expense		$105,282	$112,660	$118,362	$100,931	$437,235			
Less noncash expense:									
Depreciation—furniture & fixtures		600	600	600	600	2,400			
Sales department payments		$104,682	$112,060	$117,762	$100,331	$434,835			

[a] Quarterly fixed payroll cost equals annual fixed payroll cost (Exhibit 10.8) divided by 4: $14,400 = ($45,000 × 1.28)/4.

[b] Variable payroll cost equals 1% (plus payroll tax, fringe benefits) times sales revenue, where 1.28% = 1% × 1.28.

[c] For later use in budgeted cash receipts and payments (Exhibit 10.17).

CURRENT PRACTICE

Determining a Marketing Budget

The marketing budget for Altschuler, Melvoin, and Glasser, a CPA firm, ranges from 2 to 2.5 percent of gross revenue, based on a company guideline. Budget approval, however, is not automatic, and the firm's partners demand a cost-benefit analysis of marketing and media programs. Marketing has responded by tracking every form of output available, such as seminars, speaking engagements, articles published, and newsletters. The firm's budget objective is to try to link revenue with specific marketing efforts. In some areas, such as public relations, the link evolves only over the long term and is generally impossible to identify in the short term. Still, the director of marketing contends that tracking the number of articles placed or times mentioned in the media builds a case that marketing efforts are improving the firm's reputation. Other marketing costs, such as telemarketing or direct mail, can be more closely connected with new business generated.

Source: Fern Lentini, "Accounting for Marketing Success," *Journal of Accountancy,* Mar. 1993, pp. 44–48.

EXHIBIT 10.13 HEALTHFIRST YOGURT CO.

Administration and Finance Department Expense Budget for 1997

		Quarter					Fixed Costs
	Reference	1	2	3	4	Total	per Quarter
Administration & finance payroll:							
President[a]	Exh. 10.8	$42,188	$42,188	$42,188	$42,188	$168,750	$42,188
Controller[a]	Exh. 10.8	24,000	24,000	24,000	24,000	96,000	24,000
Clerical worker[a]	Exh. 10.8	4,650	4,650	4,650	4,650	18,600	4,650
Secretary[a]	Exh. 10.8	6,200	6,200	6,200	6,200	24,800	6,200
Travel		2,500	2,500	2,500	2,500	10,000	2,500
Facility rent		2,400	2,400	2,400	2,400	9,600	2,400
Supplies & utilities		850	850	850	850	3,400	850
Depreciation—furniture & fixtures		900	900	900	900	3,600	900
Total administrative expense		$83,688	$83,688	$83,688	$83,688	$334,750	$83,688
Budgeted cash payments:							
Total administrative expense		$83,688	$83,688	$83,688	$83,688	$334,750	
Less noncash expense: Depreciation—furniture & fixtures		900	900	900	900	3,600	
Administrative dept. payments		$82,788	$82,788	$82,788	$82,788	$331,150	

[a] Quarterly payroll cost equals annual payroll cost (Exhibit 10.8) divided by 4: $42,188 = $168,750/4.

EXHIBIT 10.14   HEALTHFIRST YOGURT CO.

Budgeted Income Statement for the Year Ending December 31, 1997

		Quarter				
	Reference	1	2	3	4	Total
Sales revenue	Exh. 10.4	$662,406	$732,875	$789,250	$634,219	$2,818,750
Cost of goods sold[a]	Exh. 10.11	399,345	441,829	475,816	382,352	1,699,342
Gross margin		$263,061	$291,046	$313,434	$251,867	$1,119,408
Selling expense	Exh. 10.12	105,282	112,660	118,362	100,931	437,235
Administrative expense	Exh. 10.13	83,688	83,688	83,688	83,688	334,750
Operating income preinterest, pretax		$ 74,091	$ 94,699	$111,385	$ 67,248	$ 347,423
Interest expense[b]	Exh. 10.17	23,265	23,265	21,200	21,200	88,930
Income pretax		$ 50,826	$ 71,434	$ 90,185	$ 46,048	$ 258,493
Income tax @ 34%		17,281	24,288	30,663	15,656	87,888
Net income		$ 33,545	$ 47,146	$ 59,522	$ 30,392	$ 170,605

[a]   Cost of goods sold equals units sold times $0.332 unit cost (rounded): $399,345 = 1,204,375 × $0.331579 (Exhibit 10.10).

[b]   Interest is calculated in budgeted cash receipts and payments (Exhibit 10.17).

Budgeted Cash Collections.   The first step in budgeting for cash receipts (and for cash payments, as we'll see next) is to determine the timing of collections from sales. HealthFirst Yogurt bases its collections on a 30-day lag from the time of sale (because of the 30-day credit terms it offers all customers). The accounts receivable balance at the end of a quarter represents credit sales from the last month of the quarter.

Projecting the effects of collection time lags can be especially important to firms such as HealthFirst, which are affected by seasonal sales fluctuations. According to the budgeted cash collections schedule (Exhibit 10.15), managers should be aware that cash collections will fall short of sales revenue—by about $20,000 or more—in each of the first three quarters of 1997.

Budgeted Cash Payments for Direct Materials Purchases.   The budgeted cash payments for direct materials (Exhibit 10.16) follows a format similar to that used for cash collections. HealthFirst's purchases are all based on credit payment terms of 30 days. The accounts payable balance at the end of a quarter represents credit purchases during the last month of the quarter.

Note the cash excesses during the first three quarters, as budgeted payments are about $4,000 to $8,000 less each quarter than purchases on account. Nonetheless, this cash payment advantage fails to make up for the firm's shortfall in quarterly cash collection.

Budgeted Cash Receipts and Payments.   The budgeted cash receipts and payments schedule (Exhibit 10.17) summarizes the firm's cash receipts and

---

EXHIBIT 10.15 HEALTHFIRST YOGURT CO.

Budgeted Cash Collections for the Year Ending December 31, 1997

	Reference	Quarter 1	2	3	4	Total
Beginning accounts receivable[a]	Exh. 10.18	$201,339	$220,802	$ 244,292	$263,083	$ 201,339
Plus sales on account	Exh. 10.4	662,406	732,875	789,250	634,219	2,818,750
Total amount receivable		863,745	953,677	1,033,542	897,302	3,020,089
Less ending accounts receivable[b]		220,802	244,292	263,083	211,406	211,406
Budgeted collections		$642,943	$709,385	$770,458	$685,896	$2,808,683

[a] Quarter 1 beginning accounts receivable is taken from December 31, 1996, balance sheet (Exhibit 10.18).

[b] Ending accounts receivable is based on 1-month collection terms: $220,802 = $662,406/3 mo (Exhibit 10.4).

EXHIBIT 10.16 HEALTHFIRST YOGURT CO.

Budgeted Cash Payments for Direct Materials Purchases for the Year Ending December 31, 1997

	Reference	Quarter 1	2	3	4	Total
Beginning accounts payable[a]	Exh. 10.18	$ 74,636	$ 78,359	$ 86,558	$ 92,037	$ 74,636
Plus purchases on account	Exh. 10.6	235,078	259,673	276,111	225,137	995,998
Total amount payable		$309,714	$338,032	$362,668	$317,174	$1,070,634
Less ending accounts payable[b]		78,359	86,558	92,037	75,046	75,046
Budgeted cash payments		$231,354	$251,474	$270,631	$242,128	$ 995,588

[a] Quarter 1 accounts payable is taken from December 31, 1996, balance sheet (Exhibit 10.18).

[b] Ending accounts payable is based on 1-month payment terms: $75,046 = $225,137/3 mo (Exhibit 10.7).

---

payments for each quarter. The detail in the schedule can be resolved into the following simplified format:

> **Beginning cash**
> *Plus or minus* cash from operations
> *Plus or minus* cash for nonoperating needs (investments, financing)
> *Equals* **cash excess or deficiency**
> *Plus or minus* short-term financing
> *Equals* **ending cash**

This format contains the same information given in the traditional end-of-period statement of cash flows. However, this chart is prepared in a way that helps managers easily plan for short-term financing.

Referring again to the exhibit, we find data for cash receipts and cash payments for operating activities taken from previous exhibits. Nonoperating cash items include preplanned investments and financing—for example, the $60,000 equipment investment in quarter 4, which was approved

EXHIBIT 10.17 HEALTHFIRST YOGURT CO.

Budgeted Cash Receipts and Payments for the Year Ending December 31, 1997

	Reference	Quarter 1	2	3	4	Total
Beginning Cash[a]	Exh. 10.18	$ 45,000	$ 20,074	$ 44,389	$140,870	$ 45,000
Cash from operations:						
Cash collection from sales	Exh. 10.15	642,943	709,385	770,458	685,896	2,808,683
Cash payments from operations:						
Production department:						
Raw materials purchases	Exh. 10.16	$ 231,354	$251,474	$270,631	$242,128	$ 995,588
Direct labor	Exh. 10.9	40,920	40,920	40,920	40,920	163,680
Manufacturing overhead						
Plant manager	Exh. 10.9	27,200	27,200	27,200	27,200	108,800
Materials handling	Exh. 10.9	7,161	7,161	7,161	7,161	28,644
Repair & maintenance payroll	Exh. 10.9	11,424	11,424	11,424	11,424	45,694
Purchasing, shipping, & receiving	Exh. 10.9	10,742	10,742	10,742	10,742	42,966
Insurance[b]	Exh. 10.9	16,000	0	16,000	0	32,000
Supplies, parts, tools	Exh. 10.9	12,741	13,506	14,073	12,437	52,758
Power & water	Exh. 10.9	26,172	28,251	29,791	25,345	109,559
Sales department payments	Exh. 10.12	104,682	112,060	117,762	100,331	434,835
Administrative dept. payments	Exh. 10.13	82,788	82,788	82,788	82,788	331,150
Estimated income tax payments[c]	Exh. 10.14	12,420	17,281	24,288	30,663	84,651
Total payments from operations		$ 583,604	$602,806	$652,778	$591,139	$2,430,326
Net cash from operations		$ 59,339	$106,580	$117,681	$ 94,757	$ 378,357
Cash for nonoperating needs:						
Purchase of yogurt packing equipment[d]					(60,000)	(60,000)
Pay beg-of-yr installment on long-term debt[e]		(120,000)				(120,000)
Interest payments						
Notes payable at 12%[f]		(4,200)	(4,200)	(4,200)	(4,200)	(16,800)
Long-term debt at 10%[g]		(17,000)	(17,000)	(17,000)	(17,000)	(68,000)
Total cash for nonoperating needs		$(141,200)	$ (21,200)	$ (21,200)	$ (81,200)	$ (264,800)
Cash excess or deficiency		$ (36,861)	$105,454	$140,870	$154,427	$ 158,557
Short-term financing (at 14%)[h]		59,000	(59,000)			
Interest payment for short-term financing[i]		(2,065)	(2,065)			(4,130)
Ending cash (minimum = $20,000)		$ 20,074	$ 44,389	$140,870	$154,427	$ 154,427

[a] Quarter 1 beginning cash taken from December 31, 1996, balance sheet (Exhibit 10.18).

[b] Insurance premiums paid semiannually.

[c] Income tax payments for quarter 1 equals December 31, 1996, tax payable on balance sheet (Exhibit 10.18); Tax payments for quarters 2 through 4 equal budgeted tax expense from end of previous quarter (Exhibit 10.14).

[d] Capital budget purchases approved during long-term planning.

[e] Maturing long-term debt requires January 1, 1997, payment.

[f] Interest payment based on notes payable is taken from December 31, 1996, balance sheet (Exhibit 10.18): $4,200 = 0.12 \times (3/12) \times \$140,000$.

[g] Interest payment based on long-term debt at December 31, 1996, is taken from balance sheet (Exhibit 10.18) less January 1, 1997, payment (per note e): $17,000 = 0.10 \times (3/12) \times (\$800,000 - \$120,000)$.

[h] Short-term financing is needed to maintain $20,000 minimum ending cash and is available in increments of $1,000.

[i] Interest payments at 14% are made at end of each quarter: $2,065 = 0.14 \times (3/12) \times \$59,000$.

during the long-range planning process. The yogurt division plans to pay off a portion of its maturing long-term debt ($120,000) in quarter 1. Also scheduled are quarterly interest payments on notes payable ($4,200) and on remaining long-term debt ($17,000).

When quarterly cash flows are added algebraically, the result is a quarterly excess or a quarterly deficiency. HealthFirst's management decides it must have an end-of-quarter minimum cash balance of $20,000 in order to meet its payroll and working-capital needs. Short-term financing, available in multiples of $1,000, may be necessary to make up any shortfalls. In quarter 1, for example, we find that the firm must plan to secure a loan for $59,000 on January 1. Thus, it will pay additional end-of-quarter interest ($2,065). In quarter 2, the budget shows a cash excess ($105,454) that will enable the firm to pay off its short-term loan and quarterly interest, while providing it with an ending cash balance of $44,389.

Balance Sheets.   The firm's financial position at the beginning of the current budget year is shown on the beginning balance sheet in Exhibit 10.18. The budgeted balance sheet for the end of the year is shown in Exhibit 10.19. The budgeted balance sheet incorporates all the budget changes projected in Exhibits 10.4 through 10.17. A budgeted balance sheet generally contains less-meaningful information than is contained in the budgeted income statement and budgeted cash receipts and payments schedule. Nonetheless, projection of the financial ratios it provides, such as return on investment and debt to equity, can reveal obscured but significant insights.

Budgeted Statement of Cash Flows.   We close our analysis of HealthFirst Yogurt's profit plan with the budgeted statement of cash flows (Exhibit 10.20), which was prepared in conformance with the generally accepted

---

EXHIBIT 10.18   HEALTHFIRST YOGURT CO.

Beginning Balance Sheet (Historic Data) December 31, 1996

Assets			Liabilities		
Cash		$ 45,000	Accounts payable		$ 74,636
Accounts receivable		201,339	Income tax payable		12,420
Inventory:			Notes payable, 12%		140,000
Raw materials[a]	$ 6,276		Long-term debt, 10%		800,000
Finished goods[b]	8,431				$1,027,056
Total inventory		14,706	*Shareholder equity*		
Production machinery (net)	750,000				
Furniture & fixtures (net)	48,000		Common stock	$900,000	
Factory (net)	830,000		Retained earnings	51,989	
Land	90,000				951,989
Total plant		1,718,000			
		$1,979,045			$1,979,045

[a] Containers: $6,276 = 241,379 × $.026 (Exhibit 10.7).

[b] See Exhibit 10.11.

EXHIBIT 10.19 HEALTHFIRST YOGURT CO.

Budgeted Balance Sheet December 31, 1997

Reference	Assets			Reference	Liabilities		
Exh. 10.17	Cash		$ 154,427	Exh. 10.16	Accounts payable		$ 75,046
Exh. 10.15	Accounts receivable		211,406	Exh. 10.14	Income tax payable		15,656
	Inventory:				Notes payable, 12%		140,000
	Raw materials[a]	$ 6,590			Long-term debt, 10%[e]		680,000
Exh. 10.11	Finished goods	8,874					$ 910,702
	Total inventory		15,464				
	Prod. machinery (net)[b]	$728,000			*Shareholder equity*		
	Furniture & fixtures (net)[c]	42,000					
	Factory (net)[d]	792,000			Common stock	$900,000	
	Land	90,000			Retained earnings[f]	222,595	1,122,595
	Total plant		1,652,000				
			$2,033,297				$2,033,297

[a] Containers: $6,590 = 253,448 × $.026 (Exhibit 10.7).

[b] $728,000 = $750,000 (Exhibit 10.18) + $60,000 (Exhibit 10.17) − $82,000 (Exhibit 10.9).

[c] $42,000 = $48,000 (Exhibit 10.18) − $2,400 (Exhibit 10.12) − $3,600 (Exhibit 10.13).

[d] $792,000 = $830,000 (Exhibit 10.18) − $38,000 (Exhibit 10.9).

[e] $680,000 = $800,000 (Exhibit 10.18) − $120,000 (Exhibit 10.17).

[f] $222,595 = $51,989 (Exhibit 10.18) + $170,605 (Exhibit 10.14)—rounding.

accounting principles (GAAP) format used for published statements. The change to cash ($109,427) agrees with the change to cash in the budget for cash receipts and payments [Exhibit 10.17—ending cash ($154,427) − beginning cash ($45,000) = $109,427]. The budgeted statement of cash flows in Exhibit 10.20 reorganizes cash changes by the type of organizational activity—operations, investing, and financing—making it more useful to investors and creditors outside the firm as a tool for identifying long-term patterns.

PLAN APPROVAL AND ADDITIONAL RECYCLING

After the HealthFirst Yogurt division manager is satisfied with the budget, it is sent to the corporate budget director. If the expected outcome of a divisional budget is unsatisfactory with respect to contributing toward meeting corporate financial objectives, the corporate budget director returns the budget to the division, which must make changes to revenue, cost, or income targets. After all detailed division-level profit plans are reviewed and approved, they are integrated into the corporate plan.

TYPES OF COSTS

In deciding where and how to cut costs, managers must recognize that costs differ according to their cause-effect relationship to outcomes.

EXHIBIT 10.20 HEALTHFIRST YOGURT CO.

Budgeted Statement of Cash Flows for the Year Ending December 31, 1997

Reference			
	Cash from operations:		
	Net income		$170,605
	Add depreciation:		
Exh. 10.9	Factory	$38,000	
Exh. 10.9	Production machinery	82,000	
	Furniture & fixtures[a]	6,000	126,000
	Adjust for changes to current accounts:[b]		
	Increase to accounts receivable[c]	($10,067)	
	Increase to inventories[d]	(757)	
	Increase to accounts payable[e]	410	
	Increase to income taxes payable[f]	3,236	(7,179)
	Cash from operations		289,427
	Cash for investing:		
Exh. 10.17	Purchased production machinery		(60,000)
	Cash for financing:		
Exh. 10.17	Pay long-term debt		(120,000)
	Change to cash		$109,427

[a] $6,000 = $2,400 (Exhibit 10.12) + $3,600 (Exhibit 10.13).

[b] Increases to current asset accounts are deducted from net income to derive cash from operations; increases to current liabilities are added. For more information, refer to a financial accounting text that covers the fundamentals of the statement of cash flows.

[c] $(10,067) = $201,339 (Exhibit 10.18) − $211,406 (Exhibit 10.19).

[d] $(757) rounded = $14,706 (Exhibit 10.18) − $15,464 (Exhibit 10.19).

[e] $410 = $75,046 (Exhibit 10.19) − $74,636 (Exhibit 10.18).

[f] $3,236 = $15,656 (Exhibit 10.19) − $12,420 (Exhibit 10.18).

Engineered Costs. Some budgeted costs are largely determined by levels of expected activity. These are called *engineered costs*. In the purest case, engineering specifications prescribe the relationship between cost inputs and product or service outputs. For example, each 8-ounce cup of HealthFirst Yogurt requires ⅔ cup of whole milk, budgeted at $2.65 per gallon. Some other engineered costs, such as power and water, are based on less precise input-output connections and might have both variable and fixed components. When looking for ways to reduce budget costs, managers will have great difficulty cutting engineered costs—other than seeking changes in the operations process or its component parts.

Discretionary Costs. Some budgeted costs show no clear relationship between cost inputs and product or service outputs. These are *discretionary*, or *managed*, *costs*. They include the costs of most activities in general administration and sales, plus many indirect production costs. For example, virtually all items included in HealthFirst Yogurt's sales department budget might be considered discretionary, except for shipping cost.

The division manager exercises judgment in deciding upon levels of spending. As might be expected, discretionary costs are prime candidates for cutting when budgets are rejected and returned for revision. Alas, cutting some costs (e.g., research and development or maintenance) can help the firm meet its short-term profit goals but will pose a hazard to its long-term strategies.

Committed Costs.   Fixed costs that are part of a responsibility center's long-range plan are considered **committed costs**. For example, the yogurt division's investment in advanced manufacturing technology resulted in a machinery depreciation charge of $82,000 (Exhibit 10.9). Similarly, the $108,800 compensation for the plant manager is a committed expense, since it cannot be eliminated or reduced without a change in plan. When searching the budget for costs to cut, subunit managers do not have the option of reducing such costs. A contemplated cut in committed costs requires reevaluation of the responsibility center's strategic objectives or operational processes and is also subject to capital-budgeting analysis.

SENSITIVITY ANALYSIS

Because a budget represents linkages between resources consumed and results achieved, it can serve as a tool for a sensitivity analysis of the effect of changes in budgeting assumptions. The idea here is to show how sensitive changes in results (meaning *profit*) are to changes in inputs (meaning costs of *resources*). Assume HealthFirst Yogurt was targeted to meet a 9.0 percent *return on assets* (ROA), defined as "net income divided by beginning-of-year book value." Unfortunately, its divisional profit plan reveals that the ROA is expected to be only 8.6 percent ($170,605/ $1,979,045).

Exhibit 10.21 shows three alternative *what-if* approaches for meeting the division's 9.0 percent ROA objective.

Alternative 1 indicates the effect of buying fresh fruit at a price lower than the $1.85 in the original budget. However, the high ($1.85) price reflects the firm's commitment to high quality and nontoxicity—by its purchase of domestic fruit, despite opportunities to buy third-world-imported fruits at a significant saving. If the firm were able to buy the same quality fruit at $1.78 per pound (while maintaining its asset investment of $1,979,045), the exhibit reveals that the ROA would increase to the 9.0 percent goal.

Alternative 2 reduces the asset base. HealthFirst Yogurt's low ROA reflects a high book value, resulting from its recent investment in state-of-the-art food-processing equipment. A 9.0 percent ROA can be reached if assets are reduced by $80,000 (assuming a net income of $170,605 is maintained). Understanding this relationship can help management recognize the importance of reducing its investment in assets. For example, the firm might decide to initiate new policies to decrease investment in receivables and inventory or to eliminate idle equipment. This relationship also reveals how the passage of time affects the ROA, since HealthFirst will surpass a 9.0 percent ROA in the next year, once it reduces its asset base through depreciation ($126,000 budgeted this year, in Exhibit 10.20).

EXHIBIT 10.21 HEALTHFIRST YOGURT CO.

Sensitivity Analysis for Increasing Return on Assets

Objective: Earn 9.0% ROA for Budget Year, 1997
Current Budgeted ROA = 8.6%

Alternative 1—Effects of Cutting Fresh Fruit in Increments of $0.01

Fruit Cost	Net Income	Beginning-of-Year Assets	ROA
$1.85	$170,605	$1,979,045	8.6%
$1.84	171,662	1,979,045	8.7%
$1.83	172,719	1,979,045	8.7%
$1.82	173,776	1,979,045	8.8%
$1.81	174,833	1,979,045	8.8%
$1.80	175,891	1,979,045	8.9%
$1.79	176,948	1,979,045	8.9%
$1.78	178,005	1,979,045	9.0%
$1.77	179,062	1,979,045	9.0%

Alternative 2—Effects of Reducing Asset Base in Increments of $10,000

Net Income	Beginning Assets	ROA
$170,605	$1,979,045	8.6%
170,605	1,969,045	8.7%
170,605	1,959,045	8.7%
170,605	1,949,045	8.8%
170,605	1,939,045	8.8%
170,605	1,929,045	8.8%
170,605	1,919,045	8.9%
170,605	1,909,045	8.9%
170,605	1,899,045	9.0%

Alternative 3—Combined Effect on ROA of Reducing Cost of Fresh Fruit and Reducing Asset Base

Fruit Cost	$1,979,045	$1,969,045	$1,959,045	$1,949,045	$1,939,045	$1,929,045	$1,919,045	$1,909,045	$1,899,045
$1.85	8.6%	8.7%	8.7%	8.8%	8.8%	8.8%	8.9%	8.9%	9.0%
$1.84	8.7%	8.7%	8.8%	8.8%	8.9%	8.9%	9.0%	9.0%	9.0%
$1.83	8.7%	8.8%	8.8%	8.9%	8.9%	9.0%	9.0%	9.0%	9.1%
$1.82	8.8%	8.8%	8.9%	8.9%	9.0%	9.0%	9.1%	9.1%	9.2%
$1.81	8.8%	8.9%	8.9%	9.0%	9.0%	9.1%	9.1%	9.2%	9.2%
$1.80	8.9%	8.9%	9.0%	9.0%	9.1%	9.1%	9.2%	9.2%	9.3%
$1.79	8.9%	9.0%	9.0%	9.1%	9.1%	9.2%	9.2%	9.3%	9.3%
$1.78	9.0%	9.0%	9.1%	9.1%	9.2%	9.2%	9.3%	9.3%	9.4%
$1.77	9.0%	9.1%	9.1%	9.2%	9.2%	9.3%	9.3%	9.4%	9.4%

Assets

Alternative 3 assumes reductions both in fruit cost and in the asset base. The shaded area shows a wide range of combined decreases that result in an ROA of 9.0 percent or more. For example, if fruit is purchased for $1.82 (a $0.03 reduction) and assets are decreased to $1,939,045 (a $40,000 reduction), the firm earns 9.0 percent. This type of analysis discloses the interactions and trade-offs between two (or more) alternatives for reaching a goal.

CORRECTIVE ACTIONS

When a division's budget does not meet corporate expectations, three things can be done:

1. Managers can *change operations* by devising better ways to employ resources to deliver outcomes. For example, they might decide to use different materials or labor, or to reconfigure the production process.
2. Managers can *question the budget model* itself as an accurate portrayal of cause-effect relationships. Improvements to the model may be needed in order to enable them to predict more accurately the division's financial performance.
3. Managers may need to *reexamine goals and strategies.* Perhaps these are unrealistic and need revision.

Note that these are the same three possible corrective actions to be taken *after* receiving feedback on actual results (as discussed in Chapter 9).

The sensitivity analysis for HealthFirst Yogurt shows how a well-designed budget model can help managers plan corrective actions. Assume the budget model is accurate. We found, according to the model, that reductions in fruit cost or assets, or both, would offer viable operational changes that would enable the division to reach its financial objective of a 9.0 percent ROA. However, if such operational changes do not produce the ROA returns required, managers will need to reexamine long-term goals and strategies. For HealthFirst, this might involve such diverse options as looking for new types of products (e.g., frozen yogurt), new channels of distribution (e.g., food wholesalers), or a new geographic focus (e.g., Mexico).

BEHAVIORAL IMPLICATIONS

Having studied the technical aspects of budgeting, we now look at the budget as part of a *management control system*, whose fundamental purpose is to implement strategy. And good control enables employees to satisfy their personal goals while acting in the company's best interest—that is, it promotes *goal congruence.* Let's see how the budget helps, and hinders, the firm in its attempts to motivate employees to work together to achieve the corporate purpose.

PARTICIPATIVE BUDGETING[4]

We have seen that short-term operating plans need to accommodate long-term strategies. Corporate managers, who are concerned with the corporate environment and competition, develop the higher-level strategies that must take into account local market conditions. In developing a **participative budget,** corporate managers and division managers share information in a short-term plan that melds their differing outlooks.

ADVANTAGES

Researchers have found that participative budgeting improves communication and motivation among managers and employees at all levels. The process of sharing information up, down, and across the organization structure helps managers and employees understand their roles in achieving corporate goals. When budget changes are necessary, universal participation helps further companywide understanding of and commitment to the changes.

DEGREES OF PARTICIPATION

A *bottom-up* participative budget starts at the lowest-level responsibility centers, where each manager sets targets and functional strategies. A *top-down* budget starts at the corporate level, where senior management sets specific revenue and cost targets for responsibility centers. In turn, responsibility center managers are concerned with following the directives implied by the budget. Most budgets are neither totally bottom-up or top-down, but rather call for setting some targets at lower levels and having some targets set or revised by senior management. The extent of participation most useful for a firm depends on its own situation.[5] A firm having one or more of the following characteristics, for example, will likely steer toward a top-down budget:

- An autocratic team of top managers
- A small firm size, especially a firm run by an owner-manager
- An experience of economic crisis, especially where survival depends on cost cutting
- A supply-driven business, such as utilities or mining, which is more concerned with productivity than with market strategy

Given the dynamic markets we face today, we would expect less top-down and more participative budgeting by lower-level managers, who best understand their customers' needs.

---

[4] For further information see Edwin H. Caplan, *Management Accounting and Behavioral Science,* Reading, Mass.: Addison-Wesley, 1971; G. H. Hofstede, *The Game of Budget Control,* New York: Barnes & Noble, 1968; V. Bruce Irvine, "Budgeting: Functional Analysis and Behavioral Implications," in A. Rappaport, ed., *Information for Decision Making,* 3d. ed., Englewood Cliffs, N.J.: Prentice-Hall, 1982, pp. 192–207.

[5] P. Brownell, "Participation in the Budgeting Process: When It Works and When It Doesn't," *Journal of Accounting Literature,* no. 1, 1982, pp. 124–153; Frank Collins and John J. Willingham, "Contingency Management Approach to Budgeting," *Management Accounting,* Sept. 1977, pp. 45–48.

NECESSARY CONDITIONS

There are certain conditions that must exist in order for participation to be effective:

- The culture of the firm must support it. Managers and employees together must have a *positive attitude* toward company goals.
- Employees must perceive their *participation as real.* Lower-level managers will become resentful if they think their input is merely a mechanical exercise.
- Managers must believe the *result of participative budgeting is fair.* Corporate managers should avoid making what seem to be arbitrary changes to division managers' targets.

THE BUDGET: A SOURCE OF GAMESMANSHIP

Even if all conditions for successful participation are in place, budgets are often blamed for motivating behaviors that run counter to achievement of corporate goals. Managers depend on budget approvals in order to secure operating resources they need to meet their performance objectives. Managers are held responsible for meeting their targets and are compensated accordingly. These two considerations could partially explain why division managers—and corporate managers, as well—sometimes "play games" with the budget. (See "Current Practice: Budget Game Playing.")

IDENTIFYING PROBLEM AREAS

Here are some ways managers can more easily meet their budget targets.

Create Budget Slack.[6]   *Slack* is the deliberate underestimation of budgeted revenue or overestimation of budgeted costs. Managers create budget slack in their targets as they prepare their budgets. Subordinate managers don't mind slack, because it means they won't have to expend as much effort to reach performance expectations. However, budget slack means failing to control inefficiencies, and it can also cause problems elsewhere in the organization. Underestimated sales, for example, can result in companywide shortages in equipment, personnel, or supplies.

Avoid Paying for Resources.   Managers may take special efforts to evade charges for the resources they use, causing problems for managers of other responsibility centers. For example, the sales department may fight for enhanced product features, the cost of which will be charged to another department—say, production or R&D. Or a design group may avoid making needed quality enhancements by approving a project too early, in the hopes that the work still needed will be done at a later stage of development.

---

[6]   For more information see Michael Schiff and Arie Y. Lewin, "The Impact of People on Budgets," *Accounting Review,* Apr. 1970, pp. 259–268; and Kenneth A. Merchant, "Budgeting and the Propensity to Create Budget Slack," *Accounting, Organizations, and Society,* vol. 10, no. 2, 1985, pp. 201–210.

CURRENT PRACTICE

Budget Game Playing

Once a budget has been "committed to paper"—as they used to say in the days before computers and modems and faxes—it often becomes what *must be*, instead of a tool to help achieve what should be. Worse, managers may be motivated to do stupid things in order to meet their budget targets. One manager met his sales budget through "sales" to a fictitious company—he stored the goods in his basement and then returned them the next year. Another manager, who feared losing an unused expense authorization, prepaid consultants in December for work he wanted done the next year.

Budgets can also influence managers knowingly to make bad decisions, such as curtailing current expenses in their own departments even though it's clear that the expense reduction will mean higher costs later. For example, manufacturing might want long production runs for a new product in order to reduce setup cost. Marketing has no reason to oppose the longer runs, because more finished units guarantee product availability. When a senior corporate manager spots a growing inventory problem, he orders inventories of all finished goods cut by 25 percent. Then the older, popular items sell out, while the new, overproduced items accumulate. As a result, because inventory space is not available to store the more popular product, loyal customers must wait to buy it.

Source: Thomas A. Stewart, "Why Budgets Are Bad for Business," *Fortune,* June 4, 1990, p. 179.

Postpone Discretionary Costs. Some costs, such as maintenance and employee training, can be avoided in the current period without immediately jeopardizing sales. This technique is frequently used when cost overruns are imminent at year-end. Managers can impose freezes on spending, or they can shift budgeted costs to other, more-pressing categories in order to meet profit targets. Unfortunately, such cost reductions can often cost the firm more than is saved—especially in the long run—when delayed spending results in falling sales or causes extraordinary emergency expenditures.

Accelerate Year-End Spending. A manager who has resources that are budgeted but unspent at year-end may look for ways to spend these resources so that all the allotment is used. Cost center managers, who may want to justify inclusion of the same, or higher, budgeted costs for their centers in the following year's budget, often act this way. In fact, independent business consultants report they are besieged with late-autumn project requests from managers who are looking for ways to spend discretionary funds.

Accelerate Year-End Sales. Managers sometimes go to great effort to meet their targeted sales figures, even if it means the sales will be undone early in the new year. Sometimes, they sell to customers who have poor credit histories, or they cut prices too deeply. Or they may "sell" to distributors by promising to take back the goods when the new year starts. Often these tactics prove useless.

COUNTERING GAME-PLAYING BEHAVIOR

When it seems to managers that they are being measured by how well they meet the numbers in the budget rather than how well they are working toward achieving corporate strategies, then managers will play games with the budget. Here are some ways managers can be motivated to not play games.

Improve Superior-Subordinate Communication. The supervising manager should understand the lower-level manager's operation and environment. The time for the supervising manager to understand this is during early budget negotiations, so that the targets set for the subordinate manager are realistic and achievable.

Correct Cost Charging Systems. The accounting system should charge managers for the resources they consume. These costs can be charged using cost allocations or direct charges (discussed earlier in Chapters 3 and 4) or using transfer pricing (which will be covered in Chapter 14).

Broaden Evaluation Criteria. Managers who are evaluated and rewarded solely on budgeted financial results will tend to do all they can to meet their targets. This can motivate wrong behavior in the short term. A single measure of performance, such as profit, is easy to manipulate. Managers know this. Therefore they may be tempted to do so, making decisions that are not in the best interests of the organization.[7] The solution is to design evaluation systems that include more than one measure of financial performance (e.g., profit *and* cost reduction). Some would argue that the advantages of using multiple measures can be increased by including measures focused on the long term (e.g., 3-year sales growth) or on nonfinancial performance (e.g., quality, on-time delivery).

COMPARING ACTUAL RESULTS WITH THE BUDGET

The accounting system compiles and reports actual results and compares them to the budget. It is up to each manager to interpret differences between actual results and budget estimates in order to correct deficiencies and to eliminate their causes, as well as to learn from budgets whose targets were achieved. Hence, the budget is pivotal in the reporting-and-analysis and corrective-action phases of management control.

---

[7] V. F. Ridgway, "Dysfunctional Consequences of Performance Measurement," *Administrative Science Quarterly*, Sept. 1956, pp. 240–247.

We return to the HealthFirst Yogurt example and assume the budget year is now complete. The division manager has received the year-end report shown in Exhibit 10.22. The first column of data shows the actual results for the year. The center column shows the budgeted estimates, from the income statement (Exhibit 10.14).

REPORTING VARIANCES

The last column shows line-by-line dollar variances between actual results and the budget estimates. Note that each variance is designated either "F" for *favorable,* meaning actual data turned out to be more than the budget estimate, or "U" for *unfavorable,* meaning the opposite. Comparing actual to budget in this way is helpful to those who *manage by exception*—those who intervene only where there are *U*s and in such a way as to turn them into *F*s.

Looking down the variance column, we find that operating income (before interest and taxes) is $48,565 U. (It is unfavorable because actual income results were below the budget target.) The major cause is sales revenue, which resulted in a $58,750 U variance and echoes the 125,000-unit U variance in unit sales.

The difference between actual and budgeted cost of goods sold is $308 U, which indicates a small (unfavorable) production cost variance.

The variances for selling expense ($4,243 F) and for administrative expense ($6,250 F) show that both of these expense budgets were underspent, which contributes toward more income.

EXHIBIT 10.22 HEALTHFIRST YOGURT CO.

Profit Variance Analysis Based on Original Profit Plan for the Year Ending December 31, 1997

	Actual Results		Budget		Variance	
Unit sales	5,000,000		5,125,000		125,000	U
Units produced	5,000,000		5,126,338		126,338	U
Sales revenue[a]	$2,760,000	100.0%	$2,818,750	100.0%	$ 58,750	U
Cost of goods sold	1,699,650	61.6%	1,699,342	60.3%	308	U
Gross margin	$1,060,350	38.4%	$1,119,408	39.7%	$ 59,058	U
Selling expense[b]	432,992	15.7%	437,235	15.5%	4,243	F
Administrative expense	328,500	11.9%	334,750	11.9%	6,250	F
Operating income preinterest, pretax	$ 298,858	10.8%	$ 347,423	12.3%	$ 48,565	U

[a] $58,750 U means income decreased because actual sales revenue was less than that budgeted.

[b] $4,243 F means income increased because actual selling expense was less than that budgeted.

This report also displays each statement line item as a percent of sales. Here we find, for example, that the budgeted gross margin was 39.7 percent, but the actual margin was 38.4 percent. Despite its favorable dollar variance, selling expense as a percent of sales was estimated at 15.5 percent but turned out to be higher (15.7%). Administration expense, which also showed a favorable dollar variance, was budgeted at 11.9 percent of sales and came in at the same figure.

INTERPRETING VARIANCES

Using variances such as those shown in Exhibit 10.22, managers can gain some insight into overall results of the division and can identify potential problem areas. In the example, it is apparent that the drop in sales volume caused the division's income shortfall. And because the gross margin was budgeted at 39.7 percent but was lower, at 38.4% actual, the variance indicates some combination of sales price decrease and production inefficiencies. Both sales and administration report favorable dollar variances, suggesting operating efficiencies. These are basic conclusions, however. Management will need more-specific information in order to guide improvements.

SUMMARY

There are many different facets to a budget—and they all relate to management control.

The budget enables the firm to convert its long-term strategic plans into short-term targets for each responsibility center manager. It is also instrumental in coordinating actions among subunits, motivating managers toward achieving profit targets, and providing managers with signals for taking corrective action.

In this chapter, we examined the many calculations needed to prepare a budget. The beginning point is the sales budget, which is needed to plan the level of production. Then, resources must be committed. The budget specifies, in detail, the firm's need for human resources, raw materials, factory overhead, and sales and administrative support. The end result is a set of pro forma financial statements, the most important of which are the income statement and the statement of cash receipts and payments.

To ensure subordinate managers' commitment toward their budget targets, senior managers often use participative budgeting. Regardless of the amount of authority lower-level managers are given to prepare their budgets, senior management must approve targets and ensure that, when all subunit budgets are combined, the firm meets its corporate objectives.

Because of the importance often placed on achieving budget targets, subordinate managers may resort to undesirable behavior—such as creating budget slack or postponing discretionary expenditures—to ensure they "make their numbers." The firm can guard against such behavior by improving communication between levels of management, by correctly charging for resources consumed, and by broadening the criteria for evaluating performance.

Budgets are used for providing periodic feedback consisting of comparisons between targets and actual results. Such information is needed if management is to correct deficiencies and to learn from actions that lead to successful outcomes.

CHAPTER 10 ASSIGNMENTS

DISCUSSION PROBLEMS

D10.1　(Budget Process; Participative Budgeting)

Uniservo is an equipment maintenance company that has recently undergone a management buyout. The management team is replacing the centralized corporate financial control system with a responsibility accounting system that will increase overall participation in the budgeting process. The company is now segregated into three geographical profit centers: eastern, central, and western. Each center is responsible for the following:

- Obtaining new business and maintaining profitable contracts with older customers.
- Depreciating both existing and new assets. Included among the existing assets are technologically obsolete maintenance and repair parts that will continue to be depreciated until they are replaced. Depreciation expense is being assigned to profit centers in order to minimize the recurrence of this obsolescence problem. Furthermore, any new capital asset acquisitions must first be approved by the corporate staff.
- Recommending and implementing real estate changes, except where long-term leases are in effect. The majority of leases are annual; however, responsibility for the more costly, longer-term contracts has been assigned to the corporate real estate department. Property taxes are related to the real estate leases. All insurance is negotiated by the corporate insurance department in order to obtain the best national coverage at the most reasonable cost.

Each region's general manager, along with the subordinate managers, is required to develop an annual budget and submit it to the corporate staff for review and consolidation into an overall company budget. After undergoing the initial corporate review, the budgets are returned to the general managers, who then revise their submissions in order to reach corporate sales and profit objectives. For the coming year, the general managers and corporate staff have agreed on the corporate budget, which is presented in Exhibit D10.1.

Required:

1. Discuss why the revised budget process and the new regional breakdown are likely to receive the managers' support.
2. Which line-item accounts in the budget are managers likely to find objectionable? Explain how these particular items can be improved.

(CMA Adapted)

D10.2　(Game Playing with a University Cost Center's Budget)

Professor Carol Hammer is the chairperson of the 35-person English department at Colossal State University. One of Professor Hammer's primary responsibilities

EXHIBIT D10.1 UNISERVO

Consolidated Operating Budget
for the Year Ending December 31, 1997 ($ in millions)

	Uniservo	Eastern Region	Central Region	Western Region
Net sales	$52.8	$22.2	$11.7	$18.9
Expense controllable by regions:				
Salaries—field technicians	22.2	9.3	4.9	8.0
Salaries—supervision	3.5	1.5	0.7	1.3
Selling expense	2.5	1.1	0.5	0.9
Training	0.9	0.4	0.2	0.3
Repair & maintenance	4.0	1.7	0.9	1.4
Rents	6.3	2.6	1.4	2.3
Property taxes	1.3	0.5	0.3	0.5
Depreciation	0.8	0.3	0.2	0.3
Total expense controlled by regions	$41.5	$17.4	$9.1	$15.0
Controllable contribution	$11.3	$4.8	$2.6	$3.9
Expense controllable by corporate:				
Insurance	0.5	0.2	0.1	0.2
Corporate administration	3.6	1.5	0.8	1.3
Total expense controlled by corporate	$4.1	$1.7	$0.9	$1.5
Total contribution	$7.2	$3.1	$1.7	$2.4

is to manage the department budget. As part of this process, Professor Hammer submits a budget request. The request serves as the basis for negotiation with the dean of the College of Arts & Sciences over spending approvals for the next year. The English department budget becomes part of the arts & sciences budget and, eventually, the university budget, which is submitted to the state legislature for approval.

Through her years of experience in this process, Professor Hammer feels that she knows the realities of working within the budget process. As a result, she has formulated her own budget philosophy, upon which she bases her actions. First, she inflates the original numbers she submits to arts & sciences in the belief that the request will inevitably be cut. After she receives final budget approval, she uses the spending authority she holds over individual line items—such as equipment, professional development, and supplies—to reward the behavior of those colleagues within her department who are supporting her goals. For example, she will give the latest computer technology to certain professors who are the best teachers or most-productive researchers. Wherever possible within the mandates of the budget rules, she will try to move budget dollars from one category, such as repair, to another, such as travel, to serve her purposes. Often, however, budget rules eliminate spending latitude between line items.

One other important practice Professor Hammer follows is to make sure that she spends all dollars allotted to her for the year, regardless of actual need. For example, in the last month of the past budget year she instructed her staff to spend the remaining $1,800 in the supplies account on photocopy paper. Actually, this purchase created a tremendous storage problem, since the department did not have unused space readily available. Perhaps even more significantly, the department did not need the paper to begin with, since it had previously moved to make greater use of electronic storage and avoid the use of paper documentation. When these issues were pointed out to Professor Hammer, she explained that if the department did not spend these supply approvals this year, the amounts budgeted for the next year would be cut to reflect lower projected spending.

Required:

1. Comment on Professor Hammer's budget philosophy. Do you believe her philosophy is rational? Do her actions support the objectives of the department and the university?
2. Assume that you stepped in as a budget systems expert for the state legislature. What types of safeguards could you put into the budget approval process to help avoid the problems evident at Professor Hammer's level?

PROBLEMS

P10.1 (Budgeted Cost of Goods Manufactured)

Fashion Designs Inc. is a custom manufacturer that fills large textile production orders for wholesale distributors and large discount retailers. The company uses an actual-cost manufacturing accounting system, and it prepares a monthly budget for cost of goods manufactured. Over the next 2 months, the company will work on only one production order. It is for 220,000 sweaters—100,000 to be produced in April and 120,000 in May. Production cost projections are shown in Exhibit P10.1.

Manufacture of each sweater requires 10 minutes of direct labor time and 20 minutes of machine time. Fixed overhead costs are incurred at an even rate throughout the year.

Required: Prepare budgets for cost of goods manufactured for April and May.

P10.2 (Activity-Based Administrative Budget)

As part of its ongoing effort to reduce costs and eliminate non-value-adding activities, Western Telephone Company has revised its budget request process. All

---

EXHIBIT P10.1 FASHION DESIGNS INC.

Production Cost Projections

Variable Cost	Quantity per Unit	Unit Price
Yarn	2 yards	$1.50 per yard
Appliqué package	1 package	$2.50 per package
Direct labor-hours	10 minutes	$9.00 per hour
Variable overhead:		
Supplies		$1.20 per direct labor-hour
Repair		$0.60 per machine-hour

Fixed Overhead	Annual Expense
Management salaries	$ 240,000
Depreciation	325,000
Other	1,180,000
Total	$1,745,000

EXHIBIT P10.2 WESTERN TELEPHONE COMPANY— PAYROLL DEPARTMENT

Cost-Driver Relationships

Payroll expense:		
Department manager	1	employee
Supervisors	3	employees
Clerks	25	employees
Payroll benefits	25	% of payroll dollars
Supplies	$150	per employee per year
Occupancy	2,000	square feet
Travel	5	trips per year for dept. manager
Training:		
New employees	15	hours per employee
Supervisors	12	hours per year
Clerks	8	hours per year
Depreciation—equipment	$16,450	per year

administrative departments are now required to show cost drivers for each functional cost category for which they request funding.

The payroll department has identified the cost relationships shown in Exhibit P10.2.

The payroll department manager earns a base salary of $35,000 per year, before benefits. Department supervisors earn $24,000, and clerks $18,000. The department pays an occupancy rate, including utilities, of $15 per square foot per year. Only the department manager travels on company business, and each trip costs an average of $1,200. Only the supervisors and payroll clerks receive training during the year. Because of employee turnover, the department expects to hire six new employees during the upcoming year. Each will receive 15 additional hours of training. The payroll department is charged $24 for each hour of training.

Required: Prepare an annual budget for the payroll department.

P10.3 (Budgeted Income Statement)

Office Solutions Inc., a retailer, plans the revenues shown in Exhibit P10.3 for October, November, and December for its desk division.

The cost of making one desk is $120. Selling expense is 12 percent of total revenue, and administrative expense is $4,200,000 per year. The division's interest expense is $600,000 per year, and its tax rate is 40 percent. Selling expense and interest are incurred at even rates throughout the year.

EXHIBIT P10.3 OFFICE SOLUTIONS INC.— DESK DIVISION

Projected Revenues

	October	November	December
Number of units	20,000	22,000	30,000
Average selling price per unit	$200	$190	$195

Required: Prepare a monthly budgeted income statement for the desk division for October, November, and December. Include a monthly projection for return on sales.

P10.4   (Preparing a Cash Budget)

(*Note:* This problem builds on the revenue and expense projections given in problem P10.3.) The desk division of Office Solutions Inc. extends credit on 50 percent of the goods it sells, and it normally collects receivables in 30 days. Purchases for cost of goods sold are made in the month prior to sale and charged to accounts payable. One-quarter of all purchases are paid in the month after purchase, and the remainder are paid within 60 days. Interest is paid biannually, in June and December.

Selling and administrative expense is paid in cash each month. Administrative expense includes a depreciation expense of $110,000 per month. Taxes are paid at the beginning of each month, based on the estimate of taxes owed for the previous month. The ending cash balance in October is budgeted to be $500,000.

Required: Prepare a cash budget for the desk division of Office Solutions for November and December.

P10.5   (Budgeting Materials Purchases and Cash Disbursements)

Variety Balloons Manufacturing Company produces balloons made of synthetic latex. The company's plant manager has prepared the following finished-goods production budget for the next 2 months:

December	1,342,000
January	904,000

He now wants to budget the amount of raw materials he will need to purchase for December. Information needed to complete this analysis is presented in Exhibit P10.5 and in the next paragraph.

EXHIBIT P10.5 VARIETY BALLOONS MANUFACTURING COMPANY

Information on Inventory and Accounts Payable

	December	January
Budgeted units of production	1,342,000	904,000
Average latex required per balloon	1 square foot	
Budgeted cost of latex	$0.90 per square yard	
Raw materials inventory, December 1	7,500 square yards	
Desired ending raw materials inventory	5% of next month's needs	
Accounts payable, December 1	$60,000	

Note: Budgeted balance at end of each month = 50% of the month's budgeted purchases.

On average, each balloon requires 1 square foot of latex. The company buys latex in lots measured in square yards. A square yard is expected to cost $0.90 during December. (*Note:* 9 square feet = 1 square yard.) At December 1, there is an inventory balance for raw materials of 7,500 square yards of latex. At December 31, the production manager would like to have adequate raw materials on hand to meet 5 percent of January's production needs. At December 1, the accounts payable balance is $60,000, and the company normally ends each month carrying 50 percent of its purchases for the month as payables.

Required: Prepare the following schedules for the month of December:

1. Materials purchases budget for latex (include both the number of yards to be purchased and the expected dollar amount of the purchase).
2. Budgeted cash payments for the latex purchase after considering changes to accounts payable.

P10.6 (Preparing a Sales Department Budget)

United Air Products, Inc., is a distributor of industrial gases—such as oxygen, nitrogen, carbon dioxide, and helium. The firm's sales department is responsible for generating new business and for servicing existing customers. The sales manager is preparing the 1997 annual budget for the sales department, but she is a bit perplexed because of some scheduled changes. The facts she has available are these:

1. As shown in Exhibit P10.6.1, the department has already received a preapproved human resource budget for 1997. The sales manager feels fortunate, because the department is expanding and will add two salespersons, thus allowing for a total of eight in 1997. Details concerning 1997 payroll, including commissions and payroll taxes, are provided in the exhibit.
2. Exhibit P10.6.2 offers details about the actual expenses, other than payroll, incurred by the department in 1996.
3. In providing for changes in 1997, the following spending increases need to be considered:
   a. The travel and entertainment budget for salespersons is expected to rise proportionately for the two new members.
   b. Office supplies will go up by 20 percent because of increased sales activity.
   c. Education and training will cost an additional $3,000.
   d. Inflation is expected to cause a general price increase of 3 percent for all nonpersonnel operating expenses, except for depreciation. The sales manager

EXHIBIT P10.6.1 UNITED AIR PRODUCTS, INC.—SALES DEPARTMENT

Preapproved Human Resource Budget for 1997

Position	Number	Base Salary	Sales Commission	Payroll Tax and Benefits
Sales Manager	1	$70,000	0.75% of sales revenue	38%
Salespersons	8	$30,000	2.0% of sales revenue	32%
Secretary	1	$17,500	None	25%

EXHIBIT P10.6.2 UNITED AIR PRODUCTS, INC.— SALES DEPARTMENT

Operating Expenses for the Year Ending December 31, 1996

	Total
Travel & entertainment:	
Sales manager	$ 34,700
Salespersons	181,440
Total travel & entertainment	$216,140
Other operating expense:	
Office supplies	10,870
Presentation materials & software	3,690
Education & training	18,600
Depreciation—office equipment	7,300
Total operating expense	$256,600

---

believes that the inflation adjustment should be applied *after* making the changes noted above for travel and entertainment, office supplies, and education and training. (Inflation has already been considered in deriving the 1997 payroll approvals shown in Exhibit P10.6.1.)

4. Sales revenue for 1997 is budgeted at $7,500,000.

Required: Prepare a budget for the sales department for 1997. Your answer should be broken down into three separate sections:

1. The human resource budget
2. The travel and entertainment budget
3. Other operating expense

P10.7 (Budgeted Sales and Cash Receipts)

The Wild Mane is a hairstyling and manicure shop. The business has developed a unique marketing twist in an otherwise overcrowded and competitive service industry. Regular customers, who account for 70 percent of sales, are billed and sent end-of-month statements. Terms are net/end of month, meaning that customers are expected to pay their statements in full in the month following receipt of service. While these liberal credit terms have helped the Wild Mane to expand its sales rapidly, some collection and cash flow problems have arisen.

In order to help the business get a handle on expected cash receipts, you have been asked to project monthly cash collections of credit sales for the next quarter. A historical analysis of past sales and collection activity is presented in Exhibit P10.7. Panel 1 shows the budgeted monthly unit sales for February through June of 1997. Panel 2 gives a breakdown of the expected rates of collection for each month's credit sales.

Required: Prepare the following monthly projections for April, May, and June of 1997:

1. Sales revenue
2. Cash collections

EXHIBIT P10.7 THE WILD MANE

Budgeted Monthly Sales for February through June, 1997

Type of service:	Service fee	Feb.	Mar.	Apr.	May	June
		Budgeted Units of Service				
Haircuts	$20	600	625	650	700	775
Manicures	$14	150	160	170	200	250

Collection terms: Payment due by end of month

Collection history:
Percent collected by end of following month	81%
Percent collected by end of 2nd month	15%
Percent never collected	4%

P10.8 (Budgeted Costs for Invoicing and Delivery Activities)

The general manager of Tapa Wholesale Company is scrutinizing the invoicing and delivery functions as part of the budget preparation process for 1997. The following are the activity levels for the year just ended (1996) and the projections for the year just begun (1997):

	1996	1997
Number of sales	20,000	24,000
Number of items per sale	4	5

The activity and expense report for Tapa's invoicing function in 1996 is shown in Exhibit P10.8. All invoicing variable expenses are driven by the total number of items invoiced. Sales invoices are handled by clerks whose wage rate is $6 per hour. Labor negotiations have resulted in a 10 percent increase in their hourly wage rate for 1997. It is expected that Tapa's invoicing function will maintain the same level of productivity in 1997 that it had in 1996. Payroll tax rates and workers' compensation insurance rates, which are charged on the basis of total wages expense, will be the same in 1997 as they were in 1996. Unit prices for supplies are also expected to be the same in 1997.

Tapa sells three products: Arcil, Balo, and Cacha. While differences in size and weight among these products do not affect invoicing cost, variable delivery cost depends completely on the particular product being delivered. For example, truck capacity is 10 units of Arcil, 5 units of Balo, or 4 units of Cacha. A truck will carry only one of the three products on each delivery run and will only operate at full capacity. Units projected to be delivered in 1997 are as follows:

Arcil	60,000
Balo	40,000
Cacha	20,000
Total	120,000

EXHIBIT P10.8 TAPA WHOLESALE COMPANY

Invoicing Function—Activity and Expense Report for 1996

Number of sales	20,000
Average number of items per sale	4
Total number of items priced	80,000
Variable expense:	
Wages	$40,000
Payroll taxes	4,000
Workers' compensation insurance	2,000
Supplies	1,000
Total variable expense	$47,000
Fixed expense	3,400
Total expense	$50,400

Projected 1997 cost for the delivery function are $30,000 for fixed cost and $228,000 for variable cost. Fixed cost is allocated equally to all units when determining the unit cost of delivery. Variable costs, however, will differ according to product and will depend on the number of product delivery runs.

Required:

1. Prepare the budgeted 1997 activity and expense report for Tapa's invoicing function.
2. Calculate the total 1997 standard delivery cost per unit for each of the three products sold by Tapa. Include both variable and fixed costs in your calculations.

(AICPA Adapted)

P10.9 **(Pro Forma Schedule of Cash Flows: 3 Months)**

CrossMan Corporation, a rapidly expanding crossbow distributor serving retail outlets, is in the process of formulating plans for 1997. Joan Caldwell, director of marketing, has completed her 1997 forecast and is confident that sales estimates will be met or exceeded. The following sales figures show the growth expected and will serve as the planning basis for other corporate departments. (All dollar amounts in this problem are in thousands.)

Month	Forecasted Sales	Month	Forecasted Sales
January	$1,800	July	$3,000
February	2,000	August	3,000
March	1,800	September	3,200
April	2,200	October	3,200
May	2,500	November	3,000
June	2,800	December	3,400

George Brownell, assistant controller, has been given the responsibility for formulating the cash flow projection, a critical element during a period of rapid expansion. The following information will be used in preparing the cash analysis:

- CrossMan has an excellent record in accounts receivable collection and expects this trend to continue. Sixty percent of billings are collected in the first month after the sale and 40 percent in the second month after the sale. Uncollectible accounts are nominal and will not be considered in the analysis.
- The purchase of the crossbows is CrossMan's largest expenditure; the cost of these items equals 50 percent of sales. Sixty percent of the crossbows are received 1 month prior to sale, and 40 percent are received during the month of sale.
- Experience shows that 80 percent of accounts payable are paid by CrossMan one month after receipt of the purchased crossbows, and the remaining 20 percent are paid the second month after receipt.
- Hourly wages, including fringe benefits, are a factor of sales volume and are equal to 20 percent of the current month's sales. These wages are paid in the month in which they are incurred.
- General and administrative expense is projected to be $2,640 for 1997. The composition of the expense is given below. All of the expenses shown are incurred at a uniform rate throughout the year, except for property taxes. Property taxes are paid in four equal installments in the last month of each quarter.

Salaries	$ 480
Promotion	660
Property taxes	240
Insurance	360
Utilities	300
Depreciation	600
Total	$2,640

- Income tax payments are made by CrossMan in the first month of each quarter and are based on the income for the prior quarter. CrossMan's income tax rate is 40 percent. CrossMan's net income for the first quarter of 1997 is projected to be $612.
- CrossMan has a corporate policy of maintaining an end-of-month cash balance of $100. Cash is invested or borrowed monthly, as necessary, to maintain this balance.
- CrossMan uses a calendar-year reporting period.

Required:

1. Prepare a pro forma schedule of cash receipts and disbursements for CrossMan Corporation, by month, for the second quarter of 1997. Be sure that all receipts, disbursements, and borrowing and investing amounts are presented on a monthly basis. Ignore the interest expense and/or interest income associated with the borrowing and investing activities.
2. Discuss why cash budgeting is particularly important for a rapidly expanding company such as CrossMan Corporation.

(*CPA Adapted*)

P10.10   (Revising the Budget for a Service Operation)

The Mason Agency, a division of General Service Industries, offers consulting services to clients for a fee. The corporate management at General Service is pleased with the agency's performance for the first 9 months of the current year. It has recommended that the division manager of the Mason Agency, Richard Howell, submit a revised forecast for the remaining quarter, as the division has exceeded the annual plan year-to-date by 20 percent of operating income. An unexpected increase in billed hour volume over the original plan is the main reason for this gain in income. The Mason Agency's original operating budget for the first three quarters is presented in Exhibit P10.10.

When comparing the actuals for the first three quarters to the figures in the original plan, Howell analyzed the variances. His revised forecast for the fourth quarter will reflect the following information:

- The division currently has 25 consultants on staff—10 for management consulting and 15 for EDP consulting—and has hired three additional management consultants. The new staffers will start work at the beginning of the fourth quarter in order to meet the increased client demand.
- The hourly billing rate for consulting revenue is market acceptable and will remain at $90 per hour for each management consultant and $75 per hour for each EDP consultant. However, because of the favorable increase in billing-hour volume (when compared to plan), the hours for each consultant will be increased by 50 hours per quarter. There is no learning curve for billable consulting hours for new employees.
- The budgeted annual salaries and actual annual salaries, paid monthly, will remain the same: $50,000 for a management consultant and 8 percent less for an EDP consultant. Corporate management has approved a merit increase of 10 percent at the beginning of the fourth quarter for all 25 current consultants, while the new consultants will be compensated at the planned rate.
- The planned salary expense includes a provision for employee fringe benefits that amounts to 30 percent of the annual salaries. However, the improvement of some corporatewide employee programs will increase the fringe benefit allocation to 40 percent.

EXHIBIT P10.10 THE MASON AGENCY

1996–1997 Operating Budget

	First Quarter	Second Quarter	Third Quarter	Total (Nine Months)
Revenue:				
Consulting fees				
Management consulting	$315,000	$315,000	$315,000	$ 945,000
EDP consulting	421,875	421,875	421,875	1,265,625
Total consulting fees	$736,875	$736,875	$736,875	$2,210,625
Other revenue	10,000	10,000	10,000	30,000
Total revenue	$746,875	$746,875	$746,875	$2,240,625
Expense:				
Consultant salary expense	$386,750	$386,750	$386,750	$1,160,250
Travel & related expense	45,625	45,625	45,625	136,875
Gen'l & administrative expense	100,000	100,000	100,000	300,000
Depreciation expense	40,000	40,000	40,000	120,000
Corporate allocation	50,000	50,000	50,000	150,000
Total expense	$622,375	$622,375	$622,375	$1,867,125
Operating income	$124,500	$124,500	$124,500	$ 373,500

- The original plan assumes a fixed hourly rate for travel and other related expenses for each billing hour of consultations. These are expenses that are not reimbursed by the client, and the previously determined hourly rate has proved adequate to cover these costs.
- Other revenues are derived from temporary rentals and interest income and remain unchanged for the fourth quarter.
- General and administrative expense has been favorable, at 7 percent below the plan. This 7 percent savings on fourth-quarter expense will be reflected in the revised plan.
- Depreciation for office equipment and microcomputers will stay constant, at the projected straight-line rate.
- Because of the favorable experience for the first three quarters and the division's increased ability to absorb costs, the corporate management at General Service Industries has increased the corporate expense allocation by 50 percent.

Required:

1. Prepare the Mason Agency's revised fourth-quarter operating budget that Richard Howell will present to General Service Industries. Be sure to furnish supporting calculations for all revised revenue and expense amounts.
2. Discuss the reasons that an organization would prepare a revised forecast.

(CMA Adapted)

P10.11 **(Preparing an Activity-Based Budget)**

Recreational Explorers, Inc., is a small firm that leads exploration trips into West Virginia for rock climbers and white-water rafters. Only two types of trips are offered: One is a 3-day rock-climbing adventure, and the other is a 2-day white-water rafting trip. Both require customers to have an intermediate level of skill and a desire to face some rugged terrain. The firm attracts its customers through word of mouth and through advertisements in specialty magazines for persons known to have an interest in these activities.

Although Recreational Explorers has been in business for 5 years, it has had very little success in preparing budgets that are useful for guiding actions and predicting results. This year the firm's founder and president, Joe Condola, is determined to prepare a budget that works. The beginning point for the budgeting process is Exhibit P10.11.1, which reports Condola's activities and revenue targets for the upcoming year, 1997. Condola believes his firm will conduct 90 climbing trips and 250 rafting trips. Both types of trip are budgeted for six customers, who

EXHIBIT P10.11.1 RECREATIONAL EXPLORERS, INC.

Expected Activities and Revenues for 1997

	Three-Day Rock-Climbing Trip	Two-Day Rafting Trip
Number of trips	90	250
Revenue per person per trip	$220	$125
Average number of persons per trip	6	6
Average miles driven per trip per vehicle (1 vehicle for rock climbing, 2 vehicles for rafting)	220	90

will pay $220 each for climbing and $125 each for rafting. For every expedition party, Recreational Explorers provides all transportation, camping and adventure gear, and food. Because of differences in equipment used, rock-climbing trips require only one vehicle, whereas rafting trips require two. Roundtrip mileage per vehicle averages 220 miles for a climbing trip and 90 miles for a rafting trip. Each rock-climbing trip is led by one expert guide and one assistant, but a rafting trip requires two of each.

Condola has compiled cost targets for 1997, as shown in Exhibit P10.11.2. He has tried to associate costs with the types of activities that cause these costs to occur. Four costs categories were accumulated: (1) companywide cost, (2) product cost (for the two types of trips), (3) trip cost, and (4) customer cost. Companywide cost includes the salaries for Condola and his secretary-bookkeeper, office supplies, rent and utilities, and depreciation of furniture and fixtures. Product cost identifies resources associated with each of the two types of adventure trip and

EXHIBIT P10.11.2 RECREATIONAL EXPLORERS, INC.

Targeted Costs for 1997

	Per Year	
Companywide costs:		
President's salary	$45,000	
Secretary-bookkeeper	22,500	
Office supplies	2,500	
Rent & utilities	16,500	
Depreciation—furniture & fixtures	3,160	

	Per Year	
	Climbing	*Rafting*
Product costs:		
Advertising	$ 6,200	$ 8,700
Expedition leaders—1 for climbing, 2 for rafting	24,500	45,000
Assistants—1 for climbing, 2 for rafting	12,000	24,000
Vehicle depreciation—1 for climbing, 2 for rafting	5,500	13,500

	Per Year	
	Climbing	*Rafting*
Trip costs:		
Depreciation—tents, cooking supplies	$1,500	$3,000
Depreciation—climbing gear	1,333	0
Depreciation—rafts & vests	0	4,000

	Per Mile	
	Climbing	*Rafting*
Vehicle gas, oil, & maintenance	$0.415	$0.480

	Climbing	*Rafting*
Customer cost:		
Food—per person, per day	$12.50	$10.00

includes advertising, salaries for the expedition leaders and their assistants, and depreciation of vehicles. Trip cost includes depreciation for tents and cooking supplies and depreciation for climbing or rafting gear. Also included is the gas, oil, and maintenance cost incurred, by the mile, for each trip. Customer cost is the food cost incurred by each person for each day out.

Required:

1. Prepare a company budget for 1997 that includes direct profit margins for the two product lines.
2. What observations can you make that might be useful for improving the firm's financial performance?

P10.12 (Continuous Budgeting)

Lexicon Services Inc. provides word-processing services to local public schools and public accounting firms. It charges clients $25 per billable hour of word-processing production. Because of the nature of its clientele, the company has cyclical business and is subject to wide quarterly swings in financial performance. To get a better handle on short-term planning, senior management has instituted a system of continuous rolling budgets that involves using updated financial targets prepared on a quarterly basis. Revisions are made to each of the next four quarters, and, thus, management always has a fresh 12-month budget at the beginning of each quarter.

Bridget Collins, Lexicon's controller, had prepared the quarterly budgets, shown in Exhibit P10.12.1, about 3 months earlier. Now, as the first quarter of

EXHIBIT P10.12.1 LEXICON SERVICES INC.

Quarterly Budget

	Quarter 1	Quarter 2	Quarter 3	Quarter 4	Total
			1997		
Sales pattern, %	15%	20%	30%	35%	100%
Billable hours	6,600	8,800	13,200	15,400	44,000
Hourly rate	$ 25	$ 25	$ 25	$ 25	$ 25
Revenue	$165,000	$220,000	$330,000	$385,000	$1,100,000
Expense:					
Administrative salaries	$ 50,000	$ 50,000	$ 50,000	$ 50,000	$ 200,000
Word processing operator wages	108,000	108,000	108,000	108,000	432,000
Benefits	23,700	23,700	23,700	23,700	94,800
Temporary help	0	0	63,000	96,000	159,000
Depreciation—equipment	5,000	5,000	5,000	5,000	20,000
Equipment rental	0	0	2,000	3,000	5,000
Rent & utilities	6,000	6,000	6,000	6,000	24,000
Supplies	6,960	8,280	10,920	12,240	38,400
Advertising	4,500	4,500	4,500	4,500	18,000
Other costs	1,000	1,000	1,000	1,000	4,000
Total expense	$205,160	$206,480	$274,120	$309,440	$ 995,200
Earnings before tax	$ (40,160)	$ 13,520	$ 55,880	$ 75,560	$ 104,800
Tax expense	(16,064)	5,408	22,352	30,224	41,920
Net earnings	$ (24,096)	$ 8,112	$ 33,528	$ 45,336	$ 62,880

1997 is coming to a close, she is gathering the information needed for preparation of a new budget. While results for the current quarter have closely paralleled the budget estimates, many changes will be implemented over the next budget year. Bridget has called upon you to help her prepare the next four quarters of budget data, beginning with the second quarter of 1997.

The following information has been gathered to help you in this process:

- Sales for the past year were based on a target of 44,000 billable hours, distributed into a sales pattern of 15, 20, 30, and 35 percent in each of the respective quarters. Bridget expects this pattern to continue but notes that total hours for the next four quarters should increase by 20 percent because of an aggressive advertising campaign. She also expects the company to raise its rates from $25 to $28 at the beginning of the fourth quarter of 1997. The rate will remain at $28 for the first quarter of 1998.
- Lexicon maintains 20 full-time work-processing operators. Each operator produces 450 hours per quarter. All other billable hours are covered with temporary employees, who are hired at a $15-per-hour flat rate from an agency.
- Word-processing equipment owned by Lexicon includes 20 word-processing stations. Additional workstations are rented at a cost of $200 per quarter for each station. Exhibit P10.12.2 provides information on the calculation of expenses for equipment rentals and for temporary workers.
- Payroll increases of 4 percent for administrative staff and 5 percent for word-processing operators are scheduled to take effect on January 1, 1998. Benefits are expected to continue at the same percentage rate of total payroll expense.

EXHIBIT P10.12.2 LEXICON SERVICES INC.

Supporting Calculations for Overflow Work

	1997			
	Quarter 1	Quarter 2	Quarter 3	Quarter 4
Temporary workers needed:				
Total billable hours	6,600	8,800	13,200	15,400
Number of core employees	20	20	20	20
Productive hours per employee	450	450	450	450
Hours available	9,000	9,000	9,000	9,000
Hours of temporary help needed	0	0	4,200	6,400
Hourly rate	$ 15	$ 15	$ 15	$ 15
Total expense	$ 0	$ 0	$63,000	$96,000
Workstations needed:				
Total billable hours	6,600	8,800	13,200	15,400
Hours per workstation	450	450	450	450
Fractional workstations needed	14.7	19.6	29.3	34.2
Required workstations	15	20	30	35
Workstations owned	20	20	20	20
Rentals needed	0	0	10	15
Rental cost per workstation per quarter	$ 200	$ 200	$ 200	$ 200
Equipment rental expense	$ 0	$ 0	$ 2,000	$ 3,000

- Rent and utilities expense will increase by 3 percent at the beginning of the second quarter of 1997. Supplies are estimated at $3,000 per quarter, plus an incremental cost of $0.60 per billable hour.
- Advertising expenses will be increased by 50 percent at the beginning of the second quarter of 1997. Other costs are also expected to increase by 50 percent at that time.
- Tax expense has been running at 40 percent and is expected to remain at the same rate. In determining net income, the company offsets its quarterly losses with income tax carrybacks and carryforwards.

Required:

1. Prepare a budget for the four quarters, beginning with the second quarter of 1997.
2. Discuss how Lexicon benefits from the implementation of a continuous-budgeting process.

(CMA Adapted)

CASES

C10.1 (Gourmet Kitchen Supply, Inc.)

Tom Sanders, the owner-operator of Gourmet Kitchen Supply, Inc., is concerned about his firm's performance prospects—and, particularly, his cash flow—for the next 6 months. Since he started the business 7 years ago, Tom has earned a modest salary, and his company has generated small, but consistent, profits. Still, he considers the business a success because it has survived while many other small retail shops in the area have had to close their doors. Nonetheless, as the 1997 year begins, Tom is once again worried about the outlook for the coming year. He has called upon you to help him set up a spreadsheet for preparing pro forma monthly income and cash flow statements for the next 6 months.

The first bits of information he provides you with are income statements for the past 2 years, 1995 and 1996, and a balance sheet for 1996 (Exhibit C10.1.1). The income statements show signs of both revenue and income growth, and the firm seems to have good liquidity. The only long-term debt carried by the business is a mortgage note for $145,000 that Sanders just took out on December 1, 1996, when he refinanced the land and building (Exhibit C10.1.2). Despite these positive signs, Sanders mentions that income numbers are deceiving, because of the seasonal nature of sales. He also expresses fear of repeating the experiences of the last 2 years, when he had to scramble to pay his bills for the first 6 months. He thinks a monthly budget will better prepare him to handle his cash shortfalls.

Insight on the Next 6 Months of Operations
Sanders begins to explain some of the detail behind the operating data.

- He used results for the past 2 years to project what he thinks are reasonably attainable sales revenue goals for the next 7 months. His monthly targets are as follows:

January	$15,000
February	15,000
March	18,000
April	20,000
May	25,000
June	28,000
July	28,000

EXHIBIT C10.1.1   GOURMET KITCHEN SUPPLY, INC.

Income Statements for the Years Ending December 31

	1995	1996
Sales revenue	$208,885	$227,800
Cost of goods sold	112,232	120,022
Gross margin	$ 96,653	$107,778
Operating expense:		
Advertising	$ 1,590	$ 1,850
Depreciation	9,460	9,965
Insurance	2,370	3,109
Interest	13,900	13,250
Office expense	970	1,162
Repair & maintenance	1,760	2,064
Supplies	2,053	2,279
Taxes & licenses	8,790	9,650
Utilities	5,703	6,072
Wages	45,670	49,700
Total expense	$ 92,266	$ 99,101
Income, pretax	$ 4,387	$ 8,677
Income tax	1,316	2,603
Net income	$ 3,071	$ 6,074

Balance Sheet December 31, 1996

		1996
Assets		
Cash		$ 4,230
Accounts receivable		16,500
Inventory		27,680
Total current assets		$ 48,410
Plant assets		
Less accumulated depreciation	$246,250	
Total plant assets	48,321	
Total assets		197,929
		$246,339
Liabilities and Shareholder Equity		
Accounts payable		$ 17,390
Income tax payable (due March 15th)		751
Total current liabilities		$ 18,141
Notes payable		145,000
Total liabilities		$163,141
Common stock	$ 80,000	
Retained earnings	3,198	
Total shareholder equity		83,198
Total equity		$246,339

EXHIBIT C10.1.2 GOURMET KITCHEN SUPPLY, INC.

Notes Payable—Amortization Schedule for First 6 Months, 1997

Month	Balance, Beginning of Month	Payment	Interest	Reduction of Principal	Balance, End of Month
January	$145,000	$1,213	$1,088	$125	$144,875
February	144,875	1,213	1,087	126	144,748
March	144,748	1,213	1,086	127	144,621
April	144,621	1,213	1,085	128	144,493
May	144,493	1,213	1,084	129	144,364
June	144,364	1,213	1,083	130	144,234

EXHIBIT C10.1.3 GOURMET KITCHEN SUPPLY, INC.

Plant Assets—Depreciation Schedule

At December 31, 1996

	Cost	Accum. Deprec.	Deprec. Expense for 1996
Building	$180,000	$36,000	$ 6,000
Land	37,500	0	0
Equipment & furniture	28,750	12,321	4,107
	$246,250	$48,321	$10,107

He explains that purchases are tied very closely to sales projections. He wants to keep inventory at its present level, and he orders just enough goods each month to meet sales. He also mentions that he increased gross margin percentages over the past 2 years and is planning on a 1997 target of 48 percent.

- As a way to boost sales, Sanders promoted the use of open accounts for regular customers, who make up about 50 percent of all sales. On the last day of each month, he sends credit customers a statement, the balance of which is due by the end of the following month. He says he has been fortunate, because he has had no significant problems with late payments.
- All inventory purchases are made on credit terms, n/30, and Sanders is conscientious about paying bills on time. He feels that the credit he has received from suppliers has been his lifeline when cash flow was at its worst, and he does not want to jeopardize these relationships.
- Advertising is paid monthly and is budgeted at the same level as in 1996. Additionally, some special radio spots costing $400 per month will run during February, March, and April. Payment for this special promotion is due in full by February 15th.
- The firm's bookkeeper has supplied the annual depreciation schedule for 1997, as shown in Exhibit C10.1.3.
- The insurance bill for 1997 has already been received. The amount due for the year is $3,250 and is payable in two equal installments on January 20th and on July 20th.

- Interest expense is related to the mortgage note shown in Exhibit C10.1.2. Payments are due by the 10th of each month, beginning January 1997.
- Wages relate to the salary paid Sanders and the hourly pay earned by two part-time employees. Exhibit C10.1.4 provides details on wages planned for 1997. Payroll is prepared two times per month—on the 15th and on the last day of the month.
- Exhibit C10.1.5 offers details about the firm's taxes and licenses account. All wages are subject to a payroll tax of 15.6 percent, which is paid when payroll checks are cut. This account also includes property tax, which is budgeted at $2,800 and payable in full in November. Additionally, fees for occupational licenses, costing a total of $360, are due by January 31.
- The business follows federal tax regulations for payment of estimated income tax. The current balance in the income taxes payable account is due by March 15. The next payment will be made on June 15 for tax owed on income earned through May 31. If income is negative, no tax is paid. The income tax rate is 30 percent.
- The remaining accounts shown on the income statement—office expense, repair and maintenance, supplies, and utilities—are each paid monthly and the amounts are expected to remain the same.

Financing and Capital Expenditures

Sanders plans to purchase in late June a new counter display that will cost $4,875. He hopes to have this fixture installed and paid for by June 30. No depreciation will be taken until July, when the display is expected to be put into use.

Finally, Sanders has set up a line of credit with his bank in order to handle negative monthly cash balances. He will be charged at the prime rate, now 7.5 percent, plus two points (for a total rate of 9.5 percent). He will take out loans in $1,000 increments on the first day of a month for which he expects a deficit and

EXHIBIT C10.1.4 GOURMET KITCHEN SUPPLY, INC.

Monthly Wages Budgeted
For First Six Months of 1997

Employee	Rate	Hr/Mo	Total
Janice Jones	$7	80	$ 560
Bob Larabee	7	80	560
Tom Sanders (salaried)			3,500
Monthly total (paid in equal amounts on the 15th and on the last day of month)			$4,620

EXHIBIT C10.1.5 GOURMET KITCHEN SUPPLY, INC.

Taxes and Licenses Budgeted for 1997

	Rate or Amount	Time of Payment
Payroll taxes	15.6%	With payroll
Property taxes, per year	$2,800	November
Occupational licenses, per year	$ 360	January

will repay each loan (in $1,000 increments) at the end of the first month in which he has a surplus. He will pay interest monthly. He wants to maintain a minimum cash balance of $2,000.

Required: Prepare monthly income statements and monthly statements of cash receipts and disbursements for the first 6 months of 1997. Assume all expenses are paid in the month in which they are incurred, unless it is indicated otherwise.

C10.2 (KAUS Television)[8]

Note: This case requires the use of an accompanying spreadsheet.

KAUS television is the number one station in the Austin, Texas, market. Many people believe the reason for the station's recent success is its owner, Rex Communications. Rex owns 18 TV stations. When it took over the Austin station in 1985, after President Reagan's deregulation of the broadcasting industry, KAUS was the perennial number three station in the market. It was being referred to as "Chaos" by both its competition and its employees. The station's profit margins were about 20 percent of income—abnormally low for the broadcasting industry.

When Rex took over Channel 7, it hired new directors for the sales, news, promotion, and production departments. It also hired a new general manager, Walter Forsythe. New people were hired at the department level as well. Knowing that news is the most visible and profitable part of a local station, KAUS's management lured popular anchors away from the competition with salaries that often approached a million dollars. The station was criticized in the newspapers for its actions, but moved forward—helped by the financial support of Rex. In the end, the investments in talent proved to be a shrewd business decision. By 1992, the Arbitron rating service reported that the KAUS 10 p.m. newscast received the highest market rating of all local news programming. (Nielsen had it ranked number two.)

Rex Communications was understandably pleased with the improvements at KAUS and had supported most of the strategic plans that the general manager, Forsythe, had suggested. As the years passed, Rex increased the percent profit margin that it expected from Forsythe. He had always come through—often exceeding the parent company's expectations. For example, in fiscal year 1996 (FY96), Rex set a goal of 32.0 percent profit for KAUS. And, after the eleventh month of the fiscal year, it appears that 32.52 percent profit will be delivered (Exhibit C10.2.1). Forsythe and his staff have just completed the budget for FY97 (Exhibit C10.2.2).

Budget Strategy

This year, as always, all KAUS directors prepared budgets for their departments. The directors went over their budgets with Forsythe and the KAUS accountant, Phyllis Kucharski. Each director had to explain any increases in their expenses. If the increases could not be justified, the budget was reworked. Forsythe and Kucharski prided themselves on the many times they had been complimented by the management of Rex Communications for submitting solid, no-fat budgets. They had gained the respect of their superiors, which has led to the acceptance of many of their initiatives.

The news director, Miguel Pumerejo, has been with KAUS for 6 years—relatively long by industry standards. He has heard that a competitor, Channel 4, is considering the addition of a 5 p.m. newscast to its news programming. It now

---

[8] Prepared by Blane Huppert under the direction of Ralph Drtina.

EXHIBIT C10.2.1 KAUS TELEVISION

Income Statement
Latest Estimate for the Year Ending June 30, 1996

	Rate	Employees		
Income:				
Advertising (see panel below)				$80,217,600
Production				600,000
News:				
Stories sold to network			$ 300,000	
Video sold			250,000	550,000
Total income				$81,367,600
Expense:				
Utilities				$ 500,000
News:				
Wages & benefits—talent		20	$ 1,940,000	
Wages & benefits—crew		25	1,375,000	
Newswire services			240,000	
Automotive			100,000	
Videotape			70,000	
Supplies			50,000	3,775,000
Production:				
Wages & benefits		20	$ 600,000	
Videotape			30,000	
Automotive			20,000	
Supplies			10,000	660,000
Programming:				
Wages & benefits		1	$ 50,000	
Programming			44,982,000	
Supplies			5,000	45,037,000
Sales:				
Salary wages & benefits		2	$ 131,068	
Commission wages & benefits	9.0%	8	721,958	
Automotive			100,000	
Sales expense			60,000	
Supplies			10,000	1,023,026
Promotion:				
Wages & benefits		1	$ 75,000	
Advertising			1,000,000	
Other promotion			20,000	
Supplies			5,000	1,100,000
Engineering:				
Wages & benefits		10	$ 600,000	
Supplies			10,000	610,000
General & administrative:				
Wages & benefits		3	$ 300,000	
Insurance ($150/employee)			14,100	
Taxes ($0.25/payroll dollar)			1,488,257	
Maintenance			100,000	
Legal			100,000	
Supplies			30,000	2,032,357
Traffic:				
Wages & benefits		4	$ 160,000	
Supplies			10,000	170,000
Total expense		94		$54,907,383
Profit before tax and depreciation				$26,460,217
Profit margin before tax and depreciation				32.52%

(continued)

EXHIBIT C10.2.1   (CONTINUED)

Advertising Income

	Ads/Hr	Days	Hours	Rate	Potential	Fill Ratio	Expected Sales
News	40	365	1.0	$1,000	$14,600,000	90%	$13,140,000
Prime time	40	365	3.0	$ 800	35,040,000	75%	26,280,000
Day	40	261	11.0	$ 200	22,968,000	70%	16,077,600
Night	40	365	8.0	$ 50	5,840,000	60%	3,504,000
Weekend	40	104	12.0	$ 500	24,960,000	85%	21,216,000
							$80,217,600

offers newscasts at 6 p.m. and 10 p.m. Pumerejo explained that the new newscast could make more viewers commit to Channel 4—and thus jeopardize KAUS's number one status. "I believe we need to add a five o'clock," explained Pumerejo. "We should be able to put it on the air with the addition of one more reporter and one more photographer." Because of the crew's contract, every time a new talent position is created, a new crew position must be created, too. Likewise, if a crew position is eliminated, a talent position must be eliminated as well. Kucharski agreed that they could fill the two positions with experienced people for $60,000 and $50,000, respectively. The only other increase Pumerejo foresaw for the operating budget was $30,000 for videotape.

The sales manager, Terri Russell, liked the idea of the new show: "It might be easy to sell, but even with a local news focus, I can't guarantee advertising sales of over 60 percent of the programs." Forsythe realized that the added sales would take the station's *fill ratio* (the average percentage of commercial time sold) down to 80 percent for newscasts. However, sales would increase by more than $4 million. Forsythe asked about increasing the advertising rates. Russell did not want to raise rates, because ads are then more difficult to sell. "You can't expect our salespeople to keep sales up with across-the-board rate increases, especially if you are asking them to sell an extra newscast." After much discussion, they compromised by increasing the daytime and weekend rates, and adjusting the fill ratios accordingly.

Production manager Tom Smith said that if a new show were added, he would need two more experienced people in the studio (at a cost of $35,000 each) to help with the production of the show. "In addition to the advertising increases that Russell can give us, I think we in production can expect about a 10 percent increase in our outside production business. In a couple of years, outside work should really take off." After further discussion of the new show, Smith added an extra $10,000 to his budget for more videotape—half for the new show and half for production.

Promotions director Maria Sudler threatened to quit unless an assistant were hired for her. "I can't take the 60- and 70-hour weeks any more. Get me an assistant or I am gone." Because she sounded serious, and because she really did need the help, Forsythe and Kucharski put in for an assistant.

The budget changes to the other departments seemed pretty standard. Most importantly, there was a $5 million increase in programming, but it was justified because several syndicated contracts were running out. To get the programs that were needed in order to bring in high viewership, KAUS has to spend top dollar. Assuming the station will continue with its current market focus, this increase is considered to be a committed cost that cannot be avoided.

EXHIBIT C10.2.2 KAUS TELEVISION

Budgeted Income Statement
for the Year Ending June 30, 1997

	Rate	Employees		
Income:				
Advertising (see panel below)				$88,069,000
Production				660,000
News:				
Stories sold to network			$ 300,000	
Video sold			250,000	550,000
Total income				$89,279,000
Expense:				
Utilities				$ 550,000
News:				
Wages & benefits—talent		21	$ 2,058,200	
Wages & benefits—crew		26	1,466,250	
Newswire services			240,000	
Automotive			110,000	
Videotape			100,000	
Supplies			50,000	4,024,450
Production:				
Wages & benefits		22	$ 688,000	
Videotape			40,000	
Automotive			25,000	
Supplies			10,000	763,000
Programming:				
Wages & benefits		1	$ 51,500	
Programming			49,675,000	
Supplies			5,000	49,731,500
Sales:				
Salary wages & benefits		2	$ 135,000	
Commission wages & benefits	9.0%	8	792,621	
Automotive			100,000	
Sales expense			60,000	
Supplies			10,000	1,097,621
Promotion:				
Wages & benefits		2	$ 97,250	
Advertising			1,200,000	
Other promotion			50,000	
Supplies			5,000	1,352,250
Engineering:				
Wages & benefits		10	$ 618,000	
Supplies			10,000	628,000
General & administrative:				
Wages & benefits		3	$ 309,000	
Insurance ($150/employee)			14,850	
Taxes ($0.25/payroll dollar)			1,595,155	
Maintenance			100,000	
Legal			100,000	
Supplies			30,000	2,149,005
Traffic:				
Wages & benefits		4	$ 164,800	
Supplies			10,000	174,800
Total expense		99		$60,470,626
Profit before tax and depreciation				$28,808,374
Profit margin before tax and depreciation				32.27%

(continued)

EXHIBIT C10.2.2 (CONTINUED)

Advertising Income

	Ads/Hr	Days	Hours	Rate	Potential	Fill Ratio	Expected Sales
News	40	365	1.5	$1,000	$21,900,000	80%	$17,520,000
Prime time	40	365	3.0	$ 800	35,040,000	75%	26,280,000
Day	40	261	11.5	$ 250	30,015,000	60%	18,009,000
Night	40	365	8.0	$ 50	5,840,000	65%	3,796,000
Weekend	40	104	12.0	$ 600	29,952,000	75%	22,464,000
							$88,069,000

Once the other department budgets were settled, Kucharski went through the salaries and the general and administrative budget. She increased all salaries 3 percent, which is the base to be used for union negotiations next month. In general and administrative (G&A) she allocated $150 per employee for insurance and set aside 25 percent of wages for payroll taxes. Other expenses were figured in and the budget completed. Although the profit margin was down, it was still above 32.0 percent, and profits were expected to increase by more than $2 million.

Forsythe was pleased and submitted the budget.

Corporate Discussion

Forsythe submitted the budget in person to a panel that was headed by Richard Recksolva III. This was the first budgeting cycle since Recksolva took over complete control of Rex Communications from his father. Although corporate management assured Forsythe that things would be no different under the new leadership, Forsythe has heard otherwise from other Rex-owned-station general managers. As he and Kucharski entered the conference room to submit the budget, Forsythe noticed many new faces.

Forsythe presented the entire budget without interruption or question. When he concluded and opened up the floor for questions, the room fell silent, and all eyes turned to Recksolva. "That's a very interesting analysis," he said. "Interesting, but I'm not sure how realistic for us at this time. First off, I don't like the idea of a new newscast. KAUS has not made a name for itself by reacting to what its competition does. We need to be more proactive, and, besides, I'm not sure this five o'clock show can offer the type of return that we at Rex Communications expect. We have coddled you long enough and now expect a 35 percent profit margin. I can honestly say I'm a bit disappointed. With a 32.52 percent return for FY96, I expected that you would come forward with a 35 percent margin on your own. I think you need to rework your numbers and—for the sake of your station—I hope your revisions are more realistic than your original proposal."

Forsythe was stunned, but managed to respond with, "I'm sorry you feel that way. Have you considered the future implications of stunting our growth today? All the progress we have made during my tenure has been based on long-range planning. If you take away my ability to plan for growth, it will be difficult for KAUS to make budget in the future."

"I agree that growth and long-term planning are important. My only request is that you don't jeopardize the viability of Rex Communications by mishandling your current responsibilities. The bottom line is that we expect higher profits this year than we did in FY96, and a profit margin of at least 35 percent."

"But ..."

"I believe our negotiations are over Mr. Forsythe."

Forsythe had never been treated so rudely at a budget meeting before. He knew that the 5 o'clock newscast was a good idea and a profitable idea. The only question was how to get it into the budget while keeping a 35 percent profit margin. When he returned to Austin, Forsythe called a meeting of directors to discuss their options. The easy thing to do would be to cancel the five o'clock show. This option was considered but discarded, because everyone wanted to be the first in the market with an early newscast. The other options include:

- *Changing advertising rates.* Russell estimated that changes were inversely proportional to the cost. For every percent change in price, there would be roughly a 0.5 percent change in the fill ratio. (These changes were applied to numbers in the FY97 budget, not to past—FY96—rates.) For example, if the weekend rate were changed from $600 to $612 per 30-second ad (an increase of 2 percent), the fill ratio could be expected to fall from 75 to 74 percent (a decrease of 1 percent point). Russell reiterated that she did not want to make additional changes to the KAUS rate structure but would do so if it helped to save the show. Forsythe said he would consider raising each of the five advertising sources by as much as 24 percent if more income could be generated thereby.
- *Increasing production work.* Smith believed that, if pressed, production could speed up its increases in outside business: "I will need some more nontechnical help. Let's say, four full-time people at about $15,000 per year. And I'll need someone in sales to give me a few hours a week to call on accounts. If we can hire someone half-time for about 20 grand a year, I think we should be able to double the business we originally planned for FY97. We'll probably need another $10,000 worth of videotape beyond what we already budgeted. But if you can get me that, we should be able to make the sales."
- *Cutting newsroom personnel.* Pumerejo did not want to start the 5 o'clock show without new staff members but agreed that to save the show he might consider it. "Miguel," Forsythe said, "News is the most highly staffed area in the building. You know that we are one of only four of the stations owned by Rex Communications that don't have reporters shoot their own video. Be aware that, if we need to, we will cut some staff from the news department." Pumerejo commented no further during the meeting.
- *Decreasing sales commission.* The current budget shows about 90 percent of the sales coming from Russell and one inside sales representative who deals solely with statewide and national accounts. The two work on straight salary, which totals $135,000 in the FY97 budget. The eight outside salespeople work on a straight commission of 9 percent. Much to the dismay of Russell, Forsythe also suggested decreasing commissions. Russell argued that the fill ratios would decrease, because the salespeople would be less motivated, but Forsythe said that in order to save the 5 o'clock show drastic changes would need to be made.
- *Eliminating promotions assistant.* Forsythe also said that, as a last resort, he would consider eliminating the position of promotions assistant, leaving responsibility for the department again entirely on Sudler's shoulders.

The meeting broke up. Forsythe and Kucharski returned to Forsythe's office, where they considered how to salvage the 5 p.m. newscast while meeting the corporate goal of a 35 percent profit margin. After discussion, they decided to use the following seven-step methodology to achieve their goals:

1. Optimize sales revenue by increasing rates by as much as 24 percent for each of the five sources of advertising income. An increase of 2 percent in rate means a decrease of 1 percent in fill ratio.
2. Increase the revenue of the production department, as suggested by Smith.
3. Cut the two new positions in the news department that were proposed in the FY97 budget by Pumerejo.
4. Cut the proposed promotions assistant position.
5. Cut sales commissions from 9 percent to 8.5 percent.
   And, if necessary:
6. Decrease sales commissions further, from 8.5 to 8 percent.
7. Cut more pairs of news positions until the profit margin reaches 35 percent. Recall that one talent position must be cut for every crew position cut (one talent—wage and benefits of $75,000; one crew—wage and benefits of $50,000).

Required:

1. Using the spreadsheet accompanying this problem, apply Forsythe's seven-step methodology to achieve the 35.0 percent profit margin objective. For step 1, find the maximum revenue per advertising source by increasing rates in increments of 2 percent, up to a maximum increase of 24 percent. (Data tables such as those shown in Exhibit 10.21 in the text can also be used.)
2. Based on the trade-offs implicit in your budget calculations for requirement 1, do you think the station should begin producing a 5 p.m. newscast? Explain.

CHAPTER 11

PROFIT VARIANCE ANALYSIS AND ENGINEERED COST CENTERS

The two basic things just learned about budgets are (1) they are tools for setting targets and for planning, and (2) they are compared to operating results in order to determine where improvements are possible. Now we'll see how the budget is used for identifying and correcting problem areas of operations. We'll focus on engineered cost centers, which represent the most predictable type of resource consumption.

Engineered costs show specific, predictable relationships between a department's product outputs and its resource inputs. These costs are common in repetitive manufacturing such as occurs in production of, say, bags of potato chips and even assembly-line cars. Engineered costs also occur in repetitive service processes, such as payroll preparation or insurance claims processing.

This is the first of three chapters explaining how managers make decisions about cutting costs, improving efficiency, and becoming more competitive. The first

part of this chapter focuses on standard costing systems in manufacturing. It shows how standard costs are derived and how they are used to measure, report, and correct deviations. The second part examines standard costing systems in today's complex production environment.

In this chapter we'll see what role this kind of cost data plays in determining the type of information managers need in order to help their organizations succeed in today's global marketplace. We will also look at how cost information changes because of competition and changes in technology. Within this broad framework, we'll focus on phases three through five of the management control system:

1. Long-range planning
2. Budgeting
3. *Measurement*
4. *Reporting and analysis*
5. *Corrective action*

EXHIBIT 11.1 CREATING A FLEXIBLE BUDGET		
When Actual Unit Sales Exceed the Master Budget Figure by 10 Percent		
	Master Budget	Changes	Flexible Budget
Number of sales units	10,000	1,000	11,000
Sales revenue	$100,000	$10,000	$110,000
Variable expense	60,000	6,000	66,000
Contribution margin	40,000	4,000	44,000
Fixed expense	30,000	0	30,000
Operating income	$ 10,000	$ 4,000	$ 14,000

ENGINEERED COSTS AND CHANGES IN VOLUME

As actual levels of sales volume vary from budgeted volume, managers are expected to adjust their resource consumption to accommodate changes in activities as needed to support actual sales volume. These new levels of expected resource use—and their related profits—are calculated in the flexible budget.

PROFIT VARIANCE ANALYSIS USING A FLEXIBLE BUDGET

A **flexible budget** is a budget prepared *after actual sales are known.* Budgeted income statements must first be reorganized, by cost behavior, into a variable expense format before they can be converted to a flexible budget. A flexible budget, then, is a revision of the original, or master, budget that reflects the amount of income that should have been earned on actual units sold.

In Exhibit 11.1, a flexible budget is created from a master budget. It is now known that actual unit sales increased from 10,000 units budgeted to 11,000 units actually sold—an increase of 10 percent. Sales revenue and variable expense in the flexible budget are each increased by 10 percent. Fixed expense remains constant, since no changes in operating capacity are needed to support increased volume.

Managers rely on flexible budgets to explain differences between actual operating results and the original budget. The process of isolating differences on items contained in the income statement is called *profit variance analysis.*[1] The flexible budget helps in this process by separating out income differences that arise because of changes in sales from those that arise as the result of other causes—such as operating inefficiencies.

---

[1] We'll find that many of the methods and techniques discussed in this chapter use terminology that seems inconsistent with other terms we use today. A good example is *"profit"* *variance analysis,* which we will use to explain differences in operating *"income."* Over the years, accounting language has changed, but some older terminology is still in use in the areas of standard costing and variance analysis.

For example, if an actual variable expense of $70,000 was incurred in our example, but the flexible budget targeted a variable expense of only $66,000, then the department manager must determine what caused the $4,000 cost overage.

Preparing a profit variance analysis based on a flexible budget involves two steps: (1) Convert the master budget to a flexible budget, and (2) calculate variances by comparing actual results with the flexible budget data. Exhibit 11.2 illustrates these two steps for Certified Block, Inc., a maker of concrete building blocks. The analysis of this exhibit moves

---

EXHIBIT 11.2 CERTIFIED BLOCK, INC.

Profit Variance Analysis Based on a Flexible Budget

Step 1. Convert the Master Budget into a Flexible Budget.   (*Note:* Analysis moves from right to left.) ◄

	(4) Standard per Unit		(3) Flexible Budget	(2) Sales Volume Variance	(1) Master Budget
Units sold & produced[a]			1,275,000 ◄	75,000 F	1,200,000
Sales revenue	$0.750000		$956,250		$ 900,000
Variable expense:					
Manufacturing	$0.303148		$386,513		$363,777
Selling & administration	$0.100000		127,500		120,000
Contribution margin	$0.346852		$442,237		$416,223
Fixed expense:					
Manufacturing overhead			$106,500		$106,500
Selling & administration			197,500		197,500
Operating income			$138,237	$26,014 F	$112,223

Step 2. Calculate Flexible Budget Variances.   (*Note:* Analysis continues from right to left.) ◄

	(4) Standard per Unit	(3c) Actual Results	(3b) Flexible Budget Variance	(3a) Flexible Budget	(2) Sales Volume Variance	(1) Master Budget
Units sold & produced		1,275,000	0	1,275,000	75,000 F	1,200,000
Sales revenue	$0.750000	$956,250		$956,250		$900,000
Variable expense:						
Manufacturing	$0.303148	$397,234	$10,721 U	$386,513		$363,777
Selling & administration[b]	$0.100000	127,500		127,500		120,000
Contribution margin	$0.346852	$431,516		$442,237		$416,223
Fixed expense:						
Manufacturing overhead		$108,100	$ 1,600 U	$106,500		$106,500
Selling & administration[b]		197,500		197,500		197,500
Operating income		$125,916	$12,321 U	$138,237	$26,014 F	$112,223

[a] *U* = unfavorable effect on operating income; *F* = favorable effect on operating income.

[b] Selling & administration expense actual results can also vary from those shown in the flexible budget. However, these variances are not the focus of our present discussion; they are assumed to be zero.

from right to left, because the conventional format of a profit variance report shows actual results on the left and the master budget—our starting point for discussion—on the right.

1: CONVERT THE MASTER BUDGET TO A FLEXIBLE BUDGET

In a flexible budget the budgeted amount for each variable expense item is recalculated using the actual amount of unit sales achieved. In column 3 in the upper panel of Exhibit 11.2, we see that the flexible budget is based on actual sales of 1,275,000 units. The budgeted sales volume, shown in column 1, is 1,200,000 units. A standard unit sales price of $0.75 and standard unit variable costs of $0.303148 and $0.100000 are given in column 4.[2] These were the unit-level targets used to calculate the master budget. We will use these same standard unit amounts to calculate targeted totals for revenue and variable expense in the flexible budget. How these standards are developed will be discussed in detail later in this chapter.

Multiplying actual units sold by the standard unit price (sales revenue) in column 3, we derive the flexible budget revenue, $956,250. Multiplying the actual units sold by the standard cost and deducting the result from the flexible budget revenue, we get the flexible budget contribution margin, $442,237. From that we deduct fixed expense; this results in $138,237 in operating income. More specifically, we obtain the flexible budget operating income—the amount that should have been earned at the actual level of unit sales.

The difference between the operating income in the master budget and that in the flexible budget is called the **sales volume variance.** It's the amount by which actual income is expected to differ from the master budget amount solely as the result of the difference between actual and budgeted unit sales. In Exhibit 11.2, column 2, the sales volume variance is $26,014 F (favorable). This is the amount by which income should exceed the master budget as a result of selling 75,000 units more than were budgeted.

2: CALCULATE FLEXIBLE BUDGET VARIANCES

Not only can the amount of units actually sold differ from budgeted sales units, so also can the actual results and the flexible budget for any of the various revenue and expense items differ. For example, a company may have sold 75,000 more units than expected, but the cost to produce and distribute those additional units could well have varied from the allowable unit cost standard. And the company may have created a revenue variance by charging more (or less) than the unit sales price standard.

---

[2] Six decimal places are used in order to prevent rounding errors in the income statement. Rounding errors increase in size when the rounded number is multiplied by a large amount—as, for example, occurs in this chapter when volumes exceed 1,000,000 units. Nonetheless, unit costs will be rounded to three places throughout the chapter for ease of illustration.

Let's see how all this fits into Certified Block's profit variance analysis. Look down the Actual Results column in the lower panel of Exhibit 11.2, column 3c. These are the revenue and expenses reported in the end-of-period income statement. Actual operating income (in column 3c) is $125,916 and its **flexible budget variance** (in column 3b), is $12,321 U (unfavorable). This variance is the difference between actual income and the flexible budget income in column 3a—income that should have resulted from actual units sold.

Although the firm sold 75,000 more units than budgeted, inefficiencies in operations increased variable and fixed costs. Unfortunately, the total of these cost overruns exceeds by $12,321 U the income produced by the 75,000 additional units sold.

Exhibit 11.2 provides an overview of the components of profit variance analysis. The sales volume variance (column 2) and the flexible budget variance (column 3b) offer information about why actual operating results differ from budget expectations. When managers know why actual income differed from the budget income, they can take steps to either improve their operations or alter their plans and expectations. Now we discuss standard costing systems, which are used to set unit cost standards and to report cost variance in more detail.

STANDARDS ARE ENGINEERED-COST TARGETS

A *standard cost*, as defined earlier, is the (budgeted) cost of making one unit of product (output). It is made up of two types of input standards:

1. **Standard quantity**—the budgeted amount of resources needed to make one unit of product
2. **Standard price**—the budgeted purchase price for one unit of resources

Production of a small pleasure boat might call for a standard quantity of 30.0 labor-hours for fiberglass lamination at a standard price of $10 per hour. A restaurant may prescribe for its lobster dinner a standard quantity of 1.25 pounds of lobster at a standard price of $6.75 per pound. From these examples, you should get the idea that standards for quantities and purchase prices of resources are commonly assigned to the variable costs of production—that is, to materials, labor, and variable overhead. These are also examples of *engineered costs*, which, by definition, *exhibit a highly predictable relationship between resource inputs and product outputs*.

On the other hand, standards for fixed costs—such as rent, insurance, and depreciation—are set by cost totals, since such costs are expected to remain constant for the period.

THE HISTORY OF STANDARD COSTS

Resource input standards originated during the industrial revolution, at the end of the nineteenth century. Managers had unprecedented levels of resources and technology at their disposal, but they lacked methods to plan, organize, and control operations. Despite advances in machinery, production was mainly driven by labor. Managers failed to understand how labor and machines could work best together.

Largely because of the influence of Frederick Taylor, a mechanical engineer known as the "father of scientific management," U.S. managers began looking for systematic approaches to performing tasks. Taylor's *time-study analysis* became a tool for scientific management. It broke down an operation into its component parts in order to find how each part could be performed most efficiently. Taylor even developed an accounting system that tracked inventory and reported differences (or exceptions) between actual results and standards which he had determined by timing workers' movement.

These historical approaches still influence the choice of production cost systems. Recall from Chapter 5 that product costs can be accumulated in one of three basic ways—using actual costs, normal costs, or standard costs. One survey revealed that 87 percent of U.S. manufacturing firms use standard costing systems, while noting that companies are focusing more attention on production by smaller work units, such as work crews and even individuals.[3] Despite changes in production technology, standard costing systems are still widely used today because of two basic advantages:

1. *Easier bookkeeping.* In standard costing systems, all inventory is recorded at standard cost, regardless of cost fluctuations from unit to unit, thereby making recording much simpler.
2. *Isolates variances.* A standard cost accounting system identifies (a) the source of variances from standard, (b) why actual results differ from the budget, and (c) areas needing improvement.

STANDARDS AND COST CONTROL

Controllable costs are costs that can be influenced by the responsibility center manager within a given time. Because engineered cost centers are closely linked to daily, repetitive activities, they have cost structures that are among the most controllable within the firm. Managers rely on cost standards to isolate cost variances so that they can determine where corrective actions are needed. Managers can control variable production costs through two factors:

1. *Shorter time span.* Engineered costs are incurred daily, hourly, and by the minute. These shorter time spans offer the opportunity for quickly implemented corrective actions and quickly realized efficiencies in operations. A production manager, for instance, might change the procedures used for adding raw materials to the manufacturing process. Accounting reports on quantity variances can provide prompt feedback on whether the changes are, in fact, effective.
2. *Direct manager influence.* Production center managers have direct influence over engineered costs. They can often experiment with operational processes without awaiting the approval or cooperation of other managers—at any level.

---

[3]   Bruce R. Gaumnitz and Felix P. Kollaritsch, "Manufacturing Variances: Current Practices and Trends," *Journal of Cost Management,* spring 1991, pp. 58–64.

HOW STANDARD COSTS ARE DEVELOPED

Successful development of a standard cost depends on the extent to which its cause and effect can be predetermined. In routine operations, time and motion studies or engineering formulas prescribe the amount of a resource needed. In some cases, these engineering techniques are especially helpful in defining standard input quantities—such as pounds of material or hours of labor. In other cases, historical cost-data analysis, including linear regression, is more helpful. In these cases, cost trends are identified from past data and are used to set standards for variable overhead costs—such as kilowatt-hours of electricity or hours of repairs. Sometimes, however, neither engineering techniques nor historical information is helpful. For example, establishing price standards for raw materials will likely require an understanding of economic conditions and supply availability.

Types of Standards.   Two types of standards are commonly distinguished from one another according to how difficult they are to attain. The ideal standard can be met only under perfect working conditions. The attainable standard takes into consideration expected deviations—such as normal spoilage, downtime, and idle capacity. An attainable materials quantity standard allows for normal amounts of unuseable raw materials and spoilage in a production process. An attainable standard for labor typically includes allowances for lost time from machinery breakdowns.

Difficulty and Commitment.   The accuracy of an attainable standard depends on senior management's success in deciding what level of operating efficiency to expect. We saw in Chapter 10 that the level of difficulty entailed in attaining budget targets has implications for employee motivation. Researchers say targets should be set so that they can be achieved, but only with some difficulty. This is frequently interpreted to mean that standards inspire the greatest motivation when they can be accomplished—but only somewhat less than 50 percent of the time.

Operating managers should feel that standards are attainable. One way of gaining operation managers' commitment is to involve them in standard setting as the budget is prepared. A participatory approach such as this enables the standard setters—engineers, statisticians, and accountants—to receive feedback from the production personnel, giving the latter a chance to "buy into" their operating targets and see how these targets relate to broader strategic objectives. (See "Current Practice: Springfield Remanufacturing Corp.")

CREATING STANDARD COSTS FOR CERTIFIED BLOCK, INC.

Let's see how Certified Block, Inc., sets its standard costs. Concrete block is manufactured in a line-flow production operation, in which raw materials are taken from inventory, premixed, and then discharged by gravity feed into a production mold. Three blocks, 8 by 8 by 16 inches on each side, are produced every 9 seconds. Blocks are moved on steel pallets by forklift into a kiln, where they remain for a 24-hour curing period. Cured blocks are moved by conveyor to a machine that arranges them to form a

CURRENT PRACTICE

Springfield Remanufacturing Corp.

The Springfield Remanufacturing Corp. (SRC), a division of International Harvester, was failing when employees took control of it in 1983 through a leveraged buyout. The new CEO expected all employees to understand the accounting numbers and initiate improvements. The company's accounting reports are based on standards developed by engineering and approved by the employees who work in the shops at the most basic level.

Study of variances is at the core of SRC's efforts to improve costs. Results are monitored continually. Shop workers know they can act in one of four ways in order to produce favorable variances: (1) work faster, (2) produce more, (3) avoid waste, and (4) use overhead frugally. Each Wednesday, all employees attend meetings to discuss production variances and their relation to company profit. Subsequently, teams of workers meet to identify unfavorable cost variances and to plan how to resolve them. The substance of these meetings—what the employees discuss, what they resolve to do, and what they do—is founded on the employees' understanding of the connection between their individual actions and company profits.

Results have been impressive. Sales grew from $16 million in 1983 to $66 million in 1990, when profit exceeded $2 million. The accounting and variance systems are seen as key elements in communicating to employees their roles in meeting the company goals.

Source: Olen L. Greer, Stevan K. Olson, and Marty Callison, "The Key to Real Teamwork: Understanding the Numbers," *Management Accounting*, May 1992, pp. 39–44.

"cube" of 90 finished blocks. Forklifts then carry the cubes to the finished-goods storage yard, where they are kept 7 more days for additional curing.

Two raw materials are needed—cement and filler. The latter is made up of refined concrete sand and small pulverized rock. Direct laborers run the production machinery, while indirect manufacturing workers—meaning *overhead*—provide support in the areas of materials handling, storage, repair, and maintenance. Other plant overhead includes costs for depreciation, occupancy, tools, supplies, and utilities.

The standard cost for one unit of output—that is, a concrete block—is made up of two standard cost components: (1) standard variable cost and (2) standard fixed overhead cost.

DEVELOPING STANDARD VARIABLE COST

Exhibit 11.3 shows how the standard variable cost for producing one 8 by 8 by 16 block is calculated. How the standard variable cost is developed is discussed below.

Direct Materials. First we need to establish the amount and cost for each of the two materials used to make one block. After talking with suppliers

---

EXHIBIT 11.3 CERTIFIED BLOCK, INC.

Standard Cost Card for an 8 by 8 by 16 Concrete Building Block

	Standard Cost per Ton	Standard Pounds per Block		Standard Cost per Block[a]
Direct materials:				
Cement	$ 42.00	3.70		$0.078[b]
Filler sand & screenings	$ 6.24	34.75		0.108
				$0.186

	Standard Hourly Pay Rate	Standard Seconds per Block		
Direct labor	$ 12.50	14.12		0.049[c]

	Annual Budget	Budgeted Production (No. of Units/yr)	Standard Cost per Block	
Variable factory overhead:				
Tools & supplies	$ 21,600	1,200,000	$0.018	
Utilities	48,000	1,200,000	0.040	
Repair & maintenance	12,000	1,200,000	0.010	
Total	$ 81,600	1,200,000		0.068
Standard variable cost per unit				$0.303

	Annual Budget	Budgeted Production (No. of Units/yr)	Standard Cost per Block	
Fixed factory overhead:				
Depreciation	$ 12,500	1,200,000	$0.010[d]	
Taxes	3,500	1,200,000	0.003	
Rent	18,000	1,200,000	0.015	
Nonmanufacturing labor	72,500	1,200,000	0.060	
Total	$106,500	1,200,000		$0.089
Standard absorption cost per unit				$0.392

---

[a] Per-unit costs are rounded to three decimal places throughout this chapter, except as noted. Rounding errors may sometimes occur as a result.

[b] $0.078 = \dfrac{\$42.00/\text{ton}}{2,000 \text{ lb}} \times 3.70 \text{ lb/block}$

[c] $0.049 = \$12.50/\text{hr} \times \dfrac{14.12 \text{ sec/block}}{60 \text{ sec/min} \times 60 \text{ min/hr}}$

[d] $0.010 = \$12,500/1,200,000 \text{ units}$

---

about projected prices for next year, the plant manager forecasts standard prices for 1-ton-lot purchases. For example, the standard price for cement is set at $42 per ton. Standard quantities of materials per block are based on average materials used to produce a "good" block—that is, one that passes inspection. The standard quantity of 3.7 pounds of cement per block takes into consideration a normal materials loss factor of 0.05 percent, plus an additional expected 0.75 percent in spoilage of materials from defective output.[4]

Direct Labor.   The plant manager constructs the budget so as to allow for a standard pay rate of $12.50 per hour, which includes 25 percent for fringe benefits and payroll taxes. Standard labor time, measured in seconds per block, is the target for the total production labor time allowed per block. It is based on an engineering study of realistically attainable production time. In this case, the calculation for labor time allows for time losses resulting from start-up activities at the beginning of a run, cleanup at the end of a run, and normal amounts of defective units.

Variable Overhead.   How reliable a standard variable overhead cost will be depends on the extent to which its variability can be predicted by the level of production output. Standard variable overhead costs are frequently based on historical data and the insights of operational personnel. Negotiation can also play an important role—especially when dealing with mixed and semivariable costs that are partially determined by subjective judgment—as indicated in the following example.

Certified Block uses regression analysis to associate monthly costs for tools and supplies with the number of blocks produced.   Based on the resulting information, the maintenance supervisor prepares a schedule of the budgeted costs of tools and supplies for several different annual levels of production volume. The plant manager and maintenance supervisor then negotiate on a budgeted cost for tools and supplies during the year for the expected annual level of output. In the example, this budgeted annual total is $21,600, and the budgeted output (in units) for the year is 1,200,000 blocks. That makes the annual standard unit cost equal to $0.018.

Other costs, such as utilities, can be more precisely predicted from the level of production activity. Standards for these costs are estimated from historical data and then adjusted for anticipated price changes. Projection of Certified Block's total utility cost depends first on predicting a per-unit cost, $0.040. Since annual budgeted volume is 1,200,000 units, total utility cost is expected to be $48,000 for the year.

DEVELOPING STANDARD FIXED OVERHEAD COST

Adding fixed factory overhead per unit to the standard variable cost results in a standard absorption cost per unit. (See the lower panel of Exhibit 11.3.)

---

[4]   Another way to look at allowance for lost materials is to calculate the amount of cement needed should the standard quantity not provide for any normal loss. Assuming no loss, good output, in this example, would only require

$$3.7 \text{ lb} \times [(1.0 - (0.0005 + 0.0075)] = 3.6704 \text{ lb.}$$

Making cement blocks requires four fixed cost items. Certified Block's management considers each a committed cost that is needed for the planned level of output—1,200,000 units.

The predictability of each of the four fixed overhead annual operating costs can vary in the budget estimates:

1. Depreciation costs are taken from asset depreciation schedules set up for each plant asset used in production. Actual depreciation may vary from the budget as the result of unplanned new asset purchases or disposals.
2. Taxes are often highly predictable based on the history of payments. Variations in prediction can arise because of changes in appraised values of property and in government tax rates.
3. Rent is likely to be highly predictable when the terms of the rental lease and the company's ability to negotiate lease terms with the property owner are used as the bases for predictions.
4. Nonmanufacturing labor includes the expense of the plant manager and of indirect labor, such as forklift drivers and yard workers. Management considers even these hourly paid workers a fixed expense, since corporate policy at Certified Block assures full-time employment unless unforeseen circumstances halt production. Compensation amounts are relatively certain but may vary because of unexpected changes in pay schedules, fringe benefits (e.g., health insurance or payroll taxes), or the number of hours worked.

Dividing the total fixed component of plant overhead ($106,500) by the number of budgeted blocks (1,200,000), we get the standard fixed overhead rate, also called the *predetermined rate,* of $0.089. Because fixed overhead cost represents a long-term total cost commitment, we must keep in mind that the standard fixed overhead rate will not change much in the short term.

REPORTING AND INTERPRETING A PRODUCTION PERFORMANCE REPORT

Certified Block's budgeted and actual costs for the past year are summarized in what is called a *production performance report,* shown in the upper portion of Exhibit 11.4. We examine it by looking first at the bottom-line variances in total production cost.

First, the sales volume variance ($22,736 U) reports the difference between production cost budgeted for the 1,200,000 units targeted and the flexible budget cost for the 1,275,000 units actually produced. Second, the flexible budget variance ($12,321 U) reports the difference between actual cost and the flexible budget cost.

In the detailed analysis that follows, the variable cost portion of the flexible budget variance ($10,721 U) is broken down into separate variances for direct materials, direct labor, and variable overhead.

The panel below the report in Exhibit 11.4 shows how to resolve each variable production cost variance into its two component variances, price variance and quantity variance.

Price variance is the part of the production cost variance that results

EXHIBIT 11.4 CERTIFIED BLOCK, INC.

Production Performance Report for the Year Ending December 31

	Actual	Flexible Budget Variance	Flexible Budget	Sales Volume Variance	Master Budget
Units produced	1,275,000	0	1,275,000	75,000 F	1,200,000
Variable cost:					
Direct materials	$243,518	$ 6,215 U	$237,303	$13,959 U	$223,344
Direct labor	62,486	24 F	62,510	3,677 U	58,833
Variable factory overhead	91,230	4,530 U	86,700	5,100 U	81,600
Total variable cost	$397,234	$10,721 U	$386,513	$22,736 U	$363,777
Fixed cost:					
Fixed factory overhead	108,100	1,600 U	106,500	0	106,500
Total production cost	$505,334	$12,321 U	$493,013	$22,736 U	$470,277

General Model for Explaining Variable Production Cost Variances

Actual Results				Flexible Budget	
Actual price (AP)	× Actual quantity (AQ)	Standard price (SP)	× Actual quantity (AQ)	Standard price (SP)	× Standard quantity (SQ)

———— Price variance ———— ———— Quantity variance ————

Caution on terminology: *Actual price* and *standard price* refer to the producer's purchase prices, which are really costs to Certified Block.

from the difference between the actual price and the standard price for the quantity of resources purchased during the reporting period. Price variance is also called *rate variance* or *spending variance.* Quantity variance is the part of the production cost variance that results from the difference between the actual quantity of resources used and the standard amount that should have been used—both stated in terms of standard price. Quantity variance is also called a *usage variance* or an *efficiency variance.*

The calculation of price variance and quantity variance depends on four separate resource input factors:

- Actual price is the amount actually paid per unit of resource input. This term is conventionally used in standard costing, but it can be confusing, since *actual price* really means the producer's purchase price—what we would normally call *cost.*
- Actual quantity is the total amount of resources actually used in production.
- Standard price is the budgeted amount to be paid per unit of resource input. As with actual price, *standard price* means budgeted price to be paid, which is really the producer's cost.
- Standard quantity is the total amount of resource inputs budgeted for the number of units produced.

DIRECT MATERIALS VARIANCES

A separate cost variance analysis must be prepared for each of the two direct materials used—concrete blocks and filler. Exhibit 11.5 provides a complete cost variance analysis for both materials and a summation of total direct materials. We'll explain how to calculate cost variances for the cement (the same method can be used to calculate the variance for the filler, or for any direct material.)

Calculating Variances for Cement.   To perform a cost variance analysis for any direct resource, we need to know the resource's actual and standard prices and actual and standard quantities. Starting at the left of the diagram representing cost variances for cement (the first diagram), we find that Certified Block paid an actual price (AP) of $41.50 per ton. The standard price (SP) allowed in the budget was $42 per ton. Actual quantity (AQ) of cement purchased was 2,400 tons. Therefore, $99,600 was the total expenditure for cement during the year.

The center of the top diagram shows that the standard price allowed was $42 per ton for the 2,400 tons actually purchased. That makes the allowable total purchase price for the actual quantity of cement purchased $100,800. The difference between the actual price and standard price for the actual quantity purchased results in a total price variance of $1,200 F for the cement.[5] This relationship can also be expressed in equation form:

$$\text{Price variance} = (\text{standard price} - \text{actual price}) \times \text{actual quantity}$$

$$= (42.00 \text{ per ton} - \$41.50 \text{ per ton}) \times 2,400 \text{ tons}$$

$$= \$1,200 \quad \text{F}$$

Whether the variance is favorable or unfavorable depends on whether less or more, respectively, was actually spent in comparison with the budget. Here, actual price is less than standard price; hence, a favorable variance results.

At the far right of the cement cost-variance-analysis diagram (the top diagram), under "Flexible Budget," we see that standard price ($42 per ton), and standard quantity (SQ, 2,358.75 tons) results in an allowance of $99,068 for cement. (Note the $1 rounding error.) Both this calculation and the SP × AQ calculation ($100,800) rely on standard price. Therefore, comparing the two really involves only differences in the quantity of cement used. Because the $100,800 of actual usage is more than the $99,068 standard allowed, the $1,733 variance is unfavorable. We could have calculated this using the following equation:

---

[5]   Material price variances are often identified at time of purchase rather than at time of use. For example, if 6,000 tons were purchased but only 2,400 tons used, the price variance would be

$$(SP - AP) \times AQ = (\$42.00 \text{ per ton} - \$41.50 \text{ per ton}) \times 6,000 \text{ tons} = \$3,000 \text{ F}$$

The materials quantity variance would not be affected. It would still be calculated based on the 2,400 tons actually used.

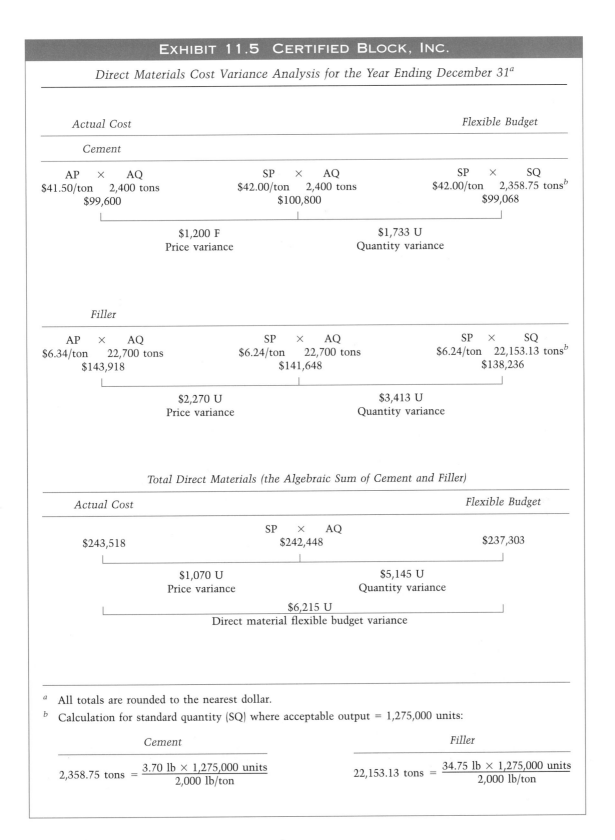

EXHIBIT 11.5 CERTIFIED BLOCK, INC.

Direct Materials Cost Variance Analysis for the Year Ending December 31[a]

Actual Cost   *Flexible Budget*

Cement

AP × AQ	SP × AQ	SP × SQ
$41.50/ton 2,400 tons	$42.00/ton 2,400 tons	$42.00/ton 2,358.75 tons[b]
$99,600	$100,800	$99,068

$1,200 F $1,733 U
Price variance   Quantity variance

Filler

AP × AQ	SP × AQ	SP × SQ
$6.34/ton 22,700 tons	$6.24/ton 22,700 tons	$6.24/ton 22,153.13 tons[b]
$143,918	$141,648	$138,236

$2,270 U $3,413 U
Price variance   Quantity variance

Total Direct Materials (the Algebraic Sum of Cement and Filler)

Actual Cost   *Flexible Budget*

	SP × AQ	
$243,518	$242,448	$237,303

$1,070 U $5,145 U
Price variance   Quantity variance

$6,215 U
Direct material flexible budget variance

[a] All totals are rounded to the nearest dollar.

[b] Calculation for standard quantity (SQ) where acceptable output = 1,275,000 units:

Cement	*Filler*
$2{,}358.75 \text{ tons} = \dfrac{3.70 \text{ lb} \times 1{,}275{,}000 \text{ units}}{2{,}000 \text{ lb/ton}}$	$22{,}153.13 \text{ tons} = \dfrac{34.75 \text{ lb} \times 1{,}275{,}000 \text{ units}}{2{,}000 \text{ lb/ton}}$

$$\text{Quantity variance} = (\text{actual quantity} - \text{std. quantity}) \times \text{std. price}$$

$$= (2{,}400 \text{ tons} - 2{,}358.75 \text{ tons}) \times \$42.00 \text{ per ton}$$

$$= \$1{,}733 \text{ U}$$

Beware: Standard quantity can be the most confusing aspect of a variable production cost analysis and is often not clearly understood. *Standard quantity represents standard resource inputs allowed for the number of good units actually produced.* In the case of Certified Block's cement calculation, the standard quantity for cement, 2,358.75 tons, is derived by multiplying the unit standard of 3.7 pounds per block by the 1,275,000 blocks that passed final quality inspection. Because the cement price is in dollars per ton, we divide by 2,000 to convert pounds to tons (2,000 pounds = 1 ton).

Interpreting Direct Material Variances.   The bottom part of Exhibit 11.5 analyzes the cost variances—not for each of the direct materials separately, but for the aggregate direct materials. Production ran over its flexible budget both in price ($1,070 U) and in quantity used ($5,145 U). The production manager must determine why the variances happened and how to prevent them in the next budget period.

Looking at the individual direct materials price variances, the variance for filler is $2,270 U. It's probably unfavorable because prices rose faster than expected, a condition that is out of management's control. Other factors can also cause price variances. Perhaps poor planning necessitated hurried purchases from lower-level suppliers (distributors, not wholesalers) or the use of more-expensive transport. Poor planning could also result in having to buy smaller quantities than were budgeted, causing higher handling charges or loss of quantity discounts. Favorable price variances, such as that for cement ($1,200 F), in our example, should also be explained, since they might offer clues about successful actions that could be taken elsewhere. On the downside of a favorable price variance, lower direct materials prices may have been the result of purchasing poorer-quality materials.

Both the cement and the filler cost variances that resulted from quantity produced—the quantity variances—were unfavorable, as shown in Exhibit 11.5. There could have been several causes. Perhaps workers were sloppy and wasted materials, or perhaps they were poorly trained. Old or poorly maintained machinery might have created unexpected problems. Or it may be that an abnormally high percentage of defective concrete blocks were produced.

Sometimes insights can be gained by combining different types of variances for analysis. For instance, poor materials quantity variances can be tied to favorable materials price variances arising from the purchase of lesser-quality materials.

Production variances help managers explain why actual operating results differed from flexible budget targets. It is up to managers and their frontline employees to determine the exact causes. In fact, variance investigation might reveal no problem with operations. Instead, *it may be the standards that need repair.* Information contained in production variances is reliable only if the standards used for comparison are correct. (See "Current Practice: Standard Pricing During a Worldwide Oil Crisis.")

DIRECT LABOR VARIANCES

The top part of Exhibit 11.6 shows the direct labor cost variance analysis for Certified Block. Calculations for the price variance and quantity variance of direct labor are much the same as they are for those variances for direct materials. The labor price variance is also called the *labor rate variance,* and the labor quantity variance is often called the *labor efficiency variance.*

Calculating Direct Labor Variances. At the left of the upper diagram (Exhibit 11.6), multiplying the actual price of $12.56 per hour by the actual quantity of 4,975 labor-hours gives us the actual total labor cost of $62,486.

The center of the diagram shows the $12.50-per-hour standard price that should have been paid for the 4,975 hours actually worked, or $62,188. The difference between the two totals for labor cost ($62,188 − $62,486) results in the labor price variance of $299 U, due solely to the fact that the actual labor rate paid exceeds the standard.

At the right of the diagram, we calculate the direct labor flexible budget, which is the total labor standard cost allowed for all units that passed inspection. Multiplying the standard price ($12.50 per hour) by the standard quantity (5,000.83 hours) we see that the total direct labor cost should be $62,510, according to the flexible budget. (See footnote *b*, Exhibit 11.6, where 1,275,000 blocks at 14.12 seconds per block converts to 5,000.83

CURRENT PRACTICE

Standard Pricing During a Worldwide Oil Crisis

In the 1970s, Warner Lambert Corporation owned a small toiletries manufacturer of specialty fragrances, such as Bay Rum, which were typical of its location in St. Thomas, U.S. Virgin Islands. The toiletries manufacturer reported financial results, including direct materials price variances, on a monthly basis to its U.S.-based parent company. In 1973, oil prices increased by 400 percent over 6 months as the worldwide oil cartel—the Organization of Petroleum Exporting Countries—limited supply. These price increases were severely felt in the Virgin Islands, since all of the firm's resource inputs were imported and dependent on transportation. Monthly performance reports submitted to the parent company during this period contained huge direct materials price variances, which resulted from the manufacturer's quickly outdated price standards.

Source: Authors' consulting experience.

EXHIBIT 11.6 CERTIFIED BLOCK, INC.

Cost Variance Analysis for Direct Labor and Variable Overhead
for the Year Ending December 31[a]

Direct Labor

Actual Costs			*Flexible Budget*

AP × AQ	SP × AQ	SP × SQ
$12.56/hr 4,975 hr	$12.50/hr 4,975 hr	$12.50/hr 5,000.83 hr[b]
$62,486	$62,188	$62,510

$299 U
Price variance

$323 F
Quantity variance

$24 F
Direct labor flexible budget variance

Variable Overhead

Actual Costs			*Flexible Budget*

	SP × AQ	SP × SQ
	$17.337/hr 4,975 hr	$17.337/hr[c] 5,000.83 hr
$91,230	$86,252	$86,700

$4,978 U
Price variance

$488 F
Quantity variance

$4,530 U
Variable overhead flexible budget variance

---

[a] All totals are rounded to the nearest dollar.

[b] Calculation for standard quantity (SQ) for direct labor where acceptable output = 1,275,000 units:

$$5,000.83 \text{ hr} = \frac{14.12 \text{ sec} \times 1,275,000 \text{ units}}{60 \text{ sec/min} \times 60 \text{ min/hr}}$$

[c] Calculation for standard price (SP) for variable overhead where budgeted output = 1,200,000 units:

$$\$17.337 \text{ hr} = \frac{\$81,600 \text{ (see Exhibit 11.3)}}{\left(\frac{14.12/\text{unit} \times 1,200,000 \text{ units}}{60 \text{ sec/min} \times 60 \text{ min/hr}} \right)}$$

labor-hours.) Because both the $62,188 and $62,510 total labor costs were calculated using the same standard price, then the difference ($62,510 − $62,188) is the labor quantity variance ($323 F).

Interpreting Direct Labor Variances. Labor price variances result when the actual labor rate differs from the standard labor rate. Certified Block, for example, actually paid $12.56 per hour but had only expected to pay $12.50. The effect of supply and demand on pay rates for comparably skilled labor is a probable reason for this difference. Differences can also arise from changes to rates for fringe benefits, such as health insurance, if these are included in the standard rate. While Certified Block may have paid its workers, say, the direct hourly rate of $10, charges incurred for health insurance rates may have changed. Pay rates can also vary as the result of hiring workers of a different skill level than was provided for in the standard.

Managers pay attention to labor quantity variances because such variances signal levels of worker efficiency. This is an area that managers can control directly and immediately. Laborers might be inefficient because of poor work habits. Unskilled workers may have been hired—possibly causing a favorable labor rate variance but an unfavorable labor quantity variance. Other possible factors contributing to labor inefficiency are poorly maintained machinery or use of substandard materials.

VARIABLE FACTORY OVERHEAD VARIANCES

The cost variance analysis for variable factory overhead in Exhibit 11.6 uses the same kinds of calculations as those used to obtain the price variance and quantity variance for direct materials and direct labor. However, we need to be aware that variable overhead is composed of many different types of costs that are unrelated to each other. Accounting systems have long grouped together overhead into diverse overhead cost pools, which are then applied to units produced by some common activity base— such as labor dollars or machine-hours—based upon a predetermined, or standard, overhead rate.

Calculating Variable Overhead Variances. Total actual variable overhead cost is $91,230. There is no actual price or actual quantity for pooled overhead cost. Since Certified Block's overhead comprises three different types of costs—tools and supplies, utilities, and repair and maintenance—there is no single unit actual price for pooled overhead. Each component of the pool has its own unique standard price—for example, utilities might be charged at $0.0743 per kilowatt-hour. Similarly, there is no single quantity measure for variable overhead, either.

However, total overhead cost is normally applied to output by means of a common activity base, assuming that the activity base is the driver (the cause) common to all variable overhead costs. For example, Certified Block uses an AQ of 4,975 actual direct labor-hours (the same amount used in the direct labor analysis). It uses an SP of $17.337 per hour (the calculation is shown in footnote c of Exhibit 11.6).

The variable overhead standard price ($17.337 per hour) is multiplied by the actual quantity (4,975 labor-hours) to get the standard variable overhead cost ($86,252) for the number of labor-hours actually used. The difference between this standard and the actual variable overhead cost ($91,230 − $86,252) is the price variance ($4,978 U).

Multiplying the standard price of $17.337 per hour by the standard quantity of 5,000.83 direct labor-hours, we get the flexible budget amount for variable overhead, or $86,700. The difference between the flexible budget overhead cost for hours that should have been used and standard variable overhead cost for hours actually used ($86,700 − $86,252) is a $448 F quantity variance. However, this variable overhead quantity variance has little or nothing to do with controlling variable overhead! *The variable overhead quantity variance identifies the amount of cost difference caused by variation in the underlying activity base*—direct labor, in this case. In other words, the quantity of variable overhead consumed is tied to the efficiency of production workers. If labor exceeds standard time allotted, the additional labor time—which means more production time was required to make the same number of units—will incur greater variable overhead costs, such as utilities needed to run machinery.

For Certified Block, direct labor performed more efficiently than the standard—that's what the $323 F direct labor quantity variance means. As a result, less variable overhead was needed to keep the factory running—indicated by the variable overhead quantity variance of $448 F. When the standard quantity for variable overhead is based on direct labor-hours, the calculation of the variable overhead quantity variance is derived from the calculation of the direct labor quantity variance. Thus, the variable overhead quantity variance will always take on the same algebraic sign—here, favorable—as the direct labor quantity variance.

Interpreting Variable Overhead Variances. In Exhibit 11.7, we see the component costs of variable overhead cost. We analyze only the price variance, because if reflects controllable differences. Using the term *"price"* variance is a bit misleading, because overhead variances can be caused by differences either in price or in efficiency. (Some authors call this a *spending variance* in order to imply a broader causal context.)

Certified Block's production manager needs to understand why actual cost exceeded by $4,978 the standard cost allotted for actual direct labor-hours. By examining the price variance for each of the three component costs, it is possible to identify utilities cost ($3,243 U) as the major source of variance. More investigation will be needed to determine whether corrective action can be undertaken. The variance may be the result of increases in utility rates or to setting a standard utilities cost that is a poor reflection of the actual cost. Perhaps machinery is running poorly and requires more electricity and water usage. Or workers might be leaving equipment turned on when it is not in use. The utilities variance can be caused by any combination of factors, but at least its identification helps management to now realize that utilities cost is a problem in meeting budget.

Besides revealing the variance in utilities cost, Exhibit 11.7 shows a $2,226 U variance for repair and maintenance. This cost item will require

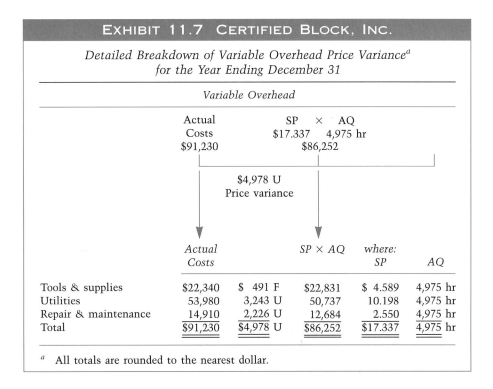

EXHIBIT 11.7 CERTIFIED BLOCK, INC.

Detailed Breakdown of Variable Overhead Price Variance[a]
for the Year Ending December 31

Variable Overhead

	Actual Costs		SP × AQ $17.337 4,975 hr $86,252		
	$91,230				

$4,978 U
Price variance

	Actual Costs		*SP × AQ*	*where: SP*	*AQ*
Tools & supplies	$22,340	$ 491 F	$22,831	$ 4.589	4,975 hr
Utilities	53,980	3,243 U	50,737	10.198	4,975 hr
Repair & maintenance	14,910	2,226 U	12,684	2.550	4,975 hr
Total	$91,230	$4,978 U	$86,252	$17.337	4,975 hr

[a] All totals are rounded to the nearest dollar.

a separate investigation and may involve many factors—for example, unexpected major repairs, more-aggressive preventive maintenance, or improperly set standards.

The third variable overhead cost item, tools and supplies ($491 F), may also require explanation. Possible causes include postponed tool purchases, more-efficient use of supplies, and lower prices paid for tools and supplies, among others.

FIXED FACTORY OVERHEAD VARIANCES

Certified Block's fixed factory overhead budget variance is $1,600 U (see Exhibit 11.4). Exhibit 11.8 is a performance report showing the breakdown of this variance into its individual cost components.[6]

Calculating Fixed Factory Overhead Variances.   Fixed cost analysis is concerned with only the variance between actual fixed cost and flexible budget fixed cost. For fixed overhead cost, there are no price and quantity variance components. Fixed overhead cost, by definition, does not vary with volume—the only reason fixed cost will differ is as the result of price differences.

Certified Block's fixed factory overhead comprises four cost components. In Exhibit 11.8, a variance is reported for each fixed cost component

---

[6]   See the appendix to this chapter for the financial reporting aspects of fixed factory overhead and for the calculation of production volume variances.

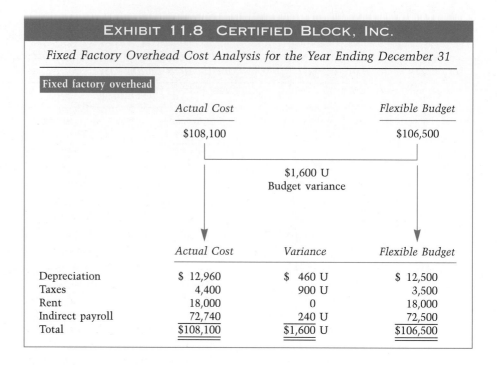

EXHIBIT 11.8 CERTIFIED BLOCK, INC.

Fixed Factory Overhead Cost Analysis for the Year Ending December 31

Fixed factory overhead

	Actual Cost		Flexible Budget
	$108,100		$106,500

$1,600 U
Budget variance

	Actual Cost	Variance	Flexible Budget
Depreciation	$ 12,960	$ 460 U	$ 12,500
Taxes	4,400	900 U	3,500
Rent	18,000	0	18,000
Indirect payroll	72,740	240 U	72,500
Total	$108,100	$1,600 U	$106,500

to help the production manager determine why the unfavorable variance occurred. For example, the variance for taxes is $900 U. This difference is explained by an incorrect forecast during budget preparation. Virtually nothing can be done to reduce this cost, which is primarily caused by property tax increases, other than to reduce property holdings. Depreciation shows a $460 U variance, perhaps the result of higher-than-expected depreciation on a machine replacement. The $240 U variance in nonmanufacturing labor (indirect payroll) can be the result of unexpected price increases to employee benefits, such as health insurance premiums.

Interpreting Fixed Factory Overhead Variances. A fixed factory overhead cost analysis won't be much use to a production manager in trying to control costs. A production manager can only control variable production costs. Decisions for controlling fixed costs are made *before the reporting period even begins.* Once management decides upon a given level of operating capacity, fixed costs needed to support that level are committed. This is the case of Certified Block, which can do little in the short run to cut depreciation, taxes, rent, or nonmanufacturing labor. Of course, any of these costs can be reduced by decreasing assets, eliminating employees, or reconfiguring the production process. However, these are long-term strategic decisions that are not addressed in the cost center's operational report.

WHEN TO INVESTIGATE VARIANCES

Variances should be investigated only when doing so is justified by the benefits expected to result. If, for example, the quantity of direct materials used is greater than the standard quantity, someone will have to spend time researching the cause. Was the variance the result of poor materials? Was it the result of poorly maintained machinery? Or was it caused by poorly trained personnel? Perhaps all of these factors—plus some others—contributed to the problem. Managers should decide to investigate only when the value of the benefits received from identifying the cause is expected to exceed the cost of gathering the information and analyzing it—the *opportunity cost* of the investigator's time.

Managers tend to use simple rules to help them determine whether to investigate financial variances—not necessarily the same rules. Some simply investigate all variances, regardless of cost trade-offs. Others investigate only variances that are not within acceptable limits. For instance, one manager may specify that all variances exceeding the standard by 5 percent or by $500, whichever is lower, must be investigated. Still others may investigate variances that they "feel" should be investigated.

There are also technical tools for analyzing financial variances, such as *control charts.* Control charts are graphs of successive observations that are bounded by a statistically determined range of acceptance. Observations that fall within the "acceptable" range are considered normal random fluctuations that require no investigation. Observations falling outside the range are signals that investigation is needed.

Assume the production manager at Certified Block is concerned with a large, unfavorable utilities cost variance reported in the analysis of variable overhead cost. Exhibit 11.9 shows a control chart that tracks utilities cost in the form of a graph of the plant's weekly consumption of kilowatt-hours. Utilities cost data from the previous year, when energy consumption was acceptable, are used to construct an acceptable control range. Observations are reported for energy consumption during the first 8 weeks of the year. The graph helps the manager to identify an apparent trend in energy consumption. Usage in each 4-week period begins at a low level and increases with each passing week. The upper control limit is exceeded in weeks 4 and 8. After investigation, the plant manager isolates the problem—equipment servicing, which is performed on the first of each month. By switching to a semimonthly service schedule in weeks 9 through 12, the production manager causes energy consumption in week 12 to fall back within the range of acceptable control.[7]

COST CONTROL IN COMPLEX PRODUCTION ENVIRONMENTS

Standards are most effective in controlling costs when the production environment is stable. Environmental changes resulting from global competition and technology undermine this premise, upon which standard cost

---

[7] For additional information on statistical process control, refer to a production-operations text. See for example J. Krajewski and Larry P. Ritzman, *Operations Management: Strategy and Analysis,* Reading, Mass.: Addison-Wesley, 1987, Chap. 19; or Norman Gaither, *Production and Operations Management,* 4th ed., Chicago: Dryden, 1990, Chap. 15.

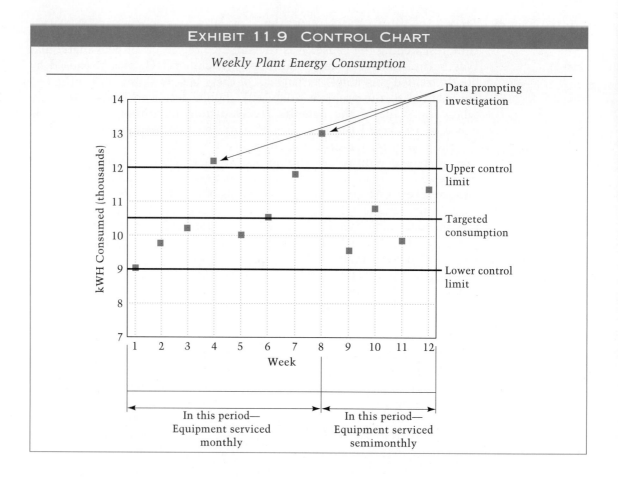

EXHIBIT 11.9   CONTROL CHART

Weekly Plant Energy Consumption

IMPACT OF COMPLEX PRODUCTION METHODS

systems are built. (See "Current Practice: Change in the Computer Industry.")

Next, we examine the use of standard costing in today's dynamic business environment and explore control alternatives.

In industrial nations, production operations are shifting from the use of human labor to automation. For many firms, direct labor cost has fallen to less than 10 percent of product cost; for some, it is now an insignificant cost. A Hewlett-Packard plant that makes circuit boards received considerable attention in the mid-1980s when it reclassified its direct labor as an overhead cost. This decision was based on labor costs that were small— 3 to 5 percent of product cost—and mainly fixed.[8] As direct labor shrinks, the cost of overhead and of support activities increases. Overhead costs in the United States are now more than three times the cost of labor.[9]

---

[8]   R. Hunt, L. Garrett, and C. M. Merz, "Direct Labor Cost Not Always Relevant at H-P," *Management Accounting,* Feb. 1985, pp. 58–62.
[9]   J. Miller and T. Vollman, "The Hidden Factory," *Harvard Business Review,* Sept.–Oct. 1985, p. 143.

CURRENT PRACTICE

Change in the Computer Industry

The personal computer market is afflicted with a mercilessly short product life cycle. Dell Computer, for example, has introduced a new product every 3 weeks during the past few years. Its longest-lasting product is 11 months old. The overcrowding in the PC-suppliers industry— an industry led by high-growth mail-order firms such as Dell, Northgate, and Gateway 2000—has resulted in razor-thin profit margins and uncertain survival prospects. Some older, established companies, such as IBM and Compaq, are finding it difficult to compete with the cut-rate prices offered by low-overhead mail-order firms. Moreover, consumers, accustomed to continual cost cutting, have come to expect the newer PCs to deliver more and more power and capacity at lower and lower prices. As computer component suppliers around the globe adjust their prices to meet those of their competition, the PC manufacturers must regularly change the standard prices they use in their cost accounting systems.

Source: Hal Lancaster and Michael Allen, "Dell Computer Battles Its Rivals with a Lean Machine," *The Wall Street Journal,* Mar. 30, 1992, p. B4; Michael Allen, "Low-Cost PC Makers Have Come on Strong But Difficulties Loom," *The Wall Street Journal,* May 11, 1992, p. A1.

Despite rapid technological changes in production, cost accounting information has not changed accordingly. In 1990 most companies were still using labor-focused costing systems. According to one study, less than 25 percent of midwestern manufacturing firms used other activity bases (e.g., machine-hours, materials cost, or cycle time) to assign indirect overhead cost to products.[10] Where cost systems do not reflect changing production processes, the manager will need to interpret cost variances as well as to recognize when additional information is needed to interpret them.

Three things make today's production cost control more difficult:

1. *Multiple product lines.* Companies often manufacture diverse product lines using the same plant and equipment. Some products are standard and mass-produced, others are specialty items. Specialty production is more complex and tends to create the need for additional support staff for activities such as engineering design, machine setup, materials procurement, and production scheduling. The cost of most of these activities is fixed or semifixed, and, thus, does not change when volume changes.

2. *Product life cycles.* Standard costing systems are normally based on targets that are developed as the annual budget is prepared. Using the same standard cost over a 1-year period is appropriate for mature

---

[10]   James R. Emore and Joseph A. Ness, "The Slow Pace of Meaningful Change in Cost Systems," *Journal of Cost Management,* winter 1991, p. 38.

products competing on cost—but not for newly developed products in markets where sales price is not the determining competitive factor. Exhibit 11.10 shows a typical product life cycle. The product is

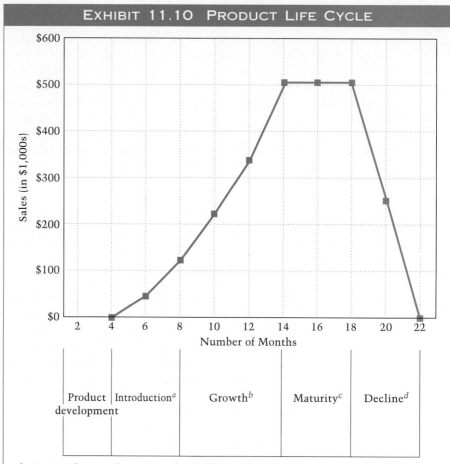

EXHIBIT 11.10 PRODUCT LIFE CYCLE

[a] During the *introduction*, as the product is brought to market, frequent design changes are made.

[b] In the *growth* phase, the product enjoys rapid sales increases, while the design becomes fairly standard.

[c] During *maturity* sales growth often continues, but at a declining rate. Eventually, sales flatten. (In this case, sales flatten immediately in the maturity stage.)

[d] During the *decline*, sales decline and the product is replaced by better products or substitutes.

Source: Definitions have been adapted from Peter R. Richardson and John R. M. Gordon, "Measuring Total Manufacturing Performance," *Sloan Management Review*, winter 1980, p. 48. The graph was adapted from Ramon L. Alonso and Cline W. Frasier, "JIT Hits Home: A Case Study in Reducing Management Delays," *Sloan Management Review*, summer 1991, p. 60, by permission of the publisher. Copyright 1991 by the Sloan Management Review Association. All rights reserved.

in the development phase for 4 months, in the introduction and growth-in-the-market phase for 10 months, and then in the mature phase, which lasts 4 months. Thereafter, product sales decline for 4 months, and the focus is on enhancing or replacing the product.

3. *Continuous improvement.* Organizations regularly seek both to reduce the costs and to improve the quality of their products and their manufacture. For instance, manufacturers focus on designing products that use common parts and interchangeable subassemblies. And they improve upon how products are made by using advanced technology, keener scheduling, and redesign of the factory floor. Standard costs must also be revised regularly in order to represent meaningful performance targets.

OPERATING CONTROLS FOR MANUFACTURING

In the past, the purpose of accounting for manufacturing process was to maximize *production efficiency*—the relationship between the value of product outputs and the costs of resource inputs. Use of standard prices helped managers to establish cost targets deemed optimal for the given operating constraints, thereby enabling them to maximize production efficiency. Production managers were evaluated according to how close they came to achieving their efficiency targets. And factory workers were not expected to do more than accomplish assigned tasks.

Today, manufacturers throughout the world have broadened the responsibility and the control of managers and production employees, and their effects on efficiency. Managers—and shop workers, as well—are encouraged to intervene in cost reduction and to search for better business practices. Workers are recognized as the experts in shop floor activities, and they are given authority to effect change. For these tactics to work—and for their success to be evaluated—there must be timely and relevant performance measures that report what work was done and the level of results achieved.

MANUFACTURING PERFORMANCE ATTRIBUTES

Managers measure their manufacturing performance against the following five attributes—each considered critical for competing in global markets[11] A more complete listing of possible measures is given in Exhibit 11.11.

1. *Quality* deals with how reliably a product is manufactured to conform to its design specifications. Assuring design conformance leads to improved customer satisfaction—the ultimate test of market acceptability. Other measures of the quality of manufacturing include assurance testing of incoming materials and of inventory during production, and tracking financial losses resulting from scrap and defects.

---

[11] Based on an article by Robert A. Howell and Stephen R. Soucy, "Operating Controls in the New Manufacturing Environment," *Management Accounting*, Oct. 1987, pp. 25–31. These concepts and their application have since been discussed in many different publications.

EXHIBIT 11.11 OPERATING PERFORMANCE MEASURES FOR COMPLEX MANUFACTURING ENVIRONMENTS

Production Attributes →	Quality	Delivery	Inventory	Materials	Machine Maintenance
Performance measures	Customer complaints Customer surveys Warranty claims Quality audits Vendor quality Cost of quality: Scrap Rework Returns & allowances Field service Warranty claims Lost business	On-time delivery Order fill rate Lead time—order to shipment Waste time—lead time less process time Cycle time—materials receipt to product shipment Set-up time Production backlog	Turnover rates by location for: Raw materials Work in process Finished goods Composite Turnover rates by product Cycle count accuracy Space reduction Number of inventoried items	Quality of incoming materials Materials cost as a percent of total cost Actual scrap loss Scrap by part, product, or operation Scrap cost as a percent of total cost	Equipment capacity utilization Availability, downtime Machine maintenance Equipment experience

Source: Reprinted from Robert A. Howell and Stephen R. Soucy, "Operating Controls in the New Manufacturing Environment," *Management Accounting,* Oct. 1987, p. 31. Copyright by Institute of Management Accountants, Montvale, N.J.

CURRENT PRACTICE

Du Pont Corporation

The polymers division of Du Pont Corporation has started a campaign to reduce its production plant downtime, thereby speeding up production and reducing costs. Reducing downtime among the dozens of its plants is expected to raise profits by $200 million a year. One plant on the Delaware River has held fixed cost constant since 1989, while sharply increasing productivity. It eliminated one production line, while reducing downtime between processing runs on the other. Workers are involved in decision making, which serves to get them to internalize the company's goals.

Source: Scott McMurray, "Du Pont Tries to Make Its Research Wizardry Serve the Bottom Line," *The Wall Street Journal*, Mar. 27, 1992, p. A1.

2. *Delivery* addresses the factory's record of consistency and reliability in meeting production schedules. Production is expected to satisfy delivery commitments. Aggressive firms often set a target of 100 percent success in achieving delivery due dates. Delivery also addresses the need for speed in the production cycle and for quick production changeovers.

3. *Inventory* of raw materials and finished goods should be set at prescribed minimum levels. How closely those minimums are adhered to is another measure of manufacturing performance. Carrying small inventory levels leads to achieving high inventory turnovers—with some manufacturers reporting as many as 100 annual inventory turnovers.[12] Physical measures are also useful—for example, counting the number of items in inventory or keeping track of the amount of space that inventory occupies.

4. *Materials* can be used in a number of ways to measure manufacturing performance. How immediately available materials are when needed, how few financial resources are tied up in them, what their level of quality is are all measures of manufacturing performance. Materials management can mean forming long-term partnerships with materials suppliers or gaining added services from suppliers. The manufacturer benefits by maintaining lower inventories or receiving defect-free materials.

5. *Machine maintenance* is the key to machine availability—downtime creates lost capacity that can never be recaptured. (See "Current Practice: Du Pont Corporation.") Firms with sound maintenance-management programs keep careful track of equipment histories, including preventive maintenance and unscheduled repairs.

---

[12] Howell and Soucy, *ibid.,* p. 29.

RELATIONSHIP TO STANDARD COST VARIANCES

Measurements of each of these five components of manufacturing performance are useful supplements to a standard costing system. Performance measurements explain those problems in the operating activities that caused the cost variances and how they may be remedied. For example, a materials quantity variance reports that income isn't what it was expected to be because of excessive scrap—that is, the dollar value of scrap is higher than was estimated when the budget was prepared. A performance measurement on the scrap itself specifically indicates a problem with one of the machines at a key point in production.

Two benefits can be gained from the use of operating performance measures:

1. *Early correction.* Referring to the example above, if the manager and shop floor workers know that materials scrap exceeds normal expectations, immediate action can be taken. Operating measures can tally the amount of scrap at frequent intervals'—by the run, the hour, or the day. These measurements are disseminated to managers and workers in the production activity affecting the amount of scrap. Prompt feedback on errant activities enables prompt investigation and correction.

2. *Better understanding.* Financial variances report the financial effects of all activities related to a cost object. Thus, a materials quantity variance can identify the impact of excessive scrap, as well as the impact of poorly maintained machines, poorly trained workers, and poor quality materials. Use of production measures helps to isolate causes. For example, separate performance measures can track levels of scrap, scrap per worker, and scrap per type of material. Understanding what caused a variance is what leads to resolving it.

REPORTING PERFORMANCE MEASURES

Through performance measures, managers and workers keep close watch on early warning indicators of any deterioration in efficiency and quality. We now look at ways that measures can be reported and how they can be used to improve factory performance.

FREQUENCY AND PRESENTATION

The frequency of performance measure reports will depend on the extent to which information is available and useful for control purposes. Recurring activities that drive highly predictable engineered costs should be reported at shorter time intervals, since the possibilities to make fine adjustments are great. Less-frequent, higher-level activities, which are more complex and can only be corrected through programmatic changes, are reported at longer time intervals. Thus, we might expect frequent, perhaps daily, reports for the number of parts scrapped during assembly. On the other hand, less frequent, perhaps monthly, reports would be adequate to control the total number of items carried in inventory.

Real-Time Measures. Highly computerized factory operations enable even-more-frequent reports using real-time measures. Manufacturers have factory floor workers constantly monitor real-time production activities. A computer terminal might display feedback, for instance, on piston ring clearances as pistons are being inserted into engine blocks. Production employees can correct even minor deficiencies before moving engines on to the next assembly station. If there is a severe problem in the production line, the line is immediately brought to a halt. Production workers—through the performance information they receive—are expected to resolve problems of quality and efficiency as they arise.

Graphic Display of Time Series. One clear way to observe performance trends is by means of a graph of performance measures over time, or a data time series. Exhibit 11.12 contains three examples. The first graph is a *weekly report* of a factory's production backlog covering the first quarter. The production manager might be expected to initiate overtime work schedules whenever the backlog exceeds 1,500 units—thereby ensuring that deliveries are timely enough to meet customer expectations. The graph also displays a rising backlog early in the year, which seems to have been corrected. The second graph is a *daily report* showing machine downtime, with a goal of zero minutes of downtime per day. This report is shared with the maintenance supervisor, who is responsible for keeping the operation running 100 percent of the time. The third graph is an *hourly report* for materials scrap, which is measured by the pound. This information is distributed to production teams, which are responsible for achieving zero-scrap-tolerance targets.

Control Limits. Managers must decide when to investigate significant variations in reported performance measures. Even when the target is to achieve zero tolerance for error, control limits will help to identify random fluctuations in performance. For example, 15 minutes or less of downtime might be tolerated. (See the machine downtime graph in Exhibit 11.12). Consequently, the manager would be required to investigate and report upon only one variance, the peak 24 minutes of downtime that occurred on the second Tuesday of the month.

The goal in a system of continuous improvement is to search for the causes of any measurements exceeding acceptable limits in order to eliminate them in the future. The long-term effect is to reduce the amount of (explained) variation in the system, and thus, to narrow the acceptable band set by the control limits. Hence, the plant manager may trace the cause of the excessive downtime to a mechanical belt-driven timing device that snaps and must be replaced after about every 1,000 hours of use. This problem can be prevented by replacing the belt at shorter intervals, perhaps every 950 hours, and thereby reducing the chances of unexpected belt snapping. By eliminating the cause of this downtime, the average range of

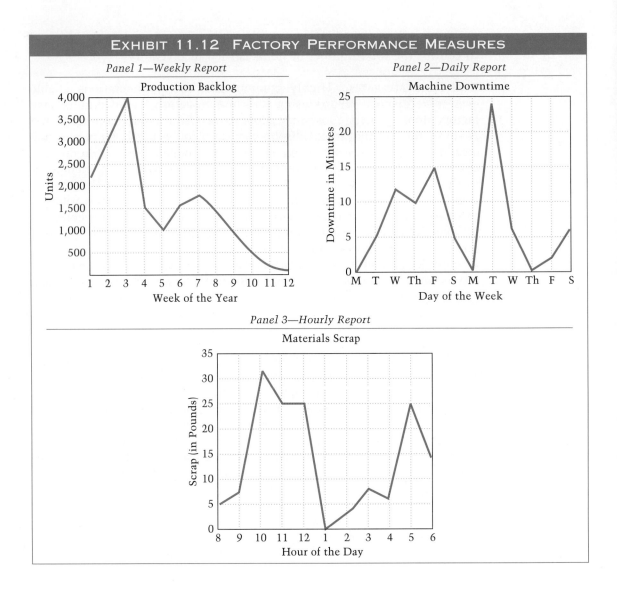

EXHIBIT 11.12   FACTORY PERFORMANCE MEASURES

Panel 1—Weekly Report   *Panel 2—Daily Report*

Production Backlog   Machine Downtime

Panel 3—Hourly Report

Materials Scrap

downtime fluctuation will be reduced below the 15-minute maximum acceptable level.

TARGETS AND BENCHMARKING

Performance-level targets should be difficult, but possible, to achieve, as noted earlier. For example, the graphs in Exhibit 11.12 are based on achieving a zero level of tolerance for error in product delivery, downtime, and materials scrap, respectively. Benchmarking—as first discussed in Chapter 7—is the means for setting performance targets that enable the firm to compete with target levels being achieved by other firms. (See Exhibit 7.15

for use of benchmarking comparisons when making outsourcing decisions.)

Types of Benchmarking.   Two types of benchmarking are common. One is *competitive benchmarking*—a direct competitor's targets are benchmarked for comparison. For example, Ford Motor Company might see Toyota as the performance leader in its field. Ford would attempt to gather data on Toyota's accomplishments from a myriad of information sources—business publications, published annual reports, trade reports, and informal business contacts, to name a few. Ford might even purchase some of Toyota's models, dismantle them, and compare details of their component parts with its own. Most who compete worldwide see no ethical problem with this approach, provided the data gathering relies on public information and not on data obtained through industrial espionage.

The other type is *world-class benchmarking*, which is based on comparisons among companies exhibiting the best available business practices. Data are gathered from firms without regard to whether or not the firms are direct competitors. For example, Xerox has examined the following as benchmark targets: how DEC assembles its workstation computers; the warehousing operations of L. L. Bean; and the service parts logistics of John Deere, a maker of farm equipment.[13] This approach generates awareness of innovations outside the industry and can help foster technology transfers. Some managers argue that firms that cannot compete with the best in the world benefit by outsourcing nonessential activities and concentrating on those processes that they do best.

Performance Gaps and Action Plans.   Benchmarking transforms the somewhat nebulous ideas of continuous improvement into measurements that are tangible and realistic. By comparing their own operating results with the results of other firms, managers and frontline workers can identify gaps in their performance, investigate them, and look for solutions. A performance projection chart, such as the one shown in Exhibit 11.13, is an attempt to forecast and compare a company's trend on a specific activity or level of output with that of a benchmarked competitor. Using historical data, managers can estimate future performance by extrapolating the past improvements of their own company and that of the benchmarked competitor. They can then establish an action plan that defines very specific improvement activities and milestone dates for their accomplishment. The exhibit shows three such actions to be taken—one now (at 0 months), one 6 months from now (at +6 months), and one 12 months from now (at +12 months). The result of this three-phase action plan is a shift—within 18 months—to a level of percent-defective output that is lower

---

[13]   See Robert C. Camp, *Benchmarking—The Search for Industry Best Practices That Lead to Superior Performance*, Milwaukee, Wis.: ASQC Press, 1989, p. 62.

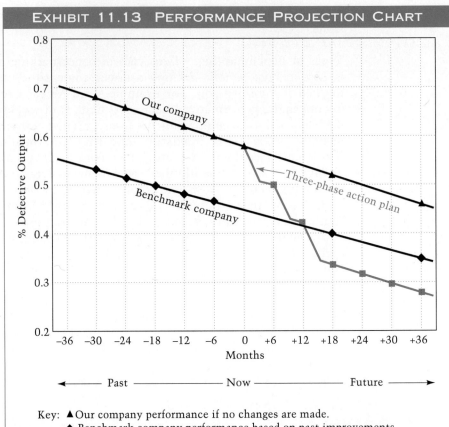

EXHIBIT 11.13 PERFORMANCE PROJECTION CHART

Key: ▲ Our company performance if no changes are made.
      ◆ Benchmark company performance based on past improvements.
      ■ Our company performance if three-phase action plan is implemented.

Source: Adapted from H. J. Harrington, *Business Process Improvement,* New York: McGraw-Hill, 1991, p. 231. Used with permission of The McGraw-Hill Companies.

than that attained by the competitor. The production manager and floor personnel now have a blueprint for improving their results.

ADVANTAGES OF USING FACTORY PERFORMANCE MEASURES

Let's look briefly at how performance measures supplement standard costing systems in controlling manufacturing environments.

Multiple Product Line.   Standard cost systems assign overhead cost to products. We often allocate factory overhead cost using a single allocation base, such as direct labor or machine-hours. And, in simple manufacturing situations, we use that single allocation base to analyze price and quantity variances in factory overhead cost. But we can't do that in manufacturing situations where the same labor and production equipment is jointly used for many products. In these cases, labor—or any other cost driver—does little to explain why activity costs go out of line. But performance measures focus on critical attributes—such as quality and inventory—of production activities for each of the different, jointly produced products. Without concern for more-exact (and expensive) cost driver identification, we can identify and analyze cost variances—with the help of performance measures.

Product Life Cycles. Here's the problem with highly competitive products' rapidly changing life cycles: In early life-cycle stages, products and processes are redesigned without regard to costs as customer needs become more clearly defined. As the product matures it becomes standardized, and the emphasis shifts to efficiency. In the declining stage, the focus is shifted from improving the efficiency of operations back to the more costly activity of product redesign or replacement.

Changing cost standards to encourage employee action that is consistent with each changing stage is difficult. Unfortunately, the standard-setting process is tied to the budget, which is often prepared at 1-year intervals. With short-lived products, the entire life cycle may be 1 year or less. Reliance on performance measures can take the pressure off solely meeting static standards by focusing attention on work activities and processes. As a product moves from early market success to maturity, performance targets are continually tightened in order to gain efficiency. In product decline, measures track the success and cost for design of product replacements.

Continuous Improvement. Performance measures help production workers understand how their daily activities affect product cost and quality. Employees who receive frequent, even continuous, feedback on the work they do have the opportunity to understand how their work relates to the output they help produce. Contrast this with the feedback that is based on financial variances, which helps managers to identify what affects income but fails to help them or their workers understand how activities can be improved. To remedy this failing, performance measures must be part of a larger management program in which greater responsibility—and decision authority—is shifted to lower-level employees, work teams where fellow employees share ideas and devise cooperative solutions. Those closest to production activity usually know best how to improve it.

SUMMARY

Engineered cost centers are characterized by predictable relationships between their product outputs and their resource inputs. Production departments that engage in repetitive activities are the most common type of engineered cost centers.

Managers prepare flexible budgets as a means of revising budget targets in the master budget to reflect the level of sales unit volume achieved. They use flexible budgets to conduct profit variance analysis, which explains differences between actual operating income and the income target contained in the master budget.

Standard costing systems account for inventory costs and report cost variances between actual operating results and the flexible budget. Standard costs are budgeted costs per unit of product output. Standards for purchase prices and resource quantities are used to derive variable manufacturing cost variances. A budget variance is calculated for fixed manufacturing costs. Managers and frontline workers use standard cost variances to identify and correct production deficiencies. Standard costing systems are the dominant accounting systems used in manufacturing.

Tracking performance in today's complex production environments often requires use of supplemental performance measures. Cost control is difficult to accomplish with standard costing systems alone, because of multiple product lines, shortened product life cycles, and the need for continuous improvement. Operating controls focus on critical performance attributes for quality, delivery, inventory, materials, and machine maintenance. The result is earlier correction of operating deficiencies and better understanding by managers and workers of the relationship between activities and performance outcomes.

Benchmarks are used to compare the firm's operations with those of its best-managed competitors. Managers use benchmarks to identify performance gaps in operating activities and performance outcomes. They develop action plans that define how operations will be changed and the time period over which improvements are expected to occur.

APPENDIX

USING STANDARDS FOR ABSORPTION COSTING

We establish standard costs so that we can calculate cost variances that help managers determine how close they come to achieving their budgeted cost targets. In this appendix, we turn from a discussion of how variances are used as a way of controlling costs to an examination of how variances are reported in published financial statements.

APPLIED FIXED FACTORY OVERHEAD

The principles of **absorption costing** require that a product's cost comprise the costs of all factory resource inputs needed for its production. Besides variable costs of production, a unit of output is charged with an allotment of the cost of fixed factory overhead (i.e., depreciation, supervisory salaries, and insurance).

For example, management of Certified Block established a predetermined factory overhead rate (or standard price) of $0.089 based on a budget expectation of $106,500 for fixed factory overhead cost and 1,200,000 units of production. (See Exhibit 11.3 for more detail.) This charge of $0.089 per unit will be correct only if two conditions are met:

1. Actual costs equal the budget of $106,000
2. Actual units of production equal the estimate of 1,200,000 units, sometimes referred to as the *denominator level of activity*

Differences between the actual and budgeted fixed overhead costs are reported as a fixed overhead budget variance in both a variable costing system and an absorption costing system. (See Exhibit 11.8 for a discussion of fixed overhead budget variances.) Differences, however, between actual and estimated production, called *production volume variances,* are unique to absorption costing. How production volume variances are calculated and reported is discussed below.

Calculating Fixed Overhead Variances.   Exhibit 11.14 shows how Certified Block reports its fixed factory overhead variances under an absorption costing system.

The left side of the diagram shows a budget variance of $1,600 U, the same budget variance amount reported by Certified Block in its flexible budget cost reconciliation (Exhibit 11.8).

What's different is the right side of the diagram. That's where we show absorption costing for the fixed factory overhead. The production volume variance shown results from the difference between the estimated output (1,200,000 units) used to prepare the master budget and actual units

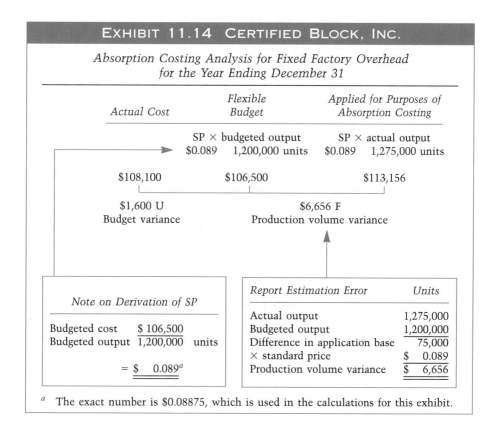

EXHIBIT 11.14 CERTIFIED BLOCK, INC.

Absorption Costing Analysis for Fixed Factory Overhead for the Year Ending December 31

	Actual Cost	Flexible Budget	Applied for Purposes of Absorption Costing
		SP × budgeted output	SP × actual output
		$0.089 1,200,000 units	$0.089 1,275,000 units
	$108,100	$106,500	$113,156

$1,600 U
Budget variance

$6,656 F
Production volume variance

Note on Derivation of SP	
Budgeted cost	$ 106,500
Budgeted output	1,200,000 units
	= $ 0.089[a]

Report Estimation Error	Units
Actual output	1,275,000
Budgeted output	1,200,000
Difference in application base	75,000
× standard price	$ 0.089
Production volume variance	$ 6,656

[a]   The exact number is $0.08875, which is used in the calculations for this exhibit.

produced (1,275,000 units). The standard price ($0.089 rounded) is multiplied by the difference in units [75,000 units = (1,275,000 units − 1,200,000 units)], resulting in the production volume variance ($6,656 F).

Interpreting Fixed Overhead Variances. The budget variance is what managers investigate in order to find out why actual fixed overhead cost exceeded the original budget by $1,600. This cost is established by management's commitment to maintain plant capacity—so there is very limited scope for cost control in fixed overhead.

The production volume variance has nothing to do with operating cost. A favorable variance of $6,656 means only that fixed overhead was overapplied (i.e., overcharged) because more units were produced than originally planned when the standard price of $0.089 was established. If it had been known that the production was actually going to be 1,275,000 units, then each unit would have been charged only $0.084 ($106,500 budgeted cost/1,275,000 units). The favorable production volume variance is the amount that was overcharged to all units produced, and it will need to be added back to income by year-end.

INVENTORY COST FLOWS

Standard costing systems assign a value for inventory on the basis of its standard cost when entered in the books. Exhibit 11.15 shows Certified Block's inventory cost flows. Across the top of the exhibit are three *T-accounts:* work in process, finished goods, and cost of goods sold. The lower part of the exhibit shows the variance accounts for direct materials, direct labor, variable factory overhead, and fixed factory overhead. The key is to understand that all costs are added to work in process at their standard costs (taken from the top T-accounts), and that variances arising during production are immediately placed in separate accounts (the bottom T-accounts).

For example, direct materials costs are entered in the work-in-process account at $237,303, which is equal to the standard price multiplied by the standard quantity for the units produced. The differences between the standard cost for materials and the actual amount spent ($243,518) was explained in the direct materials cost variance (Exhibit 11.5). The combined total for price and quantity variances ($6,215 U) is charged to the direct materials variance account. Unfavorable entries are entered as debits, which is equivalent to recording a loss.

When goods are completed, they are transferred from the work-in-process account to the finished-goods account at standard cost ($499,670 = standard price of $0.392 rounded × 1,275,000 units produced).

When the goods are sold, standard cost is transferred from the finished-goods account to expense—the cost-of-goods sold account. The result is that cost of goods sold on interim—monthly or quarterly—income statements is based on standard cost, which can cause income distortions until variance accounts are closed.

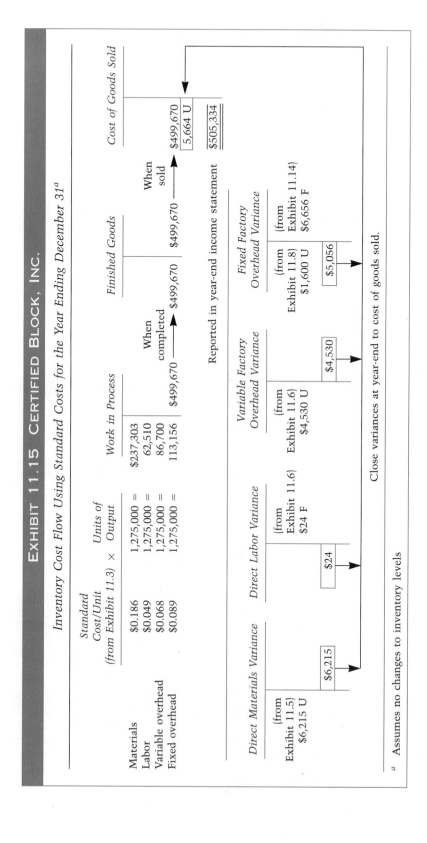

EXHIBIT 11.15 CERTIFIED BLOCK, INC.

Inventory Cost Flow Using Standard Costs for the Year Ending December 31[a]

	Standard Cost/Unit (from Exhibit 11.3)	×	Units of Output	
Materials	$0.186		1,275,000 =	$237,303
Labor	$0.049		1,275,000 =	62,510
Variable overhead	$0.068		1,275,000 =	86,700
Fixed overhead	$0.089		1,275,000 =	113,156

Work in Process

$499,670

Finished Goods

When completed → $499,670 $499,670

When sold → $499,670

Cost of Goods Sold

$499,670
5,664 U

$505,334

Reported in year-end income statement

Direct Materials Variance

(from Exhibit 11.5)
$6,215 U

$6,215

Direct Labor Variance

(from Exhibit 11.6)
$24 F

$24

Variable Factory Overhead Variance

(from Exhibit 11.6)
$4,530 U

$4,530

Fixed Factory Overhead Variance

(from Exhibit 11.8)
$1,600 U

(from Exhibit 11.14)
$6,656 F

$5,056

Close variances at year-end to cost of goods sold.

[a] Assumes no changes to inventory levels

Reporting Variances in Interim Financial Statements. Variances, such as any of the four shown in Exhibit 11.15, can build large balances during the year. Some firms report these variances on interim income statements as adjustments to the balance in the cost-of-goods sold account. Many firms report variances on interim statements as adjustments to inventory accounts on the balance sheet. Precisely where a variance goes on interim statements is a function of its nature. If a variance is seasonal, such as large-scale maintenance, and is largely expected to balance out by year-end, it is shown as an adjustment to assets. If a variance balance seems to grow over time, it will be more informative if shown as an adjustment to income.

Disposing of Variance Accounts. Regardless of the manner in which variances are handled for interim reporting, all variance accounts are closed at year-end. The common way to do this is to charge variances directly to cost of goods. Doing this will translate cost of goods sold from standard costs back to the actual costs of production. In Exhibit 11.15, for example, Certified Block closes its variance accounts and increases cost of goods sold by $5,664.

CHAPTER 11 ASSIGNMENTS

DISCUSSION PROBLEMS

D11.1 (Standard Costs and Employee Motivation)

Terry Travers is the manufacturing supervisor of the Aurora Manufacturing Company, which produces a variety of plastic products. Some of these products are standard items that are listed in the company's catalog, while others are made to customer specifications. Each month, Travers receives a performance report displaying the master budget for the month, the actual activity for the period, and the variance between the master budget and actual costs. Part of Travers's annual performance evaluation is based on a comparison of his department's performance against budget targets. Aurora's purchasing manager, Barbara Christensen, also receives monthly performance reports, and is evaluated, in part, on the basis of these reports.

The most recent monthly reports (showing last month's actual results) had just been distributed, on the 21st of the month, when Travers met Christensen in the hallway outside their offices. Scowling, Travers began the conversation:

Travers: "I see we've had another set of monthly performance reports hand-delivered by that vindictive junior employee in the budget office. He seemed pleased to tell me that I was in trouble with my performance again."

Christensen: "I got the same treatment. All I ever hear about are the things I haven't done right. Now, I'll have to spend a lot of time reviewing the report and preparing explanations. The worst part is that the information is almost a month old, and we spend all this time on history."

Travers: "My biggest gripe is that our production activity varies a lot from month to month, but we're given an annual budget that's written in stone. Last month, we were shut down for 3 days when a strike delayed delivery of the basic ingredient used in our plastic formulation, and we had already exhausted our inventory. You know that, of course, since we had to ask you to call all over the country to find an alternative source of supply. When we got what we needed on a rush basis, we had to pay more than we normally do."

Christensen: "I expect problems like that to pop up from time to time—that's part of my job—but now we'll both have to take a careful look at the report to see where charges are reflected for that rush order. Every month, I spend more time making sure I should be charged for each item reported than I do making plans for my department's daily work. It's really frustrating to see charges for things I have no control over."

Travers: "The way we get information doesn't help, either. I don't get copies of the reports you get, yet a lot of what I do is affected by your department, and by most of the other departments we have. Why do the budget and accounting people assume that I should be told only about *my* operations, even though the president regularly gives us pep talks about how we all need to work together, as a team?"

Christensen: "I seem to get more reports than I need, and I am never asked to comment until top management calls me on the carpet about my department's shortcomings. Do you ever hear comments when your department shines?"

Travers: "I guess they don't have time to review the good news. One of my problems is that all the reports are in dollars and cents. I work with people, machines, and materials. I need information *this* month to help me solve this month's problems—not another report of the dollars expended last month or the month before."

Required:

1. Based upon the conversation between Terry Travers and Barbara Christensen, describe the likely motivation and behavior of these two employees as the result of Aurora Manufacturing Company's variance reporting system.
2. Variance reporting systems, when properly implemented, should benefit both the employees and the company.
   a. Describe the benefits that can be realized from using a variance reporting system.
   b. Based on the situation presented above, recommend ways for Aurora Manufacturing Company to improve its variance reporting system so as to increase employee motivation.

(*CMA Adapted*)

D11.2 (Product Life Cycles and Production Control)

Burke Company manufactures various electronic assemblies that it sells primarily to computer manufacturers. Burke's reputation has been built on quality, timely delivery, and products that are consistently on the cutting edge of technology. Burke's business is fast-paced. The typical product has a short life. The product is in development for about a year and in the growth stage—with sometimes spectacular growth—for about a year. Each product then experiences a rapid decline in sales as new products become available.

Burke has just hired a new vice president of finance, Devin Ward. Shortly after reporting for work at Burke, Ward had a conversation with Andrew Newhouse, Burke's president. A portion of the conversation follows:

Newhouse: "The thing that fascinates me about this business is that change is its central ingredient. We knew when we started out that a reliable stream of new products was one of our key variables—in fact, it's the only way to cope with the threat of product obsolescence. You see, our products go through only the first half of the traditional product life cycle—the development stage and then the growth stage. Our products never reach the traditional mature-product stage or the declining-product stage. Toward the end of the growth stage, products die as new ones are introduced."

Ward: "I suppose your other key variables would be cost controls and efficient production scheduling?"

Newhouse: "Getting the product to market on schedule is most important. Some firms in this business announce a new product in March to be delivered in June, and they make the first shipment in October, or a year from March—or, sometimes, never. Our reputation for delivering on schedule may account for our success, as much as anything."

Ward: "Where I previously worked, we also recognized the importance of on-time deliveries. Our performance reporting system set 97 percent on-time deliveries as a standard."

Newhouse: "We now see the key to our success as production control. It took us a while to recognize that. At first, we thought that product development was the key and that profits would naturally follow. But now we know that the key is to set reasonable targets for performance and to monitor our progress continually. We are finding that our budget and standard cost reporting system just doesn't seem to meet our needs."

Required:

1. Discuss the operational characteristics for each of the four stages of the product life cycle:
   a. Development (introduction)
   b. Growth
   c. Maturity
   d. Decline
2. Describe the production control problems confronting the Burke Company.
3. Suggest techniques that Ward might implement in order to cope with Burke Company's production control problems.

(CMA Adapted)

PROBLEMS

P11.1   (Preparing a Profit Variance Analysis)

The master budget for the month of April for Global Press, a magazine publisher, is presented in Exhibit P11.1.1. Actual sales for the month of April were 135,000 units, at an average price per unit of $1.10. Other operating results for the month were as shown in Exhibit P11.1.2.

Required: Prepare a profit variance analysis for the month. Calculate the flexible budget variance and the sales volume variance.

P11.2   (Direct Labor Variances)

Specialty Eyeware, Inc., is a retailer of eyeglasses and contact lenses. The company employs optometrists and lab assistants to perform eye examinations for its customers. The company has developed standard eye exam labor costs, which are detailed in Exhibit P11.2. In the second quarter of this year, Specialty Eyeware examined 15,000 patients. Actual labor costs are also shown in Exhibit P11.2.

Required: Calculate the total labor variance for both optometrists and lab assistants, broken down into price and quantity variances.

EXHIBIT P11.1.1 GLOBAL PRESS

Master Budget for the Month of April

Budgeted units		100,000
Sales revenue (100,000 units @ $1.25)		$125,000
Less variable expense:		
Production @ $0.20	$20,000	
Selling & administration @ $0.25	25,000	45,000
Contribution margin		$ 80,000
Less fixed expense:		
Production	$46,000	
Selling & administration	28,000	74,000
Operating profit		$ 6,000

EXHIBIT P11.1.2 GLOBAL PRESS

Actual Operating Expense for the Month of April

Variable expense:	
Production	$29,000
Selling & administration	$40,500
Fixed expense:	
Production	$44,500
Selling & administration	$30,000

EXHIBIT P11.2 SPECIALTY EYEWARE, INC.

	Optometrists	Lab Assistants
Standard labor quantity per patient, in minutes	10	20
Standard labor cost per hour	$40	$16
Actual direct labor cost	$105,825	$79,200
Actual direct labor-hours	2,550	4,800

P11.3 (Variable Overhead Variances)

(This problem relies upon direct labor information for Specialty Eyeware, Inc., as first presented in P11.2) Variable overhead for Specialty Eyeware, Inc., consists of two accounts: (1) miscellaneous supplies for optometrists and lab assistants and (2) repair and maintenance cost for examination equipment. Standard variable overhead cost is applied to patients based on direct labor-hours. Standard cost and actual cost for the second quarter of the year are shown in Exhibit P11.3.

Required: Based on the direct labor-hours given in Exhibit P11.2, calculate:

1. The variable overhead price and quantity variances
2. The variable overhead price variance for each overhead account

P11.4 (Fixed Overhead Variances)

Sofas Unlimited has budgeted its fixed costs for the year based on production of 25,000 sofas. Unit costs are shown in Exhibit P11.4, along with actual costs

EXHIBIT P11.3 SPECIALTY EYEWARE, INC.

	Standard Cost	Actual Cost
Miscellaneous supplies	$1.50 per hour	$13,240
Repair & maintenance	$0.50 per hour	$ 2,590

EXHIBIT P11.4 SOFAS UNLIMITED

	Depreciation	Rent	Supervisory Salaries	Total
Budgeted unit cost	$ 2.25	$ 3.75	$ 6.50	$ 12.50
Budgeted number of units				25,000
Actual cost	$54,750	$96,500	$170,000	$321,250
Actual number of units				26,500

incurred for this time period. Because of higher demand, production was increased to 26,500 sofas.

Required:

1. Calculate the fixed overhead budget variance for Sofas Unlimited in total and for each overhead account.
2. Calculate the fixed overhead production volume variance. (See the Appendix to this chapter.)

P11.5 (Control Chart)

The Candy Center Company is a manufacturer of hard candy. It employs two shifts of workers and uses several production machines in the candy-making process. The Candy Center has begun tracking the performance of its equipment by monitoring the daily unscheduled downtime of machinery. Downtime has, in the past, been due to mechanical failure or to other operating problems.

Data for a recent 2-week period are shown in Exhibit P11.5. The Candy Center has established limits for acceptable downtime. These are expected to be useful in identifying those days of operation when downtime was unexpectedly high or low. The upper control limit is 25 minutes and the lower limit is 10 minutes. Ultimately, the company wants to reduce the upper limit and to set the lower limit at zero minutes, but the plant manager sees this as an unrealistic goal.

Required:

1. Prepare a graph showing the pattern of downtime, in minutes, for the 2-week period. Include control limits.
2. Comment on the information presented in the control chart. What actions do you suggest be taken to eliminate observations that fall outside the control limits?

P11.6 (Developing a Standard Material Cost)

ColdKing Company is a small producer of fruit-flavored frozen desserts. For many years, ColdKing's products have had strong regional sales on the basis of brand

EXHIBIT P11.5 THE CANDY CENTER COMPANY

Day	Downtime, in minutes
1	22.4
2	31.2
3	21.9
4	14.6
5	7.6
6	11.4
7	17.4
8	14.0
9	8.9
10	8.5
11	16.0
12	19.8
13	24.3
14	30.9

recognition. However, other companies have begun marketing similar products in the area, and price competition has become increasingly important. John Wakefield, the company's controller, is planning to implement a standard costing system for ColdKing and has gathered considerable information from his coworkers on production and materials requirements for ColdKing's products. Wakefield believes that the use of standard costing will allow ColdKing to improve cost control and make better pricing decisions.

ColdKing's most-popular product is raspberry sherbet. The sherbet is produced in 10-gallon batches, and production of each batch requires 6 quarts of good, fresh raspberries. The fresh raspberries are sorted by hand before entering the production process. Because of imperfections in the raspberries and normal spoilage, 1 quart of berries is discarded for every 4 quarts of acceptable berries used. Three minutes is the standard direct labor time for sorting the raspberries in order to obtain 1 quart of acceptable fruit. The acceptable raspberries are then blended with the other ingredients. Blending requires 12 minutes of direct labor time per batch. After blending, the sherbet is packaged in quart containers. Wakefield has gathered the following pricing information:

- ColdKing purchases raspberries at a cost of $0.80 per quart. Each batch of sherbet requires 10 gallons of other ingredients, costing a total of $0.45 per gallon.
- Direct labor is paid at the rate of $9 per hour.
- The total cost of the materials and the labor required to package the sherbet is $0.38 per quart.

Required:

1. Develop the standard cost for the direct cost components of a 10-gallon batch of raspberry sherbet. (Note: 4 quarts = 1 gallon.) For each direct cost component of a batch of raspberry sherbet, the standard cost should identify:
   a. Standard quantity
   b. Standard price
   c. Standard cost per batch
2. As part of the implementation of a standard cost system at ColdKing, Wakefield plans to train those responsible for maintaining the standards in the use

of variance analysis. He is particularly concerned with the causes of unfavorable variances.

a. Discuss the possible causes of unfavorable materials price variances, and identify the individuals who should be held responsible for these variances.

b. Discuss the possible causes of unfavorable labor quantity variances, and identify the individuals who should be held responsible for these variances.

(CMA Adapted)

P11.7 (Variance Analysis for a Service Business)

Tredoc Company is engaged in the business of seasonal tree spraying and, in its operations, uses chemicals that prevent disease and bug infestation. Employees are guaranteed 165 hours of work per month at a wage rate of $8 per hour. They receive a direct labor bonus equal to 75 percent of their net favorable direct labor efficiency variance. The efficiency variance represents the difference between actual time consumed in spraying a tree and the standard time allowed for spraying a tree of that height (specified in feet), multiplied by the $8 standard hourly wage rate. For budgeting purposes, there is a standard allowance of 1 hour per customer for travel, setup, and cleanup time. However, since several factors are uncontrollable by the employee, this 1-hour budget allowance is excluded from the bonus calculation. Employees are responsible for keeping their own daily time cards.

Chemical usage should vary directly with the tree footage sprayed. Variable overhead includes costs that vary directly with the number of customers, as well as costs that vary according to tree footage sprayed. Customers pay a service charge of $10 per visit and $1 per tree-foot sprayed.

The standard master budget and actual results for June are shown in Exhibit P11.7.

Required: Compute the following for June, and indicate whether each variance is favorable or unfavorable:

EXHIBIT P11.7 TREDOC COMPANY

Standard Budget and Results for June

	Basis for Measure		Master Budget	Basis for Measure		Actual Results
Service calls	200 customers		$ 2,000	210 customers		$ 2,100
Footage sprayed	18,000 feet		18,000	21,000 feet		21,000
Total revenue			$20,000			$23,100
Chemicals	1,800 gallons		$ 4,500	2,400 gallons		$ 5,880
Direct labor:						
Travel, setup, & cleanup	200 hours	$1,600		300 hours	$2,400	
Tree spraying	900 hours	7,200		910 hours	7,280	
Total direct labor			8,800			9,680
Overhead:						
Variable based on no. of customers		$1,200			$1,350	
Variable based on tree footage		1,800			1,975	
Fixed		2,000			2,075	
Total overhead			5,000			5,400
Total cost			$18,300			$20,960
Gross profit before bonus			$ 1,700			$ 2,140

1. Direct materials price variance
2. Direct materials quantity variance
3. Total direct labor variance for travel, setup, and cleanup
4. Direct labor quantity variance for spraying
5. Direct labor bonus
6. Variable overhead flexible budget variance
7. Fixed overhead budget variance

(AICPA Adapted)

P11.8 (Comprehensive Variance Preparation)

At the beginning of 1997, Beal Company adopted the standards shown in Exhibit P11.8. Normal volume per month is 40,000 standard labor-hours. Beal's January 1997 budget was based on normal volume. During January Beal produced 7,800 units. Records indicated the following:

Direct materials purchased	25,000 lb @ $2.60/lb
Direct materials used	23,100 lb
Direct labor	40,100 hr @ $7.30/hr
Variable factory overhead	$124,500
Fixed factory overhead	$171,500

Required:

1. Prepare a schedule of budgeted production costs for January 1997, based on actual production of 7,800 units.
2. For the month of January 1997, compute the following variances. Indicate whether each is favorable (F) or unfavorable (U).
   a. Direct materials price variance, based on purchases
   b. Direct materials quantity variance, based on usage
   c. Direct labor price variance
   d. Direct labor quantity variance
   e. Variable factory overhead price (spending) variance
   f. Variable factory overhead quantity (efficiency) variance
   g. Fixed factory overhead budget variance
   h. Fixed factory overhead production volume variance (see appendix)
3. Based on your answers above and the following additional information, calculate the flexible budget variance and the sales volume variance for the month of January 1997:

EXHIBIT P11.8 BEAL COMPANY		
		Standard Cost per Unit
Direct materials	3 lbs @ $2.50 per lb	$ 7.50
Direct labor	5 hrs @ $7.50 per hr	37.50
Factory overhead:		
Variable	$3.00 per direct labor hour	15.00
Fixed	$20.00 per unit produced	20.00
Total standard cost per unit		$80.00

	Actual	Budget
Sales price per unit	$ 120	$ 120
Selling and administration:		
Variable cost	$ 87,500	$ 88,000
Fixed cost	$180,000	$185,000

(AICPA Adapted)

P11.9 (Factory Overhead Variance Analysis)

Talbot Company manufactures shirts that are sold to customers for embossing with various slogans and emblems. Bob Ricker, manufacturing supervisor, recently received the November production report (see Exhibit P11.9.1). The November budget is based on the manufacture of 80,000 shirts.

Ricker was extremely upset by the negative variances in the November report, as he has worked very closely with his people for the past 2 months in order to improve productivity. He immediately asked to meet with his boss, Chris Langdon, to discuss the report and express his disappointment. Langdon, also disturbed by the November results, suggested that Ricker meet with Sheryl Johnson, Talbot's manager of cost accounting, to see if he could gain further insight into the production problems. Johnson was extremely helpful and provided Ricker with the following additional information on the annual budget and the actual results for November, shown in Exhibit P11.9.2.

- Factory overhead at Talbot includes both variable and fixed components and is applied on the basis of direct labor-hours. The company's 1997 budget includes data for the manufacture of 960,000 shirts, produced in monthly batches.
- Each shirt is budgeted for 0.25 hours of labor. Total budgeted labor for 1997 is 240,000 hours.
- The standard labor rate at Talbot is $12 per hour. During November, employees worked 20,600 hours and were paid at an actual wage rate of $12.
- Actual production for November was 82,000 shirts.

With this data, Johnson and Ricker began analyzing the November variances, paying particular attention to the factory overhead variance. Johnson knows that part of the problem is caused by the fact that Talbot does not use flexible budgeting. Nonetheless, she plans to use flexible-budget techniques to help them identify the causes of the overhead variance.

Required:

1. Determine how much of the November 1997 total factory overhead variance is the result of an increase in production volume from 80,000 to 82,000 units.

EXHIBIT P11.9.1 TALBOT COMPANY

November 1997 Production Report

	Budget	Actual	Variance
Direct materials	$160,000	$162,000	$(2,000)
Direct labor	240,000	247,200	(7,200)
Factory overhead	200,000	236,800	(36,800)

EXHIBIT P11.9.2 TALBOT COMPANY

Variable Overhead Expenditure

	Annual Budget	Actual for November
Indirect materials	$432,000	$36,000
Indirect labor	288,000	33,700
Equipment repair	192,000	16,400
Equipment power	48,000	12,300
Total	$960,000	$98,400

Fixed Overhead Expenditure

	Annual Budget	Actual for November
Supervisory salaries	$ 260,000	$ 22,000
Insurance	320,000	26,900
Property taxes	80,000	6,500
Depreciation	320,000	27,000
Heat, light, & telephone	210,000	25,600
Quality inspection	250,000	30,400
Total	$1,440,000	$138,400

2. Calculate the November price variance and quantity variance for variable factory overhead. Then calculate a price variance for each of the four accounts that constitute variable overhead. (See Exhibit 11.7, in the text, for an example.)
3. Calculate the November budget variance for fixed factory overhead. Then, calculate the budget variance for each of the six accounts constituting fixed overhead. (See Exhibit 11.8 in the text.)
4. What conclusions can you draw from your analysis of factory overhead?

(*CMA Adapted*)

P11.10 (Budgeted Production and Fixed Overhead—Appendix)

Yuba Machine Company manufactures nut shellers at its Sutter City plant. The machines are purchased by nut processors throughout the world. Since its inception, the family-owned business has used actual factory overhead cost in costing factory output. However, on December 1, 1996, Yuba began using a predetermined factory overhead application rate in order to determine manufacturing cost on a more timely basis. The predetermined rate is based on the plant's best-possible sales projection of 100,000 units. The information in Exhibit P11.10.1 is from the 1996–1997 budget for the Sutter City plant. Based on this data, the predetermined fixed factory overhead application rate was established at $1.60 per unit.

A variance report for the Sutter City plant for the 6 months ending May 31, 1997, is shown in Exhibit P11.10.2. The plant produced and sold 40,000 units for this period.

Yuba's plant controller, Sid Thorpe, is concerned because he feels that the interim income statement, shown in Exhibit P11.10.3, is being distorted by the difference between budgeted and actual production. Unfortunately, he is having trouble determining how much of the company's interim income is the result of accounting effects rather than of actual cost control.

EXHIBIT P11.10.1 YUBA MACHINE COMPANY

Budgeted Fixed Factory Overhead

Budgeted output	100,000 units

Fixed factory overhead cost:	
Salaries	$ 80,000
Depreciation & amortization	50,000
Other expense	30,000
Total fixed factory overhead cost	$160,000

EXHIBIT P11.10.2 YUBA MACHINE COMPANY

Variance Report

	Actual Cost	Applied Cost[a]	Variance
Fixed factory overhead:			
Salaries	$39,000	$32,000	$ (7,000)
Depreciation & amortization	25,000	20,000	(5,000)
Other expense	15,300	12,000	(3,300)
Total	$79,300	$64,000	$(15,300)

[a] Applied cost = standard price × actual output.
For example, applied salaries cost:

$32,000 = $80,000/100,000 units × 40,000 units
$32,000 = $0.80/unit × 40,000 units

EXHIBIT P11.10.3 YUBA MACHINE COMPANY

Interim Income Statement
for the Six Months Ending May 31, 1997

Sales	$625,000
Cost of goods sold	380,000
Gross profit	$245,000
Selling expense	$ 44,000
Depreciation expense	58,000
Administrative expense	53,000
Operating income	$ 90,000
Provision for income taxes (40%)	36,000
Net income	$ 54,000

Required:

1. Prepare a revised variance report for Yuba Machine Company using a master budget of 80,000 units as the basis for applying fixed factory overhead.
2. Prepare a revised interim income statement for Yuba Machine Company at May 31, 1997, assuming the fixed factory overhead rate was based on a budget of 80,000 units.

(CMA Adapted)

P11.11   (Performance Measures in Manufacturing)

Wymore Company produces a variety of bathroom and kitchen fixtures. In an effort to keep up with foreign competition, it has invested in advanced manufacturing equipment and computerized materials-resource planning systems. Now the firm's management finds its standard costing systems fail to provide important information on critical factors—data that are needed to reduce cost on the factory floor. Management believes the key to reducing cost and improving efficiency is to make sure that work is scheduled in such a way as to prevent bottlenecks and to take full advantage of the plant's productive capacity. The following variables have been identified as being crucial to the firm's efforts for continuous improvement:

1. *Cycle time*—tracks the average hours consumed daily to convert raw materials to finished product
2. *Machine time*—measures the percentage of time each day that the plant's machinery was in productive use
3. *Machine breakdowns*—measures lost time, in minutes per day, caused by unscheduled repair and maintenance
4. *Target completion*—measures the number of units completed per day as a percent of planned production.

Management provides you with the data shown in Exhibit P11.11, which were accumulated over the last two 6-day work weeks.

EXHIBIT P11.11   WYMORE COMPANY

Performance Measurements

		Date	Cycle Time, Avg Hr	Machine Time, %	Machine Downtime, Total Min	Target Completion, %
Week 1	March	3	14.1	0.81	5	0.82
		4	16.3	0.75	8	0.86
		5	12.1	0.82	0	0.89
		6	17.5	0.76	7	0.81
		7	18.8	0.68	6	0.77
		8	20.0	0.62	11	0.72
Week 2		10	21.3	0.54	13	0.68
		11	19.5	0.55	0	0.65
		12	18.3	0.60	10	0.70
		13	16.1	0.63	8	0.76
		14	14.3	0.83	2	0.77
		15	15.6	0.75	0	0.80

Required:

1. For each of the four critical variables, prepare a graph to report daily performance over the 2-week period. What conclusions can you draw from the outcomes reported?
2. What investigative steps would you suggest to management in order to begin improving performance on these key variables?

P11.12   (Standard Cost and Performance Measures in a Nonprofit Organization)

HomeHealth Inc. is a nonprofit organization composed of three service operations: nursing care, housecleaning, and meals on wheels. The agency's clients are non-ambulatory elderly and disabled persons who are unable to venture outside their homes. This problem addresses the cost containment concerns faced by the meals-on-wheels operation, which prepares and delivers one meal per client per day, 7 days per week.

The director of the meals-on-wheels program has been receiving a weekly performance report that monitors two major operating costs—food and labor. A food cost variance compares actual cost with standard cost for the number of meals served. It is calculated as follows:

$$\text{Food cost allowed} = \text{standard cost per meal} \times \text{meals delivered}$$

$$- \text{ actual food cost incurred}$$

$$= \text{food cost variance}$$

All of the standards used to calculate the 1997 budget are given in Exhibit P11.12.1.

The labor cost variance is broken down into a traditional standard costing format based on the standard times allowed to prepare and deliver meals. Both labor rate and quantity variances are calculated, although actual hourly rates seldom vary from standard rates. One modification in calculating labor cost variances is the adjustment made to total labor time for (unpaid) volunteers. All workers—both paid and volunteer—are expected to meet time standards, but labor variance calculations adjust for volunteer time. For example, based on data shown in Exhibit P11.12.2, the actual quantity of labor time used in the variance analysis for the second week of January 1997 is equal to 104.0 hours (67.75 + 107.50 − 71.25). The standard labor quantity calculation, based on a target of 40 percent volunteers, is as follows:

$$\text{Standard quantity} = (1 - 0.40) \times (\text{time/meal} \times \text{meals served})$$

EXHIBIT P11.12.1   HOMEHEALTH INC.

Standards Used to Build the 1997 Budget

Cost allowance per meal	$2.50
Labor rate[a] per hour (includes payroll taxes)	$9.00
Labor time:	
Meal preparation	10 min
Meal delivery	15 min
Planned volunteer time	40% of total labor

[a]   Actual labor rates were equal to standard rates.

EXHIBIT P11.12.2 HOMEHEALTH INC.

Operating Data for the Second Week in January 1997

Day	Meals Delivered	Prep Time, Hr	Delivery Time, Hr	Volunteer Time, Hr
Monday	50	9.25	17.50	10.00
Tuesday	50	8.25	16.25	11.75
Wednesday	50	11.25	15.00	7.50
Thursday	50	8.75	12.50	10.25
Friday	49	11.75	18.00	14.00
Saturday	46	11.00	15.50	8.25
Sunday	44	7.50	12.75	9.50
Total	339	67.75	107.50	71.25

Total food cost for the week	$864.45

The director has now decided that she needs daily feedback on key operating variables. She is most interested in tracking how much time is spent preparing and delivering an average meal. In other words, she wants to know whether meals are, in fact, being prepared in 10 minutes and delivered in 15 minutes and whether actual times vary from day to day. Further, she feels it is imperative to keep close track of the 40 percent target for volunteer time, which is now being buried in the weekly calculation of labor efficiency. If an adequate number of volunteers are not being retained for any one day, she wants to make sure the problem is rectified early and that volunteers are on hand the next day. She has gathered the following operating data for the second week of January 1997 (see Exhibit P11.12.2).

Required:

1. Calculate the following cost variances for the second week of January:
   a. Total cost of food variance
   b. Labor rate variance and labor quantity variance (Actual hourly rates were equal to the standard.)
2. Prepare a 7-day report comprising paid labor and volunteer labor results for the second week of January. You should include a measure for each day of the week for the following key variables:
   a. Average meal-preparation time
   b. Average meal-delivery time
   c. Percent of total labor time provided by volunteers
   (*Optional:* Present your findings for requirements 2(a) thorough 2(c) in graphical form.)
3. Based on your results for requirements 1 and 2, what two areas of operation would you suggest are most in need of improvement?

CASES   **C11.1 (Precious Dolls, Inc.—A)**

Precious Dolls, Inc., is made up of three manufacturing operations, one located in the United States and two in Mexico. The U.S. facility, called the Niceville operation, has been under close scrutiny for the past several months by corporate management.

Because of the higher costs of manufacturing in the United States, Niceville has been showing lower financial returns than have its counterparts in Mexico. Corporate management is considering closing down the plant, laying off the workforce, and expanding the two existing Mexican operations. Niceville's plant managers know the concerns of the corporate management, and they have implemented changes in the production process in order to gain greater production efficiencies. The results obtained in the first month after these changes are the subject of this case.

Niceville's strength has been its ability to change over its manufacturing operations as necessary to meet the short product life cycles of the doll market. Quick adjustments are possible because the plant uses modern, computer-driven equipment. In contrast, the Mexican sites are more labor-intensive and make some dolls, such as Sweet Suzy and Barbette, that have enjoyed stable market demand for 3 years or more. Most of Precious Dolls' products, however, are tied to market trends, and they lose sales momentum after only 3 or 4 months. If the Niceville plant is shut down, corporate management will most likely disassemble the plant's advanced manufacturing equipment and move it to the Mexican facilities.

Standard Costs and the Budget

Niceville is currently producing only one doll, named Baby Dirty Drawers, which is a big hit because of its continual need to have its diapers changed. The standard cost for each doll is $9.75, as shown below in Exhibit C11.1.1. Direct materials cost $5 per unit and consist of polyvinyl, used to fabricate the body, and fabric for making the doll's clothes. Each requires only 10 minutes of direct labor time, costing $1.50 per unit, since most of the work is automated. Variable overhead consists mainly of power and some inexpensive indirect materials (such as the doll's eyes); at $0.25 per unit, it is a very small part of total standard cost. Fixed overhead is applied at 200 percent of direct labor cost, and, at $3 per unit, it represents a sizeable portion of total cost.

The firm prepares product standard costs and operating budgets on an annual basis. Niceville's budget for the current month, June 1996, is presented in Exhibit C11.1.2. The totals for variable production expense are derived by multiplying planned production (28,000 units) by standard cost. Production fixed expense, comprising depreciation, maintenance, rent, and wages, is based on annual capacity estimates and preapproved expenditures for labor and capital investment.

Actual Results for the Month

The Niceville results for June, reported in Exhibit C11.1.3, are discouraging. Despite the improvements initiated this month, the plant has generated an oper-

EXHIBIT C11.1.1   PRECIOUS DOLLS, INC.— NICEVILLE OPERATION

Standard Variable Cost for Baby Dirty Drawers

Direct materials			
Polyvinyl	3 lb @ $1.50	$4.50	
Fabric	0.5 yd @ $1.00	0.50	$5.00
Direct labor	10 min @ $9.00		1.50
Variable overhead	10 min @ $1.50		0.25
Production variable costs			$6.75
Fixed overhead @ 200% of direct labor cost			3.00
Total			$9.75

EXHIBIT C11.1.2 PRECIOUS DOLLS, INC.— NICEVILLE OPERATION

Budget Income Statement for the Month of June 1996

Target units	28,000
Sales	$364,000
Variable production expense:	
Direct materials	$140,000
Direct labor	42,000
Variable overhead	7,000
Variable selling expense	29,120
Total variable expense	$218,120
Contribution margin	$145,880
Fixed expense:	
Production overhead	$ 84,000
Selling & administration	34,000
Total fixed expense	$118,000
Operating income	$ 27,880

EXHIBIT C11.1.3 PRECIOUS DOLLS, INC.— NICEVILLE OPERATION

Income Statement for the Month of June, 1996

Actual units produced & sold		31,500
Sales		$397,500
Variable production expense:		
Direct materials:		
Polyvinyl	97,200 lb @ $1.52	
Fabric	17,240 yd @ $.99	$164,812
Direct labor	5,900 hr @ $9.12	53,808
Variable overhead		8,000
Variable selling expense		$ 35,775
Total variable expense		$262,395
Contribution margin		$135,105
Fixed expense:		
Production overhead		90,700
Selling & administration		35,500
Total fixed expense		$126,200
Operating income		$ 8,905

ating profit of $8,905—far below the budget target of $27,880 for the month. Niceville's managers are perplexed by these results, particularly since sales for the month (31,500 units) are 12.5 percent more than budgeted. Some of the recent improvements required start-up costs that were not expected to show returns immediately, but these alone do not seem to explain the poor profit results. Improvements can be categorized into three areas:

1. *Added preventive maintenance.* In order to gain the greatest precision tolerances from production equipment, Niceville has initiated frequently scheduled maintenance and machine testing. Experiments have shown that these

preventive steps result in less materials waste and fewer product defects. It was necessary, however, to invest in test equipment and to train both direct and indirect factory workers in their use. Some workers had remarked during the month that they liked having better control over their equipment, but until they gained more experience, they were not sure whether their efforts were productive.

2. *Information sharing and improvement.* The plant's managers have initiated a series of ongoing meetings to explain to factory workers the meaning of reported cost variances. Process improvement teams were formed to examine the causes of past variances and to look for ways to improve current work practices. These steps have been looked upon favorably by Precious Dolls' corporate managers, whose quality experts advised that rank-and-file workers be given more opportunity to share in the search for improvement. As with preventive maintenance, these efforts are new at this point, and, during June, meetings have consumed employee time that could otherwise have been spent directly on manufacturing.

3. *Tightened quality control.* As part of the improvement training process, Niceville's managers have emphasized the need for all employees to inspect products for defects at every part of the production cycle. Workers are told to examine incoming materials carefully and to notify the receiving department if they find substandard parts. If, at any time during production, a worker feels that a doll does not adhere to quality output standards, then the doll should be removed from the line immediately. Rejected dolls are handed over to an employee team designated to find the source of each specific problem and to follow up on corrective actions. Although these efforts have been extremely successful in June, they have resulted in an inordinately large amount of materials that never reached final product completion.

Required:

1. Prepare a profit variance analysis using a variable costing income statement format (as shown in Exhibit 11.2 in the text). Your analysis should break out Niceville's income variance for the month into a flexible budget variance and a sales volume variance.

2. Prepare a variable cost production variance analysis showing both the price variance and quantity variance for direct materials, direct labor, and variable overhead.

3. Assume you are given the following breakdown of fixed factory overhead cost (see Exhibit C11.1.4). Based on this information and your answers to requirements 1 and 2, above, prepare a brief explanation of Niceville's poor results in June. Offer a prognosis on whether you believe June's results should be seen as an added argument for disposing of the Niceville plant.

C11.2 (Precious Dolls, Inc.—B)

The Niceville operation is one of three production facilities owned by Precious Dolls, Inc. (Refer to C11.1 for more background information.) Niceville is a capital-intensive plant whose product costs are dominated by the costs of materials and production overhead. Corporate management has notified Niceville about the possibility of its closing down the plant and moving production to two existing Mexican sites, which are much more labor-intensive. During the month of June 1996, an improvement program was begun that was designed to reduce costs and raise productivity. Results for June were discouraging, however, as Niceville's income statement fell far short of meeting targets for profit and standard costs.

EXHIBIT C11.1.4 PRECIOUS DOLLS, INC.— NICEVILLE OPERATION

Fixed Production Overhead Cost for the Month of June 1996

	Actual Cost	*Flexible Budget*
Depreciation & maintenance	$31,500	$27,200
Rent	21,000	21,000
Indirect factory wages	38,200	35,800
	$90,700	$84,000

$(6,700)
Budget variance

As the plant began its July work schedule, both the plant's managers and the workers knew that changes put into effect the previous month would be effective. The three-part program involved a participative system for preventive maintenance, widespread information sharing and problem solving, and an expanded approach to improving quality control. The plant's senior managers had earlier decided that their past attempts for increasing profitability were insufficient, and they initiated the new program, which represented a fundamentally different way of making decisions. The new approach seems to be working, since most everyone at the plant is searching for new ways to increase output and cut waste.

The factory workers soon began to show management that they could identify many possible improvements that had been overlooked. When workers were told about specific problems, such as excessive use of raw materials, they were quick to bring up their discoveries—for example, hairline cracks apparently caused by overheated machinery. They also pointed out easily remedied inconveniences, such as the height of work tables, which was a constant source of backache and frequent fatigue for those in the packaging department. Over the past month, many changes were made to correct these everyday problems, and now employees are feeling more comfortable working in teams to solve problems and implement solutions. They are also becoming adept at their new roles, which require their participation in everyday machine maintenance and continual quality inspections. Nonetheless, the only measured outcomes through the end of June are the financials, and these reports are very unsatisfactory.

Reporting Operational Measures of Performance

Rather than waiting until the end of July to receive the next monthly financial report, employees began to push for more-frequent feedback. After some discussion, the plant's manager came up with a list of four measures that seemed critical to achieving program success. Each of these could be measured and reported daily.

1. *Units produced.* Given the high degree of capital investment at the Niceville plant, an important key to profitable operation is to increase the number of output units. Since capital costs have already been committed, low volume causes lost efficiencies of scale and thus becomes a primary cause of inflated unit costs. The plant's practical daily capacity is 1,650 units.
2. *Machine downtime.* Closely tied to the number of units produced is the need to make sure that scheduled machinery is fully functional. Because of the

highly integrated nature of the production line, a breakdown in machinery can cause the whole plant to close down until the problem is corrected. Favorable outcomes for this measure depend on proper execution of the preventive maintenance program.

3. *Cost of scrap loss.* Raw materials lost in the production process have become a special target for cost reduction. In the past, Niceville's materials-use standards have allowed for a normal amount of loss during production. Thus, for example, a standard of 3 pounds of polyvinyl per doll might be based on 3.05 pounds actually being used. *Scrap* is defined as the difference between material requisitions and the standard amount needed for good output.

4. *Production backlog.* Niceville's managers and employees have long recognized the need to reduce the plant's production backlog, a cause of unnecessary customer delay. Although this backlog is closely tied to the number of units produced, the plant manager has decided to report this measure daily. Thus, it will serve as a constant reminder that further improvement is needed. No precise numeric goal has yet been established.

Results Through Mid-July

The first report for these four performance measures was presented graphically for 5 weeks' performance ending July 14 (see Exhibit C11.2). Charts were posted in highly visible locations throughout the plant so that all employees could see progress made to date. These reports were to be updated daily to report the most recent 25 working days. They were to be posted by 9 a.m. each morning. Employees could see their results from the previous day, and, most important, they could track progress over time. Each work center in the plant was expected to devote 15 minutes of the (unpaid) lunch hour to examining changes made to date and to brainstorming in order to identify further improvements. Also, frequent meetings were scheduled during working hours in order to promote the efforts of the interdepartmental improvement teams.

The mid-July charts in Exhibit C11.2 offered evidence of the plant's progress. Both managers and employees were elated by the results, which showed steady improvement over the 25-day period. The graphs also helped employees understand why financial results for June were depressed, since the rate of improvement had evidently speeded up during July. Employees were hopeful that July's financial results would reflect the strong performance outcomes shown on the factory floor. The plant's manager was also encouraged, not only by the performance report but also by the commitment and enthusiasm clearly exhibited throughout the plant. She began to think there might be hope after all that the Niceville operation could compete with the less expensive, more labor-intensive Mexican plants. Still, she knew there was more work to be done.

Required: Comment on the progress made to date by the Niceville plant and on a recommended course of action for the future. Consider the following issues:

1. What advantage is gained by reporting performance results on a daily basis? How can Niceville's managers and workers benefit by their use?
2. Do you think it is sufficient to compare performance results over time as a way to achieve improvement? Would there be any advantage at this point in using control charts with upper and lower control limits?
3. How might benchmarks be used as targets for operational performance? What benchmarks seem most appropriate for the four measures in use? How would such information be gathered?
4. Would it be useful to begin developing specific action plans with designated dates for implementation and expected results? How does such an approach differ from the one presently in use at the Niceville operation?

EXHIBIT C11.2   PRECIOUS DOLLS, INC.—NICEVILLE OPERATION

Results of Daily Production Charts

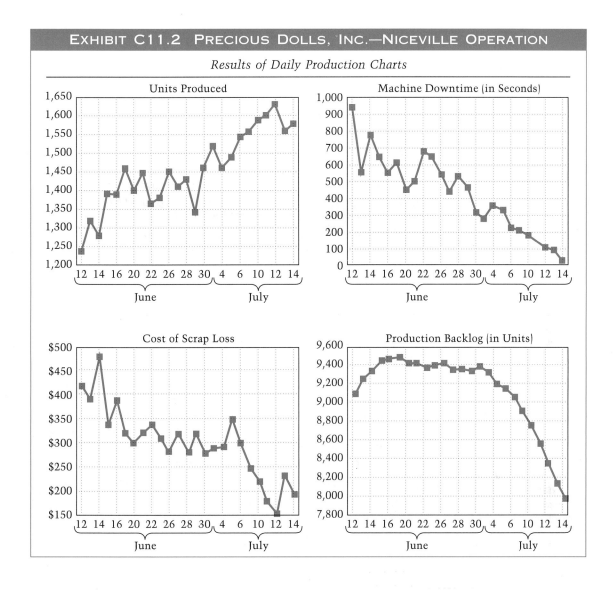

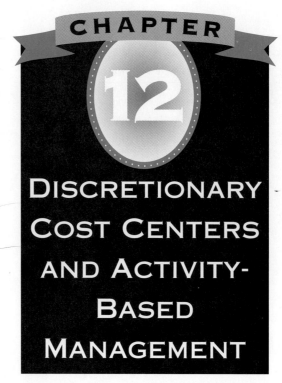

CHAPTER

12

DISCRETIONARY COST CENTERS AND ACTIVITY-BASED MANAGEMENT

— предпосылки не верне усмотрени

In Chapter 11 we discussed ways to control engineered costs, which are costs that have very specific, known relationships to product output, and which increase and decrease with the level of output. In this chapter we discuss ways to control discretionary costs, which are costs that have no clear relationship to output. Instead, discretionary costs are increased or decreased at the discretion of decision makers, based on their assessment of the costs' usefulness and effectiveness. Consider, for example, a promotional campaign to introduce a new movie. The marketing department knows that the campaign will create interest in the movie. But there is no specific relationship between output (here, attendance at the movie) and the amounts of such inputs as advertising, publicity, and product tie-ins. Instead, resources must be allocated to these inputs based on experience and judgment—that is, at the discretion of management.

Плюсоаддиция мекениа усмотрени

Activities that involve discretionary costs are becoming increasingly more important as competition—including international competition—increases. Heightened competition tends to focus customer expectations on such vital product attributes as quality, on-time delivery, and after-sale service. Improvement in these areas requires greater use of the company's internal support services. A successful product is thus dependent not only on production but also on activities such as design, materials procurement, logistics, quality control, promotion, distribution, and customer support. And all these activities involve discretionary costs.

The trend toward growth in support service activities offers many opportunities for managers to cut discretionary costs. But there is a trade-off: These same support services and discretionary costs may be the keys to sustaining a competitive advantage.

In this chapter we explore the factors involved in such a trade-off, again focusing on the last three phases of the management control framework—measurement, reporting and analysis, and corrective action.

We begin with a brief discussion of the relation between support services and discretionary costs. We then examine how discretionary costs can be controlled through the use of budget variances (first discussed in Chapters 10 and 11) and activity-based management techniques (discussed in Chapter 4). We conclude by reviewing some of the programs used by businesses in order to control discretionary costs.

NATURE OF DISCRETIONARY COSTS

Discretionary costs are costs that have no predictable relationship with outputs. They include many indirect factory overhead costs, such as purchasing and maintenance, and administrative and marketing expenses. Moreover, they generally arise from service activities within the firm—either support services offered by one department to another or services provided directly to customers.

THE CONNECTION BETWEEN SERVICES AND DISCRETIONARY COSTS

Not all services give rise to discretionary costs. Some—for example, preparing payroll checks (an internal support service) or taking fast-food orders (a customer service)—are repetitive and deliver measurable outcomes. For such services, the resource inputs that are needed to produce any desired level of output can be specified; consequently, these services can be treated as engineered costs. However, for the vast majority of service activities, there is no obvious, direct relationship between inputs and outputs. For research and development or for legal services, for example, outcomes are far from certain, and managers rarely know what resource inputs may eventually be needed. The costs of such services thus are highly discretionary, largely as a result of the nature of the services.

DIFFICULTIES IN ASSESSING THE VALUE OF SERVICES

Two fundamental characteristics of services contribute to the difficulties of relating inputs to outputs, and, hence, of controlling their costs:[1]

Lack of Standardization. Successful delivery of services often requires that activities be tailored to fit the needs of individual customers, both outside and within the firm. For example, a design engineer must work within the context of cost and size limitations that are unique to each product. As another example, the advertising department may be called upon to direct a campaign toward a new and unfamiliar market. Unfortunately,

---

[1] William J. Baumol, "A Growing Economy Can Pay Its Bills," *The Wall Street Journal*, May 19, 1992, p. A14; and Robert G. Murdick, Barry Render, and Roberta S. Russell, *Service Operations Management*, Needham Heights, Mass.: Allyn and Bacon, 1990, pp. 27–31.

such custom services do not lend themselves to the development of standardized, engineered cost relationships.

Labor Dependency.   The value of a service and the customer's perception of that value often depend on the degree of personal attention given to the customer by the service employee. The extent of the employee's personal attention, in turn, depends on the amount of time the customer demands from the employee. A retail salesclerk may be able to ring up a sale in only 1 minute, but if the customer felt that he or she was being hurried and his or her questions were not answered, the customer may leave with a bad feeling—despite the prompt service. A human resources staff member who rushes an employee's pension plan evaluation meeting will certainly convey a negative message to the employee. Curtailing service time, via engineered (i.e., forced) relationships, could easily lead to unintended customer dissatisfaction.

SERVICES ADD STRATEGIC VALUE

If services and their costs are such a problem, why not try to eliminate them, and so eliminate the problem? Mainly because services have become the primary means by which firms create their own particular advantage in the marketplace. The ready availability of technological advances has made it more difficult for firms to create a competitive advantage through their production processes alone. So firms develop a package of services to accompany their products, and they seek to differentiate their product packages by identifying and emphasizing what they do best.

Prescription drug manufacturers provide a good example. They compete in an industry where direct manufacturing costs are trivial relative to selling price, and price competition and product competition are almost nonexistent. Instead, one company maintains its strength through a powerful, research-based patent position, another gains competitive advantage by targeting rapid regulatory drug clearance, and a third is known for its system of sales and distribution.[2] Note that these are all internal support-service activities, but they provide companies with a competitive advantage just as offering customers consumer-oriented services does. (See "Current Practice: ServiceMaster Company.")

CONTROLLING DISCRETIONARY COSTS

Most discretionary costs arise from the delivery of some service activity. Given the difficulties of associating resource inputs with service outputs, developing effective control systems for discretionary costs is a challenging task. To begin, we should focus on cost centers that have the responsibility for providing services. It is at the cost-center level that senior management decides how much resource use is justified, and it is within the

---

[2]   James Brian Quinn, Thomas L. Doorley, and Penny C. Pacquette, "Beyond Products: Services-Based Strategy," *Harvard Business Review*, Mar.–Apr. 1990, pp. 58–67.

ServiceMaster Company

ServiceMaster, a $3-billion industrial maintenance firm, uses service activities to carve out its market niche through lower costs and lower prices. The firm's success is built on a sophisticated database that includes 14 years of maintenance history on 17,000 pieces of customers' equipment. ServiceMaster has set itself apart from the competition by using this database to produce customized, scientifically derived service schedules that define how each customer's facilities should be maintained, when preventive maintenance should be provided, and when equipment replacement would be cost-effective.

Source: Taken from James Brian Quinn, Thomas L. Doorley, and Penny C. Paquette, "Technology in Services: Rethinking Strategic Focus," *Sloan Management Review,* winter 1990, pp. 79–87; and "Beyond Products: Services-Based Strategy," *Harvard Business Review,* Mar.–Apr. 1990, pp. 58–67.

cost center budget that operational managers examine whether individual costs can be cut.[3]

CHARACTERISTICS OF DISCRETIONARY COST CENTERS

Discretionary costs are incurred by most cost centers. Even an engineered cost center—for example, a production department—might include in its budget an allowance for a discretionary cost such as employee training. On the other hand, the budgets of some cost centers, such as marketing, are dominated by discretionary costs. Thus, as shown in Exhibit 12.1, cost centers can be positioned anywhere along a cost-type continuum ranging from "highly engineered" (e.g., a production department) to "highly discretionary" (e.g., a marketing department) based on their proportions of discretionary and engineered costs. Those that fall to the right of the continuum are generally referred to as *discretionary cost centers.*

Most cost centers fall somewhere between the two extremes. A repair and maintenance department, for example, involves more discretionary costs than does a production department. Most repair and maintenance procedures are no doubt routine, but some require the exercise of judgment and, hence, are somewhat discretionary. A human resource department gives rise to more discretionary costs than does a repair and maintenance

---

[3] Technically speaking, *costs* refers to resources used in making tangible products—that is, to assets that are recorded as inventory until sold. *Expenses* refers to resources consumed in a period, nonassets whose value is shown immediately on the income statement. Following this same line of reasoning, *cost centers* refers to responsibility centers that make products, while *expense centers* refers to responsibility centers that provide services. In our discussion, however, we shall use the terms *cost* and *expense* interchangeably, as is common practice in business.

EXHIBIT 12.1   CONTINUUM OF THE DISCRETIONARY NATURE OF COST CENTERS

Highly engineered	Mostly engineered	Mostly discretionary	Highly discretionary
Production department	*Repairs & maintenance department*	*Human resources department*	*Marketing department*

EXHIBIT 12.2   CHARACTERISTICS OF HIGHLY ENGINEERED AND HIGHLY DISCRETIONARY COST CENTERS

	Type of Cost Center	
	Highly Engineered	*Highly Discretionary*
1. Type of cost structure	Largely variable (direct materials)	Mostly fixed (salaries)
2. Measurability of output value	Easily measurable (product sales price)	Measurable only by rough approximation (added value of training)
3. Relationship of inputs to outputs	Known relationships (direct materials cost per unit)	Unknown relationships (revenue per advertising dollar)
4. Proportion of personnel costs	Low (highly automated)	High (labor-driven activities)

department—but to fewer such costs than a marketing department does. Human resource personnel typically use routine procedures for processing job applicants and developing employee evaluations, but such activities as employee selection, training, and personal counseling are discretionary in nature.

Exhibit 12.2 compares some characteristics of cost centers at the two extremes. Generally, a cost center will be more discretionary in nature when it has the following characteristics:

• A cost structure that is dominated by fixed costs
• Outputs whose value is difficult to measure
• Input-output relationships that cannot be standardized
• Budgets that are dominated by payroll costs

IMPLICATIONS FOR COST CONTROL

We have seen that, on the one hand, service activities provide a way to create a competitive advantage in the marketplace. On the other hand, services are not easy to standardize and are very labor-intensive, requiring great amounts of employee time. There is then a trade-off between the costs of services and their benefits, and senior managers must continually evaluate that trade-off. Lower-level responsibility center managers are called upon to assess trade-offs between delivering quality service and reducing operating costs. To be worthwhile, cost control tools must be of help to both senior managers and operating managers in balancing costs and services so as to best meet the firm's objectives. (See "Current Practice: AT&T Corporation" for examples of service problems that resulted from cost cuts.) In the sections that follow, we examine the use of accounting information in controlling discretionary costs.

COST CONTROL THROUGH THE BUDGET

The budgeting process provides three stages of control for discretionary cost centers; they are summarized in Exhibit 12.3 in chronological order.

1. The first control stage is the budget review that takes place *prior to budget approval.* Since levels of discretionary costs—and, hence, spending—cannot be determined by input-output relationships, cost center managers must negotiate with top management for resources.

CURRENT PRACTICE

AT&T Corporation

AT&T is an example of a firm that cut costs and then struggled to maintain its ability to deliver quality service. One of AT&T's most important current objectives is to become more flexible and efficient. In the process of doing so, it has cut more than 100,000 jobs—a fourth of its payroll—and created 20 separate operating units. Many analysts, in praising the results, have said that the firm now runs businesses that are more agile and cost-competitive than before. Others, however, assert that the danger of such a massive restructuring is that the company risks losing its reputation for reliability. In other words, AT&T has cut its discretionary costs deeply enough to affect its ability to deliver telephone service.

One customer that has complained about its AT&T-supplied phone service is UAL Corp. (the parent company of United Airlines). UAL's telecommunications manager says that AT&T has sent in inexperienced technicians who had to ask UAL how to get into their own computer system. A separate indication is AT&T's long-distance system that, after years of reliability, failed four times in 2 years. A potentially disastrous failure occurred in September 1991—it closed down the air traffic control system for the entire northeast United States. In other cases, AT&T has outsourced its client service contracts. Customers have complained that the outsourcing firms that represent AT&T have sent technicians in who didn't know what they were doing.

Source: John K. Keller, "Some AT&T Clients Gripe That Cost Cuts Are Hurting Service," *The Wall Street Journal,* Jan. 24, 1992, pp. A1 and A5.

EXHIBIT 12.3 THREE STAGES OF BUDGET CONTROL FOR DISCRETIONARY COST CENTERS

Stage	Time of Occurrence	Activity	Objective
1	Before the budget period	Budget review and acceptance	Plan spending
2	During the budget period	Review of periodic performance reports	Constrain spending
3	After the budget period	End-of-year (or end-of-period) budget review	Promote understanding of resource needs

EXHIBIT 12.4 MONTHLY FINANCIAL PERFORMANCE REPORT FOR A DISCRETIONARY COST CENTER

Cost Account	This Month Actual	Budget	Variance	Year to Date Actual	Budget	Variance	Annual Budget
Salaries	$16,980	$17,083	$103	$49,720	$51,250	$1,530	$205,000
Supplies	300	350	50	1,120	1,050	(70)	4,200
Travel	1,230	1,042	(188)	3,300	3,125	(175)	12,500
Printing & copying	.	.	.	.	.	.	.
Telephone	.	.	.	.	.	.	.
Total	$22,878	$23,333	$455	$68,980	$70,000	$1,020	$280,000

The negotiation and review process allows senior managers to control costs by participating in the budgeting process. In order for a cost center's budget to receive approval, senior management has to agree with the cost center's objectives and the level of resources requested.

2. The second control stage occurs *during the budget time period* and consists of disseminating and reviewing periodic performance reports. These interim reports are most often distributed monthly. They tell the senior managers and the operating managers whether cost center spending is in line with monthly budget expectations and whether or not it is in danger of exceeding budgeted spending limits over the entire budget period. Periodic financial reporting helps managers keep track of past spending and, where necessary, adjust present and future spending. Exhibit 12.4 shows the form that these reports might take.

3. The third stage occurs *after the budget period has ended.* Then, an end-of-period budget review—mainly a comparison of budgeted spending with actual spending—is used to identify expense variances.

These variances become important in negotiations over the next period's budget. Information contained in end-of-period budget reports can help both cost center managers and senior managers understand how costs arise from the cost center's tasks and thus lead to more-realistic cost expectations.

In the remainder of this section, we focus our attention on these end-of-period reports.

VARIANCE ANALYSIS BASED ON THE MASTER BUDGET

Exhibit 12.5 presents the end-of-period income statement for Global Aircraft Supply, Inc., a distributor of aircraft parts and supplies. The format of this report is the same as that used for published financial statements. It is commonly used by managers to evaluate their service operations.

TWO TYPES OF COMPARISONS ARE REPORTED

The income statement format of Exhibit 12.5 provides the manager with two separate ways to examine deviations from master budget amounts—dollar variances and percentage-of-sales ratios.

Dollar Variances.   Each line item of the statement is compared with the corresponding line on the master budget, and dollar variances from the latter are listed. Dollar deviations from approved spending authority signal where and by how much the budget has been underspent or overspent. For example, the exhibit highlights as a primary concern the operating expenses of the warehousing and delivery department, which shows a $27,150 U (unfavorable) variance.

EXHIBIT 12.5 GLOBAL AIRCRAFT SUPPLY, INC.

Income Statement Analysis—Conventional Approach for the Year Ending December 31

	(1) Actual	*(2)* As % of Sales Revenue	*(3)* Master Budget	*(4)* As % of Budgeted Sales Revenue	*(5)* Dollar Variance[a] (Cols. 1 & 3)
Sales revenue	$3,000,000	100.0%	$2,800,000	100.0%	$200,000 F
Cost of sales	1,789,200	59.6%	1,610,000	57.5%	179,200 U
Gross margin	$1,210,800	40.4%	$1,190,000	42.5%	$ 20,800 F
Operating expense:					
Sales, marketing, advertising	438,000	14.6%	442,000	15.8%	4,000 F
Finance & administration	188,700	6.3%	187,600	6.7%	1,100 U
Warehousing & delivery	$ 442,350	14.7%	$ 415,200	14.8%	$ 27,150 U
Operating income	$ 141,750	4.7%	$ 145,200	5.2%	$ 3,450 U

[a]   F = favorable; U = unfavorable.

Percentage-of-Sales Ratios.   The two columns of percentages in Exhibit 12.5 show percentage-of-sales ratios. That is, the various dollar amounts appear as percentages of either actual sales revenue (for actual dollar amounts) or of budgeted sales revenue (for budget amounts). Percentage variances can be obtained by comparing the two percentages for any line item. For example, for cost of sales the actual ratio of 59.6 percent exceeded the 57.5 percent budgeted ratio, for an unfavorable variance of 2.1 percent.

APPLYING THE VARIANCES

To use this type of report effectively, managers must realize that each type of variance is appropriate to one type of cost. Specifically:

- *Dollar variances are meaningful only for fixed costs.*
- *Percentage variances are meaningful only for variable costs.*

To understand this, note that, for fixed costs, changes in sales volume have no effect on actual costs incurred. If sales increase, however, the ratio of fixed cost to sales will decline, but the decline is caused solely by economies of scale, not by an increase in operating efficiency. Next, note that, for variable costs, changes in sales volume should cause proportionate changes in actual costs incurred—that is the nature of variable costs. So the ratio of variable costs to sales should remain constant when operating efficiency does not change. A variance in that ratio, however, signals a change in operating efficiency. (A variance in the *dollar amount* of variable costs may not mean anything as regards efficiency.)

However, variance analyses such as the one shown in Exhibit 12.5 will be misleading whenever they report *semivariable (mixed) costs.* These are costs, such as utilities costs, that have both fixed and variable components. Mixed costs are almost sure to arise when department costs are aggregated for reporting purposes. The reported expenses for the warehousing and delivery department, for example, comprise fixed costs such as rent and variable costs such as supplies. If managers emphasize the dollar variance—in this case, $27,150 U—they will ignore variable cost increases that result from the increased sales volume. If they stress the percentage variance—here, 0.1 percent F (14.7 percent actual versus 14.8 percent budgeted)—they will erroneously infer that fixed costs were managed with increased efficiency. A reasonable way to solve this dilemma is to separate the operating expenses by cost behavior and then to analyze variances in a flexible budget format. We do so next.

VARIANCE ANALYSIS AND THE FLEXIBLE BUDGET

Exhibit 12.6 offers a detailed flexible budget analysis for Global's warehousing and delivery department, whose operating expenses were shown in Exhibit 12.5. For this illustration, we assume that *unit sales volume is the sole activity that drives warehousing and delivery variable cost.* Columns 1 and 5 show actual and master budget amounts. Actual total cost ($442,350) and master budget total cost ($415,200) are the beginning

EXHIBIT 12.6 GLOBAL AIRCRAFT SUPPLY, INC.—WAREHOUSING AND DELIVERY DEPARTMENT

Flexible Budget for the Year Ending December 31

	Budgeted per Unit	(1) Actual	(2) Flexible Budget Variance (Cols. 1 & 3)	(3) Flexible Budget	(4) Volume Variance (Cols. 3 & 5)	(5) Master Budget
Assumed cost driver: Number of units sold		60,000	0	60,000	4,000 F[a]	56,000
Variable cost:						
Fuel, oil, & power	$0.60	$ 37,150	$ 1,150 U	$ 36,000[b]	$2,400 U	$ 33,600
Repair & maintenance	0.18	12,200	1,700 U	10,500	700 U	9,800
Supplies	0.30	21,300	3,300 U	18,000	1,200 U	16,800
Total variable cost	$1.08	$ 70,650	$ 6,150 U	$ 64,500	$4,300 U	$ 60,200
Fixed cost:						
Payroll		$171,500	$ 9,500 U	$162,000	$ 0	$162,000
Rent		111,000	6,000 U	105,000	0	105,000
Depreciation		52,000	0	52,000	0	52,000
Insurance		37,200	1,200 U	36,000	0	36,000
Total fixed cost		$371,700	$16,700 U	$355,000	$ 0	$355,000
Total warehousing & delivery		$442,350	$22,850 U	$419,500	$4,300 U	$415,200
Total from income statement (Exhibit 12.5)		$442,350		$ 27,150 U		$415,200

[a] F = favorable; U = unfavorable.
[b] $36,000 = $0.60 variable cost per unit × 60,000 units sold.

points for the analysis. The flexible budget amounts in column 3, including the total cost of $419,500, are computed by scaling *only variable costs* up to the actual sales volume. Recall that fixed costs are not scaled up or down in a flexible budget, because they are not expected to change with volume fluctuations.

Once the flexible budget amounts are computed, we can calculate two types of variances, resulting from different sources. One, the sales volume variance in column 4, is the difference between the master budget and the flexible budget amounts. This variance of $4,300 U explains warehousing and delivery cost increases that result from the increase in the number of units sold over the budget volume. The variance is unfavorable, because flexible budget costs exceed those in the master budget. This variance can be disregarded for control purposes, since it represents a cost increase that can be explained by higher sales volume (4,000 units F). The second variance is the flexible budget variance in column 2, which is the difference between the actual budget and flexible budget amounts. It totals $22,850 U and requires further investigation.

ISOLATING CAUSES OF FIXED COST VARIANCES

Most discretionary cost centers are *dominated by fixed costs*, as is the case for Global's warehousing and delivery department, as shown in Exhibit 12.6. That department's variable cost accounts for only about 15 percent ($64,500/$419,500) of its flexible budget and 27 percent ($6,150/$22,850) of its flexible budget variance. Fixed cost, in contrast, constitutes about 85 percent of total cost and 73 percent of the flexible budget variance.

Discretionary fixed costs are budgeted so as to accommodate the level of tasks planned by the department. Two kinds of changes can reasonably and justifiably cause variances in these costs:

Changes in the Prices of Fixed-Cost Resources.   One explanation for fixed cost variances is that price changes during the year caused cost increases or decreases. In Exhibit 12.6, the payroll ($9,500 U variance) may have increased, for example, because of an unexpected increase in the cost of a benefit, such as health insurance.

Changes in Workload.   Another explanation for variances in fixed costs is changes in the department workload. While true fixed costs do not change as a result of short-term fluctuations in output, step-function fixed costs can be expected to increase when the existing operating capacity is exceeded. Consider, for example, payroll cost. During temporarily slow times, managers are reluctant to release employees because of the negative effect that can have on morale and because of the cost of rehiring. When sales exceed expectations, however, temporary workers are frequently hired in order to increase output accordingly. Payroll costs thus tend to increase in jumps as sales increase.

Thus, the unfavorable payroll variance of $9,500 in Exhibit 12.6 may have arisen because management hired an additional part-time warehouse worker to handle the increased sales activity. The other two fixed costs showing unfavorable variances—rent ($6,000 U) and insurance ($1,200 U)—may reflect other warehouse-management decisions, such as adding temporary storage and increasing risk protection. However, the flexible budget doesn't explain variances in detail. To determine specific causes for these cost overruns requires a more thorough investigation of the types of activities going on in the warehouse and their effect on resource consumption.

ISOLATING THE CAUSES OF VARIABLE COST VARIANCES

Although, for discretionary cost centers, variable costs generally have less impact than fixed costs do, variances in variable costs are often worth exploring nonetheless. As an example, consider the warehouse and delivery department's supplies account, which is broken down in Exhibit 12.6. The account shows a flexible-budget variance of $3,300 U and a sales volume variance of $1,200 U. Only the $3,300 U variance is of concern. (The $1,200 U variance is an expected variance, because it comes directly from an increase in sales volume.)

Variable-cost variances can be analyzed by means of standard costs, as we did for engineered cost centers in Chapter 11. The result is a breakdown of the variance into a price variance and a quantity variance. Exhibit 12.7 shows the breakdown for the $3,300 U supplies variance, assuming that the supplies account includes only the cost of pallets used in the warehouse. We also assume that the per-pallet average actual cost (AP) is $7.607, that the standard price (SP) used to construct the master budget is $7.50, that the actual quantity (AQ) of pallets used is 2,800 pallets, and that only 2,400 pallets are allowed as the standard quantity (SQ). The analysis in Exhibit 12.7 shows that the supplies variance in Exhibit 12.6 ($3,300 U) can be subdivided into a price variance of $300 U and a quantity variance of $3,000 U. In other words, Global's warehousing and delivery manager can now see that, of the $3,300 supply cost overrun, $300 is caused by higher pallet prices and $3,000 is caused by an excessive use of pallets.

Such detailed variance analyses are not normally performed for discretionary cost centers—except under special circumstances—because the outputs of most discretionary cost centers are not easily measurable. For example, the ultimate output of the warehousing and delivery department is the delivery of parts and supplies to customers. This output is much different from Global's unit sales volume, which is the cost driver we

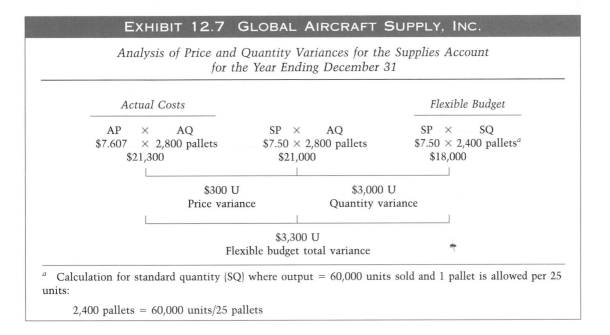

EXHIBIT 12.7 GLOBAL AIRCRAFT SUPPLY, INC.

Analysis of Price and Quantity Variances for the Supplies Account for the Year Ending December 31

Actual Costs		Flexible Budget
AP × AQ	SP × AQ	SP × SQ
$7.607 × 2,800 pallets	$7.50 × 2,800 pallets	$7.50 × 2,400 pallets[a]
$21,300	$21,000	$18,000

$300 U	$3,000 U
Price variance	Quantity variance

$3,300 U
Flexible budget total variance

[a] Calculation for standard quantity (SQ) where output = 60,000 units sold and 1 pallet is allowed per 25 units:

2,400 pallets = 60,000 units/25 pallets

assumed for warehousing and delivery variable costs. Further, in Exhibit 12.7, we allowed 1 pallet for every 25 units sold; in reality, pallet use will depend on many factors, such as the weight of the units and their bulk. As a consequence, the $3,000 U quantity variance that we computed may be mathematically precise, but it offers managers little insight into how to improve the efficiency of pallet use.

CONCLUDING REMARKS ON COST CONTROL USING FLEXIBLE BUDGETS

As noted earlier, discretionary costs are difficult to control once the operating period has begun. By then, management has already committed to a certain (budgeted) level of service and support. Consequently, most opportunities for control occur in the preparation, review, and approval stages of the budget process—that is, *before the operating period begins.* Hence, it is essential that variances for the current period be well-understood before discretionary costs are budgeted for the next period. Flexible budgets can provide useful information as to which cost accounts are out of line. They cannot, however, tell us why cost variances exist. Managers are generally left to draw their own inferences about how to increase cost-efficiency and thereby eliminate the variances.

COST CONTROL THROUGH ACTIVITY-BASED MANAGEMENT

To really control discretionary costs, managers need to look beyond budgets and budget variances. They need information about the ways in which work is actually accomplished. How do employees perform their tasks? Are their efforts productive? Do they squander resources? Where can process improvements be made? For the answers to such questions, managers need to examine work activities and their costs.

ACTIVITIES, COSTS, AND CONTROL

Recall from Chapter 4 that activities constitute the work people actually do. To isolate and identify activities, we begin with processes—the major elements of work performed in an organization—which often transcend departmental boundaries. The very broad processes (such as customer support) are broken down into subprocesses (such as distribution) and then into lower-level subprocesses, as necessary, until only very-low-level activities (such as pack orders) remain. Deciding how narrowly to define subprocesses and the point where a subprocess becomes an activity is judgmental. However, well-defined activities normally involve the conversion of inputs to outputs, and activities typically reflect actual day-to-day work for which the level of detail collected can be useful.

In Chapter 4 we saw that activities provide a focal point for collecting costs in activity-based costing (ABC) systems. Here, however, we shall use activities to control costs. The reasoning behind this use is simple: If activities drive costs, then managers can control costs by controlling activities.

ACTIVITY-BASED MANAGEMENT

The general concept of exerting control by the management of activities is referred to as **activity-based management.** A basic requirement of activity-based management is that periodic reports and the information they contain be focused on activities, rather than on functional cost objects such as payroll, supplies, and rent. The idea is to give managers the feedback they need in order to understand the activities that drive costs.

With such an understanding, managers can pursue their primary goal of improving activities that are essential to the organization's work and eliminating those that add no value. The first step is to identify activities as either value-adding or non-value-adding. Activities that provide value to the customer—for example, after-sale repair service—are essential. Activities needed to sustain the organization—for example, preparation of monthly financial statements—are also essential, since they are necessary in order to maintain the organization. Such activities should be evaluated in order to identify ways to improve their results and reduce their costs. However, activities such as inspecting incoming parts may add no value and, in that case, should be eliminated. In this example, one way to do so would be to purchase parts only from suppliers who will deliver preinspected parts.

EXPLOITING LINKAGES

Activity-based management is not focused solely within departments. Changes that occur in one department can affect others. Better communication of customer needs to engineering by the sales department, for example, can lead to improved product design and fewer subsequent engineering change orders. Changes in the maintenance department, for example, may benefit manufacturing by lowering production costs by increasing machine availability. These connections between departments (or processes) are difficult to discover when firms focus on department line-item costs such as payroll or maintenance. However, analysis at the level of subprocesses and activities very often points up such linkages, allowing management to take full advantage of their cost-control potential. And department managers will want to work closely with other departments when they find they can improve their own department's performance thereby.

Additional advantage can be gained through capitalizing on existing or newly developed linkages with external suppliers and buyers. Again, a focus on activities helps managers find areas where such linkages can provide a competitive edge—often to the benefit of external parties, as well. Many firms outsource nonessential activities—such as maintenance, payroll preparation, and freight delivery—to vendors who can often provide services at lower cost. Others work in complementary partnerships with other firms; each partner specializes in those activities in which it has unique competencies. For example, a computer hardware producer may collaborate with a systems-networking company. As another example, there is a maker of beverage containers that has even built plants close to beer breweries, thus securing considerable savings both for itself and for its customers by reducing transport cost. Linkages between buyers and suppliers—commonly referred to as *strategic partnerships*—have become part of the way of doing business in global markets. (See "Current Practice: PC Connection.")

ANALYZING ACTIVITY-BASED COSTS

Some preliminary analysis is required before operating costs can actually be reduced. This analysis can more or less parallel the steps introduced in Chapter 4 for determining costs in activity-based costing systems.

1: Identify Activities Whose Costs Can Be Reduced. Not every activity is a candidate for cost reduction. To determine which ones are, the manager begins with a process-subprocess-activity analysis for the purpose of identifying the firm's (or department's) activities. Then the manager must decide which activities will offer the greatest payoff potential. Students of management say that, as a rule of thumb, 80 percent of a company's costs result from 20 percent of its activities. It is this 20 percent of activities that should be targeted.

The way to begin targeting cost reduction is to decide which activities create value for customers (e.g., delivering after-sale service), which

---

CURRENT PRACTICE

PC Connection

PC Connection is a standout in one of the most competitive industries in the world. In the early 1990s, it was named the best mail-order company in the computer industry for 2 years in a row. The key to the company's success is its prompt and inexpensive overnight delivery. The company has a deal with Airborne Express, which delivers all of PC Connection's orders for a flat $3-per-package shipping fee. PC Connection earns this low rate by grouping orders by destination, "containerizing" them, trucking them to Airborne's airport terminal, and providing Airborne with weight and destination information while the trucks are en route to the airport. Meanwhile, Airborne concentrates on providing its core service—delivering the goods.

Source: Robert J. Berling, "The Emerging Approach to Business Strategy: Building a Relationship Advantage," *Business Horizons*, July–Aug. 1993, pp. 22–23.

create value for sustaining the organization (e.g., keeping payroll records), and which create no value at all (e.g., inspecting, reworking, or moving). Non-value-adding activities are targeted for elimination. To identify which value-adding activities are candidates for improvement, managers can benchmark their unit's performance of an activity against another department's performance of a similar activity or against outside competitors' performance, if such data are available.

2: Determine Cost Drivers. *Cost drivers* are the things (or people) that create the need for work—the objects of activities. The combination of a cost driver and an activity produces costs. Cost drivers are useful only when they are measurable or countable. They are most useful when they can be controlled. So, for example, the customer service department of a retail store might determine that costs are driven by the number of after-purchase customer complaints. That department would not want to consider customer attitude as a cost driver, however, since this is far too difficult to measure and control.

At this point it is worth recalling from Chapter 4 that activities are assigned to products and other cost objects by use of *activity drivers.* An activity driver, however, can also be a *cost driver* if it causes costs to increase or decrease. Throughout our discussion in this chapter, we use the term cost driver when discussing activity costs since our focus is on the behavioral relationships between costs and the activities that caused these costs to occur.

3: Understand Activities and Linkages. Understanding the activities, their importance to the organization and to customers, and the degree to which they are open to change comes largely as a result of the preceding two steps. Some additional analysis will likely be necessary as well. The analysis will often suggest that some investigation into connections between departments be done. Thus, the analysis may ultimately extend beyond the cost concerns of individual managers. For example, an analysis of a given organization's procurement activities may reveal that costs are driven by the number of purchase orders placed. If interdepartmental communication could be improved so that managers were better able to coordinate order placement, fewer orders would need to be placed, and procurement cost could be reduced.

ILLUSTRATION: GLOBAL AIRCRAFT SUPPLY—WAREHOUSING AND DELIVERY

We now return to Global Aircraft Supply, Inc., whose financial statements we examined in Exhibits 12.5 through 12.7. We shall continue to analyze the warehousing and delivery department data—but, now, in an ABC format. Our objective is to determine where costs can be eliminated or reduced. To do this, we must better understand the causes and nature of, and linkages between, activities.

IDENTIFYING ACTIVITIES AND COST DRIVERS

In the upper part of Exhibit 12.8, the warehousing and delivery costs listed in Exhibit 12.5 are broken down and assigned to six separate and specific activities. These activities are described as follows:[4]

Activity	Description
1. Receive shipment.	• Unload the vehicle. • Verify receipt of goods against vendor documentation. • Inspect goods for shipment damage.
2. Store goods.	• Determine storage location. • Put away goods. • Pick orders for sale from storage.
3. Inventory goods.	• Perform manual count of stored goods. • Update inventory records.
4. Repackage goods for resale.	• Repackage bulk items in smaller quantities.
5. Deliver goods.	• Load company vehicle. • Deliver orders to local customers.
6. Ship order.	• Pack orders for common carrier. • Prepare documentation for shipping.

Redistributing the costs, as shown in Exhibit 12.8, required a good bit of study in order to first determine the proportionate amount of time spent by warehouse and delivery employees at each activity and the amounts of space, equipment, and operating resources that each activity consumes. The results may not have the precision of a general-ledger cost classification, but they are precise enough to offer important insights about cost consumption and improvement. (The mechanics of preparing such an activity cost report are discussed in Chapter 4.)

The cost driver for each activity is shown in the bottom panel of Exhibit 12.8. The purpose of identifying the cost drivers is to help managers determine the causes of resource consumption. The cost drivers can be found using logic, or by observation, or by asking workers about the factors that affect their workload, or by combining these methods. Choosing the correct cost driver requires good judgment, but a consensus of what seems to be the most important trigger of activity will generally emerge. For example, Exhibit 12.8 notes that the receive shipments activity is driven by the number of orders received. Other factors will also affect receiving—such as the quantities, bulk, and weight of shipments; the need for inspection; and the verification time—but the primary determinant is still

---

[4] Adapted from Harold P. Roth and Linda Sims, "Warehousing and Distribution," *Management Accounting,* Aug. 1991, pp. 43–44; and Ernst & Whinney, *Warehouse Accounting and Control: Guidelines for Distribution and Financial Management,* Oak Brook, Ill.: National Council of Physical Distribution Management and Montvale, N.J.: Institute of Management Accountants (formerly National Association of Accountants), 1985, p. 29.

EXHIBIT 12.8 GLOBAL AIRCRAFT SUPPLY, INC.

Breakdown of Actual Costs for Warehousing and Delivery into Activities
for the Year Ending December 31

Cost per Activity

	Cost per Functional Category	Receive	Store	Inventory	Repackage	Deliver	Ship
Component:							
Fuel, oil, & power	$ 37,150	$14,860	$ 1,858	$ 743	$ 2,601	$15,230	$ 1,858
Repair & maintenance	12,200	2,440	1,830	122	122	7,076	610
Supplies	21,300	1,704	852	1,704	8,520	2,130	6,390
Payroll	171,500	34,300	42,875	17,150	25,725	25,725	25,725
Rent	111,000	3,330	99,900	0	4,440	2,220	1,110
Depreciation	52,000	9,360	13,000	2,600	7,800	18,200	1,040
Insurance	37,200	1,488	27,900	372	1,860	5,208	372
Total warehousing & delivery	$442,350	$67,482	$188,215	$22,691	$51,068	$75,789	$37,105
Percent of total cost	100.0%	15.3%	42.5%	5.1%	11.5%	17.1%	8.4%

Cost Driver

		No. of orders received	No. of square feet	No. of items in inventory	No. of items repackaged	No. of orders delivered	No. of orders shipped

the number of orders received. When there is no clear choice of a primary cost driver, it may be necessary to designate more than one.

UNDERSTANDING AND IMPROVEMENT

The understanding of warehousing and delivery that is acquired during the development of data such as those shown in Exhibit 12.8 and the identification of any linkages are put to use in the next phase of activity-based management—the cost-reduction or improvement phase. There are four specific ways in which cost reductions can be effected: (1) via activity reduction, (2) via activity elimination, (3) via activity redesign, and (4) via activity sharing.[5]

Activity Reduction. Reducing the amount of an activity that is performed, or **activity reduction**, will translate directly into a cost reduction. Consider, for example, the deliver activity in Exhibit 12.8. This is a relatively high-cost service to customers, consuming $75,789 (17.1%) of the cost center's resources. The need for deliveries arises from Global's standing policy that it will deliver all parts and supplies sold to local customers. Once company managers understand that this policy results in a high-cost activity and that the cost is directly attributable to the number of deliveries, they might question this policy. One way to reduce its cost would be to restrict its use by designating a minimum-dollar order amount for free deliveries, or by limiting deliveries to preferred customers. As a less-drastic alternative, managers could perhaps restrict delivery schedules or modify delivery routes in order to reduce the activity's cost.

Once possible changes have been identified, their potential effects should be analyzed. Global's management might expect, for example, that it could cut deliveries in half by delivering only local orders that are above some minimum dollar amount. Exhibit 12.9 provides a detailed analysis showing that the firm could save $36,580 annually if deliveries were indeed reduced by 50 percent. Cost savings are shown in the "Change in Operating Income" column, and they represent costs that would be *avoided* if the activity were cut by 50 percent.

The new delivery policy would, however, have some effect on revenue. Based on judgment alone, the marketing manager expects that the new policy will result in a loss of sales of no more than $40,000. Assuming last year's average gross margin percentage for these lost sales, a drop in expected gross margin of $16,160 can be expected. Thus, the analysis favors the new reduced-delivery policy, since it would increase annual operating income by $20,421.

Activity Elimination. A second way to reduce costs is by eliminating nonessential activities, such as unnecessary materials handling. Managers can use outsourcing to achieve **activity elimination**. Alternatively, they can make activities nonessential by changing processes or technology. For

---

[5] See Peter B. B. Turney, "How Activity-Based Costing Helps Reduce Cost," *Journal of Cost Management*, winter 1991, pp. 29–35.

EXHIBIT 12.9 GLOBAL AIRCRAFT SUPPLY, INC.

Estimated Income Effect of Reducing Deliveries by 50 Percent per Year

| | | Delivery Activity Costs (from Exhibit 12.8) | |
	Present Situation	*Projected Costs After Cutback*	*Change in Operating Income*
Component:			
Fuel, oil, & power	$15,230	$ 7,615	$ 7,615
Repair & maintenance	7,076	3,538	3,538
Supplies	2,130	1,065	1,065
Payroll	25,725	12,863	12,862
Rent	2,220	2,220	0
Depreciation[a]	18,200	9,100	9,100
Insurance	5,208	2,808	2,400
Total warehousing & delivery	$75,789	$39,209	$36,580
Projected lost sales	$40,000		
Average gross margin, percent	40.4%		
Lost gross margin			16,160
Net effect to operating income			$20,420

[a] It is assumed that equipment not needed after reduction will be sold. Any resulting gain or loss will be included in pretax income in the year of disposal.

example, the warehousing and delivery department incurs an annual cost of $22,691 for the inventory activity. This activity entails periodically counting parts and supplies in stock and continually updating perpetual records. The need to take inventory could be eliminated, however, if the firm invested $50,000 in point-of-sale terminals and bar code technology.

Because this change would require a capital investment, a favorable capital-budgeting analysis of expected changes in the firm's cash flows would be required in order to justify making the change. Note, however, that a long-term study was not needed to justify the reduction in deliveries described above, because no investment was required and the annual increase in operating income was expected to recur in future years. The short-term income analysis became, in effect, a surrogate for an analysis to determine the effect on shareholder value. Managers commonly use such changes-to-income analyses as the bases for decisions with longer-term effects, although technically it is incorrect to do so. As always, the true measure of value is the impact of the change on the firm's discounted cash flows over the term of the change.

A capital-budgeting analysis for the inventory activity is presented in Exhibit 12.10. The treatment of cash saved by eliminating the inventory activity is initially the same as in the short-term delivery-savings analysis, since it involves only resource consumption that will be *avoided* annually by making the proposed change. It differs, however, because this capital-budgeting analysis is based on cash flows. Hence, it must include all

EXHIBIT 12.10   GLOBAL AIRCRAFT SUPPLY, INC.

Capital Budgeting Analysis for Elimination of the Inventory Activity

		End of Year			
Cash from Operations	0	1	2	3	4
Annual cash savings for eliminating the inventory activity:					
Inventory activity costs (from Exhibit 12.8)	$ 22,691				
Less tax effects @ 34.0 percent	7,715	$14,976	$14,976	$14,976	$14,976
Less depreciation—a noncash expense		(2,600)	(2,600)	(2,600)	(2,600)
Net cash from operations		$12,376	$12,376	$12,376	$12,376
Tax Shield on New Investment					
Cost	$ 50,000				
Depreciation: straight-line, 4 yr, no salvage	25.0%				
Annual depreciation expense	$ 12,500				
Tax rate	34.0%				
Tax shield		4,250	4,250	4,250	4,250
Investment					
Purchase price—new point-of-sale terminals with bar code technology	$ (50,000)				
Salvage on old equipment—assume equal to book value (no gain or loss)	10,400				
Net investment	(39,600)				
Differential cash flows	$(39,600)	$16,626	$16,626	$16,626	$16,626
Discount factor at 18.0 percent (assumed)	1.000	0.847	0.718	0.609	0.516
Discounted cash flows	$(39,600)	$14,090	$11,941	$10,119	$ 8,576
Net present value	$ 5,125				

changes to cash over the assumed 4-year investment planning horizon. Consequently, tax effects for the inventory activity are included. Also included in the analysis is the tax effect of depreciation on the new equipment. The $50,000 investment in new technology occurs in year 0, and it is expected that, at the same time, the old equipment will be sold for its book value of $10,400. So there is a net outlay of $39,600 in year 0 and an annual cash saving of $16,626 in each of years 1 to 4. Assuming the firm uses an 18 percent cost of capital (or discount factor), the net present value (NPV) of $5,125 indicates that the investment is justified.

Activity Redesign. Activities can be reconfigured into lower-cost alternatives that accomplish the same results, and the most cost-effective alternative can then be utilized. For example, the warehousing and delivery department's storage cost presently totals $188,215, or 42.5 percent of total cost (from Exhibit 12.8). So the investigation of other approaches for handling and storing inventory would be worthwhile. One approach might involve reducing the storage cost driver (square footage needed) by negotiating favorable agreements with manufacturers to ship low-turnover parts and supplies by air express on an as-needed basis. Another alternative might be to make use of new storage technologies that increase capacity through the use of closely stacked shelves and specially designed narrow aisles. Still another possibility would be the purchase of high-reach forklifts that allow higher stacking of inventory in taller warehouse spaces. As before, managers should analyze the effects of such alternatives on income and, where appropriate, on discounted cash flow. (See "Current Practice: Virtual Offices.")

Activity Sharing.   Still another way to cut operating costs is to restructure work processes in order to combine or share activities. Activity sharing and combining can produce economies of scale, whereby the unit cost of an activity decreases when the volume or frequency of that activity increases. From the given activity descriptions for Global, it looks as though two activities—repackage and ship—entail much the same type of work. These activities may have been separated originally because they were seen as having different purposes: The repackage activity consists of breaking down the bulk quantities that are received into smaller ordering quantities, while the ship activity consists of preparing ordered goods for common freight carriers.

It may be possible that the same work unit—say, shipping employees—can be responsible for both activities, particularly since both activities

CURRENT PRACTICE

Virtual Offices

Companies are cutting costs by redesigning office workspace for some employees. Advances such as laptop computers, cellular phones, and fax machines have made offices portable and, in some cases, almost obsolete. Companies such as IBM, Arthur Andersen, and Dun and Bradstreet are eliminating some private office space as a way to cut rental costs while compelling salespeople and other professional employees to spend more time with customers. Employees who now normally work away from the office can reserve temporary offices when an on-site meeting with clients is necessary. One expert estimates that by converting offices from private to shared-usage facilities, companies can reduce their space requirements by 25 to 50 percent. For example, the Chicago office of Ernst & Young, an accounting and consulting firm, now maintains a five-to-one employee-to-desk ratio and has reduced its office space by 77,000 square feet in one year alone. At $40 per foot, the saving mounts up.

Source: Mitchell Pacelle, "To Trim Their Costs, Some Companies Cut Space for Employees," *The Wall Street Journal,* June 4, 1993, pp. A1 and A6.

are largely driven by the volume of outgoing orders. Some additional training would have to be provided to shipping employees, who would now be expected to repackage items to suit customer needs. But the firm would benefit by making better use of employee time, thus reducing the number of scheduled work hours. Other benefits can include reduced space requirements and reductions in related occupancy costs, such as insurance and maintenance.

PRACTICAL LIMITATIONS TO ACTIVITY-BASED MANAGEMENT

Using an activity-based approach to cost control is intuitively appealing to managers because it focuses on the daily events that cause costs to occur. If, for example, a manager wants to reduce the cost of quality control, the most fundamental strategy is to produce defect-free goods that require no inspection. Similarly, a manager trying to cut marketing cost can appreciate the importance of making sure past customers keep returning, thus reducing the firm's dependence on—and incurring the cost of generating—new customers. By concentrating on the root causes of activities in the first place, managers can find creative cost-reducing solutions that also serve the firm's broader strategic objectives—such as high-quality products and customer satisfaction.

Unfortunately, accounting systems designed to produce GAAP financial statements must often be substantially reworked in order to be used to prepare activity cost data. While the need for such information has been recognized increasingly since the late 1980s, much effort and expense is necessary in order to transform accounting reports based on functional cost categories into reports based on activity groupings. Special studies must be conducted in order to determine cost drivers and to find linkages among activities. Further, some managers may be disturbed by the subjective manner in which functional costs are allocated to activities. Moreover, activity costing is inherently less reliable than conventional financial reporting, because ABC categories are not standardized.

A lower-cost alternative to activity-based reporting is to continue generating conventional accounting reports and to use those reports to produce less-exact estimates of the effects of cost-cutting efforts. What is lost, however, is the acquisition of information that can reinforce a focus on activities, their causes, and their related costs. As with all decisions, the firm's managers must decide whether the incremental cost of generating activity cost reports can be justified by the value-adding benefits such reports are expected to produce.

CURRENT APPROACHES TO DISCRETIONARY COST REDUCTION

In this section we briefly examine several broad-scale programs that are currently used by managers to control discretionary costs. Exhibit 12.11 offers an overview of the discussion.

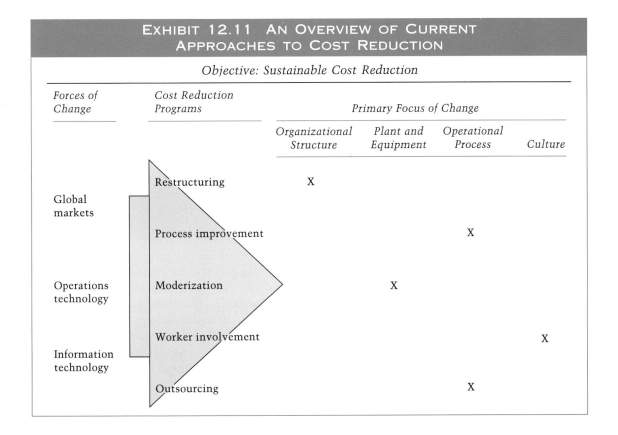

EXHIBIT 12.11 AN OVERVIEW OF CURRENT APPROACHES TO COST REDUCTION

Objective: Sustainable Cost Reduction

Forces of Change	Cost Reduction Programs	Primary Focus of Change			
		Organizational Structure	Plant and Equipment	Operational Process	Culture
Global markets	Restructuring	X			
	Process improvement			X	
Operations technology	Moderization		X		
	Worker involvement				X
Information technology	Outsourcing			X	

FORCES OF CHANGE

We begin by examining the three major forces that have brought about a widespread effort by firms to cut costs:

1. *Global markets.* International trade is growing and is expected to continue to do so. Firms in advanced countries now must compete not only with each other but with firms in countries where labor is cheap and regulation is lax. To be successful, they must reduce costs wherever possible, so as to compete effectively.

2. *Operations technology.* Newer technologies have provided means for cutting discretionary costs. They have, for example, shortened the time needed to bring a product to market and permitted more and faster customization of products. Service operations are being improved by standardizing the smallest possible levels at which a service task can be replicated. Standardization has led to improvements in ordering, inventory control, payroll, and direct-mail advertising, among other business functions.

3. *Information technology.* Computers enable information to be gathered and distributed quickly to even remote installations. For managers, this means ready access to the information on which to base cost reductions and with which to oversee the implementation of,

monitor the results of, and, where needed, correct deficiencies of such cost reductions.

Together, these three forces provide the means and motivation for cost-reduction efforts by firms. What is needed next is a plan, or program, for implementing the cost reductions.

TYPES OF COST REDUCTION PROGRAMS

We shall discuss five types of cost reduction programs: (1) restructuring, (2) process improvement, (3) modernization, (4) worker involvement, and (5) outsourcing. Each program is usually accompanied by a downsizing (i.e., reduction) in the workforce.

RESTRUCTURING

The primary focus of change in a **restructuring program** is the form of the organization. The objective is to create enterprise-oriented business units whose customers, markets, and performance measures are clearly defined, while eliminating barriers to interdepartmental action.[6] One trend of such programs is toward "flatter" organization structures, where layers of management hierarchy are eliminated and authority for many types of decisions is pushed down to frontline workers. The result is a much broader span of manager control—in some cases, with 20 to 50 employees or more reporting to one manager. Work is unified and integrated as employees focus on product delivery rather than on being concerned with meeting narrower departmental objectives.

Another trend is toward new structures, called horizontal organizations, that are driven by core business processes, such as gaining and filling new business orders or managing materials and production (see Exhibit 12.12). *Core processes* are groups of logically related tasks that span the organization and focus on customer needs. They are few in number—perhaps five or six per strategic business unit—and critical to organizational success. Core processes are linked to each other and to functional work areas (research, manufacturing, etc.) through key performance objectives, such as customer satisfaction and reduced cycle time. Teams of workers are formed around core processes—not inside functional departments—and are led by *process leaders* rather than department heads. The key to a horizontal organization is team-based work flows, with team members working as a unit to share responsibility for achieving process outcomes. (See "Current Practice: Eastman Kodak Co.")

PROCESS IMPROVEMENT

A second approach to cost reduction, called **process improvement**, focuses on, and seeks to improve, business processes. The approach generally begins with competitive benchmarking, whereby important measures of

---

[6] For more information, refer to James Brian Quinn and Penny C. Pacquette, "Technology in Services: Creating Organizational Revolutions," *Sloan Management Review*, winter 1990, pp. 67–77; and Thomas A. Stewart, "The Search for the Organization of Tomorrow," *Fortune*, May 18, 1992, pp. 92–98.

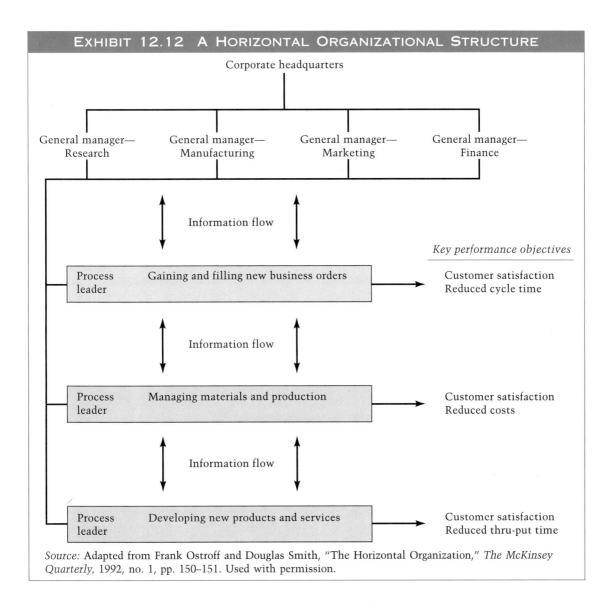

EXHIBIT 12.12 A HORIZONTAL ORGANIZATIONAL STRUCTURE

Source: Adapted from Frank Ostroff and Douglas Smith, "The Horizontal Organization," *The McKinsey Quarterly*, 1992, no. 1, pp. 150–151. Used with permission.

performance for each operation are compared with those used by similar operations both within and outside the firm. Managers whose processes turn out to be more costly or less productive than others seek to make changes that will improve quality, eliminate waste, and remove duplication. Changes in one area often produce benefits in other areas—cutting across functional lines of authority. Improved product design, for instance, to make better use of interchangeable parts, will result in procurement savings as well.

MODERNIZATION

New plant and equipment reduce costs by making available the best operations technology. In manufacturing, for example, this often requires significant investment in robotics and computer-aided manufacturing systems.

CURRENT PRACTICE

Eastman Kodak Co.

Eastman Kodak Co. has been successful in reorganizing its black-and-white film operation, a $2-billion per year business, into a horizontal organization. Approximately 1,500 employees work in what's called the "flow," a business process that is led by a 25-member multiskilled leadership team. The flow comprises product and service streams whose outcome targets are defined by the internal-business-unit customers they serve. For example, one stream makes hundreds of types of film for the health sciences division, with which it works closely in developing new products and in scheduling production. Most employees within the streams work in self-directed teams, which are evaluated on measures of customer satisfaction, such as on-time delivery.

When the black-and-white film operation was reorganized in 1989, it was running 15 percent over budget and was late in filling orders one-third of the time. Just 2 years later, the group was 15 percent under budget and was late in filling orders only 5 percent of the time, while working with more fervor. The change was the result of employees' having both the authority and responsibility for improvement. One employee-team member explained it this way: "When you create a flow and a flowchart, you find where you're wasting time, doing things twice. And because we 'own' our entire process, we can change it."

Source: Thomas A. Stewart, "The Search for the Organization of Tomorrow," Fortune, May 18, 1992, pp. 95–96; Frank Ostroff and Douglas Smith, "The Horizontal Organization," The McKinsey Quarterly, 1992, no. 1, p. 158.

For services, modernization usually means investment in advanced information technology. The key to reducing costs by modernization is increased productivity—the new equipment yields a greater output from the same (or lower) level of resource inputs. For example, Union Camp, a producer of paper and linerboard, increased productivity 26 percent by investing $1.4 billion in modernization over 5 years.

WORKER INVOLVEMENT

The fourth approach to cost reduction, worker involvement, has as its primary focus the corporate culture, and its object is to build support for continuous improvement. Some companies strive to transform the workplace into a high-involvement, self-managed operation where managers and employees share similar values and a common corporate vision. To make sure employees can and do act in ways that support corporate goals, decentralized information systems are implemented in order to report the results of key performance measures. Information still remains at the heart of control, but responsibility for learning and improvement is shifted down to the lowest operational levels.

OUTSOURCING

Another common approach to cost reduction is to purchase parts and services from outside vendors, or by **outsourcing.** Services that are outsourced can range from high-level organizational processes such as data processing or product design, to lower-level activities such as printing, delivery, or payroll preparation. The buying firm seeks the cost saving that arises from the vendor's specialized knowledge and economies of scale. Walt Disney Company, for example, now outsources vehicle maintenance for thousands of trucks and buses used for its Florida attractions and resorts.

Outsourcing often means more than a cost savings alone. For many firms, it means entering into long-term partnerships with suppliers in an effort to build a sustainable advantage through technology and new market opportunities. (See "Current Practice: UPS" for other examples of cost-reduction programs.)

CURRENT PRACTICE

UPS

UPS (United Parcel Service of America, Inc.) is the worldwide model for efficiency in the delivery industry. But, because of increasingly competitive industry conditions, UPS has initiated a series of sweeping changes intended to keep it at the market forefront. The goal is twofold: boost quality and reduce costs. Three programs are at the heart of its companywide makeover.

1. *Outsourcing customer service call centers.* UPS runs 65 service call centers where service representatives field customers' inquiries about lost packages and other delivery concerns. The call centers employ about 5,000 people. UPS has announced plans to turn to an outside company to run these call center operations.
2. *Process improvement in customer service.* UPS is seeking faster response to customer concerns. In the past, customers with lost packages called the service representatives, who called an operating center, which called a delivery office, which contacted the driver who was to retrieve and redeliver the lost package. Now service reps contact the driver directly, thus skipping two in-between calls.
3. *Worker involvement in day-to-day operations.* UPS is well-known for strict time and motion standards for its delivery workers. Formerly, workers were given the day's exact delivery schedule and were told to walk at a brisk pace of 3 feet per second and to knock on the door rather than losing time searching for a doorbell. The company is now seeking worker involvement in decision making. Delivery workers can design their own routes and decide how much time to spend with customers.

Source: Robert Frank, "Efficient UPS Tries to Increase Efficiency," *The Wall Street Journal*, May 24, 1995, p. B1; Daniel Machalaba, "United Parcel Service Gets Deliveries Done by Driving Its Workers," *The Wall Street Journal*, Apr. 22, 1986, p. A1.

SUMMARY

Discretionary costs have no clear relationship to output; instead, discretionary costs are increased or decreased at the discretion of the decision makers, which is based on management's judgment of the action's expected usefulness and effectiveness. Discretionary costs generally arise from service activities within the firm. As firms emphasize services as the primary means to create competitive advantage, their discretionary costs increase.

Discretionary costs are difficult to control, because services tend to lack standardization and their effectiveness often depends on the amount of employee labor time spent. Firms focus discretionary cost control efforts on the cost centers to which they are charged. Senior management uses the budget process to control cost center spending at three chronological stages: (1) prior to budget approval, (2) during the budget time period, and (3) after the budget period has ended. Most budget control for discretionary costs occurs when senior managers grant spending authority to cost centers in the first stage (i.e., before the budget period begins).

Analyzing variances between actual and budgeted costs helps managers understand discretionary spending. A flexible budget based on cost behavior reports variances in more detail than does a master budget based on an external reporting format. The use of flexible budgets for discretionary cost centers is limited, because most costs are fixed and standards are not easily determinable.

An alternative form of discretionary cost control relies on activity-based management. Reducing discretionary costs depends on the ability to control activities. Activity-based management involves three steps: (1) identification of activities whose costs can be reduced; (2) determination of cost drivers; and (3) an understanding of activities and their linkages. Cost reductions are accomplished by reducing activities, by eliminating activities, by redesigning activities, and by sharing activities. Deciding whether these changes are worthwhile is based on capital-budgeting analysis or, in the case of recurring annual effects, analysis of changes to income.

Managers are currently initiating several broad-scale programs designed to control discretionary costs. The need to cut costs arises from the growth of global markets and worldwide competition, along with advancements in operations and information technologies. Among the most common types of programs used to reduce costs are organizational restructuring, process improvement, modernization, worker involvement, and outsourcing.

CHAPTER 12 ASSIGNMENTS

DISCUSSION PROBLEMS

D12.1 (Comparing Engineered and Discretionary Cost Centers)

Dateway 3000 is a mail-order computer company that is trying to improve its operational efficiency. The company has been highly successful in offering a limited

EXHIBIT D12.1 DATEWAY 3000

Order of Activity	Departmental Activities		
	Assembly	*Shipping*	*Customer Support*
1	Assign resources.	Receive computers from assembly.	Answer and route incoming calls.
2	Assemble.	Fill sales orders.	Discuss problems.
3	Install software.	Pack.	Reroute calls as needed.
4	Test.	Label.	Diagnose problems.
5	Move to shipping.	Move to common carriers.	Recommend action.

variety of low-cost, high-quality personal computers that are delivered to the customers' door. Dateway makes no computer components itself; instead, it buys all necessary parts and subassemblies from outside sources. Computers are assembled and packaged by Dateway and then handed over to a freight company for delivery. Dateway offers a 24-hour toll-free "800" telephone number for all its customers for after-sale support.

To understand better where operational efficiencies might be gained, Dateway's president has decided to conduct a pilot study comparing activities in three key departments: assembly, shipping, and customer support. Information on departmental activities is shown in Exhibit D12.1. The assembly department assigns production resources, assembles components, installs software, tests the system, and then moves the finished products to shipping. Upon receiving computers from assembly, shipping fills sales orders, packs computers for shipping, prepares labels, and consigns products to outside freight haulers for delivery. After the products are sold and delivered, the customer support department answers incoming telephone calls, discusses problems, and, as needed, reroutes calls to more-knowledgeable representatives, who diagnose problems and then recommend solutions.

Dateway's president would like to use these three departments as models for a program to tighten resource consumption throughout the company. He believes that use of standard costs will help employees keep track of unnecessary waste. However, his managers have pointed out that some activities cannot be easily standardized, since no one knows just how much effort is needed to achieve the desired results. Nonetheless, the president's goal is to create standards for resource consumption wherever possible and then to hold workers accountable for meeting the standards.

Required: Discuss the possibility for standardizing activities within the three departments. To guide your response, consider whether a formula can be developed that specifies the relationship between each department's inputs and outputs. Identify which department is best-suited to standardization and which is least-suited.

D12.2 (Reengineering the Procurement Process)

General Avionics, which manufactures engine subassemblies for jet aircraft, is considering a major change to its parts procurement process. Its objective is to eliminate from its overhead those activities that do not add value to the final product. Generally, non-value-adding activities include anything to do with inspecting, storing, handling, or moving purchased parts. The process change under consideration would shift many of these responsibilities to the company's external suppliers. In return the company would commit to long-term procurement relationships with the suppliers. In effect, the supplier would be expected to make a commitment to deliver goods on a just-in-time (JIT) basis and to meet precise parts specifications without any allowance for defect or error. The suppliers would expect to benefit as well, since they could count on having a steady stream of revenue from one source.

A comprehensive analysis of procurement activities has been prepared and is shown in Exhibit D12.2. The exhibit compares the activities and costs using the traditional approach with those expected under the proposed approach. The new approach involves modifying, combining, and eliminating existing activities, but it also requires that some activities be added. For example, the new approach is expected to reduce the cost of searching for potential suppliers, since fewer will be needed. It will also reduce the cost of negotiating prices with existing suppliers, because only prices for new products will need to be discussed. Several activities and their related costs will be eliminated entirely—such as inspecting incoming goods, storage, and expediting quality. However, additional costs will be incurred for activities such as certifying new suppliers and conducting joint TQM (total quality management) training sessions.

The results reported in Exhibit D12.2 show that the new approach will reduce or eliminate many current procurement activities and will generate a cost saving of 40 percent. Still, some General Avionics managers are hesitant to make the changeover—partly because it is simply different from the old way of doing things. However, others are cautious because they fear the company will become

EXHIBIT D12.2 GENERAL AVIONICS

Procurement Activities and Their Costs

Traditional Approach		Change	Proposed Approach	
Assess materials requirements.	$ 4,000	(None)	Assess materials requirements.	$ 4,000
Search for potential suppliers.	3,900	Reduce	Search for potential suppliers.	3,100
		Add	Certify potential suppliers.	4,000
		Add	Conduct joint TQM training.	3,100
Approve new supplier procedures.	3,000	(None)	Approve new supplier procedures.	3,000
Gather price data.	3,200	Delete		
Negotiate price—old suppliers.	2,400	Reduce	Negotiate price—old suppliers.	1,500
Negotiate price—new suppliers.	1,200	(None)	Negotiate price—new suppliers.	1,200
Requisition and order.	5,900	Reduce	Requisition and order.	4,900
Carry out stock control procedures.	1,900	Delete		
Receive goods.	2,000	(None)	Receive goods.	2,000
Inspect incoming goods.	5,800	Delete		
Return defective goods.	2,500	Delete		
Store goods.	2,900	Delete		
Deliver to production.	1,800	Reduce	Deliver to production.	1,200
Expedite supplier delivery.	1,900	Delete		
Expedite supplier quality.	5,000	Delete		
Maintain documentation.	2,600	Reduce	Maintain documentation.	2,000
	$50,000			$30,000

Source: Adapted from Takeo Yoshikawa, John Innes, and Falconer Mitchell, "Functional Analysis of Activity-Based Cost Information," *Journal of Cost Management*, spring 1994, pp. 44 and 47.

overly dependent on its suppliers and perhaps lose some negotiating power regarding price changes. Finally, some are afraid that the firm will lose its freedom to shop in the marketplace for the latest technological advances offered by other suppliers.

Required: Comment on the advisability of General Avionics' changing the procurement process now in use. Do you see the threats posed by the new system as outweighing its potential saving? How can the firm protect itself against these threats?

PROBLEMS

P12.i (Using a Flexible Budget to Analyze Discretionary Costs)

Budgeted and actual human resource expenses for the East-West Manufacturing Company are given in Exhibit P12.1. Payroll and facilities expenses are fixed, benefits administration and recruitment advertising are variable, and training is a mixed cost. Variable costs are assumed to be driven by the number of full-time-equivalent employees at East-West, which was budgeted to be 400 for the year but was actually 420 because of expansion efforts. Training expense includes an attributed salaries and facilities cost of $120,000. The remainder of training expense is variable and includes the cost of supplies and materials.

Required: Prepare a flexible budget analysis that shows a flexible budget variance and an employee-driven volume variance.

P12.2 (Reducing an Existing Activity)

Globe Hopper Travel Agency has traditionally offered free delivery of all travel documents. Transactions are handled by telephone, and customers use credit cards so that Globe Hopper can send all completed documents to its customers via a commercial delivery service. In order to cut costs in an increasingly competitive industry, Globe Hopper is considering discontinuing delivery of all transactions amounting to less than $300. These customers will now have to pick up their tickets at Globe Hopper's office.

Expected annual cost reductions and lost sales are shown in Exhibit P12.2. One part-time employee will be released as a result of less time being needed for

EXHIBIT P12.1 EAST-WEST MANUFACTURING COMPANY		
Human Resource Expense		
	Budget	*Actual*
Payroll	$255,000	$252,000
Benefits administration	40,000	41,160
Facilities (including depreciation)	122,000	127,480
Recruitment advertising	4,000	8,040
Training:		
Variable & fixed	150,000	
Variable only		30,450
Fixed only		113,000
Total	$571,000	$572,130
Number of employees	400	420

EXHIBIT P12.2 GLOBE HOPPER TRAVEL AGENCY

	Current Cost	Projected Saving
Delivery cost	$ 11,000	25.0%
Packaging cost	$ 3,500	30.0%
Payroll (including benefits)	$250,000	$7,000
Lost bookings		$100,000
Average commission on bookings		10.0%
Tax rate		30.0%

EXHIBIT P12.3 GLOBE HOPPER TRAVEL AGENCY

		Year 1	Year 2	Year 3	Year 4
Estimated delivery cost saved		$ 14,500	$ 15,250	$ 16,000	$ 17,000
Estimated new bookings		$105,000	$120,000	$120,000	$120,000
Average commission rate	10.0%				
Full-time salary & benefits		$18,000			
Fuel & maintenance		$3,200			
Purchase of vehicle	$16,500				
Depreciation rate		34.0%	44.0%	15.0%	7.0%
Globe Hopper cost of capital	15.0%				

package preparation. While lost bookings seem quite substantial, the revenue lost is actually the commission received by the company, which is calculated using the average commission rate of 10 percent.

Required: Calculate the net income effects resulting from the reduction in ticket delivery for the Globe Hopper Travel Agency.

P12.3 (Redesigning Activities; Discounted Cash Flow Analysis)

The Globe Hopper Travel Agency is considering the use of its own, internal travel documents delivery service rather than using a commercial delivery service. (Refer to P12.2 for more background information.) The company would purchase a vehicle for delivery of documents for travel bookings of $300 or more. The current delivery cost of $14,500 per year would be eliminated. The hours of an employee whose part-time pay is included in the current delivery cost would now, however, be increased to full time.

Additional detail on costs, sales, and investment data is given in Exhibit P12.3. Sales are expected to increase because of this added service. Salaries and fuel and maintenance costs will increase after year 1 at 5 percent per year. The vehicle to be purchased will be depreciated over 4 years, and it is expected to be sold at the end of year 4 for $4,000. The company's tax rate is 30 percent.

EXHIBIT P12.4 NEW AGE CABLE SERVICES

Ledger Account	Cost per Ledger Account	Breakdown, by Activity		
		Identify Client Needs	Discuss Service Options	Take Service Order
Wages	$285,000	$75,000	$160,000	$50,000
Amortization expense	36,000	12,000	16,000	8,000
Computer services	70,000	4,000	46,000	20,000
Total cost	$391,000	$91,000	$222,000	$78,000
Activity driver		No. of calls	No. of call options	No. of options ordered
		30,000	120,000	70,000
Cost per activity		$3.03	$1.85	$1.11

Required: Determine the net present value of instituting the ticket delivery service at the Globe Hopper Travel Agency.

P12.4 (Reducing Activity Costs)

New Age Cable Services has completed an activity cost analysis of its sales order process, as shown in Exhibit P12.4. Management is considering the installation of a computerized telephone questionnaire in order to reduce the use of service representatives. The new system has a life expectancy of 3 years. An expected investment cost of $96,000 will be amortized over this time period by the straight-line method. Besides changing amortization expense, the new system will affect the "identify client needs" activity in two ways: Wages will be eliminated, and computer service cost will increase by $24,000 per year. The company uses a 15 percent cost of capital and pays taxes at a 40 percent rate. The costs of the other two sales order activities are not expected to change under the new questionnaire system.

Required:

1. Calculate the new cost, by component, of the identify client needs activity in year 1. Assume no change in activity driver.
2. Calculate the net present value of the new system.

P12.5 (Revising a Performance Report to Consider Activity Drivers)

Cheetah Motors Corporation, widely recognized as a leader in the production of elegant sport sedans, runs an active publications operation within its marketing department. The performance report for the publications cost center for the month of July is shown in Exhibit P12.5.

The newly appointed manager of publications is unhappy with the report, which shows that she has overspent her budget by $8,094 through July 31. Despite the fact that publications volume is spread evenly throughout the year, she says the report gives an inaccurate perspective on her department. Additionally, she thinks she does not receive information useful for making improvements.

EXHIBIT P12.5 CHEETAH MOTORS CORPORATION MARKETING—PUBLICATIONS COST CENTER

Performance Report Through the Month of July

	Annual Budget	Year to Date Actual	Year to Date Budget	Year to Date Variance[a]
Number of publications	600,000	380,000	350,000	30,000
Expense:				
Salaries	$104,500	$ 60,750	$ 60,958	$208
Office supplies	4,700	2,867	2,742	(125)
Travel	8,500	5,235	4,958	(277)
Typesetting	22,800	14,680	13,300	(1,380)
Production printing	124,900	75,360	72,858	(2,502)
Postage, freight, & handling	88,700	55,760	51,742	(4,018)
Total expense	$354,100	$214,652	$206,558	$(8,094)

[a] Variances are favorable or (unfavorable).

Three expenses budgeted for the cost center—salaries, office supplies, and travel—are basically fixed, regardless of the level of work. The other three expenses—typesetting; production printing; and postage, freight, and handling—depend directly on the number of publications produced and sent. The manager says that decisions regarding the number of publications are made by the vice president of marketing and, thus, are out of her control. She believes she could gain much more from the report if variable expenses were categorized separately from fixed expenses. She would then like to see all variable expenses shown on a per-unit basis for the number of publications sent. The manager wants two extra columns added to the report: one for unit costs based on the budget and the other for unit costs based on actual output.

Required:

1. Revise the performance report so that variable expenses and fixed expenses are each categorized separately. Report variances in a manner that complies with the department manager's requests.
2. Comment on the manager's performance through July.

P12.6 **(Evaluating a Proposal to Implement Concurrent Engineering)**

Unee Dachip, Inc., is a small custom producer of computer components. A cost study has just been undertaken in order to determine whether the firm could benefit by implementing methods of concurrent engineering. Under the concurrent-engineering approach, engineers from several distinct functional areas collaborate from the outset on product design. This represents a rather dramatic departure from the compartmentalized engineering approach used in the past, where design engineers would complete product blueprints without input from specialists in production or quality assurance (QA). Too often, the firm has encountered problems of delay on the production line—for example, when it was discovered that designs that looked fine on the drawing board created unexpected bottlenecks. Many quality conformance problems have arisen as well, but these were not discovered until the finished product had been tested against customer specifications.

One current project has been selected as a test case. Information is presented in Exhibit P12.6 showing the expected time line under the old approach versus a projected time line under the new approach. This particular component is typical in that it proceeds from design to production to QA. The new approach will require much more design time up front—an increase from 1.5 days to 4.0 days. It will also entail an increase in design engineering time from 12 hours to 32 hours. And it will call for an added 12-hour investment by production and QA engineering during the design phase. The payoff of these added costs is seen in the more efficient use of the production facility and of QA. Usage of production is expected to be cut from 8 to 5 days, and usage of QA facilities is to be cut from 8 hours to 4 hours.

Details given in Exhibit P12.6 show the expected amount of labor-hours, broken down by type of worker, needed to support the production and QA operations. For example, the cost of labor for operating the production facility, which employs

EXHIBIT P12.6 UNEE DACHIP, INC.

Projected Effect of Introducing Concurrent-Engineering Approach

Design	Old Approach	New Approach
Use of design facilities	1.5 days	4 days
Personnel:		
Design engineer	12 hr	32 hr
Production engineer	0 hr	12 hr
Quality assurance engineer	0 hr	12 hr

Production		
Use of production facilities	8 days	5 days
Personnel—2 production workers	8 days each at 8 hr/day	5 days each at 8 hr/day

Quality Assurance		
Use of quality assurance facilities	8 hr	4 hr
Personnel:		
2 technicians	8 hr each	4 hr each
1 engineer	2 hr	1 hr

Resource Cost		

Personnel	Hourly Rate	
Design engineers	$28.50	
Production engineers	$27.00	
Quality assurance engineers	$28.00	
Production workers	$12.00	
Quality assurance technicians	$14.25	

Opportunity Cost of Facilities	Rate	
Design facility	$500/day	
Production facilities	$1,000/day	
Quality assurance facilities	$150/hr	

two full-time production workers, is reduced from 8 days to 5 days each. The QA facility is run by two technicians and one engineer, whose time requirements for this project will be cut in half as a result of concurrent engineering.

In the lower panel of the exhibit, information is provided about the cost of resources to be used. The hourly rate for engineers ranges from $27.00 to $28.50, depending on the type of function they perform. Production workers are paid $12.00 per hour, while QA technicians earn $14.25. Unee Dachip is operating at full capacity. Thus, management views the cost of a facility as its opportunity cost, approximated here by the cost to the firm of renting similar facilities in the local community. For example, a design facility could be rented for $500 per day. For purposes of calculation, one day is considered an 8-hour time period, and partial days are charged out based on pro rata allocations of 8 hours.

Required:

1. Calculate the expected savings on this order if the concurrent-engineering approach is used.
2. What other factors might affect the decision?

P12.7 (Using Standard Cost Variances to Evaluate Travel Expenses)

The national sales manager of Ecosweepers, Inc., is very concerned about travel expenses incurred by the sales force for the past year. Sales efforts for the nation are broken down by district territory. The territories generally encompass the area within a 300-mile radius of the district office. Based on a geographic grid of potential customers within all districts, the sales manager has found that, on average, each sales call should require 50 miles of travel. The firm reimburses its sales personnel for the actual number of miles driven at the travel rate used by the U.S. Internal Revenue Service. This rate was budgeted at $0.30 per mile for the past fiscal year (ending on April 30). It is expected that each sales contract written will require six sales calls. For the year just ended, 14,800 sales contracts were budgeted. Calculations used to develop the companywide travel budget of $1,332,000 are shown in Exhibit P12.7.1.

Actual results were far different from the master budget estimates, however

EXHIBIT P12.7.1 ECOSWEEPERS, INC.

Master Budget for Travel Expense

Number of sales contracts budgeted	14,800
Number of sales calls per contract	6
Total sales calls budgeted	88,800
Number of miles allowed per sales call	50
Travel miles budgeted	4,440,000
Budgeted travel allowance per mile	$ 0.30
Travel expense budget	$1,332,000

Actual Results Reported for the Year

Travel mileage expense incurred	$1,615,000
Quantity of sales miles driven	5,200,000
Number of sales calls made	89,600
Number of sales contracts written	15,000

EXHIBIT P12.7.2 ECOSWEEPERS, INC.

Flexible Analysis for Travel Expenses

	Actual	Flexible Budget Variance	Flexible Budget	Sales Volume Variance	Master Budget
Number of sales contracts written	15,000		15,000		14,800
Number of sales calls per contract	5.97		6		6
Total sales calls	89,600		90,000		88,800
Number of miles allowed per sales call	58.04		50		50
Travel miles	5,200,000		4,500,000		4,440,000
Travel allowance per mile	$ 0.310577		$ 0.30		$ 0.30
Travel expense	$1,615,000	$265,000 U	$1,350,000	$18,000 U	$1,332,000

(see the lower section of Exhibit P12.7.1). Total travel expense was $1,615,000, and the sales force logged a total of 5,200,000 miles. What seems to have caused some confusion in assessing the causes and impacts of the variance is the number of actual sales contracts written (15,000), which exceeded the budget by 200. As might be expected given the favorable results in sales, the firm also made more sales calls—89,600, as compared with the 88,800 originally budgeted. Still one other complication is the travel reimbursement rate, which was increased from $0.30 to $0.325 during the year, when the IRS changed the rate it uses.

With the help of the firm's accountants, the sales manager has prepared a flexible budget analysis to adjust for changes in sales activity (see Exhibit P12.7.2). The information in the flexible budget offers some important insights. The sales volume variance explains that $18,000 of the unfavorable results can be attributed to the increase in the number of sales contracts written. Still, the sales manager cannot understand the large $265,000 unfavorable flexible budget variance. She feels she could gain more understanding if this number were broken down into a price variance, showing effects of changes in the reimbursement rate, and a quantity variance, showing effects of additional miles driven for each sale.

Required:

1. Break down the flexible variance budget for travel expenses into a price variance and a quantity variance. (Note that the output determinant of standard quantity is the number of sales contracts written.)
2. What seems to be causing the travel expense variance? Is the sales force meeting its target of writing one contract per six calls? How many miles, on average, are being driven per sales call?
3. Suggest actions that the sales manager might take to correct the deficiencies identified above.

P12.8 (Evaluating a Proposal to Outsource an Activity; Discounted Cash Flow)

Senior management at RKM Machined Parts, Inc., is deciding whether to outsource part of the company's maintenance function. The maintenance department performs three types of work: (1) preventive maintenance, (2) scheduled repairs, and (3) unscheduled repairs. Senior management has been approached by an independent auto and truck firm that is seeking a contract on all of RKM's vehicle repair.

This includes both scheduled and unscheduled repairs, as well as emergency roadside repair. At this point, RKM is not considering eliminating any preventive maintenance activities, which it will continue to perform in-house whether or not this contract is signed.

One of the young MBAs working in the accounting department has been assigned to the task of analyzing the financial effects of the outsourcing proposal. If repairs are outsourced, RKM will have to sign a 2-year contract and then will have the option to renew for 1 year thereafter on the same terms. Hence, after 3 years, the terms will be renegotiated. If RKM decides to go ahead with the outsourcing proposal, it plans to make a 3-year commitment, which is the time frame for which the analysis will be conducted. The outsourcing arrangement will commence on January 1, 1997.

Exhibit P12.8.1 presents information on the projected annual saving if vehicle repairs are outsourced. A reduction in services will result in the elimination of 1.5 full-time-equivalent positions, at a saving of $29,625 per year. Other annual operating costs that are expected to be eliminated include gas and oil ($3,150), supplies and parts ($9,200), and training ($1,080). One roadside repair vehicle, with a book value of $36,900, will be sold immediately at its market value, estimated at $38,600. As a result of the sale, the firm will not incur depreciation expense ($12,300 per year) for the remaining 3-year life of the asset. The only other operating item affected is the maintenance department's use of facility space, for which it is charged $16,800 per year. About 10 percent of the department's space is allocated to the vehicle repair function, but the department will merely shift use of this space to its other maintenance and repair activities. Neither its cash flow nor its occupancy expense will change.

The terms of the outsourcing contract call for the supplier to provide parts and service at 20 percent below the published guideline prices commonly used in the industry. (See Exhibit P12.8.2.) Based on RKM's repair history, the firm expects to need 265 repairs per year, 5 percent of which will be emergency roadside repairs. It has agreed to pay a surcharge of $35 for these roadside repairs, which require that the vendor dispatch a tow truck to the site of the emergency. RKM estimates that its repairs will average $190 each, after deducting the 20 percent parts and labor discount.

Several other bits of information have also been supplied. RKM uses a discount rate of 16 percent in making its investment decisions. Inflation over the next 3 years is expected to be negligible and will be ignored in this analysis. Finally,

EXHIBIT P12.8.1 RKM MACHINED PARTS, INC.

Projected Annual Saving If Vehicle Repairs Are Outsourced

		Annual Saving
Eliminate 1.5 full-time-equivalent employees—annual wages		$29,625
Eliminate one roadside vehicle (3-year remaining life)		
Book value, as of December 31, 1996	$36,900	
Market value, end of 1996	$38,600	
Annual depreciation		$12,300
Annual saving:		
Gas & oil		$ 3,150
Supplies & parts		$ 9,200
Training		$ 1,080

EXHIBIT P12.8.2 RKM MACHINED PARTS, INC.

Contractual Cost of Outsourcing Vehicle Repairs

	Expected Mix
Types of repairs expected:	
Drive-in repairs at the garage for parts & labor	95%
Emergency roadside calls @ $35 plus parts & labor	5%
Estimated cost of average repair for parts & labor	$190
Total number of vehicle repairs expected per year	265

RKM's marginal tax rate on both operating items and capital gains is 35 percent. Any tax saving generated by this proposal will be used to help offset the firm's profitable operations.

Required:

1. Prepare a discounted cash flow analysis of the outsourcing proposal for the 3-year period.
2. Based on your calculations for requirement 1 and on other qualitative considerations, what course of action do you recommend?

P12.9 (Evaluating Reengineered Offices; Discounted Cash Flow)

In their continuing efforts to cut discretionary costs, companies that employ service professionals—such as salespersons, consultants, and real estate agents—are redesigning office space and reconfiguring work activities. Employees with laptop computers, cellular telephones, and portable printers are instructed to use their homes, their cars, and customers' offices as *virtual offices.* When employees need to spend time at the corporate home offices, they are assigned use of "nonterritorial" shared space. For example, one major accounting firm in Chicago keeps available for common use 125 well-equipped offices, which must be reserved in advance by its auditors or by consultants who wish to spend more than half a day at the home office.[7] Those using the temporary offices hang their nameplates on the office doors, bring along their work files, and reprogram telephone numbers. Both work and personnel have proven to be easily transportable.

Consider the case of one large, 1,500-employee firm, Bronwin Consulting, whose senior management is now considering a major office space reconfiguration. Presently, the firm is completing a 5-year lease on a 337,500-square-foot property, for which it pays an annual rent of $26 per square foot.[8] Use of space in this facility averages out to 225 square feet per employee. Bronwin has the option of renewing the lease for another 5 years at the same rate. Should Bronwin renew, it will continue its policy of providing extensive use of private offices for its employees.

---

[7] Mitchell Pacelle, "To Trim Their Cost, Some Companies Cut Space for Employees," *The Wall Street Journal,* June 4, 1993, pp. A1, A6.

[8] Commercial rents are frequently quoted at a rate per square foot per year. For example, at $28 per foot, a 1,000-foot property would rent for $28,000 per year or $2,333 ($28,000/12) per month.

The firm has the opportunity to sign a 5-year lease for a new, largely unoc-cupied office building of 225,000 square feet, at $32 per square foot. The advan-tage of this new location is that Bronwin can redesign space to make better use of common offices, thereby cutting the average use per employee to only 150 square feet. The owner of the building has agreed to pay a one-time refurbishing allowance of $22 per square foot to help defray the costs of setting up a fiber-optics network and of building the interior office space. Bronwin Consulting has obtained esti-mates of $2,500,000 for the fiber-optics network and $3,800,000 for the interior office construction. In addition, it will incur a moving cost of $750,000. All refur-bishing and moving costs will be incurred and paid for in the year prior to occu-pancy, on January 1, 1997. Also, the landlord will pay Bronwin the $22-per-square-foot refurbishing allowance as these costs are incurred. Lease payments begin in 1997.

All lease payments and moving costs are expensed in the year in which they are paid. Costs that Bronwin incurs beyond the refurbishing allowance for network setup and interior construction are considered leasehold improvements and are amortized using a straight-line method for the term of the lease. Bronwin Con-sulting incurs taxes at a 35 percent rate and uses an 18 percent discount rate for all long-term cash flow analysis.

Required:

1. Calculate the net present value of moving into the new property.
2. How do you think the use of a virtual-office work environment will affect employee productivity and corporate culture? Should these issues be factored into the NPV calculation?

P12.10   (Assessing Alternatives for Cost Reduction; Activity-Based Management)

Over the past several years, Greater Midwestern Bank has been faced with the problems of mounting costs and stagnant revenues. A task force has been orga-nized and assigned the task of finding new and creative ways to reduce or elimi-nate some of the bank's existing expenses. The group has focused especially on reducing activities in many of the bank's clerical functions. One of the areas where the team found opportunity for improvement is the accounts payable department. As seen in Exhibit P12.10.1, the expense of running this department has increased at an average rate of about 6 percent over the past three years. Most of the costs of this department are in payroll. Payroll expense constituted 78 percent of the total department expense in 1996. This department is typical of many processes in the bank in that it has become more costly over the years. Yet financial reports have provided little insight into the reasons for such growth.

The task force began its investigation by talking with the manager of accounts payable, Clyde Trumbley III, who now manages a workforce of seven employees. Trumbley was quick to explain that the department's work has increased because of the increased number of specialized purchases by the bank for equipment, supplies, and outsourced services. Greater scrutiny is needed in order to verify the amounts billed, and his staff frequently ends up resolving dis-crepancies over invoices. He points out that this is a very time-consuming process and involves prolonged discussions with vendors and with the bank employees who initiated the purchases in question.

The task force decided to examine the specific activities that constitute the accounts payable process. The department's expenses for 1996 were distributed by the five types of activities performed. The five activity types are:

EXHIBIT P12.10.1   GREATER MIDWESTERN BANK— ACCOUNTS PAYABLE DEPARTMENT

Expense Reports

	1994	1995	1996
Payroll	$136,600	$145,300	$153,000
Depreciation—equipment	11,600	12,300	13,100
Occupancy expense	14,400	15,400	16,500
Training	4,800	5,200	5,500
Supplies	6,700	7,150	7,600
Total	$174,100	$185,350	$195,700
Rate of increase	6.1%	6.5%	5.6%

EXHIBIT P12.10.2   GREATER MIDWESTERN BANK— ACCOUNTS PAYABLE DEPARTMENT

Report on Actual Costs for 1996

	Cost per Functional Category	Cost per Activity				
		Process Mgmt	Invoice Processing	Coding and Keying	Control and Attesting	Vendor Inquiry
Payroll	$153,000	$36,000	$55,000	$27,000	$ 9,000	$26,000
Depreciation—equipment	13,100	1,300	4,500	4,500	1,300	1,500
Occupancy expense	16,500	6,600	3,300	2,475	1,650	2,475
Training	5,500	2,200	1,375	0	825	1,100
Supplies	7,600	3,800	1,140	1,140	760	760
Total	$195,700	$49,900	$65,315	$35,115	$13,535	$31,835
Percentage of department cost	100%	25.5%	33.4%	17.9%	6.9%	16.3%
Cost driver		Oversight of dept. operations	No. of invoices	Line items of code	No. of data entries	No. of discrepancies

1. Managing the accounts payable process
2. Processing invoices
3. Coding and keying data into the computer system
4. Controlling for errors by attesting to the accuracy of data entered
5. Making vendor inquiries and resolving differences

An activity cost analysis was performed in order to distribute the department's functional costs to the five activities. The results are reported in Exhibit P12.10.2. This report, along with discussions with Trumbley and other department employees, helped the task force to understand what changes could be made.

In its search for ways to reduce department costs, the task force has come up with two options:

1. The first option entails forwarding all discrepancies over invoices back to the bank employee who authorized the purchase. This person would be responsible for resolving all problems. When a solution is reached, proper documentation

would be submitted to accounts payable, which would then process the invoice. Under this proposal, 1½ positions used for vendor inquiry would be eliminated, saving $26,000. The department could also eliminate all equipment, training expense, and supplies now used for vendor inquiry. Occupancy expense, however, would probably not be cut, since the department would shift use of the newly available space to other purposes.

2. The second option involves making a programmatic change to the way the bank deals with its vendors. Any invoice for which there is a discrepancy would be returned immediately to the vendor, who would be expected to take charge of resolving all problems. Only after full agreement was reached by both the vendor and the authorizing bank employee would the invoice be processed by accounts payable. Although this option would result in only a partial elimination of the vendor inquiry activity, it would also cause a partial reduction in process management. Payroll would be reduced by $17,500 in vendor inquiry and $9,000 in process management. Equipment depreciation would fall by $1,000 for each activity. Occupancy expense would be reduced by 10 percent for the department. Both training and supplies costs would fall by about 33⅓ percent in the process management activity and by 80 percent in the vendor inquiry activity.

Required:

1. Calculate the annual pretax cost saving for each of the two alternatives proposed.
2. What other factors should be considered in making this decision? Do you support either of the two options?

P12.11   (Identifying Opportunities for Cost Reduction; Activity-Based Management)

The chief financial officer (CFO) of Healthy Snacks, Inc., has been selected to head a major corporate restructuring. She has decided to begin by focusing on one of her own departments, general accounting, which has shown a tendency to increase costs despite recent improvements to its business processes. Exhibit P12.11.1 presents a cost report showing expenses charged to the department for each of the

EXHIBIT P12.11.1 HEALTHY SNACKS, INC.— GENERAL ACCOUNTING DEPARTMENT

Cost Center Reports for 3 Years

	1994	1995	1996
Salaries & wages	$310,000	$317,750	$327,283
Depreciation	22,000	22,900	24,200
Occupancy	9,000	9,500	10,000
Supplies	4,200	4,800	5,500
Training	6,400	6,720	6,854
Travel	2,600	2,704	2,812
Total cost	$354,200	$364,374	$376,649
Cost increase	4.2%	2.9%	3.4%
No. of employees	16	16	16

past 3 years. Expenses are categorized into functional accounts, such as depreciation and supplies, as is normally seen in published GAAP financial statements. The report shows that the department has employed 16 workers throughout the 3-year time period. It also shows that costs have increased steadily at rates (ranging from 2.9 to 4.2%) that have been close to each year's rate of inflation. These increases occurred despite the introduction of advanced computing equipment and training programs on cost reduction and total quality improvement.

The CFO is concerned because the functional format of cost data provides no information on the type or amount of work performed. She assigns two analysts from the budgeting department to the task of reconstructing the 1996 functional costs into an activity-costing format. The results, reported in Exhibit P12.11.2, broke costs down into six separate work activities. The analysts conducting the study distributed costs from functional categories to the activities these costs helped to support. For example, they charged $102,276 of salaries and wages to the activity called *general ledger*, based on their estimations of the amount of time the department's employees spent on analyzing and recording general ledger transactions. The total cost charged to the general ledger activity from all functional cost categories accumulated to $114,446, which the analysts felt was a fair indication of resources consumed in accomplishing this activity.

The analysts also identified what they thought was the best cost driver for each activity, and they counted the number of occurrences for each cost driver for the year. For example, they found number of entries to be the primary cause of work for the general ledger activity. In 1996, 297,600 entries were recorded. Finally, they gathered activity and cost driver data for each of the 3 years reported in general accounting's cost report. The activity cost data for the 3 years are reported in Exhibit P12.11.3.

Required:

1. Calculate for each year the unit cost and the rate of change in unit cost for each of the department's six activities.

EXHIBIT P12.11.2 HEALTHY SNACKS, INC.— GENERAL ACCOUNTING DEPARTMENT

Breakdown of Costs into Activities, 1996

	Per Functional Category	Cost Breakdown, by Activity					
		General Ledger	Accounts Receivable	Accounts Payable	Fixed Assets	Payroll	Financial Reporting
Salaries & wages	$327,283	$102,276	$40,910	$40,910	$20,455	$40,910	$81,821
Depreciation	24,200	6,050	3,025	2,269	3,025	5,294	4,538
Occupancy	10,000	2,500	938	625	1,875	2,188	1,875
Supplies	5,500	1,203	344	344	688	1,203	1,719
Training	6,854	1,714	428	428	428	1,714	2,142
Travel	2,812	703	176	176	176	703	879
Total Cost	$376,649	$114,446	$45,821	$44,752	$26,647	$52,011	$92,973
Cost driver		No. of entries	No. of entries	No. of entries	No. of entries	No. of paychecks	No. of pages sent
No. of cost driver units		297,600	149,690	114,260	13,790	153,400	55,760

EXHIBIT P12.11.3 HEALTHY SNACKS, INC.— ACCOUNTING DEPARTMENT							
Comparative Data on Activities for 3 Years							
			Activity Cost				
	Total Cost	*General Ledger*	*Accounts Receivable*	*Accounts Payable*	*Fixed Assets*	*Payroll*	*Financial Reporting*
1996	$376,649	$114,446	$45,821	$44,752	$26,647	$52,011	$92,973
1995	$364,374	$112,956	$51,012	$43,725	$32,794	$43,725	$80,162
1994	$354,200	$113,344	$47,817	$44,275	$40,733	$37,191	$70,840
			Number of Cost Driver Units				
1996		297,600	149,690	114,260	13,790	153,400	55,760
1995		279,744	142,206	109,690	13,376	152,633	50,742
1994		274,149	133,673	108,044	12,707	151,107	45,667

2. Look for trends over the 3-year period, and identify the most-troublesome activities. Given the limited information offered in the problem, offer a reasonable explanation for the cost increases.
3. What actions should the CFO take in order to reduce the cost of the general accounting function? What information is needed in order to make a more-informed analysis?

P12.12 (Evaluating Opportunities to Reduce Costs; Activity-Based Management)

Having gathered cost information on the activities performed by the general accounting department, the CFO of Healthy Snacks, Inc., has decided to consider two cost-reduction opportunities. (Refer to P12.11 for more background information.) The first opportunity involves payroll preparation and the second focuses on financial reporting. Details of the 1996 cost makeup for each of these two activities are presented in Exhibit P12.12.1, along with data on their cost drivers and average costs per unit.

The CFO has contacted a vendor that specializes in providing outsourced payroll services. As noted in Exhibit P12.12.1, Healthy Snacks currently cuts 153,400 paychecks per year, most of which are prepared weekly. The payroll vendor has agreed to take on this service for a cost of $0.28 per check, which includes maintaining detailed payroll records for each employee and filing all necessary payroll-related tax forms. If Healthy Snacks outsources its payroll, virtually all costs incurred in 1996 to perform the payroll activity would be eliminated. This includes the cost of two full-time employees and all the expense incurred for supplies, training, and travel. The firm would dispose of its specialized computer payroll equipment, carried on the books at $12,400, for its market value of $9,000. Occupancy expense now used for payroll would be converted for other corporate purposes but would no longer be charged to the general accounting department.

The second opportunity under consideration entails reducing the number of financial reports being distributed. The CFO surveyed the firm's 35 managers who receive reports internally, and she found that much of the information is either duplicated or not used. A calculation showing the number of report pages now being sent is given in Exhibit P12.12.2. Based on feedback she gathered from the

EXHIBIT P12.12.1 HEALTHY SNACKS, INC.— GENERAL ACCOUNTING DEPARTMENT

1996 Cost Report for Two Departmental Activities

	Activity	
	Payroll	Financial Reporting
Salaries & wages	$40,910	$81,821
Depreciation	5,294	4,538
Occupancy	2,188	1,875
Supplies	1,203	1,719
Training	1,714	2,142
Travel	703	879
Total cost	$52,011	$92,973
Cost driver	No. of paychecks	No. of pages sent
No. of cost driver units	153,400	55,760
Cost per unit	$0.34	$1.67

EXHIBIT P12.12.2 HEALTHY SNACKS, INC.— GENERAL ACCOUNTING DEPARTMENT

Financial Reporting—Calculation of Number of Pages Sent in 1996

	Reports for Internal Use		External Quarterly Reports	Grand Total
	Weekly	Monthly		
No. of reports prepared	6	6	2	
No. of reports per year	52	12	4	
	312	72	8	
Average pages per report	4	4	10	
Total pages prepared	1,248	288	80	1,616
No. of copies distributed	35	35	25	95
Total pages sent	43,680	10,080	2,000	55,760

managers, she believes the firm could cut back the number of reports to four weekly and three monthly, and report pages could be reduced to an average of three pages each. The reduced number of internal reports would be distributed to all 35 managers, and the external quarterly reports would remain at their current level. The CFO believes that these changes would allow her to make significant cutbacks to the financial reporting activity expense. Two of the four persons employed for financial reporting would be eliminated, resulting in a 50 percent saving in salaries and wages. Expenses for supplies, training, and travel would be cut by 40 percent. The general accounting department would reduce its depreciation by 25 percent by sending its computers and other office equipment to the marketing department. Occupancy costs for general accounting, however, are not expected to be cut at all.

The CFO has some misgivings about both of these courses of action and about the entire restructuring program. She knows the firm has to cut its costs in order to remain competitive, but how these cutbacks will affect morale is largely unknown. On a more personal level, the CFO has worked closely with the two employees who would most likely be released, and she feels badly about the prospect of letting them go.

Required:

1. Calculate the first-year after-tax income effects to the firm for each of the two cost-reduction options being proposed. Assume a tax rate of 35 percent. What actions do you recommend?
2. Calculate the new cost per unit for the financial-reporting activity, given the new set of costs and number of pages being sent. How should this information be interpreted?
3. What special considerations do you think might be undertaken to preserve the morale of employees who are not released when a company downsizes?

CASES

C12.1 (Household Supply Company)

Jim Meyers, the manager of the receiving and shipping department at Household Supply Company, is searching for ways to reduce operating expense. Despite increased revenue, the firm is running behind its income targets for the first 4 months of the current year (see Exhibit C12.1.1). Meyers, along with all other cost

---

EXHIBIT C12.1.1 HOUSEHOLD SUPPLY COMPANY— RECEIVING-SHIPPING DEPARTMENT

Performance Report at April 30

| | | | Year to Date | | |
| | | | | Variance[a] | |
	Annual Budget	Actual	Budget	Dollar ($)	Percent (%)
Company sales revenue	$4,000,000	$1,560,000	$1,333,333	$226,667	17.0%
Salaries & wages—					
full time	$ 88,000	$ 29,600	$ 29,333	$ 267 U	−0.9%
Wages—part-time	6,500	3,500	2,167	1,333 U	−61.5%
Depreciation expense	4,500	1,500	1,500	0	0.0%
Packing materials	14,500	5,630	4,833	797 U	−16.5%
Freight & mail expense	24,800	9,940	8,267	1,673 U	−20.2%
Telephone:					
Local	900	295	300	5 F	1.7%
Long-distance	1,200	480	400	80 U	−20.0%
Supplies	3,200	1,150	1,067	83 U	−7.8%
Corporate charges:					
Occupancy	6,600	2,200	2,200	0	0.0%
MIS support	1,800	560	600	40 F	6.7%
Total department expense	$ 152,000	$ 54,855	$ 50,667	$ 4,188 U	−8.3%

[a] Variances are favorable (F) or unfavorable (U).

center managers, is being called on the carpet by the company president, who expects him to explain the unfavorable expense variances. He is also expected to come up with corrective actions to get department operating expenses back in line.

Meyers has already taken some preliminary steps to get ready for the meeting. He has met several times with the firm's chief accountant, and the two have worked together to prepare an activity-cost performance report through April 30. The report, presented in Exhibit C12.1.2, summarizes the first 4 months of this year's operations. It also breaks down the department's receiving and shipping activities into five subactivities:

1. *Check and count*—Goods being received are counted against the vendor's packing slip.
2. *Move to storage*—Goods received are moved by forklift and pallet jack to inventory control.
3. *Match to sales order*—Goods being shipped are compared item by item against the customer sales order.
4. *Packaging*—Goods being shipped are put into boxes or mailing envelopes.
5. *Sending*—Shipping arrangements are made with the post office or freight carrier, and charges are checked for accuracy.

Department expenses, which are normally reported on a functional basis, are listed on the left side of the exhibit. Expenses have been distributed to the five subactivities based on the extent of support given to each.

EXHIBIT C12.1.2 HOUSEHOLD SUPPLY COMPANY— RECEIVING-SHIPPING DEPARTMENT

Performance Report of Year-to-Date Expense in an Activity Cost Format at April 30

	Actual YTD	Count and Check	Move to Storage	Match to Sales Order	Packaging	Sending
		Receiving		Shipping		
Salaries & wages—full time	$29,600	$4,440	$10,360	$2,960	$8,880	$ 2,960
Wages—part-time	3,500	350	1,400	1,050	700	0
Depreciation expense	1,500	50	1,200	50	200	0
Packing materials	5,630	0	0	0	5,630	0
Freight & mail expense	9,940	0	0	0	0	9,940
Telephone:						
Local	295	59	59	59	59	59
Long-distance	480	0	0	0	0	480
Supplies	1,150	115	690	115	115	115
Corporate charges:						
Occupancy	2,200	220	550	220	660	550
MIS support	560	140	140	140	0	140
Total expense	$54,855	$5,374	$14,399	$4,594	$16,244	$14,244
Percent breakdown of activity expense	100.0%	9.8%	26.2%	8.4%	29.6%	26.0%
Total for receiving & shipping			$19,773			$35,082
Number of orders processed			239			3,598
Average cost per order			$ 82.73			$ 9.75
Industry average cost per order			$ 72.00			$ 12.50

Benchmarking Activities

After compiling activity cost data, Meyers decided he needed some type of benchmark in order to assess his department's performance. After doing some searching, he came across a trade publication that showed separate average costs for receiving and for shipping for other firms in the mail-order industry. Meyers noticed that average-cost calculations were based on the number of orders received for the receiving activity and on the number of orders shipped for the shipping activity. He decided these were reasonable drivers for his company's receiving and shipping activities, and he was able to gather comparable information for the first 4 months of this year.

The results of his data analysis are shown on the bottom part of Exhibit C12.1.2. Total cost for receiving through April was $19,773, and 239 orders had been received. Dividing the total cost by the number of orders results in a cost per order of $82.73, which unfortunately, exceeds the industry average of $72 by more than $10. Results for shipping put Meyers' operation in a more favorable light, since his costs averaged $9.75, compared to the industry average of $12.50 per order shipped. Meyers was somewhat skeptical of the comparisons' value—because of differences between the companies, the types of products they dealt with, and the composition of the costs used to calculate the averages. Nonetheless, he felt the comparisons were somewhat useful in that they encouraged him to think more creatively about options for lowering his costs, particularly in receiving.

Evaluating a New Conveyor System

Most disturbing to Meyers was the high cost of the move to storage activity. He had not realized how much of his labor and his budget went to support the movement of goods to inventory. He believed he might have a solution to the high cost of this activity, but it involved a rather significant capital expenditure that would have to be approved by the president.

Meyers knew that other mail-order firms had installed conveyor systems in order to move goods from the receiving dock to the inventory storage area. He had already investigated the possibility of installing such a system, which would cost $40,000. He believed use of this system would cut his costs significantly. First of all, he could reduce his workforce by the equivalent of one-half of a full-time position, which meant decreasing the current 4-month salary expense of the move to storage activity ($10,360) by one-third. He also expects to cut part-time wages in this activity by at least 50 percent.

Upon further investigation, Meyers obtained some other pertinent information. Use of a conveyor means he could sell a forklift and a pallet jack, whose book value is $13,500, for about $12,000. The sale would result in the elimination of 75 percent of depreciation expense in the move to storage activity shown on the performance report. He would also reduce 80 percent of the $690 supplies expense, as the result of savings in gas, oil, and parts. All other activity expenses would remain unchanged.

Now Meyers needed to initiate a study that would justify the purchase of the conveyor equipment. The chief accountant informed Meyers that she would have to prepare a capital-budgeting analysis. She also said the tax effects of the transaction must be considered, since the firm was in a 40 percent tax bracket. Besides the tax effects on operating expense, there would be tax consequences on the expected loss on sale of the old equipment and on the change in depreciation expense. Meyers pointed out that the new conveyor would be used for 5 years—about the same amount of life expected for the forklift and pallet jack.

Meyers thanked the accountant for all her help and expressed confidence about his intuitive feel for modernizing the operation. He went on to express his gratitude to the chief accountant for preparing the new activity-cost performance report, which gave him the chance to view his operations in a totally different light. Meyers closed by saying:

> I know that report has some mixed blessings. I think Carlos (the firm's president) will see that we are really keeping our costs down in the shipping department. On the flip side, I know he'll want some explanations for our high receiving costs—and suggestions on how to solve this problem. But at least there seems to be a solution with the new conveyor. Let's just hope your calculations support my arguments for this important investment.

Required:

1. Prepare a capital-budgeting study of the conveyor system. Assume the following for your calculations:
   - Sale of the old equipment and purchase of the new will take place on May 1 of this year.
   - Existing equipment is being depreciated on a straight-line basis, with no salvage value.
   - The conveyor will be depreciated on a straight-line basis, with no salvage value.
   - The cost of capital is 18 percent.
2. Calculate the average receiving cost per order for the 4 months ending April 30 if the new conveyor system had been in place.
3. What action do you recommend?
4. How was the activity cost analysis useful in identifying the problems in the receiving and shipping department?

C12.2 (Nebraska Chemical Company)

Upon leaving the planning meeting for next year's budget, Sarah Walters feels as if her back is against the wall. As manager of order processing and collection, Walters has received acclaim over the past 3 years for her contribution in helping the firm increase sales and improve its collections. Despite increased competition in the chemical industry, she has been instrumental in building customer relations and helping to establish Nebraska Chemical Company as the state's leading supplier of commercial and industrial chemicals. With today's budget meeting, she feels that the vice president of sales and marketing, to whom she reports, wants to undo all that she has established. The VP claims that her costs are beginning to outstrip her accomplishments and that she can no longer use a disproportionate amount of department resources.

Nebraska Chemical is organized along functional lines. Sales and marketing forms one of the firm's four major departments (see Exhibit C12.2.1). The department is divided into four cost centers, one of which is order processing and collections (or OP&C), headed by Walters. As the firm has grown, this subunit has expanded its duties well beyond the more-mechanical functions implied in its name. It now works closely with field sales representatives in establishing the credit qualifications of new customers. It also plays an important role in the function of order taking, which includes helping customers define product needs before a sale and expediting shipment afterwards. As the company's receivables and collections agent, OP&C keeps close tabs on outstanding account balances, and it works actively to obtain prompt payment of overdue accounts. Most significantly, the OP&C staff has earned a reputation among field sales reps and customers as being knowledgeable, courteous, and extremely helpful.

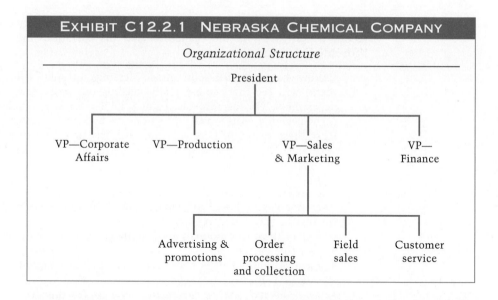

EXHIBIT C12.2.1 NEBRASKA CHEMICAL COMPANY

Organizational Structure

President

VP—Corporate Affairs | VP—Production | VP—Sales & Marketing | VP—Finance

Advertising & promotions | Order processing and collection | Field sales | Customer service

EXHIBIT C12.2.2 NEBRASKA CHEMICAL COMPANY—
ORDER PROCESSING AND COLLECTION

Cost Center Reports

	Actual		Budget
	1995	1996	1997
Payroll	$330,000	$362,000	$402,000
Payroll taxes	36,300	41,630	48,240
Payroll benefits	14,850	17,376	20,100
Supplies	18,300	22,380	25,500
Occupancy	25,000	27,400	30,000
Depreciation	22,000	23,900	26,500
MIS charges	6,000	6,800	8,000
Total	$452,450	$501,486	$560,340
Cost increase	9.7%	10.8%	11.7%
Sales revenue increase	4.6%	5.3%	8.4%
Headcount	17	18	20

Nature of the Problem

The problem facing Walters can best be seen by looking at the numbers for the OP&C cost center. Exhibit C12.2.2 reports actual expenses for the past 2 years (1995 and 1996) and the budget for 1997. Costs show sharp increases over the 3 years—even exceeding the growth rate of sales revenue. Included in the budget for 1997 is a cost increase of 11.7 percent, even though revenue is expected to rise by only 8.4 percent. The continual increase in costs can be attributed to the increase in the number of personnel, which has grown from 17 in 1995 to a projected 20 in 1997.

Walters defends her position by saying that the financial data do not capture the contributions made by her staff in generating sales. She asserts that the field representatives have become more dependent on OP&C for analyzing credit of new customers and for extending the credit line of existing customers. She also claims that OP&C is doing much of the actual sales work of the field reps, since her staff is spending more time on the phone discussing product options, encouraging the customer to try other products, and tracking down late deliveries. Further, she argues that her staff's close work with customers has done much to increase the firm's cash flows. In the past 3 years, the average number of days in accounts receivable has fallen from 45 to 35, and Walters is quick to remind the VP of sales and marketing that her cost center's handling of credit approvals and collections has made the difference.

Activity-Based Cost Reports
In an attempt to resolve these issues, the VP has called upon the accounting department to report OP&C costs by activity. The first step in this process is to identify activities and their cost drivers. Based on conversations with Walters and her staff, the accountant in charge of the project reported the results shown in Exhibit C12.2.3. Walters agreed that these categories seemed to explain better the types of work being done.

The accountant then began analyzing the cost drivers for each activity. He gathered data for 1995 and 1996 in order to spot trends over the 2 years. The results, reported in Exhibit C12.2.4, show that the rates of growth exhibited by the cost drivers did, in fact, differ. Perhaps most striking is the growth in requests by field reps to set up new accounts (up by 23.5%) and the direct requests by customers (up to 19.7%). The more-routine activities, measured by number of customer-order line items and collections by treasury, showed a smaller increase. The fifth cost driver, overdue accounts, showed little change.

EXHIBIT C12.2.3 NEBRASKA CHEMICAL COMPANY— ORDER PROCESSING AND COLLECTION

Breakdown of Activities

Activity	Cost Driver
Credit analysis	Requests by field rep to set up new account
Customer support	Direct requests by customer
Customer order entry	No. of customer-order line items
Accounts receivable posting	Collections by treasury
Collections	Overdue accounts per month

EXHIBIT C12.2.4 NEBRASKA CHEMICAL COMPANY— ORDER PROCESSING AND COLLECTION

History of Cost Drivers Over the Past 2 Years

Cost Driver	1995	1996	% change
Request by field rep to set up new account	1,220	1,507	23.5%
Direct requests by customer	3,210	3,843	19.7%
Number of customer order line items	167,532	192,308	14.8%
Collections by treasury	23,460	26,470	12.8%
Overdue accounts per month	340	351	3.2%

The final step performed by the accountant was to reassign OP&C's functional breakdown of accounts for 1996 into an activity format (see Exhibit C12.2.5). This was necessary in order to determine how much time was actually spent by OP&C employees on each of the cost center's five activities. For example, the accountant found that about 30 percent of employee time was spent on customer order entry. Thus, he assigned to that activity 30 percent of department payroll, or $108,600 (30% × $362,000). Similarly, he estimated by activity the resource consumption for payroll taxes, payroll benefits, supplies, occupancy, depreciation, and MIS. While the resulting cost assignments were not exact, both he and Walters felt that they were reasonable approximations.

The activity costs reported in Exhibit C12.2.5 presented new insights about the use of cost center resources. Most striking was that nearly 60 percent of OP&C's resource consumption involved direct contact with customers—that is, customer support (18.5%), customer order entry (30.6%), and collections (8.9%). Also interesting was the fact that 17.5 percent of the cost center's resources were used on the front end of new customer transactions for preapproval of credit. These breakdowns seem to give credence to Walter's arguments on the important role her staff plays in customer service. They also raise some questions about the shifting responsibilities between cost centers and the need to establish procedures for qualifying customers for credit, for providing information on products, and for handling customer inquiries.

In writing a follow-up report to the vice president of the department, Walters offered some specific recommendations for reducing OP&C's costs. She offered three suggestions:

1. Field sales representatives should be responsible for gathering critical information on the customer's creditworthiness before requesting that a new account be set up. Information must be gathered in a standardized form, and the rep should first prequalify the customer in order to determine whether OP&C's help is even needed.
2. The field sales reps should take more responsibility for servicing customer accounts. When customers call orders in, OP&C staff should be expected to

EXHIBIT C12.2.5 NEBRASKA CHEMICAL COMPANY— ORDER PROCESSING AND COLLECTION

Redistribution of 1996 Costs to Activities

	Per Functional Category	Credit Analysis	Customer Support	Customer Order Entry	Accounts Receivable Posting	Collections
Payroll	$362,000	$61,540	$72,400	$108,600	$90,500	$28,960
Payroll taxes	41,630	6,245	7,493	13,322	11,240	3,330
Payroll benefits	17,376	2,606	3,128	5,560	4,692	1,390
Supplies	22,380	4,476	1,119	12,309	2,238	2,238
Occupancy	27,400	6,850	2,740	7,535	7,535	2,740
Depreciation	23,900	4,780	4,780	4,780	4,780	4,780
MIS charges	6,800	1,360	1,360	1,360	1,360	1,360
Total	$501,486	$87,857	$93,020	$153,466	$122,345	$44,798
	100.0%	17.5%	18.5%	30.6%	24.4%	8.9%

enter orders and ensure prompt processing, but they should not be expected to explain differences between products, nor should they be expected to encourage the customer to try new lines.

3. Some of OP&C's work concerning follow-up of order delivery should be handled by the customer service cost center. This department normally handles after-service inquiries and warranty claims with products, but it has access to delivery schedules and could easily take over the job of expediting orders.

Walters explains that, without these changes, she doesn't understand how it is possible to cut her costs. That is, of course, unless the firm is willing to allow its commitment to strong customer relations to slide.

Required:

1. Refer to OP&C's trends in costs (Exhibit C12.2.2) and cost drivers (Exhibit C12.2.4) for the past 2 years. Are these data sufficient to support Walter's arguments concerning the department's growing need for resources?
2. Now consider the added information provided by the activity-cost report (Exhibit C12.2.5). Does this information help to justify Walter's arguments? Explain.
3. Evaluate the three recommendations for reducing OP&C's workload.
4. Offer suggestions to resolve the budget controversy surrounding OP&C.

CHAPTER

13

PERFORMANCE MEASUREMENT AND STRATEGIC COST ANALYSIS

To this point we have examined only the use of budgets and budget-based measures to analyze and control cost center spending. Such financial measures are essential to management control, because they focus attention on the resources consumed in generating profits. But firms have strategic goals other than profit generation, and the exclusive use of these budget-based measures draws managers' attention away from those other, equally important, goals.

Consider the cost center manager who puts workers under such intense pressure to speed production and thus lower costs that the result is products of lower quality. Or the harried hotel clerk who has survived a large-scale personnel cutback but no longer has the time to offer customers courteous service. Both are doing all they can to meet their firms' profit goals. But in order to do so they must work in such a way that the result

drains their firms of customers. The profit goals have not been properly balanced against performance goals involving quality of service.

In this chapter, we explore ways in which the accountant can satisfy managers' needs for information regarding such goal-related factors as customer satisfaction, product quality, and timely delivery. We first discuss the selection of measures with which to communicate such information. Then, because much of this information already exists in the cost accounting system—but perhaps not in a useful format—we examine how cost data can be reorganized by strategy or by objective. Again, as in Chapters 11 and 12, our focus is on the last three phases of the management control framework: measurement, reporting and analysis, and corrective action.

1 class

BUILDING A PERFORMANCE MEASUREMENT SYSTEM

If you want people to work toward several objectives, then you need to measure their performance in terms of achieving those objectives. If a department store manager is evaluated on attaining customer courtesy targets as well as cost targets, then a clear signal is sent to subordinate sales clerks that both the customer and the sale are important. Similarly, a production manager who is evaluated on both cost standards and inventory turnover goals will be careful not to build up excess inventory while cutting costs. These examples lead us to a central theme in this chapter. _People will act in accordance with the way their actions are measured._ So, the first step in designing a performance measurement system is to select the proper measures—measures that are congruent with all of the firm's interests. By a _measure_ we mean a scale on which to evaluate performance.

In the following discussion, we focus on performance measures mainly at the operational, cost center level. Recall from Chapters 9 and 10 that organizations form higher-level goals and objectives at the corporate and business-unit levels. _Goals_ are broad statements of purpose (e.g., to build shareholder value), while objectives amplify goals numerically (e.g., to achieve a 12% return on assets). In our discussion, we use the term _objectives_ broadly to include the goal statements upon which they are based. Strategies are then the action plans for achieving these objectives. Responsibility centers at all levels use performance measures and targets in order to determine whether strategies are being achieved.

THE TWO TYPES OF PERFORMANCE MEASURES

There are two general types of measures that are used for evaluating the performance of an organization: (1) efficiency measures and (2) effectiveness measures. Exhibit 13.1 offers examples of each type, generated for a specific cost center.

EXHIBIT 13.1 EXAMPLES OF EFFICIENCY AND EFFECTIVENESS MEASURES

Cost Center	Efficiency Measure	Effectiveness Measure
Insurance investigation unit	Cost per case	Number of cases settled per year
Appliance service center	Average time per service call	Percent of orders resolved on first call
Training center	Time per trainee	Percent of trainees that meet learning objectives
Dairy production unit	Pounds of milk per cow per year	Percent of on-time deliveries
Advertising department	Advertising cost per sales dollar	Percent of sales target achieved

EFFICIENCY

The **efficiency** of a responsibility center is a ratio between an input and an output. Thus, efficiency measures indicate how well a resource is transformed into a product or service. For an insurance company's investigation unit, for example, operating cost (input) can be divided by the annual number of cases settled (output) to obtain the ratio of dollars per case. Thus, this efficiency measure indicates the average amount of resources consumed per unit of output.

One advantage of efficiency measures is that they can be used to assess operations over time or to compare operations of diverse responsibility centers. A second advantage is that they need not be computed in dollar (or currency) amounts—an important issue for responsibility centers that do not earn revenue. For instance, a reasonable efficiency measure for an appliance service center would be the average time spent per service call.

EFFECTIVENESS

The **effectiveness** of a responsibility center is the degree to which its objectives have been met. Effectiveness measures may or may not be ratios. However, they must be comparable to the department's or firm's targets, and they must tie operating results to the performance goals that satisfy external demands. For example, a dairy product might have the objective of delivering products within 1 day of receiving a customer's order (Exhibit 13.1). Hence, it could measure its effectiveness either as the percent of on-time (1-day) deliveries or as the average number of days between order receipt and delivery. Both measures can be easily translated into the language of the firm's delivery objective.

Effectiveness measures—for example, the percent of on-time deliveries—offer the same two advantages as efficiency measures. First, the measure can be used to assess operations over time and to compare operations of different responsibility centers. Second, it need not be computed in dollar (or currency) amounts.

OVERCOMING MEASUREMENT LIMITATIONS

Efficiency and effectiveness are difficult to measure when output is not easily quantified. The best examples of applications for which these measurements are greatly limited are service centers with intangible or varied outputs—for examples, reception centers and corporate public affairs offices in the business world, or school systems and drug rehabilitation clinics in the public sector. An alternative efficiency measurement in these cases—as long as output can be assumed to be constant—would be costs. A reduction in costs implies an increase in efficiency. Such measures do not, however, indicate whether or not targets were met, so they provide no indication of effectiveness.

Many different measures of efficiency and effectiveness can be devised for most responsibility centers. Those that are chosen should reinforce the company's main objectives. For example, a car production facility might be very efficient as measured by cost per unit and production

CURRENT PRACTICE

Federal Express Corporation

Federal Express Corporation, an overnight package delivery service, is a 1990 recipient of the Malcolm Baldrige National Quality Award, a prestigious and competitive award administered by the U.S. Department of Commerce. Federal Express has been very successful in meeting high standards of quality performance and customer satisfaction, and it continues to set higher targets. A 12-component index of service quality indicators (SQIs) is used by the firm to describe how its performance is viewed by customers. Included are such measures as missed packages, damaged packages, abandoned calls, and invoice adjustments requested. Data on these measures are gathered by computer tracking systems. The systems record each time that a package changes hands between pickup and delivery. Rapid analysis of these data yields daily SQI reports, which are transmitted to workers at all Federal Express sites.

Source: Adapted from materials published by Federal Express Office of Public Relations.

time per unit, but its output may be of low quality unless a measure of quality is included among the effectiveness measures. Managers must be made aware that outcomes other than cost outcomes are also significant and must be monitored. (See "Current Practice: Federal Express Corporation.")

SELECTING APPROPRIATE PERFORMANCE MEASURES

Performance measures are selected in a two-stage process: (1) Derive key variables based on objectives and (2) attach measures to the key variables. This process is useful for selecting both financial and nonfinancial performance measures. The data needed to compute values for the measures can come from within the accounting information system or from outside. In some cases, accounting data must be restructured for use in performance measures that have been designed to meet a manager's specific control needs.

1: DERIVE KEY VARIABLES BASED ON OBJECTIVES

Characteristics of Key Variables. The key variables chosen determine what is and is not to be tracked by the performance measurement system. Selection begins by identifying the important high-risk activities that could cause operations—and thus strategies—to go out of control. These activities include variables that can be monitored in order to gauge both external (market) expectations and internal (firm) operations.

For example, suppose an automobile-bumper manufacturer sets an objective of low-cost production. Its management is worried about—actually, cannot afford—downtime on a new $25-million flexible-manufacturing system. This firm would identify effective machine management and maintenance as a key variable, because such a measure is necessary in order to prevent operational bottlenecks. As another example, suppose a bank, with an objective of a high level of customer retention, finds that too many of its customers become upset and close their accounts after repeatedly waiting in long, slow lines. The bank might establish prompt customer service as a key variable for evaluating the effectiveness of its branch operations. Thus, key variables are tailored to fit the needs of the specific responsibility center.

Here are some characteristics to look for in choosing key variables:[1]

- Ability to *explain* success or failure in attaining objectives.
- *Volatility*—The key variable is subject to quick changes in performance.
- *Lack of predictability*.
- Key variables identify quantities that *require prompt action* upon changing.
- *Measurability*—The variable must be measurable, either directly or by measuring a closely related surrogate variable.

After managers identify activities that exhibit most or all of these characteristics, they can develop an information system that monitors their variables' performance over time.

Categories of Key Variables. As noted earlier, key variables are, by definition, unique to their specific responsibility centers. Nonetheless, they can be grouped into five broad categories, distinguished by the objectives they are meant to promote. (Note that from this we can infer that there are categories of objectives as well as of key variables.) Not every key variable fits precisely in one of these categories, and some may straddle more than one category to an extent.

Nonetheless, identification of the categories provides a place to start a search for key variables. The categories and examples are discussed below.

- *Variables concerned with shareholder value.* An important objective for business corporations is to increase shareholder value. Projections of reported *cash flows* can serve as indicators of value creation. Also useful for this purpose is *profitability* (which can be measured in several ways, such as net income or ROI), as well as the *market value* of outstanding stock.
- *Variables concerned with quality.* One important variable that is obviously dependent on quality is *customer satisfaction*. Other vari-

---

[1] Robert N. Anthony and Vijay Govindarajan, *Management Control Systems*, 8th ed., Chicago: Irwin, 1995, p. 428.

ables that might be used to focus attention on quality include *process improvements, product defects,* and *waste.*

- *Variables concerned with market position.* The market-position category of variables focuses attention on the competition. One commonly used variable in this group, *market share,* requires careful definition of a firm's products. Another variable useful for firms competing on a differentiation strategy is *product leadership,* whereby a firm compares the innovativeness of its own products with that of industry leaders' offerings. Use of *product development* as a variable requires managers to look more closely at the research and development activities that presage product leadership. On an operational level, market position can be indicated by financial variables such as *sales growth.*

- *Variables concerned with flexibility.* By *flexibility* we mean the ability to revamp operations quickly in order to meet new market opportunities or to respond to changing market conditions. *Time to bring products to market* has become one of the most important key variables related to flexibility. Other variables in this group, such as *production setup time* and *on-time delivery* focus attention on production and delivery systems.

- *Variables concerned with productivity.* Many of the variables discussed throughout this text—such as *output, costs,* and *variances*—are related to productivity. Other variables, such as *cost reduction* and *inventory reduction,* may be used to monitor improvement. *Downtime* and *maintenance cost* focus on the availability of equipment for production. *Cycle time* for business processes is important for tracking overall improvement.

Integrating Variables Among Organizational Levels.   The key variables chosen at each level of the organization must be integrated with those selected for all other levels. Each responsibility center should identify the key variables it will use to assess its progress toward achieving its strategies. All variables chosen for all responsibility centers must support attainment of the corporate objectives. As each lower level of the organizational hierarchy is reached, the key variables become more specifically defined, in operational terms, relative to production and sales expectations. The lower the organizational level, the greater the importance key variables place on cost control. Just as with financial budgeting, this reflects the shorter planning horizons and increased emphasis on efficiency that exists at lower levels.

Exhibit 13.2 shows a typical corporate hierarchy and illustrates certain key variables that require integration among levels. At the corporate level, senior management chooses market value as the key variable. The product group then selects market share as the key variable that is most instrumental in achieving corporate market value. The division then focuses on sales growth as the most important factor in achieving the product group's targeted market share. Next, the operational group identifies on-time delivery as a key variable for ensuring divisional sales growth. A well-integrated system of key variables thus focuses attention on those

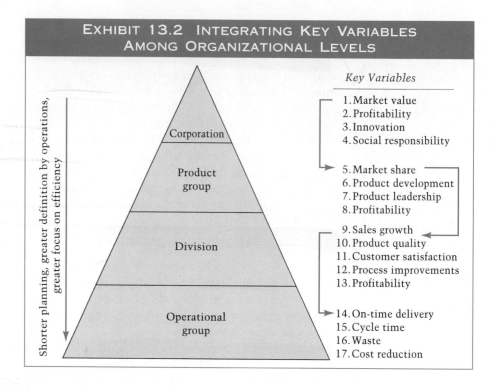

EXHIBIT 13.2 INTEGRATING KEY VARIABLES AMONG ORGANIZATIONAL LEVELS

Key Variables

1. Market value
2. Profitability
3. Innovation
4. Social responsibility
5. Market share
6. Product development
7. Product leadership
8. Profitability
9. Sales growth
10. Product quality
11. Customer satisfaction
12. Process improvements
13. Profitability
14. On-time delivery
15. Cycle time
16. Waste
17. Cost reduction

Shorter planning, greater definition by operations, greater focus on efficiency

Corporation / Product group / Division / Operational group

specific lower-level actions needed for achieving success at higher organizational levels.

Integrating Variables at the Same Level. Responsibility centers at the same level of a firm's structure can find that their key variables cause them to work at cross-purposes. Hence, variables should also be integrated across levels of the organization. For example, consider the plight of a product design group that must occasionally rely on manufacturing to help it build prototype subassemblies. Meanwhile, manufacturing is being monitored using productivity variables such as output. Manufacturing suffers if it takes time out to help product design, but product design suffers if it doesn't. Inclusion of a common key variable such as customer satisfaction ensures that both product design and manufacturing focus on delivering products that are both up-to-date and produced in adequate volume. Thus one key variable combines the objectives of both responsibility centers. Some firms have tried to resolve this particular issue by holding all managers accountable for an internal-customer-satisfaction variable.

2: ATTACH MEASURES TO KEY VARIABLES

Once the key variables are selected, one or more specific measures must be associated with each variable. These measures determine exactly how the variable will be evaluated. Consider the customer-satisfaction variable. It is possible to survey customers and to use the direct responses as a mea-

CURRENT PRACTICE

GM's Divisional Measures

In 1994, the CEO of General Motors, John F. Smith, Jr., focused on a turnaround strategy for the behemoth automaker. One important element in this strategy involved changing the measurement of the profitability variable for each operating unit from income to return on assets (ROA). Managers were expected to produce a return of at least 12.5 percent on the value of net assets invested in their operation. For example, the Saturn subsidiary, which had an asset base of $2.5 billion, was expected to generate a minimum profit of $300 million. By using an ROA measure, Smith expected to motivate managers to spend less on equipment and buidings, thereby minimizing the asset base used in the measurement.

Source: Robert L. Simison and Joseph B. White, "Strike Fears Imperil GM's Bid to Rev Up Its Turnaround," *The Wall Street Journal*, Jan. 7, 1994, p. B4.

sure of this variable. Alternatively, the degree of customer satisfaction could be inferred from the number of customer complaints. An indirect (or surrogate) measure could also be used—such as the percentage of deliveries that are on time. (See "Current Practice: GM's Divisional Measures.")

Characteristics of Performance Measures. Ideally, performance measures should have all of the following characteristics:

- *Appropriateness.* A measure should capture the meaning of the key variable with which it is associated, and the unit responsible for the measure should be able to influence its outcome. Managers of different departments will often evaluate the same variable, using different measures. Each measure must also be appropriate to the organizational level at which it is used, with those at lower levels reflecting narrower, operational objectives and those at higher levels reflecting broader, organizational objectives.

- *Freedom from measurement error.* Two types of errors, random variation errors and bias errors, can enter into measurements; both should be reduced, where possible. *Random variation* consists of differences between measurements and the *true value.* These differences are scattered on both sides of the value and result from the limitations of the measuring instrument. Random variation can be minimized by measuring the variable at hand with a reasonable degree of precision. *Bias errors* are systematic differences that tend to fall to one side of the true value. Bias errors may or may not be the result of limitations of the measuring instruments. For example, workers may continually underreport work stoppages in order to appear more productive. Such bias errors can be controlled by having a third party, such as the controller, collect data, whenever possible.

Technology, Barcodes...

ex-accountants:- $
production floors:- pounds, N units

how much it costs to
(measure)
take the number.
Do we benefit more if we
have that measurement.

- *Timeliness.* The sooner the results of measurements are available for use, the better they will serve their control purposes—especially as a means of fending off impending problems. The recent emphasis on flattening organizations and pushing decisions to the operating level makes the timeliness of this information especially important. The degree of timeliness desired depends on the level of reporting—higher levels need information less frequently, perhaps monthly, whereas lower operational levels may need feedback daily, hourly, or continually as the work is done.

- *Understandability.* The most effective measures are those that are easiest to understand. While this idea is simple, its importance should not be underestimated. Certainly, it is easier to comprehend and use a direct performance measure—such as percent of deliveries on time—than it is to use a synthetic, indirect measure that involves several activities, gives them weights, and reports an index of performance.

- *Cost-effectiveness.* The cost of implementing the measure—that is, of obtaining measurement data—should not be prohibitive. If necessary, in order to reduce the cost of obtaining the data, less-costly measurements can be substituted and can often be just as helpful. For instance, a manager may want to measure customer satisfaction directly by surveying customers, but because of the high cost of survey research, may choose instead to rely on a measure of customer complaints.

Example of Measures Attached to Key Variables. Exhibit 13.3 lists examples of performance measures for the key variables given in Exhibit 13.2. Many other measures may, however, be appropriate in a given situation. (See "Current Practice: The Balanced Scorecard.")

ILLUSTRATION: ON-LINE COMPUTER COMPANY

We now examine how On-Line Computer Company, a producer of business software, translates its objectives into cost-center performance measures. As shown in Exhibit 13.4, On-Line is a firm with four organizational levels and three product groups.

On-Line's senior management has set three corporate objectives to be used as guidelines for all internal decision making:

1. To lead the industry in its business lines
2. To offer the most-efficient software production
3. To ensure full customer satisfaction

These unifying objectives guide business-line strategies and their implementation at lower levels. We shall focus on the southwest systems support operations unit, a cost center at the operations-unit level of the firm's business software product group. Specifically, we shall look at the way this unit (which we shall refer to simply as "southwest") developed the four key variables and corresponding performance measures shown in Exhibit 13.5. (Note that each variable relates to a corporate objective.)

EXHIBIT 13.3   EXAMPLES OF PERFORMANCE MEASURES

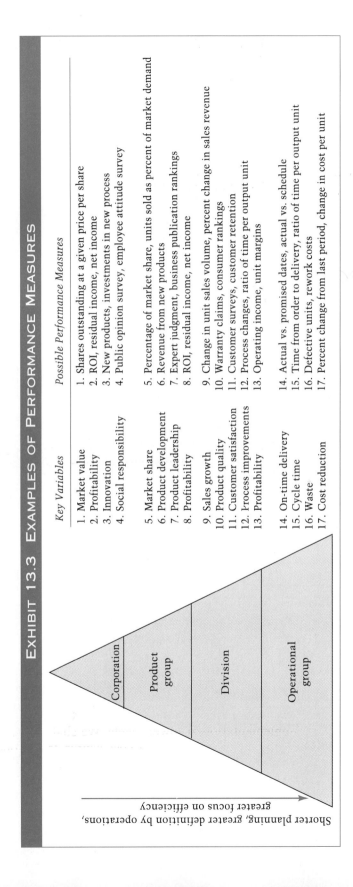

Key Variables	Possible Performance Measures
Corporation	
1. Market value	1. Shares outstanding at a given price per share
2. Profitability	2. ROI, residual income, net income
3. Innovation	3. New products, investments in new process
4. Social responsibility	4. Public opinion survey, employee attitude survey
Product group	
5. Market share	5. Percentage of market share, units sold as percent of market demand
6. Product development	6. Revenue from new products
7. Product leadership	7. Expert judgment, business publication rankings
8. Profitability	8. ROI, residual income, net income
Division	
9. Sales growth	9. Change in unit sales volume, percent change in sales revenue
10. Product quality	10. Warranty claims, consumer rankings
11. Customer satisfaction	11. Customer surveys, customer retention
12. Process improvements	12. Process changes, ratio of time per output unit
13. Profitability	13. Operating income, unit margins
Operational group	
14. On-time delivery	14. Actual vs. promised dates, actual vs. schedule
15. Cycle time	15. Time from order to delivery, ratio of time per output unit
16. Waste	16. Defective units, rework costs
17. Cost reduction	17. Percent change from last period, change in cost per unit

Shorter planning, greater definition by operations, greater focus on efficiency

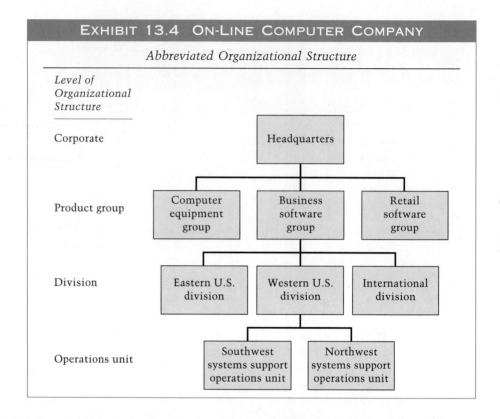

EXHIBIT 13.4 ON-LINE COMPUTER COMPANY

Abbreviated Organizational Structure

Level of Organizational Structure

Corporate	Headquarters
Product group	Computer equipment group — Business software group — Retail software group
Division	Eastern U.S. division — Western U.S. division — International division
Operations unit	Southwest systems support operations unit — Northwest systems support operations unit

EXHIBIT 13.5 ON-LINE COMPUTER COMPANY— SOUTHWEST SYSTEMS SUPPORT OPERATIONS UNIT

Key Variables and Attached Measurements

Hierarchical Level	Type of Structure	Corporate Objective	Key Variable	Measurement
Operations level: Southwest systems support operations unit	Cost center	The most-efficient software production	Cost reduction	Percent change from approved budget
		The most-efficient software production	Cycle time	Days from order to installation
		Full customer satisfaction	On-time delivery	Percent attainment of promised delivery date
		Full customer satisfaction	Product quality	Percent of additional work hours necessary after installation

[handwritten margin notes: "Some of the majors are lead indicators"; "It's better to innovative business"; "Here are trying to differentiate our product."]

CURRENT PRACTICE

The Balanced Scorecard

The *balanced scorecard* is a systematic approach for organizing performance measures into an integrated and understandable framework. It is based on four different *perspectives* (or key variables) that define a firm's objectives. Firms select performance measures that display characteristics such as those discussed in the text: appropriateness, freedom from measurement error, timeliness, understandability, and cost-effectiveness. Below is a sample of the measures used by Rockwater, a world leader in underwater engineering and construction, along the four perspectives.

The balanced-scorecard approach offers several advantages over reliance on performance evaluations that are based on financial information alone:

- It offers early warnings for a wide range of potential problem areas.
- It ties qualitative corporate objectives—such as innovativeness—to quantitative measures.
- It gives feedback on trade-offs when measures conflict with each other.
- It focuses attention on both current and future success.

The Four Perspectives	Performance Measures
1. Customer perspective	Customer satisfaction index
	Pricing index
2. Financial perspective	Sales backlog
	Cash flow
3. Innovation and learning perspective	Revenue from new products
	Staff attitude survey
4. Internal-business perspective	Project closeout cycle
	Rework

[handwritten margin notes: "demand for product"; "the trend?"; "new metrics that last"]

Source: Adapted from Robert S. Kaplan and David P. Norton, "The Balanced Scorecard—Measures That Drive Performance," *Harvard Business Review,* Jan.–Feb. 1992, pp. 71–79; and "Putting the Balanced Scorecard to Work," *Harvard Business Review,* Sept.–Oct. 1993, pp. 134–142.

BACKGROUND ON SOUTHWEST SYSTEMS SUPPORT OPERATIONS UNIT

Southwest is at the lowest organizational level of the business software product group, and it has the most contact with customers. Once a sale of software has been made by the western U.S. division, southwest takes over. It determines in detail what system capabilities the customer requires, modifies packaged software accordingly, installs it, and makes as many follow-up visits as are necessary to ensure the customer's satisfaction. Southwest plays an important role in assuring that the corporation meets two of its three corporate-level objectives—most-efficient software production and full customer satisfaction. The third objective—leadership in business software packages—is accomplished at the group and divisional levels of the firm.

Southwest has run into some difficulties recently in meeting delivery schedules and fulfilling customer expectations. Problems occur because customers are usually unaware of their own specific needs. Budget overruns result when employees must consequently spend extra time on software modifications after installation. Southwest's manager and employees are working together to formulate key variables and performance measures that will allow them to track improvements in carrying out these further modifications. All agree that the key to operating success lies in understanding what the customer wants *prior to design.*

DERIVING KEY VARIABLES FROM OBJECTIVES

Southwest is concerned with the prompt and satisfactory completion of software modification. The unit derives the four key variables (Exhibit 13.5) from the corporate objectives in order to help it monitor improvements in the software modification process.

***Corporate Objective:* To Offer the Most-Efficient Software Production.** Two of southwest's key variables emphasize attaining high efficiency in its software systems production:

1. *Cost reduction.* The key variable cost reduction is chosen in order to emphasize the expected gains from reducing the time spent on postinstallation modification.
2. *Cycle time.* Cycle time is a "natural" variable with which to monitor the promptness of delivery.

***Corporate Objective:* To Ensure Full Customer Satisfaction.** Two other key variables track customer satisfaction:

1. *On-time delivery* monitors a major determinant of customer satisfaction that also has become a major concern of southwest—delivery on the promised date.
2. *Product quality* is another major determinant of customer satisfaction and one that tends to suffer when emphasis is placed on cost and time variables. It will be monitored in order to ensure retention of high product quality.

ATTACHING MEASURES TO KEY VARIABLES

Having established the key variables, southwest must decide how they should be measured.

Cost Reduction. During preliminary meetings, corporate management directed that cost reductions be measured in terms of percent change from the approved budget. Monthly performance reports showing spending variances from budget are already in use. They will now also be used to track the percent changes from approved budget over time.

Cycle Time. The manager chooses to measure days from order to installation. Exhibit 13.6 presents 6-month graphic displays of southwest's three nonfinancial performance measures (i.e., those other than the budget measure). Data are reported for the 6 months, ending with December, but the program emphasizing early software redesign did not begin until October. Panel 1 in Exhibit 13.6 shows that jobs completed over the last 6 months took anywhere from 8 to 15 days. However, since October, when the software improvement program was begun, cycle time was steadily reduced to as few as 8 days.

On-time Delivery. Southwest will measure on-time delivery as the percent attainment of promised date. Senior management believes that full customer satisfaction means delivering software when promised. Examination of panel 2 in Exhibit 13.6 shows positive movement in meeting delivery schedules, particularly since October.

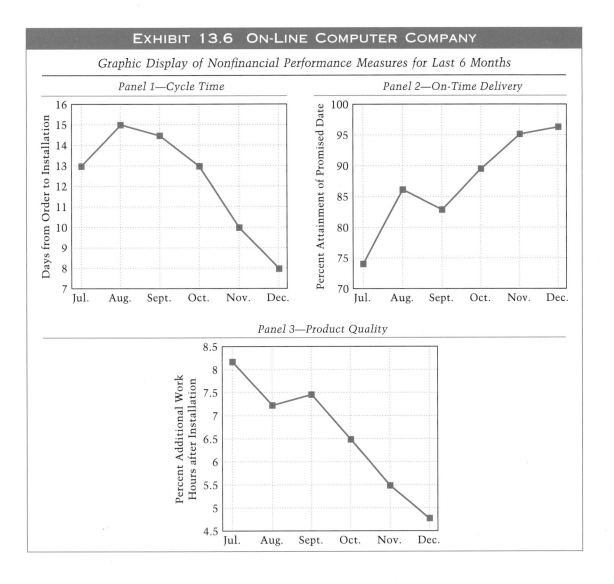

EXHIBIT 13.6 ON-LINE COMPUTER COMPANY

Graphic Display of Nonfinancial Performance Measures for Last 6 Months

Panel 1—Cycle Time

Panel 2—On-Time Delivery

Panel 3—Product Quality

Product Quality. The key variable product quality is measured by tracking additional work hours necessary after installation, as a percent of total. It was not unusual for system support units to continue working on projects long after installation. Panel 3 of Exhibit 13.6 shows tremendous progress on this measure over the past 3 months. Before October, follow-up work had ranged from 8.5 to about 7 percent of the unit's total working hours. Since October, there has been a continuous decrease in additional work hours, to below 5 percent in December.

PUTTING MEASURES TO USE

Successful use of performance measures at the operational level normally requires that front-line workers are committed to their use. Thus, department employees—not just their managers—should see the measures as tracking those activities that define critical performance outcomes. The preferred way to achieve workers' commitment is to gain their *involvement* during the measurement selection process. As a result, workers can help to choose the most appropriate measures, thereby creating among them a sense of ownership in the measurement system.

Not only should workers be involved in the selection of measures, but they should take the lead in tracking performance results. Graphic reports like those shown in Exhibit 13.6 should be displayed prominently so that all employees can see them. It is, after all, the workers on the front line who know best what changes in their actions may have contributed to changes in reported outcomes. Measures thus become tools by which both managers and their workers can learn from their actions, while striving for operational improvements.

RESTRUCTURING COSTS FOR STRATEGIC PURPOSES

Managers often want to know how much of their resources are being used for a particular purpose. For example, the manager of the southwest unit may want to know how much it is spending to produce the software, by type of customer. To obtain this information, On-Line's accountants would have to assign to each customer its appropriate share of the cost center's general ledger expenses—salaries, supplies, and travel, for examples. Such information can be of help generally in spotting costly trends associated with certain types of customers. It can also be useful in evaluating efficiency or in negotiating contract terms with new customers. (See "Current Practice: Braintree Hospital.")

Restructuring cost data to suit the unique strategic needs of managers is referred to as **strategic cost analysis.** The methods used to develop strategic costs are the same as those used for activity-based costing, discussed in Chapter 4. The main difference is the cost object for which the data are generated. Activity-based costs focus on activities, which involve groupings of the work that must be done in order to deliver business processes. However, in strategic cost analysis activities are not the only type of cost

Braintree Hospital

Strategic cost analysis was used at Boston's Braintree Hospital for disaggregating fixed-cost nursing allocations. There is wide variation in the amount of nursing services consumed by different types of patients, as well as in the skill levels among the nursing staff (i.e., RNs, LPNs, and NAs). Nurses were asked to keep track of the time they spent performing various activities, patient by patient. Their data were then reconfigured in order to determine the nursing skill level needed to deliver care, by type of patient. The result was a cost report that shows the cost of services actually required by each type of patient. Besides improving control, these finely tuned cost data are useful to the hospital when it negotiates fees with insurance providers.

Source: Lawrence P. Carr, "Unbundling the Cost of Hospitalization," *Management Accounting*, Nov. 1993, pp. 43–48.

object. Instead, the strategic costs can focus on any strategy or objective that a manager considers important. For example, managers might use products, programs, territories, customers, or marketing distribution channels as cost objects.

There are two types of strategic-cost-data application. The first makes use solely of information contained in the existing accounting system. The same total amount of costs is reported, but the costs (all of them) are reassigned to categories of strategic importance. The second is used to determine the amount spent to create and maintain quality throughout the organization. It also reassigns data in the existing accounting system to categories of strategic importance. However, it does not require that *all* costs be reassigned, and it allows the use of additional cost information that is gathered from outside the accounting system.

RESTRUCTURING EXISTING ACCOUNTING COST DATA

Existing cost data, which are usually reported by department, may be fully restructured to reflect strategies, using a four-step process:

1. Identify the new strategic cost categories.
2. For each department (or other unit), break down resource use by each new strategic cost category, as a percentage of total use.
3. Use the percentage breakdown to assign costs to the new strategic cost categories.
4. Organize the results into a breakdown of resource costs for each new category.

We illustrate the use of these steps in the example that follows.

ILLUSTRATION: CUSTOM SCROLL STEELWORK, INC.

Custom Scroll Steelwork, Inc., is a job-order shop that manufactures custom and prefabricated steelwork for homes, stores, and office buildings. It makes and installs gates, fences, staircases, and other building-related steel structures. The firm's organization is simple, consisting of two functional units—sales and administration, and production. Production has three operating subunits: (1) fabrication, which designs and makes specialty pieces; (2) assembly, which preassembles major components at the factory; and (3) installation, which stores, transports, and installs the structure at the customer site. Financial recordkeeping for the three production subunits (or departments) has been simple and follows traditional job-order accounting methods. The three departments use standardized cost categories, and operational control in the past has been based on management's cost estimates.

Not long ago, senior managers identified process improvement as an objective (and a key variable) they consider critical for long-term success. The strategy for achieving process improvement involves developing a cultural ethic among the production workforce, in which employees continually seek to improve work processes. Employees have been encouraged to attend training sessions in order to learn how they can draw from past experience to identify potential job-site improvements. Department managers have been urged to encourage—both morally and financially—employees to make improvement suggestions. Despite all this, however, senior managers have seen few (if any) changes being made to the production process. To gain some insight on the problem, they have asked their accountant to reshape financial data in order to include information on spending, by department activities.

1: Identify Strategic Cost Categories. The firm's top managers asked their accountant to fully reassign cost data to new, activity-based categories so that they can better examine departmental spending priorities. After some discussion, they agreed that reports should include three basic groupings of information.

Department	Cost Category	Activity Category
Fabrication	Materials	Conversion
Assembly	Labor and supervision	Storage and movement
Installation	Machine cost	Conformance with specifications
	Occupancy	Process improvement
	Power	
	Maintenance	

Management was especially pleased with the four-way breakdown of activities, since traditional reports, which show spending by department and cost category only, imply that all department resources are used solely for converting inputs to outputs. The proposed report should show how much of each department's resources are used for other purposes and, of more immediate concern, how much emphasis is being given to process improvement.

2: For Each Department, Break Down Resource Use by New Category, as Percentages of Total Use. In step 2, each department prepares a percentage breakdown, by new activity cost category, of its resource use. For example, the accountant worked with the lead supervisor of the fabrication department to determine what portion of materials were used to convert inputs to outputs, to store and move inventory, to conform the product to specifications, and to improve the process. By analyzing materials requisitions, they found that fabrication used only 80 percent of total materials for initial conversion and a whopping 20 percent to correct conformance problems. They then did the same for the other cost categories. It was difficult to find percentages for labor and supervision, since no time records are kept by activity. So workers were asked to keep track of how they spent their time for 2 weeks. This information, with some subjective adjustment by the lead supervisor, showed that 50 percent of labor and supervision resources were spent on conversion, 30 percent on storing and moving materials, 15 percent on conformance, and 5 percent on discussions of and meetings on process improvement. While these percentage assignments might not be precise, they seemed to be reasonable. This technique was used to assign percentages to every new cost category in each of the three departments. The result is shown under steps 1 and 2, in the middle columns of Exhibit 13.7.

3: Use the Percentage Breakdown to Assign Costs to the New Categories. The right-hand side of Exhibit 13.7 assigns dollar amounts to activities. These costs are simply the product of each percentage and the associated cost-category totals. The spreadsheet format makes the assignment of costs to new categories a very simple, repetitive task. Next, after dollar amounts are assigned to each new cost category (i.e., activity), the columns are added for each department, and resource use by activity is calculated as a percentage of total department spending.

The activity-cost assignments in Exhibit 13.7 proved to be very telling, as a wide diversity between departments became apparent. For example, conversion activities consumed 71 percent of the assembly department's resources but only 34 percent of the installation department's resource. Installation spent 52 percent of its resources on storing and moving inventory—which is understandable, since its basic tasks include storing finished product and delivering it to customers. Discussion with department personnel further revealed that installation's "Store & Move" column contained large amounts spent on use of machinery (mainly delivery vehicles) and on power (mostly vehicle gasoline). One of the most strategically important statistics that emerged from comparisons of the three departments was the variations in the levels of—and the general lack of—improvement activities. These range from a low of 2 percent of resources used by fabrication to a high of 7 percent by installation.

EXHIBIT 13.7 CUSTOM SCROLL STEELWORK, INC.

Worksheet for Breaking Down Production Costs
by Department, Cost Category, and Activity Category

Existing Data		Steps 1 and 2 — Assigned Percentages					Step 3 — Assigned Dollar Amounts				
Cost Category, by Department											
Fabrication	Total	Convert	Store & Move	Conform	Improve Process	Total	Convert	Store & Move	Conform	Improve Process	Total
Materials	$ 120,000	0.80		0.20		1.00	$ 96,000	$ 0	$ 24,000	$ 0	$ 120,000
Labor & supervision	192,000	0.50	0.30	0.15	0.05	1.00	96,000	57,600	28,800	9,600	192,000
Machine cost	96,000	0.65	0.20	0.15		1.00	62,400	19,200	14,400	0	96,000
Occupancy	38,400	0.70	0.05	0.25		1.00	26,880	1,920	9,600	0	38,400
Power	14,400	0.30	0.30	0.40		1.00	4,320	4,320	5,760	0	14,400
Maintenance	19,200	0.50	0.20	0.30		1.00	9,600	3,840	5,760	0	19,200
Total fabrication cost	$ 480,000						$295,200	$ 86,880	$ 88,320	$ 9,600	$ 480,000
Total as percent of dept. total cost[a]							62%	18%	18%	2%	100%
Assembly	Total	Convert	Store & Move	Conform	Improve Process	Total	Convert	Store & Move	Conform	Improve Process	Total
Materials	$ 600,000	0.95		0.05		1.00	$570,000	$ 0	$ 30,000	$ 0	$ 600,000
Labor & supervision	120,000	0.20	0.45	0.15	0.20	1.00	24,000	54,000	18,000	24,000	120,000
Machine cost	276,000	0.40	0.30	0.30		1.00	110,400	82,800	82,800	0	276,000
Occupancy	120,000	0.80	0.05	0.10	0.05	1.00	96,000	6,000	12,000	6,000	120,000
Power	36,000	0.50	0.25	0.20	0.05	1.00	18,000	9,000	7,200	1,800	36,000
Maintenance	48,000	0.65	0.15	0.10	0.10	1.00	31,200	7,200	4,800	4,800	48,000
Total assembly cost	$1,200,000						$849,600	$159,000	$154,800	$36,600	$1,200,000
Total as percent of dept. total cost[a]							71%	13%	13%	3%	100%

(continued)

EXHIBIT 13.7 (CONTINUED)

Cost Category, by Department	Existing Data	Steps 1 and 2 — Assigned Percentages					Step 3 — Assigned Dollar Amounts				
Installation	Total	Convert	Store & Move	Conform	Improve Process	Total	Convert	Store & Move	Conform	Improve Process	Total
Materials	$ 5,700	1.00				1.00	$ 5,700	$ 0	$ 0	$ 0	$ 5,700
Labor & supervision	199,500	0.40	0.40	0.10	0.10	1.00	79,800	79,800	19,950	19,950	199,500
Machine cost	42,750	0.20	0.80			1.00	8,550	34,200	0	0	42,750
Occupancy	5,700		1.00			1.00	0	5,700	0	0	5,700
Power	22,800	0.05	0.95			1.00	1,140	21,660	0	0	22,800
Maintenance	8,550	0.20	0.80			1.00	1,710	6,840	0	0	8,550
Total installation cost	$ 285,000						$ 96,900	$148,200	$ 19,950	$19,950	$ 285,000
Total as percent of dept. total cost[a]							34%	52%	7%	7%	100%

[a] Amounts shown as percent of department total cost are rounded to the nearest whole number. Thus, as in the fabrication department, the same percentage (18%) is reported for different total costs ($86,880/$480,000 = 18.1%; $88,320/$480,000 = 18.4%).

4: Organize the Results into a Breakdown of Resource Costs, by New Category. Exhibit 13.8 is a breakdown of resource costs, by activity, for Custom Scroll's production unit. The bottom line of this combined cost report indicates what percentage of resources is spent on each of the four basic activities. Managers were surprised to find that only 63 percent of production resources actually go to conversion, with 20 percent spent on storing and moving inventory and 13 percent on making certain the product conforms to customer specifications. Most alarming of all is the mere 3 percent of resources devoted to the firm's process improvements—the single activity that management has identified as crucial for its long-term success.

Armed with this information, managers and other employees at Custom Scroll Steelwork can debate whether the factory departments are making proper use of their resources. Historically, discussions would have centered on whether costs could be cut in functional cost categories, such as materials or power. It was not unusual for department lead supervisors to say that all the fat had already been cut and that further reductions would result in more quality problems. Information on costs, by activity, can broaden the focus of these discussions to encompass the costs of accomplishing specific objectives or strategies. If the firm, in fact, is committed to process improvement, then actions can be taken to make sure a greater percentage of resources are directed toward it. For example, senior management might insist that a minimum of 10 percent of resources be spent on process improvement and that resources be shifted from other activities in order to achieve that target.

EXHIBIT 13.8   CUSTOM SCROLL STEELWORK, INC.

Production Cost Categories Broken Down by Activity

		Activity			
Cost Categories	*Convert*	*Store & Move*	*Conform*	*Improve Process*	*Production Total*
Materials	$ 671,700	$ 0	$ 54,000	$ 0	$ 725,700
Labor & supervision	199,800	191,400	66,750	53,550	511,500
Machine cost	181,350	136,200	97,200	0	414,750
Occupancy	122,880	13,620	21,600	6,000	164,100
Power	23,460	34,980	12,960	1,800	73,200
Maintenance	42,510	17,880	10,560	4,800	75,750
Total	$1,241,700	$394,080	$263,070	$66,150	$1,965,000
Total as percent of production total cost[a]	63%	20%	13%	3%	100%

[a] Amounts shown as percent of production total cost are rounded to the nearest whole number. For example, "Convert" is rounded to 63 percent from 63.19 percent ($1,241,700/$1,965,000).

OTHER APPLICATIONS OF COST RESTRUCTURING

The cost groupings we used in the Custom Scroll example—department, cost category, and activity category—are effective only if they satisfy the organization's needs. Many other ways of defining information blocks are possible. Custom Scroll could have reorganized its costs by product group—for example, gates and fences, stairways, window security bars, and specialty designs—instead of by department. These product groups or categories could then have been combined with the new activity categories and the traditional resources-cost categories in order to offer an alternative to the matrix shown in Exhibit 13.7.

The Custom Scroll Steelwork example shows how standard accounting information can be recategorized in order to deliver strategically important information. In the next subsection, we look at a variation of this approach, one that is used most often to calculate the cost of creating and maintaining quality throughout the organization. For that purpose, additional cost data must be gathered from outside the accounting information system.

RESTRUCTURING EXISTING COST DATA AND GATHERING NEW COST DATA

DETERMINING THE ELEMENTS OF QUALITY

This second procedure for reassigning costs is used for finding the costs that are added when firms seek quality improvement. Before examining the procedure itself, we need to clarify what is meant by *quality* and to consider how the accounting information system can help managers work toward improving it. *Quality* usually means different things to different people. For example, one car buyer may say that the Jaguar XJ6 is a quality automobile because of its luxurious appointments, elegance, and style. Another may say that the Honda Accord is a quality car because of its reputation for customer satisfaction and dependability. Both are seeking the same thing—quality—but each is interpreting it from his or her own perspective. Experts in the quality field recognize the vagueness of the concept and tend to evaluate the quality of a product by its ability to conform to customer expectations.

Some precision can be added to the concept by separating quality into two elements. The first, called **quality of design**, focuses on the degree to which the product's design specifications fulfill customer expectations. Proper definition of this element requires a knowledge of who the intended customers are and an understanding of what they expect in a product. Such a definition is critical to the proper evaluation of quality, yet it relies on information that must be collected outside the firm. Some firms assign the responsibility of determining basic design features to the marketing department, which might use focus groups, test marketing, or other means to determine what potential customers expect. Other companies use an internal, team approach in which people from marketing, management, engineering, and other technical units use their particular knowledge and judgment, as well as collective insights, to produce basic designs. Regardless of how design-related information is gathered and assessed, design features can only be offered subject to resource and production constraints, and designed products are expected to meet profit objectives.

The second element of quality, **quality of conformance**, refers to the extent to which a product matches, or conforms to, its design specifications. Responsibility for quality of conformance falls on the service and production operating units, which must transform the design into a marketable item. Much of this responsibility has traditionally been given to quality control groups within operating units. Today there is a wide range of in-process controls available to ensure that quality is built into the product at every stage of production. For example, many firms use *statistical process control,* in which samples are checked throughout the production process—rather than waiting to check only finished products—so as to isolate and resolve problems of quality as they arise. Vendors are now evaluated on the basis of their shipments' quality, and materials are often subjected to strict conformance tests before they enter the production cycle. Nowadays, too, employees are expected to take an active role in evaluating work activities and suggesting means for improving quality.

DETERMINING THE COST OF QUALITY

As managers become increasingly concerned about quality, they need to know the costs of maintaining and increasing quality—and the investment trade-offs involved. Obtaining that information is not an easy job, since accounting records are not organized so as to enable quality to be reported as a separate cost account. The costs of quality are, in fact, embedded in many existing accounts, and no generally accepted principles for determining quality costs have been established. Raw materials that cannot be used because their quality is low will probably be charged to inventory. Tests of quality compliance performed by an internal audit team will probably be reflected in the cost of running an internal audit department. Investments in expert information systems designed to define more clearly a customer's (unspecified) job or product requirements will likely be amortized as software costs. All of these issues are concerned with quality, but their costs are hidden in other accounts. How, then, can the accountant determine the separable costs of quality?

Most efforts at accumulating the costs of maintaining quality have centered on its second element, quality of conformance—perhaps because the cost of quality of design is very difficult to separate from the cost of design itself. However, even these efforts are not without problems, since they require not only that existing accounting data be reassigned but often that special studies gather data from outside the accounting system. Generally, such costs are grouped into three categories, according to when they occur within the production cycle, as follows:

1. Cost of preventing quality problems before operations begin.
2. Cost of appraising quality during and after operations.
3. Cost of failures to meet expectations. The cost of failures can be further broken down according to whether these costs are internal to

the firm (i.e., incurred within the production facility) or external (i.e., incurred after delivery).

A list of quality cost elements that typically fall into each of these categories is presented in Exhibit 13.9. The restructuring of quality costs is illustrated in the example that follows.

ILLUSTRATION: JUSTRIGHT PRINTING COMPANY

Exhibit 13.10 shows the quality cost reports for Justright Printing Company for the three calendar years, from 1994 to 1996. (Note that all figures in this example are expressed in thousands.) Senior managers were

---

EXHIBIT 13.9 BROAD CATEGORIES OF QUALITY COSTS WITH SOME EXAMPLES FOR EACH CATEGORY

Cost of Prevention

Quality training
Quality circles
Supervision of prevention activities
Development of systems to enhance conformance with design specifications
Development of in-process operational control systems
Auditing the effectiveness of the quality control system
Rewarding employees for process quality enhancement

Cost of Appraisal

Inspection and testing of incoming materials purchases
Component inspection and testing
Review of sales orders for accuracy
In-process or final product inspection
Field inspection at customer site prior to release of final product
Depreciation of test equipment
Reliability testing

Cost of Failures

Internal Failures	*External Failures*
Net cost of scrap or spoilage	Responses to customer complaints
Rework labor and overhead	Investigation of customer claims on warranty
Reinspection or reworked product	Warranty repairs and replacement
Retest of reworked product	Product recalls
Downtime because of quality problems	Legal costs related to product liability claims
Data reentered because of data entry errors	Returns and allowances because of quality problems
Revision of in-house computer programs because of software errors	Opportunity cost of lost sales because of reputation for poor quality

Source: Adapted from Morse, Roth, and Poston, *Measuring, Planning and Controlling Quality Costs,* Montvale, N.J.: National Association of Accountants (now called Institute of Management Accountants), 1987, p. 20.

EXHIBIT 13.10 JUSTRIGHT PRINTING COMPANY

Quality Cost Reports for Years Ending December 31 (in thousands)

	1994		1995		1996		
	Dollar Amount	Percent of Total	Dollar Amount	Percent of Total	Dollar Amount	Percent of Total	Source of Data
Cost of prevention:							
Quality training workshops	$ 12		$ 48		$ 98		Allocated payroll of trainers
Process improvement projects	18		59		109		Allocated payroll of team members
Auditing the quality system	24		62		91		Allocated cost of internal auditing
Total prevention cost	$ 54	5%	$ 169	17%	$ 298	30%	
Cost of appraisal:							
Clarifying customer expectations	$ 32		$ 86		$ 109		Allocated payroll of project managers and staff
Proofreading	115		164		192		Payroll of proofreaders
Inspecting by quality control	43		118		137		Quality control payroll, depreciation
Total appraisal cost	$ 190	19%	$ 368	37%	$ 438	44%	
Cost of internal failure:							
Press downtime	$ 125		$ 89		$ 55		Payroll for idled production workers
Correction of typos	104		92		67		Allocated payroll for data reentry
Bindery waste	63		35		21		Allocated production payroll, spoiled materials
Total internal-failure cost	$ 292	29%	$ 216	22%	$ 143	14%	
Cost of external failure:							
Responding to customer complaints	$ 112		$ 66		$ 45		Allocated payroll of project managers and staff
Investigating customer claims	116		66		39		Allocated payroll of project managers and staff
Lost sales because of unresolved problems	235		109		29		Estimation based on past experience
Total external-failure	$ 463	46%	$ 241	24%	$ 113	11%	
Total estimated quality cost	$ 999	100%	$ 994	100%	$ 992	100%	
Ratio of quality cost to sales	21.7%		19.2%		16.6%		
New sales revenue	$4,604		$5,177		$5,976		
Sales growth	7.3%		12.5%		15.4%		

prompted by concerns about customer complaints and dissatisfaction when they first requested a report for 1994. Their objective was to determine where in the production cycle quality-control efforts were being directed and why those efforts seemed to be ineffectual. The accounting staff first identified all cost elements that were concerned with quality and sorted them into prevention, appraisal, internal failure, and external failure cost categories, using a list similar to that shown in Exhibit 13.9. Then they obtained a cost for each element, using actual costs (where available), estimating costs (where necessary), and gathering outside cost data (as necessary).

Cost of Prevention.   The cost of prevention consists largely of employee training cost and the cost of developing new quality processes. Three such cost elements are included in Exhibit 13.10: (1) quality training workshops to educate employees; (2) process improvement projects, such as implementing a performance measurement system; and (3) audits of the quality system, whereby production workers review other departments' quality procedures. Some of these costs can be gathered easily—such as the cost of having outside trainers conduct quality workshops. However, estimating such costs as the lost productivity of employees attending, say, quality workshop sessions requires subjective judgment. One possibility is to allocate to these costs a portion of the payroll cost of those employees who attend the workshops. Similar allocations should be made for employees who are present during meetings on process improvement, or those involved in quality audits. If the accountants know beforehand that this information is needed, they can request all who are involved to keep track of their time. A direct charge of that time to quality costs is then possible.

Cost of Appraisal.   This category involves the cost of testing and inspecting for quality during and after operations. The clarifying customer expectations element, for example, includes more-frequent preproduction meetings with customers. As with the cost of prevention, most of the costs of appraisal activities are derived from payroll records. The jobs of proof-readers and quality inspectors, for examples, are defined in terms of quality assurance activities, so 100 percent of their payroll is a quality cost. All appraisal-support costs, such as the depreciation of test equipment, should also be included. It is more difficult, however, to determine the dollar cost of time spent with customers (clarifying expectations), since this is only one of the activities performed by project managers. Estimates of time spent in this activity can be used to allocate a percentage of the project managers' salaries.

Cost of Internal Failure.   The cost of internal failure comprises the costs of correcting defects before delivering the product to the customer. Just-right incurs such costs for press downtime and the correction of typographical errors. Machine downtime, sometimes called *idle time,* is one cost that some firms already record separately in ledger accounts. It is a recognized production overhead cost, and it typically includes an allocation of direct labor (for the time during which the machine is down). Internal failure cost also includes the cost of materials lost because of quality prob- lems (here, bindery waste), another cost that is already captured in many cost accounting systems.

Cost of External Failure.   The cost of external failure comprises the costs of correcting quality problems *after* the product has been delivered to the customer. All three cost items listed here must be estimated. The costs of responding to customer complaints and investigating customer claims are allocations of payroll cost and are based on estimates of time spent. Lost sales because of unresolved problems is an opportunity cost, and thus is not found in accounting records.[2] However, it is perhaps the most important indicator of the effectiveness of quality efforts, since the firm's success is most affected by it. Accountants gather data on lost sales by estimating the amount of sales that would have been earned if customers were more satisfied with service or product quality. It consists of sales lost when dissatisfied customers take their business elsewhere (which may be estimated from past records) and sales lost when unknown potential cus- tomers are dissuaded by a reputation for poor quality (which is very diffi- cult to estimate). (See "Current Practice: Xerox Corporation's Omaha Dis- trict.")

---

[2]   Opportunity cost is measured by lost contribution margin. Service firms such as the one in this illustration can measure lost profits by estimating lost sales alone, based on the assumption that variable costs did not change as a result of the effect on sales.

Interpreting Justright's 1994 Quality Cost Report. The "Percentage of Total" column for 1994 in Exhibit 13.10 shows that Justright's 1994 approach to quality control was oriented more toward fixing problems than toward preventing them. The cost of internal failure accounted for 29 percent of the total annual quality cost, and the cost of external failure accounted for 46 percent. In contrast, only 19 percent was invested in quality appraisal—the category that includes inspection and testing. Even worse, only 5 percent of the 1994 quality cost was spent on prevention—the activity that is absolutely required if the firm is to move toward zero defects.

An analysis of quality-cost information such as that given in Exhibit 13.10 shows not only where quality efforts have been concentrated in the past but also where further improvements are possible. The 1994 report for Justright demonstrates an overemphasis on the correction of quality defects—which is an expensive way to maintain quality. Theoretical models and experience both indicate that the cost of quality is highest when quality conformance is lowest—that is, the cost of correcting failure is greater than the cost of preventing it in the first place. For Justright, containing the cost of quality means shifting quality cost components (and Justright's attention) toward prevention and appraisal activities.

Changes in Justright's Quality Emphasis Over Time. In 1995, Justright management began a three-pronged effort to enhance quality. First, it sought to better understand customer needs, second, to place more emphasis on proofreading, and third, to arrange for additional inspecting. Programs also were implemented that were intended to encourage employee involvement in identifying needed improvements. Employees began to look for faulty work and to make sure that jobs were halted when defective work was spotted. The results were encouraging—the cost of failures decreased and the ratio of quality cost to sales revenue fell from 21.7 percent in 1994 to 19.2 percent in 1995. (The actual quality costs, which are listed in Exhibit 13.10, by category and ratios, are graphed in Exhibit 13.11.)

In 1996, management extended the quality improvement program. Justright now began to encourage more-creative thinking by its employees at every stage of the printing process. This was tantamount to saying, "You know the job better than anyone else does, so help us find better ways of doing things." The quality-training programs were expanded, as were collaborative projects to improve work processes. Employees were persuaded to submit suggestions for process improvement. This continued redirection of the firm's efforts, from correcting errors to doing the job properly the first time, resulted in a further drop in quality cost, to 16.6 percent of sales in 1996.

Some Limitations of Quality Cost Reports. While quality cost data can help managers spot trends in spending on quality, some rather apparent limitations should be noted. Like all cost reports, quality cost reports, by themselves, offer information only on the input portion of performance

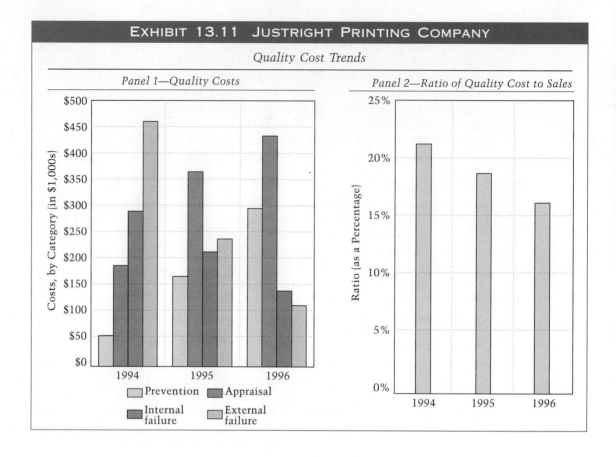

EXHIBIT 13.11 JUSTRIGHT PRINTING COMPANY

Quality Cost Trends

Panel 1—Quality Costs

Panel 2—Ratio of Quality Cost to Sales

measurement. That information must be combined with data on output, such as units produced, if it is to provide insight on efficiency. Justright Printing has included in its cost reports a measure of the cost of quality as a percentage of sales revenue. This, too, is a measure of efficiency and, when displayed over a 3-year period, offers a useful means for evaluating trends in quality spending.

Even more important, however, are measures of effectiveness that show how close the firm comes to achieving its objectives. Here, we must refer back to market-related key variables, which, if properly derived, indicate the extent to which objectives are accomplished. For example, even if Justright Printing improves its quality-spending efficiency, other problems may cause its market share to decrease. It may lose sales as a result of the replacement of commercial printing services by desktop publishing or CD-ROM technology. A cost-of-quality report does not provide enough information to enable management to discover these outside market trends. Key variables can, however, be tracked by a performance measurement system, so that managers and employees stay focused on the need for innovation and improvement in dealings both inside and outside the firm.

SUMMARY

Performance measurement systems provide managers and employees with feedback on how well organizational objectives are being attained. The theme underlying the use of measures is that people's actions will reflect the way in which their actions are being measured. There are two general types of performance measures. The first type, efficiency, is a ratio of input to output; it indicates how well a resource is transformed into a product or service. The second type, effectiveness, compares a responsibility center's outputs with its targets; it indicates the degree to which objectives are achieved.

Organizations developing a performance measurement system follow a two-step process. The first step is to use organizational objectives as the basis for deriving key variables for each responsibility center. Key variables gauge high-risk activities that can disrupt the accomplishment of corporate strategies. There are five broad categories of key variables. They concern (1) shareholder value, (2) quality, (3) market position, (4) flexibility, and (5) productivity. Key variables at lower organizational levels have shorter planning horizons, more-specific operational definitions, and more of an efficiency focus.

The second step in setting up a performance measurement system is to associate specific measures with each key variable. Ideal measures should be appropriate—meaning that they should capture the significance of the key variable, they should be tailored to the department's situation, and their outcomes must be controllable by department actions. Measures chosen should also be free from measurement error, and should be timely, understandable, and cost-effective. The same key variable might be measured in different ways by different departments.

Restructuring cost data to suit the unique strategic needs of managers is referred to as *strategic cost analysis*, of which there are two types. The first type requires that existing general ledger costs be assigned to new categories that are defined by activities, products, programs, customers, or distribution channels, which function as cost objects. To achieve restructured costs, departments break out resource use for each new cost category. Managers and other department employees can examine restructured costs in order to determine whether they are making proper use of resources for accomplishing objectives and strategies.

The second type of strategic cost analysis is used for calculating the cost of creating and maintaining quality throughout the organization. Quality costs concentrate on achieving product conformance to design standards. There are three quality cost categories: (1) prevention, (2) appraisal, and (3) failure. The third category, failure, comprises two subcategories—internal failure and external failure. Total quality cost is expected to decline when spending shifts from correction of failures to failure prevention and quality appraisal. Some of the cost of external failure must be estimated based on an assessment of lost sales revenue. Cost-of-quality information is used to monitor spending trends among the quality cost categories and for tracking quality cost as a percentage of sales revenue.

| CHAPTER 13 ASSIGNMENTS |

D13.1 (Corporate Objectives and Department Measures)

John Maynard, president of Fuel Injection Systems, Inc., cannot understand why his departments do not work well together. Although his firm is set up with a functional organization structure, he has tried to evaluate department performance on both financial and nonfinancial criteria. The selected performance measures include what Maynard sees as the number one determinant of company success—speed to market. Still, department managers seem to make decisions that are based solely on the best interests of their own individual departments, rather than on the interests of the company as a whole. Although managers have met performance targets, problems between departments have hampered the development of new products. One recently delayed new product was a jet flow restrictor, which was expected to be a breakthrough product because of its ability to reduce fuel consumption. However, because of unanticipated problems in coordinating efforts between departments, product sales were delayed 6 months behind target projections.

After some investigation of the delay, Maynard found that bottlenecks had originated in two places. The first was in production, where problems arose in extruding nozzle components to comply with tight tolerance specifications. A second problem became evident in marketing, where the salesforce kept pushing existing lines and discouraged customers from trying the new product "until all the problems are ironed out." The manager of R&D explained to Maynard that this was to be expected, since the production manager would not cooperate in building a prototype early in product design because, he claimed, such efforts would interfere with his ability to meet his production targets. The R&D manager also pointed out that the salesforce did not want to jeopardize meeting their service targets because of late deliveries of the new product. Hence, the salesforce encouraged customers to postpone buying the new offering.

Maynard began to reexamine the criteria he uses for evaluating the three department managers. Surely, he thought, there must be something he had overlooked in the performance measures he used that motivated managers to think first of their department outcomes. The performance measures he has been using to evaluate the three department managers are as follows:

Department	*Performance Measure*
1. Production	Percent of production achieved Standard cost targets achieved Percent of product defects
2. Research & Development	Number of new products Speed to market Percent of budgeted cost targets achieved
3. Marketing	Sales in dollars Customer satisfaction Percent of budgeted cost targets achieved

Required:

1. Explain why the measures currently in use at Fuel Injection Systems might encourage managers to choose to promote their department's interests instead of targeting corporate objectives.

2. Offer suggestions for improving the company's system of performance measurement.

D13.2 (Distribution Channel Profits and Strategic Costing)

It seemed like a nightmare come true. Carol Minelli, president of Zeeko Fishing Supply, had just received the results of a study by Price-Waterbridge, an outside consulting firm. Her suspicions were confirmed. It has been less than 3 years since Zeeko became a supplier of Mega-Mart Stores, which agreed to put Zeeko's products in its more than 1,500 discount retail locations throughout the United States, Mexico, and Canada. Minelli has witnessed a tremendous 55 percent jump in sales over this period—along with a nearly 70 percent decline in operating income (Exhibit D13.2.1). Now the consultant's strategic cost report shows that it is Zeeko's relationship with Mega-Mart that is the cause of the profit slide (Exhibit D13.2.2).

EXHIBIT D13.2.1 ZEEKO FISHING SUPPLY

Income Statements for the Years Ending December 31

	1994	1995	1996
Sales	$85,987,000	$120,381,800	$133,503,416
Cost of sales	49,872,460	72,229,080	84,021,710
Gross profit	$36,114,540	$ 48,152,720	$ 49,481,706
Operating expense:			
Advertising	$ 7,308,895	$ 9,991,689	$ 9,762,170
Distribution	9,458,570	13,964,289	15,071,201
Promotion	4,299,350	5,778,326	6,386,870
Administration	11,178,310	16,010,779	17,071,082
Total operating expense	$32,245,125	$ 45,745,083	$ 48,291,323
Operating income	$ 3,869,415	$ 2,407,637	$ 1,190,383

EXHIBIT D13.2.2 ZEEKO FISHING SUPPLY

Strategic Cost Report Showing Income by Distribution Channel for the Year Ending December 31, 1996

	Sporting Goods Retailers	Specialty Goods Wholesalers	Mega-Mart	Total
Sales	$53,401,366	$38,715,991	$41,386,059	$133,503,416
Cost of sales	32,415,964	22,842,435	28,763,311	84,021,710
Gross profit	$20,985,402	$15,873,556	$12,622,748	$ 49,481,706
Operating expense:				
Advertising	$ 4,645,919	$ 3,046,948	$ 2,069,303	$ 9,762,170
Distribution	6,247,960	4,684,635	4,138,606	15,071,201
Promotion	3,230,783	1,914,506	1,241,582	6,386,871
Administration	6,675,171	4,684,635	5,711,276	17,071,082
Total operating expense	$20,799,833	$14,330,724	$13,160,767	$ 48,291,324
Operating income	$ 185,569	$ 1,542,832	$ (538,019)	$ 1,190,382

Before landing the deal with Mega-Mart, Zeeko Fishing Supply had traditionally supplied two customer-distribution channels—sporting goods retailers and specialty goods wholesalers. Over the years, however, it began to see its profit margins slide as the sporting goods retail market became more competitive. After trying to get its products into the Mega-Mart chain for 4 years, Zeeko's management was jubilant when the deal was finalized. While Minelli and her staff knew that sales margins would be cut thin at Mega-Mart, they also expected their operating cost to fall. What Minelli had not anticipated, however, is that Mega-Mart would not accept price increases from Zeeko, regardless of the cause. Mega-Mart made it clear that it had five suppliers waiting to take Zeeko's place, and, presumably, willing to sell their goods at the current supply prices. Consequently, when Zeeko was stung with price increases from its own suppliers, with labor rate increases, and with increased cost of complying with environmental regulation, it was forced to absorb the added costs.

Looking over the consultant's report, Minelli is considering her options. She could drop the Mega-Mart account, but that would mean a decline of more than 30 percent in sales, and she would be faced with the prospect of instituting a tremendous downsizing program. Further, she thought, it would not be easy to avoid all costs charged to Mega-Mart, even if these sales were eliminated, since many involve depreciation and corporate allocations. Another alternative would be to initiate a cost-cutting campaign targeted at conforming to the Mega-Mart cost structure. But, in fact, Zeeko has worked hard over the past 2 years to cut its costs and has been generally successful. The next round of cost cuts would be even more difficult to realize, and would likely meet with resistance throughout the organization. Perhaps she could replace the Mega-Mart sales with another customer channel, but, in today's competitive market, this seems more a pipe dream, than it does an attainable goal. Clearly, some action is necessary, but the options are not attractive.

Required: Discuss the options facing Minelli. What suggestions would you offer? (No computations are needed.)

PROBLEMS

P13.1 (Efficiency and Effectiveness Measures)

The Sun Tea Company recently introduced a new product, diet lemonade. The marketing campaign promoting the product relied heavily on the use of consumer advertising and on the placement of discount coupons in publications read by potential customers. Data on initial sales and marketing expense are given in Exhibit P13.1.

The Sun Tea Company has decided to measure the efficiency of the campaign by examining:

1. The advertising cost per net sales dollar
2. The advertising cost per unit sold
3. The average unit discount per coupon redeemed

It will measure the effectiveness of the campaign by examining:

1. The percentage of sales targets achieved, in dollars
2. The percentage of sales targets achieved, in units
3. The percentage rate of coupon redemption
4. The market share of unit sales

Required: Calculate each of the efficiency and effectiveness measures using the actual operating results (Exhibit P13.1).

EXHIBIT P13.1 SUN TEA COMPANY		
Initial Sales and Marketing Expense Data		
	Budgeted	*Actual*
Gross sales revenue (before coupon)	$1,210,000	$1,430,000
Cost of coupon redemption	3,375	4,050
Net sales revenue	$1,206,625	$1,425,950
Size of market, in units	15,000,000	15,255,000
Number of units sold	1,100,000	1,375,000
Number of coupons redeemed	22,500	27,000
Total advertising expense	$120,000	$135,000
Number of coupons distributed	225,000	225,000

EXHIBIT P13.2 PC COMPUTER COMPANY— CUSTOMER SERVICE CENTER	
Operating Data	
Total no. of calls	260,000
No. of days open during period	300
Average total time per call, minutes	21.0
Average time spent with customer representative per call, in minutes	16.5
Total expense	$1,450,250
No. of employees	42
No. of callers requiring further assistance	13,500
No. of customers satisfied with service received	241,750
No. of calls resulting in product refunds	3,200

P13.2   (Constructing Efficiency and Effectiveness Measures)

PC Computer Company has recently opened a customer service center in order to respond to customer inquiries relating to computer installation and operation. The service is offered to all customers via a toll-free telephone number. Although senior management believes the added service is needed in order to retain its customers and to increase future sales, it has not yet devised a means of evaluating the cost center's performance. It must identify measures that allow it to gauge the performance of the service center to date. Relevant cost, revenue, and operating data for the center are given in Exhibit P13.2.

Required: Identify at least two efficiency measures and two effectiveness measures for PC Computer's customer service center. You may find it necessary to create new measures from data shown in Exhibit P13.2.

P13.3   (Restructuring Costs by Production Operation)

Color Graphic, Inc., designs and prints commercial print materials, such as brochures, newsletters, and restaurant menus. The company offers a full range of services. Normally, the firm stipulates that it must perform all design, layout, and

			EXHIBIT P13.3 COLOR GRAPHIC, INC.	
		Production Cost Allocations		
	Setup	Production Process	Quality Control	*Total*
Initial design cost:				
Labor & supervision	24%	58%	18%	$165,000
Materials	5%	80%	15%	$15,000
Occupancy	15%	70%	15%	$42,000
Equipment	0%	74%	26%	$2,300
Typesetting & layout cost:				
Labor & supervision	12%	45%	43%	$265,000
Materials	31%	50%	19%	$64,000
Occupancy	17%	62%	21%	$87,500
Equipment	11%	70%	19%	$8,100
Printing cost:				
Labor & supervision	20%	70%	10%	$725,000
Materials	5%	92%	3%	$469,550
Occupancy	15%	73%	12%	$214,000
Equipment	25%	72%	3%	$17,500

print operations for each job. Recently, however, Color Graphic has become involved in a number of projects of limited scope that require it to perform only one or two operations. The CFO of the company wants to determine the breakdown of costs within each operation in order to assess the profitability of such piecemeal business.

Production has thus been broken down into three separate operations: initial design, typesetting and layout, and printing. Each operation involves three stages: setup, which includes time spent with the customer; the production process itself; and quality control. Costs for each operation include labor and supervision, materials, occupancy, and equipment. Percentage allocations of these costs are given in Exhibit P13.3.

Required: Break down the costs, by stage, for each of the three production operations.

P13.4 (Quality Cost Report)

Additions, Inc., produces hand-held calculators. The company has recently begun a total quality management (TQM) program for which it is tracking the cost of quality in its manufacturing process. Additions has identified the quality costs for the 6 months just before and the 6 months after the program was initiated (Exhibit P13.4). The CEO of the company is shocked at the costs associated with TQM and wants to cancel the program. He believes the company was already spending too much on quality. He has stated that the company's customers are not willing to pay more for higher quality and that quality costs are a drain on profitability.

Required: Prepare a quality cost report for the 6 months before and 6 months after the TQM program was begun. Your report should categorize quality costs and report relevant percentage breakdowns.

EXHIBIT P13.4 ADDITIONS, INC.

Quality Costs for 6 Months Before and 6 Months After TQM Program

	Before TQM Program	After TQM Program
Testing of materials purchased from outside suppliers	$10,000	$32,700
Returns because of poor quality	$67,900	$35,000
Quality training for production employees	$0	$44,150
Depreciation of equipment used to test products	$0	$22,750
Product inspection	$12,000	$32,300
Scrap cost	$45,000	$17,500
Warranty repairs	$75,000	$62,250
Development of quality control system	$0	$39,000
Rework of defective products	$55,800	$28,650
Lost sales because of poor quality	$215,000	$125,000
Total sales	$4,621,500	$5,251,240

P13.5 (Tracking Quality Costs Over Time)

Innovations, Inc., is a supplier of computer components. The company began a total quality management program 1 year ago and has been tracking its quality costs for the cost categories listed in Exhibit P13.5. The results shown are for the two quarters prior to the institution of the TQM program and for the four quarters just after the program was begun.

Company officials are worried because the total cost of quality has been increasing over this time period. When the program was started, the cost of quality was expected to decrease over time as the costs for external and internal failures were reduced. While these costs have decreased, the increased costs of prevention and appraisal have more than offset the saving due to fewer failures. The production manager is satisfied with the progress of the program, but the controller wants additional support to justify continuing the TQM program.

EXHIBIT P13.5 INNOVATIONS, INC.

Quality Costs Before and After TQM Program Implementation

Cost Category	1	2	3	4	5	6
	Before TQM		After TQM			
Prevention	$0	$0	$14,500	$23,400	$29,850	$35,400
Appraisal	$6,200	$6,400	$12,500	$22,450	$25,025	$28,300
Failure:						
Internal	$26,550	$28,475	$19,440	$17,600	$14,500	$12,250
External	$45,800	$52,900	$42,300	$28,000	$22,625	$16,360
Total Revenue	$802,500	$810,750	$850,100	$926,150	$995,820	$1,176,400

conformance
non-conformance

Required: For the six quarters shown in Exhibit P13.5, calculate the percentage breakdowns of quality cost categories and the quality-to-sales ratio.

P13.6 (Measuring Performance for Insurance Operations)

NationState Insurance Company has recently begun tracking monthly performance measures for its claims processing operation. These data, presented in Exhibit P13.6, offer a range of information dealing with such areas as the number of claims processed, time of processing, number of errors, customer satisfaction ratings, and hours of training per employee. The problem now confronting Helen Blackwell, manager of operations, is how to use these data to evaluate results and pinpoint areas for improvement. She believes that 4 months of comparative measures should provide an adequate basis for making some preliminary judgments about operational effectiveness and efficiency.

When the performance-measures system was first discussed last summer, Blackwell's boss reminded her that the bottom line for the claims processing operation entailed two key success areas—productivity and quality. As Blackwell worked with the accounting staff to identify relevant measures for claims processing, she had little idea how to translate these two key targets into meaningful numbers. Since the system was new to the accountants, they relied mainly on Blackwell's suggestions in selecting which measures to monitor. Now that the data have been collected for the past 4 months, Blackwell is feeling some pressure to come up with interpretations and a plan for action.

She decides that, as a beginning point, she should try to identify those measures that deal mainly with productivity and those that mainly concern quality. Second, she wants to narrow her selection down to not more than two measures in each area, so that she will not be overwhelmed with data at this early stage of analysis. Next, she wants to determine whether the measures chosen best address operational efficiency or departmental effectiveness. From some of the recent seminars she has attended, she has learned that being efficient is of little good if the

EXHIBIT P13.6 NATIONSTATE INSURANCE CO.— CLAIMS PROCESSING OPERATION

Monthly Performance Measures for July through October

	July	August	September	October	Average
Beginning inventory of outstanding claims	1,900	1,670	1,560	1,300	1,607.5
No. of claims received	2,340	2,760	2,430	2,540	2,517.5
No. of claims processed	2,570	2,870	2,690	2,970	2,775
Ending inventory of outstanding claims	1,670	1,560	1,300	870	1,350
Cycle time for processing claims, in days	30	35	37	33	33.8
No. of customer complaints	79	112	153	105	112.3
No. of contested claims	45	31	12	35	30.8
No. of claims resulting in litigation	3	0	1	4	2.0
No. of errors found during claims verification	298	476	254	318	336.5
Percent of customers rating service as satisfactory	87%	85%	81%	81%	84%
No. of fraudulent claims discovered	21	14	8	17	15.0
Average personnel headcount	21	19	20	21	20.3
Average hours of training per employee	0.75	1.50	2.00	2.50	1.7
No. of claims processed per employee	122	151	135	141	137.3

outcomes lead to a loss of future business. Finally, she wants to use this information to evaluate her department's performance and to identify areas needing improvement.

Required: Help Blackwell make sense out of the performance-measure data for the last 4 months. Specifically, you should:

1. Categorize each measure into either a productivity or quality grouping. Then choose two measures that seem most informative for each of the two key variables (i.e., productivity and quality), and justify your choice. Do your measures address efficiency or do they address effectiveness?
2. Prepare graphs for the four measures you chose in requirement 1. Based on these measures, evaluate the operation's performance for the past four months. What areas are most in need of improvement?

P13.7   (Choosing Performance Measures for Key Variables)

Industrial Pumps and Motors is a mid-sized, publicly held company that is facing increased market pressure from overseas competitors. The firm's CEO, Bill Konchak, has always relied on financial reporting and budget-variance analysis data as a means of gauging the firm's performance. In the beginning of 1996, however, Konchak informed the accounting department that he would like to use some other performance measures, as well. He believes this would help him to better understand how the firm is competing in the market and where it is experiencing operational problems. Furthermore, he wants this information reported monthly, along with the usual financial reports, so that he can gain early insight into where the firm seems to be headed. The accounting department responded with the information presented in Exhibit P13.7, which it has tabulated for the first 6 months of 1996.

Despite having received these additional monthly performance reports, Konchak does not feel he is using these data to their maximum potential. Nor does he feel confident about interpreting the data. Some of these measures seem to show improvement, while others seem to indicate an increase in difficulties. Some are in dollar amounts, some in percentages, and others in absolute numbers. And the biggest problem is that they are not organized in any order or in categories of importance. He would like to have this information reported in some form that would help him gain the extra insight he has been seeking.

Since the time when Konchak first instructed the accounting department to construct the new measures, he has been engaged in a strategic planning process with the firm's executive committee. After much debate, the committee has agreed that the success of the firm depends on accomplishing three overriding goals:

1. Building shareholder value
2. Strengthening market position
3. Continually improving productivity

Konchak now realizes that he needs to focus employee attention on specific measures that indicate whether progress is being made toward achieving the company's goals, which can serve as key variables. At the same time, after his experience with the array of measures reported in Exhibit P13.7, he feels that only two or three of the most important measures should be attached to each key variable. Use of too many measures might take away from the importance and clarity of the report. The main problem he faces now is trying to figure how to regroup the current measures and deciding which to use.

EXHIBIT P13.7 INDUSTRIAL PUMPS AND MOTORS

Performance Results for the First 6 Months of 1996

	January	February	March	April	May	June	Average
Corporate net income	$43,290	$21,330	$(11,350)	$36,500	$47,600	$42,600	$29,995
Market share	14.3%	12.6%	10.3%	13.5%	13.9%	13.4%	13.0%
Cycle time, in hours	5.3	5.7	5.5	5.4	5.0	4.2	5.2
Percent on-time delivery	68%	78%	82%	86%	88%	97%	83%
Percent of revenue from products less than 3 years old	34%	40%	28%	35%	42%	51%	38%
Percent change in sales revenue	6.5%	−5.0%	−9.8%	15.6%	13.2%	0.5%	3.5%
Percent of satisfied customers	75%	70%	68%	77%	86%	85%	77%
No. of new products introduced	2	0	1	4	2	3	2
Residual income	$20,790	$830	$(26,350)	$21,100	$33,520	$30,100	$13,332
Market value of outstanding stock (in 000s)	$865,800	$843,800	$835,600	$834,600	$863,200	$895,900	$856,483
Rework costs	$8,740	$10,450	$13,280	$6,490	$4,370	$8,350	$8,613
Cost of quality as a percent of sales revenue	23.2%	25.4%	26.7%	25.4%	19.3%	21.0%	23.5%
Warranty claims	238	154	321	376	215	152	242.7
Factory downtime, in minutes	348	780	1,008	549	320	460	577.5
Percent of orders filled	96%	91%	88%	94%	99%	95%	94%
Percent change in operating cash flows	7.6%	0.3%	−2.1%	−4.1%	9.6%	6.4%	3.0%
Inventory carrying cost (in 000s)	$9,348	$8,943	$8,857	$8,450	$7,958	$7,750	$8,551

Required:

1. Select from Exhibit P13.7 those two or three measures that seem to best capture each of the firm's key variables. Be prepared to explain the reasons for your choice.
2. Analyze the trends shown in each key variables category. Evaluate the firm's performance over the past 6 months, and identify those areas where improvement is most needed.

P13.8 (**Restructuring Cost Data by Type of Customer**)

LD Communications offers long-distance telephone service to commercial and residential customers in North America and Europe. The firm has been profitable during the past 3 years of operation, and senior management is now considering expanding its services to the Pacific Rim. Meryl Hightower, the firm's vice president—finance has questioned whether the firm could better position itself by offering only commercial or only residential services as it expands. At present, however, the internal financial reports show results by geographic location—that is, North America and Europe—but not by customer (see Exhibit P13.8.1). Hightower decides that more information is needed in order to determine how resources are currently being used and which customer segments generate the greatest profit margins.

In the new income statement format, revenues and expenses will be broken down by type of customer in North America and in Europe. Upon first analysis, the finance staff is able to find the following information on sources of sales revenue (in thousands of dollars):

	North America		Europe	
Commercial	$10,632	40%	$15,120	70%
Residential	15,948	60%	6,480	30%
Total	$26,580	100%	$21,600	100%

Satellite hookup fees are directly proportional to these costs, since they are paid on a per-user basis. The relationships for other costs, however, are not so clear. Consequently, a special study was conducted in order to determine where use of resources other than satellite hookup fees was most closely linked to customers. Results are presented in Exhibit P13.8.2, which shows a high degree of variability. In many cases, there is apparently not much relation between expenses and the amount of sales generated.

EXHIBIT P13.8.1 LD COMMUNICATIONS

Operating Results by Geographic Location (in $ thousands)

	North America	Europe	Total
Revenue	$26,580	$21,600	$48,180
Production expense:			
Satellite hookup fees	$ 3,680	$ 2,560	$ 6,240
Transmission maintenance	1,200	980	2,180
Field maintenance	2,980	3,140	6,120
Total production expense	$ 7,860	$ 6,680	$14,540
Finance & administration expense:			
Billing & collections	$ 2,260	$ 1,430	$ 3,690
Accounting	540	320	860
General administration	1,540	1,230	2,770
Total finance & administration expense	$ 4,340	$ 2,980	$ 7,320
Marketing expense:			
Advertising	$ 5,400	$ 3,290	$ 8,690
Field sales	3,660	2,360	6,020
Customer service	2,200	1,870	4,070
Total marketing expense	$11,260	$ 7,520	$18,780
Total expense	$23,460	$17,180	$40,640
Operating income	$ 3,120	$ 4,420	$ 7,540
Operating margin	11.7%	20.5%	15.6%

EXHIBIT P13.8.2   LD COMMUNICATIONS

Percentage Breakdown of Resource Consumption

	North America		Europe	
	Commercial	*Residential*	*Commercial*	*Residential*
Production expense:				
Transmission maintenance	45%	55%	80%	20%
Field maintenance	60%	40%	60%	40%
Finance & administration expense:				
Billing & collections	20%	80%	40%	60%
Accounting	50%	50%	55%	45%
General administration	45%	55%	60%	40%
Marketing expense:				
Advertising	35%	65%	75%	25%
Field sales	70%	30%	80%	20%
Customer service	35%	65%	65%	35%

When Hightower met with those of her staff members responsible for the study, she wanted more information on the derivation of the percentages shown in Exhibit P13.8.2. She found that some of the costs, such as advertising, were assigned directly to the customer. Based on an analysis of activities in North America, it was determined that 35 percent of advertising cost was used for mailings sent to commercial enterprises, while 65 percent was spent for mailings and for telephone soliciting of prospective residential customers. On the other hand, some costs, such as billing and collections, were estimated based on the number of accounts maintained for each type of customer. Yet other costs, such as field maintenance, were assigned based on approximations of the time personnel spent dealing with commercial or residential issues. Still other costs, such as general administration, do not always involve a particular type of customer. In such cases, costs were allocated by activity, where possible, and remaining costs were assigned by a "most reasonable" activity driver, such as sales revenue. After some discussion, Hightower agreed that the percentage breakdowns seemed reasonable.

Required:

1. Prepare a companywide income statement for each geographic location that also includes a breakdown by type of customer for each location.
2. Which of the income segments that you prepared for requirement 1 shows the best performance results, and which shows the worst performance results?
3. If you were to meet with senior managers in order to decide whether the firm should embark on a new operation in the Pacific Rim, what questions would you ask?

P13.9 (Using Strategic Costing in Production)

Ms. Carla Alvarez, vice president—operations at HinneyWare Co., a maker of men's undergarments, has initiated a new monthly cost report. After attending a total quality management seminar last summer, she realized that she had little understanding of the way her resources were consumed on a day-to-day basis. The seminar stressed the importance of reducing non-value-adding activities, especially the moving and storing of inventories and the cost of quality failure. It also offered suggestions on ways to focus attention on these activities by assigning them a monthly dollar cost. The goal of doing so is to reduce—as much as possible—the time and money spent on non-value-adding activities by either redirecting resource inputs to more-productive uses or by eliminating them entirely.

Alvarez has instructed her three department heads to break down all their monthly costs into one of three strategic cost categories:

1. *Conversion.* Included in the conversion category are only those resources directly consumed in the translation of a department's inputs into its outputs. For instance, conversion costs for receiving and shipping include employee time, floor space, and supplies needed to load and unload incoming and outgoing goods.

2. *Moving and storing.* Included in the moving and storing category are resources used in the internal transport and storage of inventory. For example, the production department uses forklifts to move fabrics from the finishing station to the packaging station, and thus incurs moving and storing costs.

3. *Quality failure.* Included in the quality failure category are resources consumed in order to fix errors and defects. In maintenance, for example, a worker makes an emergency call to correct a machine defect causing excessive fabric damage. Because it is not provided for as part of preventive maintenance, this repair is considered a failure.

The results of these cost recategorizations are presented in Exhibit P13.9.1. The functional accounts, such as salaries & wages or depreciation, have been examined and assigned percentages for each of the three strategic cost categories. Thus, the receiving and shipping department has determined that 45 percent of its employee salaries and wages are incurred on the dock to receive and ship goods. Another 25 percent is used for moving and storing goods, and the remaining 30 percent is used for dealing with quality-failure problems, such as damaged goods. Following this same type of thinking, the department heads have assigned percentages to functional cost categories for their respective departments.

Additional information, presented in Exhibit P13.9.2, summarizes the breakdown of operations costs by strategic cost categories over the past eight months. Alvarez has been pleased with the shift in use of resources over this time. She attributes the program's success to the feedback that the new system provides. She looks forward to receiving results for the latest month, March 1996, and hopes to see that further progress has been made.

Required:

1. Prepare a cost report that distributes costs for March 1996 into the designated strategic cost categories for each department and for operations as a whole. Calculate the percentage breakdown, by strategic cost category.

2. Compare the results obtained in requirement 1 with the results for the last 8 months, as reported in Exhibit P13.9.2. Has progress been made this month?

3. How might this type of approach help a manager redirect the actions of employees?

EXHIBIT P13.9.1 HINNEYWARE CO.

Breakdown of Department Costs into Strategic Cost Categories for the Month of March 1996

| | March Expense | Percent Assignments for Strategic Cost Categories | | | |
		Convert	Move & Store	Quality Failure	Total
Receiving & shipping:					
Salaries & wages	$ 15,000	45%	25%	30%	100%
Depreciation	25,000	0%	90%	10%	100%
Occupancy	5,000	75%	25%	0%	100%
Supplies	12,000	75%	15%	10%	100%
Total receiving & shipping	$ 57,000				
Production:					
Materials	$240,000	98%	0%	2%	100%
Salaries & wages	90,000	50%	25%	25%	100%
Depreciation	160,000	65%	20%	15%	100%
Occupancy	10,000	70%	25%	5%	100%
Supplies	8,000	85%	10%	5%	100%
Total production	$508,000				
Maintenance:					
Salaries & wages	$ 24,000	50%	30%	20%	100%
Depreciation	18,000	30%	40%	30%	100%
Occupancy	2,500	75%	15%	10%	100%
Supplies	4,800	65%	5%	30%	100%
Total maintenance	$ 49,300				
Total production cost	$614,300				

EXHIBIT P13.9.2 HINNEYWARE CO.

Breakdown of Operational Costs into Strategic Categories for the 8 Months Ending February 1996

| | | Percent Breakdown, by Strategic Cost Category | | |
		Convert	Move & Store	Quality Failure
1995	July	58%	24%	18%
	August	61%	25%	14%
	September	63%	26%	11%
	October	65%	23%	12%
	November	64%	20%	16%
	December	66%	22%	12%
1996	January	68%	22%	10%
	February	69%	20%	11%

P13.10 (Preparing Quality Cost Data)

The general manager of your division, which produces textile materials and fibers, has assigned you the task of organizing and reporting changes in the cost of quality. You have decided to use a "bottom-up" approach. That is, you ask individual accounting staff members most familiar with discrete phases of the operation to provide you with detailed information on the past year. The data shown in Exhibit P13.10 represent the results of the accounting staff's efforts. Now it is up to you to examine the quality accounts, assemble them, and then compile a quality cost report.

Admittedly, this is unfamiliar territory for you. Nonetheless, you decide to follow the classification format you have often seen in quality cost publications, in which costs are categorized as (1) prevention, (2) appraisal, and (3) failure, which has (a) an internal and (b) an external component.

Required:

1. What questions might you have about the validity of the data given you by the accounting staff? Specifically, explain how you think dollar amounts were derived for the first three quality accounts—rework, product testing, and waste storage.
2. Prepare a quality cost report showing total cost columns for the three quality cost categories mentioned above. Show which failure costs are internal and which are external. Include a percentage breakdown for each cost category in relation to sales revenue.
3. What suggestions would you offer the plant general manager when you drop off your report? How can this information be helpful, and what additional or future information do you think is needed?

EXHIBIT P13.10 INFORMATION NEEDED TO COMPILE QUALITY COST REPORT

Quality Account	Amount
Rework of defective output	$ 19,450
Product testing during production	6,980
Waste storage	5,380
Customer claims for defective goods	11,340
Preventive maintenance	4,550
Energy management program	8,700
Quality process inspections during production	3,400
Idle time because of machine breakdowns	14,770
Depreciation on quality improvement equipment	6,500
Capital expenditures on quality improvement equip.	31,900
Inspection of incoming materials	9,800
Defective raw materials returned to vendor	1,700
Reliability testing of equipment	1,300
Repairs following machine breakdowns	1,850
Follow-up calls to clarify customer-order specs	6,420
Sales-effectiveness staff training	3,200
Total expense	$137,240
Sales revenue	$527,846

P13.11   (Interpreting Quality Cost Data)

It was with great fanfare that, 18 months ago, The Unified State Bank initiated a total quality management program. The central focus of the program was the bank's tellers, because, as the bank's president explained:

> These are the folks that handle 90 percent of the bank's daily transactions. Our customers know us through our tellers. We can only succeed if our front-line people are committed to gaining the full satisfaction of every customer on every transaction. The bank's quality program is designed to ensure that this will happen.

By conducting surveys of its customers, the bank identified several elements considered crucial to increasing the tellers' effectiveness. Most important on the list was the need for short waiting lines. Also on the list of requirements was speedy and accurate service. Another expectation was that tellers conduct business in a friendly and courteous manner.

The TQM program included several features. First was a series of ongoing seminars intended to make every bank teller a disciple of TQM principles. Data was to be gathered on a regular basis in order to monitor customer waiting time and to track customer satisfaction. Employee seminars could then be held at which this information could be shared, allowing all employees to use it as a means for improvement. Tellers were expected to become expert at solving problems—as these arose—and the program took great pains to make sure that tellers were empowered to make on-the-spot decisions. The program seemed to work. Tellers changed their work schedules in order to provide more coverage at the busiest times of the week, thereby minimizing customer waiting time. They also initiated preventive maintenance on equipment at each teller window and instituted special recognition awards to reward their colleagues for work well done.

Now, after 18 months have passed, the president would like some reassurance that the time and money spent on the TQM program are paying off. Throughout the program period, the accounting staff has collected and reported the bank's quarterly costs of quality. As seen in Exhibit P13.11, these data break costs down into four categories: (1) prevention, (2) appraisal, (3) internal failure, and (4) external failure. (The failure category's two components are given separately here.) The bank president has remarked, however, that it seems to him that the cost of quality has not really changed that much. He also points out that he has had some doubts about the precision of the quality cost data, since no information is given on changes in lost sales. He goes on to say that, although preventing customers from changing banks was the main reason he supported the TQM program, the cost report does not say anything about the program's effect on sales revenue. Sales revenue has, in fact, increased, but many other factors, such as economic growth or lower lending rates, could have contributed to the change.

Required:

1. Prepare a graph showing trends of the four quality cost categories over the past six quarters. Calculate the quality-cost-to-sales-revenue ratios for this same time period.
2. Evaluate the progress to date of the TQM program. Does it seem to be paying off?
3. Respond to the president's comments about effects of excluding sales revenue from the quality cost report.

EXHIBIT P13.11 THE UNIFIED STATE BANK

Quarterly Cost of Quality Data for the Past Six Quarters (in $ thousands)

	Quarter					
	1	2	3	4	5	6
Prevention cost:						
Preventive machine maintenance	$ 1,200	$ 970	$ 1,440	$ 1,230	$ 1,860	$ 1,560
TQM seminars	2,600	2,480	3,440	3,280	4,580	5,960
Quality recognition awards	900	1,400	800	1,300	2,100	2,900
Total prevention cost	$ 4,700	$ 4,850	$ 5,680	$ 5,810	$ 8,540	$ 10,420
Appraisal cost:						
Monitoring customer queues	$ 1,170	$ 1,460	$ 1,740	$ 1,590	$ 1,920	$ 2,460
Surveying customer satisfaction	3,510	3,900	4,690	4,360	4,260	4,270
Total	$ 4,680	$ 5,360	$ 6,430	$ 5,950	$ 6,180	$ 6,730
Internal-failure cost:						
Correcting process errors	8,640	9,350	7,450	6,350	5,460	4,800
External-failure cost:						
Handling customer complaints	6,750	7,290	7,200	6,130	4,320	3,940
Total cost of quality	$ 24,770	$ 26,850	$ 26,760	$ 24,240	$ 24,500	$ 25,890
Sales revenue	$191,133	$179,335	$188,300	$206,088	$220,358	$242,945

P13.12 (Examining Trends in Quality Spending; Budget Justification)

Since late 1992 Barbara Richfield has held the position of head quality manager at Black Top Equipment Co., which manufactures products for road construction and maintenance. During her first 3 years on the job, Richfield guided Black Top through a major corporate culture readjustment geared toward implementing total quality management. As verified by the data shown in Exhibit P13.12.1, the results were impressive. During the 1993–1995 time period, the company actually reduced its spending on quality, while increasing sales revenue—this at a time when the road construction and maintenance industry was beset by economic cutbacks. Yet it also enhanced the firm's quality image, which went from being among the lowest to being the very best in the industry.

Black Top's quality results were achieved by shifting its priorities from failure correction to failure prevention and quality appraisal. Richfield is seen as a relentless crusader who has instilled in each employee an understanding that the customer comes first and that the best way to meet customer needs is to do the

EXHIBIT P13.12.1 BLACK TOP EQUIPMENT CO.

Trend in Quality Spending (in $ thousands)

Year	Prevention	Appraisal	Failure		Total Quality Cost	Sales Revenue
			Internal	External		
1993	$7,500	$9,700	$15,400	$12,600	$45,200	$210,100
1994	$10,800	$11,400	$11,400	$7,500	$41,100	$228,000
1995	$14,600	$12,100	$9,400	$4,300	$40,400	$243,700

job right the first time. Black Top's employees and its suppliers have been actively involved in ongoing training and seminars that reinforce these basic tenets of the quality philosophy.

Despite Richfield's accomplishments, the quality programs she initiated are now being threatened. When Black Top brought in a new president from the outside in January 1996, the quality improvement campaign lost its support from senior management. The new president disregarded the budget originally approved for the year and directed spending away from training and inspection (Exhibit P13.12.2). The latest estimates for 1996 show that the original quality cost budget will be underspent by $4,670, a 12.6 percent decrease. When Richfield and the CEO met recently to discuss these results, the president was emphatic in his desire to cut costs and improve profits. He said the spending on continuous quality training and inspections was a luxury the firm could no longer afford. To put it simply, the president said, "We all need to trim our sails, Richfield, and you're not exempt. The key is to meet the expectations of our shareholders. They have to come first."

Now, however, as Richfield prepares her budget for 1997, she knows the problem she faces. Given the new direction of the firm, employees are being pressed to get the finished product "out the door." It is evident to Richfield that this is a path to disaster, despite the favorable quality cost variances reported for 1996. The

EXHIBIT P13.12.2 BLACK TOP EQUIPMENT CO.

Quality Cost Spending in 1996 (in $ thousands)

	Budget	Latest Estimate of Actual Cost
1. Prevention:		
Quality training	$ 7,425	$ 3,050
Seminars with suppliers	3,300	2,100
Process improvement project	4,125	0
Audits of quality effectiveness	1,650	1,200
Total prevention expense	$ 16,500	$ 6,350
2. Appraisal		
In-process inspections	$ 3,150	$ 3,300
Field inspections at customer sites	5,250	2,200
Depreciation of test equipment	2,100	2,100
Total appraisal expense	$ 10,500	$ 7,600
3. Failure		
Internal:		
Scrap	$ 3,195	$ 3,800
Rework	1,775	2,450
Downtime	2,130	3,140
Total internal failure expense	$ 7,100	$ 9,390
External:		
Responding to after-sale problems	$ 1,450	$ 3,690
Warranty repairs	1,450	5,300
Total external failure expense	$ 2,900	$ 8,990
Total quality cost budget	$ 37,000	$ 32,330
Sales revenue	$266,300	$263,500

cost to fix problems brought on by poor product conformance grew considerably last year. Richfield is determined to try once more to show the president that quality spending does pay, and the 1997 budget request is the place to start.

Required:

1. Prepare graphs to report trends on the following relationships for the 4-year period from 1993 through 1996 (use the latest estimates for 1996):
   a. Quality cost components
   b. Quality-cost-to-sales ratio
2. Discuss the results shown in the two graphs you prepared for requirement 1. Why has the quality-cost-to-sales ratio fallen in 1996? What are the implications of the information in the quality-cost components graph?
3. What arguments can Richfield make in support of an expanded quality budget for 1997? Do you think she will be successful?

CASES

C13.1 (United Electric Corp.—Power Generating Division)[3]

The power generating division is one of five business units that constitute United Electric Corporation. The power generating division is headquartered in Gainesville, Georgia, and employs approximately 2,000 people worldwide. The division has five manufacturing plants in the eastern United States and Canada. The division manufactures industrial turbines and jet engines, and it provides a variety of operating-plant services. Sales for the unit increased 35 percent in 1995 and are expected to increase steadily through the year 2000.

Total Quality Commitment

After experiencing a rash of product quality problems in the 1980s, the power generating division began a continuous-improvement program in 1988. Total quality is now recognized as one of three primary strategic goals of the division, yet each year the focus on total quality is modified in order to meet changing needs. The aim for 1996 is to implement a "total quality approach," in order to achieve the results diagrammed in Exhibit C13.1.1. The keys to success are (1) to ensure that the division employs systematic processes for interpreting customer needs, (2) to ensure a commitment by all employees to meet these needs at every phase of a project, and (3) to deliver a product that satisfies customer expectations.

The commitment to quality is implemented through a multiphase plan that is based on broad participation by employees. As outlined in Exhibit C13.1.1, strategies are identified by *total quality councils*, which are also charged with implementing and monitoring improvement plans. Six success measures have been identified; these are distributed to functional teams comprising employees that have production responsibilities. The teams are expected to translate the six success measures into lower-level measures tied to specific strategies. These lower-level measures must reflect the activities most critical for achieving day-to-day operational success.

In addition to the measurement system, employees are immersed in quality training and quality philosophy. A "Quality Week" is held once a year, at which time the importance of quality and management's commitment to it are emphasized. Every employee is involved in training seminars individually and as a member of a team, both during Quality Week and throughout the year. During Quality

---

[3] Prepared with the assistance of Kelly Newman and Amy Tonnessen.

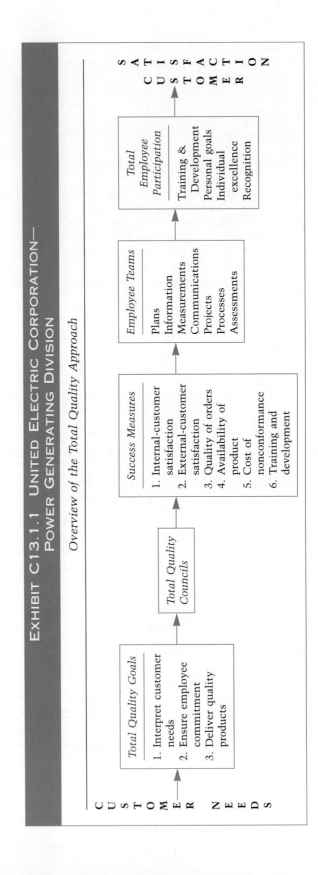

EXHIBIT C13.1.1   UNITED ELECTRIC CORPORATION—POWER GENERATING DIVISION

Overview of the Total Quality Approach

Week, employees are expected to fill out a goal card on which they describe their personal targets for the coming year and to devise a schedule for implementing these targets. Goals must address the six success measures. During the year, employees or teams are nominated for Total Quality Awards in recognition of exceptional performance in the key success measures. Nominated employees receive desk plaques and lapel pins, and are eligible for special recognition awards presented during Quality Week.

Internal-Customer Satisfaction

Internal-customer satisfaction (ICS) became one of the division's six success measures because of a close union vote at the Ashville plant in 1994. Reorganization of manufacturing facilities—including shutdown of the plant—resulted in new job functions for 80 percent of the shop employees. Management felt that the focus needed to be changed from tasks to people. Plant management was changed, and the ICS committee was formed, with the mandate of creating a more cooperative work environment.

An ICS program was initiated in order to achieve three goals: (1) to increase employee involvement, (2) to decrease the employee turnover rate, and (3) to create a focus on quality issues at the lowest level of the organization. Employees were expected to help identify important measures that signal the extent to which local departments serve the needs of other departments within the division. Because this was a new measurement area, one primary expectation of the ICS program was continued improvement in identifying key activities and in measuring results. In 1995, the ICS committee began a series of half-day workshops that all employees were required to attend. Rank-and-file employees attended workshops taught by members of their own departments, so that courses could be tailored to address local key issues.

The ICS committee developed 16 measures in order to address key issues. Most issues centered on the timeliness of interplant shipments and quality of orders administered. Responsibility for achieving outcomes was assigned to specific managers, and target performance measures were developed and agreed upon by local teams. These measures were to be summarized in index form and reviewed monthly by the staff of the division's general manager. The use of customer satisfaction surveys was also encouraged, although the surveys have thus far been used only by service units, such as the cafeteria, word processing, and human resources.

Central Problem

Although much thought and preparation went into the ICS program, follow-up has been haphazard. Actual measures data have been published only once, late in February 1996, and these consisted of the monthly results for December 1995 (Exhibit C13.1.2). Employee response to the ICS workshops has been mixed and is often characterized by ambivalence. Workshops have been designed around the Golden Rule—that is, employees are encouraged to respond to other employees' work needs as they would like to see others respond to *their* needs. Exercises conducted during the workshops are intended to make employees think personally about giving or receiving poor service. No effort has been made to give employees an understanding of the interconnectedness of departments' operations.

Employees generally agree that internal-customer satisfaction is a good idea, but they are busy meeting their own job-task targets and are less concerned about going out of their way to help someone else. While senior management appears to be committed to the quality process and places great emphasis on ICS, employees get mixed messages from their superiors. The department managers must submit team reports on ICS measures monthly. However, as noted above, top management

EXHIBIT C13.1.2 UNITED ELECTRIC CORPORATION— POWER GENERATING DIVISION

Internal Customer Satisfaction—December 1995
Team Reports

Team No.	Team Name	Team Leader	Measurements	Target	Current Month Total	Satisfaction Rating[a]
4	Contract requirements	A. P. Balao	Timeliness of order administration	100%	84%	1
			Timeliness of sourcing	100%	93%	1
10	Engineering requirements	R. Northwill	Design request turn-around time in days	2.0	1.8	5
			Percent of change orders delivered by promised date	90%	98%	5
			Percent of change orders delivered by required date	80%	79%	3
11	Purchased materials	S. Elder	On-time delivery to original promised date	92%	90%	3
			On-time delivery to required date	75%	66%	1
			Supplier quality performance	85%	85%	3

[a] The meanings of the ratings are as follows:
5 = exceeds target by 5 percent (or meets target of 100%); 3 = meets target within ±5 percent; 1 = falls below 5 percent of target.

has published only one report so far and offered no comment. Employees are further discouraged by a lack of follow-up on the individual quality goals submitted during Quality Week for the current year. Progress reports on achieving these goals are seldom updated, and the goals are not reviewed at all by immediate superiors.

Required:

1. Compare the three sets of team measures for internal-customer satisfaction shown in Exhibit C13.1.2. Which of the three teams seems to be doing the best? Does it seem that standards across departments are equally difficult to achieve?
2. Given the problems with the ICS system, what suggestions can you offer to improve implementation of the measurements system? How can senior management ensure employee commitment to the ICS system?
3. Refer to Exhibit C13.1.3, which shows newly reported monthly data for the engineering requirements team. What additional insights about the team's ICS performance can you gain from this exhibit? What improvements to the measurement system can you suggest?

EXHIBIT C13.1.3 UNITED ELECTRIC CORPORATION— POWER GENERATING DIVISION

Team 10 (Engineering Requirements)— Performance Report for the 6 Months Ending June 30, 1996

		1996					
	Target	January	February	March	April	May	June
Design request turnaround time, in days	2.00	1.78	1.93	2.03	1.98	1.84	1.96
Percent of change orders delivered by promised date	90%	92%	89%	99%	94%	95%	91%
Percent of change orders delivered by required date	80%	87%	81%	78%	80%	77%	75%

C13.2 (Tri-State Office Supply Co.)

Lawrence "Mr. Money" Monroe, president of Tri-State Office Supply Co., is fuming. He has just received comparative income statements for 1996 (Exhibit C13.2.1). He cannot understand how his company increased its sales revenues by more than $500,000—or about 12 percent—only to see operating profits fall by some $15,000. He has called in his chief financial officer, Peggy Robbins, who now finds herself on the receiving end of a tirade. Unfortunately, she is hard-pressed to explain what has happened. She can only say, "The sales mix has shifted somewhat from the more-lucrative commercial market to government and institutions, where gross margins tend to run a bit lower." At this point, though, she notices that the veins on Monroe's forehead look as if they are beginning to pop, and he is turning purple. She decides it is time for a quick departure. She mentions something about more-detailed data and promptly excuses herself.

Background Information

Tri-State Office Supply is a small, but growing, wholesale distributor of all types of office supplies—including photocopier paper, computer supplies, pens, pencils, paper clips, adhesives, stationery, and envelopes. The firm is 6 years old and is located near Harper's Ferry, West Virginia, where it runs a storage warehouse and distribution facility that services West Virginia, Virginia, and Maryland. Tri-State has enjoyed substantial sales growth, which has largely been fueled by the area's booming development. It is well-positioned to meet the demands of anticipated growth.

Beginning last year (1995), Monroe had requested more information on the breakdown of company sales. Robbins responded by breaking out sales into two market segments—government and institutions, and commercial. This information has proved helpful in disclosing market differences in sales discounts and gross margin percentages. Despite the lower returns in the government and institutional markets, however, the firm has continued to pursue sales in these markets because of their high-volume advantages. The average dollar sale per government or institutional order is generally much larger than that seen in the commercial market. And, as Monroe and Robbins reason, sales in the first segment are likely to generate a greater return because they require less freight, handling, customer service, and the like. Unfortunately, the firm's income statements do not provide any information on use of resources per market segment, so it is not clear whether these higher returns are being realized.

EXHIBIT C13.2.1 TRI-STATE OFFICE SUPPLY CO.

Comparative Income Statements

| | Fiscal Year Ending December 31, 1995 | | | | Fiscal Year Ending December 31, 1996 | | | |
	Government & Institutional	Commercial	Total		Government & Institutional	Commercial	Total	
Sales revenue	$1,389,050	$3,245,200	$4,634,250	101.7%	$1,712,664	$3,477,226	$5,189,890	102.0%
Sales discounts	20,141	60,036	80,177	1.7%	26,572	75,565	102,137	2.0%
Net revenue	$1,368,909	$3,185,164	$4,554,073	100.0%	$1,686,091	$3,401,662	$5,087,753	100.0%
Cost of sales	972,335	2,158,058	3,130,393	68.7%	1,216,230	2,293,414	3,509,644	69.0%
Gross margin	$ 396,574	$1,027,106	$1,423,680	31.3%	$ 469,862	$1,108,247	$1,578,109	31.0%
Gross margin percent	29%	32.2%			27.9%	32.6%		
Operating expense:								
Freight & handling			$ 185,390	4.1%			$ 196,590	3.9%
Warehousing			431,651	9.5%			451,600	8.9%
Customer service			81,973	1.8%			143,270	2.8%
Commissions			55,143	1.2%			78,124	1.5%
Advertising & promotion			209,487	4.6%			240,036	4.7%
Other sales & administration			136,622	3.0%			160,024	3.1%
Total expense			$1,100,267	24.2%			$1,269,644	25.0%
Operating profit			$ 323,413	7.1%			$ 308,464	6.1%

Redesigning the Income Statement

Based on an article about strategic costing that she recently saw in a management publication, Robbins decides that the firm's income statement should be completely revamped. As she understands it, a more strategic financial report would disclose how the firm's resources were being consumed differently by different customer segments. The place to begin is with a reexamination of the breakdown of sales revenue. Although the government and institutions segment sales differ greatly (qualitatively) from commercial sales, there can be differences between customer types *within* each of the present market groupings. Robbins prepares information, shown in Exhibit C13.2.2, that creates more-detailed distinctions: government is separated from institutions, and, in the commercial market, distributors are separated from retailers. Although she knew that sales discounts and costs of sales would differ between these markets, she had not before realized just how much variance there was between customers. In fact, she was surprised to see that the cost-of-sales ratio for government agencies ran 7.5 percent higher than the same ratio for commercial retailers.

The next task was to figure out how costs were related to the four customer types. First, she looked at the costs that were directly linked to each customer. The most obvious connection was with commissions, which were paid to salespersons as a percent of net sales revenue (after all discounts). Robbins was well-aware that Monroe paid at different rates, depending on the type of customer sales he was trying to motivate. She further realized that advertising and promotion expense was actually composed of three different types of activities—co-op advertising, sales promotion, and catalog expense—each of which could be directly related back to customers. The only other expense that seemed direct was bid preparation for government agencies and for institutions, which together accounted for 20 percent of the total cost incurred for other sales and administration. Details on these and all other operating expenses are provided in Exhibit C13.2.3.

Next, she decided to employ activity-based costing methods in order to identify the most-appropriate drivers of other expenses shown on the income statement. In many cases, she had to approximate the amount of resources consumed. For example, the freight and handling activity was evaluated based on the number of freight-tons distributed to each of the four customer classes, and warehousing expense was assigned based on the approximate cubic footage of warehouse space used to support each customer. She found that both of these expenses tended to be rather closely related to the approximate mix of dollar sales, by customer—although some variation was evident. Institutions, for example, accounted for 13 percent of sales revenue, but they tended to use proportionately more resources overall: 19 percent of freight and handling and 18 percent of warehousing.

EXHIBIT C13.2.2 TRI-STATE OFFICE SUPPLY CO.

Breakdown of Sales Revenue for 1996

	Government & Institutional		Commercial		
	Government	Institutional	Distributors	Retailers	Total
Sales revenue	$1,037,978	$674,686	$1,972,158	$1,505,068	$5,189,890
Percent breakdown on gross sales	20.0%	13.0%	38.0%	29.0%	
Sales discounts	1.0%	2.4%	2.0%	2.4%	
Cost of sales (on net revenue)	73.5%	70.0%	68.5%	66.0%	

EXHIBIT C13.2.3 TRI-STATE OFFICE SUPPLY CO.

Breakdown of Expenses by Type of Customer

	Cost Driver or Allocation Base	Government & Institutional		Commercial		
		Gov't.	Institutional	Distributors	Retailers	Total
Freight & handling	Tons shipped	15%	19%	42%	24%	$196,590
Warehousing	Cubic feet	20%	18%	38%	24%	$451,600
Customer service	No. of orders	6%	20%	29%	45%	$143,270
Commissions	% of net sales $	0%	3%	1.5%	2%	$78,124
Advertising & promotion:						
Co-op advertising	Cost incurred	0%	0%	68%	32%	$ 45,607
Sales promotion	Cost incurred	0%	12%	54%	34%	122,418
Catalog expense	Cost incurred	10%	20%	35%	35%	72,011
Total advertising & promotion						$240,036
Other sales & administration:						
Bid preparation	Cost incurred	60%	40%	0%	0%	$ 32,005
Order taking	No. of orders	6%	20%	29%	45%	80,012
General administration	Sales revenue	20%	13%	38%	29%	48,007
Total sales & administration						$160,024

One of the areas where costs had grown the most over the past year was customer service, which Monroe had purposely increased in order to meet the firm's commitment to total customer satisfaction. As Robbins began to look for connections between sales revenue and customer service, she decided the best measure at this time was the number of orders processed. In her discussions with customer representatives, she was told that the amount of work was closely related to orders processed, regardless of the number of items within each order. Based on this information, she found that the amount of service given a customer differed from the amount of customer sales revenue generated. Government, for example, generated 20 percent of sales revenue but only accounted for about 6 percent of customer service. On the other hand, retailers represented 29 percent of sales but were linked to 45 percent of service.

The only other costs that needed to be assigned were order taking and general administration, both of which were included in the income statement as part of Other Sales and Administration. Order-taking costs could easily be assigned to customers by using the number of orders processed as the basis. General administration, however, would have to be rather arbitrarily assigned, on the basis of the (gross) sales dollars generated by each customer.

Strategic Choices
Having gone through this information-gathering exercise, Robbins knew that the most-difficult part was yet to come. The information would have to be put together in an income statement that would yield new insights on the company's downturn in income. Once Monroe calmed down, he would want some specific explanations of what went wrong last year. Robbins hoped the new statement would help them understand the relationships between their markets and costs. Most importantly, she needed to come up with some suggestions on how they might do things differently next year in order to avoid this same occurrence.

Required:

1. Prepare an income statement broken down by the firm's four types of customers. Show the direct profit and operating income for each.
2. What conclusions can you draw from the new income statement? What caused the downturn in income in 1996?
3. What changes in strategy should Tri-State Office Supply consider? How would you expect the consumption of resources to differ if your suggestions were implemented?

Sh. Term what happens to if we quit selling to institutions.

Long Term → (we are dropping all segment of our market
   → ? implication)

           where to concentrate?

What is unique about I sales.

who are you as a supplier on the market. who do we wanna be

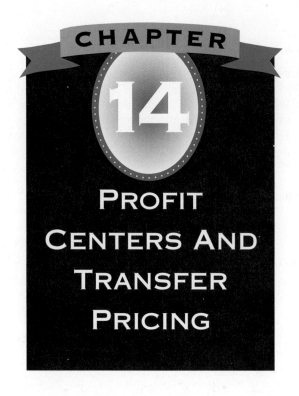

CHAPTER 14

PROFIT CENTERS AND TRANSFER PRICING

The idea of shifting business-level decision authority—along with responsibility for attaining business profit targets—down to lower organizational levels is called *decentralization.* The idea has been popular since the end of World War II. It has, however, grown in importance recently because of the increase in global competition and advancements in information technology. Decentralized structures are designed to give lower-level managers the freedom to make their own business decisions, to implement changes without corporate interference, and thus to respond quickly to changes in the business environment. A lower-level responsibility center that has been given business-level decision-making authority is generally called a *profit center* since the subunit manager decides how best to generate revenue and incur expense.

Profit centers within a corporation often depend on each other for support and for resources. For example, a computer hardware unit might rely on the microchip unit to supply its products' internal components, on the transportation subunit to deliver its products, and on the corporate legal subunit to defend it against a patent infringement charge. Questions immediately arise about how each unit or subunit should be "paid" for its products or services, and how its performance should be measured. The answers can be critical to the operation of both the profit centers and the overall organization.

A common answer to the first of these questions is that each subunit should pay an internal (fictitious) transfer price for using another subunit's goods or services. Each seller thus generates revenue by selling its goods or services to other subunits and is evaluated strictly on the basis of its own profitability. Transfer prices let each manager buy, sell, and price internally as if doing so in the free market.

In this chapter, we examine issues that arise in designing an accounting information system for use by profit centers. The primary control objective, as always, is to ensure that managers and their employees act so as to promote the goals of the firm. We begin with a short discussion of the pros and cons of decentralization. Then we look at some performance measures that are applied to profit centers and the effects they can have on managers' motivation. Finally, we examine transfer prices and the methods that are used to set them.

PROFIT CENTERS AND DECENTRALIZATION

The degree to which an organization is decentralized indicates the extent to which decision authority has been shifted down to lower operating levels. The more decentralized the organization, the further down the decision-making authority extends in the corporate structure. In a highly centralized organization (with little or no decentralization), all decisions are made at the upper levels. In a highly decentralized organization, managers at even the lowest levels decide how to achieve their objectives.

A firm's organizational structure (first discussed in Chapter 9) reflects the degree to which it is decentralized (see Exhibit 14.1). In organizations using a function-based structure, where responsibility for such functions as marketing, manufacturing, research, and finance is assigned separately to managers of the respective functional areas, senior managers at the corporate level decide on resource trade-offs between activities. In such centralized firms, the managers of functional subunits (which may be set up as revenue centers or as cost centers) are expected to meet budget targets but are held responsible for only a part of the profit equation. In more-decentralized firms, with either divisional or matrix structures, managers are held responsible for profits. The right-hand side of the lower panel of the exhibit identifies which decentralized responsibility centers are profit centers (where managers are responsible for profit outcomes) and which are investment centers (where managers' responsibility extends to both profit and investment outcomes, or ROI). The focus of this chapter is on profit centers, while the focus of the next, Chapter 15, is on investment centers.

Ideally, in a decentralized structure, a profit center manager should be given authority to decide *what to make and how to make it* and should control decisions concerning both revenue and cost. Profit centers can, however, differ considerably in type, size, form, and degree of autonomy. Large, independent subunits are commonly called *divisions* or *strategic business units* (SBUs). These sovereign units generally are responsible for manufacturing, marketing, and distributing one or more complete product lines. For example, General Motors Corporation includes the independently run Saturn division. As a rule, other, smaller profit centers—sometimes called *business units*—concentrate primarily on marketing and distributing the products and services of other subunits. In the matrix structure shown in the exhibit, each project is a business unit which draws its personnel from the functional departments—marketing, production, and finance. Each unit is responsible for its project's profitability. Still other profit centers may be set up—as, say, a print shop or a vehicle maintenance center—to provide particular services. Some may actually be

EXHIBIT 14.1 TYPES OF ORGANIZATIONAL STRUCTURES

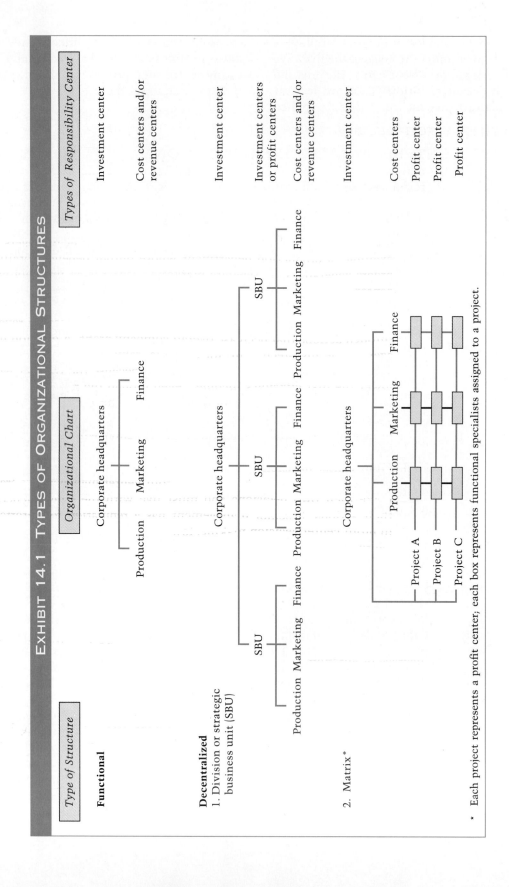

Type of Structure	Organizational Chart	Types of Responsibility Center
Functional		Investment center
		Cost centers and/or revenue centers
Decentralized 1. Division or strategic business unit (SBU)		Investment center
		Investment centers or profit centers
		Cost centers and/or revenue centers
2. Matrix*		Investment center
		Cost centers
		Profit center
		Profit center
		Profit center

* Each project represents a profit center; each box represents functional specialists assigned to a project.

nothing more than cost centers, as are most production plants that work only for other subunits of the firm. Senior management can convert cost centers into profit centers simply by instituting a transfer-price policy for intracompany transactions.

CONDITIONS FOR DECENTRALIZING INTO PROFIT CENTERS

To be successful, profit centers have to operate in an environment that allows their managers to *influence actions* so as to achieve the profit center objectives. Ideally, these conditions should be met:

1. *Profit centers should be independent*. A profit center's manager is in the best position to influence actions when his or her decisions are not contingent on those of other responsibility center managers. For example, a production department whose output depends totally on orders generated by a separate marketing center is an unlikely profit center.
2. *Profit center goals should be congruent with corporate goals*. More specifically, a profit center should not be able to increase its revenue through actions that decrease overall company profit. A division manager at one high-tech firm, for example, refused to transfer a newly developed microchip to another division, because the transfer would lower the first division's income—even though the resulting product would have dominated a new market for the consumer product. There must be decentralization guidelines and operating guidelines to ensure that actions benefiting a profit center will also benefit the corporation.
3. *Profit center decisions should be free of corporate interference*. One premise of decentralization is that profit center managers are free to make their own decisions and must live with the consequences of their actions. If senior management has a reputation for interfering in profit center decision making, lower-level managers will view their "autonomy" with skepticism.

BENEFITS AND COSTS OF DECENTRALIZING

Unfortunately, it is virtually impossible to satisfy all three of these requirements for effective decentralization. As a result, top management must consider the trade-offs between the costs and benefits of various degrees of autonomy when deciding how much authority should be given to profit center managers. (See "Current Practice: Decentralizing IBM.")

BENEFITS

By creating profit centers, senior management attempts to bring lower-level managers more directly into the competitive environment in which the firm exists. The benefits of doing so are the same as those that arise from any free market where individual businesspeople must generate profits in order to survive. The most important of these benefits are as follows:

CURRENT PRACTICE

Decentralizing IBM

In 1988 IBM began decentralizing its corporate structure in order to combat a slow-moving bureaucracy that had caused it to lose touch with customers. Specifically, the giant computer firm had continued to concentrate on mainframe computers when the market was shifting to desktops, to emphasize hardware even as software was growing in importance, and to produce proprietary software when the trend was toward compatible software.

IBM was reorganized into thirteen autonomous profit centers. Nine business units were organized around products, such as personal systems and storage devices; each of these units could control manufacturing and set prices. The other four business units were organized as regional marketing and service operations for geographic areas—such as North America and Asia Pacific. Their mission was to buy goods from the nine producer units and then resell them to earn a profit.

Reaction to the decentralization by those inside and outside the firm is mixed. On the upside, the head of IBM North America has said: "This [restruc-turing] has unleashed an unbelievable amount of energy and creativity like I've never seen before. It's exciting. It leaves me breathless." An investment manager with a large IBM portfolio commented that the firm might be able to accelerate its revenue growth if all divisions can sell whatever products they like. Others expect greater cost-efficiencies and market responsiveness, which had often been difficult to attain in the past because of the layers of approval through which new ideas had to be filtered.

However, the potential downside of such a massive organizational change is still largely unknown. What, for example, will be the long-term effects of product overlap? The personal systems business manager asserted: "I'm going to make whatever is competitive in the industry, period." Those are challenging words to a corporation whose primary product, mainframe computers, can now be "cannibalized" by business units that sell workstations and networks. Profit margins may, in fact, begin to slide as competition between divisions accelerates.

Source: Adapted from David Kirkpatrick, "Breaking Up IBM," *Fortune,* July 27, 1992, pp. 44–58; and Paul B. Carroll, "IBM Announces Details of Plan to Break Its Business into More Autonomous Pieces," *The Wall Street Journal,* Dec. 16, 1991, p. B3.

- *Better information and more timely response.* Managers at local sites are in a better position to understand customers, employees, suppliers, and the regulatory environment. They are also in a position to respond quickly to changes in the business environment.
- *More entrepreneurial spirit.* Profit center managers make their own decisions and are held accountable for their own results—a connection that encourages entrepreneurial thinking. A manager who is free and accountable, and is rewarded for favorable outcomes, is likely to be better motivated.

- *Better focused and trained corporate managers.* Because decentralized systems empower local or lower-level managers, top-level corporate managers are freed from the demands of many detailed oversight tasks. They can concentrate on corporate goals and objectives, while leaving business and functional strategies to those at lower levels. Also, profit centers serve as useful training grounds for future corporate-level managers.
- *Better decision making.* The essence of decentralization is the belief that it will enable better decision making. This is expected to be a natural outcome of the benefits listed above.

COSTS

Decentralization brings with it the possibility of dysfunctional behavior and additional costs, including the following:

- *Misplaced loyalties.* Managers who are concentrating on their own profit center's performance do not always consider the effects of their decisions on others within the corporation. When profit centers are highly interdependent, gains by one subunit can mean greater losses by another. This is often a sign of dysfunctional corporate performance.
- *Less corporate control.* Surrendering decision authority to profit centers means having less control over decisions that may affect other responsibility centers or the corporation as a whole. When such decisions are dysfunctional because of a lack of information at lower levels, they can only be rectified through intervention by corporate-level managers. Such intervention, however, undermines the goals and structure of the decentralization.
- *Unnecessary duplication.* With decentralization often comes the need to create division-level administrative support services that already exist at the corporate level. As a result, these *back-office functions*—such as payroll processing, computer services, and product distribution—are frequently duplicated throughout the firm, thus eroding some economies of scale.

WHEN TO DECENTRALIZE

The key rule governing the decentralization decision is that *organizational structure should follow corporate strategy*—the game plan for accomplishing the firm's goals.[1] Top management's strategy must address such fundamentals as the firm's lines of business, resource commitments, target markets, and geographic locations. (See "Current Practice: Moving SBU Headquarters Abroad.") The firm's structure is then the organizational design through which this plan—that is, the strategy—will be administered.

---

[1]   See the classic management treatise on organizational structure: Alfred D. Chandler, Jr., *Strategy and Structure*, Cambridge, Mass.: MIT Press, 1962, especially pp. 13–16.

CURRENT PRACTICE

Moving SBU Headquarters Abroad

Decentralized multinational companies are finding that senior managers of business units must be located close to their units' centers of operations. Only thus can managers relate to key customers and understand fast-changing markets. Many large companies are now transferring the headquarters of major business units abroad. In 1992, for example, Du Pont moved its worldwide electronics business from the United States to Tokyo, Japan, AT&T moved its corded phone unit from the United States to France, and Hyundai moved its personal computers division from South Korea to the United States.

Source: Joann S. Lublin, "Firms Ship Unit Headquarters Abroad," *The Wall Street Journal,* Dec. 9, 1992, p. B1.

If the firm has a single mission—that is, if it operates only one business and sells to a homogeneous market—then a functional, centralized form is suitable. Responsibilities delegated along functional lines such as marketing and production will best support the central mission of the firm. However, if the firm expands its mission by adding business lines, a decentralized structure becomes more appropriate for dealing with the added complexity of product selection, production, and delivery. If the firm competes in multiple markets or deals in multiple lines of business, a divisional or matrix form is probably best.

HOW MUCH TO DECENTRALIZE

It is important to realize that decentralization is not an all-or-nothing proposition. Firms of the same general size may have hundreds of profit centers or only a handful. A firm may decentralize to any degree that best suits its corporate strategy. Moreover, there is no single way to determine the correct number of profit centers for a given firm. Some subunits seem to be natural candidates for profit centers—for example, a subunit whose manager controls virtually all phases of production, marketing, and resource procurement. Sometimes, designation as a profit center is desirable for creating a more entrepreneurial spirit even though the subunit's manager has only limited decision authority over one or more of these functions. This would be the case for a sales distribution profit center that sells goods produced by other subunits, for example. In general, having more profit centers is often a result of top management's desire to become more decentralized.

You should also realize that all firms—even highly decentralized ones—are organized functionally within each profit center. In other words, each profit center likely will have its own cost centers for activities such as marketing and production.

MEASURING A PROFIT CENTER'S PROFIT

One important advantage of a decentralized structure is that performance can be evaluated by looking at each business unit's bottom line. Senior management can influence the actions of profit center managers by defining what components will be included in this bottom line and by specifying how they will be measured. Although we may call this "bottom line" the profit center's *profit*, it may actually be defined differently from the standard corporate profit. It should—perhaps, most importantly—be a reasonable measure of the performance of the profit center and its manager.

REVENUES AND EXPENSES

Profit center revenues include revenue from two sources: from customers external to the firm and from other (internal) corporate subunits. No problems are involved in assigning to profit centers revenues that are generated from external customers. The measurement of revenues when business units sell to each other can, however, lead to problems. These problems are resolved using transfer pricing, to be discussed shortly.

Two expense issues are important in choosing an appropriate measure of a profit center's operating performance:

1. *The measure should reflect the manager's ability to influence the results.*[2] Undoubtedly, any expense that is controllable by the manager should be included in determining the profit. The difficulty enters in deciding whether to include expenses over which a manager may exercise some influence but may not in fact have complete control. From a motivational standpoint, the manager must view the profit measure as being a fair indicator of performance; consequently, it should exclude charges initiated by other business units or by corporate officers.

2. *The performance measure sends a powerful message about the degree to which profit center managers should utilize certain resources.*[3] The method by which internal charges are levied will determine the extent to which corporate resources are used. If, for example, corporate management wants profit center managers to be mindful of the cost-benefit trade-offs for central services—such as legal services or employee training—it charges managers according to their use of these services. If, on the other hand, corporate management sees the use of such services as beneficial and wants them used extensively, it can lower or even eliminate the internal charge for these services.

---

[2] John Dearden, "Measuring Profit Center Managers," *Harvard Business Review*, Sept.–Oct. 1987, pp. 85–87.

[3] Richard F. Vancil, *Decentralization: Managerial Ambiguity by Design*, Homewood, Ill.: Dow Jones-Irwin, 1979, chap. 5.

TYPES OF PROFIT MEASURES

Exhibit 14.2 shows four types of profit-center profit, as well as four methods of measuring them—one for each type. The profit types are discussed below.

Controllable Profit. Controllable profit is a profit measure that begins with sales revenue (as do all four profit types) and takes into account the use of controllable variable expenses plus those fixed expenses that are controllable by the business unit manager. Many of these expenses, such as salaries and insurance, are controllable only in the short term. Others, such as depreciation, are committed costs that are controllable mainly when the decision to invest is being made. In addition, direct charges for the use of corporate services are included if the profit center manager controls the use of those services.

Direct Profit. The direct profit performance measure is derived from controllable profit by deducting a charge for all corporate services that can be traced directly back to the business unit but that were not requested by its manager. These services are corporate-level activities—for example, a CPA audit or a human resource study—whose expenses can be assigned to business units based on an allocation for services they receive. Although they are not immediately controllable by the division manager, by including them in the profit measure, senior management can encourage lower-

---

EXHIBIT 14.2   FOUR WAYS TO MEASURE PROFIT FOR A PROFIT CENTER

	Examples of Expense
Sales revenue	
Less controllable variable expense:	
Outside purchases	Materials, supplies, and wages.
Purchases from other divisions of the corporation on a per-use basis	Parts, printing, and maintenance.
Equals contribution margin	
Less controllable fixed expense:	
Discretionary charges controllable in the short to intermediate term	Salaries and insurance.
Committed costs controllable in the long term	Depreciation of plant assets.
Controllable corporate services allocated by use	Corporate MIS provides service upon request.
1. Equals controllable profit	
Less noncontrollable, but traceable, corporate charges	CPA audit of division's financial statements. Rent negotiated by corporate office.
2. Equals direct profit	
Less noncontrollable, nontraceable corporate overhead	Corporate staff expense and public relations expense.
3. Equals pretax profit	
Less assignable portion of corporate income tax	Tax of subsidiary.
4. Equals net income	

level managers to take steps that might reduce their costs. For example, a subunit manager who will be charged for the subunit's portion of a CPA audit will be motivated to take steps—such as preassembling supporting documentation—to lower audit expense.

Pretax Profit. Direct profit less an indirect charge for general corporate overhead yields pretax profit. This measure is not as effective as the others for evaluating business unit performance, because it includes an expense—overhead—that business unit managers cannot control and that is often assigned arbitrarily. Nevertheless, it does offer several benefits:

- It gets business unit managers to think about overhead and to complain if overhead expense becomes excessive. This provides a check on runaway corporate overhead.
- It gets business unit managers to include their share of corporate overhead in the pricing formulas. This ensures that profit is net of all company expense.
- It assigns all company expense to business units. This ensures that the total profit for all business units will equal the total corporate profit.

Thus, despite its shortcomings as a measure of performance, pretax profit is useful for raising managers' concern about the allocation and use of resources. Surveys have shown it to be very popular in practice; it is used by more than 50 percent of all firms.[4]

Net Income. The net income measure is derived by deducting from pretax profit a portion of corporate income tax expense. Like pretax profit, net income charges managers with responsibility for corporate overhead expenses over which they exert no control. It is useful, however, in getting managers to consider the effects of income taxes when they make business decisions. Despite its cost allocation problems, net income seems to be widely used as a performance measure.[5]

Different Measures, Different Uses. Every profit measure should promote behavior that is in keeping with corporate goals. Some measures, such as controllable profit and direct profit, are more effective than the others as measures of business unit and manager performance; they provide reasonable bases for determining compensation and rewards. Other measures,

[4] James S. Reece and William A. Cool, "Measuring Investment Center Performance," *Harvard Business Review*, May–June 1978, pp. 28–46, reported that 49 percent of 351 companies did not allocate corporate administrative expense to profit centers. Vijay Govindarajan, "Profit Center Measurement: An Empirical Study," referenced in Robert N. Anthony and Vijay Govindarajan, *Management Control Systems*, 8th ed., Chicago: Irwin, p. 152, reported that 64 percent of 593 companies *did* allocate corporate general and administrative expenses. Thus, both surveys imply use of pretax profit by over 50 percent of firms.
[5] Reece and Cool, op. cit., reported that 71 percent of firms did not assess taxes to profit centers. Govindarajan, ibid., reported that 40 percent of firms *did* charge income taxes in computing business unit profit.

such as pretax profit and net income, are more useful for evaluating the economic viability of a business unit than for evaluating the performance of its manager. Senior managers should be careful to distinguish between these two reporting objectives—but often are not.

EFFECTS OF FOREIGN CURRENCY TRANSLATION

When a firm has profit centers that are located in different countries, it faces special difficulties in evaluating the performance of business units and managers. The problem lies in the uncertainty of world currency values, which are determined by market forces that can change quickly. Operating profits that have been calculated in local currencies can erode when they are converted to the parent firm's currency—the standard used in consolidated corporate reports. Exhibit 14.3 shows an example of this effect. The budget at the left, prepared in dollars (the parent firm's currency) and then converted into the profit center's local currency, calls for a profit of £150. The results at the right show that the subunit made its local target profit of £150. But, because the exchange rate dropped from $2.00 per pound to $1.50 per pound during the accounting period, the subunit *did not* meet its dollar profit target of $300. This underbudget effect is due entirely to **currency translation**, the conversion of financial reports from one currency to another.

The decision as to whether to include currency translation in a decentralized financial report should be made based on the purpose of the report. If a profit center's income report is being used to evaluate the subunit as an economic enterprise or to compare it with other profit centers, then results should be measured in a single currency, usually that of the par-

EXHIBIT 14.3 EFFECT OF CURRENCY TRANSLATION ON DIVISIONAL INCOME

	Budget Prepared in Parent's Currency			Results Reported in Parent's Currency		
	Parent's Currency, U.S. Dollars	Beginning Exchange Rate, Dollars per Pound	Local Currency, U.K. Pounds	Local Currency, U.K. Pounds	Ending Exchange Rate, Dollars per Pound	Parent's Currency, U.S. Dollars
Sales revenue	$2,000	2.0	£1,000	£1,000	1.5	$1,500
Less						
Cost of sales	$ 800	2.0	£ 400	£ 400	1.5	$ 600
Rent	200	2.0	100	100	1.5	150
Advertising	400	2.0	200	200	1.5	300
Salaries	300	2.0	150	150	1.5	225
Total expense	$1,700	2.0	£ 850	£ 850	1.5	$1,275
Direct divisional profit	$ 300	2.0	£ 150	£ 150	1.5	$ 225

$(75)
Currency translation variance

ent firm. Profit-center income reports should be translated into that unit of currency wherever necessary. However, if the purpose of the financial report is to evaluate the business unit's manager, then currency translation effects should be included only if the local manager is to be held accountable for them. Here are the two possibilities in greater detail:

1. *Hold the profit center manager responsible for operating results only.* This approach allows profit center managers to concentrate on what they do best—directing daily business operations—while leaving currency translation concerns to the corporate treasury office. Financial reports for business units then *do not* include translation effects; they are prepared either in the local currency or in the parent firm's currency. (A fixed and predetermined exchange rate is assumed for this purpose.) Either way, the manager's performance ends up being evaluated only on the basis of unchanging targets that are unaffected by currency translation. This does not, however, relieve managers of responsibility for controlling the currency effects involved in buying and selling goods across national lines. A French subunit that reports in French francs and buys British parts, for example, will show lower income when the franc weakens against the pound sterling. As part of normal subunit operations at such times, the manager should consider alternative sources of supply that are less costly in terms of French francs.

2. *Hold the profit center manager responsible for results of operations and of currency translation.* The advantage here is that corporate managers can evaluate local subunit managers in terms of their direct contributions to corporate profits (which are, of course, denominated in the parent firm's currency). In this case, local financial reports are translated into the parent firm's currency. The local profit center manager must control both operations and currency translation effects. One common strategy managers use for protecting their unit's income against the effects of local currency fluctuations is to purchase currency options. (See "Current Practice: Monsanto Corporation.")

INTERPRETING PROFIT CENTER PERFORMANCE REPORTS

After corporate management has decided on an appropriate measure of business unit profit, it must decide on a standard against which to evaluate the manager's performance. The budgeted profit normally serves this purpose, but it should only be used along with other indicators. To get a feel for the quality of the manager's decisions, corporate managers must look beyond the bottom line. Specifically, corporate managers should seek answers to the following questions:[6]

1. Did forecasting errors in the budget affect profit results?
2. Were the market share and efficiency targets achieved?
3. Did the manager spend as planned for the long term?

---

[6] This discussion draws from Dearden, op. cit., pp. 87–88.

We now discuss each of these questions, using as an example the profit center income statement of Exhibit 14.4. That statement is in the flexible budget format discussed in Chapters 11 and 12, which is helpful in obtaining answers to such questions.

1. DID FORECASTING ERRORS IN THE BUDGET AFFECT PROFIT RESULTS?

Even when a profit measure that includes only controllable expenses is chosen, factors outside the manager's influence can significantly affect measured results by affecting budgeted amounts. The budget is built on forecasts of such variables as industry sales and materials purchase price, and inaccuracies in those projections will produce variances in revenue and expense. Corporate management should identify and separate out the effects of forecasting errors, so that it can judge managers solely on their ability to manage.

Returning to our example, senior management will want to know why actual sales volume was 400 units below budget (Exhibit 14.4)—a shortfall of 4 percent. The "Sales Volume Variances" column (column 4), which reports the income effect of decreased unit sales, shows that $2,480 of the total $7,000 U (unfavorable) profit variance is due to this sales volume shortfall. The "Master Budget" column (column 5) was built on an industry sales forecast of 50,000 units, but investigation indicates that actual industry sales were only 45,000 units. The profit center manager should not be held responsible for the $2,480 U profit variance resulting from that drop in industry demand, since he or she had no control over demand.

The "Flexible Budget" column (column 2) shows unfavorable variances for the variable expenses and for two of the three categories of fixed

EXHIBIT 14.4 EXAMPLE OF A PROFIT CENTER INCOME STATEMENT—FLEXIBLE BUDGET FORMAT

	(1) Actual	(2) Flexible Budget Variance	(3) Flexible Budget	(4) Sales Volume Variance	(5) Master Budget
Units sold	9,600 units	0 units	9,600 units	(400) units	10,000 units
Sales revenue	$95,000	$(1,000)	$96,000	$(4,000)	$100,000
Less variable expense:					
Production	$29,000	$(2,120)	$26,880	$1,120	$28,000
Sales	12,000	(2,400)	9,600	400	10,000
Total variable expense	$41,000	$(4,520)	$36,480	1,520	$38,000
Contribution margin	$54,000	$5,520	$59,520	$2,480	$62,000
Less fixed expense:					
Production	$23,000	$(1,000)	$22,000	0	$22,000
Administration	13,000	(3,000)	10,000	0	10,000
Marketing and advertising	13,000	5,000	18,000	0	18,000
Total fixed expense	$49,000	$1,000	$50,000	0	$50,000
Direct profit	$5,000	$(4,520)	$9,520	$(2,480)	$12,000

$(7,000)
Total profit variance

Achieved when actual industry sales were only 45,000 units

Based on industry sales forecast of 50,000 units.

Unfavorable sales price variance is due to lower average prices.

Unfavorable variable cost variances can be explained by detailed price and efficiency variances

Cost cuts may cause unfavorable long-run strategic impacts.

Unfavorable fixed expense variances can be explained by a detailed activity analysis.

Variance caused by actual unit sales falling short of master budget.

expense. Each of these variances can be broken down into individual expense components (as we did in Chapters 11 and 12) in order to identify those that are the result of errors in forecasting purchase prices. The $2,120 U variable production-cost variance, for example, would likely be broken down into materials, labor, and overhead components, each of which is composed of price and quantity (efficiency) variances. Again, here, the profit center manager is not responsible for variance components that arise because of differences between forecasted and actual prices.

2. WERE MARKET SHARE AND EFFICIENCY TARGETS ACHIEVED?

To be successful, a profit center manager must constantly look to the subunit's market share and efficiency. Exhibit 14.5 shows a detailed method of analysis that can be used to evaluate each of these business components; the analysis of the components is an extension of the flexible budget.

The analysis in panel 1 of Exhibit 14.5 breaks the profit variance due to sales volume into two parts: a market share variance and a market size variance. Three contribution margins are calculated. Each is based on the company's budgeted contribution margin per unit. The left-hand column shows that actual industry sales volume is multiplied by the company's actual market share in order to derive the contribution margin ($59,520) shown in the flexible budget. The right-hand column shows forecasted industry sales volume multiplied by the budgeted market share in order to derive the contribution margin ($62,000) shown in the master budget. Variances are obtained by comparing each of these two amounts with the corresponding amount in the center column. The budgeted contribution margin ($55,800) shown in the center column is derived by multiplying actual industry unit sales by budgeted market share.

Only the market share variance is controllable by the business unit manager. On the right-hand side of the analysis we compute the noncontrollable market-size variance ($6,200 U), which is the result of the 5,000-unit shortfall in sales. On the left-hand side of the analysis we compute the controllable market share variance ($3,720 F), which the business unit achieved by surpassing the revised target (9,000 units) by 600 units. Thus, the unit's outcome surpassed the budgeted market share of 20.0 percent by 1.3 percent. Obviously, the subunit manager did well to increase the subunit's market share in the face of a shrinking market that otherwise would have reduced profit by $6,200.

The analysis in panel 2 of Exhibit 14.5 breaks the variable production-cost variance into a combined price variance and a combined quantity variance; only the quantity variance is controllable by the business unit manager. The price variance ($1,400 U) is primarily the result of forecasting errors during budget preparation and thus is outside the manager's control. The quantity variance ($720 U) is indicative of actions initiated within the business unit and for which the manager should be held accountable. Similar analyses should be performed for the other expense variances shown in Exhibit 14.4.

EXHIBIT 14.5 DETAILED ANALYSIS OF SALES VOLUME VARIANCE AND VARIABLE COST PRODUCTION COST VARIANCE

(An Extension of Exhibit 14.4)

Panel 1—Breakdown of Sales Volume Variance

	Flexible Budget		Master Budget
Actual industry unit sales	45,000	Actual industry unit sales 45,000	Forecasted industry unit sales 50,000
Actual market share	21.3%	Budgeted market share 20.0%	Budgeted market share 20.0%
Actual unit sales	9,600	Budgeted share of actual sales 9,000	Budgeted share of forecast sales 10,000
Budgeted contribution margin/unit	$ 6.20	Budgeted contribution margin/unit $ 6.20	Budgeted contribution margin/unit $ 6.20
Budgeted contribution margin for actual company sales	$59,520	Budgeted contribution margin for actual company sales $55,800	Budgeted contribution margin for forecasted sales $62,000

$3,720 $(2,480) $(6,200)

Market share variance   Market size variance   Market size variance

Sales volume variance

Panel 2—Breakdown of Variable Production Cost Variance[a]

	Actual Results	Actual quantity × standard price	Flexible Budget Standard quantity × standard price
Combined material, labor, and variable overhead cost	$29,000	$27,600	$26,880

$(1,400) $(720)

Combined price variance   Combined quantity variance

$(2,120)

Variable production cost variance

[a] *Recall the following definitions from Chapter 11: Actual quantity is actual resource inputs used. Standard price is the budgeted cost per unit for resource inputs. Standard quantity is the budgeted amount of resource inputs allowed for the actual number of units produced.*

Although our analysis of expense variances is not complete, it already indicates that the subunit manager's performance was more effective than the $7,000 profit shortfall would imply. First, the subunit's market share was expanded at a time when industry sales fell. Second, we have already identified two noncontrollable variances—market size variance and variable production-price variance—that, if taken alone, would reduce the profit target by $7,600 ($6,200 + $1,400). One other question must, however, still be considered.

3. DID THE MANAGER SPEND AS PLANNED FOR THE LONG TERM?

Some discretionary expenses—such as research, product development, and maintenance—can be cut in the short term without hurting business unit profits. Underspending on these strategic expenses can cause tremendous harm over the longer term, however, as the subunit's unique market competencies begin to erode. Managers who are feeling pressured to meet profit targets can easily be tempted to scale back on such discretionary expenses.

In Exhibit 14.4, the fixed marketing and advertising expense stands out as one expense item with the potential for long-term consequences. The below-budget spending ($5,000 F) should be investigated. From one perspective, it is encouraging that this business unit was able to increase market share while cutting back so substantially on marketing and advertising expense. However, senior managers need to determine what types of expense items were cut and why. If, for example, product development expenses necessary to long-term profitability were cut in order to produce higher current earnings, corporate management would do well to deal harshly with that imprudent decision.

TRANSFER PRICING

Transfer pricing is the assignment of prices to the goods and services that are exchanged among responsibility centers. The *transfer prices* of goods sold to one corporate subunit by another determine the revenue recorded by the selling subunit as well as the cost of the purchase to the buying subunit. While transfer prices can apply to any type of responsibility center, they are of special interest to profit center managers, since transfer prices directly affect subunit revenue, expense, and income. Hence, fairness in transfer pricing becomes an important issue.

TRANSFER-PRICING PRINCIPLES

TRANSFER PRICING VERSUS COST ALLOCATION

Transfer pricing may be viewed by some as just another form of cost allocation, since transfer prices are used to charge one subunit for using the resources of another. According to this view, a transfer price is an artificial mechanism that allows the firm to distribute costs internally, and transfer prices have no effect on corporate profits. In fact, however, transfer prices differ from cost allocations in at least two important ways:

1. *Transfer prices offer choice.* In keeping with the main purpose of decentralization, transfer prices offer a mechanism that allows managers who buy resources the freedom to choose their own supply sources—internal or external. Consider, for example, a firm that has its own freight-shipping subunit. A truly decentralized organization would permit each profit center manager to decide whether to use this in-house transportation service or to seek shipping services from some outside firm. Transfer prices enable the buying manager to compare the values offered by in-house *and* outside vendors, and to choose a supplier based only on value (and the bottom line).

2. *Transfer prices allow profits, which measure competitiveness.* Transfer prices allow the intracompany seller of goods or services to earn a profit—*in addition to* recouping costs—whereas cost allocations are concerned only with recouping costs. Reasonable profits indicate that the intracompany seller is able to compete effectively with outside firms, but lower profits may indicate the need for corrective action. Suppose, for example, that a subunit's profits are low because other managers prefer to use external suppliers. Then corporate managers must determine why the internal operation cannot compete with similar operations of external suppliers.

Transfer prices are thus the means by which a firm allocates not only costs but also profits to its component subunits.

ILLUSTRATION: TIRE AND BICYCLE DIVISIONS

The bicycle division of Carrier Corporation is considering whether to buy tires from the tire division. The buyer division needs 10,000 tires for a limited-edition model planned to commemorate the firm's 50th anniversary. As panel 1 of Exhibit 14.6 shows, the seller division sells these tires in the market at $12 each. Its production cost is $8 per tire—$3 variable and $5 fixed—so its gross margin is $4 per tire. The buyer, however, has received a price of $11 per tire from an outside supplier. Let's examine this situation under two circumstances: when the seller division is operating at full capacity and when it is operating below full capacity.

Seller Division at Full Capacity. The buyer division is better off if it selects the lower-cost option—buying at $11 from the outside supplier. The seller division is better off if it sells its entire capacity at the higher price of $12 to outside customers. This means that the two divisions—and the firm as a whole—will maximize their income by buying and selling externally, rather than making an intracompany sale, when the seller is at full capacity.

The easiest way to demonstrate that buying and selling externally is the most-effective course of action is to assume now that subunits are required to buy and sell internally whenever possible. Panel 2 of Exhibit 14.6 shows the effects of two likely transfer prices. In case 1, the price is

EXHIBIT 14.6 CARRIER CORPORATION

Transfer Pricing for Tire Division (Seller) and Bicycle Division (Buyer)

Panel 1—Basic Information

Seller Division (Tire Division)			Buyer Division (Bicycle Division)	
Market price/tire		$12	Tires needed	10,000
Production cost:			External bid/tire	$11
Variable	$3			
Fixed	5	8		
Gross margin/tire		$ 4		

Panel 2—Goods Sold Internally with Seller Division at Full Capacity

Case 1. Transfer Price = $12 (Seller's Outside Price)

Differential Effect to Seller	Per Unit		
Lost outside sales price	$12		
Gained inside sale price	12		
Differential income	$ 0	× 10,000 units =	$ 0

Differential Effect to Buyer			
Outside cost avoided	$11		
Inside cost incurred	$12		
Differential income	$ (1)	× 10,000 units =	$(10,000)
Combined effect on corporate income			$(10,000)

Case 2. Transfer Price = $11 (Buyer's Outside Cost)

Differential Effect to Seller	Per Unit		
Lost outside sales price	$12		
Gained inside sale price	11		
Differential income	$ (1)	× 10,000 units =	$(10,000)

Differential Effect to Buyer			
Outside cost avoided	$11		
Inside cost incurred	11		
Differential income	$ 0	× 10,000 units =	0
Combined effect on corporate income			$(10,000)

$12 per tire, the seller's external price. At $12, the seller division receives its normal revenue, but the buyer division must pay $1 more than the outside price per tire, thus incurring a $10,000 added cost. In case 2, the price is $11 per tire, the buyer's external cost. At $11, the seller foregoes the $1 per tire that could have been earned by selling externally and incurs a $10,000 revenue decrease. The cost to the buyer is thus the same as its external cost. In both cases the effect on corporate income is a reduction of $10,000, calculated by adding the effects on the two divisions. In fact, no matter what transfer price is chosen, the firm will always lose $10,000 as a result of the internal transaction when the seller is operating at full capacity. The transfer price merely allocates the loss among the divisions.

Seller Division Below Full Capacity.   Exhibit 14.7 shows data for the below-full-capacity scenario. In all other respects, it is based on the same conditions as above. Panel 1 shows that the seller (the tire division) is producing and selling only 125,000 tires, which is 25,000 tires below its capacity. Thus, it can produce the 10,000 units needed by the buyer (the bicycle division) without decreasing its sales to external customers. Now the differential effect of an internal sale is positive: The buyer avoids the outside cost of $11 per tire, while the seller incurs a differential production cost (which we assume is approximately the variable cost) of $3 per tire. The effect on the firm is an increase in income of $80,000.

What transfer price would apportion this increase in income between the two divisions fairly and reasonably? The seller's normal market price is irrelevant to the transfer price, since no market currently exists for the 10,000 tires in question. Instead, what is needed is a price that leaves the seller in no worse a position than it would be in if it did not produce the tires. That is, the transfer price should allow it to recover the differential cost of producing the 10,000 tires. At the same time, the transfer price should leave the buyer in no worse a position than it would be in if it bought the tires externally, at the $11 purchase price. What we find, then, is that there is a **range of acceptable transfer prices**, bound at the upper limit by the buyer's outside price of $11 and at the lower limit by the seller's differential cost of $3. Any price within these two extremes will leave each division in the same—if not a better—position than it was in before the internal sale of the tires.

Panel 2 of Exhibit 14.7 shows the effects of two possible transfer prices within the $3-to-$11 range. The first, a transfer price of $9, results in the seller's earning a differential income of $6 per tire (the difference between the $9 transfer price and the differential cost of $3); the buyer earns a differential income of $2 per tire (the difference between the $9 transfer price and the $11 price the buyer would have paid to its outside supplier). Multiplying these unit earnings by 10,000 tires, we see that the seller earns $60,000 and the buyer saves $20,000. The sum ($80,000) equals the differential income to the firm, calculated in panel 1 of Exhibit 14.7. The second transfer price ($6) results in earnings to the seller of $30,000 and a saving to the buyer of $50,000, the sum of which is again the total differential income to the firm ($80,000).

THE MINIMUM TRANSFER PRICE

Our analysis in the Carrier Corporation illustration can be extended in order to derive a general guideline for determining the **minimum transfer price** to be set in order to leave the seller subunit in the same position that it would be in if the internal sale were not made:

EXHIBIT 14.7 CARRIER CORPORATION

Transfer-Pricing Illustration When Tire Division (Seller) Has Excess Capacity

Panel 1—Additional Information and Acceptable Transfer Prices

Capacity	No. of Tires
Seller's operating capacity per month	150,000
Present level of outside sales	125,000
Excess capacity	25,000

Differential Effect

Differential effect to corporate income from internal sale:	Per Unit		
Outside cost avoided	$11		
Differential production cost	3		
Differential income	$ 8	× 10,000 units =	$80,000

Transfer Price Range

Buyer's *maximum* acceptable unit price = outside market price	$11	Range of acceptable transfer prices
Seller's *minimum* acceptable unit price = differential cost per tire	$3	

Panel 2—Effects of Interdivisional Sale at Two Possible Transfer Prices

Case 1. Transfer Price = $9

Differential Effect to Seller	Per Unit		
Transfer price	$ 9		
Differential production cost	3		
Differential income	$ 6	× 10,000 units =	$60,000

Differential Effect to Buyer			
Transfer price	$ 9		
Outside cost avoided	11		
Differential income	$ 2	× 10,000 units =	20,000
Combined effect on corporate income			$80,000

Case 2. Transfer Price = $6

Differential Effect to Seller	Per Unit		
Transfer price	$ 6		
Differential production cost	3		
Differential income	$ 3	× 10,000 units =	$30,000

Differential Effect to Buyer			
Transfer price	$ 6		
Outside cost avoided	11		
Differential income	$ 5	× 10,000 units =	50,000
Combined effect on corporate income			$80,000

Minimum transfer price = differential cost to seller (approximated by variable unit cost) + unit opportunity cost of the internal sale

In the illustration, the variable unit cost was $3. When the seller was operating *at full capacity*, the opportunity cost of selling one tire internally was the difference between the external sale price ($12) and the variable unit cost. So the minimum transfer price would have been

$3 + ($12 − $3) = $12

In other words, the minimum transfer price in this situation should be the seller's outside price. Then, as we determined, the buyer division should purchase from the supplier—either internal or external—who offers the lowest price.

When the seller had *excess capacity*, the opportunity cost of selling internally was $0, since additional tires could not be sold outside the firm. Then, the minimum transfer price would have been

$3 + $0 = $3

In this situation, the minimum transfer price is the seller's variable cost. At that price, the seller just recovers the additional cost of making the internal sale—again, as we concluded in the illustration.

TRANSFER-PRICING METHODS

The minimum transfer price helps management to determine whether the seller should sell internally. To establish a transfer price that both the buyer and the seller subunits see as fair may, as a rule, require some allocation of profit as well. Senior management can choose among three transfer-pricing methods that serve to guide subunit managers in setting transfer prices:

1. *Market pricing.* For **market pricing**, use as the internal price the same price that is charged by external suppliers. Profit centers then are subjected to the same market factors as their external competitors.
2. *Cost-based pricing.* For **cost-based pricing**, use a price that is based on the cost of the resources needed to produce the good or service. The transfer price can also include an amount that allows the seller to share in firmwide profits.
3. *Negotiated pricing.* For **negotiated pricing**, let the buyer and seller agree on an equitable transfer price. This method simulates a competitive free-market system within the firm, since both parties will be aware of alternative external prices, suppliers, and buyers.

Surveys have shown that about one-third of the U.S. corporations that use transfer prices set them by using market pricing, about half use cost-based pricing, and the rest use negotiated pricing.[7]

---

[7] Vancil, op. cit., p. 180; Roger Y. W. Tang, "Transfer Pricing in the 1990s," *Management Accounting*, Feb. 1992, p. 24.

CRITERIA FOR CHOOSING A TRANSFER-PRICING METHOD

Senior management must choose a transfer-pricing method that balances three often-conflicting criteria for controlling decentralized companies:

1. *Goal congruence.* An effective management control system must motivate subunit managers to make decisions that further the organization's objectives while furthering the subunit's objectives. As applied to transfer pricing, this means that transfer prices that increase profit center income should also increase corporate income.

2. *Autonomy.* In a decentralized structure, profit center managers are free to act in their own best interests. An effective management control system should allow the selling manager to set the subunit's transfer prices and allow the buying manager to accept or reject the transfer price offered—regardless of the effects on overall corporate income.

3. *Fairness.* Effective control systems include measures for evaluating the performance of profit centers and their managers. Since transfer prices are recorded as revenue to the seller and cost to the buyer, they directly affect subunit profit—the key performance indicator. Thus, the chosen transfer-pricing method should result in prices that both buyers and sellers consider fair.

APPLYING THE TRANSFER-PRICING METHODS

We now examine the effect each of the three transfer-pricing methods has on the criteria for controlling decentralized companies.

MARKET-BASED TRANSFER PRICING

For *identical goods,* the transfer-pricing method that best satisfies all three selection criteria is market pricing. Here, subunit managers base their decision to transfer goods internally on market prices. The illustration involving Carrier Corporation's tire and bicycle divisions demonstrates this point, since both divisions used outside market price to guide their actions. In Exhibit 14.6, no internal sale is made when the seller is operating at full capacity and the buyer has lower purchase-price opportunities outside the firm. In Exhibit 14.7, when the seller is operating below capacity, both buyer and seller benefit by the transfer; the market price sets the maximum price the buyer is willing to pay.

The *goal congruence* criterion is thus satisfied, as both subunits rely on market price to decide which actions best increase their own income—and, as a consequence, corporate income. Use of market prices in such cases also meets the *autonomy* criterion, since buyers are free to choose suppliers, and sellers free to set prices. Managers faced with unacceptable market prices can look outside the firm for other supply sources in order to increase their subunit's profit. The *fairness* criterion is met by market pricing as well, since subunit managers are evaluated on the basis of profits that result directly from their own actions. They compete against market forces and are free to look for more-profitable alternatives, rather than being told by senior management that they *must* buy or sell goods internally.

Unfortunately, market prices are limited in their use. In general, they work best when the selling subunit is operating at capacity *and* when like goods are traded in a free, competitive market. Even when these conditions are met, the following factors may make it difficult to determine the market price of a particular product to be sold between subunits:

- As a result of product differentiation, either through offering unique product features or attached services (e.g., warranties), each competing product—and its price—may be different from all the others. Then, neither a comparable product nor a single price may be found in the market.
- The product to be sold internally may not be available from outside suppliers.
- Market prices may vary because of oversupply or undersupply, promotions, or "product dumping" by foreign competitors, whereby exported goods are priced below cost or below the home-country price.

COST-BASED TRANSFER PRICING

In cost-based transfer pricing, the transfer price is set so as to allow the seller subunit to recover its production costs. The transfer price may also include a profit margin to compensate contributing subunits for the value they add to the product. The effectiveness of cost-based transfer prices largely depends on the accuracy with which costs can be allocated among products within subunits and profits can be allocated among subunits. Since the process of allocation is by nature judgmental, conflict inevitably arises in setting transfer prices. These conflicts usually result in prices that reflect compromises in weighing the importance of the three criteria for choosing a transfer-pricing method.

Which Cost to Use.   Correct use of cost-based transfer pricing relies on a proper definition of *cost,* by which we mean the seller subunit's product cost. Two decisions are important in that regard. The first is whether standard or actual cost should be used. The second is whether the transfer price should be based on the full cost of production or only on the variable cost.

Use of standard cost is preferable to use of actual cost. Use of standard cost offers management the advantage of being able to set efficiency targets for the manager of the producing subunit. That manager is responsible then for explaining variances from the targets. Using actual cost gives the manager the opportunity to pass inefficiencies on to the buyer. Then the buyer becomes responsible for the seller's cost overruns. There is, of course, one condition that applies to the use of standard costs for cost-based transfer pricing: it must be possible to establish reasonable cost estimates prior to production. (See "Current Practice: Cost-Plus Defense Contracts.")

Use of variable cost is preferable to use of full cost. In Exhibit 14.7 we saw that, when the seller subunit has excess capacity, any transfer price

Cost-Plus Defense Contracts

Using actual costs for transfer pricing parallels the pricing dilemma encountered by the U.S. government when it engages contractors to produce defense systems. The government has steadily moved away from *cost-plus contracts*, in which a weapons supplier bills the government for actual costs, including all cost overruns beyond the original estimate, plus a set percentage for profit. A more favorable arrangement to the government is to set contracts on a fixed-price basis, wherein the contractor is held responsible for delivering the project at the agreed-upon price. When costs are highly uncertain, however, as with very experimental projects (e.g., the Star Wars space-based defense program), contractors may be unwilling to work on a fixed-price basis—preferring instead that the government share the risk.

Source: Authors' unpublished research.

above the seller's variable cost will benefit both the seller and the corporation as a whole. It is the variable cost of production, then—and not the full cost—that determines whether the transfer price is a viable one. It is unwise, however, to always set prices exactly at the variable cost of production, since such prices do not provide for the replacement of fixed assets that are used up during production. Variable cost must be modified in order to account for other pricing factors when it is used to set either internal prices or market prices.

Adding a Share of Profit. Once the cost basis for a transfer price has been decided upon, an amount may be added to the price in order to allow the company to allocate profits among its subunits. The intent is to increase the seller subunit's profits, thereby rewarding it for making the internal sale. The allocation mechanism should be a systematic one, in order to prevent squabbles among subunit managers. Even a systematic allocation method can, however, seem fair to some managers and unfair to others. Two popular approaches to profit allocation are cost plus normal markup and cost plus value added, and both can lead to such problems.

1. *Cost plus normal markup.* In the cost-plus-normal-markup approach, the seller subunit's manager adds a markup that approximates the subunit's normal markup for outside sales. This seems fair to the seller subunit, which then earns a normal return. It can, however, cause goal-congruence problems if the resulting transfer price is so high that the buyer subunit cannot earn a reasonable profit and thus decides not to sell its product in the open market.

   Suppose a subunit receives a product proposal that requires that some work first be done by two other subunits. Exhibit 14.8 provides

EXHIBIT 14.8 TRANSFER PRICING BASED ON VARIABLE COST PLUS NORMAL SUBUNIT MARKUP

	Division			Total Company
	A	B	C	
Variable cost added by each division	$10.00	$10.00	$10.00	$30.00
Add:				
Markup by div. A @ 40%	4.00			
Transfer price from A to B	$14.00	14.00		
Total variable cost of div. B		$24.00		
Markup by div. B @ 40%		9.60		
Transfer price from B to C		$33.60	33.60	
Total variable cost of div. C			$43.60	
Markup allowed div. C to				
meet market price			6.40	20.00
Market price for final product			$50.00	$50.00
Markup over total variable cost	40.0%	40.0%	14.7%	66.7%

an illustration in which three subunits work on a product that has a $50 market price and generates a differential income of $20 per unit ($50 selling price − $30 variable cost) for the firm. The product moves from division A to division B and then to division C. Two seller divisions, A and B, each charge a 40 percent markup over their respective variable costs. When division C adds its variable cost to the cost of the goods transferred in, its contribution margin is squeezed by the product's $50.00 outside market price; division C can add a markup of only $6.40, or 14.7 percent, versus the 40 percent markups added by the other divisions. As a consequence, the manager of division C might decide to reject outside sale of this product, despite the favorable outcomes such sales would provide divisions A and B and the company as a whole.

2. *Cost plus value added.* Another reasonable basis for allocating corporate profits to subunits that help earn it is based on the value each division adds to the final product, or the **cost-plus-value-added** approach. Referring again to the example in Exhibit 14.8, suppose that the same product is to be worked on by the same three subunits. However, instead of using normal markup, the firm allocates profits in proportion to the value added (using variable cost added) by each subunit. The result is shown in Exhibit 14.9. Divisions A, B, and C will each incur a variable cost of $10—for a total variable cost of $30. As shown in panel 1 of Exhibit 14.9, each division will be allocated 10/30, or one-third, of the firmwide profit of $20.00. This results in a transfer-price markup of $6.67. This approach does take the autonomy of the markup decision away from subunit managers, but it ensures goal congruence and offers fairness when a profit measure is used to evaluate subunit managers.

EXHIBIT 14.9 TRANSFER PRICING WITH PROFIT ALLOCATION BASED ON VALUE ADDED

Panel 1—Markup is Proportional to Direct Variable Cost of Each Division

	Division A	Division B	Division C	Total Company
Variable cost for each division	$10.00	$10.00	$10.00	$30
Markup @ 10/30 of total	6.67			
Transfer price from A to B	$16.67	16.67		
Markup @ 10/30 of total		6.67		
Transfer price from B to C		$33.33	33.33	
Markup @ 10/30 of total			6.67	20
Outside sales price for final product			$50.00	$50

Panel 2—Effects of Cost Cutting by Division A

	Division A	Division B	Division C	Total Company
Variable cost for each division	$ 6.00	$10.00	$10.00	$26
Markup @ 6/26 of total	5.54			
Transfer price from A to B	$11.54	11.54		
Markup @ 10/26 of total		9.23		
Transfer price from B to C		$30.77	30.77	
Markup @ 10/26 of total			9.23	24
Outside sales price for final product			$50.00	$50

Panel 2 of Exhibit 14.9 shows, however, that the value-adding approach can motivate the wrong behaviors. Suppose the manager of division A lowers that division's variable cost by improving its efficiency with new, advanced machinery. Division A's variable cost now falls to $6 per unit, and total variable cost falls to $26 per unit. The profit increases from $20 to $24 per unit. But when that profit is distributed in proportion to divisional variable costs, division A earns a lower profit (down from $6.67 to $5.54 per unit), while divisions B and C earn a higher profit (up from $6.67 to $9.23 per unit). Obviously, division A adds the same value to the product in both cases; it is actually the use of variable cost as a measure of the value added that can cause problems and discourage improvements in efficiency.

NEGOTIATED TRANSFER PRICING

A manager's freedom to act in his or her own best interest is the very foundation of a decentralized profit center structure. Negotiated transfer pricing offers managers a mechanism that extends their authority for setting prices and choosing suppliers. In this pricing method, buyer and seller subunits are given the opportunity to agree on an acceptable transfer price. The method does not, however, guarantee that the three transfer-pricing criteria (goal congruence, autonomy, and fairness) will be satisfied. Consider the following two circumstances that involve negotiated transfer pricing:

1. *When managers have complete freedom to act.* When decisions concerning intracompany transfers are left completely to subunit managers, the company is assured that two of the three control criteria—autonomy and fairness—are met. There is, however, no guarantee of goal congruence—that decisions which optimize subunit income will also optimize corporate income. Consider, for example, a manager whose subunit is a monopoly supplier of a new computer component. While the subunit might gain the most by selling externally at a premium price, the company as a whole might be more profitable in the long term if outside sales of the component are initially restricted in order to allow another subunit to develop products that use it.

2. *When managers must act within limitations set by corporate directives.* When corporate management decides that an internal transfer is preferable to an outside purchase or sale, it can instruct subunit managers that they *must* make the transfer but they may negotiate the transfer price. This might occur, for example, when corporate management wishes to use one subunit's idle capacity to supply another subunit with components, so as to increase overall efficiency. In the process, the firm appropriates some of its division managers' autonomy.

A major problem with the use of negotiated transfer pricing is that it increases the potential for unresolved conflicts—along with the time delays and hard feelings that can result. Some firms counter these problems by setting up arbitration committees that act as referees or judges in such negotiations. However, these conflict-resolution mechanisms themselves can be the cause of even more inefficiency and delay. The key to devising a successful negotiation policy is to *establish corporate ground rules* that clearly identify the conditions, expectations, and procedures for negotiations among subunits. Managers involved in negotiation must know what type of outcome upper management expects and what the time limits are for conflict resolution. Moreover, both the buying and selling managers must understand the circumstances in which they are permitted to stop negotiating internally and to deal instead with outside parties.

TRANSFER PRICING IN A GLOBAL ENVIRONMENT

Most companies that operate globally have profit centers located in many countries throughout the world. These multinational corporations often use transfer pricing for purposes other than performance evaluation—such as to minimize total corporate tax liability, to repatriate currency, to minimize customs duties, and to overcome import restrictions. The corporation then must ensure that its transfer-pricing policies are in compliance with the laws of the countries in which it operates.

Exhibit 14.10 shows income statements for three divisions of Multi-National Corporation. Goods are shipped from division A in Germany to the United States via Ireland. Corporate headquarters has set an intracorporate

EXHIBIT 14.10 MULTI-NATIONAL CORPORATION

Using Transfer Prices to Minimize Corporate Tax

Flow of Goods Between Divisions (Divisional Tax Rate)

Division A—Germany (48%) → Division B—Ireland (4%) → Division C—United States (35%)

Determination of Taxable Income

Production		Packaging		Distribution		Total Company (Effective Rate = 4%)	
						Consolidated Report	
Revenue	$1,000	Revenue	$3,000	Revenue	$3,800	Revenue	$ 3,800
Cost of goods sold	(900)	Cost transferred in	(1,000)	Cost transferred in	(3,000)	Production costs	(900)
Other expenses	(100)	Other expenses	(400)	Other expenses	(800)	Other expenses	$(1,300)
Taxable income	$ 0	Taxable income	$1,600	Taxable income	$ 0	Taxable income	$ 1,600
Income tax @ 48%	0	Income tax @ 4%	64	Income tax @ 35%	0	Income tax	64
Divisional income	$ 0	Divisional income	$1,536	Divisional income	$ 0	Divisional income	$ 1,536

CURRENT PRACTICE

Toyota Motor Corporation

One of the U.S. Internal Revenue Services' biggest victories ever involved a transfer-pricing settlement with Toyota Motor Corporation of Japan. The agency accused Toyota of systematically inflating the intracompany prices it charged its subsidiaries for cars, trucks, and parts sold in the United States. Toyota denied any impropriety. Still, Toyota agreed to a reported $1-billion settlement, representing taxes the U.S. government claimed had been evaded.

Source: Larry Martz, "The Corporate Shell Game," *Newsweek,* Apr. 15, 1991, pp. 48–49.

pricing policy that minimizes the amount of profit reported in Germany, which carries the highest tax rate (48%). The goods are produced in Germany and transferred in bulk to Ireland at $1,000 per unit, which equals the cost of sales plus operating expense and yields no taxable income. The division in Ireland packages the goods for eventual sale in the U.S. market. Since the Irish division operates in a low-tax environment (only 4%), the firm sets a high transfer price from Ireland in order to shift as much corporate profit there as possible. In the exhibit, the Irish transfer price of $3,000 results in divisional taxable income of $1,600. This turns out to be the total taxable income per unit, because the selling price in the United States is just enough to cover the U.S. transfer price plus expense. The U.S. division reports zero taxable income and thus pays no tax at the 35 percent U.S. corporate rate. The net result for the firm, as shown at the far-right-hand side of the exhibit, is a tax of $64 on $1,600 of taxable income—a corporate tax rate of only 4 percent.

Global corporations that shift profits through the use of transfer prices create a worldwide problem for tax authorities. Surveys indicate that when selecting transfer-pricing policies, multinational firms seek above all to increase corporate profit and minimize taxes.[8] Since the late 1980s, many nations—including the United States, Canada, Japan, and the members of the European Union—have enacted transfer-pricing regulations that deal with this issue. The United States, for example, now requires that firms provide strict documentation that demonstrates that transfer prices are truly "arm's length"—that is, comparable to market prices that would be paid by independent, third-party buyers. When it suspects transfer-pricing abuses, the Internal Revenue Service actively pursues both domestic and foreign-owned companies. (See "Current Practice: Toyota Motor Corporation.")

---

[8] See, for example, Roger Y. W. Tang, op. cit., pp. 22–26; and Wayne A. Johnson and Robert J. Kirsch, "International Transfer Pricing and Decision Making in United States Multinationals," *International Journal of Management,* June 1991, pp. 554–561.

When global firms use transfer-pricing in order to meet corporate profit and tax goals, they compromise the use of subunit profits for evaluating performance; subunit profits no longer reflect the actions of their managers. Under these circumstances, corporate management should use measures other than profit to evaluate the performance of subunits and their managers.

SUMMARY

Decentralization is the handing down of decision authority over products, prices, production, and sourcing to the business unit managers who are closest to local markets and customer needs. A lower-level responsibility center that has been given business-level decision-making authority is generally called a *profit center*, since the subunit manager decides how best to generate revenue and incur expense. Three conditions should be met in order for decentralization to be successful: (1) Profit centers should be independent, (2) profit center goals should be congruent with corporate goals, and (3) profit center decisions should be free of corporate interference, to the extent possible.

One important advantage of a decentralized structure is that performance can be evaluated by looking at each business unit's bottom line. Senior management can shape the actions of profit center managers by choosing among four definitions of profit: (1) controllable profit, (2) direct profit, (3) pretax profit, and (4) net income. Defining *profit* involves deciding how much profit center managers should be charged for resource use that falls outside their control. In evaluating performance, senior management should understand which factors affecting profit could be influenced by the profit center manager.

Transfer pricing is the assignment of prices to the goods and services that are exchanged among responsibility centers. Transfer prices are of special interest to profit center managers, since they directly affect subunit revenue, expense, and income. Minimum transfer price to the seller equals differential cost plus the opportunity cost of making an internal sale. No internal sale is made when the seller is operating at full capacity and the buyer has lower purchase price opportunities outside the firm. When the seller is operating below capacity, both buyer and seller benefit by selling internally. In such cases, the market price determines the maximum price the buyer is willing to pay.

Senior management can choose among three transfer-pricing methods to be used as guidelines for subunit managers in setting transfer prices: (1) market pricing, (2) cost-based pricing, and (3) negotiated pricing. Choosing the best method entails balancing three often-conflicting criteria for controlling decentralized companies: (1) goal congruence, (2) autonomy, and (3) fairness. The transfer-pricing method that best satisfies all three selection criteria is to use the market price for identical goods. Unfortunately, market prices are limited in their use. The effectiveness of using cost-based transfer prices largely depends on the accuracy with which costs can be allocated among products within subunits and profits can be allocated among subunits. Negotiated transfer pricing offers a mechanism for buyer and seller subunits to agree on an acceptable transfer price, but this method offers no guarantee of satisfying the three selection criteria, and it can result in unresolvable conflicts between subunit managers.

Multinational corporations often use transfer pricing for purposes other than performance evaluation—such as to minimize total corporate tax liability, to repatriate currency, to minimize customs duties, and to overcome import restrictions. Under these circumstances, corporate management should use measures other than profit to evaluate the performance of subunits and their managers.

CHAPTER 14 ASSIGNMENTS

DISCUSSION PROBLEMS

D14.1   (Decentralizing for International Expansion)

Latest Styles Inc. (LSI) supplies a limited range of garments to several boutiques in New York. LSI produces these garments in a small factory that it owns and operates in Mexico. LSI has been more responsive to the boutiques' needs for timely delivery of changing styles than have been the Asian garment producers, whose shipments typically take 30 days. As a result, several other boutiques interested in LSI as a potential supplier have approached the firm. Victoria Johnson, president of LSI, has decided that the firm must expand in order to meet the needs of these additional boutiques.

Johnson discussed the situation with her colleagues—Frank Corrigan, controller, and Tom Conway, production and shipping manager. It was agreed that the expansion should be undertaken. Since Johnson makes most of the decisions that involve day-to-day operation and does most of the designing, Corrigan and Conway are concerned about her ability to manage the expansion at the same time. Corrigan and Conway expressed this concern in a meeting with Johnson, who agreed that the additional workload resulting from the planned expansion would be too great for her to handle alone. Accordingly, Johnson has decided to delegate some of these additional functions to Corrigan and Conway.

During these discussions, Johnson stated that, in view of the North American free-trade zone, she is considering even further expansion in order to increase the range of garments produced and to supply boutiques in Philadelphia and Boston. As a consequence, she is considering further decentralization of the business. Expanded operations in Mexico, increased product lines, and supplying two new geographical areas will necessitate hands-on operational management at these locations if the firm is to keep up with inventory needs and differing local fashion trends. Both Corrigan and Conway are capable of handling these operational duties, although they will need to hire new managers to assist them in the expansion and decentralization.

Required:

1. *Decentralization,* as discussed in the text, is the extent to which power and authority are systematically delegated throughout an organization.
   a. Discuss the factors that generally determine the degree of decentralization in an organization.
   b. Describe several benefits that an organization can generally derive from decentralization.

c. Discuss several disadvantages to an organization that decentralizes.

2. Discuss at least two behavioral issues that may result from Johnson's plan to decentralize Latest Styles Inc.

(CMA adapted)

D14.2   (Behavioral Effects of Value-Adding Transfer Pricing)

Earth's End is a mail-order retailer that specializes in ladies' dresswear. The company is organized into three production departments—cutting, assembly, and packing. These departments were recently converted from cost centers to profit centers. While each of these departments does some outside contract work, most of their cutting and assembly work is for internal transfer. With the new budget year, problems have begun to emerge over the transfer-pricing system used to credit departments for intracompany sales.

Departments have been allocated a fair share of profit from each outside sale based on the value they add to a particular dress. Value added has been based on the standard variable cost per product allowed each department. For example, Exhibit D14.2.1 shows the variable cost ratios for dress 54031 for each of the three departments. Given a selling price of $24 and a standard cost of $16, the dress generates a company profit of $8. The cutting department is given credit for a $4 profit, as it incurs $5 of the $10 standard variable cost of the dress.

The cause of the recent transfer-pricing controversy stems from the cutting department's new cost-saving modernization program. As seen in Exhibit D14.2.2, the cutting department has reduced its variable cost from $5.00 to $4.00 and has increased its fixed cost from $2.00 to $2.50. As a result, the profit on the dress increased to $8.50. Based on the new standard variable-cost structure, however, the cutting department has seen its measure of value added fall because of the decrease in variable cost. It now receives credit for $3.78 of allocated profit, a decrease of $0.22 from its $4.00 profit before the cost-saving improvements. Meanwhile, the assembly department has seen an increase in profit, from $2.40 to $2.83.

Required:

1. Comment on the behavioral outcomes motivated by this type of cost-plus transfer-pricing system. What actions would you expect a manager to take in order to increase department profit?
2. What transfer-price alternatives are possible for Earth's End?

EXHIBIT D14.2.1 EARTH'S END				
Profit Allocation for Dress 54031				
	Department			*Dress Total*
	Cutting	*Assembly*	*Packing*	
Outside sales price				$24.00
Standard cost:				
Variable	$5.00	$3.00	$2.00	$10.00
Fixed	2.00	3.00	1.00	6.00
Total standard cost	$7.00	$6.00	$3.00	$16.00
Dress profit	$4.00	$2.40	$1.60	$ 8.00
Allocation basis	5/10	3/10	2/10	10/10

EXHIBIT D14.2.2 EARTH'S END

Profit Allocation for Dress 54031
After Cutting Department Efficiency Improvements

	Department			Dress Total
	Cutting	Assembly	Packing	
Outside sales price				$24.00
Standard cost:				
Variable	$4.00	$3.00	$2.00	$ 9.00
Fixed	2.50	3.00	1.00	6.50
Total standard cost	$6.50	$6.00	$3.00	$15.50
Dress profit	$3.78	$2.83	$1.89	$ 8.50
Allocation basis	4/9	3/9	2/9	9/9

EXHIBIT P14.1 DESIGNER KIDSWEAR

Financial Results for Two Divisions

	Infant Wear	Toddler Wear	Company Total
Sales revenue	$650,000	$1,240,000	$3,690,000
Variable production cost	$220,000	$485,100	$1,337,100
Depreciation and advertising	$173,800	$256,200	$856,400
Sales commissions	$32,500	$62,000	$184,500
Market research	$45,000	$32,000	$130,000
Corporate overhead			$216,000
No. of employees	42	56	165

PROBLEMS

P14.1 (Alternative Measures of Divisional Profit)

Designer KidsWear is a manufacturer of clothing for children. The company has four divisions. The divisions are based on children's age groups—for example, toddlers. Each division operates independently, even incurring its own advertising expense. KidsWear's chief financial officer wants to compare the performance of the infants and toddlers divisions.

Financial results for the two divisions are shown in Exhibit P14.1. Included, along with expenses for each division, is an allocated charge for the market research performed at corporate headquarters for each division. The results of the research are used to determine future strategies. Corporate overhead is also shown. It is allocated based on a given division's proportionate number of employees. The corporate tax rate is 30 percent.

Required: Calculate controllable divisional profit, direct divisional profit, pretax profit, and net income for each division.

P14.2 (Transfer-Pricing Basics: Seller Below Capacity)

Bookmakers, Inc., manufactures books for various publishers. The company is made up of two divisions: the print division, which typesets and prints books, and the binding division, which binds and covers books. Although each division has its own outside customers, from whom it takes orders independently, most work involves a joint production effort. Because of the growing use of CD-ROM in place of traditional, hardbound text material, both divisions are plagued with excess capacity.

The binding division recently obtained an order to print and bind 2,000 books at a unit price of $31.50. It has received two price bids on the print portion of the job: one for $22.50 per book, from the print division, and another for $18.50 per unit, from an outside firm, The Print Shop. The print division estimates its costs will be $19.25 per book, including a fixed unit cost of $9.00. When informed of the outside bid price of $18.50, the manager of the print division said there was no way he could price the units that low, since he would end up with a loss. The president of Bookmakers wants both division managers to work harder at getting an agreeable internal price, since she believes the company will end up saving money by keeping all the work within the firm.

Required:

1. What is the differential income effect to the firm if the print division performs the work?
2. What is an acceptable range for a negotiated transfer price?

P14.3 (Transfer-Pricing Basics: Seller at Capacity)

Cinturon Electronics is made up of four divisions: components, consumer, military, and commercial. A dispute has arisen between the components division, which is running at full capacity (175,000 units), and the consumer division, which buys 15,000 units of part A10Z4 from the components division at a per-unit price of $3.75. The consumer division uses these parts in its production of stereo equipment and VCRs.

The components division sells part A10Z4 on the open market at a unit price of $3.75. The variable cost associated with A10Z4 is $1.00, and the applied fixed cost is $1.50. The consumer division manager argues that the $1.25 markup, or 50 percent over cost, charged by the components division is excessive. The consumer division manager points out that the average markup earned by components for sales on all of its products is only 40 percent, which, if applied to part A10Z4, would result in a price of $3.50. Further, the consumer division manager notes that the division has been approached by an outside supplier that offered to supply it with as many units of part A10Z4 as it needs—at a per-unit price of $3.50.

The consumer division is now requesting that Cinturon's senior management require the components division to lower its price on part A10Z4 to $3.50.

Required: Calculate the differential income effect to the components division, the consumer division, and Cinturon Electronics if senior management forces the sale at $3.50 per unit. What is the correct transfer price for part A10Z4, given that the components division is at full capacity?

P14.4 (Transfer Prices Based on a Cost-Plus Markup)

PC Parts Inc. sells custom personal computers, which are produced by three autonomous divisions: chip, motherboard, and computer. Divisions are permitted to sell subcomponent parts to outside manufacturers when they have surplus capacity. On internal sales, PC Parts uses a cost-plus method of transfer pricing.

Each division charges a transfer price of variable cost plus 25 percent markup, to allow for fixed cost and profit. Variable cost for the chip division is $75 per unit. Variable cost for the motherboard division consists of the price paid to the chip division plus $225 per unit. Variable cost for the computer division consists of the price paid to the motherboard division plus $450 per unit. Through a new purchase contract with its suppliers, the motherboard division has reduced its variable cost to $205 per unit. The market price for an average sale by the computer division is $1,040 per unit.

Required: For each division, calculate the sales price and average markup percentage before and after the cost reduction by the motherboard division.

P14.5   (Differential Income Due to Alternative Sourcing Arrangement)

Sail Away, Inc., recently obtained a patent for an extremely quiet and fuel-efficient engine. The engine division, which manufactures the new engine, has thus far limited sale of the engine to the pleasure boat division, exclusively. The engine division is producing at its full 10,000-unit capacity. Its internal sales price is $450 per unit, and unit variable cost is $325.

The pleasure boat division can sell boats with deluxe engines for $6,500, which is $1,000 more than the price of any boat in its standard line. The pleasure boat division, which is also producing at capacity, is making 10,000 deluxe boats and 4,000 standard boats. All engines for standard boats are purchased from an outside supplier, Power Company, for $300 each. Variable cost, excluding engines, is $5,250 for the deluxe boat and $4,600 for the standard boat.

The manager of the engine division has just received a proposal that it supply 10,000 engines to a competing firm, SeaGlider Inc., for $500 each. If the engine division accepts the offer, the pleasure boat division will sell only its standard boat line. The pleasure boat division has projected it can sell a total of 12,000 standard units at a unit price of $5,500. Power Company has informed the pleasure boat division that it can supply all the engines the latter will need in order to meet this stepped-up level of standard boat production.

Required: Calculate the differential income to Sail Away if the engine division sells deluxe engines to SeaGlider rather than to the pleasure boat division.

P14.6   (Preparing Alternative Measures of Divisional Profit)

Empire Corporation is a highly decentralized company whose core business is building and distributing construction materials and supplies. While its corporate offices are located in New York City, Empire's 20 divisions are dispersed throughout the United States and Canada. Each division tends to be focused on a particular niche of products or services within the construction industry. The firm's corporate management is now in the process of reevaluating the profit center measures used for evaluating its division managers. The information presented in this problem is concerned with measurement of income for one profit center, the windows and doors division.

The income statement for the division is shown in Exhibit P14.6. The division manager's performance has been evaluated based on net income, which is net of deductions for many expenses not controlled by the manager or traceable to the division. Unfortunately, use of division net income to gauge performance has created acrimony and squabbling among division managers, who frequently complain about being charged for expenses over which they have no say. Empire's corporate

EXHIBIT P14.6 EMPIRE CORPORATION—WINDOWS AND DOORS DIVISION

Income Statement for 1996

Sales revenue		$4,532,900
Cost of goods sold:		
Materials	$1,040,754	
Labor	177,690	
Production overhead:		
Rent expense (paid to corp. HQ)	368,071	
Depreciation—equipment	228,458	
Utilities	139,613	
Supervisory salaries	304,611	
Indirect labor	190,382	
Production supplies	88,845	
Total cost of goods sold		2,538,424
Gross margin		$1,994,476
Selling & administrative expense:		
Rent expense (paid to corp. HQ)	$ 184,036	
Depreciation	151,172	
Salaries	617,834	
Corporate charges on services requested:		
MIS	92,018	
Legal fees	59,154	
Allocated corporate overhead:		
Marketing	78,872	
Audit fees	46,009	
General corporate overhead	85,445	
Total selling & administrative expense		1,314,541
Profit before tax		$ 679,935
Income tax expense		237,977
Net income		$ 441,958

managers are now considering two other divisional measurement options: direct profit and controllable profit. They have asked for your help in preparing these new income measures.

Upon investigation of the windows and doors division's expenses, you obtain some added information. Empire's corporate offices own all the division's facilities, and rent expense is unilaterally set by headquarters. You also find that an expense identified as allocated corporate overhead is charged to divisions based on a sales-revenue-allocation formula that has little to do with actual services rendered. Corporate *does* charge for MIS and legal services rendered, but these services are only provided upon the request of division managers. Decisions for plant asset purchases and disposals are initiated by the division managers, but large transactions are subject to corporate approval. All other expenses are directly controllable by the division managers.

Required:

1. Calculate the direct pretax profit for the division.
2. Calculate the division's controllable pretax profit.
3. Which do you think is the preferable measure for tracking a division manager's performance? Why?

P14.7 (Evaluating the Manager of a Foreign Profit Center)

Todo Telefónica, S.A., is a Spanish division of International Telephones, Inc., a multinational corporation headquartered in the United States. The senior managers of the corporate entity have adopted a policy of evaluating all division managers based on the managers' ability to meet annual budgeted profit targets. All budgets and all comparisons between actual results and the budget estimates are in U.S. dollars, the currency used for reporting consolidated corporate results.

The 1997 budget for the Spanish division manager, Jorge Ramon-Gonzalez, is shown in Exhibit P14.7.1. Data were originally prepared based on targets set in Spanish pesetas, the currency that Todo Telefónica uses in its daily transactions. These amounts were then converted to U.S. dollar amounts, which became the basis for negotiation and approval by corporate headquarters in the United States. The profit budget in U.S. dollars ($322,000), as presented in Exhibit P14.7.1, is the agreed-upon target used for evaluating Ramon-Gonzalez. The budget is converted back to pesetas, using the 1997 expected conversion rate (142 pesetas to the dollar). The budget in pesetas is used as the basis for the division's reports when dealing with the Spanish financial community.

Todo Telefónica faced a tumultuous year during 1997, as the lingering recession throughout Europe restricted the division's projected sales growth. Ramon-Gonzalez was pleased, however, that the peseta grew in strength during the year, and thus made purchases of U.S. goods much less costly. He also knew that the stronger peseta would help make his financial results look better when the income statement figures were translated back into U.S. dollars—the figures on which his annual performance review would be based.

The final 1997 profit numbers reported to corporate headquarters are shown in Exhibit P14.7.2. The division ended the year with a net income of $334,000, which exceeded by nearly 4 percent the budgeted target of $322,000. Ramon-Gonzalez felt relieved and believed that he could expect a rather healthy bonus

EXHIBIT P14.7.1 TODO TELEFÓNICA, S.A.

Budgeted Income Statement for 1997
(All Numbers in thousands)

	Spanish Pesetas[a]	U.S. $
Sales revenue	843,054	$5,937
Cost of goods sold	347,048	2,444
Gross margin	496,006	$3,493
Operating expense:		
Salaries	130,640	$ 920
Advertising & promotion	63,190	445
Distribution	88,466	623
Occupancy	42,174	297
Warehousing	92,726	653
Total operating expense	417,196	$2,938
Operating income	78,810	$ 555
Income tax	33,086	233
Net income	45,724	$ 322

[a] Converted at 142 pesetas to the U.S. dollar.

EXHIBIT P14.7.2 TODO TELEFÓNICA, S.A.

Income Statement for 1997
(All Numbers in thousands)

	U.S. $[a]
Sales revenue	$6,716
Cost of goods sold	2,789
Gross margin	$3,927
Operating expense:	
Salaries	$1,049
Advertising & promotion	504
Distribution	716
Occupancy	336
Warehousing	746
Total operating expense	$3,351
Operating income	$ 576
Income tax	242
Net income	$ 334

[a] Converted at 125 pesetas to the U.S. dollar.

---

payment—notwithstanding the fact that his division did not meet its unit sales volume expectations. The average exchange rate for 1997 turned out to be 125 pesetas to the dollar. This rate was far lower than the rate of 142 to 1, upon which the budget was originally based.

Required:

1. Calculate, in Spanish pesetas, the profit made by Todo Telefónica in 1997.
2. What problem is there in using U.S. dollars to evaluate the performance of Ramon-Gonzalez? Evaluate his 1997 performance.
3. Should the evaluation system now in use be changed? Explain why or why not.

P14.8 (Interpreting a Division Manager's Profit Summary)

The president of Sunnyvale, Inc., has just received a copy of the new performance report for the firm's division managers, but he is having some difficulty interpreting the results. In the past, performance has been evaluated by simply comparing actual profits against budgeted profits. If a manager met the budget, then the manager's performance appraisal was positive, but if he or she did not meet the budget, the appraisal was negative. Those managers who exceeded their budgets by the greatest proportionate amounts were considered to be the best performers.

The president initiated changes in performance appraisal after several "star" performers left Sunnyvale to go to other firms, and in the process, left behind divisions that had been stripped of future profit potential. As was later discovered, these managers had achieved high profits by making short-term cuts in discretionary cost categories such as maintenance, employee training, and product development; such cuts had negative long-term impacts. They also managed to look good by getting approval for conservative budget targets that were rather easily

EXHIBIT P14.8 SUNNYVALE, INC.— ELECTROMETER DIVISION

Divisional Income Statement for 1996

	Actual	Flexible Budget Variance	Flexible Budget	Sales Volume Variance	Master Budget	Master Budget per Unit
Units sold	123,600		123,600		120,000	
Sales revenue	$5,673,240	$(105,060)	$5,778,300	$168,300	$5,610,000	$46.75
Less variable expense:						
Production	1,550,562		1,532,640		1,488,000	
Selling	863,964		838,008		813,600	
Total variable expense	$2,414,526	$ (43,878)	$2,370,648	$ (69,048)	$2,301,600	$19.18
Contribution margin	$3,258,714	$(148,938)	$3,407,652	$ 99,252	$3,308,400	$27.57
Percent contribution margin	57.4%		59.0%		59.0%	
Less fixed expense:						
Production	$1,270,750		$1,276,480		$1,276,480	
Selling	834,590		915,480		915,480	
Administration	638,310		650,480		650,480	
Total fixed expense	$2,743,650	$ 98,790	$2,842,440	$ 0	$2,842,440	$23.69
Pretax profit	$ 515,064	$ (50,148)	$ 565,212	$ 99,252	$ 465,960	$ 3.88
Profit margin	9.1%		9.8%		8.3%	

attainable. The new performance report was designed to prevent such misinformation and misconduct in the future by keeping the president aware of spending trade-offs and budget-forecasting errors.

Looking at the report shown in Exhibit P14.8, however, the president is not sure what to make of the income statement for the electrometer division. The division's pretax profit of $515,064 surpassed the master budget target by almost $50,000—surely a positive indication of performance. According to the flexible budget, however, the manager could have generated $565,212 in profit if price and efficiency standards had been met. Does this mean the manager actually did a poor job in running the day-to-day operation? The president calls upon you to help him sort out the meaning behind the numbers.

Required:

1. Identify the most-significant variances in the performance report, and discuss the importance of each. Fill in the missing figures in the division's income statement in order to increase your understanding of the manager's performance.

2. What information do you think is still needed in order to respond to the president's concerns?

3. Based on the information available, rate the division manager's performance.

P14.9 (**Calculating Market Size and Market Share Variances**)

Despite having instituted the use of a new income statement format, the president of Sunnyvale, Inc., is still having difficulty evaluating the performance of division managers. (See Problem P14.8 for background information.) The new flexible report form, shown for the electrometer division in Exhibit P14.8, has helped him understand better how managers can defer some long-term expenditures, such as product development, in order to boost the current year's income. Because the new statement also reports a favorable sales volume variance of $99,252 for the electrometer division, the president can see how much of the budget variance can be attributed to the number of units sold. The question still remains, however, as to whether sales variances were due to factors within the control of the division manager or to noncontrollable economic factors.

Using the electrometer division's 1996 income statement (Exhibit P14.8), you are to calculate the market share and market size variances. You have been able to find that the division's target for sales revenue was based on the following calculation:

Forecasted industry unit sales, 1996	2,000,000
Budgeted market share	× 6.0%
Budgeted share of unit forecast sales	120,000

Data published by the industry's leading trade association have reported that actual industry sales for 1996 were 2,112,821 units. The electrometer division earned a 5.85 percent market share, with sales of 123,600 units. Based on its market share target of 6.0 percent, the electrometer division should have realized unit sales of 126,769 in 1996.

Required:

1. Break down the division's 1996 sales volume variance of $99,252 into a market share component and a market size component.
2. Evaluate the division manager's sales performance for 1996.

P14.10 (Evaluating Alternative Transfer-Pricing Options)

Ajax Consolidated has several divisions; however, only one division transfers products to one other division. The mining division refines toldine, which is then transferred to the metals division. There, the toldine is processed into an alloy and is sold to customers at a price of $150 per unit. The mining division is currently required by Ajax to transfer its total yearly output of 400,000 units of toldine to the metals division at total manufacturing cost plus 10 percent. Unlimited quantities of toldine can be purchased and sold on the open market at $90 per unit. While the mining division could sell all the toldine it refines at $90 per unit on the open market, it would incur a variable selling cost of $5 per unit in doing so. However, the mining division avoids the $5 unit cost on all internal transfers.

Brian Jones, manager of the mining division, is unhappy with having to transfer the entire output of toldine to the metals division at 110 percent of cost. In a meeting with the management of Ajax, he said, "Why should my division be required to sell toldine to the metals division at less than market price? For the year just ended in May, the metals division's contribution margin was over $19 million on sales of 400,000 units, while mining's contribution was just over $5 million on the transfer of the same number of units. My division is subsidizing the profitability of the metals division. We should be allowed to charge the market price for toldine when transferring to the metals division."

Presented in Exhibit P14.10 is the detailed unit-cost structure for both the mining and metals divisions for the latest fiscal year.

EXHIBIT P14.10 AJAX CONSOLIDATED		
Cost Structure per Unit		
	Mining Division	Metals Division
Mining division's transfer price		$ 66
Direct materials	$12	6
Direct labor	16	20
Manufacturing overhead	32[a]	25[b]
Total cost per unit	$60	$117

[a] Manufacturing overhead cost in the mining division is 25 percent fixed and 75 percent variable.

[b] Manufacturing overhead cost in the metals division is 60 percent fixed and 40 percent variable.

Required:

1. Explain why transfer prices based on cost are not appropriate as a divisional performance measure.
2. Using the market price as the transfer price, determine the contribution margin for both the mining division and the metals division for the latest fiscal year.
3. Assume Ajax Consolidated were to institute the use of negotiated transfer prices and to allow divisions to buy and sell on the open market. Determine the product price range that would be acceptable to both the mining division and the metals division. Explain your answer.
4. Identify which one of the three types of transfer prices—cost-based, market-based, or negotiated—is most likely to elicit desirable management behavior at Ajax Consolidated and thus benefit overall operations. Explain your answer.

(CMA adapted)

P14.11 **(Revising Cost-Based Transfer Prices to Market-Based)**[9]

Mobley Inc. is a manufacturer of small consumer electronic products. Last year, Mobley's senior managers approached DryCell Company and expressed their interest in a friendly takeover. It was well-known within the industry that DryCell, a manufacturer of a wide range of consumer batteries, had run into financial difficulties. After considerable negotiation, Mobley consummated the purchase of DryCell.

One of the main reasons for DryCell's financial problems was its unfocused offering of battery products. Mobley decided it could strengthen its own market position—and that of DryCell—by selling all of its consumer products complete with rechargeable batteries. In support of this new strategy, Mobley's senior management decided to shut down all DryCell operations except rechargeable battery production. While Mobley managers felt that this would provide the greatest combined market advantage, they realized it would probably take 2 or 3 years before

---

[9] Prepared with the assistance of Gregory Goates.

DryCell could increase its outside sales in order to make use of available capacity. Meanwhile, Mobley management directed all of its consumer products divisions to use only DryCell rechargeables. In exchange, DryCell would transfer batteries to other divisions at manufacturing cost alone—without markup. Through the first year of operations, the major customer of DryCell batteries has been Mobley's cordless telephone division. Early in the second year, however, DryCell was able to sign two large outside contracts—guaranteeing battery sales to other companies. As a consequence, DryCell now expects to produce close to capacity.

Last year's internal operating statements for DryCell, the cordless telephone division, and other Mobley divisions are presented in Exhibit P14.11.1 (prepared before corporate consolidation). Additional information regarding the results of operations for these divisions is as follows:

- Included in DryCell's sales revenue was $1,000,000 that represented sales made to other divisions of Mobley ($600,000 in sales were made to the cordless telephone division).
- Cost-of-goods-sold expense amounts incurred by DryCell and the cordless telephone division are shown in Exhibit P14.11.2.
- Manufacturing costs per battery amounted to $1.25. In total, DryCell transferred 800,000 batteries to the other divisions at this internal price.
- DryCell sold 250,000 batteries to other companies for $2 apiece.

Todd Mansell, manager of the DryCell division, is concerned about his division's operating results for the first year since being acquired by Mobley. Because of supplying 800,000 units to other divisions at cost, DryCell reported a loss of $37,500. Mansell feels that DryCell did not receive the credit it deserved for its contribution to Mobley's profit. Now that DryCell is selling to outside companies, he feels that all internal transfers should be at market price. Mansell is curious to see how the operating statements would have changed for last year if market price had been used.

EXHIBIT P14.11.1   MOBLEY INC.

Internal Operating Statement for the First Year of DryCell Acquisition

	Cordless Telephone Division	DryCell Division	Other Divisions	Total
Sales revenue	$14,400,000	$1,500,000[a]	$7,500,000	$23,400,000
Cost of goods sold	9,600,000	1,312,500	5,000,000	15,912,500
Gross profit	4,800,000	187,500	2,500,000	7,487,500
Operating expenses:				
Administrative	750,000	150,000	400,000	1,300,000
Selling	1,200,000	75,000	625,000	1,900,000
Total operating expense	1,950,000	225,000	1,025,000	3,200,000
Income from operations before taxes	$ 2,850,000	$ (37,500)	$1,475,000	$ 4,287,500

[a] Breakdown of DryCell sales revenue is as follows:
   Internal: 800,000 units @ $1.25 = $1,000,000
   Outside: 250,000 units @ $2.00 =   500,000
   Total $1,500,000

EXHIBIT P14.11.2 MOBLEY INC.— CORDLESS TELEPHONE AND DRYCELL DIVISIONS

Schedule of Cost of Goods Sold

	Cordless Telephone Division	DryCell Division
Direct materials	$5,400,000	$ 984,375
Direct labor	2,520,000	157,500
Variable overhead	960,000	91,875
Fixed overhead	720,000	78,750
Total cost of goods sold	$9,600,000	$1,312,500

Required:

1. Using a market-based transfer price, prepare a revised operating statement for Mobley for last year.
2. Discuss the income effects to the divisions by changing to market-based transfer pricing. Do you think that the other divisions of Mobley will go along with this decision?
3. Under what conditions should market price be used for internal transfers?

P14.12 (Transfer Pricing in an Engineering Services Firm)

Hardaway and Associates, P.E., is an environmental engineering firm with 450 employees and 12 independent offices located throughout the state of Texas. Each office is set up as a profit center whose manager has complete freedom to bid on jobs, set prices, and determine the overhead structure for the office. Complications arise, however, over the use of the workforce, which is predominantly composed of highly trained engineers and technicians. Offices must frequently rely on each other for specialized engineering talent and for temporary use of each other's personnel when any one office is shorthanded for a job. Although the firm instructs managers to charge market price for the interoffice use of services, many managers feel that the market price is too high. The firm is now reexamining its transfer-pricing policy and seeks a pricing mechanism that will serve to indicate to the buying office when to seek support, while fairly compensating the selling office for loaned personnel.

There is considerable disparity in pricing and costing among the firm's offices. Exhibit P14.12.1 offers a comparison of some of the services offered by three offices: Austin, El Paso, and Galveston. Environmental assessment in Austin, for example, carries a standard cost[10] of $15 per hour and is priced at $45, while the same service at Galveston costs $18 and is priced at $55. Accounting data for some services are based on completely different price structures: For example, soil testing is billed on the basis of a price per hour plus a charge per cylinder by the Austin and El Paso offices, versus a higher, all-inclusive charge per hour billed by Galveston. Moreover, some very specialized services are offered only from the corporate headquarters. As seen in Exhibit P14.12.2, wastewater analysis and toxic

---

[10] Standard costs are equal to the average payroll cost of personnel who supply the service.

EXHIBIT P14.12.1 HARDAWAY AND ASSOCIATES, P.E.

Standard Fee Schedule for Three Offices

Type of Work	Austin Office		El Paso Office		Galveston Office	
	Standard Cost	Market Price	Standard Cost	Market Price	Standard Cost	Market Price
Environmental assessment	$15	$45/hr	$16	$48/hr	$18	$55/hr
Soil testing:						
Per hour	$10	$25/hr	$22	$43/trip	$30	$65/hr
Per cylinder	$ 4	$8/cylinder	$ 4	$10/cylinder		
Hydrology analysis	$22	$70/hr	$30	$90/hr	$27	$80/hr
	$ 5	$10/sample			$ 4	$8/sample

EXHIBIT P14.12.2 HARDAWAY AND ASSOCIATES, P.E.

Specialty Services Offered Only by Corporation Headquarters (Dallas)

Type of Work	Standard Cost	Market Price
Wastewater analysis, per hour	$25	$85/hr
Toxic substance cleanup:		
Per hour	$32	$95/hr
Per barrel	$22	$50/barrel

EXHIBIT P14.12.3 HARDAWAY AND ASSOCIATES, P.E.—AUSTIN OFFICE

Details of Proposal for Job 11-1052

Type of Work	Job Estimate	Item Price	Total Bid Price	Resource Availability		
				In-House	Sourcing Need	Sourcing Location
Environmental assessment	100 hr	$45	$4,500	50 hr	50 hr	El Paso
Soil testing	40 hr	$25	1,000	24 hr	16 hr	Galveston
	40 cylinders	$ 8	320	40 cylinders	0 cylinders	
Wastewater analysis	30 hr	$85	2,550	0 hr	30 hr	Corp. HQ (Dallas)
			$8,370			

substance cleanup are available only from headquarters. Generally speaking, the largest cost incurred by the firm is for personnel, and the vast majority of all costs incurred are fixed in nature.

The Austin office is putting together a bid on job 11-1052, the details of which are presented in Exhibit P14.12.3. The left-hand side of the exhibit shows an estimate of the types and quantities of services required and the Austin office's market prices for each. The total bid price of the job will be $8,370. As often happens, however, Austin will not have the personnel to complete the job on its own, and it will have to rely on corporate headquarters and other branch offices to supply it with the needed human resources. Details of the breakdown of the amounts of services that can be provided by Austin in-house and the amounts that must be procured from other offices are shown on the right-hand side of the exhibit. Except in rare cases, office managers are not permitted to purchase needed services outside the firm, since the firm markets itself as a full-service operation.

The manager of the Austin office is debating whether it is even worthwhile to pursue the project. He argues that job 11-1052 is so heavily dependent on services purchased from other offices that there is no way to generate a satisfactory profit. He has brought this job to the attention of the corporate president and has asked him to consider the profit effect for the Austin office if different transfer prices were used. In his transmittal letter to the president, the Austin manager states:

> It seems silly to let such highly qualified personnel sit idle in other offices when we have work for them in Austin. As we all know, most office managers deliberately keep their workforces underutilized so that there are always enough idle employees to help with meeting project deadlines as the need arises. I know you will agree that we should set a companywide transfer-pricing policy that best contributes to overall profit.

Required:

1. Prepare the total cost of the job to the Austin office under each of the following three transfer-pricing options. For each option, use standard costs to calculate the cost of resources used by Austin.
   a. Market price of the office supplying the service
   b. Standard cost of the office supplying the service
   c. Standard cost (from requirement 1b) plus a markup of 25 percent
2. Using the criteria of goal congruence, autonomy, and evaluation, which of the three methods do you think is preferable?
3. Would negotiation help office managers reach a more favorable transfer price? In general, what is the minimum price that sellers should be willing to accept?

CASES

Case C14.1 (ABC Maintenance Company)

In early 1997, Paula Knox, owner and president of ABC Maintenance Company, Inc., was reviewing the firm's 1996 operating results (Exhibit C14.1.1), industry statistics (Exhibit C14.1.2), and variance reports (Exhibit C14.1.3). She was pleased that the commercial division exceeded its target of 25 percent of market share, but was concerned that the residential division fell short of its target of 6 percent of market share. She was also very concerned about the alarmingly low net income for 1996—the second year in a row for which the company recorded such low profits. The decrease in profits began when ABC entered the residential housecleaning business. Knox wondered whether she should close the residential division. She decided to seek the advice of a management consultant.

Company History

ABC was formed by Knox in 1975. Its goals were to provide cleaning services and to sell maintenance products to the business sector of Toronto, Canada. Throughout the 1970s and into the early 1980s, Knox personally hired and trained all workers and supervised the three-person commercial office-cleaning teams. Business grew steadily because of successful direct-mail campaigns and word-of-mouth recommendations.

EXHIBIT C14.1.1   ABC MAINTENANCE CO.

Income Statements for the Year Ending December 31, 1996

	Budgeted				
	Commercial		Residential		
	Total	Per Unit	Total	Per Unit	Total
Expected sales volume (units)	1,200,000		24,000		1,224,000
Revenue:					
Cleaning	$4,200,000	$3.50	$600,000	$25.00	$4,800,000
Maintenance products	900,000	0.75			900,000
Total revenue	$5,100,000	$4.25	$600,000	$25.00	$5,700,000
Variable cost:					
Direct cleaning labor	$3,600,000	$3.00	$384,000	$16.00	$3,984,000
Cleaning overhead	300,000	0.25	6,000	0.25	306,000
Cost of maintenance products	720,000	0.60			720,000
Total variable cost	$4,620,000	$3.85	$390,000	$16.25	$5,010,000
Contribution margin	$ 480,000	$0.40	$210,000	$ 8.75	$ 690,000
Fixed selling & administration:					
Direct—manager salary, marketing	75,000	0.06	45,000	1.88	120,000
Direct divisional income	$ 405,000	$0.34	$165,000	$ 6.88	$ 570,000
Companywide selling & administration					130,000
Pretax operating income					$ 440,000

	Actual				
	Commercial		Residential		
	Total	Per Unit	Total	Per Unit	Total
Actual sales volume (units)	1,320,000		21,000		1,341,000
Revenue:					
Cleaning	$4,290,000	$3.25	$525,000	$25.00	$4,815,000
Maintenance products	1,030,000	0.78			1,030,000
Total revenue	$5,320,000	$4.03	$525,000	$25.00	$5,845,000
Variable cost:					
Direct cleaning labor	$4,039,200	$3.06	$392,000	$18.67	$4,431,200
Cleaning overhead	264,000	0.20	63,000	$ 3.00	327,000
Cost of maintenance products	824,000	0.62			824,000
Total variable cost	$5,127,200	$3.88	$455,000	$21.67	$5,582,200
Contribution margin	$ 192,800	$0.15	$ 70,000	$ 3.33	$ 262,800
Fixed selling & administration:					
Direct—manager salary, marketing	81,200	0.06	42,000	$ 2.00	123,200
Direct divisional income	$ 111,600	$0.08	$ 28,000	$ 1.33	$ 139,600
Companywide selling & administration					136,800
Pretax operating income					$ 2,800

By 1985, the company had grown to such an extent that Knox could no longer personally supervise all cleaning teams. Therefore, for each cleaning team, she appointed one of the cleaners to act as supervisor. Supervisors were made responsible for controlling the quality and efficiency of their teams. For this increased responsibility, supervisors were paid a higher wage than were the other cleaning-

EXHIBIT C14.1.2 INDUSTRY STATISTICS

	ABC Maintenance	Quick Cleaning	Others
	Commercial Segment—		
	Average Cleaning Charge per Unit		
1994	$3.50	$3.50	$3.50
1995	$3.50	$3.60	$3.65
1996	$3.25	$3.70	$3.80
	Market Share		
1994	20%	20%	60%
1995	22%	20%	58%
1996	30%	18%	52%
	Residential Segment—		
	Average Cleaning Charge per Unit		
1996 Regular clients	$25	NA	$25
1996 Periodic clients	$25	NA	$40
	Market Share		
1995	2%	NA	98%
1996	5%	NA	95%

EXHIBIT C14.1.3 ABC MAINTENANCE CO.

Variance Reports[a] for the Year Ending December 31, 1996

	Commercial	Residential	Total
Sales price variance	$330,000 U	$ 0	$330,000 U
Sales volume:			
Market share	$ 55,000 F	$36,750 U	$ 18,250 F
Market size	$ 25,000 U	$10,500 F	$ 14,500 U
Total sales volume variance	$ 30,000 F	$26,250 U	$ 3,750 F
Direct cleaning labor:			
Price	$237,600 U	$ 0	$237,600 U
Efficiency	$158,400 F	$56,000 U	$102,400 F
Total direct cleaning labor variance	$ 79,200 U	$56,000 U	$135,200 U
Cleaning overhead:			
Price	$ 10,000 F	$ 2,000 F	$ 12,000 F
Efficiency	$ 56,000 F	$59,750 U	$ 3,750 U
Total cleaning overhead variance	$ 66,000 F	$57,750 U	$ 8,250 F
Direct fixed selling & administration:			
Manager salary	$ 0	$ 500 F	$ 500 F
Marketing	$ 6,200 U	$ 2,500 F	$ 3,700 U
Total fixed selling & administration variance	$ 6,200 U	$ 3,000 F	$ 3,200 U

[a] U = unfavorable; F = favorable.

team members. Knox also adopted an informal budgeting system that based labor and overhead usage standards per cleaning unit on the previous year's average actual usages. (A *cleaning unit* is defined as each time a cleaning team cleans a 100-square-meter area.) Without Knox's personal supervision, the efficiency of the cleaning teams slowly regressed, as evidenced by the increased average amount of time required for each cleaning unit. By 1995, commercial office-cleaning teams required an average of 7.5 minutes per cleaning unit, up from 7.2 minutes in 1985.

Recent Strategy

In 1995, to compensate for a decreasing growth rate in the office-cleaning market, Knox decided to pursue aggressively an increased market share by undercutting her competitors' prices. She also opened a residential cleaning division in order to take advantage of the growing housecleaning market. Further, she assigned the operating responsibilities of the new divisions to two of her best cleaning-team supervisors, who would still be expected to spend a sizeable portion of work time on the job supervising their cleaning teams. Knox's long-term goal is to capture a 50 percent share of the office-cleaning market and a 20 percent share of the house-cleaning market.

Traditionally, the housecleaning market had been serviced by self-employed individuals, such as housewives, whose rates varied according to the type of job performed (i.e., routine weekly cleaning jobs versus infrequent jobs, such as spring cleaning). Knox decided that, because of the success of the commercial division, she would set prices and operating standards for the new divisions based on those used for the commercial division. Thus, a flat rate per housecleaning unit was charged, regardless of the type of job. Unlike the three-person office-cleaning teams, each housecleaning team was made up of only two people: a supervisor, who had the same responsibilities as the office-cleaning supervisors, and only one cleaner. One other difference with housecleaning jobs is that Knox will not be supplying maintenance products, such as garbage bags, paper towels, and toilet paper, which are billed to commercial customers at a 25 percent markup.

Operational Control

Knox prepares a detailed annual budget that is based on her sales revenue targets and standards for operational performance. She sets standard prices per cleaning unit, and she determines the standard variable cost allowed for each commercial and residential job. For example, the 1996 standard price to clean a residential unit is $25. The price is based on a standard time allowance of 40 minutes per residential job. Direct labor per job is $16, which includes one supervisor at $10 and one cleaner at $6. Cleaning overhead consists of cleaning supplies (such as detergents, rags, and mops) and is budgeted at $0.25 per job, a charge that is based on an actual average of past commercial cleaning overhead costs. Overhead also includes travel time between jobs. Income statements are prepared on a monthly basis, and variance reports, such as those shown in Exhibit C14.1.3, are prepared quarterly. As Knox points out, she wants to keep the reporting system simple and to minimize unnecessary paperwork.

Knox has always emphasized to her cleaning supervisors that ensuring customer satisfaction is a way to achieve desired market share. Twice each year, clients are asked to complete evaluation report forms, comment on the cleaning team's performance, and provide suggestions for improvement. Division managers review these reports and then give them to team supervisors for their consideration and comments. Generally, the clients' reports regarding the office-cleaning teams have been extremely favorable. Client reports on the housecleaning teams, however, have been mixed. For most housecleaning teams, the regular clients complained that the cleaning job was often not thorough enough, while the periodic customers were satisfied. For other housecleaning teams, it was the periodic customers who complained and the regular clients who were satisfied. These complaints, as well as the comments by the team supervisors (Exhibit C14.1.4) have contributed to Knox's concerns.

Knox has asked that you analyze ABC's operation and make recommendations that can help it improve future profits.

Required:

1. Explain why the firm has fallen so far short of its 1996 annual profit objective. Discuss the variances of each division separately.
2. Can the division profit be used to evaluate the performance of the division managers in 1996? Over which revenue and expense items do the managers seem to have the greatest influence?
3. Offer suggestions for improving operating performance in the future. Should the residential division be eliminated?

(SMA adapted)

EXHIBIT C14.1.4 ABC MAINTENANCE CO.

Summary of Comments Made by Team Supervisors in Response to Clients' Evaluation Reports

Commercial Division

1. Most workers perform their jobs well.
2. All workers take pride in their work and feel that they do an exceptional cleaning job.
3. All teams spend as much time as needed on each job in order to maintain high quality standards.

Residential Division

1. Many workers complain that the jobs are too difficult.
2. Some workers have asked to be transferred to the commercial division, despite having to work nights instead of days, because the pay is higher and the work easier.
3. Many workers have quit in order to work for other housecleaning companies, despite ABC's superior pay scale. Reasons given include the following:
   a. There are too few routine jobs where cleaners can become familiar with the house and can do heavy jobs over a number of visits.
   b. There are too many "one-time" jobs, where the locations often have not been properly cleaned in months and involve heavy cleaning jobs such as washing windows, walls, and floors.
   c. Quality standards cannot be attained within the standard time targets set for the one-time jobs.
4. Many workers take little pride in their work. Some feel guilty for rushing through the routine jobs in order to allow themselves more time to attend to the periodic jobs. Others, who spend the standard time per cleaning unit on the routine jobs and try to spend some extra time on the periodic jobs, are satisfied with their performance on routine jobs, but not on the periodic ones.
5. The overall number of routine jobs has decreased steadily over the past year, and the number of periodic jobs has increased steadily.

C14.2   (The Fashion House, Inc.)

The Fashion House, Inc., is a vertically integrated company that produces and distributes clothing merchandise. The company is composed of three independent divisions: fabric division, production division, and designer division. Exhibit C14.2.1 provides an overview of the normal flow of goods within the company and with outside suppliers and outside customers.

Corporate Structure

The fabric division, located in Los Angeles, buys raw materials in large quantities from outside suppliers in southeast Asia, China, and Indonesia. It then finishes the product by subjecting it to dyeing, printing, and other treatments in accordance with customer specifications. This is a highly successful operation that is working at full production capacity. One important reason for the division's success is its established, long-term relationships with a critical core of external buyers and sellers, who share information with the firm and help it to identify emerging market trends. The fabric division also supplies goods internally to Fashion House's production division, located in South Carolina.

The production division is of special interest to corporate management because of the corporation's recent commitment to staying in the domestic garment-manufacturing business—this at a time when the trend is for U.S. firms to have garments produced abroad. Corporate management approved a complete overhaul of the production division's only plant facility, which now has the most technologically advanced equipment in the industry. However, because of global competition, the plant has yet to capture enough production orders outside the firm to make it profitable. It is presently running substantially below its production capacity.

The third profit center is the designer division, located in New York City's garment district. Its role is to design and distribute garments in quantity to retail outlets. Production work is predominantly done by the South Carolina production division, but the designer division also uses external textile manufacturers when it is more profitable to do so. The designer division typically sells in bulk quantities to retail giants, such as Walmart and Sears, and to specialty clothing chains, such as the Gap and Chess King. The designer division is well-established in the retail industry, but it must constantly battle for orders in this extremely competitive market. It is now working below capacity.

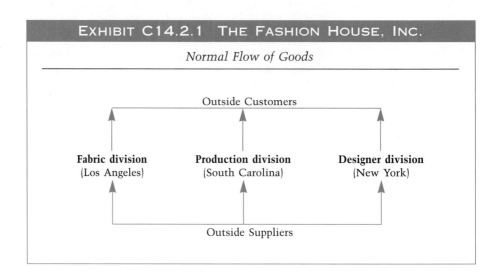

EXHIBIT C14.2.1   THE FASHION HOUSE, INC.

Normal Flow of Goods

Outside Customers

Fabric division   Production division   Designer division
(Los Angeles)   (South Carolina)   (New York)

Outside Suppliers

Pricing Dilemma on a Specialty Order

Senior corporate managers have found themselves in the middle of a transfer dispute for a specialty order received by the designer division. They have been given information on three different sourcing options and have been requested to instruct the divisions as to which course of action should be taken.

Option 1: All Transfers Are Made within Fashion House

An external retail chain has offered a price of $85,000 for a lot order of specialty dresses. Exhibit C14.2.2 shows income effects when transfers are made at prices based on normal markup. The designer division finds that it will lose $1,900 on the order if it fully allocates overhead of $20,000. At the same time, the division's managers recognize that overhead consists of unavoidable fixed cost and that the division will actually earn $18,100 in differential income if this overhead is not considered.

The designer division's income estimate is based on a garment production bid of $57,500 made by the production division. This transfer price includes a $28,000 charge for materials supplied by the fabric division and a differential production cost of $6,000. After adding its absorption overhead of $12,000, production adds its standard markup of 25 percent, to obtain the $57,500 transfer price. The fabric division followed a similar cost-plus pricing scheme to calculate its transfer-price offer to production. Its differential cost for purchasing, printing, and treating raw materials is expected to be $13,000. To this it assigned an absorbed overhead of $7,000, and then charged its standard 40 percent markup over full cost, to obtain its $28,000 transfer price.

On the right-hand side of Exhibit C14.2.2 is shown this order's differential income effect to the firm as a whole. The net amount ($41,600) is calculated by adding the differential income of each division and deducting the opportunity cost of lost sales for the fabric division from the total. Although both the production and designer divisions are working under capacity, the fabric division, which is operating at capacity, will forego sales that would have generated a total normal

---

EXHIBIT C14.2.2 THE FASHION HOUSE, INC.

Option 1—Income Effects If All Transfers Are Made Internally and Price Includes Normal Markup

	Fabric (At Capacity)	Production (Under Capacity)	Designer (Under Capacity)	Differential Corporate Income	
Differential cost:				Fabric division	$15,000
Materials transferred in	$　0	$28,000	$57,500	Production division	23,500
Added by division	13,000	6,000	9,400	Designer division	18,100
Total differential cost[a]	$13,000	$34,000	$66,900	Total	$56,600
Allocated overhead	7,000	12,000	20,000	Less fabric division	
Full absorption cost	$20,000	$46,000	$86,900	opportunity cost	15,000
Markup[b]	8,000	11,500	(1,900)	Net increase	$41,600
Price[c]	$28,000	$57,500	$85,000		
Divisional incomes:					
[b]　Absorption income	$ 8,000	$11,500	$ (1,900)		
[c − a]　Differential income	$15,000	$23,500	$18,100		

Division

markup of $15,000. This amount must be deducted in order to determine the differential effect to the firm.

Despite the immediate increase of $18,100 to designer division's income, the division manager does not feel this order is beneficial in the long term. The manager is dissatisfied that the division cannot earn its targeted markup of 22 percent over full cost, particularly since other divisions will earn their normal markups. He feels he is being overcharged, and wants lower production-cost estimates. Also, there is a timing problem, since the fabric division will delay delivery of materials to the production division. Because of existing commitments to outside customers, the fabric division will cause the production division to deliver the final goods 3 weeks after the date on which they are scheduled to be produced. The designer division's manager is most concerned about meeting the customer's deadline, and hopes this sale will lead to a long-term relationship with the retail chain.

Option 2: Designer Division Buys from an Outside Supplier
The designer division manager has sought other sources of garment supply. A Mexican textile producer offers to guarantee timely delivery of the finished dresses to the division at a total cost of $43,000—$14,500 less than the $57,500 bid price of the production division. As shown in Exhibit C14.2.3, this cost-saving goes directly into the division's bottom line. Its absorption income now increases to $12,600 and differential income to $32,600. The absorption markup is 17.4 percent over cost for this order and still falls short of the target of 22 percent. However, the manager believes that the difference can be made up with higher markups on other orders.

Despite the good fortune of the designer division in finding the Mexican supply option, Fashion House as a corporate entity will suffer financially if garments are made outside. As shown in the right-hand side of Exhibit C14.2.3, the designer division's purchase from Mexico will result in differential corporate income of only $32,600—a drop of $9,000 from the option 1 income of $41,600 (Exhibit C14.2.2). The designer division's manager argues, however, that this loss is counterbalanced by quicker delivery and the potential for additional future sales to its retail-chain customer. In order to avoid suboptimal decisions such as this, the corporate transfer-pricing policies require that divisions be given the opportunity to meet outside bid prices.

EXHIBIT C14.2.3   THE FASHION HOUSE, INC.

Option 2—Income Effects If Designer Division Buys from Mexican Supplier

	Designer Division		Differential Corporate Income	
	Differential cost:			
External supplier ⟶	Purchases	$43,000	Fabric division	$ 0
	Added by division	9,400	Production division	0
	Total differential cost[a]	$52,400	Designer division	32,600
	Allocated overhead	20,000	Net increase	$32,600
	Full absorption cost	$72,400		
	Markup[b]	12,600		
	Price[c]	$85,000		
Divisional incomes:				
[b] Absorption income		$12,600		
[c − a] Differential income		$32,600		

At the corporate level - 9000 less?

EXHIBIT C14.2.4 THE FASHION HOUSE, INC.

Option 3—Income Effects If Production Division Meets Mexican Supplier's Price

		Production Division	Designer Division	Differential Corporate Income	
External	Differential cost:				
supplier →	Purchases	$32,000	→ $43,000	Fabric division	$ 0
	Added by division	6,000	9,400	Production division	5,000
	Total differential cost[a]	$38,000	$52,400	Designer division	32,600
	Allocated overhead	12,000	20,000	Net increase	$37,600
	Full absorption cost	$50,000	$72,400		
	Markup[b]	(7,000)	12,600		
	Price[c]	$43,000 —	$85,000		

4000 lower

Divisional incomes:			
[b] Absorption income		$(7,000)	$12,600
[c − a] Differential income		$ 5,000	$32,600

Option 3: Production Division Meets Mexican Supplier's Price
Exhibit C14.2.4 shows the income effects if the production division meets the Mexican supplier's price of $43,000. The designer division is thus in the same position it would be in if it were to buy from Mexico, and its differential income of $32,600 is the same as for option 2. Moreover, the production division has agreed to use an outside supplier of fabric in order to speed up delivery of finished dresses by 3 weeks, so the designer division will satisfy its need to have on-time delivery to its retail-chain customer. The production division will, however, have to pay a premium of $4,000 above the original price offered by the fabric division in order to ensure this timely delivery.

The net effect of these changes to the production division is a negative $7,000 absorption income, but a positive differential income of $5,000, as seen in Exhibit C14.2.4. Because production is operating below capacity, and assuming it has no better outside sales options, the division would increase its reported income by $5,000 by selling to the designer division at the $43,000 price. However, as shown on the right-hand side of Exhibit C14.2.4, corporate income would be $37,600, which is $4,000 less than under option 1, where all transfers are made within the firm.

Corporate Management Seeks a Solution

Senior corporate managers are unsure which of the three transfer options is in the best interests of each division and of the corporate entity as a whole. They ask for your advice and stress the importance of balancing both the autonomy of division managers with the strategic interests of Fashion House. Ultimately, the right decision is the option that would result in the greatest companywide increase to shareholder value over the next 5 to 10 years.

Required:

1. Recommend an appropriate course of action. Support your conclusion by including a list of strategic advantages and disadvantages to each division and to the company.
2. If you were called in as policy consultant, how would you suggest that the company handle such transfer disputes in the future? Should all decisions be fully decentralized, with each division setting its own transfer prices?

CHAPTER 15

INVESTMENT CENTERS AND COMPENSATION

Recall that the managers of investment centers are responsible both for earning a profit and for deciding how and where to invest the organization's assets. The evaluation of investment center performance thus requires the use of measures of profitability and measures that evaluate investment effectiveness. We discussed measures of profitability in Chapter 14; here we discuss the means by which capital investment effectiveness can be evaluated.

The importance of including investment in overall performance evaluation was understood almost as soon as organizations began to decentralize. In the 1920s the Du Pont Corporation and General Motors formulated the concept of *return on investment* with which to evaluate their newly created divisions. When the trend toward de-

centralization accelerated after World War II, General Electric Corporation developed and used *residual income,* an alternative measure that includes an interest expense for the use of invested capital. Both these measures were (and still are) used widely: One often-cited survey of Fortune 1000 firms reported that, by 1978, 77 percent of respondents had created investment centers, and of these, 95 percent used either return on investment or residual income (or both) as an evaluation measure.[1]

In the early 1980s these "traditional" measures for evaluating investment center performance came under attack. In a classic article that appeared in the *Harvard Business Review* in 1980, the heavy use of return on investment was pointed to as a cause of managers' concentration on short-term re-

[1] James S. Reece and William R. Cool, "Measuring Investment Center Performance," *Harvard Business Review,* May–June 1978, pp. 28–49.

sults and risk-averse behavior.[2] Since that time, management experts have sought other measures that are better able to show the alignment of short-term interests of investment center managers with the long-term goals of the organization as a whole. The emphasis has begun to shift from the exclusive use of financial results to include measures of quality, productivity, and customer satisfaction. Nonetheless, return on investment and residual income remain the most widely used measures of investment performance.

In this chapter, we examine these two measures in some detail. Then we conclude the chapter, and this book, with a discussion of the relationships between organizational strategy, performance evaluation, and employee compensation.

FINANCIAL MEASURES FOR INVESTMENT CENTERS

Much of our discussion of return on investment and residual income will be illustrated using the case of Environmental Enterprises, Inc., a (hypothetical) multidivisional corporation whose organization chart is shown in Exhibit 15.1. The firm is composed of three divisions, each of which is managed as an autonomous investment center. Our current focus is on the manufacturing division, whose abbreviated financial statements are presented in Exhibit 15.2.

RETURN ON INVESTMENT

Return on investment (ROI) is a rather generic financial concept that is broadly defined as

$$ROI = \frac{profit}{investment}$$

The profit and investment components of ROI can be interpreted in various ways, depending on the purpose for which an organization uses this measure. We will discuss some of these interpretations later in this chapter. For the present, however, we assume that Environmental Enterprises defines ROI as

$$ROI = \frac{operating\ income}{average\ assets}$$

For the manufacturing division, this becomes[3]

$$ROI = \$28\ /\ [(\$110 + \$138)/2]$$

$$= \$28\ /\ \$124$$

$$= 22.6\%$$

---

[2] Robert H. Hayes and William J. Abernathy, "Managing Our Way to Economic Decline," *Harvard Business Review*, July–Aug. 1980, pp. 67–77.
[3] All figures for this example are expressed in thousands of dollars here and later on in this chapter.

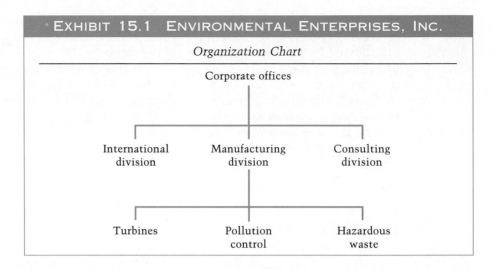

EXHIBIT 15.1 ENVIRONMENTAL ENTERPRISES, INC.

Organization Chart

Corporate offices

International division — Manufacturing division — Consulting division

Turbines — Pollution control — Hazardous waste

EXHIBIT 15.2 ENVIRONMENTAL ENTERPRISES, INC.— MANUFACTURING DIVISION

Abbreviated Financial Statements

Balance Sheet—Beginning and End-of-Year Data
(in $ thousands)

	Assets			Liabilities and Shareholder Equity	
	Beginning	*End*		*Beginning*	*End*
Current assets	$ 30	$ 40	Current liabilities	$ 18	$ 24
Plant:			Long-term debt	30	52
Cost	100	100	Shareholder		
Accum. deprec.	(40)	(50)	equity	62	62
Other	20	48			
Total	$110	$138	Total	$110	$138

Income Statement
for the Year Just Ended
(in $ thousands)

Sales revenue	$130
Cost of goods sold	66
Gross margin	$ 64
Selling & admin. expense	36
Operating income	$ 28

CHOOSING A COMPARATIVE BENCHMARK

To determine whether computed ROI percentages are acceptable, it is necessary to establish a standard, or benchmark, with which to compare them. As Exhibit 15.3 indicates, some benchmarks are useful for evaluating the

EXHIBIT 15.3 BENCHMARKS FOR COMPARISONS OF ROIS		
Possible Benchmarks	*Use to Evaluate the Manager?*	*Use to Evaluate the Entity?*
Budgeted target ROI	Yes	Yes
ROIs from past periods	Possibly	Yes
ROIs from other divisions	No	Yes
ROIs from comparable companies or from industrywide averages	No	Possibly

performance of the manager, and others are useful for evaluating the performance of the investment center.

Benchmarks for Evaluating the Manager.   If an ROI is to be used to evaluate the manager's performance, it is best to negotiate a target (or benchmark) ROI during budget preparation. The benchmark should take into account any special circumstances that the manager is expected to face. For example, if a new product line is being introduced, allowances should be made for the expected low sales and increased investment during the start-up period.

A manager may also be evaluated by comparing the current ROI with past ROIs computed for the same investment center, but only if current operating circumstances are similar to those of the past.

When a subunit's return on investment is being used to evaluate the subunit's manager, the ROIs of the other subunits should *not* be used as benchmarks. Suppose, as an example, that Environmental Enterprises' divisions earned the following ROIs:

Manufacturing division	22.6%
International division	12.0%
Consulting division	28.5%

These numbers do tell us which division had the highest ROI, but they tell us nothing about the division managers' performances. The circumstances faced by the three managers are likely to have been very dissimilar. The differences between the divisions' ROIs were probably caused by such factors as the amounts of capital invested in the divisions (e.g., much more would be invested in manufacturing than in consulting), the age of the capital equipment (perhaps international is a newer division whose assets carry a higher book value), and economic conditions (there could be recessionary pressures overseas).

Similarly, a manager's ROI *should not* be evaluated by comparing his or her subunit's ROI against those of comparable outside firms or against industrywide averages. Even if a very similar external operation could be identified, its accounting methods would also have to be comparable, as would its methods for allocating corporate expense and assets. It would be extremely difficult to determine whether that was indeed the case.

Benchmarks for Evaluating the Division. When a subunit's return on investment is used as a measure for evaluating the subunit as an economic entity, the objective generally is to determine the subunit's potential for profitable *future* performance. Allowances may be made in evaluating a manager who stepped into a poorly performing division, but allowances will likely not be made in determining whether the firm should continue to invest in a subunit with a poor ROI. Using ROI as a diagnostic tool, senior management can compare the division's returns with other benchmarks as a way of determining whether the investment is justified. Clearly, comparisons with budgeted target ROIs and with past ROIs are useful in determining whether subunit expectations are being met. Comparisons with the ROIs of other investment centers are also useful—especially to determine whether continued investment in the subunit is wise. For example, senior management at Environmental Engineering may question whether the international division's meager 12.0 percent return is a cause for concern in terms of the unit's ability to meet reasonable future expectations. Comparisons with the ROIs of outside firms or with industrywide averages may also prove helpful, but such comparisons must be used cautiously because, again, accounting methods and expense and asset allocations may differ between firms.

SALES MARGIN AND INVESTMENT TURNOVER

The ROI formula can be rewritten in a way that provides additional useful information. To do so, we write it as

$$\text{ROI} = \frac{\text{profit}}{\text{sales revenue}} \times \frac{\text{sales revenue}}{\text{investment}}$$

The first factor on the right is called the **sales margin**, or **return on sales**, and is usually given as a percentage. It indicates the effectiveness of the business unit in earning income from its sales revenue. For the manufacturing division, we have

$$\text{Sales margin} = \frac{\text{operating income}}{\text{sales revenue}}$$

$$= \frac{\$28}{\$130} = 21.5\%$$

Thus, the manufacturing division managed to retain 21½ cents of every sales dollar it generated.

The second factor is called the **investment turnover** (or turn). It is a measure of investing efficiency. For the manufacturing division,

$$\text{Investment turnover} = \frac{\text{sales revenue}}{\text{average assets}}$$

$$= \frac{\$130}{\$124} = 1.05$$

So, every dollar invested by the division was turned over 1.05 times, meaning it generated $1.05 in sales revenue.

The sales margin and investment turnover measures serve to highlight the subunit manager's approach to generating a return on investment.

More specifically, they indicate how the manager has decided to combine the two fundamental means for creating competitive advantage—low cost and differentiation. A strategy that leans most heavily on low cost will show a small sales margin and high investment turnover. This pattern is typical of fast-food restaurants such as Burger King or discount retail stores such as Walmart. At the other end of the spectrum, a strategy that emphasizes differentiation—say, for a five-star restaurant or an upscale department store such as Nordstroms—will show a high sales margin but rather low investment turnover.

Sales margin and investment turnover can also be used to identify opportunities for improving operations. Suppose the manager of the manufacturing division found the following trend over the past 3 years:

	Sales Margin		Investment Turnover		ROI
2 years ago	15.0%	×	1.20	=	18.0%
Last year	17.7%	×	1.15	=	20.4%
Current year	21.5%	×	1.05	=	22.6%

The division's investment turnover has steadily worsened, but improvements in its sales margin have been great enough to produce increases in its ROI. Changes in sales margin can be explained only by changes in sales revenue and changes in operating expense. In other words, the manufacturing division has managed to either increase sales or decrease expense, or perhaps it has done both. The decline in investment turnover is the result of an increase in the division's investment base for the amount of sales it generated. (See "Current Practice: Sales Margin in Japanese Firms.")

CURRENT PRACTICE

Sales Margin in Japanese Firms

Many Japanese companies emphasize sales margin as a primary measure of financial performance. This ratio is particularly useful in tracking two important elements of Japanese product strategy—continuous cost reduction and, whenever possible, price reduction. When prices are being maintained or reduced, the only way to drive up the sales margin is to increase cost efficiency and sales volume.

Hence, the sales margin serves to monitor these two factors.

On the other hand, Japanese companies do not emphasize ROI, and their investment turnover is generally not as high as that of U.S. firms. Instead, they reinvest—almost religiously—in order to keep the advantages of productivity-enhancing technology.

Source: Robert A. Howell and Michiharu Sakurai, "Management Accounting (and Other) Lessons from the Japanese," *Management Accounting*, Dec. 1992, pp. 28–34.

STRENGTHS AND WEAKNESSES OF ROI

The use of return on investment offers important advantages over the use of profit alone for evaluating manager and subunit performance. Most important, it is a means for assigning to subunit managers the responsibility of ensuring that improvements and additions to operating assets result in increased profit. It tells managers that they will be evaluated more positively when they take action to reduce investments, such as decreasing average collection time for receivables or reducing inventory stocks. Overall, ROI does a remarkably good job of reporting, in a single performance measure, the efficiency with which an investment center uses its resources.

Nonetheless, overreliance on ROI, particularly as the sole measure of performance, can motivate investment center managers to take the following kinds of dysfunctional action.

To Do All Within Their Power to Meet Short-Term Targets. ROI, like profit, is a performance measure that can be manipulated in order to meet the current period's expectations—at the expense of meeting long-term goals. Managers may feel compelled to "make their numbers," which they can do in the short term by foregoing discretionary long-term expenditures. For example, a manager may cut outlays for personnel training, equipment maintenance, or new product development, knowing that the effects of such cuts would not likely be felt in the current year.

To Avoid High-Risk, Entrepreneurial Investment. Product and process breakthroughs are often successful because someone with vision was willing to commit to an entrepreneurial project and bring it to fruition. As an example, Ted Turner's all-news television station (the very successful Cable News Network, or CNN) was seen by many as a fiasco-in-the-making when it was introduced in the early 1980s. Critics of the use of ROI as a performance measurement have argued that the widespread use of that measure in large corporations has encouraged managers to take the "safe route" and avoid breakthrough projects. Such projects carry a higher-than-average risk of investment loss—especially in the short term—and threaten to reduce the ROI of a subunit manager who may well transfer out of the subunit before any future returns can be realized.

To Forego Acceptable Corporate Investments That May Reduce ROI. Managers with high ROIs will generally be motivated to pursue only those investments that at least maintain the subunit's existing ROI. To demonstrate, we return to the Environmental Enterprises, Inc., example. We now assume the company wants division managers to invest in all such projects that come their way with expected ROIs of at least 18 percent. Further, we assume that the manager of the manufacturing division has the opportunity to invest in a project with the following estimated return:

$$\text{Project ROI} = \frac{\text{project income}}{\text{project average investment}}$$

$$= \frac{\$10}{\$50} = 20.0\%$$

This ROI is above the company-specified minimum and so should be financed. But note the effect it will have on the division's overall ROI:

$$\text{Current ROI} = \frac{\text{operating income}}{\text{average investment}}$$

$$= \frac{\$28}{\$124} = 22.6\%$$

$$\text{Expected ROI} = \frac{(\$28 + \$10)}{(\$124 + \$50)} = \frac{\$38}{\$174} = 21.8\%$$

Because financing the project will cause the division's ROI to fall from its current level, the manager of the manufacturing division may well decide not to pursue it. On the other hand, the manager of the international division, which is now generating an ROI of only 12 percent, would gladly accept an investment generating a 20 percent ROI. Reliance on ROI alone can thus motivate different business units to act differently regarding comparable investments and can cause the firm as a whole to miss desirable investment opportunities.

RESIDUAL INCOME

Residual income offers what is generally regarded as a conceptually superior means for capturing, in a single measure, the relationship between profit and investment. Unlike ROI, which is reported as a percentage, residual income is an absolute dollar amount. It is defined as follows:

Residual income = profit − capital charge

Where: Capital charge = imputed interest rate × investment

As with ROI, the definitions of profit and investment are left to the discretion of each firm. Residual income includes a third term—the imputed interest rate, which represents the opportunity cost of investment capital.[4] For the manufacturing division of environmental enterprises, with an assumed imputed interest rate of 18 percent, residual income is calculated as

Operating income		$28.0
Capital charge:		
Average investment	$124.0	
Multiplied by imputed interest rate	18%	22.3
Residual income		$ 5.7

---

[4] The words *imputed interest* suggest that corporate management decides on an interest rate that it will charge its business units for the use of corporate funds. Some argue that the corporate cost of capital, as used in capital budgeting, should always be used as the imputed interest rate, since this rate represents the parent corporation's cost to acquire funds, and the business units are inseparably tied to the parent for financing. See David Solomons, *Divisional Performance*, Homewood, Ill.: Irwin, 1965, pp. 154–159. Others argue that different implicit rates can be set as a means of reflecting differences in risk. See Robert N. Anthony and Vijay Govindarajan, *Management Control Systems*, 8th ed., Chicago: Irwin, 1995, pp. 232–236.

INTERPRETING RESIDUAL INCOME

Residual income is a unique number that is difficult to compare between time periods or divisions. A zero residual income for a period indicates that all costs—including the carrying cost of capital—have been covered by revenues during the period. Thus, residual income is useful for evaluating business units, because it shows whether they are adding to the company's overall shareholder value. (See "Current Practice: Economic Value Added.")

When residual income is used to evaluate a business unit and its manager, the only meaningful benchmark is the budget target residual income for that unit for the period in question. Comparisons between different business units' residual income or with outside firms' are not meaningful, since the units or firms will have different levels of capital investment. It would not be fair to compare the residual income earned with, say, $1 million of assets to that earned with $10 million of assets. And even within the same business unit, changes in the investment base can make period-to-period comparisons unreliable.

STRENGTHS AND WEAKNESSES OF RESIDUAL INCOME

The fundamental strength of residual income as a measure is that *it ensures that the same investment profit objective is applied to all subunit managers.* Earlier, we saw that the manager of a successful division would not be motivated to take on a project that generated an ROI lower

---

CURRENT PRACTICE

Economic Value Added

One of today's hottest financial concepts for evaluating business units of major corporations is EVA—short for economic value added. Many companies—including Coca-Cola, Briggs and Stratton, CSX, Quaker Oats—are using EVA to determine whether their businesses are adding shareholder value. So, what is EVA? It's really nothing more than a variation of residual income. A business unit's EVA is equal to its net income less its cost of capital. If the EVA is positive, the unit adds value. If not, it is destroying value and becomes a candidate for elimination.

The railroad company CSX offers a good example. The managers of its Intermodal freight unit, which reported a $70-million loss in 1988, were told to break even by 1993 or the unit would be sold. In response, the managers came up with several creative ways to increase their EVA, such as reducing the fleet from 150 to 100 locomotives, running some routes with fewer locomotives, and reducing speeds when existing schedules included slack time. As a result, Intermodal generated an EVA of $10 million in 1992, and the EVA was expected to hit $30 million in 1993.

Source: Shawn Tully, "The Real Key to Creating Wealth," *Fortune,* Sept. 20, 1993, pp. 38–50.

EXHIBIT 15.4 ENVIRONMENTAL ENTERPRISES, INC.— MANUFACTURING DIVISION

Calculation of Residual Income (in $ thousands)

	Without Proposed Investment		*Proposed Investment Alone*		*Total, Including Proposed Investment*	
Operating income		$28.0		$10.0		$38.0
Capital charge:						
Average investment	$124.0		$50.0		$174.0	
Imputed interest rate	18%	$22.3	18%	$ 9.0	18%	$31.3
Residual income		$ 5.7		$ 1.0		$ 6.7

than the division's current ROI, even if the expected ROI were reasonable. The residual income measure solves this problem, because an investment that produces any residual income at all increases the division's total residual income.

Consider again the $50 investment that was likely to be rejected by the manufacturing division because its very acceptable 20 percent ROI was less than the 22.6 percent return currently being earned. The calculation of residual income illustrated in Exhibit 15.4 shows that the proposed investment alone will generate a residual income of $1.0. Because the project will also increase total residual income by that same amount, the division manager will be motivated to accept it, in accordance with corporate management's wishes.

Although use of the residual income measure leads to more goal-congruent investment decisions, it fails to overcome other weaknesses of ROI-based measurement. That is, managers will still strive to attain short-term budget targets and, in the process, may cut spending for such discretionary items as training, maintenance, and product development. Further, they will be no more motivated to pursue higher-risk, breakthrough investments with residual income measures than with ROI (because now residual income is decreased by additional capital spending). And, because residual income is reported as a dollar amount rather than as a ratio, it provides no yardstick for comparing performance between divisions.

ROI AND RESIDUAL INCOME: TWO ADDITIONAL ISSUES

MEASURING PROFIT AND INVESTMENT

Earlier, we noted that there are several ways to define (or measure) the profit and investment that are used to compute return on investment and residual income. The different definitions—and interpretations of these— will convey different messages to subunit managers, thereby motivating them to act in different ways. The proper definitions are those that motivate desired actions from subunit managers as they attempt to optimize their own results.

DEFINITIONS OF PROFIT

Panel 1 of Exhibit 15.5 shows the definitions of profit that can be used in ROI and residual income computations. They are the same four profit measures that we used in Chapter 14 to evaluate profit center managers (see Exhibit 14.2). Choosing among them means deciding which kinds of expenses investment center managers should be concerned about. Ideally, a profit measure should reflect only the manager's influence in producing profits. This would suggest the use of either controllable profit (i.e., profit for which managers have full control over costs) or direct profit (i.e., profit for which managers at least exert considerable influence over costs). Nonetheless, survey data indicate that two other measures—pretax profit and net income—are the most commonly used.

DEFINITIONS OF INVESTMENT

Panel 2 of Exhibit 15.5 lists three common definitions of investment-center investment. The choice of which definition to use depends on which

---

EXHIBIT 15.5 ALTERNATIVE DIVISIONAL MEASURES FOR PROFIT AND INVESTMENT

Panel 1—Profit

Sales revenue
Less controllable variable expense
Less controllable fixed expense

1. Equals controllable profit
   Less noncontrollable, but traceable, corporate charges

2. Equals direct profit
   Less noncontrollable, nontraceable corporate overhead

3. Equals pretax profit
   Less assignable portion of corporate income tax

4. Equals net income

Panel 2—Investment

Possible Definitions of Investment	Possible Asset-Valuation Methods
1. Total assets available	1. Current assets:
2. Total assets employed	Begin with book value, modify as needed.
3. Assets less accounts payable	2. Plant assets:
	Net book value
	Gross book value
	Current cost:
	Via replacement cost
	Via price level adjustment

factors corporate management wants its investment center managers to focus on. The alternatives and their definitions are discussed below:

1. *Total assets available.* The total assets available measure of investment includes all assets available to the investment center, regardless of their investment purpose. The manager is motivated to add high-return assets and eliminate unproductive assets in order to boost results. This measure is reasonable only if the manager really has the autonomy to influence the purchase and disposal of assets. (See "Current Practice: Borg-Warner Chemicals.")

2. *Total assets employed.* The total-assets-employed measure of investment does not include assets that are not in use, such as land held for future expansion or idled assets. The danger here is that a manager will deliberately not use marginally productive assets in order to boost results—when, in fact, these assets represent *sunk costs* that could generate positive cash flows.

3. *Assets less accounts payable.* To derive the assets-less-accounts-payable measure, accounts payable are deducted from either assets available or assets employed. The measure rewards the manager for extending the subunit's non-interest-bearing debt. In cases where the manager can influence the terms of payment to vendors—possibly by selecting the vendors—this measure encourages full use of available supplier credit.

CURRENT PRACTICE

Borg-Warner Chemicals

In 1986, senior management at Borg-Warner Chemicals implemented a residual-income reporting system for evaluating and rewarding its 10 business unit managers. The new system rated managers on the basis of their unit's earned profit less a capital charge for average total assets, the bulk of which were inventory and receivables. The residual income that remained after the capital charge was then split between the parent, which received 75 percent, and the business unit manager, who was awarded 25 percent as a bonus. The results of this approach were very promising. Not only did sales increase by 20 percent in the first year of implementation, but all profit objectives were exceeded. The key was motivating managers to internalize the financial goals of the business unit. The managers—whose goal in the past was to generate sales—now needed to control overhead and investment. Managers found new ways to increase sales and profit margins while reducing investments and operating expenses such as freight, entertainment, and rent.

Source: Adapted from James F. Mosberg, "Managing for Profit," *Management Accounting,* Aug. 1991, pp. 50–53.

ASSET VALUATION

Once senior managers have defined *investment*, they must specify how its components will be valued for use in ROI and residual income computations. This process is called **asset valuation**. The two components of investment are described below:

1. *Current assets.* The value of **current assets** is already reported on the division's balance sheet. This book value may not, however, be useful for performance appraisal purposes as is and, thus, may require modification. A good example is inventory. Inventory that is valued by the LIFO method for financial statements tends to be undervalued, and so book value does not reflect the true cost of inventory buildups. To remedy this for performance appraisal purposes, inventory should be valued using either the FIFO (first-in, first-out) or average cost method. Accounts receivable may also require some adjustment in cases where the investment center manager has no control over credit approval and collection policies. (This is true for organizations such as J. C. Penney and Allstate Insurance Company, which have centralized credit and collections departments that handle all aspects of all accounts receivable.) Then each subunit's receivables may be evaluated according to some artificial, but equitable, formula—for example, 30 days' worth of subunit sales.

2. *Plant assets.* The value assigned to an investment center's **plant assets** figures heavily in its ROI and residual income computations. Three reasonable valuation options are available: *net book value*, which is the value reported on the external financial statements, *gross book value*, which is the asset's acquisition cost, and *current cost*, which is the cost to purchase on the date of the performance report.

Net Book Value and Gross Book Value. Panel 1 of Exhibit 15.6 shows some details of an investment being considered by the international division of Environmental Enterprises, Inc. The investment has an acquisition cost of $28 and a 4-year life, and is expected to generate operating cash flows as indicated in the exhibit. After the annual straight-line depreciation of $7 is deducted, the investment will generate pretax income of $2 in year 1, $3 in year 2, $8 in year 3, and $6 in year 4. Panel 2 of Exhibit 15.6 shows two annual ROI calculations for the investment. One (in column 3) is based on **net book value** and the other (in column 5) is based on **gross book value.** In this example the ROIs based on net book value begin low—at 8.2 percent—and increase in each successive year, *primarily because the net book value decreases as the result of depreciation.* The ROIs based on gross book value begin at 7.1 percent and are lower than the net-book-value ROI in each subsequent year, although they also increase annually.

Two different decisions concerning the investment can be reached, depending upon which of the two plant-valuation methods is used. Suppose Environmental Enterprises requires an 18 percent return on divisional investments. The ROIs based on both valuation methods are below this

EXHIBIT 15.6 ENVIRONMENTAL ENTERPRISES, INC.— INTERNATIONAL DIVISION

Effect on ROI of Plant Asset Valuation
Using Gross Book Value and Net Book Value Methods
(in $ thousands)

Panel 1—Assumptions and Data

Acquisition cost of equipment	$28.0
Useful life	4.0 years
Expected salvage value	$0.0
Annual depreciation (straight-line method)	$7.0

	Year 1	Year 2	Year 3	Year 4
Incremental cash inflow from operations	$9.0	$10.0	$15.0	$13.0
Annual depreciation	(7.0)	(7.0)	(7.0)	(7.0)
Pretax income	$2.0	$ 3.0	$ 8.0	$ 6.0

Panel 2—Calculation of Annual ROI Using Two Valuation Methods

	(1)	(2)	(3)	(4)	(5)	
Year	Pretax Income	Average Net Book Value[a]	ROI on Net Book Value[b]	Average Gross Book Value[c]	ROI on Gross Book Value[d]	Division manager might reject.
1	$2.0	$24.5	8.2%	$28.0	7.1%	
2	3.0	17.5	17.1%	28.0	10.7%	
3	8.0	10.5	76.2%	28.0	28.6%	
4	6.0	3.5	171.4%	28.0	21.4%	

[a] Average net book value = (beginning-of-year balance + end-of-year balance)/2
In year 1 for example: ($28.0 + $21.0)/2 = $24.5
[b] The result of dividing the figure in column 1 by that in column 2.
[c] Average gross book value equals acquisition cost.
[d] The result of dividing the figure in column 1 by that in column 4.

benchmark in the first 2 years, and those derived from both methods exceed it in years 3 and 4. However, in the last 2 years, the net-book-value ROI far exceeds both the 18 percent benchmark and the gross-book-value ROI. Thus, if the international division manager plans to stay at the division for more than 2 years, an ROI based on net book value may motivate purchase of the asset. An ROI based on gross book value may not. The choice of valuation method chosen by corporate managers should be the one that motivates an investment decision that is in keeping with corporate goals, but neither of these methods may actually do that.

Exhibit 15.6 points out other problems in using net book value and gross book value to determine plant asset value. Both methods produce somewhat arbitrary results that have little to do with the true economic return of an investment (which should be calculated using discounted cash flows). ROIs based on net book value overstate the returns earned by older assets, whose net book value has been reduced by depreciation. Consequently, net-book-value ROIs reward managers in the short term for keeping old assets rather than for replacing them with newer, higher-cost assets. In contrast, ROIs based on gross book value understate the returns of older assets, whose value is kept artificially high, and so are less of a deterrent to asset replacement. Since residual income calculations use the same investment base as ROI, their results will be similarly affected by the choice of asset-valuation method.

Despite these shortcomings, surveys indicate that most firms use net book value in determining plant assets value, while only a few use gross book value.[5]

Current Cost.   One way of avoiding the problems inherent to the use of net book value and gross book value as valuation methods is to value plant assets at their **current cost**, which is the cost now of purchasing similar assets that would generate identical cash flows. Properly assigned current values approximate the true economic value of plant assets and thus promote investment decisions that are in the corporate best interest. There are two basic ways to go about determining current value:

1. *Estimate replacement cost.* In this method, each of the investment center's assets is appraised by experts in order to determine the **cost of replacement**. However, rapid technological change often makes such appraisals difficult, particularly with older assets, for which exact replacements may no longer be available. It then becomes necessary to find an asset that performs a similar function, adjust its value for differences in productive output, and then adjust its value further in order to account for differences in the current asset's remaining useful life.

2. *Adjust cost using an inflation index.* The value of the division's existing assets can be adjusted by using their original acquisition costs as the starting point and then applying a general price-level index, similar to the consumer price index. An alternative form of this method consists of adjusting asset costs based on a more specific index, such as the geographic-area construction cost indexes used by insurance companies. **Inflation-adjusted costs** are further adjusted to reflect asset age. The use of such indexes is especially helpful in computing ROIs for business units that operate in countries with high inflation rates, such as Peru, Brazil, and Russia.

---

[5]   Two older surveys reported that about 85 percent of firms use net book value and 14 to 15 percent use gross book value. See Reece and Cool, "Measuring Investment Center Performance," p. 42, and Richard F. Vancil, *Decentralization: Management Ambiguity by Design,* Homewood, Ill.: Dow-Jones Irwin, 1979, p. 351. More recently, Govindarajan, "Profit Center Measurement: An Empirical Study," as reported in Anthony and Govindarajan, *Management Control Systems,* p. 233, found that 93 percent use net book value and 6 percent use gross book value.

Despite its conceptual appeal, current-cost valuation is seldom employed by businesses. In fact, survey data have reported the use of replacement-cost valuation by no more than 2 percent of responding firms.[6] There are several possible reasons for this. Perhaps the most apparent is that accounting records already report book values that managers accept as reliable. Even though more-relevant data can be gathered, it is costly to do so, and gathering those data increases the potential for error. Moreover, replacement costs are, by nature, subjective—especially if exact replacement assets cannot be found. Also, the use of price-level indexes presupposes that the subunit's asset values mirror the *average* asset values for which the index was calculated. Differences in technology or in special features, for example, are not considered. Finally, some say that the effects of asset-valuation problems are overstated. Through the process of budget negotiation, they argue, managers set reasonable ROI targets that bring together the objectives of the subunit and those of the corporation.

ROI, RESIDUAL INCOME, AND DISCOUNTED CASH FLOW

At this point, we need to step back and examine how ROI and residual income relate to the main purpose of management control—that is, to promote goal-congruent behavior. We do so by looking for compatibility between these financial measures, which are used to evaluate past performance, and **discounted cash flow (DCF)** models, which are used to determine whether a proposed investment should be funded.

COMPARING THE FINANCIAL MEASURES WITH DCF MODELS

Exhibit 15.7 extends the investment decision illustration of Exhibit 15.6. Panel 1 reviews the assumptions and data from Exhibit 15.6, and supplies the assumed corporate income tax rate (35 percent), which we shall need to know later. Pretax income is calculated by deducting the annual depreciation of $7 from annual cash inflows. Panel 2 of Exhibit 15.7 shows the annual pretax ROIs calculated based on net book value—which, for year 1, is only 8.2 percent and, for year 2, is 17.1 percent. It also shows that the average ROI is 33.9 percent. (Recall that the firm's target return is 18 percent.) Panel 2 also shows the computation of pretax residual income (column 5), which totals a positive $8.92 over the asset life but is a negative $2.41 in year 1 and a negative $0.15 in year 2. The low ROI and residual income in years 1 and 2 would dissuade a manager who is concerned with short-term results from proceeding with the investment.

Panel 3 of Exhibit 15.7 shows a DCF analysis for the investment, using an after-tax discount rate of 13.96 percent. (ROI and residual income are computed from operating income, a pretax measure that is controllable by the division manager. However, DCF calculations involve taxes and must be discounted at an after-tax cost of capital. The mechanics of converting the 18% *pretax* cost of capital to the 13.96% after-tax rate are

---

[6] See Reece and Cool, op. cit., p. 42; Vancil, op. cit., p. 351; and Govidarajan, op. cit., p. 233.

EXHIBIT 15.7 ENVIRONMENTAL ENTERPRISES, INC.— INTERNATIONAL DIVISION

Comparing Financial Measures and Discounted Cash Flow
(in $ thousands)

Panel 1—Assumptions and Data (from Exhibit 15.6)

Acquisition cost of equipment	$28.0
Useful life	4 years
Expected salvage value	$ 0.0
Annual depreciation (straight-line method)	$ 7.0

	Year 1	Year 2	Year 3	Year 4
Incremental cash inflows from operations	$ 9.0	$10.0	$15.0	$13.0
Annual depreciation	(7.0)	(7.0)	(7.0)	(7.0)
Pretax income	$ 2.0	$ 3.0	$ 8.0	$ 6.0
Tax rate	35%			

Panel 2—Calculation of Pretax ROI and Residual Income

		(1)	(2)	(3)	(4)	(5)	
			Average	ROI on			
		Pretax	Net Book	Net Book	Capital	Residual	
	Year	Income	Value	Value[a]	Charge[b]	Income[c]	Division manager
							might reject
	1	$2.00	$24.50	8.2%	$4.41	$(2.41)	
	2	$3.00	17.50	17.1%	$3.15	$(0.15)	
	3	$8.00	10.50	76.2%	$1.89	$ 6.11	
	4	$6.00	3.50	171.4%	$0.63	$ 5.37	
Averages		$4.75	$14.00				
Average ROI (= $4.75/$14.00)				33.9%			
Total residual income						$ 8.92	

[a] The result of dividing the figure in column 1 by that in column 2.

[b] 18% × the figure in column 2.

[c] The result of deducting the figure in column 4 from that in column 1.

(continued)

---

shown in the footnote to Exhibit 15.7.) The investment has a net present value (NPV) of $0.88, and an internal rate of return (IRR) of 15.4 percent, as shown in panel 3 of the exhibit. Both of these measures indicate that the proposed investment surpasses corporate cost-of-capital requirements and thus is desirable. What is interesting here, though, is the lack of relationship between the conceptually correct DCF calculations and the accrual-based financial measures. The average ROI of 33.9 percent (from panel 2) far exceeds the asset's true return of 15.4 percent (panel 3). And the investment's total residual income of $8.92 (panel 2) is much greater than the $0.88 NPV, which is the correct measure of value creation for the firm.

EXHIBIT 15.7 (CONTINUED)

Panel 3—Calculation of Expected Discounted Cash Flows

	Year 0	Year 1	Year 2	Year 3	Year 4
Investment	$(28.00)				
Operations—cash		$9.00	$10.00	$15.00	$13.00
Less tax @ 35%		3.15	3.50	5.25	4.55
Net cash from operations		$5.85	$ 6.50	$ 9.75	$ 8.45
Tax shield:					
Depreciation/yr	$7.0				
Tax rate	35%	$2.45	$ 2.45	$ 2.45	$ 2.45
Salvage					$ 0.00
Net cash	$(28.00)	$8.30	$ 8.95	$12.20	$10.90
Discount factor @ 13.96[a]	1.0000	0.8775	0.7700	0.6757	0.5929
Discounted cash	$(28.00)	$7.28	$ 6.89	$ 8.24	$ 6.46
Net present value (NPV)	$ 0.88				Project passes
Internal rate of return (IRR)	15.4%				hurdle rate.

[a] ROI and residual income were both calculated based on pretax operating income. The pretax cost of capital was assumed to be 18 percent. However, the DCF model includes tax effects, and its cost of capital must be based on an after-tax rate. We assume the corporate capital structure indicated in the following computation:

	Pretax			After Tax of 35 Percent		
	Rate	Weight	Cost of Capital	Rate	Weight	Cost of Capital
Long-term debt	0.1650	0.7	0.1155	0.1073	0.7	0.0751
Stockholder equity	0.2150	0.3	0.0645	0.2150	0.3	0.0645
Total			0.1800			0.1396

Refer to Exhibit 8.13 and the accompanying discussion for more information on deriving the cost of capital.

This simple case demonstrates the underlying conceptual flaw in the use of ROI and residual income for performance evaluation: They don't match DCF calculations to any significant extent. The problem stems from the fact that DCF cash-based calculations are inherently different from accrual-based financial measure calculations. In the past, when business environments were more stable, results were more predictable and the effects of this difference were less of an issue. Today, however, accrual-based accounting systems that measure results of past periods do not usually reflect the expected cash benefits to be earned in future years. As a result, managers who are evaluated on accrual-based measures may be short-term oriented—guided only by the results they expect in the first year or two of a project's life. For the corporation, this translates into a lack of investment in strategically important projects that could build the overall competitive position and ensure the long-term survival of the firm as a whole.

PERFORMANCE MEASUREMENT ALTERNATIVES

Accrual-based and DCF-based measures can be reconciled in two ways:

1. *Evaluate investment center performance on a discounted cash basis.* This option makes sense theoretically, since it uses a single measurement basis—discounted cash flow—to evaluate future investment *and* current performance. Unfortunately, before this method can be used in evaluating periodic performance results, future cash flows must be estimated. The result is a performance evaluation based not on what has been done in the immediate past, but rather on what is expected to be done in the future. Predictions of future results are extremely relevant to investment decisions but they are generally not relevant to performance evaluation—especially since the necessary data are only projections.

2. *Use accrual-based financial measures, but adjust budget targets in order to reflect the effects of new investment.* Certainly, the effects of capital budgets can be reported as accrual numbers, as was done in Exhibit 15.7. A subunit manager who justifies an investment based on DCF methods can present senior management with projections for subunit ROI or residual income should the new investment be made. These projections can be part of the negotiation process of setting budget targets that will be later used for evaluating performance. If senior management agrees that the investment is the correct strategic decision, then the subunit manager should be evaluated based on accrual-based budget targets consistent with the cash outcomes expected.

ACCOUNTING INFORMATION FOR REWARD SYSTEMS

In this final section we discuss the use of accounting information, including performance measures, to reward desirable behavior in employees. Like all elements of management control, the *reward system* (i.e., the system for determining who gets how much of which rewards) has as its objective the merging of employees' self-interest with the goals of the organization.[7]

REWARD SYSTEMS GENERALLY

Organizations reward their employees with pay, promotions, fringe benefits, perquisites (or "perks"), and status. Accounting feedback plays an

---

[7]   This section draws heavily from the classic work of Edward E. Lawler III, "Reward Systems," chap. 4, pp. 163–226, in J. Richard Hackman and J. Lloyd Suttle, *Improving Life at Work: Behavioral Sciences Approaches to Organizational Change*, Santa Monica, Calif.: Goodyear Publishing, 1977.

important role in helping management to determine how these rewards are to be distributed among managers and employees. Before exploring this role, we take a brief look at the two basic facets of all reward systems.

PAYING EMPLOYEES—TWO APPROACHES

The pay component is, for most employees, the most important part of their reward, or compensation, for working. Employees can be compensated using either a fixed-pay or performance-based pay approach.

In the fixed-pay approach to compensation, the firm pays each employee an agreed-upon amount per pay period; in return, the employee is expected to perform his or her job in an effective manner. Exceptional performers may be rewarded with promotions, larger-than-average pay raises, or special recognition. The amount of pay is not, however, tied to the quality of performance within any pay period. This approach is used to compensate factory and service workers who are paid an hourly wage, teachers who agree to annual contracts, and many managers and rank-and-file workers who are paid an annual salary. Research suggests that fixed-pay plans are especially appropriate in situations when performance cannot be reliably measured or when subjective evaluations are necessary.[8]

With performance-based pay, the firm pays each employee an agreed-upon base rate per pay period plus an increment that depends on some measure of performance (also agreed to beforehand). The employee's pay per period is thus uncertain, but the compensation can be higher than normal if performance is superior. Unlike a fixed-pay approach, in which pay is guaranteed, a performance-based pay plan requires employees to show results first. The nature of the results then determines their pay. Consequently, the fortunes of the employee are more directly tied to the fortunes of the firm. Some examples of employees whose pay is performance-based are salespeople who are paid a percentage of their sales volume as a commission, managers who can earn a bonus, and factory workers who participate in profit-sharing or other methods of apportioning corporate financial gains. Research has shown that performance-based pay plans can contribute to organizational effectiveness.[9]

Surveys show that more companies are using performance-based pay plans each year and that such plans are being extended to encompass more levels of the organization.[10] One survey reports that more than 25 percent of large companies use such plans to compensate employees other than managers and salespeople. Another found that 51 percent of firms surveyed use some sort of pay-for-performance program.

COMPENSATION MODELS

For performance-based pay plans and for distribution of other rewards, as well, a basic issue concerns what quality of performance is to be rewarded

---

[8] Ibid., p. 199.
[9] Ibid., pp. 191–193.
[10] Joseph Spiers, "Wages Are Starting to Inch Up," *Fortune*, June 1, 1992, pp. 17 and 20; Amanda Bennett, "Paying Workers to Meet Goals Spreads, But Gauging Performance Proves Tough," *The Wall Street Journal*, Sept. 9, 1991, p. B1+.

EXHIBIT 15.8 THREE COMPENSATION MODELS

Degree of Worker Involvement in Business Decision Making

Low ◄──► Very High

	Linear	*Adaptive*	*Interpretive*
		Model	
Process for forming strategy	Routine, systematic	Dynamic, with frequent modification	Highly participative, linked to operations
Person in charge of forming strategy	Mainly corporate management	Business unit managers	Business unit managers, but objectives depend on worker input and customer input
Driving force	Forecasts and budgets	Continual competitive analysis and timely change	Shared values and continual learning
Selected types of measures	Profit, ROI, residual income, variances	Profit, ROI, cash flow, quality, market share, revenue growth	Profit, ROI, cash flow, cycle time, quality, time for new products, customer partnerships, business process improvement
Characteristic industries	Utilities, mining	Apparel, autos	Computer systems, commercial airlines

at what level and how performance is to be measured. The answer actually begins with the strategic planning process, which gives rise to three different compensation models. The model chosen is a function of the nature of that process. Exhibit 15.8 compares the essential characteristics of these three models.[11]

1. *Linear model.* The first model shown in Exhibit 15.8 is linear, because it relies on strategies that are largely derived from extrapolations of past performance. Corporate strategies are primarily developed by senior management through a planning process that is itself routine and systematic. The key document for the implementation strategy and for management control is the budget, which is used to evaluate managers' performance. Attention is focused mainly on internal operations, and the competitive environment is of lesser concern. The measures that are used to set corporate and subunit managers' compensation are tied to outcomes. These measures include ROI, residual income, and profit. They can also be used to reward lower-level managers and workers, but tying pay to performance is generally not of importance at those levels. A linear compensation

---

[11] Based on Ellen Hufnagel, "Developing Strategic Compensation Plans," *Human Resources Management*, spring 1987, pp. 93–108.

model seems best-suited to firms that operate in stable environments with predictable demand, such as utilities and mining operations.

2. *Adaptive model.* This **adaptive model** begins with decentralized strategic planning at the business-unit level and relies on the judgment of the business units' managers. Planning is based on the understanding that the firm's markets are complex and can change rapidly. Continual environmental scanning and timely strategy modification are required. A manager's success is measured by results in the current period and, where appropriate, by the likelihood that his or her actions will produce future value. Measures of performance include ROI and profit, as well as cash flow, market share, and product quality. These measures tend to vary with the product life cycle, so the performance of a subunit with many mature products would be measured primarily by using profit and cash flow, and the performance of one with more products in the development stage would be measured by using revenue growth and market share. This compensation model is useful in competitive industries, such as apparel, autos, and defense.

3. *Interpretive model.* The **interpretive model** stems from a much more participative planning process. The business unit manager is responsible for his or her strategic planning but relies on input obtained internally from the subunit's workers and externally from customers and suppliers. The key here is an organizational culture with a shared set of values and a commitment to learning and improvement. The performance measures used here are similar to those used for the adaptive model but lean more heavily on process and operational feedback considerations. Examples of the measures used include ROI, cash flow, cycle time, product quality, the time needed to bring new products to market, and business process improvement. Rewards must be widely distributed in order to ensure recognition of the many sources of contribution. This model is especially appropriate for firms adopting TQM methods. It may be used by—but is not limited to—industries such as computer software development firms and commercial airlines.

REWARD SYSTEM DESIGN FACTORS

We have seen that the use of performance-based compensation systems is on the rise and can be an effective means for promoting goal congruence, that these systems are an important part of management control, and that their design should be tied to the firm's strategic planning. Our next step is to look at some of the requirements that must be met in order for a compensation system to be effective.

FUNDAMENTAL DESIGN PRINCIPLES

No single compensation plan is suitable for all—or even most—organizations. A reward system should be *tailor-made to match the unique situation of each firm.* Whether or not the system is effective will ultimately depend on whether the behavior it motivates helps the firm to achieve its goals. At the minimum, a successful reward system must be able to convince the employees being rewarded that (1) their actions can influence the performance measures and (2) their own rewards are equitable.

Research has found that it is not enough merely to link pay to performance. Organizations must link pay to performance in such a way that employees perceive the relationship. Further, employees see objective performance measures, such as sales dollars or number of defects, as more credible than subjective evaluations.[12] If these basic design criteria are not met, employees are likely to become cynical about the connection between work effort, outcomes, and rewards.

CONSIDERATIONS IN REWARD SYSTEM DESIGN

As a way of systematically approaching reward system design, we will look for answers to the following four basic questions:

1. Who is to be rewarded?
2. What performance measures are needed?
3. When should rewards be given?
4. How much reward should be given?

We shall now examine each of these questions.

Who Is to Be Rewarded?   All employees should be rewarded for their efforts. The compensation models in Exhibit 15.8 offer a framework from which to discuss the degree to which rewards should be based on performance. At the top of the model chart, we see a scale indicating that employee involvement ranges from low in the linear model to very high in the interpretive model. Generally, the greater the amount of involvement required of employees, the greater the power of employees to make decisions that influence outcomes, and the greater the degree to which these employees should be rewarded when those outcomes are favorable. We can expect, for example, that a firm with a linear approach to rewards will restrict performance-based pay primarily, if not exclusively, to key executive officers. At the other extreme, a firm using the interpretive approach will likely distribute performance-based rewards to many employees throughout the organization. In both cases, pay raises may also be based somewhat on performance.

What Performance Measures Are Needed?   Knowing what positions are rewarded and the type of activities they involve will help management to determine what performance measures are needed. As we saw in Chapter 13, these measures should be associated with specific key variables derived from corporate objectives. Exhibit 15.9 shows how performance measures are linked across the levels of the corporate structure for the On-Line

---

[12]   Lawler, "Reward Systems," p. 171 and pp. 195–196.

EXHIBIT 15.9 ON-LINE COMPUTER COMPANY

Some Performance Measures Across the Organization[a]

Organizational Level	Type of Responsibility Center	Key Variables	Measure	Annual Target
Corporate	Investment center	Market value Profitability Cash flow Innovation	Shares outstanding × (price/share) Net income/book value of assets Cash from operations Revenue from new products	$200 million at year-end 12.5% $27.8 million 25% of revenues from products < 1 yr old
Product group— business software	Investment center	Profitability Product leadership Customer loyalty Cash flow	Net income/book value of assets Percent of revenue from new products Retention rates of past customers Cash from operations	16.4% 25% of revenues Retain 96% $9.8 million
Division— western United States	Profit center	Profitability Customer satisfaction Market share Cash flow	Income before tax Percent of satisfied customers Percent of share in competing markets Cash from operations	$1.8 million 95% 20% $0.54 million
Operations— southwest systems support	Cost center	Cost reduction Cycle time On-time delivery Product quality	Percent change from approved budget Days from order to installation Percent attainment of promised date Percent additional work hours necessary after installation	4% cost reduction 7 days 100% Less than 4% of total hours

[a] This exhibit is an extension of the On-Line Computer Company example that was discussed in Chapter 13. See Exhibits 13.4 and 13.5 for background information.

Computer Company. At lower levels, the measures become increasingly specific, with shorter planning horizons and greater emphasis on cost control.

The head of a responsibility center is ultimately responsible for achieving all appropriate measurement targets. Thus, in Exhibit 15.9, performance-based rewards for the manager of the business software product group, an investment center, can be based on four key variables. These variables contain information both on *results,* such as profitability and cash flow, and on *process,* such as product leadership and customer loyalty. Alternatively, the investment center manager could be evaluated on a single, comprehensive, results-oriented measure such as ROI, but that would introduce a bias toward short-run decision making, as discussed earlier in this chapter.

These same measures and corresponding key variables are useful for evaluating operational employees. However, it is important to first determine which measures relate to the work effort of each individual. For example, in Exhibit 15.9, employees of the southwest systems support cost center may be evaluated on the basis of four measures: (1) cost reduction, (2) cycle time, (3) on-time delivery, and (4) product quality. It may be possible to isolate some of these measures and to link them to individual jobs within the cost center. However, as the level of involvement increases, employees will more likely be evaluated as *small teams* responsible for working together on certain tasks.

When Should Rewards Be Given?   Behavioral experts note that frequent rewards are more effective than infrequent ones in terms of sustaining employee motivation.[13] Nonetheless, performance-based rewards are almost always distributed for designated time periods—for example, a month, a quarter, or a year—for which performance data have been collected. In general, the lower the organizational level, the more repetitive the required activities, the more frequently they can be monitored, and the more frequently performance-based rewards may be distributed.

Even at higher levels, where decisions may affect operations over several years, bonuses are typically paid to managers annually. One way of focusing managers' attention (and of basing rewards) on periods longer than a year is through the use of *deferred compensation plans,* in which the collection of performance rewards is delayed. Under such plans, managers have to "bank" their rewards and can withdraw only a limited portion—perhaps 25 or 33 percent of each annual reward—in any one year, except upon retirement. Some firms can also make deductions from a manager's rewards bank account in years in which performance results fall below targets. Thus, the manager shares in the risks as well as the rewards of long-term strategies. Deferred compensation plans can be useful in conjunction with single financial measures, such as ROI, as a means of motivating long-term thinking.

---

[13]   Lawler, op. cit., p. 173.

How Much Reward Should Be Given?   Cost to the firm is, of course, an important consideration in successful compensation-system design. The cost cannot exceed the benefits expected because of the organization's increased effectiveness. At the same time, however, employees must perceive their rewards as being great enough to justify their taking the desired action. One survey of employers found that average performers (employees and unit managers) received 4.7 percent pay increases, while outstanding performers received 7.7 percent. For a $40,000-a-year employee, the 3.0 percent difference means about $17 more per week in after-tax pay. As one compensation expert commented, that is "hardly enough to push someone to excel."[14]

Performance-based reward systems typically expect employees to initially relinquish part of their total compensation in exchange for the promise of greater rewards if target outcomes are met or exceeded. However, such trade-offs can create resentment with employees, who often see the new system as taking away some of their existing pay. A solution is to *involve employees* at all levels in the design of performance-based systems. This approach will help employees understand the connection between their compensation and the work they do and to accept the risk-reward trade-offs that such pay plans entail. In the final analysis, how much compensation is put at risk depends on the particular situation of a given firm. But, again, if employees feel they can influence performance outcomes and are being treated fairly, the reward system is likely to succeed.

INCENTIVE-BASED COMPENSATION PLANS IN USE

Exhibit 15.10 describes three general types of **incentive-based compensation** plans, which are in essence the means for distributing performance-related rewards. The plans are broadly categorized as (1) companywide, (2) group-level, and (3) individual, but there can be a good deal of overlap between the categories.

COMPANYWIDE PLANS

Incentive plans that include all (or most of) the employees of a firm generally reward employees by giving them shares of ownership in the company. These are most often distributed in one of three forms: (1) stock options, which permit employees to buy shares at reduced prices; (2) employee stock ownership plans (ESOPs), which grant shares to employees based on a prescribed formula; or (3) a component part of a retirement benefit package. One important advantage of encouraging employees to own company stock is that, as owners of the company, they have a vested interest in its performance. Additionally, there is an expectation that they will identify more with the company, develop a company spirit, and increase productivity. Unfortunately, the degree to which any one

---

[14]   Amanda Bennett, "Caught in the Middle," *The Wall Street Journal,* Apr. 18, 1990, p. R9.

Exhibit 15.10	Incentive Compensation Plans		
	Type of Plan		
	Companywide	*Group*	*Individual*
Degree of influence by each worker on performance measures	Low	Medium to high	High
Some examples of compensation	Employee stock options ESOPs Retirement plans	Profit sharing Gain sharing Team-based incentive plan	Executive stock options Bonuses Recognition awards
Advantages	Employee ownership Builds company spirit	Builds teamwork and cooperation	Close link between reward and achievement
Disadvantages	Stock price not linked to individual achievement Deferred payment Devaluation	Rewards free riders Poor discriminator between group members (These also apply to companywide plans.)	More subjective performance evaluation Can cause suboptimal decisions
Types of measures	Market value Discounted cash flow	Division income Group results on quality, delivery, etc.	Division income Sales booked Performance appraisal
Example companies	PepsiCo Merck & Co. Waste Management	Whirlpool Corp. Adolph Coors Kroger Grocery	Federal Express Corp. Ford Motor Corp. Valvoline, Inc.

employee—except, perhaps, the most-senior executives—can influence the market price of the stock is quite low. Thus, there is only a very weak connection between an individual's performance and the value of the reward. Further, many stock plans restrict the conversion of the stock into cash, and thus defer actual payment of the reward. (See "Current Practice: PepsiCo's Stock Option Plan.")

Group-Level Plans

Group-level plans reward all employees with a subunit for their accomplishments as a group. Profit-sharing plans, in which employees receive a percentage of their business unit's income results, are among the most popular of these plans. So are gain-sharing plans, in which the business unit divides with its employees any greater-than-expected profits or productivity gains. An individual's ability to influence group results (and, hence, his or her reward) will vary depending on the size of the group being evaluated. In general, though, individual performance is secondary to that of the group, and, typically, any one employee's accomplishments are not closely tied to the reward. On the downside, group-level rewards also compensate free riders (nonperformers) within the group, and they generally do not provide special rewards to individual group members for their superior personal achievements. (See "Current Practice: Gain Sharing at Whirlpool's Benton Harbor Plant.")

CURRENT PRACTICE

PepsiCo's Stock Option Plan

In 1989, Pepsico began offering stock options to all its employees worldwide who work at least 30 hours per week. Under this program, called Sharepower, employees receive grants for stock options equal to 10 percent of their annual compensation. The options allow them to buy stock at a locked-in price at any time for the next 10 years, but no more than 20 percent of the option can be exercised in any one year. That is, employees must parcel out their stock purchases over a minimum of 5 years. PepsiCo has implemented this plan as an incentive in order to encourage employees to take actions that build teamwork and enhance productivity in the course of their work. As the logic goes, these improvements will lead to increased stock value, and thus will benefit each employee personally.

Source: Jolie Solomon, "Pepsi Offers Stock Options to All, Not Just Honchos," *The Wall Street Journal,* June 28, 1989, p. B1.

CURRENT PRACTICE

Gain Sharing at Whirlpool's Benton Harbor Plant

The Benton Harbor plant of Whirlpool Corp. produces parts for washers and dryers and employs 265 people. This is an old operation that does not use high-tech machinery. Nonetheless, over a recent 3-year period, productivity steadily increased, while quality improved greatly. Results of two measures emphasize these changes: (1) Parts produced per worker-hour increased by 19 percent to 110.6, and (2) the incidence of rejected parts plummeted from 837 per million to 10 per million. As a result of these gains, the cost of production fell. An agitator shaft decreased in cost by 13 percent, and the cost of a spin pinion fell by 24 percent, for example.

Institution of a gain-sharing program seems to have been a major factor in the plant's newfound success. The program is structured so that employees receive no automatic wage increases. Instead, they accept the risk of relying on their ability to find ways to increase productivity. In return, they share in gains obtained thereby, which are determined using a formula that includes measures of productivity and quality. Basically, the bigger the gains in output, the larger the pot of money the workers share with the company. The employees' portion is divided equally among all employees. The 3-year result for employees has been an average annual wage increase of almost 4 percent—this at a time when real wages actually fell for most U.S. factory workers. The company's gains have helped it keep its prices low, increase its market share, and show better profits than its rivals have shown.

Source: Adapted from Rick Wartzman, "Sharing Gains: A Whirlpool Factory Raises Productivity—and Pay of Workers," *The Wall Street Journal,* May 4, 1992, p. A1.

CURRENT PRACTICE

Federal Express Corporation

Federal Express Corporation evaluates each of its 50,000 hourly workers twice a year using lengthy proficiency tests and various measures of performance. Based on the evaluation results, hourly workers can receive either raises or, if their pay already exceeds a certain level, bonuses. Managers can also distribute small "spot" awards—normally less than $100—to individuals as a reward for exceptional achievements. After this plan was implemented in 1989, company performance improved substantially, according to measures such as the number of lost packages, the number of late deliveries, and customer response time.

Source: Joann S. Lublin, "A New Track," *The Wall Street Journal*, Apr. 22, 1992, pp. R5 and R7.

INDIVIDUAL INCENTIVE PLANS

Individual incentive plans measure and reward the performance of individual employees. Commission salespeople are rewarded by means of such plans. Individual plans are also used to reward senior-level executives by giving them stock options, periodic bonuses, and special recognition awards for outstanding achievements. The main advantage of individual plans—an important advantage—is that rewards are closely linked to accomplishments. The main disadvantage is that this may be so only for top-level managers—for example, the CEO whose stock or stock options increase in value as her or his efforts result in an increase in the market price of the company stock. For lower-level managers and employees, measures of individual effort and outcomes may be difficult to design, and the measures that are used are more likely to reflect group effort than individual effort. Or, where individual evaluation is required in such cases, it tends to be more subjective than objective. (See "Current Practice: Federal Express Corporation.")

INDIVIDUAL NEEDS

The ultimate success of a company's reward system depends on whether or not it satisfies employees' needs. Research has found, however, that satisfaction is a complex reaction that is influenced by a number of factors.[15] To close the topic of compensation, we look briefly at three of the findings relevant to our discussion.

1. *Satisfaction depends on comparisons.* Employees are bound to compare their compensation with that of other workers, both inside and

---

[15] Lawler, "Reward Systems," pp. 164–166.

outside the organization. If their compensation compares favorably, they tend to be satisfied.

2. *Both intrinsic and extrinsic rewards influence employee satisfaction.* Our discussion has concentrated on *extrinsic* rewards, such as salary and bonus. *Intrinsic* rewards—for example, involvement in exciting work and in decision making—also affect satisfaction. This is especially important in TQM environments, which can create many opportunities for intrinsic rewards.

3. *Employees differ greatly in their needs for reward.* Many employees are satisfied with mainly extrinsic rewards, but others—because of background or situation—prefer more in the way of intrinsic rewards. Further, individual needs change over time. Thus, any broad-scale compensation program will satisfy some employees more than it will satisfy others. Similarly, it may satisfy different groups at different times.

All of this adds to the challenge of designing a successful reward system, especially one that includes performance-based rewards. Again, the key is to involve employees when the plan is created, so that a sense of ownership in the plan is widespread throughout the firm.

SUMMARY

Return on investment and residual income are two financial measures that are often used to evaluate performance of investment centers. ROI measures the efficiency of investments in generating profits. ROI is broken down into two parts—sales margin ratio and investment turnover—in order to reveal more about competitive strategy and opportunities for improvement. Residual income (which is equal to profit minus a capital charge) measures the amount of economic value added by an investment center.

ROI and residual income are accrual-based measures that report outcomes differently from measures that rely on the use of discounted cash flow methods, such as IRR and NPV. The use of a residual-income measure encourages managers to make investment decisions that are more congruent with corporate objectives than are those based on the use of an ROI measure. However, both ROI and residual income measures can discourage managers to invest for the long-term. One feasible way to reconcile the dilemma is to use accrual-based financial measures but to adjust budget targets to reflect effects of new investment.

Reward systems, which help to direct employee action toward congruence with corporate objectives, determine how much compensation (pay and benefits) is distributed to which employees. They should be tailor-made to match the unique situation of each firm. Effective reward systems depend on the firm's ability to convince employees that their own actions influence their performance measures and that their own rewards are equitable. The key is to involve employees when the pay plan is being created so that a sense of ownership in the plan is widespread throughout the firm.

Firms must answer four basic questions when designing reward systems. Who is to be rewarded depends on the extent of employee involvement in business decision making. What measures are needed depends on the key variables derived from corporate objectives. When the reward should be given depends on the repetitiveness of employee actions. How much reward should be given depends on the benefits expected by the firm, but the reward should be large enough to motivate desired actions.

There are three general types of incentive compensation systems in use: companywide plans, group-level plans, and individual plans. Individual plans offer the greatest link between rewards and personal influence, but individual accomplishments are difficult to measure and are more likely to reflect group efforts.

CHAPTER 15 ASSIGNMENTS

DISCUSSION PROBLEMS

D15.1   (Using Benchmarks to Evaluate Manager Performance)

Nero's Contemporary Resorts, Inc., is a privately held company that is made up of three divisions: hotels, restaurants, and hotel management. Each of these is run as an investment center whose division manager has broad authority to make virtually all business investment and operating decisions. Nero's CEO has just received the final reported results (Exhibit D15.1) for the year just ended and is now trying to rank the performance of the three division managers.

The hotels division is the firm's original business line and its oldest business segment. Most of the hotels are 10 to 15 years old. However, only 2 years ago, all of the hotels were modernized in order to better meet the rising market trend of competition. During the past 12 months, the hotels division conducted a

EXHIBIT D15.1   NERO'S CONTEMPORARY RESORTS, INC.

Actual Performance Results (All in $ thousands)

	Division		
	Hotels	*Restaurants*	*Hotel Management*
Net income (*A*)	$ 19,090	$ 4,295	$1,890
Asset balances:			
Beginning of year	$136,780	$44,320	$6,060
End of year	$138,750	$65,420	$6,480
Average balances (*B*)	$137,765	$54,870	$6,270
ROI (*A/B*)	13.9%	7.8%	30.1%
Benchmark Measures			
Budgeted target ROI	15.0%	10.0%	30.0%
Leading competitor's ROI	14.6%	9.1%	34.7%
Division's actual ROI last year	9.1%	9.4%	24.5%

major restructuring campaign designed to boost efficiency and to cut unneeded personnel. The division's current ROI is an improvement over the rate reported for the previous year, but it failed to meet its budgeted target rate.

In the firm's early days, the restaurants were located on-site at the hotels. The restaurants division was originally started in order to free the restaurant managers from the control of the managers of the respective hotels. The concept seems to have proven successful. Restaurants are now being built at new locations, independent of hotels. The division is expanding at a rapid clip. Despite the apparent success of the division, restaurant's ROI has fallen from the previous year's rate and is now below that of its leading competitor. Furthermore, the division failed to meet its targeted ROI rate, and its ROI ratio is the lowest of the three. The CEO cannot understand why this is so.

The hotel management division is the firm's newest business segment and, perhaps, the division with the greatest profit potential. Its ROI this year was by far the best of all three divisions, and it was the only one to meet its target ROI ratio. Still, the division's ROI was several percentage points behind that of its leading competitor. Furthermore, the firm's CEO has heard the other two division managers argue that it is unfair to evaluate their division returns on the basis of the same measures and criteria used to evaluate hotel management, since making such comparisons is "like comparing apples to oranges."

Required:

1. Evaluate the benchmarks used to judge each division manager's ROI results. Which are most valid?
2. What differences between the firm's three divisions might cause direct comparisons between the three's ROI results to be invalid?
3. Rank the three division managers' performance. Explain.

D15.2 (Evaluating Incentive Plan Alternatives)

Renslen Inc., a truck-manufacturing conglomerate, has recently purchased two divisions, Meyers Service Company and Wellington Products Inc. Meyers provides maintenance service for large truck cabs for 18-wheeler trucks, and Wellington produces air brakes for the 18-wheeler trucks.

The employees at Meyers take pride in their work, as Meyers is said to offer the best maintenance service in the trucking industry. Prior to the acquisition by Renslen the management of Meyers, as a group, received additional compensation from a 10 percent bonus pool that is based on income before taxes and bonus. Renslen plans to continue to compensate the Meyers management team on this basis, as this same incentive plan is used for all other Renslen divisions.

Wellington offers a high-quality product to the trucking industry and is the premium choice—even when compared to foreign competition. The management team at Wellington strives for zero defects and minimal scrap costs; current scrap levels are at 2 percent. The group incentive compensation plan in place for Wellington management has been a 1 percent bonus based on gross profit margin. Renslen plans to continue to compensate the Wellington management team on this basis.

The condensed income statements for both divisions for the fiscal year ending May 31, 1996, are shown in Exhibit D15.2.

Renslen has invited the management teams of all of its divisions to an off-site management workshop in July, at which time the bonus checks will be presented. Renslen is concerned that the different bonus plans at the two recently acquired divisions may cause some heated discussion.

EXHIBIT D15.2 RENSLEN INC.

Divisional Income Statements
for the Year Ending May 31, 1996

	Meyers Service Company	Wellington Products Inc.
Revenue	$4,000,000	$10,000,000
Cost of product	$ 75,000	$ 4,950,000
Salaries (before bonus)	2,200,000	2,150,000
Fixed selling expense	1,000,000	2,500,000
Interest expense	30,000	65,000
Other operating expense	278,000	134,000
Total expense	$3,583,000	$ 9,799,000
Income before taxes and bonus	$ 417,000	$ 201,000

Required: Having two different types of incentive plans for two operating divisions of the same corporation can create problems.

1. Discuss the behavioral problems that could arise within management for Meyers Service Company and for Wellington Products Inc. as the result of each having a different type of incentive plan.
2. Formulate arguments that Renslen Inc. can present to the management teams of both Meyers and Wellington that will justify their each having a different incentive plan.

(*CMA adapted*)

PROBLEMS

P15.1   (ROI and Residual Income)

The Clean Bee is a manufacturer of household cleaning products. The detergent division prepared an annual budget, as shown in Exhibit P15.1. During the year, the division made unexpected investments in new machinery. Consequently, actual results shown in Exhibit P15.1 differ greatly from the budget estimates. ROI and residual income are determined by using operating income and average assets. Residual income is computed by deducting a 15 percent capital charge from operating income.

Required: Calculate ROI and residual income based upon both budgeted and actual data. For ROI, include calculations for sales margin and investment turnover.

P15.2   (Investment Bases for ROI and Residual Income)

American Delivery Service (ADS) transports packages across the United States for its customers. ADS is examining an investment intended to make sorting packages more efficient, thereby resulting in decreased sorting time and speedier delivery times. The equipment costs $60,000 and will be depreciated at $20,000 in the first year. Other budgeted effects to income and balance sheet accounts are given in Exhibit P15.2.

EXHIBIT P15.1   THE CLEAN BEE—DETERGENT DIVISION

Annual Budget

Statement of Income

	Budget	Actual
Revenue	$1,625,000	$1,806,300
Less expense:		
Cost of goods sold	568,750	614,142
Selling expense	450,000	480,000
Administrative expense	300,000	350,000
Operating income	306,250	362,158

Balance Sheet

	Beginning of Year	Budgeted End of Year	Actual End of Year
Current assets	$ 345,000	$ 460,000	$ 572,800
Plant assets, net	1,235,500	1,310,000	1,760,000
Other assets	210,000	225,000	220,000
Total assets	$1,790,500	$1,995,000	$2,552,800
Current liabilities	$ 237,500	$ 246,000	$ 252,100
Long-term liabilities	960,000	860,250	1,356,042
Shareholder equity	593,000	888,750	944,658
Total liabilities & equity	$1,790,500	$1,995,000	$2,552,800

EXHIBIT P15.2   AMERICAN DELIVERY SERVICE

Budgeted Effects to Income and Balance Sheet Accounts

	Beginning of Year	Budget Before Investment	Budget After Investment
Revenue		$ 645,000	$ 700,000
Cash operating expense		$ 431,500	$ 453,000
Current assets	$ 214,000	$ 234,500	$ 242,000
Property, plant, & equipment	$ 550,000	$ 590,000	$ 650,000
Accumulated depreciation	$(115,000)	$(160,000)	$(180,000)
Other assets	$ 50,000	$ 62,000	$ 62,000
Current liabilities	$ 110,000	$ 115,000	$ 114,000
Long-term liabilities	$ 306,500	$ 219,475	$ 259,200
Shareholder equity	$ 282,500	$ 392,025	$ 400,800

Required: Calculate residual income and ROI both before and after the investment. Use the following as the investment bases: (1) average net assets and (2) average gross assets. Use net income for the earnings measure. The tax rate is 35 percent. The rate for imputed interest is 16 percent.

EXHIBIT P15.3 THE WRITE COMPANY— LEAD PENCIL DIVISION			
Anticipated Investment Data			
Effects of Investment	Year 1	Year 2	Year 3
Number of units sold	595,000	675,000	815,000
Average price per unit	$ 0.55	$ 0.58	$ 0.62
Variable cost of goods sold per unit	$ 0.22	$ 0.23	$ 0.25
Cash operating expense	$150,000	$156,000	$160,000

P15.3 (DCF, ROI, Residual Income on New Investment)

The Write Company manufactures pens and pencils. The lead pencil division has the opportunity to purchase a machine that produces a new type of mechanical pencil. Anticipated income and cash data from the sale of this product are given in Exhibit P15.3. Because of "cannibalization," sales of the current line of mechanical pencils will decrease by 65,000 units per year. This older product has a contribution margin of $0.14 per unit.

Acquisition cost of the new equipment is $150,000. The asset will be depreciated over 3 years using the straight-line method, with no residual value. The company's after-tax cost of capital is 14 percent, and its tax rate is 30 percent.

Required: Calculate the net present value (NPV) and internal rate of return (IRR) for the proposed investment. Calculate the ROI for years 1 through 3 using the beginning-of-year net book value.

P15.4 (Alternative Bonus Plans)

The Simpson Company manufactures consumer food products. Each product line is produced and sold by independent divisions. Corporate management wants to institute a pay-for-performance bonus plan for its division managers. Two plans are under consideration. In the first, the managers will receive 20 percent of residual income as a bonus, on top of salary. Simpson uses a capital charge of 18 percent, which is applied to average total assets. In the second plan, the division manager's bonus will be based on the average of the percentage achievement of market share and ROI. For example, if a division's budgeted market share was 9.1 percent and its achieved market share was 7.5 percent, then the division manager's percentage of achievement would be 82.42 percent (7.5%/9.10%). Percent bonus awards, along with other performance data, are shown in Exhibit P15.4. The resulting bonus percentage is applied to the manager's base salary. In both plans, underachievement means that no bonus is awarded, according to the bonus formula.

Required: Calculate the bonuses for the managers of divisions A and B under the two bonus plan proposals.

P15.5 (Individual vs. Group Bonus Plan)

Executive management at Welcome Hotel wants to improve sales and service by offering a comprehensive bonus plan covering all employees. Two types of plans

> ### EXHIBIT P15.4 THE SIMPSON COMPANY— DIVISIONS A AND B
>
> *Performance and Bonus Award Data*
>
> | Average Percentage of Budget Attained | Bonus as a Percentage of Salary |
> |:---:|:---:|
> | < 100% | 0.0% |
> | ≥100% to 105% | 5.0% |
> | >105% to 115% | 10.0% |
> | >115% to 130% | 15.0% |
> | > 130% | 20.0% |
>
> | | Division A | Division B |
> |---|:---:|:---:|
> | Fixed salary of manager | $ 45,000 | $ 52,000 |
> | Operating income | $125,520 | $194,593 |
> | Average total assets | $675,000 | $840,200 |
> | Market share: | | |
> | Budgeted | 9.1% | 6.6% |
> | Achieved | 7.5% | 7.0% |
> | ROI: | | |
> | Budgeted | 12.5% | 22.5% |
> | Achieved | 18.6% | 23.2% |

are under consideration, an individual plan and a group plan. Under each plan, current employee salaries will be cut by 5 percent. All bonus calculations are based on salaries after the 5 percent reduction. The particulars of each plan are given below:

1. *Individual plan.* A bonus of up to 15 percent will be available under the individual plan. The bonus will be based on the average of two performance scores—one given by the employee's supervisor, the other given by the employee's immediate colleagues. Criteria for performance scores include several factors, such as meeting job expectations, promoting customer satisfaction, and working as a team player.
2. *Group plan.* Under the group plan, employees will share 50 percent of hotel net profit in excess of the budgeted targets. The profit bonus will be distributed to employees based on each person's salary as a percent of total hotel payroll.

Exhibit P15.5 offers additional information needed to calculate the two bonuses for two sample employees—a housekeeper and a desk clerk.

Required: Calculate bonuses for the housekeeper and desk clerk under both the individual and group bonus plans. Further, calculate total compensation for the two employees under the two plans. Then compare each of these amounts with the original fixed salaries for each employee, respectively.

P15.6 (ROI, Sales Margin, and Investment Turn)

The public accounting industry has experienced tremendous pressure regarding profitability and survival over the past several years. Large international firms (e.g.,

EXHIBIT P15.5 WELCOME HOTEL		

Individual versus Group Bonus Plan

Company Operating Data

Company net income	$565,450
Company budgeted net income	$530,000
Total hotel payroll before 5% reduction	$450,000

Basis of Bonus Awards for Individual Plans

Average Evaluation Score	Bonus as a Percentage of Salary
< 85%	0.0%
85–85.9%	1.0%
86–86.9%	2.0%
.	.
.	.
.	.
98–98.9%	14.0%
99–100%	15.0%

Information on Two Employees

	Housekeeper	Desk Clerk
Salary before 5 percent reduction	$13,500	$16,000
Supervisor evaluation score	88	97
Colleague evaluation score	87	94

the Big Six) have intensified their efforts to attract and maintain Fortune 1000 clients. Meanwhile, the pool of potential clients has shrunk because of mergers and corporate restructurings. These large firms have generally managed to grow their consulting businesses, while trying to maintain their traditional audit and tax base. Small local firms have often succeeded in this highly competitive environment by focusing on the audit and tax needs of local businesses and by charging reasonable prices. The regional firms have often encountered difficulties, however, since they carry more overhead than do local firms but cannot offer the extensive services of the large international firms.

Chastain, Greenberg, and Trowel, CPAs, is one such regional firm, located in the midwest. Since 1994 it has redirected its operating strategies. The firm is made up of a central office located in Indianapolis and four branch locations. Each branch is run by a managing partner, who decides how the branch will invest in personnel and assets and how it will structure its operations. Managing partners are evaluated on the basis of their ability to reach profit objectives and on the basis of their ROIs. Further, the central office keeps close track of the sales margin and investment turnover components of ROI in order to monitor the actions of managing partners and to discover whether managers are meeting their branch's strategic objectives.

The results for the last 3 years of operation for the Kansas City office are shown in Exhibit P15.6. This office has been faced with a regional glut of overcapacity in public accounting services. The environment has been highly competi-

EXHIBIT P15.6 CHASTAIN, GREENBERG, AND TROWEL, CPAS—KANSAS CITY OFFICE

Comparison of Financial Results for 3 Years

	1994 Total	1995 Total	1996 Quarter 1	Quarter 2	Quarter 3	Quarter 4	Total
Revenue	$10,327,350	$9,746,124	$2,300,480	$2,436,800	$2,387,590	$2,563,850	$9,688,720
Operating expense	9,201,669	8,985,926	2,153,249	2,288,155	2,272,986	2,424,120	9,138,510
Operating income	$ 1,125,681	$ 760,198	$ 147,231	$ 148,645	$ 114,604	$ 139,730	$ 550,210
Asset book value (end of period)	$ 5,589,034	$3,957,890	$3,345,780	$3,154,320	$3,056,740	$2,887,543	$2,887,543

tive. Many CPA firms have recently gone out of business or have been absorbed by other firms. Since accounting fees have been flat during this period and billable hours have fallen, this branch office has focused on running more efficiently and keeping its current clients. A building was sold in 1995, and efforts to reduce outstanding receivables are ongoing. Supplies inventories and office equipment have also been reduced. Professional and support staff are expected to work longer hours, and all overtime pay has been eliminated. Still, the branch's managing partner contends that his operation is on the right path and is well positioned to "ride out" the industry's realignment. In his annual review, he argues that the branch's financial results bear out his assertion of success to date.

Required:

1. For each of the years and quarters shown in Exhibit 15.6, calculate the following:
   a. Sales margin
   b. Investment turn
   c. ROI
   (*Note:* You will have to convert quarterly results to annual equivalents to make the results comparable. Use end-of-period asset book value in your computations.)
2. Comment on the results achieved in the Kansas City branch over the past 3 years. Do your calculations in requirement 1 confirm that the managing partner has been successful in positioning the branch for the future?

P15.7 (ROI Asset Valuation)

Herbert Dumars, president of Quality Foods, is concerned about the impact that ROI is having on the morale of his division managers. Over the past 5 years he has relied on ROI—which is equal to the quotient of division net income divided by division assets—as a means of assessing manager performance and as the basis for determining bonuses. Increasingly, however, his division managers are complaining that the ROI measure does not accurately gauge the value they have generated for their divisions and for the firm as a whole. For one thing, they say the methods used by the corporate office to calculate division income include arbitrary cost assignments for corporate charges, which are clearly out of the managers' immediate control. Further, they contend that ROI encourages them to take actions that are not in the best interests of the firm. They argue that they are penalized whenever they make new investments—even when actual cash flows meet the capital budget expectations that were used to justify the investments in the first place.

Mr. Dumars understands the gravity of these concerns, but still he is generally satisfied with the information conveyed in the ROI measure. Instead of doing away with the use of divisional ROI, he decides to try some alternative measures for calculating the numerator and denominator of the ROI ratio. He wants to begin by examining the numeric outcome and possible behavioral implications of calculating ROI under several different numeric combinations for one of his divisions, frozen foods. He asks you to help derive the numbers and to comment on their usefulness.

The most recent year's financial statements for the frozen foods division are given in Exhibit P15.7. Upon further investigation, you also discover the following:

- Current cost can be estimated using replacement value. You find that the replacement of current assets is approximately equal to the book value. However, the replacement value of plant assets has recently been estimated by the firm's insurance agents at $21,350,000.

EXHIBIT P15.7 QUALITY FOODS— FROZEN FOODS DIVISION

Financial Statements

Income Statement
for the Year Ending December 31, 1996
(in $ thousands)

Revenue		$12,080
Cost of goods sold		5,850
Gross margin		$ 6,230
Operating expense:		
Salaries, wages, & commissions	$1,254	
Occupancy	920	
Depreciation	2,073	
Travel & entertainment	430	
Corporate charges:		
Marketing & public relations	235	
General overhead	180	5,092
Pretax income		$ 1,138
Income tax		455
Net income		$ 683

Balance Sheet
at December 31, 1996
(in $ thousands)

Assets:			Liabilities & shareholder equity:	
Current assets		$ 5,340	Current liabilities	$ 3,870
Plant assets	$18,654		Long-term debt	8,560
Accumulated depreciation	6,210	12,444	Shareholder equity	5,354
Total		$17,784	Total	$17,784

- The firm uses straight-line depreciation on its books. Depreciation expense under replacement value will also be calculated using the straight-line method and will use the same estimated lives.
- Divisions are currently assigned corporate charges for marketing and public relations, and for general overhead. Division managers have no authority in decisions related to these expenses.
- Corporate-level income taxes are managed at the corporate level. Division managers are assigned a fair portion of the corporate tax expense.
- The average corporate tax rate is 40 percent.

Required:

1. Using divisional net income as the numerator, prepare three separate ROI calculations using the following denominators. (Be sure to recalculate net income when replacement cost is used.)
   a. Assets using net book value of plant assets
   b. Assets using gross book value of plant assets
   c. Assets using replacement cost of plant assets
2. Repeat requirement 1, using direct divisional profit (before tax) as the numerator in the ROI ratio.
3. From the six ratios calculated, choose two that seem to be most useful for evaluating the performance of division managers. Explain your reasoning.

P15.8 (Designing an Appropriate Divisional Investment Basis)

By what means can we assign managers a capital investment number that captures their performance? This was the question that opened a recent meeting at the office of the corporate controller of Sound Systems International, Inc. The focus of concern was the evaluation mechanism used to track performance of the firm's 32 division managers, who were located throughout the world. Both ROI and residual income have been used in the past, but the firm's president has often raised questions about the effects of differences between divisional operating practices. The major controversy seems to focus on the definition and valuation of each division's investment. In the past, these have been based on net book values taken directly from the balance sheet.

To illustrate the issues, the controller offers the following examples of one division located in New Zealand (see Exhibit P15.8).

- *Cash balance*—The firm's corporate office keeps careful control over cash flows and generally tries to minimize cash holdings at foreign locations. Consequently, divisional cash balances are often much smaller than they would be for a comparable independent company. To alleviate this problem, the controller suggests using an across-the-board carrying value for divisional cash equal to 5 percent of net sales revenue.
- *Accounts receivable*—Accounts receivable represents an accurate estimate of amounts collectible and is totally under the division manager's authority. The book value is thus considered a useful indicator of accounts receivable.
- *Inventory valuations*—Inventory valuations vary, depending on types of inventory and local tax regulations. The New Zealand division uses a LIFO method, whereas others apply FIFO or weighted averages. If New Zealand's inventory were valued at today's replacement cost, the value would increase by about 75 percent. However, cost of sales would not change, since LIFO approximates replacement value.

EXHIBIT P15.8   SOUND SYSTEMS INTERNATIONAL, INC.

Example of New Zealand Division's Balance Sheet

Assets

Current assets:		
Cash		NZ$ 159,850
Accounts receivable		1,214,200
Inventory		2,154,700
Total current assets		NZ$ 3,528,750
Plant assets:		
Land		NZ$ 3,745,500
Buildings	NZ$ 9,875,400	
Less accumulated depreciation	7,406,550	2,468,850
Machinery & equipment	NZ$13,908,000	
Less accumulated depreciation	8,413,300	5,494,700
Total plant assets		NZ$11,709,050
Total assets		NZ$15,237,800

Liabilities and Shareholder Equity

Current liabilities:	
Accounts payable	NZ$ 1,756,800
Notes payable	425,000
Taxes payable	225,300
Total current liabilities	NZ$ 2,407,100
Long-term liabilities—bonds payable	4,000,000
Total liabilities	NZ$ 6,407,100
Shareholder equity:	
Common stock	NZ$ 6,500,000
Retained earnings	2,330,700
Total shareholder equity	NZ$ 8,830,700
Total liabilities & shareholder equity	NZ$15,237,800

- *Plant asset accounting*—Plant asset accounting varies considerably from division to division. Much of the problem stems from fluctuations in asset value since the division's inception and from the variability of ages of its assets. Also, depreciation methods vary between divisions due to differences in tax codes from country to country. Generally, older divisions have assets that would be much more costly to replace than is indicated by the values in the books.

  If the New Zealand plant assets were revalued for their current replacement cost, their net book values would have to be increased by approximately NZ$7,800,000. Moreover, depreciation expense for the current year would increase by NZ$1,200,000.

- *Accounts payable*—Accounts payable are completely under the division manager's control. The problem here is that some division managers, such as New Zealand's, are able to push their outstanding values very high—which, in effect, translates into an interest-free loan to the division. The controller wants to reward these actions by deducting the accounts payable balance from the investment base.

- *Other factors*—Other liabilities and shareholder equity accounts have not been seen as problems. Notes payable, which carry interest, and taxes payable, which carry interest and fines if paid late, are the responsibilities of the division manager. Bonds and shareholder equity accounts are completely controlled by the central office. Regardless, all these accounts are excluded from the division's capital investment basis.

New Zealand's income statement for the year just ended reveals an operating income of NZ$2,545,500 on net sales revenue of NZ$16,431,680. Depreciation expense reported on the income statement is NZ$2,100,100. For determining residual income, assume that the division is charged a rate of 15 percent of capital investment.

Required:

1. Calculate the New Zealand division's ROI and residual income based on data originally reported in the financial statements. Recalculate the division's ROI and residual income based on the changes suggested by the corporate controller.
2. Which of the two sets of measures does a better job of capturing the manager's performance for the past year? Why?

P15.9 (Using DCF, ROI, Residual Income to Evaluate New Investment)

The headquarters of biomedical division of Comprehensive Health Company has recently been the site of a heated dispute between the division's manager, Sandra McCord, and her marketing manager, Bob Arnoff. The controversy began when Arnoff proposed investing in a new product that, according to his projections, would surpass the division's required 13 percent investment hurdle rate. Nonetheless, McCord rejected the proposal and refused to approach the corporate committee for funding approval. McCord said that she would only accept proposals that began paying for themselves immediately—meaning that she would only support new investments that would boost the division's current ROI of 16 percent. She left Arnoff with the gentle reminder that her annual bonus—and her future— was tied first and foremost to the division's ROI. She did not wish to jeopardize either by accepting marginal investments.

Arnoff plans to meet with the division's controller, who originally helped with preparation of the new product proposal. First, Arnoff wants to get a better handle on the proposal and to understand why McCord is so adamantly against it. He begins by examining Exhibit P15.9, which contains detail on projected product performance and a DCF analysis. Based on a five-year life and a 13 percent discount rate, the $250,000 investment is expected to generate a positive NPV of $3,592.

Reflecting on McCord's comments, Arnoff also realizes that the primary measure of her division's performance is ROI, which is calculated as divisional net income divided by the average book value of investment. He also knows that McCord is seen as a rising young star within the company, and it has been rumored that she could be next in line to lead the firm's vanguard business unit—the hospital division. He decides he should ask the controller to calculate the project's ROI in order to see if it meets the division's required current return rate of 16 percent. Further, he thinks the controller may know of other ways to present the data in order to make the proposal more acceptable.

Required:

1. Calculate the project's ROI for each year of its expected 5-year life. Why is McCord rejecting the project?

EXHIBIT P15.9 COMPREHENSIVE HEALTH COMPANY— BIOMEDICAL DIVISION

DCF Analysis of New Program Proposal

Assumptions

Initial investment, end of 1996	$250,000
Expected residual value, end of life	$ 0
Projected life of program	5 yr
Expected annual revenue	$140,000
Variable cost for delivery @ 40%	56,000
Annual contribution margin	84,000
Annual depreciation, straight-line method	50,000
Income, pretax	34,000
Tax @ 35%	11,900
Net income	$ 22,100
Discount rate (net of tax)	13.0%

DCF Analysis	Year					
	1996	1997	1998	1999	2000	2001
Investment	$(250,000)					
Annual cash flow:						
Net income		$22,100	$22,100	$22,100	$22,100	$22,100
Add depreciation		50,000	50,000	50,000	50,000	50,000
Net cash flows	$(250,000)	$72,100	$72,100	$72,100	$72,100	$72,100
Discount factor @ 13.0%	1.0000	0.8850	0.7831	0.6931	0.6133	0.5428
Discounted cash	$(250,000)	$63,805	$56,465	$49,969	$44,220	$39,133
NPV	$ 3,592					

2. Calculate the project's residual income for each year of its life. (Use net income and average book value of assets). Is it likely that this measure of performance will justify the investment to McCord?
3. Assume that McCord becomes persuaded that the new project is a good idea. Under what circumstances will she try to have the project accepted by senior management? How will the current method for evaluating her performance have to be changed?

P15.10 (Evaluating Division Managers on Multiple Measures)

Waste Disposal, Inc., is a waste industry giant that operates eight separate divisions. Each division manager has considerable autonomy in deciding upon his or her unit's strategic direction, operating plans, investment, pricing, and cost structures. Past performance appraisals of division managers have been based on comparisons between actual results and budgeted objectives and have assessed both financial and nonfinancial outcomes.

Because of an impending reorganization of the corporate structure, the firm's CEO wants to promote a division manager to a new position as leader of the newly formed commercial services group, which will oversee five of the firm's divisions. The list of candidates has been narrowed to two managers—one of whom presently heads the residential division and the other, the medical division. Both persons

EXHIBIT P15.10 WASTE DISPOSAL, INC.

Comparison of Performance in Two Divisions
(All in $ thousands)

	Residential			Medical		
	1994	1995	1996	1994	1995	1996
Estimated industry sales	$98,500	$101,947	$104,802	$17,240	$18,533	$20,034
Divisional performance:						
Sales	$ 5,043	$ 5,617	$ 6,257	$ 3,534	$ 3,725	$ 3,967
Expense:						
Operations	2,905	3,303	3,829	2,166	2,239	2,352
Sales & administration	1,725	1,910	2,121	1,067	1,128	1,173
Total expense	$ 4,630	$ 5,213	$ 5,950	$ 3,234	$ 3,367	$ 3,525
Income, pretax	$ 414	$ 404	$ 307	$ 300	$ 358	$ 442
Assets, net book value	$ 3,335	$ 3,148	$ 2,780	$ 1,586	$ 1,864	$ 2,168
Percent of satisfied customers	72.3%	75.6%	79.2%	84.3%	85.7%	88.1%

have been with the company in their present positions for at least 3 years. Comprehensive operating results for the past 3 years of operation are reported in Exhibit P15.10.

The corporate CEO is having a difficult time deciding which of the two candidates has been more effective. He knows that both have generated huge profits for the firm and have been highly successful in meeting their budgeted targets. Now, however, he needs someone who can establish Waste Disposal as the recognized leader in the commercial-waste-management sector. The industry is experiencing tremendous growth, which is being driven by an increase in regulatory pressures and added complexity in the area of environmental compliance. Furthermore, the competition is becoming highly specialized, and market position is largely dependent on being at the cutting edge of technology. The person selected must be a strategist who can position the firm to take advantage of future opportunities. At the same time, the CEO knows that the firm will face huge capital-financing needs, and he wants a manager who can keep profits up and maintain operating efficiency.

Required:

1. Prepare the following annual measures of performance for each manager:
   a. ROI
   b. Sales margin
   c. Investment turnover
   d. Operations expense ratio (operations expense/sales)
   e. Sales and administration expense ratio (sales and administration expense/sales)
   f. Sales growth
   g. Market share
   h. Industry growth
2. Which of the two managers seems better-qualified to meet the CEO's requirements? Justify your position.

EXHIBIT P15.11.1 ALLIED PLASTICS COMPANY

Calculation of Bonus Payout in Year 1

Revenue		$2,945,000
Expense		2,356,000
Income before tax		$ 589,000
Income tax @ 35.0%		206,150
Net income		$ 382,850
Capital charge:		
Capital investment	$1,800,000	
Required rate of return	12.0%	216,000
Economic value added		$ 166,850
Bonus rate		25.0%
Bonus earned		$ 41,713
Bonus-bank transactions:		
Opening balance		$ 0
Add bonus earned		41,713
Available for payout		$ 41,713
Bonus paid at ⅓ of available		13,904
Closing balance		$ 27,808

P15.11 (Using Bonus Banks to Defer Bonus Payments)

Allied Plastics Company is a diversified parent company made up of 23 highly decentralized business units. The firm has just completed its first year of using a bonus plan based on economic value added (EVA)—a method widely used by such corporate giants as Coca-Cola, AT&T, CSX, and Quaker Oats. While new under that name, EVA is actually a variation of the residual-income method long advocated by management accountants. At Allied Plastics, a business unit manager is awarded a bonus equal to 25 percent of the unit's annual EVA. The actual payout, however, is limited to one-third of the manager's bonus bank balance, which includes all previous years' unpaid bonus earnings.

Consider the case of one of the company's unit managers, whose bonus payout calculations are shown in Exhibit P15.11.1. The manager generated net after-tax income of $382,850, and was charged a required rate of return of 12.0 percent on the unit's capital investment or $1,800,000.[16] Based on an EVA of $166,850, the manager is awarded a 25 percent bonus, equal to $41,713. In the lower part of the exhibit, the manager's bonus-bank transactions are disclosed. Since these figures are for the first year of the bonus plan, the manager had no previous unpaid bonus balance. Thus, the total available for payout this year is the amount just earned, $41,713. However, only one-third (or $13,904), can actually be paid out. The remaining balance becomes the opening balance for the next year's bonus calculation.

The bonus-bank system is designed to make managers act as owners. A key element to the system is that managers are awarded bonus earnings only when their business units have increased the firm's total wealth, as approximated by

---

[16] Several accounting adjustments were made for investment expenditures, such as R&D and employee training, which had been expensed for the company's external financial statements. No detail is provided on these adjustments.

EXHIBIT P15.11.2 ALLIED PLASTICS COMPANY		
Results of Operations for Years 2 and 3		
	Year 2	Year 3
Revenue	$3,681,250	$3,239,500
Expense	$2,742,531	$2,931,748
Capital investment	$1,965,000	$2,112,375

cumulative EVAs. Not only are bonus earnings deferred over 3 years, but the manager is charged with a negative bonus whenever EVA is a loss amount. If, for example, a business unit reports a negative EVA of $100,000, the manager's bonus-bank balance is reduced by $25,000, which is equal to 25 percent of the company's loss in value. Furthermore, should a manager leave the firm before retirement, the outstanding balance in the bonus-bank account is either foregone or settled at a fraction of the total. The bonus-bank concept thus results in business unit managers' sharing in both their units' good fortune as well as in their failures. Moreover, a manager must implement both short-run and long-run business plans in order to be truly successful.

To continue with the case of the Allied Plastics business units, assume the manager's operating results for years 2 and 3 of the EVA-based bonus plan are as shown in Exhibit P15.11.2.

Required:

1. Calculate the business unit manager's bonus, bonus payout, and closing bonus balance for years 2 and 3. Assume a tax rate of 35 percent.
2. Evaluate the effectiveness of the EVA-based bonus system used by Allied Plastic Company. What shortcomings can you foresee?

P15.12 (Evaluating a TQM Pay-Plan Proposal)

"Our people will rise up in revolt." These were the sentiments of Bob Larson, manager of the military division, concerning the new pay plan proposed by the corporate human resource group. Larson continued by agreeing with the basic thrust of the plan—to encourage teamwork, to have workers focus on quality and cost reduction, and to put the division's interests above the individual department. Nonetheless, he asserted, "These are all the things we are trying to accomplish with TQM in our division, but the plan is inequitable. Its standards are the same for all departments and all divisions, and it penalizes those who have already been successful in improving their past operations. We'd be better off using fixed pay, as we've always done in the past, and letting supervisors reward employees through pay raises."

The outline of the proposed pay plan is given in Exhibit P15.12.1. Basically, the plan is composed of two elements—fixed pay set at 88 percent of an employee's former pay and a variable component worth 24 percent of former pay. The variable-pay portion depends on the performance of one's department and division. If all were to go well, an employee could earn 112 percent of the previous year's pay. To do so, the person's department would have had to improve its quality measures by 6 percent over the past year and to reduce its unit costs by 6 percent as well. Furthermore, the division would have had to earn 12 percent more in profit than it earned the previous year.

EXHIBIT P15.12.1   PROPOSED PAY PLAN

Component	Amount	Basis	
Fixed pay	88.0%	Former pay	
Variable pay	24.0%	Former pay broken down into three elements, shown below.	

Variable Pay Element	Amount	Bonus for Each 1.0% Gain over Last Year	Maximum Bonus Percentage
Department level:			
Quality	6.0%	1.0%	6%
Cost reduction	6.0%	1.0%	6%
Division level—profit	12.0%	1.0%	12%
Total variable pay	24.0%		

EXHIBIT P15.12.2   PAST YEAR'S OPERATING RESULTS FOR TWO EMPLOYEES

Component	Design Engineer— Consumer Goods Division		Production Worker— Military Division	
	Last year's pay	$65,000	Last year's pay	$30,000
Department outcomes:				
Quality	1.7% improvement in delivery time		9.2% reduction in defects	
Cost reduction	0.5% reduction in cost/engineer		4.5% reduction in cost/unit	
Division outcome—profit	10.7% profit improvement		1.1% profit improvement	

The calculation is straightforward: For each percent gain (or fraction thereof) in quality, cost, or profit, the employee earns an equal percent (including fractions) in bonus payment, based on last year's pay, to the limits prescribed. For example, an employee who earned $50,000 last year would start with a base salary of only $44,000 under the plan. If the department improved quality and cost by 6 percent each, the employee would earn two bonuses of $3,000 ($50,000 × 6%). If the division improved profit by 12 percent, the employee would earn another bonus, equal to $6,000 ($50,000 × 12%). Total annual pay under the proposed plan would then be $56,000.

Upon the urging of Larson, human resources has gathered information on two employees to see how the proposed plan would have affected compensation for the past year. This information, presented in Exhibit P15.12.2, reports on the operating results of a design engineer in the consumer goods division and a production worker in the military division. For each person, information is provided on last year's pay, departmental outcomes in quality and cost reduction, and divisional profit.

Required:

1. Calculate the total earnings for each of the two employees if the proposed pay plan had been in effect last year.

2. What problems are evident from the proposed plan? Do you agree with Larson that the plan is inequitable? Explain.

3. Should a pay plan such as this reward only the performance of the group—that is, the department and the division? Or should the plan also include a component for awarding individual performance?

CASES

C15.1 (Syndicated Builders, Inc.)

A heated argument has developed between senior managers at the corporate headquarters of Syndicated Builders, Inc., and managers at one of its three business units, the equipment division. The firm is going through its annual capital project approval process. A new product proposal by equipment was rejected by corporate on the grounds that it did not adequately increase the firm's ROI. As Syndicated's finance director, Jeremy Irony, explained, "We plan to go to the capital markets within two years. If we accept this project, it will end up hurting the numbers we report in our banking prospectus. At this point, we can only consider taking on investments that boost our ROI and earnings-per-share numbers. Otherwise, we'll be cutting off our nose to spite our face."

Equipment's division manager, Janella Blunt, was incredulous. True to her reputation as a no-nonsense woman, she went right to the heart of the matter:

> You have got to be kidding! What is our purpose here—are we playing games with numbers or are we trying to build value for the company? I was under the impression the market was smart enough to see through the "smoke and mirrors" of reported financial statements. Shouldn't we be focused on cash flows and our competitive position in the market? Let's go over these arguments one more time and ask Mario Marino (the corporate CEO) to sit in this time. I think he will look at the project with a different view.

More on the Firm and Its Operations

Syndicated Builders is a 65-year-old firm that has its roots in the construction of large public projects—buildings, bridges, monuments, dams, and the like. Over the past 25 years, the company expanded into equipment manufacturing and then architecture. Now the firm comprises three separate business units, each considered an investment center. Division managers are authorized to make virtually all operating and investment decisions, but they are required to gain approval for investments over $2,000,000 from the capital budget committee, headed by Irony from finance.

Selected results of operations over the past 3 years for the firm and its divisions are reported in Exhibit C15.1.1. These data have been used by the corporate finance director to support his argument that equipment's product proposal should be turned down. He maintains that the company must boost its ROI to at least 15 percent for the next year (1997) in order to look impressive in the market. The firm's major competitors have kept their ROI percentages at 15 percent or higher over the past 2 years, and Irony believes the market will respond unfavorably if Syndicated cannot do the same. On more than one occasion, he has pointed to the equipment division as the cause of low corporate ROI. Furthermore, Irony wants to make sure the firm's reported earnings per share improves in the next year, especially since latest estimates for 1996 show this figure taking a downturn.

Arguments similar to this have arisen in the past. Inevitably, discussions about divisional investment and business performance evaluation involve differences between the three divisions, each of which roughly accounts for the same amount of revenue. Construction is the oldest of the three, and it has a very large

EXHIBIT C15.1.1 SYNDICATED BUILDERS, INC.

Operating Summaries for the Past Three Years

	1994	1995	Latest Estimate (1996)
For the company as a whole:			
ROI	12.9%	14.6%	14.5%
Earnings per share	$2.85	$3.64	$3.38
ROI for each division:			
Construction	11.9%	13.3%	15.6%
Architecture	19.4%	21.4%	20.7%
Equipment	8.2%	9.8%	8.5%

inventory of vehicles and equipment, which are housed at its 15 regional site locations. Its assets have substantially longer remaining lives than do the other divisions' assets. Architecture is mainly a design and engineering operation whose main asset base is its highly skilled and specialized employees. Equipment is a manufacturer and marketer, whose strength stems from its ability to produce specialized equipment aimed at the construction trade. It maintains an edge by investing heavily in latest production technology and by making its state-of-the-art construction products widely available in the marketplace. As reported in Exhibit C15.1.1, architecture generated the highest ROIs over the past three years and equipment the lowest.

The New Product Proposal

The product proposal offered by equipment's Blunt involves a highly innovative portable pressure-sprayer–painter combination. Not only is this unusual in that it combines what are normally two separate pieces of equipment, but it also offers the equipment division an opportunity to break into a new market—independent commercial painting contractors. Blunt has presented several arguments asserting that this product will help the division position itself in a new market segment. Admittedly, however, strategic position is not a benefit easily translated into hard numbers.

What the division has come up with are the projected financial expectations shown in Exhibit C15.1.2. The new project has a 6-year life and requires an investment of $2,400,000 at the beginning of 1997 (or year 1, for analysis purposes). It is expected to generate sales revenue of $2,650,000 in the first year. Sales projections for all six years are shown in the exhibit. Variable expenses will run at 50 percent of sales revenue. Fixed expense is budgeted at $675,000 in year 1 and will increase with inflation at a rate of 4 percent per year. Other information concerning taxes, residual values, and depreciation is given in the exhibit.

Before attending the capital-budgeting meeting, Blunt had asked her divisional controller to put together the cash flow expectations for the new product. She was quite pleased to see that the calculations yielded a very favorable NPV after they had been discounted at the corporate hurdle rate of 15 percent (after tax). She mistakenly assumed that NPV would be the number that counted and that the project would easily sail through the committee. As Blunt soon discovered, the

EXHIBIT C15.1.2 SYNDICATED BUILDERS, INC.

Financial Data Projections for the New Product Proposal

Investment requirements at the beginning of 1997:

Plant assets	$1,800,000
Land	600,000
Total	$2,400,000

Projected sales revenue (includes growth factor and 4.0% inflation rate):

Year (Calendar Year)

	1 (1997)	2 (1998)	3 (1999)	4 (2000)	5 (2001)	6 (2002)
Sales revenue	$2,650,000	$2,893,800	$3,250,316	$3,785,968	$4,134,277	$4,299,648

Expense relationships:

Variable expense	50.0% of sales revenue for all years
Fixed expense (excluding depreciation)	$675,000 in year 1 of project; increases with inflation @ 4% per year

Other important assumptions:
1. Tax rate is 35.0 percent, due at year-end.
2. Expected life of product is 6 years.
3. Land will be sold at the end of the project for its inflation-adjusted price of $759,191. However, plant assets will carry no residual value and will be scrapped at that time.
4. For financial statements, plant assets are depreciated by the straight-line method.
5. For tax purposes, plant assets are depreciated on a 5-year MACRS basis, using the midyear convention. (Midyear convention presumes that the asset is purchased on July 1 of year 1 and sold on June 30 of year 6.) Annual rates are year 1, 20.0 percent; year 2, 32.0 percent; year 3, 19.2 percent; year 4, 11.52 percent; year 5, 11.52 percent; and year 6, 5.76 percent.

[handwritten annotations: "assume → in the middle", "modified accelerated con-"]

corporate finance director was more concerned about the division's ROI, which Blunt had not looked at. Still, she was well aware that corporate headquarters calculated ROI by dividing a division's net income by its end-of-year net book value. She decided to go back to the controller and ask him to do a little more homework before she argues the issue any further.

Required:

1. Calculate the net present value for the product proposal and the annual ROIs during the product's 6-year life. In calculating ROI, assume that the land will be sold at the beginning of year 7. Thus, it is still technically on the books at December 31st, year 6.
2. Based on your calculations in requirement 1 and on nonquantifiable factors, should the equipment division be permitted to pursue the new product being proposed? Do you believe the market will, in fact, penalize the corporation if its divisions take on projects such as this?
3. Discuss the differences between the three divisions' ROIs. Can the divisions and their managers be properly evaluated by comparing these financial measures?

EXHIBIT C15.2.1   QUAKER OATS PET FOODS— LAWRENCE PLANT

Pay Plan's Strategic Components and Percentage Payouts

Strategic Components	Maximum Payouts
Financial	2.0%
Safety	1.0%
Quality	1.0%
Sanitation	1.0%
Annual focus	1.0%
Divisional performance	0.5%
	6.5%

C15.2   (Quaker Oat's Pet Foods Division)[17]

This case focuses on a pay-for-performance plan in use at one of Quaker Oat's pet foods production plants. The facility is a small, modern plant located in Lawrence, Kansas, and it was first put on-line in 1978. It employs a stable, nonunion work-force of about 165 persons and has built an excellent record of operations since its inception. The plant produces dog food, and its principal product line is Kibbles n' Bits n' Bits n' Bits. Its product strategy is to be *the* low-cost supplier of high-quality, good-value products.

In the early 1990s, the firm's management decided to initiate a compensation plan that would tie employee pay to the success of the plant's operations. Previously, employee pay had been based on comparisons of the plant's outcomes with those of a market group comprising national pet food suppliers, Quaker's other pet food plants, and local manufacturing firms. The plant's managers found, however, that this external reference resulted in worker pay adjustments that were driven by factors unrelated to plant performance. If, for example, the Lawrence plant had a very good year but the external reference firms did poorly, pay adjustments would provide no reward. The new plan was designed to overcome the lack of a performance linkage by tying pay to controllable plant outcomes.

Plan Overview

The plant's cultural climate, characterized by openness and a high level of trust, was important in the development and implementation of the plan. A series of meetings was held, at which managers worked side by side with hourly employees in devising the plan. While plant management had a good idea of the criteria that must be used in order to drive the plan, it was necessary to get the approval of all parties involved, including the Quaker Oats corporate home office, in order to make the plan work. Eventually, it was agreed that the plan would be made up of six strategic components, as shown in Exhibit C15.2.1. Payout percentages were attached to each component, resulting in a payout bonus that could reach 6.5 percent of worker earnings.

---

[17]   Based on James P. Guthrie and Edward P. Cunningham, "Pay for Performance for Hourly Workers: The Quaker Oats Alternative," *Compensation and Benefits Review*, Mar.–Apr. 1992, pp. 18–23.

EXHIBIT C15.2.2 QUAKER OATS PET FOODS— LAWRENCE PLANT

Application of Bonus Percentage Payout

Case 1: Average plant wages are greater than or equal to 5 percent of market average; payout is as a lump sum.

Case 2: Average plant wages are less than 5 percent of market average; payout is added to hourly pay.

Example employee: Joan Jackson Total annual earnings		Hours	*Hourly* *Rate*	*Total*
	Regular	1,900	$14.00	$26,600
	Overtime	100	$21.00	2,100
				$28,700

Assume bonus payout earned = 5.5%

Case 1: Plant wages are 6.25% greater than market average, then pay in lump sum:
$28,700 × 0.055 = $1,578.50

Case 2: Plant wages are 4.25% greater than market average, then payout is added to hourly pay rate in the following year:
$14.00 × 1.055 = $14.77

In addition to the bonus portion of the new plan, the agreement also contained a provision that sprang from the old, market-based pay policy. The performance-based plan provided that the plant would continue to pay its workers a rate that exceeded by at least 5 percent the average wage of the market. In the past, this had been an important plant policy, for two reasons: It ensured that top-quality employees were attracted and retained, and, as the plant's managers openly explained, it demonstrated their commitment to remaining nonunion. By including the 5 percent guaranteed premium, the pay plan would minimize risk to hourly workers.

The way in which the bonus percent is applied to a worker's pay depends on whether or not average plant wages exceed the 5 percent market premium. Bonuses are paid to employees either in the form of lump-sum payments or as adjustments to their base wage rates. These two alternatives and an example of each are summarized in Exhibit C15.2.2. Assume that Joan Jackson, who earns a base rate of $14 per hour, earned a total of $28,700 for the year. Further assume that all workers earned a bonus of 5.5 percent on the basis of the plant's performance outcome. In case 1, the Lawrence plant's hourly pay rate of $14 is 6.25 percent greater than the market average. Jackson then qualifies to receive the 5.5 percent performance bonus as a lump-sum payment of $1,578.50. In case 2, however, the plant's average hourly wage is only 4.25 percent greater than the market average. Under these circumstances, Jackson would receive an hourly wage adjustment of 5.5 percent, thereby increasing her base rate to $14.77. Note that including the performance bonus in base pay has the effect of raising one's annual base pay in the future, as opposed to the one-time effect of a lump-sum payment.[18]

---

[18] The plant's pay structure was highly egalitarian, with each employee within a pay category receiving the same pay.

Determination of pay outcomes is conducted once a year for the period of July 1st to June 30th. A running summary of plant performance is tabulated and reported to all employees each month. A meeting for each shift of workers is also held once a month to discuss updated results. This periodic feedback is vital for providing guidance on improving outcomes, for creating feelings of ownership among employees, and for eliminating the possibility of year-end surprises.

Details of the Performance Plan
The strategic components of the performance plan (as seen in Exhibit C15.2.1) were each defined by one or more performance measures. The measures link specific plant outcomes to worker pay. Exhibit C15.2.3 provides information on the composition of these measures, along with the targets, maximum bonus percentages, and actual results associated with each. The following is a brief description of plan components:

Financial
The financial component includes two measures: raw materials usage and raw materials conversion. Standard yields, developed from historical data, are used to set targets for each measure. For example, raw materials usage has a low goal of 97.0 percent of standard and a high goal of 98.5 percent of standard. If the plant achieves the low goal, employees earn a 0.5 percent bonus; for achieving the high goal, they earn a 1.0 percent bonus. Actual results for the year were 98.9 percent.

Safety
Three measures are used for the safety component: the OSHA (Occupational Safety and Health Administration) incidence rate, a days-away severity rate, and a lost workdays case-incident rate. Targets are established for each, as shown in Exhibit C15.2.3, based on historical data and the plant's excellent safety record. If the plant achieves two of the three target measures, hourly employees earn a 0.5 percent bonus; if it achieves all three, employees earn a 1.0 percent bonus.

Quality
Two quality measures are included: moisture content and controllable plant complaints. If moisture is held to less than 5.0 percent, employees earn a 0.5 percent bonus. If complaints that result from truly controllable plant actions are reduced by 3.0 percent, another 0.5 percent bonus is earned. Excluded would be complaints arising from external events, such as having a product bag torn by a stockperson at a retail outlet.

Sanitation
Two measures are taken to monitor plant cleanliness. The first involves spot inspections conducted two or three times per year by a corporate audit team. The target is an "excellent" rating, which earns a 0.5 percent bonus. The second measure is a quarterly inspection conducted by the plant's quality assurance function. If a 94 percent target rating is met, employees earn another 0.5 percent bonus.

Annual focus
The annual-focus strategic component is based on special needs, and may change from year to year. In Exhibit C15.2.3, two such measures are included for this year: employee training, targeted at meeting 99.5 percent of planned sessions, and departmental mission statement preparation, with a goal of 100 percent completion. Each of these measures can earn employees another 0.5 percent bonus.

Divisional performance
Corporate management sets a budgeted target profit for the year, here shown as $482,500. This measure is the furthest removed from the immediate control of

hourly employees. Nonetheless, if the target is met, employees earn a 0.5 percent bonus.

Required:

1. Prepare the payout percentage earned by hourly plant employees based on the information presented in Exhibit C15.2.3.
2. Based on your answer to requirement 1, determine the bonus payout to a plant hourly employee, Grant Highland. His hourly pay rate for the past year was $15.40, and he worked 2,000 hours at straight time and 142 hours overtime. Assume that the plant wages are 5.28 percent greater than the market average.
3. Evaluate the program instituted by the Quaker Oats Lawrence plant. Identify its strengths and its weaknesses.

EXHIBIT C15.2.3 QUAKER OATS PET FOODS— LAWRENCE PLANT

Payout Plan Measures, Targets, and Results

	Target	Actual Results	Maximum Payout
Financial:			
Raw materials usage	Low goal ≥ 97.0% of std		0.5%
	High goal ≥ 98.5% of std	98.9%	1.0%
Raw materials conversion	Low goal ≥ 96.5% of std		0.5%
	High goal ≥ 98.3% of std	97.6%	1.0%
Safety:			
OSHA incidence rate	< 6.0 per year	5.0	Achieve 2 out of 3,
Days-away severity rate	< 13.5 per year	15.6	earn 0.5%
Lost workdays case-			Achieve 3 of 3,
incident rate	< 0.85 per case	0.80	earn 1.0%
Quality:			
Moisture content	< 5.0% per unit	3.67%	0.5%
Controllable plant complaints	Decrease by 3.0%	2.85%	0.5%
Sanitation:			
Corporate audits	"Excellent" rating	excellent	0.5%
Quality assurance audits	≥ 94.0% of std	96.4%	0.5%
Annual focus:			
Employee training	Meet 99.5% of planned sessions	93.5%	0.5%
Departmental mission statement preparation	100% completion	100.0%	0.5%
Divisional performance	Operating income ≥ $482,500	$322,460	0.5%

Disclaimer: Information presented in this exhibit is purely hypothetical and is presented solely for purposes of illustration. Neither the targets nor the actual results are meant to represent the operations of Quaker's Lawrence, Kansas, plant.

Name and Company Index

SUBJECT INDEX